ENVIRONMENTAL DISASTERS

ENVIRONMENTAL DISASTERS

A CHRONICLE OF
INDIVIDUAL, INDUSTRIAL, AND
GOVERNMENTAL CARELESSNESS

LEE DAVIS

Facts On File, Inc.

To Amy

Who is, herself,

an environment that ceaselessly

thrives and endures and prevails

ENVIRONMENTAL DISASTERS: A Chronicle of Individual, Industrial, and Governmental Carelessness
Copyright © 1998 by Lee Davis

Facts On File, Inc.
11 Penn Plaza
New York NY 10001

Davis, Lee A.
Environmental disasters / Lee Davis.
p.   cm.
Includes bibliographical references and index.
ISBN 0-8160-3265-3 (alk. paper)
1. Environmental degradation.   2. Nature—Effect of
human beings on.   3. Industrial accidents—
Environmental aspects.   I. Title.
GE140.D383   1998
363.73´2—dc21   98-29134

Facts On File books are available at special discounts when purchased in bulk quantities for businesses,
associations, institutions, or sales promotions. Please call our Special Sales Department in New York at
(212) 967-8800 or (800) 322-8755.

You can find Facts On File on the World Wide Web at http://www.factsonfile.com

Cover design by Semadar Megged

Printed in the United States of America

VB Hermitage 10 9 8 7 6 5 4 3 2 1

This book is printed on acid-free paper.

♦ ♦ ♦ ♦ ♦

CONTENTS

♦ ♦ ♦ ♦

◆ ◆ ◆ ◆ ◆

ACKNOWLEDGMENTS

◆ ◆ ◆ ◆ ◆

There is always a staggeringly abundant population of people who make a book possible, from those who inspire to those who conspire, those who contribute the software of ideas and those who supply the hardware of information, those who comfort and those who shame an author into getting down to work and staying there. Some of all of these will be left out, so I apologize to them ahead of time.

But to those who still swim in the now environmentally safe waters of my memory, my gratitude:

To Jean Kaleda and her crew in the Riverhead Library, who dug till they found what I wanted, then made it available when I needed it; to Selma Kelson and the research staff of the Patchogue-Medford Library, who were endlessly helpful; to the research staff of the Library of Congress, who brought a little reality and some reward to my search for documentation.

To Alexandra McCarty of National Public Radio in Washington, who, in the oddest and most fortuitous of ways, directed me to a semiburied treasure of environmental resources.

To Nora McCarthy of Greenpeace, who not only supplied me with astonishing illustrations but tirelessly and patiently opened countless doors that led me to sources she didn't immediately possess.

To the patient and no-nonsense Steve Delaney of the EPA in Washington, who broke through the bonds of his agency and his call of duty to supply me with richly rewarding resources.

To Petty Officer Brown of the U.S. Coast Guard Picture Division in Washington, whose cooperation, efficiency, and graciousness were indispensable.

To all my friends in London, and particularly to Liz Dew and her imaginative and creative and munificent supplying of some of the most dramatic visual images in this book.

To the unnamed but enormously generous and helpful people at UNEP, who supplied me with mountains of material that had a way of smoothing out conflicting theories and multiple interpretations of the major environmental issues of our age.

To Annie of Squires, who provided me with esoteric reference material that lent color and wonder to some of the tougher entries.

To the editors of the *Sierra Club* magazine, whose information and expertise were invaluable.

To my agent, Ed Knappman, for helping this to happen.

To Tony, my canine companion, who kept me company and probably sane during the long and weary winters of the writing of this book.

And most of all, to my remarkable and resourceful and compassionate and complex editor, Anne Baxter, who set me straight and kept me going.

To all of you, and to all the rest of you whom I've neglected to mention, my deepest and most heartfelt gratitude.

Lee Davis
Westhampton, New York

INTRODUCTION

A great number of scientists agree that the earth began with a bang. What is unclear, even in the scientific community, is whether or not it will end with a whimper. Considering the present state of environmental disturbance caused by the needs and determinations of Earth's human inhabitants, the evidence seems to point that way. "No witchcraft, no enemy action had silenced the rebirth of new life in this stricken world. The people had done it themselves," wrote Rachel Carson in *Silent Spring*, the book whose publication gave birth to the environmental movement.

From the first 14 robins dead of DDT poisoning that Ms. Carson observed and which sent her on her own expedition of discovery, through Love Canal, the *Torey Canyon, Exxon Valdez,* and Gulf War oil spills, Bikini, Eniwetok, Minamata, Bhopal, Chernobyl, and the rape and plunder of the Brazilian rain forests, it is human beings who have been busily fouling their own nests.

"Man is the only animal who blushes—or needs to," said Mark Twain, and in no single destructive activity other than war have human beings done more about which to be ashamed than in their destruction and devastation of the environment that provides them a living place.

Land, water, and air have long been in abundant supply for humans, though not in equal amounts. Wars have largely been fought, in fact, over real estate, and the "conquest of the seas" and the "conquest of the air" have become coined catchphrases designed to romantically describe technological dominance. "Taming the Wilderness" is another phrase that describes the forward march of civilization. "Subduing the elements" is a dramatic arrangement of words that weather forecasters use to describe their newfound ability to track storms by computer.

And yet, has the environment actually been conquered, tamed, or subdued? The answer is sometimes—particularly through the dangerous games we have played with it in the past 50 years.

Once, there was plenty of natural bounty for the comparatively small number of humans on Earth, and the supply was sustained by periodic wars, outbreaks of fatal disease, and natural disasters that controlled human population. The eruption of volcanoes, the coming of floods, the cycle of drought, the awesome power of wind and rain when they are collected together in storms all must have seemed to these early humans like an assertion by the elements that they were, after all, visitors in nature's domain.

Imitating the wildlife that helped to keep them alive, primitive peoples lived in comparative peace with their environment, using it judiciously and respecting it, lest it really lash out at them.

And then came the industrial world with its demands for raw materials, and for centuries, the environment accommodated it; there was enough to be destroyed and still regenerate itself, enough to meet the needs of civilization and have plenty left over to provide the beauty that made life more than mere existence.

As we developed improved means of survival, the need to combat natural forces rose, too. Storms became not awesome spectacles to be sheltered from or tremble before but annoying inconveniences. Floods became steeds to harness and turn into power. And even volcanoes became models, whose principles were studied to create some of the more terrible weapons of war.

And so the "battle," metaphorical and otherwise, between humankind and the environment was joined, and it has raged on, chipping away at the life force that sustains our own life force. For centuries, the consequences have been either bearable or unnoticeable. But now, as we invent new ways of remaining alive, as our demands for longevity and comfort and profit proliferate, so does our destruction, intentional and unintentional, of the planet increase and, alas, accelerate.

Finally, it has been necessary to own up to the responsibility of maintaining, rather than destroying, the only living place we have. And that is what we have been doing, for the past three decades.

Well that we have, for in the past 50 years the assault upon our planet has so rapidly compounded that an atomic winter, an eternal, tropical, greenhouse summer, or the prospect of the air we breathe leaking out into space through a hole in the ozone layer have become possibilities that deserve public as well as scientific attention.

The primitive peoples were right. We *are* guests on this earth, and we had better begin to learn how to be guests who appreciate their status, not merely endure it or, worse, abuse it.

The only hope that this philosophical change will occur is the fortuitous fact that, added to the multiple conflicts that humankind has managed to devise, this, its most potentially cataclysmic one has come to occupy at least a healthy portion of the center stage of our attention. It has all the drama and darkness of a Greek tragedy, but with the ennobling possibility that it all could turn out well, provided that we learn before it is too late.

And so, the following chronicle of environmental disasters is a compilation of human error and misjudgment, of irresponsibility, of shortsightedness, and of a failure to value what must be valued if life itself is to continue on this planet, in addition to some of the efforts that have been made to correct the errors and misjudgments. The hope—despite considerations of politics, commerce, blindness, and avarice—seems to be gathering light and heat and energy. In other words, we may be learning.

The criterion for inclusion in each of the units is constant: The disasters that have been most abusive to and have had the most far-reaching effects on the environment are detailed, whereas others, not quite as dreadful or long-lasting or widespread, are merely listed. A balance was attempted between the various types of environmental disasters, but this was a secondary consideration to effect and scope.

ENVIRONMENTAL DISASTERS

COLLECTIVE AND INDIVIDUAL ASSAULTS AGAINST THE ENVIRONMENT

Africa
* Madagascar (deforestation, biodiversity destruction) (1960–present)
* River valleys of Central Africa (deforestation, desertification) (1960–present)
* Southern (deforestation, land degradation) (17th century–present)

Australia
* Southeast coast (crippling brushfires) (1983)

Bangladesh
* (flood, water pollution, disease) (1970)
  (flood, water pollution, disease) (1974)
* (flood, water pollution, disease) (1988)
* (flood, water pollution, disease) (1991)

Brazil
* Amazon River basin (rain forest destruction) (1964–present)
  Paraná (plantation fire) (1962)

Canada
* British Columbia, Fernie (forest fire) (1908)
* Northern Ontario (forest fire) (1916)

China
* Hankow-Han-yang-Wu-ch'ang area (flood) (1954)
* Shantung (flood) (1933)
* Yangtze River (flooding) (1931)

Costa Rica
* La Selva area (deforestation, biodiversity destruction) (1980–present)

Egypt
* Aswan (water pollution, land degradation) (1953–70)
  (brushfires) (1970)

Eurasia
  Aral Sea (coastal destruction) (1960–present)

France
  Les Landes (forest fire) (1949)
  Mediterranean coast (water pollution) (1980–present)

Greece
  Rhodes (forest fires) (1987)

India, Nepal, Pakistan
* Himalayan foothills, plains (deforestation, water pollution) (1960–present)
  Punjab (flood) (1972)

Indonesia
  West Kalimantan (forest fire) (1982)

Italy
  Adda valley (floods) (1987)
  Adriatic coast (water pollution) (1980)
* Savona (forest fire, explosion) (1921)

Japan
  Hakodate (forest fire) (1934)
  Hiroshima (forest fire) (1920)
* Saghalien (Sakhalin) (forest fire) (1929)
  Tokyo (wetland drainage) (1964–present)

*Detailed in text

1

Mexico
  * Pachuca de Soto (dam burst) (1921)
    Xochilapa (forest fire) (1929)

Peru
  * Upper Huallaga River valley (deforestation) (1974–present)

Southeast Asia
  * Malaysia, Indonesia, Papua New Guinea (deforestation, water pollution) (1976–present)

Spain
    Almería (pesticide contamination) (1981)

Suharto
    Burkit (air pollution from coal fire) (1982–83)

Tasmania
  * Hobart, Mt. Wellington (forest fire) (1967)

United States
    Alaska
  * Tongass National Forest (deforestation) (1950–present)
    California
  * Cleveland National Forest (fire) (1956)
  * Entire state (Medfly infestation) (1980)
  * San Francisquito valley (dam collapse and flood) (1928)
  * Minnesota (forest fire) (1918)
  * Northwest (forest fires) (1910)
  * Oklahoma, Texas, Kansas, Colorado, New Mexico (Dust Bowl drought) (1933–38)
    West Virginia
      Logan County (coal mine flood) (1972)

<h1 style="text-align:center">◆ ◆ ◆ ◆ ◆
CHRONOLOGY
◆ ◆ ◆ ◆ ◆</h1>

17th century–present
* Africa: southern portion, deforestation and land degradation

1908
* Canada: British Columbia, Fernie, forest fire

1910
* USA: Northwest, forest fire

1916
* Canada: Northern Ontario, forest fire

1918
* USA: Minnesota, forest fire

1920
 Japan: Hiroshima, forest fire

1921
* Italy: Savona, forest fire and explosion
* Mexico: Pachuca de Soto, dam burst

1928
* USA: California, San Francisquito Valley, dam collapse and flood

1929
* Japan: Saghalien, forest fire
 Mexico: Xochilapa, forest fire

1931
* China: Yangtze River, flood

1933
* China: Shantung, flood

1934
 Japan: Hakodate, forest fire
* USA: Oklahoma, Texas, Kansas, Colorado, New Mexico, Dust Bowl drought

*Detailed in text

1949
 France: Les Landes, forest fire

1950
* USA: Alaska, Tongass National Forest, deforestation

1954
* China: Hankow-Han-yang-Wu-chang area, flood

1956
* USA: California, Cleveland National Forest, fire

1960
 Africa
* River valleys of Central Africa, desertification and deforestation
* Madagascar, deforestation
* Egypt: Aswan, water pollution and land degradation
 Eurasia: Aral Sea, coastal destruction

1962
 Brazil: Paraná, fire

1964
 Japan: Tokyo, wetland drainage

1967
* Tasmania: Hobart, Mt. Wellington, forest fire

1970
* Bangladesh: flood, water pollution, and disease
 Egypt: brushfires

1972
 India: Punjab, flood
 USA: West Virginia, Logan County, coal mine flood

1974
 Bangladesh: flood, water pollution, and disease
* Peru: Upper Huallaga River valley, deforestation

1976
* Brazil: Amazon River basin, rain forest destruction
* Southeast Asia: Malaysia, Indonesia, Papua New Guinea, deforestation and water pollution

1980

* Costa Rica: La Selva area, deforestation and biodiversity destruction

France: Mediterranean coast

* India, Nepal, Pakistan: Himalayan foothills and plains, deforestation and water pollution

Italy: Adriatic coast, water pollution

1981

Spain: Almería, pesticide contamination

1982

Indonesia: West Kalimantan, forest fire

Suharto: Burkit, coal fire

1983

* Australia: Southeast coast, brushfires

1987

Greece: Rhodes, forest fires

Italy: Adda valley, floods

1988

* Bangladesh: flood, water pollution, and disease

1991

* Bangladesh: flood, water pollution, and disease

COLLECTIVE AND INDIVIDUAL ASSAULTS
AGAINST THE ENVIRONMENT

"Lord, let me die, but not die out . . ." wrote poet James Dickey, and his prayer is one that probably could, if they could speak, be uttered by every wilderness, every body of water, every habitable climate, and every living being who yearns to breathe free.

The extensive and unfolding chronicle of planetary destruction is not new; there is archaeological evidence that conservation was practiced by the earliest known civilizations. That the nature that they sometimes preserved, sometimes destroyed outlasted these civilizations is a sobering truth; that we have apparently learned something, but have forgotten more about the destructive experiences of the past is an even more sobering truth.

The view that there was a limit to the largesse of nature by 19th-century American scientist, politician, and diplomat George Perkins Marsh expressed in his book *Man and Nature* went against the prevailing Western philosophy of the relationship of human beings and the earth that nurtured them. The accepted thought of the time was that Earth provided unlimited resources for human growth and expansion. This idea was put to use by European settlers of Africa, Asia, and the Americas. Whereas native civilizations had respected, to the point of worship, the earth upon which they depended for sustenance and shelter, colonists regarded it as an enemy to be fought and subdued. And if in the conquest of nature, the destruction of nature was necessary, so be it. Someone—or something—had to lose.

What is astonishing to contemporary minds is the hardiness and longevity of this perception and philosophy. It would be more than 100 years from the publication of *Man and Nature* before Rachel Carson would publish *Silent Spring,* the wakeup call for Western civilization and the book that would make her literary midwife of the environmental movement.

Though Carson focused her book on the environmental damage done by pesticides and herbicides, it struck a nerve in the public consciousness, which was, in 1962, becoming slowly but increasingly aware of the widespreading ancillary effect of nuclear bomb testing. Graphic evidence of the destructive, often disastrous, effects of modern technology upon the natural environment began to rise to the surface of waters polluted—to the point of marine death—by hydrogen bombs set off on atolls in the Pacific. Contemporaneous oil spills that had the same effect upon both the waters and adjacent coastlines, warnings that fossil fuels might be running out, and population statistics showing that certain parts of the earth were being exhausted of their ability to feed growing populations furthered the belief that we might be going too far in our subjugation of our natural environment, that perhaps there were limits, and perhaps we were moving inexorably toward them.

Not that there weren't voices in and for the wilderness from 1862 to 1962. In 1916, President Theodore Roosevelt, sensing that preservation was the antidote for industrial greed and carelessness, established the National Park System in the United States. But it was not until the 1960s that a worldwide concerted effort was mounted to study the effects of human activity upon the planet.

In 1972, the United Nations Conference on the Human Environment in Stockholm, the first worldwide convocation dedicated to the state of the planet and ways to sustain it, raised Rachel Carson's warning cry to a level that everyone, even politicians, could hear. The immediate result was the formation of the United Nations Environment Programme (UNEP), which gave rise to a growing group of national environmental agencies and private groups dedicated to the salvation of the environment through public awareness and protective legislation.

One such group, the World Wildlife Fund, issued a startling warning at the conclusion of its fourth meeting, in San Francisco, in November 1976. Present was Dr. Raymond F. Dasmann, the senior ecologist for the International Union for the Conservation of Nature, who noted feelingly that "humanity is rapidly draining the earth of those materials which it requires for survival, and carries on with a childlike trust that its two great magicians, science and technology, will perform the necessary rituals to change a finite planet into an infinite cornucopia."

Nowhere has that "finite planet" defined itself more dramatically than in its forests, both temperate and tropical. "These forests have been stable for 60 million years, up to now," said Sir Peter Scott, the head of the World Wildlife Fund, at the same meeting. "Now they are disappearing, under the various incursions of man, at a worldwide rate of 50 acres a minute, day and night."

By the 1990s, that figure appeared conservative. In 1990, it was estimated that at the rate of loss indicated that year, by the end of the decade 2007–17, Nigeria, the Ivory Coast, Sri Lanka, Costa Rica, and El Salvador would eliminate their tropical rain forests completely. Worldwide, 1990 figures concluded, 40 to 50 million acres of tropical forest—an area the size of Washington State—are disappearing each year. "We were saying [in the 1980s] that we were losing the forests at an acre a second," said James Gustave Speth, president of the United Nations Food and Agriculture Organization in June of 1990, "but it is much closer to an acre and a half a second."

Deforestation occurs in a variety of ways. It can be by forest fires either begun or spread through human carelessness. It can happen through clear cutting of timber by timber interests or burning of timber by farmers; it can be brought on by indigent populations whose only heating and cooking fuel is wood or by developers, mining interests, or agricultural concerns that practice irresponsible farming methods.

The cumulative effect is manifold, for forests perform a multitude of duties. For one, they are binders of soil. Cut them down and the soil erodes. Heavy rains then cause gullying, which can wash silt into streams and rivers, which can clog waterways or lead to downstream flooding.

For another, the forest floor is notoriously bereft of nutrients. Most of these are contained in the trees and plants themselves. Thus, cleared forest land becomes untillable within three years of its clearing and simply erodes.

Rain forests, the tropical forests of the world, are the abodes of countless thousands of animals and useful plants. While they cover only 6 to 7 percent of the earth's land mass, they house 40 to 50 percent of all living species, thus making them the richest biological environments on Earth. In fact, one quarter of the prescription drugs used in the United States, including potent cancer and cardiac medications, were originally derived from or inspired by rain forest plants. There are still hundreds, perhaps thousands, yet to be discovered.

The plant species contained in forests are not merely medicinal. Many important crop plants, such as corn, originated in tropical rain forests. Wild parent plants still grow there, and they are sources of genes that confer such economically important characteristics as pest resistance to a variety of plants.

Finally, though the greenhouse effect is caused mostly by industrial emissions, forests play a vitally important role in the modulating of global climate. They can store from 20 to 100 times more carbon than other vegetation on the same land area, or around 30 to 60 tons of carbon per hectare (a hectare is roughly equal to slightly less than 2.5 acres). The current destruction of forests may be contributing up to 30 percent of the carbon dioxide and nitrogen oxides being released into the atmosphere. Further breakdown of the soil after clearance also releases these oxides.

Conversely, large-scale reforestation could, according to UNEP, help to slow or halt the current trend in global warming caused by the release of carbon dioxide, methane (from decomposing vegetation in wetlands and as a byproduct of digestion by ruminant animals), and chlorofluorocarbons into the atmosphere.

And so, nature's credentials are impressive and in order. Yet civilized humankind has seemed, through its actions, to doubt the authenticity of the balance and mastery of nature. Despite irrefutable scientific evidence, individuals, individual industries, and individual governments continue to be responsible for the wholesale destruction of the environment. Indigent countries like Brazil realize millions from timber interests; the need for hydroelectric power in many developing countries, such as Egypt, have resulted in 120,000 square miles of land worldwide being flooded by dam building; cattle ranching and timber and oil interests in developed countries like the United States threaten ancient growth forests; ancient habits and modern industry send emissions that spread disease and death into waterways.

These are some of the worst individual and collective assaults against the environment, and this unit deals with some of the most egregious examples of them.

AFRICA
(MADAGASCAR)
DEFORESTATION AND DESTRUCTION OF BIODIVERSITY
1960–Present

Madagascar, which was once carpeted with tropical rain forest, has destroyed its natural resource at a rate that, unchecked, will eliminate it entirely by the year 2025. Soil erosion and gullying already scar its landscape. Mindful of Madagascar's role as a repository of nearly boundless biodiversity, international organizations have helped to form forest preserves, the latest of which, the Ranomafana preserve, is also the most ambitious.

The elimination of the earth's necessary biodiversity is a particularly tragic consequence of the deforestation of the earth's rain forests. Nowhere is this more dramatically demonstrated than on Madagascar, an island nation situated in the Indian Ocean, 250 miles off the coast of Mozambique, on the southeastern part of Africa.

In prehistory, Madagascar was part of the African continent. But more than a million years ago, it broke off and floated out to sea. Some geologists say that it was once part of what is now Mozambique; others contend that it was a portion of what is now Tanzania and drifted southward to its present position.

When Madagascar took its trip to sea, the flora and fauna on it were still in a primitive stage of evolution. Thus, unthreatened by higher forms of life—notably monkeys—they developed freely. Today, in fact, there are no predators on Madagascar except human beings, and so, in the small pockets of undisturbed vegetation, more than 80 percent of the island's flowering plant species grow, uniquely. They are found only on Madagascar.

Of these, Rosy periwinkle (*Catharanthus roseus*) is a prime example of useful natural fauna. It, like many plants, is the source from which a natural medicine is derived that is used to treat a range of serious illnesses, from diabetes to Hodgkin's disease to leukemia, and a series of other cancers.

In the fauna category, Madagascar has been termed a "nirvana for frog lovers." One hundred forty-eight of its 150 frog species are endemic.

This is why, with some 100 species of plants and animals disappearing every day from the world because of rain forest destruction, the plight of Madagascar is so dramatic and devastating. Its central plateau, once lushly covered with tropical rain forest, is now a scarred moonscape, rife with gullies and pockmarked by eroding soil.

The entire eastern portion of the island was once thickly blanketed with evergreen and deciduous forest. Now, only one-fourth of this forest remains.

As of 1990, the cutting of the rain forest in Madagascar was progressing at such an alarming rate that scientists predicted that it would be completely eliminated by the year 2025.

Mindful of this, less industry-oriented, more ecologically dedicated minds prevailed, and with a $3.2 million grant from the United States Agency for International Development (USAID), the Ranomafana National Park, a forest

A mother, carrying her child, plants rice in the ashes of the felled Ranomafana forest, currently under rehabilitation.
(PAUL HARRISON/STILL PICTURES)

7

preserve, was established in the remaining rain forest on the southeast coast.

United States, UN, and African researchers determined that, within an island that contained an encyclopedic collection of flora and fauna, the Ranomafana forest contained one of the greatest unexplored diversities of life left in the world. It was the fourth area to be preserved in Madagascar, and it has been greeted by governments and environmental groups with applause and expectation. The 80,000 people who reside in it, use it as a source of fuel, and clear it for their rice fields are considerably unhappy, however, and pose a universal problem for environmentalists: the care and feeding of populations who have legitimately—if negligently—lived within and upon rain forests.

In Madagascar's Ranomafana Preserve, much of the USAID money is going toward building schools in villages, delivering health services, and searching for broad-scale, alternative sources of income for its residents. The results may well determine the direction of further worldwide experiments in the creation of extractive reserves.

AFRICA
(RIVER VALLEYS OF CENTRAL AFRICA)
DEFORESTATION AND DESERTIFICATION
1960–Present

....

Accelerating population growth, indiscriminate burning of forests and savannas, destructive farming and grazing methods, and rapacious industrial uses of the ecology have joined to ravage the not altogether friendly environment of Central Africa. The United Nations and local governments have joined to alleviate the problem and deflect the plunge toward total demolishment.

It seems to be axiomatic. Native and primitive peoples have treated the earth as a benevolent provider to be cared for and worshiped. European conquerors and settlers, on the other hand, have treated the environment as an enemy to be subdued. And nowhere is this more dramatically—and perhaps complexly—evidenced than on the continent of Africa. For thousands of years, native farmers and herdsmen dealt with the rain forests and savannas of Africa with respect and judiciousness. As in South America (see Brazil, Amazon River Basin, pp. 19–28), they slashed and burned the rain forest, but only in small, manageable chunks. The ashes were left as fertilizer, and forest crops such as yams were planted in these temporary clearings, ritually, for three years only, which was the maximum the tropical forest soil could be farmed and still yield crops. The farming family then moved on, and the forest grew again over the cultivated plot.

But 350 years ago, when the first European colonists came to Africa, they brought their industrial ideas with them. Huge areas of the forest were permanently cleared in order to establish plantations of rotating crops of coffee and cocoa. Other parts of the forest were logged heavily, cleaning out rich stores of mahogany in such wholesale fashion that few of these trees—or of any other tropical hardwoods—still survive, except in three threatened portions of Africa: the Ivory Coast, chiefly in Sierra Leone and Liberia; Central Africa in Gabon, Congo, Democratic Republic of the Congo (Zaire), Equatorial Guinea, Cameroon, portions of Rwanda; and on Madagascar (see pp. 6–8).

In 1900, Ivory Coast possessed 55,970 square miles of dense and lush rain forest. By 1980, only one-third of the rain forest remained. In all of West Africa, the forest is shrinking at the rate of 4 percent per year, which means that, at the present rate, by 2010, it will have disappeared entirely.

The reasons are not merely industrial. As independence came to Africa during the 1960s and 1970s and countries, each with their own agendas and ethnic traditions and cross-traditions became established, huge migrations of people began to call upon the environment for sustenance. Firewood is still the main source of heat and cooking power throughout Africa, and it is not unusual for members of families to be sent on 10-mile walks to gather this firewood.

Political boundaries set in place by European administrators disrupted the nomadic routes of the pastoralists of the savannas, who since ancient times had observed an environment-friendly ritual of moving their cattle, in the dry season, to the south where they fertilized the fields with their droppings. When the rainy season returned, and with it the dreaded tsetse fly, these pastoralists and their herds would return to the north, where the pastures had had time to regenerate themselves.

In addition, new farming methods, such as rototilling and the addition of chemical fertilizers and pesticides, which ignore the wisdom of the ages, have been instituted, and so, because of the introduction of chemicals, the fertility of forest soils has been lost forever. Severe erosion has been the result (see Africa, Madagascar, p. 7).

In modern times, forests have been cut down and grass set on fire to create new forest growth, which, because of overgrazing and out of control bush fires, makes new growth more difficult, not easier.

Furthermore, the soil, deprived of tree roots to bind it, erodes, and desertification takes place. Because of this, encroachment of the Sahara in both the south and the north has accelerated in the past two decades to its present advancement of 250,000 acres per year. In Nanka, Nigeria, half a million tons of soil are eroded every year during the rainy season because the area has been deprived of its protective cover through deforestation, overgrazing, and the continuous cultivation of marginal lands.

The overgrazing comes about as a direct result of the advantages (turned to disadvantages) of civilization. With the introduction of modern veterinary medicine to the continent, there has been a veritable explosion in the animal

Deprived of binding tree roots, the Sahara has encroached on formerly tillable land in both South and North Africa at the rate of 250,000 acres a year.
(UN PHOTO #154843/E. DARROCH)

population. Huge, often unmanageable herds are now kept as much for status as for income. In the inland delta of the Niger River, an ecologically fragile part of Africa, equally enormous herds have been pushed, to feed on and soon decimate whatever grazing land is left.

But the greatest threat to the environment of Central Africa is the exploding population. In 1990, the area was populated by 310 million people. By 2015, that number is expected to double. As more people enter an area, urbanization, and overcultivation and overutilization of limited natural resources become the inevitable result.

With the exception of the rich alluvial soils found in rare locations like Lake Victoria in Uganda, Kenya, and Tanzania, there is little in the land of Africa to support continual cultivation. High in iron content, these soils lose their fertility rapidly, and once stripped of vegetation, they either drift from the wind or gully from rainfall—when the rainfall arrives.

Since bare earth reflects solar radiation, the encroachment of this depleted land upon the remaining forests produces less rainfall and hence drought conditions. And drought, in turn, increases desertification.

So much for the soil. The influx of huge populations and the requirements of industrial agriculture have also placed huge demands upon the rivers of Central Africa, and this, in a perverse way, has increased the incidence and severity of disease.

The building of dams produces ecological consequences such as the silting up of reservoirs and the increased salinization of soil in irrigated areas (see Egypt, Aswan, pp. 38–42). The dam projects designed to provide hydroelectric power for urban areas and irrigation for cultivated areas along the Congo, Volta, Zambezi, and Niger Rivers have produced still, silt-clogged reservoirs. These in turn have become natural habitats for malaria-spreading mosquitoes and water snails that spread both malaria and schistosomiasis (also known as bilharzia), a parasitic infection that invades the bloodstream and ultimately consumes the flesh of the affected person.

The urbanization of areas along rivers also pollutes these natural life support systems, filling them with untreated human and industrial waste, which endangers human and animal life alike.

And then there is the extinction of wildlife and plantlife. The mammals of the savannas—the black rhinoceros and the elephant—are being destroyed by poachers despite international agreements that limit the export of ivory. Within the forest dwell rare primates, such as Mountain gorillas, which are rapidly becoming extinct. Scientists estimate that over a million species, or a quarter of the total biological diversity on Earth are at risk of complete extinction by 2010.

Plant species in the forest, specifically *zanthosylum* (Fagara), indigenous to West Africa, which shows promise in controlling problems relating to sickle-cell anemia, are being eliminated.

Central Africa also exports pollution in large quantities. A West German team of scientists, headed by Dr. Paul Crutzen, a leading atmospheric scientist, released startling findings in 1989. The burning of savannas and forests in the region, according to Dr. Crutzen, was pumping three times more gases and particles into the air than all the fires set by farmers and settlers in South America, including the Amazon. In fact, he noted, of all the carbon dioxide (which causes global warming and acid rain) released by worldwide burning or deforestation, at least half comes from Africa.

Satellite readings confirm that, although less rain forest is destroyed by burning in Africa than in other depositories of tropical forests, the savanna fires cover a great area; burn a greater volume of dry grass, shrubs, and trees; and are set more frequently than anywhere else in the tropics.

"The forest burns once and it is destroyed, but the savannas and the grasslands become larger and are burned regularly," concluded Dr. Crutzen.

Since 1989, the contribution of burning forests and savannas to global warming has been modified but not by any means eliminated; and, at any rate, the role of the burning of the rain forest in the destruction of the ecology of Africa remains undisputed.

Not that the continent was ever a terribly friendly place for the human species. The Great Rift Valley of eastern Africa and the highlands of Cameroon contain crater lakes that erupt now and then with lethal gases. On August 21, 1986, Lake Nyos in Cameroon spewed forth a deadly cloud of carbon dioxide that had percolated up from the volcanic depths of the lake. The cloud hugged the ground and blanketed an area 10 miles from the lake, smothering some 1,700 villagers to death.

The river waters and jungles also contain microorganisms that kill and debilitate both cattle and humans, particularly children. Besides the tsetse fly, which causes sleeping sickness in humans, and nagana, a wasting disease in cattle, there is onchocerciasis, known by the natives as river blindness, carried by the black fly, which breeds in fast-flowing river water. And then there is AIDS, which, although there is some dispute about it, is generally considered to have

originated in the African green monkey, which inhabits the rain forest and savannas of Central Africa.

And so, a compounding of industrialization, overpopulation, and modern, ecologically unsound damming, cultivating, and deforestation techniques, plus the inherent unfriendliness of the ecology, threatens—particularly if the theory of origin of the AIDS virus is true—to turn the cradle of human life into its tomb.

However, all is not entirely bleak. Family planning efforts, under the tutelage of the United Nations, are being advanced by individual governments to curb out of control population growth. Reforestation and land reclamation plans are in use in the area stretching from Senegal to northern Kenya. Desertification and gullying are being fought with the planting of trees, which not only hold the soil but provide leaves for livestock, which in turn reduces the overgrazing of pastureland.

In particular, the Green Belt Movement of the National Council of Women of Kenya, begun in 1977, has worked well enough to become a model for other reclamation projects. In it, villages and urban communities plant trees on any open space. By the early 1990s, the movement had established 21,000 green belts and set up 65 village-based plant nurseries in Central Africa.

The introduction of the ceramic-lined jiko, a stove for cooking that provides a 50-percent saving in fuel has alleviated, somewhat, the destruction of the forests for wood fuel.

And the introduction of "corridor planting," in which rapidly growing, nitrogen-fixing trees that return nutrients to the soil are planted on either side of alleys of food crops is a revolutionary change in farming methods that has a number of ecologically sound side effects. The leaves of the trees provide food for livestock; the branches are a source of wood fuel and building poles.

This, plus the establishment by the United Nations of the headquarters of its Environment Programme, with remote sensing technology and monitoring equipment that gives advance warning of impending degradation and land loss, as well as advice and planning funneled in from its onsite and worldwide network of contributing environmental scientists, bode better for the survival of both humans and the ecology of Africa.

AFRICA
(SOUTHERN)
DEFORESTATION AND LAND DEGRADATION
17th Century–Present

Three hundred and fifty years of overfarming, overgrazing, irresponsible land and forest clearing, and replacement of wise and judicious use of a varied but delicate ecology with land use for profit has resulted in severely damaged land in southern Africa. The crisis of drought is the greatest problem, and this is finally being addressed by the various governments of the various countries of southern Africa.

The pastoral and farming Bantu-speaking peoples and the nomadic hunter-gatherers who once inhabited the southern portion of Africa (from the region represented by present-day Angola and Zambia on the north and South Africa on the south) had a working relationship with the environment. It supplied them, and they respected it.

But, within a few decades of the first Dutch settlement of Cape Town in 1652, all of the hardwood forests that had blanketed the slopes of Table Mountain in lush green had been totally and unceremoniously cleared. The colonists used the timber for fuel and for building homes, wagons, ships, and furniture.

By the 1880s, a further industrialized society exploited the remaining supply of endemic yellowwood, stinkwood, and cedar.

By the end of the 19th century, European farming methods had so damaged soil fertility and stability that there was hardly any part of the area that could yield crops of consequence. To add to this situation, overgrazing removed the natural vegetable cover after which wind and water eroded it, leaving deep gullies where flat green pastureland once stood.

The Land Apportionment Act of 1930 in Southern Rhodesia (now Zimbabwe) set aside the more fertile portion of the country for whites. The other part became "Native Reserves," which in 1960, with independence from colonial rule established throughout most of Africa, became known as "homelands." Forced to exist in marginal territories, kept out of some of South Africa's cities, the pastoralists and farmers who worked these Native Reserves soon rendered them infertile at worst and overcultivated at best. Today, they are ravaged by drought, overgrazing, erosion, and a general state of neglect.

Urban sprawl has created demands upon the environment that it simply cannot sustain. The coalfields and power stations east of Johannesburg have produced discharges of sulfurous air pollution that rival Eastern Europe at its worst. Tourist resorts, free of meaningful governmental regulations, presently discharge untreated or semitreated sewage into coastal estuaries, lagoons, and inshore waters. The resultant damage and frequent destruction of plant and animal life is widespread. In addition, much of the coastal wetlands, which include estuaries and mangrove swamps, have been cleared for tourist developments or are polluted by sewage and industrial effluent. These estuaries and swamps are natural barriers to coastal erosion, and their removal has hastened this erosion.

On the southwestern Cape of Africa, *Acacia* tree species have been imported from Australia and planted in an effort to stabilize the coastal dunes. This they have done, but they have also suffocated native vegetation, since their proliferation is unchecked by the natural process of feeding by native wildlife and insects, who ignore the *Acacias*.

In the cities, burgeoning populations have created their own environmental problems. The majority of the huge indigent urban population of South Africa depends upon wood and charcoal for heating and cooking. Thus, huge areas surrounding the shantytowns that exist on the fringes of the Cape Town metropolitan area (which is a home of sorts to nearly 3 million people) have been stripped bare of trees. The air is heavy with pollution caused by wood smoke. In Lusaka, Zambia, and Harare, Zimbabwe, an effort has been made to introduce electricity in order to alleviate the air pollution from wood burning and coal, but it has had little effect. Only the very wealthy living in these areas can afford the electric rates.

What remains of the forests has also fallen prey to the constant armed conflict that rages across this troubled landscape. In Angola, prior to the ceasefire declared in mid-1991, guerrilla troops felled and smuggled out huge amounts of hardwood timber to foreign powers in exchange for weapons and supplies.

The exploiting of mineral resources, in which the region was once unusually rich, has further ravaged the environment. Wholesale and indiscriminate copper, iron, gold, and diamond mining have left their marks upon the landscape and their pollution within the waterways. The open cast diamond mines of South Africa have leached enormous quantities of toxic chemicals into the soil and water supply, as have the copper mines of Zambia and the uranium mines of Namibia. The slag heaps from these mines, the crushing plants, and reduction works have disfigured the landscape and have spewed toxic fumes into the air.

A constant casualty of the atomic age has been the groundwater near the enormous uranium works at Rossing in Namibia's Namib Desert. Environmentalists contend (and the mine owners deny) that toxic and radioactive effluents have entered the most subterranean parts of the underground water system of the Khan and Swakop Rivers, on Namibia's western fringes. The rivers flow into and supply the coastal towns of Swakopmund and Walvis Bay, thus contaminating their water supplies and affecting the wildlife that inhabits the region surrounding these towns.

This is a major environmental disaster, since water is a precious commodity in all of Africa. But this portion of the continent has treated its water supply in a particularly cavalier way. In addition to the pollution of water supplies through poor sanitation and primitive waste disposal methods, chemical pesticides such as DDT and dieldrin are still widely used in South Africa. As in other parts of the world where these pesticides are no longer employed in such vast quantities, these chemicals have run off farmland into rivers, thus entering the food chain through the fatty tissues of animals. The toxicity of African eagle eggs, for instance, is so high that they have become thin enough to crack before hatching.

In rural areas, water contamination and drought conspire to deprive the people of safe drinking water. Cholera and wasting-type intestinal diseases are rife. Rural inhabitants must sometimes walk miles for water, balancing jerry cans on their heads. Nearly 21 million Africans do not have enough water in which to bathe, wash their clothes, or run a flush toilet.

In Zimbabwe, more than 8,000 storage dams have been built to provide domestic, agricultural, and industrial water. All of this is to the good; but, as with all dams, siltation occurs, and in the case of the large dams built in the 1960s, particularly on the Zambese River, reservoir lakes have become blocked by weeds and silt, which in turn become breeding grounds for insects carrying such diseases as malaria and bilharzia.

The combination of drought and misuse of land reaches its most critical condition in Madagascar (see Africa, Madagascar, pp. 6–8), the mountain slopes such as the Drakensberg range, and the semiarrid savannas of areas like Botswana. In the mountain kingdom of Lesotho, southeast of Johannesburg and west of Durban, nearly 90 percent of the land has been eroded. In 1994, the annual loss of soil was estimated at 18.5 million tons from only 6.7 million acres of land. Since the early 1980s, 80 percent of southern Africa's 750 million acres has suffered the effects of desertification, brought about by irresponsible use of the land and drought.

Drought, in fact, is a continuing and pervasive problem, perhaps the core environmental trouble of this part of the world. A quarter of the population of southern Africa, or about 12 million people, does not have easy access to drinking water. Although the period between October 1995 and February 1996 was wetter than usual, with actual floods washing cars from roads and drowning people and cattle, and an Indian Ocean cyclone landing in Zimbabwe and meandering across the continent, these climatic changes represented, as those who study such phenomena contended, only a brief respite from preexisting conditions. Growth rings in trees show a regular drought cycle in which nine wet years are followed by nine dry ones. And 1996 was the eighth year of a wet cycle.

In precolonial times, this would bode well. But since the appearance of whites in Africa 350 years ago, colonists have leveled the forests and overfarmed and overgrazed the land, removing drought-resistant, indigenous thorn trees and baobabs and replacing sorghum and tuber crops with drought-sensitive corn. In addition, farms of imported pines and eucalyptus have sucked underground aquifers dry.

And so, the years of drought have been and will continue to be years of disaster. Although a project designed to import water from the mountains of Lesotho has been under construction for 10 years, government ministers in South

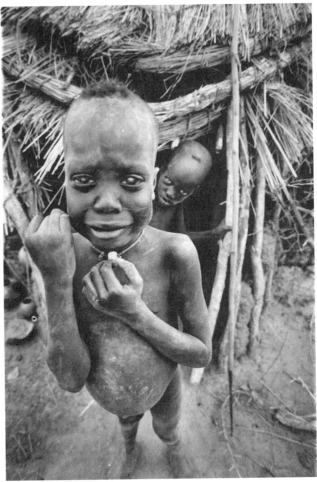

Starvation is the inevitable and repeated price of land degradation from the destructive farming habits that have proceeded, unabated, in southern Africa from the 17th century through the present.
(ANDREW STUWICKI/UNEP)

Africa know it simply will not be enough and that, sooner or later, South Africa will have to import water, at a tremendous cost, from what remains of the rain forests of Angola and Zaire. All of this gives credence to the prediction of futurists that the wars of the next century will be fought over water, not oil.

There is a growing awareness of the necessity to either forestall or postpone this eventuality—or prove the futurists wrong. Conservation preserves—for wildlife, land, and people—are thus coming into being throughout southern Africa.

In Zimbabwe, the Rural Afforestation Project has established 70 state nurseries that provide rural inhabitants with seedlings at subsidized prices.

Zambia, in an effort to turn back time and cultivate ancient ways of preserving land and wildlife, implemented a plan in 1987 in the Luangwa valley in the southeast portion of the country to provide its people and wildlife with a self-sustaining future involving hippo cropping, a game meat and forest cooperative, and facilities for safari tourism.

In July 1991, the Richtersveld National Park on the Orange River border with Namibia became South Africa's newest reserve. Its most telling feature was the allowing of the Nama—the indigenous but impoverished people of the area—to stay on their traditional lands. Furthermore, they were given financial assistance to help sustain their pastoral way of life.

Some national and international corporations, in pursuit of positive public images, have established nature preserves. The South African Nature Foundation, affiliated with the World Wide Fund for Nature, has influenced large landowners to register important areas as natural heritage sites, and some smaller farmers have established their own, smaller conservancies, although many of them have been set up as tourist attractions, complete with nature trails. Small matter. In order to build the trails, respect for the environment has had to be practiced.

And finally, Kader Asmal, South Africa's new minister of Water Affairs and Forestry, has embarked on a massive program to conserve, purify, and disseminate pure water. "Everyone should be entitled to six gallons of water a day that does [sic] not have to be carried more than 200 yards," he has proclaimed.

This has been brought about by the drilling of bore holes in communities, a method of water gathering that is not endorsed by many ecologists who decry the tapping of underground water reserves. Mr. Asmal has met this objection by restricting private drilling for water.

Minister Asmal has drafted legislation that would abandon the system under which rivers have been owned by the landowners on their banks. He has set the price of water at its market value, created water rights that can be bought and sold, legislated how much water must be kept in rivers so the environment and downstream users do not suffer, and required conservation.

His plan is a bold attempt to turn back centuries of neglect and rapacious assassination of an ecology that was once recognized—and worshiped—for its delicate and precarious nature. Its existence is encouraging; its success is necessary.

AUSTRALIA
(SOUTHEAST COAST)
CRIPPLING BRUSHFIRES
February 16–20, 1983

....

From February 16 to 20, 1983, in fires deliberately set and fanned by winds that sometimes reached 60 mph, 71 people died, equaling the record of Australia's worst brushfire until that time. More than 2,500 square miles of forest, farm-, and brushland, and towns were burned, and more than 3,000 homes destroyed.

Thousands of sheep and cattle died, and entire crops of wheat were blackened and burned.

"The fire came up the highway like a fireball. The roar of the wind and the flames was horrific, like a train," said 39-year-old postmistress Eleanor Gray to a Reuters reporter on Thursday morning, February 17, 1983. Her town, Macedon, which is west of Melbourne, near the border between Victoria, Australia's southernmost state, and its western neighbor, South Australia, had been gutted by wildfire. She and approximately 160 others had survived the night of February 16, 1983, in Macedon's single hotel. Built of brick, it was one of the few remaining structures in the scorched village, which in turn was one of hundreds that would become scorched ruins before week's end.

The Australian summer of 1983 was extraordinarily dry. The brush and vegetation in Victoria and along the coast of the Indian Ocean west of Tasmania and into South Australia was as brittle and receptive to fire as weathered kindling. In some parts of the area, it had not rained in nearly four years.

On Wednesday, February 16, the temperature was 104 degrees Fahrenheit, and heavy winds came in off the northern mountain ranges. It was enough to drive most of the considerable population indoors.

That simple defense became a fatal decision for many. Within hours, scores would be injured and scores more would die as three huge brushfires caught, then raged with express-train speed across the drought-parched countryside.

Thousands fled to the beach, but hundreds more were trapped in their cars or homes. Within hours, seven towns along a 500-mile stretch of coastline had been destroyed, and the fires were encircling the South Australia capital city of Adelaide.

Every fire brigade in the two states leaped into action. By the end of the day on the 16th, more than 4,000 firefighters battled the blazes in suffocating heat and managed to put out the fires surrounding Adelaide quickly. "People are dying as they try to reach their homes," a firefighter in the coastal town of Lorne, Victoria, told reporters. In South Australia, near the Victoria border, a family of five was incinerated in their car as they tried to flee the flames. Near Cockatoo, 30 miles from Melbourne, 12 volunteer firefighters were killed when the fires trapped them in a closing circle. "We're resigned to the fact that more bodies will be recovered when we finally get inside cars which were trapped by the fires and houses where the residents had nowhere to run," said an exhausted firefighter on the night of the 16th.

The next day, an unrelenting summer sun was haloed by acrid smoke. Dust and smoke clouds had closed both the Adelaide and Melbourne airports. The national government, alerted to the catastrophe, sent troops into the region to relieve the exhausted volunteers. Flying over the furiously burning area, Prime Minister Malcolm Fraser likened the scene to one after a "panzer division [went] through," and Victoria governor Brian Murray noted that "the fire-hit areas looked as though they had been attacked with napalm."

On the ground, walls of flame, whipped by continuing winds, were racing along the coastline, consuming cattle, sheep, farms, and residents at an alarming speed. By the end of the day, a 19-year-old unemployed man, Andrew Mervyn Davey, had been arrested and charged with unlawfully and maliciously setting fire to scrub at Kersbook, 22 miles northeast of Adelaide. He had had nothing better to do, he confessed.

By the next day, some of the worst fires had been extinguished, but others still burned out of control. In forest land near Warburton, 50 miles from Melbourne, more than 700 firefighters and 50 water tankers took hours to finally conquer the spreading flames.

Milder weather and tamer winds came to the aid of the exhausted battlers of the flames on the 20th, and by the end of the week, the fires, most of which had been deliberately set, were brought under control, though the dryness of the landscape, the caprices of the weather, and the unpredictability of arsonists failed to allay fears of reignition.

Seventy-one people died, making this equal to Australia's worst brushfire to date: the 1939 fires, when an equal number were killed by fire in Victoria. Hundreds were injured, and more than 3,000 homes were destroyed. The property damage amounted to nearly $400 million. No new fires ignited for the rest of the summer. Apparently the devastation had sobered the other, still unidentified arsonists.

BANGLADESH

(EAST PAKISTAN)

FLOOD, WATER POLLUTION, AND DISEASE
November 12, 1970

....

The cyclone of November 12, 1970, in Bangladesh is widely considered to be the worst natural disaster of the 20th century. Between 300,000 and 500,000 residents of this dangerously poised, ecologically unsound country were killed by a combination of wind and water.

On November 12, 1970, five months before it became Bangladesh, East Pakistan experienced the worst disaster of the 20th century. The combination of a killer cyclone and a tidal wave said to be 50 feet high caused a death toll of between 300,000 and 500,000 (reliable statistics were hard to come by in the new country; estimates were combinations of governmental releases and International Red Cross observations). Winds of up to 150 mph lashed the East Pakistan coast, the Ganges Delta, and the offshore islands of Bhola, Hatia, Kukri Muktri, Manpura, and Rangabali.

Bangladesh is roughly the size of Wisconsin, with an enormous population, exceeding 95 million people. It borders on India and Burma and consists mainly of low plains cut by the Ganges and Brahmapurtra Rivers and their delta. A portion of India until 1947, the area became part of East Pakistan and remained so until its declaration of independence from Pakistan in March 1971. Alluvial and marshy along the coast, with hills breaking this monotony only in the extreme Southeast, it has one of the rainiest climates in the world and is thus a breeding ground for tropical monsoons.

Ironically, this, the worst disaster of the century was first dismissed as a false alarm. Barely a month earlier, on October 23, 1970, a small cyclone had frightened the inhabitants of the Ganges Delta into evacuating the environs, and only minimal damage resulted. But this false alarm brought with it a false sense of confidence; and when, on November 11, 1970, an American weather satellite warned of a giant cyclone heading toward the same region, Radio Pakistan ignored it. Uninformed, the huge population slept blissfully as this meteorological monster pounded inexorably toward it.

The storm hit in the middle of the night of November 12. Cyclonic winds pushed a tidal wave of at least 20 feet—some said 50 feet—in height toward islands whose highest ground level rested a maximum of 20 feet above the sea's surface. Thus, when the wave curled over and crashed upon the thatched roof houses and paddies of these islands, it absolutely consumed them, and only the second stories of the manor houses of a few well-to-do farmers were saved.

Most houses were smashed into piles of soaked straw, and the fleeing inhabitants were swept out to sea by the roaring current. Moments later, the storm itself made landfall, with winds of 150 mph. Houses, hospitals, power lines were instantly collapsed, cutting off communication with the outside world. It would be two days before the rest of Pakistan would know of the calamity, and by then the tragedy would climb to monumental proportions.

More than 20,000 inhabitants of one island alone disappeared into the sea without a trace; corpses covered the land like grim cobblestones. They were scooped up from the islands and thrown into the sea, where they floated toward the land. There, inhabitants lined the beaches, shoving the beached corpses back out to sea with bamboo poles.

Disease spread rapidly. Cholera ravaged the island of Rangabali. Rice paddies turned the color of blood. Vultures circled constantly, and the smell of death and decaying corpses hung like a sickly sweet mist over the entire area. Water was unobtainable; food supplies were spoiled or tainted by disease.

Within two days, medical supplies, personnel, and food began to be airlifted into the region from the rest of the world. America and Great Britain ferried in the largest amount of supplies and engineers to reconstruct the trans-

Every year the cyclones return to Bangladesh. And every year, the islands are bitten away by the river floods that are the storms' consequence.
(PAUL HARRISON/STILL PICTURES)

portation and health-support systems. But air drops of food supplies caused further misery in the form of food riots.

It would be months before the dead would be collected from the streets of the demolished city of Patuakhali and its surrounding fields and paddies, and months more before the International Red Cross would be able to stem the rampant spread of cholera and typhoid in the region.

BANGLADESH
FLOOD, WATER POLLUTION, AND DISEASE
September–November 1988

Though a 1990s reevaluation of the role of Himalayan defor-estation in the repeated flooding of Bangladesh seemed to indicate that the loss of binding forest floor was not its overwhelming cause, the wholesale loss of forests in the foothills of India and Nepal undoubtedly contributed to the devastation of Bangladesh by the cyclone-induced flooding of September through November

1988. Five thousand died, half the population of the country was rendered homeless, and three quarters of Bangladesh disappeared under water.

Despite the words of Indian environmentalist and writer Bittoo Sehgal, that ". . . forest cover brakes the first burst of rains, giving people in the area of rainstorms or down-stream just those few minutes that are critical between life and being swept away in flash floods" (see India, Nepal, Pakistan, pp. 42–45), new evidence collected by the Inter-national Centre for Integrated Mountain Development in Katmandu and the UN Project in Nepal has led environ-mentalists to conclude that deforestation in the Himalayas had less to do with the regularly repeated tragedies of cata-clysmic flooding in Bangladesh than was originally thought. Although massive soil erosion does take place during the rainy season, it is also caused in great part by seismic activ-ity and consequent landslides created by the unstable youth of the Himalayas. A further cause for the terrible destruc-

City streets become canals, carrying people, debris, and disease during Bangladesh's monsoon season.
(CARE PHOTO)

that feed the rice paddies. By 1988, wholesale forest destruction, brought about by an increased population in Nepal that took down trees to provide wood fuel, had reached a peak.

Second, there had been a steady increase in population in Bangladesh itself between the 1974 flood disaster and 1988, with no change in the living or farming habits of this populace. The fact that one devastating flood every 4 years had become the norm in the past 40 years had done nothing to change living habits in Bangladesh.

Third, international cooperation among Bangladesh, India, Nepal, Bhutan, Tibet, and China was virtually impossible. Distrust and fear, particularly between India and China, prevented a sharing of technical assistance and the wisdom of experience with centuries of flooding from the Yangtze and Yellow Rivers.

Finally, 1988 was a particularly rainy year. The monsoon rains came early, and stayed. And then the multiple cyclones of August, September, and October struck. There was just too much water, too much wind for the frail structures and low-lying countryside of Bangladesh to absorb.

Villages like Nickhasia, in the Bhola district, disappeared along with their hundreds of inhabitants. Some refugees lived for days on the tin roofs of their homes; others climbed trees. But the trees often turned into lethal abodes when poisonous snakes, attempting to survive the flood, climbed them, too.

The floodwaters washed away entire settlements. In Bhola alone, 70,000 people lost their homes, their farms, their possessions, and all hope of making a living. Practically all of the livestock and crops of the entire country were destroyed.

With the floodwaters came pollution in the form of raw sewage. An estimated 3 million people became afflicted with diarrhea or dysentary; 5,000 died of this and drowning. When the floodwaters receded, half the population of the country was homeless and more than 85 percent were without work. Farms were untillable; factories and equipment were destroyed.

It was a tragedy of monumental proportions, made more so by the fact that Hurricane Gilbert, which struck Jamaica at exactly the same time, occupied the attention of world relief agencies. Japan finally came to the rescue, sending $13 million and rescue workers to Bangladesh, where they joined private and UN relief agencies in the mind-numbing task of rehabilitation.

When the monsoon season ended in January, several flood control studies were launched. All proved to be either too expensive, impractical, or unworkable. The French plan involved the construction, over 20 years, of 2,500 miles of embankments, 15 feet in height, along the three largest rivers of the Bangladesh delta. The cost: $10 billion.

Critics immediately asserted that since the combined discharge of the Ganges and Brahmaputra is two and a half times that of the Mississippi, the embankments would be

tion of these floods, conclude the new studies, is the interrelationship between the people of Bangladesh and its environment. In a country that is drastically overpopulated, achingly poor, and located below sea level, the studies note, this sort of environmental disaster is nearly inevitable.

Still, as Mr. Sehgal stated, the ecology of Bangladesh is so delicately poised, so thoroughly dependent upon undependable natural behavior, even a slight influence is enough to cause a cataclysm. All influences must be taken into account in order to develop plans to alleviate their effects. The horrible floods that inundated over three quarters of the country from September through November of 1988 were caused, not by one but by multiple circumstances.

First, there was the deforestation of the foothills of the Himalayas. During the monsoon season every year, huge quantities of rain pummel the countryside and wash silt and runoff water into the Brahmaputra, Ganges, and Meghna Rivers, and some 250 smaller, unnamed streams and rivers washed away by even a small increase in this water flow. Furthermore, the erection of high embankments would impede the movement of fish that breed in the rivers and then swim into the flooded paddy fields. These fish are then caught by inhabitants and form their main source of animal protein.

Still, some embankments were built in order to protect coastal paddy fields from seawater incursion. They lasted only until the next bout of cyclones, in 1991, when 260 miles of them collapsed, drowning more than 13,000 people and injuring half a million.

BANGLADESH
FLOOD, WATER POLLUTION, AND DISEASE
April 30, 1991
....

A staggering 131,000 residents of southeastern Bangladesh died, and an equally overwhelming 9 million were rendered homeless by floods during an eight-hour cyclone that struck on April 30, 1991. Thousands of survivors perished of water-borne diseases and starvation, swelling the effects of a disaster whose causes were multiple, and included upstream soil erosion, overpopulation, and poverty in a fledgling democracy.

What was termed the worst disaster of the 20th century befell Bangladesh in 1970. This was a disaster that, had it occurred before the industrial age, could only be blamed upon nature. But by the end of the 20th century, other forces had arisen to make the naturally threatened ecology of the region even more vulnerable to cataclysm—a vulnerability that made the disaster of 1991 nearly inevitable. There was, first of all, the continuing erosion, from logging, of the lower foothills of the Himalayas. Not as serious an environmental threat as it was once thought to be (see Bangladesh, pp. 15–17 and India, Nepal, Pakistan, pp. 42–45), it was nevertheless the source of silt that washed down the Ganges, Meghina, and Brahmaputra Rivers. This silt formed small islands in the Bay of Bengal and in estuaries of the rivers, which were increasingly inhabited by the population of the overcrowded Bangladesh, mainland.

As soon as grass began to sprout from the silt, squatters arrived, building mud and straw shacks, establishing homes from which they could pursue whatever industrial, fishing, or farm work they could find.

It was these inhabitants of the offshore and estuarial islands who suffered most dramatically at 6:30 P.M. on April 30, when the cyclone of 1991 arrived. For eight terrible hours, it pounded Bangladesh with winds of up to 145 mph—7 mph harder than those of the 1970 storm. Waves cresting at 20 feet thundered across the islands off the southeast coast of the country, demolishing everything on the islands, drowning their inhabitants and, in some cases, eradicating the islands themselves.

There was ample announcement of the storm's arrival. In Manpura, one of the islands off the ragged southern coastline 108 miles from the large city of Dhaka, cyclone warnings were sounded over megaphones and announced by beating drums.

Several hours before the cyclone hit, 20,000 of the island's 50,000 inhabitants sought safety in recently erected cyclone shelters. Built after the last great cyclone in 1985, they were buildings composed of concrete and set upon three-story-high columns. In Moghnama, a coastal village on the island of Maheshkhali, more than 3,500 women and children squeezed into a shelter built for 1,000. On several parts of the islands of Kutubdia and Maheshkhali, shelters were flooded with seven feet of water, forcing the refugees in them to ascend to the second floors of the structures. These people survived.

But others, who had heard 11 cyclone warnings prior to this one, none of which were followed by real storms, ignored the announcements. And so they perished, or survived miraculously, as Mufizur Rahman, of the island of Kutubdia did. "I saw waves as high as mountains coming at me," he told reporters afterward. When he first regained consciousness, hours after the waves hit, he called out for his wife and three daughters, but they had been swept into the sea by the waves.

Nearby, the husband of Rabeya Begum died from being bitten by a poisonous snake as he tried to snag a floating banana tree to convert into a makeshift raft for his infant son. In another part of the island, Shafi Alam managed to save one of his sons by tying him to a coconut tree, but six other members of his family drowned.

And so it went, through eight nightmare hours of relentless pounding by waves and winds that carried torrential rains sideways before them. The storm raced inland, and while it was still ravaging the coast, it unleashed mountain torrents that fed the rivers that ran like muddy veins through Bangladesh, swelling them so they flooded the bordering paddy fields long after the storm had abated.

The next day, the revealed destruction was appalling. "I saw deaths, devastation, agony, and misery of a magnitude I have never seen before," an Associated Press photographer who flew over the area wrote. Bodies by the thousands began to wash up on the beach. Five thousand fishermen, caught in the Bay of Bengal when the storm struck, were unaccounted for until their bodies began to appear along the coastline. For days, relatives picked their way through the sentried rows, trying to identify brothers, fathers, sons, and husbands.

The most heavily damaged stretch of the shoreline was near the seaside town of Cox's Bazar and on the nearby islands, where 95 percent of the houses were destroyed. Hospitals and schools that might have served as shelters for the homeless and treatment centers for the injured simply disappeared or were reduced to rubble. Rice fields, ready for

The mud and straw shacks that constitute shelter for farmers, fishermen, and squatters are destroyed annually by recurrent floods like the one that tore through southeastern Bangladesh in 1991.

(CARE PHOTO)

the harvest that was a mere week away, were filled with a mixture of brackish seawater and heavily polluted river water. The crops were ruined. Drinking water supplies were polluted and unusable. Roads no longer existed, nor did telephone lines.

In the port of Chittagong, eight ships, one of them belonging to the infinitesimal Bangladesh Navy, sank, blocking the only harbor that could accommodate large vessels with relief supplies.

On the morning after the cyclone, two light planes dropped dry food and clothing in plastic bags. There was no landing room for the planes anywhere in the area.

By the end of four days, almost no food supplies had reached Bangladesh, and now water-borne diseases—dysentery and cholera—and starvation began to add to the death toll.

"Babies are the first to die," wrote Barbara Crossette in the *New York Times*. "Everywhere—on the muddy shoulders of roads, in the remains of bamboo houses, on empty wind-torn patches that once were shelter—there are weeping mothers and fathers clinging to infants too weak to hold up their heads, cradling their children in the desperate hope that love might save their lives."

Helicopters hovered over some knots of survivors, attempting to drop plastic containers of water. Most of them exploded upon contact with the ground. And there were precious few of them. Bangladesh only owned six helicopters, and they and the men who flew them were taxed to the breaking point. When three C-130 cargo planes finally arrived from Saudi Arabia with food and medical supplies, members of the Bangladesh Air Force who had neither eaten nor slept in days fell upon some of the food, elbowing starving children out of the way. It was evident that poverty—of the people and the country—contributed in large degree to the burgeoning toll.

Outside help was desperately needed, but it was slow in coming. Famine in Africa and Kurdistan were stretching the resources of private relief agencies, and so it fell to the United Nations and CARE to take on the burden of relief for Bangladesh. This they did, with the help of some international private and religious agencies. The Salvation Army, the Catholic Relief Service, B'nai Brith, Church World Service, and the Save the Children Fund all collected money to buy and send food and medical aid.

On May 4, Mother Teresa arrived from Calcutta with 1,630 pounds of milk powder and biscuits, and the government of India, an unfriendly neighbor of Bangladesh, nevertheless offered $750,000 in aid and 3 helicopters.

Nature continued to thwart the rescuers. Foul weather interfered with relief efforts, and refugees, battling with poisonous snakes for whatever high ground was left, continued to die. Rotting livestock added to the pollution problem, and disease began to spread, particularly among the children. On the fifth day after the storm struck UNICEF arrived with plastic sheeting for shelters and oral-rehydration kits for the victims of diarrhea. But disaster continued to stalk the survivors. A CARE vessel, loaded with supplies for the offshore islands, capsized in the Bay of Bengal, drowning one of the CARE workers.

Some of the refugees from this and the 1988 cyclone wondered aloud if democracy helped or hindered them in times of crisis. The preceding military government of Lieutenant General H. M. Ershad had been more efficient in its relief efforts, they recalled, than the present democracy. And, under the former military regime, prices were kept under strict control so that the poorest could afford to restock their ruined rice crops and buy basic food. Within days of the 1991 flood, opportunists had driven up the price of rice by 30 percent.

This, however, with its death toll of 131,000 and millions made homeless, was, though not as severe as the tragedy of 1970, far worse than that of 1988, and once the waters receded, this was realized by the populace. But the continuing problems facing people who live under the threat of constantly returning cyclones had still not been squarely met—not by the government of Bangladesh, not by its people, not by international relief and environmental agencies. What was needed, and what is still needed, is systematic control of upper-river pollution; raised homes, schools, and roads; high-ground shelters; and environmentally sound embankments that will hold against the floods and still afford the people of Bangladesh an interchange between agriculture and nature that allows these people to live.

They will, it seems, never live well. There are too many people in a small part of the world that should never have been settled as thickly as it is today, and certainly not as it will probably be tomorrow.

BRAZIL
(AMAZON RIVER BASIN)
RAIN FOREST DESTRUCTION
1964–Present
....

Brazil continues to lead the world in rain forest destruction. From the 1970s through the 1980s, its forests, burned by ranchers, indigent farmers, miners, and road builders, were disappearing at a rate of 50 acres a minute. The murder of Chico Mendes in 1988 and new world awareness of the dramatic difference between the public pronouncements of the Brazilian government and the practices it permitted, slowed the destruction. But the present state of the Brazilian economy has allowed a steady upward creep of destruction of one of the last great repositories of biodiversity and a rich potential resource for medicines to facilitate world health.

"Is there a land in the temperate zone which can show, through all its length and breadth, the living beauty that exists in one acre of tropical jungle?"

So observed Royal Geographic Society Fellow Frederick Boyle, as he visited the Rajang, the tropical rain forest of Borneo, more than a hundred years ago. Had he lived until now, Boyle would have been struck dumb by the conditions in the Rajang and in all of what is left of the rain forests of the world.

Called recently by environmentally aware Prince Bernhard of the Netherlands ". . . the last great untouched ecosystem in the world . . . the product of tens of millions of years of undisturbed evolution," the rain forests of the world disappeared at the rate of 50 acres a minute from the 1970s through the 1980s. And had it not been for the dramatic and gruesome events in the Amazon region of Brazil in the late 1980s, this atrocious and irresponsible consumption of a vitally necessary resource might have continued unabated.

The world's tropical rain forests, located principally in Africa, New Guinea, Borneo, and Latin America, cover about 4 million square miles, an area a little larger than the United States. They account for approximately 7 percent of Earth's surface, but they harbor at least 40 percent of Earth's species.

Of the several reasons for the destruction of tropical rain forests (see Introduction, pp. vii–viii), the causes in Brazil center largely in the clearing of forests for agricultural and ranching purposes, the gathering of wood for fuel, and rapacious commercial timbering. But, as in each of the locations of the world's tropical forests, Brazil has its unique and dramatic characteristics.

The largest of the Latin American countries (it occupies half of the continent of South America) Brazil is a federation of 22 states, 4 territories, and Brasilia, the federal district and capital of the country. Latin America has more than half of the world's remaining tropical rain forest, and three-fifths of it is in Brazil, whose rain forests spread from the northeastern mouth of the Amazon River to the Andes on the west. The greatest, richest, and most exploited portions of them are to the west, in the large state of Amazonas, and the relatively smaller states of Acre, on the border of Peru, and Rondonia, which borders Bolivia.

For generations, this area, which makes up 42 percent of the land mass of Brazil but houses only 5 percent of its people, was ignored. But when a series of military upheavals culminated in the instituting of a military regime in 1964, the Amazon became the site of ambitious settlement programs. In order to move huge numbers of Brazilians from the impoverished northeast into the Amazon, roads were cut through the rain forest, leveling some 12,000 square miles of it and contributing mightily to the extinction of

indigenous tribes who had lived there for thousands of years. In fact, only 10 percent of the people alive in the forests at the beginning of the century still survive, and their numbers are shrinking, even as this is being written.

In the same way that generations of human beings, once destroyed, find it difficult to regenerate, the forest itself, once cleared, will not regenerate. The reason is explained in the cycle of birth and death and rebirth that takes place in it. Chemical nutrients are stored in the rain forest's vegetation, passing directly from decaying plants to live ones without entering the soil. Robbed of its protective cover, the earth quickly dries up and becomes useless for either planting or pasturage.

Furthermore, the forest itself induces half of its own moisture. Studies conducted in Panama, where forests were felled prior to 1960, showed that rainfall decreased one-third of an inch every year after the forests were destroyed.

Bright sunlight turns to twilight as the Brazilian rain forest burns. Robbed of its protective cover, the earth quickly dries up and becomes useless for either planting or pasturage.
(HERBERT GIRADET/STILL PICTURES)

What was once lush rain forest in Acre has been reduced to charred ruins by indiscriminate burning. Its misguided mission: to create pastures for cattle.
(UN PHOTO #157447/P. SUDHAKARAN)

Archaeological findings in 1990 showed that from the Pleistocene Age, 10,000 years ago, the rain forests of Brazil were farmed delicately and intelligently by the native peoples. Conventional crops were planted in reclaimed swamps and on alluvial plains along rivers. Yams, corn, manioc, and tubers were sown near burned trees felled to accommodate the small plots of planted crops.

But the planting only lasted for a few consecutive years, within the soil's capability of sustaining crops. Then, by degrees, the forest was allowed to encroach upon the area, bringing with it fruit trees, palms, medicinal herbs, and berries that attracted wildlife, which in turn was hunted for food. Thus, a cycle of life and death and regeneration was established and sustained, enough to support an agricultural economy that lasted until the 1500s, when Europeans colonized Brazil and destroyed its native culture.

Now, 20th-century destruction has accelerated, first with the large-scale slash-and-burn methods of modern farmers, then, in the last half of the century, by the methodical intensity of large agribusinesses, cattle ranchers, miners, and timber concerns collecting single-species hardwoods.

As for official inhibition of the wholesale slaughter of the environment, in 1964 the military government of Brazil declared that conservation was a luxury a developing nation could not afford.

And so, for 15 years, the rain forests of Brazil were fair game for agriculture, industry, and road builders. But by 1980, the world began to take notice of the accelerated destruction in Brazil. By 1985, international scientists, aware that the carbon dioxide collecting ability of forests was being eroded by their destruction, and the release of carbon into the atmosphere from burning forests was possibly contributing to global warming, made public their concerns. The government of Brazil was unresponsive.

But 1987 was a year of monumental changes. First, an international scientific expedition sanctioned by Brazil's National Institute for Space Research and partially funded by the U.S. National Aeronautics and Space Administration (NASA), arrived in the Brazilian rain forest to examine and measure its influence on atmospheric chemistry. The study concluded, with firm evidence, that the giant trees of the rain forest not only absorb carbon dioxide as they grow but also release it into the atmosphere when they burn or rot.

Furthermore, and equally important, these scientists found that although some plants in the forest soils and waters produced nitrous oxide—which can transform into an ozone destroyer in the upper atmosphere—they were outstripped by forest vegetation, which destroys ozone near the ground, where it is a pollutant. In other words, rain forests help to control the greenhouse effect by absorbing ozone and carbon dioxide.

"Burnings to clear forests and fields produced a lot of ozone in the dry season," concluded NASA's Dr. Robert Harris. "But the rain forest is unique in destroying the polluting ozone. When it comes in contact with a surface like a leaf, it oxidizes and is consumed."

And so, a direct role in controlling the greenhouse effect in rain forests was established.

But the most dramatic environmental change in Brazil occurred in the state of Acre. For centuries, rubber workers there depended upon the rain forest for a livelihood that peaked in the 1940s. Real rubber was still in international demand, and the tapping of the abundance of rubber trees provided a healthy living for these workers. But then, to compound the problem of the increasing popularity and practicality of synthetic rubber came the steady, relentless encroachment of large cattle ranches and the exacerbation of the construction of a huge highway. With the destruction of the rubber trees came the destruction of their sole source of support. By the 1980s, both would destroy enough of the rain forest in Acre to bring economic ruin to the rubber workers.

Mindful of the huge international trade in beef, the Brazilian government provided tax relief for cattle ranchers, and the road projects were widely seen as a quicker way to get the product to market. Between 1965 and 1983, 469 large cattle ranches, averaging 23,000 hectares each, were established in the Amazon region. (A hectare is equivalent to 2.5 acres.)

In September of 1987, Francisco Alves Mendes Filho (known as Chico Mendes), a rubber worker and president of the local rubber tappers union surrounding his native village of Xapuri, traveled to Washington to meet with environmental groups, and to lobby members of the U.S. Congress and the Inter-American Development Bank. His object was to require the Brazilian government to scale back its highway project through Acre and to persuade other international organizations to finance projects other than highways in Brazil. His plan was to substitute initiatives that, instead of cutting down trees, would make use of rubber, nuts, medicinal plants, and other products furnished by the rain forest itself.

A spokesman for the Inter-American Development Bank acknowledged that Brazil had not lived up to some of the environmental requirements of its loan contract,

including areas for rubber trees, and that if these requirements were not met, the loan would be reconsidered.

It was a victory for Mendes that was fraught with danger. Life, in fact, for all rubber workers in Brazil was a perilous experience. The small group of wealthy cattle ranchers in Brazil (in Acre, which is roughly the size of Illinois, a mere 130 people still own practically all of the land) made a practice of hiring gunmen, *pistoleiros,* who systematically murdered activists like Mendes. The reason: These activists sometimes organized groups of native peoples and rubber workers to block, with their bodies, bulldozers trying to clear land for the highways or for new ranches.

The landowners' terrorism campaign even had a name, *limpeza,* which, freely translated, means "cleaning." Cleaned land still fetches higher prices than uncleaned land for foreign logging or mining interests, and in the furtherance of this grim equation, Brazilian landowners have contracted, in the past 20 years, more than 1,600 killings of environmental activists, indigenous peoples, and rubber tappers.

Mendes had survived five attempts upon his life; the latest had occurred at a union meeting just before his departure for Washington. The would-be assassin had slipped on a loose board while climbing up the side of the union hall, and the noise had alerted those inside. But the gunman had escaped into the dark of the jungle.

Now, Chico Mendes had become an international figure. The United Nations Environment Programme presented him with the Global 500 Award for environmental protection. He was mentioned as a possible Nobel laureate. Though the union he headed in the small village of Xapuri had only 3,000 men, he became the de facto spokesman for 165,000 families making a living as rubber tappers in Brazil.

On the other side of the argument, the cattle ranchers stepped up their campaign of terror. Fourteen Tukano Indians, peacefully drifting in their canoes on the neutral Amazon, were shot by the gunmen of a local landowner. Immediately after the declaration of a forest preserve, four rubber tappers were killed by two large landowners, Darly and Alvarino Alves da Silva. Though the identity of these and other murderers was widely known, none was arrested.

As 1988 approached, further international pressure was put on Brazil and its president, Jose Sarney. At the end of June, largely through the efforts of Chico Mendes and international environmental groups, a meeting of delegates from 42 nations of the International Tropic Timber Organization was held in Rio de Janeiro. The two-year-old group brought together the producers of hardwoods and the wealthy nations who purchased them in hopes of bringing about an understanding that would preserve, rather than gut, rain forests.

By the end of its 10-day conference, the organization had adopted a plan that realized much of Mendes's pleas to establish a 247,000-acre preserve in Acre state, designed to study the rate at which forest products—rubber, nuts, spices, and medicinal plants—can be responsibly exploited or replanted, and to create companies to handle them.

This would be a small start, but it would take place in Acre, where hundreds of trees were felled daily, but only 5 percent were sold for lumber. The rest were burned, or left to rot.

In neighboring Rondonia, during that same summer of 1988, the torching of the rain forest reached epidemic proportions. A NASA satellite sensitive to heat sources reported 170,000 separate fires in the western Amazon during the preceding year. Estimates from NASA scientists stated that fully one-tenth of the global production of carbon dioxide, which contributes to global warming, was coming from these fires.

In Rondonia, as in Acre, cattle ranchers were responsible for 80 percent of the destruction. In addition to the ranchers, half a million new settlers had funneled into the Rondonian forest because of the construction of the Cuiba-Porto Velho road, which had been paved with a $250 million World Bank loan.

The loan had come with a stipulation that the forest and its tribes be protected. Obviously, the stipulation had been ignored, and when the road was completed, the area of forest destruction tripled.

By October 1988, the fires in the rubber-producing portions of the Amazonian rain forest had increased to 6,000 a day. To add to this, thousands of gold miners in the forest continued to leach ore containing mercury into its rivers. The 40 tons of this fearful poison that were dumped annually promised a lethal legacy as they worked their way through the food chain. But nothing was done to stop it, though President Sarney made public statements decrying "predatory development."

They were empty rhetoric. And now, Antonio Jose Guimaraes, the head of Brazil's Forest Service complained that he lacked the money, men, and helicopters to protect the forests, and Roberto Messias Franco, the head of the Secretariat for the Environment, resigned in angry frustration.

Then, on Thursday night, December 22, 1988, the incident that would, if not halt, at least inhibit the destruction and forever change the attitude of the world toward its rain forests occurred.

It happened at the end of a particularly bloody autumn and early winter. Six rubber tappers in Acre had been gunned down between September and December. On December 6, a state legislator in the Amazon town of Belem who had defended landless peasants revealed in a speech that he had received death threats. That same night, he was murdered in his garage.

On the ninth of December, at a meeting of his union, Mendes said, "If a messenger came down from heaven and guaranteed that my death would strengthen our struggle, it would even be worth it. But experience teaches us the opposite. Public rallies and lots of funerals won't save the Amazon. I want to live."

To assure this, Mendes employed two armed guards to remain with him wherever he went and to stay in his four-room shack on Dr. Batista da Moraes Street, five minutes from the town square and 40 paces from the police station. This spartan living space was, as Andrew Revkin described it in his book about Chico Mendes, *The Burning Season*, "little bigger than a single-car garage, raised on stilts 2 feet off the tamped, grassless soil. . . . As with most of the houses in town, the only running water was in the outhouse in the backyard."

At 5:00 P.M. on the night of December 22, Mendes and the two bodyguards assigned to him by the military police sat at his kitchen table, playing dominoes. On the television set in the living room was *Anything Goes*, one of Brazil's most popular soap operas.

At 6:00 P.M., his wife Ilzamar asked them to stop, so that she could set the table for dinner. They reluctantly concluded the game, then moved to the living room to watch the end of *Anything Goes*.

Dinner was set out, and the guards who were not required to stay with Mendes after dark, but, since they were friends, too, sat down to eat. It was unbearably hot in the house. One of the guards had shut the blinds for safety's sake, and Mendes decided he would go to the outhouse to throw some cold water on his face.

He opened the back door. It was engulfingly dark in his backyard, and he went back to the bedroom to get a flashlight.

Near a palm tree, opposite the outhouse, two men crouched in the brush. One was Darly Alves da Silva; the other was his son Darcy. The Alves clan had come north to Acre from the state of Parana in 1974 to occupy a 10,000-acre cattle ranch. They trailed a long history of murder, beginning from the time they began their travels from state to state in the early 1950s.

They had already threatened Chico Mendes. In September, a lawyer working with the tappers had unearthed a 15-year-old arrest warrant for murder from the family's earlier days in the south. Darly Alves da Silva and his brother Alvarino were forced to go into hiding.

On the night of December 22, Chico Mendes opened the back door a second time, and swept the backyard with the beam from his flashlight. Simultaneously, a shotgun blast erupted from the undergrowth. It hit Mendes in the chest, and spun him around, toward the bedroom. He collapsed and died almost immediately in the arms of one of his guards. The other leaped through a window and sprinted toward the military barracks for help. Ilzamar ran into the street screaming, "They've killed Chico!" but her screams failed to move the group of policemen in the sheriff's office 40 paces away. They remained where they were, otherwise and studiously occupied.

Rubber worker and activist Chico Mendes's home. It was here that he was murdered by rancher Darly Alves da Silva and his son Darcy. The assassination became a worldwide outrage, finally forcing the Brazilian government to enforce its own environmental—and criminal—laws.
(CAMPBELL PLOWDEN/GREENPEACE)

The rest of the world would not be as unmoved. More than a thousand people braved torrential rains to attend Chico Mendes's funeral on Christmas Day. That same evening, Brazil's Roman Catholic Church accused the government of President Jose Sarney of adopting policies that could lead to the extinction of the Yanomami Indian tribe by allowing gold prospectors to overrun their homeland.

The following day, Darcy, Darly Alves da Silva's son, turned himself into police, confessing that he had hired a professional assassin to kill Chico Mendes.

Worldwide, editorial writers seized upon the murder of Mendes to plead the cause for the Brazilian rain forest. Their indignation coincided with new findings that emissions of carbon dioxide into the atmosphere had increased, in the 1980s alone, from 1.5 billion tons to more than 5 billion tons annually, thus contributing mightily to the admittedly disputed Greenhouse effect (see Introduction, p. vii, and unit II, pp. 71–132).

On December 27, in the *New York Times*, Tom Wicker brought the blame home to the United States, zeroing in on the importing of Brazilian beef, and decrying the "rising demand in the United States for cheap beef to make the Big Macs and Whoppers on which the new fast-food industry [is] thriving." It would not be long before Burger King would publicly sever its ties with the Brazilian cattle industry.

In Brazil, President Sarney, mindful of the international implications of remaining silent, ordered a rapid investigation of Mendes's murder. Romeo Tuma, national head of the federal police, visited Acre personally. It was, according to environmentalists, a paper turnaround. Repeated telegrams to Mr. Tuma during the previous month, warning of threats upon Mendes's life, had gone unanswered. Now, four arrests were made, and Darcy Alves da Silva revised his story to an admission that he had personally shot Chico Mendes. Police were skeptical.

In January 1989, a fact-finding mission arriving in Brazil from the United States received a warm welcome from environmentalists and rubber tappers, a plea for help in opening up tropical hinterlands to development from businessmen, and a statement from President Sarney that Brazil would not permit its sovereignty to be threatened by a foreign role in protecting the Amazon. Besides, he added, the industrialized nations had no right to criticize Brazil, since they had destroyed much of their own environment and were responsible for most of the world's pollution. In that accusation, President Sarney had some justification (see USA, Alaska, pp. 52–55).

Meanwhile, a gothic drama was playing itself out in Acre. A local judge indicted Darly Alves da Silva as one of the instigators of Chico Mendes's murder, and his son Darcy as the killer. Armed guards were immediately assigned to protect the judge. A week earlier, the son of the chief state prosecutor had been kidnapped by hooded men, who later released him near the Alves ranch. At the same time, one of the reportedly 30 mistresses who lived with Darly Alves da Silva committed suicide by cutting her own throat. Before killing herself, she told others that she was frightened of Darly Alves da Silva because she had given information about him to the police. Now, with the indictment, three other union leaders received death threats and police bodyguards.

Internationally, pressure began to build against Brazil. The World Bank and the Inter-American Development Bank postponed several loans vital to Brazil for highways and energy production, through the building of dams on the Amazon. West Germany, Japan, the Netherlands, and the United States offered "debt-for-nature swaps," deals that would buy off a portion of Brazil's $115 billion foreign debt and channel the funds toward environmental protection measures.

In February, the Brazilian government announced that it would be willing to accept international funds to protect the rain forests of the Amazon, provided that they were supervised by the Brazilian government. It was a major policy reversal that was in no way universally endorsed within the military-industrial-political structure of Brazil. General Leonidas Pires Goncalves, the army minister, lashed out against "that tiresome grinding on and on" about forest destruction. "Those who think they can exercise influence over the Brazilian Amazon are deceiving themselves," he said.

He apparently meant what he said. By the end of the month, much to the consternation of environmentalists worldwide, Brazil was negotiating with Japan to build a new highway link from Rio Brando, at the border between Acre and Rondonia, across Acre northward and westward across the Andes to Pucalipa, in Peru, where it would join the Peruvian highway to the seacoast city of Lima, the gateway to Asia from South America.

Opposing this was a tough decision for the rubber tappers of Acre. Transportation was primitive at best within their state, and a highway would help them to get their products of latex and nuts to market. But they were also mindful of the catastrophe of building highway BR 364 over which more than a million migrants had moved through Mato Grosso and Rondonia, razing the jungle along its 880-mile route.

Acre governor Flaviano Melo, an environmentalist who had negotiated the contract with Japan, and Thomas Lovejoy of the Smithsonian Institution, who visited Rio Branco, tried to allay these fears. "In many ways, this may be Brazil's last opportunity to show they can do things right in the Amazon by putting in the proper protection beforehand," he stated, adding in qualification, "if not, it could be a final turning point. If 40 percent of the Amazon is deforested, the rest may unravel."

The seesaw of conflicting actions continued to rise and fall, as other projects were announced. A five-day meeting of world environmentalists, organized by the Kaiapo Indians and blessed by Pope John Paul II, was convened to oppose a big dam planned for the Xingu River, a tributary of the Amazon in the northeast, and the result was the Charter of Altamira, vowing to protect the rain forests. On the other hand, the 4 percent of the rain forests that still existed on the eastern coast of Brazil, thousands of miles from Acre, were being systematically torched. More than 74,000 acres burned along a 420-mile stretch of coast, most set by local politicians and developers. As in Acre, those who opposed them were threatened with death by hired gunmen.

Now the Brazilian government joined in the complex of contradiction. Obtaining the concurrence of Bolivia, Colombia, Ecuador, Guyana, Peru, Suriname, and Venezuela, it issued a joint statement denouncing foreign pressure to save rain forests and averring that none of the seven countries would take orders from abroad concerning their environmental policies.

In order to enhance its image and erase from public memory the fact that its subsidies of more than $1 billion to ranchers and settlers had resulted in massive deforestation between 1975 and 1986, the Brazilian government announced a new environmental program slated to take effect in April. It included drastic changes in the tax system, which had favored ranchers, miners, and loggers, a ban on deforestation for agriculture and cattle, controls on the sale of mercury, and the enlistment of the army and air force in the coming dry season to diminish fires set by ranchers to clear—and often increase—their land.

As to the trans-Acre highway: Japan had cooled on the idea; President Bush offered American aid; Brazil declared that it was a national priority and would be built with or without foreign financing and interference.

All of this added up to a setback for the rubber tappers, who seemed to themselves to be the only ones in the world dedicated to saving the rich resources of the rain forests, which, they pointed out to visiting journalists, provided not only latex and Brazil nuts (harvested from January to March and their main source of income now) but also medicinal herbs and plants—leaves that could numb a toothache and trees whose resin could seal a skin wound or an ulcer—and for food, wild honey, soursop, cashew, and banana and jackfruit trees.

"But," said Pedro Rocha, a tapper, "the ranchers want empty land. We want more forest reserves. It still rains death threats in Xapuri."

On the conflict raged throughout the month of April. A group of Latin American intellectuals, meeting in Mexico City, issued a proclamation indicting, in no uncertain terms, the government of Jose Sarney for "massive deforestation" and other "acts of barbarism." Brazil's nationalistic stand against foreign intervention was dismissed out of hand. "To invoke national security to justify crimes against nature seems to us to be puerile and dishonest," the statement noted. "Ecocide and ethnocide cannot be excused with chauvinist, jingoist words and sentiments," it continued. "We, as Latin Americans, would like to see you, with your love for national sovereignty, defend the Amazon from local and foreign predators."

Almost simultaneously, while continuing its nearly xenophobic defense of its right to control its own environment by denouncing foreign interference and ruling out debt-for-nature swaps, the Sarney administration released details of a $100 million, five-year program designed to zone the 1.9 million square mile forest basin for "economic and ecological use." Financed partially by the United Nations Food and Agriculture Organization ("We accept international aid but we don't accept conditions," stated President Sarney) the program involved 49 environmental decrees, including new parks and investments of $76 million in localized environmental programs.

While pointing out holes in the plan that still allowed massive exploitation of the forest, governments of the world evinced cautious and realistic optimism. They had not forgotten Chico Mendes—an Italian environmental group sustained a movement for a Nobel prize for him; filmmakers from Brazil, Europe, and the United States chose the meeting of the National Council of Rubber Tappers to approach his wife, Ilzamar, about making a film of the life and death of her husband. (A Brazilian company was awarded the contract; eventually an original HBO movie was also made.)

The months went by, and the dry season arrived in Brazil. The rate of the burning of the forest slowed because of three factors: suspension (but not total loss) of tax incentives for the ranchers; enforcement of the relative inviolability of the new preserves; and the 1988 dry season, which was not very dry (it in fact rained during a considerable part of it).

International studies of the Amazon rain forest continued through the end of 1989. The extraordinary diversity of it was revealed in one joint Brazilian and American study: identified were 320 different species of birds, 800 species of trees, and 460 species of butterflies. It was a veritable garden of biodiversity.

In December 1989, new elections were held in Brazil, and the government of Jose Sarney was replaced by another, headed by Fernando Collor de Mello. A conservative, whose strongest backing came from Amazonian states, where miners, loggers, and ranchers were most powerful, Mr. Collor gave Brazil's environmental movement little with which to be happy.

In March, shortly before the inauguration of Mr. Collor, Fernando Mesquita, the head of the Government Institute of Environment and Renewable Natural Resources, stepped down. He had, under Sarney, done heroic work despite a possibly purposeful lack of support from the government he represented. In a country that had no fire-fighting airplanes whatsoever, he had managed to impose $10 million in fines for illegal burning, shelve 5,000 applications for deforestation by burning, and had established a 1.2 million–acre reserve to be managed along the lines advocated by Chico Mendes. He was interviewed by reporters as he left office. "While we have been talking," he said, "hundreds of trucks have carried illegal logs, hundreds of lumberjacks have been cutting trees in nature reserves. Our budget is small and our needs are great."

But again, the seesaw tilted. Surprising everyone, president-elect Collor de Mello appointed Jose Antonio Lutzenberger, a pioneer conservationist, to the newly created post of secretary of environment. Lutzenberger was a man who, for two decades, had assailed the Brazilian government over the burning of the forest, uncontrolled use of pesticides, and invasions of Indian lands.

Equally as stunning as the appointment was the concession that was made in order to achieve it: President Collor agreed to abandon the building of the Acre-spanning highway designed to transport hardwood from the western Amazon to Peru's Pacific ports. "The only people really interested in the road are the Japanese wood industry [sic]," said Mr. Lutzenberger, after his appointment. "It would be disastrous for the Amazon." It seemed that Brazil's sorry record of rain forest destruction and violence, which had earned it the unenviable title of third-largest creator of greenhouse gases in the world, behind the United States and the Soviet Union, was about to be amended.

Now, in December 1990, the trial of the Alves da Silvas, father and son, was about to begin. That it had come to trial at all was something of a miracle. First, Darcy recanted his original confession and was remanded, with his father and brother Oloci, to the Rio Branco penitentiary. Hardly a maximum-, or even minimum-, security prison, it possessed only 10 guards to oversee 240 prisoners. At night, one guard stood duty.

The Alves da Silvas had a color television set and most of the amenities they desired in their cell. That they desired to stay at all was their choice; the going price for an escape in 1989 was $800. In August, Darly's nephew, in prison on a murder conviction, joined 20 other prisoners who walked away from the prison while the guards watched Brazil play Chile in a soccer match on television.

Finally, the Alves da Silvas' patience ran out. On December 30, 1989, Darly and Oloci overpowered a guard and took his pistol. Then, with two other revolvers that had been smuggled in to them, they walked through the front gate of the prison. But Darcy, only 59 years old, was chronically ill and could barely walk. They had chosen the wrong time, and the authorities had no other choice but to recapture them.

They remained in prison until the trial, confident that there would be no trial. Potential jurors had been suitably terrorized by their fellow ranchers. But, astonishingly, a jury appeared. And even more astonishingly, Darcy Alves da Silva reversed himself again, and announced, to the surprise of the courtroom and his own attorneys, "I killed Chico Mendes." His father, however, maintained his innocence.

Four days later, Darly Alves da Silva was convicted of planning Mendes's murder, and his son was convicted of firing the shotgun that killed the union leader as he stood in the back door of his house on the night of December 22, 1988. Each received a 19-year sentence. It was a clear reversal of the tradition of ignoring the other, more powerful, tradition in Brazil of ranchers killing and intimidating with impunity those who opposed them.

Why was a conviction possible? International interest in the outcome of the case certainly played a role. But internally, it seemed to be a direct consequence of overreaching, and of a deep-seated tunnel vision among the ranchers. On the very night of the verdict they killed Indians without, apparently, feeling a shred of either guilt or remorse. To them, Chico Mendes was an indigent peasant, not—as he was to the rest of the world—an international symbol.

Still, from this point onward, the momentum in Brazil seemed to be with the environmental movement. Jose Antonio Lutzenberger, who had been a friend of Mendes, was actually enforcing the inviolability of the three extractive reserves—in Acre, Rondonia, and the eastern Amazon state of Amapa—that were decreed during the final week of the Sarney administration.

Shortly after his inauguration, President Collor had accompanied Lutzenberger on a helicopter tour to witness firsthand the devastation wrought by miners on the forest. After seeing the dozens of airstrips that ranchers and miners had built at the expense of the forest, he told Romeo Tuma, still the federal police chief, "Dynamite them, and be quick about it."

However, three months later, when Collor came to Washington to boast a bit about his environmental policies and to lobby Congress for money to implement them, it was pointed out to him that not only were the airstrips still in place, but up to 8,000 gold miners had reinvaded the lands of the Yanomami Indians. He professed surprise and promised that the miners would be expelled and the dynamiting would begin in earnest.

Collor pressed his suit by noting that he had now abolished the tax subsidies that had heretofore made cutting down the forest profitable, and that he would now allow $100 million of Brazilian debt to be exchanged every year for financing for environmental projects.

His presence was persuasive. The West German government soon joined the United States in proposing an ambitious Amazon project that would cost $1.6 billion over a five-year period. The project would create a massive Amazon reserve in which business would be restricted or banned, and new ways would be found to find environmentally sound work for ranchers, farmers, prospectors, loggers, and other exploiters of the rain forest and the Amazon.

Back in Brazil, however, environmentalists charged that President Collor had not followed through with his promises to demarcate native lands and had slashed money appropriated for Amazon preservation projects. In Acre, the conviction of Darly Alves da Silva was overturned on appeal, but he was retained in the state penitentiary because of murder charges from earlier years, when he lived in the south of Brazil.

In 1992, the first Earth Summit was scheduled to take place in Rio de Janeiro. It was encouraging, perhaps a public sign that times, for all the difference between presidential rhetoric and rain forest reality, had changed in Brazil.

Or had they?

There had been a 63 percent drop in annual deforestation rates since 1985, from 11,580 square miles of destruction to 4,229 square miles, or an area roughly the size of Delaware. That was a positive sign. But scientists in Brazil and the United States warned that the dramatic decline was due, not to a concerted concern for the environment, but to a series of other causes. Certainly, the suspension and then abolishment of tax incentives for ranchers and increased fines levied against violators of forest laws were laudable government factors. But two others—increased rainfall during the dry season and most important, the precipitous decline in Brazil's economy—were not.

The last factor was a particularly thorny problem. The economic decline had hit the rubber tappers particularly hard. Life had never been easy for them. From 1890 to 1911, the Amazon had been the domain of the rubber barons, who treated their workers like serfs and drove rubber prices high enough to prompt the British to sneak rubber tree seedlings to Ceylon and Malaya.

The insatiable demands for rubber by the Allies in World War II and the unavailability of Asian rubber gave the industry in Brazil a huge boost upward. But now, in 1992, the bottom had again dropped out of the market, and Asia was supplying the world with just about all it needed of rubber.

The jungle was full of skilled tappers who had been recruited by the United States and Brazil during World War II and who were promised lifetime pensions for the work they did. Neither government had paid out the promised pensions.

Settlers still flooded into the rain forest; loggers' roads were still begun; opponents of the despoilment like Pedro Ramos, a state representative of the National Council of Rubber Tappers, were visited in their offices and beaten up by hired goons.

Finally, the inevitable end to the Chico Mendes story occurred. Darly and Darcy Alves da Silva were now living high in the Acre state penitentiary. Their cells were outfitted with a color television, a refrigerator, a freezer, a stove, and a radio. They had overnight visiting rights with women, which resulted in the birth of a baby boy to Darly and one of his paramours, Maragareth Goes.

With the Earth Summit bringing world publicity to Brazil, their high-living, state-subsidized presence was proving to be an embarrassment for the authorities, and the two were slated to be moved to a facility in the south of Brazil, which was less posh and more secure.

But the move never took place. On Monday, February 15, 1993, father and son and seven other prisoners sawed through some rickety bars in the Acre penitentiary and jogged to a waiting pickup truck. They were last seen headed toward the Bolivian border.

The search for the escapees was halfhearted at best. Romildo Magalhaes, Acre's governor, did not even abbreviate his summer vacation on a South Atlantic beach to supervise it. And as of this writing, neither father nor son has been found.

The burning of the Brazilian forests goes on. In September 1993, astronauts, peering out of the windows of the Discovery space shuttle, commented publicly on the fact that Brazil was obscured by wood smoke. Brazil shot back that the 111,000 fires that burned in Brazil that month had taken place in existing pastureland.

The destruction of species of insect, animal, and plant life in the Brazilian rain forest continues. But the moratorium by the World Bank on further road construction along the Amazon also continues. New findings in 1993 removed some of the force of environmentalists' preservation arguments when it was confirmed that the burning of rain forests contributes less to the greenhouse effect than the burning of fossil fuels.

Meanwhile, the economy of Brazil continues to sputter, and the lives of the followers of Chico Mendes and his successor, Antonio Macedo (who has survived three assassination attempts so far and travels with a bodyguard) grow worse. Until 1994, a living was possible for rubber tappers. But in 1995, the bottom dropped out of both the rubber and Brazil nut markets. Though today there are some scattered companies in the world, such as the U.S.'s Deja Shoe, who still buy Brazilian latex, not many do. Even Brazilian manufacturers import Asian latex. New warehouses built after Mendes's death are empty.

Photographer-journalist Bill Gann, exploring the rain forest for a magazine article in 1995, half-jokingly suggested that "with the right marketing, Amazonian rubber could give some manufacturers the competitive edge: California surfers could boast that their wet suits were made of 'like, you know, Amazon rubber.'"

Still, the stark reality is that this rubber cannot compete with Asia's, and so the possibility exists that the Indians and rubber tappers who preserved the rain forest in Brazil will soon cease to exist. For now, there are those in Brazil like Chico Mendes was, and like Antonio Macedo is, who know and will do everything they possibly can to preserve it. "Enter the forest respectfully," he told Gann, then turned to the river within it. "Let the water know you are in harmony with it and nothing will hurt you. Put your hands flat. Raise your arms to the sky, and the water will know your spirit."

CANADA
(BRITISH COLUMBIA, FERNIE)
FOREST FIRE
August 1–3, 1908

A forest fire that began in the Rocky Mountains in the extreme southeast portion of British Columbia in July 1908 was ignited by heavy winds on August 1. In a three-day rampage, it destroyed the town of Fernie completely, threatened several other nearby settlements, killed 74, and caused $10 million in damage.

For the entire month of July 1908, the forest floor in the Crows Nest section of British Columbia smoldered. Small fires rose and died in this extreme southeastern corner of the province, just across Crows Nest Pass from Alberta and north of Idaho and Montana.

The countryside was extremely mountainous, its peaks jutting up several thousand feet, its settlements in the Kootenay valley, a natural bowl nestling within the mountain range. Above the ground, lush forests coated the mountainsides; beneath the ground, the huge stores of coal that brought a determined prospector named Fernie to the area in 1863 had turned the countryside into one vast million-dollar mining industry.

Fernie had made his way north from Butte, Montana, and returned, half-starved and haggard, several months later with wild stories of limitless coal waiting for the taking. His tales were generally thought to be the ravings of a man who hadn't eaten in a while, but Fernie was determined. He formed a mining company and convinced several other down-at-the-heels prospectors from Montana, Idaho, and Colorado mining camps to buy shares at—appropriately—rock-bottom prices.

Forty-five years later, historian W. A. Fraser would write, "It has been said of Fernie that he sat down on a lump of coal and made a million." Fernie made more than that, once he convinced businessman James J. Hill, Toronto senator Robert Jaffray, and Sir William Van Horne that the Canadian Pacific Railway should connect the area to the outside world.

From that point forward, the growth of the valley was explosive. The town of Fernie was its center; Cove Creek and Hosmer soon formed around the burgeoning mines that, by 1908, were producing between 2,000 and 3,000 tons of bituminous coking coal a day. Experts predicted that if the oven capacity of the mines were increased four times, the supply would last a thousand years.

The town of Fernie, with a population of between 6,000 and 7,000 people, had gained a reputation as a thriving little city with a hard luck streak. In its early years, it was burned out twice by careless miners. In 1901, 123 men lost their lives nearby in a Crows Nest Pass Coal Company mine. Nevertheless, in the spring of 1908, a brand-new post office and custom house, costing $40,000, were begun. By late July, they were nearly complete. The simmering, smoking forest floor in the impenetrable underbrush of the mountains to the east was an annoyance but not a perceivable danger.

And then, on the morning of August 1, the forest floor suddenly erupted into an inferno. Fed by sudden winds from the west, it scurried up the 3,000-foot peaks and, early that afternoon, like an army of fiery skiers, plunged toward the Kootenay valley's mines, settlements, and settlers. Flames leaped from tree to tree until a solid sheet of flame, 100 miles in length, roared into the village of Fernie, igniting every building, and sending its inhabitants scurrying for their lives. It all happened so quickly, a fire guard could not be formed, and the residents of Fernie simply took to the fields, left everything behind, and ran for their lives.

The Fort Steele Brewery was the first large building to go, and it then ignited every house in its neighborhood. The Elk River Lumberyard exploded in flames, wiping out the homes neighboring it.

Individual tales spread as rapidly as the flames. In one part of the town, a crippled elderly woman was carried for a short distance by two relatives, until the heat became so intense she begged to be left behind. She was wrapped in wet blankets and laid down gently in a front yard, where she burned to death.

In West Fernie, another elderly woman collapsed of a heart attack as she was leaving her front gate. Neighbors risked their own lives to bury her before they left and headed toward the bridges over the Elk River. By the time they reached them, they had been burned through, the charred corpses of those who had tried to outrace the flames still astradle some of the timbers that had not been consumed.

Clumps of refugees waded from the riverbanks to the Canadian Pacific tracks, where a hastily assembled train took scores of hysterical people aboard. The train was then cleared when it was learned that the railroad bridge between Hosmer and Michel had been burned out.

By that night, between 5,000 and 7,000 refugees were camped on a small prairie three miles south of Fernie. Flaming cinders, carried by the wind, continued to rain on them, even as the wind began to die down.

The next morning, residents worked their way back to their devastated town. Hardly a house stood, and those that did were uninhabitable. The Canadian Pacific Railroad station, a score of coal bunkers, its water tank, its freight store, and 100 railroad cars had burned to oblivion. Over 25 million feet of manufactured lumber was gone, and a half million tons of coke went up in flames in the railroad yards. Not a store, not a bank, not a hotel, not a business stood. The new post office and custom house had been burned to their foundations. All that was left of the town of Fernie was the Great Northern train station and water tank, and the concrete warehouse of Trito's Lumber Company.

Meanwhile, the fire continued eastward, following the tracks of the Canadian Pacific Railroad. Small fires started in the town of Michel, but the local firefighters had had a warning, and put out most of them. In Hosmer, a magazine holding dynamite for the mining operations around it blew up spectacularly as the flames reached it, but, miraculously, the town itself escaped extensive damage.

Through the night of August 2, the air was filled with fragments of burning wood and bark, while sheets of flame played across the hills above the valley. "It seemed as if the very air were on fire," reported an exhausted firefighter from Michel who had watched as two of his companions were incinerated.

The forest around the towns burned unchecked. Thousands of acres of pine, spruce, cedar, and redwood, surrounded by enormous undergrowth, continued to burn, but now, with the dying of the wind, the fire began to diminish. It continued eastward, out of the valley, into the uninhabited brush to the east, where it slowly began to burn itself out, until, on August 10, fresh northwest winds began to reawaken it. Banff, Kimberly, Marysville, Sullivan, and Portous, with a combined population of between 2,000 and 3,000, were threatened. Refugees were trapped in the towns because an engineers' strike at Cranbrook prevented the dispatching of an escape train.

A wind change on the 15th, however, saved the towns, though the Sullivan Lumber Company was destroyed.

Meanwhile, at Fernie, the residents started to drift back, and the clearing of the ruins began. There were few women and children; they had taken trains provided by the Great Northern Railroad to Cranbrook. Seventy-four known dead would be reported, though some of the miners who disappeared near the mines in the hills would never be counted.

The damage to the burned-out town and surrounding forest would exceed $10 million.

But Fernie would be rebuilt, and signs that, even in tragedy, the distrust among ethnic groups that characterized the frontier became immediately apparent. On August 2, while the fires were still visible from the ruined town, concern rose that the Slavs, employed in the mines to do labor the other miners refused, might make trouble. Officials in Fernie requested that all the guns and leg irons that could be sent from Cranbook be dispatched immediately. The message was received, and a special train was sent from Cranbrook bearing all the guns that could be rounded up. Life was back to normal.

CANADA
(NORTHERN ONTARIO)
FOREST FIRE
July 28–31, 1916

....

One hundred and eighty-four settlers, farmers, prospectors, and workers in the paper mills of the towns along the Abitibi River in Northern Ontario lost their lives in a gigantic, three-day forest fire that raged from July 28 to July 31, 1916. The origin of the fire was never proved, though informed speculation blamed it on careless campers.

A forest fire roared out of the wilderness south of James Bay and along the Abitibi River in Northern Ontario on July 28, 1916, annihilating settlers' encampments—most of which serviced the Abitibi Power and Paper Company, Ltd., a sprawling business devoted to lumbering and pulp making—laying waste to nearby towns and destroying scattered farms in a three-day conflagration.

The fires began as smoldering undergrowth fires, a normal occurrence customarily ignored by the settlers. But this July, the smoldering, fed, in some unsubstantiated postmortems, by careless campers, burst into raging flames.

Still, the vast majority of settlers in the French Canadian conclaves of Nushka, Matheson, Cochrane, Iroquois Falls, Ramore, and Porcupine Junction, and prospectors at Tashota and Kowcash treated the fire more as an annoyance than an imminent calamity. As a result, many were trapped in their homes as the flames encircled farms and settlements, cutting off escape on every side.

The score of frame buildings and stores at Nushka caught fire on the afternoon of the 28th, as did those in nearby Monteith. Residents who tried to escape were walled in by fire, and 98 perished in the resulting inferno.

At Matheson, 34 residents were burned to death trying to reach the railroad station. It and two houses were all that remained of the settlement after the fire swept through it.

Residents of Cochrane were more fortunate. Lake Abitibi served as a refuge for some, and the Temiskaming &

Northern Ontario Railway carried others south. The town fared far worse; only two streets survived.

By the night of the 29th streams of refugees, their clothing burned, their farms and dwellings consumed, began to pour into the southern towns of Cobalt, Haileybury, and Englehart.

A relief train with physicians, nurses, and supplies aboard set out on the 30th from Cobalt but only traveled a little north of Englehart. The long trestle bridge over the Blanche River there was totally burned out.

Finally, on the evening of July 31, rain began to fall over the entire area, and the fires sputtered and died. The heavy rains turned the ashes of burned-out buildings into black mud. In South Porcupine, the sawmill burned to the ground, and although most of Iroquois Falls was incinerated, one store and the paper mills remained, untouched. Several hundred square miles of farmland and bush were reduced to ashes, and 184 residents were burned to death.

CHINA
(HANKOW-HAN-YANG-WU-CH'ANG AREA)
FLOOD
August 1954

....

An inadequately designed dam meant to contain the flood stages of the Yangtze River collapsed under torrential rains and river waters that reached a record 97.51 feet of depth in August 1954. More than 40,000 drowned, and more than a million were rendered homeless by the worst flood in China since 1931.

Approximately 41.6 percent of China's total food output in 1954 consisted of rice. Forty percent was composed of millet, corn, kaoliang, and potatoes; 10 percent was wheat.

In 1953, there was a wheat blight in north-central China as a result of a series of natural calamities, including unseasonable frost, insect and pest infestations, and hailstorms.

And so, there was a more than average dependence upon the rice crop of China that year—to carry out the lagging agricultural component of the first part of a five-year industrialization plan, and to feed the populace.

But once more, nature, neglect, and bad choices would conspire to make matters considerably worse. The rich and abundant rice fields of the Hankow-Han-yang-Wu-ch'ang triangle have always had a double-edged meaning to their inhabitants. During normal cycles of flood and withdrawal of the Yangtze River, they form the heart of the food supply for much of China. But they are flood plains. Their soil content results from flooding. And nature does not ration its floods.

Thus, for millennia, rice farmers have been alternately made wealthy or destitute by the monsoon seasons and cruel capriciousness of the Yangtze, the sixth largest river in the world.

Between April and July of 1954, the heaviest rainfall in a hundred years swelled the Yangtze and Hwai Rivers to overflowing and beyond. Dikes built by Communist workers after the takeover of China in 1948 had been raised to a height of 98 feet—more than ample, their builders felt, to contain the most extreme floods of the Yangtze. The great flood of 1931, after all, had only reached a height of 92.76 feet.

In addition, under the guidance of leading Chinese Communist architect Chien Chen-ying, 3 million workers constructed a Soviet-style dam above the region.

But both proved inadequate. As the rains fell and the river rose, human walls were pressed into service to reinforce crumbling dikes. In Hupeh Province, toward the end of July, 200 soldiers and 10,000 peasants stood together with mats on their backs for three hours, forming a human wall while other workers thickened and strengthened a portion of dike.

During the first week of August, strong winds began to raise the river waters even higher, breaking through dikes, reducing them to sand. An inland sea the size of Indiana formed over the region, and was spotted by Japanese diplomats flying home from conferences in Peiping (Peking). The government of China, which, until that time had downplayed the flood, was forced to admit imminent catastrophe.

By August 3, floodwaters had reached a height of 95.5 feet in Wuhan, in central China. A week later, they had climbed to 96.06 feet, surpassing heights reached in 1931.

Sometime during the middle of August (the official government news agency kept a tight lid on details) the new dam gave way. Designed in the Soviet way, entirely above the ground, it was no match for the Yangtze, and now, at 5:00 P.M. on August 18, the flood crest rose to 97.44 feet at Wuhan—a statistic, speculated the AP, that was probably an indicator of the day the dam burst. It was a mere half foot less than the height of the highest dikes along the Yangtze. The disaster spread rapidly.

The International Red Cross was refused admission to the flood area by the Chinese government. The United States, partially immobilized by cold war fears of communism, did nothing to aid the refugees of the disaster (the U.S. State Department reasoned that aid should not be given to an enemy nation that shipped badly needed foodstuffs out of the country in exchange for armaments, and which had rebuffed offers of American aid during a lesser flood in 1950). Nationalist airplanes, however, airdropped 60 tons of rice and leaflets in five flood-stricken areas.

Finally, as August gave way to September, the flooding abated. A massive rebuilding process began. Thirty locomotives, 650 freight cars, more than 1,000 trucks, 55 ships, 300 barges, and 500 boats were pressed into service to haul earth, stone, and other repair materials to the affected dikes. Sixty-three million dollars were appropriated by the Peiping government to help peasants re-sow their land

and, as the government put it, "engage in other forms of productive work."

At the end of September, China released final disaster figures. They were, as the rest of the world had divined, larger than those of the cataclysmic 1931 flood, which had inundated 34,000 square miles (see p. 32) of the same area. Approximately 41,665 square miles of farmland, villages, and towns disappeared under floodwaters in 1954. More than 10 million people were evacuated from the area.

The only figures withheld by the Chinese government were those of casualties. "Few persons drowned," was as near to a tally the Chinese government gave reporters, which would make the death toll considerably less than the 3.7 million of the 1931 flood. Later estimates by international agencies, including the International Red Cross, exceeded 40,000, but they were still only estimates. The true figures would never be known.

CHINA
(SHANTUNG)
FLOOD
August–September 1933

Governmental misconduct and the need to utilize floodplains in China accounted for the devastation of the 1933 China flood, which ruined more than 3,000 square miles of farmland, sent 3 million refugees into other areas of China, and inundated more than 2,000 towns and villages.

Since recorded antiquity, China has had a history of governmental interference in the natural order of the earth. Ancient dynasties both built and destroyed dikes along the Yellow River (Hwang Ho) to protect themselves and divert floodwaters to areas inhabited by peasants. In 1938, during the Sino-Japanese War, an anticipated invasion of China by Japan was purportedly avoided by diverting the Yellow River southward, thus flooding 20,000 square miles of farmland and killing several hundred rural residents of the area.

The great flood of 1933 was blamed by officials in 18 counties in western Shantung Province on the governor of Honan Province. According to the charges filed with the national government in Nanking, the governor ordered troops to cut the dikes in strategic places along the course of the Yellow River in order to protect areas of Honan inhabited by wealthy families. The openings in the dikes allowed the rain-bloated waters of the Yellow River to surge into Tsinan, Shantung's capital, a city of 600,000 people, and over the surrounding countryside, peppered with hundreds of small villages.

Rains had fallen steadily throughout the summer; by the end of August, the Yellow River was rising at the rate of 12 feet a day. Probably no dikes could have held it, but certainly, the man-made destruction of key sea walls exacerbated an already tragic situation. Within days, 3 million people were deprived of their homes; hundreds of thousands drowned.

In their petition to Nanking, the officials detailed the incidents leading to the tragedy: "Rumors have been set afloat," the petition stated, "to the effect that bandits were responsible for the collapse of dikes, but meantime Liu Shih, the civil governor of Honan, has openly dispatched a brigade of troops to the Lanfeng district [bordering on western Shantung].

"Under the pretext of safeguarding the province, his men cut the dikes at Lanfeng, and the result was a gruesome inundation extending over western Shantung. The people are now in the midst of consternation and ravages.

"It is a most curious incident in history for a high official to employ his soldiers in cutting dikes to make a neighboring State inundated, thus rendering the slaughter of people an amusing pastime . . . ," he concluded.

Other dikes crumbled along the Yellow River at Tunga, above Tsinan, where 200 villages disappeared under the waters of the river. Alarm guns and enormous temple gongs were placed along the dikes to warn farmers and their families that a break in the dike had occurred. Kaifeng and other walled cities, located more than 20 feet below flood level, barricaded their gates with sandbags.

As the water began to subside, the homeless began to populate the landscape. In western Shantung alone, more than 3 million formerly productive farmers and their families were displaced. Where there were once rice fields, layers of sand, deposited by the floodwaters, choked all vegetation.

By the end of August, the floodwaters slowly subsided, but not the rains. Less intense than they had been, they nevertheless continued to fall, and there were disconcerting reports of flooding in the gorges on the upper river.

Meanwhile, Liu Shih, the Honan Province governor, denied the charges of cutting the dikes to save his province, and asked Nanking to appoint an investigating commission with power to punish his accusers if he were exonerated.

By the beginning of September, over 3,000 square miles of crops had been destroyed by the floods; more than 2,000 towns and villages were inundated. The cost of repairing ruined dikes was estimated at $10.6 million.

CHINA
(YANGTZE RIVER)
FLOODING
July–October 1931

In conservative estimates, more than 140,000 people died, more than 2 million were rendered homeless, and $50 million in property damage was caused by the flooding of China's Yangtze and Yellow Rivers from July through October 1931. Three

thousand years of deforestation and careless farming took its most severe 20th-century toll in a continuing situation that would not receive a partial solution until the construction of several small dams on the Hwang Ho (Yellow River) in the 1950s, and the planning of the Three Gorges Dam on the Chang River in 1991.

Once, 3,000 years ago, the upper valley of the Yangtze and Yellow Rivers was the fertile life source of China. Originally populated by nomadic herdsmen, the floodplains on either side of the Yangtze were gradually filled by farmers, who took advantage of the rich soil that was irrigated by floods each year.

Flat, traversed by meandering rivers that at first were easily contained by earthen dikes, these plains were, in early, agricultural centuries, abundant suppliers of food. Rice became the principal crop in south and central China; wheat, millet, and sorghum were raised in the north. Every inch of space not occupied by a dwelling or a grave mound was given over to raising crops.

But, as the centuries progressed, the landscape became far less benign. Years of torrential rains and unwise clearing of timber on the slopes of hills above the plains caused fast-moving and powerful rushes of water to cascade into the streams and rivers, filling them beyond capacity. The runoff became so rapid that huge quantities of silt began to accumulate in the riverbeds, making a constant heightening of the dikes a yearly necessity.

As years and silt accumulated, the beds of the streams sometimes grew higher than the land outside the dikes. By the 20th century, there were stretches of the Yellow River in which its water level was actually 30 feet above the plain through which it flowed.

When the rains and the floods abated, the flatness of the land prevented the water from running off rapidly, more often than not preventing farmers from planting their next crops. And, since the floods usually occurred in the growing season, two successive harvests were often lost.

Today, overpopulation, climate changes, and misuse of the land have altered this part of China even more dramatically. Deforestation over a thousand years has allowed the Gobi desert to expand southward; winds have carried sand in the same direction, which in turn has buried fertile soil, rendering it unusable. Further erosion from overfarming and deforestation has turned the land into gullies of mud during the rainy season, and this topsoil in turn has washed into the Yangtze River.

But back to history: As the population increased, as more and more farmers began to work the Yangtze valley, disasters from the river's annual floods increased. The Grand Canal, linking Peking and Shanghai, was designed and built to divert water during flood times.

But the Yangtze, dubbed "China's Sorrow," refused to be tamed. And the population continued to grow at an alarm-

The consequences of 3,000 years of deforestation and careless farming converged in a moment in the monumental floods of the Yangtze and Yellow Rivers in 1931. Since then, despite dams and dikes, the Yangtze continues to overflow its banks during flood season.
(UKA/STILL PICTURES)

ing rate. In 1887, over 2,500,000 lost their lives to floodwaters, and in the late summer and fall of 1931, with an even greater population inhabiting the flood plains, an equal disaster occurred.

China was a troubled country in 1931. There were threats from Japan and clashes with it in Manchuria; there were armed uprisings and civil wars within the country itself. In a way, the abnormally abundant and far-reaching flooding from the Yangtze in July and August was a peacemaker—and perhaps the beginning of the eventual Communist takeover of the country. Both sides in the civil conflict abandoned warfare, reasoning that any warlike activity would be translated by the populace into heartless preying on a distressed people. Communists were active in preying upon the suffering of the masses, convincing them that in some circuitous way, the Nanking government was responsible for the flood.

Meanwhile, aided by torrential tropical rains and windstorms, the waters of the Yangtze and Yellow Rivers swelled rapidly, eventually bursting their banks. Floodplains were inundated; dwellings were swept away. The population scattered, searching for higher ground, but the higher ground continued to disappear beneath the floodwaters.

Finally, at the end of August, the dikes along the Grand Canal gave way, and more water poured into the farmland on either side of it. By September 1, more than 100,000 people had drowned and 2 million others, huddled in oases and on the tops of houses, were in imminent danger of starvation.

The areas hardest hit at this time were four: The first was along the middle Yangtze River above and below Hankow, 31 million people lived in this area (chiefly in the provinces of Hunan, Hupeh, and Kiangsi). By September 1, approximately 10 million—a third of the populace—had been driven from their homes and were destitute.

The second area was the lower basin of the Hwai River, which had been protected by the dikes of the Grand Canal. As the dikes burst, the basin was covered by the roiling, silt-thick waters of the canal.

The third area was along the Tientsin-Bukow railway from Nanking north to Hauchufu, which ran along the bed of the Yellow River.

And the fourth was along the Shanghai-Nanking Railroad, where the large cities of this portion of China were normally protected from floods by high walls and dikes.

But not this time. Nanking was threatened, as three dikes collapsed simultaneously near the west gates of the city. Hundreds of refugees encamped within the city walls suddenly found themselves knee-deep in water. They climbed the walls and watched as the waters swirled through the gates.

The city of Hinghwa in the lowlands of northern Kiangsu Province, 30 miles east of the Grand Canal, became part of a lake 35 miles in radius, encompassing multitudes of villages that had already disappeared beneath the floodwaters. Portions of Hinghwa disappeared under 20 feet of water, and its district offices, on the highest ground within the city, were soaked by 3 feet of water.

Taichow and Tungtai, the other major cities in the area, suffered similar fates.

By the second week in September, floodwaters had spread to the provinces of Honan, Shensi, and Kiangsu, and the northwestern province of Anhwei. In Sinti, 75 miles southwest of Hankow, 80,000 refugees from the flood huddled next to the few dikes that had not burst. In Hankow itself, temporary raised sidewalks and pontoon bridges provided the links that allowed the city to function as normally as possible. Train service to Peiping (Peking) was restored, but it ran only intermittently.

Now starvation became as pressing a problem as the flood itself. With so much land underwater, it was becoming imperative to import relief shipments of grain. About 50 million persons in the flood area were immediately without food; another 10 million had to be fed within the following eight months, or they would die of starvation. The international community responded, but slowly.

And into this holocaust of horror, on September 18, dropped Colonel and Mrs. Charles A. Lindbergh, on a diplomatic visit that rapidly turned humanitarian and nearly ended in disaster.

The Lindberghs were on a flight, from New York to the Far East, that had already met its quota of trouble. On August 18, shortly after takeoff from Petropavlovsk, Russia, their Lockheed monoplane developed engine trouble over Avatcha Bay on the southern end of the Kamchatka Peninsula.

The engine trouble was repaired, and the Lindberghs set off again for the 987-mile flight to Nemuro, Japan. Midway through the Kurilie Island chain, they ran into a heavy fog bank and were forced to land on choppy seas off Ketoi Island, known as the "black hole" of the Kurilies. There, they spent what Colonel Lindbergh later described as "one of the worst nights in my experience."

The next day, the Japanese steamer *Shimushiru Maru* arrived and towed the Lindberghs to a safer anchorage. From there, they took off, only to experience motor trouble again. Once again, they were towed by ship to Buroton Bay, where the engine was repaired, and they resumed their journey. And once more they ran into an impenetrable fog bank, which forced them down on the southernmost island of the Kurilies, where they spent the night before finally resuming—and completing—their journey to Nemuro.

The Lindberghs were apparently not discouraged by their multiple mishaps. They had, after all, in February 1929, when Mrs. Lindbergh was still Anne Spencer Morrow, flipped over at Valbuena Field, near Mexico City, when they attempted a landing minus a wheel that had fallen off in the air. They were not easily dissuaded. So now, in 1931, they proceeded on to China.

The two celebrities, on a sight-seeing trip to Shanghai and Peiping, were scheduled to be met at 1:30 in the afternoon of September 19 at a wharf on the Yangtze River in Nanking. The wharf was decorated in bunting; Chinese and American diplomats were at the ready. At 1:35, Chinese military planes took off to escort the Lindbergh plane.

But the Lindberghs were late, and when, in their Lockheed monoplane, they arrived, they merely circled over the wharf and then disappeared upriver. The swift current of the Yangtze, combined with a strong upriver wind was deemed too dangerous a combination. Hence, the Lindberghs chose to land on Lotus Lake, beyond the city walls of Nanking.

The stunned diplomats were informed by telephone at 3:10 P.M. of the whereabouts of the world-famous couple and immediately dashed over improvised board sidewalks to a squadron of two-score limousines, hub-deep in water, which sloshed them across the city to Lotus Lake, where the Lindbergh plane was serenely floating, surrounded by sampans.

Willis Peck, the U.S. consul to Nanking, commandeered another sampan, officially greeted the couple, and transported them to the consulate.

The following day, Lindbergh announced that he was putting his plane and himself at the service of the Chinese government to aid in meeting the flood emergency, and he immediately embarked upon a series of aerial surveys, the first of their kind. The findings were devastating. The flood zone was thought to extend 20 miles southward from Nanking. But the Lindberghs flew over 60 miles of submerged countryside, including the city of Taipingfu, which was under 10 feet of water.

Westward from Taipingfu, they found similar scenes of relentless flood, with only a few mountains, thick with refugees, emerging like islands in a water-filled world. Worst of all, there was no sign whatsoever that the flood was receding.

On the 22nd of September, the Lindberghs made another reconnaisance flight over the area between the Grand Canal and the Yellow Sea. They found 8,000 square miles of flooded countryside, dotted by villages in which only the roofs of houses were visible and whose inhabitants were living in small boats moored in the streets.

"When we flew over this area," Colonel Lindbergh later reported, "the wind had whipped up the waves over the fields and the few remaining dikes were being eroded away rapidly. Thousands of refugees had congregated on dikes lining the Grand Canal and on an uncompleted road just south of the flood area."

The cities of Hinghwa and Fowning were under water; water poured unchecked through breaks in the Grand Canal; on the east and northeast, floodwaters had nearly reached the Yellow Sea.

The only positive note in their survey dealt with the area west of the Grand Canal in the upper section of the Hwai River, where the water had withdrawn within the banks of the river. Farmers had immediately begun to replow their land and repair what was left of their homes, but, in the words of Lindbergh, "crops in the area of the . . . flood have been completely destroyed."

On September 26, Colonel Lindbergh and Dr. J. Heng Liu, the head of the Department of Hygiene and Sanitation of the Floor Relief Commission, took off from Lotus Lake with a small amount of drugs and antiplague vaccines. Their destinations were the cities of Hinghwa, Yangchow, Taichow, Fowning, and Yencheng.

The mission was aborted after a near disaster in the waters outside of the ancient walls of Hinghwa. No sooner had the plane landed when it was surrounded by thousands of sampans containing starving boat people who thought that the plane was loaded with food. Dr. Liu attempted to enter a sampan with a bundle of drugs, but the boat was immediately swamped by scores of men leaping into it, again mistaking the bundles for food. Dr. Liu stepped into three other sampans, which were similarly sunk beneath the weight of hungry refugees. The drugs sank along with the last sampan, and Dr. Liu had to swim back to the plane, which took off immediately before it, too, was swamped and sunk.

It was a numbing experience for Colonel Lindbergh, who later described the frenzied occupants of the sampans as men and women and children driven to madness by hunger. When the plane took off, he related, and the people realized that no relief had arrived for them, they retreated into hopeless stillness.

On September 28, at the request of the National Flood Relief Commission, the Lindberghs and a Dr. Borcic, a League of Nations health expert on plague prevention, left Nanking for Hankow in order to survey further unexplored flood regions along the Han River and south of the Yangtze. After spending a night in the city of Wuhu, they landed, on the 30th of September, in the Yangtze near the British aircraft carrier *Hermes*.

Their groundbreaking aerial reconnaisance flights came to an abrupt halt, however, on October 2, when, attempting to take off from the deck of the *Hermes*, Lindbergh misjudged his distance and crashed into the water. A launch was immediately dispatched from the carrier and plucked Mrs. Lindbergh from the plane. Lindbergh and Dr. P. Z. King, a Chinese relief worker, ended up in the water for a short time when the plane flipped over, but they were soon rescued by another launch. The plane, too damaged to be easily repaired, was carried, with the Lindberghs, to Shanghai, where the famous couple caught a boat for home.

Through the remainder of the autumn and into the early winter of 1931, the flood remained in place. The number of homeless climbed to 50 million. Relief supplies of basic grain began to arrive, but the distribution of it was painfully slow.

Aid teams, with supplies and medicines to fight nascent plague, found appalling sights. In Black Hill, a small rise of ground near the outskirts of Hankow, 20,000 refugees shivered in approximately 4,000 crude shelters made of bark, straw matting, tree branches, and bits of flotsam snatched from the waters. Flies were as thick as swarming bees. Dysentery was rampant. The only water supply was the river, which was stagnant and foul. Lining the river were unburied corpses, most of which had been stripped by shivering refugees of whatever clothing they had been wearing. Most of the survivors, reported relief teams, had passed beyond despair and into an apathetic acceptance of a grim and inevitable fate.

Thousands of other camps duplicated the conditions in Black Hill. Relief workers attacked hunger first, then proceeded to dig wells, chlorinate the water, build shelters, and start the long process of innoculating tens of millions against smallpox and cholera.

Appeals were sent out to the international medical community; in all of China, there were not enough trained medical personnel to begin the task. In a desperate attempt to provide stopgap measures, the Nanking government closed all of the nation's medical schools for three months, so that the faculties and advanced medical students could assist in treating refugees for cholera, typhoid, malaria, dysentary, and smallpox and attempt to prevent epidemics of influenza, typhus, and pneumonia that would inevitably occur with the coming of cold weather.

As the floodwaters began to slowly recede, it was apparent that it was too late for the fall planting. Nothing edible would be possible in the flooded regions until after the May planting, and millions would die in the interval. "The ghastliness of the situation can hardly be exaggerated," wrote missionary J. L. Buck, husband of author Pearl Buck. Appeals to the world for relief came, but the supplies were slow in arriving. There was a worldwide depression, and America withheld most of the $2,500,000 it had pledged until after November 25, to avoid conflict with a nationwide unemployment relief campaign.

When the final figures were tabulated, more than 140,000 people had died, and more than 2 million were left permanently homeless. The cost of rebuilding property destroyed by the flood was $50 million.

The heritage of years of bad and destructive habits continued unabated after the tragic 1931 flood. And there were more floods. Only two years later, in 1933, the Yellow River again rampaged over its banks, killing 50,000 (see p. 31). As late as 1991, floods along the Huai, a tributary of the Hwang (Yellow) River drowned more than 2,000 people and left a million homeless.

To this day, overwatering has led to waterlogging and salinization of the arable land in China, which has shrunk, in the northwestern provinces, by one-third since 1949.

In the 1950s, China began an effort to control flooding and simultaneously create badly needed hydroelectric power. The plan was to dam every one of China's major rivers. In 1960, a dam was constructed at Sanmenxia on the Huang River. At first, it seemed to be an ideal solution for both floods and an inadequate electricity supply. But by the end of four years, its reservoir had filled with silt, and its power station had to be closed down.

The massive flood of 1991 reinvigorated the government's taste for damming China's rivers, and so the latest, gargantuan dream began: A massive $20 billion, 650-foot-high dam titled the Three Gorges Dam, on the Chang River. It would be the largest hydroelectric project in the world, capable of producing one-sixth of China's electricity output.

The dam, however, remains unbuilt, probably for excellent reasons. First of all, its gigantic, 370-mile-long reservoir would not only destroy a breathtakingly beautiful part of China's natural landscape, it would increase markedly the risk of the flooding it was designed to inhibit. The reason: Much of the water that reaches the Chang floodplain comes from tributaries *below* the planned location of the dam.

Then, too, vital food production for many rural areas would be lost because of the submersion of large areas of land, and the displacement of the people who work it and live on it. The Sanmenxia dam forced 300,000 people out of their homes. The Three Gorges project would displace 1,700,000 productive farmers and their families. Thus, the cure seems as bad, if not worse, than the problem, which nevertheless still exists, as it has for thousands of years.

COSTA RICA
(LA SELVA AREA)
DEFORESTATION, BIODIVERSITY DESTRUCTION
1980–Present

Rain forest devastation in Central America still exists at an unacceptable level. But the establishment and continuance of the La Selva Research Station is an example of an environmental disaster averted. Its studies of the tropical rain forest in Costa Rica have produced invaluable information regarding the biodiverse content of rain forests, their potential to save human life, and, most recently, the astonishing discovery that rain forests are not, as previously thought, primeval, but have been shaped by human intelligence.

It must be stated at the outset that this is an isolated, if monumentally important, success story occurring in a worldwide jungle of tragedy. Central America is a particularly poignant example of destruction by greed and ignorance. Illegal logging combined with squatting by peasants ground down by a brutal economy have reduced Central America's tropical forests by more than 60 percent.

Mexico, Nicaragua, Guatemala, Honduras, Panama, and Costa Rica have all been guilty of enormous destruction of their natural environments. Costa Rica in particular has one of the highest rates of deforestation in the world: 3.9 percent per annum. Of the 3.7 million acres of forest that now remain, 148,000 acres are destroyed every year.

And yet, in the midst of the carnage, a hope not only for Central America, but for the remainder of the world, has flourished. In fact, if there is cause for good cheer in the fight against deforestation, it is in Costa Rica, the small Central American democracy that is roughly the size of Vermont.

Until the early 1980s, Costa Rica, like all countries rich in rain forests, was busily slashing and burning its tropical hardwood strongholds. Indeed, until 1989, the country was rife with loggers ravaging its rain forests, farmers clearing land indiscriminately, and Costa Rica's most indigent people, forced because of the Costa Rican economy into felling trees for fuel to heat their homes and cook their food. In 1940, more than 80 percent of the land of Costa Rica was covered by forest. By 1977, 20 percent was forest, and it was disappearing.

But, in La Selva, located near the border of Nicaragua, 100 miles north of the Costa Rican capital of San Jose, there was hope. Here, in the midst of 1,800 acres of untouched rain forest, the La Selva Biological Station, an oasis of construction in a desert of destruction was established. Biologists from all over the world now gather there to study the local ecosystem—its biodiversity, its possibility of providing a clue to the origin of life itself, its potential to save life by providing medicines to cure the world's diseases, and its present and future role as a provider of food and energy to the world's ever-growing population.

Biologists under the direction of Drs. David and Deborah Clark are utilizing the rain forest by uncovering and exploring its natural riches for medicinal purposes.
(CAMPBELL PLOWDEN/GREENPEACE)

The station was established in 1968, when research grants were easy to obtain, by the Organization for Tropical Studies. Since then, more than 2,000 scientists from all over the world have journeyed here to conduct their research.

To biologists, the rapid, worldwide disappearance of the inhabitants and interior structure of the rain forest is very real. According to estimates released by the La Selva Station, it is possible that, at the present rate of destruction, approximately 1 million species of animals, insects, and plant life will have been lost without ever being identified or studied.

"It's a salvage operation," explains Dr. David Clark, who, with his wife, Dr. Deborah Clark, head the research station. "We're trying to identify useful species and preserve them, though preservation is not that easy. A while back, the National Cancer Institute requested more information on one plant, but [the plant] had already disappeared."

By the early 1980s, the area around the station was also at risk; land was being sold off at a furious rate. In 1981, the Organization for Tropical Studies purchased an adjoining 1,500-acre plot containing one-third virgin forest, one-third secondary forest, and one-third pastures.

But timber interests were threatening to close in on the station from other directions, and the government of Costa Rica, while sympathetic, was unable to provide the money to buy up the privately owned land that would link the research center to the existing 124-square mile Braulio Carrillo National Park.

"We're too small to talk about species preservation," said Dr. Clark at the time. "Only national parks can do that. If we're surrounded by pastures, 100 of the 120 interior forest bird species would disappear."

The Clarks' dream was to create a new reserve to link La Selva to the national park and form an unbroken stretch of tropical forest 21 miles long, rising from 115 feet above sea level to 9,500 feet. It would afford unprecedented study that might convince other world nations to halt the rampant destruction of the planet's biodiversity.

The biologists worked, not only in the forest, but on world consciousness, and in mid-1986, the John D. and Catherine T. MacArthur Foundation in Chicago offered a grant of $1 million, which was matched with funds from other donors mobilized by several conservation groups, chief among them Washington's World Wildlife Fund.

The land was bought; the link was forged. Now 24,700 acres of diverse rain forest from nearly sea level to 9,500 feet has become a laboratory for the study of biodiversity and the nature of the rain forest.

The world movement has gained momentum. In late 1987, the Costa Rican lumber company that had leveled much of Costa Rica by clear cutting, the most destructive of all logging methods, was ready to cross the border into Nicaragua. But suddenly, a contract with the Nicaraguan government was canceled. By February 5 of 1988, Nicaragua and Costa Rica completed a plan to protect and manage an international "peace park" on both sides of their common border along the San Juan River. The park contained a rain forest slated for destruction by Nicaragua's $2.5 million a year logging industry. At the same time, Costa Rica arranged, with Panama, to establish another "peace park" along their mutual borders. Shortly before this, Guatemala, Honduras, and El Salvador had agreed to create a preserve in the mountain forests along *their* borders.

The preserves, modeled on La Selva but on a larger scale, would become "biosphere reserves," that is, totally protected core areas surrounded by buffer zones for sustainable economic development ranging from forestry to subsistence agriculture to more efficient use of misused ranch and farm lands.

This, in turn, brought moneys from environmental organizations worldwide and ecologically aware world govern-

ments, which proved to more than one Central American government that deteriorating environment meant deteriorating economics. The Netherlands and Sweden were generous; the American government, opposed to the Sandinistas in Nicaragua, was noticeably silent about offering aid.

In Costa Rica, the linking of preserves, begun at La Selva, continued. The Monteverde reserve was established in the mountains linking the Caribbean and the Pacific. A repository of huge amounts of wildlife, its protected area was widened in 1988 through the efforts of the Monteverde Conservation League. Buying up farmland linking the Monteverde reserve with the Guanacaste National Park in the Pacific lowlands would establish a continuous refuge, linked by forest paths, of 51,900 acres.

Meanwhile, on the fringes of this refuge, abandoned and bare farming plots were bought up and replanted with forest trees propagated in special nurseries, and farmers were paid to give over parts of their land for replanting, in order to provide windbreaks and renewable sources of timber and firewood.

The extensiveness of this project brought economic advantages to Costa Rica: in 1988 and early 1989, debt-for-conservation arrangements, through American banks and the Nature Conservancy, retired debt in exchange for the conservation that Costa Rica was now practicing.

In July 1993, biologists working in the La Selva forest made an astonishing discovery. The jungle of La Selva, along with other rain forests, was thought to be pristine, untouched by human hands. It was, so some thought, a living example of the prehistoric, prehuman world.

But studies in La Selva yielded the astonishing news that, on the contrary, rain forests go through both natural and human-induced changes and have done so for many thousands of years. Few patches of rain forest are long lived, they found. Enormous trees topple, creating spots of open sunlight within which new plants sprout, new creatures who feed upon them develop, and so, area by area, the forest is reborn, in a rapid dynamic of change.

Not only this. Evidence was discovered of small scale slash-and-burn agriculture. Through radiocarbon dating, charcoal found in the soil was determined to be between 1,200 and 2,000 years old. Stone hearths, burial sites, and tools indicate that the La Selva forest was worked by farmers, circa A.D. 800, who planted yucca and corn, both of which had been previously considered unfriendly to the rain forest.

These ancient farmers did, it was found, utilize slash-and-burn techniques to clear the forest, but only in small areas, consisting of a few acres. The land was allowed to remain fallow, and then, after a few years, replanted.

In the same way, natural disturbances, in which trees fell and new species were formed, took place in areas no larger than 200 square yards. The pattern, then, that modern inhabitants of the forest have not followed but that their ancestors did, is obvious: Less results in more conservation.

The discovery that a jungle previously thought to be pristinely primitive was not was unnerving, particularly to Dr. Deborah Clark, who had lived in it so long. "One thing it does is it makes you humble," she announced, after the findings were made public. "I think it's really important that we all get adjusted to the idea. . . . It's time to overcome this lack of comprehension of humans as part of the ecosystem."

EGYPT
(ASWAN)
WATER POLLUTION, LAND DEGRADATION
1953–1970

The Aswan High Dam project was designed as a panacea for Egypt's agricultural and energy needs. The energy needs have been met; one-third of the nation's electricity demand has been satisfied through hydroelectric power from the dam. But side effects—loss of silt, salinization of land, and the spread of aquatic disease organisms—have had a devastating effect upon Egypt's agriculture, fishing industry, and national health.

From long before the 20th century B.C., Nubia was a powerful and formidable state, extending north to south from the First Cataract of the Nile (near the present city of Aswan) to Khartoum, in the Sudan. Regimes came and went; Egyptian pharoahs lived and died. Egypt occupied Nubia for most of the Middle Kingdom period (2000–1786 B.C.); Nubians from the Kush Kingdom occupied Egypt during the eighth and seventh centuries B.C. That, however, was merely a temporary state of affairs. Through most of history, Egypt has dominated the Nubians, enslaving them and gutting their gold and copper mines.

Although archaeological treasures abound along the Nile in the part of Egypt bordering Sudan, the glory of ancient Nubia is most dramatically represented by the settlement of Abu Simbel, where Rameses II, usurper of the throne of Egypt from 1292 to 1225 B.C. and probably the oppressive pharoah mentioned in the Old Testament, built a great rock temple that contained an immense statue of his queen, the Hittite princess Neferati, and not one, but four, versions of the royal presence. All of it was carved out of a sandstone mountain. And as grand as his mortuary was at Thebes, and as elegant as his temple was at Luxor, the Abu Simbel constructions were the greatest, most expensive, and most impressive signatures that Rameses left on the landscape of the Nile valley.

Though his excesses led to the downfall of Egypt, his creations remained, as did the Nubian islands of Elephantine and, particularly, Philae—so lovely that Cleopatra moored her barge there. What did not remain was the wealth of the area.

By the 20th century, the old kingdom of Nubia had become an arid plain that waited for the yearly flood of the Nile to support whatever crops it might grow in its preciously brief season.

In 1902, the British built a dam three miles south of the city of Aswan, and its reservoir became the chief source of irrigation water storage for the southern, or upper, Nile basin.

By the early 1950s, the plans of Gamal Abdul Nasser and his United Arab Republic (UAR) could obviously not be served by the 50-year-old dam. What was needed was not only a larger source of irrigation, but a dam large enough to provide hydroelectric power for the burgeoning economy of Egypt. And so, in 1953, with all good intentions, the planning of the High Dam at Aswan began.

It was an immense design, worthy of the pharoahs whose monuments would be threatened by it. The dam would be built seven miles upstream from the city of Aswan, and five miles upstream from the old dam. It would be 370 feet high and more than 2 miles long. Lake Nasser, the dam's reservoir, would be 300 miles long and would contain 9.8 billion cubic yards of water. Water from it would, for the first time, provide irrigation to cultivate 1 million acres of desert land, mostly in Upper Egypt, and water 700,000 acres that were only tillable during flood time. Three crops a year would replace the once-a-year crop yield of the area. In addition, the hydroelectric power provided by this massive but leashed amount of water would provide power for fully one-third of the country's electricity.

At first, the one billion dollars the dam would cost was planned as a joint venture between the United States, Great Britain, and the United Arab Republic. But political differences between the United Arab Republic and the western powers led to a withdrawal of British and American support. Shortly after this, Nasser announced the nationalization of the Suez Canal Company, whereupon Britain and France invaded Egypt in October of 1956. The former Soviet Union filled the gap left by the withdrawal of French, British, and American aid and financed the first two stages of the construction of the dam.

The first stage was signaled by a ceremony on January 17, 1960, in which President Nasser, before an audience of 2,000 invited guests, pressed a plunger detonating 20 tons of dynamite. Following this, work was begun on a concrete-lined open channel that would divert the waters of the Nile around the construction area. A coffer dam, built of waste rock from the project with great quantities of sand to make it watertight was designed to keep the diverted waters from backing up to the construction site.

The second stage involved building the main dam and the erection of eight turbines in the power station.

The third stage dotted the i's, crossed the t's, and connected the power lines that completed the dam's power-producing capacity.

The first stage, the diversion of the Nile, aroused consternation among archaeologists and protecters of Egypt's artistic heritage. The Great Temple at Abu Simbel was squarely in the path of the diverted Nile and would be inundated by its waters. Even as Soviet equipment and engineers were moving 400 miles up the Nile from Alexandria, scientists were negotiating the spending of $25 million of the $93 million loan from the former Soviet Union to build a protective dam around the Great Temple at Abu Simbel.

Meanwhile, a new airport was constructed at Aswan, and in the nearby sandy plain between brown granite hills, a fertilizer plant, destined to be operated by power from the dam's turbines, began to take shape. A railroad bed was chiseled out of granite wastes on the Nile's east bank.

On January 10, 1960, President Nasser opened the first hydroelectric plant in Egypt. Attached to the old dam, it was a minor preview of its coming forceful incarnation.

Caught between the engineers and the archaeologists were human beings—33,000 Nubians, whose ancient homeland and present dwelling place was about to be flooded out of existence. They were poor agrarians—date farmers, primarily—but they were proud. Four thousand of them lived in lowly, if neatly kept, huts on Elephantine Island, within easy sight of the best rooms in the Cataract, one of Egypt's most luxurious hotels.

Ever since 1902, when the first dam was built, their living space had been steadily given over to development. Now it was about to disappear altogether.

The Nubians proposed relocation to the upper Egyptian desert east of the Nile where an area that could be cultivated existed. The government of President Nasser took this under advisement and suggested that in addition to this relocation, several thousand Nubians could be transported to Kom Ombo, near Aswan, where the Egyptian government had completed a large sugar refinery. The Nubians could work in the cane fields, it was reasoned. But the Nubians were not overly receptive to the idea.

As January drifted into February, the United Nations Educational, Scientific and Cultural Organization (UNESCO) announced a worldwide funding drive to preserve the threatened antiquities along the Nile. Some of the treasures could be moved, UNESCO announced, but not Abu Simbel. Not a statue or a rock had been carried to this site; ancient artists, working with hammers and chisels, had hewn the four statues and the temple from the inside of a sandstone mountain.

The first proposal for preserving the site, put forth by a group of French architects, involved the building of a 2,200-foot wall of rock and sand circling the site 1,000 feet into the river. The plan proved far too costly; it would have used up fully half of the $93 million Soviet loan for the first stage of the dam.

Meanwhile, work on the dam itself progressed slowly. By the end of 1960, 1.5 million tons of rock had been cleared

for the diversion canal, leaving 25.5 million tons to go. Three thousand laborers and 350 engineers (65 of them from the former Soviet Union) had moved some rock; constructed a laboratory for testing silt, sand, and rock; raised transmission lines; built a six-mile railroad spur; and had half completed a plant to purify Nile water for drinking purposes.

Meanwhile, a timetable was announced in the resettlement of Nubians living in the district of Wadi Halfa. In 1967, the government announced that they would be moved 500 miles southeast across the desert to a yet-to-be-built reclamation project. Once more, the Nubians protested. None of them had been consulted about the move.

Now a new plan to preserve the temple at Abu Simbel was put forth by Italian engineer Pier Gazzolo. Instead of building a separate dam around the site, and erecting a wall that would block the sunrise from striking the god Re-Harakti (as Rameses had planned it), he proposed to saw the temple enclosures loose from the rock, encase them in steel and concrete crates, remove the rock above the temples, and, through a system of gigantic hydraulic jacks, raise the 400,000-ton, 16-story-high temple from its present location on the Nile to a safer and drier location 200 feet higher, at the edge of the new Lake Nasser. UNESCO immediately pronounced the plan more feasible than the building of a wall.

Meanwhile, a new administration had assumed office in Washington. Distinctly less Soviet-phobic than the Republican congress and presidency of Dwight Eisenhower, the new president, John F. Kennedy, asked the U.S. Congress for $10 million to rescue the monuments to Isis and Osiris on the island of Philae. The proposal had a rough trip through a congress still not ready to forgive Cairo for accepting Soviet aid in constructing the dam. When it finally emerged, the funds had shrunk to $4 million and were earmarked as a general fund to help the preservation of all Egyptian monuments, regardless of location.

Now work on the dam ground to a halt while the Egyptian government made plans to follow through with the Italian plan for the salvation of Abu Simbel. The price for lifting the temples on 300 hydraulic jacks: $70 million—a sum that produced worldwide argument. Was the preservation of any historic site worth that much money, its detractors asked, while archaeologists and artists answered in the definite affirmative.

While the argument raged and work stopped, in Kalabsha, a few miles upstream from Aswan, the West German government quietly dismantled a temple, and French teams began work on the dismantling and moving of Amada, 100 miles farther south.

Richard Nixon visited the site of the dam in June 1963 and stated that, in retrospect, the Eisenhower administration might have made a mistake in withholding aid for the project in 1956.

While work on the dam lagged, the United Arab Republic pressed ahead with plans to reclaim the desert at Kom

Ombo as a resettlement area for the soon to be displaced Nubians. Thirty-five thousand acres of land suitable, when irrigated, for the production of sugarcane was punctuated with 17,000 new stone houses, schools, shopping centers, and mosques. Forty new villages were formed from the freshly bulldozed valley floor, and water for drinking and irrigation was piped in. The coming of electricity, when the new dam's turbines became activated, was captured in a song sung by Nubian boatmen:

Welcome to the High Dam;
For your sake we left the land
* where our dead are buried.*
We always looked at you, from
* old Daboud.*
But now we are not too far
* from you.*
It's not too far, and we have
* electricity.*
Before we had only the sun.

What it lacks in poetic translation, the song makes up for in capsulized history. As ancient Egypt had plundered the gold mines of ancient Nubia, now contemporary Egypt was expanding its sights beyond the dam to the surrounding desert. Unlocking natural resources was high on its list of priorities. Oil exploration in the western desert and ore mining in the Aswan region were begun, while the dam languished at midpoint. Tangentially, a steel plant was projected to use iron mined from the desert, giving credence to the prediction of the United Arab Republic Information Department that Aswan would soon be known as "the Pittsburgh of Egypt."

Crop diversification plans were a second priority. Much of the new land to be watered by the high dam would be turned over to sugarcane and rice. Within five years, Dr. Aziz Sidky, the Minister of Industry for the United Arab Republic predicted that sugar production would be increased annually from 300,000 to 500,000 tons.

The third priority focused on tourism. The old and Victorian and legendary Cataract Hotel (whose rooms rented for $10 a night, with meals) was refurbished. Nearby, a colony of tourist bungalows, slated to rent for $5 a night with meals, was constructed. Elephantine Island would, if plans went forward, be the site of a tall hotel. Amon Island would contain a country-club-type guest house, with a swimming pool and casino.

It was quite a contrast to the region's previous, prosperous age, 3,000 years before, when caravans skirted the shores of the river and its cataracts, carrying gold, ivory, ostrich feathers, leopard skins, slaves, and tamed animals, and leaving behind their temples, the—as C. L. Sulzburger described it in the *New York Times*—"precious depositories of collective human memory."

While President Kennedy and Congress fought over the United States' $12 million contribution to the preservation of antiquity, UNESCO, funneling funds from 45 other world governments plus the Knightly Order of Malta and the United Arab Republic, signed contracts with a consortium of West German, Italian, French, Swedish, and UAR firms to move 19 temples, including those of Rameses II.

Finally, in October 1964, Congress and the president agreed, and the United States contributed the final $12 million, which would allow the work at Abu Simbel to begin. Engineers, working like surgeons, supervised the cutting up of the temples into 1,200 stone blocks, each weighing from 20 to 30 tons apiece. The blocks, numbered for reconstruction, were then carefully and meticulously hauled uphill along beds of sand to their new site, 211 feet above the old one.

There, 2,000 workers hollowed out a new, 55-foot deep cavity in the rock face, in careful imitation of the original site.

In gratitude for its final gift, Cairo presented the 2,000-year-old Temple of Dendur, already dismantled and ready for shipment, to the United States. This sparked yet another internecine argument, this time between the Smithsonian Institution and the Metropolitan Museum of Art. The Metropolitan Museum won the fight, and by 1968, the temple had been installed, with great ceremony, on the grounds of the museum.

By 1967, the temples of Abu Simbel were in place (they would be rededicated in September 1968) and work resumed on the high dam. By 1968, the first turbines were churning out electricity to Cairo, and Egyptian newspapers were lauding the role of the former Soviet Union in financing the dam, and condemning America for its lack of support.

A year later, the second turbines were in use, Lake Nasser was filling up, and the sluiceways in the dam were in full function. In 1970, the Aswan High Dam was officially declared open.

It was a boon to Egypt's economy, certainly. But what of its environment? In 1965, during the fifth year of its 10-year construction, scientists began to notice that the phytoplankton—the minute plants that directly or indirectly feed fish and other marine animals of the eastern Mediterranean—were noticeably absent. The fish, they reasoned, were hungrier than they had been in perhaps a million years, and the reason was the building of the Aswan High Dam.

For millennia, there had been a yearly flushing of the great African Watershed during the September and October rains. The billions of tons of floodwater that had rolled to the sea contained millions of pounds of organic matter and such mineral nutrients as phosphates, nitrates, and nitrites—all of which had produced the life-giving phytoplankton.

The advantage of supplying energy for Egypt by the construction of the Aswan High Dam has been offset by the enormous ecological damage, loss of priceless antiquities, and gigantic displacement of hundreds of thousands of Nubians.
(UNITED NATIONS/FAO/P. PITTET)

Now, however, this organic matter was being trapped in Lake Nasser, and phytoplankton, the base of a food pyramid in the Mediterranean, was missing.

Other changes were noted. North and northeast of the Nile delta, flood-borne sediment historically settled and smoothed the coastal contours of the Levant and lined the river bottom with muddy sand, which formed the environment of bottom-dwelling life, including mollusks and such crustaceans as shrimp and lobsters.

Once again, without the yearly influx of new sediment from the Nile, other currents along the Levantine coast were beginning to scour the depths, removing the sand that was already there and leaving a rocky base upon which no bottom-dwelling life could live. And so, the fishing industries of Israel, Lebanon, and Syria were all affected.

Further damage was noticed. Increased evaporation from Lake Nasser, newly irrigated land, and dispersion through the sub-Sahara water table was decreasing the freshwater flow through the Suez Canal, thus forcing a biological change in its waters and the sweeping of fish through it to the Mediterranean and Atlantic.

As the years following the opening of the dam accumulated, more environmental damage began to present itself downstream of the structure. The silt of the Nile, historically and dependably fertile and vital to the agriculture along the river was now being diverted to Lake Nasser. Fully 92 percent of this silt remained in the reservoir, and the river, less impeded by its natural fertilizer, began to flow faster. The result was a deeper channel downstream of the dam, which necessitated the digging of deeper irrigation channels to receive the water in the fields.

The fields themselves, and the land on the Nile's Mediterranean seacoast, shrank. Robbed of the silt that customarily builds up at the delta, the sea advanced steadily inland, thus reducing the productivity and acreage left for agriculture. Not only that: Without the nutrients that laced this silt (specifically the phytoplanktons warned of in the 1960s) nearly 30,000 jobs were lost from the shrinking of the Egyptian fishing industry that once thrived at the mouth of the Nile. More than the industry was deprived: A major source of protein to the people of Egypt also became a victim of the high dam.

Salinization of the soil is another price that was paid for hydroelectric power. In the early 1980s, the amount of salinized land in Egypt was between 28 and 50 percent of all irrigated land, and growing. In the early 1990s, 10 percent of agricultural production was lost each year through the decline in soil fertility that salinization causes. And so, though more land was admittedly opened to agriculture through the Nile diversion, more than 13,000 tons of calcium nitrate fertilizer had to be added to this land to replace the annual loss of 60 to 80 million tons of fertile silt.

The changed formulation of the water running into the irrigation ditches has now allowed disease microorganisms to affect the farmers who daily wade in these ditches. In the early 1990s, roughly 30 percent of the population was infected by schistosomiasis and 50 percent suffered from bilharzia.

And so, what was to be the greatest boon of many ages to the people of Egypt has become a mixed blessing. Power, increased land for agriculture, and new sites for mining have come at a terrible and rising price to the environment, economy, and health of the people. And the continuing power of the dam itself is now in question. The Sudanese have built dams on the Atbara river and Blue Nile; the Ethiopians are planning a dam on Lake Tana, the source of the Blue Nile, which provides 85 percent of Egypt's water. If all this happens, Lake Nasser will become as arid as the land it was built to irrigate, the turbines that lit Cairo will slow, and one more grand plan that failed to fully explore both its ecological impact and its vulnerability to the environmental carelessness of others will crumble.

INDIA, NEPAL, PAKISTAN
(HIMALAYAN FOOTHILLS, PLAINS)
DEFORESTATION, WATER POLLUTION
1960–Present

....

Widespread destruction of forests in the Himalayan foothills of India and Nepal and on the plains of Pakistan have caused pervasive flooding and water pollution downstream of the forests. The wholesale clearing of 3.75 million acres of forest annually in the area has been brought about by foreign loggers, unwise farming methods, overgrazing of livestock, overuse of wood fuel, and the growing needs of a rising population that has gravitated to the area's urban centers. The solutions, with international aid, have been largely local, ranging from the Chipko, or "tree-hugging" tactics of Indian peasants to the "village forestry" methods of Nepal.

Careless farming, irresponsible overgathering of wood for fuel, and overlogging has produced severe erosion in the Himalayan foothills, which in turn has become one of the multiple causes of flooding in Bangladesh.
(UN PHOTO #157446/P. SUDHAKARAN)

For a very long time, it was thought that the wholesale destruction of the forests in the lower Himalayas was responsible for the yearly floods in Bangladesh. According to the best scientific theory from 1960 to 1990, the astonishing population growth in the mountains of India and Nepal, the overuse of wood for fuel, overgrazing, the advance by Chinese armed forces into the Indian Himalayas during the 1962 war and the roads (later used by loggers) that were cut through their forests during this invasion, and the destructive farming methods they themselves practiced led to erosion and gullying, which in turn unleashed floods that washed into the lowlands of Bangladesh, killing thousands.

According to this theory, the removal of the binding of forests, plus the overgrowing and overgrazing on the denuded slopes led, in monsoon season, to wholesale floods and landslides, which, in turn, disrupted the hydrological cycle, in which the trees of the forest bind the soil, absorbing rainwater and only sending clear water into the downhill streams and rivers. Deprived of the binding nature of the forests, silt and water ran unchecked toward the lowest part of the land that formed the country of Bangladesh.

Downstream, there was (and still is) evidence that the silt washed downhill also clogs irrigation channels and reservoirs used in hydroelectric generation. And, the absence of firewood forces the dwellers on the Himalayan slopes, particularly in Nepal, to use dung as their main fuel, thus depriving the soil of its natural fertilizer.

While all of this is true, recent research has brought into question the weight of the role of deforestation and farming in the Himalayan foothills upon the horrendous floods in Bangladesh. Such research groups as the United Nations University Project in Nepal and the International Centre for Integrated Mountain Development in Katmandu have discovered, in the 1990s, that the centuries-old method of terrace farming actually mitigates flooding, and that the deforestation in Nepal and northern India is less than it was originally thought to be. The floods in Bangladesh, these groups found, were probably caused more by abnormal rainfall on the lower plains, high incidences of cyclones along the coast, and the naturally vulnerable nature of the below-sea-level, heavily populated country of Bangladesh than by the misuse of the Himalayan slopes.

This in no way mitigates the suffering of the people of Bangladesh or the necessity to build raised homes, high ground shelters, and embankments there. Nor does it ignore the large-scale and irresponsible deforestation in the Himalayan foothills. "There is no doubt that forest cover brakes the first burst of rains, giving people in the area of rainstorms or downstream just those few minutes that are critical between life and being swept away in flash floods," wrote Bittoo Sehgal, the editor of *Sanctuary,* an Indian environmental magazine, in 1991, in an effort to challenge the downplaying of Himalayan deforestation.

And so, though the link to the Bangladesh flooding has become more complex and less dramatic than it was originally thought to be, the undeniable fact of cavalier misuse of the tropical forests of India and Nepal, the ones that are rich in teak and oak, still exists.

The historic fact is that tropical forest once covered most of the Indian subcontinent. Settlement changed that long ago. Slash-and-burn cultivation destroyed more than 19,300 square miles of the richest vegetation, leading to landslides on the lower slopes of the Himalayas in India. By 1990, it was ascertained that 3.75 million acres of forest were being destroyed annually, some for agriculture, some for logging, some by urbanization, some by native fuelwood gatherers.

Since there is no unified national environmental policy in either India or Nepal, local rule largely determines conservation or exploitation of the land. This seems unjust, considering that the greatest pressure upon the ecology of this part of the world is from overpopulation.

Consider the case of Sri Lanka, for instance: Once, tropical rain forest covered the entire southwestern portion of this island off the southeastern tip of the Indian continent. Today, the forest has almost entirely disappeared in order to accommodate rice and coconut plantations on the lowlands, and tea and teak on the hillsides.

In the same way, Bangladesh has done away with its rain forests, swamps, and mangroves to provide various forms of shelter for a population that presently tops 2,000 people per square mile (in comparison to Sri Lanka, which is 734, or Canada, which is 8).

In fact, the aptly named "Green Revolution" of the mid-1960s, as in Indonesia and other parts of Southeast Asia (see pp. 47–52), which was designed to feed a burgeoning population, did great harm to the environment. Introducing new, high-yielding species of rice and wheat, expanding irrigated areas, and practicing intensive agriculture techniques have joined to form an appropriate response to the needs of an exponential population explosion. But all of this has also reduced the productivity of the land. Waterlogging from overirrigation has rendered over 42 million acres of land in India and Pakistan unusable. In addition, one-third of the tillable land in Pakistan has been affected by salinization.

With the coming of modern agricultural techniques, chemical fertilizers and pesticides have also arrived in India and Pakistan, and the runoff from intensely treated land has polluted numerous rivers and groundwater, from which drinking water is also pumped.

In a related problem, sewage from the increasingly crowded urban centers creates horrendous pollution of rivers and lakes. India has 3,119 towns and cities, but only 8 of them are able to treat their sewage fully before discharging it into nearby lakes and rivers. In Pakistan, only Islamabad and Karachi have sewage treatment plants.

Add to this industrial effluent and oil from Karachi's oil terminals and slicks that drift across the Arabian Sea from the gulf, and the situation becomes threatening to both fish and humans.

Several projects have been undertaken to control these problems. Some seem plausible; all will cost more than these developing countries can possibly afford. Pakistan has attempted to codify a National Conservation Strategy, under the tutelage of the World Conservation Union.

One of the first steps in this process has been to attack the salinization problem by lowering the groundwater level in order to prevent salt water from penetrating the ancient bricks of the historical site of Mohenjo-Daro. Similar erections of rings of wells have worked well in controlling salinization in the northern Indian states of Uttar Pradesh, Harvana, and Punjab.

Because of the sheer magnitude of it, the control of flooding in Bangladesh has been much more complicated.

The Green Revolution, dramatically successful elsewhere, foundered in Bangladesh. The depth of the water produced by seasonal rains was so deep that the stems of new rice varieties were too short to take root. Though the water brought down from the Himalayas by the Brahmaputra, Ganges, and Meghana Rivers is vital for agriculture, the monumental amounts that appear during the monsoon season turn necessity into tragedy.

After the tremendous floods of 1988 (see pp. 15–17), a 20-year, $10 billion plan of erecting embankments was proposed by the government of Bangladesh, but the combination of its cost and its problems, most particularly, the blocking of the movement of fish, which form Bangladeshis' main source of animal protein, from migrating from rivers into the flooded paddyfields, stopped the project from going forward. Well that it was aborted, since the 1991 floods and cyclones demolished 260 miles of earth embankments (see Bangladesh 1991, pp. 17–19).

And so, if the far-reaching effects of deforestation in the Himalayan foothills are not quite as devastating as have heretofore been presented, they nevertheless exist, in roughly the same proportion and certainly for the same reasons that they do in South and Central America, Africa, Southeast Asia, and the northwestern United States.

A lack of a unified national policy further exacerbates the problem in India and Nepal. In the lower Himalayan hills of Tehri and Uttar Kashi, 150 miles northeast of New Delhi, there is no state-produced regulation of the forests. As a result, there are very few forests still standing. Foreign logging contracters have simply entered the area through the roads cut through Tibet by its Chinese conquerers or directly from China, and felled wholesale.

But the destruction is scattershot, for a reason that on the surface seems contradictory. The local villagers are themselves guilty of indiscriminate and widespread devastation of the forest, slashing and burning it for both farming and fuel. However, in 1973, in this very area, the villagers of Gopeshwar, in the state of Uttar Pradesh, which includes New Delhi and the village of Tehri, began an environmental movement that spread quickly and proved highly effective in discouraging outside loggers.

Borrowing their method from the Passive Resistance Movement of Mohandas Gandhi, the villagers placed themselves ahead of the encroaching bulldozers, extended their arms around individual trees, and placed their bodies between the tree and the machinery. They appeared to be hugging the tree, and thus the name Chipko ("hugging," in Hindi) was adopted by other villagers to describe the movement that they in turn spread to neighboring villages. Within days, men and women from the village of Raini, 40 miles farther up into the Himalayas, wrapped their arms around trees marked for cutting by a logging concern. The loggers retreated; the trees were saved.

The movement expanded and sometimes turned violent, in contradiction to its original model. In the eastern state of Bihar, tribal people challenged police protecting loggers. Twenty-five tribal people were killed by the police, and scores were arrested. In the central state of Madhya Pradesh, 300 members of the Bastar tribe attacked a logging convoy with bows and arrows, forcing it to unload trucks carrying timber. When police attempted to arrest the tribal members, they, too, were attacked.

Both native uprisings and the Chipko movement, for all their effectiveness against outside logging interests, have failed to stem the forest destruction by native Indians, who use wood for 60 percent of their fuel needs. Once the forest in which these native Indians live is stripped, or their pastureland overgrazed, the natives themselves have been forced to migrate to urban centers, where they exist as poorly paid, unskilled building workers.

In Nepal, north and east of Uttar Pradesh, higher up in the Himalayas, the devastation is dramatic. In 1985, world environmental experts concluded that whereas in 1960, Nepal possessed 16 million acres of forest, it now had a mere 10 million acres. At that rate, the experts concluded, there would be no forests at all in Nepal within 25 years.

Authorities and villagers are aware of this, and a solution, unique to Nepal because of its history and its culture, is under way.

The governmental role has been complicated by past history. In 1956, all of Nepal's forests were nationalized, a decision that, present authorities concede, probably hastened deforestation. Previously, local constraints on cutting prevented this destruction; with the constraints removed, wholesale clearing occurred. Thus, in 1978, this decision was reversed, and legislation was passed that returned close to half of the country's forest estate to village ownership.

In 1980, international donors—the International Development Association, which is a branch of the World Bank (which provided a five-year, $15 million loan); the United Nations Development Programme (which donated $2 million); and the governments of Australia, the United States, Switzerland, and West Germany—supplied financial underpinning. The United Nations Food and Agriculture Organization provided equipment and supplies; foresters from voluntary programs such as the Peace Corps provided muscle and expertise.

The program, which centers around individual villages, involves the establishment of plantations, usually on barren grazing grounds or steep untillable slopes, and nurseries to nurture seedlings. Each village must agree to maintain these plantations and nurseries and to protect and manage the area of degraded forests within their purvue. Seedlings are distributed free to the villages and in many areas, new clay woodstoves that conserve up to 50 percent of wood during cooking are allocated.

The individual needs of individual areas are thus served, and local involvement contributes to local compliance. "When we started this program," stated Dutch forester Egbert Pelinck to environmentalist and author Erik Eckholm, "everyone said that sociological obstacles among the villagers would be our undoing. But our monitoring surveys have revealed just the opposite."

Technical glitches and budget delays have brought about such setbacks as the death of thousands of seedlings because of late sowing caused by late delivery, which was in turn brought about by international politicians squabbling over budget amounts.

Still, by 1984, 350 nurseries were in operation and more than 7 million seedlings had been planted. The survival rate was an encouraging 65 percent. If not a solution, it was a beginning, which has proved, if only in a small way, that the spread of farming to produce food destroys much of the forest, and then the shortage of forest threatens food production, can be broken.

ITALY
(SAVONA)
FOREST FIRE, EXPLOSION
October 25, 1921

Several hundred residents of Savona, Italy, lost their life on the night of October 25, 1921, when flames from a forest fire ignited a powder magazine in the fortress of Santa Elena.

Savona is located on the western arc of the Gulf of Genoa, in the northwestern ankle of the boot of Italy. Before it, the sheltered waters of the gulf spread serenely. Not so serene is a series of forts, some of them medieval, some more recent, that line the shore like a lethal necklace. Behind the forts and stretching up the slopes of the Alps behind Savona is a scrub forest that blazed out of control in the dry October of 1921.

The flames had licked at the sky for a week; on October 25, they reached out more dangerously toward the forts on the shore.

Firefighters from Savona and Vado formed a line between the flames and the forts, and for slightly less than 24 hours, were able to contain them. But as night fell on October 25, a gust of wind carried the flames downward from the hills, and one ignited the powder magazine at Santa Elena fortress, between Savona and Vado. It exploded with a roar that was heard in Florence and Bologna, more than 150 miles away.

The night sky turned to dawn as repeated explosions decimated the fort and the dwellings surrounding it. Hundreds of soldiers and civilian residents of the countryside around the fort, assured by firefighters that the flames would not reach them, perished.

JAPAN
(SAGHALIEN)
FOREST FIRE
May 28–June 4, 1929

Forty-one people died, 163 were seriously injured, and 4,710 were rendered homeless by a raging forest fire on the island of Saghalien, Japan, from May 28 to June 4, 1929.

Drought and high winds were the twin culprits in the forest fires that raged, sputtered, then raged again across the northern Japanese island of Saghalien (now Sakhalin) from May 28 to June 4, 1929. A sparsely inhabited island, Saghalien was woefully unequipped to battle the blaze that broke, like fiery waves, over the towns of Otodari, Shikika, Mochika, and Toyohara (now called Yuzhno-Sakhalin). In the early stages of the fire, Hama and Esutorimachi were nearly destroyed. Scores of houses, a school, a hospital, and a factory were the first to disappear in the flames in Hama; heroic work by firemen managed to finally control the fire in that neighboring town.

By May 30, more than 50 percent of the forests on Saghalien were engulfed or destroyed, and several coastal villages were gutted, forcing their inhabitants to flee in boats.

By June 2, most of the conflagrations were either under control or burned out, and inhabitants of villages returned to their homes, only to be forced away again by fires, reignited by new bursts of wind that also fanned forest fires on the large island of Hokkaido, where 4,000 acres of timberland were destroyed in 48 hours.

Finally, on June 4, the winds decreased and were replaced by heavy, healing rains. Nervous authorities feared reigniting fires, once the ground dried, but the rains continued, soaking out the embers, turning scorched fields into mudflats and damping down the smoking ruins of most of Saghalien's forests.

Forty-one died, 163 were seriously injured, 1,206 houses were destroyed, 4,710 residents of the island were rendered homeless, and more than $3,250,000 in property damage was assessed.

MEXICO
(PACHUCA DE SOTO)
DAM BURST
January 18, 1921

Fifty people died, 200 were injured, and more than 1,000 were rendered homeless when two dams burst above the mining center of Pachuca de Soto, Mexico, on January 18, 1921. The deaths were caused not merely by drowning, but by the chemically contaminated waters released by the sudden absence of the dams.

In the early part of January 1921, torrential rains pounded the waters of the Moctezuma River in Mexico's Sierra Madre Oriental range, on the Mexican Plateau north of Mexico City. The thriving mining center of Pachuca de Soto was protected by two dams, both built by the Rosario Fresnillo company to hold back the waters used in the chemical treatment of ores mined in the mountains above Pachuca.

On January 18, 1921, without warning to the thousands of miners' families and tradespeople in the city, both dams burst, and thousands of gallons of chemically contaminated water plunged through streets and houses and into a score of mine shafts.

It was a brief flood; the streams feeding into the reservoir above the dams were only moderately swollen by the rain, and the flimsy construction of the dams would be blamed for the tragedy.

In the city itself, the destruction was palpable and appalling. Hundreds of houses were flattened by the force of the water and the silt and mud it pushed before it. More than a thousand people would be rendered homeless. Two hundred residents of the city and miners were injured by the force of the water or collapsing buildings. And 50 died, not merely from drowning or battering, but from swallowing the poisonously contaminated water that submerged the town and flooded the mines.

The mining company paid damages to the victims and their families; the dams were reconstructed, and today, more than 85,000 people live in Pachuca de Soto. But above the dams, the water is still rife with contamination, as poisonous as it was in 1921.

PERU
(UPPER HUALLAGA RIVER VALLEY)
DEFORESTATION
1974–Present

....

Peru possesses perhaps the most unique and bizarre case and cause of deforestation in the world. Its rich rain forest in the Upper Huallaga River valley is threatened not by loggers, but by producers of a $540 million a year coca crop for the international drug trade. Efforts to control the deforestation have become dangerous exercises because of the presence of the Shining Path guerrillas, acting on behalf of the Colombian drug cartel.

Severe pollution, deforestation, and serious erosion have gutted the rich, genetically diverse rain forest of the Upper Huallaga River valley in the Andes in central Peru. Called "the eyebrow of the jungle" because of its altitude and lushness, it has, since 1974, also become the center of the coca growing plantations of Peru, providing about 75 percent of the nation's coca harvest.

Coca is the major ingredient in cocaine, and the rising American and European demand for the drug has resulted in the chopping down of more than 500,000 acres of lush, biodiverse rain forest and the dumping of millions of gallons of toxic chemicals into the waters of the Huallaga, which empties into the Amazon. The location, where the Andes meet the Amazon, at elevations ranging between 3,000 and 6,000 feet, is particularly suited to this activity, since the soil has a high content of alkaloid, also an active agent in cocaine.

The fact that great portions of this rain forest encompass two national parks and two national forests seems to be of little consequence to the slashers and burners of the area. Coca leaves are Peru's leading crop today, and the one that brings in the most money.

In fact, Peruvian farmers, whose ancestors preserved the forest for 7,000 years with wise cultivation, are, in pursuit of easy wealth, ignoring the lessons of the past. Inca and pre-Inca civilizations were acutely aware of the danger of erosion in this delicately balanced ecology, and so they cultivated coca bushes in two-foot-deep trenches dug in stone-walled terraces. Shade trees were planted around this, and yucca was intercropped to further prevent topsoil erosion. Today, all of these methods are discarded in favor of instant destruction of the forest and wholesale planting of coca bushes by farmers and wage laborers who are paid about $12 a day—which is eight times what other Peruvian farmworkers earn. The annual value of the coca crop is estimated at $540 million.

"Today, the ancestral practices have been abandoned with deathly results," was the observation, in 1991, of Carlos F. Ponce, the president of the Peruvian Foundation for Nature Conservation. The deathly results have a two-pronged nature: First, there is the cutting and burning of the forest itself. It has been estimated that, since the early 1970s, when the coca boom began, roughly 1.7 million acres of forest, or an area approximately twice the size of Rhode Island, have been laid bare.

Large sections of Tingo Maria, Cutervo, and Abiseo National Parks and Alexander von Humboldt and Apurimac National Forests have been virtually stripped of their trees and undergrowth to provide for not only the billions of coca plants but also landing strips for small airplanes and fields for corn, bananas, and manioc to feed the workers.

The slapdash nature of the farming process has produced severe soil erosion. Ordinarily, the leaves and roots of covering vegetation keep the jungle's heavy rainfall from eroding the topsoil on the steep slopes. But, between the wholesale clearing of the area, regular weeding, and a four-times-a-year harvesting schedule, furrows and gullying are rampant, and much of the topsoil is washed downhill into the valley, where it clogs streams and waterways.

The other prong of the destruction involves the river itself. Clandestine laboratories are clustered under the rain

*As a consequence of the cocaine trade, which depends on coca plant cultivation, some of Peru's richest forests have been stripped,
necessitating huge reforestation projects like this one, near Lima.*
(UN PHOTO #153871/SHAW MCCUTCHEON)

forest canopy, in which growers refine coca leaves, first into coca base, then into coca paste. The final processing step, into white cocaine powder, is usually done in Colombia. All of this involves a rich array of toxic chemicals, and in a 1987 study by Peruvian forest engineer Marc J. Dourojeanni, it was estimated that farmers and processors annually dumped 15 million gallons of kerosene, 8 million gallons of sulfuric acid, 1.6 million gallons of acetone, 1.6 million gallons of the solvent toluene, 16,000 tons of lime, and 3,200 tons of carbide into the Huallaga River and its ancillary streams.

And that was just from the processing. Large amounts of fertilizers, including Agent Orange and paraquat, were used to clear and care for the estimated 5 billion coca bushes planted in the area, and there was runoff from these. Thus, the pollution of the Peruvian Amazon has become legion. "Many species of fish, amphibians, aquatic reptiles, and crustaceans have already completely disappeared from the rivers and streams," notes Marcelo T. Buenaventura, another forest engineer.

Efforts to stop the deforestation and eradicate the coca crop have proven extremely dangerous. "Nobody dares go study there—you not only have to deal with the mafia, but also the Shining Path," states Livia Benavides, an environmental engineer associated with the Association of Ecology and Conservation, a private environmental group.

United States officials in Peru, anxious to destroy the coca crop without destroying the rain forest, attempted to test herbicides that would kill the coca bushes without harming the rest of the ecology. Hexazinone, marketed by Du Pont under the name Velpar, and tebuthiron, marketed by Eli Lilly and Company under the name Spike, were tested, but both chemical companies, because their scientists feared further contamination of the local water and possible ancillary ecological contamination and, like other drug companies, were fearful of lawsuits, halted the supply of these two herbicides.

Meanwhile, the Shining Path has suppressed opposition through fear. In May 1989, Peru's best known environmental journalist, Barbara D'Achille, was captured and stoned to death by Shining Path guerrillas, who were determined to maintain their role as protectors of the coca plantations and liaisons between their farmers and the Colombian drug lords.

And so, the forest continues to disappear, and the pollution of the Amazon has risen to a life-threatening level. Apparently, only international intervention by more than environmental engineers and agencies is needed to solve a situation whose continuance carries with it danger that is multifaceted and far reaching.

SOUTHEAST ASIA
(MALAYSIA, INDONESIA, PAPUA NEW GUINEA)
DEFORESTATION, WATER POLLUTION
1976–Present

Wholesale and indiscriminate logging is destroying the last and lushest rain forest in the world, in Southeast Asia. Up to 80 percent of these forests have already disappeared in Thailand, Vietnam, and the Philippines. Now, with an exploding world market demand for tropical hardwoods, the attention of international logging interests has turned toward Malaysia, Indonesia, and, Papua New Guinea.

The pervasive confrontation between politicians with monetary ties to logging interests and defenders of the environment has run amok in Southeast Asia. Between 1976 and 1980, 3.7 million acres of forest were cut down each year; from 1986–90, the figure had more than doubled, to 8.4 million acres a year, and there is no plausible end in sight.

Indiscriminate logging has brought about devastation and drought in Malaysia, as well as severe river pollution. Nevertheless, the poor collect water from disease-carrying waters.
(CHUCHAT KUNBUA/UNEP)

It is plainly a magnified clash of cultures that has caused such cataclysmic and irreversible destruction. On one side are the natives, who have passed down, through hundreds of generations, a needed and natural conservancy of the forests that cover such parts of Southeast Asia as Malaysia, Indonesia, and the Papua forest of the Pacific Island of New Guinea. On the other side are, in the words of anthropologist Evelyne Hong, author of *Natives of Sarawak: Survival in Borneo's Vanishing Forests,* "the people who gain from the export of logs, [who] are the timber owners, the state in terms of revenue, the foreigners who obtain the wood and the timber workers who earn wages from the industry."

Malaysia is a country divided: a peninsula that drifts southward from Thailand to Singapore, and, 400 miles eastward across the South China Sea, the former British colonies of North Borneo (now Sabah) and Northeast Borneo (now Sarawak).

The indigenous forest dwellers of Southeast Asia, particularly in Sarawak and in West Kalimantan (the southern half of Borneo, belonging to Indonesia), developed—and still practice—centuries-old agriforestry systems that established managed forests of useful trees, which in turn provided the dwellers with shelter and sustenance. Tengkawang nuts and fruits such as durian and rambutan fed them; thorny rattan vines, used to make furniture and mats, were planted on cleared forest plots to be harvested seven or more years later as the forest regrew.

In Sarawak, the traditional ethnic groups—Iban, Bidayuh, Penan, Kenyah, Kayan, and other "orang ulu," or people, of the interior fish, farm, and hunt in much the same way as the natives of Brazil have (see Brazil, Amazon River Basin, pp. 19–28) through selective burning and clearing and planting, which allow the forest to regenerate.

But from the early 1980s onward, the vast stores of tropical hardwood, prized particularly by Japan because of their textures and colors and because they are impervious to pests that easily invade and damage woods from temperate forests, became fair game for loggers. Much of this hardwood came from Thailand, where environmental laws prevented the sort of wholesale felling of primeval, triple-canopy forests that was unabashedly encouraged in Sarawak.

By 1987, the value of hardwood had climbed high on the international market, and the waters of the Rajang River, a major route for centuries into the heart of the forest of Borneo, had turned the color of light coffee from the pollution dumped into it by loggers. "The fish are almost gone," said a superannuated headman to Barbara Crossette of the *New York Times.* "And when we find some, they are different, with cloudy eyes."

Unsurfaced roads had been slashed through the forests to haul out huge loads of timber, eroding hills leading to the riverbanks, disrupting animal habitats, flattening protective vegetation, and sending silt and discarded wood into the river from which native inhabitants drank and in which they bathed, fished, and washed their clothes.

Where the triple canopy of trees once created an environment friendly to the growing and continued life of vegetation, sunlight blasted the earth, killing the vegetation and turning the underbrush to kindling that too often ignited.

The Penan, a group of hunter-gatherers, succeeded in blocking bulldozers by erecting barricades across logging roads and petitioning the government to protect their rights, but they were only small, and unmotorized, and the forces of industry and government apparently counted considerably more than the voices of environmental reason. Still, they managed, through the international publicity their blockades caused, to secure an area of wilderness in the eastern part of the state for their own use, in which logging would not be permitted.

But James Wong, Sarawak's minister of Environment and Tourism stated to reporters, "We can't cocoonize Sarawak and keep it from being affected by the big, wide world."

That big wide world brings nearly $500 million a year in timber sales to Sarawak, mostly from Japan, South Korea, and Taiwan, "[and]," noted a local anthropologist to Western reporters recently, "the people who gain from the export of logs are the timber owners, the state in terms of revenue, the foreigners who obtain the wood, and the timber workers who earn wages from the industry."

Meanwhile, Indonesia, noting that most of the timber that leaves Sarawak leaves it as unsawn logs, attempted to base an international tropical hardwoods organization in Jakarta, so that decisions about the forests could be made in the area in which they were situated. They lost out to Japan, which, in effect, put the largest consumer of the area's hardwood in charge of the conservation of it, a situation akin to putting a fox in charge of a chicken yard.

Indonesia itself is a part of the world rife with riveting contrasts and contradictions. In West Kalimantan (the southern half of Borneo), for instance, the centuries-old agriforestry system that involved managed forests and cleared forest plots of rattan vines was nevertheless the scene of one of the world's largest forest fires, the 1982–83 conflagration that destroyed 20 percent of its forest reserves. It is axiomatic that logging severely increases the intensity of forest fires by leaving flammable detritus on the forest floor and cutting access roads, which act as funnels for moving fires.

More than 70 percent of Indonesia is forested, and this places an inordinate amount of pressure upon its environmental agency to preserve this forest against overwhelming pressures from a burgeoning population. There are more than 3,700 islands in Indonesia, and there are 178 million people—65 percent of them under 35 years of age—living on them. The economy of the area is getting better, but there are 2.3 million young people still seeking jobs every

Aware of the gigantic destruction of the rain forest by logging interests, Penan tribespeople gather together to form human blockades on logging roads in the Malaysian forests.
(LIBMAN/GREENPEACE)

year. The gross domestic product of Indonesia calculated, in 1990, to $450 per person per year, and there is a heavy foreign currency debt. It is not a place in which conservation is easy.

And yet, despite seemingly insurmountable obstacles, it does take place, in greater abundance than in Malaysia. Indonesia, for instance, is the world's largest exporter of tropical plywood, and thus there is that industry to employ its people.

The negative side of this has been the failure on the part of its industrialists and its government to adopt more stringent pollution standards. Though Indonesia does not have the monumental problem of Bangkok, in nearby Thailand, with its population of 6 million, 50,000 factories, no sewerage system, and the wholesale dumping of industrial waste and household garbage into the Chao Phraya River, the industrial pollution of its waterways is enough to cause great concern.

First, mass deforestation has caused widespread runoff of eroded soil into Indonesia's waterways. Second, industrial waste adds further pollution. Third, the success of the

"Green Revolution," which turned Indonesia from a nation dependent upon imported rice to one of the world's leading rice exporters, also resulted in the leaching of large amounts of agricultural chemicals (necessary for the survival of new strains of rice) into the waterways.

Finally, it has been proved that the mass deforestation in Indonesia and in other parts of Southeast Asia has increased global warming. Tracts of forest anywhere act as sinks for carbon dioxide, which is lost during major clearance. The burning that precedes the clearing releases carbon into the atmosphere. The breakdown of organic matter in the soil afterward releases still more carbon into the air. Add to this the release of methane, produced by decomposing vegetation in the paddyfields and a byproduct of digestion from cattle, and the emission of greenhouse gases from Southeast Asia, particularly Indonesia, is abundant indeed.

Nevertheless, there is an effort to enforce longstanding environmental laws by the Indonesian government. The regulations state that only trees larger than 19.7 inches in diameter may be logged; that the average concessionaire who holds 864,500 acres may log only 24,700 acres a year, which means that each block is cut only once every 35 years; and that concessionaires must maintain nurseries and must engage in systematic reforestation. The exporting of raw logs has been banned since 1985. Since 1990, these regulations have been enforced by aerial photography and additional forestry police.

Indonesia has announced its intentions to reforest the 50 million acres of land that has been most grievously devastated, but, since it can only spend about $300 million—enough to plant 740,000 acres—a year, this will take 65 years to accomplish.

And this is one of the greatest problems facing the preservers of forests in Southeast Asia. Emil Salim, Indonesia's state minister of population and the environment stated its position forcefully in an interview with the world press in 1990: "While the developed world screams about the forests," he said, "it puts quotas on the imports of textiles and shoes." Charging higher export duties on processed wood products, which Indonesia exports, than on raw logs, which Malaysia exports, makes it more difficult to pay back their debts, he said. "If people in the West want to help the tropical forests, help us to plant trees and speed it up," he concluded.

The banning of the export of raw logs in 1985 drove the logging industry from Malaysia and Indonesia to Papua New Guinea, the eastern half of the main island of New Guinea plus an archipelago of 600 smaller islands, and the repository of what has been called by conservationists "the last rain forest." Last or not, it is a miraculously green and lush cloud of greenery that houses walnut and Borneo mahogany trees that rise a hundred feet in the air, and cover 80 percent of Papua New Guinea—a total of 145,000 square miles, or an area roughly the size of California. Within its lush recesses, it shelters and nurtures one of the most diverse collections of wildlife on the earth, including the world's largest butterfly and 38 of the 43 species of birds of paradise.

Isolated from the rest of Southeast Asia and thinly populated, this part of the world has made only short strides from the Stone Age. Its inhabitants speak a brand of Pidgin English, dress in minimal, natural attire, and trade the teeth of animals.

Thus, when foreign loggers, many of them from a gutted Malaysia, arrived on the beaches of Papua New Guinea in 1985, clutching great wads of money, it was very much like a replay of 17th-century colonists dealing with natives whose way of life was based upon trust.

"This is a battle that pits people wearing loincloths and bird feathers against fast-talking, fast-moving foreign loggers," explains Tim Neville, an Australian who is the forests minister of the area. "The loggers turn up on a beach with a handful of money and tell these gullible landowners, 'I'm here to help you if you let me just take down a few of these old trees.' And they leave the landowners with nothing."

Law in Papua New Guinea is clear; the land belongs to those who have settled it since antiquity, and so the government cannot legally step in and block these sales. The loggers offer provocative inducements: new schools, health care, roads, bridges. For this, they shipped out of the area, in 1993 alone, $500 million worth of logs, for which they paid $15 million.

They often make deals with entire villages, paying an average of $24 per tree, then selling the felled trees for $600 apiece. The village of Sembam, on the eastern coast of New Britain, the largest of the offshore islands, sold off all of its forest in 1991 to a Malaysian logging company, which immediately brought in its bulldozers and chain saws. It made short work of the forest, sweeping the landscape clean.

Without trees to hold it together, the topsoil soon eroded, and ran into nearby creeks that were once used for drinking water. The streets of the village turned to rivers of mud. Two years later, each inhabitant of the village had received approximately $57, which added up to $14,000 for the entire settlement. The company hauled off more than $3 million worth of timber. As for its promise to build a schoolhouse, three new first-aid stations, and a permanent bridge: Only the schoolhouse was built, a rickety open-air structure with two classrooms and housing for two teachers.

Not only did the bulldozers take down the trees, they carved roads through the farms of the village people, rendering the farms untillable, and therefore destroying the future way of life for the villagers.

And all of this occurred despite a government commission finding in 1989 that concluded that, because of government incompetence and corruption, which included bribes from loggers to officials, logging in Papua New Guinea was "out of control." The report likened the loggers to "robber barons—bribing politicians and leaders, creating social disharmony, and ignoring laws."

After the release of the report, gangs of unidentified men gathered near the homes of its authors. Judge Ross Barnett was attacked in the streets of Port Moresby, the capital, and repeatedly stabbed with sharpened screwdrivers. Mr. Neville also came under repeated attack. The windshield of his car was smashed, and men with guns surrounded his house several times.

The loggers shrug off responsibility for any of this. "The resources in this country are owned by the landowners," one of them told New York Times reporter Philip Shenon, "and they have to decide for themselves whether they are happy. We think they are happy."

A handful of villages have, as of 1994, signed up with the Pacific Heritage Foundation, a creation of environmentalist Max Henderson. Villagers who do are put to work for about $6 a day, which is a good wage in Papua New Guinea. They chop down trees but leave enough standing so the forest can grow back quickly. The trees are then processed by them and shipped to a chain of English hardware shops that sell only "environmentally sensitive" lumber.

It is admittedly not enough to stem the terrible tide of destruction in Papua New Guinea. The tribal chief of a New Britain village articulated the reason. "Many of these people," he said, referring to his fellow villagers, "want fast money. Some of them have been so poor all of their lives that they have never eaten tinned meat. And that's what they tell me. They say that they want tinned meat before they die."

The supply of money and meat and forest will not last forever, or even nearly forever. Environmentalists have reported to the government of Papua New Guinea that, at the present rate of destruction, all of the timber with commercial value will be felled within a generation, possibly within a decade.

And this is the situation throughout all of Southeast Asia. Thailand, Vietnam, and the Philippines have already lost 80 percent of their forest cover and will have to replant. Indonesia and eastern Malaysia still retain enough forest to be able to rely on natural regeneration to stabilize their ecology—if they can control the logging interests.

Meanwhile, governments of these areas are slowly coming to the realization that they are destroying not only their richest natural wealth, but seriously jeopardizing their future income and stability, too. But new regulations, however admirable, are often selectively and almost always gently administered. Environmental agencies are understaffed and underfunded.

It appears that action is taken only after periodic natural disasters such as the 1988 flash flood in southern Thailand, in which mud and cut logs cascaded down a mountain and killed 350 villagers. Immediately following this, the Thai government instituted a complete ban on all logging. But the ban proved temporary. Within months, illegal cutting resumed.

And so, environmental awareness comes, it seems, slowly in Southeast Asia, which is why it has become a prime target area for logging interests, international environmental organizations, and the United Nations Environment Programme.

TASMANIA
(HOBART, MT. WELLINGTON)
FOREST FIRE
February 7–13, 1967

The most destructive forest fire in Tasmania's history destroyed 860 homes, 12 small towns, and 3 of the state's biggest industries from February 7 through February 13, 1967. Fifty-two residents of the city of Hobart and the surrounding area died, hundreds were injured, and thousands were made homeless.

"We have just gone through the most horrible day of our history and we need help," entreated Mabel Hiller, the Deputy Lord Mayor of Hobart, the capital city of Tasmania, on the morning of February 8, 1967, the heart of the southern hemisphere's summer. The night sky had been turned to a feverish daylight by the most extensive and destructive forest fire in the history of the small (26,383 square miles) island state, located 150 miles south of Australia, and the flames, fanned at times by 70 mph winds, would continue to consume the area on either side of the Derwent River and on the slopes of Mt. Wellington for the next week.

Bordered on the east by the Pacific Ocean and the west by the Indian Ocean, and ringed by a constellation of smaller islands, Tasmania is a relatively unspoiled and undeveloped part of the world, looking very much as it did when it was discovered by Dutch navigator Abel Tasman in 1642.

Taken over by the British in 1803, the island state was used as a penal colony until 1853, when local opposition and a growing nationalism removed the prisoners and their medieval-seeming penitentiaries. By 1901, when Tasmania was federated as a state in the Commonwealth of Australia, there were only two sizable cities, Hobart and Launceston. In 1967, the same two cities were the only centers of population that exceeded 50,000 people, but the harnessing of hydroelectric power from the abundant waters of Great Lake, in its interior, promised new industry and prosperity for the area.

But on the night of February 7, the three largest industries to be built since the arrival of adequate hydroelectric power—a brewery, a carbide company, and a huge fish cannery—were reduced to blackened rubble by the fire.

It began on the agricultural slopes of Mt. Wellington, a small mountain in southern Tasmania, on the afternoon of February 7. The summer dryness, exacerbated by high winds, turned a small fire into a conflagration in a matter of hours.

The small sheep farms on the lower slopes of Mt. Wellington were the first to feel the fury of the fire. An Australian Broadcasting Commission reporter later recounted scenes of depressing devastation, of house after house in ashes and the carcasses of hundreds of cattle, sheep, and wild animals littered along country roads. Families sat by the sides of these roads, weeping as their farms were consumed by the racing wall of flames.

By nightfall, the fire had reached the outskirts of Hobart. In Ferntree, a suburb of the city, 44 homes and a hotel were destroyed; in Lenah Valley, four men were burned to death in a useless attempt to fight back the advancing fire.

By daybreak, the atmosphere was thick with black ashes, hanging on the air like suspended beetles of dark dust. The ground was charred to a stygian, crumbling consistency, and the fire raced through Hobart, then southward to the sea. Twelve small towns in its path were wiped entirely off the map. More than 600 homes, both in Hobart and in the countryside, were totally destroyed; hundreds more were damaged. More than 6,000 people, at final count, were rendered homeless by the fire.

Aid, in the form of medical and food supplies, was immediately shipped from Australia by the ironically named destroyer *Derwent*. The supplies arrived as more fires ignited on the other side of the Derwent River from Hobart.

For a solid week, the brush on either side of the river would suddenly ignite, as firefighters patrolled the area. Finally, on February 15, the last flames of a fire that began as several nearly insignificant seasonal summer smolderings but which united into one of Tasmania's worst tragedies was extinguished. The final count: 52 dead, hundreds injured, thousands made homeless, and more than $12 million in property damage.

UNITED STATES
(ALASKA, TONGASS NATIONAL FOREST)
DEFORESTATION
1950–Present

··

For slightly more than 40 years, the Tongass National Forest in Alaska has been a hotly contested piece of natural real estate— the last great tract of northwest temperate forest in the United States, and therefore a place to protect (according to environmentalists), or a place to exploit (according to timber, mining, and oil interests). The Endangered Species Act, itself endangered by a less-than-sympathetic majority in the Congress of the United States, has so far preserved the area, but there are strong forces currently at work to remove this protection.

The panhandle of Alaska, which drifts downward and eastward from its major bulk, biting slightly into British Columbia and encompassing the elegant, icy blueness of Glacier Bay National Monument, does not offer an expected picture of the nation's largest and coldest state. True, its glaciers are spectacular and are thus a stop on the itinerary of cruise lines. But overall, it has mild winters, with heavy rainfall and little snow, which is why, if it were wider and less mountainous, it would probably contain more of Alaska's population than it does.

As it is, its climate has produced the Tongass, the largest national forest in the United States, and, with the Chilean frontier, one of two surviving temperate rain forests in the world. But, like the forests of Chile, the Tongass National Forest is under siege from commercial interests who see, not great natural beauty, but great amounts of money to be made from logging, mining, and oil exploration.

And so, the saga of the Tongass has turned into one of the most hard-fought environmental conflicts in the United States.

The Tongass, like almost everything in Alaska, is big. It meanders over a 17-million-acre archipelago, an area the size of Indiana. For centuries, largely because the panhandle of Alaska is difficult to get into or out of, it remained pristine and untouched. Its spruce trees grew to skyscraper heights, its salmon streams were undisturbed except for Indian and sport fishermen. Its stock of grizzly bears, seals, and bald eagles multiplied and maintained themselves without danger or challenge.

Then came the drive toward statehood and the development mania of the 1950s, and with them two major timber companies, the Alaska Pulp Corporation and Louisiana-Pacific Ketchikan, Inc. Both deal in the clear cutting of spruce forests, then the grinding down and squashing of the wood into pulp, which in turn is sold primarily to Japan to produce textiles, such as disposable diapers.

At the time, seasonal fishing was the main occupation of the residents of the area, and the prospect of two major logging interests setting up shop carried with it promises of high and rewarding employment. And so, a 50-year contract between the logging companies and the U.S. Forest Service was hammered out. In it, the timber interests were guaranteed a profit, which meant that when the bottom dropped out of the timber market—which it did in the 1980s—the government would make up the difference, thus handsomely subsidizing the profits of the two lumber outfits.

Ordinarily, Congress, in 1980, might have tried to buy its way out of the arrangement. But Alaska's senator Ted Stevens successfully fought to lock in the 50-year contract, arguing that some 1,500 logging jobs would be lost, and the honor of the United States of America would be compromised if it reneged on its guarantees. A deal was, after all, a deal.

The Alaska National Interest Lands Conservation Act of 1980 provided that the Forest Service spend as much as $40 million a year to assist in harvesting 4.5 billion board feet of lumber over a 10-year period.

To conservation groups such as the Southeast Alaska Conservation Council, the act was corporate welfare personified. In 1986, Bart Koehler of the council told reporters that the Tongass timbering industry was a "juggernaut grinding away at wildlife habitat. It is incredible," he continued, "that the overall management of the forest since 1982 had an average cost to the taxpayers of $882 million a year, primarily for building timber roads."

The promise of building these roads so that the pulp companies could get their equipment in and their logs out was one of the main inducements to the timber industry in the 1950s, and their maintenance was crucial to the continuance of their operations. "Nature here is pretty forgiving," noted David Morton, a Forest Service supervisor, "What looked like godawful places a few years ago are now pretty nice places."

Not necessarily so, countered Sylvia Geraghty, a local critic of timbering. "We're losing the Tongass and we are losing our way of life and we feel it's unjust and unfair," she told Philip Shavecoff of the *New York Times* in 1986. "It is a big giveaway to the mills. They pretend it is for multiple use—good for fishermen and tourism. It's not true. It's just sugar coating on a bitter pill."

More sugar-coated give aways went to the pulp companies. From 1982 through 1986, the Forest Service spent $234 million on roads and subsidies. The pulp companies paid $2 per 1,000 feet (the yield of one tree), which they sold on the open market for from $200 to $600 per 1,000 feet. It was an easy way to make a very good living, and American taxpayers were supplying much of the means to do it, while simultaneously depleting a natural resource.

Finally, in 1988, public and conservationist pressure forced Congress to reexamine the locked-in provisions of the logging contract.

By 1989, the mills in the Tongass were entitled to buy up to 15,000 acres of Tongass timber a year at $2.19 per 1,000 board feet, which was less than 1 percent of the market price, which was $100 to $400 per 1,000 board feet, depending upon the grade of wood.

Without that sort of arrangement, the two companies working the Tongass asserted that they would have to pull out, eliminating 1,800 jobs.

"What they're saying," observed Joe Mehrkens, a member of the Wilderness Society in Alaska, to reporters, "is that they need a monopoly, they need the very best timber and they need $40 million a year in taxpayer money to keep them going."

The House of Representatives ignored the timber companies' threat and pressure from Alaska's congressmen, and passed a bill that required annual appropriations for logging subsidies, forcing a renegotiation of the timber harvest contracts and limiting cutting in areas of the forest where wildlife was particularly vulnerable.

In addition, Representative Robert J. Mrazek of New York introduced, for the second time, a bill that would entirely end the 50-year contract, make the $40 million yearly appropriation subject to annual review, set up additional protected wilderness areas, and redirect the Forest Service to put its energies into wildlife and recreational enhancements and get out of the timber business.

This time, the bill passed. In July 1989, the House canceled the 50-year deal, designated 1.8 million acres of the Tongass as wilderness area free from roads and commercial development, banned logging within 100 feet of salmon streams, and subjected future timber sales to competitive bidding.

Nearly a year later, the Senate modified the House bill. The new version, instead of canceling the 50-year deal,

The Tongass National Forest, the last great tract of northwest temperate forest, could be reduced to this if antienvironmental forces in industry and the U.S. Congress have their way.
(UNEP)

merely modified it, barring logging from only 637,000 acres and, even within that reduced acreage, allowing mining.

It was a clear setback for environmentalists. "The Senate bill doesn't protect enough lands, doesn't designate them as wilderness, doesn't include as tough a buffer zone provision as the House passed bill, and doesn't terminate the long-term contracts," complained Alaska Conservation Council director Bart Koehler.

On and on the debate raged, with the two pulp companies, and especially the Japanese-owned Alaska Pulp Corporation threatening to pull out of Alaska entirely, thus throwing a considerable number of workers out of work.

But the Alaska Pulp Corporation broke its own contract. In 1993, it shut down a pulp mill in Sitka, citing as its reason a worldwide glut in pulp products. In January 1994, the Clinton administration seized upon this action as proof of a breach of the original contract and, through the National Forest Service, canceled the 50-year deal.

It was a major victory for environmentalists. "This egregious contract has long been the driving force in mismanagement of the Tongass National Forest," stated Representative George Miller of California, the chairman of the House Natural Resources Committee.

But the battle was far from over. Only 10 months later, in November 1994, the monumental Republican election victory that swept Republicans into control of both the House of Representatives and the Senate swept out environmentally conscious committee heads in both houses. In a quirk of politics and history, all three members of Alaska's congressional delegation were awarded significant committee chairmanships.

Representative Don Young was appointed head of the House Resources Committee; Senator Frank Murkowski was awarded chairmanship of the Senate Energy and Natural Resources Committee; and Senator Ted Stevens became the number two man on the Senate Appropriations Committee.

The three immediately went to work to not only reinstate the 50-year contract but to knock down the regulations passed by the previous Democratic Congress, toss out the breach of contract suit against Alaska Pulp Corporation, up the limit of timber that could be cut by the other two Alaska companies, and, while they were at it, open up the Arctic Wildlife Refuge to oil drilling (see Alaska, unit III, pp. 164–166).

The Alaskan delegation was totally dedicated to industry, and apparently invincible. When Senator Murkowski went home to Alaska with an announcement that he was going to create 2,400 timber-related jobs in the Tongass with his legislation—and encountered unified and overwhelming opposition from his constituents—Senator Stevens merely attached a Tongass rider, which was less conspicuous than the Murkowski bill, to an Interior Department appropriations bill.

By September 1995, the new Congress's legislative attack upon the environment, written partly by lobbyists representing timber, mining, energy, and ranching interests, had succeeded in drawing up bills that would not only open the Tongass, but vast stretches of forests in Montana, the Carolinas, and Maine to near total destruction. A bill designed to help balance the federal budget by cutting the budget of the Department of Interior carried far-reaching provisions that would spell ecological disaster for Alaska. Among much, the bill would place a moratorium on listing new species for protection under the Endangered Species Act by eliminating financing for such activities, and curtail a major assessment of the regional ecology of the Columbia River Basin, thus sharply limiting studies of how logging would affect endangered fish species.

In the Tongass specifically, the rider that Senator Stevens attached to appropriations legislation would increase by approximately one-third the allowable timber harvest in the Tongass National Forest and direct the Forest Service to restore the original 50-year plan of subsidized logging in the Tongass.

President Clinton promised a veto, and the threat forced the withdrawal of the rider. But the assault against the Tongass was still far from over.

In May of 1997, the Forest Service dropped its own environmental bombshell. In its long-awaited land management plan for the Tongass, it authorized what amounted to a 10-year program of clear-cutting of 220 million to 267 million board feet of timber annually, which is enough to load 50,000 logging trucks or build over 20,000 houses a year. The plan also established buffer zones along streams and beaches and at the mouths of rivers, and protected 500 miles along 32 rivers, under the terms of the Wild and Scenic Rivers Act.

While less than loggers and Alaska's congressional delegation had sought, and a slight reduction over past logging levels, it was attacked vigorously by environmentalists and editorial writers. "If you take a watershed and punch it full of clear-cuts that only cover a total of one-third of the watershed, you have ruined it for everyone who does not have a chain saw in their hands," wrote Nathaniel Lawrence, forestry director at the Natural Resources Defense Council.

"The volume of timber to be made available annually under this plan will clearly be inadequate to sustain an integrated timber industry in southeast Alaska," countered Jack Phelps, executive director of the Alaska Forest Association, an industry group.

As of this writing, the battle simmers, while Secretary of Agriculture Dan Glickman reviews the proposal. Meanwhile the two senators and one congressman from Alaska promise a fight, a predictable action. In a little over two years, they accomplished more potential damage than thousands of years of careless destruction has done in the rain and temperate forests of the world. Time and future elections will write the outcome.

UNITED STATES
(CALIFORNIA, CLEVELAND NATIONAL FOREST)
FIRE
November 24–28, 1956

Eleven firefighters died and hundreds of homes burned in a five-day forest fire that gutted the land along the San Diego River in the Cleveland National Forest in California from November 24–28, 1956. The fire was begun by a 15-year-old boy who confessed that he wanted to "see if the grass would burn."

"I've never seen anything like this fire," Ralph L. Fenner, a specialist in backfiring technique said as he mopped charred wood bits from his face. He and hundreds of other firefighters, including volunteer sailors from the San Diego Naval Base, were battling an enormous forest fire that consumed 40,000 acres of the Cleveland National Forest, located between San Diego and Anza Desert State Park in California.

"It burns without a sound. There isn't a bit of moisture in the underbrush to cause crackling," he went on. "Until the winds die down or shift, or unless it rains, the whole United States Air Force and one hundred million dollars can't stop this fire."

Hundreds of homes were burned, 11 firefighters died, and 40,000 acres of the Cleveland National Forest were consumed after a 15-year-old boy dropped a match in dry grass "to see if it would burn."
(ROUGIER/UNEP)

The timber in the Cleveland National Forest was, as he noted, as dry as the dust of the desert to its east. No rain had fallen in weeks, and near gale-force winds were whipping both flames and treetops.

A week earlier, north of San Diego, in the San Bernardino Mountains, another brushfire had consumed 15,296 acres of watershed. But a force of 1,235 firefighters had brought that under control.

The new blaze, fanned by the same winds that had made the earlier fire so destructive and difficult to control, consumed 10,000 acres of timber and brush in the first four hours of its life, on November 24. It continued to spread its fiery fingers westward, consuming the countryside at a rate of 2,000 acres an hour.

By November 25, nearly 2,000 firefighters were battling the blaze, but their efforts had to be concentrated along a 20-mile stretch of the 73-mile perimeter of the fire.

Its eerie silence mystified veteran firefighters like Mr. Fenner. A group of them, including United States Forest Service employees, sailors, and prisoners from a county honor prison camp in the path of the fire, were trapped on the night of November 25 against a sheer cliff wall. Flames spread before them, parallel to the cliff, and they were making steady progress against them until the wind suddenly shifted. Without a sound, the flames caught on both sides of the group, forcing them back against the cliff.

A score of men dropped their shovels and raced through a space that was not entirely consumed by flames. But 11 of the group, including three Forest Service employees and seven prisoners of the camp were pinned against the cliff wall. They tried frantically to scale the wall, but it was too steep, and there were neither foot nor handholds in it. All 11 burned to death.

On the fire raged for another two days, consuming 44,000 acres, until finally, on the night of November 27, 1956, tanker planes dousing burning brush and timber with a fire-stopping solution and 500 men setting backfires along the San Diego River canyon brought it under control.

That same night, the Forest Service arrested 15-year-old Gilbert Paipa, a native American of the Inaja tribe, who lived on the Inaja Reservation, and attended high school in the mountain town of Julian, bordering the Cleveland National Forest.

"I just got a crazy idea to throw a match in the grass to see if it would burn," he told Forest Service investigator Elwood Stone who brought the youth before Judge Robert B. Burch the following day. The judge, taking testimony from the boy's high school principal who described him as a "sad little character," circled the boy with his arm and said, "Gilbert, we're going to try to help you."

The judge remanded the youth who, despite his high school attendance could neither read nor write, to San Diego Juvenile Hall, where he received an education and was paroled the following year.

UNITED STATES
(CALIFORNIA)
MEDITERRANEAN FRUIT FLY INFESTATION
June 1980–September 1982

··

A horrifically destructive and costly outbreak of Mediterranean fruit fly infestation occurred in southern California in June 1980, reached its height in December of that year, and was not brought under control until September 1982. In the interim, the $14 billion agricultural industry of California was temporarily crippled and depleted, and 4,000 acres of California were placed under quarantine. Fourteen hundred and forty-five square miles were subjected to regular aerial spraying, and the cost of it all amounted to $95 million—$74.7 million from the state of California and $20.6 million from the federal government. Confrontations between environmentalists and aerial sprayers, between the federal and state governments, between Japan and the United States, between states in the United States, and among politicians turned this into a full-scale war waged on many fronts.

The "Medfly" as it is unaffectionately called, first made its presence known in the United States in 1921, when it was discovered in Florida citrus fruit. It invaded the coffee plantations of Hawaii in the 1940s and first appeared in California in a San Diego suburb in 1974, probably imported by a tourist from Hawaii. In each case, the pest was eradicated. But these confrontations were merely skirmishes compared to the all-out war that began with the appearance of the Medfly in the residential northern California county of Santa Clara in June 1980.

By December of that year, the Medfly had withstood every effort to eradicate it, and on Christmas Eve of 1980, California governor Edmund G. Brown Jr. declared a state of emergency, ordering 1,000 state workers, including a contingent from the California Conservation Corps, to form a task force to join state, local, and federal workers in stripping trees of fruit that might be contaminated.

The emergency was declared after Taiwan banned fruit imported from the Santa Clara valley unless the state certified that the produce had been fumigated and was free of fruit flies, and threats by Mexico and Japan to follow Taiwan's example. "I can't overstress the impact," Martin Muschinske, an economic entomologist for the state of California, stated at the time. "The Medfly is for all practical purposes the greatest threat to tree fruit that we have. There isn't a 'beastie' that I can think of that even comes close to the Medfly, primarily because of its ability to withstand a wide temperature range and its huge selection of host plants."

The fly, called *Ceratits capatata* by entomologists, is part of the Tephritidae and Drosophilidae families of flies (the Tephritidae family alone contains about 1,200 species). Floppy winged, with blue translucent eyes, a little larger than fruit flies native to the United States, a little smaller than the ordinary housefly, and considerably more destructive than both, the female of the species spreads havoc by puncturing a fruit and injecting an average of 300 to 400 eggs under its skin. Highly nonselective, the Medfly chooses at least 250 plants as hosts for its egg laying.

Its first infestation of the Santa Clara valley occurred in 1975, when that part of California justifiably reflected its original title as "the Valley of the Heart's Delight." Square mile upon square mile of valley was rich in fruit trees, as far

In 1980, fertile "Medflies" invaded the Santa Clara valley of California, shredding its crops, then spread to the San Joaquin valley, one of the nation's richest sources of fruits and vegetables.
(AP/WIDE WORLD)

as the eye could see. By 1980, urbanization and industrialization had combined to produce a name change for the area from Valley of the Heart's Delight to Silicone Valley. Still, 530 square miles of fruit trees were first threatened in the 1980 invasion.

How the fly migrated to the Santa Clara valley in 1980 is unknown. The eggs deposited by females are almost invisibly small, as is the maggot that emerges from the egg. It is at this stage that the fly is usually transported on fruit and, according to Robert Marburger, assistant regional director for the United States Department of Agriculture, "possibly someone unknowingly brought it in from Hawaii. . . ." In other words, the fly might have come in on an illegally imported piece of fruit concealed in someone's carry-on.

In 1975, the outbreak of Medflies was controlled naturally by the introduction of sterile male flies. The impotent males, made sterile by bombardments of radioactive cobalt, were interjected in huge numbers, and so supplanted the fertile males. As a result, the females produced unfertilized eggs.

Unfortunately, though California and the federal government had joined funds to construct a $3.8 million facility in Hawaii to increase the supply of sterile male fruit flies, it was still unfinished in December 1980, and there were not enough sterile males to control the latest invasion.

Ground spraying with pesticides had proved ineffectual, so federal and state authorities proposed aerial spraying, a recommendation that was met with immediate opposition from the cities of Palo Alto, Mountain View, and Santa Clara, as well as the Santa Clara County board of supervisors.

Dr. Theodore Feinstadt, professor of obstetrics and gynecology at the Stanford University Medical School, warned at a San Jose city council meeting that December that the proposal to spray the pesticide Malathion from the air risked "cellular poison" in newborns, and called the proposal "a cruel biological experiment."

And so the three-sided battle was joined: On one side were the advocates of spraying, on another those against it, and on the third side of the triangle was the Medfly, merrily multiplying.

California Governor Jerry Brown chose to take the middle ground and declare a state of emergency during which he launched a blanket stripping of fruit trees in the affected area. One thousand state workers, including a contingent from the California Conservation Corps, were mobilized to join local and federal workers in stripping the trees. Some 300,000 residences were visited by this army, which climbed and shook all manner of fruit-bearing trees, gathered up the fallen fruit, stuffed it into plastic bags, and hauled it off to landfills.

Behind the tree strippers, other crews followed, lacing the earth where the fruit fell with the larvicide Fenthion, and spraying the denuded trees with Malathion to kill any residual flies.

Simultaneously, four light planes blanketed the area with sterile male fruit flies imported from Peru by the U.S. Department of Agriculture, and reared by the tens-of-millions in an empty school. At least 200 million sterile males were released by January 31, which meant at least 100 sterile males for each fertile female.

"We've been a step behind the fly," said Jerry Scribner, the leader of the eradication effort. "Now we're working against a biological deadline, the end of February when the fruit starts ripening and the fly becomes much more active."

Meanwhile, other fronts were opening in the war. By the end of February, state officials in Texas issued an order to ban all California fruit that had not been fumigated from entering their state. While California already required Texas fruit and vegetables to be fumigated against the Mexican fruit fly, California nevertheless decided to fight the Texas ban against its produce in the U.S. Supreme Court. The Court refused to hear the case.

By July 1981, it was apparent that the $22 million program of stripping trees and dropping sterile male fruit flies had failed. Fifty-six separate infestations of the fly larva in northern Santa Clara County proved it. There appeared to be only one way left, and that was through aerial dropping of Malathion over 500 square miles of Santa Clara County.

Governor Brown, mindful of the demonstrations of the previous December against aerial spraying, did nothing. And the infestation spread, from 530 square miles to 620, including part of southern San Mateo County, near the town of Mountain View.

New stripping ordinances followed. Local residents of Santa Clara County were ordered to strip the trees on their property, or face a $500 fine and/or a six-month jail sentence. Two thousand more California Conservation Corps members were mobilized to follow up with ground spraying. In addition, roadblocks were set up on the perimeters of the contaminated area to confiscate any contaminated produce being carried out.

The demonstrations against aerial spraying were revitalized. Angry mothers, some with children in their arms, stormed the state house in Sacramento. Governor Brown listened and stated that he would forgo the "unacceptable health, human welfare and environmental risks" of "subjecting 500,000 people, including pregnant women, infants and children, to six or more aerial applications of a toxic pesticide."

But as July wore on and new information surfaced, the governor began to backtrack. The Peruvian sterile males had, it turned out, not been sterile at all and had mated with females to introduce a new generation of Medflies. The state's entire $14 billion produce crop was now threatened, and the U.S. Department of Agriculture announced a quarantine of the whole state.

Calling the order "politically motivated sabotage" by the Reagan administration, Governor Brown reversed himself, and ordered aerial spraying. The Department of Agriculture rescinded its order, awaiting the results of the spraying.

Now the Environmental Protection Agency entered the picture, vowing that the exposure levels to be expected from spraying posed no health hazard. The American Cancer Society also noted publicly that Malathion, developed by Germany as a nerve gas in World War II, and now a staple in household pesticides, did not induce cancer in rats or mice.

Beverlee Meyers, California's Health Director, issued a statement assuring citizens that "there is no significant health risk" in Malathion, which had been cleared for a variety of home uses.

Environmental groups, on the other hand, were far from sanguine about the prospects of aerial bombardment. Friends of the Earth stated that "the decision to go to aerial spraying . . . represents a cynical effort that will poison people, not the Medfly."

But, after a 5:00 A.M. call to President Reagan that was unreturned, Governor Brown issued the order to begin aerial spraying at midnight on July 11, a deadline that passed with no takeoffs because of efforts by attorneys for citizen and environmental groups set upon blocking the spraying.

A Superior Court judge in Santa Clara issued a stay order until the following Monday, and over the weekend a condition of supreme discontent seemed to settle over the afflicted area. Though California agricultural officials continued to insist that Malathion spray posed no threat to human health, they nevertheless urged residents to stay indoors, to cover their cars, and not to leave children's toys outdoors during the sprayings, which were scheduled to take place between 2:00 and 6:00 A.M. Other medical authorities advised people with respiratory problems to leave the area.

As the time drew nearer, the International Red Cross, in anticipation of the possible worst, set up four shelters containing a total of 4,000 beds in Alameda, San Mateo, and Santa Cruz Counties, on the rim of the target area. Meanwhile, roadblocks leading out of the quarantined region yielded startling results. In four days, State troopers reported stopping approximately 82,000 vehicles and confiscating fruit or vegetables from 4,700 of them.

Meanwhile, a parallel political battle raged, as Secretary of Defense Casper Weinberger first rescinded, then reinstated an agreement reached earlier between California officials and Secretary of the Navy John Lehman to allow the use of Moffet Field, a navy air base near San Jose, as a staging area for the spraying aircraft.

However, because of threats to shoot down the helicopters used for spraying (the threat proved real, after bullet holes were later found in one of them, police helicopters were launched as escorts), the aircraft were ultimately kept at a secret location.

At public meetings, demonstrators held up signs stating, "We oppose death from the skies." At one of these, in San Jose, Governor Brown addressed a crowd of 500 and conveyed assurances from experts, including Dr. Donald Kennedy, president of Stanford University and former head of the Federal Food and Drug Administration, that the spraying would be safe.

On Monday, July 13, both the California Supreme Court and the Santa Clara County Superior Court refused to issue restraining orders against the spraying, and the orders to begin the operation were issued. Simultaneously, the Federal Agriculture Department expanded the quarantined area from 630 square miles to 2,082 square miles, which represented all of Santa Clara, San Mateo, and Alameda Counties.

At 2:00 A.M. on July 14, the first helicopter took off with its cargo of molasses-like liquid-protein bait, coated with Malathion. The object was to kill the Medfly not by inundating it with a cloud of pesticide but rather by attracting it to the poison. The first sortie was aborted after 48 minutes, however, because of a malfunctioning spray pump. Only five to six square miles were covered in the first night, and hardly any of the 575,000 residents in the target area seemed to notice the mission, with the exception of a small group of demonstrators who discovered the secret launching site of the helicopters, rushed it, and managed to nick one workman with a knife.

Meanwhile, across the country, 11 southern states announced that they were also quarantining unfumigated produce from the three California counties.

The following day, crews checking plums stripped from trees in an area 20 miles from San Francisco and outside of the quarantine zone, found fertile Medflies, and Governor Brown asked President Reagan to declare the three quarantined counties federal disaster areas—a request that would be denied a week later.

The aerial assault was still sputtering. One more helicopter ascended into the skies above Santa Clara county on July 14 and covered another six square miles. The following night, as more square mileage was added to the quarantined area, more clogging of another helicopter's spraying mechanism occurred, and a mere 18 square miles more were covered.

As word of what appeared to be fumbling attempts to control the epidemic were printed, Texas, Alabama, Florida, Mississippi, and South Carolina widened their quarantine on California crops from the three counties and threatened to boycott all California produce.

Finally, on July 18, the aerial sprayers got it right. Six helicopters took to the air and covered more area than they had in the previous four nights. But now, the fear that motorists might carry contaminated fruit into the fertile San Joaquin valley, the heart of California's $14 billion agriculture industry, began to complicate the situation even further.

On July 20, Louisiana, North Carolina, and Arkansas announced that they would also quarantine California produce shipped from the three counties, and California promptly added these states to the enjoinment suit it had already begun against Texas. The charge: these quarantines were in violation of the Constitution and federal regulations, since they attempted to regulate interstate commerce. On July 22, the suit was carried to the Supreme Court. By the 23rd, a federal judge had ordered Florida to lift its quarantine and four other southern states announced that they would not enforce theirs. But Texas still ordered inspection points for California produce, and Mexico announced a ban on importing produce from the three affected counties. Meanwhile, back in California, the federal government increased the quarantine to more than 2,000 square miles.

By the beginning of August, some fears about the spread of the Medfly infestation were realized. Three dead Medflies, presumed to have come from California, were discovered in Tampa, Florida. The bodies were so decomposed, it was impossible to determine their origin, but Florida agriculture commissioner Doyle Connor approved limited local ground spraying, and Florida appealed the Supreme Court decision that had prohibited its previous ban on California produce.

On August 14, the worst fears of California's farmers were also realized. Three Medflies were found in an insect trap in the small town of Patterson, located in the San Joaquin valley, and a day later, 56 more were discovered in nearby Wesley.

Now the battle was resumed in earnest. Four C-130 transport airplanes were dispatched to saturate the area with Malathion, and the quarantine was extended to 264 square miles of the lushest farmland in the San Joaquin valley. The crop loss was estimated at up to $567 million, and to forestall further damage, the harvest of tomatoes, pears, and bell peppers was accelerated. Eight billion of the state's $14 billion annual agriculture business was put at risk by the latest infestation.

And now the problem became international. Japan, California's biggest agricultural customer, asked the United States to restrict shipments of some California fruits, a move that produced a sharp rebuke and a threat by Governor Brown to retaliate by embargoing Japanese goods in California and preventing them from being shipped through his state to the rest of the United States.

The crisis was important enough to involve the U.S. State Department, which managed to allay Japan's fears. On August 19, Japan reversed its decision and agreed to accept produce from all of California except the three quarantined counties.

This did not, however, stop the spread of the infestation. Farmers in the northern San Joaquin valley discovered Medflies in apricots and hired aerial sprayers. In Newark, a 32,000 home community near San Francisco, two fertile flies were discovered, and aerial spraying was instantly ordered. A Medfly was discovered in a small walnut orchard outside of Hollister in San Benito County. Another was discovered in the northern end of San Benito County, about 80 miles south of San Francisco, an area in which bell peppers were grown. The quarantined area was now enlarged to more than 3,000 square miles.

On August 26, an infestation of Medflies was confirmed in Los Angeles County, 280 miles south of the original sighting. This was enough for Japan. It reinstated its embargo on all unfumigated produce from California, and widened its demands to require that any shipments of fruits and vegetables from any other states be certified as free of pests, and any shipments of produce going through California be shipped in sealed containers.

The infestation seemed to be out of control. More and more fertile Medflies were found in Los Angeles, and fears that the Medfly had flown beyond eradication began to surface. It would be autumn before the success or failure of the initial aerial spraying could be assessed, and in the interim, while individual farmers furiously built fumigating centers, the state of California turned its attentions to assessing blame for the mixup in fertile and infertile flies, which seemed to be a major cause for the July explosion of the pests. On September 1, Jerry Scribner, director of the project to eradicate the flies, declared publicly, "It is now undisputed that at least 50,000 wild, nonirradiated Peruvian Medflies were released on June 14 in the Mountain View area of Santa Clara County." Then, in a twist designed to deflect blame from California and on to the federal government, he added, "[The shipments of Medflies], like those from labs in Costa Rica, Mexico and Hawaii, all were arranged and paid for by the United States Department of Agriculture. Because the U.S.D.A. did not maintain on-site supervision of the lab in Peru, all pupae were sampled for sterility *prior* to release [by them]." Mr. Scribner stated that only 72 flies were tested and found sterile, whereas several million supposedly sterile flies from the same batch were released, and accounted for "the subsequent explosion of larvae in the Mountain View Gap, followed by satellite infestation in San Jose and elsewhere."

As autumn deepened, it seemed as if the Medfly had finally been stopped. A full six-week cycle had passed for most of the areas without any new discoveries.

By the end of the month, Mr. Scribner was forced to modify his accusations of fumbling by the U.S.D.A. when California scientists announced that in all probability, the similarities between the dye used to identify sterile flies and the natural color of the Medfly might have led to the release of fertile flies. Furthermore, they reasoned, the dye from a sterile fly could have rubbed off on fertile flies after contact.

By the 1st of October, 3,935 miles of California remained under quarantine; 1,131 square miles had been sprayed at least once; and about a third of that area, approximately 340 square miles, had been sprayed 12 times. The fight to eradicate the Medfly had cost $50 million, but the end seemed to be in sight. Spraying was diminished to once a month in most areas until March, when a weekly schedule would be instituted, and until the departure of the fly had become a certainty.

All through this, officials were at pains to assure residents of the infested and therefore sprayed areas that the spraying was harmless to humans. This some residents accepted, though others still resisted bitterly, citing, along with the doubt expressed by Stanford University pharmacologists, a statement by the California State Department of Fish and Game that Malathion in a creek near Freemont killed approximately 2,000 fish.

Through the autumn and winter of 1981 and early 1982, there were small satellite sightings of Medflies that were swiftly controlled by tree stripping and ground spraying. On October 11, a Medfly was trapped in the LaPuente area of Los Angeles; two days later a larger, 27 square mile area of the San Gabriel Valley resumed aerial spraying.

But as 1981 gave way to 1982, it became clear that the Medfly was once more under control. By June 5, the quarantine was lifted on fruits and vegetables in Los Angeles, Stanislaus, and San Benito Counties, with promises of an imminent lifting of the quarantine in Santa Clara and Santa Cruz counties.

Three weeks later there was a scare. A single Medfly was discovered in a loquat tree in a residential area of Stockton, in the midst of the San Joaquin valley. An immediate, 81-square-mile quarantine was instituted, to guard against infestation and damage to the nearby early peach harvest, and to the tomatoes, apricots, apples, plums, and bell peppers in the immediate area. Airplanes arrived and sprayed Malathion over a nine-square-mile area.

There were no recurrences as spring gave way to summer, and finally, at the end of September, after a period that was equivalent to four full life cycles for the fly from the time of the last large infestation on November 20, 1981, the U.S. Department of Agriculture, represented by its deputy Richard Jackson, gave the state a clean bill of health. Jerry Scribner, the head of the Medfly project and the remaining 171 employees of a 4,000 person task force, retired.

While the environmental war ended, the political war raged on. At one time during the conflict, farm area legislators called for Governor Brown's impeachment. California senator S. I. Hayakawa, whose seat in the Senate Governor Brown had announced he would seek the following year, visited the area and stated that the governor "sat on his hands [for 13 months, and then encouraged] a climate of hysteria so intense that people got sick from the pure power of suggestion."

And in Texas, Reagan Brown, the commissioner of Texas agriculture, who had been locked in legal combat with California throughout most of the Medfly crisis, minced no expletives. "That moonbeam, that idiot out there they've

got for a governor," he told international reporters, "is not any kin to me. I want to put that in the record. All the time he said his hands were tied trying to please all the elements. And all the time the Medfly was threatening the food supply of this nation."

Governor Brown's spokesperson replied in kind: "Another Texas idiot, and we're not responding to him."

Eventually, tempers cooled and statistics were gathered. The two-year struggle with an insect half the size of a housefly cost $95 million, $74.7 million from the state of California and $20.6 million from the federal government. From the time the first flies were found in San Jose in June 1980, more than 1,445 square miles were subjected to regular aerial spraying and approximately 4,000 square miles were placed under quarantine. During that time Florida and Texas and some other southern states briefly quarantined produce from California, and Japan refused to accept unfumigated crops from most areas. All in all, it was the most costly and contentious insect eradication program in the history of the United States.

UNITED STATES
(CALIFORNIA, SAN FRANCISQUITO VALLEY)
ST. FRANCIS DAM COLLAPSE AND FLOOD
March 12, 1928

....

Four hundred and twenty inhabitants of the Santa Clara valley were drowned when the St. Francis Dam collapsed at two minutes before midnight on March 12, 1928. Human error caused the destruction of 79 million acres of rich farmland and $15 million in property damage.

More than the St. Francis Dam collapsed at 11:58 P.M. on March 12, 1928. The career of its creator, engineer William Mulholland, was washed away through its disintegrating wings, along with 12 billion gallons of water. Although an earthquake was the first reason given for the failure of the two-year-old dam spanning the San Francisquito Canyon above Los Angeles, and sabotage by dynamite was the second, and despite the fact that Mulholland first blamed the tragedy on heavy rains and then landslides, the distraught and guilt-ridden engineer finally concluded that the fault was his. The dam had been built on a red conglomerate rock composed of decomposed or altered cranite, which geologists describe as mica schist.

Testifying in the long investigation that followed the tragedy, Ventura County engineer Charles Petit characterized the countryside into which the dam's concrete abutments had been anchored as strata which "when [it] is subjected to water pressure, it crumbles. . . . The decomposed rock at the sides weakened by the water gave way and then the structure went." A weeping Charles Mulholland agreed, admitting also that leaks had been reported for days at the locations that first gave way at two minutes before midnight of March 12.

In fact, farmers had, according to Mrs. A. M. Rumsey, the postmistress of Saugus, "talked of nothing else but the leaks in the dam for ten days. . . ." A week of steady downpours swelled the huge reservoir beyond its capacity, and muddy water gurgled through cracks in the retaining wall and into the dry riverbed of the Santa Clara River.

Everyone had trusted Mulholland's judgment. It was he, after all, who had thought of and supervised the building of the 233-mile-long aqueduct that pierced the Sierra Nevada and carried both water and hydroelectric power to Los Angeles. And at the time of the tragedy, he was working on a preliminary survey for a much larger and longer aqueduct designed to bring water from the Colorado River 250 miles across deserts and through record-length tunnels to Los Angeles.

In the San Francisquito Canyon, an enormous, 1,000-foot-long waterfall emptied into two concrete power stations, which turned the plunging waters into hydroelectric power for the city. To add to the water supply for an ever-growing Los Angeles, Mulholland again put his expertise to work, constructing a huge dam that would be located midway between the power stations and capture the surplus water roaring out of the aquaeducts in one enormous reservoir.

But this time, possibly heady with the success of his first venture, Mulholland ignored the advice of a panel of geologists who warned him that not only was he building on a combination of insubstantial conglomerate and mica schist; he had located his dam along a geologic fault.

And so the dam was built, and it was enormous—205 feet high, with a span of 600 feet across the mouth of the canyon and an additional dike nearly as long on the spur of the hill. Its nominal capacity was 1.655 billion cubic feet of water, and almost from its inception, it began to leak. A motorist, driving past its base on the morning of March 12, noted an unusual amount of water pouring through cracks in the base of it. That very morning, Mulholland himself had been summoned to inspect that fissure, and he pronounced it safe.

And then, at 11:58 that evening, while a substantial number of residents of the Santa Clara valley slept, the two wings of the dam suddenly gave way, and a wave of water 88,000 acres in circumference, 2 billion gallons in volume, and 78 feet high, split the 3,000-ton sections into fragments and cascaded into the dry riverbed of the Santa Clara River.

When the dam collapsed, it did so with a thunderous roar. There was no time for the residents of the Santa Clara River valley to escape the wall of water.

Within minutes, it geysered over the riverbanks and through the ranches and construction camps of the sixty-mile-wide valley. The hydroelectric plant exploded as if it had been detonated. Further down the valley, the unwarned victims of the flood were caught in their beds. Some were wakened by the thunder of the approaching flood; most

were swept forward or consumed by the roiling waters. Houses were crushed like eggshells, farmland was turned to seas of mud, roads were uprooted, and the cars on them were tossed around like toys.

A 60-mile-wide swath of land was swept clean of everything in its path—buildings, trees, rocks, crops, animals, and humans. The natural slope of the land carried the flood toward the Pacific Ocean, 75 miles south of the dam. Along that track lay the city of Los Angeles and the crop-rich San Fernando valley. Both were spared by a low mountain range, 35 miles north of Los Angeles, that offered protection from the floodwaters.

But in the Santa Clara valley, chaos and destruction turned the night into unmitigated horror. Eighty-year-old C. H. Hunick described the scene as his ranch house, a mile and a half below the dam, blew apart like a house of cards. "I couldn't see a thing in the darkness," Mr. Hunick related, "but found myself clinging to what turned out to be a part of the roof of our house.

"Down, down with the current we went. I held on desperately. I kept saying to myself every second was my last. . . . Then—I must have floated for miles—somebody grabbed my arm in the darkness.

"'Is it you, Dad?' I knew that it was one of my sons. He got me over to the plank he was on. . . ."

Mrs. Russell Hallen, wrapped in a vivid red sweater, stared vacantly at the dawn-streaked sky as reporters climbed over yellow silt to interview her. She was standing on the site of the ranch house in which her mother and daughter had been spending the night. There was nothing but a flat tabletop of yellow sand, near a cottonwood tree that had been stripped of its bark by the floodwaters.

"Why did I have to live?" inquired a hysterical woman whose three-month-old baby had been torn from her by a whirlpool. The same whirlpool had deposited her on dry land.

In a construction camp composed of tents, 66 of 150 men rode the wave of the flood to safety; the others, including Edward Locke, the watchman at the Southern California Edison Company's power switching station, who ran into the camp shouting a warning just before the wave reached them and consumed him, perished.

Rescuers who arrived with pack trains of supplies shortly after dawn were faced with unbelievable destruction. Where lush farms and orchards and open ranches once stood, there was a succession of running rivers and rivulets, interspersed with mud holes. So much silt had been carried down the valley that the Santa Clara River bed had been raised 30 feet above its former level in some places.

Roadside morgues were set up, and the International Red Cross tended to the survivors. Immediate precautions against typhus were begun.

The ancillary destruction was equally vast. All power to the area departed with the obliteration of the powerhouse, and lights flickered and went out in parts of Los Angeles.

Ten important bridges were demolished. Seventy-nine thousand acres of citrus orchards and farmland lay buried under mud and silt. Telegraph and telephone lines were wiped out. Property damage was estimated at $15 million. Two hundred seventy-three homes were destroyed; 35 families, numbering 768 persons, were made homeless and destitute. And the final death count mounted to a staggering 420.

Inquiries began immediately, and the first theory, dynamiting, was fed by the discovery of a sheet of note paper near the dam with a roughly outlined chart of the structure and a short piece of newly frayed rope. "The strand was asserted to be the same type as used by aqueduct dynamiters who in the past have blasted sections of the waterway," said a report in the *New York Times*. "The chart was said to be written in the same handwriting that sketched charts found at the previous dynamitings."

The theory was discarded when no physical evidence was presented at the hearings.

While these hearings, which would eventually place the entire blame upon the faulty judgment of William Mulholland went on, old and new dam projects were rushed to the forefront of public consciousness. The 1889 Johnstown Flood, which killed more than 2,500 people and was also attributed to human neglect—in that case the damming up of a spillway in order to create fishing grounds for a club of wealthy sportsmen—was resurrected abundantly and dramatically.

Senators opposed to the building of Boulder Dam, the largest dam project yet in the United States, had a field day of purple oratory—which was not confined exclusively to the halls of Congress. "Mother Nature may have nodded on the job while her children perished . . ." posited one national newspaper.

But the conclusion was far more scientific. Mulholland disappeared in disgrace from the public arena, and the mayor of Los Angeles admitted "moral responsibility" for the calamity, promising that "Los Angeles will put this valley back as nearly as possible as it was."

This it did, minus the lives of 420 of those who had established it.

UNITED STATES
(MINNESOTA)
FOREST FIRE
October 12–14, 1918

....

A monumental forest fire roared through northeastern Minnesota from October 12–14, 1918, killing more than 800 persons, destroying 26 settlements, leaving 13,000 homeless, and causing more than $175,000 in personal and property damage.

The peat and underbrush of the forest of northeastern Minnesota bordering on Lake Superior fumed and smoked through the late summer of 1918. Had the settlers of that particular area of the Midwest been there longer, or had they been as sensitive to the environment as the Native Americans they had displaced and who were now confined to the Fond du Lac Reservation, the signs of a potential disaster would have been apparent.

But they let the forest smolder, and early in the afternoon of Saturday, October 12, a 60-mile-per-hour gale tore through the area, igniting the smoldering undergrowth into a roaring fire that, within an hour, had turned into a solid wall of flame, 25, then 50, and finally nearly 200 miles wide. From the slopes of the Mesaba Range northwest of Duluth to the open land south of the city, and southeast to Two Harbors, on Lake Superior, the fire rushed at express-train speed, laying waste to thousands of acres of forest and swallowing up settlements, some of them before their inhabitants had time to flee.

Moose Lake, some 50 miles southwest of Duluth, was incinerated in minutes, along with all of its inhabitants, and nearby Barnum suffered the same fate. Kettle River, Lawler, Adolph, Munger, Five Corners, Harney, Grand Lake, Maple Grove, Twig, Mathews, Atkinson, French River, Clifton, Brookston, Brevator, Pike Lake, Pine Hill—all were either completely destroyed on the fiery night of October 12, or ravaged enough to require rebuilding.

The two neighboring lumbertown settlements of Cloquet and Carlton were leveled, too, but because they were on a railroad spur, a large percentage of their inhabitants escaped. Safely in Duluth, Albert Michaud, a special policeman from Cloquet, repainted the scene for reporters.

"At six o'clock last night, a forest ranger gave warning that unless the wind died down the townspeople would have to flee," he related. "A thick pall of smoke hung over the town, and at seven o'clock the special trains were called.

"The scene at the station was indescribable. There came a rush of wind, and the entire town was in flames. The trains pulled out with the fires blazing closely behind them. Women wept and clung to their children, while others cried frantically for their missing ones. The flames licked at the cars. Windows in the coaches were broken by the heat. The engineers and firemen alternately stoked, to give the boilers all the fuel they could stand.

"Other trains were hurriedly made up of flat cars, box cars and anything that would roll. But even then all did not get away. . . ."

Cloquet's population totaled around 7,500. More than 4,700 were aboard the train, which stopped in Carlton, six miles away, long enough to load the survivors of that settlement, which also disappeared in fire. Eventually, the groaning, overloaded train reached Superior, Wisconsin, 50 miles away.

Meanwhile, the roads from the outer reaches to Duluth became clogged with cars, many of which never reached

The great Minnesota forest fire of 1918 raged along a 200-mile front, killed more than 800 people, and left more than 2,000 square miles of forest looking like this.

(LIBRARY OF CONGRESS)

their destinations. The next day, rescuers encountered scores of burned out automobiles populated by incinerated corpses.

As in any panicked escape from a fire, refugees took to the water. Some were scalded to death. A family that climbed into a thirty-foot-deep well in Moose Lake was found dead at the well's bottom. In Pike Lake, outside of Duluth, scores drowned when their boats capsized. An eight-year-old boy held the heads of his three small brothers and three small sisters underwater, and saved himself and them, while the bodies of their parents floated nearby.

Duluth itself was threatened. On its rim, the Duluth Country Club and the Children's Home, one of the largest structures in the state went up in flames, and fire swept through Woodland and Lester Parks, the city's major recreation areas. Rescuers in automobiles drove through a wall of flame to rescue 200 tuberculosis patients at the Nopeming Sanitarium.

A cacophony of bells and horns warned the residents of Duluth of the advancing wall of fire that was rapidly enclosing the city from the west and the north. But before the flames entered Duluth, the wind abruptly shifted, and the city was saved.

Elsewhere, the conflagration roared on, and it reignited itself in earnest on Tuesday, the 15th. Five trains of firefighters were ready this time, but the wind died, and with it the fire.

The destruction was appalling: a 2,000-square-mile tract of forest was reduced to cinders; 26 towns were either totally or partially destroyed. Eight hundred known dead were reported, but because of the nature of the terrain, scores more were thought to have perished. Thirteen thousand settlers were left without homes.

World War II had another month to go; German saboteurs were immediately charged with starting the blaze. ENEMY AGENTS SUSPECTED, shouted the subhead in the *New York Times,* and F. J. Longren, Duluth's fire marshall, reported that "incendiaries were driven away from a local shipyard when the fires in Duluth and Superior were burning at their height."

But, in the cleansing coolness of afterthought, it became apparent that ignorance and neglect were the culprits. Frank J. Bruno, of the American Red Cross, wrote about the blaze in *Survey,* the organization's magazine, and concluded that "this calamity, which is the greatest the state of Minnesota has ever suffered . . . is not without its benefits . . . fire protection and the treatment of the peat bogs, the ever-present menace, will be more carefully studied. . . ."

UNITED STATES
(NORTHWEST)
FOREST FIRES
August 1910

....

A monster forest fire that destroyed 2 million acres of trees in Idaho, Montana, Washington, and Oregon, left 85 dead and caused an estimated $10 million in damage, began on the Montana-Idaho border and raged for three weeks in the dry and windy August of 1910.

Two theories about the origins of the cataclysmic forest fires that roared through the American Northwest in August 1910 pointed accusing fingers at careless campers and the Northern Pacific Railroad. The third part of the equation, an unusual drought, was the only culprit that could be proved guilty, although public opinion, expressed in letters to various editors of various newspapers, suggested that the sparks belching from coal burning locomotives were a continuing danger to the environment and should be replaced by oil-burning engines.

Whatever the cause, the result was enormous and discouraging. Two hundred firefighters and settlers died. The economy, heavily dependent on timber, suffered over $10 million in losses. The indirect damages, the retarding of forest growth, the erosion of the sponge of forest humus that might have retained snow, rain, and mud and prevented the floods of the following spring, were incalculable.

The fire began on the Montana-Idaho divide around the first of August, 1910. An eight-mile-long wall of flame ate its way from the head of Cedar Creek, Missouri, toward the settlement of Missoula, which immediately went into attack mode. Street runners and officials of the U.S. Forest Service began assembling the first recruits of what would eventually become a huge army of volunteer firefighters. On the evening of the first of August, 60 men left Missoula and headed their horses toward Saltz, where a pack train loaded with supplies waited for them.

Their numbers would increase dramatically within a week when President Taft authorized the use of U.S. Army troops to be moved from as far away as San Francisco to join in battling the fires—which had, by now, consumed 200,000 acres of forest.

On August 10, a mile-wide wall of flame swept toward Yellowstone National Park from the mountains southeast of Yellowstone Lake. The night sky was lit with skyrocketing embers and willowing flames that resembled earthbound Northern Lights, and hundreds of tourists, attracted by the rumble of the approaching fire, gathered to watch the destruction as if it were another natural spectacle.

During the day, the relentless sunlight was auraed and dimmed by the heavy smoke clouds that preceded the fire, now ascending with rising roars, mountain after mountain. Thousands of deer, elk, and antelope died rushing into high country to escape low-lying fires and dashing headlong into the flames that had taken over most of the mountains in the area.

By August 11, the fires that had been thought to be under control on the Flathead Indian Reservation in Montana had begun to burn again, and the Coeur d'Alene National Forest in Idaho was consumed in flame. The settlers in Wallace, Murray, and Mulian, Montana, were enveloped in heavy smoke. Their nervousness gradually turned to terror as the smoke increased and the gunshot reports of snapping branches from the advancing fires grew closer. Knots of weary firefighters disappeared, and rumors ran rampant about their incinerations.

All during the following week, as the skies remained rainless, new fires sprang up, in the farmlands near Bellingham, Washington, and near Butte and the Flathead Reservation and Glacier National Park in Montana. By August 14, General Leonard Wood, chief of staff of the army, had dispatched 5,000 troops to the affected areas.

Then, on August 15, high winds began to rise in the St. Joe district of Washington, whipping the flames out of the control of the firefighters there. Elk City, Idaho, was cut off from the outside world when its power lines went down, and the entire countryside surrounding it burned like the landscape of an active volcano.

As quickly as the fires were extinguished in Missoula, where the first fire reports originated, they would reignite. Near Spokane, Washington, the fires extended for 30 miles over a strip 10 miles wide. Soot-covered refugees began to appear on dirt roads extending out from the most heavily burned areas.

More and more firefighters were reported missing or trapped in pockets of fire. Near St. Joe, Montana, 2 men from a group of 200 took a horse and rode it to death searching for help. They eventually found a camp of weary fighters at Bird Creek and returned with them, rescuing the trapped men at St. Joe.

By August 22, all of northern Idaho, eastern Washington, and western Montana seemed to be engulfed in flames. Half of Wallace, Washington, was burned to the ground, and three nearby villages were completely consumed. The Chicago, Milwaukee, and Puget Sound Railroad attempted to send relief trains into the region, but wooden bridges over ravines were torched and eliminated by fire, and the rescue trains were forced to turn back.

New dangers developed in the mining regions of Montana. Cars of dynamite, reached by the fires, exploded, generating still more fire. More and more villages were being abandoned, and finally, on August 23, a series of trains on the Northern Pacific's Coeur d'Alene line began to transport refugees out of burned towns. More than 250, including patients from the burned-out Sisters' Hospital in Wallace, were transported to Missoula, which escaped the fires. A woman who had fled from her home just before midnight on the 24th gave birth to a child in a boxcar just before it arrived in Missoula.

More refugees, many of them blinded by fire and smoke, began to arrive from the St. Joe region, bringing death statistics and tales of terror. Two men told of spending two days and two nights in Trout Creek, only raising their heads to breathe, while fire raged on either side of them and giant cinders fell into the water around them. Steve R. Marquette of Independence, Iowa, one of 37 firefighters working with a Forest Ranger at Beauchamp's Ranch on the Big Fork of the Coeur d'Alene River, 10 miles from Wallace, arrived in the town with most of his clothes burned away.

"When the flames swept up the canyon of the Big Forks," he told reporters, "we found ourselves surrounded by fire. We ran back to the clearing at Beauchamp's ranch. Ranger Bell ordered us to lie down in a pool. Joseph Beauchamp, Roderick Ames, and the others who perished sought shelter in a cave that Beauchamp had dug for his valuables. The water in the pool was only five inches deep, and the sparks and hot wind compelled us to turn over every few minutes to avoid being roasted. We breathed through wet garments. Tobacco boxes and razors in the pockets of the men cracked on account of the heat. We lay two hours in the water before the flames blew over enough to allow our escape."

The women of Elk City were credited with saving it while most of the men were out in the surrounding territory, fighting the blaze. The women remained on the roofs of houses, beating out flaming cinders that dropped like incendiary bombs around them.

Finally, a soft rain began to fall on Wallace, and the terrified residents and exhausted firefighters began to breathe more easily.

The mist turned to a full-fledged rainstorm by Thursday the 25th, and the fires seemed to lessen, then go out. Stunned and scalded survivors, thought dead, began to drift back into Wallace and Missoula. Most of the loss of life had taken place on the afternoon and night of Saturday, August 20, when hurricane-force winds developed and flames overwhelmed most of the camps. Twenty-five men were imprisoned in a mine tunnel near Wallace. As the flames advanced on the tunnel, the men worked in shifts, some holding a blanket over the mouth of the tunnel, and others writing farewell messages. Eight succumbed to the heat and fumes; the rest survived.

In Idaho, on the same day, 75 men huddled together in the tunnel of the J.J.C. Mine. When the heat began to draw the air out of the space, Forest Ranger Pulaski took 30 of them to the War Eagle Mine, a quarter of a mile away.

An unidentified survivor described the scene to reporters: "The flames swept over the mouth [of the tunnel] like a blast. The smoke was suffocating. About an hour and a half after we had been in the tunnel, Pulaski, who was nearest the mouth, lost consciousness.

"Two men who got scared rolled around in the middle of the tunnel instead of keeping by the edge on the floor, and they died across my knees.

"Nearly all of us during six hours were lying in water that dripped from the roof and walls of the tunnel.

"When the fire finally passed and the tunnel cleared a little, nearly half of us were unconscious. The eyes of the others were gummed together from smoke and tears so that we could hardly open them. Five were dead.

"We found a sixth man burned to a crisp, a short distance up the creek from the tunnel. Our two horses were nearly suffocated . . . . We had to shoot them."

As snow was added to the rain, pack trains with hospital equipment and detachments of U.S. Army Medical Corpsmen from Fort Robinson, Nebraska, began to arrive in Montana.

By August 25, the fires in Montana and Idaho were deemed to be under control. Not so the ones in Washington, and new fires began to ignite in Oregon and California. They would burn for several more weeks, and the smoke clouds from them would drift as far east as Boston.

The War Department was urged by the Washington Forest Fire Association, the Washington Conservation Association, and other organizations of lumbermen and loggers to fire all its guns on Puget Sound and at the mouth of the Columbia River in hopes of bringing rain to douse the Washington fires, but cooler heads and some sage advice from the U.S. Weather Bureau prevailed, and the plan was never implemented.

Varying estimates of fatalities from the fires began to emerge, and with them, accusations of official malfeasance. Gifford Pinchot, a Forest Service head deposed by President Taft, lashed out at Senators Heyburn, Mondell, and Carter, three conservative senators from western states. "The men in Congress like Heyburn, Carter, and Mondell, who have made light of the efforts of the Forest Service . . . have, in effect, been fighting on the side of the fires against the general welfare," he said, in a press statement.

"If even a small fraction of the loss from the present fires had been expended in additional patrol and preventive equipment some or perhaps all of the loss could have been avoided," he continued. "I believe our people will take this lesson to heart and insist that the settlers and their wives and children, the lumbermen and the miners, and the $2 million worth of National property in the National Forests shall be adequately protected.

"Forest fires are preventable. It is a good thing for us to remember at this time that nearly or quite all of the loss, suffering, and death these fires have caused is wholly unnecessary. A fire in the forest is the same kind of a thing as a fire in the city. There is only one way to fight either. The fire department of every city is organized with the prime idea of getting to the fire when it is young."

Montana senator Thomas Carter shot back at Pinchot, accusing him of misappropriating the Forest Service funds he had been given in "his absurd campaign for the presidency of the United States."

Chief Forester Graves of the Northern Idaho and Montana districts assessed the damage and concluded that the combination of extreme drought and high winds, plus the fact that many of the fires began in inaccessible places, had led to the huge loss of trees and lives. In the Missoula district alone, more than 90 large and 3,000 small fires had to be extinguished.

In the final tally, more than $10 million in timber was lost, and 85 people—most of them firefighters, but some of them settlers—died. For years, the loss of the forest humus resulted in ruined crops from the wash of rain from the forests to the fields.

In Congress, new bills were introduced to reduce the disposal of slash by loggers and for the establishment of roads, trails, fire lines, and telephone communication through the damaged forests and national park sites. The lessons that had been learned and then unlearned from the cataclysmic Wisconsin fire in October 1871, which killed 2,682 people, were dramatically reiterated and turned into action.

UNITED STATES
(OKLAHOMA, TEXAS, KANSAS, COLORADO, NEW MEXICO)
DUST BOWL DROUGHT
1933–1938

In the 1930s, the entire Southwest of the United States was turned, through irresponsible farming practices combined with five unusually dry years, into a shifting desert. Abandonment of family farms and mass migrations of displaced farm families made this a bleak, symbolic chapter in the story of America's Great Depression.

"It is plain that the age-old forces that made the earth what it is are still at work. Rock and rill, plain and mountain, are not yet 'finished' in the sense that a sculptor would use the term. Indeed, if Nature were satisfied with the planet, if there were no dust storms, no winds or rains, no earthquakes to shift deep-lying strata, we would not be here. Stagnation is death."

So pontificated an editorial writer for the *New York Times* in the spring of 1934, just past the depth of the Great Depression, but in the middle of the Dust Bowl drought that moved over 10 million tons of soil, pollen, spores, diatoms, bacteria, and the remains of birds and animals caught in the swirling winds of multiple dust storms. It was the most dramatic and damaging drought in the history of the United States.

There have been other prolonged periods of arridness in the long history of the world, enough to give the editorial writer some credence, among them: the great biblical famine in Egypt of 1708 B.C.; the multiple famines of India, China, and Africa—particularly the 1883–88 droughts in Ethiopia and Sudan. Dust storms abounded in the South American drought reported by Charles Darwin in 1830, in the great Australian drought of 1902 and the 1928 drought in southern Ukraine, during which 15.4 billion tons of earth were rendered airborne by high winds.

None of these made as much of an imprint, however, on the collective conscience of the Western world as the Dust Bowl tragedy. Thousands of families, immortalized by John Steinbeck in his 1939 novel *The Grapes of Wrath* as "Okies" (though they as often came from Colorado, Texas, Kansas, or New Mexico as they did from Oklahoma), set to words and music by Woodie Guthrie, and to flight by Carl Sandburg's poetic epic *The People, Yes*, were forced off their land when it would no longer yield the crops that offered them even marginal living.

Eastern banks, holding the mortgages for these properties, often bulldozed homes in order to force out squatters, who had lived in the homes for generations. And so, a forced migration of millions of people, the largest since the settling of the West, resulted.

Families used to simple comforts were decimated by disease, exposure, and exploitation by entrepreneurs who saw them as cheap, and frequently free, labor. It was the worst human suffering of the Great Depression magnified and thus, eventually, mythologized.

As in most of the famines that have resulted from droughts, the Dust Bowl was created, not because of a cycle of nature, but by human carelessness and disregard for the rhythms of the environment.

The natural ecology of the prairie before the West was opened to European settlement was stabilized by short grasses that held the sandy soil in place. But farmers plowed the binding vegetation away, year after year, without regard to the increasing amount of dust ascending into the air. At the same time, the forests that existed in the Midwest were felled. The soil was being broken up, its binding elements eliminated. And the inevitable occurred.

But not all at once. The soil particles in the 97 million acres that made up the land that would eventually be dubbed the "Dust Bowl" were large enough not to travel very far. Still, continuous plowing, compounded by a string of dry spells, gradually began to break up the soil into smaller and smaller units, which became, because of the periodic stalling of the jet stream to the north of the Great Plains, combined with strong El Niño winds from the Pacific. Over a period of time, they were carried aloft and spread over larger and larger areas.

In the winter of 1860, a protracted drought hit the region, and the snow falling in Oberlin, Ohio, turned black with the dust that had been loosed from the Dust Bowl. That same winter, black snow fell in Syracuse, New York.

On April 5, 1895, the first "snuster" hit the region. A combination of icy winds, dust, and driving snow, it killed three children and scores of cattle and coated the ground with a patina of mud that took weeks to dissipate.

The beginning of the 20th century, however, seemed to mark the end of the plague of dust on the Western Great Plains. Rain fell regularly, the soil became enriched, and the farms began to proliferate and prosper. Modern technology brought the power tractor and what was to become a menace to the earth—the one-way disk plow.

For the first 30 years of the century, farmers planted straight, military rows of crops, ignoring the logic of digging strips of grain and arranging ridged rows planted at right angles to the prevailing winds. The abundant rains forgave their folly. Still, as the rains fell and the soil yielded bumper crop after bumper crop, more and more grass, trees, and shrubs were stripped away to accommodate more fields of grain. By 1929, more than 650 million bushels of grain were harvested in the area, and the stock market crash and abrupt onset of the Great Depression existed only as a distant story to its inhabitants.

Then, in 1930, the worst drought in U.S. history struck. Month after month without rain began to take its toll. The

In the 1930s, during the Great Depression, more than 10 million tons of soil were lifted into the atmosphere and swirled into blinding, choking dust storms that killed livestock and humans and buried the farms and dreams of hundreds of thousands. The once-fertile rural portions of five southwestern states became "Dust Bowls."
(LIBRARY OF CONGRESS)

topsoil, less than an inch thick in various overfarmed areas, began to be lifted in swirling clouds, until it became impossible to sow, much less grow crops.

Dust storms were unknown and unnamed by the bewildered settlers. The pulverized soil they had been plowing and replowing became ideal fuel for a dust storm, which is born when one particle of soil becomes airborne, then bounces off another particle, which in turn bounces off another, until a chain reaction is set up. It takes only a slight breeze to begin the action of the chain and to lift a small quantity of dust off the ground; the process takes care of the rest, until millions of particles of dry soil form a midnight black cloud that hugs the ground and roars along it like a roiling sea, with waves that crest at heights of 5,000 feet.

Static electricity, set up by the crashing of dust against dust, renders the ignition systems of cars and tractors inoperable, and thunder and lightning shooting through the black cloud turn it into a frightening, nearly otherworldly experience. One woman, in Hooker, Oklahoma, described the oncoming cloud in poetic metaphor: "At the top of the

storm were plumes that danced in the sunlight and emblazoned the colors of the rainbow across the sky before plunging savagely toward the ground," she told Associated Press reporter Robert Geiger, based temporarily in Guymon, Oklahoma. It was he who coined the term *Dust Bowl,* but that was in 1935, the same year that Woody Guthrie witnessed the huge dust storm that hit Pampa, Texas, and began writing the first of his multiple ballads about the Dust Bowl and its inhabitants.

Before that, much occurred. As is often the case, the drought brought ancillary and unexpected horrors to the people who experienced it. Birds died by the thousands, weighed down by the dust until they coated yards and fields with their dead bodies. Battalions of spiders, grasshoppers, and rabbits, deprived of their usual feed, overran farms, consuming whatever vegetation had not shriveled up or been buried.

Rabbit drives, sometimes participated in by thousands of men, women, and children swinging whatever makeshift weapons they could devise, would corner jackrabbits into fenced enclosures. The dead rabbits were then sold to meat packers, who shipped the meat east to be eaten in fancy French restaurants.

The drives reflected the desperation of a people whose livelihood was being either blown away or buried. The harvests, bountiful in 1930, shrank to nearly nothing by 1933. Texhoma, Oklahoma, which thrived on buying grain from farmers and which possessed grain elevators that had been overloaded with between 2 and 3 million bushels of wheat in 1931, became a ghost town, its elevators housing a mere 200 bushels by 1933.

The ripple effect spread to the cattle industry. Without feed, cattle ranchers were forced to find whatever roots or plants they could to feed their cattle; but there was not enough. Hundreds of head of cattle starved, and the cattle market shrank.

Nineteen thirty-three was one of the worst years. Seventy separate dust storms were reported. There was no escaping the dust. Within farmhouses and commercial buildings alike, a layer of white dirt coated everything. Wet towels were stuffed into the cracks around windows and doors, but they became so heavy with dust after a day or so that they fell away.

In May 1934, the dust storms multiplied so vigorously, they finally reached the East Coast of the United States. Three hundred million tons of topsoil from the valleys of the Missouri and Mississippi Rivers swept up in a strong northwest wind formed a pale yellow cloud, which rose more than 20,000 feet into the atmosphere and headed eastward at a speed of between 60 and 100 mph.

On May 9, the atmosphere was so dense in the north central states that airplane service between Chicago and St. Paul had to be halted because of the zero visibility, and night crowds at the Chicago Exposition were stung by billows of dust swept down the avenues and into the concessions by 50-mile-per-hour winds.

By May 11, the cloud had reached New York City, and by 3:00 P.M. of that day, the light over the city resembled the semitwilight of a three-quarter eclipse of the sun. Observers at the top of the Empire State Building could not see Central Park, 25 blocks to the north. Dr. E. E. Free of New York University, testing the air on the 17th floor of the Flatiron Building, 11 blocks south of the Empire State Building, announced that it contained 40 tons of dust per cubic mile. North of the city, in Westchester County, New York, state troopers became irked by dust settling on the freshly waxed hardwood floor of their lounge in the Hawthorne Barracks.

Washington, D.C., measured a denser atmosphere than any previously on record. In Boston, scientists sent airplanes aloft equipped with plates to which bacteria would adhere. Later that year, Bernard E. Proctor, addressing the Society of American Bacteriologists, affirmed that bacteria were present in the dust cloud to a height of 20,000 feet.

Meanwhile, the great migration westward, out of the unyielding earth of the Dust Bowl, persisted and grew. Between 1935 and 1937, the California Department of Agriculture counted approximately 221,000 people entering the state to look for jobs. Of the 221,000, 84 percent were farmers and their families from the Dust Bowl states. What they found was sometimes comforting. At other times, they entered compounds of exploitative entrepreneurs who paid them in scrip, redeemable only at company stores, where inflated prices were charged for the bare necessities of life.

And still they came, 50,000 a month during the summer of 1936. Those who stayed suffered further. The American Red Cross handed out dry filter masks, but they proved useless. Moisture from the wearer's breath formed mud between his or her mouth and the mask. Dust-related illnesses swept through the area like a plague. The term *dust pneumonia* was coined to describe the particularly virulent and mostly fatal respiratory ailment that afflicted most patients in area hospitals. Farmers with collapsed lungs coughed up solid dirt in their doctors' offices.

Finally, in the fall of 1938, meaningful rain returned to the Dust Bowl. It had fallen all during the years of the Great Drought, but in amounts so small and in areas so isolated that the rains merely momentarily turned the dust into mud.

But by 1939, the empty grain elevators at Texhoma were filling up again. A million bushels of wheat poured into them that year, and the *Texhoma Times* stated in print that DUST BOWL IS A TERM TO BE DISCARDED AND FORGOTTEN.

It would not be forgotten by either the government or those who survived it. The government put part of the army of depression-unemployed to work planting seed in ridged rows at right angles to the prevailing wind direction. In Washington, the Department of the Interior undertook massive reforestation, planting a new forest belt 1,000 miles long and 100 miles wide, to act as a dam against further dust storms.

Those who survived the storms had plenty to remember and relate to newspaper reporters and future generations. Carl Sandburg, in his epic *The People, Yes*, captured their spirit and their economy of complaint tellingly, authentically, and lastingly:

"How do you do, my farmer friend?"
"Howdy."
"Nice looking country you have here."
"Fer them that likes it."
"Live here all you life?"
"Not yit."

INDUSTRIAL AND GOVERNMENTAL DISASTERS

Belgium
Limbourg Province (chemical factory explosion) (1942)

Brazil
Cubatao (natural gas explosion) (1984)
Rio de Janeiro (oil refinery fire) (1972)

Canada
Mississauga (chlorine gas leak) (1979)
St.-Basile-le-Grand (toxic cloud from waste dump) (1988)

Chile
* Sewell (Braden copper mine fire) (1945)

China
Hong Kong (chemical warehouse fire) (1948)
* Shanghai (rubber factory explosions) (1933)

France
St.-Auban (chemical electrometallurgical works explosion) (1926)
Tours (Protex plant chemical fire) (1988)

Germany
Ludwigshafen (I. G. Farben chemical works explosion) (1948)
* Oppeau (Badische Anilinfabrick Company explosion) (1921)
* Saar Basin Territory, Neunkirchen (Neunkirchen Ironworks explosion) (1933)

India
* Bhopal (Union Carbide pesticide plant explosion) (1984)

Iraq
Al Basrah (mercury-tainted grain) (1972)

Italy
* Seveso (Icmesa chemical plant emission of TCDD) (1976)

Japan
* Minamata (Chisso chemical plant mercury contamination) (1932–79)

Korea
Pusan (chemical plant fire) (1960)

Mexico
Guadalajara (sewer explosion) (1992)
* Mexico City (gas storage tank explosion) (1984)

Netherlands
Lekkankerk (discovery of toxic waste dump) (1980)

North Africa
Lake Nyos (gas cloud) (1986)

Norway
Oslo (Aker River acid leak) (1980)

Poland
* Łódź (Fuks and Hagria chemical factory explosion) (1928)

Rhenish Prussia
Saarlous (Nobel Dynamite Works explosion) (1921)

Romania, Bulgaria, etc.
* Black Sea (industrial pollution) (1960–present)

Spain
* Madrid area (toxic cooking oil scandal) (1981)

Switzerland
* Basel (Rhine River pollution) (1986)

*Detailed in text

Syria
    Homs (fuel depot explosion) (1950)

Thailand
    * Bangkok (chemical explosion and fire) (1991)

United Kingdom
    England, Camelford (chemical plant accident) (1989)
    * England, London (fog) (1952)
    * England, London (fog) (1962)
    England, Scunthorpe (chemical plant explosion) (1974)
    Witten (Roburite factory explosion (1906)

United States
    Iowa
      * Cedar Rapids (Douglas Starch Works explosion) (1919)
    Michigan
      * (PBB contamination of livestock) (1973–74)
      Detroit (sodium cooling plant explosion) (1956)
    * Mississippi (pesticide contamination of chickens) (1974)
    Missouri
      * Times Beach (dioxin contamination) (1971–86)
    New Jersey
      * Newark (Butterworth and Judson Chemical Works explosion) (1918)

New York
    * Niagara Falls (Love Canal pollution) (1978)
    Rochester (gas explosion) (1951)
    Rochester (Ginna steam plant explosion) (1982)
Ohio
    * Cleveland (Cleveland clinic explosion and fire) (1929)
    * Cleveland (East Ohio Gas Co. explosion) (1944)
    Dunsmuir (pesticide spill) (1991)
Oklahoma
    Gore (Sequoyah Fuels Corporation plant explosion) (1986)
Pennsylvania
    Fairchance (Rand Powder Mills explosion) (1905)
    * Oakdale (Aetna Chemical Co. explosion) (1918)
    * Pittsburgh (Equitable Gas Co. explosion) (1927)

USSR
    * Ufa (gas pipeline explosion) (1989)

The World
    * Acid rain contamination (1852–present)
    * Global warming greenhouse effect (prehistory–present day)
    * Ozone layer depletion (1928–present)

Prehistory
  * The World: global warming/greenhouse effect

1852
  * The World: acid rain

1905
  Fairchance, Pennsylvania, USA: Rand Powder Mills explosion

1906
  Witten, England, UK: Roburite factory explosion

1918
  * Newark, New Jersey, USA: Butterworth and Judson Chemical Works explosion
  * Oakdale, Pennsylvania, USA: Aetna Chemical Co. explosion

1919
  * Cedar Rapids, Iowa, USA: Douglas Starch Works explosion

1921
  * Oppeau, Germany: Badische Anilinfabrick Co. explosion
  Saarlous, Rhenish, Prussia: Nobel Dynamite Works explosion

1926
  St.-Auban, France: chemical electrometallurgical works explosion

1928
  * Łódź, Poland: Fuks & Hagria chemical factory explosion
  * The World: ozone layer depletion

*Detailed in text

1929
  * Cleveland, Ohio, USA: Cleveland clinic explosion

1933
  * Shanghai, China: rubber factory explosion
  * Neunkirchen, Germany: ironworks explosion

1940–60
  * Minamata, Japan: Chisso chemical plant mercury contamination

1942
  Limbourg Province, Belgium: chemical factory explosion

1944
  * Cleveland, Ohio, USA: East Ohio Gas Co. explosion

1945
  * Sewell, Chile: Braden copper mine fire

1948
  Hong Kong, China: chemical warehouse fire
  Ludwigshafen, Germany: I. G. Farben chemical works explosion

1950
  Homs, Syria: fuel depot explosion

1951
  Rochester, New York, USA: gas explosion

1952
  * London, England, UK: fog

1956
  Detroit, Michigan, USA: sodium cooling plant explosion

1960
  * Romania, Bulgaria, etc.: Black Sea pollution
  Pusan, Korea: chemical plant fire

1962
  * London, England, UK: fog

1972

Rio de Janeiro, Brazil: oil refinery fire

Al Basrach, Iraq: mercury-tainted grain

1973

* Michigan, USA: PBB contamination of livestock

1974

Scunthorpe, England, UK: chemical plant explosion

* Mississippi, USA: pesticide contamination of chickens

1976

* Seveso, Italy: Icmesa chemical plant emission of TCDD

1978

* Niagara Falls, New York, USA: Love Canal pollution

1979

Mississauga, Ontario, Canada: chlorine gas leak

1980

Lekkankerk, Netherlands: discovery of toxic waste dump

Oslo, Norway: Aker River acid leak

1981

* Madrid, Spain: toxic cooking oil scandal

1982

Rochester, New York, USA: Ginna steam plant explosion

* Times Beach, Missouri, USA: dioxin contamination

1984

Cubatao, Brazil: natural gas explosion

* Bhopal, India: Union Carbide pesticide plant explosion

* Mexico City, Mexico: gas storage tank explosion

1986

* Basel, Switzerland: Rhine River pollution

Lake Nyos, North Africa: gas cloud

Gore, Oklahoma, USA: Sequoyah Fuels Corporation plant explosion

1988

St.-Basile-le-Grand, Canada: toxic cloud from waste dump

Tours, France: Protex plant chemical fire

1989

Camelford, England, UK: chemical plant accident

* Ufa, USSR: gas pipeline explosion

1991

* Bangkok, Thailand: chemical explosion

Dunsmuir, Ohio, USA: pesticide spill

1992

Guadalajara Mexico: sewer explosion

INDUSTRIAL AND GOVERNMENTAL DISASTERS

As it has aged, this sometimes benevolent, sometimes malevolent Earth is being put to the test more and more, as each new person is born, as each new country begins to develop itself. And the biggest shock to its ecosystem came with the beginning of the Industrial Revolution. When the population of the world turned its attention from the earth to the goods it could manufacture, that population's priorities changed, and its carelessness seemed to increase.

Consider the last half of the 20th century: In 1960, the population of the world was 3,000 million. In 1987 it was 5 billion. By 2025, it will probably be 8 billion.

Earth's population demands goods and services, and industry provides both. In the 1990s, it produced seven times more goods than it did in 1950. It handles 80,000 chemicals and introduces 1,000 to 2,000 new ones every year.

And all of this has more and more impact on the environment by extracting natural resources, utilizing them, and disposing the materials that are unwanted or not needed in the final product.

The disposal of industrial waste is the most obvious, dramatic, and pervasive problem facing the environment. Gaseous waste generates air pollution. Liquid wastes seep into the ground and infest surface water. Hazardous solid wastes cause soil contamination and the pollution of both surface and underground water supplies.

For decades, from the beginning of the Industrial Revolution to World War II, hardly any attention was paid to the disposal of industrial and chemical waste. But as World War II produced an intense industrial expansion throughout much of the world, the impact upon the environment of this expansion began to become apparent, and what had heretofore been hidden by its comparative rarity and by an ignorance of the connection between waste and contamination, took many by surprise.

Some of the earliest manifestations of this happened during the 1950s, with the crippling, often lethal, London fogs, which carried in their picturesque contents soft-coal smoke, sulfur dioxide, and chemical fumes. Every winter, the city's transportation system was brought to a standstill, and throughout the 1950s, thousands died.

In Japan, mercury and cadmium, concentrated by edible fish in estuaries and lakes used by industry, killed and maimed thousands in Minamata, Japan, and elsewhere. In Europe, industry poured other pollutants into the Rhine River, until it became nearly uninhabitable by fish, plant life, and amphibians, and absolutely unswimmable by humans.

DDT residues spread to the most remote sites, even invading the ice of Antarctica, and writer Rachel Carson warned that unless DDT and other pesticides were controlled, the world could look forward to a "silent spring."

In Sweden, acid rain from western Europe, and in Canada, acid rain from the United States, killed off life in thousands of each country's lakes.

Throughout the world, industrial accidents that discharged fatal doses of chemicals into the environment and, as a result, into the people who lived near or worked in these industries, increased.

By the 1970s, industry was being assaulted from a number of sides. Populations, as they grew, demanded more and better products. But at the same time, there was pressure from this same public to clean up and preserve the environment.

Governments responded by imposing regulations on industry, and industry was forced, mainly at its own expense, to install clean-up technologies and pollution control equipment. As varying ideologies came into and left power in various countries, the controls lessened or increased, and profit-driven industries either conformed to regulations or used their political muscle to have them relaxed.

Overall, since the 1970s, and particularly since the UN Conference on the Human Environment held in Stockholm in 1972, there has been a widely contrasting reaction to the accumulating knowledge of the cataclysmic effect of industrial pollution—pollution that could, if left unchecked, render the earth uninhabitable.

Industrialized, developed countries have reduced pollution levels or held them steady in many areas. Progress is

75

due to government regulation, a decline in heavy manufacturing industries, public awareness, and a trend toward service and information industries.

However, in the developing countries, where some of the heavy industry from developed countries has gone, the trend toward saving the environment has gone in exactly the opposite direction. Pollution levels are increasing and heavy industry is expanding. For example, the developing countries' share of world iron and steel production rose from 3.6 percent in 1955 to 17.3 percent in 1984. Between 1982 and 1990 alone it expanded by 38 million tons. Clean technologies, no matter how effective, simply cannot compensate for this rate of expansion.

In both developed and developing countries, there has been little or no noticeable progress in the avoidance of industrial accidents. In fact, the scale and frequency of industrial catastrophes is increasing, particularly in developing countries. Counting only disasters with more than 100 dead, 400 injured, 3,500 evacuated, or 70,000 deprived of drinking water, the last three five-year periods recorded have seen the worldwide numbers of major accidents rise continually. There were 4 in 1974–78, 10 in 1979–83, and 16 in 1984–88. Of the 16 accidents in the last period, 13 were in developing countries.

In isolated instances and in selected countries, there has been a dramatic change for the better once industries became convinced that cleaning up pollution also increased profits. In France, for instance, over the past 10 years, the chemical industry has cut pollution levels in half while increasing production by 25 percent. In the past 20 years, French chemical plants have nearly halved the numbers of accidents involving illness or injury. In Japan, since the terrible tragedy at Minamata, the "Polluter Pays Principle" has caught on with a vengeance. In 1974, its steel industry devoted 21.3 percent of all new investment to pollution control, and as of 1994, investment in controls still stood at 5 percent.

Other industries in other countries have discovered that pollution prevention can be cheaper than cleaning up messes made by ignoring the problem. And so, prevention has replaced control, particularly in air pollution.

Although globally 180 million tons of sulfur dioxide are released into the atmosphere annually, some countries have been able to reduce their individual emissions significantly. In the years 1974–84, Sweden reduced its emissions by 55 percent, France by 41 percent, and the United States by 16 percent.

Water pollution is decreasing more slowly, but there are positive signs. Fish have recently appeared in the Thames for the first time in decades.

A survey released by the United Nations in 1984 concluded that expenditures on environmental measures had a positive short-term effect on growth and employment, and the benefits greatly exceeded the costs.

Large industries and developed countries—depending upon the vulnerability of their governments to industrial pressures—have generally heeded these statistics and lessened their assault on the environment.

Smaller industries and smaller, developing countries, however, have not. And it is to this problem that world concentration should turn. Financial help, information, and instruction in the development of clean technologies would not only help to preserve the ecology of the earth, but to improve it. At the same time, these clean technologies would improve the quality of life for both those who depend on these industries for goods and services and those within the industries who depend on the bottom-line profits that environmental awareness has proved to increase.

CHILE
(SEWELL)
BRADEN COPPER MINE FIRE
June 20, 1945

Three hundred eighty-three miners died in a flash fire that began in an underground car repair shop in the Braden Copper Mine in Sewell, Chile, on June 20, 1945. Hundreds more were injured.

The copper mines of Chile were furiously active during World War II. One of the first minerals known to man (it was probably mined in the Tigris-Euphrates valley in the fifth century B.C.), copper is a wartime necessity and priority, not only as the chief conductor of electricity, but as an alloy in bronze, gun metal, and Monel metal.

Although the United States is the chief world supplier of copper, South America, particularly Chile and Peru, have proved to be rich sources of the widely used metal. In 1945, as today, mining copper in Chile had the added advantage of cheap labor.

On June 20, the Braden Copper Company's mine at Sewell, near Santiago, Chile, was working at full capacity. Hundreds of Chilean workers, overseen by American engineers, toiled during its morning shift. At 8:10 A.M., a fire broke out in the underground car repair shop in Teniente No. 1, its largest shaft. The huge scoop-shaped railcars that transported workers deeply into the bowels of the earth and carried copper ore to the surface were maintained in this fully equipped shop, whose underground location helped maintain the flow of work unimpeded by delays of distance.

An acetylene torch ignited trapped gases, and the fire roared out of control instantaneously. There was inadequate ventilation in the mine; even the day-to-day work of the miners brought on respiratory problems. Now, the inadequate ventilation sealed the fate of 383 miners. Some of the 100 men who worked in the car repair shop were burned by

Families of the 383 victims of the Braden Copper Mine fire witness the evacuation of the bodies.
(AP/WORLD WIDE)

the flames, but the overwhelming majority of deaths in the mine were caused by asphyxiation. Rolling clouds of toxic smoke roared like discharged ammunition through every tunnel in the shaft.

Firefighters had the fire under control by 2:30 that afternoon, but it would be weeks before the smoke cleared. Hundreds would be hospitalized with smoke inhalation.

It would be several months before the mine resumed full production. When it did, no safety improvements had been made.

CHINA
(SHANGHAI)
RUBBER FACTORY EXPLOSIONS
February 21–27, 1933

Ninety-eight workers were killed and 150 were injured in two explosions in two rubber factories in Shanghai, China, during the week of February 21, 1933.

Today, most of the rubber in the world is synthetic. Not so in 1933. From 1770—when Joseph Priestley discovered that this odd and bouncy substance could be used as an eraser and thus named it "rubber"—until World War II, rubber was obtained chiefly from the Para rubber tree, which originally grew only in South America's Amazon basin. It was raised there, harvested there, and manufactured there until 1839, when Charles Goodyear discovered vulcanization, a process that revolutionized the rubber industry.

In vulcanization, gummy, elastic rubber from the trees (or elsewhere now) is turned strong, resistant to solvents, impervious to ordinary heat and cold while maintaining its elasticity. The process involves the addition of varying

quantities of sulfur and heat. Not a very pleasant process to be around, its factories employed, through the 19th century and into the 20th century, natives who could stand extreme heat and the overpowering stench of heated sulfur.

In the Orient, the workers were usually young girls, pressed into service for very little money. In fact, the history of the movement of the rubber industry out of Brazil and into Ceylon and the East was a dismal and underhanded one. Seeds of the Para tree were smuggled into England in 1876, and from there, British plantation owners shipped it to colonies in Ceylon, the Malay area, Java, and Sumatra. By the end of the 19th century, the Brazilian rubber industry had all but disappeared, while the Far Eastern industry had become enormous.

Shanghai in the 1930s was a manufacturing center, and it contained several vulcanizing plants. One of the largest of these was in the eastern, exclusively Chinese, section of Shanghai. Its hundreds of employees, working the multiple gasoline vulcanizers, were young girls, who were paid paupers' wages.

On February 21, 1933, two of the vulcanizers exploded, spewing molten rubber, flames, jagged steel, and toxic sulfur fumes into the factory and the surrounding residential area. Flames licked at surrounding roofs, igniting the sparely made residences around the factory. Walls collapsed and rubble buried workers trying to flee from the blast.

Eighty-one workers, 79 of them young girls, were killed. One hundred twenty other workers suffered varying injuries. The bodies of the dead were carried to a vacant lot near the factory and laid on the ground for relatives to identify. The injured were carried on stretchers to hospitals.

Police attempted to determine the cause of the blast, but workers were at a loss to explain it, and the owner of the factory disappeared, never to reappear. Police reasoned that he feared damage claims from relatives of the victims, who never collected.

Six days later, another blast demolished another vulcanizer in the Yunghao Rubber Factory, a sister plant nearby. This time, 17 workers, 15 of them young girls, were killed, and 30 were injured. But this time, the police captured the owner, who was similarly at a loss for the reason for the blast, though he admitted, as in the case of the previous explosion, safety checkups and maintenance of the machines were elementary to the point of nonexistence.

Ironically and perhaps prophetically, Irish playwright George Bernard Shaw, visiting China during the very same month, commented to an Associated Press reporter in Peiping, "The Chinese should study Communism. . . . Cheap labor is the ruin of China. What she needs is industrial progress."

Communism certainly wouldn't have prevented Shanghai's rubber explosions, or its exploitation of natural resources and labor. But industrial progress might have avoided the twin disasters at the two vulcanizing plants.

GERMANY
(OPPEAU)
BADISCHE ANILINFABRICK COMPANY EXPLOSION
September 20, 1921
....

Five hundred died and 1,500 were injured in a mammoth explosion that occurred because of an error in mixing chemicals at the gigantic Badische Anilinfabrick Company plant in Oppeau, Germany, on September 20, 1921. The poisonous cloud of ammonium sulfate released by the explosion sickened rescuers and made living hazardous for survivors in the demolished plant and town.

The horrendous green cloud that erupted from the cataclysmic explosion at Oppeau, Germany's Badische Anilinfabrick Company plant at 7:30 A.M. on September 20, 1921, was not the first potentially lethal pollution of the atmosphere for which the plant was responsible. The first poison gas used by either side during World War I was manufactured there. Throughout the war, chlorine, phosgene, and lachrymatory gases were manufactured in Oppeau for the German army.

Before the war, the works were known as the largest dye and high explosive concern in the world. More than 10,000 people were employed among its several plants on huge acreage at the village's outskirts. After the war, between 15,000 and 18,000 workers toiled in its dye works and nitrate plants. The French Army of Occupation still maintained a guard barracks near the gate.

What neither the French garrison nor the rest of the world knew was that there were military experiments going on in the plant. Most of the evidence was destroyed and all of those involved in it were killed in the gigantic blast that occurred just as shifts were changing on the clear early morning of September 20. Like the cloud that hung over the area for days afterward, the mystery of what was going on at Oppeau remains just that, though speculation that nuclear experiments were being carried on stubbornly persists.

The plant was built in 1913, and its first task was to save Germany from military collapse. In 1915, the British blockaded German ports, preventing the import of saltpeter from Chile. In counteraction, the Badische plant manufactured artificial nitrates, which substituted for the saltpeter in explosives. Once the war began, it expanded its activities to its principal manufacture, poison gas.

After the war, its more peaceful pursuits involved employing the Haber process, in which nitrogen was extracted from the air and in the presence of a catalyst mixed under high compression with hydrogen to produce ammonia, nitric acid, nitrates, fertilizers, and ammonium sulfates.

The plant had a sorry safety record. German engineers had perfected for use in the compression tanks a new type of steel that would withstand the pressure of more than 2,000 pounds per square inch when the hydrogen and nitrogen gases were compressed under a temperature running from 500 to 600 degrees Fahrenheit. But on at least two occasions, the steel failed to hold. In September 1917, one of the compression tanks exploded, killing approximately 100 workers, one of whom was blown off a bridge half a mile away from the eruption.

Still, the plant grew to its eventual 200 to 250 acres. The nitrate plant was laid out on a rectilinear plan. The roughly 100 buildings were built of brick, two stories high at the eaves, three at the center.

On the morning of September 20, 1921, the population of the buildings was in busy transition. Most of the 6,500 inhabitants of the village of Oppeau either worked in the plant or were related to plant workers.

At 7:30 A.M., the scheduled hour of the change of shift, three trains, belching clear white steam into the unusually cold morning air, pulled onto the siding alongside the plant, preparatory to discharging fresh workers and receiving those from the night shift.

At exactly that moment, the main building exploded in one horrific roar. According to eyewitnesses, the entire building lifted from its foundations, flew apart in the air, then descended in a thousand pieces, crushing some of those who had managed to survive the original blast.

The three trains at the siding were hurtled skyward. They sank back onto the siding and were immediately buried under bricks, torn pieces of steel, and wooden girders. A short distance away, another train that had just left the Eisenheim station, located next to a barracks of French Occupation troops, was driven by the force of the explosion into and through the barracks, killing 12 French soldiers as it continued crazily through the opposite wall.

The dust had scarcely settled from the first explosion when a second, slightly lesser one, followed, which leveled more factory buildings and unleashed a noxious cloud of thick green smoke that blanketed the entire area and spread into the village and adjacent countryside.

The village of Oppeau was no more. It had been leveled as surely and effectively as if it had been bombed from the air. Throughout the 50-mile radius of the Mannheim-Ludwigshafen district, buildings were blown off their foundations. The nearby villages of Franenthal and Edigheim were leveled; store fronts collapsed at Worms, were smashed at Frankfurt, and Heidelberg experienced enormous damage.

Fires immediately spread outward from the central explosion site. Firemen wearing gas masks entered the area, fighting their slow way to an immense funnel-shaped hole where the plant had once stood. Mutilated animals wandered through the ruins and were put out of their misery by policemen; bodies and pieces of bodies littered the site; groundwater rapidly filled the crater, making it impossible to retrieve the bodies of those who might still have been at the center of the explosion. And over it all, an ammonia-drenched cloud hovered.

The funeral for the 500 dead was held in Ludwigshafen Cemetery in Mannheim, and more than 70,000 attended it. It was bewildering to some of the local relatives and survivors; the outpouring of grief came from far beyond local borders.

But now it was time for questions.

The previous explosions had been caused by experimentation in wartime. The sheer magnitude of this one and the conclusion by Berlin scientists that the cause of the catastrophe was "extreme heat, generated by some hitherto unknown gas explosive" sounded suspiciously familiar. Of course, the explanation went on to speculate that the first explosion "must have led to the decomposition and subsequent explosion of a large quantity of ammonia and sulphate of saltpeter which forms the basis of artificial fertilizer," thus shunting the explanation off in a peaceful direction.

Still, there was the "hitherto unknown gas explosive." Its identity was never explained, nor were the experiments, nor the reason for the occurrence of the second explosion. Nor, and this was most immense, was there an explanation given for the devastation, the likes of which had never until now been seen, in Germany or anywhere else, for that matter.

The explanation for the lack of explanation became manifest a little more than a decade later. Germany went to war again, and Oppeau once more became a place of explosive experiment. Speculation without confirmation continues that the beginnings of the triggering devices for atomic and hydrogen bombs received their first public airings in September of 1921 in Oppeau. It was, those who speculate say, the first of many failures that led to the winning of the race to atomic weaponry by the Allies.

Again, there is no hard proof of this. Nor is there proof otherwise. The mystery of the 1921 explosion in Oppeau remains a mystery.

Survivors and families of those missing in the Badische Anilinfabrick Company explosion are fed from a portable soup kitchen.
(LIBRARY OF CONGRESS)

GERMANY
(SAAR BASIN TERRITORY, NEUNKIRCHEN)
NEUNKIRCHEN IRONWORKS EXPLOSION
February 10, 1933

....

Sixty-eight people were killed and more than 300 injured when a gas storage tank exploded in the Neunkirchen Ironworks in the Saar on February 10, 1933. The explosion occurred on the same day that Adolf Hitler assumed his role as chancellor of the Third Reich, and his government hastened to exploit the incident in order to absorb the environmentally rich Saar during a March 1935 plebiscite.

Like Alsace-Lorraine, the Saar is a territory that, since its formation, has been the focus of a tug-of-war between Germany and France, except for a brief time after 1815 when the Treaty of Paris divided it between Bavaria and Prussia. After World War II, it became an autonomous territory administered by France under League of Nations supervision, pending a plebiscite to be held in 1935 to determine its ultimate status.

The fight over the Saar was understandable. Bounded by France on south and west, Luxembourg on the northwest, and the Rhineland on the north and east, it is a land of low hills, drained by the Saar River. But it is what is under the hills that has been at the root of the fighting. There are enormous deposits of coal there, particularly coke, which, from the early part of the 20th century onward, was necessary to the manufacture of steel. Overlaying the vast coal fields of the Saar, were and are huge iron- and steelworks.

One of the largest of these was the Neunkirchen Ironworks, located in the town of Neunkirchen, some 130 miles north of Basel, Switzerland, 150 miles south of Cologne, Germany, and 70 miles west of Heidelberg. The Neunkirchen works, formerly known as the Stumm Brothers Plant, consisted of blast furnaces, steel mills, a coking kiln, a benzol factory, and the largest gas tank in Europe. Built in 1931, it had a capacity of 4.2 million cubic feet; it was 262 feet high, 147 feet in diameter, and covered 17,050 feet. This enormous and imposing globe supplied a great part of the Saar Basin with gas through long pipelines, as well as fuel for the ironworks and its incorporated benzol works, designed to extract benzene from coke, which in turn would be used to produce dyes and—it was believed—synthetic rubber.

The tank was explosion proof, said its designers and manufacturers. But the boast, like that of the designer of the *Titanic,* turned out to be vastly overstated. At exactly 6:00 P.M. on February 10, 1933, as shifts were being changed and the streets of the town were crowded with workmen going to or coming from work, the gas tank exploded with a volcanic roar, launching shards of steel 40 feet long into the air, sending shock waves for miles, showering rubble and flaming debris into the town, collapsing buildings, and setting immediate fire to the adjacent benzol works, which in turn set fire to the town.

The pressure of the explosion forced fire out of the blast furnaces in the plant, incinerating men who were working near them. The electricity in the town disappeared immediately, plunging the area into a Stygian darkness deepened by the thick and acrid black smoke that poured from the explosion site. The scene was punctuated by the spreading flames from the benzol factory fire.

In the town, the roof of a movie theater was blown in, killing three patrons and injuring scores. A streetcar that was passing not far from the tank was blown into oblivion, its wheels, which remained in place on the track, the only evidence that it had been there at all. The roof of the large hall of the Catholic Hospital collapsed, enfolding patients and medical personnel under its rubble. The railroad station and its adjoining tracks were buried beneath boulders of displaced stone, and shards of steel, which were pieces of the tank, landed over 350 feet from the explosion site. Windows were blown out within a radius of five miles of the city, and the sound of the explosion was heard in Basel, 130 miles away.

As fires ignited throughout the ironworks, smaller explosions followed the first, and lethal gas forced an evacuation of all the homes left standing in the immediate vicinity of the plant. More than 2,000 persons were involved in the mass exodus into the woods surrounding the city.

Within an hour of the first explosion, four truckloads of injured persons were rushed to the hospitals that were still standing. Police, firemen, and rescue workers arrived during the night from Saarbruecken and other nearby towns.

Workmen toiled around the clock, clearing away debris and cutting away enormous steel girders, which had snapped like matches from the force of the explosion.

Daylight revealed the enormous extent of the damage and summoned forth a chronology of the events leading to the blast. Shards of steel were discovered spread over a distance of two miles. The huge cover of the tank was found a half mile away, near the ruined railroad depot.

Eyewitnesses determined that shortly before the major explosion, a smaller one occurred in one of the tar reservoirs in the benzol plant. Pockets of flaming tar were flung into the air, and some of them fell on the gas tank.

Alarm whistles had sounded after the benzol plant explosion, and a rescue squad had rushed to the plant. None of its members survived; they were blown asunder by the major explosion of the gas tank.

Survivors told stories of coincidence and miraculous occurrences. A watchman went off duty a mere two minutes before the second blast and survived. A six-month-old child was found asleep in the street in the immediate vicinity of the gas tank, unharmed.

The benzol plant and the adjacent tar reservoirs burned for several days, spewing acrid ebony smoke, which in turn coated the scene in black silt.

If the explosion had happened at any time other than during the changing of shifts, more of the 4,000 workers in the ironworks would have been killed or injured. As it was, 68 in the plant and the adjacent residential area were killed, and more than 300 were injured.

Ironically, at the very moment that the gas tank exploded, Adolf Hitler was addressing a huge throng of followers at the Sportspalast in Berlin in his first public appearance since the Nazi Party had come into power and Hitler was appointed chancellor of the Third Reich.

In his speech Hitler declared war on the "parliamentary-democratic system," and exclaimed, "It is to be either the German nation or Marxism!"

Four days later, a huge police force surrounded the funeral of the victims, as the official news release stated it, "to prevent demonstrations which Communists . . . have planned."

None took place, but all over the Reich, flags at public buildings were flown at half staff, and when France sent condolences directly to the League of Nations Commission rather than through the French Embassy in Berlin, they received a sharp rebuke from the Nazis, who immediately poured money and materials into a nearly instant rebuilding of the ravaged city of Neunkirchen, obviously with an eye on the coming plebiscite.

When it occurred, 90 percent of the occupants of the Saar voted reunion with Germany, and Hitler acted immediately to bring it about. After World War II, the Saar again reverted to France, and its coal riches flowed toward that country until 1959, when the Saar was once again made part of West Germany (now Germany), which it remains today.

Questions persisted: Was the German government conducting synthetic tire experiments in the benzol plant, and was that the cause of the 1933 blast? Was it a staged incident, to offer the new Nazi-controlled government of Germany a show of sympathy and solidarity? Or was it simple carelessness? No solid answers were ever offered to counteract the last analysis, provided by the only eyewitnesses. But one conclusion was undeniable: The rich environment of the Saar would, as long as coal and steel were important to the world, be a place to be fought over, exploited, and sometimes carelessly handled.

INDIA
(BHOPAL)
UNION CARBIDE PESTICIDE PLANT EXPLOSION
December 3, 1984

....

The worst industrial accident in history, and possibly the most irresponsible, was the explosion at the Union Carbide pesticide plant in Bhopal, India, on December 3, 1984. The multiple causes included faulty maintenance, lax management, outdated equipment, misguided judgment, and societal factors. At least 2,000 died; 200,000 were injured.

India has been a place where a patina of the present is layered over an ancient civilization accustomed to conducting itself in ancient ways. The teachings of Kashmir Shaivism go back 3,000 years. The words of Brahmin chants that accompany contemporary religious services are in ancient Sanskrit. Oxen carts still haul produce, electricity is still unavailable in parts of the country. Although television now permeates India as thoroughly as it does the rest of the world, the most popular program—the one that brought the entire country to a virtual standstill when it was shown—was a dramatization of the great and ancient Hindu spiritual epic, the *Mahabharata.*

Thus, there is always a sense of pure difference, which allows only accommodation, not compromise, when Western ideas or industries introduce themselves into India. And sometimes these accommodations carry with them a certain detachment that can manifest itself in dangerous carelessness.

Although Western industries find that locating their industrial plants in Third World countries is profitable because labor is cheap, there are also trade-offs. The labor is usually both cheap and unskilled. And because of the distance from supply sources, some equipment in these plants goes far too long without updating, replacement, or even maintenance. Finally, there is the danger that a kind of casualness, a slowing down of the metabolism, more in tune with the pace of ancient life than of modern life, works against the constant, concentrated vigilance necessary to prevent industrial disaster by guarding against it.

All these factors contributed to the complex series of events that led to the worst industrial accident in history early in the morning on December 3, 1984. The disaster took place in the Union Carbide pesticide plant in Bhopal, a small city in the north central region of Madhya Pradesh, midway between New Delhi and Bombay.

The plant, a boon to this economically depressed city, was located in its slum section, a community called Jai Prakash Nagar.

At 2:45 P.M. on Sunday, December 2, while children played in the dirt outside the huts crammed together near the plant's entrance, about 100 workers reported for duty for the eight-hour late shift.

The plant, which manufactured the pesticide Sevin, had been closed down for some time and had been reactivated only a week before. It was still making the pesticide, which consisted of a mix of carbon tetrachloride, methyl isocyanate, and alphanapthol, at a partial pace.

The methyl isocyanate, commonly shortened to MIC, was stored in three partially buried tanks, each with a 15,000-gallon capacity.

One of the tanks, numbered 610, was giving the workers trouble. For a reason they could not determine, the chemical could not be forced out of the tank. Nitrogen was pumped in to force the MIC into the Sevin plant, but each time this was done, the nitrogen leaked out.

There was a greater problem with tank number 610, however, and this, plus a leak that had not been repaired in seven days, would set the stage for a major catastrophe.

First of all, MIC must, to maintain stability and be non-reactive, be kept at a low temperature. A refrigeration unit designed to maintain it at low temperature had, for a still-unexplained reason, been turned off. The chemical was thus warmer than the four degrees Fahrenheit recommended in the plant's operating manual, but just how much warmer was impossible to tell, since the instruments monitoring it were old and unreliable.

In addition, the money-losing plant had undergone further cost-cutting procedures in recent months, and these included the curtailment of maintenance on the noncomputerized, behind-the-times equipment. And finally, long-time supervisors and operators in key positions had just been replaced.

As a result of this laxity and unfamiliarity, tank number 610, besides having a faulty valve and not being maintained at the proper temperature, was also overfilled.

Other pieces of the scenario began to assemble themselves. At approximately 9:30 P.M., a supervisor ordered a worker to clean a 23-foot section of pipe that filtered crude MIC before it went into the storage tanks. The worker did this by connecting a hose to the pipe, opening a drain, and turning on the water. The water flowed into the pipe, out the pipe drains, and onto the floor, where it entered a floor drain. It flowed continuously over this route for three hours.

All of the workers and presumably the new supervisor knew that water reacts violently with MIC. They also knew that there was a leaky valve not only in tank number 610, but also in the pipe that was being washed. Rahaman Khan, the worker who washed out the pipe, later told the *New York Times*, "I knew that some valves leaked. I didn't check to see if that one was leaking. It was not my job."

It is generally conceded that it was the water flowing from the hose that triggered the horror that was to follow.

At 10:30, a pressure reading was taken on tank 610. It was two pounds per square inch, which was normal.

At 10:45, the next shift arrived. The water was still running.

At 11:00 P.M., the pressure had climbed to 10 pounds per square inch, five times what it had been a half hour before. Something was obviously wrong. But no one did anything about it, because it was still within acceptable limits. In fact, some workers later testified that that was the usual temperature and pressure of the MIC at the plant.

Then, too, there was the problem of the instruments. Shakti Qureshi, the MIC supervisor on duty, later noted that he thought that one of the readings was probably

wrong. "Instruments often didn't work," he said. "They got corroded. Crystals would form on them."

But around this time, the natural alarms contained in the bodies of the workers informed them that something was indeed wrong. Their eyes began to tear. They knew MIC was leaking, but this happened on the average of once a month. They often relied on these personal, primitive symptoms to inform them that a leak had occurred. Suman Dey, a worker, later told reporters, "We were human leak detectors."

V. N. Singh, another worker, discovered the leak at approximately 11:45 P.M. He noticed a drip of liquid, accompanied by some yellowish white gas, from a pipe about 50 feet off the ground. Mr. Singh informed his supervisor, Mr. Qureshi, who said that he would look into it after his tea break.

The tea break began for everyone at 12:15. And while this ancient custom went on for 20 minutes, the disaster continued to unfold, unchecked.

From 12:40 A.M., events began to accelerate with lightning rapidity. The smell of gas rose alarmingly. Workers choked on it. The temperature gauge on tank number 610 rose above 77 degrees Fahrenheit, the top of the scale. The pressure gauge was visibly inching upward toward 40 pounds per square inch, a point at which the emergency relief valve on the MIC tank was scheduled to burst open.

At 12:45 A.M., the pressure gauge read 55 pounds per square inch, 15 points from the top of the scale. The tea break was over, and supervisor Qureshi read the gauges. He immediately ordered all the water in the plant turned off, and it was only then that the water in the hose that had been running for three hours was finally found and shut down.

But it was far too late. The water mixed and reacted with the MIC, and the leak burst forth, into the air. Panicked workers dashed to and fro, blinded and coughing.

An alarm sounded, and within minutes the fire brigade arrived to place a water curtain around the escaping gas. But the curtain reached only 100 feet in the air. The top of the stack through which the gas was now spewing into the atmosphere was 120 feet high, and the gas fountained another 10 feet above that.

A vent gas scrubber, a device designed to neutralize the escaping gas, was turned on. But its gauges showed that no caustic soda was flowing into it. Or, perhaps the gauge was broken. Who knew at this point? In either case, the gas, instead of being neutralized, was shooting out of the scrubber stack and was being carried on the high winds southward from the plant and into the surrounding slums.

There were four buses parked by the road leading out of the plant. Drivers were supposed to man them in an emergency to load and evacuate workers and people who lived near the plant. But no drivers appeared. They, along with the terrified workers, were dashing, full speed, from the plant.

At 1:00 A.M., Mr. Qureshi ran out of ideas. He called S. P. Choudhary, the assistant factory manager, who instructed him to turn on the flare tower, which was designed to burn off escaping gas.

But, explained Mr. Qureshi, with all that gas in the air, turning on the flare would certainly cause a huge explosion. At any rate, a four-foot elbow-shaped piece of pipe was missing from the flare. It had corroded and was due to be replaced as soon as the part arrived from the United States.

An alternative would have been to dump the MIC into a spare storage tank. There were two spares that were supposed to be empty for just such an emergency. But they were not. Both were full of MIC.

The workers who remained and tried to control the leak now donned oxygen masks. It was the only way they could breathe. Visibility was down to one foot. Mr. Qureshi, the supervisor, unable to find a mask, he said, opted to run away from the plant. He found a clear area, scaled a six-foot fence topped by barbed wire, vaulted over it and fell to the other side, breaking his leg. He was later transported to a hospital along with many, many others.

The gas continued to pour unchecked out of the leak until 2:30 A.M., when it stopped of its own accord. Jagannathan Mukund, the factory manager, arrived at 3:00 A.M. and only then, because, he later stated, the telephones were out of order, did he send a man to inform the police about the accident. The company had a policy, he said, of not involving the local authorities in gas leaks.

And to be fair, the sleeping populace *did* hear the emergency sirens going off, but these sirens sounded so often in false alarms that the residents of the surrounding slums ignored them and went back to sleep—some of them for the last time.

Outside the factory, people were dying by the hundreds, some in their beds. Others, panicked, choking, blinded, ran into the cloud of gas, inhaling more and more of it until they dropped dead. Thousands of terrified animals perished where they stood.

The outside temperature was only 57 degrees Fahrenheit, which kept the lethal cloud of gas close to the ground, rather than allowing it to rise and dissipate into the atmosphere, as it would have under warmer conditions.

The gas crept into open shacks, killing the weak and the frail immediately. Others woke, vomited, and groped blindly to get outdoors, where they filled their lungs with the searing chemical vapor.

"I awoke when I found it difficult to breathe," said Rahi Bano to a reporter afterward. "All around me my neighbors were shouting, and then a wave of gas hit me."

She fell, vomiting, and her two infant sons, whom she was carrying, rolled onto the floor. She revived herself and grabbed one son. He and she would survive; the son she left behind would die.

A choking, lethal cloud of methyl isocyanate (MIC) was unleashed, without warning, upon the populace that lived next to the Union Carbide plant in Bhopal, on December 3, 1984.
(PRAKASH TILOKANI/UNEP)

Rivers of humanity, tens of thousands of people, stumbled about. Some were trampled. Others simply gave up and sat down. As the cloud spread southeastward, it enveloped the Bhopal railroad station. Ticket takers, trainmen, and passengers died where they stood or sat.

A hill was located in the center of the city, and thousands rushed toward it, thinking they could climb above the gas. "There were cars, bicycles, auto-rickshaws, anything that would move on the road trying to get up the hill," said one survivor. "I saw people just collapsing by the side of the road."

New hazards presented themselves; many of the fleeing refugees were run over by cars, buses, and emergency vehicles. The police, instead of helping, heightened the panic by roaring through the crowds in police vans shouting, "Run! Run! Poison gas is spreading!" over their loudspeakers.

Hospitals were immediately filled. Doctors and nurses tried to save as many as they could, but Hamida Hospital recorded a death a minute until it finally gave up trying to keep count. Dr. N. H. Trivedi, deputy superintendent of the hospital told the *Times*, "People picked up helpless strangers, their best friends, their relatives, and brought them in here. They did far more than the police and official organizations."

Most hospitals placed two stricken people in one bed, until there was no more room, and emergency clinics were set up in stores and on streets.

When dawn finally broke over Bhopal, it lit a scene of cataclysmic destruction. Thousands of bodies—human and animal—littered the streets. No birds sang. The only sounds and movement were from trucks sent out to pick up the dead and to search houses for more dead and dying.

Most of the dead had come from Jai Prakash Nagar and Kali Parade, the two slum neighborhoods adjacent to the plant, but the brisk night breeze had carried the fatal fumes much farther than that.

Between 2,000 and 2,500 had perished, and more than 200,000 would be afflicted for years, possibly for the rest of their lives, with the aftereffects of the Bhopal tragedy. Some were permanently blinded. Others could not sleep, had difficulty breathing or digesting food, and had trouble functioning.

For a week, the suffering continued in Bhopal's hospitals and clinics. Children between one and six years old seemed to suffer most. The tragedy was made worse by the inability of either medical specialists or parents to do anything. Relatives watched mutely from doorways as doctors placed intravenous feeding tubes into the children's arms and oxygen tubes into their noses and mouths.

For weeks, sirens wailed, single cremations took place, one after another, and other bodies were buried in mass graves. The worst panic took place 10 days after the accident, on December 13, when Union Carbide announced that it would start the plant up again on Sunday, December 16, to neutralize what remained of the MIC.

Bhopal, normally a city of 900,000, was already depleted. Besides the 2,000 dead and the 200,000 injured, 100,000 others had fled after the disaster. Now, 100,000 more took to trains, buses, cars, planes, auto-rickshaws, two-wheeled tongas, and their own feet to put distance between themselves and what they perceived to be the site of another possible catastrophe.

In an effort to prevent the looting of vacated homes and to maintain order in the clinics and refugee camps, 2,000 paramilitary troops and special armed police officers were brought in by the Indian government to supplement the local police force.

A year after the accident, residents of Bhopal who had been affected by MIC were still suffering. According to authorities in India, an estimated 10 to 20 percent of the 200,000 people injured were still seriously affected. Many were having trouble breathing, sleeping, digesting food, and undertaking simple tasks, just as they had right after the leak occurred.

They suffered memory loss, nausea, nerve damage, including tremors, and injury to kidneys, liver, stomach, and spleen. A year after the tragedy, 40 percent of those afflicted were in the same condition, 40 percent had improved, and 20 percent had worsened. Medical studies predicted that those who had worsened would be victims of long-term, perhaps lifelong, afflictions.

The relief effort had become bureaucratic and sometimes contradictory. Cortisone injections were given by one medical team; cough medicine and aspirin by another. One health expert, Rashmi Mayur of the Urban Institute in

Bombay averred that he had come across one victim who had been able to get 250 pills in one day from seven different doctors.

What ultimately became apparent in the tragic unfolding of this disaster was that ignorance—real and generated—was also a culprit. Even as people were dying, Union Carbide factory doctors were telling local physicians that MIC, used in 20 to 25 percent of all of the world's pesticides, only caused lung and eye irritation. And none of these company doctors had informed local medical workers ahead of time that a simple antidote for the effects of the chemical was to merely cover the face with a wet cloth. "Had we known this," police superintendent Swaraj Puri later told reporters, "many lives might have been saved."

Six months before the accident, the U.S. National Academy of Sciences had said that little or nothing was known about the health effects of most of the 54,000 chemicals used in commercial products, making treatment and prevention difficult at best.

Afterward, concerted efforts were made to find causes and assign blame, and there was more than enough to go around. Officials of Union Carbide were arrested when they arrived in India, then freed. They were later charged with criminal negligence, as was the plant supervisor.

The Indian government filed suit against Union Carbide in the federal district court in Manhattan, seeking compensation for victims of the disaster. But the court threw out the suit, claiming that the government of India had no jurisdiction.

It was an interesting decision, and one fraught with possible political influences. Was it, as some charged, a payback to Union Carbide for its role in the development and sustenance of American atomic power? Or was it, as others charged, a case of the United States government protecting United States companies against foreign lawsuits?

Whatever the reason, the scenario now became confusing and complex, particularly for victims of the tragedy. First, an army of American lawyers descended upon Bhopal intent upon making a lot of money at the expense of the victims. Lawyer John Cole was the first to arrive, and before the bad news that the Indian government's suit had been dismissed was handed down from the Indian government, he had signed up no less than 60,000 clients.

All these lawyers, expecting an appeal from the Indian government, continued to merrily accumulate clients. But no appeal came. And furthermore, while the Indian government agreed to proceed with the prosecution of Union Carbide in India, it forbade the victims from being represented by United States lawyers, who thereupon deserted their clients.

The grim charade continued. Union Carbide CEO Warren Anderson accepted full responsibility for the tragedy; then, two months later, he blamed the Indian management of the plant and strongly suggested that a disgruntled plant employee had purposely attached a water pipe to the MIC tank.

There was, however, no evidence of sabotage, and workers blamed cutbacks and shoddy equipment at the plant. Still, to this day, no legal conclusions have been reached.

Now, without consulting the victims, the Indian courts, through the government of Rajiv Gandhi, reached an out-of-court settlement with Union Carbide of $470 million—a bargain for Union Carbide when placed side by side with the $5 billion settlement with Exxon for the *Exxon Valdez* disaster (see pp. 166–169).

Furthermore, victims were required to settle all claims—and there were nearly 600,000 of them, including 15,000 death claims—in special regional courts. The plaintiffs were required to be represented by lawyers, but hardly any of them could afford a lawyer. Not only were they residents of Bhopal's poorest slum, but most of them had exhausted whatever money they had on medical bills before the regional courts were even established.

And so the process dragged on. And on. The paperwork was monumental and often slipshod. In the 12 years that the courts have been in existence, three judges have been dismissed for corruption. In the same 12 years, most of the victims are still waiting for settlement. Only 30 percent of the claims have been heard, and only half of these have been resolved. The other half of the 30 percent have been excluded because of draconian requirements for proving injury by industrial accident set by the Indian government—requirements that the victims often cannot even comprehend. The average settlement has been $750—and often the victims are badgered into accepting either that or nothing at all.

A demonstration in 1994 at which tombstones were erected around the shuttered Union Carbide plant did nothing to correct an inhuman situation that the world, now apparently bored with Bhopal, failed to notice.

Meanwhile, there is a strong suspicion that the Indian government is withholding information that is far more terrible in its indictment of Union Carbide than has previously been known, and which is furthermore rife with predictions for long-term effects, much like those at Hiroshima and Minamata. To this day, the Indian Council of Medical Research refuses to release its reports on the tragedy.

Tuberculosis and gynecological problems still rack the survivors, and doctors, who could benefit from the council's research, are powerless to treat the thousands and thousands of cases.

And the tragedy spreads. Union Carbide has spent $5 million on increasing safety measures at its plants, but only in the United States. It and hundreds of other American industries continue to move their plants to developing countries where labor is cheap and pollution standards are lax.

As for Bhopal, which is now an ongoing and seemingly never-ending tragedy: All that is generally and obviously acknowledged is that the seeds of the tragedy were planted in 1972, when, under Indian government pressure to reduce imports and loss of foreign exchange, the company proposed to manufacture and store MIC at the plant in Bhopal. Both the local government and the company agreed, at that time, that the risks would not be high.

Dr. S. R. Kamar, a prominent Bombay expert on industrial health and the hazards of development, probably summed it up most succinctly and accurately: "Western technology came to this country but not the infrastructure for that technology," he told the *New York Times* on March 2, 1985. "A lot of risks have been taken here," he went on. "Machinery is outdated. Spare parts are not included. Maintenance is inadequate. Bhopal is the tip of an iceberg, an example of lapses not only in India but in the United States and many other countries."

If ever there was an iceberg that needs melting, or an example of international government and industry irresponsibility and coverup, it is the example of Bhopal.

ITALY
(SEVESO)
ICMESA CHEMICAL PLANT EMISSION, TOXIC CLOUD
July 10, 1976

On July 10, 1976, an explosion in the Icmesa chemical plant in Seveso, Italy, released a toxic cloud containing dioxin, one of the most lethal substances known to humankind, and the principal ingredient in the defoliant Agent Orange, dispersed by United States forces in Vietnam. Thousands of animals and birds died, and hundreds of residents of the contaminated area were made ill. The release of the cloud and the eventual disposal of the contaminants is a tangled tale of intrigue and coverup.

According to Corrado Salvatore, a spokesperson for the Italian Ministry of Health, something "went mad" on July 10, 1976, at the Swiss-owned Icmesa chemical plant in the small town of Seveso, 13 miles north of Milan, on the road to Lake Como. Without warning or reason, temperatures rose, causing pressure to build within the plant's system. Then a safety valve opened, and a white cloud of trichlorophenol, carrying crystals of dioxin, was released into the atmosphere.

The plant, owned by the pharmaceutical and chemical concern Hoffman-LaRoche, manufactured trichlorophenol, a chemical used to make hexochlorophene, an ingredient in cleansers and germicides. But there is another, more lethal and frightening use of one of the ingredients in tricholorophenol: Dioxin, also known as TCDD, is the contam-

On the afternoon of July 10, 1976, a cloud containing dioxin—an ingredient in the defoliant Agent Orange—billowed out of the Icmesa chemical plant in Seveso, Italy, obscuring the towns of Seveso, Desio, and Cesano Maderno, an area populated by 1,500 unwary residents. The cloud lasted for half an hour before coming apart and dispersing droplets of dioxin to the ground.

(Tim Alipalo/UNEP)

whitish cloud southward for about half an hour before it came apart and dispersed droplets of dioxin to the ground.

Because chemical and medicinal odors constantly emitted from the plant, the residents of the area were used to it. And so they dismissed the increased chemical smell in the summer air. But then, two days after the cloud first appeared, animals began to die. Plants started to wither. And, alarmingly, children who were playing in the fields around the plant began to develop skin rashes that manifested themselves in severe blemishes and islands of angry eruptions.

It rained, and company officials apparently felt that the rain might wash away the contaminant. It didn't. Finally, one week after the valve in the plant opened, Icmesa managers alerted local officials to the toxic dangers carried in the mysterious white cloud that had hovered over the landscape for days after it had been released from the plant.

The officials were outraged. It was as if the plant managers and the federal government were conspiring, criminally, against the populace. Italy was in a depressed state economically in the mid-1970s. In the hunger for jobs and industrialization, safety regulations in its factories and other corporate structures were often ignored, or never adopted. The Icmesa plant had, in fact, been the subject of previous complaints from workers and residents about unsafe conditions.

Local officials issued immediate warnings about eating, or even touching, local produce. "The factory tried to hide the situation," Dr. Vittorio Rivolta, chief medical official for the Lombardy region, later asserted. It would be a week before evacuations and hospitalizations would begin.

Fourteen children were taken to Milan with skin rashes, and plans were made to send hundreds more from the contaminated zone to summer camps in the south of Italy. More than 100 pregnant women were admitted to the same hospitals. Although no women had been involved in previous dioxin accidents, the immediate concern of medical authorities was the fate of the fetuses. Would they be born dead or deformed? No one knew. "What we have here are human guinea pigs," said Professor Francesco Pocchiari, director of the National Institutes of Health.

Scientists and officials swarmed over the area, testing, but uncertain of what results to expect. Aside from the rashes on the children, no residents showed evidence of contamination, but the doctors and scientists really did not know what signs would establish a connection to contamination. In some previous cases, workers exposed to dioxin had suffered liver, kidney, and heart ailments. As for the pregnant women: None had ever, so far as the officials knew, been involved in a dioxin spill. But some doctors, mindful of the children who had been born with birth defects to women who had been affected by Agent Orange contamination in Vietnam, wanted to perform abortions immediately. Others, and hospital officials, demurred. The Vatican had just renewed its

inant used in 2-4-5, or Agent Orange, the defoliant that was employed by American forces in Vietnam (see pp. 226–29).

Dioxin is one of the most toxic substances yet known—so deadly that a dose of less than a billionth of a gram is fatal to guinea pigs. It is usually present in tricholorophenol in harmless quantities, but extremely high temperatures can produce dangerous amounts. Apparently, there were extremely high temperatures present on the afternoon of July 10, 1976, in the Icmesa plant; otherwise, the safety valve would not have opened.

All of this happened secretly and silently, beyond human notice. The valve opened; the valve closed; the white cloud spread out in a conelike pattern south of the city of Meda, touching the towns of Seveso, Desio, and Cesano Maderno, an area populated by more than 1,500 unwary residents. The wind was north that day, and it carried the thick, attack on government plans to provide abortions for women who might give birth to deformed children.

Finally, two weeks after the accident, wholesale and organized evacuations began. An area of approximately 285 acres, called "Zone A" was evacuated and sealed off. The 2,580 residents of "Zone B," farther away from the plant and presumably less contaminated, were allowed to remain at home, though parents were urged to send their children away, even in this area. "Zone C" was not evacuated, but residents were warned against eating produce grown in the area.

The factory's technical director, Giovanni Radice, and two other executives were taken into custody. In Switzerland, Hoffman-LaRoche officials announced that they would pay damages, but denied criminal culpability.

As July drew to an end, Italian officials pushed the boundaries of the contaminated area outward, and began to evacuate more and more families. The countryside was now littered with dead animals. One cow and hundreds of rabbits, cats, birds, and chickens—all of whom presumably either ingested the TCDD or ate plants on which it had settled—lay dead where they had fallen.

It reminded some scientists of the case of waste oil sprayed on the earthern floor of a Missouri stable to keep dust down in 1974 (see United States, Missouri, Times Beach, pp. 108–11). In that case, the oil had been contaminated with a concentration of dioxin that was 60 parts per million. Over a period of years, 48 horses, 70 chickens, several dogs, a dozen cats, and hundreds of wild birds died within the sprayed area. The animals had merely walked over the oil-soaked earth, some up to two years after the soil had been contaminated. No humans had died in that incident, though several had become ill.

Near Seveso in 1976, barbed wire now began to be placed around the zone of heaviest pollution, which meant that a heavily traveled road between Milan and Lake Como was blocked. The total area of contamination was increased to include 10,000 acres.

Interviews with executives and the technical director of the factory revealed that about four and a half pounds of dioxin had escaped from the factory, an amount that could kill several thousand people.

Doctors were now even more concerned about pregnant women; the parallel to Vietnam was dramatically close. Carlo Sirtori, a leading Italian obstetrician advised women in the area against pregnancy for at least three months.

Awareness began to spread, albeit as slowly as the toxic cloud. Warnings were issued to medical examiners to look for telltale evidence of contamination: skin lesions; kidney, liver, and pancreas disorders; decreased immunization factors in the blood; and/or an alteration in chromosomal makeup.

By August, more than 500 persons had been treated for skin rashes and liver disorders, and the Italian government contacted Hanoi for advice in detoxifying the area and treating the symptoms of those exposed to the toxin. North Vietnamese doctor Ton That Thut of the Viet Duc hospital had developed a treatment method for persons afflicted by chemicals United States forces had used to defoliate jungle hiding places of the Vietcong during the war. Three hundred of every 1,000 people affected by TCDD in Vietnam had died, and Dr. Thut recommended the use of natural soap as an antidote, because the animal fats and natural oils neutralized dioxin. Large quantities of natural soap were shipped into the region in which no human beings had yet died.

On August 2, Italy's Christian Democratic government issued a statement agreeing to change Italy's strict law against abortions to allow the procedure for women affected by the toxic cloud in the Seveso area.

As August wore on, the contaminated area was again widened, this time to an area 4.5 miles long, encompassing more than 100,000 persons. All children up to the age of 15 and all pregnant women were ordered out.

Clinics were set up near the city of Meda, and the decision by the Italian government to relax the national abortion laws was challenged by an adamant statement from the Vatican. "Even in difficult, very painful situations, the fundamental principle of absolute inviolability of every innocent human life, including the unborn, must remain," L'Osservatore Romano, the Vatican newspaper declared.

This gave rise to an immediate flurry of anecdotes from the contaminated area. Three women from Seveso had miscarriages in Milan's Mangiagalli clinic over the weekend following the Vatican announcement, but it could not be determined if the miscarriages were the consequences of the dioxin poisoning. A week later, three women from the area, aged 21 to 37, defied the order, and, fearing that their babies might be deformed by the gas, had abortions, in clinics that were willing to defy, or at least ignore, the Vatican.

In Meda, health officials rounded up children, who tearfully boarded buses and waved good-bye to their equally tearful families, and the chorus of complaints against the plant began to grow. It was always a hazard, said Antonio Creviso, a construction worker. He had first become suspicious about the goings on there, he said, when a neighbor's sheep died after drinking water near the factory. Others chimed in with protests about the refuse and odor that the factory dispensed into the neighborhood.

If these statements were tinged with individual interpretations of reality, the decline in the economy of the region was becoming undeniable. Many residents raised their own produce and livestock and consumed it themselves. Now they could not touch, much less eat anything grown locally.

Cesano Maderno was a center for the furniture industry, but customers were canceling orders or demanding large discounts. Some shipments from the area were stopped and turned back at the Swiss border.

On August 17, the Swiss company Givauden, which owned Hoffman-LaRoche, announced that it had developed an antidote, developed in laboratory experiments, that would accelerate the disintegration of the dioxin. Plans went forward to spray a mixture of olive oil and water over the polluted area.

But this was deemed inadequate by some international scientists, and other plans proceeded to remove all vegetation and the earth itself to a depth of one foot from directly affected areas. This vegetation and soil would then be processed in special incinerators capable of producing temperatures high enough to disintegrate the dioxin. Hoffman-LaRoche pledged to pay for the decontamination process.

Six more women underwent abortions at the end of August, and squads of soldiers were dispersed throughout the area to kill dozens of domestic animals, mainly rabbits and chickens suspected of being contaminated by the fumes.

By the beginning of September, regional authorities and trade union officials announced that the Icmesa plant would be permanently closed. "Icmesa can no longer be made operational," stated a trade union official representing the 170 workers in the plant. "The degree of pollution inside the factory is so high that it can hardly be decontaminated."

The area around the plant resembled a war zone. Soldiers armed with rifles and wearing protective clothing, rubber boots, and gas masks, patrolled the barbed-wire boundaries. Rumors spread, fed by an article in the Italian magazine *Panorama*, that not 4 pounds, but 22 pounds—perhaps 132 pounds—of dioxin had been released into the atmosphere. The number of people treated for skin rashes and internal complaints climbed.

"No one knows what will happen," Claudio Meroni, a 55-year-old furniture maker who employed 20 workers in a shop in the area, told freelance journalist Melton Davis. "We're in constant fear of being poisoned; we undergo continual laboratory tests; our lives are destroyed."

More bad news was disseminated. Although the cloud of contamination had dissolved about half an hour after the accident, the dioxin continued to be spread, carried by human beings, animals, birds in flight, the tires of cars, and what was most disturbing, waters, both subterranean and aboveground. The Seveso River flows through the area and moves into the Po, which runs through the richest industrial and farmland in Italy. The possible consequences were staggering.

In late September, Dr. Vittorio Carreri, an official in the Lombardy region, announced that mass checks of 10,000 people most exposed to the cloud revealed "a decrease of lymphocytes in the blood" in several hundred of them. The loss was particularly pronounced in children. A reduction in lymphocytes, he went on to explain, means a reduction in the body's immune response, that is, its ability to fight infection.

By October, residents of the area had lost patience with the glacial pace of the decontamination process. More than 500 of them, driving cars, trucks, and motorcycles, overran the protectively clothed guards, broke through the barbed-wire barricades, and returned to their still-contaminated homes.

As autumn wore on, 20 more people, exhibiting boils on their faces and necks, which indicated that they were suffering from chloracne, the skin disease caused by dioxin, were admitted to Milan clinics.

Meanwhile, the indicted Hoffman-LaRoche executives were acquitted of criminal wrongdoing, but the company was required to pay restitution to contaminated families and to clear all contamination from the closed plant.

As with all tales of pollution, the story dragged on for years. No human deaths occurred, although there were reports of hundreds of cases of illness caused by the contamination. But the postscript to the disaster was bizarre enough to qualify as either an international tale of intrigue or an ecological nightmare. For some observers, it qualified as both.

In 1982, Italian officials, exasperated by delays, warned Hoffman-LaRoche that it would have to transport 41 steel drums containing the collected dioxin contamination from the Icmesa plant out of Italy. In June of that year, Mannesmann Italiana, a subsidiary of the West German steel products company Mannesmann, agreed to transport the wastes.

But time passed and nothing happened, and Senator Luigi Noe, charged with handling what the Italian government now dubbed "the Seveso Problem," pressured Mannesmann to turn the transport over to Bernard Paringaux, the president and only employee of Spelidec, a company based in Marseilles.

On September 10, 1982, the chemical wastes, under the care of Mr. Paringaux, left Italy and entered France, by way of the Italian border town of Ventimiglia. From there, they proceeded to a customs depot in Saint-Quentin, in northern France, near Anguilcourt. And there, they disappeared.

Now Greenpeace entered the picture, along with other environmental groups. They discovered the trail and Mr. Paringaux, and made their discovery public. Their revelations of the mysterious disappearance of 41 barrels of dioxin brought about the arrest of Mr. Paringaux. He refused to reveal the whereabouts of the barrels.

The French government now became involved, and Huguette Bouchardeau, France's secretary of state for environment and quality of life hinted, in April 1983, that the barrels "were in a neighboring country," specifically, Germany. The Bonn government vehemently denied this, and ordered Mannesmann to join it in a search for the dioxin.

Mannesmann, it turned out, paid off "persons close to Mr. Paringaux" to find out where the barrels were, and Agence France-Presse reported in an article in the West German paper *Die Welt* that the wastes were discovered on

Thursday, May 19, at 4:34 P.M., stored in a slaughterhouse in Anguilcourt.

The date the barrels were located became important when accusations were flung back and forth between the French and German governments. Germany accused France of knowing, long before the announcement, of the whereabouts of the barrels. France denied this. Mr. Paringaux muddied the waters by stating that he had told authorities of the dioxin's whereabouts before May 19. He had intended, he stated to the press, to keep the barrels out of view "until all the excitement calmed down. Unfortunately," he added, "it never did."

What Mr. Paringaux apparently planned to do was to extract more money from Hoffman-LaRoche; he failed. He was released from jail in June 1983. Meanwhile, former senator Noe was investigated by the Italian government for complicity in the scheme, trying to force Mannesmann to move the wastes before the company had received the authorization required. France promised prosecutions, but they never materialized.

The 41 barrels of dioxin were finally moved, under heavy guard, to Switzerland, where they were incinerated at a Hoffman-LaRoche plant.

The Italian publication *Corriere della Sera*—in a front-page editorial titled "A New Era After Seveso?"—encapsulated the disaster, its causes, and its repercussions. "Seveso," it said, "has shaken public opinion much more than a hundred speeches about ecology: It has increased people's awareness of the malignity and power of a semiclandestine enemy, namely pollution, which can hit anywhere or anyone. . . . The incident . . . [shows] us that defense of the environment . . . must be a fundamental and permanent exigency in any government program . . . although chimneys smell like jobs, if the stink is dioxin, we now know that no increase in employment can make up for the social harm it does."

Back in 1976, when the first news of the initial dioxin drops released by the toxic cloud from Icmesa began to reach the public, Cesare Golfari, president of the Lombardy region of Italy, had articulated this and a little more: "This is a warning to all the advanced systems of the world to take another look at their industry," he said. "We have to see if there are limits beyond which we cannot go."

JAPAN

(MINAMATA)

CHISSO CHEMICAL PLANT MERCURY CONTAMINATION
1932–1979

Between 1932 and 1968, contaminants containing mercury were dumped into Minamata Bay in uninhibited quantities by the Chisso chemical plant. Fish consumed the pollution and were eaten by the populace. Two hundred eighty-three persons died from what became known as "Minamata Disease." More than 7,000 were injured, and of those children poisoned, 283 suffered birth defects.

"Mad as a hatter" is an expression that came about in the 19th century to refer to workers in hat factories who became contaminated by mercury used in the manufacture of hats. But how to succinctly describe the insane behavior in 1953 of the cats of the coastal city of Minamata on the southern island of Kyushu in Japan? They were certainly mad, catapulting noisily through the streets, running blindly into obstacles, frightening children, adults, and other cats; then, reaching the end of the streets, racing onto the docks and flinging themselves into the harbor, where they drowned.

The link between cause and manifestation was a long and grim one. The workers in English hat factories and the cats of Minamata had been contaminated by the same chemical substance. The workers had touched it. The cats had ingested it from fish that had been swimming in the waters of Minamata Bay, which, for decades, had been slowly filling with contamination from the mercury dumped into it by the Chisso chemical plant.

At first, the link between the crazed cats of Minamata and what was to come was not understood by the general public. It might have been, had the management of the Chisso chemical plant been motivated by human, rather than business considerations. But it was not, and, like Bhopal and its Union Carbide plant (see pp. 81–85), Minamata was about to become a city under ecological siege by the industry that supported it.

Minamata itself is a combination farming-fishing-factory city, reached by train from Tokyo by traveling through Hiroshima, past Nagasaki, and from there down the west coast of Kyushu island. The town itself is ideally suited for fishing, since the Shiranui Sea is placid, and Minamata Bay, which flows into and out of the Shiranui Sea, is sheltered.

The Chisso factory, built in 1907, was originally designed to produce fertilizer (*chisso* in Japanese means "nitrogen"). But in 1932, the factory converted to the production of acetaldehyde, sometimes called ethanol. Made by the addition of water to acetylene in the presence of sulfuric acid and mercuric sulfate, it is used as a reducing agent for silvering mirrors and in the manufacture of synthetic resins and dyestuffs. Thus, the fertilizer factory became a petrochemical factory, turning out material for the plastics industry.

Apparently, Jun Noguchi, who founded the company and built the factory, established, early on, a negative, or, at best, love-hate, relationship between the factory and the town of Minamata. "Treat the workers like cows and horses," was an oft-quoted remark that Chisso's founder once made.

As early as 1925, there was evidence of damage to the fishing industry, and small indemnities were paid by the company to local fishermen to offset the relentless diminishment of their heretofore abundant catches. But it was not until the 1932 conversion to acetaldehyde that the contamination began to become lethal.

By 1952 the factory was in full production. For the next eight years it would employ 50,000 local workers, and cats would begin to fling themselves off the piers and into the bay. In April 1956, the first case of what would eventually be termed *Minamata Disease* entered the local hospital. A five-year-old girl was brought in by her parents; she was suffering from severe brain damage; she could neither walk nor speak and was in a state of delirium.

Several days later, her two-year-old sister entered the same hospital with the same symptoms. Within a week, neighbors, suffering identical manifestations began to appear, and a long drama of horror and obfuscation began.

On May 1, 1956, Dr. Hajime Hosokawa of the Chisso Company Hospital reported, "An unclarified disease of the central nervous system has broken out." By the end of the year, Dr. Hosokawa had determined that the disease was not contagious but that it could undeniably be traced to the fish consumption of each of the patients.

This meant that wide contamination was inevitable, since the abundance of fish in the town and the custom of feeding more fish to those who were ill to make them well was an age-old custom, and, to the poor, a necessity.

The case of Sohachi Hamamoto was typical. A sturdy, energetic, and mildly successful fisherman, he spent a social evening with friends in mid-September of 1956, then went to bed as usual. But the man who went to sleep that night and the man who woke the next morning seemed to be two different people.

In the morning he stirred and sat on the edge of the bed, but his eyes looked odd, and he stared blankly around him. His hearing was not as clear as it had been the day before. Tsuginori, his son with whom he fished, told him what time it was, but he seemed to have difficulty understanding the concept. When he rose to walk, his feet refused to act properly. Told by Tsuginori not to fish that day, he flew into an uncontrollable and unaccustomed rage.

On his son's arm, he tottered to his boat, was helped into it, then fell into the sea when the wake of another passing boat rocked his. He was led back to his home, where, for the next few days, he weakened and became more distracted and enraged. Four days later, when his wife could no longer hold him down by herself, she took him to the hospital at Kumamoto University, where he died.

As the sickness increased, theories were floated as to the cause of the infection, and all these theories pointed toward the dumping of chemical garbage into Minamata Bay. Manganese, thalium, and selenium were blamed; some investigators said as many as 60 poisons were thrown into the bay by the factory, which vehemently and systematically denied each allegation.

By 1958, Chisso temporarily shifted its dumping activities to the Minamata River delta, in the Hachimana district, where the river flowed into the Shiranui Sea. It was only a matter of months before both the residents and the cats of Hachimana began to show the same symptoms.

In July 1959, a group of researchers from Kumamoto University reported that, undeniably, organic mercury was at fault, and methyl mercury poisoning was occurring in Minamata.

Independent committees were formed to examine the evidence further and, in some cases, to refute the Kumamoto findings. Some committees, such as one sponsored by the Japanese Chemical Association, of which Chisso was a member, met once, announced bluntly that the contaminant was definitely mercury, then disappeared.

Meanwhile, Dr. Hosokawa, the company physician for Chisso, was conducting his own experiments. First, he established that poisoning was the cause of the illness. Next, he confirmed that fish were the carriers of the poisoning, and he began to understand that his company might be responsible. Sensing perhaps that the results might not be what the company wished, he told the younger doctors serving under him that all the experiments were his doing, and not theirs.

For months, he would feed cats all of the poisons that might have produced the same symptoms as fish from Minamata Bay contained—manganese, selenium, thalium, and finally, mercury. Further investigation unearthed the information that the factory's acetaldehyde facility used mercury, and this in turn produced some anxiety within Dr. Hosokawa. "I was a bit hesitant and found it difficult to begin that [particular part of the] experiment," he later testified. "I did not talk about it."

But proceed he did, with cat number 400 of those he tested. At the beginning of October, he fed the cat waste water from the acetaldehyde facility. On October 7, 1959, the cat became ill, and while Dr. Hosokawa watched, it convulsed, salivated, and suddenly turned insane, whirling around the laboratory, crashing into objects and walls and behaving exactly as the mad cats who had flung themselves into the bay had, and as the victims of Minamata Disease had, too.

In the words of W. Eugene Smith, the American photographer who, with his wife, is the foremost chronicler of the Minamata disaster: "[Dr. Hosokawa] reported the result to Chisso management. The next time his assistant went out to get acetaldehyde waste water, he was stopped by a guard. In a November meeting, Hosokawa was told that there would be absolutely no more experiments connected with Minamata Disease."

There was a reason for the coverup. A growing but respectful group of fishermen and patients were demanding restitution from Chisso for their suffering, which was both monetary and physical. Knowing full well their own culpability, but hiding the results of Dr. Hosokawa's own in-house experiments, the management of Chisso negotiated a settlement with the fishermen and patients that was distinctly favorable to Chisso.

"There is no scientific proof that Minamata Disease is caused by Chisso," the agreement began, in direct contradiction to Chisso's own knowledge. Relying—rightly, it turned out—on the scientific and legal naïveté of the fishermen and residents of Minamata, Chisso drew up a contract that specified that payments made to the victims would not be regarded as indemnity but merely as *mimai,* which translates as "consolation" for a misfortune for which Chisso accepted no responsibility. Furthermore, the contract stated, if Chisso were later proved guilty, the company would not be liable for further compensation.

The fishermen were not pacified and, as a union, stormed the factory. There were numerous injuries, and the local government warned the fishermen that if they did not accept Chisso's offer, they might end up with nothing. It was a possibility they could ill afford, and so patients and fishermen alike accepted the meager arrangement, and what would later be described as "industrial genocide" proceeded, unimpaired.

Meanwhile, Dr. Hosokawa pleaded with the Chisso management to allow him to resume his study of animals affected by acetaldehyde waste water. "I asked them to please let me continue the experiments," he later testified, "but it was no good after all . . . the answer was not affirmative."

Dr. Hosokawa told no one of his findings and resumed his work as head of the Chisso hospital. Then, in mid-1960, the management of Chisso reversed itself and allowed him to start his experiments again, provided he only used waste water that the new factory manager sent to him. "I don't know whether it was or was not the real—the same waste water as before," he recalled.

Judging from the further interference with his experiment that occurred, it probably was not. Papers he prepared vanished, and the bodies of cats he sent to Tokyo University to be autopsied disappeared. Finally, Hosokawa retired, without publicly blaming Chisso for what would eventually widen into confrontation and worldwide publicity.

For the next eight years, in a quiet induced by intimidation, Chisso continued to dump poisonous effluent into Minamata Bay, while at the same time, with some fanfare, it installed a "cyclator." The gadget, they stated, would treat waste water. But it was purely a public relations gesture. Those who manned it later testified that it was ineffective against mercury.

During these eight years, Chisso continued its polluting ways and only stopped the mercury method of production in 1968, not because it felt a sense of responsibility to the hundreds of residents of the area that it was killing every month, but because the system had become outmoded.

However, in 1967, an incident that was exactly like the tragedy of Minamata occurred in Niigata. The chemical company Showa Denko had also polluted waters in that city with mercury, causing the same sort of terrible disease and death that had stalked Minamata. But the Niigata victims went to court, and sued, and won.

And so, inspired by the Niigata victory, on July 14, 1969, 29 families that included victims took to the courts in Minamata, and the story, now public, began to unfold in all its terrible detail. There was anything but a simple showdown. On one side was Chisso. On the other side there were, first the 29 families, who only represented one-third of the 1959 signers to that year's settlement with Chisso. And then there was the remaining two-thirds, who, too ill or lacking the will to fight, renegotiated with Chisso through government intermediaries, and in so doing, became known as the "leave it up to the other people group."

As the trial ached forward for four years, more victims of Minamata Disease began to surface. Some of them settled, and thus joined the "leave it up to the other people group." Others forged an alliance with those in the pre-1959 cluster and with a new, forceful "direct negotiations" group.

On May 25, 1970, the "leave it up to the other people" group signed a settlement with Chisso, and the company claimed a moral victory. But two months later, Dr. Hosokawa, now mortally ill, gave testimony from his deathbed regarding his experiments and their suppression, thus opening old wounds and destroying Chisso's credibility. In November 1970, the Central Pollution Board was formed by the Japanese government to handle all complaints and oversee settlements.

Chisso had hidden behind outright lies and small assurances at the beginning of the Minamata tragedy. It now erected iron bars and barbed wire in front of the entrance to its Tokyo headquarters. These would remain for well over a year, while the trial wended its way slowly through the Japanese legal system.

Across from the barred headquarters, a small tent-city, presided over by activist Teruo Kawamoto, was set up to forward the demands of the "direct negotiation" group. This, in contrast to the more accommodating "old," or pre-1959, contaminees, was confrontational and impatient, though not given to breaking the law. All they desired, they said on their banners, was "vengeance," which in Japanese translates not into simple revenge, as it does in English, but into a more complex process involving pursuit to a just end, after which the original reason for the pursuit is never forgotten.

Kawamoto was a former Chisso employee who had been fired by the company for union activity, and had then become a nurse in a mental hospital. When his father contracted Minamata Disease, he applied to the Kumamoto Minamata Disease Verification Committee for certification, but his father died before the certification came. When, after several months, it still did not arrive, Kawamoto came to the conclusion that his father was one among many whom both the company and the government were systematically hiding, in order to minimize the number of victims of the disease. When Kawamoto disinterred his father's body and took it to Kumamoto University for an autopsy and the body mysteriously disappeared, he was galvanized into action.

In September 1971, the Niigata verdict in favor of the plaintiffs was announced, and the "direct negotiations" group gathered new determination. Platoons of supporters gathered around their tents, and the media began to cover the confrontation widely. Kawamoto and his followers turned physical, jamming the gates before the Tokyo headquarters of Chisso with their bodies.

Finally, on November 13, 1971, President Kenichi Shimada of Chisso came to Minamata and signed a paper accepting moral—but not legal—responsibility for causing Minamata Disease.

It was not enough for the tent dwellers and their supporters. The confrontations between the demonstrators and police escalated.

On January 7, 1972, Kawamoto set a meeting between the management of Chisso's factory in Goi and himself. When his supporters and he arrived, the management became suddenly unavailable. A small riot ensued, during which several journalists and photographers, among them American photographer W. Eugene Smith, were seriously injured. Their cameras were either seized or smashed by security police and workers.

Ironically, in the midst of this, Japan sent diplomat Shinobu Sakamoto and Tsuginori Hamamoto, the wife of afflicted fisherman Sohachi Hamamoto, to the first United Nations Environmental Conference in Stockholm, Sweden. Now the story became an international one that the entire environmental movement heard.

The Minamata trial finally came to an end, and it was announced that the verdict would be pronounced in March. But the Central Pollution Board would be issuing its findings earlier.

That, however, was not the agenda the "direct negotiation" group wished. On January 10, 1973, they crowded into the hearing room of the Pollution Board, demanding to see the absolving documents signed by—or "chopped," which is a signature with a rubber stamp, and accepted as binding in Japan—a large group of Minamata patients. The patients themselves verified that the signatures and chops were forgeries. The scandal forced the Central Pollution Board to delay its findings.

On March 20, 1973, the trial verdict by the Kumamoto District Court was announced. Its preamble excoriated Chisso. "No plant can be permitted to infringe on and run at the sacrifice of the lives and health of the regional residents . . . ," it said.

"The defendant's plant discharged acetaldehyde waste water with negligence at all times, and even though the quality and content of the waste water of the defendant's plant satisfied statutory limitations and administrative standards, and even if the treatment methods it employed were superior to those taken at the workyards of other companies in the same industry, these are not enough to upset the said assumption . . . ," it continued, "the defendant cannot escape from the liability of negligence."

The plaintiffs were awarded a maximum of $68,000 for deceased patients or severe cases, and a minimum of $60,000 for less severe cases. Chisso immediately issued a statement announcing that it would not appeal the verdict.

But the confrontation was not yet over. The verdict had set damages, but had said nothing about the continuation of life: medical fees, medicines, therapeutic massages and hot baths, nursing for the bedridden, transportation to and from treatment, an allowance upon which to live. And the settlement had only applied to 29 of the 1959 patients who had filed suit.

Two days after the verdict was handed down, the "direct negotiations" group met with officials of Chisso in their Tokyo offices. The outcome of the first day of negotiations was positive; President Shimada agreed that all damages arising from Minamata Disease should be paid by Chisso.

The next day, the iron gates in front of Chisso headquarters were dismantled and carried off.

But arriving at a meeting of the minds regarding specific amounts of restitution proved a more difficult task. For days, demands and counterdemands ricocheted across the table. Kawamoto climbed up on the table and confronted President Shimada eye to eye.

The deciding incident was one involving a heretofore unknown patient, Kimito Iwamoto. He had been newly verified, and, after several hours of bickering, he rose, shaking violently. "I can't stand this anymore!" he shouted. "You can see for yourself. If I don't get the indemnity money, I can't live!" And he grabbed a glass ashtray, smashed it to bits on the table and slashed his wrist.

Bedlam. Supporters, guards, reporters rushed toward him, and through the din, President Shimada's voice could be heard: "Yes, yes, yes—we will pay."

The precedent had been set, and now it would apply to new patients, too. And a few weeks later, the Central Pollution Board added its findings, which coincided with the court and Chisso's latest offer: $68,000 maximum, $60,000 minimum, and a monthly allowance for all patients. By the end of 1975, Chisso had paid out more than $80 million.

Life returned to a quiet normalcy in Minamata. But the patients' symptoms did not abate. Some died; some survived. The Chisso factory remained closed. The Japanese government ruled, for safety's sake, that the Minamata Bay area, where the bottom mud contained 25 parts per million or more of mercury, should be filled in. To assure that the

Shiranui Sea would not be contaminated, Minamata Bay was turned into a closed harbor, lost forever as a fishing area.

Two hundred eighty-three deaths would occur as a direct result of Minamata Disease. Exactly the same number of children—283—were born with birth defects of contamination-afflicted parents. The certification of infected residents of Minamata was a slow process. More than 7,000 asked to be certified, to be eligible to receive the $68,000 or $60,000 plus benefits from Chisso.

In 1979, Kiichi Yoshioka, the president of Chisso in 1959, when the worst contamination and coverup occurred, and Eiichi Nshida, the plant manager at the time, were convicted of the deaths of 2 of the 283 who died and sentenced to two years in prison and three years' probation. It was a slap on the wrist for a cataclysmic condition brought about because of industrial irresponsibility, which was in turn caused by a not altogether incorrect belief that there would be no punishment for Chisso's actions. And, perhaps, if a worldwide awareness of the consequences of worldwide practices of rampant pollution by industry had not begun in the 1960s, Minamata, too, would have gone unnoticed by all but those afflicted by the practices of many international companies using contaminating substances to produce their products.

Minamata did provide some positive results, chiefly in a change of attitude in Japan toward the pollution of Earth's natural resources. A governmental environmental agency was established in 1971. Shortly after the Chisso-Minamata verdict, more stringent controls over toxic emissions from all Japanese factories were instituted. Official encouragement was given to developing "lean-burn" engines, which burn fuel more efficiently and produce cleaner exhaust emissions than older engines. In 1973, the use of catalytic convertors in all car engines was made mandatory—a measure that caused a significant drop in air pollution initially, but, as the number of automobiles on Japan's roads in the 1990s exponentially increased, clean air again became a scarcity.

"Feelings cannot remain intense forever," said Aileen Smith, the journalist, who, with her husband, moved to Minamata to live with those they chronicled and photographed. "Life goes on, and one tries to cope day by day." Still, the reminders remained. The tragedy at Minamata was the first classic example of the consequences of water pollution through irresponsible industrial wastes. Or perhaps it was the first to be recognized and publicized. Unfortunately, it is also not the last.

MEXICO
(MEXICO CITY, TLALNEPANTLA)
GAS STORAGE TANK EXPLOSION
November 18, 1984

Four hundred fifty-two people were killed, 4,248 were injured, and 31,000 were displaced as the result of a huge gas explosion

in the San Juan Ixhuatepec gas storage plant in Tlalnepantla, a suburb of Mexico City, on November 18, 1984.

At exactly 5:42 A.M., in an explosive echo of the Bhopal disaster in India, where a slum neighborhood was also decimated by an industrial catastrophe (see pp. 81–85), a slum section of Tlalnepantla, located eight miles northwest of Mexico City, was transformed into a roaring inferno by an explosion in the San Juan Ixhuatepec gas storage plant in the predawn moments of November 18, 1984.

The catastrophe began with the explosion of a gas truck, which ignited a series of explosions at holding tanks of the Unigas Company. These, in a matter of minutes, ignited tanks of butane and liquefied gas at the Pemex storage facilities, which were located next to those of Unigas.

The sound of the explosion, equal to a volcanic eruption, was heard and seen for miles. A jogger, setting out on his early morning run, later told an American reporter, "All of a sudden it was not dark. For a few seconds the sky was orange."

Thirty acres of gas facilities and living quarters were flattened as if a tornado had run through them. Residents of Tlalnepantla told reporters that they had been shaken out of their beds by a huge eruption followed by what seemed to be a dozen smaller ones.

One survivor stated that "there was an explosion, then more explosions, and we all started running toward the hill. There were balls of fire going up in the sky and rocks started rolling down from the hill."

"I felt as if there was an earthquake," said another. "It shook the earth and then huge flames shot up."

"Every home in the area burned down," added a third, and one of the first rescuers to enter the area spoke of broken glass, burning timbers, debris blocking the streets, and pools of standing blood on the sidewalks.

Firefighters rushed into the area and battled the flames for seven hours before finally taming them. Even then, Pemex technicians burned off 80,000 barrels of gas to avoid new explosions.

Emergency aid stations were set up to accommodate the hundreds, then thousands, of injured and homeless. At the nearby 18th-of-March Sports Center, 1,200 people were fed and cared for. A hundred thousand more were handled at makeshift rescue stations and local hospitals. Army patrols arrested 20 looters who used the chaos to ply their spontaneous trade. Barricades were ultimately set up around the devastated area, manned by soldiers.

By noon, the International Red Cross and other rescue agencies began broadcasting calls for blood, plasma, and medical supplies that were running short in the seven hospitals treating the injured. Rescue teams foraged for blankets, clothing, food, and other essentials. A spokesperson at Traumatology Hospital told a reporter, "We are saturated with wounded and injured. We even have them in the corridors."

The customary pollution of the air over Mexico City was increased exponentially by the multiple explosions in the San Juan Ixhuatepec gas storage plant in November of 1984. Pemex, the government oil monopoly, and one of the worst polluters in Mexico, compounded the tragedy by denying responsibility for the death and injury by fire, explosion, and suffocation of nearly 5,000 people.
(JULIO ETCHART/REPORTAGE/STILL PICTURES)

On Tuesday night, the 20th, firefighters and police officers began the grim task of burying 275 people whose bodies were charred beyond recognition. The headlights of a jeep and 10 flashlights held by police officers guided a bulldozer, which stacked the coffins in layers, then lowered them into a huge excavation.

By Wednesday, November 21, health crews began fumigating the burned-out neighborhood. Bodies of dead animals and some open sewers, blown apart by the explosion, had already contaminated the district, and rodents and flies posed an imminent threat to the returning refugees.

Four storage tanks holding more than 3 million gallons of liquefied gas had each exploded, and two others burned. The operation and main pipeline were closed to prevent further explosions. Pemex, the government oil monopoly, met with the press and announced that its $1 million facility was a total loss. Plans, according to a company official, were being made to rebuild the plant elsewhere, away from populated areas.

The government of Mexico hastened to promise shelter for those displaced by the blast. Governor Alfredo del Mazo

of Mexico State promised to build 130 new houses by the weekend, available to families that lost their homes. More houses, each worth about $10,000 would be built and given free to those left homeless by the explosions.

But, as in Bhopal and Minamata (see pp. 81–85), promises did not necessarily result in just settlements. Although there were multiple, touching stories of neighbor helping neighbor, and though the government sent mattresses and blankets for the displaced and promised to rebuild homes and provide other social services usually not found in San Juan Ixhuatepec, anger and distrust began to rise. Even health workers, walking the neighborhoods, giving inoculations against typhoid and tetanus, and the workers in a mobile government dentist's office set up in a side street, were met with fury.

"We never even had a health center here," said one woman to a *New York Times* reporter. "But this is a special occasion, no?" she added, sarcastically.

There was ample graffitti expressing the feelings of the dispossessed and the grieving: "November 19—day of blood," and "Pemex guilty—assassins," were two prominent ones. But the accusation that was whitewashed away almost immediately was aimed at Mario Ramon Beteta, the general director of the oil giant: "Beteta—Don't look for the guilty—Pemex exists and is close at hand."

"We have lived with the smell of gas for years," said Leon Ramirez Avila, one of the workers dispensing blankets and mattresses to refugees at a relief station. He and others agreed that a fire had broken out at the Pemex gas plant the previous March, but was little reported, partly because security guards smashed the cameras of reporters who attempted to cover it.

There were many missing from this most recent accident, and the fact that they were still missing kept the inhabitants of the area angry.

Meanwhile, Pemex denied responsibility for the explosion and attributed it, somewhat disingenuously, to an accident at the neighboring plant of Unigas, S.A.—a foolish and insulting shifting of responsibility, according to protesting citizens, who pointed out many pristine, white storage tanks of Unigas, still standing entire next to the ruined Pemex plant.

Pemex eventually backed down and said that it would face up to any responsibility established by "competent authorities."

That authority turned out to be the Mexican attorney general's office, which placed the blame squarely and singly upon Pemex, for mismanagement and arrogant disregard of safety precautions, and ordered it to pay damages to those filing suits. Ultimately, those suits would climb into the hundreds of millions of dollars, for damage to homes and compensation for injuries and deaths.

An interagency commission reported to President Miguel de la Madrid in December 1985, that 452 were killed, 4,248 were injured, 88 homes housing 179 families were destroyed, and 1,300 damaged. Thirty-one thousand people were displaced.

POLAND
(LÓDŹ)
FUKS AND HAGRIA CHEMICAL FACTORY EXPLOSION
July 29, 1928

More than 50,000 residents of Łódź, Poland, were driven from their homes by toxic fumes released when the Fuks and Hagria chemical factory exploded on the morning of July 29, 1928. Forty plant workers and patients in two nearby hospitals were killed; more than 100 were injured.

Łódź, the large industrial city located at the mouth of the Bzura River, southwest of Warsaw, was home to the Fuks and Hagria chemical factory, one of Poland's manufacturers and storers of munitions. The region had been a battleground on which Germans and Russians fought each other for territory in the early part of World War I.

Since that time, the residential area surrounding the plant, and the two hospitals that were situated in uneasy proximity to the plant had been rebuilt. But on the morning of July 29, 1928, for those old enough, it was as if the war had returned, in one cataclysmic explosion.

Chemicals used for peacetime agricultural purposes ignited, which in turn ignited wartime munitions stored in the chemical plant. The entirety went up in one volcanic roar, which shattered windows, leveled apartment houses, and severely impacted both hospitals. Walls caved in on patients; water mains erupted; windows were shattered.

Flames and toxic fumes spread out like fingers from the explosion site, forcing not only workmen in the medium-size plant but also 50,000 refugees from the hospitals and residences surrounding it to flee.

Controlling the fire would be an all-day job for firemen, who were forced to don masks to dig through the rubble for survivors. Twenty-five died; more than 100 were injured, and it would be years before the city of Łódź would be rebuilt.

ROMANIA, BULGARIA, RUSSIA, TURKEY, MOLDOVA, UKRAINE
(BLACK SEA)
INDUSTRIAL POLLUTION
1960–Present

A combination of political turmoil and poverty is prolonging the steady and potentially disastrous transformation of the Black Sea from a viable supporter of marine life to a destroyer of it. Pollution from industry and cities is robbing this inland sea of its preciously small layer of oxygen, thus upsetting a delicate balance that even nature has had difficulty sustaining.

Change is natural to the Black Sea, which was once the water highway between Europe and Asia. Some 8,000 years ago, give or take a hundred years, its most monumental geological shift took place. The Black Sea was a freshwater lake at the time and some sort of upheaval—possibly an earthquake or possibly an undersea volcanic eruption—raised the sea level of the Mediterranean, whose waters slipped through the strait of Bosporus.

The salt water that poured into the Black Sea killed the life there that had adapted to freshwater, and this wholesale slaughter—a sort of marine genocide—produced an enormous mass of hydrogen sulfide, which to this day remains trapped in the deep waters beneath a thin surface lid of oxygen.

Thus, only the top 100 yards or so of the Black Sea is oxygen-bearing water; more than nine-tenths of it has such high levels of hydrogen sulfide that no life can dwell in it. "A geological freak," is the way Dr. David Aubrey, a senior scientist at the Woods Hole Oceanographic Institution in Massachusetts describes it. "If you put a piece of metal in deep enough, it will come out black. If you turned the Black Sea over, it would smell of rotten eggs."

The smell would be more than offensive. If, for some reason, either a natural or man-made calamity would capsize the Black Sea or break its skin of oxygen, the escaping gases could kill every person on its shore.

And so, according to Dr. Aubrey, "In this fragile setting, man has now created an environmental catastrophe."

The worst phase of the catastrophe actually began nearly four decades ago, with the frantic proliferation of industry along the rivers in Eastern Europe. More than 60 rivers and streams empty into the Black Sea. The four largest are the Danube, the Don, the Dnieper, and the Dneister, all of which travel through a region that is generally considered to be one of the most polluted in the world. Every year, these rivers alone transport tons of toxic materials, including oil, lead, phosphorous, nitrates, chromium, and cadmium. And in the spring, when the melting snow washes the land, the Dnieper picks up radioactive fallout from the Chernobyl nuclear plant (see pp. 194–200) and ferries it into the Black Sea.

But this is only part of it. In Russia, Georgia, Moldova and Ukraine, former Soviet dams and irrigation projects have diverted so much river water that, by their own estimates, the Black Sea is receiving one-fifth less freshwater and becoming more salty than it was two decades ago.

As a result, some scientists say, the poisonous hydrogen sulfide customarily trapped beneath the oxygen is now welling up, reducing the oxygen layer and causing fish kills.

This, plus the dumping of detergents and fertilizers into the 60 rivers and streams that also deliver waste from a catchment area of 160 million people has caused a virtual collapse of the Black Sea fishing industry. Along its 2,500-mile coastline, fishing boats that once bulged with catches of sturgeon, mackerel, and anchovies, sit in port, idle.

In the estuary of the Danube, a 70-mile-wide wetland of channels, lakes, and swamps, algae blooms—which are population explosions of algae caused by an increase in plant nutrients—have grown wildly since the beginning of the 1980s.

"By the end of the summer much of the delta is covered in spume," Romanian biologist Mircea Staras has noted. "When the algae die, everything else is killed," she continues, "even the underwater plants. This was an important spawning ground for sturgeon, for carp, for pike. We lost all the big fish."

Turkey has a 700-mile coastline on the Black Sea, and its fishermen have been hit the hardest by the Black Sea's contamination. Anchovy fleets lie at anchor, immobilized at Trebizond, Samsun, and Sinop. According to the Ankara government, the catch dropped almost 95 percent between 1987 and 1989, from 340,000 to less than 15,000 tons. The anchovy catch shrank enough to drop off the bottom of the calculation scale.

Turkish oceanographers are philosophical and quizzical. "Nobody really knows why all this is happening," stated Umiot Unluata, a member of the Turkish Institute of Marine Sciences. "It may be a combination of overfishing, pollution, climate change, and shifts in the food chain."

"I know of no other inland sea under such pressure," noted Stansilav Knovalov, the director of the Soviet Institute for Biology of the Southern Seas at Sebastopol. "This is much more degraded than the Baltic."

Meanwhile, bathing beaches near Constanța in Romania and Odessa in Ukraine have been closed since 1989 because of chemical pollution and the odiferous froth of algae blooms. A large and luxurious bay at Burgas, Bulgaria,

As in the Aral Sea in Uzbekistan, the Black Sea has become so polluted that once prosperous fishing fleets now lie idle and rotting.
(ANATOLY RAKHIMBAYEV/UNEP)

The fouling of the Black Sea from industrial waste has created wholesale poverty in the coastal cities and towns of Romania.
(VALERIU BOGDANET/UNEP)

once a popular beach resort, has fallen victim to the waste from the chemical plants that were erected near it two decades ago. Today, the bay is off-limits to bathers, and water and air vie with each other for designation as more polluted. Each is equally greasy and opaque with contaminants. Every town, industry, and mine along its shores uses the Black Sea as a dump and a sewer.

Petrochemical plants at Midia and Navoderi, Romania, pour effluent into the water, and it in turn is carried south by currents to threaten the tourist resort of Mamaia.

In 1992, a chemical plant in western Romania was monitored as discharging ammonia, nitrates, and phosphates at 10 times the permitted rate. The plant was located only two and a half miles from a major water source for the city.

And so, this once bountiful though precariously balanced inland sea is rapidly losing its oxygen and its ability to purge itself.

That something will be done soon to reverse a terrible plunge into pollution is questionable. Political turmoil in the new Russia and the new independent states that surround the Black Sea have blocked a new international agreement to stop the marine pollution that is already banned off other coasts. As a consequence, ships from a

multitude of nations clean their oil tanks, flush their ballasts, and dump tons of dangerous sludge and toxic waste into the Black Sea.

There is also the uncomfortable reality of poverty. Awareness of the degradation of the Black Sea is rising. A convention for the control of pollution in the Black Sea has been planned for years, but lack of funds and political will have repeatedly sidetracked it.

The situation is desperate. Yuvenaly Zaitsev, a Russian biologist who is willing to blame much of the collapse of the fishing industry on overfishing, is skeptical regarding a long term solution to the precipitous decline in the purity and viability of the Black Sea. "Even if we stopped all the pollution as if by magic," he stated, "it would be impossible to go back to the 1950s. Nature has its own laws."

Still, while acknowledging this, international biologists and ecologists, under the aegis of the United Nations Environmental Programme, which itself is undergoing a severe budget reduction, are willing to try.

SPAIN
(MADRID AREA)
TOXIC COOKING OIL SCANDAL
May 1, 1981—May 20, 1987

....

The longest trial in Spanish history ended in dissatisfaction and riots as sellers of contaminated cooking oil were acquitted of murder in the death of 700 and the sickness of 25,000 consumers of cooking oil that some experts, including the World Health Organization, said was tainted with rapeseed oil. Others said the cause was tomato crops contaminated by organophosphate pesticides used in Almería.

On May 1, 1981, an eight-year-old boy died mysteriously in a poor section of Madrid. He had been healthy, as had been a lengthening parade of people being felled, in increasing frequency and abundance, by a syndrome that began with fever, headache, and nausea, then escalated to racking muscle pains, numbness of limbs, skin rashes and sores, collapsing of the lungs, bodily spasms or overall paralysis, and death.

For weeks, the deaths and terrible debilitation were treated as isolated cases and named, for want of a better description, "atypical pneumonia." But then, as the Madrid hospitals began to fill with victims, a pattern began to emerge. Practically all of the affected victims had consumed quantities of a certain inexpensive brand of cooking oil, which had been sold door to door by salesmen, mostly to poor families in Madrid, Castile, and León, who, while used to cooking, as most Spaniards do, with large quantities of oil, found it difficult to afford the more expensive commercial brands.

The oil, it turned out, upon analysis and investigation, had been illegally imported from France, where it was treated with aniline to make it fit solely for industrial use. The importers then reprocessed the oil at a high temperature to rid it of the chemical taste and color and mixed it with animal fats, which in turn produced analide, a poisonous, oily derivative of benzene. It was the analide, reasoned investigators, that had caused the toxic syndrome.

But their findings were far from conclusive. The disease, now renamed "toxic oil syndrome," seemed to strike at random, without a pattern. It would attack some members of a family and spare others, strike down a young boy in one house, an elderly woman in the next, and none in a third. As the toxic oil syndrome spread, scientists experimented with animals and analide, but they found no parallel reactions. Furthermore, analysis of the cooking oil showed that analine reaction products were not present in all of the oil.

While the analysis was going on, panic began to spread in Spain and elsewhere in Europe. By mid-June, 43 had died, and a consumer stampede had begun. By August, domestic sales of canned seafood preserved in oil had plummeted 25 percent. Seventeen canneries were closed, leaving some 4,000 workers idle. The government of Prime Minister Leopoldo Calvo Sotelo seemed to be immobilized until early October, when Italy closed its borders to Spanish edible oil products. Several weeks later, France followed with a three-month ban on canned foods containing oil from Spain.

Faced with international condemnation and plummeting sales, Jorge Jordana, the vice president of the National Food and Beverage Federation, accused the government of mishandling what had now become a national scandal, and, furthermore, aggravating the loss of consumer confidence by doing nothing.

On October 12, the European parliament in Strasbourg, France, voted in favor of a system that would permit the rapid withdrawal of contaminated products sold in the Common Market. It was time to act, and the Spanish government declared 21 brands of cooking oil toxic and began to make arrests. By the end of October, they had arrested 22 businessmen and accused them of selling tainted cooking oil. Four known vendors of the cheap oil had fled the country.

Panels of doctors were appointed by the government to try to pinpoint the toxic agent, and indemnity was promised for the victims and punishment assured for those responsible. But doctors and scientists, both in Spain and elsewhere, were baffled, and they remained so.

Two years later, with a new, Socialist government in place in Spain, and a new name, *los afectados*, for the growing number of victims of the syndrome, researchers were no closer to an analysis, much less a cure.

"This is something absolutely new in the history of medicine," said Dr. Luis Soldervilla of the National Plan for Toxic Syndrome, in May 1983. "It is a new illness. There is no pool of symptoms like this existing in the world's medical knowledge."

The spraying of tomato crops with organophosphate pesticides in Almería by methods like this in Italy's Po valley, was the reason, according to some scientists, for the contamination of cooking oil that caused 700 deaths in Spain. Others blamed it on rapeseed tainting.
(Mark Edwards/Still Pictures)

The number of dead had swelled to 400 by now, and victims began to hold sit-ins to protest the fact that no one had yet been punished for their involvement in the scandal. The fact of the matter was that, in addition to the voluminous testimony that was being collected, much uncertainty over the identity of the disease was complicating the prosecution.

Pedro César Sanz Orosco, who, with two of his three children had contracted the disease while taking his family to Valencia on vacation, and whose wife lost a baby to the syndrome, enunciated the frustrations of the survivors. "Here we are, two years after the outbreak of this syndrome, and we, the sick people, feel we are just as uncertain as we were at the beginning," he said.

It would be four more years before the trial would actually be held, and in the interim, international groups, including the World Health Organization, would become involved in trying to find both a cause and a cure. The cure was not found, and it has not been found to this day. The causes proved to be largely circumstantial, which fueled the controversy swirling around the trial when it finally began, on March 28, 1987.

By that time, 627 people had died and 25,000 had been affected in various ways by the toxic syndrome. Forty importers, two of whom were tried in absentia, since they had fled the country, were charged with manslaughter and fraud.

The lines were drawn by two authorities. The prosecution's argument depended solely on rapeseed as the culprit. "The correlation between the illness and the oil is so impressive, it is the only viable theory," said Dr. Manuel Posado of the National Health Research Center in an interview with the newspaper *El País*.

On the other hand, defense lawyers, backed by such authorities as Dr. Luis Frontela, professor of legal medicine at the University of Seville, challenged this. "I have not observed animals falling ill with denatured rapeseed oil," he told the same paper. Instead, he and the defense asserted that the blame lay elsewhere, specifically in the pesticides Nemacur and Oftanol, used widely in spraying tomatoes in Almería, in southern Spain, in 1981.

The trial dragged on for months. The investigative report totaled 250,000 pages, and 2,500 people, including Prime Minister Felipe González and his deputy, Alfonso Guerra, were examined. Two hundred experts testified, and 1,500 witnesses appeared, including Leopoldo Calvo Sotelo, Spain's prime minister at the time of the outbreak of the disease. Before a recess was called in August, more than 100 experts had testified, mostly to refute the pesticide theory, but none could absolutely establish that the rapeseed oil was the sole culprit.

Two other possibilities were advanced by the defense: One was herbicide contamination of the tanks in which the oil was transported; the other was an accident involving biological weapons at a United States air base at Torrejon, outside Madrid. Both were dismissed.

Finally, on May 20, 1989, eight years after the first reported case of toxic oil syndrome, three Spanish judges handed down a decision that ignited an explosion of protest by victims. All murder charges were dismissed against the importers. Only two of them would serve lengthy prison terms.

Prosecutors had asked for sentences of more than 60,000 years for eight of the accused, even though Spanish law limits prison terms to 30 years. But the judges sentenced one man to 20 years, another to 12 years, and several others to suspended sentences of between 6 months and 10 years. Twenty-four were acquitted.

Crowds shouting "We want justice!" rioted outside of the courtroom, and heavily armed police fired at least one tear gas canister into the crowd to quiet it.

The 25,000 injured who recovered were not comforted by the judges' awards of the equivalent of $125,000 to relatives of each of the 700 persons who died of poisoning, and sums ranging from $1,250 to $750,000 to survivors, depending upon the severity of their permanent injuries.

Still, though the syndrome disappeared with the consumption or destruction of the rapeseed-tainted cooking oil, doubts that were expressed from the very beginning failed to disappear. Defense lawyers and medical experts alike noted that an undeniable link between the oil and the syndrome was never established. No animals contracted the syndrome from the oil. And there were some regions in which the oil was distributed where no victims were reported, and some victims claimed they had never consumed the oil. And so the pesticide-in-Almerían-tomatoes theory gained weight not only with the judges but with the public, too.

There has been no definitive solution to this, one of the most tragic environmental conundrums of modern times.

SWITZERLAND
(BASEL)
RHINE RIVER POLLUTION
November 1, 1986

In the early morning of November 1, 1986, 30 tons of toxic chemicals and 440 tons of mercury spilled into the Rhine River after a fire in a storage warehouse owned by the Sandoz chemical company in the Basel, Switzerland, suburb of Schweizerhalle. Half a million fish died, and ecologists pronounced it the worst chemical spill in Europe in several decades.

Switzerland's reputation for neat efficiency and the Rhine River's reputation for Wagnerian romance both suffered severe blows when a fire in a chemical storage warehouse belonging to the Sandoz chemical company became the flashpoint for the spillage of 30 tons of toxic chemicals and 440 tons of mercury into the Rhine. The warehouse, located in Schweizerhalle, six miles southeast of Basel, Switzerland, caught fire in the early hours of November 1, 1986.

The primary concern of the residents of Basel and its surrounding suburbs (one of which was Schweizerhalle) was the thick, fetid cloud that settled over the city. But a few days later, the Rhine turned a sickly brownish green, and thousands of dead fish and eels began to float on its surface. The few live ones were grotesquely mutilated, their eyes bulging, their gills collapsed, their skin covered with wounds and sores.

Firemen fighting the blaze, which totally destroyed the warehouse, were the ones who washed 30 tons of agricultural chemicals, dyes and solvents, and what was worse, 440 pounds of mercury into the Rhine. Contained in the warehouse were 12 metric tons of liquid ethoxyethyl-mercury-hydroxide, a fungicide, normally used in low concentrations to treat sugarcane and cotton.

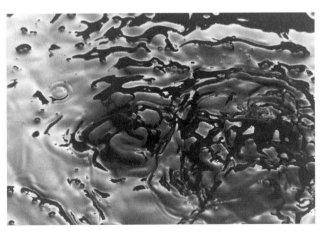

The once romantic Rhine River looked anything but romantic after 30 tons of toxic chemicals and 440 tons of mercury from the Sandoz chemical company in Basel, Switzerland, spilled into it.

It would be nine days—long after the first dead and deformed marine life began to surface—before Switzerland would admit that the tragedy had occurred, and then, a firestorm of protest erupted immediately from France, West Germany, and the Netherlands, through which the Rhine flows on its way to the North Sea.

Water treatment plants in the villages of Unkel and Bad Hönningen in West Germany immediately closed their floodgates and trucked in fresh water through their fire departments.

In Basel, Sandoz executives, who called a public meeting to discuss the accident, were forced to flee from the conference hall when angry crowds rioted. Meanwhile, outside, more than 10,000 protesters marched through the city, shouting such slogans as "We don't want to be tomorrow's fish" and "Chernobale!" a bilingual pun linking the French version of the city's name with the Chernobyl meltdown (see pp. 194–200).

A more logical relationship was voiced when protesters exhumed the ghosts of Minamata, Japan, where a prolonged mercury spill caused death and disfigurement (see pp. 89–93) and of Seveso, Italy, where a huge and deadly toxic cloud was released during a chemical explosion in 1976 (see pp. 85–89). The resultant movement toward cleaning up the environment of Europe was dubbed the "Seveso Directorate."

The demonstrations escalated in the next days. Banners stating that "Fish are powerless, we are not," and "This time the fish, next time us" blossomed. At a panel discussion by city officials and a Sandoz director, protesters pelted the officials with dead eels and bottles of river water, and one zealous demonstrator rushed to the dais and spit in the face of Sandoz chief of safety and ecology Hans Winkler, who fled the premises.

Finally, on November 12, after European ecologists pronounced the spill one of the worst environmental disasters in Europe in modern times, Switzerland formally accepted responsibility for the accident, offered to pay compensation to other affected countries, and pledged to study ways of tightening existing antipollution rules to bring them closer in line with stricter standards already adopted by neighboring countries.

By November 15, mercury levels had reached three times their normal elevation at the Dutch–West German border. The cloud of contamination in the Rhine stretched for 185 miles and was drifting slowly toward the sea. On its way, it was killing more and more fish (it would slay over half a million before finally emptying into the North Sea) and infecting others that contained the potential of making thousands of residents of the bordering countries sick from eating contaminated fish.

There was also the problem of the whereabouts of the mercury. The possibility existed that it would eventually settle to the bottom of the river and form a more toxic substance that would interrupt the life cycle of the river.

Meanwhile, while the Common Market was blaming Sandoz, seven other chemical spills took place on the Rhine. Sandoz is only one of three major chemical companies on the Rhine in Basel. Ciba-Geigy and Hoffman-La Roche are both situated nearby, and several days after the Sandoz fire and spill, Ciba-Geigy admitted that it had accidentally released 88 gallons of Atrazin, a weedkiller, into the Rhine just hours before the Sandoz spill.

A month later, 2.7 tons of polyvinyl chloride leaked into the river from the Lonza chemical factory at Waldshut, Germany.

Two months later, two barges collided near Düsseldorf, dumping 540 tons of nitrogen fertilizers into the river. Shortly after that, a Dutch barge, the *Minstreel*, rammed a tanker near Krefeld, Germany, pouring 10 tons of a highly explosive benzene into the water. Small wonder that swimming had been prohibited in the Rhine since the 1960s, though its low point in terms of purity is generally considered to have occurred in the 1970s, when chemical and pharmaceutical companies—among them BASF and Baer, along with steelmakers Mannesmann and Krupp, had largely replaced mining and manufacturing factories that had heretofore rimmed the river.

The BASF complex at Ludwigshafen, Germany, for instance, comprises 330 factories and plants, employing 53,000 people. Their pumping stations suck in between 750 million and 935 million gallons of water a day, chiefly used to cool and wash the various processes. The more polluted the river becomes, the more equipment for filtering it must be added to these factories. Thus, pollution has also become an economic problem along the 820 miles of the Rhine.

Though France and Germany criticized Switzerland vociferously for the Sandoz spill, they themselves had been slow to implement the Seveso Directorate. Germany had only banned a fraction of the 200 chemicals considered toxic by the convention.

Now, around Basel, divers raked the river bottom with vacuum hoses. Sandoz cut production at a nearby pesticides plant by 60 percent in order to reduce hazards involved in the storage of toxic ingredients for pesticides, herbicides, and fungicides.

Industries became fearful of increased governmental regulation; politicians, mindful of the pro-environmental mood of the electorate, began to listen. On December 19, two Swiss protesters associated with Greenpeace climbed a smokestack in Basel and, despite a driving snowstorm, vowed to stay there until Christmas. The Greens, an environmental political party in Germany, conducted mock funerals along the Rhine for the dead river and held a tribunal that found the chemical industry guilty of murder. In the German elections that January, the Green Party increased its share of the popular vote from 5.6 percent to 8.3 percent, largely because of the Swiss chemical spill.

Finally, on January 10, representatives of the Federal Institute for Water Planning, Purification and Protection, a group of independent Swiss technical experts, issued the first extensive report on the condition of the Rhine. It stated that the microbiology of the already heavily polluted river had survived the chemical spill. The river seemed to be washing out pollution residues from the Sandoz spill, and the survival of small invertebrate water life and plants seemed to be providing the basis for a rapid regeneration of fish and other life.

Still, the report warned, failure to continue the removal of chemical residues from the river near the plant and providing safeguards against a repeat of the November leakage was important to maintain the fragile balance in the river.

Basier Zeltung, a newspaper in Basel commented, "Calcutta still sits on the Ganges, Paris still sits on the Seine, Basel still sits on the Rhine. Only utopia still remains somewhere to be found. That it is found, has recently been shown to be a fundamental imperative."

THAILAND
(BANGKOK)
CHEMICAL EXPLOSION AND FIRE
March 2, 1991

....

Three residents of Klong Toey, a slum section of Bangkok, Thailand, were killed, hundreds were injured, and more than 6,000 were rendered homeless on March 2, 1991, by a fire caused by explosions in warehouses holding 23 chemicals, some of them toxic.

In an eerie resemblance to the Bhopal disaster (see pp. 81–89), chemical storage warehouses located in Klong Toey, a slum section of Bangkok, exploded on the afternoon of March 2, 1991, setting fire to the neighborhood, killing three unsuspecting residents of the area, injuring hundreds, and rendering more than 6,000 homeless.

It was a classic case of industrial and governmental negligence and denial of responsibility. It would be more than two weeks before any effort was made to care for the injured and dispossessed, and even then some officials denied any responsibility whatsoever, whereas others acknowledged that little care was taken to keep slum dwellers a safe distance from poisonous chemicals or warehouses. In fact, an official continued, chemicals supposed to be kept in cool areas were sometimes left unattended in metal warehouses under the tropical sun, where they had the potential of exploding. "We're a fast-developing country," the official told international reporters at a news conference. "This is one of the prices we pay."

The explosions occurred shortly after lunch on March 2, 1991, ripping rapidly through the warehouses and spreading

fire in rings outward from these sites, which were surrounded by the houses of those who lived in this area of Bangkok that had a reputation as a "tough part of the city."

For hours, smaller explosions echoed through the surrounding city as cooking gas canisters in the fire-gutted houses ignited and exploded. An oily mist rose from the fire and settled onto parts of the city, peppering windshields, swimming pools, windowsills, and clothes.

An immediate veil of secrecy was thrown over the incident by the military junta that had overthrown Thailand's democratic government just a week before. Sabotage was suspected and investigated until doctors, desperate to know just what to treat among the hundreds of wounded survivors, pressed for answers. What, they wanted to know, was stored in the warehouses?

The answer was slow in coming. But finally, the Port Authority of Thailand acknowledged that there were 23 different chemicals in the warehouses, including methyl bromide, an insecticide poisonous to humans; trichloroisoyanuric acid, an industrial and household disinfectant and deodorant; and phosphoric acid, used to make fertilizer and an ingredient in soft drinks and sulfur.

Even with the contents of the warehouses made public, the government of Thailand continued to behave as if no explosion had occurred, nobody had been killed, no homes had been destroyed. For two weeks, absolutely nothing was done to clean up the damage wrought by the explosion.

But doctors and medical aids quietly entered the area, ministering as they could to the wounded, helping to rig makeshift shelters for the thousands without housing, silently attending to the former owners of homes who were, overnight, turned into squatters.

While they treated the ailing, the doctors from the Siriraj Medical College Faculty of Medicine conducted a series of tests among 215 of the 6,000 displaced refugees of the fire. The tests indicated high levels of methyl bromide in their blood—a finding verified later when it was admitted that this toxic chemical—which can be fatal in large doses and in smaller quantities can cause rashes, numbness, speech difficulties, convulsions, and stomach cramps—was indeed present.

Now refusing to abide by the official code of silence and avoidance, Dr. Pradit Charoenthaithawee, dean of the college, announced publicly that 148 of the 215 people tested showed a degree of methyl bromide in their blood of between 6.14 to 16.34 milligrams per 100 milligrams of blood—well above the maximum safety level of 5 milligrams per 100 milligrams of blood.

Faced with this charge, the military junta's leader, General Sunthorn Kongsompong, declared that the area around the fire would be labeled contaminated, and its inhabitants evacuated. The Bangkok Metropolitan Administration warned those living outside of the area to stay at least a half

As in the Mexico City gas explosion, thousands of residents of Klong Toey, the slum section of Bangkok, were made homeless by fires caused by the explosion of chemical warehouses located in their midst.
(YOG JOY/UNEP)

mile away from it, and finally, on March 18, 16 days after the explosion, the government began to clean up the site.

UNITED KINGDOM
(ENGLAND, LONDON)
FOG
December 1952

London's deadliest fog occurred in December 1952. Twelve thousand people died from ingesting soft-coal smoke, sulfur dioxide, chemical fumes, and gasoline fumes contained in the fog.

London's fogs are legendary, literary, and picturesque—to all but those who have experienced them. Formed by a combination of stalled warm air masses and smoke given off by

thousands of soft-coal stoves and factory chimneys, they have, for centuries, literally strangled a large part of the populace of this city, brought its commerce to a stop, hospitalized many, and killed more.

Even the interiors of theaters, restaurants, and other public places whose doors to the street opened and closed frequently were not exempt from the notorious and noxious fog. The dense, pungent, opaque air would roll into movie theaters, obscuring screens and making auditoriums uninhabitable. Stores would be forced to close in order to preserve their merchandise. Restaurants, offices, and schools were no match for the invasion of fogs that turned ordinary days into strange dreams.

The deadliest fog ever to settle over London arrived in December 1952. Soft-coal smoke, sulfur dioxide, chemical fumes, and gasoline fumes collected in the atmosphere, intensifying as the warm mass lingered. Four thousand people died from ingesting the fumes, and another 8,000 eventually died from its aftereffects.

Enough was enough. This catastrophic fog brought about the four-year study that would produce England's Clean Air Act in 1956.

UNITED KINGDOM
(ENGLAND, LONDON)
FOG
December 3–7, 1962

One hundred thirty-six people died and 1,000 were hospitalized in the last lethal London fog, from December 3 through 7, 1962.

Great Britain's Clean Air Act of 1956 had scoured the London air of most pollutants. But certain industries were still sending great quantities of sulfur dioxide into the air in and around England's capital city.

Thus, when another air inversion brought about a heavy fog on December 3, 1962, 136 elderly persons succumbed to the fumes and another 1,000 persons were hospitalized.

The *New Yorker*'s London correspondent gave the following colorful description of the aftermath of the event: "The fog floated visibly, like ectoplasm, into theatres, cinemas, and shops, where sales assistants stood around gossiping among the sparsely populated wastes of Christmas presents. In the evenings, the West End was as empty as on a night in the blitz. . . . If you had felt the urge to do so, you could have danced in the eerie middle of Piccadilly in safety, if not in comfort."

That, apparently, was after the first casualties of the fog conditions, and after London's 5,000 red double-decker buses were pulled from the streets when two of them collided, injuring 13 passengers. A train motorman was drowned when he stepped from his cab and, not realizing he had stopped on a bridge, plummeted into 40 feet of water. Scores of pedestrians were run down by motorists, driving blind.

Still, the fog produced two positive events. One was the use it was put to by the British Ministry of Aviation, who

The statue of Prince Albert and municipal buses become murky silhouettes during London's last enveloping and lethal fog, caused by industrial emissions of sulfur dioxide.
(AP/WORLD WIDE)

successfully tested a new blind flying system at London Airport. The other was a final and successful tightening of the regulations of the Clean Air Act—so successful that no such lethal fog has occurred since.

UNITED STATES
(IOWA, CEDAR RAPIDS)
DOUGLAS STARCH WORKS EXPLOSION
May 22, 1919

Thirty-two workmen in the Douglas Starch Works in Cedar Rapids, Iowa, were killed and 40 more were injured when dust trapped in a boiler caused a huge explosion, demolishing the starch works and causing extensive damage to the city of Cedar Rapids on the evening of May 22, 1919.

Dust was certainly a problem in the factories of the early 20th century. And dust was the culprit in the huge explosion that blew apart the Douglas Starch Works at Cedar Rapids, Iowa, on the evening of May 22, 1919. The preparation of commercial starch, a white, carbohydrate powder, is a simple process; and in 1919, it was a widespread and profitable one. Compounded from corn and potatoes, and used as a sizing in paper (which was in great demand to be written upon) and in textiles (which everyone wore in stiff neatness), starch was a staple.

But the boilers used in the formation of the starch had to be kept scrupulously clean; they had a habit of clogging, and the backed-up pressure could cause them to blow. Vacuums were run, particularly in the starch dryers, which eliminated the danger of dust explosions.

For some reason, the vacuum was turned off in one of the major boilers at the Douglas Starch Works when the six o'clock night shift arrived on May 22. It was fatal neglect. At 6:40, without warning, the boiler exploded, decimating the entire plant, flinging heavy machinery against walls, tearing gaping holes in floors and roofs, flinging human beings 50 feet into the air or away from the explosion's center, and setting fire immediately to the Starch Works, which were located in the heart of Cedar Rapids.

Office buildings and businesses had let out for the day; it was a balmy spring evening; the streets were crowded with pedestrians. Scores of these people were cut cruelly by flying glass, as every window in the central part of the city was blown out. A Chicago businessman in a hotel lost most of his nose as the window near his restaurant table turned to knives. J. D. Boorman, another Chicago businessman, was blown through a window of his hotel but suffered only cuts and bruises.

The front of the city hall and the facade of the YMCA were demolished. Chimneys caved in on families sitting down to dinner.

But the carnage in the city was minimal compared to that within the plant. Heavy machinery had crashed through ceilings and landed on workers, who were blinded by steam escaping from the wrecked boilers and trapped by the fire that ignited immediately and burned with a furious intensity.

Firemen fought their way into the tangled mess of twisted wreckage, looking for survivors. There were few. Engineer Frank Sodoma, his legs blown off, was carried from the ruins by firemen. He pleaded with soldiers from the reserve officers' training corps, who were hastily assembled to control the crowds surrounding the plant, to kill him.

Scores of relatives pressed against the lines of soldiers, asking for some word. By nine o'clock, rescuers were able to pull some of the wounded out of the debris and carry them to first-aid stations set up by the American Red Cross.

The fire burned all night, but shortly before daylight, a heavy rain began to fall. By 7:00 A.M., the pall of black smoke that had covered the city and obscured the starch works had disappeared, and the fire was under control. Thirty-two workmen were killed and 40 were injured. The monetary loss at the plant and in the city was more than $3 million in 1919 dollars.

UNITED STATES
(MICHIGAN)
PBB CONTAMINATION OF LIVESTOCK
1973–1974

In the nation's greatest agricultural disaster, 30 thousand head of cattle, 1.5 million chickens, and 7,700 other farm animals were slaughtered, and 10,000 pounds of cheese and 1.5 million eggs were destroyed because of feed accidentally contaminated by polybrominated byphenyl (PBB), a flame retardant normally applied to carpets and fabrics. Over a decade, severe neurological and biological poisoning occurred in human beings and animals who consumed food contaminated by the chemical.

Before June 1973, farmers and ranchers in Michigan who raised poultry and livestock for slaughter and the production of cheese, butter, and milk routinely purchased their feed through Michigan Farm Bureau Services, Inc. Because of a magnesium deficiency in the soil of Michigan, eight pounds per ton of magnesium oxide, manufactured by the Michigan Chemicals Company, was routinely added to one ton of feed, to help increase milk production.

However, in 1973, there was a paper shortage in Michigan, and the Michigan Chemical Company packed and shipped both magnesium oxide and polybrominated byphenyl (PBB), a toxic bromide that is used as a flame retardant in fabrics and carpets, in identical brown bags separated only by the stenciled brand names (Nutrimaster for the magnesium oxide; Fiermaster for the PBB) on the tops of the sacks.

Sometime in the spring of 1973, the PBB, instead of the magnesium oxide, was mixed with tons and tons of grain distributed to Michigan farmers by Michigan Farm Bureau Services, Inc. By late winter and early spring of 1974, the toxic compound began to have its effect on livestock that had eaten it. They began to sicken and become disoriented. Some showed abnormalities of the skin and hair, swollen joints, weeping sores, and infections that would not heal. Although their appetites increased, they lost weight and stopped milking and reproducing.

Some of the livestock died precipitously. Later analysis indicated that they died metabolic chemical deaths. Preliminary testing in June 1974 by Michigan and federal health authorities indicated that the bromine compound had lodged in their fatty tissues, which meant that dairy cows were secreting the compound in milk fat. And this meant that millions of milk-drinking residents of Michigan had consumed contaminated milk, butter, and cheese over the past year.

Not only that. Sales records of the Michigan Farm Bureau Service and the Michigan Chemicals Company showed that 28 dairy herds, including one sold for slaughter in January 1974, three beef herds, three poultry flocks, and one herd of pigs, all marked for slaughter, had been contaminated.

Dr. Harold Humphrey, the Michigan public health disease control specialist, issued a statement that would eventually prove to be false comfort. He emphasized that there was no danger to persons who ate or drank the dairy products because the contaminated milk was diluted with pure milk from dairy herds that did not use the contaminated feed.

The doctor was mum about the meat, because neither state nor federal authorities and researchers knew for certain the toxicity or effects of PBB in humans or animals. What was certain was that it had entered the food chain in Michigan.

And so, 115,000 laying hens, 3,000 dairy and beef cattle, and 150 pigs were immediately quarantined, and more than three tons of cheese and butter were seized. Tested, they all showed evidence of a 5 to 7 parts per million containment of PBB, far in excess of 1 part per million, the hastily set allowable level put in place arbitrarily by the United States Food and Drug Administration (FDA), which had understandably never dealt with animal feed containing flame retardant.

By November, the acknowledged number of contaminated livestock was raised and the acceptable contamination level was lowered. The FDA now imposed an acceptable level of 0.3 parts per million in meat, poultry, and milk and 0.05 parts per million in eggs. Five thousand more head of cattle were slaughtered. By the beginning of November 1974, farmers had also destroyed 1.5 million eggs, 900,000 chickens, 2,200 hogs, 1,000 pheasants, 348

sheep, 10,000 pounds of cheese, and 351 tons of contaminated feed.

The economic losses to farmers were estimated at between $10 million and $15 million, and lawsuits were instituted against the Farm Bureau Services agency and the Michigan Chemical Company. Over the next two years, the 534 Michigan farmers who received contaminated feed and fed it to their livestock received a total of $28 million in compensation from insurance companies representing the agency and the company responsible.

But the greatest, most pervasive and most mysterious toll was upon the people who consumed food contaminated by PBB. Since no such contamination had ever occurred before, health experts were at a loss in predicting the effect it would have upon human beings. Federal and state public health authorities were unduly cavalier in the beginning, contending that there was no threat to public health. But after two years, they changed their attitude and their predictions.

The effects of the contamination were beginning to make themselves known. The PBB had begun to insinuate itself into the food chain, into the soil, streams, and swamps. Laboratory tests disclosed high levels of PBB in wild bears and coyotes.

And now, anecdotal evidence began to surface showing that consumers as well as farm families who ate contaminated eggs, pork, beef, and dairy products were beginning to show definite signs of poisoning. Dizziness, lassitude, headaches, swollen joints, stomach cramps, and sores began to surface.

But health authorities were cautious to the point of near denial. And this produced a backlash. A Peoples Action Committee on PBB was formed, and its chief objective was to force legislation that would require the FDA to lower the tolerance level for PBB to zero and stop the sale of the poisoned feed, which, astonishingly, was still being sold in cooperative stores.

Furthermore, these committees contended that Michigan was treating PBB as an economic problem rather than a health hazard. To dramatize this, some farmers sported bumper stickers that said "PBB—Cattlegate Bigger Than Watergate," and others, like Douglas Green, shot their herds of dairy cattle. (Milk production had dropped so far that it no longer paid the cost of feeding the cows in much of Michigan.) "I saw my cows and calves dying," he said. "My conscience would not let it go on the market and be put into humans."

This in turn attracted the attention of the national media and Senator Edward Kennedy's subcommittee on health. Members of the Public Action Committee and other farmers went to Washington and testified about their grievances to the committee and the public at large.

As a result of public and national pressure, a mass testing of Michigan farmers and their families who had been

Public pressure has become an increasingly effective weapon against industrial pollution. Without it, the mass testing of PBB-contaminated Michigan farmers never would have taken place.
(JAYMES E. PAPPAS/UNEP)

exposed to PBB finally took place. One thousand one hundred people participated in what was the nation's first mass health survey to determine the effects of an environmental contaminant. Funded by the National Institute of Environmental Health Sciences, it was conducted for six days at Kent Community Hospital in Grand Rapids, by a 35-member medical team organized by Dr. Irving J. Selikoff, director of the Environmental Sciences Laboratory at Mount Sinai Center, aided by dozens of Michigan volunteers.

This team had conducted more than a dozen health surveys in various industries, including asbestos, lead, and vinyl chloride. Moreover, this was the team's first survey among the general population to assess the effects of a chemical in the environment and the first to include whole family groups.

It was new territory. All that was known was that PBB was a close chemical relative of PCB, the industrial environmental pollutant known to cause liver and thyroid abnormalities, bronchitis, nerve damage, skin lesions, pregnancy problems, and in animals, growth retardation and cancer.

The case of Chris and Donald Rehkopf, who had moved to Washington State but returned for the survey, was typical. Chris, who was 23 years old and pregnant, had had a baby in 1973 who died at the age of six weeks. "She was sick and jaundiced the whole time, but the doctors couldn't figure out what caused her death," Mrs. Rehkopf told *New York Times* reporter Jane Brody, then went on to relate that her son Thorin, born the next year, had a constant round of infections and occasional jaundice.

Leonard, the grandfather, had been unable to work since the contamination took place. Though an impressively muscular-looking fifty years old, Mr. Rehkopf had suffered from arthritis-like problems in his joints, excessive sleepiness, clumsiness, and almost continual headaches. All of these symptoms had begun shortly after the 1973 contamination.

All in the family had suffered broken bones in the past year. Donald, the father, had difficulty remembering such things as what he ate for breakfast, why his wife was angry with him, or what a car salesman had just told him.

A pattern of effects emerged during the conducting of the survey: joint problems, fatigue, dizziness, memory problems, excessive sweating, wounds that would not heal, darkening of the skin, sensitivity to sunlight, muscular weakness, diarrhea, visual disturbances, sores, and rashes. Some children, duplicating the effects on animals, had grown thin despite having good appetites. Some had lost patches of hair. Over and over, participants complained of having to stop work or driving because of fatigue or a loss of coordination.

The conclusion was that in humans as well as in animals, the chemical was stored in body fat and became mobilized when the body used or lost fat.

The study also revealed severe neurological and psychological damage. Card players could no longer keep track of their playing hands, longtime farmers could not plow a straight furrow, and drivers with formerly spotless records suddenly began to accumulate tickets and have minor accidents. Some families were living on welfare because no one in the family was able to work.

Dr. Sidney Diamond, the neurologist of the team, also addressed the psychological effects after examining dozens of participants who suffered from a loss of confidence and ambition and diminished sexual activity.

"How much of the problems are organic and how much is emotional overlay may be a valid scientific question," he said, "but in terms of the lives of these people, it's really not a relevant issue. These people's lives are destroyed, and that is as important as pain in their joints. You can't take fluid out of the soul and show PBB levels."

No firm conclusions, other than these, were drawn from the survey.

UNITED STATES
(MISSISSIPPI)
PESTICIDE CONTAMINATION OF CHICKENS
March 1974

The cancer-causing chemical dieldrin found its way into the food supply of millions of chickens being raised as broilers on four Mississippi farms during the winter of 1974. Discovered by inspectors from the Agriculture Department and the Environmental Protection Agency, they were ordered destroyed, over some initial protests by Congressman Jamie L. Whitten of Mississippi.

On March 22, 1974, the story broke in major newspapers that the Environmental Protection Agency (EPA) had been informed by the Agriculture Department that upward of 22 million chickens, grown in Mississippi for sale in midwestern markets such as Detroit and Chicago, had been contaminated with the pesticide dieldrin. Dieldrin, with its sister pesticide aldrin, is manufactured by Shell Oil Company and is used primarily to rid corn of parasites. It has also proved to cause cancerous tumors in laboratory mice when a mere 0.1 parts per million of dieldrin is digested.

Actually, the tainting of the chicken supply had been discovered in February, during a periodic spot check of the 2.9 billion broilers raised annually in the United States. The 22 million chickens represented 14 percent of the nation's eight-week supply of chickens, and it was thus pos-

sibly the magnitude of the problem that caused the EPA to momentarily freeze, and not withdraw them from the market. Their explanation was that it was important to verify the initial findings.

Reaction was swift and angry. "In light of human health aspects, I am disgusted that the decision in this matter should take more than 10 minutes," said Anson Keller, associate general counsel of the EPA.

He and several employees of the agency fumed that pressure from Congress was delaying the decision on whether or not to destroy the chickens. It was a believable assumption, considering that Mississippi ranks fifth in the nation in chicken production, all of the contamination occurred in Mississippi, and the chairman of the House Appropriations subcommittee that controlled the funds for the EPA in 1974 was Jamie L. Whitten, Democrat of Mississippi.

As if further cause for alarm were needed, Congressman Whitten examined the evidence and promptly informed the press that "nothing that I know of can endanger human health. . . ."

Meanwhile, representatives of Morton Broilers, of Morton, Mississippi, and McCarty Poultry Farms, of Magee, Mississippi, two of the five broiler concerns who raised the chickens (the others were Quad County Co-op of Sebastopol and Fred Moore and Fred Gaddis of Forest, Mississippi), met in closed session with the congressman.

The following day, it was announced that 8 million, rather than 22 million chickens had been contaminated. The sampling, by the Agriculture Department's Animal and Plant Health Inspection Service, determined that dieldrin existed in a ratio of 3.0 parts per million, which was 10 times the allowable level of 0.3 parts per million set by the Agriculture Department and used as a guideline by the EPA. Three veterinarians were sent to south central Mississippi to aid in finding the cause of the dangerous levels of dieldrin.

The contaminated chickens were breeder hens, scheduled for slaughter on February 11, 1975, and were in various stages of development before being sent to market.

Preliminary inspections, which later turned out to be accurate, pointed toward animal fats and vegetable oils added to the chicken feed as the source of the dieldrin contamination, and so scrutiny now turned to the Mississippi Vegetable Oil Company of Blendon, Mississippi, and Central By-Products of Forest, Mississippi, which produced the oils used in the chicken feed.

A tug-of-war ensued between the Agriculture Department and the EPA on one side and the broiler representatives, who continued to insist that the cutoff level of the pesticide was well below minimum standards, and that, anyway, slaughtering would remove most of the tissue in which the chemical was concentrated.

The two departments, again citing the statistics of laboratory tests with rodents, continued to insist upon the destruction of the contaminated chickens, and the broiler representatives finally agreed that they would do all that was possible to comply. "Our first priority is the consumer, and we will protect him at all cost," T. H. Eldridge, a broiler operator and chairman of the Board of the National Broiler Association told the press on March 24.

On March 27, the destruction, by gassing and burial, of 4 million chickens—down from the 22 million estimate four days before—began. The evidence that the contamination had come from vegetable fat in the feed was confirmed, but how it got there was a mystery and still remains so.

UNITED STATES
(MISSOURI, TIMES BEACH)
DIOXIN CONTAMINATION
1971–1986

....

In 1982, all of the 2,242 residents of Times Beach, Missouri, were forced to leave their homes and evacuate their village after a flood revealed extensive soil contamination from dioxin-tainted waste oil bought from the North Eastern Pharmaceutical Company in Verona, Missouri, and sprayed on dirt roads, driveways, and horse rings by Russell Bliss, a private contractor. Hundreds of animals died from the contamination, and the results of long-term health effects upon the town's residents are still inconclusive.

"Hey, look at those spacemen over there," said Ernest Hance, Jr., to a reporter in late January 1983. "Looks like we been invaded, don't it?"

He was referring to Environmental Protection Agency (EPA) researchers in white protective garments, plastic hoods, rubber gloves, and insulated boots, designed to protect them from the dioxin contamination that had forced the evacuation of Times Beach, a small village of 2,400 people on the southern shore of the Meramec River, 30 miles southwest of St. Louis, Missouri.

The problem for Times Beach and other locations in Missouri had begun in 1970, with the brief, two-year production span of the North Eastern Pharmaceutical and Chemical Company, in Verona, Missouri. The plant, which manufactured hexachlorophene for antiseptic purposes, and most importantly, Agent Orange for the U.S. government, generated some 120 pounds of dioxin during the 21 months of its operation between 1970 and 1972. Some of the waste was disposed of properly, but from February to October of 1971, about 55 pounds of dioxin hidden within 18,500 gallons of sludge was removed from the plant site by a waste hauler named Russell D. Bliss.

If the 20th century had produced a Johnny Appleseed of contamination, it was Russell Bliss. This small businessman

from Ellisville, Missouri, saw an easy way to make money when the North Eastern Pharmaceutical and Chemical Company went belly-up. He mixed the waste sludge with waste oil and went around the countryside, spraying roads, horse arenas, and driveways for very little money. The oil kept the dust down, and in 1971, Times Beach had no paved roads, just dirt byways that sent spumes of dust into the air whenever traffic moved over them.

So, Russell Bliss brought clear skies and dioxin contamination to Times Beach and scores of other towns and horse rings all over Missouri.

"I have lived here 48 years, since I was five years old," continued Mr. Hance to the reporter, "and I used to cut wood for my stove right over there at City Park where they say most of that stuff is.

"What got me to thinking was when a woman who ran a stable here had 62 horses and some cats and dogs just drop dead. She said the last thing that happened was their hair started falling out."

It was dioxin poisoning, the sort that turned Agent Orange into a lethal weapon in the Vietnam War (see pp. 226–230) and contaminated the soil in Love Canal in 1978 (see pp. 112–116).

The name *dioxin* is a common term given to a large group of compounds, the most toxic of which is 2,3,7,8-tetra-chlorodibenzo-para-dioxin, or TCDD, a compound that has been linked to mutations, birth defects, cancer, skin disorders, kidney and liver failure, and a host of other problems in laboratory animals. In fact, doses as small as 5 parts per 1,000 billion have caused statistically significant increases in cancer in rats.

All told, dioxin is one of the most lethal compounds known to humankind, 150,000 times as toxic as cyanide and as much as 670 times as lethal as strychnine. Nearly insoluble in water, it clings tightly to soil particles and dissolves in organic solvents such as alcohol or oil. It can enter the body by direct skin contact, ingestion, or inhalation, and in 1983, it was as close as the earth to the entire population of Times Beach, and to parts of the population of hundreds, possibly thousands of other residents of Missouri serviced by the Bliss Waste Oil Company.

Mr. Vance, brushing his hands through his thinning gray hair, ruminated. "My dad was seventy-one years old when he died and he had lots of hair and very little of it was gray," he told reporters, and confessed his suspicions about the white blotches on his skin and the cracks that ran insistently through his fingernails.

"I am not trying to get anything out of this," he said, "I just want to know what's what."

This had been the often and respectful inquiry of many inhabitants of Times Beach, ever since the Meramec River overran its banks during the first week of December 1982, inundating the village, damaging a large portion of its inhabitants' homes and businesses, uprooting water mains, and cracking the pavement in the roads.

The EPA had been in the village before the flood, and their findings had been alarming. Four of 114 soil samples taken were found to contain levels of dioxin as high as 100 parts per billion—100 times what federal officials regard as safe.

It was then eleven and a half years after the first horse died from dioxin sprayed on its exercise ring by Mr. Bliss, and six years from the time that the attention of federal authorities was elevated from concentration on animal deaths to possible human deaths. Even the Centers for Disease Control and the EPA's suggestion in 1975 to the Missouri department of health to reexcavate and thoroughly dispose of soil in one horse farm had gone unheeded, both in Washington, D.C., and Missouri.

Now, however, there were piles of potentially contaminated flood debris upon which children were delighted to play, and that needed to be cleaned up and shipped off to a nearby landfill. The EPA reentered the village, and its spaceman-clad inspectors began to take further soil samples from the land displaced by the flood. Their findings alarmed them enough to warn the residents of Times Beach to evacuate the town immediately.

Most of the residents needed little encouragement, provided they were compensated for the move. The flood had devastated the village. The only building in town that had escaped flood damage was one restaurant, and its owner was more than willing to sell out and move on.

By the second week in December 1982, roadblocks were set up on the edge of town, first to prevent residents from removing trailers or cars possibly contaminated with dioxin, then—after it was determined that these vehicles could be removed if they were washed down—to keep nonresidents out.

Fifty-eight families remained through December, unwilling to accept the sudden concern of authorities. One of those remaining was Mayor Sidney K. Hammer, whose reply to the Army Corps of Engineers' suggestion that the town be abandoned, razed, and rebuilt on higher ground, was "I think it stinks."

As news of the possible contamination spread through the national media, Missouri governor Christopher S. Bond ordered a halt to plans to move the debris out of Times Beach and to the Warren County landfill, 40 miles away.

In January, the remaining residents of Times Beach breathed a little more easily when the Missouri Department of Natural Resources released the news that initial results of tests of soil samples taken from inside two homes showed no traceable levels of dioxin. On the other hand, the agency cautioned, there was no conclusive evidence that the floodwaters had washed away the contamination already discovered, and tests were continuing.

Meanwhile, Russell Bliss was denied a renewal of his hauling license and called before the Missouri House Energy Committee. He broke down in tears, vowing that "I swear to all of you I had no idea that oil was bad."

On January 13, 1983, the governor relented, and the first of what was expected to be 100 truckloads of flood debris was hauled from Times Beach to the Warren County landfill. Fifty residents of Warren County peacefully protested the move.

Back in Times Beach, the remaining residents were growing restive and began to advertise their plight to the traveling public by waving signs and banners at cars and trucks passing on nearby Interstate 44. Their complaint: They were told to move out, but there had been no official compensation, nor promises of it.

"Everyone's with us but the government," unemployed automobile worker Ralph Penn told reporters. "They poisoned us ten years ago and left us sitting there. They let me buy a house in this town and now I can't get rid of it."

In the rest of the state, fears were rising that, out of the 55 pounds of dioxin that Russell Bliss had hauled away from the defunct chemical plant, he could not account for 43 pounds. He ran a small business, he said, and kept few records, and his memory was none too good.

The Verona plant apparently was not very responsible about its activities, either. James Denney, a farmer who lived near it, was paid $150 to allow the Verona plant to bury drums of dioxin on his farm. It cost the EPA nearly $2 million to clean up the site.

Further incidents surfaced. Bill Davis, a dairyman near Verona, was forced to dump 1,400 gallons of milk after Kraft, a distributor, refused to buy it. The reason: His Guernsey cattle drank from the Spring River, a declared contamination site, and many of his cows were suffering from bovine leukemia.

On the nearby dairy farm of S. B. Erwin, the tissue of a dead cow was found to contain close to 100 parts of dioxin per 1,000 billion, four times the amount allowed by the FDA for edible meats and fish. On still another Verona farm owned by Bill Davis, 23 head of cattle died from bovine leukemia in the six-month period from July 1982 through January 1983. And most dramatically, in testimony before the Missouri Hazardous Waste Management Commission, Judy Platt, the co-owner of Shenandoah Stables, a horse farm whose ring Russell Bliss had sprayed with contaminated oil in 1971, testified that "[Russell] told me there was special stuff put in the oil for special customers that would kill flies." This, plus the testimony of a former manager of the Verona chemical plant that Bliss drivers were always furnished protective gear and warned about the hazards of the sludge as they pumped it into their trucks, seemed to indicate that, for all his later protestations, Bliss knew that he was spreading contamination with his waste oil.

By the end of January, 15 sites throughout southwest Missouri were confirmed to have been contaminated with dioxin. When members of the EPA joined other state and federal government agencies to come to Hillsboro, Missouri, to reassure residents that they were doing all they could to control the situation, they were met with anything but friendly acquiescence, especially when Fred Lafser, state director of natural resources coupled this news with an announcement that Missouri had run out of funds to clean up contaminated sites, including Times Beach, and that there were 240 sites in the state contaminated with hazardous waste—100 of them probably containing dioxin. (This was later proved to be an inflated figure.)

The EPA continued testing and in February came up with seven more polluted sites in the St. Louis vicinity: three truck companies, a lumber yard, a stable in High Ridge, a house near Fenton, and—most disturbingly—a church day-care center.

The situation was obviously at a crisis juncture, and now Missouri's two U.S. senators, Republican John C. Danforth and Democrat Thomas F. Eagleton, began to bring pressure to bear on the federal government to buy out residents of Times Beach.

This was good news to the 400 families that had returned to Times Beach while the investigations continued. For many, it was a little too late in life to think of beginning all over again somewhere else. For others, the indecision forced upon them by dithering state and federal agencies was immobilizing. "It's very depressing and quite a stress on us," said Elizabeth Hagen to reporters. "We don't know what to do. There is a lot of work that needs to be done, but we are reluctant to make any repairs [on our house] because we don't know that we would have to just turn around and move. It is a shame we have to wait so long for an answer."

Meanwhile, the town of Times Beach seemed to be fading into the shadows. Its equivalent of a town hall was a couple of cramped trailers at the outskirts of town, alongside barricades that sported skulls and crossbones. The lack of property owners in town forced layoffs of 4 of its 11 municipal workers. Property taxes, water bills, even fines from traffic court—which could no longer be held—had evaporated. Worst of all, looting in the town had increased alarmingly just as the entire police force of one full-time and one part-time policemen was laid off.

Elizabeth Hagen confessed that she and other residents were now afraid to leave their homes for more than a couple of hours at a time. Looters, she said, had begun to break into homes and steal the copper plumbing.

"We are in a bind," she concluded. "Our home is worthless because we can't sell it, and the government won't tell us whether we should fix things up or that they will buy us out."

Finally, on February 22, 1983, the federal government announced that, for the first time, it would evacuate and

All that is left of the village of Times Beach and its 2,242 residents is a ghost town, cleaned out and made uninhabitable by soil contamination from dioxin-tainted waste oil.
(SAM KITTNER/GREENPEACE)

buy out an entire town threatened by chemical wastes. Thirty-three million dollars from the new federal Superfund for the cleanup of toxic waste would be allocated for the purpose.

Residents of Times Beach were jubilant. The 437 owners of permanent homes, 364 mobile homes, and 40 or 50 businesses were eligible to participate in the buyout.

The federal government's decision had come after undeniable and unavoidable findings by a team from the National Centers for Disease Control. Although there seemed to be no increase in dioxin pollution as a result of the flood, the town was still considered by the team to be uninhabitable. The highest levels of dioxin were found to still rest under the macadam of the streets. Samples of the capped soil frequently showed concentrations of more than 100 parts per billion, and some as high as 300 parts.

It was, in retrospect, a good deal for the government. Not many towns in the United States could be bought out for $33 million, but Times Beach was built on a floodplain. When most of its population moved in, a 20-by-100-foot lot cost between $300 and $700, and the average value of the homes was $40,000. The plan was one that placed no serious strain upon the Superfund.

Still, the government was concerned. Of the original 240, there were still 21 contaminated sites left in the state of Missouri alone—one of them the horse ring at the St. Louis Police Academy. And then, there was the problem of the Meramec River emptying into the Mississippi. Dioxin did not adhere to water, but there were other chemicals in the polluted mix of Times Beach.

And there was still confusion in what was left of the town. Some 400 families lived in mobile homes. Even with the buyout, they could not afford the $400 to $600 a month it would take to buy a new home elsewhere. And where would that elsewhere be? Six families that had moved from their mobile homes in Times Beach to Quail Run Mobile Manor in Gray Summit, Missouri, 35 miles southwest of St. Louis, discovered, after they had settled in, that their new site was also contaminated with dioxin to as much as 1,100 times the tolerable level.

As Russell Bliss's memory cleared under questioning by federal investigators, more and more sites in Missouri were discovered to be contaminated. By April 1983, the number had swollen from 21 to 30.

Then, as spring arrived, it appeared that the $33 million pledged to Times Beach for relocation and buyouts would not be enough. All summer, the state and federal governments waded through conflicting regulations that slowed the buyout.

By August, 14 families still lived in Times Beach, which was now redolent with huckleberry and isolated from the rest of the world by concrete barriers. Approximately 800 other families had been placed in temporary government-sponsored housing.

Over the summer, animals continued to die in the town. "A number of dogs at the Minker site died this summer," Lin Sproull, one of the hangers-on in the town, told officials in October, "and there were small birds and things lying all over the place."

The buyout inched forward. By the end of October, the government had bought only 43 properties and had processed the claims of approximately 150 other families. Most of the 800 Times Beach families were still living in temporary housing elsewhere, waiting to have their properties appraised, offers made, or sales contracts closed.

In the middle of December 1983, a lawsuit seeking $1.8 billion in damages was filed for 183 people from Times Beach and nearby Castlewood, who claimed serious health problems as a result of exposure to dioxin.

The defendents in the suit were Syntex Agribusiness Inc., of Palo Alto, California; the Charter Company and the Charter Oil Company of Jacksonville, Florida; the Independent Petrochemical Corporation of St. Louis; the North Eastern Pharmaceutical and Chemical Company of Verona, Missouri and five of its trustees.

Over the next four years, as agreements were reached between the government and the afflicted residents of Times Beach, properties were vacated and people moved out, some bitterly. Many felt that the government had not paid them enough to live elsewhere; others realized that living on a floodplain had its short-term advantages but ultimate drawbacks.

By April 1986, only two people—George and Lorene Klein—still lived in Times Beach, and they confessed to *New York Times* reporter E. R. Shipp that life was indeed lonely. The elderly couple had rejected three offers from the government for their property.

"It's not that we don't want to leave," Mr. Klein told Mr. Shipp, "but they haven't offered us enough money."

In late November 1986, an out-of-court settlement was reached in the lawsuit against the polluting corporations, for $19 million. And Times Beach now became a totally deserted piece of real estate, never very valuable, but never deserving of the total destruction it received as a result of irresponsibility and the profit motive.

Every year now, many of the former residents of Times Beach meet in a park in nearby Eureka, Missouri, to reminisce and compare notes. Most of the notes are the same: In Missouri, at least, former Times Beach occupants who were forced to relocate had been greeted with outright hostility, rejection, cruelty, and fear from their new neighbors. A sign at the city limits of Catawissa, Missouri, read, according to one refugee, "Times Beach trash unwelcome."

"Most of the people [who come back for the reunions] just want to sit down and chat with one another, especially people that were longtime neighbors in the community," noted former mayor Marilyn Leistner of Times Beach at the 1995 reunion. Part of the subject matter of these chats seemed to be the as yet inconclusive results of long-term studies of the residents' health.

UNITED STATES
(NEW JERSEY, NEWARK)
BUTTERWORTH AND JUDSON CHEMICAL WORKS EXPLOSION
March 24, 1918

Approximately 23 people were killed and 60 were injured when friction in machines—or possibly sabotage—destroyed a great deal of the Butterworth and Judson Chemical Works near Newark, New Jersey, at 11:30 P.M. on March 24, 1918.

Picric acid, or 2,4,6-trinitrophenol can be used as a yellow dye, as an antiseptic, and in the synthesis of the insecticide chloropicrin. But in itself it is also a powerful explosive, of the TNT class, and serves as a basic ingredient in the explosives lyddite, melinite, and shimose. And in March 1918, with the United States at war, all of the activities of the Butterworth and Judson Chemical Works on Canary Island in the Passaic River, near Newark, New Jersey, turned away from dyes and insecticides and toward the manufacture of explosives. Part of the plant produced TNT; part produced picric acid.

The picric acid works were contained in one wooden building and the entire plant was running at full capacity at 11:30 P.M. on March 24.

One of the workers in the picric acid building ran from the building at precisely that moment, shouting a warning. A small tongue of flame licked out from under a corner of the building, and, hearing the commotion, the plant's chief electrician and part owner, William Butterworth, left his office and ran toward the building.

He was only a few steps from it when it exploded with an earthshaking roar. Mr. Butterworth was lifted off his feet and blown backward. He landed, severely injured, against a building nearly a hundred feet from the blast. It and three more structures were flattened by the explosion, and three smaller ones that followed, as was the original building.

Fortunately, most of the workers in the building escaped, and firemen brought the blaze under control rapidly. The official explanation was that friction from a machine in the building produced the spark that ignited the flame that resulted in the explosion.

The *Newark Star-Ledger*, however, reported that the Newark police had discovered an electric wire extending from the meadows adjacent to the plant to the shop in which the fire started. Sabotage was suspected, but no follow-up stories were ever printed. It was wartime, and even the casualty figures were given in approximations: 23 dead and 60 injured—approximately.

UNITED STATES
(NEW YORK, NIAGARA FALLS)
LOVE CANAL POLLUTION
1978–1985

No single case of industrial contamination awakened more of the public, nor was more representative of the inevitable conflict and coverup that results when industry, the public, and politics mix, than the consequences of the dumping of toxic waste into a 16-acre ditch dubbed "Love Canal," in the City of Niagara Falls, New York. The Hooker Chemicals and Plastics Corporation dumped 21,800 tons of chemical wastes, including polychlorinated biphenyls, dioxin, and long-lasting pesticides, into the former piece of a canal from 1942 to 1958. Conflicting scientific studies, evacuations, multi-million-dollar lawsuits, and the establishment of the Superfund resulted.

LOVE CANAL
Another Product From
Hooker Chemical

. . . proclaimed the T-shirts sold by the Love Canal Homeowners Association and its activist head, Lois Gibbs. The homeowners were angry and publicity minded, and these twin energies kept the Love Canal controversy alive for decades, assuring its rightful place in the annals of industrial contamination and evasion, along with Bhopal (see pp. 81–85), Times Beach (see pp. 108–11), and Minamata (see pp. 89–93).

It all began in 1892—or the 1880s, depending upon the historical source—when William T. Love proposed that a canal be dug as a connection between the upper and lower Niagara Rivers. The canal would be part of a huge industrial complex and a city of 200,000, with an array of industries stationed along it, generating electric power from the rushing waters that dropped 280 feet from the upper Niagara to the lower Niagara. Since direct current was the only current then, and since DC only traveled short distances, this line of industries would, he reasoned, be a revolutionary moneymaker.

New York State was so excited by the prospect that it gave Love the right to condemn property and start digging immediately. This he did, but just as his workers began to carve out the canal, alternating current, which traveled long distances, was discovered, and Mr. Love's project was abandoned. The grand canal amounted, then, to a mere ditch, three long blocks long and three short blocks wide, a rectangular area of 16 acres, some eight miles north of the falls.

For a while, until late in the 1930s, the piece of canal bearing Love's name was a swimming hole for local youngsters. And even then, it was becoming slowly polluted. In the 1920s, the land that included the canal was sold at public auction. The high bidder was the Niagara Power and Development Corporation, who used it as a municipal dumping site.

Long before this, in 1905, shortly after the collapse of William T. Love's grand design, the Hooker Electrochemical Corporation, which later became the Hooker Chemical and Plastics Corporation, and, in 1969 was absorbed into Occidental Petroleum, set up business in Niagara Falls. It manufactured industrial chemicals, fertilizers, and plastics. The company thrived, and, in 1942, it signed an agreement with the owners of Love Canal to use it as a dump for chemical wastes. Nobody was living there; it seemed like a good, safe idea.

Four years later, in 1946, Hooker bought the canal from the Niagara Power and Development Corporation, and between 1947 and 1952, it dumped more than 43 million pounds of industrial chemical wastes into it, including more than 13 million pounds of benzene hexachloride, a carcinogenic chlorinated hydrocarbon pesticide; more than 4 million pounds of chlorobenzenes—known to induce aplastic anemia and leukemia; and half a million pounds of TCP, which is used in the manufacture of herbicides.

The TCP was heavily contaminated with several hundred pounds of TCDD, better known as dioxin. Less than three ounces of dioxin is enough to kill the entire population of New York City. The most potent known carcinogen and teratogen (deformity-causing agent), it produced cancers in experimental animals at concentrations as low as 10 to 100 parts per trillion.

Added to this mix were dumpings by the U.S. Army of drums of toxic chemicals from various defense contractors. Altogether, it amounted to a lethal cocktail, and Hooker knew it when it filled in and sealed Love Canal in 1953.

Meanwhile, the city of Niagara Falls was growing and needed space for suburban homes and the schools to service them. The Board of Education planned to condemn the property around and including Love Canal, so that it could construct a school at 99th Street and Wheatfield Avenue, on the brink of the ditch.

In April 1953, Hooker sold the land to the Board of Education for $1, provided that the board sign a proviso that absolved Hooker of any and all responsibility for injury or property damage from the dump's contents. Nowhere in the contract was there any description of those contents.

Nevertheless, the Board of Education signed, and the school was built, and more families moved in, particularly after realtors assured them that the Love Canal site would soon be turned into a public park. As it was, it was an unkempt field of swamp, grasses, and gullies—ideal as a location for local children to play.

Almost immediately, however, the area began to exhibit strange and distinctive qualities. The shoes the children wore to play around the canal, once soiled, were impossible to get clean. Dogs who played with the children began to lose their hair in clumps. Some developed severe skin rashes; others died. By June 1958, several children came home with burns from chemicals that had begun to surface in the northern section of the canal.

A so-called "Black Lagoon" of sooty water started to develop by the mid-1960s, and one child, Joey Bulka, who fell into it, emerged with a punctured eardrum. A pervasive chemical odor began to rise from the old canal, and plants and vegetables refused to grow in nearby backyard gardens.

By the early 1970s, the situation had worsened considerably. The average rainfall in the Niagara Falls area is 36 inches a year, and after each of these rains, the homes closest to the canal, on 99th and 97th Streets, began to flood—not with water, but with a black, oozing sludge. Sump pumps were bought and installed, but they only lasted a few months before the black sludge corroded them beyond use. In the spring, when the snow left and the ground thawed, a foul chemical odor, so strong that prolonged exposure brought tears to residents' eyes, began to seep out of the ground and into cellars.

Then, in-ground swimming pools began to crack, elevate, and fill with the same dark liquid that was appearing in yards and basements.

Finally, in June 1977, the city of Niagara Falls turned to Calspan, a Buffalo-based engineering consulting firm, to investigate the scene and the complaints. Hooker offered to aid in the effort.

The Calspan investigation not only confirmed the complaints of the citizenry, it also discovered contamination in the groundwater. Apparently, drums of chemicals nearest the surface of the canal had worked their way to the surface of the dump and had then corroded and leaked. Samples of

ground- and surface water revealed heavy contamination by a number of toxic chemicals, among them hexachlorocyclopentadiene, a precursor of the pesticide mirex; hexachlorobenzene, a fungicide; and a wide range of other carcinogenic chlorinated hydrocarbons.

This was enough for some of the residents of the Love Canal area. Lois Gibbs, who would eventually become the most famous of them (a made-for-television movie about her would air on CBS in February 1982) had begun collecting signatures on a petition to close the Ninety-ninth Street School, the school that had been built on the brink of the canal-landfill.

As the petition drive intensified, more and more stories surfaced of miscarriages, birth defects in children recently born, skin rashes, and bronchitis.

Simultaneously, the New York State Department of Health and the State Department of Environmental Conservation initiated their own tests of groundwater, soil, and air. Their findings were alarming. The air, water, and ground were all found to be heavily contaminated with a wide range of toxic and carcinogenic chemicals obviously oozing from the Hooker dump. The air in basements close to the dump was rife with these chemicals. In a creek running close to it, the water was found to be contaminated with 31 parts per billion of dioxin, a level about 700 million times greater than that calculated by the Environmental Protection Agency (EPA) to produce one cancer death per million population. Chloroform was discovered in the air of one home at a level more than 100 times that considered by the EPA to cause a significant cancer risk.

The state urged the county to close the school, but the county refused, forcing the state to step in and close it. Not only that. The state would, it was announced, buy up the most seriously contaminated houses and evacuate the families from these houses. Panic spread like a plague through the neighborhood.

Lois Gibbs and her petition committee, which had now grown and become the Love Canal Homeowners Association, pushed the state to conduct a full-scale health survey. The state brought a van and some technicians in to take blood tests, but within an hour, they were overwhelmed by the crowd, shut up shop, and distributed questionnaires for those still waiting.

Frustrated, the Homeowners Association hired Beverly Paigen, a cancer researcher from Buffalo to conduct a telephone survey. An overwhelming percentage of children with birth defects were found to have been born to families in the most contaminated areas. Nervous disorders, resulting, in some cases, in institutionalization and suicide, were also reported.

On February 8, 1979, the New York State Department of Health issued a directive recommending that all pregnant women and children under two be "temporarily" removed from the canal area. But there were 200 other families living

Boarded up, bulldozed, and bitterly abandoned, the once thriving but thoroughly contaminated community of Love Canal, near Niagara Falls, New York, is a grim monument to industrial irresponsibility, governmental collusion, and corruption.
(LISA BUNIN/GREENPEACE)

in the most contaminated part of Love Canal who were not advised to move.

The anger in the area mounted, and claims against the city of Niagara Falls of $3 billion were filed.

Now, politicians began to become involved. The so-called "Rall panel" convened by Congressman John LaFalce and headed by David Rall, director of the National Institute of Environmental Health Sciences, issued a mild report suggesting that the remaining residents should be evacuated.

Faced with this publicity, New York State began a cleanup of the site, which turned out to cause further contamination through the appearance of new holes spewing black ooze, and contaminants carried on the tires of trucks spreading the pollution to other neighborhoods.

Finally, on August 7, 1978, President Jimmy Carter declared Love Canal a limited Disaster Area. Throughout the month of August, 239 families living on the border of the canal were evacuated and relocated. Their homes, purchased by the state for $10 million, were demolished.

Now it was time for the Department of Justice to become involved. On December 20, 1979, it filed a federal suit against Hooker Chemical, the city of Niagara Falls, the Niagara County Health Department, and the Board of Education of the city of Niagara Falls. The suit, which for the first time revealed that toxic chemicals from the dump had entered the pipes in several households and contaminated drinking water, called for an immediate cleanup of the site, funds for medical research, the relocation of remaining residents if necessary, and compensation of $7 million to the government for money it had already expended on the canal. It was the largest environmental pollution suit yet filed by the Justice Department.

But throughout the winter of 1979–80, no funds arrived, and nothing was done for the occupants of the contaminated homes.

In May, the EPA leaked a news bombshell to the national press. A pilot study had revealed that 11 of 36 residents tested had suffered chromosome damage. On May 21, the EPA followed this with an announcement that all remaining residents would be temporarily evacuated pending further tests. On May 22, President Carter declared a federal emergency area extending up to six blocks from the canal, and 400 more families were evacuated. Their homes were bought with state and federal funds.

By this time, several congressional committees had become involved with Love Canal, and politics began to muddle matters. Governor Hugh Carey of New York organized a special scientific panel that concluded that all efforts and conclusions before its formation had been botched. For instance, calling the Love Canal tragedy an "environmental nightmare" that "threatened profound and devastating effects" was too dramatic and only succeeded in frightening area residents. It called the Paigen investigation "literally impossible to interpret" and reserved its harshest words for the EPA chromosome study, calling it poorly designed and a mistake to have been conducted in the first place.

These conclusions, in turn, were called to task for their scientific objectivity by other independent biostatisticians, Irwin Bross, in particular.

Now Hooker issued its own rebuttal, which stated that the company had done all it could and should have done to contain the chemicals and to warn the Niagara Falls city School Board against any activity that would disturb the cap on the canal.

In 1981, the New York State Health Department conducted its own research at Love Canal, and reported findings of dioxin in storm sewers and creeks, but not near houses.

By January 1982, New York State had filed a $200 million lawsuit against Hooker and its parent company, the Occidental Petroleum Corporation, charging that not only Love Canal but also other sites in the city of Niagara Falls had led to pollution of the river. At the same time, the EPA began to conduct what was hoped to be a definitive health study of Love Canal.

By May, a federal judge had settled part of the New York State suit with an agreement by Hooker to clean up the offending sites. But by now there were 1,300 individual suits against Hooker, involving billions of dollars in claims.

May was also a month of compounded confusion. Although most of the Love Canal site was now a vandalized ghost town, and even though the results of the federal health study had not been released, the Love Canal Area Revitalization Agency was formed by Niagara Falls city officials, and more than 160 people had put their names on a waiting list to buy or build houses there. "No one denies that there are chemicals in the ground," stated Mayor Michael C. O'Laughlin, who was chairman of the agency, "But if the report [of the federal health study] says they are contained, it's like living near a factory anyplace else in the city."

Former residents and their supporters opposed the "revitalization" movement, citing the fact that Mayor O' Laughlin had complained publicly that local government had lost hundreds of thousands of dollars in tax revenues since the evacuation of Love Canal. The motivation for the project was, then, based on political and economic needs, not scientific assurances. Furthermore, opponents feared that the federal study, when it was released, would be a whitewash, watered down and sanitized by local and federal politicians.

On July 12, two days before the results of the EPA-sponsored study were to be released, New York State attorney general Robert Abrams released details of the 1980–81 state study that had discovered dioxin in the area, and which had not been fully released until now because the state was using it to pursue its lawsuit against Hooker. The levels of dioxin in abandoned homes (the original report had said there had been no dioxin in the homes) were "among the highest ever found in the human environment," the new portions of the report stated. The level, Mr. Abrams went on to say, was eight times greater than levels discovered in Seveso, Italy, after its chemical plant explosion (see pp. 85–89)—in the sumps of homes abutting the canal, dioxin levels ranged as high as 17.2 parts per million. (The chemical is known to be toxic to animals at levels as low as 0.0002 per million.)

This seemed to take the wind out of the sails of the revitalization movement.

But now the EPA study conducted by the Centers for Disease Control and two major national laboratories was released, and it contradicted the 1980 state study. It found "no increase in abnormalities" among 46 residents or former residents of the area surrounding the canal compared to 50 residents of a control area roughly a mile away.

"This suggests," concluded the study, "that no specific relationship existed between exposure to chemical agents in the Love Canal area and increased frequency of chromosome damage."

It went on to state that the study could find no firm evidence of increased disease incidence or mortality from cancer, birth defects, or other reproductive abnormalities.

"I'm horrified," said former Love Canal resident Barbara Quimby after the release of the report.

Homeowners Association head Lois Gibbs was less economical in her reaction. The study, she told reporters, "had been released deliberately to confuse and cause a smoke screen around the canal" in order to allow efforts to revitalize the area to proceed.

The Revitalization Commission was indeed vitalized by the report. But its good luck ran out swiftly. In July, the journal *Archives of Environmental Contamination and Toxicology* challenged the scientific validity of the EPA study, as did the Congressional Office of Technology Assessment.

Both challenges were based upon a four-year study of meadow voles, the field mice that lived near the now fenced-off Love Canal site. In it, the voles were found to have shortened life spans and organ damage similar to that caused by the kinds of toxic chemicals that had been dumped into the canal. The most severe contamination and health damage was found in mice that lived along the edge of the inner ring, an area accessible to children and pets living in the Emergency Declaration area, which Niagara Falls officials, energized by the EPA study, were hurriedly preparing for resettlement.

It was back to the drawing board, until September 27, 1983, when the EPA, agreeing that its findings in 1982 were incomplete (but not admitting any political reasons for them) announced that it had found unexpected leaking of chemicals at Love Canal. It would, said assistant administrator for solid waste and emergency response Lee Thomas, once again determine the habitability of the area. Its first report would be issued in March 1985, and assessment would continue into 1988. In the interim between 1982 and 1983, approximately 550 single-family homes, of which 150 were still occupied, and an apartment building were being cleaned up in preparation for what the Love Canal Revitalization Agency had hoped would be a clean bill of health. Using state and federal funds, the agency had bought 400 of the 550 homes. Now, once again, work was halted.

The new EPA announcement was based upon findings during the summer of 1983, of a "significant migration of chemicals" beyond a containment wall that Hooker said was impregnable. Now, Love Canal, with its 227 demolished homes in the most heavily contaminated zone, was becoming more and more of a ghost town, and local politicians, hoping for a resumption of tax revenues from the area, were growing increasingly nervous.

Their woes were compounded when, in December 1983, state investigators unearthed $5 million in overcharges by Newco Chemical Waste Systems of Buffalo, the company charged with cleaning up the site in 1978. There was, furthermore, evidence that Newco's contract was bought through former Niagara Falls city manager Donald J. O'Hara, and state attorney general Robert Abrams moved swiftly to sue both Newco and Mr. O'Hara for $15 million.

The evidence of collusion was overwhelming. Two months after the contract between the city of Niagara Falls and Newco was signed, Mr. O'Hara resigned his city post and moved to Florida, where, with a "loan" from Newco of

$8,500 and a guarantee by Newco of a $60,300 mortgage on a new home in Lake Park, he began work at a $40,000 job at the Heavy Equipment Leasing Services Company of Buffalo, a subsidiary of Newco. For two years, then, Love Canal had turned into a cash cow for Newco and Donald J. O'Hara.

Meanwhile, another lawsuit, that of the federal government against Hooker and Occidental Petroleum for cleanup of the so-called S-Area, near Love Canal, was settled with an agreement by the companies to spend $36 million in cleaning up the site, since, if left as it was, it threatened the drinking water of the entire city of Niagara Falls.

Questioned by reporters at the time, Richard J. Morris, the formerly exuberant director of the Love Canal Revitalization Agency, turned considerably pessimistic. It would take up to five years to complete the project, he said, "[And] when that's complete, we are talking about a long period of monitoring—maybe fifteen years, maybe three generations," he added.

The EPA released a further report in January 1984, stating that Hooker obviously knew about the presence of dioxin in the three dump sites in Niagara Falls from 1950 forward but did not reveal this until 1980. However, because of a change in wording in the disposal permit issued by the EPA, the company had not violated the law.

On and on the saga of Love Canal spun. In October 1984, the new depository sites for the contaminants from Love Canal were themselves found, by the EPA, to be leaking. Families who had moved from Love Canal to housing near the new site were called on to relive nightmares.

Finally, in December 1985, six years after it was filed, the lawsuit brought by 1,300 Love Canal families against the Hooker Company and Occidental Petroleum, the city of Niagara Falls, Niagara County, and the Niagara Falls school board, was settled. The federal court ordered the defendents to pay $20 million to the plaintiffs, who had charged that cancer, birth defects, emotional upset, and property damage had all resulted from negligence and collusion.

In February, the families lined up in the snow outside of a local bank to receive checks ranging from $2,000 to $400,000. Pat Brown, who had had two miscarriages and had given birth to a daughter with a number of abnormalities, reflected upon the bittersweetness of the settlement to Lindsey Gruson of the *New York Times*. "We still have all our children and our grandchildren to worry about," she said.

"They could give me the whole $20 million and it wouldn't compensate me for the mental anguish I face every time I look at my daughter," added Marie Pozniak, who had had several cancer operations. "I put a smile on my face and say it's okay. But deep down I'm scared."

It had been a long, bruising fight that would never really end. Lois Gibbs, for all her notoriety and efforts and worldwide television fame, had no more family. Her husband had been taunted by fellow workers at Hooker Chemical until he had lost his job, as had she. The marriage ended soon after.

None of those compensated would ever set foot in the Love Canal area again, though some few residents had, all along, continued to live in what had become a true 20th-century ghost town, overgrown, eerily still, and enclosed by a green cyclone fence.

To this day, the Revitalization Agency still survives, and as time extends itself, an increasing number of inquiries and down payments trickle in, asking for settlement in what is still an abandoned, unsafe area. When the agency attempted to sell some houses and erect a market, the state attorney general immediately sued the agency, stopping the transactions.

The mayor of the city of Niagara Falls, acknowledging that Love Canal had been an obstacle in his program of urban redevelopment, put a happy face on the $20 million settlement. "It's a milestone," he told reporters. "It ends the hysteria. That's all behind us now. We hope the younger generation doesn't remember Love Canal. We want them to remember us as the City of Romance, a great place to visit, a great place to have conventions, and a great place to live."

But the reality was visible to anyone who came near the former bustling suburb of Love Canal, now flattened by bulldozers and boarded up. In the end, Love Canal is a primer in the familiar pattern of industrial irresponsibility and governmental collusion that not only leads to but complicates the contamination of the earth through carelessly disposed wastes. Its legacy has been an awakened national concern about the dumping of toxic chemicals, and that concern is widely credited with bringing about the creation of state and federal Superfunds for toxic waste cleanup.

UNITED STATES
(OHIO, CLEVELAND)
CLEVELAND CLINIC EXPLOSION AND FIRE
May 15, 1929

One hundred and twenty-three patients, health workers, and rescuers died from carbon monoxide and nitrogen dioxide poisoning, released by the explosion and burning of 2 tons of X-ray film in the Cleveland Clinic on May 15, 1929. Hundreds more were injured.

A carelessly strung light bulb, an overheated steam pipe, and ignorance about the exact procedure for the safe storage of X-ray film combined to produce an explosion, a fire, and a tragic mass poisoning of patients, doctors, nurses, hospital aides, and rescuers in the famed and respected Cleveland Clinic on May 15, 1929.

"I never hope to look at anything so horrifying again," said fireman Louis Hildebrand, who had climbed to the roof of the burning clinic, and had a clear view down through a skylight to the stairwell below. "Lord help me," he continued, "as far down the stairway as you could see were bodies, bodies, bodies. Twisted arms and legs, screaming men and women. Bodies and screams."

It was a horror that, as in most terrible happenings, began peacefully and uneventfully. The clinic, founded in 1921 by nationally famous surgeon Dr. George W. Crile, who had discovered a cure for postsurgical shock, and other doctors who had served with Crile in France during World War I, was busily seeing to more than 200 chronically ill patients, some in beds, some on operating tables. More than 300 people were in the clinic that day, and among them was Bofferty Bogg, a steamfitter, who had been called in at 9:15 that morning to repair a leaking steam pipe.

The pipe was located in the basement, in a small, brick-lined room, off the furnace room. More than 75,000 pieces of X-ray film, with clinical notes attached to them, were stored in 300 pigeonholes, each about two feet on a side, and open to the air.

For four years, the small room had gradually been filling up with films put there by Enid Critcher, an X-ray technician charged with filing old films. Originally, it had been a dingy, unlit room, but, four months before the tragedy, Miss Critcher, in order to be able to see to file the film, either installed or ordered installed a bare bulb attached to an extension cord.

"I realized the danger from having it too close to the films," she later told investigators, "so I looped it over a spike which stuck out from the end of the filing cabinet and pulled it tight so that the bulb was in a slanting position to give more light."

Her motives were sound; the execution turned out to be less so. Sometime between the installation of the light and the explosion, the cord leading to the light, with its exposed and extremely hot bulb, loosened, and by the morning of May 15, the bulb was resting directly and dangerously on some of the X-ray film protruding from one of the pigeonholes.

But that was only one part of the cause of the catastrophe. The second cause was the overcrowded condition of the room. W. R. Yant, the supervising chemist of the United States Bureau of Mines estimated later that the amount of film stored in the small room was enough to generate approximately 1 million cubic feet of a variable mixture of nitrogen peroxide, carbon monoxide, and other gases—enough to kill 4 million persons in less than 20 seconds.

The third and final cause was the most obvious, and the only one at first cited by investigators. This was the steam released by the leaking steam pipe.

Bogg, called to the clinic that morning, traced the leak to the storage room and removed approximately 18 inches of the casing around the pipe. He reached out to touch the metal, and immediately retreated. It was too hot to handle, and so Bogg left the room in search of the clinic's chief engi-

neer, R. A. Mullinaux. Mullinaux was the only one who could shut off the steam to allow the pipe to cool enough to be repaired.

He found Mullinaux; the engineer agreed to turn off the steam, and Bogg went back to his shop.

He returned an hour and a half later, with an assistant. When he entered the room, he was momentarily taken aback. There was a cloud of escaped steam that was condensing into water droplets on the ceiling, but there was a plume of yellow smoke hugging the ceiling, too. It was still ungodly hot in the room, a situation that should have triggered the closing of a heavy metal fire door positioned at the storeroom's entrance. But for some reason, the automatic door failed to close.

It was not because of a lack of electricity. Just outside the storeroom door, the beginning of the clinic's ventilation system, a huge ceiling fan, was spinning at full speed, cooling the hallway and sucking some of the steam up through its vent, which led to the rest of the building. It would be a fatal selection of what worked and what did not work.

Bogg turned and walked to the boiler room, where he asked for a fire extinguisher. "When I got back in that storage room with my pal," he later told reporters, "I heard a sort of sputting hiss and up near the ceiling we saw a big patch of yellow stuff, probably four or five feet in diameter. It was sticky looking and puffs of yellow smoke shot out of it at intervals, going downward and then up as though it was lighter than air. . . ."

Bogg discharged the fire extinguisher, but it was already too late. Suddenly, there was a flash, and an explosion that felt, according to Bogg, "as if a million cushions hit you all at once." He and his companion were blown down the hall by its force. "Now the place got full of yellow smoke, and we couldn't see," he continued. "Finally, we found a window. Just then, a loud roar sounded behind us and the next moment we were lying outside."

The chemicals in the film, liberated by the combined heat of the light bulb and the steam pipe, had ignited; their mixture with air after the first small explosion in turn ignited the second, cataclysmic one. Bogg and his companion, crawling along the floor, stood up at that moment, and the concussion from the explosion blew them through the open window at the end of the corridor and into an alleyway.

That corridor had been instantaneously transformed into a blast furnace. The flames, the concussive force, and what was most lethal, the poisonous fumes from the films' chemicals shot up the ventilating ducts. The skylight and part of the roof were ripped asunder, and flew a score of feet into the air.

From cellar to roof, the clinic was converted instantaneously into a huge chemical retort, with a tumbling succession of chemical reactions, all taking place at once. Unstable organic compounds built up and broke down, in rapid succession, in rooms, in corridors, in the lungs and the

Explosion, fire, carbon monoxide, and nitrogen dioxide poisoning converged in an instant to document the price of carelessness and ignorance at the Cleveland Clinic. New standards for storing X-ray film resulted from the tragedy.
(LIBRARY OF CONGRESS)

bloodstreams of the persons breathing the noxious fumes. They fell where they stood, some poisoned by nitrogen peroxide, others by carbon monoxide, others by hydrocyanic acid and bromine gas. Not one of them was burned.

Others, the ones observed by Hildebrand, the horrified fireman, were saved momentarily by the rush of air from the exploded skylight, which had once allowed sunlight into the main stairwell, in front of the main elevator. Other panicked patients trampled each other on the stairs and died not from poisoning but from shock and the crushing weight of bodies piling up in the stampede toward the bottom of the stairwell.

Fire traveled through the ventilation system, too, bulging walls, blowing out windows, robbing some of the survivors of air. "I glanced over at the clinic and saw the roof lift as the explosion tore through," said F. B. Conklin, who was standing on his lawn a hundred yards away from

the clinic when the second explosion occurred. "The doors were hurled open and nurses in their white and blue dresses and patients fled screaming from the building. About a score of girls appeared at the first- and second-story windows and jumped to the ground.

"Pedestrians ran over to the building and caught some of the girls as they leaped. . . . Some limped away, but others apparently had broken ankles and legs and lay squirming where they fell.

"Everything was confusion. Flames shot from the windows. The screams of men and women rent the air. The whole building seemed to catch fire at once. Faces of men and women appeared at the windows, but some withdrew when the flames licked at them."

The force of the explosion burst windows and collapsed ceilings. Compression buckled steel doors. Most of the victims were trapped and asphyxiated, but others were crushed beneath heavy diagonistic apparatus or operating tables.

Firemen shot ladders to the roof of the clinic and lowered themselves through gaps in the roof and the smashed skylight. Some, donning oxygen masks, were able to enter the clinic, but most, even with masks, were driven away by the deadly fumes.

Fire chief James H. Flynn, surrounded by his men on the roof, looked down through a skylight at the other end of the clinic from the burst one. "I looked for signs of life and I saw one man struggling," he said. Flynn lowered himself on a rope, and pulled the man—Dr. J. L. Locke, the first to be rescued from the building—up through the skylight.

There were heroes who lived and those who died trying to save others. Dr. Wilson J. Pearl, the head of the dental clinic, was one who survived. The third floor was the scene of the worst carnage; bodies piled up at the entrance to the elevator. Patients in his clinic tried to make their way to the fatal stairwell. His technician and a girl elbowed their way through them, flung open the door, and dashed into the hallway. But Dr. Pearl managed to close the door behind them, and keep the rest of his patients and other health workers from leaving his suite.

He and Dr. Wallace Duncan of the orthopedic department opened the windows of the suite and kept hysterical patients from jumping before firemen reached them with ladders. All of the patients and workers who remained in the suite of offices survived; the bodies of the technician and girl were later found in the hall, steps away from the door.

Robert Chares, a huge and muscular laborer in a nearby car wash rushed to the scene and grabbed a ladder to rescue terrified patients who were at a second-story window. The ladder was too short. Undaunted, he lifted the ladder to his shoulders and held it while 10 people climbed down it to safety. When they were safe, he threw down the ladder, dashed into the building, and saved 10 more victims of the blast.

Others were less fortunate or hardy. Ernest Stabb, an emergency policeman, repeatedly battled his way into the gas-filled clinic, and pulled out 21 victims, some of whom died after he rescued them. As he was dragging the 21st person to safety, he collapsed and died himself.

"Don't have to do a thing for me," one man said to firemen as they put an oxygen mask over his face and attempted to clear his lungs. "The gas didn't bother me. Get the others who are dying."

Five minutes later, he collapsed, and firemen lifted him into an ambulance that left immediately for a hospital. He was dead before they reached it.

X-ray salesman Paul Roguemora of East Dallas, Texas, who had been in the building when the explosion occurred, worked side-by-side with firemen, pulling bodies and survivors from the wreckage.

"Better go to a hospital," one of the rescue squads told him, "You don't know what that gas can do."

He ignored them and worked for a few minutes more, then went to a hospital, where he requested treatment. Ten minutes later, he, too, was dead.

Through it all, clinic head Dr. Crile tended to the wounded and the dying, directing police and firemen in how to treat the afflicted. The next day, he would open the clinic in an empty schoolhouse across the street, paid for by a committee of 36 influential and wealthy men. By the end of the first day after the tragedy, Dr. Crile had removed six thyroid glands.

The rescue efforts went on into the night. The city morgue was filled to overflowing, and some doctors performing autopsies were overcome by the gases rising from the bodies. The local hospitals were packed, and they would be besieged by other victims who would become ill two and three days later.

The explanation for this would come weeks later, after an investigation by a commission headed by General Harry L. Gilchrist, chief of the U.S. Chemical Warfare Service. The investigation concluded that there were no wartime gases involved. Carbon monoxide and nitrogen dioxide suffocated those who died immediately. Those who collapsed and died hours or days afterward were victims of pneumonia, which resulted from lung edema brought on by the gas poisoning.

Fevered, condemnatory articles appeared in national publications regarding the tragedy. World War I, with its poison gas, was still fresh in the minds of a great many Americans, and Elvira Fradkin, a well-known and well-read advocate of the abolition of chemical warfare, published a long reaction to the explosion. "Once again humankind suffers a terrible lesson before preventable action is taken," she wrote. "The tragedy at Cleveland brings near to home the inescapable facts concerning poison gas. . . . Its wider implications must be explored, especially in the present and future of poison gas in warfare, so that the Cleveland tragedy will serve not only as a lesson to the world in handling X-ray films but also will bring home to all the imminent tragedy in store for us if the chemical warfare, so carefully developed, is persisted in.

"The warfare of the future will not be confined to trenches," Ms. Fradkin continued, with accuracy, then veered into speculation: "The whole area of the combatant territory will be the battleground, and all within that area will suffer untold agonies—untold as the Cleveland tragedy must remain untold, because they were killed who suffered most. Willie going to war will wear stiff oiled clothing, oiled gloves, and a gas mask, which he will not dare to take off. . . .

"There is only one grain of comfort for the combatants," she concluded, "by airplane attacks, defensive and offensive, the centres of civilization will be so quickly paralyzed that the war will be over before they get to the front."

The investigation, sticking to the facts, found no evidence of a link to military poison gas. "There has been a tendency to connect the accident at Cleveland with chemical warfare," the report stated. "It is important that our citizens should [sic] know that there is no connection with these gases formed by the burning of film and the agents used in chemical warfare."

The fire and explosion were blamed on both the gerry-rigged light bulb and the leaking steam pipe. "In the present investigation," the report stated, "it was ascertained that X-ray film can be ignited by coming into contact with a hot steam-pipe, with an electric light bulb, or in general by any source of heat that will raise the temperature of the film to about the boiling point of water for a considerable length of time. . . ."

No fire extinguisher could put out such a fire, the report stated, nor was there a gas mask that would have saved any of the victims, and no criminal act or negligence was found, since there were no building code regulations in Ohio regarding the storage of X-ray film.

As a result of the Cleveland disaster, new national regulations were instituted by the U.S. Senate, in a resolution introduced by Senator Royal Sami Copeland of New York, and states and municipalities throughout the country issued stiffer guidelines for the storage and manufacture of X-ray film.

One hundred and twenty-three died, most from suffocation. It was a lesson learned at an extraordinarily high price. "I really believe the people who died here must be regarded as sacrifices to experience rather than victims of negligence," concluded Major General Gilchrist, and his judgment was accepted.

UNITED STATES
(OHIO, CLEVELAND)
EAST OHIO GAS COMPANY EXPLOSION
October 21, 1944

One hundred twenty-nine people were killed by fire and toxic smoke when a holding tank of liquefied gas exploded on the afternoon of October 21, 1944, at the East Ohio Gas Company in Cleveland, Ohio. Nearly 200 were injured, and 1,500 were rendered homeless. More than 300 homes and offices were demolished, and the ultimate monetary cost was over $15 million.

In 1944, the East Ohio Gas Company maintained a storage and liquefying plant at the foot of East Sixty-second Street and the New York Central tracks in Cleveland, Ohio. Natural gas pumped into the plant over pipelines was converted to liquid and stored in four tanks containing a total of 300 million feet of liquefied gas.

At exactly 2:50 P.M. on October 21, 1944, one of these tanks exploded. The gas within it immediately caught fire, sending flames 2,800 feet into the air, and spewing choking, blinding fumes and smoke after them. Within minutes, a second tank, ignited by the fire from the first, blew up with a slightly less thunderous roar, and the flames, as if fanned by some inward wind, leaped outward, into the 50-block area of residences and offices surrounding the plant. It would, within the hour, become the worst fire in the history of Cleveland, a holocaust that turned the East Side of the city into a war zone.

Gas mains began to erupt, first in the plant and then, spreading like waves from a rock dropped in a lake, over a 30-block area adjoining it. Sheets of flame raced through the neighborhood, forcing motorists on Lake Shore Boulevard to abandon their cars and wade into Lake Erie. The police commandeered sound trucks and raced through the streets shouting a strident warning: "The neighborhood is on fire! Get out! Run eastward!"

If this technique was designed to avert panic, it didn't. Just the opposite occurred. Traffic was snarled as residents emptied houses and stores and ran through the streets, away from the advancing fire and smoke. New explosions punctuated the chaos, as water mains blew and manhole covers spiraled into the air. Fire raged through thickly populated neighborhoods, igniting building after building. Walls and roofs collapsed on residents frantically gathering their belongings in order to flee.

Every piece of fire equipment in the city and the neighboring suburbs was pressed into service. Firemen and police were supplemented by army, navy, and Coast Guard personnel stationed in the city. At least 50 ambulances, including army, navy, American Red Cross, police, and private vehicles were pressed into service. Every hospital in Cleveland rapidly filled with the injured and the dying.

The fire burned through the night, and small explosions still echoed through the district into the following afternoon. Soldiers armed with rifles and bayonets, armed naval militia and Coast Guardsmen patrolled the district as county engineers directed the search for bodies. Eighty men, formed into 20 four-man crews, worked with picks, shovels, and bulldozers.

It was a monumental task. Thirty businesses and more than 300 dwellings were leveled or so damaged that they would remain uninhabitable. Fifteen hundred residents were made homeless, and the Red Cross immediately set out to establish shelters in schools, churches, and meeting halls.

This was wartime, and the Red Cross had to obtain special shoe-ration stamps from the Office of Price Administration (OPA) in Washington, to clothe, and further food-ration stamps to feed 1,500 refugees three times a day. Agents of the Federal Bureau of Investigation descended upon the area to check the possibility of sabotage.

But apparently there was none. Although no conclusive reason was ever given for the blast, a spokesperson for the company gave the clearest indication of its origin the day after it happened. The "holder," as he put it, that exploded had developed a leak during tests immediately after its completion in May 1943. But, the spokesperson added, repairs were made and in subsequent tests it was judged to be satisfactory.

Apparently, satisfactory was not good enough.

When the body count was completed, 129 people were recorded to have died, and nearly 200 had been injured. The monetary damage totaled more than $15 million.

UNITED STATES
(PENNSYLVANIA, OAKDALE)
AETNA CHEMICAL COMPANY EXPLOSION
May 18, 1918

....

Two hundred and ten were killed, 400 were injured, and 31 were reported missing and presumed dead in an explosion in the Aetna Chemical Company plant in Oakdale, Pennsylvania, on May 18, 1918. The plant, which manufactured TNT, exploded in sections, burned for hours, and released a deadly and noxious cloud of gases that lingered for days over the countryside adjacent to the shattered plant.

Oakdale is a small town 16 miles from Pittsburgh on the Panhandle Division of the Pennsylvania Railroad. On the afternoon of May 18, 1918, a large parade of American Red Cross volunteers and officials marched in downtown Pittsburgh, in a patriotic show of resolve to end the war in Europe. The march never officially ended. Long before reaching its appointed conclusion point, all of the Red Cross personnel had broken ranks to care for scores of terribly wounded men being discharged from rescue trains, hastily put together to remove the dead and dying from one of the grisliest chemical explosions ever to occur in the eastern United States.

At noon, a sound not much more impressive than a pistol shot occurred in the Aetna Chemical Company's "soda house," where portions of chemicals that go into the formulation of TNT were mixed. The magnitude of the sound was unimportant; its implications were immediately apparent to the men who worked there, who rushed toward the nearest exits.

Most of them never made it. The space between the prelude and the explosion was only seconds long; the air in the soda house burst into flames, and with a horrendous roar that was heard for miles, all of the buildings in the complex suddenly catapulted skyward, carrying with them both men and equipment.

"I was sitting with two friends about a hundred feet from the TNT stock room," said one survivor, "when the blast came. I started up and up. I lost consciousness. When I hit the ground I came to. My two friends landed about a hundred feet from me. I got to my feet and was hurrying away when I came to an injured man. I put him on my back and started from the plant, when the second explosion occurred."

It was the second of many rapid-fire explosions that hurled iron girders, heavy machinery, walls, roofs, and rafters into the sky and rained them down on survivors frantically trying to flee the carnage.

Each time the flames reached a new tank of chemicals, a ground-rattling explosion would follow. Each explosion unleased a new cloud of noxious gas that spread out from the site and into the nearby valley and town. Firemen donned oxygen masks to penetrate the wreckage and try to control the flames, which now rose several hundred feet in the air.

A hellish heat drove back most rescuers; one group was caught at a small stream into which acid and oil had poured. It exploded as they crossed it, killing some of them and maiming the rest. Meryl Aschelman, a young nurse from New Philadelphia, Ohio, and a member of the staff of St. John's Hospital in Pittsburgh, was one of these. She lost a leg in her efforts to reach the wounded.

Telephone and telegraph wires were downed by the explosion, and the tracks of the Pittsburgh, Cincinnati, Chicago and St. Louis Railroad, which utilized the Panhandle, were blocked by falling debris. The wreck and relief trains were assembled in Carnegie, four miles away; ambulances were dispatched immediately from every hospital in Pittsburgh, and company guards and the country constabulary set up a cordon around the burning site, which continued to belch fire and gases, punctuated by repeated explosions.

Dr. J. A. Hanna, a Pennsylvania Railroad surgeon, who was in charge of the first relief train leaving the scene described it as a "living hell." Flames three and four hundred feet high shot into the air and seemed, according to the doctor, to be engulfing the town of Oakdale, though they never did. The train itself was forced to race through the flames to pass an unexploded tank of TNT.

Finally, at 6:30 P.M. one final, rending explosion scattered debris over a widening circle of destruction, blackening the countryside, but extinguishing some of the fire. The sickening brownish cloud of chemical pollutants failed to lift, and later that night, a detail of mine rescuers from the arsenal station of the United States Bureau of Mines arrived in Oakdale. Outfitted with oxygen helmets, they began to penetrate the dense cloud to search for survivors and to haul out bodies and pieces of bodies.

A morgue was set up in Oakdale, and late in the afternoon, Adam Partz, one of the coroner's workers collapsed. He had discovered, in a bundle of belongings, a ring of keys and a penknife that belonged to his son, a worker in the plant.

The cleanup was monumental and grim. Two hundred and ten persons died; nearly 400 were injured, some terribly, and 31 employees of the plant were never accounted for and presumably blown apart by the blast.

It was wartime, and the FBI and local police made the usual arrests of suspicious characters. Two men who were photographing the ruins and who were charged by a woman with making seditious remarks were arrested. Two more were arrested as they were about to hurry away from the plant on a motorcycle. Ultimately, the fire from an electrical short circuit was deemed to be the culprit.

UNITED STATES
(PENNSYLVANIA, PITTSBURGH)
EQUITABLE GAS COMPANY EXPLOSION
November 14, 1927

....

Twenty-eight residents of Pittsburgh, Pennsylvania, were killed, 600 injured, and 5,000 made homeless when workmen's torches ignited gas in a supposedly empty tank at the Equitable Gas Company on the morning of November 14, 1927.

Elwood Carroll, the foreman of a crew of 13 workmen, hired from the Riter Conley Company to perform repairs on the gigantic gas storage tank at the heart of the Equitable Gas Company works in Pittsburgh, turned to his father as he left for work on the morning of November 14, 1927. "That job is the worst I've ever been ordered out on," he said. "It's practically suicide to work on that tank with electric torches."

An hour later, Elwood Carroll and his entire crew would be dead, blown a hundred feet into the air and hundreds of feet away from the explosion that their torches ignited as they worked at the 208-foot-pinnacle of the largest natural gas reservoir in the world, the Equitable Gas Company's 5-million-gallon central tank.

The usual precautions had been taken before the workers mounted the girders surrounding the tank at 8:00 A.M. It had been drained of natural gas. Following this, air had been blown through it to purge it of any residual gas. Still, the workers, Carroll among them, were aware that even a minute amount of the inflammable fumes mixed in a ratio of 1 part gas to 8 parts air, could ignite. They were being paid well for their dangerous work, but this time, all of the pay in the world proved to be tragically useless.

At exactly 8:43 (clocks in the neighborhood stopped at that moment, pinpointing the time of the catastrophe), sparks from one of the workmen's torches ignited a tiny amount of gas, and the tank blew with a thunderous roar. It ascended like a balloon, and the fireball accompanying it shot a thousand feet into the air. Observers said it seemed to ascend higher than the tip of Mount Washington across the Ohio River from the scene. Two adjacent tanks, filled with gas, ignited, and their flames added to the inferno, spewing flame and choking black smoke over a square-mile area. Pieces of the steel framework descended like thousand-pound arrows, piercing roofs, walls, roads, and sidewalks. Water mains burst, flooding the area to the height of adult waists.

The plant was located on the north side of Pittsburgh, in a thickly populated section fronting on the Ohio River and centering in Reedsdale Street. One of the oldest districts in the city (the tank itself was erected in 1899), it was heavily built, with old-fashioned brick-and-frame dwellings crowding upon each other, interspersed by factories, warehouses, and industrial plants.

Engine Company Number 47, at Fulton Street, was in the midst of this. Firemen sitting in the station house were knocked to the floor by the blast, which blew out every window in the building. "The boys hurriedly regained their feet and leaped upon the already moving fire apparatus," said battalion fire chief Daniel Jones. "As we reached the street, great waves of black smoke swept up the street and there was a whining noise in the air."

The Pittsburgh Clay Pot Company was located directly across the street from the gas works. One hundred and forty men were at work when the explosion occurred. Immediately after the blast, only 40 of them could be found.

Sixteen hundred children in the Conroy public school were either in school, playing in the playground, or just arriving. Flying glass rained down on them like shrapnel, and many were severely cut.

Seconds before the blast, Patrolman Sylvester Stoehr, walking his beat, noticed a small boy playing on the bank of the Ohio River. The patrolmen had walked half a block past the boy when the tank blew. He turned and raced to the river, into which the unconscious child had been thrown and was now floating. The policeman tore off his coat, jumped into the river, and saved the boy.

Farther downtown, skyscrapers shuddered and moved as if an earthquake had struck. Weather forecaster W. S. Brotzman, whose office was on the 26th floor of the Oliver Building, noted that his barometer was forced upward five hundredths of an inch by the wave of air that struck the building.

Rescuers groped their way through the flames and heavy smoke that turned day into night. Dynamite was used by a team of rescuers to move the steel braces surrounding the exploded tank, and the team found three of the workmen who had been at the top of the tank, huddled together in death. Firemen following the rescuers ordered them out, as girders began to shift and pieces of flaming debris fell around them.

On the fringes of the blast area, survivors were pulled from beneath collapsed buildings and taken to hospitals. As night fell, thousands of homeless persons were cared for and fed in police stations, warehouses, and improvised barracks.

It would be a long time before the district returned to anything resembling order. Twenty-eight died, 600 were injured, and 5,000 were made homeless. A grand jury investigation found no neglect, merely bad luck in a dangerous job.

USSR
(UFA)
GAS PIPELINE EXPLOSION
June 3, 1989

A leak in a liquefied petroleum gas pipeline was ignited by a spark from a passing passenger train near Ufa, USSR, on June 3, 1989. The explosion killed 190 and injured 720. Another 270 were presumed dead.

Early in the morning of June 3, 1989, partway between the two Soviet cities of Asha and Ufa in the Ural Mountains of the USSR, a liquefied petroleum gas pipeline erupted. It was a Sunday morning, and the gas, which was being transferred from oil fields in Nizhnevartovsk to refineries in Ufa, was being monitored, presumably by a skeleton crew. Pressure gauges undoubtedly showed a drop in pressure, an indication of a leak. But for some unexplainable and unexplained reason, instead of investigating the leak, the pipeline operators on duty simply turned up the pumps, thus feeding a mixture of propane, butane, and benzene vapors into a ravine leading to a nearby railroad. By the time the vapors had settled into the valley surrounding the train tracks, they were composed mainly of methane, the highly volatile gas responsible for a multitude of mine explosions.

Shortly after this, two trains traveling in opposite directions between the Siberian city of Novosibirsk and the Black Sea town of Adler, passed each other in that ravine. The trains, loaded with vacationers, were not scheduled to pass at that particular point at that particular moment, but one was behind schedule, and as fate would have it, the two were parallel when they entered the valley. The heavy aroma of gas, hanging like a fog to the level of the train windows, became sickeningly apparent to the engineers of both trains as they sped through the pass.

Suddenly, a spark from one of the trains ignited the gas, which exploded with a deafening roar and bright orange flashes of flame. Its force—that of 10,000 tons of TNT—felled every tree within a three-mile radius and blew both locomotives and the 38 cars of the two trains completely off the tracks. Pieces of metal smashed windows. Fragments of bodies were blown in several directions.

A metal-melting fire instantly followed, incinerating the surviving passengers before they could extricate themselves from the mangled coaches.

Speaking later to Tass, the Soviet news agency, a Soviet army officer who was a passenger on one of the trains noted that he had been standing at an open window when he noticed the acrid petroleum smell coming from the gas leak.

"I sensed that something must be wrong," he said, "but before I could do anything there was a glow and then a thunderous explosion." The officer escaped from the burning car through a broken window.

Rescue squads immediately poured into the region from both Ufa and Asha, and surgeons, burn specialists, and medical supplies were airlifted from Moscow throughout the day and night. The final casualty count was appalling: 190 were known dead, at least 270 were missing and presumed dead, and 720 were injured seriously enough to be hospitalized.

THE WORLD
ACID RAIN CONTAMINATION
1852–Present

Acid rain, which results from the release of industrial and automotive pollutants such as sulfur dioxide, nitrogen oxide, and hydrocarbons into the atmosphere, threatens the very life-sustaining forces of Earth. Found in bodies of water, in soil, and on the leaves of trees and plants, acid depositions have the ability to disrupt entire ecosystems. Despite the seriousness of the situation, individual governments have busied themselves with more fingerpointing than cures.

Separating out the various stresses upon ecosystems created by pollution in the air is not easy, and the proponents of cleaning up the acid rain, as those who propose that the greenhouse effect is a great danger to the atmosphere (see pp. 126–28) have had to battle not only industry and government but also conflicting scientific theories about just what causes ecosystems to wither and die.

This is certain: Acid rain and acid deposits, drifting down from the atmosphere upon soil, lakes, plants, and forests have caused death and damage and will continue to do so if they proceed unchecked.

Their source is industrial and motor vehicle pollutants, mainly sulfur dioxide, nitrogen oxide, and hydrocarbons. When these pollutants react with sunlight and water vapor in the atmosphere, they create sulfuric and nitric acids. These acids in turn descend to Earth through wet deposition (rain, snow, fog, mist, or dew) or dry deposition (in gases or particulate matter). For the sake of simplicity, all of these depositions—wet or dry—have been collected under the general title of acid rain.

The first connection between air pollution and acid rain was made in 1852; by 1911, there was a report of a disruption of the nitrogen cycle in the soil by acid rain around the city of Leeds, England. In 1959, Norway announced to the world that a connection had been discovered between losses of fish from freshwater lakes and acid rain, and in 1968, Norwegian scientist Svante Oden extrapolated data and noted that acid rain knew no national boundaries; it migrated easily and naturally from polluting countries to nonpolluting countries. In the early 1970s, this was brought home to the United States by ecologist Gene Likens and his colleagues, who pointed at fossil-fuel combustion as a cause of acid rain in eastern North America.

While governments fritter and politicians argue, acid rain falls on the forests and fields of the world, causing immense disruptions in entire ecosystems, and making them more vulnerable to climate changes.
(VLADIMIRE ILICH NIESENBAUM/UNEP)

The effect of acid rain is precise and far reaching. It reduces soil fertility and releases heavy metals such as aluminum, copper, and cadmium into the soil, which hinder the growth of trees and crop plants. It attacks and corrodes buildings, bridges, and railroad tracks. It raises the acid levels in lakes and rivers, making them uninhabitable. In northeastern North America, Britain, and Scandinavia, a great number of lakes are already heavily acidified and have lost much of their former animal life, including valuable fish species such as trout.

Birds such as loons, the American black duck, and British breeding dippers that depend upon aquatic systems for their food supply are declining, and acidification is the cause. Other birds, such as the Netherlands' resident titmice, nuthatches, and great spotted woodpeckers, show the same sort of evidence of thinning eggs, crushed by incubating parents. The effects are the same as those that the overuse of DDT produced in the 1950s and 1960s.

Forests in Germany showed such extreme effects of acid rain in the late 1970s and 1980s that a word, *Waldsterben*—forest death—was coined to describe it. At present forests throughout central Europe are beginning to show symptoms of attack by acidification: a yellowing and dropping of needles and leaves and the ultimate death of the trees. Generally speaking, this has followed a long period of soil acidification that creeps into the roots of the trees and robs them of needed magnesium.

In the eastern United States, a marked deterioration of forests in areas in which a high degree of air pollution is present have also been detected, despite the general attitude of industry and politicians that other, natural forces are causing the decline.

In formerly Communist Central and Eastern Europe, where pollution controls have been nonexistent, the combined assault of industrial pollutants as well as acid rain have had devastating effects. In Czechoslovakia and the former East Germany, nearly 500 square miles of forest have disappeared or been so ravaged that only stands of dead and dying trees are left. And what is worse, where these forests are most damaged, the hydrologic cycle has been disrupted, allowing widespread flooding and erosion in the spring and water shortages in the summer.

Certainly, some soils are more vulnerable to the effects of acid rains than others. Generally, the more highly alkaline the soil, the less susceptible it is to acid rain. North America and central and southern Europe contain neutral and acidic soils and the air in these regions contains high emissions of sulfur dioxide and nitrogen oxide. Other parts of the world that will become more vulnerable as industrialization increases are southern China, equatorial Africa (particularly Nigeria), southeastern Brazil, northern Venezuela, and southwestern India.

Cures, beyond the obvious ones of decreasing pollutants in the atmosphere, are problematic. In Norway and Sweden, where more than half the lakes have become devoid of fish, and in Britain and North America, lime has been dumped into these lakes to reduce their acidity. The fishkill has not diminished, chiefly because the lime does not reach the inflow streams, were fish breed.

And so, these lakes are already affected, and perhaps beyond redemption, but what about the others? By the time they are contaminated, it may be too late to reverse the process.

The problem is exacerbated, and frustrating to ecologists, because probably no other source of ecological contamination has engendered more politically inspired problems than acid raid. It freely crosses national boundaries and pollutes where pollution does not originate, and does not pollute where it does.

Various European nations have pointed fingers at each other without lessening the problem. During the Reagan administration's years in the United States, the country stoutly refused to admit to Canada's charges that its lakes and forests were being contaminated with acid rain from America's industries. The U.S. government, at that time, consciously did nothing to inhibit industrial pollution. In 1984, Sweden and Norway formed the "30 Percent Club," which aimed at reducing emissions by at least that figure by 1993. Many countries joined, but four of the largest producers of acid rain—the United States, Britain, Spain, and Poland—refused.

Regimes do change. But the arguments persist, and while they do, so does the damage done by acid rain. It disrupts ecosystem processes, which cause losses of species and make the systems more vulnerable to climate changes.

There is interaction between acid rain and the production of greenhouse gases, too. Deposits of nitrogen compounds in air pollution can lead to accelerated releases of nitrous oxides from soils while reducing these soils' ability to absorb methane. The result: greenhouse gases ascending into the atmosphere.

Perhaps the growing awareness that acid rain can be an economic as well as an ecological disaster will bring about more action on the parts of the governments of the world. For instance, in 1990, the International Institute for Applied Systems Analysis determined that if emissions of sulfur and nitrogen compounds are not sharply reduced, acid rain will cost Europe some 118 million cubic meters of wood, worth about $30 billion per year, for the next century.

The cost is equal to two and a half times as much as European governments have so far agreed to spend annually to abate air pollution, and with increased industrial production and population growth, the conclusions are probably conservative. If they are, the ability of the earth to sustain life will be severely threatened.

There are positive signs, subject to political revision as governments rise and fall. In the United States, for instance, the Bush administration did what it could to reverse some of the damage to the environment brought about by the laissez-faire approach of the previous administration, and a new amendment to the Clean Air Act was passed in 1990 to strengthen the nation's ability to reduce air pollution. Aimed at both ozone depletion and acid rain, it decreed that all production of chlorofluorocarbons (CFCs), the cause of ozone depletion, must be ended by the year 2000. Other ozone-damaging chemicals were put on a phase-out schedule. Sulfur dioxide emissions were to be reduced by half by 1995 and total emissions from all power plants halved by 2000, after which a cap on total emissions would apply. And oxides of nitrogen emissions from stationary sources and vehicles were to be reduced by half or more by 2000.

All of this constitutes a step in the right direction, though its relatively modest demands are currently, as of this writing, under attack by a U.S. Congress heavily pressured by industrial lobbies. By 1997, a new phrase had crept into the national vocabulary: "pollution politics." At the end of June 1997, Gail McDonald, president of the Global Climate Coalition, a euphemism for an industry group dead set against Clean Air Standards, noted publicly that she and her group were ". . . encouraged by the fact that President Clinton seems to be taking a slightly more cautious approach to climate issues than he appeared to be taking several months ago.

"There are many vested interests pushing very hard for an agreement that would have dire consequences for the economy," she concluded, obviously targeting environmental groups and using industry's prevalent argument, an argument that has apparently worked.

In the United States, industry has prevailed. Energy taxes to lower fuel consumption and regulations to enforce fuel-efficiency on automakers have fallen out of favor, and an economic boom that has outpaced and diminished industrial energy efficiency may be largely to blame. Add to this an echoing boom in the sale of gas-guzzling sports-utility vehicles (mostly used for neither) and it seems that the United States is likely to increase emissions of carbon dioxide by 13 percent by the end of the decade of the 90s. It will be just the reverse of what it promised in Rio de Janeiro.

It isn't all bleak. There is some effort in the world toward wider use of photovoltaic solar cells, electric cars, fuel cells that run on hydrogen, and other energy efficient methods of locomotion, motor movement, and production. But this experimentation has failed to have any noticeable impact on the hunger and demand for fossil fuels. At least not yet, and the contentions that crackled through the Kyoto convocation in December 1997 proved it. Economic considera-

Too much industrial burning of fuels and dumping of waste foul the atmosphere and contain the potential of creating uninhabitable wastelands in vast parts of the world.
(UNEP)

tions have, because of intense lobbying and campaigning by the interest groups that will benefit from continued fossil fuel consumption and the status quo in clean air standards, remained in control.

But the clock is ticking. Unless the Clean Air Act in the United States and other models like it in the rest of the industrialized world are put in place and kept in place, and unless new technologies are developed soon to improve the air quality of the earth, the consequences could be catastrophic.

THE WORLD
GLOBAL WARMING/THE GREENHOUSE EFFECT
Prehistory–Present Day
....

Global warming, through the burning of fossil fuels and their release of the greenhouse gases of carbon dioxide, nitrous oxide, chlorofluorocarbons, ozone, and methane into the atmosphere is already under way, according to scientists who subscribe to the greenhouse effect theory. There is resistance from governments and industry, and conflicting solutions to the problem. Meanwhile, the earth grows warmer.

When, on June 10, 1991, in the greatest volcanic eruption of this century, Mount Pinatubo blew part of the Philippine Islands asunder, approximately 15 million tons of sulfur dioxide were catapulted into the atmosphere. Once elevated, these tons of sulfur dioxide were converted into aerosol droplets of sulfuric acid, which remained in the sky, circling Earth, for three years. That, plus the volcanic ash that the mountain released during the three days of its repeated eruptions reflected the sun's rays away from the earth, cooling it as much as it had heated up in the previous 100 years.

To the critics of scientists who have warned of the greenhouse effect, which our reliance upon the burning of the fossil fuels oil, coal, and natural gas has caused, this was proof that the earth merely goes through a series of heating and cooling cycles and that such meetings as the Sundance Conference, convened in Utah in 1988 to warn of imminent global warming, were nothing but gatherings of misguided scientists, celebrities, and world politicians such as Norway's Prime Minister Gro Harlem Brundford and the United States's vice president Albert Gore.

The controversy rages, as industry and conservative politicians line up with the naysayers, and environmentalists and world governments align themselves with the doomsayers. Still, the fact remains, as it did in 1896, when Swedish scientist Svante Arrhenius first warned of the effect that carbon dioxide might have upon world temperature, that the earth does warm, and that levels of carbon dioxide, plus methane, nitrous oxide, chlorofluorocarbons, and ozone in the atmosphere do influence it. The predominant present thinking, as of 1998, is that, indeed, this

warming is taking place and that it is not a mere cycle in the evolution of Earth, but a product of the activity of human beings, burning fossil fuels and burning off tropical rain forests.

The prognostication is that before the end of the next 40 years, which is easily within the life spans of many of us, the climate of the earth could be warmer than it has been at any time in the past thousand years. By the middle of the next century, which would be within the lifetimes of our children, or certainly of their children, it is possible that the earth will be warmer than it has been at any time in the past 125,000 years.

Decades are, of course, mere eyeblinks in geologic time. Still, if the prognosticators are correct, the present rate of warming brought about by the greenhouse effect—that is, the trapping of radiant heat within a shield of carbon dioxide, much the way that heat is trapped inside a greenhouse or an automobile on a summer day by glass—could cause catastrophic results such as those already making themselves felt by extremes of weather—more hurricanes, more rain, more heat.

To understand this it is necessary to understand the way the earth is warmed. Energy from the sun is absorbed as heat by the earth, and this heat is bounded back, or radiated, toward its source, the sun. However, most of the radiated heat does not reach the sun but rather is bounced back to the earth because of the presence of carbon dioxide and methane in the lower atmosphere. These so-called greenhouse gases are necessary. Without their ability to prevent the escape of radiated energy, the surface of the earth would be a chill minus 65 degrees Fahrenheit.

For thousands of years, this preventive, gaseous greenhouse has remained fundamentally constant. The carbon dioxide balance has been maintained by the absorption of the carbon dioxide by phytoplankton in the sea and trees in the forests. However, in the last 100 years, since the Industrial Revolution, forests have been cleared and seas have become polluted, and concentrations of carbon dioxide in the atmosphere have increased dramatically, from 250 parts per million to 370 parts per million. In the same time span, global temperatures have risen by 3 degrees Fahrenheit, and many scientists perceive an undeniable link between the two.

If the present trend continues—and allowing for momentary disruptions like the three-year respite caused by the eruption of Mount Pinatubo—carbon dioxide levels could reach 500 parts per million by the middle of the 21st century. This could mean a rise in temperature of from 3 to 8 degrees Fahrenheit—an increase in temperature that has not occurred since the ending of the last ice age, between 10,000 and 18,000 years ago. And what is more dramatic and disturbing is that the present cycle of warming will take place from 10 to 100 times faster than the warming trend that produced the melting of the last world-consuming glaciers.

The 15 million tons of sulfur dioxide catapulted into the atmosphere by the eruption of Mount Pinatubo in 1991 cooled the world for three years, and nonbelievers in global warming were heartened. The cooling didn't last.
(ROBERT T. WELLS/UNEP)

In January of 1996, the British Meteorological Office and University of East Anglia issued a report stating that the years 1991 through 1995 were warmer than in any similar five-year period, including the two half-decades of the 1980s, the warmest decade on record up to that time. And this included the three years of cooling that Mount Pinatubo's eruption caused. And this appeared to be just the beginning. The years 1995–97 were, taken together, the hottest since records were first kept in 1856.

In 1995, an iceberg the size of Rhode Island broke off from the polar cap and floated northward, and flowers bloomed on it. Seas rose, inundating the shores of southern California and killing off huge amounts of fish-sustaining plankton. Floods raged across northern Europe. Eleven hurricanes—the most since 1933—roared through the Caribbean. More than 800 died in a heat wave that roasted the Midwest. London had its hottest summer in 200 years. Siberia was a full 5 degrees Fahrenheit hotter than normal.

Northeast Brazil had its worst drought of the century, and the worst winter rains in memory. While snow fell as far south as Florida, Alaska's tundra was visible in January.

And so it went. "The more rapidly we force changes in the [climate] system," said climatologist Stephen Schneider of Stanford University in January 1996, "the more likely it is to exhibit inscrutable behavior."

To some meteorologists, the current behavior of the climate is far from inscrutable. Since hurricanes derive their energy from heat, a warmer world will naturally spawn more—and more intense—hurricanes. The heating of the oceans also releases more water into the air in the form of evaporation. And when the water vapor condenses, becoming liquid again, the process releases heat. Thus, the warm moist air that feeds rainstorms in the summer and blizzards in the winter parks itself over the larger seas, delivering rain or hurricanes or cyclones when a warm air mass merges with them and snow when cold air does. "The greenhouse effect alters the probabilities [for storms]," said James E. Hansen, the director of NASA's Goddard Institute for Space Studies to *Newsweek* magazine in early 1996. "In that sense, the greenhouse effect is changing our climate now."

Mr. Hansen has long been a proponent of the greenhouse theory, and in December 1995, he was joined forcefully by the Intergovernmental Panel on Climate Change (IPCC), sponsored by the United Nations. The IPCC forecast a rise of temperature of 1.8 to 6.3 degrees Fahrenheit by 2100. Kuwait and China, who have heretofore resisted even mentioning the greenhouse effect, since their economies depend upon oil and coal, concurred.

And so the scenario seems to be gaining more and more substance. If all goes as it seems to be going, rainfall will increase over moist areas, like coasts, and be rarer in the interiors of continents. "As you get more global warming," says Mr. Hansen, "you should see an increase in the extremes of the hydrologic cycle—droughts and floods and heavy precipitation."

As global warming continues, melting will take place at the polar icecaps, and glaciers will turn liquid, thus causing the sea level to rise by between 2.6 and 6 feet, which could be disastrous for such low-lying countries as Bangladesh, the Netherlands, and many Pacific islands.

Ocean currents could change, thus causing stormier seas and rainfall or flooding where it has not occurred before. The Pacific Ocean current known as El Niño, which brings torrential rain to the Southeastern United States and unusual heat to the Pacific Northwest has already increased its effect. Global warming, according to Kevin Trenberth of the National Center for Atmospheric Research, has made and will continue to make El Niño effects stronger and more frequent.

The repeated, calamitous floods and storms that ravaged the California coastline and tracked across the United States from west to southeast during the first half of 1998 form a grim testament to the power of natural phenomena that are sensitive to the changes in atmospheric and ocean currents that can be—and possibly already have been—brought about by the greenhouse effect.

Since the warming would take place far more dramatically toward the poles than at the equator, the world's ecology would change. Tundra might replace forests, causing drought in farmlands and improving growing conditions in the tropics.

On the other hand, there are stabilizing influences in the atmosphere, and their role in global warming has not been entirely assessed—which gives those who minimize or chastize those scientists who warn of global warming and urge preparation now much comfort and some ammunition.

For instance, since 1990, the cooling effect of sulfates, which are released into the air when dirty high-sulfur coal and other fuels are burned, has been noted by the Global Climate Coalition, an industry-sponsored group fighting efforts to require cuts in the emissions of carbon dioxide by industry.

Furthermore, it is known that the seas absorb up to 50 percent of the carbon dioxide created by humans, and this might counteract global warming. Also, a warming sea might encourage greater photoplankton growth, which would trap and absorb even more carbon dioxide. And, even if this didn't occur, say scientists and governments in opposition to the greenhouse effect theory, the increased evaporation in a warmer world would create clouds, which would also have a cooling effect.

Still, the predominance of evidence seems to point toward an inevitable warming of the world at an increasingly rapid rate if we continue our industrial habits as we have for the past 100 years.

In light of this, the 1992 Earth Summit in Rio de Janeiro brought national governments together to plan a scenario that could avoid cataclysm. The developed nations, which produce three-fourths of the world's pollution, are depending upon new technology—solar power and hydrogen, for instance—to reduce or reverse global warming.

Progress is often slow. Immediate steps, like an energy tax or government regulations to force industry to burn fewer fossil fuels are dangerous politically, since they might reduce the standard of living and/or increase prices for voters. And so, the United States, for instance, is relying upon industry to voluntarily reduce emissions by using less energy or making more fuel efficient cars, etc.

Developing nations, on the other hand, add an entirely different complication. In a changeover from agrarian to industrial economies, much as the developed nations did at the beginning of the Industrial Revolution, these countries argue that their increasing populations make it impossible for them to either halt or slow industrialization. They lack both the money and the resources to develop clean technology, and they need to earn currency from their forests and other natural resources and cannot afford largescale replanting schemes.

But the 1992 Earth Summit, although acknowledging the catch-22 situation of many countries and the political ramifications that global warming implies, agreed to a multinational pledge to cut releases of greenhouse gases so that emissions in the year 2000 will not exceed those of 1990.

It is an admirable, reachable pledge, but there is still enough opposition to it to probably prevent it from occurring—a situation that scientists like Dr. Hansen find, at the very least, uncomfortable. Time is running out, Dr. Hansen told reporters in January of 1996. "The climate system is being pushed hard enough that change will become obvious to the man in the street in the next decade," he added. And that, he concluded, might make us more serious about meeting our responsibilities in avoiding potential chaos, disruption, and destruction.

THE WORLD

OZONE LAYER DEPLETION

1928—Present

The assault upon the ozone shield that keeps cancer-causing, agriculture-crippling, and potentially blinding ultraviolet radiation from reaching the earth has been increasing since the discovery of chlorofluorocarbons (CFCs) in 1928. However, since the signing and implementation of the Montreal Protocol, industry and governments have cooperated in reversing the destruction, which could have become catastrophic.

Chlorofluorocarbons, or CFCs, were invented, more or less by accident, in 1928 and immediately put to use as a coolant in refrigerators. From 1950 forward, CFCs served primarily as propellants in aerosol cans, and with the advent of the computer, their use widened still further (as solvents they were ideal because they cleaned, without damage, the plastic mountings of delicate circuitry). And with the advent of fast food, their use was expanded still further. They were necessary in the blowing up of the foam for polystyrene cups and hamburger cartons.

There is an amazing and indestructible stability about CFCs, which makes them enormously useful on Earth and enormously destructive in the stratosphere. Unchanged, they drift upward, where intense UV-C radiation severs their chemical bonds, releasing chlorine, which strips an atom from each ozone molecule, turning the ozone into ordinary oxygen, thus causing a hole in the thin but necessary ozone layer.

The ozone layer is actually a wall of poison that has been safeguarding the earth for thousands of years by protecting it from ultraviolet radiation, which emanates from the sun. In fact, ozone, a form of oxygen with three atoms rather than two, is, because of its extra atom, poisonous enough to be lethal if inhaled.

It does exist near the earth's surface, as a pollutant. Chemical smog contains ozone, and so does acid rain. But in the stratosphere, it becomes a fragile and thin shield, no thicker than a shoe sole, stretching around the earth. Vulnerable to destruction by natural compounds containing nitrogen, hydrogen, and chlorine, it has a singular effect upon ultraviolet rays: The shorter the wavelength of ultraviolet radiation, the greater the harm it can do to life, but the better it is absorbed by the ozone layer.

UV-A, the sort of ultraviolet light that bakes us in summer and that causes the insidiously destructive tanning we now regard as ultrafashionable, is relatively harmless, and is almost entirely allowed through. However, in the middle wavelength is UV-B, less lethal than UV-C, but damaging enough, in combination with UV-A, to cause non-melanoma skin cancers and a rare but virulent cutaneous malignant melanoma. The ozone layer absorbs most of this UV-A–UV-B combination. UV-B, ultraviolet radiation,

and clouds and tropospheric pollution screen out what it does not absorb.

However, as the ozone layer is destroyed, more UV-B gets through, and, in a perverse equation, as ground-level pollution is cleaned up, still more UV-B reaches and threatens human life on Earth.

By the year 2000, scientists predict that the summertime loss of the ozone layer in the mid-latitudes will be 5 to 10 percent, a situation that would lead to about a 26 percent increase in the incidence of skin cancer.

An increase in UV-B in combination with UV-A reaching the earth would also lead to the following:

1. Increased incidents of eye damage, including cataracts, deformation of the eye lens, and oldsightedness. A 1 percent decrease in protection by the ozone

A nightmare vision of a future with an unbreathable atmosphere is, fortunately, being ameliorated by clean air laws. But the pace toward less pollution is a slow one, made tortuous by industrial and governmental forces that profit from processes that produce a fouling of the air we breathe and the earth that supports us.

(ANATOLY SHDANOW/UNEP)

shield may result in 100,000 to 150,000 additional cases of cataract blindness worldwide.

2. A suppression of the body's immune system. This would be particularly devastating in developing countries, where the population depends upon immunization programs to maintain a minimum health level.

3. Changes in the chemical composition of several species of plants, which would result in decreased crop yields and damage to forests. Among the most vulnerable crops are those related to peas and beans, melons, mustard and cabbage; the quality of tomatoes, potatoes, sugar beets, and soya beans is also affected by UV-B.

4. Damage to ocean life, which carries with it an enormous number of echoes: Most obviously, UV-B works destructively on aquatic organisms to a depth of 20 meters (66 feet) in clear waters. It particularly affects small creatures such as plankton, fish larvae, shrimp, crabs, and aquatic plants. But this is only part of the story. These creatures and organisms form part of the marine food web, and a decrease in their numbers might, in turn, lead to a decrease of fish up the food chain. And this, in turn, would be particularly damaging to countries that rely heavily on fish as an important source of food.

   Furthermore, a decrease in the number of small marine phytoplanktons would rob the oceans of their ability to function as carbon dioxide sinks. Without them, there is the potential of an increase in carbon dioxide in the atmosphere, which in turn would cause global warming (see pp. 126–28).

5. Materials used in buildings, paints, and packaging would also be degraded by ozone depletion and a consequent increase in UV-B.

6. And finally, the already oppressive photochemical pollution brought about by automobile exhaust fumes and industrial emissions, and now potentially bombarded by more ozone, would become extreme enough to affect human health, damage crops, and disrupt ecosystems, even more than it already does.

As new chemical compounds are developed and old ones used in greater profusion, the ozone layer is subjected to increased assault. The process is straightforward and relentless: The stable structure of CFCs, which makes them immensely useful on Earth, allows them to drift, unchanged, upward into the stratosphere, where, as explained earlier, the intense UV-C radiation severs their chemical bonds, releasing chlorine, which strips an atom from the ozone molecule, turning it into ordinary oxygen.

The chlorine acts as a catalyst, accomplishing this destruction without undergoing any permanent change

itself, so it can go on repeating the process, over and over and over. Every CFC molecule thus destroys thousands of molecules of ozone.

And although this is the largest threat to the ozone layer, it is by no means the only one. There are small assaults, such as the release into the stratosphere of nitrogen oxides and chlorine by supersonic aircraft and the space shuttle, and the presence of methyl bromide, used as a multipurpose fumigant and in some chemical processes and organic synthesis. Because organic synthesis happens in natural processes and has for thousands of years with virtually no effect upon the ozone layer, it, too, has a minimal effect. And nitrous oxides released by nitrogenous fertilizers and by burning coal and oil, while long-lived and destructive, are by themselves not catastrophe-causing—though their cumulative effect is obviously dangerous.

But there are other highly perilous substances and processes. Methyl chloroform, largely used for cleaning metal, is less of a threat to the ozone layer than CFCs, but its danger lies in its proliferation: its use is doubling every decade. Carbon tetrachloride, used in firefighting, pesticides, dry cleaning, and grain fumigation is slightly more damaging than CFCs.

And then there are halons, which are similar to CFCs in structure, but which contain bromine atoms rather than chlorine and are considerably more dangerous to ozone than CFCs. Used mainly as fire extinguishing agents, they are benign to people on Earth escaping from burning buildings, but concentrations of them in the stratosphere have the same effect as CFCs on the ozone layer, and—what is most important—their concentration doubles every five years.

New strains of CFCs are being discovered, and they also multiply the longer they live. Concentrations of CFC 11

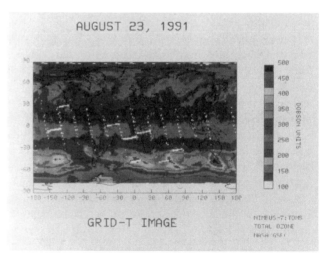

A NASA satellite image indicates progressive and widespread ozone damage to the atmosphere.

(NASA/GREENPEACE)

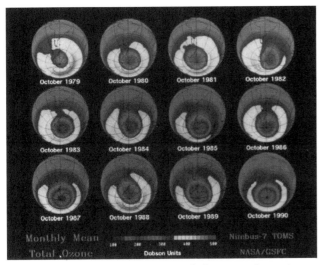

NASA charts show progressive ozone depletion over Antarctica from October 1979 to October 1990. Prohibition of the use of chlorofluorocarbons and methane in some countries has shrunk the hole in the atmosphere.

(NASA/GREENPEACE)

doubles every 17 years and lasts for an average of 74 years in the atmosphere. CFC 12 doubles every 17 years and lasts for 111 years. Concentrations of CFC 113 double every 6 years and last for 90 years. And halon 1301 lasts an average of 110 years. Thus, all of these compounds have the potential of eating away at the ozone layer for generations.

The most dramatic manifestation of this has been the so-called Antarctic Hole—one of the starkest examples yet of man's interference with the natural atmosphere. Every southern spring, a hole as big as the United States and as deep as Mount Everest occurs in the ozone layer over Antarctica. Visible and noticeable since 1979, it has appeared every year except 1988.

It grew to its largest circumference, from an average 17 million square miles to 23 million square miles in 1992, probably, say researchers, because of the explosion of Mount Pinatubo, which increased ozone destruction by CFCs enormously. Some stations reported complete destruction of the layer between the heights of 8.7 and 12.4 miles.

The importance of the Antarctic Hole has not yet been assessed, but it has been proved beyond a doubt that it is caused by CFCs, as are other reported thinnings of the ozone layer. In January 1993, for instance, the amount of ozone over the entire 45 degrees to 65 degrees northern latitudes belt was 12 percent to 15 percent below normal. And during most of February 1993, levels over North America and most of Europe were 20 percent below normal.

Further observations show that the depletion of the ozone layer is increasing in all latitudes except over the tropics, that the overall decline in the layer is about 3 per-

cent per decade, and that the decrease was greater in the 1980s than in the 1970s.

Researchers estimate that if emissions of CFC and halons continue to grow as they have in the past, the ozone layer will be depleted by roughly 20 percent within the lifetimes of today's children. Just half this loss would cause 1.5 million extra deaths from skin cancer and 5 million extra cataract cases in the United States alone.

What, then, is to be done?

Since 1974, and the Stockholm United Nations Conference on the Human Environment, there has been an increased awareness of and concentration on reversing the potentially catastrophic depletion of the ozone layer. The first conference focused its attention on damage done by supersonic aircraft, space flights, and the release of nitrous oxides from fertilizers. It was a small but necessary beginning.

In March 1977, the World Plan on Action on the Ozone Layer was adopted after a meeting in Washington, D.C., of experts from 32 countries. The conference resulted in the immediate banning by the United States, and later Sweden, Norway, and Canada, of aerosols, which at that time accounted for half the total global use of CFCs. (Non-aerosol uses of CFCs 11 and 12, however, began to rise at the beginning of the 1980s.)

In March 1985, the Framework Convention for the Protection of the Ozone Layer was adopted in Vienna. The convention was designed to produce "cooperation between nations for scientific research and observation to improve world understanding of atmospheric processes. . . ." Most important, it provided for future protocols and specified procedures for amendment and dispute settlement.

In September 1987, the most important document in the protection of the ozone layer was signed. The Montreal Protocol on Substances that Deplete the Ozone Layer called for a 50 percent reduction in the production and consumption of specified CFCs by 1999 and a freeze on the consumption of halons.

Subsequent meetings adjusted the protocol. In June 1990, in a London gathering, the schedules were adjusted so that the five CFCs and three halons initially included would be phased out by 2000, other fully halogenated CFCs and carbon tetrachloride were to be controlled and eventually phased out by 2000, and methyl chloroform would be controlled, then phased out by 2005.

As it became apparent that ozone depletion was accelerating, other meetings were held, and in the Copenhagen gathering in November 1992, an agreement was signed to phase out all CFCs, carbon tetrachloride, and methyl chloroform by 1996, halons by 1994, methyl bromide by 1995.

New technologies have been developed by industry, some of it independent and prefiguring the various international conventions and protocols. Aerosols, the worst offenders in ozone depletion, have been replaced by hydrocarbons, deimethyl ether, and compressed gases, by finger pumps, trigger pumps, and mechanical pressure dispensers.

In drycleaning, aqueous cleanings, hydrocarbons and chlorinated solvents have made their appearances, and in the solvent industry, "no clean" processes, aqueous cleanings, hydrocarbons, and chlorinated solvents have come into being.

In firefighting, halon replacement chemicals have been developed, as well as inert gas mixtures. Water mist technology, fine particulate technology, water sprinklers, carbon dioxide systems, foam systems, and dry powder systems have been introduced.

Hydrocarbons are now used in domestic refrigeration; hydrocarbons and ammonia are used in commercial refrigeration; and hydrocarbons have been introduced in mobile air-conditioning.

By May 1996, it was reported that the quantity of ozone-destroying chemicals in the atmosphere had, for the first time, declined, which meant that by the end of the decade, ozone destruction should peak, provided there are no major volcanic eruptions before then.

"This is the very beginning of a change," said Dr. Stephen A. Montzka of the National Oceanic and Atmos-

pheric Administration to the Associated Press. "This is the first step toward the goal of closing the ozone hole [in the Antarctic]."

The optimistic report was based on developments since 1993, when U.S. government scientists reported a reversal in the buildup of industrial chemicals responsible for ozone depletion. Extensive and comprehensive ground-level measurements on three continents and on two Pacific islands detected reduction in chlorine concentrations. The conclusion was that residual destructive elements should cause a peak of ozone destruction in the stratosphere sometime between 1997 and 1999, followed by a slow recovery of the ozone shield.

"A detectable signal for ozone recovery is expected around 2005 or 2010," continued Dr. Montzka.

However, Dr. Montzka cautioned that the presence of CFC 12, which is the CFC that is most commonly used in cooling compressors, continues to increase, presumably because many old refrigerators and air conditioners still in use contain CFC 12, and the chemical itself has an atmospheric lifetime of more than a century.

However, he concluded, so long as most countries observe the restrictions of the Montreal Protocol, the worst seems to have passed, and the decline in the assault upon the ozone shield will continue.

OIL SPILL DISASTERS

Brazil
* Cubatão (oil pipeline explosion) (1984)

Canada
* Nova Scotia, Port Hawkesbury (*Arrow* oil spill) (1970)
* Thousand Islands (see United States, New York)

France
* Portsall-Kersaint (*Amoco Cadiz* grounding) (1978)

Ireland
River Mersey (barge oil spill) (1989)

Italy
* Gulf of Genoa (*Haven* burning) (1991)

Lithuania
* Klaipeda (*Globe Asimi* foundering) (1982)

Mexico
* Campeche Bay (Ixtoc 1 oil platform blowout) (1979)

Norway
Alesand (*Arisan* grounding) (1992)
* North Sea (oil rig blowout) (1977)

Russia
* Usnisk (oil spill in the Arctic) (1994)

Saudi Arabia
* Dhahran (oil field fire) (1977)

*Detailed in text

Spain
* La Coruña (*Aegean Sea* grounding) (1992)

Tobago
* Coast (*Atlantic Empress* and *Aegean Captain* collision) (1979)

United Kingdom
* England, Cornwall (*Torrey Canyon* oil spill) (1967)
Scotland
  * North Sea (Piper Alpha oil rig explosion) (1988)
  * Shetland Island (*Braer* grounding) (1993)
* Wales, Milford Haven (*Sea Empress* grounding) (1996)

United States
Alaska
  * (Trans-Alaska Pipeline explosion) (1977)
  * Valdez (*Exxon Valdez* grounding) (1989)
California
  * San Francisco (*Arizona Standard* and *Oregon* collision) (1971)
  * Santa Barbara Channel (oil platform spill) (1969)
* Florida, St. Petersburg (*Delian Apollon* oil spill) (1970)
Gulf of Mexico (oil platform blowout) (1974)
* Hawaii, Honolulu (*Hawaiian Patriot* explosion) (1977)
* Louisiana, Gulf of Mexico (oil platform fire) (1970)
* Massachusetts; Nantucket (*Argo Merchant* oil spill) (1976)
* Midway Island (*Irenes Challenger* breakup) (1978)
* New York, Thousand Islands (St. Lawrence Seaway barge spill) (1976)
* Pennsylvania, Pottstown (oil spill in Schuykill River) (1972)

◆ ◆ ◆ ◆ ◆

CHRONOLOGY

◆ ◆ ◆ ◆ ◆

1967
* United Kingdom: England, Cornwall, *Torrey Canyon*
oil spill

1969
* USA: California, Santa Barbara Channel, oil platform
spill

1970
* Canada: Nova Scotia, Port Hawkesbury, *Arrow* oil spill
* USA: Louisiana, Gulf of Mexico, oil platform fire
* USA: Florida, St. Petersburg, *Delian Apollon* oil spill

1971
* USA: California, San Francisco, *Arizona Standard* and
Oregon collision

1972
* USA: Pennsylvania, Pottstown, oil spill in Schuykill
River

1974
Gulf of Mexico, oil platform blowout

1976
* USA: New York, Thousand Islands, St. Lawrence Sea-
way barge spill
* USA: Massachusetts, Nantucket, *Argo Merchant* oil spill

1977
* USA: Midway Island, *Irenes Challenger* breakup
* USA: Hawaii, Honolulu, *Hawaiian Patriot* explosion
* Norway: North Sea, oil rig blowout
* Saudi Arabia: Dhahran, oil field fire
* USA: Alaska, Trans-Alaska Pipeline explosion

*Detailed in text

1978
* France: Portsall-Kersaint, *Amoco Cadiz* grounding

1979
* Mexico: Campeche Bay, Ixtoc 1 oil platform blowout
* Tobago: *Atlantic Empress* and *Aegean Captain* collision

1982
* Lithuania: Klaipeda, *Globe Asimi* foundering

1984
* Brazil: Cubatão, oil pipeline explosion

1988
* United Kingdom: Scotland, North Sea, *Piper Alpha* oil
spill

1989
* USA: Alaska, Valdez, *Exxon Valdez* grounding
Ireland: River Mersey, barge oil spill

1991
* Italy: Gulf of Genoa, *Haven* burning

1992
Norway: Alesand, *Arisan* grounding
* Spain: La Coruña, *Aegean Sea* grouding

1993
* United Kingdom: Scotland, Shetland Islands, *Braer*
grounding

1994
* Russia: Usnisk, oil spill in the Arctic

1996
* United Kingdom: Wales, Milford Haven, *Sea Empress*
grounding

OIL SPILL DISASTERS

God placed these things [oils and minerals] beneath the surface for a purpose, for us to use. To say that we shouldn't use them is to be anti-god.

—Julian Rice, mayor of Fairbanks, Alaska,
to a *New York Times* reporter, 1972

Although land spills exist in great profusion, spills at sea are more abundant, dramatic, and destructive. Thus, government and environmental organization efforts at controlling oil spills have concentrated upon those on water.

Quite a while ago, there was a cartoon in the *New Yorker* magazine that showed a ship's bridge. On its wing was a bearded character in a sou'wester. Inside the wheelhouse, the captain was saying to his officers: "From now on, the company wants no more excuses. We have radar, sonar, radio-direction finder, autopilot, gyrocompass repeaters, and, as of today, an old salt from Gloucester."

From all indications, in cartoons, in the *apologia* of the oil companies, in the statements of captains of tankers, in the pronouncements of spokespersons for environmental and citizens' groups, it is, to quote former president George Bush, "the vision thing."

"On almost any past spill there is a spectrum of views ranging from the judgment that impacts were negligible to the contention that they were calamitous," stated John Robinson, the scientific coordinator of a federal oil spill task force after the Ixtoc 1 oil platform fire and resultant catastrophe of the summer and fall of 1979. "Judgments seem to vary with obvious biases of people making them—how close they are to the oil industry, what research grant they may be after. . . ."

Two conclusions seem to be safe, however: Oil spills are part of doing business in a world dependent upon fossil fuels, and oil spills are a constant, hammering threat to the ecology of the planet. Seventy percent of the world is water, and that water is bordered by land masses. Ever since the abandonment of sails and steam, we have been fouling these waters and this land at an amazing and irresponsible rate of speed and extravagance. And not just with tanker oil spills.

A National Academy of Science study conducted in 1983 estimated that only one-third of marine oil pollution comes from ships (the rest comes from exploration), and of that, 85 to 90 percent comes not from wrecks but from routine operations such as flushing tanks.

Still, it is the concentrated spectacle of millions of gallons of oil washing up on a beach, entering a lagoon, coating a rockface within a circumscribed period of time that captures our attention and raises our hackles. That these oil spills are merely intermediary punctuations in a long story of continuing contamination of our waters is an acknowledgment of a manageable human attention span, and no less abominable for the statistical rarity of the individual disasters.

Oil spills, for all their apparent simplicity of impact, are complex entities. They are, like the difficulty in reporting them objectively, a perplexing mass of variables. Oil itself has many constituents, ranging from tar to elements that are almost as evaporative as gasoline. The form the oil takes can range from an evanescent film to a persistent emulsion three times the volume of the oil itself.

And then there are the many grades of oil, ranging from the heaviest, crudest crude to a light variation that is near to gasoline in texture, look, and behavior.

The course of oil slicks contains another bushel of variables. Wind conditions can spread a slick wide and thin and thus make it amenable to such dissipative mechanisms as evaporation and the oxidation process promoted by sunlight. The thin film of oil absorbs ultraviolet light, and activated molecules react readily with oxygen to form more soluble materials. Nutrients in the water can degrade oil slicks by microbial and photochemical processes, depending upon light, temperature, and water velocity.

Still, much, much oil survives, and this causes monumental environmental damage. The late Jacques Cousteau, at a conference following the fouling of the Brittany Coast by the *Amoco Cadiz*, described a five-month journey through the Mediterranean, a sea fecund with 7,000 marine species. Visiting 16 sites suggested as deep-sea nature preserves, he found all but five ravaged and beyond protection.

And so, by extension, the most dramatic effect of oil spillage is to the flora and fauna that live under and at the edge of the polluted seas. These can be analyzed scientifically, as they have been by the likes of an M.I.T. study, which discovered, not surprisingly, that the recovery of areas of ecosystems damaged by oil spills depends on a host of variable factors.

These include the type and chemical composition of the oil, the time of year of the spill, the amount of oil spilled, the weather conditions, and the evaporation, oxidation, and bacterial action rates.

Certain plants and animals are more resistant to toxic chemicals than others, and some species are more capable of returning to their ecological niches than others. Such animals as mussels and barnacles can rebound quickly in their oil-disturbed environments, but many other species of shellfish and many kinds of marsh grasses—essential to prevent shore erosion and to provide spawning areas for oceanic fish—are more sensitive and take much longer to return to their former areas and state of health.

Generally, the type of area—silty, sandy, or rocky—determines the rapidity with which species can restore themselves. The more silt and sand in an area, the study showed, the longer the damaging effects of an oil spill lasts. The more rocky, the more quickly the environment restores itself.

All well and good. But to anyone who has seen, firsthand, the suffering and death of the wildlife that oil has attacked and defeated, this is small comfort. A diving bird that surfaces through oil is a sorry sight. Fouled on back and wings, it cannot fly and must await either a predator, drowning, or starvation.

There are some few birds who reach shore, and there, they try desperately, through instinct, to preen themselves. And in so doing, they swallow some of the oil on their feathers, and die.

If this does not happen, there is another fate awaiting them. In cold weather, a spot of oil the size of a quarter may cause death. The oil mats the protective feather layers into strings, permitting the frigid water to seep in against the skin, thus dissipating body heat faster than it can be restored.

There is another dimension to the destruction of wildlife. There is a chain in nature, and water birds are a link in it. Many are scavengers, patrolling the beaches as natural sanitation squads. Without them, the stench on the beaches would be gut-wrenching; ships' garbage would float on the waves and clutter the harbors; foulness and disease would choke the inlets and the bays. And so, with the chain broken, the death of a bird causes untold ancillary damage.

Despite this knowledge, the carnage continues. In a single year, the Newfoundland coast has numbered its waterbird kill in the hundreds of thousands. The razor-billed auk, once a common sight, has been killed off at the rate of a million birds in two years. It is now extinct. Thirty thousand birds were washed up on the shores of Sweden in a single pollution event. One bad winter, and the English shoreline has been littered with 100,000 dead or dying birds.

Mammals fare no better. In 1967, after the *Torrey Canyon* disaster, Dr. Harry R. Lillie, a surgeon to an Antarctic whaling fleet, described a devastating meeting. "I have found half-grown seals covered in a tarry mess, their eyes bloodshot with irritation," he said, "and penguins hopelessly clogged, waiting for a slow death."

Oysters, shrimp, fish. As they feed upon the food chain, which can be contaminated at any point, they become either too polluted to eat, and so decompose, or die of the effects of the pollution. Entire fishing areas on the North Sea, the Black Sea, and the Mediterranean have become barren.

And yet, say the oil companies, how can we pass up huge, unexplored motherlodes of oil beneath the seas, on countless continental shelves? People want it. People demand it. And we merely meet the demand.

True. But people do not demand a wasteful way of doing business. Consider one of the two major causes of the fouling of water, that of offshore drilling. Major well blowouts, which spew oil into the water both from above and below the surface, sometimes simultaneously, as in the famous 5-million-gallon Santa Barbara Channel fiasco, have occurred in all of the major offshore drilling regions. In the Gulf of Mexico, off Australia, and in Middle Eastern waters, enormous offshore platforms, as tall as two-thirds the height of the Empire State Building, and serving as control points for as many as 25 wells at a time, have dumped hundreds of millions of gallons of all sorts of oil into every body of water into which they have been introduced.

Environmentalists complain of wholesale devastation of marine life and cite as their primary examples the Santa Barbara spill and the Mexican Ixtoc 1 oil platform disaster, which produced an 800-square-mile slick that contaminated beaches and fishing grounds in both Mexico and Texas.

Oil companies counter with the argument that they must meet the undeniable need for more and more energy by a burgeoning world population. And if this is where the oil is, they say, this is where they must go. Regulations? They only impede the flow of oil to a needy world. To get it there, there must be tankers. And so, there are more than 97 million tons of tankers of all nationalities sailing the waters of the world today, totaling about 4,000 ships, and they have been built specifically to carry liquids, some in double hulls, some in single hulls. There are, admittedly, tankers that carry vegetable oil, animal fats, petrochemicals, molasses, grain alcohol, simple syrup, and orange juice.

There are tankers that are refrigerated in order to keep propane and butane in a liquid state. There are the so-called drugstore tankers that carry a little bit of everything.

But the tankers that carry oil have been the most destructive to the environment. Orange juice does not kill birds and mammals.

As the demand for fuel and the need to transport it has grown, so have the ships that carry it. The *Torrey Canyon* was 974 feet from bow to stern. New tankers today exceed 1,200 feet and could accommodate two or three normal freighters within their dimensions.

Over the course of a year, more than 100 million tons of petroleum products, mostly crude and heavy oils, are shipped to American ports alone. The procedure is that the ship travels one way loaded with oil, and the other way loaded with seawater for ballast, which means that it must dump this seawater before it reaches port to load up with oil again. The water that goes over and into the sea is, of course, contaminated with the residue oil left in the tanks after the previous unloading. And that is part of the fouling of the seas that results from the ordinary conduct of business.

Other steps in the process include washing the tanks down when the cargo goes from heavy to light crude. Legally, this is supposed to be done with the help of a separator. The oil is supposed to run from one tank to another through a mechanical separator, and the residue is supposed to be hauled onto land for disposal. But, according to the U.S. Coast Guard, the mess is usually tossed overboard.

Slop water contaminated by oil also regularly goes over the side. And there is careless refueling of all ships.

All of this mounts up. The oil industry itself admits that an average tanker of 50,000 tons may spew, after unloading, 1,400 barrels of petroleum residue into the sea. Traffic to American ports alone, then, would account for the disposal of 2.8 million barrels of oil a year. That is not inconsiderable.

Factor in accidents, groundings, collisions, explosions, fires, and it all totals up to quite a threatening mess.

What is at least a little encouraging is the fact that after (or sometimes during) one of these periodic catastrophes, the conscience of governments seems to be rediscovered, and the favor of the public, at least temporarily, outweighs the favors dispensed by oil companies and new regulations come into being. And so one part of a three-part equation that is the only solution to the current dilemma created by the gathering and transporting of fossil fuels for human consumption and the cost in environmental spoilage is realized.

This three-part equation for cure is a straightforward one: National Laws + International Treaties + Technological Advancement = Stability.

The United States has forbidden the dumping of oil and oily refuse from shore establishments since 1899 and the Harbor and Harbors Act. The Oil Pollution Act of 1924 prohibited discharge of oil into the streams and territorial waters of the United States. But these laws have been traditionally broken in a wholesale fashion. To correct this, Congress, in 1972, passed the Ports and Waterways Safety Act, charging the Coast Guard with developing adequate standards for all tankers entering United States waters. But the Coast Guard has done next to nothing in carrying this out.

Internationally, there was the 1953 London conference to initial the Pollution of the Sea by Oil Convention. Twenty nations, including the former Soviet Union, signed, but the United States did not, because American oil companies convinced the State Department that technological developments, rather than regulation, would cure the problem. When nothing improved, the United States finally signed the treaty in 1961.

Since then, the United Nations has attempted to develop treaties that would safeguard the world ecology against oil spills, with varying results. In 1972, 91 nations, including the United States, agreed to stop dumping pollutants into the world's oceans, and yet, in 1982, it was Third World countries who were the largest supporters of the Law of the Sea Convention, signed by 119 nations, but not the United States, and not the United Kingdom.

To its credit, the United States Congress passed, in 1990, in the wake of the *Exxon Valdez* disaster, the Oil Pollution Act, which established a network of regional oil spill response centers, promoted better navigational safety, and demanded crew licensing and new tanker construction standards.

Ultimately, large settlements against oil companies, made easier in the United States by the Comprehensive Oil Pollution and Compensation Act, have done more than attempt to impose moral values. And, to be fair, several major American oil companies have imposed safety standards and rules for tank washing.

Yet, all of this cannot provide for the vagaries of life at sea, which is probably why we surround our best sailors with an aura of romantic courage. Bad weather, fog, and tight harbors are the acknowledged enemies of safety at sea. Mix them with a peculiar blight among tanker captains and oil companies of carelessness, pigheadedness, recklessness, overreliance on technological aids, and greed, and a separate and effective formula for disaster is enhanced and elongated.

As the world population explosion continues, the oceans, through artificial desalinization, will probably become a major source of humankind's water supply. Then, what will we do with the oil pollution?

Something, it is fondly hoped, before what we now regard as the birthplace of human life becomes its graveyard, too.

BRAZIL
(CUBATÃO)
OIL PIPELINE EXPLOSION
February 25, 1984

....

A rupture, instant explosion, and fire occurred in a pipeline passing through a shantytown on the outskirts of Cubatão, Brazil, on the night of February 25, 1984. More than 100 residents of the town were killed, and 150 were injured.

Cubatão is, by any definition, a poor place, located in one of the most polluted areas in Brazil. Just off the Santos–São Paulo highway, the town is trapped between, on one side, 23 belching factories, many of which produce petrochemicals, and on the other, the 2,500-foot *Serra do Mar* range. The topography, the factories, and the predominantly cloudy weather conspire to trap the fumes emitted by the factories.

Nature reacts to the contamination in a graphic way. Thousands of trees stand bare on surrounding hills, stripped of vegetation and lifeless. No birds sing. Where brooks once ran, there are occasional pools of stagnant waste.

As a result, the 90,000 indigent factory workers who live in Cubatão and put up with its pollution in order to eke out a meager existence produce children with an abnormally high incidence of birth defects. Other health problems, particularly respiratory disorders, abound. It is not a healthy or profitable place in which to live.

Nor was it a safe place on February 25, 1984. Shortly after midnight, a pipeline pumping diesel oil from the nearby Atlantic Ocean port of Santos to a refinery in Cubatão, which belonged to the state oil company, *Petroleo Brasileiro*, exploded. The pipe ran directly under a shantytown on the outskirts of Cubatão, a place of huts built mostly of wood and cardboard poised on stilts over a swamp.

The blast atomized the shacks directly above it, then sprayed oil on the surface of the swamp, which instantly caught fire. The flames raced across the entire circumference of the swamp, setting fire to the other huts and incinerating the inhabitants as they slept within.

More than 100 men, women, and children were killed, and another 150, some with terrible burns, were taken to the hospital in São Paulo, 30 miles northwest of the town.

The medical bills were paid by the refinery owners, the shacks were rebuilt much the way they had been, and life resumed in one of the world's most contaminated areas, a place called, by Brazil, in a 1975 presidential decree, "an area of critical pollution." It is still critical, and still polluted.

CANADA
(NOVA SCOTIA, PORT HAWKESBURY)
ARROW OIL SPILL
February 4, 1970

....

Just 40 miles short of its destination, at Port Hawkesbury, Nova Scotia, the ill-kept, ill-equipped 11,379-ton tanker Arrow ran aground, on February 4, 1970, on Cerberus Rock. Three million eight hundred thousand gallons of oil spilled along the coast when the ship broke apart.

At the beginning of January 1970, the 11,379-ton tanker *Arrow* left Venezuela with 3.8 million gallons of Bunker C oil, a heavy crude normally burned by ships and factories. The ship was bound for Canada to deliver its cargo to a pulp mill at Port Hawkesbury, Nova Scotia. The oil belonged to Imperial, a subsidiary of the Standard Oil Company of New Jersey; the ship was owned by Sunstone Marine, Ltd. of Panama, one of the companies of the late Aristotle Onassis, the Greek shipping magnate.

The *Arrow* was well known along the St. Lawrence River, which she regularly sailed. Glen W. Stead, Canada's assistant deputy minister of transport later characterized her as having "a reputation among pilots as a dirty ship, badly maintained. She was certainly far from a luxury liner. She was rusted and careworn. Her radar system was faulty. Her echo sounder was disabled. Her gyro compass read several degrees off course." In other words, she was an accident waiting to happen.

And happen it did, just 40 miles from the *Arrow*'s destination. On Wednesday, February 4, she ran hard aground, on Cerberus Rock, three-quarters of a mile off Arichat, 190 miles northeast of Halifax and 40 miles from Port Hawkesbury.

The weather was its usual dreadful February self, but there was no gale blowing. It was merely cold, gray, and foggy, with about a mile visibility. And so, there was really no excuse for the grounding, other than the multiple inoperative necessities of navigation aboard the ship.

Captain George Anatasobolos testified at the hearing that followed the accident and its aftermath that the ship's radar, which he had just had repaired in January, had functioned normally until about an hour before the grounding.

As for the echo sounder aboard: That had not really worked since the first day Captain Anatasobolos had taken charge of the *Arrow*, on December 14, 1969. He had not told the owners about it, he confessed, but he had planned to have it fixed when the ship called at Aruba a year ago January. However, there were no technicians available in Aruba, so he decided to put it off for a future time in a future port.

When the crash occurred, Captain Anatasobolos was on the bridge with his third officer, a young man who was unlicensed, though he had graduated from navigation school.

It was apparent by the end of the first hour of grounding that the tanker was going nowhere except to the bottom of the Atlantic. The captain and his crew of 34, realizing this, abandoned ship, which was already leaking oil at a furious rate, early. Divers who inspected the vessel on Sunday the 8th returned with the news that only 8 of her 27 tanks were intact.

The oil that gushed from her hull had formed a slick 3 miles long and 100 yards wide. The only good news was that most of the slick was drifting out to sea, but this was hardly a comfort to those living on the coast in a two-mile section near Arichat. Here, patches of oil had drifted in and despoiled the snow- and ice-covered beaches.

By February 7, the constant pounding of the waves of the North Atlantic had begun to break the *Arrow* in two. At first, the plan was to use explosives to cut the stern free, but this was abandoned as too polluting, and so tugs threw lines around her stern, which held 3.6 of the 3.8 million gallons of oil. The revised plan was to haul the stern out beyond the Continental Shelf and the Gulf Stream. There, it would be bombed, and its cargo set afire, and it would sink.

As for the oil still in her forepart: There was some hesitation and disputation. It might not burn. And if chemical dispersants were brought in, they probably would not work because of the arctically low temperatures. On the other hand, if she were left on the rocks till spring, greater contamination to fish and shellfish during the fishing season might occur.

On February 11, the weather worsened considerably. A southeasterly gale drove the oil that was headed out to sea toward the Nova Scotia shore. The 40-to-50-mile-per-hour

The North Atlantic pounds the tanker Arrow *into its aquatic grave. The mast was the last to go under after the hull broke in two, spilling more than 1 million gallons of crude oil into the sea and thence onto the shore of Chedabucto Bay and Cansco Strait.*

(AP/WORLD WIDE)

winds foreclosed plans to pump out the oil in the stern section before the section could be towed out to sea.

But most alarmingly, the wind and the sea and the storm kicked up and began to nudge the ship along the rocky ledge, a distance of a full 150 feet in one morning. A third tug was brought in to secure a line to the stern, and a compressor was brought alongside to pump air into the stern and increase its buoyancy.

While the gale raged, a scheme was formulated to bring on a boom to contain the oil in the water around the stern and set fire to it with the help of seabeads, which are glass beads about a quarter inch in diameter that have a pitted exterior and act as a wick for the fires.

But before any of the grand plans could be realized, on February 12, the worst happened. The tugs were no match for the winds and the sea. The stern of the *Arrow* edged off the rocky ledge and sank into the roiled waters of the Atlantic. As she sank, huge quantities of oil poured forth, more than could be contained, more than could be burned. And the prevailing winds drove the oil directly at the shore. Twenty to 30 miles of the shore of Chedabucto Bay and Cansco Strait took on a thicker coating of oil by the hour.

Learning the lesson of the *Torrey Canyon* (see pp. 155–6), the cleaners of this coast brought in straw rather than detergent. When the weather cleared, thousands of workers arrived to begin the cleanup, but officials acknowledged that it would be weeks, months, and possibly years before the effects of the pollution would be dissipated.

As February turned to March and then to April, and the seas calmed, tugs surrounded the stern section, now resting in 95 feet of water, and began the laborious and altogether new project of trying to pump out the remaining oil in the stern section's tanks, thus stemming any further pollution of land and water.

It was a first, and largely successful venture. Canadian navy divers attached flanges to the ship's deck. Valves were secured to the flanges. Then, through the open valves, the divers drilled holes in the *Arrow*'s deck and threaded rubber hoses about eight inches in diameter through the valves and into the ship's cargo tanks. Steam was then pumped through flexible metal hoses within the rubber hoses to heat and make the oil less viscous.

In an effort to reassure eaters of fish from Nova Scotia, Donald C. Jamieson, the Canadian minister of transport, had himself photographed on April 14 eating a freshly caught lobster. The minister of fisheries, ignoring Mr. Jamieson's photo-op, ordered a temporary suspension of the gathering of clams, mussels, and periwinkles because of the risk of contamination. The fishing industry in Nova Scotia suffered a severe economic loss.

Since the *Torrey Canyon*, the International Tanker Owners Pollution Federation, Ltd., a voluntary insurance pool, was set up by ship owners. Because of its regulations, the liability of the owners was limited to $1,137,900.

A board of inquiry was set up, and the $1,137,900, plus cleanup expenses and damages for negligence were awarded to the Canadian government. The *Arrow* probably never should have been sailing on any sea at all, considering its customary condition.

FRANCE
(PORTSALL-KERSAINT)
AMOCO CADIZ GROUNDING AND BREAKING UP
March 16, 1978

The worst oil spill until that time occurred on March 16, 1978, in the English Channel off the coast of Portsall-Kersaint, Brittany, when the supertanker Amoco Cadiz, *carrying 68 million gallons of Middle East crude oil and bound for Le Havre, lost control of its steering mechanism and ran aground on coastal rocks. The spill eventually fouled nearly 200 miles of Brittany coastline, killed more than 1,000 birds, and diminished the fishing industry of the area permanently.*

"We were fully booked for the summer, but now it looks like the season will be ruined," complained a hotel owner on the Brittany coast in mid-March of 1978. Fishermen made plans for a demonstration on the streets of Brest. On a wall near the sea someone scrawled "*Petrol—ras le bol!*"—"Oil—we're fed up!"

The reason: the grounding on the rocks three miles offshore, near Portsall-Kersaint, 25 miles north of Brest, on France's Brittany coast, of the American-owned supertanker *Amoco Cadiz,* and the beach-, fish-, and wildlife-consuming oil slick that resulted.

It all began on Thursday, March 16, 1978, a stormy day on the Brittany Coast. A high sea was running, and the winds were gusty. At approximately 12:30 P.M., the French naval radio station at Le Conquet received a distress call from the *Amoco Cadiz,* sailing north to Le Havre from the Persian Gulf. It had just entered the English Channel. Its steering had failed, and it requested a civilian tug.

Aboard the ship, life had become extremely tense. Late that morning, the helmsman, fighting the storm and the sea, complained that when he steered to starboard, the rudder went to port. The chief engineer, Salvatore Melito, went down to investigate. What he found appalled him. Two engines and two hydraulic pumps had failed, and the steering mechanism was inoperable. "The rudder was moving substantially from side to side," he later testified. "The bolts must have sheered under tension induced by pressure." Five bolts had broken loose, and almost the entire 211 gallons of oil that cushioned the steering system had leaked into the sea.

What might have been a difficulty on a smaller, more easily maneuverable ship became a crisis condition. Supertankers move at a terrific momentum, which makes them

Evidence of the worst oil spill until that time (1978) floats onto the resort beaches of Brittany, mixing with the flora, killing the fauna.
(PHILIPPE MARTINZ/UNEP)

several times more susceptible to collisions or groundings than smaller ships. Anchors cannot stop them. It takes at least three miles and 21 to 22 minutes to stop a 250,000-ton tanker doing 16 knots, and this is aggravated if the ship has lost power or steering.

The *Amoco Cadiz* was a 228,513-ton tanker, loaded with 68 million gallons of Middle East crude oil, and its length—1,067 feet, meant that the metal plates of the hull were under vastly more pressure than those of an ordinary freighter as the ship flexed under the pounding of the sea. And if it were to run aground, it, like other supertankers, was more prone to breaking up than shorter ships.

By 1:15, the West German tug *Pacific* had arrived and had the tanker in tow. But for three precious hours, during which a tragedy might have been averted, the two captains argued over the cost of the salvage operation and where the tanker should be taken.

At 4:15, after relentless pounding by the sea on both ships, the towline broke, and the *Amoco Cadiz* drifted onto the rocks off Portsall-Kersaint. The hull was ripped open, and three of its 15 tanks, containing 24 million gallons of oil, began to pour it into the channel. A 15-mile slick immediately developed, and by evening, 3 miles of beaches had been blackened.

French navy helicopters evacuated 41 crew members, leaving the captain, Pasquale Bardari and its first officer to be rescued the following morning. By then, the tanker had split in two, and the oozing of oil into the English Channel had turned into a torrent. By midmorning, 80,000 tons of oil had fouled beaches, harbors, and fishing grounds along 70 miles of the Brittany coast, and what had begun with a quarrel between captains had turned into a terrible oil spill.

Ironically, it had happened almost 11 years to the day from the date of the grounding of the *Torrey Canyon*, the

first supertanker disaster, which occurred nearby, on the coast of Cornwall (see pp. 155–6).

The mess on the beaches became indescribable. Three to four inches of oil covered the walled harbor of Portsall-Kersaint, and the smell hung on the air for miles inland. Local leaders of the village demanded that the ship be blown up immediately and the oil still in its tanks burned. Their arguments were cogent ones. It would take at least 10 days to pump out the oil that was left in the *Amoco Cadiz,* and bad weather and the approaching spring high tides might break up the tanker completely, spilling more oil onto the beaches and fishing grounds.

The authorities responded in odd and small ways. They arrested the captains of the tanker and the tug and began to install barriers across river estuaries to protect the oyster beds. Officers at the French naval headquarters at Brest vetoed the burning idea because of danger to nearby villages but acknowledged that nothing much had been done to stop the oil spillage, which had now increased to a slick 4 miles wide and 70 miles long.

The weather turned from bad to horrendous. Gale force winds and mountainous seas assaulted the tanker. One hundred twenty thousand tons of oil had already escaped, and the battering was certain to open up more gashes in her hull. In the channel, the oil slick was moving toward the British Channel Islands of Jersey and Guernsey. In France, fishermen began to turn in their fishing licenses in angry protest over the inaction of authorities.

As the storm in the channel worsened, conditions deteriorated on land, too. None of the three principals in the incident assumed responsibility—not Amoco, not the owners of the tug, and not the French navy, who charged that the captain of the tanker did not ask for emergency assistance until the vessel had foundered.

Finally, on Wednesday the 22nd, vacuum-cleaner type machinery was moved onto the beaches from Portsall to the Isle of Batz, and the cleanup began. Five hundred troops and civilian volunteers assisted on land, and 30 ships began to treat the oil slick with chemical solvents that were described as harmless to marine life.

By the end of the day, it was reported that all of the tanks of the *Amoco Cadiz* were open to the sea and only 50,000 tons of oil remained in them.

On the 23rd, the French navy reversed its original pronouncements and, resigning itself to the fact that the weather was not going to change for the better, weighed the option of burning what was left of the oil in the tanker. Meanwhile, the slick continued to drift eastward, along the French coast, reaching Brehat Island and the port of Paimpol, at the entrance of the bay of St.-Brieuc.

Still, anger simmered. One marine pollution expert, called in to help, commented, "This is the only oil spill disaster in the world where cleanup responsibility is divided between rival officials and everyone knocks off at 5:30 P.M."

In Paris, members of the environmental group Friends of the Earth occupied the offices of Shell International, the company that owned the oil in the *Amoco Cadiz,* and, from their vantage point, urged the French to boycott Shell products for a month.

The next day, March 24, the last strut holding the *Amoco Cadiz*'s bow and stern sections together snapped, and the stern swung around to face the open sea, which was still churning from the same storm that had raged for a week. Brown spray cascaded from both sections of the tanker.

Across the channel, mindful that the oil slick was approaching at the rate of approximately 10 miles a day, British tugs loaded with detergents cruised near the Channel Islands. Nineteen other vessels were standing by in port ready to put to sea, and two crop-spraying planes were being prepared for antipollution action.

By the 25th, every commercial radio station in France began to appeal for help in cleaning up the beach pollution. Residents of villages along the coast bombarded city halls with heavy rubber gloves, thigh boots, raincoats, garbage cans, buckets, shovels, rakes, and rags. Within six hours of the first announcement, a second followed, stating that three times the amount of equipment that was needed had been collected.

The wreck of the *Amoco Cadiz* was anything but buried. Geysers of oil 20 feet high spewed out of her shattered hull as waves slammed into her at high tide. More than 180,000 tons of oil had already poured into the channel; 30,000 tons still remained, and the French navy now determined that dynamiting would be the best way to free up the oil. Endless repetitive cleanups would result, they argued, if it was left to seep onto the 110 miles of already-polluted beaches during the next month.

And so, French divers were assigned to attach dynamite charges to the hull of the *Amoco Cadiz* as soon as the weather cleared.

But again, the weather refused to cooperate, and so navy helicopters flew over the ship and bombarded it with depth charges, in a slightly less efficient effort to free up the last 10 percent of the oil.

The coast of Brittany was devastated. The harvest of oysters, lobsters, fish, and seaweed, worth millions of dollars, was destroyed. The tourist season was over before it began.

There was, however, a little light in the darkness. Environmentalists generally agreed that, in contrast to the inaction of the authorities, the quick response of fishermen, farmers, and other residents helped to minimize environmental damage. Furthermore, the oil was a light crude that broke up and dispersed in the high seas and high winds. Then, too, new and improved chemical dispersants, rather than the detergents used in the *Torrey Canyon* disaster, which were more potent than the oil in damaging marine life, had been developed and were pressed into use.

Yves Le Gall, the assistant director of the Marine Biology Laboratory in Concarneau on the southeast Brittany coast did disagree to an extent, countering that the plankton upon which marine life fed would be diminished and overwhelmed, and that the possibility existed that a thin layer of oil left on the sea would block photosynthesis.

But generally, environmentalists agreed with A. J. O'Sullivan, a consultant with Cremer and Warner, a British firm of consulting engineers and scientists. "If one was [*sic*] to make a long-range guess—given the rate at which cleanup operations will continue—within three months there should be no immediately visible signs of the oil, [though] there will still be oil present—under stones, possibly buried in the sand—and there will still be oil present in the ecosystem, in the tissues of marine organisms." But with regeneration, he concluded, the environmental impact of the spill would disappear.

The scientists' views, of course, were uttered in laboratories. On the beaches, more than a thousand dead birds were uncovered, and many more were assumed to have died out of sight. The pollution persisted and would not leave the beaches or the waters. Fishing would be ruined for a year, and the beaches would not be clear for years after that. More than half a million tourists canceled their vacations that summer, while 6,300 volunteers from France, Belgium, and the Netherlands pumped slime into trucks and sprayed rocks throughout the entire month of June.

The oyster crop was devastated and would not recover for years. That summer, 4,600 tons of oysters were destroyed by the government. Fishing never returned to the abundance it had enjoyed before the disaster. There were fewer fish in the sea and fewer birds in the air, though the beach, swept and swept again, was probably cleaner than it had been before the spill.

Boards of inquiry were held, the two captains were let off with reprimands, and the government of France and local governments of Brittany were the recipients of hundreds of millions of dollars in settlements from Royal Dutch Shell, Amoco, and their insurance companies.

Other improvements in regulating the traffic in supertankers resulted from the *Amoco Cadiz* grounding. Instead of remaining five miles from the coast of France, tankers entering the English Channel were required to remain seven nautical miles off the coast. They were also required to announce their presence when entering the channel, whether they were in difficulty or not. Any trouble within 50 miles of France was required to be reported, and tugs going to the aid of tankers were required to report the fact to French authorities.

When it was all over, a headline in a local newspaper in Brittany summed up the catastrophe succinctly and accurately: "The causes of the tragedy [were two]: delays and a sordid question of money," it said.

ITALY
(GULF OF GENOA)
BURNING OF TANKER *HAVEN*
April 11, 1991

....

The supertanker Haven, *carrying 41 million gallons of Iranian crude oil, exploded and burned in the Gulf of Genoa on April 11, 1991. Three crewmen were instantly killed and three were reported missing. The oil slick was minimal, and the Italian and French Rivieras were spared an ecological disaster by the quick action of the combined Italian and French Environmental Services.*

Yet another supertanker burst into flames, sank, and released a potentially polluting oil slick on April 11, 1991, near Arenzano, a resort town in the Gulf of Genoa.

As the 109,000-ton supertanker, the Cypriot-registered *Haven* rested at anchor 2,000 yards off Arenzano on the night of the 11th, an explosion suddenly tore through her hull. Three crewmen were instantly killed; three more were blown overboard and never found. Some of the 41 million gallons of crude oil immediately ignited, and the tanker became a torch that burned for five hours, while the remainder of its crew and officers were evacuated.

At the end of the five hours, shortly before dawn, a second, larger explosion ripped through the tanker, blowing it apart down to and below the waterline. She began to founder, but fortunately, a relatively small amount of oil spilled.

Even before the second explosion, a flotilla of boats surrounded the flaming tanker. Booms and floating barriers were dispersed in a ring by Italian and French officials, who were justifiably horrified and concerned about the possibility of one of the worst ecological disasters in the Mediterranean developing. Just as the season was beginning, both

The supertanker Haven *turned into a torch that burned for five hours after an explosion tore through her hull.*
(ANTONIO AMATO/UNEP)

wildlife and the livelihood of resorts along the French and Italian Rivieras were threatened.

Three days after the first explosion, a third ripped through the *Haven*, totally submerging her except for her flaming stern. Tugs were attached to the wreck and it was towed into water 300 feet deep on the orders of experts from the Italian Environment Ministry. Remote operated mini-submarines were then dispatched with video cameras to film the wreck and test a theory that three days of intense fire had turned the heavy Iranian crude oil into a nearly solid syrup, which kept it from dispersing in great quantities into the gulf.

The strategy worked; the slick was minimal, as was the environmental damage, and the remaining oil was pumped out of the wreck and into an oil carrier.

LITHUANIA
(KLAIPEDA)
FOUNDERING OF *GLOBE ASIMI*
November 21, 1982

....

The British oil tanker Globe Asimi *foundered on rocks off the Lithuanian port of Klaipeda, on the Baltic Sea, in a storm on November 21, 1982. Causing a record $900 million in damage, 4.8 million gallons of oil spilled into the Baltic.*

When Russia was part of the Soviet Union, disasters went largely unreported. There were, as far as the rest of the world was concerned, no airliner crashes, no train wrecks, and no oil spills. For reasons equally unknown, the Baltic Coast of Soviet Lithuania, north of Poland, was a portion of the world more firmly locked against Western journalists than other parts of the USSR.

And so, when the 20,000-ton British tanker *Globe Asimi*, carrying 4.8 million gallons of boiler fuel, ran aground in a heavy storm on the night of November 21, 1982, and broke up, spilling its cargo into the Baltic, only the residents of the port of Klaipeda, where it occurred, knew of the disaster.

Tass, the official Soviet newspaper, was mum until January, when news of the wreck began to filter out, through Reuters and through Lloyd's of London, which had insured the ship. Some few details emerged in Lithuanian regional newspapers, and Reuters picked up more news of the catastrophe. But some of the details of the grounding and its consequent oil spill would remain forever murky.

What is known is this: There was a steadily worsening, raging storm buffeting the coastal city of Klaipeda on November 21, 1982, and the fully loaded tanker *Globe Asimi*, scheduled to leave early in the day, when the storm was relatively small, put off her departure while the crew members amused themselves ashore.

By early evening, when the ship prepared to depart, the sea was a ferocious froth and the winds were enormous. The captain was warned not to leave, but he did anyway, and had no sooner cleared the breakwater when he and his ship were driven aground. The seas and winds hammered the *Globe Asimi* hard upon some rocks, and within an hour, she had broken up into three pieces and had poured her cargo of oil into the Baltic.

The crew was apparently saved, though no particulars of this ever reached Western news bureaus.

The effects of the oil spill were, however, experienced by thousands of ordinary citizens, who were not loath to give their stories to the world. Twenty-five miles of the lush Lithuanian coast north of Klaipeda and extending into Latvia were blackened. A resort area of sandy beaches backed by dunes, the region included the summer resorts of Palanga, Giruliai, and Sventolji, all of them thinly populated in November, all of them heavily coated with oil.

Klaipeda itself was invaded by the oil slick. Docks were fouled and several cargo ships anchored there had to be cleaned before they could leave in order to avoid further spreading of the oil pollution.

The area south of Klaipeda, a broad shallow embayment known as the Courland Lagoon, was penetrated by the slick for 12 miles, as far as the village of Dreverna. But because of the prevailing winds, the resorts on the 60-mile-long Courland sand spit, which separates the lagoon from the Baltic Sea, emerged unscathed.

There were, reportedly, no floating booms, pumps, or skimmers available to clean the oil slick, and calls for help had to be sent to other ports. Cleanup teams and the needed equipment arrived from the Latvian port of Ventspils; from Baku, the oil-producing center on the Caspian Sea; and from Novorossisk, an oil harbor on the Black Sea.

Coastal residents commandeered trucks and other equipment to help remove the oil-impregnated sand; ecological damage to grasses, wildfowl, and fish was never revealed.

As news of the oil spill drifted out from the Soviet Union, West Germany supplied its new catamaran *Thor*, a vessel specializing in the cleanup of oil spills. *Svetlomor*, the flagship of the Soviet Union's oil cleanup fleet, was sent from the Black Sea port of Ilyichevsk, near Odessa.

According to Soviet news sources, the 35-mile-long oil slick resulted in an astonishing $900 million in damage. No explanation of why such a small cargo of oil caused so much havoc was ever reported.

MEXICO
(CAMPECHE BAY, OFF THE YUCATÁN PENINSULA)
IXTOC 1 OIL PLATFORM BLOWOUT AND FIRE
June 3, 1979

....

One hundred and thirty-four million gallons of crude oil gushed from the Ixtoc 1 oil platform in the Gulf of Mexico 50 miles off *the Yucatán Peninsula during the nine months after its blowout, on June 3, 1979. During that time, an oil slick that could have covered the entire Gulf of Mexico formed, fouling beaches in Mexico and Texas. The total cost: $580 million.*

Sedco, Inc., was a multi-million-dollar Dallas oil-drilling conglomerate that had leased an offshore drilling rig to a private Mexican contractor who was, in turn, hired by the Mexican national oil company Pemex to drill the Ixtoc 1 well 50 miles off the Yucatán Peninsula. On June 2, 1979, an official of Sedco had a problem. The problem went beyond the byzantine business of oil leases and concerned the recently built floating city that is an offshore oil rig. It had a malfunctioning drill. The Sedco official, who knew his machinery, suggested filling the hole into which the drill was sunk with salt water to bring it under control. The Mexican supervisor ignored his directions.

At least, this is what Stephen Mahood, the vice president of Sedco said in his testimony before two committees of the United States Congress after the disaster that followed—a disaster that still stands in the record books as the worst oilfield accident of all time.

The worldwide hunt for new sources of fossil fuel is an endless and inventive one, often conducted in unlikely places, at least in the perception of the layperson. One such search took geologists and Pemex, the Mexican government oil monopoly, to the Bahía de Campeche area of the gulf of Mexico, off the Yucatán Peninsula. Ixtoc 1 would be the conduit for the discovery of oil under the Gulf of Mexico in this area, if there was oil there.

There was. In the early hours of June 3, the malfunctioning drill on Ixtoc 1 cut into a porous, oil-containing rock 12,000 feet beneath the platform. And almost immediately, the troubles began. The drilling "mud"—a clay, water, and chemicals mixture that lubricates and cools the drilling bit, carries cuttings to the top, and keeps oil and gas from gushing upward—stopped circulating.

This is not an unusual phenomenon, and the customary cure is to pump heavier mud immediately into the shaft, in order to counter the pressure of the ascending oil. But the supply of heavier mud aboard Ixtoc 1 was too small to make a difference. What was there was pressed into immediate service, but it was like trying to close a three-foot rip with a six-inch patch.

The next step in preventing the onset of a disaster would be to put a blowout preventer in place, by activating a ram, which closes in on the drill pipe, squeezing it together and capping it. The ram was activated, but instead of closing on the pipe, it closed on the heavy collar that encircled it. And nothing happened. The pressure built. And shortly before dawn of June 3, the well blew in a spectacular explosion of oil, gas, and fire.

The natural gas ignited; the oil geysered 25 feet into the air, then fell back into the Gulf of Mexico, launching an oil slick that would eventually be nearly unimaginable in its gargantuan proportions.

There were 63 crewmen aboard the Ixtoc 1 when the well blew. Aside from being coated from head to foot and in every orifice with oil, they were unharmed and were evacuated immediately and then replaced by emergency crews intent on stemming the fountain of oil that was fouling the waters surrounding the platform. Recovery vessels were drawn up to the site. A million bales of hay were ordered for the Vera Cruz coast, toward which the oil was drifting. And Red Adair and his crew of oil daredevils from Houston (see p. 215) were called in to work miracles, fast.

But this was going to be a tough one that would eventually defeat even the indominatable Red Adair. Still, early in the long saga that was about to unfold, he utilized underwater television cameras to study the valves of the blowout preventers through which oil was gushing underwater. The valves had jammed open when the oil blew, and the plan was to shut them before the oil reached the Mexican coast 50 miles away, or—and this seemed a remote possibility—the Texas coast 800 miles north.

Ten days later, oil was still fountaining out of the well and escaping underwater. Fifteen million gallons had already surged to the surface of the gulf or fallen into it from the tower of oil.

On June 24, Adair and his crew succeeded in closing the blowout preventer. For two hours, it seemed that a catastrophe had been averted. But the defect in the drill pointed out by the Sedco man had caused a leak in the drillpipe. The pressure, focused on the tiny leak, would almost certainly cause the pipe to blow at that point. And so, Adair opened the well once more.

Meanwhile, a strange sort of schizophrenic fear pervaded in Ciudad del Carmen, on the Mexican coast nearby. The 400 shrimp boats in its harbor identified it as one of the world's biggest shrimping centers. But its economy had boomed with the arrival of offshore oil drilling. Its inhabitants wanted both, but it appeared that they might end up with neither.

The spill, now 300 miles long and 25 miles wide, was clearly drifting northward, toward Texas, and more shrimp grounds, fishing grounds, and a million-dollar resort complex. The slick's volume of oil had already surpassed the record 1.3 million barrels dumped upon France's Brittany coast a year before by the *Amoco Cadiz* (see pp. 140–42).

The only cure for it was to sink another parallel well to relieve the pressure that was barreling the oil and gas up through the gusher that had taken over the oil platform. But that would take months. Forty-nine days had already passed, and the slick just kept floating along.

To those able to appreciate the aesthetics of the moment, the oil did have a certain beauty to it. It had come apart into seven major patches, and its leading edge resembled a muted rainbow, while the rest of it was as brown as crop-supporting soil.

The U.S. Coast Guard cutter *Valiant* was now pressed into service to transport marine scientists to the area to study the currents in the gulf, and through computer models, attempt to predict the location and time of the slick's landfall on the Texas coast.

In Tampico, Mexico, the Federal Fish and Wildlife Service made preparations to work with the Mexican government to airlift thousands of young Kemp's Ridley turtles, an endangered species, from their hatching grounds north of Tampico.

Meanwhile, the scientists who had been aboard the *Valiant* were growing optimistic. On July 24, they predicted that the oil would probably reach Texas in 10 to 14 days, but they also noted that it was beginning to break up into tar balls, or pancakes of oil, and they also predicted that orthodox skimming methods and the geographic fortuitousness of the barrier islands would keep it from entering the salt marshes and mangrove swamps behind them.

This was a situation fondly to be wished, for the Laguna Madre, a 130-mile-long lagoon behind the barrier islands off South Texas was a breeding ground for crab, shrimp, and fish and such birds as egrets, cormorants, roseate spoonbills, royal terns, and another endangered species, the brown pelican.

Padre Island had another sort of richness. It was just coming into its own as a summer resort, and its beaches were some of the widest and cleanest in the south. An oil spill would nip this resort in its elegant bud. Just behind it were the flats of Corpus Christi Bay, the site of Port Aransas's sport-fishing business, which was another mainstay of the local economy.

A week later, the oil washed ashore on the Mexican beaches 30 miles south of Brownsville, Texas. Now it was apparent that it was only a matter of time before it would hit Texas, and Steve Frishman, owner and editor of the *South Jetty*, Port Aransas's newspaper, summed up the prevailing mood. "It's like everything else," he said. "They really don't believe it until they see it. It's not going to be pretty when we see it, and I have a pretty good feeling that one way or another, we're going to."

He was right. The next day, the slick was visible offshore, and the more pessimistic among Fort Aransas's inhabitants noted that it was the height of the hurricane season, and one good surge from a hurricane could drive the offshore oil across the barrier islands and into the wetlands. "If you really want to be horrified," said city manager Dana Bennett to reporters, "think about that."

A floating barrier was erected between the slick and Brownsville.

By August 6, the slick, now united into one mass with silvery fingers reaching out ahead of it, extended from the mouth of the Rio Grande into the Gulf of Mexico, and tar balls began to mix with the surf and wash ashore north of Padre Island. The Coast Guard began to deploy containment booms in the South Bay area south of the Brownsville Ship Channel and near the Port Mansfield area in an effort to block off the channel to the wetlands. The oil, however, was 40 feet deep in some places, and no amount of booms could contain oil that deep. And if screens were added to the booms, they would block out both oil and marine life.

Dr. Patrick Parker, an oceanographer for the University of Texas Marine Science center at Port Aransas, worried aloud about the birds in the estuaries. "[They would be almost] one hundred percent destroyed," he said, and at his urging, the Federal Fish and Wildlife Service brought youths from the Conservation Corps at McAllen, Texas, in to set up a bird-cleaning operation.

Finally, the oil arrived at South Padre Island, in the form of baseball-size tar balls, formed by the chemical breakdown of the crude in salt water. Behind the tar balls were 55 million gallons of oil. And the slick was still building.

The following day was hot and calm, and this temporarily halted the advance of the oil. It was still pouring from the well into the gulf at the rate of 20,000 barrels a day, but its appearance on the Texas coast was proving to be spasmodic and unpredictable. If there was to be damage to the coastal ecology, scientists said, it would likely come not all at once, but in erratic, uneven stages. And then, too, in September, the "blue northerns," winds that came from the north in the autumn, could push the oil offshore.

Meanwhile, Texas politicians were losing sleep. Governor William Clements was a founder of Sedco, and he asked for calm and a "good neighbor policy" toward Mexico, which, translated, meant no lawsuits.

The U.S. State Department said it was looking into the matter of compensation from Mexico for the spill, but the international legal waters were murky, too. At the United Nations Conference on the Human Environment in Stockholm in 1972, participants agreed that international measures had to be taken to minimize ocean pollution.

But, aside from regional meetings concerning the Mediterranean and the Baltic, fulfillment of the concept, including oil spillage abatement, had devolved largely on the United Nations Law of the Sea Conference, which was still going on when Ixtoc 1 blew.

By August 13, the pollution of the beach at Padre Island increased, as a solid slick six inches deep washed ashore. It was now threatening Corpus Christi, too, but so far, only negligible and extremely light spots of oil were sighted in the environmentally sensitive area of Laguna Madre.

Day after day now, front after front of oil began to reach the beaches, staining them a filthy brown. By August 16, more than six miles of resort beaches at South Padre Island were covered. Heavier, 500-foot booms were brought in by the Coast Guard to install across the 1,550 foot wide Aransas Pass, the boat channel into the Port of Corpus Christi.

By the beginning of August, the Mexican well had emitted enough oil to cover the entire Gulf of Mexico, at a rate of 1,000 gallons per square mile. Six hundred miles of the Gulf Coast were contaminated by it. By August 19, 100 million gallons had gushed from the still-flowing well, which had calmed somewhat and was only belching forth 420,000 gallons a day, down from the original 1.25 million gallons.

By the end of August, Texas officials estimated that 120 metric tons of mixed oil, water, and sand had been deposited along the Texas barrier-island strand, and 25 percent of its 137-mile length had been soiled to a few yards above the waterline. It was unsightly but not necessarily serious. So far, the visible environmental damage had been limited to a dozen dead birds and a ravaged beach. What was invisible was yet to be studied.

On August 20, several DC-6's, piloted by Canadians, sprayed chemicals on seven of the largest patches of oil, two of them off the Texas coast.

On August 27, a tropical depression hit the Texas coast, and fears ascended. Heavy backup booms were stretched out from both sides of the Santiago Pass jetties leading to the Laguna Madre, to keep the oil from being forced into it. The booms held.

Airplanes and helicopters, directed by oceanographers, made daily flights from Mexico to New Orleans, mapping ecologically sensitive areas, surveying them, and directing teams to deflect the oil. Samples taken indicated that the oil had "weathered" during its long journey, and the combined forces of wind, sun, and water had removed many of the most toxic substances from it.

September arrived, and with it Hurricane Elena, which did not force the oil ashore but rather scrubbed some of the beaches clean. When it was over, Hans Stuart, of the United States Fish and Wildlife Service reported that "very little oil has gotten into the bays," which provided the winter nesting ground for more than 4 million water fowl.

Meanwhile, $225 million in damage suits began to pile up against Sedco, despite Governor Clements's soothing words. Now, he absolved Sedco of responsibility, stating that its equipment lay in 165 feet of water after being blown off the platform. Nothing was wrong with the equipment; it was the way it was used, he affirmed.

On a higher level, President Jimmy Carter and President Jose Lopez Portillo of Mexico met and agreed to have their governments begin negotiations concerning compensation for damages.

The goodwill lasted for only a week. On October 2, President Portillo, citing the United States's refusal to pay Mexico for damages resulting from the salting of the Mexicali Valley, announced that Mexico "will pay nothing" for the damage done to the Texas coast.

Meanwhile, the oil continued to leak into the Gulf of Mexico. More bad luck dogged the workers. A "sombrero," or

collecting funnel, was erected over the blown well to pull off the oil and burn the gas. But no sooner had it been set in place when heavy seas dislodged it. "We haven't had a single good bounce since this thing started," moaned a worker, after the sombrero failed. "At every step we've been confronted by Murphy's Law. If something can go wrong, it did go wrong."

In Mexico, that also meant damage to the environment. Thousands of dead fish were reported to have washed ashore west of Ciudad del Carmen, the rich fishing grounds. Shrimping was halted.

On October 13, 108,000 steel and lead globes the size of tennis balls were pumped into the mouth of the Ixtoc 1 well to reduce the pressure. The strategy seemed to work. The flow was beginning to lessen when, on November 12, Murphy's Law struck again. A ship dropped anchor on the pipeline of the platform, puncturing it. The oil gushed forth through the hole.

North of the rig, winter currents were beginning to take over and push the slick away from the Texas coast, but scientists worried that, at the rate the workers on the rig were inching toward the capping of the well, it was entirely possible that the danger would return with the spring.

Finally, midway through December, the relief well was finished, and a second had already been started. The flow of oil lessened, noticeably.

But oddly enough, neither the American nor Mexican governments did anything about cleaning up the spill during the winter. Scientists pointed out that now was the ideal time; it was easier to scoop up the oil in the sea than it was to scrub it from the beaches. Furthermore, skimming it at the source would prevent the slick from spreading beyond its already monumental size. But nothing was done, on land or sea.

Pemex assured the world that there had been no significant environmental damage in Mexican waters, but U.S. scientists were skeptical. John Robinson, the head of a task force evaluating the damage from the spill noted that "we have already observed impacts. The shore bird population is down considerably from what it's been in previous years."

Finally, on March 24, just as the spring tides were turning, a spokesperson for Pemex announced that engineers had finally capped the well on Ixtoc 1. Prior to the capping, seawater, mud, and thickening substances had been pumped through the two directional wells, and a cement plug, consisting of approximately 200 sacks of cement, was poured into the hole on the oil rig. The cement hardened into a plug 685 feet long.

A few hours later, a second batch of 200 sacks of cement was poured, and it hardened into a plug 550 feet long. Finally, the third and last batch of cement, this time consisting of 500 sacks of the quick-hardening cement, was poured into the opening. It formed a plug 1,650 feet long, and shortly before midnight on the 24th, the oil stopped flowing completely.

Nineteen seventy-nine had been a very bad year for sufferers from oil spills. There had been 38 accidents, resulting in the death of more than 250 people, 50,000 birds, and 270,000 fish. Just how much of this could be traced to Ixtoc 1 would never be definitely known. The Mexican government consistently underestimated everything. A U.S. study that might have presented the truth was aborted because of lack of funds.

What was known was that 134 million gallons of crude oil poured out of Ixtoc 1 during the nine months that it released its cargo into the Gulf of Mexico and onto the gulf's beaches. The total cost of emergency expenses, capping, and cleanup expenses, lost oil, and damage awards amounted to $580 million, making it the world's most expensive, as well as the largest, oil disaster to that time.

NORWAY, DENMARK, UNITED KINGDOM (NORTH SEA)
OIL RIG BLOWOUT
April 22, 1977

Eight and a half million gallons of crude oil geysered into the North Sea on April 22, 1977, when the Bravo oil rig, located in the Ekofisk oil field in the North Sea, halfway between Norway and the United Kingdom, blew. It would take more than a week to cap the well.

The economies of both Norway and the United Kingdom were depressed in the late 1960s. But oil was a catalyst upon which both countries decided they would depend to revive their fortunes. And revive them oil did. The Ekofisk field, the largest offshore oil area in Europe, located in the center of the North Sea, was discovered just before Christmas, 1969. A joint venture between Norway and the United Kingdom, the rigs were installed and operated by Phillips Petroleum, a U.S. company.

It would be five years before the wells serviced by the three rigs were established, with their innards sunk deeply into the sand of the sea bottom and their towers either majestically or foolishly (depending upon your environmental orientation) soaring skyward. Part of the agreement between Norway and the United Kingdom (Britain in 1977), included a 220-mile undersea pipeline through which oil from the field flowed directly to the United Kingdom.

It would signal the end of soft coal as a fuel for the U.K.'s industry, and, because of this, the end of the polluting, intense London fogs. For the coastal towns of Norway, it would be a revival, a change of support and a new life. Stavanger, a coastal city of 100,000, which celebrated its 850th birthday in 1975, was typical. A fading sardine port in the early 1970s, it was transformed by the oil field into the Houston of Norway.

There had been some small leaks in the construction of the rigs, but nothing that even remotely warned of the huge blowout that occurred on the night of April 22, 1977. It happened on the Bravo rig, which was located about 160 miles from the coast of Norway and approximately 180 miles from the coast of Denmark. Ironically, the catastrophe occurred as workmen, during a routine workover, were installing a safety device that was designed to prevent the sort of blowout that occurred.

The men performed the process leading up to the capping in a prescribed manner that day. The flow of oil into the well was stopped by closing the valves at the top end of the pipe on what is called by oilmen the "Christmas tree."

Next, they pumped drilling fluid, known as "mud" into the pipe, forcing the oil that had already entered it back down into its underground reservoir. The buildup of the mud and its constituent minerals, or barites, gradually equalled the pressure of the oil spurting up in the opposite direction.

Now, with the mud holding the oil back, the workers removed the Christmas tree valves from the top of the pipe and began to install a blowout preventer, to seal it.

But they then proceeded to commit a series of grievous, fatal errors. First, mud began to seep out of the valves and the tubing—a sure sign that pressure was building up in the pipe. No one paid any attention to this definite warning signal. Then, a "down hole safety valve" that was supposed to be firmly locked into place was not. After this, a plug was to be installed. But the parts of it were not properly marked and became scrambled. The installed plug was useless. Finally, the two parts of the blowout preventer, one weighing 4 tons and the other weighing 13 tons, were positioned on different decks of the platform.

For a few nervous and critical moments during the temporary stoppage of production on an oil rig, most of the safety devices on a well must be removed or disconnected. During those moments, according to a Houston oil production expert later called in to clean up, "everybody holds their breath" until the blowout preventer is secured to the top of the pipe.

At the precise time that this breath-holding moment occurred on the Bravo rig, underground pressures began to build. But the workmen on the rig continued to ignore the accumulating warning signals from the leaking valves. The first part of the blowout preventer was raised, then lowered into place and 2 of its 12 bolts were attached but not tightened.

And then it happened. The oil and mud thundered up through the pipe, reached the rig, and tossed men and blowout preventer parts onto the platform deck. With an ear-shattering roar, the combination of oil and gas shot 180 feet into the air, then fountained down on the rig and the sea around it. Forty-nine thousand gallons of crude oil an hour would pump out of the blowout well from then until it was finally capped.

The 112-man crew on the rig was evacuated immediately. Fire was a distinct possibility, and the men were taken off in tugs, as gale force winds began to rise. Phillips Petroleum immediately called in Paul "Red" Adair, one of the world's leading experts on the repair of blowouts and the man later given the responsibility of capping the Iraqi oil wells after the Gulf War (see Kuwait, pp. 211–16).

A huge oil slick began to form around the rig. Phillips officials acknowledged that it would only take six and a half days for its bulk to contain enough oil to equal the 7.6 million gallons spilled from the wrecked tanker Argo Merchant, which had split apart off Nantucket Island the preceding December (see pp. 176–79).

Several boats with firefighting apparatus and pumps aboard positioned themselves around the rig, pumping water steadily on it to avert fire.

By the following day, the oil slick measured 2 miles wide by 10 miles long and was moving in an easterly direction. The forecast was for the wind to turn west, which would move it directly toward Norway's southern coast and the southern part of Jutland, on the west coast of Denmark.

By April 24, the American experts from Houston arrived and boarded the rig, but 1.6 million gallons of red-brown oil had already been sprayed into the North Sea from a geyser that now topped 150 feet.

Phillips spokespeople maintained an optimistic stance, predicting a capping within two days. But just in case, they added, plans were going forward to drill a new well parallel to the original, to relieve the pressure.

Meanwhile, environmental specialists of the Norwegian government began to arrive on the scene with wooden booms. Their progress was slow and impeded by the capricious and dangerous winds and waves of the North Sea. If the wind velocity continued and the slick progressed as it was, it was predicted by experts to affect the Norwegian fishing industry within five or six days.

On April 24, the crew from Houston, headed by Red Adair, began their work full of confidence and determination. Told that Norwegian experts predicted that it would take 35 days to cap the well, Adair's assistant, Boots Hansen, commented that he was in the habit of working only 35 days a year—a profitable schedule, considering that Adair and his crew were paid tens of thousands of dollars a day for their admittedly terribly dangerous work.

In the case of the Bravo platform, the problem was to cap the well without striking any sparks that would turn it and the sea around it into a roaring inferno. In fact, the men who worked on capping the wellhead, under a constant rain of oil, could not speak to each other, only signal silently. Their teeth might create a spark. Furthermore, only brass tools, which do not set off sparks when they strike steel, are used in this process, which approaches brain surgery in its specialization and precise demands.

The plan, then, was to moor a huge barge carrying pumps and tanks of mud alongside the rig, far enough from the gas fumes to provide the necessary power without the sparks. A pipeline with flexible couplings was rigged from the barge to the platform, to be connected to the wellhead by the Houston crew, after which hydraulically activated rams would be attached to pinch the well pipe shut.

Everything was in place by April 25, including the 400-foot barge Choctaw, carrying Adair and his men. But once again, the vigorous and unpredictable North Sea weather intervened. Twenty-foot waves and 60-mph winds made the delicate and dangerous work unthinkable.

Meanwhile, there was mounting pressure from Norwegian fishing interests upon Odvar Nordi, whose Labor government faced a general election in the fall. In London, energy secretary Anthony Wedgewood Benn assured the House of Commons that dealing with pollution at sea was "the first priority."

On April 26, the sea flattened and the wind diminished to a gentle breeze, enough to keep the gas moving and thus lessen the chance of fire and/or asphyxiation. The men from Houston went to work. In pairs, according to a meticulously rehearsed plan, they attached the blowout protector that had only been partially bolted on when the blowout occurred.

But the job took longer than anticipated because of a startling discovery. The original protector had been attached upside down, a mistake that probably spelled the difference between escaping oil and capped oil. With all of the extra work that was necessary to correct the error, too much time was consumed, and as the afternoon waned, the wind died utterly, making it too dangerous to remain on the platform. Plans were made to resume the job the following day, provided that the weather cooperated.

Meanwhile, 20 tons of oil were skimmed from the surface of the sea around the platform. It was a small beginning. The remainder of the oil slick extended 250 square miles outward into the North Sea and contained more than 350 million gallons of crude in varying degrees of thickness. Fortunately, the waves seemed to be breaking it up, and the winds were keeping it offshore.

It would be April 28 before weather conditions turned favorable again. This time, the capping moved forward throughout the morning, and at noon the rams were attached to pinch off the pipe. But they did not hold and, eventually, under pressure, cracked.

Twice more, the Houston team made adjustments and tried to cap the well, and each time, they failed. The amount of oil in the water now totaled more than 4.5 million gallons, and more was cascading seaward every hour.

On April 29, Phillips moved a floating platform, the Borgny Dolphin, close to Bravo to begin the 40-day process of drilling a relief well, in case one more try at capping the original well did not work.

Now, Red Adair personally took charge of the operation, and apparently his presence made a difference. On the fifth try, a computer-generated plan from Rucker-Schaeffer, one of the manufacturers of "blind rams"—hydraulically operated half-discs of steel with hard rubber facings—spelled the difference. More pressure was applied this time without damage to the rams, and it worked. The pressure in the pipe was equalized, the well was capped, and the valves closed.

Now boards of inquiry met, and governmental and international agencies proposed cures and cautions. The World Organization for Economic Cooperation and Development called for emergency arrangements to cope with oil pollution from offshore exploration. Mindful of the upside down installation of the safety device, the group recommended the establishment of minimum training standards for workers on offshore platforms and that member countries ensure that the best available construction and operation techniques and safety standards were applied on offshore rigs to prevent oil spills.

By the beginning of May, the oil slick had virtually disappeared. Only scattered patches of oil remained, and the currents and waves of the North Sea seemed to be breaking them up.

By the middle of September, the Norwegian Institute for Marine Research announced that there was apparently no serious environmental damage. "[There was] no obvious effect of the oil on the number or distribution of fish," stated institute representative Grim Berge. "We feared the blowout might coincide with the spring period when the plankton are developing, but it appears the plankton were slow reaching this phase because of low temperatures and lack of stable layers in the water."

On October 10, the Norwegian Royal Commission investigating the blowout issued its findings. It noted the long string of missteps leading up to the blowout and concluded that along with the human errors, "the underlying cause of the accident was that the organizational and administrative systems were on this occasion inadequate to assure safe operations."

Phillips Petroleum, Norway, and Norwegian authorities were held responsible. Phillips accepted the responsibility and announced that "valuable lessons have been learned, and [will] be applied diligently to attempt to prevent other accidents in the future."

Since no ecological damage was reported, damage suits were null and void, but the cost of the capping, repair, and cleanup ran to several million dollars.

RUSSIA
(USNISK)
OIL SPILL IN THE ARCTIC
October 1, 1994

....

A large oil spill of between 4 and 8 million gallons of untreated crude oil from the deteriorating pipeline between the Arctic oil exploration regions of Russia and Moscow on October 1, 1994, caused immense environmental damage.

"The energy production system built in the Russian Arctic during the Soviet era is a world catastrophe waiting to happen. If Russian leaders are willing, the world community will help them in the monumental task of cleaning up and modernizing that system."

So said Walter J. Hickel, former Interior secretary and governor of Alaska, after a firsthand look at the horrendous and continuing aftermath of the huge oil spill and fire caused by a ruptured pipeline near the town of Usnisk, just south of the Arctic Circle and 1,000 miles northeast of Moscow.

The Soviets had established two conflicting and overlapping entities in the 1960s. The first was an oil pipeline linking the Russian Arctic and Moscow. Sometime in the 1960s (information was very hard to come by during the Soviet reign), a large oil and gas discovery had been made in the Pechora basin. The Pechora River is one of the main rivers of the European Arctic, rising at the northern end of the Ural Mountains and flowing into the Barents Sea through a large delta at the town of Nar'yan Mar.

The field was utilized; wells were sunk and in 1976, oil production from the Pechora basin totaled about 175,000 barrels a day, comprising nearly 2 percent of the national oil production of the USSR. A transporting pipeline was built from Usnisk to Ukhta and onward toward Moscow. As with many projects in the USSR at that time, maintenance was not of paramount importance; results were. And so, over the years, the pipeline deteriorated, and a series of leaks developed. The leaks were a threat to a rich ecology.

And that ecology formed the basis of the second, conflicting establishment by the Soviet government. Usnisk lies at the northern margin of a forest within the taiga zone—a region of open woodland interspersed with short vegetation and dominated by sedges and mosses. To the north, the trees give way to open tundra and to the south, the forest becomes more continuous. Within the Pechora River basin—and this is very important—there are large regions of marshland, which is a breeding site for many waterfowl species, including Bewick and Whooper swan, geese, long-tailed ducks, northern fulmars, glaucous and ivory gulls, little auks, and other breeds.

Around this marshland is tundra, which holds one of the region's largest herds of domestic reindeer—some 65,000 to 120,000—and 6,000 wild reindeer, and in which polar bears and eider ducks live. Because of its natural riches, the 270,000-hectare area (approximately 351,000 acres) was declared a nature reserve in 1963. The declaration, in an indirect way, also protected other species. The

A lake of burning oil covers and destroys the tundra surrounding the pipeline leak near Usnisk.
WARFORD/GREENPEACE

spring migration of the wild inhabitants of the Nenetsky Nature Park, one of the main breeding sites in European Russia, arrives in the Pechora region in mid-April. The autumn migration leaves from late September to mid-October.

And there are other natural riches in the region upon which hundreds of thousands of Russians depend. Flowing into the Pechora and influenced by everything that happens in it is the Kolva River, a tributary of the Usa. The Pechora River itself flows into the Pechorskoye Sea, in the northern part of European Russia. Bordered by delta and marshes, it is a breeding site for the Bewick and Whooper swan, and geese. Ice free until late December, it supports large concentrations of sea duck, beluga or white whales, ringed seals, bearded seals, and polar bears.

Finally, for a long time during the early years of the USSR, the Pechora delta was a rich source of commercial fishing. It was, for a time, overfished, but by the late 1970s fish stocks had renewed themselves, and subsistance fishing by the local peoples was being augmented by a growing commercial fishing industry. In fact, salmon and char fish-

ing constituted one of the main industries of Nar'yan Mar and employed more than a million people. The delta was rich in Atlantic salmon, whitefish, smelt, pike, roach, turbot, perch, and arctic flounder.

In other words, it was an ecological gold mine, and precarious besides. Tundra environments are particularly susceptible to disturbance, and many of the Arctic plants that grow on the tundra, especially lichens, the main food of reindeer, are highly susceptible to pollutants.

Oil leakage is a particular hazard in the tundra, since, at low temperature, oil tends to persist for long periods because of the low rate of evaporation. The frozen ground also prevents it from seeping in, and this has the effect of allowing it to travel for long distances on the frozen surface. Furthermore, the oil can remain hidden and stabilized within the snow and ice cover of the region and then be released once the snow's cover melts in the spring. This melting coincides with the return of migrating birds, threatening their lives, and thus maximizing the impact of the oil upon the environment. Finally, there is the danger of fire igniting the dried tundra after the thaw.

All of this was undoubtedly known to the Soviet government and its inheritors, but nothing much was done to maintain the pipeline once it was built, and, save for some protective dykes erected around it, nothing was done to protect the environment from potential spills.

Apparently, small leaks occurred over many years. Some of these around Usnisk were reported in February 1994, but this was an old and continuing story to the officials responsible for it.

On October 1, heavy rains pelted the tundra and the marshes near the pipeline, which was now pouring a goodly amount of oil into its catch basins. Finally, in the midst of a downpour, the protective dyke around the pipe burst and the oil gushed forth, racing across the marshes and spilling into the Kolva River. On and on it poured, and once again, the information that came out of Russia was general and vague. To this day, the total spillage before repairs were completed is listed as between 14,000 and 240,000 tons (4 to 8 million gallons) of oil.

Finally, international pleas after international inspections, plus the willingness of the six Western companies, who, under détente, were poised to begin oil production in the region, forced President Yeltsin to begin to replace the old and corroded pipe of the pipeline, starting with the 32 miles that ran through the area of the spill.

It was not a pleasant job. It had to be completed during the cold weather, when the oil was trapped, and before the spring thaw that could, if the job was not finished, provide incoming, breeding, and migratory birds and mammals with a lethal greeting. But it was successfully completed.

SAUDI ARABIA
(DHAHRAN)
OIL FIELD FIRE
May 11, 1977

....

The environmental impact of the four-day fire caused by a pipeline rupture in the Abquaiq oil field pumping facility, owned by Aramco, in Saudi Arabia, went largely unreported. A $100 million fire, caused by corrosion in the pipe, shut down the transfer and processing of crude oil from Saudi Arabia for four days and affected world oil markets. One worker died and one was injured in the blast and subsequent fire.

For centuries, the Middle East enjoyed an ecology that, while not necessarily benign, was not self-destructive. But that was before the discovery of oil. The vastness and richness of the oil reserves, particularly in the Arabian peninsula, changed not only the economy but the ecology of the region.

There was rapid urbanization and industrialization, which brought with them sewage problems that polluted soil and rivers. There was the rising demand for food of a rising population. There was the pollution of the air brought about by a sudden glut of automobiles on urban streets, by industry spewing industrial pollutants into the air, and by oil fires that plagued the oil fields.

One of the worst of these fires took place in the Abquaiq field, 35 miles west of Dhahran, Saudi Arabia, on May 11, 1977. The field and the pipeline that ruptured and caught fire were owned by Aramco (Arabian American Oil Company), which still operates most of Saudi Arabia's oil fields. Customarily, Aramco runs an efficient enterprise. But on the afternoon of May 11, 1977, the worst fire in the company's nearly 70-year history erupted with the bursting of one of the transport pipes in the Abquaiq field.

Had it been an ordinary field, this would have been just another oil field fire, spewing benzene, hydrocarbons, hydrogen chloride, and carbon monoxide in huge quantities into the atmosphere, adding to the world's acid rain, creating photochemical smog, and compounding climate disruption by reducing solar radiation.

But this fire took place in a one-square-mile area that contained pipelines, pumping stations, storage tanks, and processing equipment through which the bulk of Saudi oil production flowed en route to tanker terminals on the Persian Gulf.

Crude oil from major oil fields to the south of Dhahran is processed at the station, then pumped north to the tanker terminals at Ras Tanura and Ju'amayah, on the Persian Gulf coast. Situated in these southern fields is Ghawar, the world's largest oil field, which supplies 5 million barrels a day of crude oil to the world market.

What took place that afternoon was, in other words, an economic conflagration as well as an oil fire. It forced the shutdown of three-quarters of the production of Saudi Arabian oil, a situation that, if prolonged, would have had a profound economic impact upon oil markets worldwide.

The explosive rupture in the pipe occurred at 3:30 P.M., while routine maintenance was being performed on the pipeline. The force of the blast killed a Saudi foreman and injured an American worker.

Within seconds, the oil geysering from the rupture sprayed over the plant area and immediately burst into flames, sending great gouts of gray smoke billowing into the sky. The sun was totally blotted out over a thirteen-square-mile area.

Initially, it was feared that the entire compound, with its processing machinery and pumping facilities, would have to be shut down and rebuilt. But the damage was confined to a single pumping station, some pipeline, and a few processing facilities.

At first, there were widespread reports of the arrival of African Communist agents in Saudi Arabia, set upon sabotaging oil operations in the conservative Arab country. But the reports turned out to be speculation, and the cause of the fire was concluded to be corrosion in the pipe that burst.

It would take four days for firemen to extinguish the constantly reigniting blaze, and it would take the installation a week to resume operations. The combined damage and losses from the fire ultimately cost Aramco more than $100 million. The four United States owners of Aramco—the Exxon Corporation; Texaco, Inc.; the Mobil Corporation; and the Standard Oil Company of California, who were in the process of turning the operation over to the government of Saudi Arabia—reduced their pumping of Saudi oil by up to 30 percent.

Thus, the Aramco oil field fire had a two-pronged impact. The assault, both short and long range, on the environment, went largely unreported. The economic impact was duly reported and widely felt by world gasoline consumers.

SPAIN
(LA CORUÑA)
GROUNDING AND EXPLOSION OF OIL TANKER
AEGEAN SEA
December 3, 1992

....

The Greek oil tanker Aegean Sea *ran aground during a storm at the entrance to the harbor of La Coruña in Spain on December 3, 1992. The resultant oil spill, nearly twice that of the* Exxon Valdez, *fouled 60 miles of the Spanish coast and crippled the huge fishing industry located there.*

The *Aegean Sea*, a 53,964-ton oil tanker, loaded with 23.8 million gallons of crude oil, set sail from Britain's North Sea oil-loading terminal at Sullom Voe in November 1992, headed for a refinery in La Coruña, a city of 250,000 in Spain's northwestern corner, approximately 280 miles from Madrid.

It was before dawn when the ship arrived at the port of La Coruña on December 3. Fog shrouded the harbor, and there were abnormally high seas of 12 to 15 feet. The captain, Constantine Stavrides, asked for authorization to enter. He was given it, and the harbor pilot was dispatched to guide the ship into the sheltered port.

But suddenly, before the pilot reached the ship, the captain, unannounced, attempted to enter the harbor himself. It was an unfortunate and foolish decision. At 5:00 A.M., the *Aegean Sea* missed the harbor entrance widely and plowed into sharp rocks outside of it, ripping long gashes in her hull. Oil immediately began to gush forth from the ruptured tanks in her hold.

That would have been bad enough, but five hours later, at 10:00 A.M., as rescue boats took the last of the 29 crew members from the ship and salvage boats fought the rain and wind to get near her, a huge explosion ripped through the tanker. It was like a simultaneous, monumental bombardment that sent residents of the city and the coastal area on either side of it running from their homes.

What greeted them was an immense pyre of flame and black smoke, roaring out of the detached stern, which was floating free of the rest of the vessel. The oil that had escaped into the water now ignited into an immense, flaming ring, which drove the rescue and salvage boats back.

It was wise to let the oil burn; it would be a better course of action than trying to disperse it with chemicals, and the seas were still too high to allow barriers and skimmers to be used. And so the ships merely laid off, and Joan Lopez de Uralde, a Spanish spokesperson for Greenpeace, worried aloud about the fishing and shellfish grounds in the Ria de Betanzos and Ria de Ares, two inlets northeast of La Coruña harbor.

The oil burned for several days; then the bow section, which contained the cargo of oil, sank, putting out its flames. The stern had stopped burning a day before, when the ship's fuel contained in it was exhausted.

And now the pollution began. A slick from the oil that had leaked before the burnoff that was variously reported as being 10 to 20 square miles in scope began to foul the beaches on each side of the harbor. All along La Coruña Bay, in inlets rich in shellfish, the black clinging mess came ashore and stuck, four inches deep.

Galicia Province, surrounding the area, is Europe's principal fishing region, a place where 20 percent of the population made a living, in 1992, from the $300 million a year fishing industry. Two-hundred fifteen boats and 800 fishermen in the area remained ashore, since fishing was banned by government decree immediately after the grounding and fire.

The effect upon wildlife became immediately apparent. Three days after the disaster, environmentalists told the international press that in the Mera beach area alone, they had found 2,000 oil-soaked seabirds that had been plucking oily fish from the dark waters off the coast.

The only good news was that the oil was light crude and could dissipate more quickly than the heavier crude that had caused horrendous devastation on the Brittany Coast after the *Amoco Cadiz* grounding (see pp. 140–42). Still, this was the place from where the fish for Europe came, and every word from the wreck produced further consternation among fishermen and restaurateurs.

Sixteen barriers were installed across estuaries east and north of La Coruña on December 6, but the oil slick continued to spread toward Cape Prior, 20 miles north. Beaches along the Betanzos and Ares estuaries northeast of La Coruña were coated by oil, and the slick bore relentlessly down on Ferrol, just south of Cape Prior.

News of the damage reached the World Wide Fund for Nature in Geneva, and its investigators journeyed immediately to Spain. Within days, they reported that coastal ecosystems were in great danger. "The first visible victims are tens of thousands of migratory birds," they stated. "Experts also expect that the damage to mollusks, cockles,

The end of the fire aboard the Aegean Sea *was the beginning of the pollution of the Spanish Coast. An oil slick nearly twice that of the* Exxon Valdez *halted fishing in the area for six months.*
(BELTRA/GREENPEACE)

oysters, clams, barnacles, and various species of fish will be irreversible in the long term, with disastrous implications for the fisheries-based economy of the region."

The storm raged on through December 7, preventing divers from inspecting the tanker's hull. But educated estimates put the spill at between 65,000 and 70,000 tons. Only about 13,000 of the original 80,000 tons of oil remained in the vessel, salvagers said.

Twelve hundred tons of oil were skimmed from the sea in the first four days, and by the end of the first week, 4.1 miles of floating barriers had been set up. The captain of the ship was blamed for the tragedy and was kept in custody by Spanish police. Authorities acknowledged the Fund for Nature's estimate of injured and dead wildlife, but noted also that the storm had driven many migratory and coastal birds inland, thus decreasing the possible fatalities.

The final assessment was calamitous. The amount of oil—21.5 million gallons—was nearly twice the amount spilled in the 1989 *Exxon Valdez* disaster. Fishing was prohibited in the area for six months. Eventually, the beaches were cleaned up and life returned to normal. The monetary damages have yet to be totaled, but Repsol, the Spanish oil

company that leased the tanker, and the tanker's captain, were both held responsible.

TOBAGO
(COAST)
COLLISION OF *ATLANTIC EMPRESS* AND *AEGEAN CAPTAIN*
July 15, 1979

The Atlantic Empress *and* Aegean Captain, *two supertankers, collided in a thunderstorm 20 miles off the island of Tobago on July 15, 1979. Twenty-nine crew members, most of them from the* Atlantic Empress, *were lost at sea; 50 were treated at a Tobago hospital. The oil slicks from both ships dissipated at sea.*

Two supertankers, each as long as three football fields, collided during a thunderstorm 20 miles off the coast of Tobago, located, along with its sister island Trinidad, 100 miles northeast of Venezuela. The *Atlantic Empress*, carrying 270,000 tons of Arabian crude oil, and the *Aegean Captain*, carrying 200,000 tons of Venezuelan crude, were traveling at full speed in opposite directions at 8:00 P.M. on July 15. The combined amount of oil carried by the two ships was 3.2 million barrels, enough to cause the largest oil slick in the world up to that point.

Both ships burst into flame upon impact, and distress signals went out, reaching the coast guard of the Republic of Trinidad and Tobago, which sent out a rescue ship immediately. The ship was joined by a Netherlands search plane from the island of Curacao.

Of the 76 crewmen aboard the ships, 26 were reported missing and 50 others, many with severe burns, were rescued and taken to a hospital on Tobago.

The *Aegean Captain* seemed to suffer the most damage. Its starboard bow was caved in and had an enormous, gaping hole in it, from which oil poured. Flames consumed its forward deck, and the oil in the water around it burned spectacularly and ceaselessly. A German tug was attached to the ship and it was towed north, away from land.

The *Atlantic Empress*, which had rammed the other ship, and was carrying faulty navigation gear, drifted northeast of Tobago, with an east wind pushing it to the west at about one knot an hour. The oil slick from its wounds spread over 10 square miles.

The *Atlantic Empress* drifted for three days while the fire spread to two-thirds of the ship and sent huge plumes of black smoke hundreds of feet into the air. The smoke could be seen for miles.

The *Aegean Captain*, which appeared at first to have been damaged more, survived better. The fire aboard her was extinguished within a day, and the captain and crew were allowed back aboard by midday. She had only lost 98,000 barrels of her 1.4 million barrels of oil, and from all indications, she would be able to sail on under her own power.

The *Atlantic Empress* was another matter. Tugs, two cutters, and several small boats hovered around her, kept at a distance by the ring of fire burning from the oil spilled on the sea. The disabled ship drifted aimlessly for another two days before two tugs were able to secure lines and begin towing her distinctly out to sea, there to scuttle her.

The ship leaked oil in a slick that extended 60 miles, but the action of wind and water dissipated the pollution, and it posed no threat to the island of Tobago or the mainland of Venezuela. Twenty thousand tons of oil were lost before Mobil, who owned the oil in her hold, extinguished the fire and pumped the remaining cargo into two other tankers that were brought to the scene.

The missing crewmen were never found. One of them was the radio operator of the *Atlantic Empress*, who stayed aboard, with his captain, Paskalis Hatzipetros, until the very last moment. Captain Hatzipetros himself was severely burned and suffered terribly from inhaling flames.

Boats with chemical detergents were stationed at the fringes of both oil slicks, but the natural movement of the Atlantic Ocean dispersed the oil, and none of it reached land. Oil-laden gulls did reach landfall, and died. But there was no land pollution. The *Atlantic Empress* was a total loss, and scuttled at sea. The *Aegean Captain* reached port in Trinidad, then proceeded on, after emergency repairs, under its own steam.

UNITED KINGDOM
(ENGLAND, CORNWALL)
TORREY CANYON OIL SPILL
March 18, 1967

....

The 98,000-ton Torrey Canyon, *one of the first of the huge supertankers, ran aground at full speed in good weather on the shoals of Seven Stones, near Cornwall, on the morning of March 18, 1967. Thirty-six million tons of crude oil spilled into the Atlantic Ocean, fouling the beaches of Cornwall in the United Kingdom and some beaches of Brittany in France. Thirty thousand birds died, the damage was in the tens of millions of dollars, and a new era of environmental damage was launched.*

Cornwall, that stippled peninsula that pokes out, like a gnarled finger, into the Atlantic Ocean from the United Kingdom, and which ends, appropriately enough, at Land's End, has always had about it a certain magical mystique, probably grounded in its Celtic origins. Its rocky reefs, their great granite statements a cold fact, echo Arthurian times, a perfect prelude to visiting the good king's castle, which is located on Cornwall's northwestern coast.

In the 18th and 19th centuries, these reefs and caves were pockmarked by tin mines, but no more. Agriculture and mining have moved elsewhere. Fortunately, however, the gulf stream warms Cornwall's shores, a situation that probably attracted Mediterranean pirates to Penzance. The palm trees that these breezes allowed in other oddly named settlements such as Tresillian and Porthleven and Nanchenoy permitted them to also become popular beach resorts, sentinaling the mildest climate in England and carving out sandy beaches and rocky coves with sleepy, quaint fishing villages threaded through by narrow, cobbled streets. The warm weather tourist rush began early.

In March 1967, in fact, preparations were being made in the resort towns of Cornwall for the imminency of Easter and its consequent flood of tourists. In the Scilly Isles, near Seven Stones and its two lighthouses and one lightship, Britain's prime minister, Harold Wilson, had already begun his Easter holiday.

A day less than a month before, on February 17, 1967, the megatanker *Torrey Canyon*, the 13th-largest ship in the world at the time—not because she was originally built that way, but because she had been stretched and added to to become a jumbo oil tanker—was partially filled with Kuwait crude oil at Mina al Ahmadi.

The 98,000-ton ship, owned by the Union Oil Company of California, on charter to the British Petroleum Company and flying a Liberian flag, was captained by an experienced ship's master, Pastrengo Rugiati, who in turn headed a 36-man Italian crew.

On February 18, the *Torrey Canyon* sailed for Milford Haven, on the southwest coast of Wales. It rounded the Cape of Good Hope, passed the Canary Islands on March 14, and by the night of March 17, had reached the Isles of Scilly.

The next morning was only slightly hazy, with a light northwest breeze. When day broke, the watch was somewhat disconcerted to discover that they were sailing east of the isles rather than west. West was open sea. East was considerably trickier, and the ship was sailing full speed ahead.

First officer Bonfiglio called the captain, who was still in his cabin, to ask if their course was correct. The captain answered that it was, and, a half hour later, appeared on the bridge. It was a little after 8:00 A.M., and they were about to pass close to the shoals of Seven Stones.

At nearly 8:20, two lobster boats were sighted to their starboard, and they maneuvered around them, placing the ship on a direct course between the isles and the shoals of Seven Stones—a course not recommended by the *Channel Pilot,* a book necessary to navigate these waters but absent from the bridge of the *Torrey Canyon.*

The channel was six miles wide. Their fathometer was not operating, nor was one of their radar sets, and this might have warned them that they were getting close to the shoals, a dangerous place to be with their speed at a half mile a minute and their steering mechanism on automatic.

At 8:30, the French lobstermen aboard their two boats, the *Mater Christi* and *Cite d'Arvor,* began shouting and waving, trying to warn the tanker to change its course. But they received no response.

There was indeed frantic activity on the *Torrey Canyon's* bridge, but most of it was counterproductive. The helmsman was ordered to correct his course, fast. But the ship was on automatic, and only an officer could operate the mechanism that would change it. The ship failed to respond to the change in course, and at 8:50 A.M., the *Torrey Canyon* plowed, at full speed, into one of the granite underwater reefs of Seven Stones, eight miles due west of Land's End and eight miles northeast of the Isles of Scilly.

The reef tore gashes 17 feet in width in her hull, and almost immediately, the first of its 36 million gallons of oil gushed forth from the ship's wounded side, into the water. And thus began the world's first—but by no means last—major oil spill.

The oil was heavy, it was beginning to spread, and it would eventually threaten all the beaches and harbors of southern England and the channel beaches of France.

Aboard the *Torrey Canyon,* now locked aground, there was nothing but confusion and paralysis. The ship was beginning to go down by its bow, and its holds were beginning to take on water. The lobster boats were the first to contact shore, radioing to Land's End. It would be a full 10 minutes before the *Torrey Canyon* would signal distress, and another 20 before the crew of the Seven Stones lightship, ascending from below, would sight the wreck and signal "YOU ARE STANDING INTO DANGER."

Now, help came quickly. The St. Mary's Island lifeboat set out. So did the Dutch Wijsmuller company's salvage tug the *Utrecht,* berthed in Penzance. If it could save the ship, it would mean a million dollars in salvage fees to the company. If not, it was a chance taken.

By 10:00 A.M., a Royal Navy helicopter had joined the tugs and boats surrounding the *Torrey Canyon.* She had run aground at high tide; there was reason to believe that she could be freed at the next high tide.

By noon, the *Utrecht,* with its towing equipment, ground tackle, pumps, cutting and welding gear, rigs for diving, and material for hard and soft patches, arrived. Her master was Hille Post, an experienced salvager. A few hours aboard, surveying the damage, breathing the fumes that were being emitted from the engine room, and he knew that it was not going to be an easy job.

That night, the weather turned worse. By dawn, the wind was blowing northwesterly at 20 knots and kicking up the sea. The ship had begun to list 10 degrees. The coast guard advised the captain to get the crew off, and shortly after dawn, 14 of them were transferred to the lifeboat.

Hille Post, realizing that the salvage job was too much for him, gladly turned it over to the Wijsmuller's best man, Captain Hans Stal. Captain Stal now had at his disposal three more tugs and a DC-3 aircraft full of compressors, hoses, generators, and other salvage gear, as well as divers and engineers.

Four tugs tried to pull the *Torrey Canyon* off the reef. Their cables snapped immediately. By now the seas were running 25 feet, and the captain was advised to evacuate the rest of his crew. He put it to a vote, and all but three men voted to abandon ship, which they did, immediately. This left the captain, three men, one of whom was a steward's mate, and the salvage crew aboard.

Meanwhile, a thick blanket of oil, 18 miles long and 3 miles wide, floated in increasing volume out of the *Torrey Canyon.* It could, stated British naval experts, hit land anywhere from the Irish coast to the coast of southwestern France.

On the first day after the grounding, British vessels began to spray the spill with detergent to break up its mass, and plans were made to free the vessel. But longtime seamen in the area, recalling that the last successful operation to free a large ship from the reef had occurred more than 50 years ago, doubted that it could happen.

"Destroy it and set fire to the oil," said a number of members of Parliament, but Denis Healey, the minister of defense, countered that the location of the grounding was in international waters, and doing this would amount to piracy.

But the very next day, March 21, a fine Tuesday, made all of this bickering academic. The mammoth vessel was grinding away at the rocks, and it was taking on water, though the oil leaving it, oddly enough, had increased its buoyancy.

But the stench from the oil had increased, and that concerned those aboard. They knew that a random spark could cause an instant explosion. And that is exactly what happened. A door slammed, and an enormous detonation ripped through the engine room. Captain Stal was blown overboard, his spine sliced in two by a piece of metal. He and three other salvors, also propelled over the side, were rescued by tugs, but Stal, bleeding terribly and in shock, his liver ruptured, died before they reached land.

It was time to evacuate everyone but a few diehard salvors from the ship.

Meanwhile, the oil slick had assumed the shape of a pear, still 30 miles in length but now 18 miles wide. Twenty-five thousand tons of oil had already spilled into the Atlantic, and the slick was still eight miles from the southern coast of Cornwall.

For the next two days, efforts were made to pry the ship loose. Nitrogen was pumped into the ship's tanks, together with a covering of plastic foam. Another attempt was made to pull her off the reef. But Easter morning, near gale winds and a huge sea forced an end to attempts to move the *Torrey Canyon,* which was beginning to break up. As each part of the ship twisted and separated, more oil gushed into the water.

It would take another five days before the oil finally reached the coast of Cornwall. By Saturday, March 25, oily waves began to break against its rocks and coat its sand.

Out at sea, a fleet of vessels was doing its best to break up the oil slick by spraying detergent on it, then churning it up with their propellers. The detergent, BP 1002, was designed to thin the oil, then coat it with an oleophobic film that would break up the drops of oil. The result was something resembling a sickly chocolate mousse—which it was eventually, grimly nicknamed. Up to 100,000 gallons of the detergent were distributed on the oil slick by 20 vessels, and it did work, somewhat.

Onshore, their Easter leaves canceled, 2,000 servicemen with buckets and a fleet of inshore vessels began to spread more detergent on the sand and rocks. An informal army of children followed, with plastic spray cans filled with the same detergent. The portion of the slick reaching shore was 10 miles in length; the spraying job would be enormous.

The slick was already embracing the Cornish coast; the entirety of Mounts Bay was covered, and the resorts of St, Just, Sennen, Newlyn, Marazion, and Mullion were feeling the effects; a 1,000-yard stretch of golden sand at Prah Sands was so densely coated, detergents had no effect upon it. Soon, 18-inch patches of the gummy mixture were washing ashore

at Penzance. The stench was horrific, and hundreds of holiday cancellations were reported by hotels along the coast.

And now, the effect upon marine and bird life was becoming obvious. Birds, their feet and feathers black with oil, struggled to come ashore. But most of them, hundreds of them, died in the attempt.

Meanwhile, at sea, Wijsmuller got the *Torrey Canyon* afloat again, but it needed another 20 feet of water to lift it from the rocks that had bitten 15 to 17 feet into her hull. It was whistling into the wind; the ship was gradually breaking up, and now decisions had to be made about disposing of her and at the same time controlling the flow of oil that was sill gushing forth.

Whatever was to happen, Prime Minister Wilson announced from the Isles of Scilly where he was still vacationing, the ship would not be allowed to enter British territorial waters—an odd statement, considering the fact that its oil had already completely occupied those waters for as far as the eye could see. More than half the cargo was in the sea now. "Given the extra oil . . . floating off Cornwall, all the extra men and equipment in the world could not deal with this problem," said Maurice Foley, the navy minister. "This is a problem no country in the world has had to face before."

The problem had the potential of turning international. A 40-mile-an-hour northwest wind was pushing the slick into the English Channel and toward France.

And now, further ecological damage was forecast by scientists. The detergent used to break up the oil had the potential, they said, of destroying myriad and minute forms of sea life and growths. The mussel and oyster farms, particularly on the Helford River, were considered in grave danger from both oil and detergents, and major efforts were made to insulate them from both.

The situation had reached crisis proportions. At first, plans were made to burn off the oil by using electrically fused oxygen tiles, or oxygenated bricks. On Tuesday, March 28, a Royal Navy helicopter dropped the oxygenated bricks. The attempt was a fizzle, literally and figuratively.

It was time for more drastic measures, and just before 4:00 P.M., a flight of eight Royal Navy Buccaneers roared over the wreck and began to drop 1,000-pound bombs on it. By the end of the afternoon, 18 tons of bombs had sent smoke 3,000 feet in the air, had blown apart much of the *Torrey Canyon's* ravaged hull, and had ignited her cargo. More than 5,000 gallons of jet fuel from the wing tanks of the planes were also dropped, to feed the conflagration.

The next day, there was some improvement, but not much. It was decided to increase the bombardment and add napalm to the mix. For two more days, the Royal Navy assaulted the ship as if she were the enemy (which, in a sense, she now was). Prime Minister Wilson, by news accounts, interrupted a golf game on the Isles of Scilly to watch the bombing. By Friday, March 30, the smoke had cleared. The bombs had appeared to accomplish their task.

Thousands upon thousands of birds, weighed down by a lethal coating of oil from the tanker Torrey Canyon, *perished. If they tried to preen their feathers to remove the oil, they poisoned or asphyxiated themselves.*

(UNEP)

Now the focus turned to the ecological effects of the oil spill. At Sennen Cove, an exquisitely sculpted crescent of sand and rock, there was nothing but brown mousse, as there was around the miniature Mont St.-Michel of St. Michael's Mount at Marazion. Even miles from the sea, a powerful stench of oil permeated the air and everything it touched.

In hundreds of locations on the coast, volunteers were working with the Royal Society for the Prevention of Cruelty to Animals capturing, cleaning, and saving some of the thousands of birds who were coated with oil and detergent. Guillemots and razorbills, gannets and puffins and shags and cormorants and divers, distinctive to the area, usually white, were now a sickly brown. The weight of the fuel oil prevented them from flying, and if they tried to preen their feathers to remove the oil, they poisoned or asphyxiated themselves.

The only help was to wash away the oil, which would also wash away the natural oils that make them buoyant. They would drown, then, if immediately released, and catch cold. So, instead, they were put under infrared lamps to keep warm, then taken to sanctuaries to spend six weeks regaining their natural oils and preening themselves clean.

Those were the captured, lucky ones. Enough others were dying in the middle of their breeding season to cause Royal Society members to predict that this might effectively eliminate the entire reproductive cycle for some species, and eliminate others entirely.

At Porth Navas, near the Helford River, there was frantic activity to protect the huge oyster beds. A dredger laid 1,000 feet of plastic hose with holes in it across the river, seaward of the oyster beds. A yellow diesel-powered compressed-air blower poured air into the hose to create currents to dissuade the oil from flowing into the beds and affecting the oysters at low tide.

A mile upstream, on the Porth Navas Creek, oystermen lashed 300 feet of straw encased in a plastic sheet and chicken wire to float as a barrier in case the bubbling pipe failed to stop the oil.

At the mouth of the River Fal, a 3,000-foot foam plastic barrier was stretched across the river's mouth to protect the beds around Penryn and Flushing.

The oil was only a secondary worry to the oystermen, who proved to be correct in fearing the chemicals in the detergent more. These were lethal to the marine life upon which the oyster fed. In many places along the coast, the tides created a detergent penetration of as much as five feet, and the use of excessive amounts of BP 1002 resulted in a structural breakdown of the beaches, turning them into quicksands. At least some of the horrifying smell that wafted through the hedgerows was due to the interaction of oil with detergent, and the detergent in turn had a caustic effect on both human skin and rubber.

Barriers were installed at Portsmouth, Weymouth, and Southampton. A 1,000-foot gap in them had to be left across the Solent, the approach channel to Southampton, to accommodate the steady flow of freighters and passenger liners that used the port, and experts hoped that only a minimal amount of pollution would enter its harbor.

On April 1, cleaning men from the London sewers and 115 airmen from the United States Third Air Force arrived at the coast, with 12 fire engines, 10 five-ton trucks, five smaller vehicles, and two water trailers with sprays. The cleanup was beginning to show results.

Now the attention shifted to the coast of France. The prevailing winds and currents were carrying the oil across the English Channel to the beaches and oysterbeds of Normandy and Brittany, and the French were frantically preparing for the worst. Not only the oysters and mussels were threatened; seaweed that farmers along the coast use for fertilizer could be destroyed or made thoroughly useless. Detergent was stockpiled at Brest, and a rush shipment of a coagulating substance called Ekoperl was imported from Germany.

By April 9, the first oil reached the French shore near Lingreville, a small village 15 miles north of Granville in the Manche department. Four minesweepers loaded with detergents rushed to the scene from Brest and found reddish globs of oil, already treated with detergents.

By April 11, a slick several inches deep and 90 miles long had fouled Brittany's channel coast from Tregastel to Erquy. *La Maree Noire,* as the French would dub the disaster, had arrived, and with it 3,000 French troops, oystermen, fishermen, and, as in Britain, crowds of the curious who hindered rather than helped the cleanup.

The detergent used by the French was a local product called Craie de Champagne, colorfully named for the province from which it came but amounting, in the end, to stearated chalk. It was effective; 3,000 tons of it sank 20,000 tons of oil in the Bay of Biscay.

But the largest assault upon the oil was waged with simple sawdust and hay. Sawdust worked on the beaches; hay was better for absorbing the oil at sea. Inexpensively made booms, constructed of an envelope of burlap holding tightly packed straw were built and installed in coves and inlets.

As simple as it seemed, the French method proved, in the end, far more effective and safer to the environment than did the British methods. Although some detergents were used at the end, the straw and sawdust coating coated, and did not kill the vegetation and shore life, as did the detergent in Britain.

There (and somewhat in France), the food chain was severely disrupted. Worms, rock pool life, crustacea, anemones, and most sublittoral fauna and flora were found dead; bivalves, starfish, and sea urchins were affected; crabs suffered severely, as did plankton. In the deeper water, fish sickened and died and were eaten by other fish. Grasses, the food of these fish, were killed, and seaweed sprouted in odd places. All of this occurred from the chemicals in the detergents, not the oil.

The French oystermen cleared out many of their beds. Still, 2,500 acres of oysters were lost and the fishing industry was hit hard: It was off 40 percent in the Paris markets.

Birds suffered horribly, in both France and Britain. Thirty thousand seabirds were estimated to have been killed by the tragedy. The spill coincided with the northerly migration of a host of these birds, whose survival rate was less than 1 percent, once they had become coated with oil. Shock, improper cleaning and handling, ingestion of oil, ingestion of toxic chemicals by preening, and pneumonia were the causes. Those who did not reach the beaches died at sea of starvation and exhaustion, or from exposure, once the insulating quality of their feathers was removed. It was a sorry sight.

And then, in France as in Britain, there was the hotel industry, just cranking up for the spring season. It would be May before the beaches resembled anything habitable.

A board of inquiry, composed of a three-man Liberian government commission, was convened on April 3 in Genoa. A week before this, *Torrey Canyon* captain Pastrengo Rugiati emoted for reporters. "I must answer for everything, for everyone!" he cried, "I must carry the cross alone!"

The board apparently agreed with him. On May 2, they placed the entire blame for the wreck upon Captain Rugiati and recommended that his license be revoked because "of his high degree of negligence and the gravity of the incident." The captain, shattered by the decision and the guilt he carried, received the news in a hospital, where he was suffering from loss of weight, hypertension, pleurisy, and a tubercular condition of one lung. The final indignity was the circulation of a picture of him huddling under his hospital bed, taken by an apparently predatory and obviously unsympathetic press photographer.

The insurance claim for the disaster was, at that time, the largest single claim in maritime history: $16 million for the lost hull. The cost to the British for cleanup and bombing was estimated by them to be $8.5 million, and they filed suit in Bermuda against Union Oil of California for this amount. Various other amounts for lost cargo, for the French cleanup, etc., entered the courts.

The *Lake Poularde,* the sister ship to the *Torrey Canyon* was seized by the British in Singapore when it pulled into that British port to pick up some cable. It cost its owners $8 million for her to leave port, and the French steamed into Singapore harbor with the same concept in mind, but missed the sister ship by a day.

On April 1, 1968, the French finally caught up with the *Lake Poularde* in Rotterdam and collected a bond of $7.5 million. In addition, Union Oil agreed to an out-of-court settlement with Britain and France of $7.2 million, to be divided equally between the two countries, plus another $60,000 to satisfy claimants not reimbursed otherwise.

It would bring the *Torrey Canyon* tragedy to a conclusion, but it would not end oil slicks and their terrible pollutions. They were just beginning.

UNITED KINGDOM
(Scotland, North Sea)
Piper Alpha oil rig explosion
July 5, 1988

One hundred sixty-six men died and 65 were pulled from the water after the Piper Alpha oil rig exploded in the North Sea, 120 miles off the coast of Scotland on July 5, 1988. It was the worst disaster ever to strike British oil rigs in the North Sea.

In the late 1960s, Britain began to tap the rich and abundant oil reserves beneath the North Sea. The amount of oil under the floor of the sea seemed enormous, and it would provide a healthy economic lift for the United Kingdom from the 1970s onward. By 1988, there were 123 British oil rigs dotting the stormy waters of the North Sea, prominent among them the huge Piper Alpha rig, 120 miles off the shore of Scotland, opposite Aberdeen.

Like all oil rigs, the Piper Alpha performed a number of duties. It not only serviced oil wells under the sea, carrying the oil by pipeline to a terminal in the Orkneys, it was also a conduit for natural gas in another pipeline that went to Norway's Frigg field. In addition, it served as a transfer point for gas from Texaco's Tartan field and supplied gas to power the nearby Claymore platform.

It was an immense, 34,000-ton structure of steel and wood, built stronger than the oil rigs of the Gulf of Mexico because of the fierce battering it would take in North Sea weather. It was 649 feet high, but most of this height was sunk, by six huge steel legs, into 440 feet of water. There was a helicopter pad above the waterline and, nestled among the rigging, with the multiple pipes that contained oil and gas running directly through them, were the crew quarters, housing the 230 workers who toiled in two shifts aboard the rig.

There had been two minor explosions in the North Sea during that week of July. On Sunday, July 2, the British Petroleum Sullom Voe terminal in the Shetland Islands blew up, causing heavy damage but no casualties. On Tuesday, July 4, the Brent Alpha platform exploded, again with no casualties.

Some of the men aboard the Piper Alpha were uneasy. For three days, beginning on Sunday, July 2, workers had complained of a heavy gas smell. On Monday, July 3, worker Craig Barclay phoned his fiancée and told her that he had refused to ignite a welding torch that day because of the strong smell of gas. On Tuesday, July 4, Thomas Stirling phoned his fiancée, Janice Stewart, in Glasgow, and complained of a sickening gas smell. He went on to tell her how some workers had donned breathing masks to work that day. It was the last either woman would hear from their fiancés.

At dusk on July 5, half of the crew were sleeping in their quarters; half were at work. Beneath the waterline, directly under the crew's quarters, a leak had developed in a compression chamber. Natural gas was forcing itself into the chamber, and it ignited. Two cataclysmic explosions geysered up from the chamber, tore through the quarters, and split the rig in two. In seconds, an inferno of fire followed, shooting flames between 300 and 400 feet into the air.

Those in the living quarters had no chance of surviving. They were either blown apart, incinerated, or tossed into the sea, then buried under the collapsing platform. One hundred sixty-six men died, most of them in their quarters, some who were too slow in escaping.

"It was a case of fry and die or jump and try," Roy Carey, a 45-year-old survivor told reporters from his hospital bed in Aberdeen. "There was no time to ask—it was over the side or nothing. I just dived—it may have been 60 feet."

It *was* 60 feet, and the survivors either slid down hoses or dove from the platform into the water, where they dodged missiles of flaming debris.

No lifeboats were launched; there was no time for that. A rescue boat that rushed to the platform caught fire during the second explosion. Two of the three rescue workers in the boat were killed.

Flames could be seen 70 miles away, and helicopters and planes of the Royal Air Force (RAF) flew to the tragic scene. By dawn, all the survivors had been picked up. The rig still burned, and would do so for a week.

The oil caught fire as fast as it spewed from the rig, and so the damage to the environment was minimal. This was more than compensated for by the devastating human loss.

Investigations were launched, safety improvements were promised, and the prime minister and the queen extended their condolences to the families of the victims of the worst oil rig explosion in the short history of British oil exploration in the North Sea.

UNITED KINGDOM
(Scotland, Shetland Islands)
Grounding of tanker *Braer*
January 5, 1993

The single-hull tanker Braer *lost power in the international channel near the Shetland Islands during a huge storm on January 5, 1993, and was driven onto the rocks at the entrance to Quendale Bay. Two weeks later, it broke apart, spilling all of its cargo of 26 million gallons of light crude oil into the bay and sea.*

There is a curious and ironic contradiction in the relationship of storms to oil spills. Though storms cause the disasters that bring about oil spills, they also cleanse the coasts of the oil that spills.

This contradiction was heavily at work when the single hulled 89,700-ton tanker *Braer* foundered on the sharp reefs of the Shetland Islands in a monstrous storm on January 5, 1993.

There was also a further ironic contradiction at work that dark and stormy night. Quendale Bay, the site of the disaster, is a rugged, sparsely populated outcrop some 200 miles north of Aberdeen, on the Norwegian Sea. One of the only signs of life, aside from the salmon fishermen and sheepherders, is a tiny settlement near Sumburgh Head, at the extreme tip of the island and just east of the wreck. Ironically, the settlement is a staging area for many of the crews that work the oil platforms scattered across the North Sea.

Those who were on land were glad of it on the night of January 5. Thirty-foot seas and hurricane-force winds out of the southwest made a fierce froth of the Norwegian Sea, and the *Braer* was sailing safely in the middle of the 22-mile-wide channel, an international shipping lane off the Shetlands. The ship had left Norway and was enroute to the Atlantic Ocean and, from there, to Canada.

And then, just off Garth's Ness, the rocky headland that guards the entrance to Quendale Bay—a graveyard of ships since the times of the Spanish Armada—the ship lost all power. No amount of frantic repair could get her engines to reengage. She was at the mercy of the sea, which was driving her relentlessly toward the rocks.

It would take five hours for this to happen, and during that time, the ship's crew, teams of helicopters, and seagoing salvage tugs fought to get a line on the drifting tanker to drag her out of harm's way. But the elements were too overwhelming, and as the waves crashed and the wind roared, she slammed sideways into the rocky coast and wedged fast.

Powerless in a storm, the single-hull tanker Braer *foundered on rocks near the Shetland Islands in January 1993. And there it remained for two weeks, steadily leaking light crude into the Norwegian Sea and Quendale Bay.*

(MARK EDWARDS/STILL PICTURES)

Battling enormous winds, the helicopters now set to evacuating the 34-man crew, which they did, within hours after the grounding.

And there the *Braer* remained, on the rocks beneath a 150-foot cliff, with oil pouring out of a hole gouged in her forward tanks. There was no hope of salvaging her while the storm raged, and rage it did, shot through with lightning, its winds rising and peaking with 115-mph gusts, and all the while the *Braer* grinding its hull on the soft sand bottom surrounding the rocks.

The best officials and conservationists could hope for was that the ship would hold together, and not break up, for this wild piece of coastline was also a winter sanctuary for birds and sea otters. Fortunately, according to Chris Harbard, a spokesman for the Royal Society for the Protection of Birds, most of the colonies of seabirds were not expected to migrate to Shetland until the following month, and so the number of birds at risk would total in the thousands, rather than the hundreds of thousands.

Still, there were longtailed ducks, common loons, eider ducks, and cormorants nesting in the cliffs. If they stayed there, they might escape the oil, but they fed on fish, and that was where the danger was. Some pitifully oil-coated sea otters, in fact, had already been seen.

And then there were the salmon farms.

It was a dicey situation, and one over which human beings had very little control. At least the storm was breaking up the spill almost as fast as it accumulated. But it was also preventing the salvors from even inspecting, much less stanching the flow of oil.

By January 6, 36 hours after running aground, the *Braer* listed sharply, with its stern virtually submerged. She had been carrying 26 million gallons of oil, but how much of that remained in the hull was a mystery that the continuing storm maintained. Five to seven miles of coast had been contaminated so far by the slick, but it was being washed down by the waves. Fortunately, the slick was still 13 miles from the nearest salmon farm.

Six British Government DC-3s flew almost constantly over the oil slick, spraying it with chemicals to disperse it. But there was no hope of erecting barrier booms to contain the oil, nor was there a possibility of boarding the heaving ship, which was surrounded by a protective pool of heavy oil.

By the seventh of January, a unique situation had begun to develop. The heavy winds blew ocean spray across the sheep pastures above the cliffs, and that was normal. But now, the spray was laced with oil. There was a black glaze of oil on all of the roads; there was oil clinging to the grass of the pasture, the hooded jackets of the sheepherders, and the wool of the sheep. It was a singular sort of contamination, but no less serious for its isolation.

Michael Howard, Britain's environment secretary, acknowledged that this particular grounding raised new issues of severe inland contamination. About 15 square miles in all, much of it pastureland used by sheepherders, had been affected by the oily spray, he noted, which had turned roads slippery, fouled meadows, and left a thick, cloying aroma in the air.

Meanwhile, salmon farmers on the west coast were busily preparing booms to circle their fish pens, and conservationists counted 235 dead birds.

For the first time, the residents of the area became aware of the constant stench of oil that hung on the normally pristine, if moist, air. Some complained of stinging eyes and throats and nausea, and oil-contaminated cabbages grown by farmers were condemned by local health authorities as unfit for human consumption. Some families sent their children inland, and evacuation plans were prepared for the rest of the population, though health officials assured them that there were no measurable total hydrocarbons in the air and "no human health risks, either chronic or acute."

By January 9, the constant pounding of the surf had begun to work the stern of the *Braer*, so that it seemed to be grappling free of the rest of the ship. This boded ill, since if it left, the rest of the ship was at risk of breaking up and spilling the remainder of its cargo of oil. Experts estimated that half the 26 million gallons had already leaked into the sea.

Local residents still concerned about toxic air, forced a suspension of the spraying of chemicals on the slick, and the DC-3s went back to the mainland of Scotland. The storm continued to dissipate the oil at sea; most of the pollution remained within the Bay of Quendale. A mixture of the ship's cargo of light crude and thick bunker oil from its own fuel tanks had blackened part of the harbor, and it was here that most of the dead birds had been found. By now 535 dead birds, 143 injured ones, and two dead gray seals had been retrieved.

On and on the storm raged, lightening momentarily and then resuming with a kind of rejuvenated fury. Patches of cappuccino-tinted foam swirled along the shore, simultaneously staining and cleaning the rocks and sand.

Finally, on January 11, it became apparent that the tanker was coming apart. Oil was spurting from broken deck hatches, and the 30-foot surf was rolling its hull back and forth, rupturing whatever tanks remained intact. The sea then entered the tanks, forcing the oil up and through the blown deck hatches. Gert Koffeman, of the Dutch salvage company Smit Tak, who had been on the scene from the first grounding, called a news conference and announced that "most of the tanks in the forward part of the vessel are open and leaking to the sea."

The stern had already begun to separate, and cranes and other equipment on the boat's deck were beginning to topple and cause further damage.

"A day ago we thought we were going to get away with it," said Paul Horsman of Greenpeace. "Now we know the area around the tanker will be devastated." Pollution control officials, however, disputed his extreme pessimism. There was no evidence that a great deal of ecological damage had occurred. The storm had washed away as much as it had set free.

Finally, on the night of January 12, one of 30-foot waves and 95-mph wind gusts and lightning, the *Braer* broke apart, spilling the remainder of its cargo.

The ecological catastrophe, because of the coincidence of the unrelenting gale that caused the crash, did not materialize, though any deaths from oil spills are regrettable and a terrible waste. The pathetic sight of 700 dead birds, untold numbers of fish and bottom-living creatures, and the surviving seals and birds with skin lesions from chemical burning was bad enough.

But the salmon farms were spared. And though the spill was twice the size of the *Exxon Valdez* outpouring, it took place in an unconfined space rather than a confined one, and the cargo was a light crude called Gullfaks, which has a consistency that resembles gasoline, rather than the tarry, toxic heaviness of the crude carried by the *Exxon Valdez*.

David Bedborough of Britain's Marine Pollution Control Unit, which oversaw the cleanup operations, summed it up: "In crude tonnage terms, quite high. In terms of immediate gross fouling, the dirty effect, quite low. In terms of subtle, long-term effects, don't know."

And that is the present situation that exists in the Shetlands.

UNITED KINGDOM
(WALES, MILFORD HAVEN)
GROUNDING OF *SEA EMPRESS*
February 17, 1996

One of the worst ecological disasters so far occurred on February 17, 1996, when the tanker Sea Empress *ran aground off Milford Haven harbor, in Pembrokeshire, Wales. Nineteen million gallons of light crude oil leaked into the sea and harbor, near some of the most delicate wildlife refuges in Europe. Wildlife and fishing were devastated.*

A winter storm raged off the coast of southwestern Wales on February 17, 1996, and the visibility was slight at best. Still, there was really no plausible excuse for the 147,000-ton oil tanker *Sea Empress* to run aground 300 yards from shore at the tip of Milford Haven harbor, in Pembrokeshire, Wales, on that day. All of its navigation equipment was aboard and functioning; there was nothing wrong with the steering mechanism or the power. It was just that old devil, unforeseen human error, that caused what would become the fifth-largest oil spill in history.

The spill of 19 million gallons—8 million more than that of the *Exxon Valdez* (see pp. 166–69), but less than that of the *Braer* (25 million, see pp. 160–63), *Torrey Canyon* (36 million, see pp. 155–60), or *Amoco Cadiz* (the worst of all time: 68 million, see pp. 140–42)—also could have been avoided, had the British government followed through with its own commission's recommendations after the *Braer* grounding off the Shetland Islands three years earlier. That commission suggested that adequately strong tugboats be stationed around sensitive oil ports to prevent similar disasters.

But in the Wales catastrophe, the *Sea Empress* remained stranded on rocks for six days because no tugboats in the vicinity were strong enough to haul her away. In the interim, planes sprayed chemicals on the slick to break it up, booms were laid around the spill near the ship, boats laid barriers at the mouths of coves, and onshore, crews of scrubbers worked feverishly to clean the rocks and sands polluted by the light crude.

There was a particular urgency in their work, since two of Britain's most important wildlife preserves, on Stoner Island and Stockholm Island, were completely surrounded by the oil slick, and the slick was also moving toward Lundy Island with its colony of puffins, 50 miles south of the wreck site. One hundred thousand birds, as well as seals and dolphins, were immediately threatened, and the fishing and tourist industries nearby were at imminent risk.

"You have . . . poison spilled into one of Europe's premier wildlife sites," said Phil Rothwell, head of policy operations for the Royal Society for the Protection of Birds, "It is not just what you can see, like seals and porpoises, but sponges and other life. This must be a disaster in anyone's terms."

Joan Edwards, a spokesperson for the Devon Wildlife Trust, echoed his sentiments. "It's the worst environmental disaster I have seen," she said.

Finally, on Wednesday, February 21, 12 tugboats, straining at their lines, pulled the tanker free and guided it to Milford Haven harbor, where it was berthed at a jetty, and divers immediately set out to plug the leak, while pumpers stood by to pump the remaining oil into a waiting tanker.

By the 26th of February, the bodies of 7,000 birds had been found, and gray seals and dolphins, covered with oil, were rescued.

As for the $11 million Welsh fishing industry: It appeared to be out of business, at least for the foreseeable future. "I've had fishermen calling me in tears," said a fisheries official.

By April, when the cleanup had supposedly ended, the environmental impact had grown. More than 120 miles of Welsh coastline had been contaminated by the oil spill. Although the figure of 7,000 dead birds still held, experts were quick to point out that for every dead bird found after an oil slick contamination, there are at least nine more whose bodies are never recovered.

The entire ecosystem, from the lowliest plankton in the sea to the hapless inhabitants of two of Europe's premier wildlife sanctuaries, was poisoned by the massive invasion of oil from the wrecked tanker Sea Empress.
(SIMS/GREENPEACE)

On Skomer Island, a bird sanctuary that sheltered half the world's population of the Manx shearwater and also provided a nesting base for such seabirds as guillemots, grebes, auks, and cormorants, oil-soaked seaweed continued to wash ashore. Scientists said that the entire ecosystem, starting with the lowliest plankton in the sea, was poisoned.

Fishermen were forbidden to catch fish or shellfish in a 300-square-mile zone off the coast. By the middle of May, the ban was lifted on fishing, but the shellfish ban was left in place indefinitely.

The cost of the cleanup and insurance was expected to total $96 million. But that was the least expensive consequence of the disaster. Paul Cowper, a spokesman for the Tenby Campaign for Clean Seas, demanded more responsibility, the basing of a tugboat near Milford Haven harbor, and the formation of an oil-spill response team. "There's no reason why it shouldn't happen again tomorrow, given the same scenario," he said. "Although we need more information about what happened [in February], it seemed to be a fiasco from start to finish," he added.

UNITED STATES

(ALASKA)

TRANS-ALASKA PIPELINE EXPLOSION
July 8, 1977

....

One worker was killed and six others were seriously injured when an explosion, caused by oil spraying from a faulty valve, rocked pump station number 8 on the Trans-Alaska Pipeline on July 8, 1977.

In 1968, oil was discovered on Prudhoe Bay on the north slope of the Brooks Mountain Range on the Arctic Ocean in Northern Alaska. It was the richest petroleum field ever discovered in North America, and visions of billions danced in the heads of those who found it and drilled it.

But the road to fulfillment proved to be a rocky one. The field was located on tundra, a fragile surface of frozen mud essential to the survival of Arctic life forms, which stretches from Alaska through Canada and through Russia and Siberia. In April 1970, environmentalists filed suits that blocked the pipeline's construction, until Congress, urged by the Nixon administration, passed the Trans-Alaska Pipeline Authorization Act in November 1973. It effectively silenced environmentalists' contentions that the construction of the huge pipeline from Prudhoe Bay to Valdez, in the Gulf of Alaska, would forever destroy the tundra through which it would pass.

They were right, but politics and economics won out, and the construction of the pipeline began. And no sooner had it begun than its troubles also began. First, there was a rash of faulty welds spotted during routine inspections. Then, the Justice Department charged that the eight oil companies that owned the pipeline through the Alyeska consortium were planning to charge about $2 more per barrel than the amount justified to transport the oil through the line.

Various troubles emerged along the line. At pump station number 8, located 38 miles south of Fairbanks, and at milepost 488 on the 800-mile, $9 billion pipeline, a nitrogen leak shut the entire line down for two and a half days. An elbow in a pipe ascending from the buried part of the line into the station was cracked when workmen inadvertently placed liquid nitrogen, at a temperature of minus 290 degrees Fahrenheit, into the pipe. *Vaporized* nitrogen was supposed to have been used, to purge the line of air.

But all seemed to be ready for a serene start of operations at the beginning of July 1977. The Alaskan summer was balmy. Early in the morning on July 8, 1977, the first North Slope oil had begun to pass through pump station number 8.

And then, at 3:45 P.M., the road turned rocky again.

Routine maintenance, the cleaning of a filter on one side of the pump, was being performed on the pipeline. Suddenly, a thunderous explosion "like a thousand-pound bomb going off in your backyard," in the words of pipefitter foreman Bill Pender, roared through the pump station. The suction valve on the pump opened suddenly, spraying crude oil in a black fountain from the pipe. Then, oil spurted through the crack that had been caused by the faulty nitrogen process two and a half days before, and that oil ignited. The explosion threw the crew working on the pump against the station's walls.

The roof blew off the pumping station's main building. It spiraled 50 feet into the air, then fell into the middle of the scurrying workmen—some 75 of them—who were wildly trying to get out of the way of flying debris.

Less than a minute later, a second explosion tore through the same building, blowing its sides out. Now fire took over, and burning oil flowed out of the pump station, across a road, and into the ditch that had been dug to repair a break in the line earlier in the week. This in turn set fire to the woods surrounding the site.

Fire raced through the hallways of the various buildings, igniting them, and the oily smoke from the fire turned day into night.

One man had been killed instantly; six more were seriously injured. It took half an hour before a military helicopter arrived to evacuate the injured and begin rescue work.

The first Northern Slope oil to pass through pump station 8 had only traveled 30 miles south when the pipeline was shut down. Heavy equipment arrived upon the scene as helicopters took the injured to Fairbanks and doctors and nurses from Fairbanks disembarked. The fire, though under control, continued to burn.

The immediate cause had been a spark from a turbine, driving the 13,500-horsepower pump, just a few feet from where the men were changing the filter screen in the pipe. The spark had ignited the spilled oil, and within seconds, it had turned the pumphouse and its machinery to rubble.

There was $5 million worth of damage in an instant, and the pipeline was shut down on the same day that it opened. The estimate of time it would take to put the station back online ranged from two weeks to five, but it was determined that the pipeline would not be shut down that long.

It was a complex procedure, involving the closing of valves in the proper sequence in order to avoid pressure that could damage the line. It had been human error that had caused the nitrogen damage and the explosion. Fortunately, the shutting down of the pipeline proceeded without mishap.

But now the enormous task of rebuilding the station began. Early estimates of cost proved to be wildly conservative. It would cost not $5 million, but $50 million to put it back together again, and it would take months. The Interior Department in Washington, D.C., decreed that the pipeline would not be reopened until all problems had been corrected. Too much haste, too little care, and too much damage had already occurred.

Finally, in the late afternoon of July 18, pump station number 8 was bypassed, and the flow of crude oil was resumed, at a reduced capacity.

But the resumption was short-lived. The very next day, a piece of heavy construction equipment, a front-loading tractor, rammed into a portion of the pipeline about 23 miles from its northern origin. The collision smashed a vent on a check valve, which allowed more oil to spew onto the tundra. Within two weeks, the environment had been subjected to pollution and fire.

Now it was subjected to sabotage. At 3:09 A.M. on July 20, three young men exploded three dynamite charges against a section of pipe that ran above the ground, supported by refrigerated metal posts designed to prevent damage to the tundra. The explosions only managed to rip the insulation off the pipe.

A day later, news came that another leak had poured oil onto the landscape at the Prudhoe field itself.

The next day, a crew drove a wooden wedge into the vent fitting on the valve, and the flow was again resumed in the line. Finally, on July 29, at 11:02 A.M., the first oil from the North Slope arrived in Valdez. It had been a clumsy start, fatal to one man, injurious to five others, and destructive to miles of the environment. And, although the crude would flow better as time went on, its effects upon the environment—from leaks, accidents, and the havoc that was about to occur in one of the supertankers tied up at Valdez—would worsen.

UNITED STATES
(ALASKA, VALDEZ)
GROUNDING OF *EXXON VALDEZ*
March 24, 1989

....

On the night of March 24, the Exxon Valdez, *a 987-foot tanker carrying 51 million gallons of oil, struck Bligh Reef, 25 miles south of Valdez, Alaska. The impact tore enormous gashes in 8 of the ship's 11 cargo tanks, through which 10.8 million gallons of North Slope crude poured into the sea. The resulting river of oil would blacken 1,244 miles of shoreline, decimate marine life, and close fisheries. It would be the nation's largest oil spill, ever.*

Oil has flowed through the Alaska pipeline since July 1977. Between then and 1989, hundreds of tankers made a total of 8,858 trips to Valdez, in weather that ranged from summerlike to arctic, from benign to perilous. They hauled 6.83 billion barrels of oil without a single spill at sea. But at 12:09 A.M. on March 24, 1989, in clear weather conditions, through waters that reportedly contained ice floes, that long and unblemished record turned suddenly meaningless. The *Exxon Valdez*, piloted by Seaman Robert Kagan, while its captain, Joseph Hazelwood, slept off a drinking binge, hit a reef and began to spew one of the largest oil spills in history into Prince William Sound.

The grounding had its roots onshore. One of the immediate causes of the tragedy took place four years earlier, in 1985, when Hazelwood entered a Long Island hospital to be treated for alcohol abuse. He was apparently released uncured, since as late as September 1988, he was picked up for drunken driving near his Long Island, New York, home.

At noon, on March 23, 1989, Hazelwood and two members of his crew debarked from their ship, which was docked in Valdez, a tiny town at the head of Prince William Sound. Their object: to pick up a pizza and do some last-minute shopping. They ended up in a saloon and drank there until 7:30 P.M. (federal regulations prohibit crew members from consuming alcoholic beverages within four hours of the sailing of their ship).

At 8:24 P.M., the partying sailors and their captain were delivered by cab to their ship. At 9:24, the *Exxon Valdez*, carrying 51 million gallons of North Slope crude from the Alaskan pipeline, pulled away from its berth, at the hands of the harbor pilot, Ed Murphy. He would later testify that

he smelled liquor on Captain Hazelwood's breath then, but that the captain appeared to be in control of himself.

At 11:25 P.M., Murphy turned the three-football-fields-long ship back to its master. The *Exxon Valdez* was in the open sound now, out of the Narrows, but not, apparently out of danger. There were reports of floating ice from the Columbia Glacier, and there was the possibility that this ice could drift into the shipping lanes toward which the *Valdez* was headed.

Minutes after taking command, Captain Hazelwood radioed the Coast Guard to inform them that he was leaving the shipping lanes to avoid floating ice. The Coast Guard acknowledged and then mysteriously took the ship off its radar screen.

Until this moment, Hazelwood acted responsibly. But from then onward, his actions seemed at least unwarranted and at most bizarre. Instead of slowing down, which would have been a prudent action if he were trying to avoid a collision with ice, he increased his speed to 12 knots, twice what the *Valdez* had been making under the piloting of Ed Murphy. And that was merely the beginning: Instead of maintaining vigilant control, Hazelwood placed the ship on automatic pilot. And then, instead of overseeing its passage through the ice, he turned over the wheel to Third Mate Gregory Cousins, who not only did not have the training or the qualifications to pilot the ship in ice-floe-infested shoal waters but, because of the pressures of loading the ship, had had only four hours sleep in the previous 24.

The captain's instructions to Cousins were to return to the traffic lanes after Busby Island, a small spit of land slightly north of Bligh Reef, which would become visible directly to their port side. He neglected to inform Cousins that the ship was on automatic pilot, and therefore could not be steered.

Having issued his instructions, he departed from the bridge and descended to his cabin. At 11:53 P.M., approximately two minutes after the captain left the bridge, lookout Maureen Jones reported Busby Island a few degrees forward to port. Off the starboard bow was a red flashing buoy, signaling the approach of Bligh Reef and dangerous waters. She reported this to Cousins, also, who acknowledged it and prepared to adjust his course. He ordered the helmsman to come right 10 degrees. But the ship failed to respond. He ordered it again, then realized, to his horror, that they were on automatic pilot.

Cousins rushed to turn off the control, just as lookout Jones entered the bridge. "The light is still flashing on the starboard bow," she said. "It should be to port."

It was now midnight, and Seaman Robert Kagan took over the helm. Kagan's service record showed that he was deficient in steering, even in calm and normal seas.

Obviously worried and thoroughly agitated, Cousins ordered right rudder 20 degrees. The ship did not respond. Cousins shouted "Hard right!" and grabbed the wheel with

The U.S. Coast Guard employs floating barriers to contain some of the gigantic oil spill from the Exxon Valdez, *foundering in the background.*
(U.S. COAST GUARD)

Kagan. Together, they spun it right as far as it would go, and Kagan held the course. Cousins rushed to the bridge phone and shouted to the captain in his cabin below. "I believe we're in serious trouble," he yelled. The clock on the bridge read 12:05 A.M.

Four minutes later, with an audible groan, the *Exxon Valdez* struck Bligh Reef. "First [there was] a slight roll," Cousins later testified, "then a series of jolts—six or seven very hard jolts." The ship stopped, dead in the water, and the impact catapulted Chief Mate James Kunkel from his bunk. He dressed and dashed to the bridge, where he found Cousins in a state of hysteria and no sign of the captain. "He's calling the Coast Guard," explained the distraught crew member.

Kunkel descended to the ship's cargo control room. The gauges were spinning like tops. More than 115,000 gallons had gushed from the rips in the *Valdez*'s hull in the first five minutes. At this rate, she could easily capsize.

A quick run through the ship's computer confirmed this. Kunkel knew they were all in danger when he smelled choking vapors in the passageways to the bridge. "I feared for my life," Kunkel later told a board of inquiry.

"Shall I ring the general alarm?" he asked a strangely detached and subdued captain Hazelwood as he entered the bridge.

"No, Jim. Stay cool," Hazelwood replied.

"The computer says the ship's not stable to move," Kunkel ventured, smelling the alcohol on the captain's breath.

Hazelwood ignored the information, started the engines, and tried to power the ship off the reef. Six times. Had he succeeded, it would have capsized and sunk, sending the disaster into astronomical realms.

Finally, at 2:30 A.M., the Coast Guard dispatched its pilot vessel *Silver Bullet* to the *Valdez*. Aboard were two top officers from the Marine Safety Office. What they saw they scarcely believed. The surface of the sea was black and boiling. There were 16 inches of oil on the water's surface, and all of it was in motion.

With a great deal of difficulty, Chief Warrant Officer Mark Delozier and Lieutenant Commander Thomas Falkenstein boarded the *Valdez*, climbed to its bridge, and encountered yet another surreal scene. The fumes were thick enough to be on the brink of fire or an explosion. Yet, Captain Hazelwood was calmly drinking coffee and smoking a cigarette.

"That's not a prudent thing to do, Captain," said Dozier, testily. One whiff of Hazelwood's breath, and both Coast Guard officers decided that a priority would be to test the captain for alcohol. They radioed for an Alaska state trooper, who arrived at 6:00 A.M., minus his testing gear. Eventually, with toxocology equipment the *Valdez* itself carried, Hazelwood was found, 10 hours after the grounding, to have a blood alcohol content of 0.061 percent, well above the 0.04 percent allowed for vessel masters by the Coast Guard. The conclusion was that Hazelwood had continued to drink while he was aboard.

Meanwhile, the *Valdez* was spewing oil into Prince William Sound at a furious rate. Eventually, 10.8 million gallons of North Slope crude would foul the beaches for 1,244 miles, from Cape Cod to Cape Hattaras and all throughout Prince William Sound.

That day, the cleanup began, but slowly. More than 10 million gallons of oil had already poured into the sound by midafternoon. Forty-two million two hundred thousand gallons were still aboard the *Valdez*, and if the ship broke up on the reef, that would go into the water, too.

Exxon, now busily practicing damage control, diverted an inbound tanker, the *Exxon Baton Rouge*, to take on the oil, but tense hours were spent searching for the fenders needed so that it could come alongside. Hours later, they were located in the town of Valdez, under four feet of snow.

Meanwhile, the Alyeska Pipeline Service Company, a consortium set up by the seven big oil companies prospecting in Alaska, was contacted to bring in a cleanup barge. The barge took days to arrive, and by that time, the spill was out of control. Gale winds were moving it down the coast at 30 miles an hour.

Exxon dispatched thousands of workers to the area and paid volunteers $16.69 an hour to clean up the beaches. The nearby Cordova fishermen, fearing that their livelihood would be destroyed if the oil fouled the Port San Juan hatchery, appealed to Alyeska. Alyeska's reply was "File a claim." So, the fishermen set about protecting their hatchery themselves and were later presented with a check for $300,000 from Exxon for their successful trouble.

Up and down Prince William Sound, the cleanup force increased to 15,000 workers, not all of them as energetic as they might have been. By the end of the summer, the beaches were still dirty, and the death toll to wildlife was appalling: 138 bald eagles, 980 sea otters, 33,125 seabirds. The price of cleanup had climbed to $2.5 billion, while the number of people assigned to the cleanup had begun to diminish.

As for the guilty: Captain Hazelwood was at first made the scapegoat for the entire spill. Alaska filed charges against him; he was publicly mocked, but by the time his trial was held in February 1990, the jury realized that he was not entirely at fault and merely convicted him of negligent discharge of oil, a misdemeanor. Fined $50,000 by a judge,

Some of the 15,000 workers attack the enormous task of cleaning and scrubbing the beaches of Prince William Sound somewhat clean of heavy crude from the Exxon Valdez.

(RICHARD NEWMAN/UNEP)

Hazelwood, through his lawyers, had the conviction over-turned by the Alaska Court of Appeals, on the grounds that the federal government offers immunity from prosecution for anyone reporting an oil spill.

As for the fishermen and native Alaskans harmed by the 11-million-gallon oil spill: A 1994 jury awarded them $5.3 billion in punitive damages.

In May of 1997, Exxon appealed this ruling, arguing that Congress had already detailed appropriate deterrents and punishments for oil spills. In addition, it argued that the 1991 $900 million settlement with the state of Alaska pre-cluded punitive damages. No decision has been rendered as of the writing of this.

Exxon was charged, in 1991, with five criminal counts, including polluting in violation of the Clean Water Act and the Refuse Act and killing birds in violation of the Migratory Bird Treaty Act. Eventually, this was plea-bar-gained down to three misdemeanors, for killing migratory water fowl and violating the Clean Water and Refuse Acts. The company was fined $125 million up front and $900 million over 10 years.

The damage statistics have still not been entirely entered. While the Cordoba fishermen did yeoman work, the salmon industry in Alaska has yet to recover. The yields of both hatchery and wild pink salmon were less than 50 percent of the expected yield in 1992. Increased deformities of marine life were reported in the same year.

Nearly half of the wildlife population of Prince William Sound was destroyed—between 3,500 and 5,500 animals. Between 375,000 and 435,000 birds were killed.

Mussels and clams which metabolize hydrocarbons very slowly, continued to exhibit contamination three years after the spill. Sea-bottom life, such as kelp, a basic food in the ecosystem, was destroyed in huge amounts. Oil displaced from the beaches washed down to the bottom, decimating this balancing life.

Farther inland, 35 archaeological sites were fouled beyond redemption; those that were not damaged were looted by cleanup crews. To this day, subsistence hunting, fishing, and gathering by 2,200 native villagers has been almost entirely wiped out, and the villages have joined in a class action suit against Exxon. Sixty-seven percent of the 10.8 million gallons of oil spilled by the Exxon Valdez was never recovered. It presumably entered the ecosystem of Prince William Sound and the Atlantic Ocean, where it will likely remain forever.

There was, at least, some justice in the form of a monu-mental financial settlement for those affected by the spill. In September 1994, a jury awarded punitive damages of $5 bil-lion to 34,000 fishermen and other Alaskans—an amount roughly equal to a year's worth of profits for Exxon.

The verdict was appealed by the oil company, but on January 28, 1995, a federal judge refused to overturn the verdict, and it stood.

UNITED STATES
(CALIFORNIA, SAN FRANCISCO)
COLLISION OF *ARIZONA STANDARD* AND *OREGON*
January 18, 1971

On January 18, 1971, the Arizona Standard *and* Oregon, *both oil tankers, collided beneath the Golden Gate Bridge in San Francisco Bay. Eight hundred and forty thousand gallons of crude oil spilled into the bay, despoiling beaches and harbors and killing thousands of birds.*

In 1971, there were several pilot groups vying for control of the waterway into San Francisco Bay from the Pacific Ocean. As a result, there was no real central control of the channel that ran under the Golden Gate Bridge, and near collisions were reported regularly. It was a situation fraught with huge danger and consequences. Ammunition ships passed regularly beneath the bridge, and late in February, one pilot of just such a ship reported having to suddenly go full astern to avoid collision with an oil tanker. "The results could have demolished the bridge and set fire to a good portion of San Francisco Bay," he later told a con-gressional inquiry panel, convened, it was hoped, to solve the problem.

This panel was set up only after an undeniable accident raised the national consciousness to potential dangers in populated waterways: Its drama began in the early morning hours of January 18, 1971. Two oil tankers owned by the Standard Oil Company of California—the *Arizona Standard* and its sister ship the *Oregon*—steamed full ahead in the main channel leading to San Francisco Bay from the Pacific Ocean. The *Arizona Standard* was heading into the bay; the *Oregon* was headed out. Both captains had navigated the narrow channel under the Golden Gate Bridge scores of times, and so carried no pilots. But in the dark, it was, to novice and veteran alike, all the same.

Both ships carried working radar, and they, and the Coast Guard, saw the converging radar blips that indicated that each was dangerously near the other.

As they got within a half mile, Captain Morris E. English of the *Oregon* blew prolonged blasts of his whistle. But the radar blip grew nearer and larger.

Meanwhile, on the *Arizona Standard*, according to later testimony from its captain, Harry H. Parnell, the same infor-mation was being received, in the opposite direction. Each ship he said, was in the proper position. His ship was entering the bay from the west on the south side of the channel, and the *Oregon* was steaming outward on the north side.

But it was dark and the radar was apparently not heeded carefully by either ship's master. At 1:41 A.M., the *Arizona Standard*'s lookout, Adam Mowinckel, heard a whistle, "not too close," he later testified. But a moment later, he saw two lights rapidly approaching, one a white light, the other red.

"I called out," he related. "There was no time to do anything else. I believe my words were 'Ship close on the starboard bow!'" And then Mr. Mowinckel, like any sane man who wanted to save his life, turned and ran.

At the same time, aboard the *Oregon*, Captain Parnell saw the running lights of the *Arizona Standard*. "I sighted him appearing almost across my bow," Captain Parnell recalled. "I went full astern. 'My God, he's crossing my bow,' I said, and I told the second mate he was going to hit us."

At the same moment, watchers in the Coast Guard's experimental harbor advisory radar project (ironically, the only one of its kind in the nation) watched in horror as the two radar blips converged, then merged into one.

The *Arizona Standard* plowed, at full speed, into the 17,000-ton *Oregon*, driving his bow into the other ship's bow, locking forces and rupturing her forward tanks.

The two ships remained, stuck together, for seven hours, while 840,000 gallons of bunker oil poured from the *Oregon* into San Francisco Bay and out into the Pacific Ocean. Before a week had passed, 60 miles of coast had been contaminated by the oil, thousands of birds had died, fishing was ruined, and conservationists were up in arms.

"Perhaps some day," said a representative of the Sierra Club, "there will be penalties for oil spills large enough to be noticed by corporation presidents."

Eventually, the Ports, Waterways and Harbors Safety Bill was adopted by Congress and made law. It would make this sort of disaster less probable, though not impossible.

UNITED STATES
(CALIFORNIA, SANTA BARBARA CHANNEL)
OIL PLATFORM SPILL
January 28, 1969

....

A Union Oil platform blew and spilled oil over an 800-square-mile area in the Santa Barbara, California, Channel for three years from the initial blowout on January 28, 1969. Thousands of birds died, and the ecological and political impacts were enormous.

Although the spill from the Santa Barbara Union Oil Company's well number 21 under drilling platform A in the Santa Barbara Channel was small by later comparisons, it deserves a place in the history books for its suggestion of things to come.

The well blew on January 28, 1969, a massive eruption of crude oil and gas, roaring up the drill casing and spewing into the channel, which was just five and a half miles off the coast of some upper-middle-class homes of some upper-middle-class Californians. The well was the fifth of a projected 20 that were to be drilled from the platform.

It would be 24 hours before Union Oil committed its first of many errors, that of not informing the media. When the announcement arrived, it came through Union's public relations department in the form of a release that prompted a Santa Barbaran to reply, "Union's P.R. people keep putting out reassurances. But more oil on already troubled waters we didn't need." The Union people, however, knew what they were doing. The last thing *they* needed was notice of the burgeoning number of oil platforms that were going up in the Santa Barbara Channel.

There was something mysterious about the blowout. Oil continued to pour out of the top of the well. But it was also coming up from the bottom of the sea. Obviously there was a leak in the buried pipe, or perhaps in the fault on the ocean floor.

And it was a true gusher. Two days after the blowout, the slick was estimated to cover 120 square miles. It was 8 miles long, and clearly a threat to the Ventura beaches.

Further examination confirmed that the oil was coming up from the sea floor, and this meant that the only lasting relief would come from drilling one or two more wells nearby to relieve the pressure, a process that could take several months.

The platform, 15 stories high with an operating deck about 125 feet square, and standing 40 feet above the water, was sunk in a shelf so rich in oil that the crude had bubbled up around the legs of the rig when they were being sunk. It should have been apparent then that extra care had to be taken in the drilling of wells. But care was not taken, and disaster was the result. "We thought we had it made," said a derrick man afterward, "only that old boy had us made!"

The usual remedies were tried. Mud was injected into the pipe. Red Adair and his men from Houston were called in, followed closely by local and national politicians.

The following day, the first grebes—small dead oil-coated birds—began to wash up on the Ventura beaches. Various conservation groups arrived upon the scene to assess the situation and try to save the wildlife. An emergency wildlife center was set up in the Santa Barbara Bird Refuge near Montecito. The birds, some alive, some not, were brought in by anyone who found them. All were appalled by the rising destruction, and a new anti-oil group, called GOO! (Get Oil Out!) was formed.

Now Washington, D.C., became interested, and Interior Secretary Walter Hickel, who would later, as governor of Alaska, establish a not very exemplary environmental record as a champion of oil drilling on the North Slope of Alaska (see pp. 164–166), announced that he was coming to Santa Barbara to see if the Sierra Club's demand that he halt drilling in the Santa Barbara Channel was justified.

President Hartley of Union Oil had a ready explanation for the tragedy: "Mother nature . . . let us down," he said. Conservationists said it was the other way around.

Hickel inspected the site and ordered a temporary halt in drilling operations in the channel until the situation could be reviewed more thoroughly by federal authorities.

Years after the first pollution of California waters by oil, a variety of other pollutants, industrial and private, turns the state's shorelines into toxic dumps.
(SHIRLEY RICHARDS/UNEP)

Tugs sprayed Corexit on the oil slick, in the hope of breaking it up. Along the various shores, hay was stacked, telephone poles for making booms were brought in, carpeting for the booms' skirts was stacked, cranes, loaders, straw choppers and spreaders, motor graders, dump and tank trucks, trailers, tractors, earthmovers, truck-mounted vacuum pumps, compressors, and miles of hose were hauled in.

As the weeks wore on, more and more wildlife died. Cormorants, gulls, loons, and pelicans followed. "Once they swallow oil, there isn't much chance," a state fish and game employee told reporters. "I say it's shaping up to be the biggest disaster ever to hit California's bird life."

In Washington, Senator Edmund Muskie's subcommittee on air and water pollution questioned Union president Hartley, who stated that the rupture had occurred between the 500- and 700-foot level, leading to seepage through fissures in the strata.

"With the benefit of hindsight," he admitted, "we might have introduced additional steel casing."

Back at the platform, mud was being pumped in at the rate of 3,700 pounds per square inch. But it seemed to be of no consequence. The slick now covered 800 square miles of channel, and fishermen were being affected, their nets fouled, their boats coated, their catches diminished.

Finally, on February 8, after a storm had buffeted the platform and halted all activity except the gushing of oil, and calm had allowed the 1,000 workers who swarmed on the platform and in the nearby boats, to work, well A-21 was plugged with concrete. The cement set at the bottom of the 3,500-foot well, and the oil stopped flowing from its top.

The wildlife devastation was dreadful. Eighteen species of birds had been affected. More than 1,000 had died.

And then, more bad news. Fresh oil appeared in the water, in a volume not unlike the original spill. A two-man submarine dove on the new spill source on February 13 and reported that oil and gas were seeping out of the shallow sand beds. More booms were readied.

By February 18, the new slick was 8 miles long and growing. And so were the claims against Union Oil. They had climbed to $1 billion and showed no sign of slowing.

Now, more discharges were reported coming from other locations under the platform. The Department of the Interior authorized Union to utilize all five of the working wells on the platform that had been shut down and open them, to relieve the pressure.

Meanwhile, seals and dolphins were washing up on the beaches, and in Washington, D.C., a witness before the Muskie committee called the granting of oil leases in the Santa Barbara Channel "an ecological Bay of Pigs."

GOO! began to collect signatures for a petition to halt all Santa Barbara oil operations. They submitted the petition, with 100,000 signatures, to President Nixon, who promised to look into the matter.

The figures at local fisheries told the tale of the spills. The receipts at Santa Barbara Fisheries Inc. for the first six months of the year were 185 pounds of halibut compared to the previous year's 9,050; 46 pounds of bonita compared to 14,779; and sea bass down from 2,072 pounds to 864.

A year went by, and the platform continued to spew oil into the channel, though with less force and volume than at the beginning. Sixteen wells were opened on it now, and Washington seemed to be unable to make up its mind about what to do. Citizens saw it as big oil once again calling the shots. GOO! responded with a boycott of Union products. It did not change things.

Over the next year, however, public pressure did have its effects. Humble Oil decided to relinquish its lease on a 9-square-mile tract south of Union's. The Los Angeles City Council passed a resolution banning all drilling in the channel and all production activities in both the tidelands and federal waters.

After 18 months of pollution, an ecological damage assessment was made. Barnacles, limpets, and intertidal algae were affected, and thus so was the food chain. The greatest loss was suffered by wildfowl. The final count was 3,587 dead birds reported, with a possibility of many times that number unreported.

Three years after the blowout, there was still seepage, but it was diminishing. In inverse ratio, new regulations were being formulated in Washington and Sacramento. All had difficult times making it through committee, but they would eventually become law.

Union got off very easily. Of 342 counts against the company, the presiding judge found it guilty on one count each,

for which it was fined $500 per infraction. But the lesson had been learned. Environmental groups now had a precedent around which to mobilize, and it would never be as easy again for an oil company to pollute an area as thoroughly as Union had polluted the Santa Barbara Channel.

UNITED STATES
(FLORIDA, ST. PETERSBURG)
DELIAN APOLLON OIL SPILL IN TAMPA BAY
February 13, 1970

....

Thousands of birds were killed, oyster beds were closed, shrimp were eliminated, and shorelines were fouled when the Greek tanker Delian Apollon *ran aground on a sandbar while edging into a slip near St. Petersburg, Florida, on February 13, 1970. Twenty-one thousand gallons of crude oil formed a 100-square-mile oil spill in Tampa Bay.*

"A travesty of errors and a circus of mistakes" was the way Florida congressman William C. Cramer described the events leading up to, during, and after the grounding of the 691-foot, 25,100-ton Greek tanker *Delian Apollon* on the morning of February 13, 1970.

The weather was foggy, but not unusually so, as the tanker, chartered by the Humble Oil Company, was being maneuvered by the Tampa Bay pilot into the Florida Power Corporation oil port on Weedon Island, adjacent to the bay shoreline in North St. Petersburg, Florida. What nobody aboard knew except him was that the pilot had never before piloted a ship into the oil port.

Just outside the slip, he ran aground, with a grinding groan, onto a sandbar. Before the ship struck fast, a three-foot gash was torn in her hull, and bunker C grade crude oil began to spurt from the wound into the water. Twenty-one thousand gallons of it would escape into Tampa Bay before several tugs hauled her off the bar and into her slip. A styrofoam boom was drawn across the entrance to the slip and divers immediately descended to plug up the hole.

It took a full three hours to get the ship into the slip, and during that time, no one reported the oil leak or the grounding. It was, in fact, a Coast Guard pilot flying a training mission who first spotted the oil slick and radioed it in.

"During this time," according to Congressman Cramer, "no one was doing anything to contain the oil. In fact it was then too late to stop it."

Informed of the problem, Humble Oil, according to the Congressman, "didn't accept responsibility, even after the president of the company was informed of what had happened."

Shortly thereafter, the company issued a press release stating that it would pay for all damages to private and public property that resulted from the spill.

Meanwhile, the oil, coagulated into a 100-square-mile slick, washed ashore, fouling the beaches and coves of the entire 10-mile St. Petersburg beachfront. From the Howard Frankland Bridge across upper Tampa Bay, southward 30 miles to west of the Sunshine Skyway, between St. Petersburg and Palmetto, the pitch-black goo coated seawalls, boats, and beaches; crippled birds; and threatened oysterbeds.

City workers were called in, and they brought hundreds of bales of straw. Polyurethane foam and suction-equipped tank trucks joined them.

The Audubon Society issued a call for volunteers, and hundreds of Boy Scouts, college students, and residents arrived to help rescue and clean birds. Hundreds of these birds, among them pelicans, gulls, grebes, and ducks, had already suffocated.

On Monday the 16th, 14 men from the U.S. Department of Interior, headed by R. W. Thieme, the deputy assistant secretary, flew in to investigate. The Florida Department of Natural Resources brought several biologists and 10 boats to survey and help, if they could.

The oil slick continued to spread, fouling the beaches of Fort DeSoto Park, St. Petersburg Beach, Treasure Island, Madeira Beach, and the Redington Beaches. Florida's attorney general, Earl Faircloth, filed a $2 million damage action against the owner of the tanker, alleging improper navigation, intentionally bringing an unseaworthy vessel into Tampa Bay, failure to maintain a proper lookout, and stranding a vessel.

Finally, on February 18, the slick was contained, but the damage continued to be assessed. The oyster beds around Hillsborough, Pinellas, and Manatee Counties were all ordered closed. Millions of shrimp were destroyed. Thousands of pelicans, ducks, grebes, cormorants, and herons were killed by the oil. Biologists predicted that the following spring's shrimp catch would be hard hit, and sport and commercial fishermen could expect smaller catches for the following few years. In addition, conservationists predicted that the oil would remain in the tangled mangrove bayous lining the bay for years to come because the dense growth would inevitably trap the oil.

In a grim postscript, David Palmer, a 26-year-old diver, drowned on February 18 while applying a cement patch to the hull of the *Delian Apollon*, preparatory to towing her into drydock.

The final monetary cost was estimated at between $10 and $12 million. The spill affected 254,400 acres of bay in varying degrees. Beneath the water had been one of the most productive bay bottoms in Florida for plant and animal life, and biologists estimated that the monetary loss of this amounted to $8 million.

On the shore, 11,298 birds were killed, shrimp catches were diminished, and private property damaged.

There was one salutory effect of the *Delian Apollon* disaster. A bill, introduced by Senator Edwin Muskie, designed to make sure that owners of offending vessels clean up and restore damaged shorelines when their ships leaked oil, had been tied up in conference committee by House of Representative Republicans who were heeding the wishes of shipping companies. When Congressman Cramer, a House Republican, returned from Tampa Bay, he had become a convert, and his vote and those of some of his colleagues finally allowed the Senate version to pass the committee and into legislation.

UNITED STATES
(HAWAII, HONOLULU)
EXPLOSION OF *HAWAIIAN PATRIOT*
February 24, 1977

....

One crewman died and several were injured when the tanker Hawaiian Patriot, *carrying 30 million gallons of oil, foundered, then exploded and caught fire 360 miles west of Honolulu, Hawaii, on February 24, 1977. Its entire cargo spilled into the Pacific.*

On the morning of February 24, 1977, the 846-foot oil tanker *Hawaiian Patriot* radioed a distress signal to the Coast Guard. An entire hull plate had become dislodged, and a huge hole had opened up under the waterline. She was foundering and leaking oil at a furious rate.

The Coast Guard sent out a C-130 reconnaisance plane immediately, and the merchant ship *Philippine Bataan*, sailing in the area, changed course and headed toward the *Hawaiian Patriot*.

Minutes before either ship reached her, just as the plane hovered overhead and after she had leaked more than 5 million of the 30 million gallons of her cargo into the Pacific, the ship exploded. An enormous cloud of black smoke spun out of the ship's midsection, and the pilot of the C-130 reported crew members scurrying from the site of the explosion. Moments later, the ship caught fire, and despite the five-foot seas that pounded at her, the crew began to abandon ship, some leaping into the sea, some lowering lifeboats.

The *Philippine Bataan* drew alongside and hauled 38 of the 39 crew members and officers aboard as the entire *Hawaiian Patriot* became engulfed in orange flames. Smaller explosions punctuated the bursting fires and rockets of burning oil shooting into the air.

Some of the crew were injured; most were merely terrified. One crew member was missing and presumed dead.

The ship burned for hours before sinking and releasing the remainder of its cargo of oil, which drifted into a slick 50 miles long before it was finally broken up by the seas. None of it apparently reached land.

The explosion of the *Hawaiian Patriot* was the ninth in a series of accidents involving Liberian-registry vessels within a two-and-a-half-month period. It was the third

All but the bow of the Hawaiian Patriot *is obscured by an immense cloud of smoke billowing from the fire that followed an onboard explosion. The entire cargo of 30 million gallons of crude oil spilled into the sea 360 miles west of Honolulu.*
(AP/WORLD WIDE)

Liberian merchant ship to be lost in the western Pacific in six weeks. The 600-foot *Irenes Challenger* broke in half January 21 and later sank, leaking 950 tons of fuel oil and drowning three crewmen (see pp. 175–78), and the 518-foot *Rose S.* disappeared, along with its cargo of logs and 31 crewmen, on February 13.

UNITED STATES

(LOUISIANA, GULF OF MEXICO)

OIL PLATFORM FIRE
February 10, 1970

....

A huge fire consumed a Chevron Oil Company platform 75 miles southeast of New Orleans, Louisiana, on February 10, 1970. The spill drifted out to sea.

Just three days before the *Delian Apollon* ran aground and released oil into Tampa Bay (see pp. 172–73), a fire was sighted on an oil platform owned by Chevron Oil Company. The platform, a collecting station for 12 oil wells, was located in international waters in the Gulf of Mexico approximately 75 miles southeast of New Orleans.

The fire, fed by crude oil spouting free from wells drilled in the seabed, burned for nearly a month before firefighters from Houston arrived, ready to douse the fire and cap the well.

It proved to be a job far more difficult than they imagined. For several days at the beginning of March, the largest concentration of equipment ever collected at the scene of an oil spill converged upon the burning platform. Seven barges and scores of boats with skimmers and vacuum machines stationed themselves in a circle around the platform, ready to receive the oil that would escape between the dousing of the fire and the capping of the wells. The U.S. Coast Guard kept aircraft five miles away from the site and boat traffic three miles away.

At noon on March 9, 300 pounds of dynamite, packed into a barrel, were lowered, via a 106-foot boom, into the heart of the flames that were roaring skyward from the platform. At 12:18, the dynamite was ignited, and, with an ear-splitting roar and a volcanic display of sparks and shrapnel, the platform blew up.

174

The fire appeared to be out. Crude oil in enormous quantities gushed 250 feet into the air, and the boats with skimmers and vacuums scurried into action, attempting to contain the spill and direct it out to sea.

More than 100,000 gallons of water a minute were sprayed on the fire to try to cool down the twisted steel casings. It appeared that the worst was over.

But it was not. Six minutes and three seconds after the explosion, the fire reignited, and, while the oil spill stopped, the entire process had to be started all over.

Several more times during the following days, the same procedure was followed until the fire was finally extinguished and the enormous fountains of crude oil were capped.

Fortunately, the chocolatey oil slick released by the exposed wells floated out to sea and away from the Louisiana beaches. What could have been a cataclysm of far-reaching consequence was averted. But in the annals of might-have-beens, this was a big one.

UNITED STATES
(MASSACHUSETTS, NANTUCKET)
ARGO MERCHANT OIL SPILL
December 14, 1976

The 640-foot Liberian tanker Argo Merchant, *bound from Venezuela to Salem, Massachusetts, ran aground on the shoals of Nantucket Island at 6:00 A.M. on December 14, 1976. Eventually, the ship split apart twice and dumped the entirety of its cargo of 7.5 million gallons of number 6 crude oil into the Atlantic Ocean.*

The 640-foot Liberian oil tanker *Argo Merchant* seemed to be a hard-luck ship, or at least an accident-prone one. By the time its captain, George Papadopoulos, drove it onto the Nantucket shoals in the early morning hours of Wednesday, December 14, 1976, she had had 18 reported accidents. Some of these involved engine failures, but others seemed suspiciously to be the work of irresponsible or

The Gulf of Mexico is dotted with oil platforms like this. The fire that consumed the Chevron Oil Company rig 75 miles southeast of New Orleans in 1970 burned for nearly a month, simultaneously leaking oil into the gulf.
(UN PHOTO/FAO/H. NULL)

A Coast Guard helicopter rescues crew members aboard the Argo Merchant, *locked tight on the shoals off Nantucket Island, and spewing all 7.5 million gallons of its cargo of crude oil into the Atlantic Ocean.*
(LIBRARY OF CONGRESS)

careless work on the part of the ship's captain and crew. In March 1971, the *Argo Merchant* was grounded off Calabria, Italy, for 60 hours; in September 1969, she spent 36 hours aground off Borneo.

And now, in the middle of December 1976, she once again plowed into disaster. Throughout the afternoon of December 14, she stayed on a course that would bypass the shoals of Nantucket and take her straight into Salem, Massachusetts. Then, she began to drift off course. By 6.00 A.M. on December 15, she was 24 miles off, and headed directly for the shoals, which were plainly marked on all navigation charts, 27 miles off the coast of Nantucket Island, a mere 15 miles away from the Georges Bank, one of the world's richest commercial fishing areas. Not only this, the shoals were squarely on the feeding grounds of the almost extinct gray seal and in the middle of the migratory route of the humpback whale. The *Argo Merchant* hit them at full speed and

rammed herself solidly aground, ripping apart her hull in the process.

Coast Guard Commandant Owen W. Siler later testified that "[Captain Papadopoulos] had all sorts of equipment that he didn't use. It's quite possible to navigate much more closely than he did."

"I was in the wrong position," the captain told the *Boston Sunday Globe*, and this seemed to be an understatement.

The ensuing crisis was caused by an immediate oil spill. Heavy crude oil gushed from a wound in the *Argo Merchant*'s hull, torn apart by the high-speed grounding. Bill Quinn, a freelance photographer who flew over the scene within hours of the grounding, described the spill as being "as wide as the ship is long and [stretching] to the horizon."

As the weather turned ugly, Coast Guard helicopters evacuated most of the crewmen. Aboard the tanker were 7.5 million gallons of number 6 crude oil, enough to fill

2,500 average oil trucks or to heat a medium-size city for an entire winter. One hundred thousand gallons of oil leaked out in the first day. Fortunately, the temperature dropped precipitously during the storm, and this in turn coagulated the oil in the tanker, slowing the leak.

By December 19, salvage experts had boarded the ship and found it basically sound, and, in their words, "not in danger of breaking up."

Even so, as the temperature warmed, the flow of oil gushing out of the ship increased to a torrent.

And then, further disaster struck. A winter storm came up on the 20th, and at 8:55 A.M. on December 21st, the *Argo Merchant*, pounded relentlessly by 15-foot waves erupting in an enormous surf, split in half. The stern wallowed around, forming a V with the bow, which now rose, riding high and pointing skyward.

The multinational crew and officers had long since departed the *Argo Merchant* and were safely in a motel on Nantucket. The salvage crew had to be rescued by helicopter. They left behind three special heavy-duty pumps, worth $50,000 apiece. All three sank when the ship broke in two.

By the afternoon of the 21st, three-quarters of the cargo had leaked into the Atlantic Ocean. By that night, nearly 5 million gallons of crude had fouled the sea, and the oil was still gushing forth at a rate of 10,000 gallons an hour.

For most of the day, the enormous oil slick had been drifting northeastward toward Georges Bank, but late in the afternoon, a fortuitous wind shift drove it to the southeast, away from Nantucket and Martha's Vineyard, the Cape Cod beaches, and the New England land mass. If nothing else occurred, and the oil slick dissipated at sea, the disaster would rank as the 10th-largest oil spill up to that time. But the potential ecological damage, if it occurred, would propel it quickly to the top of the list.

"By all odds, this is the biggest oil spill disaster on the American coast in our history," said Russell E. Train, administrator of the Environmental Protection Agency, noting also that even if the oil never touched land, it had the enormous potential of fouling the Georges Bank fishing grounds.

Bodies of oil-soaked ocean birds had already begun to drift ashore on Nantucket Island, and three bird-cleaning stations were set up.

At the same time, fishermen on Cape Cod filed a class action suit seeking $60 million for damages to the fishing grounds.

On December 22, the bow split in half, and the remainder of the oil that had once filled the *Argo Merchant*'s hold spilled into the sea. High winds and waves thwarted any attempts by the Coast Guard to retrieve the oil; it merely floated off, powered by the gale-force winds.

The slick was now in the shape of a cone, extending for approximately 120 miles, with a width of about 35 miles at its widest point. It was still moving away from land and seemed to be on a course that would allow it to miss the Georges Banks, too.

But farther north, effects of the spill were beginning to be felt. Four hundred birds, mostly seagulls, washed ashore in Nantucket and near New Bedford. One New Bedford fishing vessel reported that it had discovered a scallop bed coated with oil. The other had its net fouled with oil and had to cut it loose.

Now, the Coast Guard inquiry into the accident attempted to ferret out its causes. A day before the hearings began, the Coast Guard received a telephone call from a man identifying himself as a crew member of the *Argo Merchant*, who stated unequivocally that the ship's owners had ordered the ship deliberately run aground because the owners knew that she was "old and leaking."

Opening statements from the Coast Guard offered small comfort to the ship's master. Rear Admiral William M. Benkert, the chief of the Office of Merchant Marine Safety, opined that the *Argo Merchant*'s skipper "should never have run aground," and "must have been asleep" when she did. The admiral continued to enumerate the many navigational aids that were at the captain's disposal, including echo soundings, radio beacons, and the ability to take celestial fixes.

Celestial fixes were exactly what the captain and his crew were taking, apparently, just before the ship ran aground. The captain was supposed to sight the Nantucket Lightship in order to pursue the normal course to Salem, according to later testimony. The officers were so intent, in fact, upon looking for the lightship, that they stood on the outer deck of the bridge and failed to watch the tanker's radar and depth finder. Both could have clearly shown them that they had gone astray.

In addition to this, Captain Papadopoulos acknowledged that something must have been wrong with either the direction finder, or the way he was using it.

The rest of the equipment on the ship seemed to be malfunctioning, too. The gyrocompass had become erratic the evening before the grounding. The charts they were using in December were November charts. The boilers were malfunctioning.

And then there was human error. According to Captain Papadopoulos, the chief mate, Georgios Ypsilantis, miscalculated the ship's position a half hour before the grounding, by adding up a set of figures incorrectly.

A federal judge took the testimony under advisement, and attention turned toward a hearing held by the Senate Commerce Committee. At this hearing, the Coast Guard dropped a bombshell, stating that it had planned to seize the *Argo Merchant* when it reached Boston and hold it for unseaworthiness. It had not seized it earlier, the Coast Guard said, because the State Department had advised them that turning away a vessel would weaken the United

States in negotiations at the Law of the Sea Conference slated to take place later in the year.

Meanwhile, a bombshell of another sort drew fire from marine biologists. The Coast Guard announced that it proposed to bomb the remains of the *Argo Merchant*, whose bow, sunk just below the surface of the sea, had become a menace to navigation.

Marine biologists immediately asked for a postponement, since January, they stated, was the prime breeding month for a number of species of fish that frequented these waters, including flounder, haddock, and pollock. The species could be wiped out by a bombing, they stated, and the Coast Guard postponed the bombardment indefinitely.

The oil slick, which by January 3 had covered a 215-by-100-square-mile area of the Atlantic, began to dissipate. By the end of the month, it was broken into smaller and smaller fragments by the heavy winter seas of the North Atlantic.

On March 15, 1977, the Liberian Shipping Council ordered the master's license of Captain George Papadopoulos revoked, and placed the chief mate and second mate under suspension. Working from the findings of the federal hearings and the Coast Guard files, the council concluded that human error caused the grounding of the tanker.

As to the effects of the oil spill: The National Oceanic and Atmospheric Administration conducted exhaustive studies and reported in April 1977 that apparently minimal biological and aesthetic damage had resulted. It was possible, the report added, that the oil might have seeped into the ocean bottom sand and contaminated the zoo plankton that is ingested by fish in the area. But there was no proof of it.

The cost to the taxpayers for the cleanup was more than $5.2 million, most of which was recovered from fines and lawsuits.

UNITED STATES
(MIDWAY ISLAND)
BREAKUP OF TANKER *IRENES CHALLENGER*
January 17, 1978

Three crewmen were reported missing and were never found when the Greek tanker Irenes Challenger *broke up in heavy seas 220 miles southeast of Midway Island on January 17, 1978. The oil slick released by the ship was 150 miles long, but reached no land.*

The Greek tanker *Irenes Challenger*, flying under a Liberian flag, and sailing from Japan to Venezuela through a Pacific Ocean storm with 8-foot waves and 60-mph gale-force winds began to founder 220 miles southeast of Midway Island during the daylight hours of January 17, 1978. By

nightfall, she was sending out distress signals and reporting that she was coming apart.

Sometime during the evening of January 17, the ship split into two sections. The Norwegian ship *Rona River* reached the bow section, and the Japanese container ship *Pacific Arrow* reached the stern section shortly afterward and rescued the crewmen clinging to the wreck or floating in lifeboats in the roiling seas. The oil from the ship was pouring in great gushes from rips in the vessel's midships, and lifeboats that were lowered were immediately coated by the gummy mess that the storm prevented from coagulating.

By morning, all but three of the surviving crewmen were accounted for. The missing three were presumed drowned. All of the cargo of the ship was released into the Pacific, and it formed an oil slick 150 miles long.

The breakup of the *Irenes Challenger* was only one of three catastrophes that afflicted Liberian-flagged ships traveling in the Pacific in the winter of 1977–78, which included the disappearance, with its cargo of logs and all of its crew, of the *Rose S.* on February 13, 1978, and the explosion of the *Hawaiian Patriot* and its consequent giant oil spill on February 24 (see pp. 173–174).

UNITED STATES/CANADA
(NEW YORK, THOUSAND ISLANDS)
ST. LAWRENCE SEAWAY BARGE SPILL
June 23, 1976

Three hundred thousand gallons of number 6 oil spilled into the St. Lawrence Seaway at the Thousand Islands on the morning of June 23, 1976. A 30-mile-long oil slick killed wildlife and fish and made an oily mess of the tourist season.

At the end of June 1976, the residents of Alexandra Bay, a Thousand Islands community located at the mouth of the St. Lawrence Seaway just before it empties, on its international route from Canada to the United States, into Lake Ontario, were preparing for the opening of the summer tourist season. Trees were in full blossom, birds were singing, school was out. Everything was fresh and new except the normally sweet scent of the pure air that customarily made the Thousand Islands a northern paradise. That morning, the scent of oil was unmistakable, heavy and sickening.

At 1:30 A.M., during a heavy fog, the barge *Nepco*, towed by a tug owned by the Oswego Barge Company and carrying number 6 oil for the New England Petroleum Company, hit a shoal at Wellesley Island, which is linked to the mainland of both the United States and Canada by the Thousand Islands Bridge. The shoals ripped open 3 of the 16 storage tanks on the barge, and before it was repaired, the barge would leak 250,000 gallons of oil into the heavily traveled waterway.

No traffic at all was allowed through for 15 hours; after that, and for weeks, it inched through on a severely curtailed basis, one boat at a time.

Coincidentally, there was a Coast Guard station on Wellesley Island, and, mindful of the extensive environmental damage that the oil spill would cause, it sent workers to the scene immediately. Thereafter, Coastal Services Inc. of Boston arrived upon the scene with booms and vacuum pumps linked to large tank trucks.

The water, normally so pure that the towns along it took their drinking water from the river with only a minimum of treatment, had acquired a sickly brown aspect, like inexpertly made cappuccino. The odor was horrific, and the oil slick had spread to a smear extending nine miles eastward and six miles westward.

While the swimming beaches could be easily cleaned, the hundreds and hundreds of small coves, estuaries, and streams, which gave the area its distinctive topography, provided a more difficult problem. Marina workers struggled to lift the hundreds of pleasure craft that had just been put into the water out of it before they were covered with oil. "All the wood boats around here will have to be pulled and scraped," said one workman to reporters. "They're porous, and this oil will sink right in."

More serious was the immediate effect upon the abundant wildlife in the area. "There are a lot of young waterfowl up there that are really incapable of getting out of the way," observed Richard Koelling, of the New York State Department of Environmental Conservation. Young fish and waterbirds abounded in the area during June and early July, especially in Chippewa and Goose Bay.

Mallards, black ducks, blue tern, teals, loons, gulls, and sandpipers were all threatened and began to die from suffocation. Muskrat and mink, and bass, young during the spring season, according to the Division of Fish and Wildlife of the Department of Environment, would be next to suffer, and suffer they did.

Most heartwrenching were the young ducks and molting older birds, who could not fly and thus could not escape the encroaching oil that killed them while they remained helplessly landlocked.

As the days of cleanup wore on and the barge was repaired and towed into Lake Ontario, commercial oil spill cleaners—called, derisively, "slicker lickers" by the Coast Guard—smelled, along with the oil, money. They descended upon the area, noisily trying to outbid each other for the job.

Though clear, calm weather aided the cleanup, the slick spread for more than 30 miles by June 24, from above Wellesley Island to below Morristown, New York. Floating booms to deflect and contain the oil were rigged as far down river as Ogdensburg, New York, to stop it before it got to the Iroquois Lock, where dispersal would complicate the cleanup.

The amount of oil eventually taken from the river would be 308,000 gallons, and it would take 10 days to accomplish this. Vacuuming out the bays and inlets took weeks, and the scrubbing of the shoreline took months. For weeks, commercial traffic on the seaway was backed up, since one-way traffic up- and downriver only allowed two or three ships through at a time.

During the cleanup, energetic public meetings were held in the villages along the seaway. At one meeting in Alexandra Bay, a local businessman proposed a new law to "keep boats carrying chemicals out of the Thousand Islands area during the night and when there is fog. I know all the environmental people can clean this up . . . ," he continued, "but if they want to run at high tide in the fog, let 'em sink a load of iron ore. At least that won't hurt anyone else."

His remarks drew applause, but little else. No such legislation was drafted, not by Canada, not by New York State, not by the government of the United States.

UNITED STATES
(Pennsylvania, Pottstown)
Oil spill in Schuykill River
June–July 1972

In the worst inland oil spill in the history of the United States, floodwaters in the aftermath of a hurricane that devastated parts of Pennsylvania and the eastern United States swept 6 million gallons of used crankcase oil into the Schuykill River. The resultant oil slick contaminated 16 miles of coastline.

Nature dealt the residents of Pottstown and Douglassville, Pennsylvania, a double roundhouse punch in the summer of 1972. Spring rains and an early hurricane at the end of June brought massive flooding to a large portion of the eastern United States. Rivers overflowed their banks and inundated riverbank settlements and farms from Pennsylvania to New England.

The Schuykill River, which flows into the Delaware River south of Philadelphia, is dotted with industrial plants. A few miles northwest of Philadelphia, midway between the towns of Pottsville and Douglassville, Berks County Associates, Inc., maintained a facility that reclaimed dirty crankcase oil. This oil was kept in storage lagoons that had, for years, been safe and impervious to the rising and falling tides of the Schuykill.

But in the last week of June 1972, the river's floodwaters completely covered these lagoons and swept 6 million gallons of the heavy pitch-black sludge onto the surrounding landscape and then, as the water receded, into the river, which proceeded to distribute the oil along 16 miles of riverfront.

The damage was monumental. Oil scum clung to trees and buildings up to a height of 20 feet. Historic farmhouses were painted a sickening pitch color, and the interiors of them were similarly patinaed with the gummy residue.

If this had been all of it, it would have been merely an aesthetic problem. But, during the first week of July, the national environment research center of the Coast Guard in Durham, North Carolina, burned a sample of sludge similar to the thick coating that covered acres of land on either side of the Schuykill, and found that it polluted the air with lead fumes 10 times beyond levels considered safe for prolonged breathing.

The flora and fauna coated with oil sludge confirmed this. Bushes, trees, and evergreens withered and died from the onslaught of the oil. Thousands of birds and hundreds of animals were suffocated by it. The ground was so saturated with the oil that merely walking on plowed fields released pools of sludge that squished up underfoot.

Vacuum trucks were brought in to suck up the oil where it had formed pools deep enough and obvious enough to respond to this treatment. But this only removed 30,000 gallons of the greasy mess.

Then, hired contractors and government supervisors attempted to spread chemicals to absorb the oil, much the same way that detergents are used to break up oil spills on water. These not only did not work, they further contaminated the wildlife that had survived the initial spill.

Straw and shredded newspapers were used in an attempt to trap the oil and keep it from spreading farther, and this worked to a small degree.

But ultimately, a more primitive method was finally, successfully employed. Hundreds of young people formed bucket brigades that laboriously scooped up the sludge and moved it to collection points on the fringe of the contaminated area. It would take nearly six months of this and the healing rains of the nature that had caused the catastrophe to finally clean up what the Coast Guard called the worst inland oil spill in the history of the United States.

NUCLEAR DISASTERS

Japan
 * Tsuruga (nuclear power plant leak) (1981)

Switzerland
 Lucends Vad (underground reactor explosion) (1969)

United Kingdom
 * England, Liverpool (Windscale plutonium plant contamination) (1957)

*Detailed in text

United States
 * Alabama, Brown's Ferry (nuclear power plant fire) (1975)
 * Idaho, Idaho Falls (nuclear reactor explosion) (1961)
 Minnesota, Monticello (nuclear reactor explosion) (1971)
 * Pennsylvania, Middletown (Three Mile Island nuclear power plant leak) (1979)
 Tennessee, Erwin (nuclear fuel plant explosion) (1979)

USSR
 * Kasli (Kyshtym) (nuclear waste dump explosion) (1957)
 * Pripyat (Chernobyl nuclear power plant explosion) (1986)

♦ ♦ ♦ ♦ ♦

CHRONOLOGY

♦ ♦ ♦ ♦ ♦

1957

    * United Kingdom: England, Liverpool, Windscale plutonium plant contamination

    * USSR: Kasli (Kyshtym), nuclear waste dump explosion

1961

    USA: Idaho, Idaho Falls, nuclear reactor explosion

1969

    Switzerland: Lucends Vad, underground reactor explosion

*Detailed in text

1971

    USA: Minnesota, Monticello, nuclear reactor explosion

1975

    * USA: Alabama, Brown's Ferry, nuclear power plant fire

1979

    * USA: Pennsylvania, Middletown, Three Mile Island nuclear power plant leak

    USA: Tennessee, Erwin, nuclear fuel plant explosion

1981

    * Japan: Tsuruga, nuclear power plant leak

1986

    * USSR: Pripyat, Chernobyl nuclear power plant explosion

NUCLEAR DISASTERS

We chuckle at the fits and starts and tumblings of a toddler. We tolerate the bull-in-a-china-shop awkwardness of a teenager, the windmilling gawkiness of an adult venturing forth for the first time on a pair of skates on a frozen pond.

But we would never, for an instant, countenance a clumsy ballerina, a bumbling ballroom dancer, or a falling figure skater. From professionals we expect nothing less than perfect concentration, excellent execution, and unfailing grace under pressure.

Why then, one wonders, has a long record of bumbling clumsiness resulting in death, slovenly disregard of detail causing environmental cataclysm, senseless fouling of the air, compounding contamination of the sea, and irresponsible moonscaping of the land not only been tolerated by the judges of such performances but also hidden from the public at large?

And yet this is what has happened, over and over in the nuclear industry. Every major nuclear disaster that has occurred since the Manhattan Project joined geniuses and generals to usher in the new universe of atomic power has come about largely because of what has gently been termed "human error."

This human error has ranged from watching a baseball game on television while a nuclear reactor began to melt down, to lighting candles to test air leaks under nuclear control rooms, to allowing paper to run out in record-keeping machinery, to faulty maintenance of safety devices, to failing to design workable evacuation plans, to designing nuclear plants that are inherently ready to explode into cataclysmic chaos. All of it seems to be proof possible that in this modern world, technology frequently—too frequently—outruns those who run it.

And there is another leitmotif that threads through both industrial and nuclear accidents: the tendency to cover them up and to minimize both the human and environmental toll. Minamata (see pp. 89–93) and Bhopal (see pp. 81–85) were horribly destructive in terms of contamination of the water supply and the atmosphere. But Chernobyl,

Kasli, Windscale, Three Mile Island, and Tsuruga have been equally destructive in their unleashing of radioactive contamination into the atmosphere.

In all of these tragedies, coverup and minimization was the plan followed by the plants and factories involved and, later, by the governments that were given the responsibility of investigating and, in some cases, paying for the cleanup or the damage suits.

It is a problem that will neither go away nor diminish, particularly since, with the eventual exhaustion of fossil fuels, and the present assault on the ozone layer by these fuels, the number of backers of atomic power as a consumer energy source will grow.

At the present moment, in Sweden, for instance, half of the electricity production comes from hydroelectric power, which is opposed by environmentalists because of the flooding of wildlife habitats, and the other half is derived from nuclear power plants—which the Chernobyl disaster has rendered null and void in the future. A 1980 referendum resolved that no further reactors would be commissioned and all existing reactors would be phased out by 2010. This takes care of the contamination problem but not the electricity problem, which will be met—unless biofuel from organic waste and wind power programs can be supplemented by something new—by importing Danish or Norwegian natural gas.

Various conferences on halting pollution in the North Sea have solved some of the industrial and agricultural dumping problems, but, although all of the Nordic countries agreed to halt the dumping of radioactive waste by 1994, the United Kingdom, in which one-fifth of the country's electricity comes from nuclear power plants, refused to set a cutoff date.

No country in Europe has pursued nuclear energy to create electricity more than France. Since the early 1970s, it has aggressively built nuclear power plants. By 1992, 55 such power stations were in operation, another 6 were under construction, and fully 75 percent of the nation's electricity came from nuclear energy.

All of this abundance of building nuclear facilities has not gone unchallenged. A terrible price has been paid for reliance on nuclear power. Chernobyl is a nightmare from which thousands still cannot wake. Much of the spent uranium fuel processed for re-use at Sellafield on the northwest coast of England, where radioactive waste is stored, is being discharged into the Irish Sea, where shellfish (and thence, humans) are being contaminated. Still, the caesium-137 and plutonium in the waste has been declared relatively harmless by government authorities despite the simultaneous discovery that the rate of child leukemia in one village near the Sellafield plant was 10 times the national average.

It could have been coincidence, or it could have been caused by other factors, as could the skyrocketing incidences of thyroid cancer among the children of the survivors of Chernobyl. But until proven otherwise, the statistics of cause logically seem to point toward the waste, whether dumped or leaked into the air, from nuclear plants.

And this is of great concern. All nuclear power plants, like all factories, produce waste, and although there is enough concern to go around about the impact upon the environment of ordinary factory waste, nuclear waste belongs to another universe, one requiring an entirely different language.

Consider the term "half-life." It is a new measurement that translates into the amount of time it takes for radioactivity to subside to a non-dangerous level. Not subside entirely. But to a non-dangerous level.

The half-life of high-level wastes, the sort that routinely emerge from nuclear power plants in the person of spent fuel rods, is at least 10,000 years, and the amount of spent fuel rods in the world today is estimated at 90,900 tons, not counting the unknown amounts produced in the former Soviet Union.

But this is not all of it. Some of the spent fuel from these rods is reprocessed to recover a small proportion of the uranium and plutonium for new fuel, but most of it is discarded as nonreusable waste. And, added to this, are the liquids that are created through reprocessing. They increase the amount of radioactive waste material by nearly 60 times.

In the early, more innocent years of the atomic age, low-level wastes were dumped into steel containers from which the waste was in turn dumped into the sea, or, equally dangerous, buried, like garbage, in landfills. Both of these methods have been banned, and now wastes are stored in liquid form in steel tanks protected by concrete or lead, or buried deeply underground as solids encased in glass.

In America, these burial sites are located at the 102 commercial reactors that exist, since there is no permanent repository site. No state wants it, and every time it comes up for consideration in Congress, enough pressure from constituents forces it back into the to-be-considered pile of continuing bills.

France, in fact, is one of the only countries in the world that has met this need head on. It has the largest reprocessing plant for radioactive waste in the world, at La Hague, near the port of Cherbourg on the northern coast of the Mediterranean. France also maintains a uranium enrichment plant at Tricastin in the lower Rhone valley, in French territory but owned by a consortium of European countries.

And here, too, there is opposition to the reprocessing plants, given impetus by the Chernobyl disaster and local events, such as the plutonium contamination found in 1990 at a "decontaminated" nuclear waste site near Paris.

So, the conflict continues, between residents who live near dumpsites and environmentalists and industry, and between the two largest forms of power generation in the world: the burning of fossil fuel and the utilizing of nuclear energy. And which, finally, is better—the creation of greenhouse gases and holes in the ozone layer from fossil fuel consumption, or the continuance of the danger of radioactive contamination from nuclear power plants? Within the next two generations, at least, the twin threats will probably continue to offset each other, unless some horrible cataclysm tips the scales one way or the other.

In the meantime, what must be addressed, and what continues not to be addressed, unfortunately, is the problem of policing and planning in nuclear power plants. Policing and setting up safety policies within these plants would dramatically reduce the chance of nuclear disasters; and planning workable evacuation procedures in case one occurs would limit the casualties to human beings, if not to the environment. And more candor, before, during, and after these atomic holocausts would also be a refreshing and monumental change for the better.

Finally, governments have explained away their suppression of the truth as a desire not to create panic in the populace. But this policy has resulted in hundreds of lawsuits against governments by the families of victims who have died agonizing and puzzling deaths long after incidents that had been passed off as posing little or no danger to the public at large. Until this pervasive policy is changed, casualty figures from nuclear accidents will continue to multiply, as governments continue to use nuclear power without spending the proper amount of time and money on researching methods of preventing disasters and controlling their consequent effects.

JAPAN
(TSURUGA)
NUCLEAR POWER PLANT LEAK
March 8, 1981

A leak from a disposal building at the nuclear power plant at Tsuruga, Japan on March 8, 1981 caused widespread radiation contamination. Fifty-nine workers were exposed to radiation, and Japan's fishing industry was temporarily suspended.

The nuclear power plant at Tsuruga, Japan, a seacoast city of 60,000 located on the far west coast of Japan, opposite Tokyo, was in chronic trouble in the early spring of 1981. And the Japan Atomic Power Commission, like the atomic power commissions of the United States (see Three Mile Island, pp. 190–93) and the United Kingdom (see Windscale, pp. 186–87), spent as much time misinforming the public as it did in investigating the mishap.

On March 8, a huge leakage of radioactive waste occurred in a disposal building adjacent to the main plant. The first newspaper report did not appear until April 18, more than a month from the time that 16 tons of the waste

Sixteen tons of radioactive waste spilled from a disposal building at the Tsuruga nuclear power plant into Wakasa Bay and from there into the Sea of Japan. The contamination, unreported for six and a half weeks, spread through the fertile fishing fields surrounding Tsuruga, and, thus, contaminated fish were shipped worldwide.
(STEPHEN PERKINS/UNEP)

had spilled into the adjoining Wakasa Bay, which flows into the Sea of Japan.

The April 18 bulletin merely stated that a crack in a pipe or the storage tanks themselves "might have allowed waste water to seep into general drainage pipes into the Wakasa Bay."

Shortly thereafter, the Ministry of International Trade and Industry also announced that it had found radioactivity levels 10 times normal in seaweed near drainage outlets, and the Kyodo News Service accompanied the release with the discomforting information that the amount of cobalt-60 discovered in the seaweed and the soil surrounding the plant was "five thousand times the previous highest reading . . . the effects on the human body could be serious if the radioactive waste has spread throughout the bay."

It would not be until April 21, six and a half weeks after the mishap, that the Japan Atomic Power Commission would make its first statement, in which it acknowledged that some waste-contaminated water had leaked onto the floor of the plant and that 56 men who had been put to work mopping up the water with buckets and rags "had been exposed to radiation at levels considerably below government limits," an assessment the Ministry of Trade and Industry immediately disputed. The announcement went on to speculate that the plant's executives might be indicted on criminal charges.

Finally, two days later, the Tsuruga company released more detailed information, which had been withheld, a company spokesman avowed, because of "Japanese emotionalism toward anything nuclear."

The accident, according to the account released by the company, occurred when an operator apparently forgot to shut off a valve, which in turn let water run through a radioactive sludge tank, which overflowed and splashed onto the floor of the power plant and then seeped into the general sewage system.

Akira Machida, the plant's general manager, attempted to downplay the accident by comparing it to Three Mile Island. "[It was] nowhere near as serious as America's Three Mile Island," he told reporters, but he then acknowledged that the biggest blunder was in failing to report it to the authorities.

Further revelations came swiftly. Forty-five other workers had been exposed to radiation in January, when another pipe had broken in the plant. Thirty-one other accidents had occurred since the plant had opened in 1970.

But the worst was yet to come. Fish and fish products from the immediate area of Tsuruga had been recalled following the March 8 mishap, but no one knew how widespread the contamination of the waters of the Sea of Japan had been. (Several years later, mutant forms of fish continued to be caught in the area, indicating that there was far more contamination than first reports indicated.) Japanese officials could not have forgotten the 1954 furor when 23 fishermen and the tuna catch aboard the Japanese fishing boat *Lucky Dragon* were victims of acute radiation exposure after the U.S. test explosion of a hydrogen bomb near Rongelap Atoll in the Marshall Islands. But their silence in 1981 seemed to indicate that they had.

Finally, in May, the chairman of the board and the president of the Japan Atomic Power Commission resigned, accepting the responsibility for the leakages. A government investigation blamed human error, faulty equipment, and structural weaknesses.

It would be Japan's first and last nuclear accident, at least so far. That human carelessness and coverup would figure at all in the nuclear industry of the first country in the world to suffer a nuclear holocaust made it enormously significant, and a discouraging comment on the pervasiveness of human recklessness.

UNITED KINGDOM
(ENGLAND, LIVERPOOL)
WINDSCALE PLUTONIUM PLANT CONTAMINATION
October 10, 1957

The overheating of uranium cartridges released radioactive iodine causing widespread radioactive contamination surrounding the Windscale plutonium plant near Liverpool, England, on October 10, 1957. Thirty-three related cancer deaths have occurred; more are expected. There was a temporary suspension of the milk and beef industries of northwestern England.

The Windscale plutonium factory in the Cumberland country of northwest England manufactured plutonium for use in nuclear reactors and atomic bombs and produced certain by-products that were used in medicine. Powered by the nearby Calder Hall atomic power plant, it was thought to be, in 1957, a model of clean and efficient productivity.

But the accident that took place on October 10, 1957, which was England's first nuclear accident—and one of the first in the peacetime world—was the forerunner and prototype of hundreds of nuclear accidents that would release radioactivity into the atmosphere. In 1957, the world was naive about the hazards, and little attention was given to the accident. But as its aftermath extended and deepened, so did the awareness of its significance.

At 4:15 P.M. on Thursday, October 10, 1957, the number one pile of uranium at Windscale overheated, and as its temperature rose, it released radioactive iodine-131 vapor and some oxidized uranium particles into the air. It would be 15 minutes before the red-hot uranium pile would be discovered; that part of the plant had been shut down for maintenance.

Shortly after it was discovered, workers wearing gas masks and other protective equipment were assigned to use carbon dioxide to extinguish the fire. It was ineffectual.

A sense that this was no ordinary fire began to grow. All of the plant's off-duty safety workers were called back, and all of the roads to the plant were blocked off. By 5:15, safety experts issued conciliatory statements to the press, claiming that all danger had departed.

It, of course, had not. By 9:00 A.M. on the 11th, it was decided to use water to damp down the fire. Two plant officials and a local fire chief hauled a hose to the top of the containment dome and aimed it at the fire. No one knew quite what would happen, and plant workers all over the complex crouched behind steel and concrete barriers.

Fortunately, the water worked, but it also released huge clouds of radioactive steam through the stacks and into the atmosphere. The worst was over, everyone thought; there had been neither an explosion nor a meltdown.

By midday of October 11, nearly all of the 3,000 workers at the plant and the nearby Calder Hall atomic energy plant were sent home. They had been exposed to radiation, and it was obvious that a reevaluation of the situation was needed.

Significant quantities of radioactive iodine-131 had been released into the atmosphere over a 200-mile radius, and at 2:00 A.M. on Sunday, October 13, police began to knock on the doors of the farmhouses in Cumberland. The milk from their cows, the police warned them, might be radioactive.

By Tuesday the 15th, the milk ban was extended from a 14-square-mile area to 200 square miles, including 600 dairy farms. Approximately 30,000 gallons of milk, worth $11,000, were dumped into the Irish Sea each day until the end of October, and all distribution of milk from the contaminated area was immediately halted.

Beyond that, hundreds of cows, goats, and sheep were rounded up, shot, and buried. Farmers who slaughtered their animals for meat were told to send the thyroid glands to the Atomic Energy Commission for testing.

Farmers in the area now began to make public the tales they had exchanged among themselves. Even before the accident, sterilization had occurred in their cattle, according to W. E. Hewitson, a dairy farmer in Yottenfews. He went on to state that he had changed bulls four times in four years, but only a third of his cows either calved or gave milk.

Now, it became apparent that the radioactive iodine-131 that safety experts first said had drifted out to sea had not done so at all. There was a marked increase in the radioactivity of the atmosphere after the accident at the Windscale plant.

Several months later, British officials conceded to a United Nations conference at Geneva that nearly 700 curies of cesium and strontium had also been released into the air over England and northern Europe, in addition to 20,000 curies of iodine-131. The iodine dose represented more than 1,400 times the quantity American officials later claimed had been released during the 1979 accident at Three Mile Island (see pp. 190–93).

As was so often the case, there were no official followup studies regarding the health of residents of the 200-mile area near the plant. When a local health officer, Frank Madge, used a Geiger counter to confirm abnormal radiation levels in mosses and lichens, representatives of the British Atomic Energy Authority discouraged publication of his findings.

Private studies of health data in downwind European countries later indicated a clear impact of the accident on infant-mortality rates. Dr. Ernest Sternglass, interviewed by Harvey Wasserman and Norman Solomon for their study, *Killing Our Own,* remarked, "[It was] as if a small bomb had been detonated in northern Great Britain."

As late as 1981, while the Windscale plant continued to operate without modification, British scientist E. D. Williams stated in the January 1981 issue of *Health Physics Journal* that there were "high cesium levels in people eating fish caught in the path of the Windscale effluent."

By 1990, 33 cancer deaths in the vicinity of the Windscale plant had been directly attributed to the 1957 accident.

UNITED STATES
(ALABAMA, BROWN'S FERRY)
NUCLEAR POWER PLANT FIRE
March 22, 1975

....

An astounding number of human errors caused a near meltdown at the Brown's Ferry nuclear power plant in Alabama on March 22, 1975. No one was injured, and no local authorities were informed of the accident until long after it had happened, thus precluding an evacuation of any type.

If the control room of a nuclear facility is its heart, the cable-spreading room is the juncture between this heart and the veins and arteries of the facility. Located underneath the control room of every nuclear facility, it resembles a neatly organized web of wires, a confluence of cables, each of which has a meaning and a function in the control of the reactors. Every line of power to every part of the nuclear facility is gathered here and radiates from this point in various organized tunnels that run off into the various buildings of the complex.

If a saboteur wanted to throw a nuclear plant into cataclysmic chaos, all he or she would have to do would be to gain access to the cable-spreading room, and like an assassin severing the jugular vein or carotid artery of his victim, bring the plant to its knees and send it into panicky paralysis.

This is exactly what happened at noon on March 22, 1975, at the Brown's Ferry nuclear power plant in Brown's Ferry, Alabama. The plant possesses two reactors, which constantly kick out 2,200 megawatts of electricity to the Tennessee Valley Authority (TVA).

That morning, an inspector and an electrician were performing a task that they and their fellow maintenance workers regarded as routine. The two were sent to do the laborious job of plugging air leaks in the room with two-inch-thick spongy polyurethene foam, which they stuffed into the offending air holes by hand.

It was standard practice to search for air leaks and then to test the effectiveness of the plug by holding a candle flame next to the present or former leak. If the flame burned horizontally instead of vertically, there was a leak; if it remained steady, no air was getting through.

On that particular morning, as the inspector later described it, "We found a two-by-four inch opening in a penetration window in a tray with three or four cables going through it. The candle flame was pulled out horizontal, showing a strong draft. [The electrician] tore off two pieces of foam sheet for packing into the hole. I checked the hole with the candle."

And that was the fatal decision that caused a calamity. Again, in the words of the inspector: "The draft sucked the flame into the hole and ignited the foam, which started to smolder and glow."

Immediately, the electrician handed the inspector his flashlight, and the inspector tried to beat out the flames with the flashlight. But they merely increased. Now, the two grabbed rags and stuffed them into the hole. They caught fire, and they removed them and stomped the fire out. But by now, there were more and more flames catching and multiplying in the hole.

The inspector retrieved a carbon dioxide fire extinguisher and shot the material into the opening. The carbon dioxide blew through the hole, leaving the fire untouched.

And now, the flames were obviously spreading into the interior of the wall, while the inspector grabbed chemical extinguisher after chemical extinguisher and tried putting the fire out with them, with no success.

All of this took 15 minutes, and during that time, no fire alarm was sounded, in spite of clear orders to sound a fire alarm first, then try to extinguish a fire.

When a guard finally phoned in the alarm, he called the shift engineer instead of the two emergency numbers listed for a fire. Ultimately, when the engineer reached the control room, an automatic alarm sounded. It was 12:35, 20 minutes after the fire had begun.

And even then, the reactor operators did nothing about shutting down the reactors. They in fact seemed to be frozen into inaction. It would be another precious five minutes before they even noticed that their gauges were going haywire, that the control lights were randomly glowing and going out, and—thank heaven—the Emergency Core Cooling System had started.

But it was only momentary.

As quickly as it had begun, the cooling system stopped. And then began again. And then stopped again. Now, smoke began to ooze out of one of the control panels.

This mad display went on for a full 10 minutes before the operators decided that it might be a good idea to shut down the reactors, and the one development that finally shocked one of these operators into action was a sharp and alarming descent of power in unit one. It was enough to prompt the operator into beginning to reduce the flow of the reactor's recirculating pumps. But within minutes, they stopped, too. And so, at 12:51, he finally shut the reactor down by inserting the control rods.

At 12:55 P.M., chaos hit the control room. The electrical supply that controlled and powered the Emergency Core Cooling System and a litany of other shutdown equipment was lost, including the instrumentation that told the control room what was going on in the reactor.

Meanwhile, the bedlam had spread to reactor number two. According to a shift engineer, "panel lights were changing color, going on and off. I noticed the annunciators on all four diesel generator control circuits showed ground alarms."

Now the shutdown equipment on unit two began to fail. The high-pressure Emergency Cooling System shut off at 1:45 P.M., and control over the reactor relief valves was lost at 1:20 P.M. This control, fortunately, returned at 2:15, and the second reactor was shut down.

But now the problem of maintaining the water level in the reactors faced those in the control room. If the cores became uncovered, a meltdown would occur. Emergency, ancillary pumps were brought in, and the water level, normally 200 inches, was maintained at just 48 inches—barely enough to cover the core. And to add to the problem, the instruments that showed the water level on unit one were not operating.

By 2:43, one of the plant's four diesel generators shut down, leaving it with only part of its emergency equipment operable.

Then, the telephone system in the control room went out, isolating the operators there from the outside world. It was a bad nuclear dream.

Meanwhile, outside the reactor buildings, the tension began to rise. The Residual Heat Removal systems were not working, and unless they could be restarted, there was a danger that the water in the towers would begin to boil, which would eventually overpressurize the containment and rupture it.

Down in the cable room, where the fire started and was still burning, more mistakes were made. A shift engineer tried to turn on the built-in Cardox safety system, designed to flood the room with carbon dioxide. But it would not work. The inspector and the electrician who had started the fire had purposely disabled the system in order to carry on their maintenance work without interruption.

The engineer tried the manual backup but found that a metal construction plate had been installed, keeping him from reaching the control.

He finally got the power on, and engaged the system. All it did was send thick smoke and fumes up and into the control room.

As if those in it did not have enough trouble, now, as one observer later described it, "The control room [filled] with thick smoke and fumes. The shift engineer and others were choking and coughing. It was obvious the control room would have to be evacuated in a very short time unless ventilation was provided."

Plant safety personnel now came into the cable room and opened the windows, clearing the smoke and fumes, but at the same time fanning the fire, which was still burning. They brought in various fire fighting equipment, but it was in such poor disrepair, unit after unit broke down.

While this was going on, the local fire department arrived, but was prevented from entering the facility by the plant safety detachment. It was obvious to the local fire chief that water was necessary to put out the fire, not carbon dioxide, which had been tried twice and had failed twice. But the plant superintendent chose to ignore the fire chief. And the fire burned on, for six hours.

Finally, at 6:00 P.M., the superintendent let the local firemen and their hoses in, and the fire was extinguished in 20 minutes. As the fire chief put it: "They were using type B and C extinguishers on a type A fire; the use of water would have immediately put the fire out."

At the same time, a new crisis developed. Control on the last four relief valves on reactor number one was lost, and the pressure in the reactor began to rise precipitously. Relief pumps were inoperable. The pressure mounted, and mounted.

Finally, at 9:50 P.M., the relief valves came on again and were immediately put into operation, and the reactor was depressurized.

It would be 4:10 the following morning before both units were finally shut down, and the danger of meltdown was reduced to zero.

And so, there was no cataclysm, and no evidence of extreme radiation released into the atmosphere. But tragedy was only a whisper away, because of not one but a massive collection of human errors, which were not confined solely to the interior of the plant. On the contrary, perhaps the most egregious ones occurred in the plant's relationship to the entirely innocent outside world that surrounded the plant.

The first and most unforgivable error was one of silence. That it would have been impossible—as it has been proved in most nuclear power plants—to evacuate the residents living near it in time to save them, is not the issue in this particular case. None of the local inhabitants were informed of the accident until long after it happened.

The responsibility for evacuation of the area around Brown's Ferry belonged to the Civil Defense Coordinator for Limestone County. But he was not informed of the accident until two full days later.

Similarly, the sheriff of Limestone County was not told about the accident until it was over. Perhaps silence was golden in this case; the sheriff possessed an emergency plan of evacuation that was three years old.

Ironically, the sheriff of neighboring Morgan County did hear about the fire four hours after it started, but, as he later testified, "I was asked to keep quiet about the incident to avoid any panic."

No official notification was made to the State of Alabama Highway Patrol.

In later testimony before the Nuclear Regulatory Commission (NRC), officials at the plant stated that the Emergency Plan for the Brown's Ferry Nuclear Plant was implemented, but that if an agency didn't answer its telephone the first time, no followup calls were tried.

This was quite a policy, considering that another host of problems were unveiled after the accident: The radiation monitors on the unit one reactor building were knocked out by the fire almost immediately, and the monitors on unit two failed at 2:00 P.M. Despite the fact that smoke was observed coming from the reactor building, both the NRC and the TVA concluded that no radiation was released into the atmosphere.

The aircraft warning lights on the plant's 600-foot radioactive gas release stack were not working. Attempts to call the plant directly to report it failed, and the Environs Emergency Center had to be contacted.

At 4:30 P.M., the plant's electric sequence printer ran out of tape, so that information on the time and sequence of the restoration of control circuits after that time were lost. The tape was not replaced until 2:00 P.M. the following day.

Chaos apparently reigned in the control room while the crisis was unfolding. Normally, six people worked in it. At the hearing, one assistant shift engineer reported that "the maximum number of people in the control room at any one time I guessed to be about fifty to seventy-five."

It was not exactly a picture of an efficiently run place, which, even under normal running conditions, contained the possibility of releasing lethal doses of radiation into the environment—enough to kill thousands of people and render the general area uninhabitable. That this did not occur in Brown's Ferry was no excuse for the dangerous inspection practices, slipshod emergency measures, and apparent coverups that occurred during and after the accident. That similar situations did produce terrible tragedy in Bhopal and Three Mile Island and Chernobyl only makes Brown's Ferry, in the seemingly casual and apparently irresponsible way in which it unfolded, all the more chilling.

UNITED STATES
(IDAHO, IDAHO FALLS)
EXPLOSION IN NUCLEAR REACTOR
January 3, 1961

Sabotage was suspected but never proved in the chemical explosion that blew apart the reactor core at the Idaho Nuclear Engineering Laboratory in Idaho Falls on January 3, 1961. Three died.

The explosion that shattered the core of an atomic reactor at the National Reactor Testing Station, part of the Idaho Nuclear Engineering Laboratory at Idaho Falls, Idaho, is significant in two ways: It was the first nuclear accident to occur in the United States, and it was symptomatic of conditions that would cause future disasters at other nuclear plants around the world.

The Idaho Nuclear Engineering Laboratory is a huge complex in which research and development projects are conducted for the military, spent nuclear submarine fuel is recycled, and military radioactive wastes are stored.

Because of the military and therefore largely secret character of the operations of the facility, details remain sketchy.

But here is what is known:

At 9:02 P.M., Mountain Standard Time, on January 3, 1961, three military technicians were at work in the Idaho Falls facility, operating a new style reactor known as Stationary Low Power Reactor Number 1. The reactor was a two-year-old prototype of a small mobile unit that was being developed as a heat and power facility for the armed forces in remote areas.

Suddenly, the core of the reactor blew. A fuel rod shot out of it, piercing the body of one of the technicians and pinning him to the reactor containment, high above the core. The other two men were blown apart and had to be buried later in pieces in lead-lined coffins. The radiation level within the container building was so high that it would be weeks before officials dared enter it, even in protective garb.

The cause of the accident was eventually determined to be "human error," causing an accidental overloading of one chemical against others. In 1981, Stephen Hanauer of the Nuclear Regulatory Commission, in an interview with Harvey Wasserman and Norman Solomon, authors of *Killing Our Own*, a study of atomic radiation in the United States, indicated that "the 'accident' may have been caused deliberately by one of the technicians in a bizarre suicide-murder plot stemming from a love triangle at the plant." More atrocious happenings than this have occurred, but there has, so far as this author knows, been no further substantiation of this steamy analysis of the events of January 3, 1961.

What is known, however, is that the Idaho plant had, as have most nuclear and industrial facilities experiencing accidents, a history of sloppiness. In the late 1960s, it was

Two members of a radiological team prepare to enter the reactor at the Idaho Falls nuclear reactor plant after the explosion.
(AP/WIDE WORLD)

charged with accidentally dumping concentrated uranium on a nearby road. From 1952 to 1960, its management deliberately tossed 16 billion gallons of liquid waste into wells that fed directly into the water table, causing radioactive contamination seven and a half miles away.

During the 1978 World Series, the plant supervisor was consumed by watching the games on a portable TV, which had been sneaked into the plant against regulations, and neglected to notice a dangerous buildup of radioactivity in a small nearby uranium-processing column. It is possible that even if the game had not gobbled up his attention, he would not have noticed the imbalance in the column, since one recording chart of the plant's monitoring devices had run out of paper two weeks before, and the paper had not been replaced.

At 8:45 P.M., high-radiation alarms were tripped by a bursting force of radiation from the afflicted column. The supervisor and others escaped to uncontaminated areas, and the column was brought under control, but not before 8,000 curies of radioactive iodine, krypton, and xenon had been released into the atmosphere—an amount that could easily threaten the health of anyone downwind of the plant.

The plant supervisor was later fired, and an investigation of worker alienation and low morale at the plant indicated that these were major factors leading to both the 1961 and 1978 incidents.

UNITED STATES
(PENNSYLVANIA, MIDDLETOWN)
THREE MILE ISLAND NUCLEAR POWER PLANT LEAK
March 28, 1979

The worst nuclear disaster in the history of the United States was blamed on human error, which was in turn caused by design flaws. No deaths or injuries occurred at the plant; there is still contention over infant and fetal mortality after the radiation spread. The chief casualty was the growth of the National Atomic Power Program.

The worst nuclear disaster in U.S. history occurred in one of America's youngest nuclear power plants. The Three Mile Island Unit Two Nuclear Power Generator, owned by the Metropolitan Edison Company and located on an island in the Susquehanna River approximately 11 miles south of Harrisburg, Pennsylvania, began operation on December 28, 1978. According to a letter sent by consumer advocate Ralph Nader to President Jimmy Carter, the plant was rushed into service in order to obtain a tax break of $40 million, despite the fact that, during its initial testing period, the reactor was experiencing mechanical failures and other problems.

Nader was, and still is, opposed to public nuclear power, and that undoubtedly skewed his evaluation of the birth of the plant. Still, there must have been a basic core of truth in his accusations, for just slightly more than three months after it began operating, the Three Mile Island generator exhibited its flaws in a dramatic and terrible way, by leaking radiation over an enormous area and by narrowly missing that most dreaded of nuclear accidents, a reactor meltdown.

At 3:58 A.M. on Wednesday, March 28, 1979, the first of a chain of mishaps occurred at the plant. A pump that provided steam to the electric turbines broke down. This in turn shut down another pump that circulated water through the reactor, which in turn raised the temperature of the reactor, which opened a relief valve designed to bleed off the increased pressure brought about by the rise in temperature. Within the reactor, some of the cladding, or sheaths, around the fuel rods melted. The uranium pellets in them apparently did not.

By this time, alarms were sounding in the control room, and operators, unschooled in this sort of unprecedented emergency, began to make wrong decisions, while the system itself malfunctioned. The relief valve failed to close, and consequently pressure in the reactor dropped low enough to allow the water to vaporize.

Then, a major error was committed. An operator opened a valve allowing water from this system to enter a waste tank, where it created enough pressure to rupture the plumbing. Sixty thousand gallons of radioactive water flooded the reactor to a depth of eight feet.

A second human error followed. The emergency core cooling system kicked in, but an operator shut it off.

Now, a pump flooded an auxiliary building with contaminated water, causing a release of steam. Within moments, radioactive steam poured up the vent stack and into the atmosphere.

Inexplicably, it would take operators almost three hours to react to and act upon these events. It would be 7:00 A.M. before state authorities would be informed and another hour before the authorities would declare a "general emergency."

Even the general emergency was, as in the Windscale disaster (see pp. 186–87), minimized, presumably to prevent panic. Margaret Reilly, of Pennsylvania's Department of Radiation Protection, in one of the most monumental understatements of all time, likened the escape of radiation to "a gnat's eyelash."

Quite a gnat. Authorities were aware that a minimum of a million millirems per hour of radiation was present inside the reactor building at Three Mile Island, a lethal dose for anyone directly exposed to it. Monitors 1,000 feet from the vent stacks, where the radioactive steam was spewing into the air, showed levels of 365 millirems of beta and gamma rays per hour.

Three months later, Albert Gibson, a radiation support section chief who would coauthor the Nuclear Regulatory Commission's final report on Three Mile Island emissions, testified that "all radiation monitors in the vent stack, where as much as 80 percent of the radiation escaped, went off the scale the morning of the accident. The trouble with those monitors is they were never contemplated for use in monitoring accidents like Three Mile Island."

Besides the beta and gamma emissions, there were bursts of strontium and iodine-131, which characteristically settle on grass, are eaten by cows, and thus enter the milk supply.

On Thursday, holding tanks filled to overflowing with radioactive water were opened, pouring 400,000 gallons of water containing xenon-133 and xenon-135 into the Susquehanna River, while federal nuclear officials assured the public that the gases posed "little hazard to persons living downstream of the . . . plant."

By the end of Thursday, March 29, detectable levels of increased radiation were measured over a four-county area,

and officials at the plant admitted that, contrary to their early assessment, 180 to 300 of the 36,000 fuel rods in the reactor had melted.

At 9:00 A.M. on Friday, March 30, the Pennsylvania Emergency Management Agency reported that there had been a new "uncontrolled release" of radiation—a puff of contaminated steam. Because of intense radioactivity within the reactor, the temperature had risen high enough in places to break up the water molecules into hydrogen and oxygen, forming a large bubble of hydrogen, which, if it became large enough, could prevent further reduction of the water molecules, therefore inhibiting the ability of the circulating water to cool down the fuel rods.

Thus, a meltdown was possible, and steadily becoming more probable.

Now, Governor Richard Thornburgh issued a directive that advised pregnant women and small children to evacuate

Following an accident on March 28, 1979, radioactive steam spewed out of the vent stacks at Three Mile Island, underlining warnings by opponents to public nuclear power against locating these plants in the midst of human habitation.

(ROBERT VISSER/GREENPEACE)

and stay at least five miles away from the Three Mile Island facility.

In 23 schools, children were pulled from classes, crammed into cafeterias, and ordered not to open windows. From these gathering points, they were transported in sealed school buses to other schools 10 to 15 miles away. ("It was sure hot in that bus with all those windows up," said nine-year-old Kim Hardy, from Etters, a community within the five-mile radius.) Parents were then informed of their children's whereabouts.

Fright, but no panic, abounded. An air-raid siren shrieked in Harrisburg shortly before noon, setting off a midday traffic jam of jittery state employees. The alarm was explained away by the governor's office as either a malfunction or the overzealous response of a civil defense official to Governor Thornburgh's directive.

Meanwhile, towns near the plant, such as Goldboro, had been emptying out ever since the news of the accident first surfaced. A small leak of people from the villages had turned into a torrent by Friday the 30th. Gasoline stations were jammed; telephone switchboards were so overloaded that callers received nothing but busy signals.

Fifteen mass-care centers were established in counties surrounding the Middletown area.

Back at the plant, officials were tensely monitoring the bubble of hydrogen, trying to decide whether to allow it to sink to the bottom of the containment vessel by drawing off water—and thus risking a further increase of temperature and the consequent possibility of a meltdown—or starting up the reactor again and trying to saturate the bubble with steam, which would break it up.

A third, venting method was tried, and on Saturday the 31st, the bubble was reduced enough so that a combination of safety rods and water could hasten the "cold shutdown" of the reactor. The danger of a meltdown passed.

By Monday, April 9, the Nuclear Regulatory Commission (NRC) declared the Three Mile Island crisis at an end and said it was safe for pregnant women and young children to return to their homes, despite the fact that the reactor was still leaking small quantities of radiation into the air and that readings of radiation emissions were still above average.

Schools were reopened, government offices returned to business as usual, and the civil defense forces were taken off full alert. It would be months before the reactor would be entirely shut down, and further instrument failure would lengthen that process, too.

But the book on Three Mile Island was not closed, by any means. First, there was the business of assigning responsibility for the accident. On May 11, 1979, the NRC issued a report blaming the operators for "inadvertently turn[ing] a minor accident into a major one because they could not tell what was really happening inside the reactor." This juxtaposition of human, instrument, and design error ran through the NRC report like a descant.

The report noted that the accident began when someone forgot to reopen a set of valves, and operators failed to notice the mistake. Operators apparently paid attention mainly to the pressurizer water indicator, which was misleading them, and failed to watch other instruments that should have informed them that something was wrong. Then, operators apparently failed to follow the procedure for dealing with a jammed pressure relief valve, and so forth.

Still, in its conclusions, the NRC removed some of the onus from the operators. "Human factors engineering has not been sufficiently emphasized in the design and layout of the control rooms," it admitted in its summary.

In February 1984, Metropolitan Edison Company pleaded guilty to charges that it knowingly used "inaccurate and meaningless" test methods at the unit two reactor prior to the accident. The company then disciplined 17 employees—among them a former vice president, shift supervisors, control room operators, shift foremen and managers—for manipulating records of the tests. The penalties ranged from letters of reprimand to the loss of two weeks' pay.

So much for the plant. What of the effect upon the surrounding population and environment?

As in practically every nuclear accident, there was no evacuation plan in place when the disaster occurred. To compound this, reports released during and after the accident consisted, either deliberately or inadvertently, of misinformation. Despite the admirable motivation of preventing needless panic, the "gnat's eyelash" analogy seems irresponsible in light of the later findings of other scientists and investigators.

Although the NRC continued to maintain that there had been and was still no significant intensification of radiation as a result of the Three Mile Island accident, Dr. Ernest Sternglass, a University of Pittsburgh Medical School professor of radiology, in a paper presented at the Fifth World Congress of Engineers and Architects at Tel Aviv, Israel, in 1980, stated that figures from Harrisburg and Holy Spirit Hospitals showed that infant death in the vicinity of Three Mile Island had *doubled*, from six during February through April 1979, to 12 in May through July.

Furthermore, Dr. Sternglass observed, data from the U.S. Bureau of Vital Statistics showed that there were "two hundred forty-two [infant] deaths above the normally expected number in Pennsylvania and a total of 430 in the entire northeastern area of the United States." He based his linkage on the large amounts of iodine-131 released into the atmosphere and the peaking of infant mortality within a matter of months after the release of the I-131.

Dr. Sternglass went on to charge that, as NRC investigator Joseph Hendrie had confirmed on March 30, 1979, individual areas where the steam plume touched the ground were "husky" that is, highly contaminated, and in the range of 120 millirems per hour or more, which was easily enough to cause severe damage to a fetus in the womb.

In addition, Dr. Sternglass noted that doses of I-131 had affected people in the path of the plume in Syracuse, Rochester, and Albany, New York, and each city had suffered rising infant deaths.

"My daughter got real sick," Becky Mease of Middletown told an NRC panel. "She had diarrhea for three days straight and headaches and she became anemic. I didn't know what to do. My little girl is still getting colds and sinus problems. Now if that's not because of that power plant, you tell me what it is."

Deaths in the Middletown area from thyroid cancer (the thyroid gland is particularly affected by iodine-131) are still monitored by families and organizations. No absolute link has been established, but those who were affected feel that the cause was the accident and the radiation it released into the Pennsylvania countryside. Some cancer victims are continuing to sue the Metropolitan Edison Company.

And finally, the third reason for the continued interest in Three Mile Island is the ongoing impact it has had on the nuclear energy industry in America. Prior to Three Mile Island, antinuclear activists were relatively quiescent. But on May 6, 1979, after the accident, a crowd of 65,000 demonstrators arrived at the Capitol in Washington, D.C., to demand the cessation of further building and the closing of existing nuclear power plants in the United States.

The Three Mile Island disaster opened the door to an escalation of protest activity that became rocket powered after the Chernobyl disaster (see pp. 194–200). It was responsible for the abandonment of the Shoreham Nuclear Energy plant on Long Island, New York, and the virtual halt in construction of nuclear power plants nationwide in the 1980s.

USSR
(KASLI)
NUCLEAR WASTE DUMP EXPLOSION
1957

....

U.S. military and Soviet secrecy have muffled the details of an explosion in a nuclear waste dump near Kasli, in the Ural Mountains of the then USSR, sometime in 1957, but a chemical or steam explosion has been theorized as its cause. Hundreds were said to have died; tens of thousands were afflicted.

What was possibly the most cataclysmic nuclear disaster in the world remains, to this day, unofficially recorded and officially nonexistent. Soviet secrecy during the cold war erased it from internal record books, in hopes of erasing it from the world's public consciousness. Even the U.S. Central Intelligence Agency, which apparently knew of the disaster shortly after it occurred, suppressed any mention of it and in fact denied, for its own reasons, its existence for 20 years, until the Freedom of Information Act forced it to open its files on the subject.

So, it is only possible to piece together the fragments of this cataclysm, largely through the diligent research of Dr. Zhores Medvedev, a Soviet emigré scientist who, in 1976, first brought the news of the explosion to the West.

In an article titled "Two Decades of Dissidence" in the British journal *New Scientist*, Dr. Medvedev told of "an enormous explosion, like a violent volcano," in a radioactive waste dump in the Ural Mountains near the town of Kasli, or Kyshtym, as Dr. Medvedev called it. "The nuclear reactions had led to an overheating in the underground burial grounds," he continued. "The explosion poured radioactive dust and materials high up into the sky. . . . Tens of thousands of people were affected, hundreds dying, though the real figures have never been made public. The large 150-kilometer-square area, where the accident happened, is still considered dangerous and is closed to the public."

The official response to the article was swift and negative. *Tass* denied it. Sir John Hill, the chairman of the United Kingdom Atomic Energy Authority wrote a letter to the *Times* of London calling the story "rubbish."

But one month later, Lev Tumerman, another Russian emigré, wrote a letter to the *Jerusalem Post* relating a ride through the same countryside in the Urals in 1960. "On both sides of the road as far as one could see the land was dead," wrote Tumerman, "no villages, no towns, only the chimneys of destroyed houses, no cultivated fields or pastures, no herds, no people . . . nothing."

Signs warned him to proceed without stopping for the next 30 kilometers and to drive through at maximum speed. "An enormous area, some hundreds of square kilometers, had been laid waste," he concluded.

Finally, in 1979, Dr. Medvedev published *Nuclear Disaster in the Urals*. In it, he quoted Soviet scientists who made post-catastrophe studies of plant and animal life and subsequent weather patterns in the area. All confirmed the explosion and its consequent radiation contamination.

Within weeks, a special report was released by the Oak Ridge National Laboratory that confirmed the Soviet scientists' reports and stated that a system of 14 lakes had been contaminated by the Kasli blast and that 30 small towns that had been on Soviet maps of the southern Ural region before 1957 were no longer there.

Investigation by reporters of newly released CIA files revealed anecdotal confirmation from survivors who were in the area. One described a huge explosion that shook the ground and spewed a huge cloud of red dust into the air, which settled on the leaves of trees. "Very quickly," the eyewitness said, "all the leaves curled up and fell off the trees," as did vegetables that were covered with the red radioactive dust.

"All stores in Kamensk-Uralskiy which sold milk, meat, and other foodstuffs were closed as a precaution against radiation exposure," said another, "and new supplies were brought in two days later by train and truck. The food was sold directly from the vehicles and the resulting queues were reminiscent of those during the worst shortages during World War II."

That was only the beginning. As the effects of the widespread radiation contamination began to be felt, another witness reported, "The people in Kamensk-Uralskiy grew hysterical with fear, and with incidence of unknown 'mysterious' diseases breaking out."

Homes were burned to the ground to prevent their owners from reentering them, and these displaced people "were allowed to take with them only the clothes in which they were dressed."

"One of the current topics of conversation at the time," said another survivor, "was whether eating fish or eating crabs from the radioactive rivers of the area was more dangerous. . . . Hundreds of people perished and the area became and will remain radioactive for years."

American officials tended to soft-pedal the implications for worldwide storage of nuclear waste. Despite more realistic warnings against risks of nuclear dumping, Richard Corrigan, a spokesperson for the Ford administration in Washington, wrote in the *National Journal* of August 1979, "They [the Russians] don't know what they're doing and we do."

It was cheerful news, but disarmingly simplistic when compared with the facts of Windscale (see pp. 186–87) and two staggering and comparable catastrophes that were yet to come: Three Mile Island (see pp. 190–93) and Chernobyl (see pp. 194–200).

As to the continuing problem of the disposal of nuclear waste, its environmental and its human impact: That continues to be a legacy of the atomic age, and possibly a frightening aspect of the disposal of all waste on the planet. Nuclear waste and the pervasiveness of plastic have much in common. Both have increased; both seem to last forever; and the disposal of both is a topic that national governments seem more prone to ignore or hide than face.

USSR

(PRIPYAT)

CHERNOBYL NUCLEAR POWER PLANT EXPLOSION
April 26, 1986

The worst recorded nuclear accident in history, that of the Chernobyl nuclear power plant in Pripyat, USSR, on April 26, 1986, was the result of human error in conducting a test of the system. Thirty-one died in the explosion and fire; more than 100,000 were evacuated from the vicinity of the plant, more than 5 million were exposed to radioactive fallout, and the tally of casualties is yet to be finally calculated.

"An accident has occurred at the Chernobyl nuclear power plant as one of the reactors was damaged. Measures are being taken to eliminate the consequences of the accident.

Aid is being given to those affected. A government commission has been set up."

Two days after the stupendous disaster at the Chernobyl nuclear power plant, located 70 miles north of Kiev, the capital of Ukraine, the Soviet government released this terse, businesslike, and uninformative announcement.

Some of the facts and some of the effects of this, the worst nuclear disaster in history, had already drifted out of the Soviet Union, on winds bringing radioactive waste to Scandinavia, then Eastern Europe, then Western Europe, and finally to the rest of the world, including the United States.

The situation at Chernobyl was frightening. With four 1,000-megawatt reactors in operation, it was one of the largest and oldest of the Soviet Union's 15 civilian nuclear stations. And then, a cascade of awesome human errors was set in motion, which, as surely as uranium brought about a chain reaction, brought on a series of events the likes of which the world has yet to experience.

At 1:00 A.M. on Friday, April 25, operators of the number four reactor, which had gone on line in 1983, began to reduce its power in preparation for an operations test. The test was designed to measure the amount of residual energy produced by the turbine and generator after the nuclear reactor had been shut down. The conclusion of the test would tell these engineers how long the turbine and generator would be able to run if, in some sort of emergency, the reactor were shut down.

It was a routine test. The valves on the main steam line between the reactor and the turbine were to be closed, thus topping power to the turbine, and the residual energy would then be measured until the turbine stopped.

While this was happening, steam would still be produced by the reactor, which would be slowly reduced to a fraction of its potential power. That steam could either be released into the atmosphere through bypass valves or condensed back to water in a cooling unit. If the operators decided to rerun the test, they could open the valves to the turbine and close the bypass valves.

The difficulty with the process was that, if the reactor continued to operate, certain "perturbations," as nuclear experts euphemistically call them, could take place in the reactor, which could in turn increase the pressure and cause the unit to be automatically shut down. Or, they could reduce the pressure, causing the automatic flooding of the reactor with emergency cooling water.

In other words, no one could tell just what would happen in the reactor under these circumstances, but the operators at Chernobyl, determined to carry through their test without a shutdown of the reactor, *shut off all of the emergency safety systems.*

As astounding as that seems, this is exactly what happened at 2:00 P.M. on Friday, the 25th, as the reactor was reduced to 7 percent capacity. The reactor's emergency cooling system was shut off. Then the power regulating system and the automatic shutdown system were disconnected. It was a little like a fire department responding to a burning fire and then dismantling the fire alarms, tearing down the fire escapes, and going home.

What the operators did was in violation of all regulations, but they did it anyway—as countless other operators in other industrial and nuclear accidents had and would—and continued with their routine testing through the afternoon and evening. And all the while, the "perturbations" began to build in the reactor.

Some time during this process, a reactor operator received a computer printout that indicated the reactor was in extremely serious danger of overheating unless it was shut down immediately. He ignored it.

Control rods were withdrawn, lowering the power in the reactor below the minimum required by the unit's operating manual. Xenon gases began to build up as the temperature rose in the reactor.

At 1:22 A.M. on Saturday, April 26, these same operators noticed that the power level had risen to the point at which, had the emergency system been engaged, it would have shut down. The operators noted it and kept on testing. If they had stopped at that moment, if they had heeded the warnings the instruments were clearly giving them, and reengaged the safety system, the disaster would not have occurred. But they blundered on, ignoring the obvious.

Exactly one minute and 40 seconds later, the reactor blew. There was a loud bang as the control rods began to fall into place. At that instant, the operators knew exactly what was about to happen. They desperately tried to drop the rest of the control rods to stop the runaway chain reactions that were taking place in the reactor, the splitting by radiation of

Devastation is utter and staggering after the enormous explosion and meltdown.
(E. P. PETUNIN/UNEP)

superhot water and the reactions caused by the superheating of the reactor's graphite shell.

But it was too late. The control rods drop by gravity, and that takes time, and the operators of the reactor had used up all the time there was. Twenty seconds later, the fuel atomized. Three more explosions tore through the reactor, blowing off its top, sending its 1,000-ton steel cover plate rocketing into the air and ripping off the tops of all 1,661 channels, which were attached to the cover plate and contained the nuclear fuel. The channels became like "a thousand howitzers pointed at the sky," according to Dr. Herbert J. C. Kouts, the chairman of the Department of Nuclear Energy at Brookhaven National Laboratory on Long Island, New York. Powered by these nuclear howitzers, a huge fireball shot up into the sky. The graphite caught fire and burned, fiercely and wildly. The reactor was completely out of control and beginning to melt down.

Flames continued to shoot over 1,000 feet into the air. This would continue for two days and nights. The operators within the building were doomed. Emergency alarms went off all through the complex, in which 4,500 workers were employed.

Miles away, a startled populace witnessed a gigantic fireworks display of hot radioactive material being flung into the night sky and onto the winds that would eventually carry this material far enough to contaminate a huge nearby area and, eventually, to a lesser and varying degree, much of the rest of the world.

The reactor continued to burn, while emergency teams hauled off the dead and the radiated. Others, their boots sinking in molten bitumen, uselessly attempted to battle the blaze. But, as in other nuclear accidents around the world both before and after this one, evacuation of the populace was delayed while scientists debated the seriousness of the situation.

Finally, at 1:50 P.M., on Sunday, April 27, fully 36 hours after the accident, the local radio station at Pripyat announced that a full-scale evacuation was to begin immediately. The city of 40,000 was to be totally abandoned, and 1,100 buses, some of them commandeered from Kiev, undertook the task. To prevent panic, rallying points were not used. The city was emptied within 2 hours and 20 minutes.

The countryside around Pripyat, a region of wooded steppes, small villages, and moderately productive farms, was less thickly populated. Between Pripyat and Chernobyl lay the Kiev reservoir, fed by the Pripyat River. And at this point, radioactive matter was falling like lethal rain onto the thinly settled countryside and into this reservoir that supplied water to the 2.5 million people of Kiev, Russia's third-largest city.

Meanwhile, at the plant, workers were shutting down the other three reactors. The fire continued to burn unchecked. Twenty-five percent of the radiation leaked in

the accident was released in the first 24 hours of the fire, which would continue for eight days.

On Monday morning, April 28, Swedish monitoring stations detected unusually high local levels of xenon and krypton and concluded that, considering the prevailing winds, an atomic accident had occurred in the Soviet Union. Sweden demanded that the Soviets comply with international agreements to notify other nations immediately after a nuclear accident that might threaten those countries with radiation.

It was not until 9:00 P.M. that night that the Soviets released the terse statement quoted at the beginning of this entry, a masterpiece of obfuscation.

But the truth began to seep out. On Tuesday, Soviet diplomats in Europe and Scandinavia approached private nuclear agencies, asking advice on fighting graphite fires. United Press International, frustrated by the silence from official sources, quoted a Kiev woman who communicated with them by telephone. "Eighty people died immediately and some 2,000 people died on the way to hospitals," she told UPI. "The whole October Hospital in Kiev is packed with people who suffer from radiation sickness."

A Dutch radio operator reported a message received from a Soviet ham broadcaster. "We got to know that not one, but two reactors are melted down, destroyed, and burning. Many, many hundreds are dead and wounded by radiation, but maybe many, many more," he said, ending with a plea. "Please tell the world to help us," he concluded.

This was clearly at odds with the official version of events, which placed the dead at two and the injured at 197.

Now the heavier products of radiation, the ones that the atmosphere could not dissipate easily and were lethal to human beings, were beginning to fall on Europe. Among a score of elements detected in the fallout were cesium-124 and iodine-131, both easily assimilated by the body and both thought to cause cancer.

By Wednesday, April 30, European countries began to take steps to preserve their own people. In Austria, mothers in the province of Carinthia were being advised to keep infants and small children indoors. The Polish government banned the sale of milk from grass-fed cows and issued iodine tablets to infants, children, and pregnant women in order to protect their thyroid glands against poisoning from iodine-131. In Sweden, officials warned people not to drink water from casks that collected rainwater for summer cottages and banned the import of fresh meat, fish, and vegetables from the Soviet-bloc countries. Evacuation plans were activated for citizens who were traveling or working in the area within 200 miles of Chernobyl. A group of American students studying in Kiev boarded planes for Moscow, then London, then the United States.

By Thursday, May 1, the Soviet bulletins noted that 18 people were in critical condition and that the fire was cooling down. In an effort to further control it, civil defense forces began to drop bags of wet sand from helicopters hovering over the gaping hole in the top of the reactor. The radioactivity levels within the building were still too high to allow human beings, even in protective gear, to enter.

International help came swiftly. Dr. Robert Gale, the head of the International Bone Marrow Transplant Registry, left Los Angeles for Kiev on May 1. Two days later, his associate, Dr. Richard Champlin, and Dr. Paul Terasaki, a tissue-typing expert, joined him. They would have much work to do, considering the hundreds hospitalized from the accident.

Wind patterns were affecting the radiation levels reported in various European countries. In Sweden, it fluctuated between normal and five times normal. Traces of iodine-131 were detected in rainwater samples in the Pacific Northwest region of the United States, but they were not deemed dangerous.

By Monday, May 5, the Soviet government announced that dikes were being built along the Pripyat River to prevent potential contamination and that the leakage of radiation from the plant had virtually stopped.

Nothing could have been further from the truth, as later studies would indicate. In a report released the following September, a study prepared by the Lawrence Livermore National Laboratory in California asserted: "The nuclear disaster at Chernobyl emitted as much long-term radiation into the world's air, topsoil, and water as all the nuclear tests and bombs ever exploded." Cesium, a product associated with health effects such as cancer and genetic disease, does not break down into a harmless form for more than 100 years, and it was sent into the atmosphere in quantities, the study estimated, that were as much as 50 percent more than the total of hundreds of atmospheric tests and the two nuclear bombs dropped on Japan at the end of World War II.

As the winds continued in a southeasterly direction, radioactive contamination fell over Poland, Ukraine, Belorussia, Latvia, Lithuania, Finland, Norway, and Sweden. But then, the winds changed, and the cloud drifted over most of Europe. Rain in the central British Isles complicated the problem by washing the contamination to the earth in a more concentrated form than in other locations. Since cesium-137 accumulated on grass that livestock ate, restrictions on livestock movement and slaughter were immediately introduced in the United Kingdom and the Nordic countries.

On May 9, the Soviets began the monumental task of encasing the still smoldering wreck of a reactor in concrete. It involved tunneling under the reactor, in order to prevent a "China syndrome" style of meltdown, which would immediately contaminate the groundwater near the reactor. The massive job was begun by dropping thousands of tons of sand, boron, clay, dolomite, and lead from helicopters into the graphite core. Then the huge sarcophagus of concrete was poured and erected.

As May moved toward June, Soviet authorities attempted to protect citizens from the continuing effects of exposure to radiation. On May 15, 25,000 students in the Kiev area received an early vacation when all of the elementary schools and kindergartens were closed for the summer ahead of schedule.

Officials told residents of Kiev to keep their windows closed, mop floors frequently, and wash their hands and hair often to reduce the chance of radiation contamination. And for the first time, these authorities acknowledged the dissemination of radiation over the rest of Europe.

The Soviet children would be transported by the state to "Pioneer" camps scattered from the Moscow suburbs to the Crimea. More than 60,000 children, in fact, joined the first evacuees from Pripyat, who, like 12-year-old Olya Ryazanova, remembered a fire-blackened nuclear power plant, "a sort of mist, a misty cloud around it," and booted workers washing down the road in front of her home.

On May 15, the day the schools closed, the radioactive cloud had, after first blowing north to Scandinavia and Belorussia, reversed itself and was hovering over Kiev. Crowds had formed at railroad stations and airports, most of them women and children, and the government had added extra trains and flights out of the city.

As more accurate information began to filter out of the Soviet Union, the scope of the disaster continued to grow. Hans Blix, the head of the International Atomic Energy Agency, confirmed that at least "two hundred four persons, including nuclear power station personnel and firefighters, were affected by radiation from the first degree to the fourth degree." The government newspaper *Izvestia* revealed that more than 94,000 people had been evacuated. Eventually, the official number of dead would be set at 31, all of them workers at the plant.

It was learned that a full month before the disaster, a Ukrainian journal had reported management failures and labor dissatisfaction at Chernobyl. Because coal was becoming scarce in the Soviet Union, construction at the plant was speeded up in 1984, and it was suggested that this haste—a fifth nuclear reactor was already under construction at the time of the accident—was partially responsible for the tragedy.

But ultimately, the blame was focused on human error, and in June, *Pravda* announced that the director and chief engineer of the plant had been dismissed for mishandling the disaster and that other top officials were accused of misconduct ranging from negligence to desertion.

But, since there are no neat endings to nuclear explosions, that would not be the end of the story. If the nuclear contamination from Chernobyl changed the physical landscape around the plant, the dissolution of the Soviet Union changed its economic landscape. And this, in turn, determined the course of human and nuclear events to this day and beyond.

When the USSR ceased to exist, the independent entities of Ukraine and Belarus sprang into being, along with the economic pressure for these new countries of providing necessities for themselves and their citizenry.

That they should turn to atomic energy to supply the electricity for their countries was logical; the USSR had been in the forefront of the nations of the world in building atomic power plants; the haste with which it built Chernobyl was, in fact, part of the reason for its disaster.

In 1995, in the former Soviet Union, there were still 15 operating atomic power plants, two in Lithuania, two in Ukraine, and eleven in Russia. Forty percent of the electric power in Ukraine was provided by atomic power plants, and 7 percent of that came from Chernobyl.

The economic chaos that presently grips the area has made this relatively inexpensive way of providing electric power a reason for the government of Ukraine not to close down Chernobyl, but to keep it open and to continue with plans to add units to it, despite its terrible legacy.

And the legacy lives on. "It's not too much to say that Chernobyl helped destroy the Soviet Union and end the cold war," is the opinion of Richard Wilson, professor of physics at Harvard University.

His conclusions are based upon the particular devastation of the area that, once Belorussia, is now Belarus. More than a decade after the explosion and contamination, it is now possible to conclude that the radiation that spread over the countryside around Chernobyl on April 26, 1986, was nearly 200 times that of the combined release from the atomic bombs at Hiroshima and Nagasaki in 1943 (see pp. 206–11).

The prevailing winds carried the heaviest radioactive deposits by far over Belarus. By 1990, rates of cancer had soared, and animals were being born without heads. Even in 1998, 12 years later, 25 percent of the land is considered uninhabitable. Thousands of villages have been abandoned. The Gomel area, once the site of the most fertile farmland in Belarus, is an eerie, abandoned landscape, dotted with ghost towns, pockmarked with semiburied abandoned cars, sentinaled by polluted wells whose buckets swing, empty, in the wind. Twenty of 21 agricultural districts produce nothing.

And yet, here and there, people live, hardly any of them happily. Several thousand are scattered like sown seed, since the cloud ravaged some areas and left others nearby untouched, in the unevenly ravaged countryside of southern Belarus. Wherever they live, in a contaminated or uncontaminated area, most of those who reside here attribute every ill or problem in their lives to "the station," their name for Chernobyl.

And that is symptomatic of the three-pronged legacy of the disaster. There are, first, those who were definitely and dreadfully afflicted physically by the catastrophe. Then, there are those who were affected economically. And finally, there are those—and they are the largest group—

that are beset by and haunted by a fear that simply will not go away.

Of the first category: There is no doubt, 10 years after Chernobyl, that thousands of children in Belarus, Ukraine, and Russia were afflicted by thyroid cancer, a cancer definitely linked to exposure to iodine-131. There were seven cases of thyroid cancer among children in Belarus in the decade preceding the accident. Since 1990, there have been 300 cases, many of them like those of Pasha Bezliuodov, who was a normal two year old, playing in his sandbox 70 miles north of Chernobyl, in the months following the explosion.

What neither he nor his parents knew, or were informed of by the authorities, was that radioactive cesium, plutonium, and strontium were mixed in with the sand. Today, at the age of 14, he cannot walk for more than a few minutes without running out of breath because he has undergone surgery twice and lost 70 percent of his lung capacity after the thyroid cancer he initially contracted spread.

Many women, finally informed of the effects of the radiation, chose to abort the babies they were carrying rather than risk giving birth to deformed children, or those who would eventually be stricken with thyroid cancer. For months after the disaster, from northern Finland to the Adriatic Sea, thousands of women had abortions. In Gomel, even today, there are three abortions for every live birth, a rate more than twice that for the rest of Belarus.

"People say we are not really sicker than anyone else in the former Soviet Union," Nikolai I. Ermakov, the man in charge of Gomel's response to the accident, recently told Western reporters. "They are talking about blood diseases and death rates. That is not my interest. My interest is life in Gomel."

And that life is the subject of the second part of the legacy of Chernobyl, its economic legacy. Gomel is the most destroyed of all of the areas near Chernobyl. It includes the so-called exclusion zone, the 18-mile radius around Chernobyl that is still considered too polluted for human habitation.

For years after the accident all those in the Gomel area got extra wages and free medical care. When the Soviet government realized it could not keep up the policy indefinitely, it applied a 12 percent "Chernobyl tax" to all USSR wage-earners. Even so, the benefits are no longer available to most people.

"Here [in Gomel] we have no jobs," continued Ermakov. "The pristine forests have radiation signs posted all over them. Poor farmers cannot eat what they grow. Is it so strange that what happened here seems like a biblical curse?"

Eight times in the last decade, the leaders of Ukraine have decided to close Chernobyl's remaining three reactors. And eight times they have changed their minds because shutting the plant would strip 5,000 jobs from a region already devastated economically.

The giant sarcophagus that was erected around the smoldering wreck of the reactor at Chernobyl.
(HANS WINDECK/UNEP)

Back in Belarus, it is worse. This country, the worst affected by the disaster, does not possess any nuclear power plants. Belarus opposed the dissolution of the Soviet Union, and when it was forced to stand alone, the newly independent country was left with immense bills it could not possibly handle. An agricultural land tainted by the ultimate modern poison is of a little use to anyone, and of no use in supporting its own people.

And this leaves the people vulnerable to the third part of the legacy, that of an abiding and everlasting fear. "Nuclear energy is invisible," said Dr. Johan Havenaar, chief of emergency psychiatry at the University Hospital in Utrecht, the Netherlands. "It's treacherous. It scares people so they think it causes them to be sick."

No matter what happens to the people who were in the affected land, they attribute it to the explosion. "My teeth are falling out, and I can't see too well anymore," said Volodya Ronashev, a 48-year-old forest administrator who lives and works in the zone. "I used to be healthy. What else could it be but the station?"

Studies conducted on some of the 200,000 refugees who have been resettled in other parts of Belarus show that they

feel terribly dislocated, strangers in a strange land, and, to compound this, guilty for having left in the first place. "If I knew it would be this bad, I would have chained myself to the gates back home," Tamara Lusenko, one of these refugees, told researchers.

Meanwhile, despite the lesson learned by the rest of the world—that the Chernobyl-type reactor, which has no containment and is considered unstable at low-power levels simply should not be built, much less operated—the old, graphite-based plants in Russia and Lithuania continue to provide electricity to the populace of these regions. Ukraine has two that are working and is ready to begin building a third.

And meanwhile, the sarcophagus erected to contain the remains of the ruined reactor at Chernobyl is continuing to deteriorate—dangerously so according to Alexander Borovoi, the head of a group of scientists from Russia's prestigious Kurchatov Institute. He and his assistants have been examining Chernobyl since its holocaust, and he is far from optimistic.

Within the tomb, there are 1,300 tons of highly radioactive lava, in formations in various rooms. There is also a

The control room, where the fatal decisions were made that led to the world's worst recorded nuclear accident. So far.
(HANS WINDECK/UNEP)

growing amount of water—at last count 6,000 cubic meters. The appearance of this water has forced plant personnel to shut down electricity to the sarcophagus, which in turn has interfered with crucial systems that monitor whether the dangerous mix of water and nuclear fuel are tending toward a chain reaction.

Besides this, the water forces a breakdown in the radioactive lava, turning it into dust, which flies around the sarcophagus.

And, finally, the water itself becomes radioactive, and as it evaporates, the concentration of radioactivity increases. Well enough if it remains within the sarcophagus, but scientists, and particularly Dr. Borovoi, are concerned that it will seep into the groundwater and once again drain into the nearby Pripyat River, which supplies drinking water to Kiev, now a city of 4 million, and equally as vulnerable to contamination from the water supply as it was in 1986.

There has already been a significant increase in groundwater contamination, according to Dr. Borovoi, and plant operators are planning to drain the water to a sealed space within the building, a process that is hampered by the economy of Ukraine, which cannot afford the technology necessary to do this.

But these plant operators only accede to Dr. Borovoi and his group grudgingly. They regard him as a malcontent and a pessimist, eager to shut them down, and they are joined by Ukrainian politicians in their condemnation, much as their predecessors at the plant minimized dangers a decade ago.

An even greater threat, says Dr. Borovoi, is the collapse of the entire sarcophagus, a definite possibility. It was built to last 70 years, but a study in 1992 by the All-Ukrainian Scientific Institute for Construction Materials concluded that there was a 70- to 80-percent chance that the structure would fall within 10 years.

If it fell, two possible scenarios have been outlined: One would be the spreading of a long, narrow "tongue" of radioactive dust across the exclusion zone and beyond, depending upon the wind patterns. The dust would include plutonium and other dangerous elements that could be inhaled by people who live and work in the area.

The second scenario would involve the collapse of certain structures within the sarcophagus. The 2,000-ton reactor lid, for example, is still perched like a partly opened tin can at a 150-degree angle on the top of the reactor core. It landed there after the explosion, and its collapse would cause a smaller puff of dust to enter the atmosphere.

Sergei Parashin, the plant director, challenges Dr. Borovoi. "It still stands, and according to our measurements there's no sign that it will need to be changed until a very long time," he told reporters on the anniversary of the accident.

And so it goes. Scientists warn of continuing catastrophe, while industrialists and politicians minimize it. The Group of Seven nations at a summit in Naples in 1994 developed an "action plan" to help Ukraine avoid another disaster at Chernobyl and close down other atomic power plants. But it is still just a plan.

And meanwhile, the situation at Chernobyl deteriorates. Three days before the 10th anniversary of the disaster, a fire, started by a discarded cigarette tossed into waist-high dry grass in the exclusion area, roared out of control, laying waste to whatever wooden buildings were left, including an 18th-century church. No increase in radiation in the atmosphere was reported.

The record stands: 31 killed outright by the disaster, and more than 5 million exposed to radioactive fallout. But records do not reflect all of reality.

"We are the great guinea pigs of modern times," said Yevgeny Konoplya, director of the Radiobiology Institute of the Belarus Academy of Sciences and an expert on post-Chernobyl effects.

"We are getting to prove for the world what radiation can do to humans," he continued. "We have suffered from the policies of a country that no longer even exists. We have suffered from lies. And we have suffered from other people's belief in technology. We once had a beautiful country. What we have now is pain."

"The Chernobyl disaster taught us there are no borders to the modern world," added Ivan A. Kenik, the chief Belarus official in charge of the Chernobyl aftermath. "It taught us to question faith in technology and in ourselves. I now wonder if we as a civilization have the knowledge, strength, and wisdom to survive this nuclear century?"

WAR CRIMES AGAINST THE ENVIRONMENT

China
 * Honan Province (flooding from breaking of Yellow and Yangtze River dikes) (1938)

Japan
 * Hiroshima and Nagasaki (dropping of first atomic bombs) (1945)

Kuwait
 * Oil fields (contamination and fires during and after Gulf War) (1991)

*Detailed in text

Marshall Islands
 * Bikini and Eniwetok Atolls (atomic and hydrogen bomb tests) (1946–58)

Tibet
 * Shigatse (floods caused by breaking walls by Chinese Communist conquerors) (1954)

United States
 * New Mexico, Los Alamos (detonation of first atomic bomb) (1945)

Vietnam
 * South (defoliation campaign with Agent Orange, spread by U.S. armed forces) (1961–70)

CHRONOLOGY

1938
* China: Honan Province, flooding from breaking of Yellow and Yangtze River dikes

1945
* USA: New Mexico, Los Alamos, detonation of first atomic bomb

1945
* Japan: Hiroshima and Nagasaki, dropping of first atomic bombs

*Detailed in text

1946–1958
* Marshall Islands: Bikini and Eniwetok Atolls, atomic and hydrogen bomb tests

1954
* Tibet: Shigatse, floods caused by breaking walls by Chinese Communist conquerors

1961–70
* Vietnam: South, defoliation campaign with Agent Orange, spread by U.S. armed forces

1991
* Kuwait: oil fields, contamination and fires during and after the Gulf War

WAR CRIMES AGAINST THE ENVIRONMENT

Accidents happen. Nature brings about its own, self-inflicted catastrophes. But when the environment is purposely attacked, when the weapons of war become such that the future of life on the planet and the life of the planet itself is threatened, then perhaps the worst environmental disaster of all is the one that is caused purposely in the name of national sovereignty.

War crimes against the environment did not begin yesterday. The first firebrand flung at the first enemy, in prehistory, probably began it all. Birnam Wood moved upon Dunsinane, and so spelled the doom of Macbeth. A scorched-earth policy has been a tactic of armies ever since the times of ancient dynasties. Rivers have been dammed and their courses changed to thwart enemy invasions. Poison gas has turned the atmosphere lethal and drifted indiscriminately over and into the lungs of both the attackers and the attacked, the soldiers who fought and the civilians who were trapped, the humans who knew there was a war going on, and the animals who did not.

But these were examples of the local environment being used or destroyed. It would take the atomic age to bring about the worst instances of the use and desolation of the environment to win battles and wars.

The architects of World War II prided themselves in never using poison gas—though all sides furiously developed it, as well as biological warfare, just in case. But, though that sort of environmental warfare did not occur, a far worse one did. The race to develop the super-weapon that would make war so terrible that it would never occur again was won by the United States, and the scorched earth and radioactive air of Hiroshima and Nagasaki, the polluted ocean and atmosphere of the Pacific Ocean over, under, and surrounding the Marshall Islands are the monuments that mark the mounting of that particular plateau.

It was all going to end there. That was what the scientists thought. But they were, of course, naive, or too hopeful, or too preoccupied with scientific discovery, for, in a very strict sense, World War II never ended. It is still being fought and will probably continue to be fought for lifetimes to come. Atomic military power was discovered and developed during World War II; the atomic arms race had begun before the truce was signed, and it continues to this day. That race incorporates the cold war and every other regional military and diplomatic conflict that involves, either directly or indirectly, atomic powers or potential atomic powers.

And this race for supremacy contains a doomsday scenario. From the beginning, the scientists of the Manhattan Project were aware—though the public was never informed of this, either then or later—that the possibility of igniting the nitrogen in the atmosphere existed. If that happened, there would be a spontaneous catastrophe, and in one explosive flash, all life on Earth would be destroyed. All forests, all land would incinerate; all life would ingest flame and die, and the atmosphere itself would perish.

That Damoclean sword hangs a bit higher now, thanks to the tests of the 1950s, which pushed the atomic envelope about as far as we presently dare push it. The odds are a million to three against atomic annihilation of the planet. But they do exist, and as each new member tests its way into the Atomic Club—46 strong at this point—those odds diminish. Only slightly. But they do.

And it just may be that human beings have finally reached a point at which the terrible prospect of an atomic Armageddon is just too dreadful to risk. Even the neutron bomb, which, in a perverse reversal, is designed to kill humans and preserve the environment, is too much beyond the pale.

Meanwhile, herbicides destroy both unfriendly and friendly humans and infest the soils of countries; oil fires create their own particular hells on earth; and biological warfare waits in the wings.

It is an uneasy standoff. But it is a standoff. At least for now.

CHINA

(Honan Province)

Massive flooding from Yellow and Yangtze Rivers caused by breaking of dikes

June–August 1938

....

Chinese forces used the Yellow and Yangtze Rivers to repell Japanese forces in 1938, during the Sino-Japanese War. But it was at a price. Nearly 200,000 refugees were created, and disease became rampant.

By the middle of 1937, the civil war that raged between the Communists and the forces of Chiang K'ai-shek in China was palpably sputtering and dying. In December 1936, Chiang K'ai-shek was kidnapped at Sian by Chang Hsueh-liang, and one of the conditions of his release was an agreement to unite with the Communists against Japan.

Japan, realizing that a united China, always a threat, would be a force against which they probably could not prevail, made immediate preparations for war.

On the night of July 7, 1937, at the Marco Polo Bridge outside of Peking, Japanese garrison troops undertook what seemed to be routine field maneuvers. Someone fired a shot. The Japanese claimed they had been assaulted. And the war began.

It was clear from the outset that the Japanese possessed the more modern technology, the more up-to-date weapons of war, the preponderance of tanks and bombers. But the war was being fought on Chinese soil, in an environment that the Chinese knew well. And they knew, furthermore, that this environment was subject to the yearly floods of the Yellow and Yangtze Rivers. If the Chinese did not possess the firepower and the mechanisms to defeat their enemy, they would, as their ancestors had, turn the environment into a weapon.

Some 4,000 years earlier, attempts were made to tame the Yellow River by diverting it into several parallel channels. It was a daring thing to do. The Yellow River was always regarded as a possessor of supernatural powers, whose dynamos were the river dragons, and even today, its power and unpredictability bespeak something more than natural causes beneath its turbulent, often lethal, waters.

Twenty-seven hundred miles long, the Yellow River rises near the border between Tibet and China and runs through the Great Plains, which have been built up by the silt it has brought from the hills of Kansu, Shensi, and Shansi. Its name comes from the yellow mud it carries, which reaches, at times, 40 percent by weight. To this day, it is impossible to swim in the Yellow River unless there is a clear pool or stream nearby to wash off the mud.

The river, true to its supernatural reputation, is both a blessing and a menace. The fertility of its banks and plains, which provide work for the hundreds of thousands of farmers who till them and the 100 million people who populate them, is caused by its overflow. But its vagaries, its wanderings over thousands of years, and its almost yearly floodings have killed millions and spread famine and disease in staggering profusion.

Between 2297 B.C.—the time of the first recorded Yellow River flood—and the present, there have been 1,500 major flood catastrophes. At one time, the river flowed north to Tientsin and entered the sea at Taku. It did so for 17 centuries. Then, from A.D. 1324 until 1852, it flowed south to enter the Yellow Sea in Kiangsu Province, near Suchow. From 1852 to the present, it has flowed northeast, to its outlet on the Gulf of Po. Beyond the mouth of the river, in the Po Gulf and for miles beyond, huge sandbars composed of silt testify to its power and its presence.

Over thousands of years, the Yellow River (called also by the Chinese, the River of Sorrow, for the major emotion it seems to foster) has migrated in various directions, fashioning the swirling eddies, formed, tradition says, by the villages that disappeared beneath it in the 1852 flood. In Northern Honan, excavations near the river have produced Shang Dynasty relics, indicating that, under the present Yellow River mud, 3,500 years ago, there were once villages.

The Yellow River occasionally empties into the Yangtse, near Nanking. It did this in 1887, when a flood took 1 million lives. And it did it again in June 1938.

As the winter dry spell gave way to the inevitable rains of late spring and summer, the river rose. Since the Hsia Dynasty, dikes have, more or less, held back the floodwaters. In bad years, rising waters have broken the dikes, causing immense floods on the Great Plains.

But in June 1938, the dikes were breached not by the river, but by Chinese soldiers.

Heavy rains had pounded the plains into mud packs by the last week in May, and as June arrived, these rains intensified. Ordinarily, the rainy season arrived in late July and extended through August, and the Japanese invaders must have been aware of this, since they planned on mounting and concluding their major offensives before flood season. But this year, nature and the environment seemed to be on the side of the Chinese. The rains came early, and stayed. The Yellow River reached flood stage and beyond by the end of June.

Before this, Japanese forces generally ran rapidly through the Chinese countryside, capturing village after village, advancing relentlessly upon Chengchow and Kaifeng, the important centers of commerce and railroads in Shantung Province. The Chinese were in full retreat, until they were able to put into actuality their planned strategy of destroying the Yellow River dikes between Chengchow and Kaifeng.

They sent runners out to warn the inhabitants bordering the river, then chopped huge holes in the dikes. The Yellow River, its bed higher than the surrounding countryside, cascaded through the breaches in the dikes like angry rapids, inundating the Honan Province plains around them, drowning livestock and Japanese soldiers, covering supplies, machinery, trucks, and tanks with silt-laced floodwaters.

As the days spooled on, the Yellow River became more and more a protagonist in the war. The Japanese advance along the Lung-Hai Railway was stopped utterly. The main stream of the flood washed across its tracks, then rolled on to the southeast and into Anhwei Province. The gap between Chengchow and the Japanese invaders, pock-marked by abandoned machinery, grew wider.

More breaks, some of them 30 feet wide, were chopped into the dikes on the north bank of the river, flooding northwest Honan. And while the floodwaters rose, the rains fell, turning normally passable roads into quagmires. It was almost as if nature had sided with the Chinese and was fighting back.

As fast as the Japanese put Chinese peasants to work repairing the broken dikes, they opened again. Japanese dispatches reported 150,000 Chinese civilians drowned in the floods, but, because they reported no incidents of drowning among their troops, the contents of the dispatch seemed highly unlikely.

By June 15, the major breaks in the dikes were between Kingshui, just north of the Chengchow junction of the Lung Hai and Peiping-Hankow Railways, and at Kaifeng, 50 miles east. The Japanese were in retreat.

But it was not all good news for the Chinese defending their homeland. The winter wheat supply was clearly being destroyed by the floodwaters. Furthermore, 30 million refugees as well as Japanese troops were in the same area. But the military exigencies of repelling the invaders took precedence over everything else that spring.

Entire villages disappeared. The city of Chungmow, 25 miles east of Chengchow, was turned into a walled island, rising out of the middle of a lake.

Now, in the middle of June, other Chinese army detachments, hearing of the success of the Yellow River flood, began to destroy dikes on the Yangtze River on the outskirts of Hankow. A nameless Chinese citizen told a reporter from the *New York Times* on June 16, "If the breaks in the Yellow River dikes work for the Chinese Army, it is justified. The Japanese machine must be stopped at any cost.

"We today hold the same philosophy as the mythical Chinese sage who, rebelling against a tyrant emperor, expressed his ideas in allegory to his followers. This sage, taking a solemn vow, said: 'If I perish, the sun will perish with me.'"

To those within the reach of the floodwaters it almost seemed as if all of nature was perishing. More than 500 square miles of countryside were underwater, throughout all of Honan Province and to the walls of Chowkiakow, 100 miles from the Yellow River's normal banks. By June 17, the floodstream was between 10 and 20 miles wide, and, accord-

ing to Japanese sources, nearly 500,000 Chinese farmers had been driven from 2,000 inundated villages.

Not so, said Chinese sources. "Japanese reports of the drowning of thousands of people should be discounted," the official Chinese report noted. "Actually, there is little danger of people drowning except in instances where dikes break in the immediate vicinity of a city at night."

The report did, however, acknowledge that famine and disease were consequent dangers of the Chinese military strategy. "When this whole level plain is flooded, it means that all food is lost except what people are able to carry with them to higher land. Many times they attempt to seek food in submerged fields. . . ."

It was a large gamble. The population of the 40,000 square miles that would eventually be affected was 30 million, averaging about 800 people to the square mile.

Onward the Yellow River surged, millions of gallons of it, toward the Yangtze. The Japanese estimated that 90 percent of the Yellow River's water was roaring through quarter-mile-wide breaks in the dikes and into the countryside, which was 30 feet lower than the surface of the river.

Meanwhile, the Yangtze continued to rise. By June 18, it had climbed 20 feet, which was 5 feet from flood level. Realizing that the real flood season was yet to come, when August brought fresh surges of water from the melting snows in the high hinterlands next to Tibet, the Japanese now shifted their attention to the capturing of Kiuliang, on the south bank of the Yangtze. There, a railway ran south to Nanchang, the capital of Kiangsi Province, from which the Japanese could advance westward upon Changsha, then cut the Canton-Hankow Railway in Central Hunan south of Hankow, thus isolating the capital of China.

But the Chinese had anticipated this and were already tearing up the rails and ties on the Kiuliang branch of the railway. And they also anticipated the coming rise of the Yangtze, and were making preparations to cut the dikes around Hankow.

All through June, the floods raged across Honan Province, engulfing 2,000 communities, drowning, according to reliable international sources, more than 6,000 Japanese soldiers and causing more than 700,000 Chinese to become refugees. The rains aided the Chinese mightily, adding to the force of the flood, which now had reached a flow of nearly 1 million cubic feet per second (CFS) at the point at which the dikes were first breached, north of Chengchow.

In effect, the Japanese were stymied. There were no modern roads, and the dirt ones were now swamps. Thousands of tanks and trucks were mired in mud and useless. The only modern means of attack that was left to the Japanese was airpower, and bombing runs against the major cities were hampered by the rains.

Now attention focused on the Yangtze River. It was rapidly achieving flood stage, a boon at first to the Japanese

Navy, since the flooding made hitherto unnavigable portions of it navigable. But by the beginning of July, it was a roaring Hellespont, and that, plus the presence of Chinese mines, made it extremely dangerous for the Japanese to use.

Heavy fighting broke out near Tikang, on the south bank of the Yangtze, 300 miles east of Hankow, and the northward advance of the Japanese was halted at Taiho, 170 miles from Hankow.

The use of the environment as a weapon of war succeeded for the Chinese, but at a great cost. At the beginning of July, 3,000 Chinese refugees were marooned at Shawo, northwest of Chungmow. They were reduced to eating the barks of trees and whatever grass protruded up through the floodwaters. In Chengchow, there were 120,000 refugees and in Chungmow 20,000. Cholera was spreading, and in Shanghai, inoculation fever ran high. Truckloads of doctors and nurses moved up and down the streets by the hour, jabbing a needle into every Chinese in sight.

During the first week in July, Chinese troops, utilizing the resumed rains and inevitable flooding that would follow, began to cut the dikes along the Yangtze, midway between Anking and Kiuliang. By the beginning of August, a full-scale Japanese assault upon Hankow was foiled by a full-scale cutting of the dikes of the Yangtze, combined with concentrated guerrilla attacks upon the Japanese invaders. The Japanese were halted 100 miles downstream from Hangkow.

The major roads to Hangkow were similarly inundated. The important city of Wusueh was partially submerged, and the highway west of Hwangmei, the dominant road to Hankow, was impassable.

Ultimately, the Chinese strategy would only serve as a holding action. Japanese forces overwhelmed most of the area once the rains ceased and the floodwaters receded naturally. It would be Japan's own actions that would finally and conclusively drive them from China. The bombing of Pearl Harbor would merge the Sino-Japanese war into World War II, and that would write the final chapter of an ages-long conflict in favor of the Chinese.

JAPAN
(HIROSHIMA, NAGASAKI)
DROPPING OF FIRST ATOMIC BOMBS
August 6 and 9, 1945

Seventy-eight thousand men, women, and children were killed outright; 70,000 more would die within 5 years; 37,000 were injured; and 13,000 were reported missing in Hiroshima after the dropping of the first atomic bomb used in warfare. Three days later, 73,884 died outright, 74,909 were seriously injured, and 120,820 civilians were affected by radiation poisoning in the bombing of Nagasaki, with an even bigger plutonium bomb. And the horror of fallout, on the environment and on humans, was introduced to the world.

Leslie Marmon Silko, a Laguna Pueblo Indian whose reservation was a few hundred miles from Alamogordo, the Los Alamos site of the first atomic bomb test, utilized the event in her novel *Ceremony*. Interpreting a ceremonial sand painting, she said, "From that time on, human beings were one clan again, united by the fate the destroyers had planned for them, for all living things; united by a circle of death that devoured people in cities twelve thousand miles away. . . ."

It is one accomplishment to discover a process. It is another to test that process. And yet another to use it, as the atom bomb was, twice within 75 hours in August 1945, against the cities of Hiroshima and Nagasaki and their populations. Ironically, the destruction was so terrible, it became not a heroic act but rather a lesson etched forever into part of the collective conscience of the world. In some respects, the terrible legacy of these bombings is carried forth with every voyage of the environmentalist ship *Greenpeace*, which tries, sometimes successfully, more often unsuccessfully, to stop nuclear testing.

After the bombs were dropped on these two cities, it was, if not easy, logical to feel shame. "I made one great mistake in my life, when I signed the letter to President Roosevelt recommending that atom bombs be made . . . ," wrote Albert Einstein to Linus Pauling, after the bombs were dropped.

It was more than a solely personal feeling of guilt. In the interim between the testing of the bomb and the dropping of it, there was soul searching and indecision among some scientists versus determination among other scientists and the military. Determination won.

In Chicago, as early as July 3, Leo Szilard composed a petition, designed to be forwarded to President Truman, for his fellow scientists at the Metallurgical Laboratory to sign. "We the undersigned, respectfully petition" it urged, "that you exercise your power as Commander in Chief to rule that the United States shall not, in the present phase of the war, resort to the use of atomic bombs."

With some modifications, 70 of his colleagues signed the petition and forwarded it to General Groves. It never reached the president.

After the Trinity test (see United States, New Mexico, Los Alamos, pp. 222–26), Szilard continued his protest. Only 15 of the scientists he polled favored dropping the bomb on the Japanese. Forty-six percent favored a military demonstration in Japan before using it as a weapon; others advocated varying forms of warning demonstrations.

But the wheels of war had been in motion too long, and those in charge were not about to stop them. The target committee, which included world famous physicist J. Robert Oppenheimer, who would eventually become the director of the Los Alamos test, drew up an execution list of four Japanese cities still standing (General Curtis LeMay's B-29s had already decimated all of the major military complexes and five industrial complexes). Four cities were

Melted, tormented wreckage is all that is left of the city of Hiroshima after the dropping of the first atomic bomb.
(LIBRARY OF CONGRESS)

picked: Hiroshima, Kokura, Niigata, and Kyoto. Secretary Stimson vetoed Kyoto because it was an ancient capital and cultural mecca for the Japanese. And so, Nagasaki, the next on the list, was chosen instead.

On August 6, at 2:45 A.M., the *Enola Gay*, a B-29 loaded with an untested atomic bomb, took off from the island of Tinian, headed for the first target, Hiroshima.

In the unsuspecting city, the day began uneventfully. There had been no warning given to its residents or to the government of Japan. A weather-observation flight had flown over Hiroshima, a daily occurrence that produced an alert and a rapid all-clear.

At 9:00 A.M., the *Enola Gay* had Hiroshima in sight. At 9:15:30, Colonel William S. Parsons triggered the mechanism that dropped the bomb.

On the ground, Naoko Masuoka, a girl on a school trip heard someone cry out, "A B-29!" "Even as this shout rang

in our ears," she later said, "there was a blinding flash and I lost consciousness."

"A bright light filled the plane," said commander Paul Tibbets. "The first shock wave hit us. We were eleven and a half miles slant from the atomic explosion, but the whole airplane cracked and crinkled. We turned back to look at Hiroshima. The city was hidden by that awful cloud . . . boiling up, mushrooming, terrible and incredibly tall."

"The mushroom cloud . . . was a spectacular sight," said tailgunner George Caron, "a bubbling mass of purple-gray smoke and you could see it had a red core in it and everything was burning inside. . . . [It] looked like lava or molasses covering a whole city. . . ."

Under the lava, an inferno roared. It was as if the earth had opened up and spit flames. People, horribly blistered and burned, ran for the river. Yoshiaki Wada, who had escaped the burning, made her way through hundreds of bodies strewn across the bridge. "Some were burned black, some had blistered skin that was peeling off, and some had pieces of glass in them all over," she recalled.

The heat, as intense as the interior of the sun, had turned the city to cinders, cremated every blade of grass, collapsed hundreds of structures with its awful wind, and polluted every repository of water, so that those who drank died from the intake of the tainted water. Iwao Nakamura, who had been burned over most of her body, went to a water tank. "When I got near and was able to see into the tank," she said, "I gave an involuntary cry and backed away. What I saw reflected in the blood-stained water were the faces of monsters. They had leaned over the side of the tank and died in that position."

And then, it began to rain. To those on the ground it seemed like a cleansing, a purgation. It was not. It was merely the second chapter of hell, a black rain of radioactive dirt that had been sucked up into the mushroom cloud, then spit out and back onto the victims. "The wind got stronger," reported Yohko Kuwabara, "and it started raining something like ink. This strange rain came down hard out of the gray sky, like a thundershower, and the drops stung as if I were being hit by pebbles."

Seventy-eight thousand men, women, and children died that day; 60,000 more would die in November and another 70,000 by 1950; 37,000 were injured, and some of them would later die; 13,000 were missing and never found. The deaths were overwhelmingly civilian. The United States Strategic Bombing Survey confirmed that only 3,243 Japanese troops were killed. Rail stations, bridges, factories, homes were reduced to flaming rubble.

Nothing like it had ever happened before, but something even more terrible would happen only 75 hours later.

It was not supposed to occur quite so swiftly. The original plan had been to release the second bomb, the plutonium bomb that had been tested at Trinity, on August 11. But the meteorological forecast was for good weather on the 9th, and five days of bad weather following this.

And so, the bombing was moved up by two days. If the original schedule had been adhered to, the second bomb would not have been dropped. But the destruction of Hiroshima had been so complete and utter, there was simply no time for the Japanese to respond to it.

In fact, as soon as Emperor Hirohito learned of the devastation of Hiroshima, he told an associate, "We must bow to the inevitable. No matter what happens to my safety, we must put an end to this war as speedily as possible so that this tragedy will not be repeated."

But the agent of the repetition was, by then, preparing to leave Tinian. Another B-29, carrying "Fat Man," the plutonium bomb, accompanied by a weather plane, reached the skies over the primary target, Kokura, at 9:50 A.M.

There were heavy clouds over the city, and the two planes circled for 10 minutes, waiting for a break in the overcast. None occurred, and so they proceeded to their secondary target, Nagasaki.

This city was also obscured by clouds, and the orders were to release the bomb by radar. But then, at 11:00 A.M., the clouds suddenly parted, revealing the Mitsubishi Heavy Industries Nagasaki Arsenal, directly below. The bomb was released at 11:02, over the heart of the city.

As it had in the testing in Los Alamos, it imploded, once again releasing the energy and the heat of the interior of the sun, incinerating, with its temperature of several million degrees centigrade, every human, animal, piece of vegetation, and wooden building within a quarter mile of the impact point. It scoured out a crater one mile in circumference, in which nothing lived or stood. A firestorm abounding in infrared rays and a simultaneous shock wave radiated out, twisting and tormenting iron girders, machines, and metal structures. Because the Nagasaki bomb was more powerful than the Hiroshima bomb, the damage to concrete-reinforced buildings was three times that of the Hiroshima blast.

The firestorm raged out of control, partly because of its immensity, partly because a large percentage of the city's firefighting apparatus and facilities were destroyed outright.

Most of the hospitals were burned or demolished. Of 70 doctors in the city, 20 were dead and 20 more seriously wounded. The remaining 30 were left to care for the maimed and wounded, often in the open, sometimes in first-aid stations that were set up in schools.

Food became a problem for the survivors and sufferers. Some hardtack rations were finally distributed in the central city area in the evening of the first day, but even this was difficult, since most of the local officials and volunteers were themselves dead or injured.

The toll in Nagasaki was 73,884 dead, 74,909 seriously injured, and 120,820 affected with radiation poisoning, which would lead to a great many deaths in later years.

The environment in and around both cities was devastated. Carp in a shallow pond on the west side of Mt. Hijiyama, near Hiroshima, were killed from the blast pressure, their air bladders burst.

Dead birds littered the landscape, killed by hemorrhage and epilation. Horses died by the hundreds, from thermal injuries and leukopenia, a blood condition. The injured animals suffered from fever and suppurative conjunctivitis.

Trees and plants were reduced to ashes, and although herbs grew quickly in these ashes, they were malformed and weirdly colored. Radiation emitted by fission, fission by-products, and induced-radioactive materials remained in the soil for months.

The bombardment of the residents of Hiroshima and Nagasaki by gamma rays and neutrons was monumental, and primary and secondary radiation sickness, particularly in the suburbs, where the fallout was most intense, persisted for years. Since the spermatogonia of the testis and follicular

The heavily populated city of Nagasaki simply disappeared, leaving a flat plain of destruction and death following the explosion of the second—and last—atomic bomb to be dropped on enemy territory during a war.

(LIBRARY OF CONGRESS)

cells of the ovary are radio-sensitive, there was a severe disturbance of sexual function in men and in the reproductive capabilities of women. Leukemia, anemia, cataracts, thyroid cancer, lung cancer, breast cancer, and salivary gland cancer proliferated in the populace of both cities, far outstripping the rest of Japan. Even those who were merely burned found that their wounds took an abnormally long time to heal, and those who did heal were frequently grotesquely disfigured.

Fear stalked many of the survivors, who, though not physically scarred, carried profound, long-lasting psychological wounds.

Thirty-five years later, an exhaustive and probing report on the bombings was released by the Japanese Committee for the Compilation of Materials on Damage Caused by the Atomic Bombs in Hiroshima and Nagasaki. "An atomic bomb's massive destruction and indiscriminate slaughter involves the sweeping breakdown of all order and existence—in a word, the collapse of society itself," it stated. "The destruction of the social and environmental systems that support human life, combined with the A-bomb victims' own loss of health and resources for living, brought about a total disintegration of human life."

The effect of the bombing would reach far beyond the borders of Japan. A second plutonium bomb, another "Fat Man," was ready for shipment to Tinian on August 12. But General Groves ordered a delay; two days later, Japan surrendered and World War II was over.

The casualties of the blast reached beyond Japan's borders, too. On August 21, scientist Harry Daghlian succumbed to the radioactivity with which he had been sprayed during the test of the Nagasaki bomb. His hands swelled horribly, the skin fell from his body in patches, and he died.

In May of the following year, Louis Slotin, who had determined the size of the bomb, saved the lives of several other scientists in a new experiment by tearing apart two hemispheres of plutonium with his bare hands, to block a runaway chain reaction. He absorbed 880 roentgens (units) of radiation. Within a week, he had lost his mind; two days later, he died, in agony.

President Truman, who gave the final order to drop the two bombs, told reporters long afterward that he did not lose a single night's sleep over the decision. It was made, he said, to avoid an invasion of Japan, and to save "half a million American lives."

That the actual figure for potential lives saved that General George C. Marshall gave him was 40,000 is probably beside the point. The decision to drop the bomb arose from a complex context. There were scores of defendable reasons, but three rise to the surface: The military needed to end the war. Russia had to be challenged. And the passion of rage that powers war was at a fever pitch.

Among the scientists, Leo Szilard never faltered in his opposition to the dropping of the bomb. "Using atomic bombs against Japan is one of the greatest blunders of history," he said, the day after the Hiroshima explosion.

J. Robert Oppenheimer, on the other hand, had a complex and shifting response. On the day the bomb dropped on Hiroshima, he walked to a podium in a Washington auditorium and clasped his hands over his head like a victorious prizefighter.

A month later, he spoke more hesitantly with a newsman. "[I'm a] little scared of what I have made," he said. "But," he added, "a scientist cannot hold back progress because of fears of what the world will do with his discoveries."

Nevertheless, the feared race for atomic domination did take place. The Soviet Union had already begun work building an atomic bomb before bombs were dropped on Hiroshima and Nagasaki—the dropping of these bombs was, in fact, a partial message of warning to the Soviet Union. Ultimately, the Soviets were able to acquire a bomb of their own with the help of detailed sketches and information transmitted to them by Klaus Fuchs, a British atomic scientist who had gone to New York to assist in the development of the American bomb.

This, plus the transfer of other sketches from Los Alamos by Julius and Ethel Rosenberg, an American couple suspected of Communist sympathies, which led to their execution, marked the escalation of the cold war. And in the paranoia of those decades, Robert Oppenheimer, the man most responsible for the development of the U.S. bomb, was stripped of his security clearance and publicly humiliated.

By then, he, as most of the scientists involved, had become increasingly horrified at what he—and they—had begun. In a conversation with President Harry Truman, he expressed deep remorse over Hiroshima and told Truman that his work at the weapons laboratory meant that he had blood on his hands.

Truman reacted in such a violently negative way that the assumption that he, too, was feeling pangs of remorse, regret, and guilt becomes nearly inescapable. "The blood is on my hands. Let me worry about that," he said. Then, after Oppenheimer had exited the Oval Office, he confided to Secretary of State Dean Acheson, "I don't want to see that son of a bitch in this office ever again."

And a private letter written by Truman on the very day that the bomb dropped on Nagasaki, quoted in Ronald Schaffer's historical study, *Wings Judgment: American Bombing in World War II*, revealed more about the conversation between Truman and Oppenheimer than perhaps even the president himself knew. "I know that Japan is a terribly cruel and uncivilized nation in warfare," he wrote, "but I can't bring myself to believe that, because they are beasts, we would ourselves act in that same manner. For myself I certainly regret the necessity of wiping out whole populations because of the 'pigheadedness' of leaders of a nation, and for your information, I am not going to do it [again] unless it is absolutely necessary. My object is to save as many American lives as possible but I also have a humane feeling for the women and children in Japan."

After the second bomb was dropped, it was Truman who made certain that it was the last. He then explained this to his vice president, Henry Wallace. "The thought of wiping out another 100,000 people was too horrible," he said. He did not like the idea of killing "all those kids," recalled Wallace in his diary, then added that for days afterward, the president complained of horrible headaches. "Physical or figurative?" Wallace asked him. "Both," the president replied.

The world was aware that it had entered a new age, and scientists turned their attention to its potential effect upon the land and its inhabitants. On August 23, 1945, 14 days after the bomb exploded over Nagasaki, Japanese newspapers reported that the bombed areas would remain biologically sterile for 70 years. It was an unproved theory, but it was the first of many, fueled by the newness of the age and the horror of its birth.

In September of that year, a giant typhoon hit Hiroshima, washing away much surveyable evidence and burying the Kyoto Imperial University survey team under a landslide.

A year later, John Hersey's "Hiroshima" was published in the *New Yorker* magazine, and joint committees and facilities began to be set up between Japan and the United States. By the 1950s, the "Hiroshima and Nagasaki Maidens," the profoundly disfigured young girls who symbolized to millions the terrible price of atomic warfare had come to the United States for rehabilitative surgery, and on December 8, 1953, President Eisenhower addressed the Eighth United Nations General Assembly on the peaceful uses of atomic energy.

But, three months later, the U.S. exploded an H-bomb at Bikini Atoll in the Pacific (see pp. 216–21) and it was plain that the atomic race would continue.

Peacetime catastrophes such as Three Mile Island (see pp. 190–93) and Chernobyl (see pp. 194–200) bore an eerie resemblance to the devastation caused by the first bombs: High-level decisions resulted in the death of helpless civilians; huge areas of the earth became uninhabitable; landscapes were destroyed; long-term effects of the fallout would persist for years.

In 1998, 53 years after the dropping of the atomic bombs on Hiroshima and Nagasaki, and after it has become plain to everyone from rulers to the least educated that atomic power contains the potential of not merely eradicating the environment of the earth, but all of the life living on it, the world still does not possess a universal test-ban treaty.

The words carved into the stone of the memorial cenotaph in Hiroshima Peace Memorial Park have been called interpretable. This may be so, but the warning of their surface optimism is not. Unequivocally, it says:

Rest in peace, for the mistake shall not be repeated.

KUWAIT
(OIL FIELDS)
CONTAMINATION AND FIRES DURING AND AFTER THE GULF WAR
January 23–November 7, 1991

The largest oil spill in the history of the world, and air pollution to rival that of the Chernobyl and Bhopal disasters combined were deliberately caused by Saddam Hussein and his armed forces during the Persian Gulf War.

Iraq's Saddam Hussein has always been notoriously unconcerned about the fate of his people. At the end of the Gulf War of 1990–91, he also exhibited a callous disregard for the ecology not only of the Middle East, but the entire world. Never has a war been so purposely destructive of the environment as the Gulf War, and although Hussein's crimes were the most heinous, neither side would qualify, in the end, for an award from an environmental group.

The Gulf War began on August 2, 1990, with the invasion of Kuwait by Iraqi armed forces. Before that, Hussein had been flexing his muscles by calling for American ships to leave the Gulf region and by threatening to use chemical weapons against Israel. For both of these activities, accompanied by statements about "let[ting] our fire eat up half of Israel, if it tries to do anything against Iraq," and "[the United States] display[ing] some signs of fatigue," he was applauded by his Arab neighbors.

But his bald-faced incursion into an Arab neighbor's territory produced a gigantic negative response from Saudi Arabia, the United States, and the United Nations (UN), including Iraq's former patron, the Soviet Union.

From August through November, while reports of atrocities in Kuwait filtered out and into the international consciousness, the UN imposed sanctions upon Iraq. Finally, on November 29, after great pressure from the United States, the UN gave Hussein 45 days to either withdraw from Kuwait or expect a military attack.

There was a great deal of opposition to the move in the United States, and much debate in Congress. On January 12, 1991, Congress approved a resolution authorizing the president to use force after January 15 "if necessary." The House of Representatives voted 250 to 136 in favor; the Senate voted 52 to 47 in the same direction. It was the closest margin of support for a war since June 1812, when Congress divided regarding President James Madison's request for war with Great Britain.

On January 17, 1991, at 2:40 A.M. Iraqi time, the first American bombs and missiles struck Baghdad; at 4:00 A.M. on February 24, a full-scale ground attack in Kuwait was begun by UN forces. The air war would last 38 days, the ground war 100 hours. The truce would come on February 28, 1991.

Hussein's war against the environment, however, had a schedule and a life of its own. On January 23, six days after the first missiles fell on Baghdad, Iraqi forces began to set fire to the Kuwaiti oil fields. On January 26, they began to spill oil from Kuwait's oil pipelines into the Persian Gulf.

There was no military advantage whatsoever in doing this; it was sheer megalomania and vengeful intent that brought about direct warfare against the environment. The oil spills and the attendant ecological devastation were examples of water, ground, and air pollution to rival the Chernobyl explosion (see pp. 194–200) and the Bhopal disaster (see pp. 81–85). The final tally of environmental destruction and its human victimization will not be known for decades, but some facts and figures are educational.

The first spill came shortly after the beginning of the air war, when the Iraqis dynamited the Sea Island loading terminal, about 10 miles offshore from Fahaheel. At roughly the same time, Iraqi armed forces scuttled five tankers moored at nearby Mina Ahmadi.

Then, during February, there was Iraqi sabotage at the oil ports of Mina Ahmadi, Abu Halifa, and Shuaiba, which discharged more oil into the Gulf. In addition, oil wells were opened on land, and oil lakes formed, which drained into waterways, and thence into the Gulf, particularly from Sabriya field, north of Kuwait Bay, where a natural drainage system of dry watercourses, or *wadis*, exist in greater profusion than anywhere else in Kuwait.

Never has a war been more destructive of the environment than the Persian Gulf War. The air over the Rumaila (shown here) and Sabriya (shown on next page) oil fields was turned opaque and lethal by the wholesale and desperate uncapping and burning of the wells by Saddam Hussein's retreating forces.
(J. ISAAC/UN PHOTOS)

The oil slick created by this combination of forces was nearly twice the size of the world's previously largest spill, that of the blowout in the Ixtoc-1 well in the Bay of Campeche off Mexico in 1979 (see pp. 144–48). At places such as Brice lagoon, a north-facing sheltered flat lying along a stretch of shoreline halfway between Manifa Bay and Ras al-Zawr, there was oil both on the shore and in the water for as far as the eye could see.

Most of the characteristic brown mousse of spilled oil came ashore along a 290-mile-long strip of land on the northern coast of Saudi Arabia. The beaches, which comprise 60 percent of the area, were totally contaminated, but they were not the only affected areas. Salt marshes, mangroves, and coral island wildlife habitats—some of them the breeding shores of the rare Green and Hawksbill turtles—were coated with the oily mess.

Mangrove plants that grew close to the low-tide line died, their leaves blackened and yellowed, their trunks coated with oil. Beneath the coating, dead tissue revealed further deterioration.

The toll on seabirds was immense; that of onshore birds was even worse. Thirty thousand recorded seabirds, espe-cially wintering greves and cormorants, perished in the oil-slick, their wings coated, their bills glued shut from trying to preen away the gummy substance. The intertidal feeding grounds, frequented by 1 to 2 million shorebirds each year were choked and coated with oil, and the same sorry death overtook these birds.

In the Gulf itself, fishing is second only to oil as an industry. The fish stocks of shrimp, barracuda, king mackerel, and two distinctively Kuwaiti fish called *subaitee* and *hamour* were totally destroyed in the affected area, though it must be added that they were already in decline because of persistent pollution of the Gulf from industry and particularly from oil.

Greenpeace retrieved the carcasses of 14 dugongs, 57 bottlenose dolphins, and 13 humpback dolphins.

Up to 11 million barrels of oil were eventually purposely spilled into the Gulf, through the direct opening of tanks and through the bombing of pipelines at the Sea Island Terminal by the allied coalition—a dramatic example of a cure becoming worse than an affliction.

The sight of the oil slick was appalling. Oil covered the shore and the water as far as the eye could see from north to

south and back again. Fossils of birds, fish, crabs, and worms were created instantly.

And there was another, human, catastrophe that might have occurred from the oil spill if Saudi Arabian officials had not prepared for it. Because of the aridity of the region, Saudi Arabia relied upon three seawater desalination plants to supply 40 percent of its drinking water. Among them was the world's largest desalination plant, a 220-million-gallon-a-day giant at al-Jubail, which provided Riyadh with 60 to 70 percent of its drinking water, and which also served a huge industrial area in the region with water needed for cooling purposes.

The plants used a multistage flash distillation process, repeatedly boiling and condensing incoming seawater in a series of chambers, which allowed the condensate from each successive chamber to become purer and purer. Oil entering the plant, or even chemical dispersants, which are customarily employed to thin and break up oil slicks, would contaminate the water, distilling out with it.

Thus, only mechanical booms could be used to keep the oil from disrupting the water supply of Saudi Arabia, and they were immediately put into place. Within a day or two of the discovery of the spill, crews hired by the Saline Water Conservation Corporation had cordoned off the 360-yard-wide entrance to the intake basin at al-Jubail and encircled each of the plant's five intakes with an additional two

lengths of boom. Norway offered help soon after, modifying the floating booms to make them more efficient.

No oil seeped into the plants, but there was an immense cleanup that was necessary as the war ended. A number of countries, including the United Kingdom, the European Community, Japan, Canada, Switzerland, Luxembourg, and China, contributed money toward it.

The United States, which spent $7.4 billion to carry out the Gulf War, contributed neither money nor equipment, but some private American companies helped, for a price. O'Brien and Lippens, of New Orleans, for instance, took on the necessary job of cleaning the mangrove thicket on Gurma Island. Sixty-three thousand barrels of oil had drifted onto the narrow, three-mile-long island, a repository for wildlife and ecologically important algae.

It was a monstrous job, though not nearly so monstrous as the act that made it necessary. Experts have still not fully assessed the effect or the damage of the oil spills in the Gulf, but many fear that irreversible damage may have been done to the Gulf's biological productivity, which would lead, in the long term, to a greatly reduced species diversity.

And this was only half the environmental outrage. The oil fires were another, perhaps even worse, tragedy.

The oil fields of Kuwait contained, before the war, 1,116 working wells. Approximately 850 of them were set afire by

Hussein's forces. Many were simply blown up, which meant that not only did oil shoot upward into ignition from ruptures in the exposed pipes, it also oozed out of blasted openings in underground pipes. As the oil saturated the soil, swamps of oil formed around the wells, and when they reached the surface of the sand, they became fiery lakes of oil. The sand around and under these lakes was so hot that, when firefighters finally tried to douse them, the water they sprayed instantly boiled away.

Most obviously and devastatingly, these fires, from the wells and from the burning lakes, released a noxious plume of smoke that covered an area from Baghdad to the north to Yemen in the south, from Riyadh to beyond the eastern slopes of Iran's Zagros Mountains, and to a height of nearly 20,000 feet.

Passing over the Gulf, the smoke dropped tons of soot particles and oil droplets onto the land and into the water of the Gulf, where it killed plant life and contaminated the water supplies of humans and wildlife.

For a thousand miles downwind, the air stank. Saudi Arabia's environmental agency canceled flights intended to pinpoint the extent of the oil spill. The governor of Adana, in southwestern Turkey, forbade his citizens to use rainwater blackened by soot for their animals or themselves. Cattle, horses, sheep, goats, and camels died from breathing poisoned air and eating poisoned fodder.

There was a further fear, which later proved to be premature, of a "nuclear winter" resulting from the absorption of sunlight by the dark cloud of soot-containing smoke. But, although the following summer was the coolest on record for the area, no nuclear winter occurred.

Still, there was enormous air pollution. The abiding danger of soot from oil-well fires is its release of large amounts of carbon dioxide into the atmosphere, which, when it combines with the water in the atmosphere, forms droplets of sulfuric and nitric acids, commonly called acid rain.

Furthermore, the cloud was big enough to cause its own weather systems. Winds converged toward the middle of the plume, picking up speed as they did. Black rain fell over the area, and black snow was reported in the Himalayas. It has been conjectured that the smoke cloud from Kuwait altered other weather patterns in the world,

A slimy, shifting sea of oil greeted the peacetime army of workmen and experts sent by a multinational combination of forces to recap the Kuwait oil wells and make a cursory attempt at cleanup.

(STEPHANE COMPOINT/UNEP)

214

Red Adair and his team of Houston, Texas, oil rangers, who have been called in to cap countless out-of-control oil wells, were dispatched to Kuwait to apply their expertise to an overwhelming task of stopping an outflow of 11 million barrels a day.
(STEPHANE COMPOINT/UNEP)

too, but to date no hard proof of this has been either uttered or written.

In total, pollution fell on a wide swath, across Kuwait, southern Iran, Pakistan, and northern India. Human beings were exposed to air pollution, grazing herds ingested soot, agricultural systems were covered with it, and water systems were polluted by it.

Fully a third of the country of Kuwait was coated with an asphaltlike layer that varied from a papery crust to a tarry goo three to four inches thick. There are oil lakes that, for as long as they are there, will be deathtraps for migrating birds who mistake them for swamps, and the fumes from the lakes still make the air nearly unbreathable.

The amount of oil that soaked into the earth of Kuwait from January to November 1991 will never be precisely known, but it was definitely in the hundreds of millions of barrels. This, plus the amount rained down from the skies is equal to 6,000 times the amount spilled from the *Exxon Valdez*.

Ironically and universally, Kuwait focused more on the economic than the environmental impact of the tragedy. It was estimated that at around 11 million barrels a day, Kuwait was losing an average of $2,500 a second while the fires burned. And so, Red Adair and his band of oil cappers and firefighters were imported from Houston, Texas, and the best sort of disaster relief that a great deal of money can buy (at last count $4 billion) was turned toward damping down the fires, capping the wells, and pumping out the oil lakes in the Kuwaiti desert.

Again ironically, as the air pollution from the fires cleared, air pollution in Kuwait City from the enormous population of automobiles and buses took over. Gasoline, which is free in Kuwait, proved to be an excellent solvent for the soot raining down from the remaining oil fires, and it was used to clean windshields of cars and supply gasoline car washes.

But a far more serious threat that gasoline could not wipe away surfaced, as international teams of environmental experts descended upon Kuwait to take up the slack left by the vandalizing, by the Iraqis, of practically all of Kuwait's environmental monitoring equipment.

The Kuwaitis had long since come to the conclusion that they had to rely upon empirical evidence of environmental pollution rather than on their government, who had traditionally tailored its reports to its own political and economic agenda. In April 1991, the Gulf Pollution Task Force of the U.S. Senate Committee on Environment and Public Works reported that there were dangerous chemicals adhering to the oil particles in the soot still falling upon the people of the Persian Gulf. They included sulfur dioxide, able to cause respiratory illness, and polycyclic aromatic hydrocarbons, which are believed to cause cancer.

But these were, in large part, findings after the fact, when the fires were almost out. Nobody collected data at the height of the air pollution, and so that part of the effect of this environmental outrage will never be known, except in anecdotal form.

However, the Gulf War in general produced health crises to match the environmental crises. Kuwait's modern sewage-treatment plant, which had purified water to the point at which it could safely be used to irrigate food crops, was destroyed. For a year after the war, there was no drinking water in the country that was safe for human consumption, and even the trucked and bottled water tasted, said many in the populace, of the diesel fuel the trucks had previously carried.

In Iraq, too, there was a health crisis. The systematic destruction of Iraq's electric power plants also knocked out its water-purification and sewage-treatment plants. Irrigation systems could not function, hospitals were deprived of power, and perishable medicines spoiled. In Baghdad and Basra, the industrial city in Iraq's south, there were no supplies of fresh water from the beginning of the air war forward. The Tigris River, upstream of Baghdad, became an open sewer, and so did the Euphrates; and Basra, located in the combined outfall of the two rivers, received a double dose of pollution.

A Harvard Study Group went to Iraq and predicted, by May 1992, that 170,000 Iraqi children under the age of five would die from "delayed effects of the Gulf Crisis," that is, waterborne infectious diseases such as cholera. A UN team disputed the figures, stating that it was not quite that bad. The true tally will probably never be known, for Saddam Hussein kept no such figures.

He, in fact, was engaged in still more environmental outrage. In order to control the Kurds in the south who made their living from the marshes in which they lived, he directed his forces to dam up rivers and streams, thus drying up the marshes in order to starve and drive out the Kurds—and to simultaneously destroy the ecology of part of his own country.

And again, as in all catastrophes brought about by governments or heavy industry, a coverup from the top obscured reality. Sanctions imposed upon Iraq after the war clouded the precise amount of humanitarian aid going to its refugees, and the juggling of statistics erased the truth even more.

Beth Daponte, an analyst with the U.S. Census Bureau, blew the whistle on the bureau by stating publicly that it was deliberately dropping the true number of civilian casualties by Coalition action during the war from 13,000 to 5,000, and suppressing her calculations that Iraqi deaths in the war and its aftermath totaled 86,194 men, 39,612 women, and 32,195 children—70,000 of whom died during the 12 months following the war as a result of hunger and disease.

She was dismissed from the bureau for her public statements but was later reinstated on appeal.

And so, the final, accurate tally will remain cloudy, mired in the deliberate obfuscation of international intrigue. What remains is the evidence of a devastated ecology that only indeterminate time can cure. "We will never be able to rebuild the Kuwait we once had—the Iraqis and the oil fires have taken that away from us forever," said an unidentified man to author T. M. Hawley after the war. "We will probably never know how many days of our lives have been taken by the smoke we had to breathe. . . ."

MARSHALL ISLANDS
(BIKINI AND ENIWETOK ATOLLS)
ATOMIC AND HYDROGEN BOMB TESTS
1946–1958

The testing of atomic and hydrogen bombs by the United States from 1946 to 1958 resulted in the total destruction of the ecology of Bikini and Eniwetok Atolls, the displacement of its people, the death of a Japanese fisherman and radiation sickness for scores of others, the contamination of 264 natives and 28 technicians, and the disruption of the Japanese fishing industry for months.

A scant 10 months after the dropping of atomic bombs on Hiroshima and Nagasaki (see pp. 206–11), and before the effect of radioactive fallout on humans and the environment had been examined, much less assessed, U.S. atomic bomb tests began on Bikini and Eniwetok Atolls in the Marshall Islands.

The Marshalls, captured by the Allies from the Japanese in 1944, are located about 3,000 miles west of Hawaii in the Pacific Ocean. Bikini is a small atoll, 27 miles from east to west, a half mile from north to south. Within weeks of the end of World War II and the signing of the truce with Japan, while the Pacific fleet was still in the vicinity, the United States Navy arrived in Bikini with the news that all of the natives of the atoll were to be evacuated to the island of Rongerik, immediately.

"A great destructive force is going to be turned to something good for mankind," the officers told the native leaders on camera, for a military training film. The natives, understandably, did not understand what the soldiers were talking about, but they obediently packed their belongings and left their generations-old dwellings on the island they regarded as the largest part of the entire world.

Operation Crossroads, designed to test the effect of the atomic bomb on ships and humans, was about to take place. It involved 100 warships, 42,000 men, 22 women, several hundred sheep and goats, 104 still cameras, 208 movie cameras, and 18 tons of film.

The detritus of war is always a threat to both surviving human beings and the environment. In Kuwait, military hardware left behind possessed an added dimension. Hussein had, it turned out, used—and was prepared to use—chemical weapons to further foul the air and kill his enemies.

(JEHAN RAJAB/UNEP)

Twenty-two target ships dropped anchor in the lagoon at Bikini during the last days of June 1946. Pens and traps were secured to the decks. Goats, and sheep, shorn to the flesh and spread with sunburn lotion, were strapped into the pens and traps. "We will learn what will happen to humans," said officers on film, regarding the animal stand-ins.

Back in Washington, scientists Robert Urey and Albert Einstein issued public protests, while Atomic Energy Commission representative Bernard Baruch proposed an international non-proliferation treaty that would allow the United States to keep on testing and stockpiling atomic bombs until the other nations of the world agreed not to stockpile or test—whereupon, the United States would stop.

At the United Nations (UN), Soviet statesman Vyacheslav Molotov objected, adding—disingenuously, it later developed—that Russia had no plans to develop an atomic bomb.

On July 1, scientists, military men, U.S. senators, representatives from the UN, and newsmen boarded observer ships near Bikini. On the morning of July 2, the world's fourth atomic bomb was dropped from a B-19 over Bikini. Observers donned goggles; sailors assumed fetal positions on the decks of their ships.

A gigantic umbrella of smoke erupted over the atoll and ascended 100,000 feet into the air. From 20 miles away, some of the observers expressed disappointment. "It was a pretty poor spectacle," said one senator for the cameras.

Ten hours after the explosion, sailors aboard reconnaisance ships sailed into ground zero. An eerie, otherworldly spectacle greeted them. Dead fish floated on the surface of the water, half of them burned, half not. Blackened hulks of ships formed grim interruptions of darkness in an otherwise tropically brilliant day. Blackened corpses of animals were collapsed in some pens; in others, test animals survived in stunned shock, their bodies covered with huge blisters that eventually festered before they too died.

The sailors retrieved the corpses and injured animals for experiment and returned to their ships for rest and relaxation before the second test. They swam in water near ground zero, sunbathed, and were told nothing about the dangers of radiation that Hiroshima and Nagasaki had proved beyond a doubt.

On July 24, "Baker" test was launched. An underwater explosion, the first of its kind and therefore an unknown quantity, it produced seismic shocks around the world and sent a lethal, radioactive waterspout tens of thousands of feet in the air. The fallout spray rained debris on the observer ships, and a radioactive mist lingered for hours over the site.

Once again, sailors aboard the navy ships held at the perimeter of the test area were sent in to observe and collect data. According to official reports, scientists and special crews preceded the sailors with Geiger counters, to assure that there was no contamination left on the target vessels.

In actuality, the teams with Geiger counters *accompanied* the sailors, measuring the ships and the personnel for radiation as they worked.

After their task was accomplished, the sailors lingered, swimming in water in which dead, blistered fish floated. And all the while, they were assured by their superiors that there was no danger to them from the bomb test.

The information was of course sinisterly wrong. Within a few weeks, some of the young men became ill and were taken back to Pearl Harbor, to its naval hospital. Some were given medical discharges within the year, but it would be the 1970s before the first of the multiple cancers that would ultimately kill many of them would begin to surface. Ultimately, thousands of men would suffer slow and tortured deaths.

The first series of tests over, the natives of Bikini and Eniwetok pleaded with the U.S. military to allow them to return to their islands. But by now both atolls had been infinitely contaminated, reduced to dead moonscapes of twisted and tormented vegetation or deserts where lush greenery once grew. They would never be inhabitable again.

And the tests went on, because the most powerful bomb of all had not yet been proved. Back in the early days of the Manhattan Project, Edward Teller had become an advocate of the thermonuclear device, calling for its inspiration upon the stars, which are thermonuclear furnaces millions of times as large as Earth. It was too dangerous, too potentially uncontrollable for some of the scientists in the program, but while the major focus of the Manhattan Project continued to be fission bombs, Teller carried on with experiments in thermonuclear explosions.

The difference between the fission device, which was the atomic bomb, and the thermonuclear device, which would become the hydrogen bomb, was that, except in its fission trigger, the thermonuclear device would require no critical mass. As a fission bomb exploded, it disassembled its critical mass, at which point, fissioning stopped. This disassembly process set a natural limit to the size of fission explosions of about one megaton.

But a thermonuclear explosion would proceed like the nuclear version of a chemical explosion, burning and burning as long as it had access to thermonuclear fuel. The horrible limitlessness of this, the potential for igniting the nitrogen in the atmosphere and thus wiping out all life on the planet in one flash fire, shook most scientists in the Manhattan Project to their moral roots.

Not so Teller. He believed that this fathomless power could be controlled, and set out to prove it.

On August 29, 1949, the Soviet Union exploded its first atomic bomb, in the Ustyurt desert. It then became imperative, in order to draw ahead in the atomic race, for the United States to develop, to the point of testing, the thermonuclear, fusion-rather-than-fission bomb, dubbed the hydrogen bomb because of its use of heavy hydrogen,

The elegant, impressive, cloudy aftermath of a 1952 explosion, part of the series of atomic bomb tests conducted in the Marshall Islands from 1946 to 1958, hovers over a spot where Elugelab islet once was. More than land was lost. The Marshall Islands' ecology was totally destroyed, and hundreds of innocent fishermen and natives were killed or contaminated.

(UNITED NATIONS/USIA)

heated to a temperature greater than 100 million degrees, to form helium.

So, while work continued on reducing fission bombs to battlefield size, work on making a thermonuclear device large enough and destructive enough to show who was best, and possibly to be so terrible that it would end the arms race, was developed.

"Mike" was the answer, a hydrogen bomb fashioned by encasing an atomic bomb in a cocoon made from successive layers of frozen deuterium and tritium. The outer casing would be of metallic uranium U-238. The atom bomb would be the trigger, heating the deuterium and tritium so that their nuclei were in turn triggered. It was reasoned that 10 bombs, exploded in this way, would create as much fall-out as 10,000 atomic bombs.

Eniwetok was chosen as the site for the test. An oval ring 20 miles long and 10 miles wide, and composed of 40 small islands, it was in the northwestern quadrant of the Marshall Islands.

Dubbed the *Ivy* series, the hydrogen bomb tests involved a Joint Task Force of more than 9,000 military and 2,000 civilians, living aboard ships in the Eniwetok area, or in tent encampments on the islands. An aircraft carrier and 4 destroyers plied the area; the Air Force operated more than 80 aircraft for transport and aerial sampling; barges, motor-boats, and helicopters transported people back and forth throughout the area.

The island of Elugelab, in the northern part of the atoll, was chosen for the shot. The island was raised, to improve its sightlines. An aircraft hangar-size, six-story building was built on it to house the bomb. Out buildings around it contained equipment. A 375-foot antenna was constructed to receive and transmit radio and television control signals to the more than 500 scientific stations on 30 islands.

A 9,000-foot tunnel, or "sausage," as it was called, was directed at the bunker containing the monitoring panel, on Bogon islet, nearly two miles away.

In September, the assembly of the bomb began. Meanwhile, on October 3, the British exploded their first atomic device on the Monte Bello Islands, off Australia, thus increasing the Nuclear Club by one.

The remainder of October on Eniwetok atoll was spent in readying the first explosion of Mike. Shortly after midnight of October 31, 1952, the arming team finished its task and boarded the destroyer *Estes*, which sailed from Eniwetok lagoon at 3:15 A.M. on November 1, to a point about 10

218

miles beyond the southern rim of the atoll and 30 miles from ground zero.

H-hour was 7:15 A.M. on November 1, which was October 31 in the United States. The airplanes were in place; the thousands of military and civilian personnel were ordered to don high-density goggles.

The radio signal was sent from the *Estes*, and the process began. Within milliseconds, there was a fission fireball hotter than the center of the sun, and radiation began to penetrate the various layers of the bomb. The explosion demolished the casing, and a blinding white fireball, more than three miles across—more than 30 times that of the Hiroshima bomb—ascended into the atmosphere, spreading heat and energy in staggering profusion. For a moment, according to historian Richard Rhodes, "the fireball created every element that the universe had ever assembled and bred artificial elements as well."

Upward it swirled and boiled, glowing purple until it formed the emblematic mushroom cloud, balanced on a stem of water and debris, that slowly fell back into the sea. By the time two and a half minutes had passed—the time it would take for the shock wave to reach the *Estes*—the cloud extended from the earth upward more than 100,000 feet. Its top finally crested at 27 miles; its stem measured 8 miles across. Finally, the cloud billowed out above a 30-mile stem to form an immense umbrella more than 100 miles wide, which rained down radioactive mud, then radioactive rain.

The island of Elugelab was vaporized. In place of it was a circular crater 200 feet deep and more than a mile in diameter. More than 80 million tons of solid material was lifted from the earth, to circle it and fall all over the world. Animals and vegetation simply disappeared from the surrounding islands, and birds were incinerated in the air.

The report of the survey team read, in part: "The trees and brush facing the test site had been scorched and wilted by the thermonuclear heat. Many of the terns there were sick, some grounded and reluctant to fly and some with singed feathers, particularly the noddy terns and the sotty terns, whose feathers are dark in color. . . .

"At Engebi [3 miles from ground zero], the group went ashore on an island where the sense of desolation was deepened . . . the body of a bird was seen, but no living animals and only the stumps of vegetation. . . . Among the specimens collected were fish which seemed to have been burned. On each of these fish, the skin was missing from one side, as if, the field notes said at the time, the animal 'had been dropped in[to] a hot pan.'"

The hydrogen bomb was a thousand times more powerful than the Hiroshima bomb, and big enough to have destroyed all five boroughs of New York City.

Edward Teller observed the blast via a seismograph. Scientist Herbert York noted that the setting off of the first hydrogen bomb marked "a moment when the course of the

world suddenly shifted, from the path it had been on to a more dangerous one. . . . Now, it seemed, we had learned how to brush . . . limits aside and to build bombs whose power was boundless."

The following August, the Soviet Union exploded its first hydrogen bomb, and the race accelerated.

There were protests in New York and Rome, but sobriety seemed to escape the world atomic powers, until the exploding of the first of the new *Castle* series of hydrogen bombs, again at Bikini, on February 28, 1954.

In practically all of the tests of fission and thermonuclear devices, those who made them underestimated their power. *Castle Bravo* was supposed to explode with a force of 5 megatons. Instead, it exploded with a force of 15 megatons, the largest-yield thermonuclear device the United States ever tested.

The fireball was nearly four miles in diameter. It trapped people in their bunkers and menaced task force ships far out at sea. The crater left was 250 feet deep and 6,500 feet in diameter.

Physicist Marshal Rosenbluth recalled, "I was on a ship that was thirty miles away, and we had this horrible white stuff [calcium, precipitated from vaporized coral], raining on us. I got 10 rads of radiation from it. It was pretty frightening. There was a huge fireball with these turbulent rolls going in and out. The thing was glowing. It looked to me like a diseased brain up in the sky. It spread until the edge of it looked as if it was almost directly overhead. It was a much more awesome sight than a puny little atomic bomb. It was a pretty sobering and shattering experience."

The incidents that ultimately sobered the world occurred simultaneously, some 82 nautical miles east of Bikini. Several islands—Rongelap, Ailinginae, and Utirik—and their inhabitants were sprayed with radioactive waste. In the midst of them, a Japanese fishing boat, the *Fukuryu Maru*—which translates into *Lucky Dragon*—was also deluged by fallout from the bomb. "Snow white ashes began falling all around the ship," said Captain Isao Tsutsui later. "The ashes continued showering the ship for two hours." And as the ashes fell, the skin of the men aboard began to blister, according to the captain.

In mid-March, the sampan docked in Japan. Every one of its 23 crew members was deathly ill, and all still had white ash on their clothing. Interviewed by Japanese reporters, they told tales of a flash that was a "sudden brilliant sunrise." Their skin first reddened, they said, then turned black as if from severe sunburn, which itched terribly. Doctors examining them stated that the effects of the blast were 10 times greater than that of an ordinary atomic bomb.

A Tokyo newspaper referred to the fallout as "ashes of death," and Japan, which knew better than any other country the horror of atomic fallout, erupted.

Once again, as in industrial accidents and the earlier atomic tests, stonewalling became the order of the day.

Atomic Energy Commission chairman Lewis Strauss issued a disclaimer of responsibility. Bravo, he noted, was a "very large blast, but at no time was the testing out of control. . . ."—an absolute untruth. Even though there was documented evidence that the *Lucky Dragon* was well outside of the designated danger area, Strauss continued to maintain that it was within the area, and he told Eisenhower's press secretary that the boat was probably a "Red spy ship."

But the truth endured. Japan demanded an inquiry into what its press was calling "American atom bombing of Japanese fishermen—a second Hiroshima." Dr. John J. Morton, the director of the United States Atomic Bomb Casualty Commission at Hiroshima, traveled to Tokyo and examined the crew, pronouncing them moderately contaminated, with slightly low white corpuscle counts and radiation wounds on their scalps and skin. But, noted the doctor, they would undoubtedly all recover within a month.

On March 19, 1954, a congressional investigation of the blast began. Not only had the fishermen been victimized by the out-of-control fallout, but 264 natives and 28 American technicians on islands more than 100 miles away from the blast were also reported to have been contaminated.

Meanwhile, Japanese police tried to track down the catch of the *Lucky Dragon*. Twelve thousand pounds of shark and tuna had been unloaded and sold, and all of it was radioactive—enough, said police reports, to be fatal to any person who remained for eight hours within 30 yards of the contaminated fish. This was overstatement, but the fish did have the potential of causing severe radiation sickness to those who handled or ingested it.

The catch that had not been sold was retrieved and buried in a deep trench, but markets in Tokyo, Osaka, and Nagoya, which would receive contaminated fish, destroyed tons of it.

Eight hundred pounds of tuna from the *Lucky Dragon* reached the Katayama packing plant in Shimizu, and an unknown quantity was canned. Shimizu officials immediately impounded the canned tuna, and it was buried, along with all of the remaining unprocessed tuna.

In Tokyo, the Central Market was flushed down with a high-powered fire hose after tons of fish were similarly buried. But the number of shoppers, warned off by media publicity, were few.

In Tokyo Hospital, tests continued on the contaminated fishermen, whose skin was turning progressively blacker and whose hair had begun to fall out. Their ship was inspected with Geiger counters and found to be still heavily radioactive.

Stonewalling in Washington was no longer possible. In reply to increasingly negative news, the U.S. Atomic Energy Commission increased the danger zone to 450 miles from Bikini, and President Eisenhower admitted, in a speech on March 24, that the Bravo explosion "surpassed the expectations of the United States scientists who devised it." Representative Chet Holifield of California went further, describing the explosion as "so far beyond what was predicted that you might say it was out of control."

On March 25, U.S. ambassador John Allison assured the families of the contaminated fishermen that the United States would pay for medical care, support of the families, and wages lost by the fishermen during their hospitalization.

This was small comfort for the Japanese, who now revealed that radioactive ash had also been falling for some time on Japan from Russian atomic tests in Siberia.

Further examination of the fishermen revealed the presence of strontium 90 in their systems, which indicated that long-term effects from the radiation could be expected. Dr. Masanori Nakaizumi, the top radiation specialist at Tokyo University, examined the fishermen and noted that radioactive elements had lodged in the bones, liver, and kidneys of the victims, which indicated a more lethal power in the bomb exploded at Bikini than either of those that destroyed Hiroshima and Nagasaki, whose victims' vital organs had not been invaded by radioactivity.

On March 27, two more radiation-contaminated fishing boats, the *Myojin Maru* and the *Loei Maru*, both of which had been approximately 780 miles from the blast sight, docked near Tokyo. Although both boats registered Geiger counter readings above the danger point, only one crewman, from the *Myojin Maru*, was sick. Thirty-seven tons of tuna, carried by the fishing vessels, was found to be radioactive, and was buried.

As March turned to April, more Japanese fishing boats coming back to harbor from the vicinity of the Marshall Islands were found to be contaminated. On April 12, several boats that had been 1,000 to 1,500 miles from the blast site still retained some radioactivity. By June, five crew members of a Japanese freighter that passed 1,200 miles off the Marshalls were hospitalized, suffering from radiation sickness.

At the end of August, Aikichi Kuboyama, the radio operator aboard the *Lucky Dragon*, suddenly became seriously ill. Jaundice and brain fever beset him, and he was admitted to Tokyo Hospital. Three days later, seven crewmen from a Japanese ship that had surveyed radioactivity in the Bikini area after the spring hydrogen bomb tests began to complain of liver trouble. Their illness was considered not serious, and they were released. And the 40-year-old Kuboyama seemed to be rallying, too.

But by the end of September, he began to weaken, his heart too battered from illness to sustain his latest relapse. He spent much of the month in a coma, and on September 23, he died.

Everyone, it seemed, regretted the death of the fisherman except Representative Carl Hinshaw, Republican of California, who suggested that Communist influences in Asia were magnifying the man's death. "Warnings were posted months in advance," said Representative Hinshaw, in clear contravention of the facts, which, because he was chairman of the subcommittee on Research of the Congressional Committee on Atomic Energy, he well knew.

Now the economics of the situation began to state themselves. The Japanese fishing industry estimated its losses at several million dollars and mounting. The waters nearly 500 miles south of Bikini were tested and were found to be so contaminated that all fishing was banned in them.

It would be a year before the tally was finally made, and when it was, the United States paid $2 million in damages to the Japanese government in compensation for medical costs to the crewmen, expenses for destroying fishing catches, and losses to the Japanese fishing industry.

For years, the Japanese fishermen who had been bombarded by radioactive fallout would be beset by recurring illnesses and low blood counts. And it would be a full two years before navy physicians reported the apparent recovery of all of the 264 Pacific islanders who had been dusted by radioactive fallout. It was admitted that Rongelap Island, 100 miles downwind from Bikini, had been the most heavily hit. Fallout had not only affected the islanders, but had been absorbed into the island's food and water supply.

Despite overwhelming international evidence to the contrary, U.S. Atomic Energy Commission chairman Lewis L. Strauss maintained that the contaminated fishing boats had ignored U.S. warnings, which, he said, were ample and given in advance to all shipping interests before the test was conducted.

World figures took a more universal and long-term view. Indian Prime Minister Jawaharal Nehru decried the hydrogen bomb tests and asked for an ending to them. "These experiments show man is unleashing power which can ultimately get out of his control," said Nehru. And Dr. Hideki Yukawa, the winner of a 1949 Nobel Prize for atomic research, joined him, stating that "this is a problem of atomic energy versus mankind."

But the genie was out of the bottle, and was not about to climb back in. Theoretical physicist Herbert York, the first director of the Lawrence Livermore Laboratory, where essential research on the development of the hydrogen bomb took place, ruminated, after the Eniwetok and Bikini tests, and Edward Teller's jubilant message that "it's a boy!" had arrived, that humankind had arrived at "a moment when the course of the world suddenly shifted from the path it had been on to a more dangerous one. . . . Now, it seemed, we [have] learned how to brush . . . limits aside and to build bombs whose power [is] boundless."

And the testing goes on, despite pleas and plans for international test ban treaties.

On September 10, 1996, the 50th United Nations General Assembly was reconvened at the request of Australia for the purpose of receiving and acting upon the Comprehensive Test Ban Treaty, which had been two and a half years in the making. It was adopted, and on September 24, 1996, President Clinton was the first to sign it, for the United States.

As of April 7, 1998, 149 nations have signed the treaty, including all five nuclear-weapons states. Ratification by national parliaments—and the Congress of the United States—has been slower in coming. Only 13 have ratified it.

What is most disturbing is that three of the 44 nations whose ratification is required for entry into force have *not* signed the treaty: North Korea, Pakistan, and, ironically, the country of Nehru: India.

TIBET
(SHIGATSE)
FLOOD
August 10, 1954

....

Wholesale destruction of protective walls by Chinese Communist conquerers of Tibet allowed the Namchung River to run amok in a flood during the monsoon season of August 1954. Thousands of acres of farmland were destroyed, and more than 1,000 people drowned.

Until A.D. 821, Tibet was a warlike, half-civilized country. But by 821, its character had undergone a remarkable and miraculous change. Decades of inroads made by Buddhist monks and priests had moved the country steadily toward a more spiritual, less warlike culture, and now it became a full-fledged theocracy.

The Dalai Lamas, residing in Lhasa, maintained control of the politics of the country; the Panchen Lamas of the Tashi-ihumpo monastery at Shigatse tended to the country's religious core. From then until 1950, they maintained an isolated existence, cut off from the world by the Himalayas and the Tibetan meditative lifestyle.

Their relations with China had always been strained, but from the time of its conversion to a theocracy, Tibet was considered no more a problem to China than it was to the rest of the world. And so it was left alone.

All of this changed with the Communist assumption of power in China in 1949. Buddhism, to this government, was a belief to be conquered rather than held, and so the Chinese Communists swept into an unarmed Tibet in 1950. The powerless country pleaded with the United Nations (UN) to intervene, which the UN then did, appealing to China to cease its carnage. But China ignored the UN and proceeded to gut and destroy Tibet's ancient monasteries and capture and imprison its Dalai and Panchen Lamas.

By the summer of 1954, Shigatse, the former spiritual center of what was once Tibet but was now China, had become a center of commerce. Its location on the Namchung River made it an ideal trading post.

But that summer was one of fierce and unceasing rains for the former Tibet. Small mudslides turned into avalanches; ponds became lakes, lakes—particularly Lake Takri Troma, which fed into the Namchung River—burst their banks. By mid-July, the Namchung had become a raging torrent that inundated agricultural land, spilling into and then destroying the villages that bordered it.

The towns of Shigatse and Gyantze were protected by ancient flood walls, but these had been breached and bombed by Chinese troops in the 1950 offensive and never rebuilt. And so, when, on August 10, the Namchung roared into the two cities, there was nothing to slow its speed or destructive power.

Within hours, both cities were under water. People and animals alike were swept to their deaths or drowned by the inundation. More than 200 residents of Shigatse took refuge in the former palace of the Panchen Lama. There, they felt, the spiritual echoes would protect them. But on August 11, the palace, undermined by the floodwaters, collapsed, crushing most of the refugees within it.

Secular shelters fared no better. More than 500 Chinese troops were buried and drowned when their barracks collapsed under the assault of the floodwaters.

The rains stopped and the waters receded shortly after they leveled Shigatse and much of Gyantze, drowning rescue squads from Peking and inundating Kalimpong, India, where Gyalu Thondup, the brother of the young Dalai Lama, was on vacation.

Records were sparse and ill-kept in the two cities, recently gutted by both the Chinese military and the Namchung River. Estimates varied, but the consensus was that nearly 1,000 persons died in a catastrophe that did not really have to happen.

UNITED STATES
(NEW MEXICO, LOS ALAMOS)
DETONATION OF FIRST ATOMIC BOMB
July 16, 1945

The atomic age began with the detonation of the first atomic bomb at a site near Los Alamos, New Mexico, at 5:30 in the morning on July 16, 1945. No one who had been associated with the long development of the bomb could have predicted its power and its awful potential for physical, political, moral, and environmental destruction.

> *If the radiance of a thousand suns*
> *Were to burst at once into the sky.*
> *That would be like the splendor*
>   *of the Mighty One . . .*
> *I am become Death,*
> *The shatterer of worlds.*

According to J. Robert Oppenheimer, the director of the Los Alamos testing of the atomic bomb, and, in media parlance, the "father" of the atomic age, these words from the Bhagavad Gita reverberated in him at 5:29:45 A.M. on July 16, 1945. That was the precise instant that the first atomic bomb was detonated, and the moment that the world entered the atomic age.

It might well be so that the words found a space in him during that monumental moment. Oppenheimer, like the men around him and before him—Albert Einstein, Enrico Fermi, Klaus Fuchs, James B. Conant, Kenneth Bainbridge, James Chadwick, Ernest Lawrence, and Major General Leslie Groves, the head of the Manhattan Project—were all learned men, to whom poetry, philosophy, and music came as easily and readily as equations. That their work would change the course of civilization, that it would open the possibility of paradise or the destruction of the world itself was undoubtedly a possibility that each of these men foresaw.

And yet, the exigencies and demands of war made it logical and expedient to, if not minimize these potentialities, at least place them in a lower priority than that of winning a war.

More than that occurred with both the Los Alamos testing and the bombing of Hiroshima and Nagasaki (see pp. 206–11). The devastation of both an inner and outer environment took place, too. The land was polluted in the desert of New Mexico, and in the cities of Hiroshima and Nagasaki and would never be the same again. But a kind of spiritual pollution happened within some of the men involved with the project, too.

First, there was elation, over the discovery, and the fact that America had beaten Germany in the race for atomic knowledge. Then, there was guilt, over the horrendous carnage caused by the bomb and the radiation that, like the poisoning of a people by mercury or chemicals, was unleashed. And finally, there was fear, which came quickly, with the leaking of atomic secrets to the Russians by Klaus Fuchs, one of the scientists intimately involved with the development of the atomic bomb and the Los Alamos tests.

And that fear exists today, as more and more countries acquire what was only known to a handful of scientists in the 1940s.

The splitting of the atom in 1934 by Enrico Fermi led to the discovery of fission in uranium in 1939 by the German scientists Otto Hahn and Fritz Stassman, which in turn led to the famous letter to President Franklin Delano Roosevelt by a group of scientists including Fermi and Einstein, suggesting an atomic bomb. And finally, this led to the designation of the Manhattan Project, so-named after the Manhattan Engineer District, in which a no-nonsense general, Leslie R. Groves, was put in charge of the development of the bomb.

General Groves was given a virtually unlimited budget and control over several secret locations, which were to be used to develop various parts of the bomb. Fermi discovered and worked on the principle of self-sustaining nuclear reaction at the metallurgical laboratory at the University of Chicago, where 2 billion dollars were spent to obtain sufficient amounts of the two necessary isotopes, uranium-235 and plutonium-239.

At Oak Ridge, Tennessee, the uranium-235 was separated from the much more abundant uranium-238. At the Hanford, Washington, installation, nuclear reactors were built to transmute non-fissionable uranium-238 into plutonium-239.

All of this took place between 1941 and 1945. By the end of the preliminary work, World War II was in its sixth year. Germany had surrendered, and Japan had been set back on its heels by the combined air and naval bombardment of the U.S. Third Fleet. Simultaneously, plans for the invasion of Japan and the Potsdam conference, in which America, Great Britain, and the Soviet Union would sort out the postwar future, were formulated.

And it was at this juncture in history that the decision to drop the atomic bomb on Japan was made. Two years before this, preparations had been made to bring all of the knowledge that had been assembled so far into the reality of a test, in Los Alamos, New Mexico, in a venture that would be headed by Robert Oppenheimer, but closely overseen by General Groves.

The site was a mesa, named after the cottonwoods that covered it. On it was the Los Alamos Ranch School, a boys' school that would be appropriated, along with the 54,000 acres surrounding it, by the U.S. government. Once, Oppenheimer had confided to a friend, "My two great loves are physics and New Mexico. It's a pity they can't be combined." They would be, cataclysmically.

Work began on setting up the site in March 1943. Laboratory buildings and temporary homes, many of them nothing more than log cabins, were erected. Eventually, a huge complex would grow on the site, serviced by 20 miles of new blacktop road and a transportation fleet of more than a hundred vehicles, a complete communications network of telephone lines, public address systems, and FM radios, stockrooms to house tons of equipment, and a huge tower that would eventually contain the bomb.

Security was fearsomely tight. What the scientists were planning—and they knew this because they specifically studied this natural phenomenon—was something of the magnitude of the explosion of Krakatau, the volcano that blew itself and an entire island off the face of the earth, killed 36,000 persons, and unleashed a cloud of pumice that plunged much of the world into darkness for 16 hours and circled the earth for three years.

The bomb that would be detonated would not explode, but implode, and although the uranium, already assembled for one bomb, was plentiful in supply from Oak Ridge, it was decided to use plutonium, because it fissioned more readily,

detonated more rapidly, and was needed in a smaller amount than U-235.

The design was completed, and General Groves reported to the Joint Chiefs of Staff that several implosion bombs, with an explosive power equivalent to "several thousand tons of TNT," would be ready between March and July 1945.

The scientists at Los Alamos picked a site in the northwest corner of the army air corps base near Alamogordo and the Jornada del Muerto in southern New Mexico. They reasoned that the prevailing winds were northwest, and the only town in that direction was Carrizozo, with fewer than 1,400 inhabitants. The scientists knew that there would be radioactive fallout—how much, they were uncertain, but they knew it would occur, and the relative barrenness of the site, plus the presence of the Oscura Mountains to the east, which would deflect some of the fallout and cushion the shock wave, led them to choose it.

But further exploration led them to some decisions that would be echoed into the present, in every major atomic catastrophe, from Three Mile Island to Chernobyl. This further exploration turned up more human beings besides the inhabitants of Carrizozo, who would be directly in the line of fallout. There were 200 Apache living to the east of the site on the other side of the Sierra Oscura. And there were some 1,000 cattle and sheep ranchers scattered about the vicinity.

The problem was obvious: How could these people be evacuated if a crisis of radiation fallout should occur? There were only three exits from the site, none of them particularly passable. It was decided that evacuation would be impossible, and probably unnecessary. And it was left at that.

It was a grand plan all right, and its 432-square-mile birthplace was named, biblically, Trinity—by the same Dr. Robert Oppenheimer who would later quote the Bhagavad Gita.

If there was a sense of urgency about the assembling of the bomb at Trinity, it was only to drop it before the war in Japan ended. Intelligence and captured documents from Strasbourg and other centers revealed that the Germans had gotten nowhere with their research into atomic power, and now, with the war over for them, they never would.

The plutonium arrived, and jitters over radiation poisoning increased. If the soldiers were unaware of this new source of pollution and death, the scientists were, and they took no chances.

In February 1945, the schedule for the test was frozen, and at the same time, two mammoth plants at Oak Ridge turned out the enriched U-235 that was shipped to Los Alamos to assemble into the gun bomb that would, without testing, be dropped on Hiroshima. The plutonium bomb would prove that the process worked.

Since 1940, the raw uranium that was needed for the bomb had been mined in the Shinkolobwe mine of Katanga

Province, in the Belgian Congo. From there it had been shipped in drums in vessels that dodged U-boats in the South Atlantic. Two of the ships had been sunk, but by the end of 1944, some 3,700 tons of raw uranium had reached New York City, where it was transferred to railroad cars and taken to Middlesex, New Jersey. From New Jersey, always in secret, it traveled to Tonawanda, New York, where a Union Carbide plant refined it into a chemical compound, uranium tetrachloride. It went through three more refineries and then to Oak Ridge for final separation. And from Oak Ridge it traveled, often in hand-carried suitcases in unmarked private cars, to Los Alamos.

The other ingredient, the plutonium, was transported in secret convoys from Salt Lake City, Utah. Armed men rode in automobiles ahead of and behind converted army ambulances that were outfitted with struts and braces to hold the 20-pound cannisters of the material steady.

That same month, the island of Tinian, in the South Pacific, was being readied for the B-29s of the 509th Composite Group, from Wendover Field, Utah. Once there, the members of the group and their airplanes would await the results of Trinity.

On April 12, Franklin Delano Roosevelt died, and President Harry Truman was given the responsibility of the testing and dropping of the first atomic bombs.

The transition had no effect upon those at Los Alamos. Work plunged forward, and on April 25, a memo with enormous and lasting implications for the environment and world survival was circulated from the Department of the Army. It detailed the advantages and use of radiation fallout as a weapon of war. The concept was to render an area of 100 square kilometers uninhabitable through fallout, as the memo described it, a "thunderstorm that would rain down fallout." It was chilling in its possibilities.

In June, the tower that was to contain the bomb began to rise to its 100-foot height, with a steel stairway, a platform station every 25 feet, and a wooden stage at the top to hold the bomb.

As the test neared, Oppenheimer and the other scientists began to voice concern about the fine points of the military and political implications of the dropping of the bomb on Japan. Oppenheimer and several others, in fact, sent memos to the White House urging that the United States, before using the weapon, advise its chief allies and suggest future controls for world peace. The suggestions were rejected.

Almost at the same moment, two explosive assemblies, one at Trinity and the other at Los Alamos, were being simultaneously assembled. The tower was completed; the assembly of the bomb was proceeding, not without moments of tension. Never before had so much nuclear material been handled at one spot.

From time to time, a three-foot long hypodermic needle was inserted into the "plug," or globe, of plutonium at the core of the bomb to monitor the rising neutron count.

Swirls of sand, kicked up by the desert wind, danced around the tent housing the operation. At one point the plug stuck; at another, a thunderstorm arrived, with its possibility of detonating the bomb by a lightning strike.

On Saturday, July 14, the bomb was transported to the tower. Five tons of unknown power was grappled and hoisted, over a 12-foot-high pile of GI mattresses that had been hauled into place in case the hoisting cable broke.

Raised into place, the bomb was now coated with racks, brackets, detonators, and monitoring wires. And as the last of these was being attached, another thunderstorm grumbled and crackled around the tower, as if nature itself were making a comment about the proceedings.

Everything was in place, even a poem, titled the "Los Alamos Blues," composed for the occasion:

From this crude lab that spawned the dud,
Their necks to Truman's axe uncurled,
Lo, the embattled savants stood
And fired the flop heard round the world.

Within a five-mile radius of the tower, the desert was pockmarked with gauges and instruments designed to measure the shock wave, the heat, the fallout. Silver barrage balloons were readied to hoist more instruments into the sky; cameras were outfitted; spectographs were readied.

At the eleventh hour, it was decided to measure the effect of the blast on "buildings," and so, small boxes filled with excelsior, some with live mice strung up by their tails from signal wires, were positioned near ground zero. The boxes would remain until the blast; all of the mice would die of thirst long before the ignition.

On the night of July 15, Oppenheimer climbed the tower one last time. Shortly after that, the weather began to deteriorate. Blustery drizzle whipped at the structure and ominous lightning flashes silhouetted the scene.

At 2:30 A.M., the thunderstorm hit full force, and it appeared as if the shot would have to be scrubbed. But by 4:00 A.M., the storm abated, and plans moved forward. At 4:45 A.M., a final weather check proved optimistic. The rain had stopped; the wind was blowing generally to the east, which would put the blowout cloud squarely above a regiment of soldiers.

At 5:10 A.M. on July 16, 1945, a full-throated rendition of "The Star-Spangled Banner" was played over the public address system, and the countdown began.

At 5:20, on various slopes, scientists and reporters jockeyed for positions. They had been advised to lie or sit down on the ground and cover their eyes with pieces of dark welder's glass.

At zero minus two minutes, in the main bunker, a translucent screen became the focus of attention. A periscope jutted up from the top of the bunker. The image of the explosion would enter the periscope and then be projected

The first of many mushroom plumes was glimpsed by an awestruck and select audience with the detonation of the first atomic bomb at Los Alamos, New Mexico, on July 16, 1945.
(LIBRARY OF CONGRESS)

on the screen. The attention of everyone in the bunker except the men at the control console was riveted to it.

At the base camp, a siren wailed, long and relentlessly, directing the soldiers and scientists to their trenches.

At the same time, a B-29, sent aloft to monitor the explosion, approached the rim of Trinity. The crew members donned polaroid glasses, as instructed. Both pilot and copilot would, within a month, be in separate planes, one to deliver the bomb to Hiroshima, the other to observe that explosion.

At 45 seconds, the automatic timer engaged. At 10 seconds, a gong sounded over the public address system. At 5 seconds, motion picture cameras, stationed 10,000 yards north and west from the tower, began to whir.

At exactly 5:29:45 A.M. on July 16, a tiny pinprick of light pierced the predawn darkness. As it grew into a bell-shaped fire mass, it became the brightest light ever produced on Earth up to that moment. Heat, four times greater than that at the center of the sun, was discharged. The earth under the bomb caved in at more than 100 billion atmospheres, the most to ever occur on the earth's surface. And the radioactivity that rushed outward was equal to 1 million times that of the world's total radium supply.

Black dust boiled in all directions, and wherever it touched, everything living died. Within milliseconds, no

grass, no buildings, no organisms survived the heat, the radiation, and the shock wave.

It would take seconds for this shock wave to reach the bunkers, and when it did, it knocked some of the scientists off their feet. They scrambled up again and embraced each other in jubilation, all save Enrico Fermi, who, the eternal scientist, dribbled scraps of paper to the ground, and watched them sweep suddenly away from him as the shock wave arrived. He paced the distance to the scraps immediately, and within seconds, arrived at the estimation that the force of the explosion was the equivalent of 20,000 tons of TNT.

For an instantaneous moment, the fireball was spiked with the wires and switches of the tower. Then, they vaporized. Desert sand was scooped up into the fireball, turning it brown, then other colors, as fresh bursts of luminous gases broke through its surface.

It hurtled upward. At 2,000 feet, it turned reddish yellow, then blood red. Light filtering through it turned the landscape lavender. At 15,000 feet, it became orange, then pink, and as it climbed toward 20,000 feet it metamorphosed into the mushroom shape that would forever become the signature symbol of atomic power. At 40,000 feet, the cloud flattened into a mile-wide pancake of gray ash, haloed by purple ionized air. Above it, a nearly benign violet afterglow crowned the northward drifting dustcloud.

On the ground, the euphoria of the scientists was contradicted by speechless, dumbfounded silence among the enlisted men, and by hysteria in a few, who had to be sedated by medics.

Shortly after 6:00 A.M., Geiger counters began to record the drift of radioactive fallout directly toward a shelter to the north of the explosion area. Scientists and GIs dashed to their trucks and cars and raced ahead of the brown cloud bearing down on them. By the time they reached the base camp, several of the vehicles were riding on their wheel rims.

General Groves phoned his headquarters at 6:30. "It worked," he said.

Meanwhile, three tanks, containing George Weil, Herbert Anderson, and Enrico Fermi, approached the epicenter. The Geiger counters in the tanks went berserk. Weil and Fermi's tanks broke down a mile from the site, but Anderson drove on, into what seemed to be another world.

The crater was coated with green ceramic-like glass. The heat of the blast had fused the sand and dumped it back on the desert surface as glass bead, which would later be dubbed "pearls of Trinity," or trinitite. The tower had totally disappeared, and its concrete stumps had been driven into the dirt. The crater was 1,200 feet wide and 25 feet deep at its center.

A retriever gathered dirt samples that sent the tank's Geiger counter off the top of its scale, and it, the tank, and the tank's inhabitants, mindful of overexposure to radiation, turned and fled from the area, leaving behind a scene of inconceivable destruction.

A nearby tower, the height of a six-story building, lay crumpled like discarded wire. Nothing that could crawl, walk, or fly was alive. Carbonized shadows of tiny animals were etched into the soil. Yuccas and Joshua trees had disappeared; not a single blade of grass survived.

The gauges and cameras that were to record the event had been mangled and paralyzed. Radioactive gases had ruined equipment with condensation; the blinding light and gamma-ray emission had blackened the films in the cameras, except for a fortunate few.

The bomb had exceeded all expectations and predictions, and very nearly the imagination of its creators. There would be thousands of lessons learned from the test; the immediate, tactical one would be that a height of 100 feet for the explosion produced more radiation than blast. Since the army had decided to kill the Japanese by explosion rather than radiation, it was decided to explode the Hiroshima bomb at an extreme height.

The fallout cloud from the blast drifted northeastward at about 10 miles per hour, dropping fission products across a region 100 miles long and 30 miles wide. It settled on cattle-grazing plains and over such communities as Coyote, Ancho, Tecolote, and Vaughn. It, too, exceeded predictions and was caught in an inversion, or wind updraft, that carried it over the cattle ranches of Chupadera Mesa, west of Carrizozo, before it finally dissipated itself around Gallinas Peak, 65 miles north of Carrizozo.

For weeks afterward, discolored birds and rats, dogs and cats with crippled paws, and cattle that had been blistered and stripped of some of their hair, hobbled, then died on ranches in the area. Lawsuits followed.

On August 21, the first fatality among those testing the first atomic bomb occurred. Purdue physicist Harry Daghlian, who had assisted in the assembly of the bomb, died a painful death. His hands swelled horribly, and the skin fell from his body in patches. It would take him a month to die.

The news of the blast was sent to President Harry Truman and Secretary of State Henry Stimson, who were at Potsdam, planning the postwar rehabilitation of the world. It reached Winston Churchill the next day, and he remarked to Stimson, "What was gunpowder? Trivial. What was electricity? Meaningless. This atomic bomb is the Second Coming in Wrath."

VIETNAM
(SOUTH)
DEFOLIATION CAMPAIGN WITH AGENT ORANGE, SPREAD BY U.S. ARMED FORCES
Late 1961–April 1970

Approximately 4.2 million acres of mangroves were defoliated, 468,559 acres of crops were destroyed, 1,000 inhabitants and 13,000 head of livestock were killed by "Operation Ranch-

hand," the spraying of Agent Orange, an herbicide-containing dioxin, during the Vietnam War.

It is entirely possible that the very first use of chemical weapons in warfare occurred with the first flinging of fireballs at fortified cities in the fifth century B.C. It would be a long time—the middle of the 19th century—before this military technique would mature into the manufacture of poison gas, and the advent of World War I before it became a major weapon of war.

Chlorine gas was first released by the Germans at Ypres in 1915, followed by a more widespread use of mustard gas. The French, in retaliation, developed the gas shell, far more effective than wind-blown gas. The atrocious aftermath, the horrible, long dying of those soldiers affected by poison gas led to a proposed worldwide banning of its use, as proscribed by the Geneva Protocol of 1925.

But the proposed ban had no teeth, and poison gas was used by Italians against Ethiopians in 1935 and by the Japanese against Chinese guerrillas from 1937 to 1942. It was, however, not used at all in World War II.

That did not mean that nations stopped developing poison gas. During World War II, in fact, Germany developed and stockpiled the worst of all, nerve gas, which is odorless and kills by assaulting every nerve in the body.

It was nerve gas that Saddam Hussein used against Kurds in his own country, and now it seems that the blowing up of bunkers containing nerve gas during the Gulf War has resulted in contamination of United Nations troops, mainly Americans. The result is what has come to be known as Gulf War Syndrome.

During World War II, the United States was also developing a chemical weapon utilizing herbicides. Between 1941 and 1946, Agent Orange, named after the color-coded stripe that was painted around the 55-gallon barrels in which it was stored, was developed by the U.S. Army at Fort Detrick, Maryland.

The contents of the barrels was a combination of equal parts of two commercial herbicides, 2,4-D (n-butyl-2,4-dichlorophenoxyacetate) and 2,4,5-T (n-butyl-2,4,5-trichlorophenoxyacetate). Hidden within the numbers and formulas was TCDD, or dioxin, one of the most lethal of all substances developed by humans and deadly not only to the person afflicted but to generations following that person. In the same way that radiation enters the food chain of a country and the reproductive mechanism of its victims (see Japan: Hiroshima and Nagasaki, pp. 206–11), so does dioxin, as was proved in the United States in 1978 at Love Canal in New York State (see pp. 112–16) and Times Beach, Missouri (see pp. 108–11).

Both during and after the war in Vietnam, the National Academy of Sciences warned the military about the consequences of biological warfare. The military assured the academy that it was merely developing defoliants that

U.S. Air Force planes spraying Agent Orange over South Vietnam as part of a nine-year defoliant campaign.
(AP/WIDE WORLD)

"I really didn't know what they were spraying," explained John Green, a medic, to Fred Wilcox, author of *Waiting for an Army to Die*. "Some people thought it was for mosquitoes, but I never really gave it much thought. I do remember walking through defoliated zones. Everything was dead. The trees had literally grown to death, because that's how Agent Orange works—it accelerates growth in a plant's cells until finally the plant or tree dies. Did we drink the water? Of course we did. Where we were there was nothing else to drink. If we found a bomb crater full of water we just scooped it out and drank it, no matter how brown or scummy it looked. Some of our food was undoubtedly sprayed with Agent Orange. But how were we to know? The army told us the stuff was harmless. And we were told it was supposed to be saving our lives."

The environment was being assaulted as it never had been before. In the coastal mangroves, entire plant communities were wiped out. In the forests, trees dropped their leaves, allowing so much light to penetrate the forest floor that bamboos and tenacious grasses took hold. After the spraying, enormous "Rome plows," with blades 10 feet wide were used to plow up the soil to prevent the forest from regenerating. Meanwhile, dioxin had entered the food chain, which would spread the effect of Agent Orange to livestock and humans on both sides of the conflict.

As Operation Ranch Hand increased in its intensity, two other herbicides were added: Agent Blue and Agent White. Agent Blue was an aqueous solution containing arsenic and about 3 pounds per gallon of the sodium salt of cacodylic acid. Its mission: First, to cause the death of grassy plants by spraying enough on these plants so that Agent Blue would be absorbed by the leaves, thus killing the plants in two to four days. Second, to kill off the rice crop. The chemical had an insidious effect upon rice plants, allowing them to develop normally, but never, from the time they were sprayed forward, produce rice. Later—much later—a government memorandum was discovered by the Long Island, New York, paper *Newsday* that also described Agent Blue as a "human carcinogen."

Agent White contained 20 percent picloram and 80 percent isopropylamine salt of 2,4,-D. It killed much as Agent Orange did but was more effective than Orange on the more woody species of plants in the mangroves.

For four years, Operation Ranch Hand ranged back and forth across South Vietnam. Approximately 4.2 million acres of mangroves were defoliated; 468,559 acres of crops were destroyed.

According to writer Seymour Hersh, "A 1967 Japanese study of U.S. anti-crop defoliation methods, prepared by Yoichi Fukushima, head of the Agronomy section of the Japan Science Council, claimed that U.S. anti-crop attacks ruined more than 3.8 million acres of arable land in South Vietnam and resulted in the deaths of nearly 1,000 peasants and more than 13,000 livestock. Fukushima also reported

would "regulate" or destroy the growth of plant life, and not be injurious or lethal to humans or animals.

In 1959, the first large-scale aerial tests of Agent Orange were conducted at Fort Drum, New York, and were so successful that in 1961 Defense Secretary Robert McNamara suggested that further testing be done on jungle vegetation in Vietnam, where the war was under way.

It was a logical step. The Vietnam War was like no other war the United States had fought thus far. The enemy was hardly ever evident. Guerrilla warfare was carried out by the Vietcong under cover of the mangrove forest. The reasoning was that if the mangroves were removed, the enemy would lose its cover and be forced into the open, where American and South Vietnamese ground forces could destroy him.

Late that year, "Operation Ranch Hand" was established. Agent Orange was loaded aboard converted, twin-engine C-123 Provider transports. It was spread in daylight, in a back and forth pattern, much like the mowing of a lawn, at a height of 150 feet, which meant that there were a great many casualties. The Ranch Handers, in fact, were among the most decorated veterans of the Vietnam War.

that one village was attacked more than 30 times by C-123 crop dusters spraying agents more caustic than the arsenic-laden cacodylic acid."

But even at its height, in 1967, there were misgivings about the use of herbicides among other than antiwar activists. Arthur W. Galston, a professor of botany at Yale, warned, in the *New Republic,* "We are too ignorant of the interplay of forces in ecological problems to know how far-reaching and how lasting will be the changes in ecology brought about by the widespread spraying of herbicides. The changes may include immediate harm to people in sprayed areas. . . ."

The danger was already manifest. Not only the environment, but the people of Vietnam and, because of the nature of the war, U.S. troops were being sprayed with Agents Orange, Blue, and White. And although there had already been laboratory research 15 years previous to this that had proved that dioxin was embryotoxic, which meant that it killed embryos in pregnant rodents, and teratogenic, which meant that it caused birth defects in several strains of rats and mice, the government persisted in its claim that Agent Orange and its companions were perfectly harmless to humans.

Dow Chemical, Monsanto, Diamond Shamrock, and Hooker Chemicals also released sanguine news stories that argued that Agent Orange was winning the war without danger to American troops.

But behind the scenes, there was ample proof that the spraying of Agent Orange was a potentially catastrophic exercise. In 1965, Dow Chemical Corporation knew that 2,4,5-T was contaminated with dioxin, and as early as 1962, the government knew that dioxin was toxic. Still, none of the manufacturers of 2,4,5-T conducted further tests until 1969, when President Richard Nixon's science advisor, Dr. Lee DuBridge, proposed that, because of laboratory findings by Bionetics Laboratories in Bethesda, Maryland, which concluded that even in the lowest dose given, 2,4,5-T caused cleft palates, missing and deformed eyes, cystic kidneys, and enlarged livers in the offspring of laboratory animals, further research was advisable.

Ironically, the study that had provided this information had been conducted in 1965, three years *after* Operation Ranch Hand had begun, and five years *before* it was terminated. It was finally made public by a member of the Ralph Nader organization, who had discovered a preliminary report submitted to the Food and Drug Administration by Bionetics Laboratories. And now, the scientific proof became too overwhelming and too public to ignore. By April 1970, it had risen to a worldwide crescendo. The Hart Committee had been formed in Congress, and so the Pentagon ordered the suspension of Operation Ranch Hand. During the same month, the Surgeon General reported to the Hart Committee that he had ordered suspension of 2,4,5-T in liquid formulation for home use and

the suspension of all aquatic uses, and intended to cancel registration of nonliquid formulations for use around homes and on all food crops. Dow immediately appealed the decision to cancel dioxin's use on food crops, and the donnybrook led, later that year, to the transfer of the regulation of pesticides to the Environmental Protection Agency (EPA).

Now, the first manifestations of the effects of Agent Orange on human beings began to appear. Servicemen who had been exposed to the spraying began to develop fierce headaches, massive skin discoloration, mysterious lumps in their groins, and blood in their urine. Joint pain, dizziness, gastrointestinal ulcerations, vomiting, and diarrhea were common. Psychological effects included loss of libido, depression, violent rages, and suicide attempts.

These veterans naturally went to Veterans Administration (VA) Hospitals, and were met with something less than cordiality. In the same way that victims of radiation in Chernobyl would be diagnosed as having "radiationphobia," and soldiers suffering from exposure to poison gas in Iraq were said to be suffering from "Gulf War Syndrome," the vast majority of these Vietnam veterans were at best given pats on the head and aspirin, and at the worst accused of hypochondria.

In the early phases of reaction to those who claimed to suffer from exposure to Agent Orange, the VA claimed that these veterans could not really prove they were exposed to herbicides in Vietnam, hence they were not eligible for service-connected disability payments.

The experience of Jerry Strait, a paratrooper, was typical. After a preliminary examination, the VA doctor assured Strait that "Agent Orange and dioxin have never hurt anyone, are not hurting and never will hurt anyone." His headaches were dismissed as "war-related stress," and the skin rash he exhibited could be treated, he was assured, by a visit to the hospital's dietician.

But further, related incidents could not be so easily minimized. Evidence of birth defects began to surface. In Vietnam, Dr. Ton That Tung studied the possible effects of dioxin on North Vietnamese soldiers exposed to herbicides while serving in the South. Among the birth defects Dr. Tung observed in the children born to the wives of these soldiers after they had been exposed to the herbicides were cleft lips, an absence of a nose, shortened limbs, malformed ears, clubfeet, an absence of forearms, hydrocephaly (water on the brain), anencephaly (a condition in which all or a major part of the brain is missing), and a variety of heart problems.

At a hearing of the New York State Temporary Commission on Dioxin Exposure in 1978, the wife of a U.S. serviceman testified, "Our first son was born with his bladder on the outside of the body, a sprung pelvis, a double hernia, a split penis, and a perforated anus. . . . We have met other Vietnam veterans and their families. We have met their children. We have seen and heard about the deformities, limb and bone deformities, heart defects, dwarfism, and other diseases for which there is no diagnosis."

In 1980, Maureen Ryan, another wife, testified before the U.S. Senate Committee on Veterans Affairs that "what the United States and what our Vietnam veterans did not know was that they carried home a tremendous legacy with them. They did not know that genetically on those battlefields were their children. So Agent Orange is now reaping an additional harvest of birth defects and cancers in our children and the men. We are losing our children through spontaneous abortions, through miscarriages, and perhaps most tragically in the surviving children, with . . . horrifying birth defects."

As early as 1970, Dr. Ton That Tung had stated in a report, "In the abominable history of war, with the sole exception of nuclear weapons, has such an inhuman fate ever before been reserved for the survivors?"

Still, the stonewalling within the Veterans Administration continued, in spite of an increasing number of articles appearing in national magazines and scientific journals regarding the toxicity of Agent Orange. As late as 1978, the VA denied disability payments on the grounds that negative effects of dioxin on human beings had not been proved. It even rejected the decade of research that the Environmental Protection Agency utilized in banning domestic use of 2,4,5-T as research that did not "offer definitive evidence for an adverse effect of herbicides on human health."

Finally, in 1982, after conducting several interior investigations whose conclusions were rejected by Congress, the VA turned its studies over to the Centers for Disease Control.

On and on the controversy raged, until 1993, when Congress finally authorized benefits for Vietnam veterans with seven specific ailments linked to Agent Orange exposure.

In May 1996, this list was expanded to nine with President Clinton's addition of prostate cancer and peripheral neuropathy, a nerve affliction, and a promise to propose legislation that would ask for combat-related compensation for birth defects, specifically spina bifida.

Ironically and tragically, retired admiral Elmo Zumwalt stood at President Clinton's side when he made the announcements. Admiral Zumwalt had ordered the use of Agent Orange in Vietnam, and his son, who served in Vietnam, had died of a cancer caused by Agent Orange.

Meanwhile, to this day, the ecosystem of South Vietnam is devastated by the spreading of Agent Orange. Dioxin entered the food chain and will remain there for decades—perhaps generations—to come.

In the United States, the battles between chemical companies, agricultural interests, and environmentalists, represented by environmental groups and the EPA, over the use of herbicides continues. Until 1975, the National Forest Service routinely sprayed 2,4,5-T on government lands, and for years afterward, Dow Chemical Company sued in the courts for resumption of the spraying.

The tug-of-war continues, despite the horrific evidence of the toxicity and violent death-dealing power of dioxin. The experience of Ray Clark, a Vietnam veteran interviewed by Fred Wilcox for his book *Waiting for an Army to Die*, is perhaps a microcosm of the problem. A victim of bladder cancer, he and his wife looked forward to spending the remainder of his life near Syracuse, New York.

"I want the system changed," he told Mr. Wilcox in 1980, "so that we're not guinea pigs, and so we don't let the government, or anyone else, do this again. . . . They have completely forgotten about us. I think they're just waiting for all of us to die, and then someone can say, 'Oh dear, maybe we did make a mistake with this Agent Orange.'"

That same night, two dead owls were found a short distance from the Clarks' home. State officials later said it was possible they had eaten fish or small animals contaminated with dioxin from Lake Ontario. "Lately," Mrs. Clark told Mr. Wilcox, "we've been looking for a safe place to move. But the more we looked, the more we realized there really is no place to hide."

SELECTED BIBLIOGRAPHY

Akizuki, Tatsuichiro. *Nagasaki 1945*. New York: Quartet Books, 1981.

Allaby, M. Green. *Green Facts: The Greenhouse Effect and Other Key Issues*. London: Hamlyn, 1989.

Allan, Thomas. *Code-Name Downfall: The Secret Plan to Invade Japan and Why Truman Dropped the Bomb*. New York: Simon & Schuster, 1995.

Alperovitz, et. al. *The Decision to Use the Atomic Bomb*. New York: Vintage, 1995.

Bernard, Harold W. Jr. *The Greenhouse Effect*. Cambridge, Mass.: Ballinger, 1980.

Beyer, Dan. *The Manhattan Project*. New York: Watts, 1991.

Blumberg, Stanley A., and Louis G. Panos. *Edward Teller*. New York: Charles Scribner's Sons, 1990.

Bolch, Ben, and Harold Lyos. *Apocalypse Not*. Washington, D.C.: Cato Institute, 1993.

Bolt, Bruce A. *Nuclear Explosions and Earthquakes: The Parted Veil*. San Francisco: Freeman, 1976.

Borgstrom, Georg. *Harvesting the Earth*. New York: Abelard-Schuman, 1973.

Boyer, Paul. *By the Bomb's Early Light*. New York: Pantheon, 1985.

Bradley, David. *No Place to Hide*. Boston: Little, Brown, 1948.

Brenner, Eliot, and William Harwood, et al. *Desert Storm: The Weapons of War*. New York: Orion, 1991.

Brown, Michael. *Laying Waste: The Poisoning of America by Toxic Chemicals*. New York: Pantheon, 1980.

Brune, Lester H. *America and the Iraqi Crisis, 1990–1992*. Claremont, Calif.: Regina Books, 1993.

Campbell, M. E., and W. M. Glenn. *Profit from Pollution Prevention*. Toronto: Pollution Probe Foundation, 1982.

Collins, M., ed. *The Last Rain Forests*. London: Mitchell Beazley, 1990.

Darkoh, M. B. K. "The Deterioration of the Environment in Africa's Drylands and River Basins," *Desertification Control Bulletin*, United Nations Environmental Programme, Nov. 24, 1994.

Davidson, Art. *Endangered Peoples*. San Francisco: Sierra Club Books, 1994.

Dethier, V. G. *Man's Plague?* Princeton, N.J.: Darwin Press, 1976.

Dux, John, and P. J. Young. *Agent Orange: The Bitter Harvest*. Sydney, Australia: Hodder and Stroughton, 1980.

Ehrlich, Paul R., and Anne H. Ehrlich. *Healing the Planet*. Reading, Mass.: Addison-Wesley, 1991.

Elkington, John, Tom Burke, and Julia Hailes. *The Business of Saving the World*. London: Routledge Kegan and Paul, 1988.

Elliot, Gil. *Twentieth Century Book of the Dead*. New York: Scribner's Sons, 1972.

Ensign, Tod, and Michael Uhl. *GI Guinea Pigs: How the Pentagon Exposed Our Troops to Dangers More Deadly Than War*. New York: Playboy Press, 1980.

Epstein, Samuel S., Lester Brown, and Carl Pope. *Hazardous Waste in America*. San Francisco, Sierra Club Books, 1982.

Faulkner, Peter. *The Silent Bomb: A Guide to the Nuclear Energy Controversy*. New York, Random House, 1977.

Feis, Herbert. *Japan Subdued: The Atomic Bomb and the End of the War in the Pacific*. Princeton, N.J.: Princeton University Press, 1961.

Freeman, Leslie. *Nuclear Witnesses*. New York: Norton, 1981.

Fuller, John G. *The Poison That Fell from the Sky*. New York: Random House, 1977.

Gallagher, Thomas. *Assault in Norway; Sabotaging the Nazi Nuclear Bomb*. New York: Harcourt Brace Jovanovich, 1975.

Gann, Bill. "Heartburn of Darkness," *Sierra Magazine* 80:6 (December 1995).

Gibbs, Lois Marie. *Love Canal: My Story*. Albany, State of New York Press, 1982.

Graham, Frank, Jr. *Since Silent Spring*. Boston, Houghton Miflin, 1970.

Gribbon, John. *Future Weather and the Greenhouse Effect*. New York, Delacorte, 1982.

Grimmet, R. F. A., and T. A. Jones. *Important Birds and Areas in Europe.* Cambridge, England: International Council for Bird Preservation, 1990.

Groves, Leslie. *Now It Can Be Told: The Story of the Manhattan Project.* New York: Harper, 1962.

Hawley, T. M. *Against the Fires of Hell: The Environmental Disaster of the Gulf War.* New York: Harcourt, Brace, Jovanovich, 1992.

Hersey, John. *Hiroshima.* New York: Knopf, 1985.

Hersh, Seymour. *Chemical and Biological Warfare: America's Hidden Arsenal.* Indianapolis: Bobbs-Merrill, 1968.

Hershberg, James. *James B. Conant: Harvard to Hiroshima and the Making of the Nuclear Age.* New York: Knopf, 1993.

Jaspers, Karl. *The Future of Mankind.* Chicago: University of Chicago Press, 1961.

Lamont, Lansing. *Day of Trinity.* New York: Atheneum, 1965.

Lane, Frank W. *The Elements Rage.* Philadelphia: Chilton, 1965.

Lean, G. Hinrichsen, and A. Markham. *Atlas of the Environment.* London: Arrow, 1990.

Leslie, John. *The End of the World: The Science and Ethics of Human Extinction.* New York: Routledge, 1996.

Lifton, Robert Jay, and Greg Mitchell. *Hiroshima in America: A Half Century of Denial.* New York: Putnam, 1995.

Lilienthal, David. *Change, Hope and the Bomb.* Princeton, N.J.: Princeton University Press, 1963.

Linedecker, Clifford. *Kerry: Agent Orange and an American Family.* New York: St. Martin's, 1982.

Little, Tom. *High Dam at Aswan.* New York: John Day, 1965.

McPhee, John. *The Curve of Binding Energy.* New York: Straus and Giroux, 1974.

Makhigani, Arjun. *From Global Capitalism to Economic Justice.* New York: Apex, 1992.

Marzani, Carl. *The Wounded Earth.* Reading, Mass.: Addison-Wesley, 1972.

Miner, Jane. *Hiroshima and Nagasaki.* New York: Watts, 1981.

Morris, Christopher. *The Day They Lost the H-Bomb.* New York: Coward-McCann, 1966.

Myers, Norman. *Scarcity or Abundance? A Debate on the Environment.* New York: Norton, 1994.

Nichols, Kenneth. *The Road to Trinity.* New York: Morrow, 1987.

Pfeiffer, E. W., Arthur H. Westing, et al. *Harvest of Death: Chemical Warfare in Vietnam and Cambodia.* New York: Free Press, 1971.

Potter, Jeffrey. *Disaster by Oil.* New York, MacMillan, 1973.

Revkin, Andrew. *The Burning Season.* New York: Penguin, 1990.

Rhodes, Richard. *Dark Sun: The Making of the Hydrogen Bomb.* New York: Simon & Schuster, 1995.

Shepherd, Jack. *The Forest Killers.* New York: Weybright and Talley, 1975.

Smith, Aileen, and W. Eugene Smith. *Minamata.* New York: Holt, Rinehart and Winston, 1975.

Stephenson, Lee, and George R. Zachar, eds. *Accidents Will Happen.* Environmental Action Foundation. New York: Harper & Row, 1976.

Stevens, Mark. *Three Mile Island.* New York, Random House, 1980.

Strohmeyer, John. *Extreme Conditions (Big Oil and the Transformation of Alaska).* New York: Simon & Schuster, 1993.

Takaki, Ronald. *Hiroshima: Why America Dropped the Atomic Bomb.* New York: Little, Brown, 1994.

Teller, Edward. *Energy from Heaven and Earth.* New York: Freeman, 1979.

Tenner, Edward. *Why Things Bite Back: Technology and the Revenge of Unintended Consequences.* New York: Knopf, 1996.

United Nations Environment Programme. *Action on Ozone.* Nairobi, Kenya: UNEP, 1993.

———. *The Disappearing Forests.* UNEP Environment Brief #3. Nairobi, Kenya: 1993.

———. *Industry and the Environment.* UNEP Environment Brief #7. Nairobi, Kenya: 1993.

Vance-Watkins, Lequite, and Mariko Aratani. *White Flash, Black Rain.* Minneapolis, Minn.: Milkweed Editions, 1995.

Ward, Barbara, and René Dubos. *Only One Earth.* New York, Norton, 1972.

Webb, Richard E. *The Accident Hazards of Nuclear Power Plants.* Amherst: The University of Massachusetts Press, 1976.

White, Theodore H., and Annalee Jacoby. *Thunder Out of China.* New York: William Sloane Associates, 1946.

Whiteside, Thomas. *The Pendulum and the Toxic Cloud: The Course of Dioxin Contamination.* New Haven and London: Yale University Press, 1979.

———. *The Withering Rain: America's Herbicidal Folly.* New York: Dutton, 1971.

Wilcox, Fred A. *Waiting for an Army to Die: The Tragedy of Agent Orange.* New York: Vintage, 1983.

Winter, Georg. *Business and the Environment.* Hamburg, Germany: McGraw-Hill, 1988.

World Commission on Environment and Development. *Our Common Future.* Oxford, England: Oxford University Press, 1987.

Wyden, Peter. *Day One: Before Hiroshima and After.* New York: Simon & Schuster, 1984.

INDEX

A

Abrams, Robert, 115

Abu Simbel (Nubia), Great Temple at, preservation of, 38–40

Acheson, Dean, 210

acid rain, 123–126
  areas vulnerable to, 124
  causes and types of, 123
  cost of, 125
  effects of, 124
  in Europe and Canada, 75
  and oil-well fires, 214
  solutions to, 124

Acre (Brazil), changes in, 22–23

Adair, Paul "Red," 145, 149–150, 170, 215

Aegean Captain, collision with *Atlantic Express*, Tobago (1979), 154–155

Aegean Sea oil spill, La Coruña, Spain (1992), 153–154

Aetna Chemical Company explosion, Oakdale, Pennsylvania, U.S. (1918), 121–122

Africa, deforestation in, 6–8, 8–10, 10–13

African independence, environmental effects of, 8

Agent Blue, 227

Agent Orange, 47, 85–86, 108
  cover-up of danger of, 227–228
  defoliation campaign in Vietnam, by U.S. military (1961–70), 226–229
  physical effects of, 228–229

Agent White, 227

AIDS, origin of, 10

air pollution. *See also* acid rain; global warming; ozone layer depletion

after Aetna Chemical Company explosion (Oakdale, Pennsylvania), 121–122

after Badische Anilinfabrick Company explosion (Germany, 1921), 78–79

after chemical explosion and fire (Bangkok, Thailand, 1991), 101–102

after Cleveland Clinic explosion (Cleveland, Ohio), 116–119

after East Ohio Gas Company explosion (Cleveland, Ohio, 1944), 120–121

after Fuks and Hagria chemical factory explosion (Łódź, Poland, 1928), 95

after Icmesa chemical plant emission (Seveso, Italy, 1976), 85–89

in London (1950s and '60s), 102–104

after Pemex gas storage tank explosion (Mexico City, Mexico, 1984), 93–95

after Rhine River incident, Basel, Switzerland (1986), 99–101

in southern African cities, 11

after Union Carbide pesticide plant explosion (Bhopal, India, 1984), 81–85

Alaska, U.S., trans-Alaska pipeline explosion (1977), 164–166

Alaska Forest Association, 55

Alaska National Interest Lands Conservation Act (1980), 53

Alaska Pulp Corporation, 53, 54

Allison, John, 220

Alves da Silva, Darly and Darcy, 23–28

Alyeska Pipeline Service Company, 168

Amazon River, pollution of, 46

Amoco Cadiz oil spill, Portsall-Kersaint, France (1978), 135, 140–142

Anatasobolos, George, 138

ancient peoples
  agriculture of, 37
    in Brazil, 21
    Incas, 46
    in Southeast Asia, 49
  conservation practices of, 5

Anderson, Herbert, 225

Anderson, Warren, 84

Antarctic ozone hole, 131

Arabian Sea, pollution in, 43

Aramco Corp., 152–153

Archives of Environmental Contamination and Toxicology (journal), 115

Arctic oil spill, Usnisk, Russia (1994), 150–152

Arctic Wildlife Refuge, 55

Argo Merchant oil spill, Nantucket, Massachusetts, U.S. (1976), 149, 175–178

Arizona Standard, collision with *Oregon*, San Francisco, California, U.S. (1971), 169–170

Arrhenius, Svante, 126

Arrow oil spill, Port Hawkesbury, Nova Scotia, Canada (1970), 138–140

Asia. *See* Southeast Asia, *and specific countries*

Asmal, Kader, 13

Aswan High Dam project, side effects of, 38–42

Atlantic Express, collision with *Aegean Captain*, Tobago (1979), 154–155

ENVIRONMENTAL DISASTERS

Tasman, Abel, 52

Tasmania, forest fire (1967), 52–54

TCDD (dioxin), 108, 112, 226

TCP, 112

tebuthiron (herbicide), 47

technological advances, and global warming, 128

Teller, Edward, 217, 219

Terasaki, Paul, 197

Texas, U.S., dust bowl drought (1933–38), 67–69

Thailand

Bangkok, chemical explosion and fire (1991), 101–102

deforestation of, 52

environmental problems in, 50

Thames River, pollution of, 76

thermonuclear bombs, development of, 217–219

Thieme, R. W., 173

Thornburgh, Richard, 191–192

Thor (ship), 144

Thousand Islands, New York, U.S., St. Lawrence Seaway oil spill (1976), 178–179

Three Gorges Dam (China), 32, 35

Three Mile Island nuclear power plant leak, Middletown, Pennsylvania, U.S. (1979), 190–193

Tibbets, Paul, 207

Tibet, Shigatse, destruction of dykes by Chinese Communists (1954), 221–222

Times Beach, Missouri, U.S., Dioxin contamination (1971–86), 108–111

Tobago, collision of oil tankers *Atlantic Express* and *Aegean Captain* (1979), 154–155

tomato crops, spraying with organophosphate pesticides, 97, 98, 99

Tongass National Forest, Alaska, U.S., deforestation in, 53–55

Ton That Tung, 228, 229

Torrey Canyon oil spill, Cornwall, England, U.K. (1967), 136, 137, 140, 155–160

tourism industry, in southern Africa, and environmental damage, 11

toxic cloud emission, Icmesa chemical plant, Seveso, Italy (1976), 85–89

toxic cooking oil scandal, Madrid, Spain (1981–87), 97–99

toxic fog, London, England (1952), 75, 102–103, 103–104

Train, Russell E., 177

Trans-Alaska Pipeline Authorization Act (1973), 165

trans-Alaska pipeline explosion, Alaska, U.S. (1977), 164–166

Treaty of Paris, 80

Tree huggers, 42, 44

Trenbirth, Kevin, 128

trichloroisoyanuric acid contamination, 101

Truman, Harry S, 206, 210, 224, 226

tsetse fly, 8, 10

Tsuruga, Japan, nuclear power plant leak (1981), 184–186

Tuma, Romeo, 24, 27

Tumerman, Lev, 193

Tundra, vulnerability of, 151

Turkey

damaged fishing industry of, 96

and pollution of Black Sea, 95–97

"Two Decades of Dissidence" (Medvedev), 193

U

Ufa, U.S.S.R., gas pipeline explosion (1989), 123

Ukraine

nuclear power in, 198

and pollution of Black Sea, 95–97

UNEP. *See* United Nations Environment Programme

UNESCO. *See* United Nations Educational, Scientific and Cultural Organization

UNICEF. *See* United Nations Children's Fund

Unigas Co., 93

Union Carbide pesticide plant explosion, Bhopal, India (1984), 81–85

Union Oil Company, 156, 159–160

United Kingdom

Cornwall, England, *Torrey Canyon* oil spill (1967), 155–160

and dam at Aswan (Egypt), 38

first nuclear tests of, 218

Liverpool, England, Windscale plutonium plant contamination (1957), 186–187

London, England, toxic fog (1952), 75, 102–103, 103–104

Milford Haven, Wales, *Sea Empress* oil spill (1996), 163–164

North Sea, *Bravo* oil rig spill (1977), 148–150

North Sea, Piper Alpha oil rig explosion, 160

Shetland Islands, Scotland, *Braer* oil spill (1993), 160–163

United Nations

and flood relief to Bangladesh, 19

work in Africa, 10

United Nations Children's Fund, in Bangladesh, 39

United Nations Conference on the Human Environment, (Stockholm, 1972), 5, 72, 92, 146

United Nations Conference on the Human Environment (Stockholm, 1974), 131

United Nations Development Programme, in Nepal, 44

United Nations Educational, Scientific and Cultural Organization, 39

United Nations Environment Programme (UNEP), 5, 22, 97

United Nations Food and Agriculture Organization, 26

United Nations University Project (Nepal), 43

United States

atomic and hydrogen bomb tests at Marshall Islands, 216–221

atomic bomb development at Los Alamos, New Mexico (1945), 222–226

collision of oil tankers *Arizona Standard* and *Oregon*, San Francisco, California (1971), 169–170

dam collapse, San Francisquito valley, California (1928), 61–63

deforestation in Tongass National Forest, Alaska, 53–55

dioxin contamination

Love Canal, Niagara Falls, New York, U.S. (1978–85), 112–116

Times Beach, Missouri (1971–86), 108–111

dust bowl drought (1933–38), 67–69

explosion

244

SOMMAIRE

Bienvenue dans l'édition 2020 du livre annuel le plus vendu au monde, totalement mis à jour pour une nouvelle décennie, avec des milliers de records. Dans ces 11 chapitres écrits au superlatif, nous célébrons les exploits les plus étonnants, les plus déroutants... ceux qui donnent tout simplement envie de se dépasser. D'ailleurs, pourquoi ne tenteriez-vous pas de battre un record, vous aussi ?

Les records sont répartis en 11 catégories correspondant chacune à une couleur.

Le livre est illustré d'images saisissantes, prises dans le monde entier. Il contient également de nombreuses photos exclusives.

C'est grand comment ? Rendez-vous compte de la vraie taille de certains records grâce aux photos à échelle 100 %.

100 %

Le GWR bénéficie de l'expertise de spécialistes internationaux sur de nombreux sujets, de l'archéologie à la zoologie. Découvrez tous nos consultants aux pages 250-251.

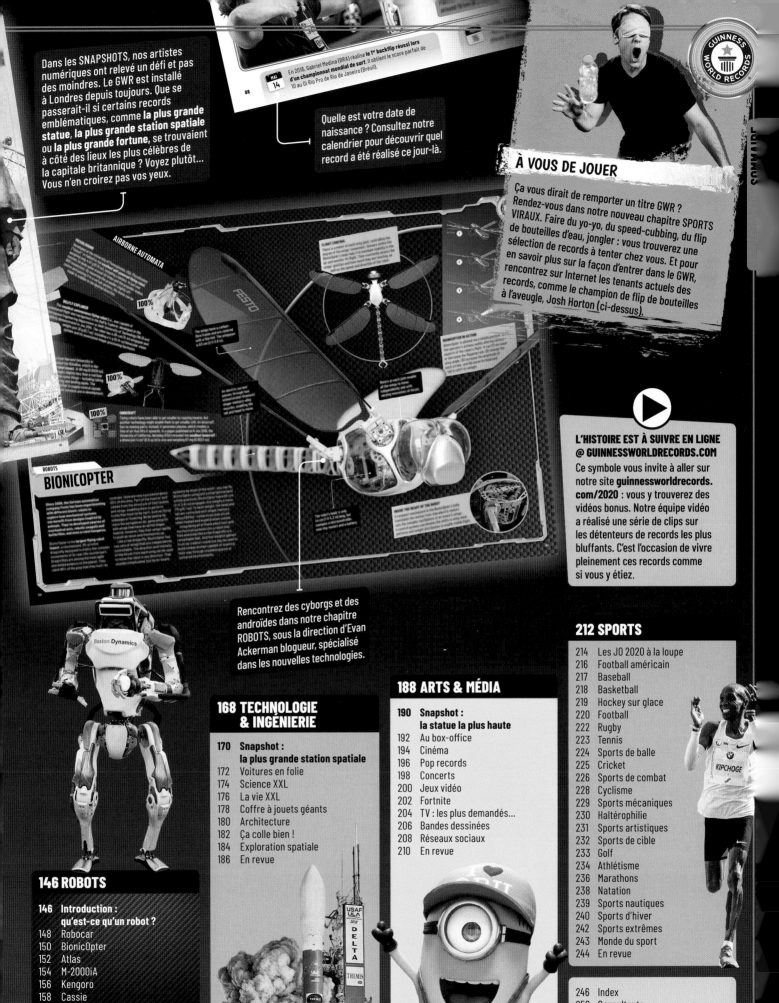

Dans les SNAPSHOTS, nos artistes numériques ont relevé un défi et pas des moindres. Le GWR est installé à Londres depuis toujours. Que se passerait-il si certains records emblématiques, comme **la plus grande statue**, **la plus grande station spatiale** ou **la plus grande fortune**, se trouvaient à côté des lieux les plus célèbres de la capitale britannique ? Voyez plutôt... Vous n'en croirez pas vos yeux.

En 2016, Gabriel Medina (BRA) réalise **le 1er backflip réussi lors d'un championnat mondial de surf**. Il obtient le score parfait de 10 au Oi Rio Pro de Rio de Janeiro (Brésil).

Quelle est votre date de naissance ? Consultez notre calendrier pour découvrir quel record a été réalisé ce jour-là.

À VOUS DE JOUER

Ça vous dirait de remporter un titre GWR ? Rendez-vous dans notre nouveau chapitre SPORTS VIRAUX. Faire du yo-yo, du speed-cubing, du flip de bouteilles d'eau, jongler : vous trouverez une sélection de records à tenter chez vous. Et pour en savoir plus sur la façon d'entrer dans le GWR, rencontrez sur Internet les tenants actuels des records, comme le champion de flip de bouteilles à l'aveugle, Josh Horton (ci-dessus).

AIRBORNE AUTOMATA

FESTO

100%

100%

100%

ROBOTS

BIONICOPTER

L'HISTOIRE EST À SUIVRE EN LIGNE @ GUINNESSWORLDRECORDS.COM

Ce symbole vous invite à aller sur notre site **guinnessworldrecords. com/2020** : vous y trouverez des vidéos bonus. Notre équipe vidéo a réalisé une série de clips sur les détenteurs de records les plus bluffants. C'est l'occasion de vivre pleinement ces records comme si vous y étiez.

Boston Dynamics

Rencontrez des cyborgs et des androïdes dans notre chapitre ROBOTS, sous la direction d'Evan Ackerman blogueur, spécialisé dans les nouvelles technologies.

GUINNESS WORLD RECORDS

SOMMAIRE

LE MOT DE L'ÉDITEUR

Bienvenue dans le *Guinness World Records 2020* — entièrement revu et mis à jour pour la nouvelle décennie...

Cette année, notre équipe de gestion des records a traité plus de 100 candidatures par jour couvrant tous les domaines imaginables. Comme toujours, en raison de notre démarche d'évaluation rigoureuse, seulement 5 à 15 % de celles-ci sont retenues tous les ans. Alors si c'était « non » pour « le plus grand nombre d'e-mails qui n'ont pas été lus » ou « le crayon le plus court du monde », je suis quand même ravi d'avoir donné le feu vert à 5 103 demandes au cours des 12 derniers mois.

En plus des milliers de candidatures que nous recevons chaque année, nous sollicitions également notre vaste équipe de conseillers et de consultants.

Ces experts extérieurs — souvent des universitaires de premier plan dans leur discipline — s'assurent que nous embrassons le plus large spectre de sujets, littéralement de A à Z, de l'archéologie à la zoologie. Norris McWhirter, qui a fondé *The Guinness Book of Records* dans les années 1950, voulait « faire du spécialiste un véritable monsieur plus » – c'est-à-dire, trouver le plus rapide, le plus grand, le plus fort grâce au conchyliologiste (spécialiste des coquillages), à l'arachnologue (spécialiste des araignées) ou au lithologue (spécialiste des roches).

Cette année, notre rédacteur en chef Adam Millward a redoublé d'efforts pour ouvrir l'équipe d'experts et je suis ravi d'accueillir l'Université des Fourmis, le laboratoire de sismologie de Berkeley et les

LE PLUS D'ABONNÉS SUR TWITTER POUR UN DJ
Au 5 juin 2019, le DJ superstar David Guetta compte 21 368 464 abonnés sur Twitter. Âgé de 51 ans, le « Parrain de l'EDM » continue de surfer sur le succès de son double album 7, paru en 2018, qui mêle morceaux grand public et pistes rappelant ses racines issues de la scène house des années 1990.

LE PLUS D'ABONNÉS À UNE CHAÎNE YOUTUBE EN FRANÇAIS
Le comédien Cyprien Iov, alias « Monsieur Dream », cumulait 13 101 051 abonnés sur YouTube au 14 mai 2019. Vidéaste web, animateur et diffuseur de vidéos de gameplay, il a commencé à publier en ligne des vidéos comiques à l'âge de 18 ans et est devenu célèbre grâce à une chronique Internet hebdomadaire, Le Rewind.

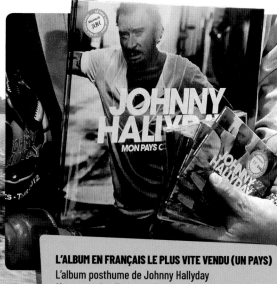

L'ALBUM EN FRANÇAIS LE PLUS VITE VENDU (UN PAYS)
L'album posthume de Johnny Hallyday *Mon pays c'est l'amour* a établi un record avec 780 177 exemplaires vendus la première semaine en France après sa sortie, le 19 octobre 2018. L'album — collaboration avec l'auteur-compositeur-interprète Yodelice — a été enregistré dans les mois précédents le décès de Johnny, le 5 décembre 2017. *Mon pays c'est l'amour* est le 79e album du chanteur.

LE PLUS DE PARTICIPATIONS AU TOUR DE FRANCE
Le vétéran Sylvain Chavanel, cycliste polyvalent, a couru son 18e et dernier Tour de France en juillet 2018, et a annoncé sa retraite l'ultime jour de la course. Âgé de 39 ans, il a participé à chaque Tour entre 2001 et 2018 et les a terminés sauf en deux occasions (en 2007 et 2012). Sur le Tour, Chavanel a marqué les esprits en finissant 19e au classement général en 2009 et en 2010, lorsqu'il a remporté le maillot jaune contre le spécialiste suisse du contre-la-montre, Fabian Cancellara.

JANV. 1 Le président Theodore Roosevelt (USA) célèbre le premier jour de 1907 en donnant **le plus de poignées de main par un chef d'État (événement unique)** : 8 513 personnes lors d'une cérémonie officielle à la Maison-Blanche.

JANV. 2 À Twickenham (GBR), en 1932, Gerhard Hamilton « Gerry » Brand a marqué **le plus long drop au rugby** — 77,7 m — lors de la rencontre Afrique du Sud — Angleterre.

LA PLUS LONGUE TABLE DE PIQUE-NIQUE

Mesurant 401,02 m pour près de 2 000 convives, cette table géante a été réalisée par le marché international de Rungis et présentée au public le 17 mars 2019. Il s'agissait de marquer le 50e anniversaire du transfert du plus grand marché alimentaire de France des Halles (Paris) vers Rungis (Val-de-Marne).

LA PLUS GRANDE PARADE DE DÉPANNEUSES

Le 13 octobre 2018, l'association professionnelle Fier d'être dépanneur a assemblé un convoi de 491 camions de remorquage lors de sa rencontre annuelle à Moulins. La collecte de fonds associée au défilé a permis de réunir plus de 9 000 € pour l'Institut Gustave-Roussy qui finance la recherche sur les traitements des cancers de l'enfant.

Fier d'être dépanneur a rassemblé 167 dépanneuses de plus que lors de la parade de l'ancien détenteur du record, qui avait eu lieu à Bridgeview (Illinois, USA) en 2011.

Jardins botaniques royaux de Kew, pour n'en nommer que trois. Vous trouverez une liste exhaustive des consultants et contributeurs aux p. 250–251. Je souhaiterais remercier toutes les personnes qui ont participé à la réalisation de cette édition 2020 : le résultat, j'espère que vous en conviendrez, constitue une collection de records fascinante et d'une ampleur inouïe.

Nous accueillons également un nouveau spécialiste, le consultant en robotique Evan Ackerman. Journaliste et blogueur, expert ès robots, Evan fait partie de l'équipe de l'Institute of Electrical and Electronics Engineers. Qui, mieux que lui, pouvait s'occuper du chapitre spécial ? Les robots

battent des records après tout et vous en découvrirez des spécimens exceptionnels sélectionnés par Evan p. 146.

Comme toujours, nos dénicheurs de talents ont parcouru la planète pour trouver des événements plus variés que jamais. Nous avons assisté à des salons automobiles, à des salons canins, à des conventions de jeux vidéo et à des marathons, et nous voudrions remercier chaque personne ayant tenté ou établi un record devant nos

LE PREMIER TRIPLE SALTO ARRIÈRE DÉPART ASSIS SUR SLACKLINE

Le gymnaste Louis Boniface a présenté un triple salto arrière départ et arrivée en position assise à Saint-Lambert, le 8 octobre 2018. Il a réalisé cette performance, certifiée par l'International Slackline Association, sur une slackline de 26 m suspendue à 3,1 m au-dessus du sol.

LE PLUS DE TOUCHES CONSÉCUTIVES AVEC DEUX BALLONS DE FOOTBALL

Le 12 mars 2019, le footballeur freestyle Norman Habri a réussi à maintenir en l'air 2 ballons de football avec 50 touches consécutives. Pour cette tentative, Habri avait le droit d'utiliser les 2 pieds, mais il détient également le record du **plus de touches consécutives avec 2 ballons de football à l'aide d'un seul pied**, soit 20, le 23 octobre 2018.

LE TEMPS LE PLUS LONG EN POSITION DE PLANCHE ABDOMINALE AVEC UNE CHARGE DE 46 KG

Tenir en planche pendant 17 min serait un véritable exploit pour beaucoup, mais pas pour Silehm Boussehaba, qui a décidé de compliquer l'épreuve en ajoutant un sac à dos de 46 kg. Il a maintenu cet effort pendant 17 min 2 s — plus de 4 fois la durée du précédent record — à Dijon le 29 décembre 2018. Cet exploit lui a peut-être paru facile, car il est également détenteur du même record avec **un sac de 90,7 kg**, pendant 4 min 2 s, le 17 mars 2018.

JANV. 3 En 1996, le photographe aérien Ryuji Furusho (JPN) se lance dans le record du **plus de lignes aériennes empruntées**. Le 13 janvier 2014, il atteint le chiffre incroyable de 156.

JANV. 4 Lakshan Wanniarachchi (LKA) a affronté **le plus d'adversaires simultanés au Scrabble** — 40 — à Colombo (LKA) en 2015. Pour réaliser ce record, il a battu 31 joueurs.

5

LE MOT DE L'ÉDITEUR

En décembre 2018, Marie-Amélie Le Fur a été élue présidente du Comité paralympique et sportif français.

découvreurs et nos juges. Cherchez nos rubriques sur les bulles (p. 90-91) et le feu (p. 92-93) pour des exemples particulièrement spectaculaires de nos derniers partenariats.

Cette année, le plus grand événement de ce type s'est produit à la SkillCon 2018 de Las Vegas (Nevada, USA). Combat de jonglerie, sabre laser et speedcubing (résolution rapide de Rubik's Cube) font partie des disciplines de cette compétition extrême. Nos juges, sur place avec notre équipe vidéo, ont certifié les records et ont également filmé des tutoriels exclusifs avec les champions. Pour cette édition, nous avons classé les records dans la rubrique « Sports viraux » — car il s'agit de sujets très populaires sur les réseaux sociaux tels que YouTube et Instagram : le chapitre consacré à ces exploits commence p. 98.
❍ Vous pouvez découvrir nos

LE PLUS DE POINTS DANS UN DÉCATHLON (HOMMES)
Le 16 septembre 2018, Kevin Mayer a rebondi ,après un championnat d'Europe d'athlétisme 2018 décevant, en battant le record du monde de décathlon au Decastar, une des épreuves combinées de l'IAAF à Talence (FRA). Son total de 9 126 points pulvérise le record établi par Ashton Eaton (USA) en 2015 de 81 points.

vidéos exclusives du SkillCon sur **guinnessworldrecords.com/2020**.

Notre équipe vidéo a enregistré des centaines d'heures de film pour la chaîne YouTube GWR. Cherchez l'icône dans les pages du livre — si vous repérez ce bouton, c'est qu'il existe des images sur le site pour accompagner le texte.

Une nouvelle section dans le *GWR 2020* s'appelle « Snapshot ». Ce sont des pages façon posters en tête de chaque chapitre. Nos rédacteurs ont travaillé avec les artistes de

55Design — et Joseph O'Neil le créateur 3D du GWR — afin de placer visuellement les détenteurs de record dans leur contexte.

Prenez, par exemple, la nouvelle **plus haute statue** du monde (p. 190-191). De nombreux lecteurs du *Guinness World Records* n'auront sans doute pas la chance de voir cette imposante structure de 182 m située dans une partie reculée de l'Inde. Alors, pour vous donner une idée de sa taille nous l'avons réinstallée sur les rives de la Tamise au Royaume-Uni.

LE PLUS LONG SAUT EN LONGUEUR (T64, FEMMES)
Au championnat d'Europe parathlétique 2018 à Berlin (DEU), Marie-Amélie Le Fur a battu son propre record du monde avec 6,01 m dans la finale du saut en longueur. Elle a également disputé les 100 m, 200 m et 400 m et est montée sur le podium. En 2016, aux jeux Paralympiques, elle a remporté une médaille d'or en établissant **le record du 400 m le plus rapide** (T64, femmes) en 59,27 s.

LA VITESSE LA PLUS RAPIDE EN KITESURF MASCULIN (SUR UN MILLE MARIN)
Christophe Ballois (à droite) a atteint 35,78 nœuds (66,26 km/h) sur un parcours d'un mille marin (1,8 km) au Speed Sailing Event de La Palme, le 21 juillet 2018. Cinq jours plus tôt, lors de la même compétition, Marine Tlattla (ci-dessous) a battu **le record féminin**, avec une vitesse de 33,60 nœuds (62,23 km/h). En plus de ces deux records, Speed Sailing Event a également vu Vincent Valkenaers (BEL) établir le record de **la vitesse la plus rapide en planche à voile** (sur un mille marin), avec 42,23 nœuds (78,21 km/h), le 21 juillet.

JANV. 5 Dans une salle de danse à Vienne (AUT), Elena Sofie Sterlini (AUT) a réalisé **le twerk le plus long** en 2018. Elle a dansé pendant 2 h 1 min.

JANV. 6 En 2017, Jon Lovitch (USA) a construit **le plus grand village en pain d'épice** — composé de 1 251 bâtiments — et l'a présenté au New York Hall of Science de Corona (New York, USA).

LE PLUS DE VICTOIRES CONSÉCUTIVES EN UNE SAISON DE LIGUE 1 PAR UNE ÉQUIPE
Le Paris Saint-Germain a entamé la saison 2018-2019 de Ligue 1 sur 13 victoires consécutives. Lors de ces matchs, l'équipe a marqué 45 buts (3,46 buts par match). Parmi les résultats notables, on compte la correction 5-0 infligée à Lyon, qui terminera troisième, et des victoires confortables contre ses rivaux de longue date : Marseille et Monaco.

Idem pour la *Station spatiale internationale*, **la plus grande station spatiale**. Nous l'avons fait atterrir sur Trafalgar Square, la célèbre place londonienne. (Et bizarrement, elle s'y intègre parfaitement !)

Pourquoi Londres ? Tout simplement parce que depuis 65 ans, la capitale du Royaume-Uni est le foyer du *Guinness World Records*. C'est ici, en 1954, que Norris et son frère jumeau Ross ont commencé à compiler des records – et depuis, nous y avons notre siège.

Le monde a bien changé depuis ! Instantané annuel de notre vie et de notre époque, le *Guinness World Records* révèle les transformations incroyables qui se sont produites durant ces 65 dernières années. À travers le prisme de l'extraordinaire, nous avons témoigné des exploits les plus étonnants : nous, humains, avons vu l'aube de l'âge des satellites, marché sur la Lune et envoyé des sondes au-delà des limites de notre système solaire ; nous avons transplanté des cœurs, déchiffré l'ADN et confirmé l'existence du boson de Higgs.

En célébrant le meilleur des réalisations humaines, nous espérons inspirer des millions de personnes et les inciter à atteindre leurs buts.

Alors, si vous voulez battre un record et lire votre nom dans le livre millésimé le plus populaire du monde, rendez-vous sur notre site **guinnessworldrecords.com**. Et comme la nouvelle décennie approche, il est temps de cocher la case « champion du monde » sur votre liste d'objectifs. Assurez-vous toutefois de nous prévenir à temps, parce que nous avons 99 autres candidatures à étudier, tous les jours...

Craig Glenday
Rédacteur en chef

LES PLUS HAUTS SCORES EN DANSE SUR GLACE
Le couple Gabriella Papadakis et Guillaume Cizeron a conservé son record en danse sur glace à la suite de la décision de l'Union internationale de patinage de mettre à jour le système de notation des difficultés techniques pour la saison 2018-2019. Au 5 juin 2019, il détient les records en danse rythmique — programme court — (88,42 points), programme libre (13,82 points) et total combiné (223,13 points).

LE PLUS DE VICTOIRES EN LIGUE DES CHAMPIONS FÉMININE
Le 18 mai 2019, l'Olympique Lyonnais (femmes) a conquis son 6e titre (et le 4e consécutif) avec une victoire 4-1 contre le FC Barcelone à la Groupama Arena de Budapest (HUN). Lors de cette victoire, Ada Hegerberg (NOR), attaquante star de Lyon et **première Ballon d'Or féminin**, a réalisé un triplé.

JANV. 7 En 1972, les Lakers gagnent leur 33e match — **le plus de victoires consécutives en NBA**. Deux jours plus tard, les Milwaukee Bucks mettent un terme à cette série, commencée le 5 novembre 1971.

JANV. 8 Ashrita Furman (USA) ajoute **le mile le plus rapide sur des échasses en boîte de conserve** à sa longue liste de titres GWR en 2011. Il termine la course en 11 min 55 s à Ottawa (Ontario, CAN).

GWR DAY

▶ LE PLUS DE SAUTS À LA CORDE DE HAUTE VOLTIGE EN 30 S

Hijiki Ikuyama (JPN) a exécuté 24 sauts mamba en 30 s à Tachikawa, Tokyo (JPN). Cela consiste à jongler avec une extrémité de la corde entre chaque saut. Hijiki lâche une poigné, fait tournoyer la corde à 360° puis le rattrape et continue à sauter.

Chaque année, des milliers de gens dans le monde relèvent les défis les plus variés pour le Guinness World Records Day. Cette journée annuelle des records a été lancée en 2005 pour célébrer le *GWR*, devenu **le livre annuel le plus vendu au monde**. C'est l'occasion de mettre en lumière une bonne cause, de recueillir des fonds pour des œuvres caritatives, de rassembler des amis ou des collègues, ou tout simplement de s'amuser. Voici quelques-uns des essais réussis en 2018...

Regardez les vidéos du GWR Day sur notre site Internet **guinnessworldrecords. com/2020**

Les Harlem Globetrotters (USA) établissent souvent de nouveaux records lors du GWR Day. Ci-dessous, Julian "Zeus" McClurkin réalise **le plus grand nombre de dunks à l'aveugle en 1 min** (5). Voir ci-dessous leurs autres exploits !

▶ LA PLUS GRANDE COLLECTION DE TIMBRES REPRÉSENTANT DES VOITURES

Nabil Karam (LBN) a amassé 3 333 timbres avec des images de voitures, record vérifié à Zouk Mosbeh (LBN). Il apparaît ci-dessus avec le rédacteur en chef du *GWR* Craig Glenday (à gauche) et le juge Talal Omar (à droite).

Ce n'est pas la première immense collection de Karam. Il possède également **la plus vaste collection de voitures miniatures** (37 777) et de **dioramas** (577).

Le plus de personnes à pratiquer le stacking (lieux multiples)
Pour son 13e "STACK UP !" – organisé le 8 novembre 2018 pour le GWR Day – la World Sport Stacking Association (WSSA) a une fois encore relevé le défi en rassemblant le plus grand nombre de personnes dans le but d'empiler et désempiler des gobelets en plastique (ci-dessous). 624 390 "stackers" se sont ainsi réunis dans 2 833 écoles et organisations situées dans 25 pays, la majorité (569 928) étant installée aux États-Unis.

La WSSA avait réussi son premier défi il y a 12 ans avec un total de 81 252 participants pour fêter le GWR Day 2006 – soit une multiplication par 7 du nombre de participants en 2018 !

▶ LA PLUS GRANDE PEINTURE À LA LUMIÈRE NOIRE ULTRAVIOLETTE (UV)

Le *Guinness World Records* a profité du GWR Day pour soutenir l'œuvre inspirée de l'association caritative YoungMinds (GBR) et mettre en lumière les défis auxquels sont confrontés les jeunes handicapés mentaux. Aidée par l'artiste Livi Gosling (GBR), une équipe de bénévoles de YoungMinds a imaginé une peinture ultraviolette de 453,22 m² à Milton Keynes, Buckinghamshire (GBR). Les peintures UV, blanches à la lumière naturelle, apparaissent à la lumière noire. Pourquoi avoir choisi l'image d'un arbre dans une tête ? Parce que "comme l'arbre, la santé mentale doit être nourrie pour être en forme et s'épanouir", explique Livi.

▶ LES HARLEM GLOBETROTTERS ET LES FLYING GLOBIES

"Zeus" McClurkin (USA) a marqué **le plus grand nombre de tirs à 3 points derrière le dos en 1 min** (3) à Atlanta, Géorgie (USA). Ses coéquipiers (tous USA) ont établi 2 autres records "en 1 min" : **le plus de cabrioles avec un ballon de basket sous la jambe (femme)** - 32, par "Torch" George - et **le panier le plus lointain** - de "Bull" Bullard marqué à 17,71 m. Pendant ce temps, les Flying Gobies (encart) réalisaient **le plus grand nombre de dunks avec un trampoline en 1 min** (28).

▶ **LE PLUS DE ROTATIONS EN GRAND ÉCART EN 1 MIN**
La monitrice de chute libre intérieure Danielle "Doni" Gales (AUS), 23 ans, a réalisé 55 rotations en grand écart avant au iFLY Downunder de Penrith, Nouvelle-Galles-du-Sud (AUS). Son autre grande passion l'a préparée à relever ce difficile défi. "J'ai dansé toute ma vie, je suis née et j'ai été élevée pour cela", a-t-elle affirmé au *GWR*. "Cela m'a vraiment aidée à progresser en vol."

Temps le plus rapide pour assembler 5 personnages PLAYMOBIL®
Hu Yufei (CHN) a assemblé 5 personnages PLAYMOBIL® en 59,88 s à la Shanghai Kids Fun Expo de Shanghai (CHN).
D'autres visiteurs chinois ont établi des records pour le *GWR*, dont : **le temps le plus rapide pour fabriquer 21 nouilles Play-Doh®** (39,32 s, par Jin Zuan) ; **le temps le plus rapide pour trier 30 voitures miniatures** (20,92 s, par Xu Qin) ; et **le temps le plus rapide pour changer l'habillage d'un siège enfant** (1 min 58,44 s, par Qi Haifeng).

Le plus de jonglages en 1 min (3 ballons de basket)
Luis Diego Soto Villa (MEX) a effectué 213 jonglages en 60 s avec 3 ballons à Mexico (MEX).

▶ **LE PLUS RAPIDE À TERMINER 3 RUBIK'S CUBES EN MÊME TEMPS AVEC LES MAINS ET LES PIEDS**
Que Jianyu (CHN) a résolu simultanément 3 Rubik's cubes avec ses mains et ses pieds en 1 min 36,39 s à Xiamen, Fujian (CHN).
Le même jour, il s'est suspendu à l'envers pour devenir **le plus rapide à résoudre un Rubik's cube la tête en bas** (15,84 s).

▶ **LE PLUS GRAND ANNEAU DE CADRAN SOLAIRE LEGO® (SOUTENU)**
Playable Design (CHN) a dévoilé un cadran solaire fonctionnel de 2,91 m de diamètre et 0,8 m d'épaisseur, fait de 45 000 briques LEGO DUPLO®. Le cadran solaire est un instrument de mesure du temps datant d'au moins 1500 av. J.-C.

Le plus de rebonds d'une balle de ping-pong contre un mur avec la bouche en 30 s
Ray Reynolds (GBR) a lancé une balle de ping-pong contre un mur et l'a rattrapée sur le rebond en se servant uniquement de sa bouche 34 fois en 30 s à Londres (GBR).

Le plus long temps sauté à la corde en faisant du hula-hoop
Zhang Jiqing (CHN) a sauté à la corde pendant 1 min 32,653 s – tout en faisant du hula-hoop – à la Beijing Chaoyang Normal School de Pékin (CHN). Zhang a tenté ce record à 63 ans afin de prouver sa forme pour le GWR Day. Il a sauté 142 fois.

Le plus de beignets empilés en 1 min (à l'aveugle)
Katie Nolan (USA) a empilé 7 beignets à l'aveugle sur le plateau d'*Always Late with Katie Nolan* d'ESPN à New York (USA) le 7 novembre 2018.

Le plus rapide à enrouler un homme dans du film alimentaire
Le youtubeur «Dekakin» (JPN) a enveloppé Ichiho Shirahata – membre du groupe idole «Gekijo-ban» Gokigen Teikoku – en 1 min 59,71 s à Minato, Tokyo (JPN).

Le plus de spots dans un spectacle son et lumière permanent
Le Wenzhou Mountain Light Show, à Zhejiang (CHN), est une attraction touristique qui utilise 707 667 lumières pour illuminer la montagne, les bâtiments et les ponts des deux côtés du fleuve Ou. Elle a été installée par Beijing Landsky Environmental Technology Co. Ltd (CHN) et confirmée record mondial officiel lors du GWR Day 2018.

▶ **LA PLUS LONGUE DISTANCE COUVERTE PAR DE LA GÉLATINE EN 30 S**
Le vloagueur japonais "Yocchi" (JPN) (ci-dessus au centre) de "BomBom TV" a étendu un morceau de gélatine sur 3,87 m à Tokyo (JPN).
Le même jour, une équipe de "BomBom TV" a couvert **la plus longue distance avec de la gélatine en 30 s (équipe de 8)** - 13,78 m.

Il a fallu plus de 3 mois de travail, impliquant des astronomes et des ingénieurs, pour réaliser ce cadran géant !

▶ **LE PLUS LONG SAUT EN FAUTEUIL ROULANT**
Aaron "Wheelz" Fotheringham (USA) a réalisé un saut de 21,35 m en fauteuil roulant au Woodward West de Tehachapi, Californie (USA). Ce même jour, il a aussi exécuté **le plus grand drop-in sur un quarter-pipe en fauteuil roulant** et **le plus haut hand plant en fauteuil roulant** (8,4 m). (Voir p. 95 pour plus de détails.)

JANV. 11 En 2016, Li Xingnan (CHN) réalise **le plus haut blackflip contre un mur** (3,70 m) sur le plateau de CCTV - *Guinness World Records Special*, à Pékin (Chine).

JANV. 12 Un ara harlequin du nom de Zac a ouvert le **plus de canettes de boisson en 1 min** en 2012 : il en a ouvert 35 en 60 s. avec son bec à San Jose (Californie, USA).

9

VIDÉOS GWR LES PLUS REGARDÉES

D'adorables animaux, de périlleuses cascades, des hommes incroyables et des talents insensés... quoi que vous aimiez, avec le GWR, vous êtes toujours au plus près de l'action. Retrouvez-nous sur les réseaux sociaux. Nous avons réuni ici nos vidéos les plus vues sur YouTube. Laquelle préférez-vous ?

Au cours des dernières années, l'explosion des réseaux sociaux a permis au *GWR* de communiquer avec des personnes du monde entier. Que vous nous cherchiez sur YouTube, Facebook, Instagram ou PopJam, vous tomberez à coup sûr sur des images d'exploits officiellement incroyables. Et nous adorons avoir les retours de notre communauté de viewers, posters et sharers, qui a toujours son mot à dire sur les records ! En novembre 2018, les vidéos GWR sur YouTube ont atteint un temps de visionnage total de plus de 1 milliard d'heures. Notre vidéo la plus populaire – montrant des responsables de la société de produits électroniques Aaron's (USA) dans **le plus grand domino humain avec des matelas** – a été visionnée plus de 46 millions de fois (voir page suivante en haut à droite). Nous sommes

toujours à l'affût du nouveau record de vues et notre équipe compile chaque mois les meilleures images.

Nous sommes très fiers de notre rubrique "Rencontrez les makers", qui va à la rencontre des talents qui se cachent derrière les exploits et qui dévoile leur incroyable histoire. Découvrez ci-dessous les vidéos les plus vues sur YouTube.

LE *GWR* DEVIENT MONDIAL

Depuis leurs débuts en 1998, les émissions de télévision officielles du *GWR* ont été vues dans plus de 190 pays – de l'Amérique du Nord au Moyen-Orient, en passant par l'Asie et l'Australie. Ici, Sultan Kösen (TUR), **l'homme le plus grand** (voir p. 58-59), est entouré d'autres détenteurs de records pour le *CCTV - Guinness World Records Special*, en Chine.

LES VIDÉOS "RENCONTREZ LES MAKERS" LES PLUS VUES SUR YOUTUBE

	VIDÉO	POSTÉE	VUES
1.	Les plus longs ongles sur une seule main	29 sept. 2015	15 317 359
2.	La femme aux plus longues jambes	9 sept. 2017	9 256 334
3.	Le plus grand chien au monde	12 sept. 2012	7 163 951
4.	Batman Cosplay bat le record du monde	24 août 2016	6 910 558
5.	Le maître des arts martiaux tente le record du monde – Tour du Japon	2 mars 2017	5 981 577
6.	Le plus de canettes collées sur la tête	31 mars 2016	4 468 971
7.	La plus haute coupe de cheveux	14 sept. 2017	4 331 221
8.	Le plus grand cheval au monde	12 sept. 2012	3 872 814
9.	Britney Gallivan : combien de fois peut-on plier un morceau de papier ?	26 nov. 2018	3 720 518
10.	"The Pull Up Guy"	5 mai 2016	3 439 371

Tous les chiffres ont été actualisés le 18 février 2019

Il n'y a pas que le *Guinness World Records* – **livre annuel le plus vendu** de tous les temps – qui recense d'incroyables exploits. Nous partageons aussi nos vidéos de records avec nos millions de fans en ligne. Repérez le symbole "lecture" dans le *GWR 2020* – une vidéo est associée à chaque défi ainsi signalé. Regardez-les tous sur le site :

www.guinnessworldrecords.com/2020

JANV. 13 En 1981, Donna Griffiths (GBR) commence à éternuer régulièrement et s'arrête le 16 septembre 1983, soit 976 jours plus tard – **la plus longue crise d'éternuements**. La 1re année, elle éternue déjà 1 million de fois.

JANV. 14 Patrick "Deep Dish" Bertoletti (USA) avale **le plus de gousses d'ail en 1 min** (36) en 2012 dans le Sierra Studio d'East Dundee, Illinois (USA).

LES 25 VIDÉOS DU *GWR* LES PLUS REGARDÉES SUR YOUTUBE

VIDÉO	POSTÉE	VUES
1. Le plus grand domino humain avec matelas	7 avr. 2016	51 446 906
2. La peau la plus extensible au monde !	12 janv. 2009	37 396 345
3. Le plus long vélo	10 nov. 2015	19 648 054
4. Le plus de tee-shirts mouillés mis en 1 min	8 juin 2015	16 606 141
5. Parkour – le plus haut saut périlleux arrière	11 nov. 2016	15 851 965
6. Les plus longues jambes de femme	11 mars 2009	15 345 386
7. Les plus longs ongles sur une seule main	29 sept. 2015	15 317 359
8. La plus haute prise d'une balle de cricket	5 juill. 2016	14 783 638
9. Le plus de dominos renversés	29 juill. 2014	14 222 140
10. L'homme le plus grand du monde : Xi Shun	14 avr. 2008	12 675 322
11. Le plus épais sandwich de lits de clous	5 févr. 2016	12 287 653
12. Le plus d'araignées sur un corps pendant 30 s	27 juill. 2007	11 882 364
13. La plus longue langue du monde	9 sept. 2014	10 990 528
14. Domino de livres	16 oct. 2015	9 473 611
15. La femme aux plus longues jambes	9 sept. 2017	9 256 334
16. Le record du créneau le plus serré battu au nouveau Mini launch	31 mai 2012	8 766 424
17. Le plus long vol en hoverboard	22 mai 2015	8 694 963
18. La plus longue course sur un mur (parkour)	30 nov. 2012	8 581 682
19. Tentative de record du monde de la plus grosse bulle de chewing-gum	31 juill. 2016	8 025 513
20. Le plus grand chien au monde	12 sept. 2012	7 163 951
21. Batman Cosplay bat le record du monde	24 août 2016	6 910 558
22. Le ronronnement de chat le plus fort	21 mai 2015	6 751 925
23. Le plus rapide pour percer 4 noix de coco avec 1 DOIGT !	11 avr. 2013	6 682 935
24. *Ultimate Guinness World Records Show – Épisode 2* : chopes de bière, bananes et cube humain	5 avr. 2012	6 660 398
25. Le plus de changements de costumes en 1 min	30 sept. 2016	6 640 954

Tous les chiffres ont été actualisés au 18 février 2019

Le plus grand domino humain avec matelas a depuis été réalisé avec 2 016 personnes, par Stylution Int'l et Ayd Group (tous 2 CHN) le 23 juillet 2016.

La durée totale passée à regarder des vidéos GWR sur YouTube par des spectateurs est d'environ 2 500 ans.

JANV. 15 En 1984, Tim McVey (USA) est **le 1er à atteindre 1 milliard de points à un jeu vidéo**. Son score est de 1 000 042 270 points après une session marathon de 44 h 45 à *Nibbler* à Ottumwa, Iowa (USA).

JANV. 16 Une équipe de 10 chirurgiens réalise **la 1re greffe de mâchoire** en 2003 à l'Istituto Regina Elena de Rome (ITA). L'opération, sur un patient de 80 ans, dure 11 heures.

LA PLANTE LA PLUS TOLÉRANTE AU SEL

L'algue verte *Dunaliella salina* peut survivre à des taux de salinité allant de 0,2 % à 35 %. C'est **l'eucaryote** (organisme dont les cellules ont un noyau) **le plus résistant au sel**. Cette algue résiste aussi très bien à la chaleur, supportant des températures de 0 à 40 °C. Elle est présente dans le monde entier, généralement dans les océans, les lacs et les marécages salés. Dans des conditions hostiles (salinité ou température extrêmes, faible taux de nutriments), *D. salina* produit plus de bêtacarotène, un pigment rouge orangé naturel qui la protège. Cette vue aérienne montre l'algue après une telle transformation dans le lac salé de Yuncheng (la "mer Morte chinoise"), dans la province de Shanxi (CHN).

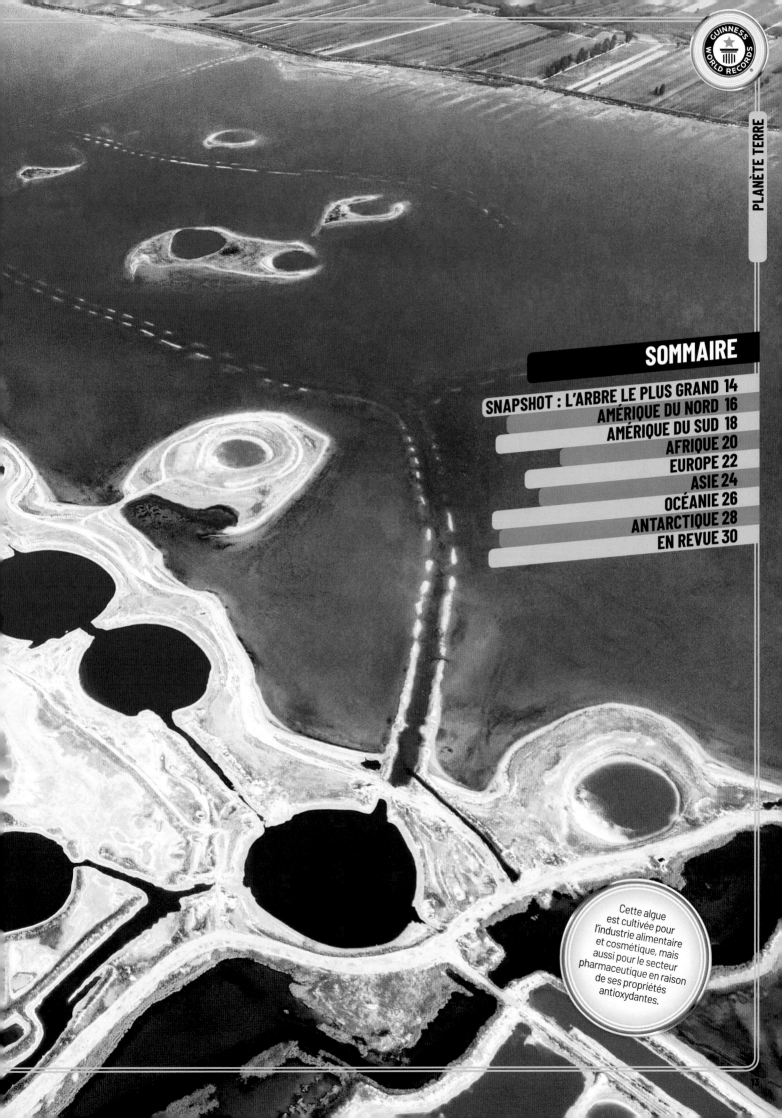

SOMMAIRE

Cette algue est cultivée pour l'industrie alimentaire et cosmétique, mais aussi pour le secteur pharmaceutique en raison de ses propriétés antioxydantes.

L'ARBRE LE PLUS GRAND

Les séquoias, arbres gigantesques, poussent dans l'ouest des États-Unis et peuvent vivre plus de 2 000 ans. Comparons-en un avec le célèbre Big Ben, la tour de l'horloge du palais de Wesminster à Londres (GBR).

Les séquoias sont de grands arbres au port vertical. Ils ont besoin de beaucoup d'humidité et ne poussent que dans une bande brumeuse de 720 km le long de la côte Pacifique des États-Unis, du sud de l'Oregon au nord de la Californie.

Trois essences se partagent le record de **la plus grande espèce d'arbre** : le séquoia, l'eucalyptus et le sapin de Douglas, qui peuvent tous dépasser 113 m. **L'arbre le plus grand** est actuellement un *Sequoia sempervirens* appelé Hyperion, qui mesurait 115,85 m en 2017. Il a été découvert par Chris Atkins et Michael Taylor (tous 2 USA) dans le parc national de Redwood, en Californie (USA), en 2006.

Les séquoias poussent aussi haut pour plusieurs raisons : climat doux, fortes pluies, brouillards estivaux réduisant l'évaporation au niveau des feuilles, sols fertiles et protection de leurs voisins contre le vent.

Les branches des séquoias abritent de nombreuses plantes, dites "épiphytes" : il peut s'agir de mousses, de lichens, de buissons de myrtilles et même d'autres arbres, comme des pins. En effet, les feuilles du séquoia tombent sur les branches quand elles fanent, puis elles se décomposent et finissent par offrir un compost fertile à d'autres plantes. Cet écosystème surélevé comprend aussi des animaux, comme des insectes, des salamandres et même de petits mammifères, le campagnol.

Hyperion fait presque 20 m de plus que la tour Elizabeth située au nord du palais de Westminster, plus connue sous le nom de Big Ben. En réalité, Big Ben est le nom de la cloche de la tour, qui pèse 13,7 t et qui a sonné pour la 1re fois en 1859. La comparaison entre Hyperion et l'édifice montre bien combien les séquoias sont majestueux, même s'ils ne donnent pas l'heure…

PETITE GRAINE DEVIENDRA GRANDE…

Ces cônes ne mesurent que 2,5 cm de long environ, mais ils donneront des arbres de dizaines de mètres de haut. Leurs écailles dissimulent 50 à 60 graines de 3 à 4 mm de long, qui mûrissent dans le cône pendant 8 à 9 mois. Le cône passe ensuite du vert au marron, les écailles s'ouvrent et les graines tombent au sol.

100 %

GUINNESS WORLD RECORDS

Les racines d'un séquoia ne sont pas si profondes, mais peuvent facilement s'étendre sur 30 m, soit presque le tiers de la hauteur de la tour Elizabeth (à gauche).

LE LONDON EYE COMPARÉ AUX ARBRES GÉANTS

Hyperion (à gauche) est le plus grand arbre actuel, mais **le plus grand arbre de l'histoire** (à droite) était encore plus haut. Difficile de l'identifier avec exactitude, mais un eucalyptus de 146,3 m décrit par G. Klein à Black Spur, près d'Healesville dans l'État de Victoria (AUS) et mesuré par le botaniste officiel de l'État, le baron Ferdinand von Mueller, en 1867, est un bon candidat. Les 2 arbres sont comparés ici au London Eye, la roue de 135 m de haut située près de la Tamise à Londres (GBR). Voir aussi p. 190-191.

AMÉRIQUE DU NORD

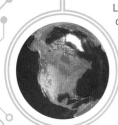

POPULATION
579 millions

SUPERFICIE TOTALE
24,71 millions de km²

PAYS
23

PLUS HAUT SOMMET
Denali : 6 190 m

PLUS GRAND LAC
Supérieur : 82 414 km²

PLUS LONGUE RIVIÈRE
Missouri : 4 087 km

La plus grande montagne

Le Mauna Kea (île d'Hawaï, USA) culmine à 4 205 m au-dessus du niveau de la mer, presque 2 km de moins que le sommet le plus haut d'Amérique du Nord (voir ci-dessous, à gauche). Mais ce n'est que la partie visible de l'iceberg, le Mauna Kea commençant plusieurs kilomètres sous l'eau. De sa base sous-marine à son sommet, il mesure en réalité 10 205 m environ, soit 1,3 km de plus que l'Everest.

Les eaux d'Hawaï abritent **la plus grande aire marine protégée** selon les critères de l'UICN. Le Papahānaumokuākea Marine National Monument a été agrandi en 2016 par le président des États-Unis de l'époque, Barack Obama, et a atteint les 1 508 870 km².

Protégée par la loi contre la pêche commerciale et l'exploitation minière, la réserve est un paradis pour les animaux marins, dont **la plus grande éponge**. Découverte par 2 véhicules robotisés en 2015, cette éponge siliceuse mesure 3,5 m de long, 2 m de haut et 1,5 m de large.

La plus grande prairie

Les Grandes Plaines forment une ceinture de 3 millions de km² du nord au sud des États-Unis. Cette vaste prairie s'étendant des montagnes Rocheuses jusqu'au Missouri est plus étendue que l'Argentine, pourtant le 8e plus grand pays du monde. C'est l'habitat naturel des célèbres troupeaux de bisons (voir p. 39).

La plante vivant à la plus grande profondeur

En octobre 1984, 2 botanistes retraités du Smithsonian, Mark et Diane Littler (tous 2 USA), ont collecté une algue corallienne rouge en sous-marin, au large de l'île de San Salvador (Bahamas). D'une couleur marron et poussant à 269 m sous la surface, elle peut réaliser la photosynthèse même si l'eau filtre 99,9995 % de la lumière du soleil à cette profondeur.

La plus grande tornade mesurée

La saison des tempêtes (juin-novembre) est redoutée aux États-Unis, notamment dans les États situés entre le Texas et le Dakota du Sud, qui forment l'Allée des tornades. Le 31 mai 2013, une tornade de 4,18 km (l'équivalent de 1 900 terrains de football) a frappé El Reno dans l'Oklahoma. Elle a été mesurée par le National Weather Service.

Durant une tempête de 4 jours, l'Organisation météorologique mondiale a enregistré 207 tornades du 27 au 28 avril 2011, soit **le plus grand nombre de tornades en 24 heures**.

Les plus grandes marées

La baie de Fundy, qui sépare les provinces de Nova Scotia et du New Brunswick sur la côte Atlantique du Canada, accueille les plus grandes marées au monde. Lors de l'équinoxe de printemps, leur amplitude peut atteindre les 14,5 m en moyenne.

LA PLUS GRANDE CONCENTRATION DE CANYONS EN FENTE

Les canyons en fente sont des gorges étroites créées dans les roches sédimentaires par les tempêtes de sable et les inondations. Le plateau du Colorado, au sud-ouest des États-Unis, en possède peut-être 10 000. La photo ci-dessus montre l'Upper Antelope Canyon en Arizona, un des canyons en fente les plus photographiés au monde.

Le volcan le plus septentrional

Le mont Beerenberg, situé dans l'île de Jan Mayen dans la mer du Groenland, mesure 2 276 m de haut. Sa dernière éruption remonte à 1985.

Plus au nord, l'île de Devon, dans la baie de Baffin (CAN), a une latitude de 75,1° N. Sa surface de 55 247 km² est largement recouverte de glace et de rigoles gelées. C'est **la plus grande île inhabitée**.

Encore plus au nord se trouve Oodaaq, un îlot au large du Groenland découvert en 1978. Situé à 83,67° N, il a été qualifié de **terre la plus septentrionale**, mais certains géologues y voient un simple banc de graviers et non une terre à proprement parler.

LE PLUS GRAND LAC D'EAU DOUCE (SUPERFICIE)

À la frontière entre le Canada et les États-Unis, le lac Supérieur (ci-dessus), un des Grands Lacs d'Amérique du Nord, couvre 82 414 km² et mesure jusqu'à 406 m de profondeur.

Le plus grand lac dans un même pays est son voisin, le lac Michigan, entièrement situé aux États-Unis et d'une superficie de 57 800 km².

LE DÉSERT LE PLUS HUMIDE

Bien que la température puisse atteindre les 40 °C l'été, le désert de Sonora reçoit entre 76 et 500 mm de précipitations par an, voire plus dans certaines régions. Situé dans le sud de l'Arizona et de la Californie (USA), le Sonora et la Basse-Californie (MEX), ce désert est inhabituel car il connaît 2 saisons des pluies : la 1re de décembre à mars et la 2de de juillet à septembre.

LE PLUS GRAND GEYSER

Situé dans le parc de Yellowstone, Wyoming (USA), le Steamboat Geyser est le plus grand geyser actif : il peut dépasser les 91,4 m de haut.

Toutefois, **le plus grand geyser de l'histoire** est le Waimangu Geyser (NZL) : en 1903, il atteignait 460 m toutes les 30 à 36 h environ. Il est endormi depuis 1904.

JANV. 17 En 1989, lors de la South Pole International Overland Expedition, forte de 11 membres, Shirley Metz et Victoria "Tori" Murden (USA) sont **les 1res femmes à atteindre le pôle Sud par voie terrestre**.

JANV. 18 En 1896, **la 1re partie de basketball universitaire** oppose l'université de l'Iowa et celle de Chicago (toutes 2 USA) au Iowa City Armory (USA).

LA PLUS GRANDE GORGE TERRESTRE

Le Grand Canyon (Arizona, USA) mesure 446 km de long. Il est l'une des merveilles naturelles les plus célèbres des États-Unis. Il a été sculpté pendant des millions d'années par le fleuve Colorado, qui le traverse toujours. La gorge plonge jusqu'à 1,6 km de profondeur et les rives nord et sud sont séparées de 0,5 à 29 km.

Il faudrait plus de 3,7 billiards de litres d'eau pour remplir le Grand Canyon. Même en y versant l'eau de tous les fleuves de la Terre, il ne serait qu'à moitié plein !

L'ARBRE À LA PLUS GRANDE CIRCONFÉRENCE

Un cyprès de Montezuma (*Taxodium mucronatum*, ci-contre et ci-dessous) vieux de 2 000 ans, situé à Santa María del Tule, Oaxacao (MEX), avait une circonférence d'environ 36,2 m en 2005. La légende veut que l'"Árbol del Tule" ait été planté par le dieu aztèque des Tempêtes.

L'arbre à la plus grande circonférence de l'histoire était un châtaignier (*Castanea sativa*) de 57,9 m mesuré en 1780 sur l'Etna, Sicile (ITA). Le tronc existe toujours, coupé en plusieurs parties.

LES PLUS GRANDS CRISTAUX DE GYPSE

La grotte des Cristaux, découverte seulement en 2000, se trouve sous le désert de Chihuahua (MEX). L'eau saturée en minéraux et l'intense chaleur dégagée par le magma sous la caverne ont engendré un climat idéal pour le gypse pendant 500 000 ans. Les plus grands cristaux mesurent 11 m de long, soit la taille d'un car scolaire.

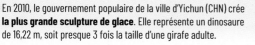

JANV. 19 En 2010, le gouvernement populaire de la ville d'Yichun (CHN) crée **la plus grande sculpture de glace**. Elle représente un dinosaure de 16,22 m, soit presque 3 fois la taille d'une girafe adulte.

JAN. 20 Le démocrate John F. Kennedy (né le 29 mai 1917) devient président des États-Unis en 1961, à l'âge de 43 ans et 236 jours. Il est **le plus jeune président élu**.

AMÉRIQUE DU SUD

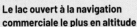

POPULATION
422,5 millions

SUPERFICIE TOTALE
17,84 millions de km²

PAYS
12

PLUS HAUT SOMMET
Aconcagua : 6 962 m

PLUS GRAND LAC
Titicaca : 8 372 km²

PLUS LONG FLEUVE
Amazone : 6 400 km

La plus longue chaîne de montagnes continentale

Avec ses 7 600 km le long de la côte ouest du continent, la cordillère des Andes est souvent surnommée "l'épine dorsale de l'Amérique du Sud". Elle compte environ 100 sommets de plus de 6 000 m.

Une étude globale sur la diversité des oiseaux dans les principales chaînes de montagnes publiée dans la revue *Nature* en janvier 2018 a montré que la cordillère des Andes accueille 2 422 espèces d'oiseaux, ce qui en fait **la chaîne de montagnes abritant la plus grande diversité d'oiseaux**.

Le lac ouvert à la navigation commerciale le plus en altitude

Le lac Titicaca chevauche la frontière Bolivie-Pérou à 3 810 m d'altitude. Il est situé sur l'Altiplano, le 2e plateau le plus haut du monde après le plateau tibétain, en Asie. Avec une profondeur maximale de 180 m, il est navigable même par de grands navires de marchandises.

La plus longue période de sécheresse continue

En plus d'accueillir **l'endroit le plus sec** (ci-dessous, à droite), le Chili, **le pays le plus étroit**, a aussi connu la plus longue période sans la moindre précipitation. D'après l'Organisation météorologique internationale, la ville d'Arica n'a pas reçu une goutte de pluie d'octobre 1903 à janvier 1918. Cela fait 172 mois, soit plus de 14 ans !

Le champ de geysers le plus actif

À 4 300 m au-dessus du niveau de la mer, El Tatio, au nord du Chili, comprend plus de 80 geysers actifs, des mares de boue et des sources chaudes. Avec ses 30 km² environ, il est le plus grand champ de geysers de l'hémisphère Sud. À cette altitude, l'eau bout à 86,6 °C au lieu de 100 °C au niveau de la mer.

El Tatio accueille aussi **le geyser le plus régulier**. En 2012, 3 531 éruptions d'El Jefe ("le chef") ont été enregistrées en 6 jours. L'intervalle moyen entre 2 éruptions était d'à peine 132,2 s.

La plus grande lagune

Lagoa dos Patos ("lac des canards") est située sur la côte du Rio Grande do Sul, au sud du Brésil. Avec ses 280 km de long et ses 9 850 km², la lagune est séparée de l'océan Atlantique par une étroite bande de sable. Elle doit son nom aux nombreux oiseaux qui s'y abritent : canards, hérons, grèbes et flamants.

Le cratère d'impact le plus récent sur Terre

Le 15 septembre 2007, une chondrite (météorite pierreuse) s'est écrasée dans un cours d'eau sec près de Carancas, au sud du lac Titicaca (PER), et a creusé un cratère de 14,2 m de largeur et d'au moins 3,5 m de profondeur. C'est l'un des rares impacts observés directement par l'être humain.

LE SOMMET DE MONTAGNE LE PLUS ÉLOIGNÉ DU CENTRE DE LA TERRE

L'Everest (voir p. 25) est **le plus haut sommet** par rapport au niveau de la mer, tandis que le Mauna Kea, à Hawaï, est **la plus grande montagne** depuis sa base sous-marine. Le mont Chimborazo (ECU) les dépasse tous les deux si on le mesure depuis le centre de la Terre. En raison d'un léger renflement au niveau de l'équateur, son sommet se trouve en effet à 6 384,4 km du centre de la planète, soit 2 km de plus que l'Everest.

La plus forte concentration d'éclairs

D'après les observations menées de 1998 à 2013, des orages se produisent 297 nuits par an près du lac Maracaibo (VEN). La foudre s'y abat 233 fois par an par km² à cause de l'interaction de l'air chaud et humide avec les montagnes environnantes.

Le plus petit désert

Avec une superficie totale de 105 200 km², soit l'équivalent du Kentucky (USA), le désert d'Atacama, au Chili, est le plus petit au monde.

LA PLUS GRANDE BROMÉLIACÉE

Puya raimondii est une plante alpine endémique des hautes altitudes en Bolivie et au Pérou, appartenant à la famille de l'ananas. Ses feuilles peuvent atteindre 4 m de haut, tandis que sa hampe florale peut mesurer 12 à 15 m. C'est aussi **la plante à la floraison la plus lente** : elle peut mettre 80 à 150 ans à fleurir, après quoi elle meurt.

LE PLUS GRAND DÉSERT DE SEL

Avec ses quelque 10 000 km², le salar d'Uyuni, au sud-ouest de la Bolivie, est à peu près 100 fois plus grand que le salar de Bonneville (Utah, USA). L'eau très salée d'un lac préhistorique géant s'est évaporée au fil des millénaires. Selon les estimations, le salar contient aujourd'hui 10 milliards de tonnes de sel.

L'ENDROIT LE PLUS SEC

Entre 1964 et 2001, les précipitations annuelles moyennes de la station météorologique située près de la ville de Quillagua, dans le désert d'Atacama (CHL), n'étaient que de 0,5 mm. Sur le même continent, le bassin amazonien (voir ci-contre) reçoit 4 260 fois plus de précipitations par an en moyenne.

JANV. 21 Lors du championnat de Scrabble d'Irlande du Nord à Belfast (GBR) en 2012, Toh Weibin (SGP) obtient **le score le plus élevé enregistré lors d'un tournoi de Scrabble** (850).

JANV. 22 Bipin Larkin (au lancer) et Ashrita Furman (au rattrapage) (tous 2 USA) établissent le record **du plus grand nombre de couteaux rattrapés en 1 min** (56) à New York (USA) en 2015.

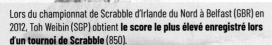

Si l'on ne compte que la partie supérieure de Kerepakupai Merú (chutes de l'Ange), comme le préconisent certains hydrologues, ce sont les chutes de la Tugela, en Afrique du Sud, qui détiennent le record à 948 m. Tugela est actuellement **la plus grande chute d'eau à plusieurs niveaux**.

LA PLUS GRANDE CHUTE D'EAU

Kerepakupai Merú (ou Salto Ángel, les chutes de l'Ange) (VEN) mesure 979 m. Jaillissant de la falaise d'Auyán Tepui, montagne au sommet plat, l'eau plonge dans le canyon à 807 m en contrebas. C'est **la plus longue cascade unique**. Le trajet est si long que l'eau se transforme en brouillard pendant sa chute. L'humidité imprègne le sol et ressort dans plusieurs cascades situées plus bas, qui justifient la hauteur totale de la chute d'eau, même si ce calcul fait débat (voir ci-dessus à gauche).

LA PLUS GRANDE FORÊT TROPICALE HUMIDE

La forêt tropicale humide amazonienne couvre 9 pays d'Amérique du Sud pour une superficie d'au moins 6,24 millions de km². Elle abrite plus de 10 % des espèces végétales et animales du monde.

Long de 6 400 km, l'Amazone serpente dans la forêt et déverse 200 000 m³ – soit l'équivalent de 80 piscines olympiques – dans l'Atlantique par seconde, ce qui en fait **le plus grand fleuve (en débit)**.

LA PLUS GRANDE ZONE HUMIDE

Le Pantanal occupe environ 160 000 km² (presque 4 fois la taille de la Suisse) à la frontière entre le Brésil, le Paraguay et la Bolivie. La région est connue pour sa biodiversité : elle abrite des anacondas verts (**les serpents les plus lourds**) et des capybaras (**les plus grands rongeurs**, voir p. 49), ainsi que des plantes exotiques telles que Victoria amazonica, **le plus grand nénuphar** (ci-dessus).

JANV. 23 Hanif Mohammad (PAK) est à la batte pendant 16 h et 10 min pour un score de 337 contre les Indes occidentales à Bridgetown (BRB) en 1958 : c'est **le plus long tour de batte individuel en Test cricket**.

 JANV. 24 En 1986, *Voyager 2* réalise **le 1er survol d'Uranus**. La sonde passe à 81 500 km du sommet de la couverture nuageuse de la planète et calcule qu'un jour y dure environ 17 h.

19

AFRIQUE

Le 1er continent à abriter l'espèce humaine

C'est en Afrique, le "berceau de l'humanité", qu'ont évolué les ancêtres des humains et des grands singes il y a des millions d'années. En 2017, des restes de crânes et de mâchoires d'au moins 5 humains modernes (*Homo sapiens*) vieux de 315 000 ans environ ont été retrouvés dans une région désolée du Maroc à Jebel Irhoud, une ancienne mine située à 100 km à l'ouest de Marrakech. Jusque-là, les scientifiques estimaient que *H. sapiens* était apparu en Afrique de l'Est plus de 100 000 ans plus tard.

L'Afrique est aussi **le continent comptant le plus de pays** (54).

La plus vieille chaîne de montagnes

Les roches des montagnes de Barberton Makhonjwa (ZAF) ont 3,6 milliards d'années. Ces monts atteignent une altitude de 1 800 m au-dessus du niveau de la mer. Selon les estimations, le mont Kilimandjaro, le plus haut sommet d'Afrique, n'a "que" 2,5 millions d'années.

La plus vieille île

Située au sud-est de l'Afrique, Madagascar est devenue une île il y a 80-100 millions d'années, quand elle s'est détachée du sous-continent indien. Avec une superficie de 587 041 km², elle est la 4e plus grande île du monde.

Le plus long système de faille

La grande faille est-africaine mesure 4 400 km de long environ et 50 à 65 km de large en moyenne. Les falaises qui la bordent mesurent de 600 à 900 m de haut. Cette formation commencerait dans le golfe d'Aden et s'étendrait jusqu'au Mozambique, au sud-est de l'Afrique. Elle se forme depuis 30 millions d'années, la plaque arabique s'éloignant de la plaque africaine.

Le plus long lac

Le lac Tanganyika mesure 673 km de long. Il est le 2e plus profond au monde après le lac Baïkal (voir p. 24). À cheval sur la Zambie, la Tanzanie, la République démocratique du Congo et le Burundi, il mesure entre 16 et 72 km de large.

Le lac le plus mortel

(ayant causé le plus grand nombre de morts hors noyade) est le lac Nyos, au Cameroun. Durant la nuit du 21 août 1986, 1 600 à 1 800 personnes et de nombreux animaux sont morts à cause d'une forte émission de dioxyde de carbone.

Le fleuve le plus profond

En juillet 2008, des scientifiques de l'Institut d'études géologiques des États-Unis et du Muséum américain d'histoire naturelle ont découvert que le Congo, qui s'écoule à travers l'Afrique centrale, a une profondeur maximale d'au moins 220 m. La profondeur maximale de la Tamise, à Londres (GBR), est de 20 m.

La plus grande mine de diamants

Avec une surface de 1,18 km², la mine à ciel ouvert d'Orapa (BWA) fait la taille de 165 terrains de football. Selon Paul Zimnisky Diamond Analytics, elle a produit environ 9,8 millions de carats (1 960 kg) de diamants en 2017.

POPULATION
1,256 milliard

SUPERFICIE TOTALE
30,37 millions de km²

PAYS
54

PLUS HAUT SOMMET
Kilimandjaro : 5 895 m

PLUS GRAND LAC
Victoria : 59 947 km²

PLUS LONG FLEUVE
Nil : 6 695 km

LE PLUS GRAND LAC TROPICAL

Avec une superficie de 59 947 km² environ (données de 2016), le lac Victoria (ou Nam Lolwe, Nyanza, Nalubaale, Ukéréoué) est le plus grand lac des tropiques. Il contient environ 2 424 km³ d'eau, soit 327 fois le volume du Loch Ness en Écosse (GBR), et forme la principale source du Nil, **le fleuve le plus long** au monde.

En 2014, le delta de l'Okavango est devenu le 1 000e site inscrit au Patrimoine mondial de l'Unesco.

LA PLUS GRANDE FORÊT DE PIERRE

Le grand Tsingy, à l'ouest de Madagascar, est une forêt de 600 km² composée de piliers de calcaire datant du jurassique. Avec le temps, la pluie a érodé la pierre et créé un paysage spectaculaire, où certaines formations atteignent 90 m de haut.

LE PLUS GRAND DELTA CONTINENTAL

Avec ses 40 000 km², le delta de l'Okavango (BWA) est une vaste zone humide alimentée par les crues des plateaux angolais. Cette région de plus de 14 000 km² est inondée au moins une fois tous les 10 ans. Ce delta abrite des lions, des éléphants, plus de 400 espèces d'oiseaux et environ 70 espèces de poissons. Le *mokoro*, sorte de canoë, est le moyen de transport traditionnel.

JANV. 25
En 2013, à Owensboro (Kentucky, USA), il est prouvé qu'Elaine Martin (USA) a un poil de 16,77 cm sur le ventre : c'est **le plus long poil d'abdomen**. "C'est quelque chose !" dit Elaine.

JANV. 26
En 1972, Vesna Vulović (YUG) survit par miracle à l'explosion de l'avion DC-9 dans lequel elle est hôtesse de l'air, à 10 160 m d'altitude. C'est **la plus grande chute non mortelle sans parachute**.

Le Sahara est plus vaste que les États-Unis et à peu près 2 fois plus grand que la forêt amazonienne.

LE PLUS GRAND DÉSERT CHAUD

Presque un huitième de la surface de la Terre est aride, avec des précipitations de moins de 25 cm par an. Aucun désert chaud n'est plus grand que le Sahara (voir p. 28 pour **le plus grand désert** dans l'absolu). Il mesure jusqu'à 5 150 km d'est en ouest, entre 1 280 et 2 250 km du nord au sud et couvre une superficie de 9,1 millions de km².

Les deux tiers de l'Afrique sont devenus désertiques ou secs, ce qui en fait **le continent le plus touché par la désertification**. Environ un tiers du continent subit une désertification modérée à sévère. Certaines causes sont naturelles, comme les variations climatiques et l'érosion, mais les activités humaines, de l'agriculture intensive à la déforestation en passant même par les déplacements de population, ont exacerbé ce phénomène. Ci-dessus, les sables du désert envahissent une maison de Kolmanskop, une ancienne ville minière au sud de la Namibie.

LE PLUS VIEUX DÉSERT

Le désert de Namibie court sur 2 000 km de long en Angola, en Nanibie et en Afrique du Sud, et reçoit moins de 10 mm de pluie par an. Il est aride ou semi-aride depuis au moins 80 millions d'années en raison de l'air sec descendant, refroidi par les eaux du courant marin de Benguela.

LA COULÉE DE LAVE LA PLUS RAPIDE

Le Nyiragongo est un volcan bouclier situé en République démocratique du Congo. Lors de l'éruption du 10 janvier 1977, la lave, qui était très fluide à cause de sa forte teneur en silice, est sortie par des fissures sur les flancs du mont et a atteint des vitesses de 60 à 100 km/h.

Le cratère du Nyiragongo abrite **le plus grand lac de lave**, qui mesure environ 250 m de diamètre et 600 m de profondeur.

JANV. 27 En 2018, le groupe scolaire de Kaligi Ranganathan Montford (IND) réunit **le plus grand nombre de personnes résolvant des Rubik's Cubes** au stade Jawaharlal Nehru (IND) 3 997.

JANV. 28 Diplom-Is (NOR) construit **la plus grande pyramide en boules de glace** à Strömstad (SWE) en 2017. Une fois achevée, la structure mesurait 1,1 m de haut et contenait 5 435 sphères de glace.

EUROPE

POPULATION
741,4 millions*

SUPERFICIE TOTALE
10,18 millions de km²

PAYS
51*

PLUS HAUT SOMMET
Elbrus : 5 642 m

PLUS GRAND LAC
Ladoga : 17 700 km²

PLUS LONG FLEUVE
Volga : 3 530 km

*Avec uniquement la partie européenne des pays transcontinentaux.

Le plus petit pays

L'État de la Cité du Vatican (*Stato della Città del Vaticano*), enclave dans la capitale italienne, Rome, occupe à peine 0,44 km², soit 8 fois moins que la superficie de Central Park à New York (USA). Le gouvernement italien a reconnu sa souveraineté par le traité du Latran du 11 février 1929. La Cité du Vatican a aussi **la plus courte frontière terrestre** : sa frontière avec l'Italie court sur 3,2 km.

Le volcan à l'éruption continue la plus longue

Le mont Stromboli, situé sur l'île éponyme de la mer Tyrrhénienne à l'ouest de l'Italie, est surnommé le "phare de la Méditerranée" à cause de la régularité de ses éruptions. Nous savons qu'il est actif de manière continue au moins depuis le VIIe siècle av. J.-C. grâce aux écrits des colons grecs. Un autre volcan record, l'Etna (ci-contre), se trouve à environ 170 km au sud du Stromboli.

Le plus profond plan d'eau souterrain

En 2015, le plongeur Krzysztof Starnawski (POL) a plongé jusqu'à 265 m dans le gouffre inondé de Hranice (CZE) sans parvenir à atteindre le fond. Un an plus tard, il a piloté un véhicule sous-marin télécommandé, qui a révélé que la profondeur y est d'au moins 404 m.

L'éclair le plus long (temps)

Le 30 août 2012, au sud-est de la France, un éclair a parcouru environ 200 km entre 2 nuages en 7,74 s. En moyenne, un éclair dure 0,2 s. L'Organisation météorologique mondiale a homologué cette distance en 2016.

Le plus long récif de craie

En 2010, le plongeur Rob Spray et une équipe d'écologistes ont découvert un récif vieux de 300 millions d'années environ. Parsemé d'arches et de rigoles creusées par la marée, il s'étend sur plus de 32 km au large du Norfolk (GBR).

Le tourbillon naturel le plus puissant

Dans le détroit séparant Skjerstadfjorden et Saltfjorden au nord de la Norvège, les courants peuvent atteindre 40 km/h. À son maximum, la marée produit de puissants tourbillons pouvant atteindre 10 m de large et 5 m de profondeur environ. Les courants atteignent leur puissance maximale durant la pleine lune.

Le plus grand marais de roseaux

Le delta du Danube, à la frontière entre la Roumanie et l'Ukraine, est une réserve de biosphère inscrite au Patrimoine de l'Unesco. C'est la plus grande zone humide d'Europe. Il comprend un marais de roseaux de 1 563 km², soit 3 552 fois la superficie de la Cité du Vatican (en haut à gauche). Il abrite un grand nombre d'espèces animales, notamment des oiseaux. Ce delta filtre les eaux du fleuve avant qu'elles ne se jettent dans la mer Noire.

La plus grande mer saumâtre

Avec ses 377 000 km², la mer Baltique, au nord de l'Europe, est le plus grand plan d'eau saumâtre (mélange d'eau douce et salée) au monde. Sa salinité oscille entre 0,23 et 3,27 %, ce qui en fait aussi **la mer la moins salée**. En général, l'eau de mer contient environ 3,5 % de sel. Cette salinité très basse est due à la grande quantité d'eau douce provenant des cours d'eau des pays qui l'entourent.

LES PLUS GRANDS ANNEAUX DE VAPEUR

Le plus grand volcan actif d'Europe (voir à droite) n'émet pas que de la lave et des cendres. Parfois, l'Etna produit de grands anneaux de vapeur pouvant mesurer 200 m de large et flotter à 1 km d'altitude. Ce phénomène rare serait dû à l'expulsion de "courtes bouffées de gaz" à haute pression émis par de petits conduits circulaires.

LE PLUS GRAND NOMBRE DE PLAGES PAVILLON BLEU

Oubliez les Caraïbes ou l'Australie : le pays recensant le plus de plages Pavillon bleu est l'Espagne, avec 590 plages au 30 juillet 2018. Ce programme de la Fondation pour l'éducation à l'environnement en Europe évalue des critères stricts, comme la qualité de l'eau, l'éducation des visiteurs et la gestion environnementale.

LA PLUS GRANDE COLONIE CLONALE D'UNE PLANTE MARINE

En 2006, une vaste prairie de posidonie de Méditerranée (*Posidonia oceanica*) a été découverte au sud d'Ibiza, dans les Baléares (ESP). Cette plante marine forme des herbiers sur le fond marin, la plus grande colonie connue mesurant environ 8 km. Selon les estimations, ce spécimen autoreproducteur aurait 100 000 ans.

LE PLUS GRAND CHÊNE-LIÈGE

Planté en 1783 à Águas de Moura (PRT), le Siffleur a fourni 825 kg de liège en 2009 - de quoi fermer 100 000 bouteilles de vin ! Ce matériau présent dans l'écorce du chêne-liège (*Quercus suber*) est récolté tous les 9 ans environ. En 2018, ce spécimen exceptionnel, qui doit son nom aux nombreux oiseaux qui s'abritent dans ses branches, a été nommé Arbre européen de l'année.

 JANV. 29 En 2013, Jim Bolin (USA) dévoile **le plus grand tee de golf** : 9,37 m de haut pour un diamètre de 1,91 m lors de sa mesure à Casey, dans l'Illinois (USA).

 JANV. 30 En 2018, 17 303 participants découvrent comment adopter un mode de vie zéro déchet durant **la plus grande leçon de recyclage**, organisée par le club Virudhunagar Toastmasters (IND) à Tamil Nadu (IND).

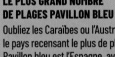

LA PLUS LONGUE HISTOIRE ÉRUPTIVE CONNUE

Bien que l'Europe soit beaucoup plus calme que la ceinture de feu du Pacifique, **la plus grande région volcanique**, elle n'est pas dénuée d'activité volcanique.

La 1re éruption documentée de l'Etna, en Sicile (ITA), date de 1 500 av. J.-C. (il y a environ 3 500 ans). Depuis, le plus grand volcan du continent, qui culmine à 3 329 m d'altitude, est entré en éruption plus de 200 fois.

Plus récemment, le strato-volcan est entré en éruption en septembre 2013 et est plus ou moins actif depuis. Le 24 décembre 2018, le flanc du volcan a commencé à cracher des cendres : c'était la 1re éruption latérale depuis plus de 10 ans. Cela a provoqué un séisme de magnitude 4,8 et plusieurs séismes plus petits.

LE PLUS GRAND RÉCIF DE CORAIL EN EAUX PROFONDES

Le récif de Røst, au large des îles Lofoten (NOR) (ci-dessous), repose sur des fonds marins ayant une superficie équivalente à 14 terrains de football. Situé entre 300 et 400 m de profondeur, il comprend surtout du corail dur *Lophelia*, qui attire des espèces marines très différentes de celles des récifs tropicaux.

LE PLUS GRAND NOMBRE DE TORNADES DANS UNE RÉGION (PAYS)

Entre 1980 et 2012, l'Angleterre a enregistré 2,2 tornades par an tous les 10 000 km², contre 1,3 par an dans l'ensemble des États-Unis. Environ 95 % des tornades anglaises entraient dans la catégorie EF0–EF1 (105–175 km/h). La photo montre les dégâts d'une tornade EF2 (jusqu'à 220 km/h) à Birmingham (GBR), en juillet 2005.

En 1920, à Québec (CAN), Joe Malone (CAN) marque 7 fois pour les Quebec Bulldogs contre les Toronto St Patricks, soit **le plus de buts marqués par un joueur dans une partie LNH de hockey sur glace**.

Le 1er studio cinématographique, un bâtiment couvert de papier goudronné surnommé "Black Maria", conçu par Thomas Edison (USA), est achevé en 1893 à West Orange (New Jersey, USA).

ASIE

POPULATION
4,463 milliards

SUPERFICIE TOTALE
44,58 millions de km²

PAYS
49*

PLUS HAUT SOMMET
Everest : 8 848 m

PLUS GRAND LAC
Mer Caspienne :
371 000 km²

PLUS LONG FLEUVE
Yangtze : 6 300 km

Sans compter les États insulaires du Pacifique en Océanie (voir p. 26-27)

Le plus grand lac

Située à la frontière entre l'Europe du Sud-Est et l'Asie, la mer Caspienne compte 7 000 km de côtes et couvre 371 000 km², soit environ la superficie du Japon. C'est un lac endoréique, c'est-à-dire que ses eaux ne rejoignent pas la mer.

Le lac le plus profond

Le lac Baïkal est un lac d'eau douce de 636 km de long situé dans une vallée en Sibérie. En 1999, une équipe internationale d'hydrographes et de limnologistes ont réévalué les données disponibles pour créer une carte bathymétrique numérique plus précise : le lac atteindrait ainsi 1 642 m de profondeur.

Le lac Baïkal contient environ 23 615 km³ d'eau, soit presque 2 fois plus que le lac Supérieur en Amérique du Nord, ce qui en fait **le plus grand lac d'eau douce en volume**.

Les dunes de sable les plus hautes (isolées)

Les dunes du désert de Badain Jaran, en Mongolie intérieure, au nord de la Chine, mesurent 330 m de haut en moyenne, mais ont déjà atteint les 460-480 m, soit plus que l'Empire State Building. Les géologues ont constaté que le sable a un taux d'humidité élevé, ce qui favorise la stabilité des dunes et explique leur taille.

Le plus grand désert de sable continu

La mer de sable du Rub al Khali ("le quart vide"), un erg, couvre une surface de 560 000 km² environ dans le désert d'Arabie. Elle est principalement située en Arabie saoudite, mais couvre aussi des régions des pays voisins : Oman, Yémen et Émirats arabes unis.

L'Arabie saoudite accueille aussi l'oasis Al-Ahsa, qui occupe environ 85,4 km² et est irriguée par plus de 280 puits artésiens. C'est **la plus grande oasis** et elle abrite plus de 2,5 millions de dattiers.

La plus longue arche naturelle

Le Xianren Qiao (le "pont aux fées"), est une arche naturelle formée par la rivière Buliu, qui a creusé le calcaire de la province de Guangxi (CHN). Selon une expédition de la Natural Arch and Bridge Society, il mesurait 120 m de long en octobre 2010.

La plus grande fleur unique

Rafflesia arnoldii, plante d'Asie du Sud-Est, peut atteindre 91 cm de diamètre et peser 11 kg, avec des pétales mesurant jusqu'à 1,9 cm d'épaisseur. Elle n'a ni feuilles, ni tige, ni racines, mais parasite des lianes dans la jungle. On l'appelle parfois "la fleur cadavre" à cause de l'odeur de moisi qu'elle émet pour attirer les mouches, une stratégie qu'elle partage avec **la fleur la plus haute** (voir p. 30-31).

La montagne grandissant le plus rapidement

Au nord du Pakistan, dans l'ouest de l'Himalaya, se trouve le Nanga Parbat, qui grandit de 7 mm par an. Avec ses 8 125 m, il est le 9ᵉ sommet le plus haut du monde.

LA PLUS PETITE MER

Une mer, généralement située en bordure des océans, est un plan d'eau salée partiellement entouré de terres. La mer de Marmara (ci-dessus) (TUR) mesure 280 km de long et environ 80 km de large au maximum. Sa superficie totale est de 11 350 km², pour une profondeur moyenne de 494 m.

La plus grande mer se trouve également en Asie : la mer de Chine du Sud mesure environ 3,5 millions de km².

LA PLUS FORTE PLUIE EN 48 H

Les 15-16 juin 1995, Cherrapunji (IND) a reçu 2,493 m de pluie en 2 jours selon l'Organisation météorologique mondiale. L'altitude de cette ville de l'État de Meghalaya, 1 313 m, explique en partie les fortes précipitations qu'elle reçoit chaque année.

LA CASCADE COMPTANT LE PLUS GRAND NOMBRE DE PONTS NATURELS

Découvert en 1952, le gouffre des Trois Ponts, à Tannourine (LBN), abrite une cascade de 255 m de haut traversant 3 ponts naturels en pierre. Elle n'est visible qu'en mars et en avril, durant la fonte des neiges. Le calcaire date du jurassique, il y a environ 160 millions d'années.

LE PLUS GRAND FRUIT ISSU D'UN ARBRE

Originaire de la région indo-himalayenne, le jaquier (*Artocarpus heterophyllus*) porte des fruits mesurant 0,9 m de long et pesant environ 34 kg, soit 250 fois plus qu'une orange. **La pomme jaque la plus lourde** connue pesait 42,72 kg le 23 juin 2016.

FÉVR. 2 Le comédien Tetsuro Degawa (JPN) se recouvre de 674 notes adhésives sur le plateau de *Grand Whiz-Kids TV* (NHK, Shibuya, Tokyo, JPN) en 2014, **le plus grand nombre de notes adhésives sur le corps en 5 min**.

FÉVR. 3 En 2014, Elisabeth Windisch (DEU) présente **le plus grand bonbon gélifié** à Schmitt Waagenbau GmbH, à Düsseldorf (DEU). Il pèse pas moins de 512 kg.

La voûte de Hang Son Đoòng est plus de 2 fois plus haute que la statue de la Liberté !

LA PLUS GRANDE GROTTE

Hang Son Đoòng ("la grotte de la rivière de la montagne") est la plus vaste grotte individuelle. Elle mesure environ 200 m de haut, 150 m de large et au moins 6,5 km de long. Elle se trouve dans le parc national de Phong Nha-Ke Bàng, dans la province de Quang Bình (VNM).

Accessible uniquement en rappel (ci-dessus), elle a été découverte en 1991 par un fermier local, Ho Khanh, qui n'a pu retrouver le chemin qui y mène que 18 ans plus tard. En avril 2009, il a guidé une équipe de spéléologues britanniques à travers la jungle pendant 6 h pour qu'ils en inspectent une partie.

LA PLUS HAUTE MONTAGNE

L'Everest (Sagarmatha ou Chomolungma), dans l'Himalaya, à la frontière entre le Tibet et le Népal, s'élève à 8 848 m au-dessus du niveau de la mer, mais n'est pas **la plus grande montagne** (voir p. 16).

L'Asie revendique **le dénivelé le plus élevé** : 9 278 m du sommet de l'Everest à la mer Morte, au pied de la vallée du Jourdain, située 430 m sous le niveau de la mer.

LE CRATÈRE DE MÉTHANE À LA PLUS LONGUE COMBUSTION

Surnommé "la porte de l'Enfer", le cratère de Darvaza, profond de 30 m, est en feu depuis 1971. Il est situé dans un champ de gaz naturel dans le désert du Karakoum, environ 250 km au nord d'Achgabat (TKM). On pense que le sol s'est effondré pendant le forage et que l'incendie a été allumé pour brûler le méthane qui s'échappait.

En novembre 2013, l'aventurier George Kourounis (CAN) a été **la 1ʳᵉ personne à explorer le cratère de Darvaza**, protégé par une combinaison en aluminium (photo).

FÉVR. 4 — En 1994, Paddy Doyle (GBR), détenteur de plusieurs records, réalise **le plus grand nombre de burpees en 1 h** (1 840) au pub Bull's Head de Polesworth, Birmingham (GBR).

FÉVR. 5 — En 2016, Didga, avec son propriétaire Robert Dollwet (USA/AUS), réalise **le plus grand nombre de tours faits par un chat en 1 min** - 24. Didga peut taper dans la main, tourner comme une toupie et faire du skate.

25

OCÉANIE

L'Océanie est une région géographique du sud du Pacifique comprenant de nombreux États insulaires, dont la Nouvelle-Zélande et la Nouvelle-Guinée. Le plus grand de ces territoires est l'Australie. Les données à gauche concernent l'Océanie dans son ensemble.

👥 **POPULATION**
38,3 millions

↗↙↘↖ **SUPERFICIE TOTALE**
8,5 millions de km²

🚩 **PAYS**
14

🔺 **PLUS HAUT SOMMET**
Puncak Jaya :
4 884 m

PLUS GRAND LAC
Corangamite :
234 km²

PLUS LONG FLEUVE
Murray : 2 508 km

Le plus petit continent
Pour la plupart des sources, dont le GWR, l'Australie est le plus petit continent, avec une largeur est-ouest de 4 042 km environ et une superficie de 7 617 930 km².

Avec une altitude moyenne de seulement 330 m au-dessus du niveau de la mer, l'Australie est aussi **le continent le plus plat**. Son point culminant est le mont Kosciuszko, à 2 228 m, soit environ la moitié de l'altitude du Puncak Jaya (ou pyramide Carstensz), en Nouvelle-Guinée, le point culminant d'Océanie.

Le plus grand lac éphémère
Contrairement au lac Corangamite, qui est permanent (voir à gauche), le Kati Thanda-Lake Eyre, en Australie-Méridionale, contient très peu d'eau, voire pas du tout, mais se remplit en cas de fortes pluies. À son maximum, ce bassin salé et plat peut devenir une mer intérieure d'environ 9 690 km².

Le plus vaste atoll
L'atoll de Kwajalein, une des îles Marshall, au centre du Pacifique, est un fin récif annulaire de 283 km de long. Il entoure un lagon de 2 850 km²,

LE PLUS GRAND NUAGE SOLITON
Les nuages solitons sont rares. Ils maintiennent leur forme tout en se déplaçant à vitesse constante. Le plus long exemple régulier de ce phénomène est le Morning Glory, dans le golfe de Carpentaria (AUS). Ce nuage peut atteindre 1 000 km de long et 1 km de haut et se déplacer à 60 km/h.

une superficie supérieure à celle du Luxembourg.

La plus longue grotte marine
Une étude menée en octobre 2012 a révélé que la grotte de Matainaka, sur l'île du Sud en Nouvelle-Zélande, mesure 1,54 km de long. Formée par l'action des vagues, elle s'allonge progressivement.

Le plus grand éperon d'érosion marine
Les éperons d'érosion marine sont des colonnes rocheuses formées par les vagues. La pyramide de Ball, au nord de l'île Lord Howe (Pacifique), mesure 561 m – plus que la tour CN au Canada. En 2001, des scientifiques y ont découvert une petite colonie de *Dryococelus australis*, **l'insecte le plus rare**. Cette espèce de

phasme que l'on croyait disparue est désormais classée en danger critique d'extinction, la population à l'état sauvage étant estimée à 9-35 individus.

La plus grande dune de sable côtière
Le mont Tempest, sur l'île Moreton, au large du Queensland (AUS), mesure 280 m de haut – 3 fois plus que la statue de la Liberté.

La plus grande source d'eau chaude (superficie)
En Nouvelle-Zélande, le lac Frying Pan, ou chaudron Waimangu, mesure jusqu'à 200 m et couvre environ 38 000 m². Son eau acide atteint les 50 à 60 °C.

La rafale de vent de surface la plus rapide
Le vent le plus rapide mesuré par un anémomètre a atteint 408 km/h selon une station météorologique automatique de l'île Barrow (AUS), le 10 avril 1996, durant le cyclone tropical Olivia. L'Organisation météorologique mondiale a homologué cette vitesse en 2010.

Uluru faisait autrefois partie d'une chaîne de montagnes. Les autres monts ont disparu à cause de l'érosion.

L'ORCHIDÉE LA PLUS HAUTE
Pseudovanilla foliata, une orchidée qui pousse sur les arbres morts dans la forêt pluviale australienne, a été retrouvée à 15 m du sol. Cette plante grimpante est un saprophyte, une plante qui se nourrit de matière organique morte.

LE PLUS GRAND MONOLITHE EN GRÈS
Uluru, aussi appelé Ayers Rock, culmine à 348 m d'altitude dans la plaine désertique du Territoire du Nord (AUS). Ce célèbre relief, qui d'après les estimations aurait 600 millions d'années, mesure 2,5 km de long et 1,6 km de large. Il doit sa couleur rouge au fer contenu dans ses roches de surface.

LE PLUS GRAND PRODUCTEUR DE DIAMANTS EN VOLUME (MINE UNIQUE)
D'après les données de Paul Zimnisky Diamond Analytics, la mine de diamants d'Argyle en Australie-Occidentale a produit 17,1 millions de carats de diamants naturels en 2017. C'est aussi la seule source connue de diamants roses. Mais les réserves diminuent, à tel point qu'elle devrait fermer en 2020.

FÉVR. 6 En 1952, la reine Élisabeth II monte sur le trône à la mort de son père, le roi George VI. Au 21 avril 2019, après 67 ans et 74 jours de règne ininterrompu, elle était **la reine au règne le plus long**.

FÉVR. 7 Au Super Bowl XLIV en 2010, le kicker Matt Stover (USA) des Indianapolis Colts a 42 ans et 11 jours : il est **le joueur du Super Bowl le plus âgé**. Il marque 5 points, mais son équipe perd le match.

LE PLUS LONG RÉCIF CORALLIEN

La Grande Barrière de corail, au nord-est de l'Australie, mesure 2 207 km de long, à peu près la distance entre le Royaume-Uni et Malte. Elle se compose d'environ 2 900 colonies de corail séparées et couvre 207 200 km². Le corail actuel pousse sur des polypes parfois vieux de 20 millions d'années.

Cet écosystème riche est fragile et exposé à de nombreux dangers, dont le blanchissement. Les eaux de plus en plus chaudes de l'océan provoquent l'expulsion des algues symbiotiques, qui ne laissent que le corail blanc. Une étude de 2018 a révélé que la forte vague de chaleur de 9 mois de 2016 a causé la mort de presque 30 % des coraux de la barrière.

LA PLUS VIEILLE FORÊT TROPICALE HUMIDE

La forêt de Daintree, dans le Queensland (AUS), couvre environ 1 200 km et fait partie des tropiques humides. Elle constitue la plus grande étendue continue de forêt humide en Australie et daterait du jurassique, il y a 180 millions d'années.

LA PLUS GRANDE PAROI ÉVASÉE

Située sur la face nord d'Hyden Rock, en Australie-Occidentale, Wave Rock mesure environ 110 m de long et jusqu'à 12 m de haut, pour une surface exposée d'à peu près 1 320 m². Le granit, vieux de 2,7 milliards d'années, a subi l'érosion provoquée par l'acidité du terrain qui le recouvrait.

FÉVR. 8 — En 2004, les chefs du Mohegan Sun Hotel and Casino d'Uncasville, au Connecticut (USA), préparent **le plus grand gâteau de mariage**. Il pèse 6,818 t.

FÉVR. 9 — L'hôtel Gevora est inauguré à Dubaï (ARE) en 2018. Ce bâtiment recouvert d'or possède 528 chambres sur 75 étages et mesure 356,33 m de haut, ce qui en fait **l'hôtel le plus haut**.

27

ANTARCTIQUE

Le continent abritant le moins de pays

L'Antarctique n'a pas de population native et aucun pays n'est reconnu sous la latitude de 60° S. Plusieurs pays y ont revendiqué des terres, mais un traité de 1959 aujourd'hui signé par 53 pays prévoit de laisser le continent ouvert à la recherche scientifique pacifique, sans aucune activité militaire.

D'après le British Antarctic Survey, l'altitude moyenne de l'Antarctique est, sans les plateformes glacières, de 2 194 m au-dessus de l'OSU91A Geoid, une mesure du niveau de la mer tenant compte de la forme irrégulière de la Terre. Il est donc **le continent le plus haut**.

Le plus grand désert

Un désert est tout simplement un lieu où il ne pleut pas, ou très peu. Le plus grand désert est donc la calotte glaciaire antarctique, qui couvre plus de 99 % des 14 millions de km² de l'Antarctique.

Chaque année, le continent reçoit à peine 50 mm de précipitations (pluie, neige et grêle). L'intérieur des terres est le plus aride. L'Antarctique est donc aussi **le continent le plus sec**.

POPULATION
0

SUPERFICIE TOTALE
14 millions de km²

PAYS
0

PLUS HAUT SOMMET
Mont Vinson : 4 892 m

PLUS GRAND LAC
Lac subglaciaire Vostok : 15 000 km²

PLUS LONG FLEUVE
Onyx : 32 km

LE VENT CATABATIQUE LE PLUS RAPIDE

Ces vents sont causés par la descente d'une masse d'air froid et dense, située à haute altitude, sous l'effet de la gravité. Les plus rapides sont situés près des escarpements côtiers antarctiques. En 1915, le géologue et explorateur Douglas Mawson, responsable de l'expédition antarctique australasienne de 1911-1914, a décrit des vents soudains de plus de 270 km/h au cap Dennison, dans la baie du Commonwealth, en Antarctique.

Sans surprise, la calotte glaciaire antarctique est **le désert le plus froid**. D'après le British Antarctic Survey, la température hivernale moyenne est de -20 °C sur la côte et de -60 °C, voire plus basse, dans les terres. C'est aussi ici qu'a été enregistrée **la température la plus basse sur Terre** (voir à droite).

Ironiquement, la calotte glaciaire antarctique abrite aussi **le plus grand plan d'eau douce**, avec environ 30 millions de km³, soit environ 70 % des réserves de la planète, mais sous forme de glace. C'est presque 400 fois le volume de la mer Caspienne, **le plus grand lac** (p. 24).

Les dunes de sable les plus méridionales

Hautes de 70 m, les dunes de sable de la vallée de Victoria, en Antarctique, se trouvent à 77,3° S environ.

La glace flottante la plus épaisse

Le courant glaciaire de Rutford se trouve à l'est des monts Ellsworth, dans l'ouest de l'Antarctique. En janvier 1975, un sondage par écho radio mené par Charles Swithinbank et des membres du British Antarctic Survey a montré que le courant mesure 1 860 m d'épaisseur jusqu'à la limite d'ancrage (point où il commence à flotter), par 77,6° S, 84,2° O, là où il rejoint la calotte glaciaire de Ronne.

Le continent le moins ensoleillé

Le pôle Sud ne reçoit aucune

LA TEMPÉRATURE LA PLUS BASSE SUR TERRE

Le 21 juillet 1983, la témparature est tombée à -89,2 °C dans la base de recherche russe de Vostok, soit 54 °C de moins que la température hivernale moyenne. En 2018, des satellites ont enregistré des températures encore plus basses : -98 °C dans le plateau antarctique oriental. Toutefois, l'Organisation météorologique mondiale rappelle que ce type de mesure doit être prise à une hauteur standard dans une station météorologique sous abri. Le GWR attend donc une confirmation sur le terrain avant d'homologuer ces records.

lumière solaire pendant 182 jours par an. Pendant 6 mois, le soleil n'apparaît pas du tout à l'horizon. Au pôle Nord, l'obscurité dure 176 jours.

Le plus vaste glacier

Le glacier de Lambert-Fisher mesure environ 96,5 km de large et 402 km de long, ce qui en fait aussi **le glacier le plus long**. Il a été découvert en 1956 lors d'une mission photographique australienne aéroportée.

L'arbre le plus isolé

Un épicéa de Sitka (Picea sitchensis) se trouve sur l'île subantarctique de Campbell, à plus de 222 km de l'arbre le plus proche, situé sur les îles Auckland. L'épicéa est surnommé "l'arbre de Ranfurly", d'après le nom du gouverneur de Nouvelle-Zélande qui l'aurait planté en 1901. Toutefois, une étude de 2017 suggère qu'il a été planté plus tard.

LA PLUS GRANDE FRÉQUENCE D'APPARITION DU POUDRIN DE GLACE

Le poudrin de glace est un nuage composé de cristaux de glace qui se forme près du sol en cas d'inversion de température, par exemple quand l'air chaud rencontre une masse d'air froid plus basse. Sur la Plateau Station, base américaine abandonnée dans le plateau antarctique central, des nuages de poudrin de glace peuvent se former 316 jours par an en moyenne.

 FÉVR. 10 En 2013, le club de saut en parachute de Dubaï (ARE) réunit **le plus grand nombre de parachutistes sautant d'une montgolfière en même temps** : 25 membres font le grand saut.

 FÉVR. 11 Mujtaba Hassan Mughal (PAK) brise **le plus grand nombre de noix avec un nunchaku en 1 min** en 2018 à Karachi (PAK) (118).

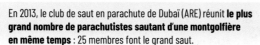

LA PLUS HAUTE MONTAGNE ANTARCTIQUE

Le sommet du mont Vinson s'élève à 4 892 m au-dessus du niveau de la mer. Faisant partie du massif Sentinel, dans les monts Ellsworth, à environ 1 200 km du pôle Sud, il a été escaladé pour la 1re fois par une équipe de l'American Alpine Club et de la National Science Foundation en 1966. Il fait aujourd'hui partie du défi des Sept Sommets, dont il est le plus reculé et le dernier à avoir été escaladé.

Le mont Vinson est le moins fréquenté des Sept Sommets à cause de la température moyenne (-30 °C) et des vents très violents.

LA PLUS GRANDE PLATEFORME DE GLACE

La barrière, ou plateforme, de Ross a été découverte par le capitaine James Clark Ross (GBR) en 1841. Avec une superficie de 472 000 km² environ sur la mer de Ross – grande baie de l'Antarctique donnant sur le Pacifique – elle constitue le plus grand ensemble de glace flottante au monde. Sa côte, quasiment verticale, mesure plus de 600 km de long et 10-15 m de haut le long de l'océan Austral.

LA MER LA PLUS TRANSPARENTE

Le 13 octobre 1986, des scientifiques de l'institut Alfred Wegener de Bremerhaven (DEU) ont mesuré la transparence de la mer de Weddell, au large de l'Antarctique. Ils ont plongé un disque de Secchi – un disque de 30 cm de diamètre conçu pour évaluer la transparence de l'eau – dans la mer jusqu'à ce qu'il disparaisse. Il est resté visible jusqu'à une profondeur de 80 m – environ 1,5 fois la taille de la colonne de Nelson à Londres (GBR).

FÉVR. 12 En 2002, une équipe de paléontologues menée par le professeur Peter Doyle (GBR) annonce la découverte **du plus vieux vomi**, un repas vieux de 160 millions d'années régurgité par un ichtyosaure, un reptile marin géant.

FÉVR. 13 Lors des Grammy Awards de 2011 (Los Angeles, Californie, USA), E ! Entertainment (USA) organise **la plus grande rencontre d'imitateurs de Lady Gaga**, qui rassemble 121 sosies.

L'éruption volcanique sous-marine documentée la plus profonde

En décembre 2015, un véhicule sous-marin autonome a recherché des cheminées hydrothermales à l'ouest de la fosse des Mariannes, **le point le plus profond des océans**, dans le Pacifique. À environ 4 450 m de profondeur, il a découvert une traînée de lave noire et vitreuse de 7,3 km de long, la trace d'une récente éruption sous-marine. Le site a été visité de nouveau en 2016 et les résultats ont été publiés dans *Frontiers in Earth Science*, le 23 octobre 2018.

Le plus long système de grottes immergées exploré

En janvier 2018, des plongeurs ont confirmé que les systèmes Sac Actún (264 km) et Dos Ojos (84 km), dans la péninsule du Yucatán (MEX), sont reliés par un canal jusque-là inexploré. En juillet 2018, il a été établi que le système mesure, dans son ensemble, 353 km, une donnée confirmée par Quintana Roo Speleological Survey. Le protocole de nomination des grottes veut que toute nouvelle grotte composée de deux ou plusieurs systèmes déjà connus prenne le nom du système le plus grand.

LE MOIS LE PLUS CHAUD (LIEU UNIQUE)

La température a été exceptionnellement élevée partout dans le monde en 2018. Du 1er au 31 juillet, la température journalière moyenne dans la vallée de la Mort (Californie, USA) a été de 42,3 °C d'après la station météo du centre pour visiteurs de Furnace Creek. Le pic de 52,7 °C a été atteint pendant 4 jours, du 24 au 27 juillet.

Pendant 24 h, le 26 juin, la température de l'air n'est pas passée en dessous de 42,6 °C dans la ville côtière de Qurayyat (encadré), à Oman : c'est **la température minimale la plus élevée**. Ce jour-là, le pic de chaleur a été de 49,8 °C.

LE PLUS VIEUX SPÉCIMEN D'ARBRE

Les plus anciens arbres sont les pins Bristlecone (*Pinus longaeva*) des White Mountains (Californie, USA). Le vent, la pluie et le gel les déforment énormément (voir ci-dessous). Le plus vieux spécimen, Mathusalem, a été découvert par le Dr Edmund Schulman (USA). Son âge a été évalué à plus de 4 800 ans en 1957.

La plus grande grotte unique (volume)

La chambre Miao fait partie du système de grottes Gebihe, dans le parc national de Ziyun Getu He (province du Guizhou, CHN). En 2013, une équipe anglaise financée par *National Geographic* l'a cartographiée au rayon laser 3D et a découvert qu'elle mesurait 10,78 millions de m³. Elle pourrait contenir 4 fois la grande pyramide de Gizeh (EGY).

La plus longue observation d'un arc-en-ciel

Le 30 novembre 2017, des membres du département des sciences atmosphériques de l'université de la culture chinoise ont étudié au moins un arc-en-ciel, et même 4 à un moment donné, pendant 8 h et 58 min, depuis plusieurs sites de l'établissement, construit à flanc de montagne dans le Yangmingshan (Taipei chinois). L'altitude, les conditions atmosphériques et l'angle d'observation du soleil étaient parfaits.

La réserve naturelle la plus en altitude

Fondée en 1988, la réserve naturelle nationale du mont Qomolangma s'étend jusqu'au sommet de l'Everest, **la plus haute montagne** (8 848 m). Située en Chine, elle couvre environ 33 810 km² au centre de la chaîne himalayenne, dans la région autonome du Tibet.

Spécimen de pin Bristlecone. L'emplacement exact de Mathusalem est tenu secret pour protéger l'arbre du vandalisme.

LA PLUS GRANDE ÉCLOSION DE MACROALGUES

Certaines algues sont appelées "macroalgues". En juin 2018, l'algue brune *Sargassum* a atteint une superficie mensuelle moyenne de 6 317 km² pour une biomasse humide estimée à au moins 8,9 millions de tonnes. Le phénomène a concerné environ 8 300 km du golfe du Mexique à la côte ouest de l'Afrique. Ci-dessus, on assiste au retrait de *Sargassum* sur la plage de la baie de Soliman, à Tulum, dans la péninsule du Yucatán (MEX).

FÉVR. 14 En 2014, 651 célibataires à la recherche de l'amour participent au **plus grand speed-dating**, dans le TELUS Spark science centre de Calgary (Alberta, CAN).

FÉVR. 15 Avec le véhicule *Oxygen*, "Slammin" Sammy Miller (USA) atteint 399 km/h sur le lac George gelé à New York (USA) en 1981. C'est **la vitesse la plus élevée atteinte par une luge à moteur.**

Environ 400 m sous le niveau de la mer, la réserve naturelle d'Enot Tsukim (ou Ein Feshkha), près de la mer Morte, est **la réserve naturelle la plus basse**. La salinité de ce plan d'eau est trop élevée pour les plantes, mais la région marécageuse de 5,8 km de long qui la borde – **la zone humide la plus basse** – est considérée comme une oasis et a une salinité plus faible grâce à l'eau douce provenant des monts de Judée. Elle est toutefois menacée par la baisse continue du niveau de la mer Morte.

La grotte de Malham se trouve au sud-ouest de la mer Morte, sous le mont Sodome (ISR). Le 28 mars 2019, elle a été reconnue comme **la plus longue grotte de sel** : elle mesure 10 km selon les estimations. L'annonce a été faite par l'université hébraïque

LA PLUS GRANDE TOURBIÈRE TROPICALE

La tourbière de la cuvette centrale du bassin du Congo occupe environ 145 500 km², soit plus de 2 fois la superficie de l'Irlande. Selon les estimations, ces marais contiennent 30 milliards de tonnes de CO_2, l'équivalent de 20 ans d'émissions de combustibles fossiles par les États-Unis. La cuvette centrale est l'un des plus importants "puits de carbone" au monde – des régions absorbant plus de carbone qu'elles n'en émettent.

de Jérusalem après 2 ans d'études. Les grottes de sel sont rares et ne mesurent généralement pas plus de 800 m de long.

La plus forte pluie en 1 min
D'après l'Organisation météorologique mondiale, 31,2 mm de pluie sont tombés sur Unionville (Maryland, USA) en 60 s, le 4 juillet 1956.

Les plus anciens pigments biologiques
Les plus anciennes couleurs biologiques naturelles sont le rose, le rouge et le violet : selon l'étude publiée dans *Proceedings of the National Academy of Sciences* le 9 juillet 2018, elles auraient 1,1 milliard d'années. Les pigments, extraits de l'argile située sous le Sahara, dans le bassin de Taoudeni (MRT), ont plus de 500 millions d'années de plus que les autres pigments naturels connus.

LA FLEUR LA PLUS HAUTE

L'arum titan (*Amorphophallus titanum*) porte la plus grande fleur. En octobre 2018, Adam Millward du GWR (ci-dessous, à droite) a délivré aux Kew Gardens de Londres (GBR) un certificat confirmant la taille exceptionnelle de cette plante. Avec ses 3 m, le spécimen de Kew a frôlé le record absolu : Louis Ricciardiello (USA, ci-dessus) a obtenu un *A. titanum* de 3,1 m, un record confirmé le 18 juin 2010 à Gilford (New Hampshire, USA).

L'arum titan est aussi appelé "fleur cadavre" en raison de son odeur désagréable rappelant la chair en décomposition et perceptible jusqu'à 800 m à la ronde. On le considère donc aussi comme **la plante la plus malodorante**.

LA GROTTE LA PLUS PROFONDE

En mars 2018, un groupe de spéléologues russes menés par Pavel Demidov et Ilya Turbanov est descendu au fond de la grotte de Veryovkina, au sud du Caucase, dans le nord-ouest de la Géorgie, et a mesuré une profondeur de 2,21 km. Pendant les 12 jours de l'expédition, l'équipe a recueilli des échantillons d'espèces troglophiles (vivant sous terre) rares, voire inconnues.

LA ZONE OCÉANIQUE LA PLUS RÉCEMMENT DÉCOUVERTE

Une étude des écosystèmes coralliens publiée dans *Nature* le 20 mars 2018 a décrit un nouveau biome de faune marine : la zone rariphotique, située entre 130 et 309 m sous la surface. Caractérisée par sa faible luminosité, elle était autrefois surnommée "la zone corallienne crépusculaire". La photo ci-dessous montre *Stichopathes*, une espèce de corail découverte ici.

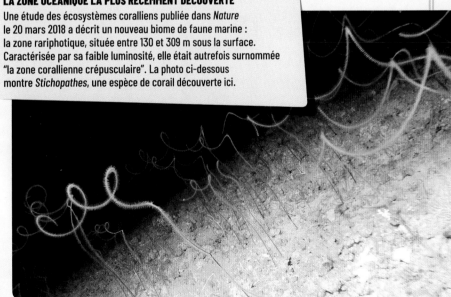

LA PRAIRIE TROPICALE AVEC LA PLUS GRANDE BIODIVERSITÉ (FLORE)

Avec au moins 6 500 espèces de plantes vasculaires, le Cerrado, savane boisée couvrant 20 % du Brésil, possède la plus forte biodiversité pour une prairie. Une étude comparative a été publiée dans *Philosophical Transactions of the Royal Society B*, le 8 août 2016. Le biome abrite aussi de nombreuses espèces animales, dont le loup à crinière (*Chrysocyon brachyurus*), le plus grand canidé d'Amérique du Sud.

FÉVR. 16 En 2008, Saeed Abdul Ghaffar Khouri (ARE) débourse 52,2 millions de dirhams (14,2 M$) pour **la plaque d'immatriculation la plus chère**, lors d'une enchère à Abou Dabi (ARE) : elle ne porte que le chiffre 1.

FÉVR. 17 En 1989, Ivan Nikolic et Goran Arsovic (tous 2 SRB) s'affrontent à Belgrade, actuelle capitale de la Serbie, pendant 20 h et 15 min, dans **la partie d'échecs comptant le plus de coups** (269).

31

ANIMAUX

▶ LE PLUS PETIT CHEVAL (MÂLE)

Bombel mesurait 56,7 cm au garrot lorsqu'il a été examiné le 24 avril 2018 au haras de Kaskada à Łódź (POL). C'est plus petit qu'un lévrier ! Il n'a d'ailleurs pas fallu plus de 2 mois à Katarzyna Zielińska (POL), sa propriétaire, pour s'apercevoir que, malgré la taille moyenne de ses parents, Bombel était hors du commun. Katarzyna a ensuite dû dénicher une toise adaptée pour que son Appaloosa miniature puisse prétendre au titre de *GWR*.

Thumbelina, qui détenait jusque-là le titre de **plus petit cheval (femelle)**, nous a malheureusement quittés en 2018. Propriété de Kay et Paul Goessling (tous 2 USA), cette jument alezane mesurait à peine 44,5 cm au garrot. Thumbelina a connu son heure de gloire en 2006 lors de sa rencontre avec Radar, **le plus grand cheval** à l'époque, qui la toisait du haut de ses 3 m (voir ci-dessous).

Katarzyna explique que, chaque mois, elle conduit Bombel dans un hôpital pédiatrique. "Les enfants adorent jouer avec lui ! Ils peuvent lui brosser la queue, la crinière."

GUINNESS WORLD RECORDS

SOMMAIRE

Retrouvez toutes nos vidéos sur
guinnessworldrecords.com/2020

LE PLUS GROS CROCODYLIFORME

Si les crocodiles sont aujourd'hui les plus lourds reptiles terrestres, ils ne sauraient rivaliser avec leurs cousins préhistoriques. Ces géants qui vivaient il y a quelque 112 millions d'années, au crétacé moyen, feraient sans aucun doute une énorme impression s'ils étaient réintroduits sur notre planète, comme dans *Jurassic Park*. Nous nous sommes amusés à imaginer ce qu'il se passerait si le plus gros d'entre eux, *Sarcosuchus imperator*, s'échappait du zoo de Londres...

Crocodiles et alligators sont parfois qualifiés de "fossiles vivants" car ils n'ont guère changé depuis la préhistoire. Cependant, si les crocodiles d'aujourd'hui ressemblent à certains de leurs ancêtres, ils ne les égalent pas en taille. Aucun n'arrive ainsi à la cheville de *Sarcosuchus*, **le plus grand crocodyliforme de tous les temps**, qui pouvait atteindre 12,2 m !

Le plus gros crocodile de l'époque contemporaine est le crocodile marin (*Crocodylus porosus*). C'est aussi **le plus lourd reptile**. Adulte, le mâle mesure en moyenne 4,9 m de long (certains spécimens pouvant atteindre 7 m) et pèse jusqu'à 1 200 kg.

La taille n'est toutefois pas le seul critère qui distingue les crocodiles d'hier et d'aujourd'hui. Certaines espèces anciennes étaient en effet toutes petites, à peine de la taille d'un chat et ne se mettaient jamais à l'eau, alors que d'autres avaient une queue de poisson et vivaient dans les mers.

Les crocodiliens ont dans l'ensemble beaucoup évolué, tout en préservant certaines caractéristiques. Cela n'est guère surprenant si l'on considère la capacité d'adaptation de ces animaux au cours des millénaires. N'oublions pas qu'ils comptent parmi les rares reptiles épargnés lorsque 80 % des espèces vivant sur Terre ont été décimées.

UN TITRE CONVOITÉ !

Sarcosuchus n'était pas le seul colosse à se prélasser dans les marécages... *Purussaurus brasiliensis*, qui vivait en Amérique du Sud il y a quelque 8 millions d'années, était peut-être encore plus imposant. Selon certaines sources, ce cousin des caïmans contemporains mesurait 10-13 m de long. Les fossiles retrouvés mettent toutefois en cause la limite supérieure de cette fourchette. Le montage ci-dessous donne une idée du rapport de taille entre l'homme, le crocodile marin et *Purussaurus*.

Sarcosuchus avait des dents de 15 cm de long !

Abstraction faite de sa taille, *Sarcosuchus*, représenté ici sous la forme d'un crocodile marin agrandi, avait une morphologie proche de celle de ses cousins contemporains, à l'exception d'un énorme rostre bulbeux peut-être avantageux pour l'odorat ou la vocalisation.

LE PLUS GROS CROCODILE EN CAPTIVITÉ

Avec ses 5,48 m de long du museau à la queue, à peine la moitié de *Sarcosuchus*, Cassius n'en demeure pas moins le plus gros crocodile vivant jamais mesuré avec précision. On a certes parfois eu vent de l'existence de spécimens sauvages plus imposants, mais ces informations reposant sur de furtives observations se sont avérées impossibles à vérifier.

Capturé en 1987 dans le Territoire du Nord australien, ce crocodile marin centenaire vit depuis dans le parc de Green Island, au large de la Grande Barrière de corail.

UN BEL OS À RONGER !

Si *Sarcosuchus* était déjà connu pour sa grande taille, c'est en 2000 que Paul Sereno (USA) en a précisé la démesure. Le paléontologue a mis au jour au Niger un crâne de 1,8 m de long, ainsi que l'essentiel d'une colonne vertébrale, révélant que l'animal mesurait au moins 11-12 m de long et pesait environ 8 t. Le fossile ci-dessus est présenté au Muséum d'histoire naturelle de Paris.

Les animaux qui résistent le mieux à la chaleur

En premier lieu, la fourmi ! Dans le désert saharien, *Cataglyphis* survit ainsi à une température corporelle de 53 °C, et la fourmi pot-de-miel australienne (*Melophorus bagoti*) a même brièvement supporté 56,7 °C en laboratoire ! Chez les humains, une température corporelle supérieure à 40 °C provoque un coup de chaleur. Parmi les stratégies développées par les fourmis du désert pour conserver un peu de fraîcheur, citons leurs longues pattes qui les éloignent du sable brûlant et leur vitesse qui limite leur exposition au soleil. La fourmi argentée du Sahara (*C. bombycina*) est **la plus rapide**, avec des accélérations atteignant 1,8 km/h, soit 100 fois la longueur de son corps à la seconde. Cela équivaut à piquer un sprint à 650 km/h pour un homme de taille moyenne !

Le plus petit renard

Le fennec (*Vulpes zerda*) mesure tout au plus 40 cm de long. De la taille d'un petit chat, il fait à peine la moitié du **plus grand renard**, le renard roux (*Vulpes vulpes*). La fourrure pâle de ce petit Sahraoui qui vit en Algérie et en Tunisie réfracte les rayons du soleil, tandis que ses grandes oreilles contribuent à le rafraîchir.

Le rongeur qui vit le plus longtemps

Vivre sous terre est un bon moyen d'échapper à la canicule. Le rat-taupe nu d'Afrique de l'Est (*Heterocephalus glaber*) évolue dans un réseau de galeries de plusieurs kilomètres. Fort de son immunité à de nombreuses maladies, dont le cancer, et de ses besoins minimes en oxygène, il atteint aisément l'âge canonique de 28 ans, quand un hamster s'estime heureux de vivre jusqu'à 3 ans.

Le mode de vie du rat-taupe, l'une des **deux seules espèces de mammifères eusociaux**, est aussi très curieux. Organisé en colonies, à la façon des abeilles, le groupe a une reine unique chargée de la reproduction, les autres individus travaillant pour la communauté.

L'habitat le plus aride abritant un crustacé

Si la plupart des crustacés connus, tels les crabes ou les homards, vivent dans l'eau ou à proximité, ce n'est pas le cas de tous ces invertébrés. Le cloporte de Réaumur (*Hemilepistus reaumuri*) arpente les zones arides du Moyen-Orient et d'Afrique du Nord, à des températures avoisinant les 37 °C. Avec une densité atteignant 480 000 individus à l'hectare, il constitue un maillon essentiel de la chaîne alimentaire du désert.

LA PLUS PETITE CHOUETTE

Endémique des zones arides du Mexique et du sud-ouest des États-Unis, la chevêchette des Saguaros (*Micrathene whitneyi*) est plus légère qu'une balle de tennis. D'une longueur moyenne de 12-14 cm, elle est connue pour nicher dans les cactus éponymes, mais peut aussi creuser son nid dans un arbre, voire un piquet de clôture.

▶ Le lézard le plus venimeux

Le venin du monstre de Gila (*Heloderma suspectum*) a une DL$_{50}$ de 0,4 mg/kg. Une dose létale médiane correspond à la quantité de toxine nécessaire pour provoquer la mort de la moitié des sujets testés. Moins d'un dixième de cuillerée à café (0,4-0,6 ml) de ce poison suffirait à tuer un humain. Fort heureusement, il est peu probable que ce grand timide morde spontanément une personne et lui injecte une telle quantité de venin. La fourmi rouge moissonneuse (*Pogonomyrmex maricopa*) est l'insecte au **venin le plus toxique** (DL$_{50}$ de 0,12 mg/kg, soit 20 fois plus puissant que celui de l'abeille commune).

L'araignée la plus rapide

L'araignée marocaine *Cebrennus rechenbergi* fait preuve d'ingéniosité pour échapper à ses prédateurs dans les dunes de sable : elle les épuise en se déplaçant à 6,12 km/h tout en enchaînant les flips, ces figures de gymnastique dont les acrobates nous régalent parfois.

Le kangourou roux met au monde **le plus gros nouveau-né marsupial**, mais ce dernier reste minuscule, avec un poids plume d'à peine 0,75 g !

LE SERPENT LE PLUS VENIMEUX

Le venin du taïpan du désert (*Oxyuranus microlepidotus*) a une DL$_{50}$ (voir plus haut) d'à peine 0,01-0,03 mg/kg. Si ses glandes ne renferment en général que 60 mg de venin, un mâle en sécréta un jour 110 mg, quantité suffisante pour tuer 125 personnes ! En dépit de la virulence de ce poison, ce serpent n'a encore fait aucune victime humaine, sans doute du fait de son habitat reculé.

LE PLUS GROS MARSUPIAL

Emblématique du bush australien, le kangourou roux (*Macropus rufus*) mesure 2,5 m de la tête à la queue. Un mâle adulte pèse 22-85 kg, une femelle un peu moins. Le kangourou est surtout connu pour son mode de déplacement par bonds qui lui permet de couvrir facilement de longues distances. C'est en 1951 qu'a été enregistré **le saut le plus long** jamais effectué par un kangourou : 12,8 m, soit l'équivalent de trois coccinelles VW placées bout à bout !

FÉVR. 18 Au Kerala, dans le sud de l'Inde, Abheesh P. Dominic (IND) **éclate le plus grand nombre de noix de coco à la main en une minute** (122 en 2017), battant ainsi le précédent record qui remontait à 2012.

FÉVR. 19 En 1994, Mark Kenny (USA) réalise le rêve de sa vie en remportant le titre de **champion GWR du 50 m sur les mains**. Mark, qui pratique la marche sur les mains depuis l'âge de 11 ans, a parcouru cette distance en 16,93 secondes.

Le plus gros crapaud cornu

Le crapaud cornu, ou plus exactement lézard cornu, vit dans les savanes et zones arides des États-Unis et du Mexique. Établi sur le littoral pacifique mexicain, *Phrynosoma asio* est la plus grosse espèce du genre (20 cm de long environ). Sa face aplatie et son corps arrondi, caractéristique encore plus marquée lorsqu'il se gonfle en présence d'un ennemi, expliquent sans doute pourquoi ce reptile est qualifié à tort d'amphibien.

Le lézard cornu dispose d'un mécanisme de défense naturel assez terrifiant : pour repousser ses prédateurs, il gorge ses sinus de sang jusqu'au point de rupture, puis en projette jusqu'à 1,5 m de distance !

La plus grosse gerboise

Les gerboises sont des rongeurs du désert qui bondissent en prenant appui sur leurs longues pattes postérieures, à la façon des kangourous (voir ci-contre). Pour tromper l'ennemi, elles sautent dans toutes les directions, effectuant des bonds allant jusqu'à 3 m. La grande gerboise (*Allactaga major*) vit dans les steppes arides d'Asie centrale. Son corps de 18 cm est prolongé par une queue de 26 cm qui lui sert de balancier.

LES INVERTÉBRÉS LES PLUS RAPIDES

Légendaires arachnides des déserts d'Afrique du Nord et du Moyen-Orient, les solifuges peuvent courir à 16 km/h. Peu d'êtres humains sont capables de cet exploit, exception faite des athlètes professionnels, et en particulier d'Usain Bolt, **l'homme le plus rapide**.

LE PLUS GRAND CAMÉLIDÉ

Avec leurs larges pattes, leurs longs cils et leur garde-manger intégré (leurs bosses sont en effet gorgées de matières grasses), les camélidés sont adaptés à la vie dans le désert. Mesurant jusqu'à 3,5 m de long et 2,4 m au garrot, le dromadaire dépasse légèrement le chameau domestique, son cousin à deux bosses. Le chameau de Tartarie, qui compte 300 000 individus en Australie, est le seul camélidé encore sauvage.

FÉVR. 20 Carolyn et Ralph Cummins (USA) sont parents du **plus grand nombre d'enfants nés le même jour** : Catherine (1952), Carol (1953), Charles (1956), Claudia (1961) et Cecilia (1966).

FÉVR. 21 Steve Fossett (USA) réalise en 1995 **la première traversée du Pacifique en ballon en solitaire**. Parti de Séoul (KOR) le 17 février, il atterrit 4 jours plus tard à Mendham, dans le Saskatchewan (CAN).

SAVANE

LE PLUS GRAND ANIMAL

La girafe mâle adulte (*Giraffa camelopardalis*) qui vit dans la savane sèche et les zones boisées ouvertes d'Afrique sub-saharienne atteint 4,6-5,5 m de hauteur. Son cou de 1,5-1,8-m (**le cou le plus long pour un animal**) compte généralement pour un tiers de sa stature. Il lui est fort utile pour parader et combattre ses rivaux, mais aussi pour atteindre, avec sa longue langue d'environ 45 cm, le feuillage frais de la canopée.

Le plus gros animal terrestre

L'éléphant de savane mâle adulte (*Loxodonta africana*) pèse 5,5 t, l'équivalent de 5 vaches laitières, et mesure jusqu'à 3,7 m au garrot.

Cet énorme herbivore a plusieurs titres de gloire : celui du **cerveau le plus lourd pour un mammifère terrestre** (5,4 kg, soit près de 4 fois le poids du cerveau humain), ainsi que celui du **nez le plus lourd** : sa trompe de près de 200 kg lui permet d'aspirer de l'eau, de communiquer avec les autres éléphants et de manipuler des objets.

Le primate le plus rapide

Le singe moqueur ou Patas (*Erythrocebus patas*) passe la plupart de son temps à fourrager dans la savane africaine semi-aride. Son squelette et sa musculature ont évolué au fil du temps pour qu'il puisse s'enfuir vite, avec des pointes à 55 km/h.

La plus longue migration animale terrestre

Les espèces essentiellement herbivores sont tenues de pratiquer le nomadisme pour trouver de nouvelles prairies à pâturer. C'est ainsi que des centaines de milliers de *Rangifer tarandus granti* parcourent 4 800 km dans la toundra et les plaines du Canada et de l'Alaska. Bien que ces troupeaux de caribous soient très denses, **les migrations terrestres qui rassemblent le plus d'individus** sont celles du gnou bleu (*Connochaetes taurinus*) : 1 à 2 millions de ces herbivores entreprennent chaque année un périple vers le nord, franchissant la rivière Mara infestée de crocodiles pour rejoindre le Kenya.

L'animal terrestre le plus venimeux

Le dragon de Komodo (*Varanus komodoensis*), dont le mâle adulte mesure en moyenne 2,59 m et pèse 79-91 kg, est aussi **le plus gros lézard**. Si le caractère pathogène de sa salive était connu depuis longtemps, la découverte de glandes à venin sous la mâchoire inférieure ne date que de 2009.

Le mammifère terrestre à la plus longue langue

Natif d'Amérique centrale et du Sud, le tamanoir (*Myrmecophaga tridactyla*) vit dans des habitats divers, mais affiche une préférence pour la pampa tempérée dans la partie sud de son territoire (Uruguay, Brésil et Argentine). Sa longue langue caractéristique est hérissée de papilles et couverte de salive collante. Cet organe déployé atteint 61 cm, soit 6 fois **la langue humaine la plus longue**. Il est parfait pour collecter fourmis et termites jusqu'au fond de leurs nids.

Avec une longueur corporelle totale de 1,2-2 m jusqu'à la pointe de sa grosse queue touffue, le tamanoir est aussi **le plus grand des Pilosa**, ordre de mammifères du Nouveau Monde qui regroupe paresseux et fourmiliers.

L'OISEAU SAUVAGE LE PLUS PRÉSENT

La population adulte du travailleur à bec rouge (*Quelea quelea*), natif d'Afrique, est évaluée à 1,5 milliard d'individus (alors qu'on estime à "seulement" 400 millions le nombre de pigeons dans le monde). On le compare souvent au criquet, car il peut comme lui ravager les plantations : une nuée d'un million d'oiseaux peut en effet détruire 10 t de cultures en une journée.

L'oiseau volant le plus lourd

Comme **le plus gros oiseau** (voir ci-contre), l'outarde kori (*Ardeotis kori*) arpente les plaines d'Afrique. Contrairement à l'autruche, en cas de force majeure, elle s'envole malgré son poids (jusqu'à 18,1 kg). Elle préfère toutefois traquer insectes et reptiles dans les herbes hautes.

Le plus petit papillon (plus petite envergure)

Oraidium barberae, que l'on peut observer dans les zones herbeuses du veld sud-africain, pèse moins de 10 mg pour une envergure de 1,4 cm.

LE PRÉDATEUR LE PLUS EFFICACE

Le lycaon (*Lycaon pictus*) vit en meutes de 10-30 individus dans la savane sub-saharienne. Alliant adaptabilité, esprit d'équipe et opportunisme, il conclut 50-85 % de ses expéditions de chasse par la capture d'une proie. Ce résultat dépasse largement celui d'autres prédateurs chassant en groupe, comme les lions et les hyènes, dont le taux de réussite avoisine 30 %.

LE PLUS GRAND ÉQUIDÉ SAUVAGE

Le zèbre impérial ou zèbre de Grévy (*Equus grevyi*), qui pèse jusqu'à 450 kg et mesure 140-160 cm au garrot, est le plus grand équidé sauvage.

Avec seulement 2 680 individus au Kenya et en Éthiopie, c'est aussi **l'espèce de zèbre la plus rare**. Les zèbres de montagne du Cap (*E. zebra zebra*) sont encore moins nombreux, mais c'est une sous-espèce du zèbre vrai.

FÉVR. 22 En 2002, le plongeur Jan Hempel (DEU) effectue **le plus long salto arrière depuis la position debout** (2,01 m), à Munich (DEU), pour le *GWR*.

FÉVR. 23 La station russe *Mir* fait face en 1997 au **1er incendie dans une station spatiale**, causé par une explosion de perchlorate de lithium utilisé pour produire de l'oxygène. L'équipage était sur le point de fuir à bord du vaisseau *Soyuz*.

L'ANIMAL TERRESTRE LE PLUS RAPIDE (COURSE DE FOND)

Si le guépard est imbattable au sprint, il ne peut cependant tenir ce rythme plus de 30 s environ. L'antilope américaine (*Antilocapra americana*), en revanche, est très endurante : cet ongulé d'Amérique du Nord a réussi à courir à la vitesse record de 56 km/h sur 6,6 km.

Le corps du guépard est aérodynamique : longues pattes fines et colonne vertébrale souple pour une foulée ample et puissante, griffes non rétractiles pour l'adhérence et longue queue en guise de balancier pour les virages serrés.

L'ANIMAL TERRESTRE LE PLUS RAPIDE (SUR UNE COURTE DISTANCE)

Adapté aux vastes espaces d'Afrique et d'Asie centrale, le guépard (*Acinonyx jubatus*) peut dépasser 100 km/h lorsqu'il poursuit une proie, une antilope par exemple. Le 20 juin 2012, Sarah, une jeune femelle, a réalisé **le 100 m le plus rapide pour un animal terrestre**. Lors de cette course départ arrêté organisée par le zoo de Cincinnati (USA), elle a couvert 100 m en 5,95 s, battant ainsi Usain Bolt (9,58 s) à plates coutures.

100 %

L'OISEAU TERRESTRE LE PLUS RAPIDE

Si le guépard court vite pour garnir son assiette, l'autruche (*Struthio camelus*) mise sur son talent de sprinteuse pour éviter de finir dans celle d'un autre. **Le plus gros oiseau** (voir **le plus gros oiseau de tous les temps**, p. 54-55) atteint ainsi 72 km/h.

Courir vite ne sert toutefois à rien quand on ne voit pas venir le danger. Heureusement, l'autruche est **l'animal terrestre qui a l'œil le plus gros**. Avec un diamètre de 5 cm de la cornée à la rétine, il est même plus gros que son cerveau !

LE PLUS GROS ANIMAL MIGRATOIRE TERRESTRE

Symbole des grandes plaines des États-Unis (voir **les plus grandes prairies**, p. 16), le bison d'Amérique du Nord (*Bison bison*) est le plus gros mammifère terrestre de la région éponyme. Cet énorme herbivore d'environ 1 t vit en troupeau et migre au gré des saisons. Après avoir frôlé l'extinction au XIXe siècle, l'espèce a été réintroduite avec succès de sorte que l'on compte aujourd'hui environ 500 000 individus.

FÉVR. 24 En 1988, le chanteur d'opéra Luciano Pavarotti (ITA) est Nemorino dans *L'Élixir d'amour* de Donizetti à l'Opéra allemand de Berlin. Le public l'applaudit 67 min. Il enregistre par ailleurs **le plus de rappels** (165).

FÉV. 25 En 1956, une Leghorn blanche pond à Vineland, dans le New Jersey (US), **le plus gros œuf de poule**. Doté d'un double jaune et d'une double coquille, celui-ci pèse 454 g, soit neuf fois plus que la moyenne.

MONTAGNES

Le plus grand des petits félins

S'il ne fait pas partie des grands félins, le puma (*Puma concolor*) se classe néanmoins juste après le tigre (voir p. 44), le lion et le jaguar. Il atteint 2,75 m de long, et un mâle adulte peut peser jusqu'à 100 kg.

C'est aussi **le mammifère connu sous le plus grand nombre de noms** (plus de 40 en anglais !). En français, on l'appelle aussi coughar (cougar au Québec) ou encore lion des montagnes.

Le plus herbivore des singes

Bien qu'il arbore d'énormes canines, le gelada (*Theropithecus gelada*) des hauts plateaux éthiopiens est herbivore, l'herbe constituant jusqu'à 90 % de son alimentation. C'est aussi l'un des singes qui passe le plus de temps à terre.

Ce n'est en revanche pas **le primate qui vit à l'altitude la plus élevée**. Le rhinopithèque brun (*Rhinopithecus bieti*), qu'abritent les forêts de conifères de la chaîne des Yun Ling au Tibet et de la province chinoise du Yunnan, s'aventure en effet jusqu'à 4 700 m.

Le rapport de taille le plus extrême entre adulte et nouveau-né chez les mammifères placentaires

Le petit, rose et glabre, du panda géant (*Ailuropoda melanoleuca*) pèse 60-200 g, soit environ 1/900e du poids de sa mère ; à titre de comparaison, un bébé humain avoisine 1/20e du poids maternel.

L'ongulé le plus austral

Le guanaco (*Lama guanicoe*) est le seul ongulé (mammifère à sabots) à vivre sous des latitudes aussi australes. Son territoire s'étend jusqu'à l'île Navarin (latitude 55 °S) située au large de la Terre de Feu argentine, à l'extrême sud de l'Amérique latine. Comme la vigogne (voir ci-contre), cet herbivore de 1,1 m de hauteur au maximum est un petit parent du lama (voir **l'ongulé le plus septentrional** p. 51).

L'OURS À L'ALIMENTATION LA PLUS VARIÉE

Natif d'Amérique du Sud, l'ours à lunettes (*Tremarctos ornatus*) consomme au moins 305 espèces de végétaux : broméliacées et fruits principalement, mais aussi cactus, mousses, fougères, orchidées, bambou, ainsi que 17 plantes cultivées, sans compter 34 espèces animales, dont 22 mammifères, 9 insectes, un oiseau, un annélide et un mollusque. Observé à 23 °S dans le nord de l'Argentine, c'est aussi **l'ursidé le plus austral**.

Le primate le plus septentrional

Le macaque japonais (*Macaca fuscata*) vit dans les montagnes de l'île de Honshu (JPN), notamment dans le parc de Jigokudani (36,6 °N). Aucun primate (l'homme excepté) ne vit plus au nord. Pour supporter le froid hivernal (-15 °C), il se baigne dans les sources chaudes de la région.

Le plus petit cervidé

Natif des Andes colombiennes, péruviennes et équatoriennes, le pudu du Nord (*Pudu mephistophiles*), qui mesure 35 cm au garrot et pèse moins de 6 kg, est le plus petit cervidé.

Le cerf-souris, ou chevrotin malais, (voir p. 45) est certes plus petit, mais il n'appartient pas à la même famille.

Le plus petit camélidé

Proche parente du lama, la vigogne (*Vicugna vicugna*) mesure quelque 90 cm au garrot à l'âge adulte, soit la taille d'un poney Shetland.

Endémique des Andes, la vigogne évolue jusqu'à 4 800 m. C'est **le camélidé sauvage qui vit à l'altitude la plus élevée**.

LE PLUS GROS RAPACE

Le condor des Andes adulte (*Vultur gryphus*) pèse 7,7-15 kg, soit le poids d'un enfant de 4 ans, pour une envergure atteignant 3,2 m. Présent sur toute la cordillère, du Venezuela à la Terre de Feu, cet oiseau de proie très robuste préfère vivre sur les hautes terres ventées, où il peut planer sur les courants thermiques.

LES FIBRES ANIMALES LES PLUS FINES

Endémique du plateau tibétain, le chirou (*Pantholops hodgsonii*) est doté sous sa toison d'un duvet soyeux composé de fines fibres de 7-10 micromètres de diamètre (1/10e du diamètre d'un cheveu), matériau isolant très prisé dans cette steppe où les températures peuvent chuter jusqu'à -40 °C en hiver. Le commerce de sa laine très recherchée (le *shahtoosh*) explique le déclin dramatique de la population, estimée aujourd'hui à moins de 150 000 individus. Le chirou figure ainsi sur la liste rouge des espèces menacées établie par l'UICN.

FÉVR. 26 — *King Rising 3* sort en 2014. C'est le 10e film de l'Allemand Uwe Boll, **le réalisateur le plus prolifique d'adaptations de jeux vidéo sous franchise**.

FÉVR. 27 — TangoTab and Friends (USA) rassemble **le plus de personnes faisant des sandwiches en même temps** (2 586 !) au Kay Bailey Hutchison Convention Center de Dallas (USA), en 2016.

▶ LES PRÉDATEURS TERRESTRES VIVANT À L'ALTITUDE LA PLUS ÉLEVÉE

Le désormais rare léopard des neiges (*Uncia uncia*, ci-dessous), dont le territoire couvre les régions montagneuses de 12 pays d'Asie centrale et méridionale, a été photographié à 5 800 m d'altitude. Dans les années 1990, un puma avait été observé à une altitude similaire dans les Andes.

Le léopard des neiges est aussi **le grand félin le moins dangereux pour l'homme** (2 attaques seulement).

Le léopard des neiges est le félin qui a **la queue la plus longue par rapport à son corps**. Atteignant 1 m, elle représente la moitié de la longueur de l'animal.

LE LÉZARD VIVANT À L'ALTITUDE LA PLUS ÉLEVÉE

L'agame à tête de crapaud (*Phrynocephalus theobaldi*) a été observé à une altitude de 5 200 m sur la face tibétaine de l'Everest et jusqu'à 5 400 m dans l'ouest du pays. Il est vivipare, une caractéristique que l'on retrouve surtout chez les reptiles des habitats extrêmes.

L'ARAIGNÉE VIVANT À L'ALTITUDE LA PLUS ÉLEVÉE

En 1924, une espèce d'araignée sauteuse de la famille des Salticidae a été découverte à une altitude de 6 700 m sur l'Everest, au Népal. Alors inconnue, elle a été décrite en 1975 et fort judicieusement nommée *Euophrys omnisuperstes*, littéralement « la plus haute de toutes ».

L'ONGULÉ VIVANT À L'ALTITUDE LA PLUS ÉLEVÉE

Présent sur les pentes abruptes et les prairies de l'Himalaya, qui atteignent 6 700 m au-dessus du niveau de la mer, l'ibex de Sibérie (*Capra sibirica*, ci-contre) évolue plus haut que tout autre ongulé. Non loin de là, sur le plateau tibétain, le yak (*Bos mutus*) broute à une altitude comparable de 6 100 m. C'est le **bovin qui vit à l'altitude la plus élevée.**

FÉVR. 28 Lors du Salon de la plongée méditerranéenne qui se tient à Barcelone en 2016, l'apnéiste Aleix Segura Vendrell (ESP) réalise **la plus longue apnée volontaire** (24 min 3,45 s, épreuve masculine).

FÉVR. 29 En 2004, Dale Webster (USA) chevauche la vague pour le 10 407e jour consécutif, soit **le plus de jours consécutifs passés à surfer**. Il poursuit jusqu'en 2015, comptabilisant 14 641 journées non-stop de surf.

41

HAUTE MER

Le plus gros poisson

La taille du requin-baleine (*Rhincodon typus*) varie énormément d'une étude et d'une région à l'autre. La fourchette est de 4-12 m de longueur, exception faite d'une femelle de 18,8 m observée au large de l'Inde en 2001. Ce poisson géant qui se nourrit de plancton apprécie les eaux chaudes de l'océan Indien, du Pacifique et de l'Atlantique.

Le plus gros poisson prédateur

Le grand requin blanc adulte (*Carcharodon carcharias*) mesure en moyenne 4,45 m de long pour un poids de 520-770 kg. L'affirmation selon laquelle certains spécimens atteindraient 10 m n'a pu être vérifiée. **Le plus gros requin connu** (16 m) est le mégalodon (*Carcharodon megalodon*), une espèce éteinte depuis 2,6 millions d'années environ. Il avait des dents impressionnantes, 2 fois plus longues que celles du grand requin blanc.

Le requin le plus récemment identifié

Planonasus indicus a été décrit pour la 1re fois en août 2018 seulement, dans la revue *Marine Biodiversity*. Ce requin évolue à 200-1 000 m de profondeur, au large du littoral sud-ouest du sous-continent indien et du Sri Lanka.

La méduse la plus lourde

Les méduses étant essentiellement constituées d'eau et de parties molles, il est difficile de déterminer leur poids avec précision. En se basant sur sa taille, son volume et la masse de ses tentacules, le poids maximal de l'énorme méduse à crinière de lion (*Cyanea capillata*) a néanmoins pu être estimé à plus de 1 t !

Le poisson le plus abyssal

Abyssobrotula galatheae a été capturé dans la fosse de Puerto Rico, à la limite entre la mer des Caraïbes et l'océan Atlantique, à 8 370 m de profondeur, à une distance du sol inférieure de 500 m seulement au sommet de l'Everest. C'est à une baleine de Cuvier marquée (*Ziphius cavirostris*) que l'on doit **le plongeon le plus profond jamais enregistré pour un mammifère** (2 992 m de profondeur !) au large du sud de la Californie (USA) en 2013.

LA PLUS LONGUE MIGRATION D'UN POISSON

Un grand nombre d'espèces de poissons entreprennent de longs périples annuels entre deux aires d'alimentation. La plus longue distance en ligne droite qu'aurait parcourue un poisson s'élève à 9 335 km. C'est le trajet qu'a effectué un thon rouge de l'Atlantique (*Thunnus thynnus*) marqué au large de la Basse-Californie (MEX) en 1958 et capturé à 483 km au sud de Tokyo en avril 1963.

Le cétacé le plus rare

En novembre 2016, on ne comptait plus qu'une trentaine de *Phocoena sinus* sauvages au monde. Estimé à 50 %, le déclin annuel de cette population s'explique par la consanguinité et le piégeage accidentel dans les filets de pêche. Cette espèce de marsouin est confinée dans la partie nord du golfe de Californie, au large du nord-ouest du Mexique.

Le mammifère à la longévité la plus longue

La baleine boréale (*Balaena mysticetus*) est une espèce à fanons native des eaux arctiques et subarctiques. Une étude réalisée conjointement en 1999 par la Scripps Institution of Oceanography et le North Slope Borough Department of Wildlife Management (tous 2 USA) a estimé à 211 ans l'âge de l'un de ses spécimens, en analysant l'acide aspartique de son cristallin. Cette technique n'étant pas très précise, l'âge de l'animal est en fait compris entre 177 et 245 ans. Pour découvrir un poisson qui vit encore plus longtemps, rendez-vous p. 55.

Le plus grand nombre de saltos aériens réalisés par un dauphin

Si tous les dauphins sont réputés aimer bondir hors de l'eau, les sauts de certaines espèces sont particulièrement acrobatiques. Le dauphin à long bec (*Stenella longirostris*) peut ainsi tourner 7 fois sur lui-même en l'air au cours d'un seul bond.

L'œil le plus gros

Le calmar géant (*Architeuthis dux*) est l'espèce animale, vivante ou éteinte, dotée de l'œil le plus gros. Le diamètre de celui d'un individu de la baie de Thimble Tickle à Terre-Neuve (CAN) a été estimé en 1878 à 40 cm, soit le double de celui d'un ballon de volley.

LE POISSON OSSEUX LE PLUS LOURD

Le poisson-lune adulte du genre *Mola* ("meule" en latin) pèse 1 000 kg en moyenne et mesure 1,8 m de l'extrémité d'une nageoire à l'autre. Le plus gros spécimen observé est un *Mola alexandrine* (voir ci-dessus) capturé au large de Kamogawa, dans la préfecture de Chiba (JPN) en 1996. Avec ses 2,72 m de long et ses 2 300 kg, il était plus lourd qu'un rhinocéros noir adulte.

Pendant de nombreuses années, on a cru que ce géant était une môle (*Mola mola*), mais une étude menée par Etsuro Sawai de l'université d'Hiroshima (JPN) et publiée dans la revue *Ichthyological Research* le 5 décembre 2017 a permis de l'identifier.

BALEINE BLEUE (*BALAENOPTERA MUSCULUS*)	
RECORD	**MESURE**
Le plus gros animal	160 t ; 24 m
La langue la plus lourde	4 t
Les poumons les plus volumineux	capacité : 5 000 l
Le cœur le plus gros	199,5 kg (1,5 m)
Le pénis le plus long	2,4 m
Le rythme cardiaque le plus lent	4-8 battements/min

LE REQUIN LE PLUS RAPIDE

Le requin mako, ou requin-taupe bleu, (*Isurus oxyrinchus*) a enregistré des vitesses supérieures à 56 km/h. Il chasse en nageant sous sa proie pour éviter qu'elle ne le détecte, puis l'attaque en piquant à la verticale.

Capable de se propulser à 6 m hors de l'eau, voire davantage, c'est en outre **le requin qui bondit le plus haut**.

 MARS 1 À Chennai (IND), Bhargav Narasimhan (IND) pulvérise en 2015 **le temps nécessaire pour résoudre 5 Rubik's Cubes (d'une main)** : à peine 1 min 23,93 s !

 MARS 2 En 2017, Lyudmila Darina (RUS) enveloppe **le plus de personnes dans une bulle de savon** (374) à Omsk (RUS). La bulle de 2,5 m de diamètre est constituée d'eau, de savon, de glycérine et d'agents épaississants.

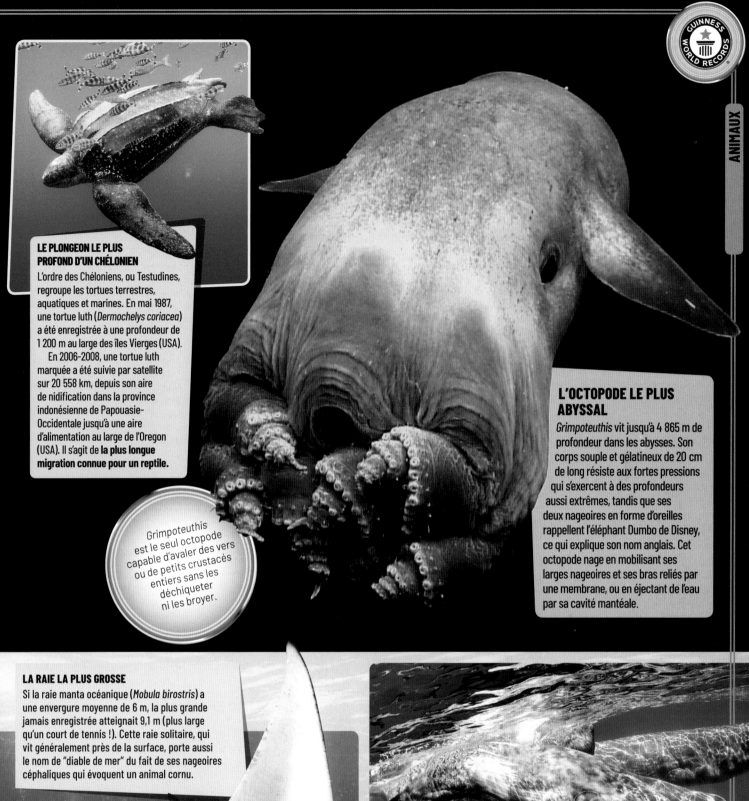

LE PLONGEON LE PLUS PROFOND D'UN CHÉLONIEN

L'ordre des Chéloniens, ou Testudines, regroupe les tortues terrestres, aquatiques et marines. En mai 1987, une tortue luth (*Dermochelys coriacea*) a été enregistrée à une profondeur de 1 200 m au large des îles Vierges (USA).

En 2006-2008, une tortue luth marquée a été suivie par satellite sur 20 558 km, depuis son aire de nidification dans la province indonésienne de Papouasie-Occidentale jusqu'à une aire d'alimentation au large de l'Oregon (USA). Il s'agit de **la plus longue migration connue pour un reptile.**

Grimpoteuthis est le seul octopode capable d'avaler des vers ou de petits crustacés entiers sans les déchiqueter ni les broyer.

L'OCTOPODE LE PLUS ABYSSAL

Grimpoteuthis vit jusqu'à 4 865 m de profondeur dans les abysses. Son corps souple et gélatineux de 20 cm de long résiste aux fortes pressions qui s'exercent à des profondeurs aussi extrêmes, tandis que ses deux nageoires en forme d'oreilles rappellent l'éléphant Dumbo de Disney, ce qui explique son nom anglais. Cet octopode nage en mobilisant ses larges nageoires et ses bras reliés par une membrane, ou en éjectant de l'eau par sa cavité mantéale.

LA RAIE LA PLUS GROSSE

Si la raie manta océanique (*Mobula birostris*) a une envergure moyenne de 6 m, la plus grande jamais enregistrée atteignait 9,1 m (plus large qu'un court de tennis !). Cette raie solitaire, qui vit généralement près de la surface, porte aussi le nom de "diable de mer" du fait de ses nageoires céphaliques qui évoquent un animal cornu.

L'ANIMAL LE PLUS SONORE

Les sons unidirectionnels que produit le cachalot (*Physeter macrocephalus*) sous l'eau peuvent atteindre 236 décibels, soit environ 44 fois le volume d'un coup de tonnerre. Le cachalot utilise en effet un système d'écholocation pour localiser ses proies dans la pénombre abyssale. Ces cétacés peuvent détecter leurs vocalisations mutuelles à des dizaines de kilomètres de distance.

 MARS 3 Le 1er numéro du magazine américain *Time* paraît en 1923. C'est le président américain Richard Nixon qui détient **le plus d'apparitions sur les unes du magazine** (55).

 MARS 4 En 2012, à Fort Myers en Floride, Happie (USA) parcourt **la plus longue distance en skateboard par une chèvre** (36 m), un exploit accompli en 25 s.

43

BOIS & FORÊTS

Le plus petit reptile

Trois espèces de caméléons nains de Madagascar se partagent le podium : *Brookesia minima* (en haut de la page), *B. micra* et *B. tuberculata*. Les mâles adultes des 3 espèces mesurent à peine 14 mm du museau au cloaque ; les femelles sont légèrement plus petites.

Le perroquet le plus lourd

C'est le kakapo ou perroquet-hibou (*Strigops habroptilus*), confiné à 3 îlots boisés au large de la Nouvelle-Zélande. Plus gros que la femelle, le mâle adulte pèse jusqu'à 4 kg. Ce poids élevé s'explique notamment par sa capacité à stocker des réserves énergétiques. L'ara hyacinthe d'Amérique du Sud (*Anodorhynchus hyacinthinus*) qui mesure jusqu'à 1 m est **le perroquet le plus long.**

L'insecte le plus lourd

Quatre espèces de la famille des Scarabaeidae endémiques d'Afrique équatoriale, le scarabée royal Goliath (*Goliathus regius*), *G. meleagris*, *G. goliatus* (= *G. giganteus*) et *G. druryi*, ont un poids supérieur à celui de tout autre insecte. La longueur moyenne observée sur un groupe de mâles atteint 11 cm de la pointe de leurs petites cornes céphaliques jusqu'à l'extrémité de leur abdomen, pour un poids de 70-100 g.

Le plus grand cervidé

En septembre 1897, un original (élan) mâle de l'espèce *Alces alces gigas* abattu dans le Yukon (CAN) mesurait 2,34 m au garrot pour un poids estimé à 816 kg. Plus petite, la femelle mesure en moyenne 1,8 m.

La plus grande ramure connue à ce jour atteint 204,8 cm. C'est celle d'un original abattu près du volcan Redoubt en Alaska (USA) en décembre 1958.

L'ANIMAL AUX YEUX LES PLUS ÉCARTÉS (PAR RAPPORT À SA TAILLE)

Les yeux des mouches diopsides (famille des Diopsidae) se trouvent à l'extrémité de pédoncules oculaires longs et très écartés, de sorte que, chez certaines espèces, la distance entre les deux yeux dépasse parfois la longueur du corps. Un gros mâle *Cyrtodiopsis whitei* (voir ci-dessus), espèce native du sous-continent indien et d'Asie du Sud-Est, mesurait ainsi 7,5 mm de long pour un écartement des yeux de 10,5 mm.

Le plus petit ours

L'ours malais (*Helarctos malayanus*) vit au nord-est de l'Inde et en Asie du Sud-Est. À l'âge adulte, le mâle ne dépasse pas 1,5 m de long et 70 cm au garrot pour un poids de 30-65 kg, soit 5 fois moins qu'un grizzly.

En dépit de sa petite taille, c'est **l'ours qui a la langue la plus longue** (25 cm). Il s'en sert pour collecter le miel et les insectes dans les arbres creux.

Le mammifère doté de la langue la plus longue par rapport à sa taille est *Anoura fistulata*, une chauve-souris glossophage des forêts andines de l'Équateur, dont l'organe atteint 8,49 cm, soit 1,5 fois la longueur totale de son corps. Pour en savoir plus sur le **mammifère à la langue la plus longue,** reportez-vous p. 38.

Le mammifère au sevrage le plus tardif

Aucun mammifère n'allaite ses petits aussi longtemps que les orangs-outans de Bornéo et de Sumatra (genre *Pongo*). Selon une étude de 2017, ces singes ne sèvrent pas leurs jeunes avant 8,8 ans.

Le pays qui abrite le plus d'espèces d'amphibiens

Sur les quelque 7 965 espèces d'amphibiens, au moins 1 154, soit 14,5 %, vivaient au Brésil en février 2019.

C'est aussi au Brésil que se trouvent **les amphibiens les plus transparents.** La peau de l'abdomen des Centrolenidae est translucide, à la façon d'un verre dépoli, laissant apparaître les organes internes et les os verts de ces grenouilles.

▶ LE PLUS GROS FÉLIN SAUVAGE

Le tigre de Sibérie mâle (*Panthera tigris altaica*) mesure en moyenne 2,7-3,3 m du museau à l'extrémité de la queue, pour un poids de 180-306 kg. Le spécimen sauvage le plus gros jamais recensé atteignait même 384 kg en 1950.

À titre de comparaison, **le plus petit félin sauvage,** le chat rubigineux (*Prionailurus rubiginosus*) de l'Inde et du Sri Lanka, mesure 35-48 cm (queue non comprise) pour un poids moyen de 1,5 kg (moins de la moitié de celui d'un chat domestique).

LE PLUS GRAND LÉMURIEN

Avec sa queue très réduite (à peine 10 % de sa longueur), l'indri (*Indri indri*) atteint 72 cm de long. Cet animal arboricole qui pèse jusqu'à 7,5 kg vit dans les forêts tropicales de l'est de Madagascar. Les quelque 100 espèces de lémuriens sont toutes endémiques de cette grande île au large de l'Afrique, où vivait aussi **le plus grand lémurien connu,** *Archaeoindris fontoynontii*, aujourd'hui éteint, qui avoisinait les 200 kg !

MARS 5 La Cámara de Comercio Santa Rosa de Cabal (COL) présente en 2011 **le plus long chorizo** (1 917,8 m) au parc Bolívar de Santa Rosa de Cabal (COL).

LE PLUS GROS PRIMATE

Évoluant dans les forêts tropicales de l'est du Congo, le gorille des plaines orientales (*Gorilla beringei graueri*) mâle mesure environ 1,75 m en position debout et pèse jusqu'à 163 kg. Si l'on comptait encore 17 000 individus environ dans les années 1990, l'espèce est aujourd'hui en danger critique d'extinction en raison du braconnage, de l'exploitation minière et forestière et de la guerre civile qui sévit dans ce pays. Selon la Société pour la conservation de la vie sauvage (WCS) et Fauna & Flora International, il resterait aujourd'hui moins de 4 000 spécimens.

Les gorilles sont **les mammifères qui construisent les plus grands nids**. Chaque jour, ces grands singes en élaborent un nouveau à même le sol, à partir de branches et de feuillage. Ces aires de repos temporaires atteignent 1,5 m de diamètre.

Le gorille de l'Est est l'une des 4 sous-espèces de ces grands singes. Son cousin, le gorille de l'Ouest (*G. gorilla*), figure parmi les espèces en danger critique d'extinction, même si sa situation s'améliore (environ 316 000 individus dénombrés en 2018).

LES PLUMES LES PLUS LONGUES SUR UN OISEAU SAUVAGE

Plus longues que l'envergure d'un aigle royal, les plumes caudales centrales du faisan vénéré (*Syrmaticus reevesii*) dépassent parfois 2,4 m ! En les dressant en plein vol, ce faisan des forêts montagneuses de Chine peut freiner son allure et rectifier habilement sa trajectoire afin d'échapper à un prédateur.

LA VISION DES COULEURS LA PLUS COMPLEXE

Selon une étude publiée en 2016, la rétine de *Graphium sarpedon* est tapissée de 15 types de photorécepteurs, sensibles à la fois aux ultra-violets et à la lumière perceptible par l'homme. Les yeux des chats, chiens et chevaux ont 2 types de photorécepteurs, ceux des humains 3, tandis que la plupart des oiseaux en ont 4. Présent dans le sud de l'Asie et en Australie, ce papillon évolue dans la canopée des forêts tropicales.

LE PLUS PETIT ONGULÉ

Le chevrotain malais, ou cerf-souris, (*Tragulus kanchil*) ne dépasse pas 55 cm de long et 25 cm au garrot, pour un poids maximal de 2,5 kg. Essentiellement nocturne, cet ongulé discret vit dans les forêts tropicales denses d'Asie du Sud-Est. On reconnaît les mâles adultes à leurs canines supérieures pointues en forme de crocs protubérants.

MARS 6 Ian Batey (GBR) écrase en 2010 **le plus de canettes avec un véhicule en 3 min** en laminant à Dubaï (ARE) 61 106 canettes de soda au volant d'un énorme camion de plus de 9 t (9 072 kg).

MARS 7 En 2010, lors de la 82e cérémonie des Oscars, Kathryn Bigelow (USA) est **la première femme à remporter l'oscar du meilleur réalisateur** pour son film *Démineurs* (USA, 2008).

LITTORAL & RÉCIFS

LE CRUSTACÉ LE PLUS RAPIDE SUR TERRE

Essentiellement présent sur les plages du littoral oriental du Pacifique et de l'océan Indien, le crabe fantôme atlantique *Ocypode quadrata* (ci-dessus) s'enfuit dans le sable au-delà de la laisse de haute mer. Malgré son déplacement latéral, ce crabe très vif a été enregistré à une vitesse de 4 m/s.

La fourrure la plus épaisse

Le pelage de la loutre de mer (*Enhydra lutris*) qui vit au nord-est de l'océan pacifique, au large des littoraux canadien, russe et américain, compte 100 000-400 000 poils au cm². Cette densité varie selon la partie du corps, la fourrure qui couvre ses pattes étant moins fournie.

Les poissons les plus goulus

Syngnathus leptorhynchus, l'aiguille de mer à bande bleue (*Doryrhamphus excisus*) et la bécasse de mer (*Macroramphosus scolopax*) peuvent détecter et avaler une proie en 2 ms à peine. S'ils sont si rapides, c'est grâce aux tendons élastiques qui permettent à leur tête tubulaire d'effectuer de vifs mouvements et d'engloutir leurs proies en un clin d'œil (généralement de petits crustacés) par aspiration.

La seiche la plus grosse

La seiche géante (*Sepia apama*) qui atteint 1 m de long, tentacules tendus, évolue à 100 m de profondeur dans les récifs coralliens, les champs d'algues et sur les fonds sableux le long de la côte sud-est de l'Australie. Comme d'autres céphalopodes, la seiche géante s'exprime et communique en changeant de couleur.

Le plus vieil oiseau de mer reproducteur

En décembre 2018, Wisdom, un albatros de Laysan femelle (*Phoebastria immutabilis*) âgé d'au moins 68 ans a pondu un œuf dans le refuge faunistique national de l'atoll de Midway à Hawaï (USA). Si tout se passe bien, ce vénérable oiseau (l'espérance de vie moyenne de l'espèce est de 40 ans), que les scientifiques suivent depuis des décennies, pourrait voir éclore son 37e poussin.

Le poisson le plus venimeux

Synanceia horrida, une synancée endémique des eaux peu profondes du littoral indo-pacifique, est le poisson doté des plus grosses glandes à venin. Une simple dose de neurotoxine injectée depuis 3 à 6 de ses 13 épines dorsales peut provoquer la mort d'un être humain.

À la différence du poison, que l'on ingère, le venin est injecté par le biais d'une piqûre ou d'une morsure.

Les poissons les plus toxiques, les poissons-globes de la mer Rouge et des eaux indo-pacifiques, contiennent de la tétrodotoxine. Bien que 16 mg à peine de ce poison suffisent pour tuer un homme de 70 kg, les Japonais continuent à se délecter du fameux *fugu*, l'un de ces Tetraodontideae, à condition qu'il soit cuisiné correctement.

Le matériau biologique le plus résistant

Pour se nourrir, la patelle gratte la surface des rochers auxquels elle est accrochée à l'aide de sa radula, dont les petites dents exercent une pression atteignant 4,9 GPa. Selon l'article publié en 2015 dans le *Journal of the Royal Society Interface*, cette force dépasse celle de toutes les matières naturelles, voire de synthèse. Ce matériau constitué de nanofibres de goéthite, une variété d'oxyhydroxyde de fer, a ainsi détrôné la soie d'araignée (4,5 GPa), elle-même loin devant le Kevlar (3-3,5 GPa).

Le manchot le plus rare

Avec une population estimée à 1 800-4 700 individus lors du dernier recensement de 2009, le manchot des Galapagos (*Spheniscus mendiculus*) figure sur la liste des espèces menacées de l'UICN depuis 2000.

Vivant, comme son nom l'indique, sur les îles Galapagos, sur l'équateur, c'est aussi **le manchot le plus septentrional**.

LE PLUS PETIT HIPPOCAMPE

En moyenne, *Hippocampus satomiae* ne dépasse pas 13,8 mm de long à l'âge adulte. Décrit comme une nouvelle espèce en 2008, cet hippocampe pygmée, plus petit qu'un ongle humain, évolue dans les eaux littorales de l'île de Derawan, au large de Bornéo (IDN).

100 %

LA PLUS GROSSE COLONIE DE TORTUES VERTES DU PACIFIQUE

Pendant la saison de reproduction, jusqu'à 60 000 tortues vertes femelles (*Chelonia mydas*) parcourent des milliers de kilomètres pour pondre leurs œufs sur l'île Raine, au large du Queensland (AUS). Plus de 15 000 individus peuvent nicher simultanément sur les 1,8 km de plage de cette petite île de la Grande Barrière, **le plus long récif corallien** au monde (voir p. 27).

L'ÉTOILE DE MER LA PLUS LOURDE

Un spécimen de *Thromidia catalai*, capturé le 14 septembre 1969 au large de l'îlot Amédée (NCL), pesait environ 6 kg. Cette énorme étoile à 5 branches a été confiée à l'aquarium de Nouméa.

LE POISSON À LA PLUS COURTE DURÉE DE VIE

Le record de longévité du goby nain décoré, ou goby nain à sept formes (*Eviota sigillata*), est de 59 jours seulement. Natif des récifs coralliens des océans Indien et Pacifique, ce poisson est également **le vertébré à la plus courte durée de vie**.

MARS 8 En 2004, Manuel Pérez Pérez (ESP) présente dans le village de Güime, sur l'île de Lanzarote (Canaries, ESP), **la patate douce la plus lourde**, d'un poids de 37 kg !

MARS 9 C'est à Los Angeles, en Californie (USA), qu'Ali Spagnola (USA) réalise en 2017 **le 100 m le plus rapide sur un ballon sauteur (épreuve féminine)** en 38,22 s.

LE PLUS GROS PÉLICAN

Le pélican frisé (*Pelecanus crispus*) atteint 1,8 m de long pour un poids de 12 kg et une envergure de 3,2 m. Sa vaste aire de répartition s'étend du sud de l'Europe à la Chine.

Ce n'est en revanche pas lui, mais le pélican à lunettes (*P. conspicillatus*) qui possède **le bec le plus long** : il mesure jusqu'à 47 cm, quasiment la taille d'un nouveau-né !

Le pélican frisé aime les zones humides (lacs, estuaires et deltas). La colonie la plus importante (1 400 couples) vit sur le petit lac Prespa à la frontière de la Grèce et de l'Albanie.

LA PLUS LOURDE MURÈNE

La murène javanaise (*Gymnothorax javanicus*) est la plus imposante des murènes. Elle atteint en effet 3 m de long et pèse jusqu'à 30 kg, soit le poids d'un enfant de 9 ans ! Les murènes géantes vivent dans les lagons et aux abords des récifs coralliens de la région indo-pacifique, où il leur arrive d'attaquer des plongeurs.

LE PLUS LONG PLONGEON D'UN SIRÉNIEN

Parmi les siréniens, ordre d'ongulés aquatiques qui regroupe le dugong et les lamantins, c'est le lamantin des Caraïbes (*Trichechus manatus*, ci-contre) qui, à ce jour, est resté le plus longtemps sous l'eau (24 min) en Floride (USA).

Le plus gros sirénien connu était la rhytine de Steller, ou vache de mer, (*Hydrodamalis gigas*). L'adulte mesurait 8-9 m de long et pesait jusqu'à 10 t, une taille sans comparaison avec les siréniens actuels. Chassé pour sa chair, sa graisse et sa peau, ce mammifère aquacole au déplacement assez lent s'est éteint en 1768, 27 ans à peine après avoir été identifié.

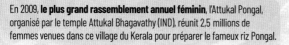
MARS 10 En 2009, **le plus grand rassemblement annuel féminin**, l'Attukal Pongal, organisé par le temple Attukal Bhagavathy (IND), réunit 2,5 millions de femmes venues dans ce village du Kerala pour préparer le fameux riz Pongal.

MARS 11 Parties de l'île Ward Hunt (CAN), Catherine Hartley et Fiona Thornewill (toutes 2 GBR) effectuent en 2001 **le trajet à ski le plus rapide pour rejoindre le pôle Nord (épreuve féminine)**, soit en 55 jours.

47

COURS D'EAU, LACS & MARAIS

Le plus petit poisson d'eau douce
C'est en 2006 qu'a été découvert *Paedocypris progenetica*, minuscule Cyprinidae transparent qui vit dans les lacs de tourbières très acides de Sumatra et de Sarawak sur l'île de Bornéo. Le plus petit adulte observé est une femelle de 7,9 mm de long. Le plus petit mâle mesure 8,2 mm.

Le plus long périple d'un poisson d'eau douce
Catadrome, l'anguille d'Europe (*Anguilla anguilla*) entreprend un marathon de 4 800 à 6 400 km pour aller frayer dans la mer des Sargasses. Après avoir passé 7 à 15 ans dans les lacs et cours d'eau d'Europe, l'anguille jaune se transforme à la maturité sexuelle en anguille argentée, dotée notamment de plus gros yeux. Elle rejoint alors la mer (c'est la dévalaison), puis traverse l'Atlantique jusqu'à son aire de reproduction, un long périple d'environ 6 mois.

Un poisson est par ailleurs qualifié d'anadrome s'il naît en eau douce, migre vers la mer au stade juvénile, puis revient frayer en eau douce. **Le plus gros poisson anadrome** (2,3 m de long en moyenne et jusqu'à 130 kg à l'âge adulte) est le bélouga, ou grand esturgeon (*Huso huso*), qui vit dans la mer Noire (et fraye dans le Danube), la mer Caspienne (fleuve Oural) ou la mer d'Azov (Don).

L'insecte au vol le plus rapide
La libellule australienne *Austrophlebia costalis* peut, sur de courtes distances, voler à 58 km/h, une vitesse supérieure à celle d'un cheval au galop.

Avec ses 12 cm de long et son envergure de 19,1 cm, le zygoptère géant *Megaloprepus caerulatus* d'Amérique centrale et du Sud est **la plus grosse libellule** connue.

Le plus long barrage construit par des castors
Le parc national Wood Buffalo (CAN) abrite un barrage de castors de 850 m de long, c'est-à-dire plus de 2 fois plus long que le Hoover Dam sur le Colorado. Le chercheur Jean Thie (CAN) fut le premier à repérer cet ouvrage en 2007, alors qu'il analysait des images satellites de la région. En comparant ces dernières à des photographies plus anciennes, Thie en a déduit que l'impressionnante structure avait dû être érigée par plusieurs générations de castors, à l'œuvre depuis 1975 environ.

L'OISEAU AQUATIQUE LE PLUS RAPIDE
Observée à 142 km/h, l'oie-armée de Gambie (*Plectropterus gambensis*), dont les articulations alaires sont munies d'éperons osseux fort utiles pour combattre ses rivaux, est l'oiseau aquatique qui vole le plus vite. C'est aussi **le plus toxique**, en raison de sa consommation occasionnelle de cantharides. Ces coléoptères renferment en effet un puissant poison, la cantharidine, dont 10 mg suffisent pour tuer un homme.

L'amphibien le plus rustique
La salamandre de Sibérie (*Salamandrella keyserlingii*) et *S. schrenckii* survivent toutes deux à -35 °C dans le permafrost sibérien. Ces animaux à sang froid supportent ces conditions extrêmes grâce à la glycérine qu'ils produisent. Cette substance agit comme un antigel naturel, empêchant leur sang de geler et leur permettant de revenir doucement à la vie au printemps. Si *S. schrenckii* vit essentiellement dans la cordillère de Sikhote Alin (RUS), le territoire de la salamandre de Sibérie est beaucoup plus vaste.

L'amphibien qui supporte le mieux la chaleur est *Buergeria japonica*, dont on a retrouvé des têtards dans les sources chaudes (*onsen*) de l'île volcanique de Kuchinoshima, dans la préfecture de Kagoshima (JPN), à une température atteignant 46,1 °C. Évoluer dans des eaux aussi chaudes pourrait accélérer la croissance de cette grenouille et booster son immunité.

▶ LE GÉNOME LE PLUS LONG
Le génome d'une espèce renferme l'ensemble de son matériel génétique. Celui de l'axolotl (*Ambystoma mexicanum*) est, avec 32 Gb ou Giga-bases (paires de bases nucléiques), 10 fois plus grand que le génome humain. Cette espèce en danger critique d'extinction est connue pour son maintien à l'état larvaire et sa capacité à régénérer ses organes endommagés.

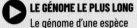

LE PLUS GROS DAUPHIN D'EAU DOUCE
Avec ses 2,6 m de long, le boto (*Inia geoffrensis*) vit dans l'Amazone et l'Orénoque. Ce dauphin doit sa teinte rose orangé aux vaisseaux sanguins sous-cutanés qui régulent sa température corporelle. Plus souples que leurs cousins marins, les dauphins d'eau douce n'ont guère de mal à contourner les arbres en cas de crue.

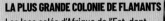

LA PLUS GRANDE COLONIE DE FLAMANTS
Les lacs salés d'Afrique de l'Est, dont le lac Natron, abritent une population de flamants nains (*Phoeniconaias minor*) de 1,5-2,5 millions d'individus. Ces oiseaux doivent leur couleur aux algues bleues qu'ils consomment, lesquelles prolifèrent dans **les lacs les plus alcalins** de la vallée du Rift (KEN et TZA). Avec son pH de 10-12, cette eau est extrêmement irritante pour l'homme.

MARS 12 Kazuyoshi Miura (JPN, né le 26 février 1967) devient à 50 ans et 14 jours **le plus vieux footballeur professionnel à marquer un but en compétition** lorsqu'il expédie la balle au fond de la cage pour le Yokohama FC en 2017.

MARS 13 David Smith Jr. (USA) parcourt en 2018 **la plus longue distance (homme), en étant propulsé par un canon**. Il a atterri 59,43 m plus loin au stade Raymond James de Tampa, en Floride (USA).

L'anaconda ci-dessus, photographié au Venezuela en 2012, mesure 6 m de long. Cette espèce passe le plus clair de sa vie dans l'eau (photo ci-contre prise à Rio Formoso (BRA).

LE SERPENT LE PLUS LOURD

L'anaconda géant (*Eunectes murinus*) vit dans les marais, cours d'eau et plaines inondées d'Amérique du Sud et de Trinidad. Le poids d'une femelle abattue au Brésil vers 1960 fut estimé à 227 kg (aussi lourd qu'un piano droit) pour 8,45 m de longueur. La plupart des herpétologistes sont cependant plus prudents aujourd'hui, avançant une longueur maximale de 7,5 m environ. L'anaconda se nourrit de poissons, d'oiseaux, de reptiles, mais aussi de mammifères, comme le cabiaï (voir ci-dessous).

LE PLUS GROS RONGEUR

Le cabiaï, ou grand cochon d'eau (*Hydrochoerus hydrochaeris*), mesure 1-1,3 m de long, à peu près la taille d'un border collie, et pèse jusqu'à 79 kg. Très sociable, ce rongeur géant des bassins du Paraná et de l'Uruguay et des zones marécageuses d'Argentine et du Brésil vit en groupes de 10 à 20 individus.

LA PLUS GROSSE TORTUE À DENTS

Endémiques du continent américain, ces reptiles sont munis d'une mâchoire puissante dont ils n'hésitent pas à faire usage s'ils se sentent menacés. Le plus gros est la tortue alligator (*Macrochelys temminckii*, USA), qui dépasse parfois 100 kg et mesure 60-80 cm de long. Pour chasser, elle agite un appendice semblable à un ver situé au bout de sa langue, leurre qui attire les poissons.

 MARS 14 En 2015, l'illusionniste Rick Smith Jr. (USA) soulève l'enthousiasme du public du Great Lakes Science Center à Cleveland dans l'Ohio (USA), avec **le plus haut lancer de carte à jouer** (21,41 m).

 MARS 15 En 2009, Takeru Kobayashi (JPN) engloutit à Kashiwa (JPN) **le plus de hotdogs en 3 min** (6) sur la chaîne privée japonaise Fuji Television, dans le cadre de son émission *Bikkuri Chojin 100 Special #2*.

49

TOUNDRA & BANQUISE

LA CHOUETTE LA PLUS SEPTENTRIONALE
Natif de l'Arctique eurasien et nord-américain, le harfang des neiges (*Bubo scandiacus*) est l'oiseau qui s'aventure le plus au nord pour chasser ses proies, essentiellement de petits mammifères ou volatiles. L'un des rares oiseaux à passer l'essentiel de l'année dans le Grand Nord, le harfang a été observé à une latitude de 82° N sur l'île d'Ellesmere (CAN), dans la nuit glaciale qui y règne au cœur de l'hiver.

Le plus gros ours de tous les temps
Ursus maritimus tyrannus, qui mesurait 1,83 m au garrot pour une longueur de 3,7 m et un poids moyen de 1 t, était 3 fois plus gros qu'un grizzly mâle (*U. arctos spp.*). Produit de l'évolution d'une population isolée d'ours bruns à la fin du pléistocène (250 000-100 000 ans avant notre ère), cette sous-espèce fossile est **le plus gros mammifère carnivore terrestre de tous les temps**. Voir ci-dessous les exploits actuels de son descendant direct.

La plus longue dent de baleine
Le narval (*Monodon monoceros*), qui vit dans les eaux froides de l'Arctique, doit son sobriquet de licorne des mers à la défense torsadée en ivoire du mâle, généralement unique.

Si une défense de narval mesure en moyenne 2 m de long, il arrive qu'elle dépasse 3 m et pèse jusqu'à 10 kg.

Les plus longues défenses de morse
Les défenses d'un morse (*Odobenus rosmarus*), qui sont en fait ses canines supérieures très allongées, atteignent généralement 50 cm de long. En 1997, 2 immenses défenses ont été découvertes dans la baie de Bristol en Alaska (USA). La canine droite mesurait 96,2 cm, tandis que celle de gauche était plus courte de 2,5 cm.

Les manchots qui pondent le moins d'œufs chaque année
Le manchot empereur (page ci-contre), qui vit en Antarctique, et le manchot royal (*Aptenodytes patagonicus*), de l'extrême sud de l'Amérique latine, pondent tous 2 1 seul œuf par an, alors que toutes les autres espèces en pondent 2.

Le lait le plus riche est celui de l'ourse polaire. Ses 48,4 % de matière grasse sont essentiels à la survie des petits dans le froid glacial.

Le gorfou huppé de Nouvelle-Zélande (*Eudyptes sclateri*) est l'oiseau qui présente **le plus fort dimorphisme entre les œufs d'une même ponte** : son second œuf (« œuf B ») est en effet jusqu'à 80-85 % plus lourd que le premier (« œuf A »).

Le manchot le plus commun
Si on compte encore quelque 6,3 millions de couples de gorfous dorés (*Eudyptes chrysolophus*), ces manchots à aigrettes des îles subantarctiques et de la péninsule antarctique figurent néanmoins sur la liste des espèces vulnérables de l'UICN du fait d'une forte chute de leur population depuis les années 1970.

La plus longue migration d'un oiseau
La sterne arctique (*Sterna paradisaea*), qui se reproduit au pôle Nord, migre jusqu'en Antarctique pour y passer l'hiver septentrional avant de revenir en Arctique. Elle parcourt ainsi quelque 80 400 km, soit près de 2 fois la circonférence de la Terre.

La plus petite sous-espèce de renne
Natif des îles Svalbard (NOR) sur le cercle polaire arctique, le renne du Spitzberg adulte (*Rangifer tarandus platyrhynchus*) ne dépasse pas 0,8 m à l'épaule pour 80 kg, un poids inférieur de moitié à celui des autres sous-espèces de rennes.

La température corporelle la plus basse chez un mammifère
En 1987, Brian Barnes, de l'université de Fairbanks en Alaska (USA), a enregistré une température corporelle de −2,9 °C chez des spermophiles arctiques (*Urocitellus parryii*) en état d'hibernation. Pour réussir à supporter des températures négatives, ce petit rongeur nord-américain refroidit ses fluides corporels avant d'hiberner, en éliminant ainsi les molécules d'eau pour éviter qu'ils ne gèlent.

LE PINNIPÈDE LE PLUS DANGEREUX
Au sein de ce clade du sous-ordre des Caniformia, qui inclut morses, phoques et otaries, le léopard de mer (*Hydrurga leptonyx*) est la seule espèce connue pour attaquer l'homme, remontant à la surface via une crevasse. Plusieurs cas de morsures au pied ont été signalés et au moins 1 cas d'agression sur des plongeurs. Ci-dessous, un léopard de mer dévore un manchot Adélie malchanceux.

LE PLUS GROS OURS
L'ours blanc, ou polaire, mâle (*U. maritimus*) pèse 400-600 kg en moyenne pour une longueur atteignant 2,6 m du museau à la queue. Cette espèce vit dans l'Arctique à des latitudes de 65-85° N. **L'ours le plus septentrional** est également **le mammifère terrestre au territoire le plus vaste** : les femelles de la baie d'Hudson (CAN) peuvent évoluer sur une aire de 350 000 km², soit environ la superficie de l'Allemagne.

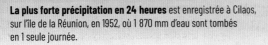

MARS 16 **La plus forte précipitation en 24 heures** est enregistrée à Cilaos, sur l'île de la Réunion, en 1952, où 1 870 mm d'eau sont tombés en 1 seule journée.

MARS 17 En 2011, Reza Pakravan (IRL) effectue **la traversée du Sahara à vélo la plus rapide** en 13 jours 5 heures 50 min et 14 s. Parti d'Algérie le 4 mars, il a terminé son périple au Soudan.

Selon une étude publiée en 2018 à propos de 20 manchots empereurs suivis par satellite dans la mer de Ross en 2013, l'un de ces palmipèdes est resté sous l'eau pendant 32 min 12 s, **la plus longue immersion pour un oiseau**.

LE PLUS GROS MANCHOT

Le manchot empereur (*Aptenodytes forsteri*) vit sur les terres gelées de l'Antarctique. Le mâle, qui atteint 1,3 m de hauteur et pèse jusqu'à 45 kg, est généralement un peu plus gros que la femelle.

Chez cette espèce, le mâle couve seul l'unique œuf du couple pendant 62-67 jours, **la plus longue durée d'incubation pour un manchot**.

L'ONGULÉ LE PLUS SEPTENTRIONAL

Le bœuf musqué (*Ovibos moschatus*) vit dans la toundra continentale, sur les îles de l'Arctique canadien et jusqu'à la pointe nord du Groenland, à 83° N. Pour survivre dans cet environnement hostile, il a développé plusieurs caractéristiques, dont de larges sabots qui rappellent des après-ski et une épaisse toison très isolante (*qiviut*), 8 fois plus chaude que la laine de mouton.

LE PLUS GROS PINNIPÈDE

L'éléphant de mer du sud mâle (*Mirounga leonina*), endémique des îles subantarctiques, est encore plus gros que l'ours polaire. Il mesure en moyenne 5 m de long depuis son large museau, évoquant une trompe d'éléphant, jusqu'à l'extrémité de sa nageoire caudale. Il pèse jusqu'à 3 500 kg, l'équivalent de plus de 7 pianos à queue !

MARS 18 Michele Fucarino et Elisa Lazzarini (tous 2 ITA) échangent en 2010 **le plus long baiser en apnée** (3 min 24 s) dans la belle ville de Rome (ITA).

MARS 19 Lorsque **le premier test-match de l'histoire du cricket** se termine au Melbourne Cricket Ground dans l'État de Victoria (AUS), en 1877, l'équipe australienne bat l'équipe anglaise en marquant 45 courses.

ANIMAUX DOMESTIQUES

Le chien qui a donné la patte le plus de fois en 1 min, en alternant pattes droite et gauche
Le 17 février 2018, Jacob, Jack Russell terrier, a donné 80 fois la patte à Rachael Grylls (GBR), sa maîtresse, à Exeter (Devon, GBR), en changeant de côté à chaque fois.

Le plus de chiens promenés simultanément par une seule personne
Le 17 juin 2018, Maria Harman (AUS), dresseuse professionnelle, a emmené en promenade 36 chiens tenus en laisse dans la réserve de Wolston Creek Bushland (Queensland, AUS).

Le plus d'objets attrapés d'affilée par un chien
Le 6 septembre 2018, à Salford (GBR), Hagrid, un leonberg, a croqué 9 saucisses lancées successivement par son maître David Woodthorpe-Evans (GBR).

Le chien à la langue la plus longue
La langue de Mochi, le saint-bernard de Carla et Craig Rickert (USA), atteignait 18,58 cm de long, le 25 août 2016, à Sioux Falls (Dakota du Sud, USA).
Cela correspond à peu près à la taille du **plus petit chat connu**, Tinker Toy,

LE PLUS DE TOURS ACCOMPLIS PAR UN COCHON EN 1 MIN
Parmi les 13 tours qu'elle a effectués en 60 s, à Newton (Iowa, USA), le 16 janvier 2018, avec Dawn Bleeker (USA), sa propriétaire, Joy, une truie miniature, a retiré un anneau de son support (ci-dessus), déroulé un tapis et même joué un air de piano à l'aide de son groin !

un himalayen bleu mâle appartenant à Katrina et Scott Forbes de Taylorville (Illinois, USA), qui ne dépassait pas 19 cm de long et 7 cm de haut adulte.

Le plus long saut effectué par un chat
En franchissant 2,13 m à Big Sur (Californie, USA), Waffle le chat guerrier (USA) a battu d'environ 30 cm le record précédent, le 30 janvier 2018.
Yabo, dressé par Maria B. Jensen (DNK), a quant à lui pulvérisé le record chez les lapins, en franchissant 3 m, le 12 juin 1999, à Horsens (DNK).

Le plus vieux lapin
Mick, un lapin agouti né le 9 février 2003, s'est vu confirmer le 16 février 2019 l'âge canonique de 16 ans et 7 jours. Recueilli en 2004 dans un centre de la SPA, il vit à Berwyn (Illinois, USA) chez Liz Rench (USA), également propriétaire d'un chien, Sheri, et de deux autres lapins.

La tortue la plus rapide
Le 9 juillet 2014, Bertie, une tortue léopard, atteint 28 cm/s dans le parc Adventure Valley de Brasside (GBR). Ce véritable bolide a ainsi parcouru les 5,48 m de la course en 19,59 s.

Le saut le plus haut d'un cheval miniature
Le 15 mars 2015, le cheval de Robert Barnes (AUS), Castrawes Paleface Orion, a franchi 1,8 m, à Tamworth (Nouvelle-Galles du Sud, AUS). Pas mal pour un animal qui mesure 93 cm au garrot !

Les plus longues cornes de yack
Jericho, un yack de l'élevage de Hugh et Melodee Smith (USA), à Welch (Minnesota, USA), présente de très longues cornes très écartées. Le 23 décembre 2018, la distance entre les deux extrémités a été mesurée à 3,46 m.

Le lama le plus rapide à franchir 10 obstacles
Le 6 septembre 2017, Caspa, qui appartient à Sue Williams (GBR), a franchi 10 obstacles en 13,96 s, à Arley Hall (Cheshire, GBR).

LE PLUS DE TOURS ACCOMPLIS PAR UN LAPIN EN 1 MIN
Taawi s'est distingué le 15 décembre 2018, à Turku (FIN) en réalisant 20 prouesses en 60 s. Ce lapin de 4 ans qui sait faire rouler une balle et franchir un obstacle (ci-dessous) illustre l'efficacité du renforcement positif que pratique Aino Kivikallio (FIN), sa propriétaire, pour faciliter le dressage.

LE CHAT DOMESTIQUE LE PLUS GRAND
Barivel, un maine coon de Vigevano près de Pavie (ITA) [ci-dessus avec sa propriétaire Cinzia Tinnirello (ITA)], atteignait 1,20 m de long, le 22 mai 2018.
Mesurant 1,23 m, Mymains Stewart Gilligan, le chat de Robin Hendrickson et Erik Brandsness (USA), surnommé "Stewie", reste le plus grand chat domestique de tous les temps.

LE PUS PETIT BOVIDÉ MÂLE
Mesuré le 27 avril 2018, à la clinique vétérinaire de Kalona (Iowa, USA), Humphrey (ci-contre), le zébu miniature mâle de Joe et Michelle Gardner (USA), atteignait 67,6 cm de haut.
Manikyam, une femelle de race Vechur appartenant à Akshay N. V. (Kerala, IND), est **la plus petite vache au monde**. Le 21 juin 2014, elle ne dépassait pas 61,1 cm au garrot.

MARS 20 En 2010, des médecins ont confirmé qu'avec 14 doigts (7 à chaque main) et 20 orteils (10 à chaque pied), Akshat Saxena (IND) détenait **le plus de doigts et d'orteils à la naissance** (polydactylie).

MARS 21 Mark Temperato (USA) de Lakeville (New York, USA) possède **la batterie la plus complète**. Il a mis 20 ans à réunir les 813 éléments qui la composent, dont plusieurs caisses claires, cymbales et cloches type "cowbells".

ANIMAUX

▶ LE PLUS DE TOURS ACCOMPLIS PAR UN CHIEN EN 1 MIN

Le 18 février 2018, Hero et sa maîtresse Sara Carson (CAN) ont ébloui le public avec 49 tours en 60 s, à Palmdale (Californie, USA). Capable de nombreux exploits, ce border collie attrape un frisbee en vol, fait du skate ou encore se tient en équilibre sur les pieds de Sara. Le duo de choc a ainsi obtenu la 5e place au concours *America's Got Talent* en 2017.

L'ANIMAL QUI PORTE LE PLUS DE CORNES

Race domestique originaire du Moyen-Orient mais présente au Royaume-Uni et en Amérique du Nord, le mouton de Jacob a la particularité de porter quatre cornes, voire six. Chez les brebis et les béliers à deux paires de cornes, l'une d'entre elles pousse généralement à la verticale et dépasse souvent 60 cm de long.

Lenny "The Batdog" a été sacré **meilleur chien skateur du monde en franchissant 5 obstacles** en 2,46 s, lors du même concours que Simba.

LE CHAT QUI A LE PLUS D'ABONNÉS SUR INSTAGRAM

Avec 4,03 millions d'abonnés au 29 avril 2019, Nala, croisée siamois tabby adoptée par Varisiri Methachittiphan (USA), reste le chat préféré de ce réseau social qu'elle a séduit avec ses grands yeux bleus, ses nombreux accessoires et son penchant pour les cartons où elle aime se blottir.

▶ LE PLUS DE NŒUDS DÉFAITS PAR UN CHIEN EN 1 MIN

Simba, un Jack Russell dressé par Valeria Caniglia (ITA), a dénoué en 1 min 8 rubans de paquets cadeaux sur le plateau de *La Notte dei Record*, à Rome (ITA), le 20 novembre 2018.

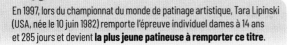

MARS 22 En 1997, lors du championnat du monde de patinage artistique, Tara Lipinski (USA, née le 10 juin 1982) remporte l'épreuve individuel dames à 14 ans et 285 jours et devient **la plus jeune patineuse à remporter ce titre**.

MARS 23 En 2012, le lycée de Morecambe (Lancashire, GBR) organise **la plus grande course à l'œuf**, avec la mobilisation de 1 445 participants. Cameron Ball a remporté l'épreuve en 28,59 s.

53

Les plus petites empreintes de dinosaure

100 %

Le 15 novembre 2018, *Scientific Reports* a annoncé la découverte près de la ville de Jinju (KOR) de traces de didactyles mesurant 10,33 mm de long et 4,15 mm de large en moyenne (voir ci-contre). Ces empreintes, laissées par un tout petit dinosaure adulte ou juvénile de la taille d'un moineau, ont été attribuées à une nouvelle espèce, *Dromaeosauriformipes rarus*, appartenant à un nouveau genre, les droméosaures, qui vivaient au crétacé (il y a 145 à 66 millions d'années).

Le plus gros oiseau de tous les temps

Selon un article publié dans la revue *Royal Society Open Science* le 26 septembre 2018, le plus gros des oiseaux éléphants de Madagascar, disparu il y a environ 1 000 ans, était le titan de Vorombe (*Vorombe titan*). Ce géant atteignait 3 m de haut pour un poids moyen de 642,9 kg (et un poids maximal de 860 kg). Reportez-vous p. 39 pour connaître **le plus gros oiseau actuel**.

Le singe le plus récent

Selon le numéro de juin 2018 de *Science*, le gibbon *Junzi imperialis*, aujourd'hui éteint, est non seulement l'espèce de singe la plus récente, mais aussi **le genre le plus récent**. En 2004, un chantier de fouilles réalisé autour d'une tombe datant de 2 200 à 2 300 ans, située près de l'ancienne capitale de la Chine impériale Xi'an dans la province de Shaanxi, a mis au jour les vestiges d'une ménagerie où des restes de gibbon ont été retrouvés. Ce fut au XVIIIᵉ siècle **la 1ʳᵉ espèce de singe à s'éteindre du fait de l'activité humaine** (déforestation, chasse et commerce des animaux de compagnie).

Le crocodilidé le plus récent

Selon une étude publiée en octobre 2018 dans la revue *Zootaxa*, le faux gavial d'Afrique centrale (*Mecistops leptorhynchus*) est l'espèce de crocodile la plus récente. Distincte de son cousin d'Afrique de l'Ouest (*M. cataphractus*), elle évolue dans les cours d'eau douce depuis le Cameroun et le Gabon jusqu'en Tanzanie.

Les 1ʳᵉˢ fourmis "explosives" connues

Le groupe *Colobopsis cylindrica* (COCY) rassemble des fourmis charpentières arboricoles d'Asie du Sud-Est. Connues sous le nom de "fourmis explosives", ces kamikazes ont la particularité de pouvoir rompre leur exosquelette et de libérer ainsi un liquide collant et irritant qui empêche les prédateurs d'attaquer leur colonie.

Le 1ᵉʳ sanctuaire pour les bélugas

Le 1ᵉʳ sanctuaire marin pour bélugas (*Delphinapterus leucas*) va être aménagé dans la baie de Klettsvik sur l'île de Heimaey au sud-ouest de l'Islande, à l'initiative de deux ONG, Whale and Dolphin Conservation et SEA LIFE Trust (toutes 2 GBR). Le bras de mer naturel qui abrite cette réserve à ciel ouvert a une superficie de 32 000 m², soit l'équivalent de 25 piscines olympiques environ, et descend à 9,1 m de profondeur au maximum.

La plus vieille araignée de tous les temps

Le record de longévité enregistré pour une araignée est de 43 ans. Selon un article publié dans *Pacific Conservation Biology* le 19 avril 2018, "Number 16" a été observée pour la 1ʳᵉ fois en mars 1974 par l'arachnologue Barbara York Main (AUS), et vue vivante pour la dernière fois en avril 2016. Cette mygale endémique d'Australie (*Gaius villosus*) évoluait dans la réserve naturelle de Bungulla dans le comté de Tammin, dans l'ouest du pays.

Les mégafossiles animaux les plus anciens

Les mégafossiles sont des vestiges organiques suffisamment gros pour être visibles à l'œil nu. Le plus ancien mégafossile animal répertorié est *Dickinsonia*, un genre regroupant des organismes ovales à corps mou d'environ 1,4 m de long qui vivaient il y a quelque 558 millions d'années. Les chercheurs se sont longtemps demandé s'il s'agissait

LE MAMMIFÈRE VOLANT LE PLUS RAPIDE

Natif du sud des États-Unis, du Mexique et d'Amérique latine, le molosse du Brésil (*Tadarida brasiliensis*) effectue en vol des pointes de 44,5 m/s (160,2 km/h). La vitesse de cette petite chauve-souris au corps aérodynamique et aux ailes délicates a été enregistrée depuis un avion en juillet 2009 à proximité de la Frio Bat Cave, située près de la ville de Concan, au Texas (USA).

LES PLUS VIEILLES JUMELLES CHIMPANZÉS

Sur la photo ci-dessous, les jumelles Golden et Glitter posent jeunes avec Gremlin, leur mère. Nées les 13-14 juillet 1998, elles avaient 20 ans et 117 jours le 8 novembre 2018.

Les deux sœurs vivent en Tanzanie, dans le parc de Gombe Stream qui abrite le centre de recherche à l'origine de **la plus vaste étude sur les primates sauvages**. Initiés en 1960 par la primatologue Jane Goodall (GBR, ci-dessous), ces travaux se poursuivent aujourd'hui, 60 ans plus tard, sous la houlette de l'Institut Jane Goodall. L'observation de près de 320 chimpanzés a donné lieu à plus de 165 000 heures d'enregistrement.

100 %

LA PLUS GROSSE ABEILLE

L'abeille de Wallace (*Megachile pluto*) atteint 4,5 cm de long, mandibules incluses. Les entomologistes craignaient l'extinction de l'espèce jusqu'à ce qu'une équipe australienne identifie en janvier 2019 la femelle ci-dessus, sur les Moluques du Nord (IDN). C'est le 1ᵉʳ spécimen vivant jamais filmé. L'abeille domestique représentée au-dessus de sa cousine géante illustre le rapport de taille entre les deux hyménoptères.

MARS 24 — Propriété de Joris Gijsbers (NLD), **le poisson rouge le plus long** se trouve à Hapert (NLD). Mesuré en 2003, il atteint 47,4 cm de la bouche à la nageoire caudale. C'est plus long qu'une quille de bowling !

MARS 25 — En 2012, le réalisateur James Cameron (CAN) **plonge le plus profondément en sous-marin en solitaire** en descendant à 10 898 m, à bord du *Deepsea Challenger*, dans la fosse des Mariannes.

LE PLUS VIEIL ANIMAL TERRESTRE

Jonathan, une tortue géante des Seychelles (*Aldabrachelys gigantea*), vit sur l'île de Sainte-Hélène (GBR) dans l'Atlantique Sud. Né en 1832 environ, ce vétéran fêterait ses 187 ans en 2019. Si ces données semblent peu fiables, c'est parce que Jonathan serait arrivé des Seychelles en 1882 "à pleine maturité", et donc âgé d'au moins 50 ans à l'époque.

La cryobiose animale la plus longue

La cryobiose est la suspension des processus métaboliques qu'un organisme met en œuvre pour faire face à des conditions environnementales défavorables. Selon une étude publiée en mai 2018 dans *Doklady Biological Sciences*, 2 nématodes (*Panagrolaimus aff. detritophagus* et *Plectus aff. parvus*), découverts en 2015 dans le permafrost arctique près de l'Azaleïa, dans le nord-est de la Russie, ont pu être réanimés après mise en culture plus de 40 000 ans plus tard.

LA PAIRE DE CORNES LA PLUS IMPOSANTE

Sato, un taureau de la race Longhorn appartenant à Scott et Pam Evans (USA), porte vraiment une belle paire de cornes. Le 30 septembre 2018 à Bay City, au Texas (USA), son envergure atteignait 3,2 m, l'équivalent de 3 battes de baseball mises bout à bout.

d'animaux, d'organismes unicellulaires géants, ou d'autre chose encore.

Le vertébré à la maturité sexuelle la plus précoce

Selon un article publié de 6 août 2018 dans la revue *Current Biology*, *Nothobranchius furzeri*, un killie natif des mares temporaires du Mozambique et du Zimbabwe, a évolué de façon à pouvoir se reproduire au bout de 14 ou 15 jours, afin de pallier la nature éphémère de son habitat.

LE MEILLEUR CHASSEUR PARMI LES FÉLINS

Selon certaines études, le chat à pieds noirs (*Felis nigripes*) réussirait, en dépit de sa taille (c'est le plus petit des chats sauvages), à tuer sa proie dans plus de 60 % des cas (voir aussi p. 44). Endémique d'Afrique du Sud, de Namibie et du Botswana, ce félin à l'alimentation variée (petits mammifères, invertébrés, reptiles, oiseaux et leurs œufs) tue en moyenne 10-14 rongeurs ou petits oiseaux chaque nuit à l'âge adulte.

Selon certains chasseurs, ce joli écureuil chasse les poules et même les cerfs ! La véracité de ces propos n'a pas été scientifiquement établie.

LE PLUS VIEUX POISSON

Selon une étude publiée en 2016, un requin du Groenland (*Somniosus microcephalus*) a vécu 392 ans, le record de longévité pour un poisson. Cet animal, qui grandit de 1 cm par an environ, est également **le vertébré à la plus longue durée de vie**. S'il n'atteint sa maturité sexuelle qu'à l'âge de 150 ans, il vit dans les eaux froides et profondes de l'Atlantique Nord, dans un environnement propice à une longue durée de vie.

LA QUEUE LA PLUS TOUFFUE

Originaire de l'île de Bornéo, *Rheithrosciurus macrotis* a une queue exceptionnellement touffue : elle représente 130 % de son poids, de sorte que cette espèce est **le mammifère doté de la queue la plus démesurée par rapport au reste de son corps**. Si l'utilité de cet appendice n'est pas clairement établie, les chercheurs pensent cependant qu'elle permet à l'écureuil de paraître plus gros, et ainsi d'impressionner ses prédateurs.

MARS 26 — En 2009, Richard Jenkins (RUS) roule **le plus vite en char à voile** sur le lac asséché d'Ivanpah en Californie (USA), conduisant son prao en fibres de carbone *Greenbird* à la vitesse de 202,9 km/h.

MARS 27 — Le maillot de football le plus cher vendu aux enchères se négocie en 2002 à 157,75 £ (225,109 $) à Londres (GBR). Il s'agit du numéro 10 que portait Pelé (BRA) pour la finale de la coupe du monde de la FIFA en 1970.

55

L'HOMME LE PLUS TATOUÉ
Lucky Diamond Rich (AUS, né NZL), jongleur avec des tronçonneuses, adepte du monocycle et avaleur de sabres, s'est fait tatouer durant plus de 1 000 h. Sa peau a d'abord été ornée de tatouages colorés du monde entier, puis entièrement recouverte d'encre noire avant que ne soient ajoutés des motifs blancs et enfin de couleurs. Sa peau est donc aujourd'hui recouverte à 200 %, y compris ses paupières, l'espace entre ses orteils, la partie externe de ses conduits auditifs ainsi que ses mâchoires. Ce portrait a été réalisé par nos soins en 2018, au cours d'une séance photo dans un hôtel londonien.

SOMMAIRE

Lucky est un homme très indépendant. "Ce que l'on pense de moi m'est égal, affirme-t-il. Mon estime de moi ne dépend pas de l'avis des autres."

L'HOMME LE PLUS GRAND

En septembre 2009, Sultan Kösen est venu à Londres, quittant pour la 1re fois son pays natal, la Turquie. Il a été photographié auprès d'éléments symboliques de la ville, tels que les cabines téléphoniques rouges ou le bus à impériale *Routemaster*. Voici le récit d'une journée mémorable, et bien plus encore !

ous avons invité au Royaume-Uni Sultan, qui mesure 2,51 m, avant la sortie du *GWR 2010* et en avons profité pour lui faire visiter Londres. Photographié ici devant un arrêt de bus, ce doux géant aurait en réalité bien de la peine à entrer dans l'un des **célèbres bus rouges, car il atteint plus de la moitié de leur hauteur !**

Issu d'une fratrie de 5 enfants ayant tous une taille moyenne, Sultan n'était pas particulièrement grand avant d'atteindre l'âge de 10 ans. Une tumeur s'est alors développée dans son hypophyse, une glande qui produit plusieurs hormones dont l'hormone de croissance, ce qui l'a fait grandir trop rapidement. En 2008, une opération qui lui a sauvé la vie lui a permis de bloquer sa croissance, Sultan étant alors devenu le plus grand homme de la planète. En réalité, il arrive en 3e position de ce classement : seuls John F. Carroll (USA, décédé en 1969), qui mesurait 2,63 m, et l'extraordinaire Robert Wadlow (voir à droite) le dépassaient. Il est aussi l'une des rares personnes à avoir dépassé la barre des 8 pieds (243,8 cm).

Évidemment, la stature exceptionnelle de Sultan le soumet à de nombreuses contraintes. Ses vêtements et son lit doivent être fabriqués sur mesure, et il n'est pas simple non plus de se procurer des chaussures lorsque vos pieds mesurent 36,5 cm ! En outre, sa grande taille a de fortes répercussions sur sa santé : Sultan se sert de béquilles pour marcher afin de soulager la pression exercée sur ses articulations.

Lorsqu'il est venu à Londres, Sultan a confié aux journalistes : "Mon plus grand rêve est de me marier… Je cherche l'amour." Ce rêve est devenu réalité lorsqu'il a épousé 4 ans plus tard à Mardin (TUR) Merve Dibo, une femme de 175,2 cm.

SULTAN ET ROBERT

Le plus grand homme du monde à côté de 2 symboles londoniens : la tour Elizabeth (surnommée "Big Ben", voir p. 14-15) et une cabine téléphonique rouge *"K2"*. La photo comporte aussi une image **du plus grand homme de tous les temps**, Robert Wadlow (USA, à gauche), qui, avec ses 2,72 m, aurait presque atteint le haut de la cabine téléphonique, qui mesure 2,74 m.

Parfois, la taille de Sultan lui offre des avantages inattendus. Dans l'avion qui le conduisait au Royaume-Uni, il a eu droit à 2 sièges pour lui seul. L'hôtel a aussi mis à sa disposition une chambre de 1re catégorie, dotée d'un lit king-size, au bout duquel un 2nd lit a quand même dû être ajouté !

LES PLUS GRANDES MAINS
Les mains de Sultan, mesurées en 2011, atteignaient 28,5 cm du poignet jusqu'au bout du majeur. Selon des mesures effectuées en 2010, il possède aussi **la plus large envergure de main**, soit 30,48 cm. Ci-dessus, vous pouvez voir quelle serait la dimension de sa main droite posée sur la double page que vous êtes en train de lire !

Voyez grand avec les vidéos de Sultan sur guinnessworldrecords.com/2020

LES PLUS ÂGÉS...

La personne la plus âgée de tous les temps

L'âge le plus élevé pour un être humain est de 122 ans et 164 jours, pour Jeanne Louise Calment (FRA). Elle est née le 21 février 1875, un an avant l'invention du téléphone par Alexander Graham Bell. Elle a commencé l'escrime à 85 ans et a fait du vélo jusqu'à 100 ans. Elle est décédée dans une maison de retraite à Arles, le 4 août 1997.

L'homme le plus âgé de tous les temps est Jiroemon Kimura (JPN), né le 19 avril 1897 et décédé le 12 juin 2013 à l'âge de 116 ans et 54 jours.

Le couple marié (âge combiné)

Masao Matsumoto (né le 9 juillet 1910) a épousé Miyako Sonoda (née le 24 novembre 1917 ; tous 2 JPN) le 20 octobre 1937. Le 25 juillet 2018, le couple était marié depuis 80 ans et 278 jours. Masao avait 108 ans et 16 jours et Miyako 100 ans et 243 jours. Leur âge combiné était de 208 ans et 259 jours.

Le coiffeur en activité

Le 8 octobre 2018, Anthony Mancinelli (USA, né en Italie le 2 mars 1911) coupait encore les cheveux à l'âge de 107 ans et 220 jours. Il travaille 5 jours par semaine, de midi à 20 h, au salon Fantastic Cuts de New Windsor (New York, USA).

Le lauréat du prix Nobel

Le 3 octobre 2018, Arthur Ashkin (USA, né le 2 septembre 1922) a reçu le prix Nobel de physique (conjointement avec Donna Strickland et Gérard Mourou)

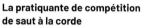

L'ÂGE COMBINÉ LE PLUS ÉLEVÉ POUR 16 FRÈRES ET SŒURS

Les 16 enfants de Louis-Joseph Blais et Yvonne Brazeau de Québec (CAN) (médaillon, assis au centre) avaient un âge combiné de 1 203 ans et 350 jours au 11 décembre 2018. Vingt et un ans séparent le membre le plus âgé de la fratrie, Jean-Jacques, 85 ans (né le 23 juin 1933), et la plus jeune, Lucie (née le 29 mars 1954). Cette famille remarquable (en photo ci-dessus, avec 15 membres) compte 6 hommes et 10 femmes.

à l'âge de 96 ans et 31 jours. Le prix récompensait son travail sur les pinces optiques.

▶ La pharmacienne en activité

Le 23 novembre 2018, Eiko Hiruma (JPN, née le 6 novembre 1923) travaillait encore à la pharmacie Hiruma d'Itabashi (Tokyo, JPN), à l'âge de 95 ans et 17 jours.

Le monarque actuel

Née le 21 avril 1926, sa majesté la reine Élisabeth II (GBR) a célébré son 93e anniversaire en 2019. Elle est devenue le monarque le plus âgé du monde le 23 janvier 2015, après la mort du roi Abdallah d'Arabie saoudite.

Le détenteur d'un permis poids lourds

Richard Thomas Henderson (GBR, né le 13 avril 1935), arrière-grand-père, continue de rouler. Il a effectué une livraison le 7 janvier 2019, à 83 ans et 269 jours, à Selkirk (GBR). Il doit

cependant passer un examen médical tous les ans pour continuer à conduire.

La pratiquante de compétition de saut à la corde

Le 23 février 2019, à Coronado (Californie, USA), Annie Judis (USA, née le 23 novembre 1943) a participé au championnat de corde à sauter toutes catégories à 75 ans et 92 jours.

L'entraîneur de football en Premier League anglaise

L'ancien entraîneur de l'équipe d'Angleterre Roy Hodgson (GBR, né le 9 août 1947) a pris la tête de l'équipe Crystal Palace à 71 ans et 255 jours pour son match de Ligue contre Arsenal le 21 avril 2019. Il a obtenu une victoire 3-2.

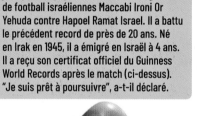

LE FOOTBALLEUR EN ACTIVITÉ LE PLUS ÂGÉ

Le 5 avril 2019, le gardien de but Isaak Hayik (ISR) avait 73 ans et 95 jours lorsqu'il a joué pour l'équipe de 5e niveau des ligues de football israéliennes Maccabi Ironi Or Yehuda contre Hapoel Ramat Israel. Il a battu le précédent record de près de 20 ans. Né en Irak en 1945, il a émigré en Israël à 4 ans. Il a reçu son certificat officiel du Guinness World Records après le match (ci-dessus). "Je suis prêt à poursuivre", a-t-il déclaré.

LE CHEF LE PLUS ÂGÉ D'UN RESTAURANT TROIS ÉTOILES AU MICHELIN

Âgé de 93 ans et 128 jours au 4 mars 2019, Jiro Ono (JPN, né le 27 octobre 1925) est le chef cuisinier du Sukiyabashi Jiro, restaurant de sushis trois étoiles au Michelin situé à Chuo (Tokyo, JPN). Installé dans une station de métro, le restaurant ne possède qu'un comptoir pour 10 personnes et le menu du jour est fixé le matin. Jiro prépare seul tous les sushis.

LA YOUTUBEUSE DE JEUX VIDÉO LA PLUS ÂGÉE

Âgée de 83 ans au 2 avril 2019, Shirley Curry (USA, née en 1936) a réalisé des centaines de vidéos pour la chaîne YouTube qui porte son nom. Sa chaîne compte plus d'un demi-million d'abonnés et totalise plus de 11 millions de vues. Shirley a été initiée aux jeux vidéo par son fils dans les années 1990 et diffuse principalement des parties du jeu de rôle *The Elder Scrolls V: Skyrim* (Bethesda, 2011).

MARS 28 En 2016, le pilote de moto Guy Martin (GBR) est **le plus rapide sur un mur de la mort**, atteignant 125,77 km/h, soit un tour en 3,41 s. L'exploit est retransmis en direct à la télévision depuis l'aéroport de Manby à Louth (Lincolnshire, GBR).

MARS 29 Gaber Kahlwai Gaber Ali (EGY) est bien secoué lorsqu'il exécute **le plus de tonneaux en 1 min** (67), au stade de l'université du Caire, à Gizeh (EGY), en 2015.

LES 10 PERSONNES LES PLUS ÂGÉES ACTUELLEMENT		
NOM	NAISSANCE	ÂGE
Kane Tanaka (JPN)	2 janv. 1903	116 ans et 73 jours
Maria-Giuseppa Robucci-Nargiso (ITA)	20 mars 1903	115 ans et 361 jours
Lucile Randon (FRA)	11 févr. 1904	115 ans et 33 jours
Shin Matsushita (JPN)	30 mars 1904	114 ans et 351 jours
Jeanne Bot (FRA)	14 janv. 1905	114 ans et 61 jours
Shigeyo Nakachi (JPN)	1er févr. 1905	114 ans et 43 jours
Haruno Yamashita (JPN)	19 févr. 1905	114 ans et 25 jours
Kame Ganeko (JPN)	10 avr. 1905	113 ans et 340 jours
Ellen Gibb ou "Dolly" (CAN)	26 avr. 1905	113 ans et 324 jours
Alelia Murphy (USA)	6 juill. 1905	113 ans et 253 jours

Source : Gerontology Research Group, au 16 mars 2019

▶ LA PERSONNE LA PLUS ÂGÉE ACTUELLEMENT

Le 16 mars 2019, à Fukuoka (JPN), nous avons vérifié que Kane Tanaka (JPN, née le 2 janvier 1903) était bien âgée de 116 ans et 73 jours. Elle est née l'année où les frères Wright ont effectué **le 1er vol motorisé**. Elle tenait un commerce familial et y vendait du riz gluant, des sucreries et des nouilles. Vivant actuellement dans une maison de retraite, elle aime faire des mathématiques ou jouer au jeu d'échecs Othello.

Kane souhaitait devenir **la personne la plus âgée** depuis ses 100 ans. Elle a fêté cela en dégustant des chocolats.

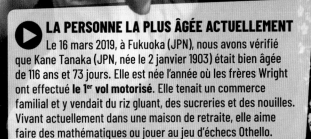

▶ LA DJ PROFESSIONNELLE LA PLUS ÂGÉE

Le 25 mai 2018, Sumiko Iwamuro (JPN, née le 27 janvier 1935), alias "DJ Sumirock", âgée de 83 ans, se produisait encore régulièrement dans le quartier de Shinjuku à Tokyo. Elle a commencé à être DJ à 77 ans. Ses morceaux de techno sont mixés avec du jazz, des bandes-son de dessins animés et de la musique classique. Sumirock s'est aussi produite en Nouvelle-Zélande et en France.

LA PERSONNE LA PLUS ÂGÉE À TRAVERSER LE CANADA À VÉLO (FEMMES)

Lynnea Salvo (USA, née le 21 septembre 1949) avait 68 ans et 339 jours lorsqu'elle a achevé sa traversée à vélo du 2e plus grand pays du monde, le 26 août 2018. Elle a parcouru 6 616 km en 70 jours.

Le 23 octobre 2016, Lynnea, enseignante à la retraite, est aussi devenue **la personne la plus âgée à traverser les États-Unis à vélo (femmes)**, à 67 ans et 32 jours.

LA PERSONNE LA PLUS ÂGÉE À TRAVERSER LA GRANDE-BRETAGNE À VÉLO JUSQU'À JOHN O' GROATS

Du 8 au 25 septembre 2018, Alex Menarry (GBR, né le 8 décembre 1932) a traversé la Grande-Bretagne et atteint l'extrémité nord-est de l'Écosse à 85 ans et 291 jours. Il a parcouru en moyenne 101 km par jour. Ancien coureur de montagne, il trouve que le voyage a été plus difficile du point de vue mental que physique.

MARS 30 — En 2012, le chanteur Tim Storms (USA) produit **la note la plus basse émise par un être humain** – le sol se trouvant 8 octaves sous le sol le plus grave d'un piano (0,189 Hz) – dans les studios Citywalk à Branson (Missouri, USA).

MARS 31 — La tour Eiffel est inaugurée en 1889 à Paris. Haute de 300 m, elle est la structure la plus ambitieuse de son époque et reste **l'édifice métallique le plus élevé** actuellement.

La plus longue chevelure (femmes)
Mesurées le 8 mai 2004, les somptueuses boucles de Xie Qiuping (CHN) mesuraient 5,62 m de long. La Chinoise a commencé à laisser pousser ses cheveux en 1973, à l'âge 13 ans. "Cela ne me gêne pas, j'ai l'habitude, nous a-t-elle confié. Mais une chevelure comme la mienne nécessite de la patience et il faut se tenir bien droite."

Longs de plus de 5 m, les cheveux de Xie Qiuping atteignent presque la taille d'une girafe adulte.

1. La crête la plus haute
Il a fallu plus de 15 ans au couturier Kazuhiro Watanabe (JPN) pour obtenir cette crête de 1,23 m, mesurée le 23 avril 2014 au studio de Dwango à Hanzomon (Tokyo, JPN). La façonner a nécessité 2 h de travail, une équipe de coiffeurs, 3 flacons de laque et un pot de gel.

2. Le plus de titres au championnat du monde "barbe et moustache"
De 1999 à 2013, Karl-Heinz Hille (DEU) a remporté 9 titres au championnat du monde "barbe et moustache". Il a été vainqueur dans la catégorie "semi-barbe impériale" à 7 reprises et sacré champion toutes catégories en 1999 et 2003. La semi-barbe impériale ne recouvre que les joues et la lèvre supérieure.

3. La coiffure la plus haute
Une pyramide de vrais et faux cheveux de 2,66 m a été échafaudée au cours d'un événement organisé par la société KLIPP unser Frisör (AUT) à Wels (AUT), le 21 juin 2009. Pour la réaliser, 2 coiffeurs ont travaillé durant 2 jours et utilisé 22 m de cheveux.

4. La perruque la plus large
Le 27 janvier 2017, la star hollywoodienne Drew Barrymore (USA) a porté une perruque de 2,23 m de large lors de l'émission *The Tonight Show* à New York (USA). Celle-ci avait été fabriquée par Kelly Hanson et la société Randy Carfagno Productions (USA). Quatre personnes ont dû l'installer sur l'actrice.

▶ 5. La plus jeune femme dotée d'une barbe complète
Harnaam Kaur (GBR, née le 29 novembre 1990) avait 24 ans et 282 jours le 7 septembre 2015 lorsqu'il a été prouvé qu'elle portait une barbe complète avec des favoris, recouvrant son menton, une partie de ses joues et sa lèvre supérieure. Sa pilosité est liée à un déséquilibre hormonal dû à un syndrome des ovaires polykystiques. Mannequin et conférencière en développement personnel, Harnaam veut montrer au monde ce que sont la véritable beauté et le fait d'être soi-même.

6. La plus longue moustache
La moustache titanesque de Ram Singh Chauhan (IND) atteignait 4,29 m le 4 mars 2010 sur le plateau de *Lo Show dei Record* à Rome (ITA). Ram la laisse pousser depuis 1970 et l'entretient avec de l'huile de coco et de moutarde. Ses bacchantes lui ont valu une apparition dans le film de James Bond *Octopussy* (GBR/USA, 1983).

AVR. 1 En 2009, 114 amateurs de football en combinaison de plongée assistent à un match diffusé dans le studio aquatique de Basildon (Essex, GBR) – **le plus de personnes regardant la télévision sous l'eau.**

AVR. 2 En 1988, Rémy Bricka (FRA) accomplit **la "marche" la plus rapide sur l'océan** grâce à ses skis de 4,2 m de long. Il parcourt ainsi 5 636 km en 59 jours.

7. La plus grande famille excessivement poilue

La famille de Jesús "Chuy" Fajardo Aceves et Luisa Lilia De Lira Aceves (MEX) compte 5 générations et 19 personnes, toutes atteintes d'hypertrichose congénitale généralisée. Cette maladie rare se caractérise par une pilosité excessive du visage et du torse. Les femmes ont une couche de poils fine ou moyenne et les hommes ont des poils épais sur 98 % de leur corps, sauf sur les paumes et la plante des pieds.

▶ 8. La plus grosse coiffure afro (femmes)

La coiffure afro d'Aevin Dugas (USA), mesurée le 31 mars 2012, atteignait 16 cm de haut depuis le sommet de sa tête et 1,39 m de circonférence. Aevin coupait alors ses cheveux 2 ou 3 fois par an et utilisait jusqu'à 5 soins lorsqu'elle les lavait.

La plus grosse coiffure afro enregistrée atteignait 25,4 cm de haut et 1,77 m de circonférence. Le jeune Tyler Wright (USA) avait 12 ans lorsque sa coiffure a été mesurée le 19 juin 2015.

9. La barbe la plus longue (homme vivant)

Le 8 septembre 2011, la barbe de Sarwan Singh (CAN) atteignait 2,49 m. Sarwan est le chef de la congrégation du temple Guru Nanak Sikh à Surrey, en Colombie-Britannique (CAN).

La plus longue barbe de tous les temps mesurait 5,33 m et appartenait à Hans N. Langseth (NOR). Elle a été mesurée après son décès en 1927.

▶ L'ADOLESCENTE À LA PLUS LONGUE CHEVELURE

La chevelure de Nilanshi Patel (IND, née le 16 août 2002), âgée de 16 ans, mesurait 1,75 m de long le 21 novembre 2018. La jeune fille laisse pousser ses cheveux depuis qu'elle a 6 ans et considère qu'ils lui portent chance. Elle les lave une fois par semaine et il faut une demi-heure pour les sécher et une heure pour les peigner. Généralement elle porte une natte, mais arbore un chignon lorsqu'elle joue au ping-pong.

AVR. 3 En 2017, le boucher Barry John Crowe (IRL) fabrique **le plus de saucisses en 1 min** dans l'émission *Big Week on the Farm* de la Radio Télévision d'Irlande, soit 78 au rythme d'une toutes les 0,76 s.

AVR. 4 En 1933, l'USS *Akron* est détruit durant une tempête au large du New Jersey (USA), entraînant la mort de 73 personnes. Il s'agit **du plus grave accident de dirigeable**. Seules 3 personnes survivent.

63

BEAUTÉ CORPORELLE

LA TAILLE LA PLUS FINE DE TOUS LES TEMPS

En 1929, Ethel Granger (GBR) a commencé à affiner son tour de taille de 56 cm en portant des corsets de plus en plus serrés. En 1939, son tour de taille mesurait 33 cm. Pionnière en matière de modifications corporelles, Ethel portait aussi des piercings sur le visage. Émilie Marie Bouchaud (FRA, 1874-1939), alias Mademoiselle Polaire, revendiquait un tour de taille identique.

Le prénom le plus de fois tatoué sur un corps
Pour fêter la naissance de sa fille, Mark Evans (GBR) a fait tatouer 267 fois le prénom "Lucy" sur son dos, un nombre vérifié le 25 janvier 2017.

▶ Le plus de modifications corporelles (couple marié)
Le 7 juillet 2014, Victor Hugo Peralta (URY) et son épouse Gabriela (ARG) totalisaient 84 modifications corporelles incluant 50 piercings, 8 implants microdermaux, 14 implants corporels, 5 implants dentaires, 4 extenseurs d'oreille, 2 barbells et 1 langue fourchue.

▶ Le plus de tunnels faciaux
Le visage de Joel Miggler (DEU) a été transformé par 11 tunnels faciaux (bijoux creux tubulaires), comme cela a été constaté le 27 novembre 2014 à Küssaberg (DEU). Ces tunnels mesurent de 3 à 34 mm de diamètre.

Le plus de personnes tatouées au henné
Le henné est une teinture brun-rouge issue de la plante *Lawsonia inermis*. Le 3 février 2018, au cours d'un événement organisé au Gujarat (IND), par Shree Ahir Samaj Seva Samiti-Surat, Natubhai Ranmalbhai Bhatu et Jerambhai Vala (tous IND), 1 982 personnes ont été tatouées simultanément au henné.

LE PLUS LONG COU
Certaines femmes de la tribu Padaung (ou Kayan), au Myanmar et en Thaïlande, utilisent de lourds colliers en laiton pour étirer leur cou. Selon une étude de 2018, certaines femmes Padaung ont un cou pouvant atteindre 19,7 cm (de la clavicule à la mâchoire inférieure). Le cou d'un adulte mesure généralement de 8 à 10 cm.

Le senior le plus piercé
John Lynch (GBR, né le 9 novembre 1930) portait 241 piercings, dont 151 sur la tête et le cou, lors d'un décompte effectué dans le Hammersmith, à Londres (GBR), le 17 octobre 2008.

Le plus de maquillages en 1 h (équipe de 5)
Le 7 septembre 2018, 5 maquilleuses de Sephora Deutschland (DEU) ont maquillé 148 personnes au centre commercial Main-Taunus Zentrum, à Sulzbach (DEU).

Le plus d'applications de rouge à lèvres
Le 9 septembre 2018, 6 900 personnes ont mis du rouge à lèvres lors du Ganda for All Music Festival, à Quezon City (Manille, PHL). Les festivaliers devaient porter une nuance de la marque Vice Cosmetics (PHL) pour entrer.

Le 27 juillet 2018, la maquilleuse Melis İlkkılıç a réalisé **le plus d'applications de rouge à lèvres en 1 min**, sur 8 mannequins, en collaboration avec Avon Türkiye (TUR).

Le plus de visages rasés en 1 h avec un rasoir électrique (individu)
Le barbier Furkan Yakar (TUR) a rasé 69 visages, à Berlin (DEU), le 31 octobre 2018. Ce rasage express a été organisé par L'Oréal Men Expert et la Movembre Foundation (toutes 2 DEU).

Le maquillage le plus épais
Le chutti est caractéristique du Kathakali, danse-théâtre traditionnelle indienne. Les personnages dotés d'une barbe rouge portent des "masques" à base de pâte de riz et de papier, dont le façonnage nécessite des heures. Ce maquillage peut atteindre 15 cm d'épaisseur.

100 %

▶ LE PLUS DE PERSONNAGES MARVEL TATOUÉS SUR LE CORPS
Rick Scolamiero (CAN) a fait tatouer 31 personnages de l'univers Marvel sur son corps, un nombre vérifié le 3 mars 2018. Black Widow est notamment tatouée sur son torse (médaillon ci-dessous) et Venom sur son genou gauche (médaillon du bas). La signature de Stan Lee est également tatouée sur son poignet.

LE MAQUILLAGE LABIAL LE PLUS COÛTEUX
Pour fêter son 50e anniversaire, le 7 septembre 2018, Rosendorff Diamonds (AUS) a orné les lèvres du mannequin Charlie Octavia de 126 diamants d'une valeur de 757 975 $ AUS (545 125 $). Ce maquillage artistique a été conçu et réalisé par la maquilleuse Clare Mac (en photo à gauche avec Charlie), qui a d'abord appliqué une couche de rouge à lèvres noir mat avant de fixer chaque diamant à l'aide de colle pour faux cils.

LE MANNEQUIN LE PLUS ÂGÉ PHOTOGRAPHIÉ DANS *VOGUE*
Bo Gilbert (GBR, née en 1916) a figuré alors qu'elle était âgée de 100 ans dans une campagne publicitaire pour le grand magasin de luxe Harvey Nichols insérée dans l'édition de mai 2016 du *Vogue* britannique. Bo a été photographiée en l'honneur du centenaire du magazine. "Je m'habille pour le plaisir", a-t-elle déclaré.

 AVR. 5 En 1930, Gandhi (IND) parvient à Dandi à la tête de 78 personnes après **la plus longue marche de protestation** – un trajet de 387,8 km à travers l'État du Gujarat destiné à protester contre la taxe britannique sur le sel.

 AVR. 6 En 1985, Lucy Wardle (USA) effectue **le plus haut saut depuis un plongeoir (femmes)**, s'élançant d'une hauteur de 36,8 m dans une piscine, à Ocean Park (Hong Kong, CHN).

LES PLUS LONGUES EXTENSIONS D'ONGLES

Créateur de chapeaux, fan de Barbra Streisand et autoproclamé "enfant terrible", Odilon Ozare (USA) a réalisé 10 extensions d'ongles de couleur de 1,21 m, mesurées le 26 août 2018, à Tampa (Floride, USA). Celles-ci se composent de 30 couches d'acrylique cosmétique recouvertes de résine polyacrylique appliquée à l'aérographe. Cela lui a été inspiré par le "yoga des oiseaux" qu'il pratique avec ses cacatoès. Il travaille aujourd'hui sur la chaussure la plus longue.

Odilon a également confectionné ○ le chapeau le plus haut (à droite), qui mesure 4,80 m. Pour valider son record, il a dû parcourir plus de 10 m en le portant.

L'INTERVENTION ESTHÉTIQUE NON CHIRURGICALE LA PLUS COURANTE

Selon l'ISAPS (Société internationale de chirurgie esthétique et plastique), l'injection de toxine botulique ("botox") est l'intervention non chirurgicale la plus courante effectuée par les chirurgiens esthétiques. 5 033 693 interventions ont eu lieu en 2017, représentant 39,9 % des interventions non chirurgicales.

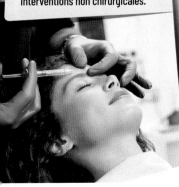

LE SENIOR LE PLUS TATOUÉ (HOMMES)

Depuis son 1er tatouage dans les années 1950, Charles Helmke dit "Chuck" (USA) est tatoué sur 97,5 % du corps, un fait vérifié à Melbourne (Floride, USA), le 9 décembre 2016.

La compagne de Chuck, Charlotte Guttenberg (USA), est ○ la senior la plus tatouée et ○ la femme la plus tatouée du monde. Le 7 novembre 2017, ses tatouages couvraient 98,75 % de son corps.

LE PLUS D'ABONNÉS POUR UNE CHAÎNE YOUTUBE MODE/BEAUTÉ

Mariand Castrejòn Castañeda (MEX), alias "Yuya", comptait 23 666 883 abonnés au 29 avril 2019, ce qui la plaçait dans le top 50 des chaînes YouTube. Également surnommée "lady16makeup", Yuya a lancé son vlog en 2009. Ses principaux sujets sont la mode et le maquillage, mais elle parle aussi de toutes les tendances.

AVR. 7 En 2014, Jack Sexty (GBR) réalise **le marathon le plus rapide sur un bâton sauteur**, franchissant d'un bond la ligne d'arrivée au bout de 16 h et 24 min, au marathon de Manchester (GBR).

AVR. 8 En 2013, l'âge du **plus vieux poirier** – une espèce de Mandchourie – est estimé à 458 ans dans l'ancien verger de la commune de Shenchuan (province de Gansu, CHN).

65

ÊTRES HUMAINS

L'HOMME AUGMENTÉ

L'exosquelette artisanal le plus puissant

Surnommé "The Hacksmith", James Hobson (CAN) a conçu et réalisé des exosquelettes motorisés pour le haut et le bas du corps qui lui permettent de soulever les roues arrière d'un pick-up de 2 272 kg ainsi que des haltères de 220 kg, comme il l'a démontré en janvier 2016. Il actionne l'exosquelette, dont la puissance provient de 2 cylindres pneumatiques.

LES PREMIERS...

Ordinateur portable

En 1961, les mathématiciens du Massachusetts Institute of Technology Edward O. Thorp et Claude Shannon (tous 2 USA) ont inventé un ordinateur de la taille d'un paquet de cartes à jouer conçu pour prédire le résultat des

roulettes. L'appareil était fixé à la taille et des boutons dissimulés dans une chaussure permettaient d'entrer les données requises avec le pied.

La 1re caméra monocle portable a été créée par le professeur Steve Mann (CAN) en 1980. Elle servait de caméra et d'écran optique, affichant des graphiques devant l'utilisateur.

"Cyborg" reconnu officiellement

En 2004, Neil Harbisson (GBR, voir page de droite), qui est achromatope (ne discerne aucune couleur), s'est fait implanter à l'arrière du crâne une antenne lui permettant de percevoir la couleur sous forme de musique. L'antenne est reliée à une caméra placée devant ses yeux qui convertit les ondes lumineuses en ondes sonores. Il porte en permanence cet implant, y compris sur la photo de son passeport.

LA 1RE PROTHÈSE DE BRAS LEGO® ARTISANALE

Né sans avant-bras droit, David Aguilar (AND) a conçu et fabriqué, à l'aide de pièces d'un hélicoptère LEGO® Technic (#9396), une prothèse de bras entièrement fonctionnelle dont il a achevé la 1re version en 2017. Surnommé "Hand Solo", Aguilar fabrique des prothèses en LEGO® depuis son enfance (médaillon) et améliore constamment ses modèles. Le plus récent (qu'il porte ci-dessus) est un membre motorisé doté de doigts qu'il commande grâce à de subtils mouvements de la partie intacte de son bras.

LE MARATHON LE PLUS RAPIDE EFFECTUÉ SEUL GRÂCE À UN ROBOT D'ASSISTANCE À LA MARCHE

Simon Kindleysides (GBR) a parcouru le marathon de Londres 2018 équipé d'un exosquelette ReWalk des membres inférieurs en 36 h et 46 min, après avoir effectué 60 373 pas et marché réellement 27 h et 32 min. Claire Lomas (GBR, en bas) – 1re personne à terminer un marathon à l'aide d'un dispositif robotisé d'aide à la marche – a effectué le marathon de Londres 2012 en 16 jours grâce au ReWalk. Le 15 avril 2018, elle a terminé le marathon de Manchester en 8 jours, réalisant **le marathon le plus rapide effectué grâce à un robot d'assistance à la marche (femmes)**.

Biohacker doté d'un dispositif de détection des séismes

Moon Ribas (ESP, voir page de droite) possède des implants dans les pieds qui l'alertent dès qu'un séisme survient sur Terre. Posés en 2017, ces implants fonctionnent grâce à une application de smartphone détectant l'activité sismique. Ils produisent des vibrations proportionnelles à la puissance du séisme.

Implant digital magnétique étanche

En 2005, Steve Haworth, pionnier de la modification corporelle, a créé avec Jesse Jarrell et Todd Huffman (tous USA) le 1er implant étanche. Cet aimant en néodyme était inséré sous la peau du bout d'un doigt et recouvert d'or et de silicone pour l'isoler du reste du corps.

Cornée imprimée en 3D

Le 30 mai 2018, des scientifiques de l'université de Newcastle (GBR) ont annoncé avoir imprimé une cornée artificielle en 3D. L'équipe a utilisé une bio-imprimante dotée d'une buse de 200 micromètres pour reconstituer une cornée scannée à l'aide de couches de bio-encre contenant des cellules de cornée, du collagène et de l'alginate. Cette technique reproduit la structure interne complexe du stroma cornéen.

La 1re côte imprimée en 3D implantée date de janvier 2019. L'implant a été fabriqué par le service d'impression en 3D 3dbgprint (BGR) en moins de 24 h à partir d'un matériau composé de nylon, et reçu par un patient, Ivaylo Josifov, à l'hôpital Tokuda de Sofia (BGR).

Les implants du futur pourraient transmettre au cerveau une impression sensorielle permettant à l'utilisateur de "sentir" sa prothèse.

LA 1RE PROTHÈSE DE BRAS ENTIÈREMENT INTÉGRÉE

En janvier 2013, un routier suédois resté anonyme, qui avait perdu son avant-bras 10 ans auparavant, a reçu une prothèse implantée dans l'os, qu'il commande directement via ses propres nerfs. Des chercheurs de l'université de technologie de Chalmers (SWE) ont en effet inséré un implant permanent en titane dans la moelle osseuse de son bras avant d'y relier la prothèse commandée par des électrodes.

AVR. 9 — Le 1er enregistrement vocal est réalisé en 1860 par l'inventeur Édouard-Léon Scott de Martinville (FRA). Il s'agit d'un extrait de 10 s d'une voix chantant *Au clair de la lune*.

AVR. 10 — En 1815, une éruption de 6 jours du volcan Tambora sur l'île indonésienne de Sumbawa s'achève après le rejet d'environ 150 à 180 km³ de matière : il s'agit de **la plus grosse éruption en volume**.

▶ LE PLUS DE COUPS DE BAGUETTE EN 1 MIN GRÂCE À UNE PROTHÈSE

Le 25 juillet 2018, le batteur Jason Barnes (USA) a joué 2 400 coups de baguette en 60 s, grâce à une prothèse de bras créée par Gil Weinberg (USA), au Georgia Institute of Technology d'Atlanta (Géorgie, USA). Sa prothèse réagit à l'activité électrique des tissus musculaires de son avant-bras, captée par une bande électromyographique.

Jason a perdu son bras après un accident électrique. "Je refuse que la perte de mon bras m'empêche de réaliser mes rêves, a-t-il déclaré. Rien ne m'arrêtera."

LES 1ᴱᴿˢ IMPLANTS DENTAIRES À FONCTIONNALITÉ BLUETOOTH

Les artistes et cyborgs Neil Harbisson (GBR, ci-contre) et Moon Ribas (ESP, à gauche) portent tous deux un implant dentaire à fonction bluetooth baptisé "WeTooth", qu'ils peuvent utiliser pour communiquer. Sous l'effet d'une pression, l'implant émet un signal faisant vibrer l'autre via une application de smartphone, ce qui permet aux 2 artistes de communiquer en morse.

LE PLUS GRAND EXOSQUELETTE TÉTRAPODE

Jonathan Tippett (CAN) a travaillé durant 12 ans sur *Prosthesis*, un exosquelette pilotable géant de course mesurant 3,96 m de haut, 5,1 m de long et 5,51 m de large, des mesures vérifiées le 26 septembre 2018. L'appareil pèse près de 3 500 kg. Ses pattes et son corps sont composés de tubes en acier chromoly, matériau très performant utilisé dans l'aérospatiale.

AVR. 11 **La plus grande portée de koalas,** composée de vrais jumeaux, Euca et Lyptus, voit le jour en 1999 dans le Queensland (AUS). La plupart des femelles ont une poche qui ne peut contenir qu'un petit.

AVR. 12 En 1998, aux championnats du monde de remplissage de wagonnets de charbon, Christine Adams (AUS) a déplacé 250 kg de charbon en 38,29 s, réalisant **le déblayage de charbon le plus rapide (femmes).**

67

QUESTION DE TAILLE

LE PLUS GRAND OU LA PLUS GRANDE...

• **danseur de ballet :** Fabrice Calmels (FRA) mesurait 199,73 cm le 25 septembre 2014. Il est danseur étoile au sein du Joffrey Ballet de Chicago (Illinois, USA).

• **homme politique :** le conseiller municipal Robert E. Cornegy Jr (USA) mesure 209,6 cm. Sa taille a été vérifiée à Brooklyn, New York (USA), le 14 janvier 2019.

• **femme :** allongée, Siddiqa Parveen (IND) mesurait 222,25 cm en décembre 2012. Elle ne peut se tenir droite, mais le médecin qui l'a mesurée a estimé qu'en se tenant debout, elle atteindrait 233,6 cm.

• **femme de tous les temps :** Zeng Jinlian (CHN, 1964-1982) mesurait 246,3 cm à sa mort.

• **homme de tous les temps :** Robert Pershing Wadlow (USA, 1918-1940) est la personne la plus grande de l'histoire de la médecine. Mesuré pour la dernière fois le 27 juin 1940, il atteignait 272 cm.

LE PLUS PETIT OU LA PLUS PETITE...

• **personne dans l'espace :** l'astronaute Nancy Currie (USA), qui mesure 152 cm, a participé à la mission STS-57 en juin 1993.

• **dirigeant :** Benito Juárez (1806-1872), qui était président du Mexique de 1858 à 1872, mesurait 137 cm.

• **mère :** Stacey Herald (1974-2018), qui mesurait 72,39 cm, a accouché de son 1er enfant à Dry Ridge (Kentucky, USA), le 21 octobre 2006. Elle a ensuite eu deux autres enfants, l'un en 2008 et l'autre en 2009.

• **femme de tous les temps :** Pauline Musters (NLD, 1876-1895), surnommée "princesse Pauline",

mesurait 30 cm à la naissance. À sa mort, à 19 ans, elle faisait 61 cm.

• **espion :** adulte, Richebourg (FRA, 1768-1858) ne mesurait que 58 cm. Pendant la Révolution, il portait des messages dans Paris déguisé en enfant porté par sa nourrice.

• ▶ **homme de tous les temps :** Chandra Bahadur Dangi (NPL, 1939-2015) mesurait 54,6 cm, une taille vérifiée à la CIWEC Clinic de Lainchaur (Katmandou, NPL), le 26 février 2012. Il est historiquement la personne la plus petite dont la taille est prouvée.

LES PLUS GRANDES MAINS POUR UN ADOLESCENT

La main droite de Mathu-Andrew Budge (GBR, né le 28 décembre 2001) mesure 22,5 cm du poignet à l'extrémité du majeur, et sa main gauche 22,2 cm, un fait attesté à Londres (GBR), le 13 février 2018. Lars Motza (DEU, né le 21 septembre 2002) est **l'adolescent aux plus grands pieds**. Son pied gauche mesure 35,05 cm et le droit 34,98 cm. Ils ont été mesurés le 19 novembre 2018, à Berlin (DEU).

▶ LES PLUS GRANDS PIEDS

Le pied droit et le pied gauche de Jeison Orlando Rodríguez Hernández (VEN) atteignent respectivement 40,55 et 40,47 cm. Nous les avons mesurés au Parc Saint Paul de Beauvais (FRA), le 3 juin 2018. Ses chaussures sont fabriquées sur mesure en Allemagne. Jeison détient ce record depuis 2014. Son pied droit mesurait alors 40,1 cm et le gauche 39,6 cm – leur croissance se poursuit donc !

Les plus grands pieds (femmes) appartiennent à Julie Felton (GBR) d'Ellesmere (Shropshire, GBR). Selon des vérifications effectuées le 23 mars 2019, son pied droit mesure 32,9 cm et le gauche 32,73 cm.

Paulo et Katyucia se sont mariés le 17 septembre 2016. Deux mois plus tard, ils étaient les invités d'honneur du GWR Day.

▶ L'HOMME LE PLUS LOURD

Pour l'instant, personne ne détient plus ce record. En 2016, Juan Pedro Franco Salas (MEX) pesait 594,8 kg lorsqu'il avait été examiné par une équipe médicale à Guadalajara (Jalisco, MEX). Après s'être fait poser un anneau gastrique, il ne pesait plus que 304 kg en novembre 2018. Le voici photographié en février 2019, montrant les effets bénéfiques de son régime. Nous aimerions le féliciter, simplement parce qu'il n'est *plus* l'homme le plus lourd du monde.

▶ LA RENCONTRE ENTRE LE PLUS PETIT COUPLE MARIÉ ET LE PLUS GRAND HOMME

Paulo Gabriel da Silva Barros et Katyucia Lie Hoshino (BRA) ont une taille combinée de 181,41 cm, une mesure validée le 3 novembre 2016, à Itapeva (São Paulo, BRA). Les voici aux côtés du ▶ **plus grand homme**, Sultan Kösen (TUR), qui mesure 251 cm. Ce remarquable trio a fait connaissance en novembre 2018 au cours d'un événement GWR à Moscou (RUS). Page 58, vous en saurez plus sur Sultan et sa taille par rapport à celle de **l'homme le plus grand de tous les temps** (voir ci-dessus).

AVR. 13 À Londres, en 2003, Paula Radcliffe (GBR) effectue **le marathon le plus rapide (record féminin)**, en 2 h, 15 min et 25 s. Elle parvient même à battre son propre record de presque 2 min.

AVR. 14 En 1986, **les plus lourds grêlons** répertoriés avec précision s'abattent sur le district de Gopalganj (BGD). Pesant jusqu'à 1 kg – environ le poids d'un ananas – ils causent le décès de 92 personnes.

Selon son père, "Khagendra était si minuscule lorsqu'il est né qu'il tenait dans le creux de la main et il était très difficile de le baigner tant il était petit".

LE PLUS PETIT HOMME POUVANT MARCHER

La taille de Khagendra Thapa Magar (NPL, né le 14 octobre 1992) était de 67,08 cm le 14 octobre 2010, lorsqu'il a été mesuré au Fewa City Hospital de Pokhara (NPL). GWR a contacté Khagendra en décembre 2018 afin de le suivre durant une journée, alors qu'il tient la boutique familiale, joue de la guitare ou se promène en ville à moto avec son frère (médaillon ci-dessus).

Junrey Balawing (PHL, né le 12 juin 1993 ; à droite) est **le plus petit homme à mobilité réduite**. Sa taille, 59,93 cm, est inférieure à celle d'une raquette de tennis. Elle a été validée le 12 juin 2011 au Sindangan Health Centre (Zamboanga del Norte, PHL).

Des vidéos GWR de grands (et petits) sur guinnessworldrecords.com/2020

LA PLUS PETITE FEMME

Mesurée à Nagpur (IND), Jyoti Amge (IND) faisait 62,8 cm le 16 décembre 2011 – jour de ses 18 ans. Elle était ainsi **la plus petite adolescente**. Jyoti est également **la plus petite actrice**. Elle interprète le personnage récurrent de Ma Petite dans la série *American Horror Story* diffusée sur FX. Elle est ici photographiée avec Erika Arvin, surnommée "Amazon Eve", actrice de 201 cm également présente dans la série, et qui a été **le plus grand mannequin professionnel**.

LE PLUS GRAND COUPLE MARIÉ

Le 14 novembre 2013, Sun Mingming **(le plus grand joueur de basket-ball)** et sa femme Xu Yan (tous 2 CHN) atteignaient respectivement 236,17 cm et 187,3 cm, soit une taille cumulée de 423,47 cm. Ils ont été mesurés à Pékin (CHN), ville dans laquelle ils s'étaient mariés le 4 août de la même année.

 AVR. 15 Le Shankweiler's Drive-in Theater ouvre ses portes en 1934, à Orefield (Pennsylvanie, USA). Il peut accueillir 275 voitures. Toujours en activité, il s'agit du **plus ancien cinéma drive-in**.

 AVR. 16 Au cours de la Tattoo Arts Convention de 2016 dans le Maryland (USA), Casey Severn (USA) bat le record **du plus grand nombre de pièges à rats libérés avec la langue en 1 min** (13).

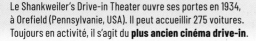

69

LES PLUS LONGUES JAMBES (FEMMES)

Les jambes gauche et droite d'Ekaterina Lisina (RUS) mesuraient respectivement 132,8 et 132,2 cm lors de vérifications effectuées le 13 juin 2017, à Penza (RUS). Ces mesures ont été prises du talon au sommet de la hanche. Avec 205,16 cm, Ekaterina est aussi **le plus grand mannequin professionnel** (voir l'ancienne détentrice du record p. 69). Elle a aussi fait partie de l'équipe russe de basket qui a obtenu la médaille de bronze aux JO de 2008.

Les plus grandes mains de tous les temps

Les mains de Robert Pershing Wadlow (USA), **le plus grand homme de tous les temps**, mesuraient 32,3 cm – plus qu'un ballon de football américain – du poignet à l'extrémité du majeur. Robert portait une bague de taille 25 (26 mm de diamètre). Wadlow avait aussi **les plus grands pieds de tous les temps** et portait des chaussures correspondant à une longueur de pied de 47 cm. Pour plus d'infos, voir p. 58-59.

Les plus longs lobes d'oreilles (étirés)

Monte Pierce (USA) peut étirer son lobe d'oreille gauche de 12,7 cm et le droit de 11,43 cm. Non étirés, ses lobes ne mesurent que 2,54 cm.

Les yeux les plus exorbités

Kim Goodman (USA) peut extraire ses yeux à une distance de 12 mm hors de leurs orbites, un exploit mesuré à Istanbul (TUR), le 2 novembre 2007.

Le plus de modifications corporelles

Rolf Buchholz (DEU) fait l'objet de 516 modifications corporelles dénombrées le 16 décembre 2012, à Dortmund

L'ADOLESCENTE LA PLUS VELUE

Le 4 mars 2010, à Rome (ITA), Supatra Sasuphan (THA), surnommée "Nat", a été reconnue comme étant la jeune femme la plus velue selon la méthode Ferriman-Gallwey d'évaluation de l'hirsutisme féminin. Nat souffre d'un syndrome d'Ambras, une affection qui n'aurait touché que 50 personnes depuis le Moyen Âge. Début 2018, nous avons appris qu'elle est aujourd'hui mariée (médaillon) et se rase régulièrement. L'équipe du GWR la félicite chaleureusement. Toute autre postulante dans cette catégorie est la bienvenue.

(DEU). Il porte 481 piercings, 2 implants sous-cutanés en forme de cornes et 5 implants magnétiques au bout des doigts de la main droite.

María José Cristerna (MEX) compte ▶ **le plus de modifications corporelles (femmes)**, soit 49 : des tatouages, des implants transdermiques sur le front, la poitrine et les bras, des piercings sur les sourcils, les lèvres, le nez, la langue, les lobes d'oreilles, le nombril et les mamelons.

100%

LA LANGUE LA PLUS LARGE

Byron Schlenker (USA) a une langue de 8,57 cm de large – plus large qu'une balle de baseball. Elle a été mesurée le 2 novembre 2014, à Syracuse (New York, USA), tout comme celle de sa fille Emily (USA, médaillon), qui a **la langue la plus large (femmes)**, soit 7,33 cm.

Sortie, ▶ **la langue la plus longue** atteint 10,1 cm de son extrémité au centre de la lèvre supérieure (bouche fermée) et appartient à Nick Stoeberl (USA). Elle a été mesurée le 27 novembre 2012, à Salinas (Californie, USA). Chanel Tapper (USA) a ▶ **la langue la plus longue (femmes)** : celle-ci mesurait 9,75 cm le 29 septembre 2010, en Californie.

L'opération de chirurgie esthétique la plus courante

Selon le rapport le plus récent de la Société internationale de chirurgie esthétique et plastique (ISAPS), l'augmentation mammaire est l'opération esthétique la plus pratiquée, avec 1 677 320 opérations en 2017. Le nombre d'opérations recensées par l'ISAPS est de 10 766 848, dont 15,6 % d'augmentations mammaires.

LA PLUS LONGUE DENT DE LAIT

Le 17 janvier 2018, une dent de lait de 2,4 cm a été enlevée de la bouche de Curtis Buddie (USA), âgé de 10 ans. Elle a été extraite par le Dr Scott Bossert (ci-dessus, à droite) du centre The Gentle Dentist à Columbus (Ohio, USA).

La plus longue dent extraite mesurait 3,67 cm et appartenait à Urvil Patel (IND). Son extraction a été réalisée par le Dr Jaimin Patel le 3 février 2017.

AVR. 17 En 2014, Philip Joseph Santoro (USA) devient **le plus rapide à manger un donut à la confiture sans les mains** (11,41 s), à San Francisco (Californie, USA). Pas le temps de se lécher les babines ici !

AVR. 18 **Le record du plus de flèches attrapées à la main en 1 min** (15) est décroché par Joe Alexander (DEU), ou "Œil d'aigle", prouesse réalisée sur le plateau de *Lo Show dei Record*, à Rome (ITA), en 2012.

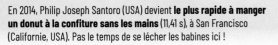

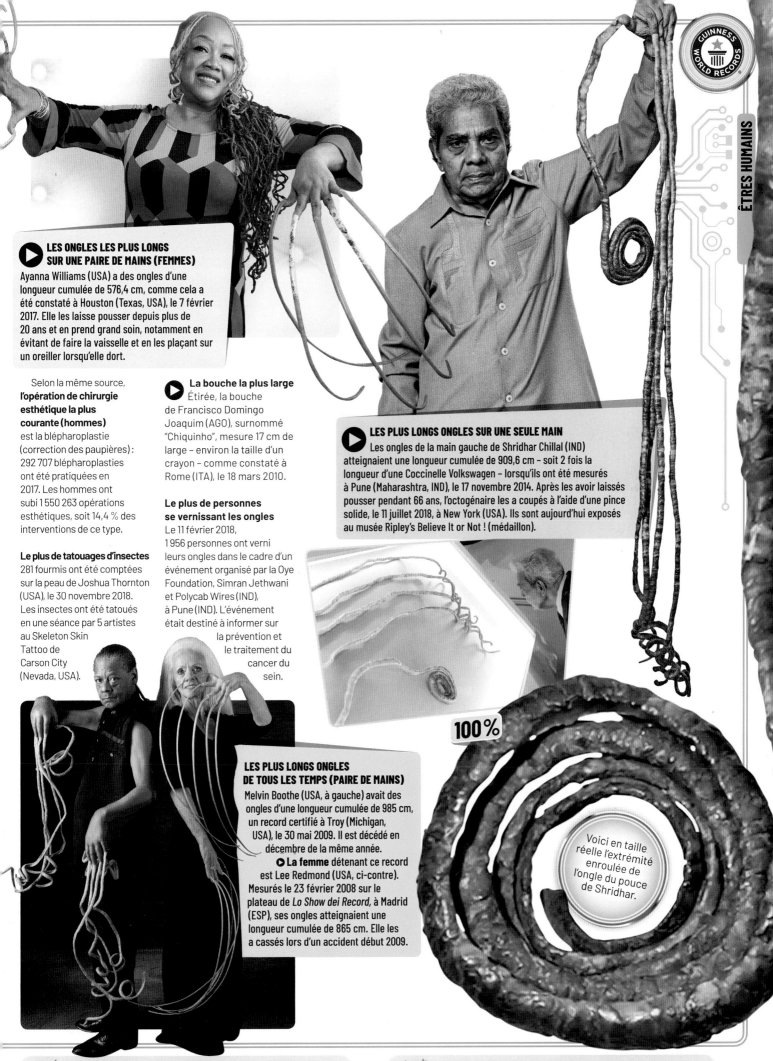

LES ONGLES LES PLUS LONGS SUR UNE PAIRE DE MAINS (FEMMES)

Ayanna Williams (USA) a des ongles d'une longueur cumulée de 576,4 cm, comme cela a été constaté à Houston (Texas, USA), le 7 février 2017. Elle les laisse pousser depuis plus de 20 ans et en prend grand soin, notamment en évitant de faire la vaisselle et en les plaçant sur un oreiller lorsqu'elle dort.

Selon la même source, **l'opération de chirurgie esthétique la plus courante (hommes)** est la blépharoplastie (correction des paupières) : 292 707 blépharoplasties ont été pratiquées en 2017. Les hommes ont subi 1 550 263 opérations esthétiques, soit 14,4 % des interventions de ce type.

Le plus de tatouages d'insectes
281 fourmis ont été comptées sur la peau de Joshua Thornton (USA), le 30 novembre 2018. Les insectes ont été tatoués en une séance par 5 artistes au Skeleton Skin Tattoo de Carson City (Nevada, USA).

La bouche la plus large
Étirée, la bouche de Francisco Domingo Joaquim (AGO), surnommé "Chiquinho", mesure 17 cm de large – environ la taille d'un crayon – comme constaté à Rome (ITA), le 18 mars 2010.

Le plus de personnes se vernissant les ongles
Le 11 février 2018, 1 956 personnes ont verni leurs ongles dans le cadre d'un événement organisé par la Oye Foundation, Simran Jethwani et Polycab Wires (IND), à Pune (IND). L'événement était destiné à informer sur la prévention et le traitement du cancer du sein.

LES PLUS LONGS ONGLES SUR UNE SEULE MAIN

Les ongles de la main gauche de Shridhar Chillal (IND) atteignaient une longueur cumulée de 909,6 cm – soit 2 fois la longueur d'une Coccinelle Volkswagen – lorsqu'ils ont été mesurés à Pune (Maharashtra, IND), le 17 novembre 2014. Après les avoir laissés pousser pendant 66 ans, l'octogénaire les a coupés à l'aide d'une pince solide, le 11 juillet 2018, à New York (USA). Ils sont aujourd'hui exposés au musée Ripley's Believe It or Not ! (médaillon).

LES PLUS LONGS ONGLES DE TOUS LES TEMPS (PAIRE DE MAINS)

Melvin Boothe (USA, à gauche) avait des ongles d'une longueur cumulée de 985 cm, un record certifié à Troy (Michigan, USA), le 30 mai 2009. Il est décédé en décembre de la même année.
○ **La femme** détenant ce record est Lee Redmond (USA, ci-contre). Mesurés le 23 février 2008 sur le plateau de *Lo Show dei Record*, à Madrid (ESP), ses ongles atteignaient une longueur cumulée de 865 cm. Elle les a cassés lors d'un accident début 2009.

100 %

Voici en taille réelle l'extrémité enroulée de l'ongle du pouce de Shridhar.

AVR. 19
En 1897, John J. McDermott (USA) remporte le 1er marathon de Boston – long de plus de 39 km – en 2 h, 55 min et 10 s. Cette course reste **le plus ancien marathon annuel**.

AVR. 20
En 2006, Joe Carlucci (USA) réalise **le plus haut lancer de pizza**, au Mall of America de Minneapolis (Minnesota, USA). Il propulse 567 g de pâte à 6,52 m de hauteur et rattrape le tout.

71

RECORDOLOGIE

LA PLUS GRANDE COLLECTION D'OBJETS LIÉS AUX *TRANSFORMERS*

Louis Georgiou (GBR) possède 2 111 objets liés aux *Transformers*, notamment des figurines et des bandes dessinées. Son record a été homologué le 11 mai 2017 à Manchester (GBR). Il a commencé sa collection en 2011 après avoir acheté à son fils un Dinobot, un Starscream et un Grimlock. Ces figurines lui ont rappelé son enfance et les dessins animés *Transformers* qu'il regardait à la télévision. Pris de nostalgie, il a alors décidé d'en faire la collection.

S'il adore trouver de nouveaux objets, il admire également la créativité nécessaire pour fabriquer les figurines : "la conception, la décoration, le travail d'artiste, la technique... et les transformations astucieuses." Il a toujours dit que, lorsque sa collection serait entrée dans le *GWR*, il cesserait de l'agrandir et la vendrait peut-être. Regardez la place qu'elle occupe !

GUINNESS WORLD RECORDS

Louis se passionne aussi pour les disques vinyles des années 1960, les montres numériques des années 1970 et 1980, ainsi que les LEGO® Technic classiques.

SOMMAIRE

LA PLUS GRANDE PIZZA

Prenez un emblème national et associez-le à un autre symbole... la cathédrale Saint-Paul de Londres par exemple et une délicieuse pizza ! Bien sûr, **la plus grande pizza** du monde n'a pas été posée sur l'édifice londonien. Si tel avait été le cas, elle aurait recouvert entièrement le dôme, pour le plus grand bonheur des pigeons de la ville !

A vec une surface de 1 261,65 m² et un diamètre moyen de 40,07 m, cette gigantesque pizza margherita pourrait recouvrir entièrement le dôme de la célèbre cathédrale Saint-Paul de Londres, mais la lanterne de celle-ci ferait un trou assez gros au milieu...

Cette gigantesque pizza sans gluten a été appelée "Ottavia" en hommage à Octave-Auguste, le premier empereur romain. Elle a été confectionnée par Dovilio Nardi, Andrea Mannocchi, Marco Nardi, Matteo Nardi et Matteo Giannotte (tous ITA) de NIPfood lors de la Fiera Roma, à Rome, le 13 décembre 2012. La pizza est un des plats vite faits les plus populaires au monde. Cependant, la confection de celle-ci n'a pas été très rapide. Pour répondre à des normes très strictes, la pâte a été préparée plusieurs jours à l'avance. Afin d'obtenir un grand disque, il a fallu assembler avec de la colle alimentaire des bases rectangulaires d'environ 4 x 6 m congelées après avoir été à moitié cuites. La cuisson de ces 5 200 bases a demandé plus de 2 jours. Pour faire cuire la garniture – 4 535 kg de sauce tomate et 3 990 kg de mozzarella –, on a soufflé dessus de l'air chaud dont la température était comprise entre 300 et 600 °C.

Les arbitres du *GWR* n'ont plus eu qu'à mesurer l'énorme pizza et à confirmer que le record précédent avait bien été battu ! Il était resté inégalé depuis plus de 20 ans ! Puis la pizza a été tranchée et les parts chauffées dans une pizzeria voisine. Un grand nombre ont été distribuées à des banques alimentaires locales.

Si vous aviez vraiment voulu recouvrir le dôme de la cathédrale Saint-Paul de cette pizza margherita, votre principale difficulté aurait été le transport aérien. Pour vous épargner le coût de la cuisson et de la location d'un hélicoptère ou d'une grue, nos génies de l'informatique ont simplement utilisé des photographies d'une pizza normale et de la cathédrale. Si vous souhaitez battre le record, vous pouvez suivre la recette ci-dessous !

LA CATHÉDRALE SAINT-PAUL

Au moins 4 églises dédiées à saint Paul furent érigées sur la colline de Ludgate dans le quartier de la City à Londres, la plus ancienne à partir de 604. L'actuelle cathédrale a été construite entre 1675 et 1710 par Christopher Wren, la précédente ayant brûlé durant le grand incendie de 1666. Son dôme de 111,3 m de haut – l'un des plus hauts au monde – pèse près de 66 040 t.

Il abrite la célèbre "galerie des murmures", appelée ainsi parce qu'un mot chuchoté d'un côté s'entend de l'autre côté, à une distance d'environ 34 m.

LA RECETTE DU SUCCÈS

Avez-vous les ingrédients nécessaires ? Vous aurez besoin de...

- 8 980 kg de farine – de préférence sans gluten
- 1 128 l de levure
- 675 kg de margarine
- 250 kg de sel gemme
- 9 387 l d'eau
- 173 l d'huile d'olive
- 4 535 kg de sauce tomate
- 3 990 kg de mozzarella
- 125 kg de parmesan
- 100 kg de roquette
- 25 kg de vinaigre balsamique

1. Pour chaque base de pizza, mélangez la farine, la levure, la margarine et le sel.
2. Ajoutez l'eau et l'huile, puis mélangez jusqu'à l'obtention d'une pâte.
3. Pétrissez celle-ci sur une surface farinée, puis tapissez-en 5 200 moules.
4. Fusionnez les bases avec de la colle alimentaire.
5. Recouvrez avec la sauce tomate, les fromages, la roquette et arrosez de vinaigre.
6. Faites cuire la garniture avec une source de chaleur très puissante !

Durant plus de 2 siècles, la cathédrale Saint-Paul fut le plus grand édifice de Londres, jusqu'à l'édification en 1939 de la centrale électrique de Battersea.

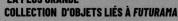

LA PLUS GRANDE COLLECTION DE TROLLS

Le 20 septembre 2018, Sherry Groom (USA) possédait 8 130 jouets représentant des trolls. Elle a battu le record en 2012 et, depuis, sa collection s'est enrichie de 5 000 pièces ! Elle est propriétaire du *Troll Hole Museum* d'Alliance (USA) où, déguisée en Sigrid la reine des Trolls, elle organise des visites et raconte des histoires sur ces créatures fantastiques.

LA PLUS GRANDE COLLECTION...

Maillots de football
Le 2 avril 2018, Daniel Goldfarb (USA) possédait 402 maillots de foot. Ils ont été comptés à Bal Harbour (Floride, USA).

Tableurs
Ariel Fischman (USA) possède 506 tableurs. Son record a été homologué à 414 Capital, à Mexico (MEX), le 15 mai 2018.

LA PLUS GRANDE COLLECTION DE SACHETS DE THÉ

Ce record est resté inégalé depuis 2013. Il a ensuite changé 2 fois de main en 2018. Il a d'abord été battu par Márta Menta Czinkóczky (HUN) qui a réussi à rassembler 743 sachets différents (sur la photo), puis par Freja Louise Kristiansen (DNK) dont la collection compte 1 023 sachets.

Baumes à lèvres
En deux ans, Bailey Leigh Sheppard (GBR), âgée de 11 ans, a amassé 730 baumes à lèvres. Son record a été confirmé à Durham (GBR), le 7 mai 2017.

Souvenirs liés aux *Jours heureux*
Le 18 février 2018, Giuseppe Ganelli (ITA) avait 1 439 objets ayant trait aux *Jours heureux*, à Codogno (Lodi, ITA). Fan du feuilleton américain depuis les années 1970, il a commencé sa collection en acquérant une figurine à l'effigie de Fonzie.

Puzzles
Luiza Figueiredo (BRA) a constitué une collection de puzzles pendant 48 ans. Le 9 juillet 2017, elle en possédait 1 047 différents, comme cela a été confirmé à São Paulo (BRA).

Pieds de sapins de Noël
Le 10 juillet 2018, Stanley Kohl (USA) avait réuni 1 197 pieds d'arbres de Noël véritables et artificiels datant du XIXᵉ siècle à nos jours. Ils sont exposés à la Kohl's Stony Hill Tree Farm de Milton (Pennsylvanie, USA).

Objets liés à Scooby-Doo
Danielle Meger (CAN) possède 1 806 objets liés au chien Scooby-Doo. Ils ont été recensés le 21 mars 2018, à Rocky View (Alberta, CAN).

Des journaux différents
La collection de Sergio F. Bodini (ITA) comprend 1 444 journaux différents. Cela a été vérifié à Rome (ITA), le 2 juin 2018.

Objets liés aux Muppets
Le 1ᵉʳ octobre 2017, à Merna (Nebraska, USA), Rhett Safranek (USA) possédait 1 841 objets ayant trait aux Muppets, son préféré étant un Gonzo grandeur nature.

Génériques de journaux télévisés
Victor Vlam (NLD) archive les génériques de journaux télévisés consacrés à l'actualité et au sport depuis janvier 2002. Le 8 avril 2019, il détenait 1 876 h, 2 min et 52 s (80 jours) d'enregistrements musicaux.

▶ Jeux de Monopoly
Le 5 septembre 2018, Neil Scallan (GBR) de Crawley (West Sussex, GBR) possédait 2 249 jeux de Monopoly différents provenant du monde entier.

Timbres représentant des oiseaux
Jin Feibao (CHN) possédait 14 558 timbres sur lesquels figurent des oiseaux, le 26 octobre 2018, à Kunming (province du Yunnan, CHN).

LA PLUS GRANDE COLLECTION DE SPATULES

Le 6 mai 2017, lors d'une fête culinaire à Everett (Washington, USA), Renee Wesberry (USA) a montré ses 1 636 spatules. Elle a commencé sa collection en 1998 après avoir célébré Thanksgiving, en constatant le temps qu'il lui fallait pour en laver une entre chaque plat. "J'aime avoir un pot rempli de spatules colorées sous les yeux, dit-elle. On dirait des fleurs qui ne se fanent pas et elles permettent de réaliser de délicieux plats !"

LA PLUS GRANDE COLLECTION D'OBJETS LIÉS À *FUTURAMA*

À Pittsburgh (Pennsylvanie, USA), le 3 septembre 2017, Adam Taylor (USA) possédait 803 objets officiels ayant trait au dessin animé *Futurama*, notamment des poupées, des vêtements, des posters, des scénarios, des œuvres d'art et des souvenirs conçus pour la production, la publicité et le marketing. Il s'est pris de passion pour le dessin animé de Matt Groening, le créateur des *Simpson*, dès sa première diffusion en 1999.

Objets liés à Cendrillon
Le 19 juillet 2018, la collection de Masanao Kawata (JPN) consacrée à Cendrillon rassemblait 908 objets, à Tokyo (JPN).

Kimono
Hironori Kajikawa (JPN) était fier de posséder 4 147 kimonos, le 22 février 2018. Son record a été certifié à Kōriyama (préfecture de Fukushima, JPN).

Takako Yoshino (JPN) se targue d'avoir constitué en 40 ans **la plus importante collection d'obis** (ceintures de kimono). Le 30 janvier 2018, à Nagoya (préfecture d'Aichi, JPN), elle en avait acquis 4 516.

Bagues fantaisie (bijoux)
Le 20 octobre 2018, Bruce Rosen (USA) possédait 18 350 bagues fantaisie, à Rose Valley (Pennsylvanie, USA). Il a débuté sa collection en 1990.

▶ LA PLUS GRANDE COLLECTION D'OBJETS LIÉS AUX *DRÔLES DE DAMES*

Depuis 1976, Jack Condon (USA) a accumulé 5 569 articles ayant trait à la série télévisée *Drôles de dames*. Jack a vu le pilote de l'émission le 21 mars 1976. Une semaine après la diffusion du premier épisode, le 22 septembre 1976, il a acheté la première pièce de sa collection : un exemplaire de la revue *TV Guide* avec les trois "dames" (Kate Jackson, Farrah Fawcett et Jaclyn Smith) en couverture.

AVR. 21 En 2014, Fred Fugen et Vince Reffet (tous 2 FRA) - et un caméraman anonyme - réalisent **le plus haut saut de BASE jump depuis un édifice** : le Burj Khalifa de 828 m de haut, à Dubaï (ARE).

AVR. 22 Né en 1937, Jack Nicholson (USA) enregistre **le plus de nominations aux Oscars (acteur)**. Entre 1970 et 2003, il est nommé 12 fois : 8 pour le prix du meilleur acteur et 4 pour le meilleur second rôle. Il a obtenu 3 Oscars.

LA PLUS GRANDE COLLECTION D'OBJETS AYANT TRAIT AU MOUTON

Le 19 février 2017, Alessia Citti (ITA) possédait 1 822 objets sur le thème du mouton, à Ciampino (Rome, ITA). Sa mère lui a offert son premier jouet représentant un mouton quand elle n'avait que 6 mois. La majeure partie de sa collection se trouve dans sa chambre qu'elle appelle *Il Vittoriale delle Pecore* ("le temple du mouton").

La prodigieuse collection d'Alessia compte 500 objets de plus que celle du précédent record.

▶ La collection de vidéos du GWR est sur guinnessworldrecords.com/2020

LA PLUS GRANDE COLLECTION D'OBJETS LIÉS À L'UNIVERS D'HARRY POTTER

Victoria Maclean (GBR) possède 3 686 objets liés à *Harry Potter* et aux *Animaux fantastiques*, comme cela a été vérifié à Neath (West Glamorgan, GBR), le 28 février 2019. Les créations de J. K. Rowling l'ont tant fascinée qu'elle a reconstitué le magasin d'antiquités de Barjow & Beurk de l'allée des Embrumes. Son objet le plus précieux est un morceau de puzzle du Vif d'Or à 24 carats provenant du Japon.

LA PLUS GRANDE COLLECTION DE GOBELETS EN CARTON

Le 5 septembre 2017, V. Sankaranarayanan (IND) possédait 736 gobelets jetables. Son record a été vérifié dans le Tamil Nadu (IND). Destinés à contenir des jus de fruits, des boissons chaudes et des glaces, ils sont en parfait état.

AVR. 23
En 1988, Kanellos Kanellopoulos (GRC) parcourt 115,11 km en pédalant à bord de son *Daedalus 88*, de Heraklion, en Crète, à Santorin (GRC), réalisant **le plus long vol propulsé par la force humaine**.

AVR. 24
En 2004, Chad Fell (USA) réalise **la plus grosse bulle de chewing-gum**. Vérifiée à Winston County (Alabama, USA), elle mesure 50,8 cm de diamètre. Il utilise 3 morceaux de Dubble Bubble.

PORTIONS GÉANTES

100%

LA MYRTILLE LA PLUS LOURDE

Pesée à l'aide d'une balance électronique le 19 juillet 2018, une myrtille "Eureka", cultivée par Agrícola Santa Azul S.A.C (PER) à Lima (PER), faisait 15 g, soit 2,6 g de plus que celle du précédent record établi en 2018 en Australie. Cette énorme myrtille d'une variété arbustive d'Amérique avait un diamètre de 34,5 mm.

LE PLUS GRAND OU LA PLUS GRANDE...

Portion de soupe aux nouilles
Le fabricant de nouilles instantanées VIFON a fêté son 55e anniversaire en confectionnant une soupe de nouilles de riz au bœuf de 1 359 kg à Saïgon (VNM), le 21 juillet 2018. La préparation a nécessité 31 personnes et 52 chefs.

▶ **Portion de fish and chips**
Le 9 février 2018, Resorts World Birmingham (GBR) a servi un filet de flétan avec des frites pesant 54,99 kg. Pour que ce record soit homologué, le poids des frites crues ne devait pas être plus de 2 fois supérieur à celui du poisson. Ce dernier a mis 90 min à cuire.

Galette de poisson
Le 30 juin 2018, le mareyeur Fonn Egersund et le chef Tore Torgersen (tous 2 NOR) ont confectionné une galette de poisson de 231 kg sur la place principale d'Egersund (NOR). Il a fallu l'aide d'un chariot élévateur pour la mettre dans la poêle, car elle mesurait 3,6 m de diamètre et était plus lourde que 50 saumons de l'Atlantique. Les habitants l'ont mangée en moins de 20 min.

Soupe Menudo
Le 28 janvier 2018, pour fêter le mois national de la Menudo, la Juanita's Foods (USA) a préparé 1 106,31 kg de cette soupe traditionnelle mexicaine à base d'estomac de vache cuit dans du bouillon. Elle pesait presque autant que 3 000 boîtes de soupe. Elle a été relevée à l'aide de 20,4 kg de purée de piment rouge, de 65,3 kg d'épices, de 24,4 kg d'oignon haché et de 875 citrons verts.

Laddu (individuel)
Mallikharjuna Rao (IND) a fabriqué un laddu, friandise indienne en forme de sphère, de 29 465 kg – soit le poids approximatif de 7 éléphants d'Asie – à Tapeswaram (Andhra Pradesh, IND), le 6 septembre 2016. Cette recette traditionnelle de *boondi laddu* comportait des noix de cajou, des amandes, de la cardamome et du ghee.

Baklava
Le 22 mars 2018, un baklava de 513 kg – plus lourd qu'un piano à queue – a été dévoilé au Sommet 2018 de la gastronomie d'Ankara (TUR). Il avait

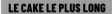

LA PLUS GROSSE PORTION DE GUACAMOLE

Le 6 avril 2018, la ville de Tancítaro, dans le Michoacán (MEX), a fêté la 7e fête annuelle de l'avocat en confectionnant une gigantesque portion de guacamole de 3 788 kg. Plus de 350 personnes ont mis la main à la pâte. La recette contenait aussi des tomates, des citrons verts et de la coriandre.

été préparé pour le gouverneur d'Ankara par la marque de glaces Mado et la Fédération culinaire Taşpakon (tous 2 TUR).

Roulé à la cannelle
La boulangerie de luxe Wolferman's (USA) a confectionné un roulé à la cannelle de 521,5 kg – soit à peu près le poids de 8 personnes – à Medford (Oregon, USA) le 10 avril 2018. On l'a fait cuire dans un plat conçu à cet effet à l'aide de brûleurs au propane.

Tarte à la patate douce
L'Honshu-Shikoku Bridge Expressway Company (JPN) a fabriqué une tarte de 319 kg à l'Awaji Service Area

de la préfecture de Hyōgo (JPN), le 7 avril 2018. Ce dessert traditionnel américain de plus de 2 m de diamètre avait été préparé avec des patates douces japonaises Naruto Kintoki.

Mazamorra aux fruits
Le 30 août 2018, à Iquitos (PER), des bénévoles ont préparé une mazamorra aux fruits (dessert à base d'*aguaje* [fruit de palmier], de sucre et de fécule de maïs) de 751,3 kg. L'événement était organisé par l'Universidad San Ignacio de Loyola et le Gobierno Regional de Loreto (tous 2 PER).

LE CAKE LE PLUS LONG

Le 7 mai 2018, la Jiangxi Bakery Association (CHN) a préparé un cake aux fruits de 3,18 km de long au Zixi Bread International Tourism Festival de la province de Jiangxi (CHN). Il a fallu aux 60 cuisiniers et 120 assistants presque une journée pour assembler le cake, plus long que le National Mall de Washington D.C. (USA).

LA PLUS GROSSE PORTION D'ŒUFS BROUILLÉS

Une énorme portion d'œufs brouillés d'un poids de 2 466 kg a été confectionnée par le producteur d'œufs Inicia (MUS) dans le centre Bagatelle de l'île Maurice, le 27 octobre 2018. Faite aussi avec du beurre, du lait, du sel et du poivre, elle a cuit plus de 2 h. Près de 250 personnes ont participé à la préparation de plus de 10 000 portions.

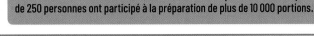

AVR. 25 Le sous-marin nucléaire américain *Triton* atteint les rochers Saint-Pierre et Saint-Paul dans l'Atlantique en 1960, après avoir effectué **le 1er tour du monde en immersion** en 60 jours et 21 heures.

AVR. 26 Samuel Bellamy (GBR) meurt quand le négrier *Whydah* coule en 1717. "Black Sam", **le flibustier le plus riche**, avait accumulé un butin de 103 millions de livres (130 millions de dollars).

LA PLUS GRANDE PIZZA COMMERCIALISÉE

Vous avez une petite faim ? Dans ce cas, dévorez des yeux "The Bus", une pizza rectangulaire de 2,438 x 0,812 m, d'une superficie de 1,98 m², mesurée le 26 mai 2018. Concoctée par le Moontower Pizza Bar (USA) de Burleson (Texas, USA), elle coûte 299,95 $ hors taxes et doit être commandée au moins 2 jours à l'avance.

La pizza cuit en seulement 30 min dans un four à pizza rotatif. Elle est livrée dans une boîte faite sur-mesure.

Découvrez des vidéos sur guinnessworldrecords.com/2020

LA PLUS GRANDE TASSE DE CHOCOLAT CHAUD

Le 6 janvier 2018, la municipalité d'Uruapan (MEX) a versé 4 816,6 litres de chocolat chaud dans une énorme tasse à Uruapán (Michoacán, MEX). La boisson avait été préparée pour fêter le jour des Rois et contenait plus de 600 kg de cacao issu de fèves locales.

LE PLUS GROS BISCUIT FOURRÉ

La biscuiterie Mondelēz Bahrain a fabriqué un biscuit Oreo® de 73,4 kg à Manama (BHR), le 16 avril 2018. Ce biscuit faisait presque 3 fois la taille du précédent détenteur du record et était 6 495 fois plus grand qu'un biscuit Oreo® classique.

LES PLUS LOURDS EN 2018

Gourde	Jeremy Terry (USA)	174,41 kg
Céleri	Gary Heeks (GBR)	42 kg
Melon Cantaloup	Danny Vester (USA)	29,89 kg
Chou rouge	Tim Saint (GBR)	23,7 kg
Poireau (à droite)	Paul Rochester (GBR)	10,7 kg
Aubergine	Ian Neale (GBR)	3,06 kg
Avocat	Felicidad Pasalo (USA)	2,49 kg
Pêche	A. et L. Pearson (USA)	816,46 g
Poivron	Ian Neale (GBR)	720 g
Nectarine	Eleni Evagelou Ploutarchou (CYP)	500 g
Piment	Dale Toten (GBR)	420 g

AVR. 27 Tel un hercule, le prêtre Kevin Fast (CAN) a porté **le plus grand nombre de personnes sur ses épaules** (11) en 2013 à Cobourg (Ontario, CAN). Chacune d'elles pesait plus de 60 kg.

AVR. 28 En 2001, l'homme d'affaires Dennis Tito (USA) a rejoint la Station spatiale internationale (ISS) à bord d'une fusée russe Soyouz. **1er touriste de l'espace**, il est resté jusqu'au 6 mai dans l'ISS.

PLAISIRS DE BOUCHE

sans les mains (19) et a été ▶ **le plus rapide à boire une tasse de café** (4,78 s). "Pourtant il ne boit pas de café !" a dit sa mère, étonnée.

Le plus de pâte à tartiner au chocolat mangée en 1 min
André Ortolf (DEU) adore battre les records liés à la nourriture. Le 30 novembre 2017, il a englouti 359 g de pâte à tartiner au chocolat en 60 s, à Augsburg (DEU).

▶ LE PLUS LONG VOL PLANÉ D'UNE SAUCISSE DE HOT-DOG
À Londres (GBR), le 24 octobre 2018, la saucisse lancée par Mark Brunell (USA, ci-dessus au centre), ex quart-arrière des Jaguars de Jacksonville, a atterri 20,96 m plus loin dans le pain fendu que tenait Ryan Moore (GBR, ci-dessus à gauche). Le hot-dog était fourni par Denny Fire & Smoke (IRL), organisateur de l'événement.

Le plus d'"oursons gélifiés" avalés en 1 min à l'aide d'une pique à cocktail
Kevin "LA Beast" Strahle (USA) a avalé 31 "oursons gélifiés" (bonbons en forme d'oursons) en 60 s, avec une pique à cocktail, à Ridgewood (New Jersey, USA), le 24 mai 2017. Il a battu 5 des 6 records du GWR auxquels il s'était attelé au cours du "Beast's Buffet". Il a notamment englouti
▶ **le plus de marshmallows en 1 min**

La plus grande pyramide de cupcakes
Le 19 janvier 2019, Preethi Kitchen Appliances et Food Consulate Chennai (tous 2 IND) ont réalisé une pyramide de cupcakes de 12,69 m de haut, à Chennai (Tamil Nadu, IND).

Le plus de personnes pour confectionner du *kimchi*
Le 4 novembre 2018, à Séoul (KOR), Mercedes-Benz et le gouvernement métropolitain de Séoul ont convié 3 452 personnes à faire du *kimchi*, plat coréen à base de légumes fermentés.

Le plus long marathon de cuisine
Ce record a été battu à 2 reprises en 2018 : du 18 au 20 septembre, dans le cadre du National Fried Rice Day, les chefs Andrey Shek (UZB) et Raymundo Mendez (MEX) de la chaîne Benihana (USA) ont tous 2 cuisiné séparément pendant 42 h d'affilée, à New York (USA).

LE PLUS DE HOT-DOGS DÉVORÉS LORS D'UN NATHAN'S HOT DOG EATING CONTEST
Le Nathan's Hot Dog Eating Contest est une compétition annuelle qui se tient le 4 juillet à Brooklyn (New York, USA). En 2018, Joey Chestnut (USA, ci-dessus à droite) a remporté sa 11e ceinture en engloutissant **le plus de hot-dogs (74)** en 10 min.
Chez les femmes, Miki Sudo (USA, ci-dessus à gauche) a enregistré **le plus de victoires consécutives** avec 5 titres, de 2014 à 2018.

Mais Rickey Lumpkin II (USA) a fait mieux en préparant du poulet frit selon la recette de sa mère durant 68 h, 30 min et 1 s afin de lever des fonds pour Vision Mondiale à Los Angeles (Californie, USA).

Le plus long baiser pimenté
Le 11 juin 2016, à Puerto Vallarta (MEX), Carly Waddell et Evan Bass (tous 2 USA) de l'émission *Bachelor in Paradise* d'ABC se sont embrassés durant 1 min et 41 s après avoir mangé des piments habanero.

La plus longue ligne de hot-dogs
Le 12 août 2018, 10 000 hot-dogs ont été mis bout à bout pour former une ligne de 1,46 km à Zapopán (MEX). Quatre marques ont fourni les ingrédients : Embasa le ketchup, Grupo Bimbo les buns, McCormick la moutarde et la mayonnaise et FUD les saucisses.

La plus longue ligne de crêpes
mesurait 110,85 m. Elle a été réalisée par Nutella Australia à l'université de Sydney (Nouvelle-Galles du Sud, AUS), le 28 février 2018.

Le plus de biscuits glacés en 1 h
Le 13 décembre 2018, l'équipe de bénévoles, de présentateurs et d'invités de l'émission *Good Morning America* a décoré 1 696 biscuits à New York (USA) avec l'aide de *So Yummy* (tous USA).

Le plus rapide à trier dans l'ordre alphabétique des pâtes lettres
Le 13 février 2018, Cody Jones (USA) de Dude Perfect a trié les lettres de A à Z en 3 min et 21 s, à Frisco (USA).

▶ LE PLUS DE BOULES DE GLACE SUR UN CORNET
Le 17 novembre 2018, Dimitri Panciera (ITA) a maintenu en équilibre 125 boules de glace sur un seul cornet pendant 10 s, sur le plateau de *La Notte dei Record*, à Rome (ITA). C'était la 5e fois qu'il battait ce record. Cela fait 6 ans qu'il rivalise avec Ashrita Furman (voir à droite) pour décrocher ce titre.

LE PLUS DE SKITTLES® LANCÉS ET ATTRAPÉS AVEC LA BOUCHE EN 1 MIN
Le 5 février 2018, Ashrita Furman (ci-dessus à droite) a attrapé avec la bouche 70 bonbons fruités lancés à au moins 4,5 m par Bipin Larkin (ci-dessus à gauche, tous 2 USA) en 60 s, à Siem Reap (KHM).
L'insatiable appétit d'Ashrita pour les records du GWR n'a pas diminué. De retour chez lui à New York (USA), il a absorbé **la plus grande quantité de moutarde (200 ml)** en 13,85 s, le 12 mai 2018.

AVR. 29 En 1989, "Jumpin'" Jeff Clay (USA) **saute par-dessus le plus de voitures en 1 h**, passant au-dessus des toits de 101 d'entre elles, à Fort Oglethorpe (Géorgie, USA).

AVR. 30 En 2013, le "Midnight Swinger", alias David Scott (USA), accomplit **le plus long stand-up jamais réalisé par un individu** en 40 h et 8 min, au Diamond Jo Casino de Dubuque (Iowa, USA).

▶ LE BOL DE PÂTES AVALÉ LE PLUS VITE

Le professeur de mathématiques Michelle Lesco (USA) mène une double vie. Sous le nom de "Cardboard Shell", elle établit des records de vitesse en mangeant. Le 18 septembre 2017, elle a englouti un bol de pâtes en 26,69 s, lors de "Carbs for a Cause", collecte de produits alimentaires, améliorant le record de 14 s. Le 13 décembre 2018, à Las Vegas (Nevada, USA), elle a été **la plus rapide à dévorer un hot-dog sans les mains** (21,60 s) et a absorbé **la plus grande quantité de mayonnaise en 3 min** (2,448 kg – environ 5 pots).

LE PLUS DE RAISINS MANGÉS AVEC LES PIEDS EN 3 MIN

Arpit Lall (IND) a mangé 53 raisins avec les pieds en 180 s, à la CNI Church de Chhattisgarh (IND), le 25 février 2018. Il fallait avoir avalé tous les grains au cours du temps imparti pour qu'ils soient comptabilisés !

Le 4 septembre 2018, il a aussi **cassé et avalé le plus d'œufs frais en 30 s** (9 œufs mesurant au moins 6 cm de long), mais c'était avec les mains !

LE PLUS DE PASTÈQUES ÉCRASÉES AVEC LA TÊTE EN 30 S

Le 6 mai 2018, Muhammad Rashid (PAK) a écrasé avec la tête 29 pastèques en 30 s, à Karachi (Sindh, PAK). Chaque pastèque pesait au moins 4 kg et était mûre et ferme selon les directives du GWR. Muhammad, fondateur et président de l'Académie des arts martiaux du Pakistan, en a cassé 4 de plus par rapport au précédent record.

 MAI 1
En 1996, la sonde spatiale *Ulysses* traverse un courant de particules chargées faisant partie de **la plus longue queue de comète mesurée**, celle de la comète Hyakutake qui s'étend sur 570 millions de kilomètres.

MAI 2
Lors des Jeux Tårnby 2015 de Copenhague (DNK), Majken Sichlau (DNK) parcourt **100 m avec des talons (femmes)** en 13,557 s. Ses talons mesuraient 9,5 cm de haut.

RECORDS DE PARTICIPATION

Le plus de personnes se douchant en même temps

Le 15 juin 2018, la marque de savon et de gel douche Irish Spring (USA) a installé des tuyaux et des pommeaux de douche au Firefly Music Festival de Dover (Delaware, USA). 396 festivaliers ont ainsi pu prendre une douche ensemble.

Le plus de personnes gardant le contrôle d'un ballon de foot

Le 14 juin 2018, 1 444 personnes ont toutes gardé le contrôle d'un ballon de football durant les 10 s requises sur la principale place de Cracovie (POL). Cet événement était organisé par le groupe de média Grupa RMF (POL) qui, le 24 août 2017, avait déjà réuni **le plus grand nombre de personnes (1 804) ayant réussi à garder le contrôle d'un ballon de volley.**

COURSE CARITATIVE

Le 6 mai 2018, 283 171 personnes ont pris part à la course de bienfaisance du groupe religieux philippin Iglesia ni Cristo (Église du Christ) à Manille (PHL). Plusieurs autres courses de bienfaisance avaient lieu en même temps dans le monde. **La plus grande course de bienfaisance organisée dans de nombreux lieux** a donc réuni en tout 773 136 participants.

Le plus de personnes dansant le "floss"

Le 4 décembre 2018, 793 écoliers de Stockholm (SWE) ont bravé une température de 2 °C pour exécuter la danse de l'année. Sveriges Television (SWE) a filmé ce "floss" géant dans le cadre des émissions pour enfants *Lilla Aktuellt* et *Lilla Sportspegeln*.

Le 12 juillet 2013, **1 527 personnes se sont brossé ensemble les dents avec un même fil dentaire.** Ce sont les Lake Erie Crushers (USA), à Avon (Ohio, USA), qui ont établi ce record en utilisant un fil dentaire de 3 230 m.

LE PLUS GRAND OU LA PLUS GRANDE...

Hackathon

Le Hajj Hackathon 2018 de la Fédération saoudienne pour la cybersécurité, la programmation et les drones (SAU) a réuni 2 950 participants le 2 août 2018. L'équipe de femmes qui a gagné le concours à Djeddah (SAU) a créé une application aidant les pèlerins à traduire les panneaux de signalisation sans connexion Internet.

Leçon d'échecs

Deux clubs d'échecs et 2 écoles de la municipalité de Muttenz (CHE) ont participé à la plus grande leçon d'échecs le 20 septembre 2018. En tout, 1 459 enfants ont appris les règles et quelques stratégies de base de ce jeu de société très ancien.

LE PLUS DE PERSONNES NUES POUR UN BAIN DE MER

Le 9 juin 2018, Deirdre Featherstone (IRL) a réussi à convaincre 2 505 femmes de se dénuder et de se baigner dans la mer d'Irlande près de Wicklow (IRL). L'objectif était de collecter de l'argent pour l'association caritative Aoibheann's Pink Tie qui aide les enfants atteints de cancer. Le soleil brillait, mais la température de 20 °C était peut-être un peu fraîche pour une baignade !

Séance de yoga

Le 21 juin 2018, Patanjali Yogpeeth, le gouvernement du Rajasthan et l'administration du district de Kota (tous IND) ont fêté la journée internationale du yoga en organisant une séance de ce sport bien-être à Kota, au Rajasthan (IND). Celle-ci a réuni 100 984 personnes, soit presque 2 fois plus de monde que 1 an auparavant à Mysore (IND).

Mêlée de rugby

Le 23 septembre 2018, 2 586 personnes se sont liées par les bras pour former une mêlée de 200 m de long à Toyota (JPN). Organisée par le Young Entrepreneurs Group Toyota (JPN), cette mêlée géante a eu lieu au Toyota Stadium, qui accueillera la coupe de monde de Rugby en 2019.

Danse Disco

Pour la sortie du DVD *Mamma Mia 2 : Here We Go Again* (GBR/USA, 2018), 324 *dancing queens* (et *kings*) de la danse ont dansé sur de la musique disco à Londres (GBR), le 26 novembre 2018. Organisée par Universal Pictures Home Entertainment (GBR), la danse était dirigée par Ola et James Jordan de l'émission *Strictly Come Dancing*.

Jeu de "chat glacé"

Le 14 septembre 2018 à Anvers (BEL), 1 393 adultes et enfants ont participé à un jeu de "chat glacé" géant organisé par la garderie IBO Duffel (BEL). C'est Alexander Dewit, âgé de six ans, qui a gagné.

Dégustation de chocolat

Le 10 août 2018, l'Universidad San Ignacio de Loyola et Gobierno Regional de Ucayali (tous 2 PER) ont accueilli une dégustation de chocolat à Pucallpa, au Pérou. 797 personnes ont goûté 3 types de chocolat noir. La région est l'un des plus gros producteurs de cacao.

LE PLUS GRAND "THÉ"

Pour son 25e anniversaire, la marque de mode et d'articles ménagers Cath Kidston (GBR) a invité 978 personnes à déguster un thé avec des scones à l'Alexandra Palace de Londres (GBR) le 1er juillet 2018. Mary Berry, juge de l'émission *Great British Bake Off*, était chargée de cette cérémonie "so british" !

RALLYE DE FOOD-TRUCKS

Une lourde et appétissante odeur de *nasi dagang* (poisson au curry et riz au lait de coco) et de *kukus berempah* (poulet épicé au riz) embaumait l'air dans le district Batu Kawan de Penang (MYS) où 158 food-trucks étaient réunis pour participer au Festival international de cuisine de Penang 2018. L'événement a eu lieu le 28 avril, l'avant-dernier jour de cette fête de 16 jours qui célèbre la cuisine de rue dans le monde.

C. B. Cebulski, éditeur chez Marvel, et l'actrice Carolina Ravassa (qui double Sombra dans Overwatch) assistaient à l'événement.

LE PLUS DE PERSONNES DÉGUISÉES EN SPIDER-MAN

Marvel Entertainment (USA) et Sony Interactive Entertainment Europe (GBR) ont réuni 547 fans de Peter Parker à Stockholm (SWE) le 16 septembre 2018. Ce défi a été réalisé à l'occasion du spectacle Comic Con Stockholm dans le cadre des manifestations organisées pour célébrer la sortie en 2018 du jeu vidéo *Spider-Man*.

SYMBOLE INTERNATIONAL D'ACCESSIBILITÉ

Le 27 février 2018, St Britto's Institutions - organisme éducatif de Chennai (IND) - a représenté le symbole international d'accessibilité à l'aide de 816 personnes qui portaient un T-shirt et une casquette identiques.

CARE FOR THE DISABLED

LE PLUS GRAND COURS AVEC UN BALLON DE GYM

Dans le cadre de sa campagne "Sweat for good", le YMCA du Grand Toronto (CAN) a organisé avec la célèbre monitrice de sport Eva Redpath, la responsable fitness de YMCA Sherry Perez et le champion olympique de natation canadien Mark Tewksbury un cours de fitness avec ballon qui a rassemblé 454 personnes le 11 janvier 2018.

 MAI 4 En 1536, le marchand Francesco Lapi (ITA) utilise **pour la 1ʳᵉ fois le symbole @** pour désigner une unité de mesure, l'amphore, à propos d'un trésor rapporté par les Espagnols après leur conquête du Pérou.

 MAI 5 Prabhakar Reddy P. et Sujith Kumar E. (tous 2 IND) réalisent **le plus de mouvements d'arts martiaux en 1 minute** (42) à Andhra Pradesh (IND), en 2018.

FORCE & ENDURANCE

Le plus de "deadlift sumo" avec la charge la plus lourde en 1 h (hommes)
Le 22 mai 2018, Walter Urban (USA) a soulevé 59 343 kg – une charge plus lourde qu'un char M1 Abrams – en effectuant près de 12 000 soulevés de terre en 1 h. Il a établi ce record en direct sur le plateau de *The Today Show*, à New York (USA). Lors de cet exercice, l'écartement des pieds est supérieur à la largeur des épaules.

Le véhicule le plus lourd tiré sur plus de 30 m (femmes)
Le 31 mars 2018, Nardia Styles (AUS), sprinteuse devenue culturiste, a tiré une dépanneuse pesant 11 355 kg sur 30,48 m, sur la Gold Coast, (Queensland, AUS). Elle cherchait à lever des fonds pour White Ribbon Campaign et Barnardo's Australia.

Le véhicule le plus lourd tiré sur 30 m par un homme pesait 99 060 kg. Kevin Fast (CAN) a réalisé cet exploit à Cobourg (Ontario, CAN), le 5 juillet 2017.

Le bateau le plus lourd tiré par les dents
Surnommé "Mr Tug-Tooth", le pédiatre Oleg Skavysh a tiré le *Vereshchagino* de 614 t sur plus de 15 m en serrant un câble avec sa mâchoire à Tchornomorsk (UKR), le 30 octobre 2018.

Le "triceps dip" avec la charge la plus lourde
Trenton Williams (USA) a exécuté une extension aux barres parallèles avec une ceinture de pesée de 106,59 kg, à Alpharetta (Géorgie, USA), le 29 septembre 2018. Pour ce vétéran de l'armée, le fitness est un moyen de soigner un stress post-traumatique.

Le plus rapide à briser 16 blocs de béton placés sur le corps (hommes)
Le 18 mars 2017, à Muğla (Turquie), Ali Bahçetepe (TUR) a placé 16 blocs de béton sur son ventre. Son assistant Nizamettin Aykemür (TUR) les a brisés avec un marteau de forgeron en 4,75 s, battant le record de 6,33 s déjà détenu par Bahçetepe.

▶ LE PLUS DE PIERRES D'ATLAS SOULEVÉES EN 1 MIN (FEMMES)
Le 1er février 2017, l'athlète de CrossFit Michelle Kinney (USA) a soulevé des pierres d'Atlas, soit en tout 539,77 kg, en 60 s, à Venice (Californie, USA). Elle est la seule femme à également avoir soulevé des pierres d'un poids total de 1 397,06 kg en **3 min** et à avoir accompli **19 burpees avec traction en 1 min.**

Le 10 km le plus rapide avec un sac de 45 kg sur le dos (hommes)
Michael Summers (USA) a fait 10 km avec un sac de 45 kg sur le dos en 1 h, 25 min et 16 s, sur la piste d'athlétisme de la Milan High School (Indiana, USA), le 7 juillet 2018.

L'équilibre le plus long sur le menton
Le 22 juillet 2018, à Sofia (BGR), Tanya Tsekova Shishova (BGR) est restée contorsionnée vers l'arrière 21 min et 26 s, menton, épaules et poitrine collés au sol.

La plus longue posture de l'échelle (yoga)
B. Prakash Kumar (IND) est resté 5 min et 28 s dans la posture de l'échelle, dans le Tamil Nadu (IND), le 15 mai 2018. Cette figure implique de s'asseoir en lotus et de se soulever dans cette position en s'appuyant sur les mains.

▶ Le plus de pompes verticales en 1 min (hommes)
Siarhei Kudayeu (BLR) a effectué 51 pompes verticales en 60 s, à Minsk (BLR), le 3 mai 2018.
Le 1er février 2017, Rachel Martinez (USA), qui représentait la marque Reebok, a réalisé **le plus de pompes verticales (femme)** avec 12 pompes, à New York (USA).

Le plus de burpees poitrine contre le sol en 24 h (femmes)
Le 23 février 2018, Eva Clarke (AUS) a accompli 5 555 burpees (pompes + saut), à Abu Dhabi (UAE). En faisant cet exercice, elle a battu aussi le record en **1 min** (31) et **12 h** (4 785).

▶ LE PLUS DE BLOCS DE GLACE BRISÉS EN 1 MIN
Le 20 novembre 2018, J. D. Anderson (USA) a cassé 88 blocs de glace lors de *La Notte dei Record*, à Rome (ITA). Conservés entiers dans un congélateur industriel à – 2 °C, les blocs mesuraient au moins 10 cm de large. Connu sous le nom d'"Iceman", J. D. détenait le record, battu depuis par Uğur Öztürk (TUR), du **plus de blocs de glace brisés par un bélier humain** (17).

▶ LE PLUS DE DÉVELOPPÉS MILITAIRES PAR UNE PERSONNE EN 1 MIN
Le 23 avril 2019, "Iron Biby", alias Cheick Ahmed al-Hassan Sanou (BFA), a soulevé 82 fois au-dessus de sa tête Emily Noakes, la responsable marketing du *GWR* qui pèse 60 kg, à Londres (GBR). Biby – strongman professionnel – a remporté le titre de Log Lift World Champion en 2019 en soulevant 220 kg.

▶ L'AVION LE PLUS LOURD TIRÉ SUR 100 M PAR DES PERSONNES EN FAUTEUIL ROULANT
Le 23 novembre 2018, 98 personnes en fauteuil roulant ont tiré un 787-9 Boeing Dreamliner de 127,6 t sur 106 m, à l'aéroport d'Heathrow à Londres (GBR). L'événement "Wheels4Wings" est le fruit d'une collaboration entre l'aéroport, British Airways et Aerobility (tous GBR) pour lever des fonds pour familiariser les handicapés avec l'aviation.

MAI 6 En 1948, Shasta naît au Hogle Zoo de Salt Lake City (Utah, USA) du croisement entre un lion et une tigresse. Il meurt à 24 ans et 74 jours. Il est ainsi **le ligre qui a vécu le plus longtemps**.

MAI 7 Réalisé par Joe Castro et produit par Steven J. Escobar (tous 2 USA), *The Summer of Massacre* (USA, 2011), projeté en avant-première à Hollywood, est **le film d'horreur où il y a le plus de morts** (155).

Le couple a frappé fort lors de sa visite au GWR en 2017, en percutant sans le vouloir notre télévision au cours d'une démonstration de taekwondo !

LES PLUS RAPIDES À BRISER 1 000 TUILES

En 2018, les moniteurs de taekwondo Chris et Lisa Pitman (tous 2 GBR) ont posé pour le GWR. Ils fêtaient leur passion : pulvériser des objets – surtout des records. Lisa est la seule **femme** à avoir brisé 1 000 tuiles en 1 min et 23,98 s. Chris détient le record **masculin** (51,08 s). Le 9 avril 2018, ils ont cassé ◯ **le plus de planches en pin en 1 min avec une main** : 230 pour Lisa (**femmes**) et 315 pour Chris (**hommes**).

LE PLUS RAPIDE À TIRER UN CHAR SUR 10 M

Le 17 mars 2018, Eddie Williams (AUS) a remporté le "*World of Tanks PC* Tank Pull", lors de l'Arnold Strongman Australia Championships, à Melbourne (Victoria, AUS). Il a tiré un FV102 Striker de 8 t sur 10 m en 36,65 s. Arnold Schwarzenegger était dans le public pour le regarder battre 11 autres hommes forts. Ancien musicien, Eddie travaille à présent avec des enfants handicapés.

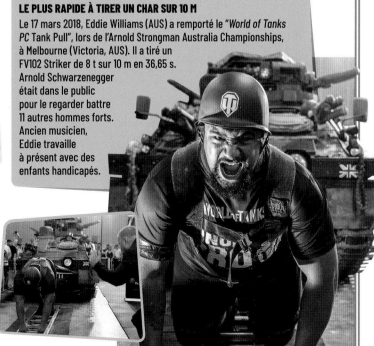

LE PLUS DE TRACTIONS CONSÉCUTIVES AVEC LE PETIT DOIGT

Le 7 octobre 2018, Tazio Gavioli (ITA) a fait des tractions à la barre fixe avec ses petits doigts 36 fois de suite, à Cavezzo (Modène, ITA), soit 23 fois de plus que l'année précédente. Grimpeur et artiste qui se baptise lui-même l'"Italian Butterfly", Tazio est aussi **l'homme qui est resté le plus longtemps en deadhang** (encadré) : 13 min et 52 s, le 14 avril 2018.

MAI 8 En 1995, un coq nommé Tugaru-Ono-94 émet **le plus long chant du coq jamais entendu**. Il s'époumone 23,6 s, à Ueda (Nagano, JPN).

MAI 9 En 2013, le parlement du Zimbabwe approuve sa nouvelle constitution, qui reconnaît 16 langues, dont le Ndau, la langue des signes et le Xhosa. C'est ainsi **le pays qui compte le plus de langues officielles**.

TALENTS INSOLITES

La plus rapide à enfiler 10 brassards gonflables
Le 25 juillet 2018, Izabelle Edge (GBR) a enfilé 10 brassards gonflables en 7,35 s, sur la Blackpool Pleasure Beach, à Lancashire (GBR).

▶ **Le plus de panneaux en verre de sécurité traversés consécutivement**
Danilo del Prete (ITA) a traversé 24 panneaux de verre de sécurité, sur le plateau de *La Notte dei Record*, à Rome (ITA), le 13 novembre 2018.

Le plus long parcours pieds nus sur des LEGO®
Le 21 avril 2018, le vlogger "BrainyBricks", alias Russell Cassevah (USA), a parcouru 834,41 m pieds nus sur des LEGO, au Brick Fest Live ! de Philadelphie (Pennsylvanie, USA).

Le plus rapide à faire un origami en forme de bateau avec la bouche
Le 2 décembre 2017, Gao Guangli (CHN) a confectionné un bateau en papier en 3 min et 34 s, à Jining (CHN).

Le plus long parcours sur des Swiss balls
Tyler Toney (USA) – un des "joyeux lurons" de la chaîne sportive Dude Perfect sur YouTube – a parcouru 88,39 m sur des Swiss balls, à Frisco (Texas, USA), le 16 octobre 2018.

LA PLUS LONGUE GLISSADE DANS UN CADDY
Le 6 juillet 2017, le speaker de la radio Richie Firth (GBR) a poussé un caddy et parcouru 10,56 m dans celui-ci, à Croydon (GBR). La tentative a été organisée après qu'il a déclaré sur Absolute Radio qu'il était un champion pour se déplacer à bord d'un caddy.

Le plus de pompes après avoir avalé une épée
Le 9 septembre 2017, Franz Huber (DEU) a effectué 20 pompes après avoir enfoncé une épée dans son œsophage, à l'exposition Tattoo & Piercing Expo d'Eggenfelden (DEU).

Le plus d'ananas fendus en 30 s
Le 20 novembre 2018, Reddy P. Prabhakar (IND) a fendu 20 ananas avec une épée de samouraï. Ses courageux assistants avaient les fruits sur la tête. L'exploit a eu lieu à Nellore (IND).

Le plus de motos roulant sur une personne
Le 28 août 2016, à Bombay (IND), 121 motos pesant chacune 257 kg *sans* pilote ont roulé sur Pandit Dhayagude (IND). Ce dernier était allongé entre deux sections de rail, son ventre étant ainsi au contact des roues des motos quand celles-ci lui sont passées dessus.

Le plus de crayons plantés dans un sac d'eau sans le percer en 1 min
Le 21 février 2018, Malachi Barton (USA) a percé un sac en plastique plein d'eau à l'aide de 15 crayons en 60 s, à Los Angeles (Californie, USA). Les crayons devaient traverser le sac de part en part sans causer de fuite.

Le plus de sauts à la corde chaussé de skis en 1 min
Le 27 novembre 2016, Sebastian Deeg (DEU) a sauté 61 fois à la corde en 60 s en tenue de skieur pour le *ZDF Fernsehgarten*, à Garmisch-Partenkirchen (DEU).

LE PLUS DE SELFIES EN 3 MIN
James Smith (USA) a fait 168 selfies en 180 s, à bord du *Carnival Dream*, le 22 janvier 2018. James est un grand amateur de croisières. Il a effectué sa tentative de record sur le pont du bateau lors de ses dernières vacances.

Le plus rapide à taper une phrase avec un doigt
Le 10 octobre 2018, Kushal Dasgupta (IND) a tapé avec un doigt la phrase *"Guinness World Records has challenged me to type this sentence with one finger in the fastest time"* en 21,99 s, à Puttaparthi (IND).

▶ **Le biscuit trempé resté le plus longtemps entier**
Le biscuit trempé dans une boisson chaude par "Mr Cherry", alias Cherry Yoshitake (JPN), est resté entier durant 5 min et 17,1 s, sur le plateau de *La Notte dei Record*, à Rome (ITA), le 15 novembre 2018.

sɹǝʌuǝ,l à sǝdɐʇ sǝɹʌil ǝp snld ǝ⅂
Le 24 mars 2018, Michele Santelia (ITA) avait tapé 77 livres à l'envers (comprenant 4 117 858 mots, 23 220 387 caractères, 31 339 pages, 291 096 paragraphes et 625 761 lignes). Son record a été homologué à Campobasso (ITA).

LE PLUS DE TRÈFLES À 4 FEUILLES CUEILLIS EN 1 H (INDIVIDUEL)
Ce symbole de chance n'est pas aussi rare que vous pourriez le penser... Katie Borka (USA) en a ramassé 166 en 60 min, à Spotsylvania (Virginie, USA), le 23 juin 2018. Ce faisant, elle en a trouvé à 5 et à 6 feuilles, et même un avec 9 feuilles, bien qu'aucun de ces derniers n'ait été retenu pour ce record.

▶ **LE PLUS DE PAILLES DANS LA BOUCHE**
Nataraj Karate (IND) a mis 692 pailles dans sa bouche, à Salem (Tamil Nadu, IND), le 25 août 2018. Le même jour, Nataraj a aussi battu le record du **plus de pailles mises en bouche (sans les mains)** : 650.

LA PLUS HAUTE TOUR EN PAPIER DÉCOUPÉ
Des employés de Haier Washing Machine Co. (CHN) ont édifié une tour de 10,08 m avec du papier découpé à Qingdao (province de Shandong, CHN), le 28 juin 2017. Il leur a fallu 4 h et 15 min pour bâtir cette tour plus haute que 5 hommes formant une pyramide. Sa base était constituée de 4 cylindres de machines à laver.

MAI 10 La Société des Magiciens américains, **la plus vieille société de magie**, naît dans un nuage de fumée dans la boutique de magie des Martinka, à New York (USA) en 1902. Harry Houdini est un de ses présidents.

MAI 11 Leigh Purnell, Paul Archer et Johno Ellison (tous GBR) rentrent à Londres en 2012 après **le plus long voyage en taxi**. Ils ont parcouru 69 716 km. Le compteur affiche 79 006,80 £ (127 530 $) !

▶ LE PLUS DE CURE-DENTS DANS UNE BARBE

Joel Strasser (USA) a piqué 3 500 cure-dents dans sa barbe à Lacey (Washington, USA), le 7 juillet 2018. Il lui a fallu 3 h et 13 min pour établir ce record. À époque de la visite du *GWR*, Joel s'entraînait à battre celui du **plus de pailles dans une barbe**. Le 18 mars 2019, il en a mis 312 dans ses moustaches (encart) alors qu'Isaac Kochman (USA) n'en avait mis que 259 le 7 juillet 2018.

Le 11 mai 2017, Dean Carter (GBR) a placé **le plus de cure-dents dans sa barbe en 1 min** (33), dans le Devon Cliffs Holiday Park de Sandy Bay, à Exmouth, (Devon, GBR).

Pour réussir cet exploit, le participant doit veiller à ce que tous les cure-dents – qu'il doit enfoncer lui-même – restent en place au moins pendant 10 s.

▶ Consultez nos meilleures vidéos sur le guinnessworldrecords.com/2020

LE PLUS DE CRAVATES AUTOUR DU COU

Jeremy Muñoz (USA) a noué 287 cravates autour de son cou, à Lubbock (Texas, USA), le 4 avril 2018. Toutes les cravates utilisées faisaient partie de sa collection. Cet exploit lui a permis d'établir un record du monde, ce qui était son rêve depuis qu'il avait commencé à collectionner les livres du *GWR* à l'âge de 10 ans.

LE PLUS RAPIDE À FAIRE ÉCLATER 20 BALLONS D'EAU AVEC LES PIEDS

Farhan Ayub (PAK) a fait éclater 20 ballons d'eau en 2,75 s en les piétinant à Lahore (Punjab, PAK), le 23 juillet 2018. Il a battu le précédent record de près de 3 s.

Le détenteur de nombreux records du *GWR* Ashrita Furman (USA) a mis 29,70 s à **éclater 100 ballons avec les pieds**, à New York (USA), le 16 décembre 2015.

LE PLUS DE TEE-SHIRTS ENFILÉS

Père de deux enfants, Ted Hastings (CAN) a revêtu 260 tee-shirts, à Kitchener (Ontario, CAN), le 17 février 2019. Au fur et à mesure de sa progression, il mettait des tee-shirts de plus en plus grands. Il est passé de la taille medium à la taille 20X. Il a eu cette idée après avoir lu le *GWR 2019* avec son fils, William, qui l'a mis au défi de battre un record. Voulant montrer à ses enfants l'importance du travail et de l'engagement, il leur a prouvé que c'était possible !

MAI 12 En 2002, le cycliste Éric Barone (FRA) pédale à 172 km/h sur les pentes raides du volcan Cerro Negro (NIC) : il est ainsi **le plus rapide à dévaler une pente sur de la terre et du gravier à vélo**.

MAI 13 Avec sa maîtresse, Samantha Valle (USA), Geronimo, croisé border collie et kelpie, réalise **le plus de sauts à la corde en 1 min** (91), en 2012.

ILS FONT DES EXPLOITS

LE PLUS DE BURPEES AVEC DES TALONS HAUTS EN 1 MIN (HOMMES)

Raneir Pollard (USA) a fait 38 burpees (pompes suivies d'un saut en l'air) avec des talons hauts en 60 s, à Los Angeles (Californie, USA), le 7 décembre 2017. Quand il ne s'entraîne pas avec des stilettos aux pieds, il est moniteur de fitness et comédien de stand-up.

(USA) a instantanément "transporté" un assistant à 285,33 m, lors du Farm Progress Show, à Boone (Iowa, USA). L'événement était organisé par Corteva Agriscience, une division de DowDuPont.

Le plus de temps à jongler avec 3 objets sur une planche d'équilibre

Yutaro Nagao (JPN) a jonglé avec 3 ballons durant 41 min et 19 s sur une planche d'équilibre, à Tokyo (JPN), le 8 février 2019.

LE PLUS DE...

Personnes faisant un saut périlleux simultanément en ski nautique

Lors du Chain of Records 2017 (USA), 11 skieurs nautiques ont fait simultanément un saut périlleux avant en s'élançant d'une rampe, sur le lac Grassy, à Winter Haven (Floride, USA), le 23 avril 2017.

Sauts périlleux arrière avec vrille en 1 min

Le 23 novembre 2018, Dakota Schuetz (USA) a réalisé 21 sauts périlleux arrière avec vrille avec sa trottinette, lors de *La Notte dei Record*, à Rome (ITA).

Plaques d'immatriculation déchirées en 1 min

Le strongman (hercule) professionnel Bill Clark (USA) a déchiré en morceaux

LA PLUS LONGUE DISTANCE SUR UN MONOCYCLE EN PÉDALANT AVEC UNE JAMBE

Le 19 juillet 2018, le monocycliste Israel Arranz Parada (ESP) a parcouru 894,35 m – plus de 8 fois la longueur d'un terrain de football américain – en pédalant uniquement avec sa jambe droite. Cet exploit s'est déroulé à Valencia de Alcántara (Cáceres, ESP).

La plus longue glissade sur la tête en breakdance

Lors de cette acrobatie, le danseur glisse sur la tête alors que son corps reste à la verticale. À Rome (ITA), le 24 novembre 2018, le champion de breakdance de 18 ans Michele Gagno (ITA) a accompli une glissade de 2,6 m.

La plus longue distance par téléportation

Selon les directives du *GWR*, ce tour de magie doit créer l'illusion qu'une personne est téléportée d'un endroit à un autre par une force invisible. Le 28 août 2018, le magicien Scott Tokar

LA FLÈCHE TIRÉE LE PLUS LOIN INTERCEPTÉE DEPUIS UNE VOITURE EN MOUVEMENT

La flèche tirée par le champion olympique de tir à l'arc Laurence Baldauff (ci-dessous) a été interceptée par l'expert en arts martiaux Markus Haas depuis le toit ouvrant d'une Škoda Octavia RS 245 que Guido Gluschitsch (tous AUT) conduisait avec dextérité. Elle a parcouru 57,5 m. Organisé par Škoda Austria, l'exploit a eu lieu le 28 juillet 2018, à Zeltweg (AUT).

23 plaques en 60 s, à Binghamton (New York, USA), le 22 août 2018.

Triathlons avec une personne en fauteuil roulant en 1 mois

Le 18 novembre 2018, l'athlète Caryn Lubetsky a accompli son 4e triathlon en 1 mois avec la journaliste tétraplégique Kerry Gruson (toutes 2 USA). Elles ont utilisé un radeau gonflable et une remorque de vélo pour tirer le fauteuil roulant de Gruson à chaque étape.

Roues en 1 min (sans les mains)

Le 15 août 2011, Zhang Ziyi (CHN) a exécuté 45 roues en 60 s, sur le plateau de *CCTV – Guinness World Records Special*, à Pékin (CHN).

Verres de vin en équilibre sur le menton

Sun Chao Yang (CHN) a gardé 142 verres de vin en équilibre sur le menton, sur le plateau de *La Notte dei Record*, à Rome (ITA), le 11 novembre 2018. Il a battu son record de 133 verres établi en 2012.

LES PLUS RAPIDES À...

Soulever et lancer 10 personnes (femmes)

Le 17 novembre 2018, Liefia Ingalls (USA) a soulevé 10 personnes au-dessus de sa tête et les a lancées en 39,5 s, sur le plateau de la *La Notte dei Record*, à Rome (ITA).

Parcourir 110 m en faisant des "hippy jumps"

Cette figure consiste à sauter de son skateboard en mouvement, franchir une haie et atterrir sur la planche qui continue à glisser. Steffen Köster (DEU) a couru un 110 m en 29,98 s pour le *Wir Holen Den Rekord Nach Deutschland*, à Europa-Park, à Rust (DEU), le 19 juin 2013.

Parcourir 100 m haies avec des palmes (femmes)

Le 8 décembre 2010, Veronica Torr (NZL) a couru un 100 m avec des palmes en 18,52 s, sur le plateau de *Zheng Da Zong Yi – Guinness World Records Special*, à Pékin (CHN).

Parcourir 100 m sur des échasses à ressort

Ben Jacoby (USA) a couru un 100 m en 13,45 s, à Boulder (Colorado, USA), le 5 octobre 2018.

Passer en limbo à rollers sous 10 barres

R. Naveen Kumar (IND) est passé sous 10 barres en 2,06 s, à Chennai (Tamil Nadu, IND), le 9 septembre 2018. Espacées de 1 m, les barres étaient à 24 cm du sol.

LA PLUS GRANDE DISTANCE PARCOURUE EN CONTRÔLANT UN BALLON DE FOOT EN 1 H (HOMMES)

Le 12 mars 2019, le footballeur de freestyle John Farnworth (GBR) a contrôlé un ballon sur 5,82 km dans le Sahara (MAR), sans utiliser les mains ou les bras. L'année précédente, il avait réussi la plus grande ascension en contrôlant un ballon en 1 h (hommes) – 197 m – en haut du Kala Patthar (NPL).

MAI 14 En 2016, Gabriel Medina (BRA) réalise **le 1er backflip (salto arrière) réussi lors du championnat du monde de surf**. Il reçoit la note maximale de 10, à Oi Rio Pro, à Rio de Janeiro (BRA).

MAI 15 En 2014, Ruan Liangming (CHN) porte **le plus lourd manteau d'abeilles** (63,7 kg), à Yichun (province de Jiangxi, CHN). Pour attirer l'essaim, il a placé 60 reines sur son corps.

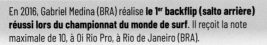

Brittany fait des acrobaties depuis des années. Après des compétitions nationales et internationales de gymnastique pendant 12 ans, elle a mis fin à sa carrière à 18 ans.

▶ LE PLUS LONG TIR À L'ARC AVEC LES PIEDS

Le 31 mars 2018, Brittany Walsh (USA) a tiré une flèche à 12,31 m à l'aide d'un arc qu'elle manipulait avec ses pieds, en se contorsionnant. Elle a touché le centre de la cible dont le rayon mesurait 30,4 cm. Elle a accompli cet exploit à la Creston School de Portland (Oregon, USA). Elle fait la démonstration de son adresse lors de spectacles au théâtre et au cirque depuis plus de 11 ans.

LE PLUS LONG PARCOURS EN RAMPANT SOUS DES BARBELÉS EN 12 H

Le 13 juillet 2018, Eric Hutterer (CAN) a parcouru 12,13 km en 12 h, rampant dans la boue sous des barbelés, à l'occasion de la 2018 Spartan Death Race, à Pittsfield (Vermont, USA). Il a fait plus de 31 fois le parcours de 386,79 m, devançant les 10 autres concurrents lors de la "course de la mort".

▶ L'ÉQUILIBRE LE PLUS LONG À L'ENVERS SUR LES MAINS

Jamie Stroud (USA) est resté en équilibre sur les mains, les jambes pliées vers l'arrière durant 60,03 s, à Las Vegas (Nevada, USA), le 15 décembre 2018. Il a battu ce record au Rio All-Suite Hotel & Casino dans le cadre du SkillCon 2018 (pages 98-107).

LE PLUS DE ROTATIONS À 180° SUR UNE PLANCHE D'ÉQUILIBRE

Silvio Sabba (ITA) a réalisé 107 rotations à 180° sur une planche d'équilibre, à Rodano (Milan, ITA), le 27 juillet 2017. Il détient de nombreux records du *GWR*, partageant celui du **plus de flexions du genou sur une planche en 1 min** (64) avec Dmytro Kharlov (UKR).

MAI 16 En 1929, des vedettes se réunissent à l'hôtel Roosevelt, à Hollywood (Californie, USA) pour **les 1ers Academy Awards**. La cérémonie dure 15 min et n'est pas diffusée à la télévision ni à la radio.

MAI 17 Après la sortie de la version alpha de *Minecraft* en 2009, il faut juste 49 min à "muku" pour poster une image de **la 1re structure construite par un joueur dans *Minecraft*** – un pont formé de 9 blocs.

ÇA BULLE !

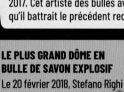

La plus longue guirlande à bulles
La guirlande à bulles se compose de petites boucles assemblées pour créer beaucoup de bulles à la fois. Le 23 septembre 2018, Alekos Ottaviucci, Anna Egle Sciarappa (toutes deux ITA) et Mariano Guz (ARG) ont créé une guirlande de 12,6 m au Bubble Daze 5 de Caernarfon, Pays de Galles (GBR) (voir p. 91).

La plus longue bulle
Alan McKay (NZL) a soufflé une bulle mesurant 32 m de plus que la baleine bleue, **le plus gros des animaux** – à Wellington (NZL) le 9 août 1996.

La plus longue série de bulles (superposées)
Le 13 janvier 2011, "Blub", alias Gennadij Kil (DEU), a formé une tour de 21 bulles superposées au Centro de Creación y Formación Joven de Guía de Isora de Tenerife (ESP).

Le plus de temps passé dans une bulle
"The Highland Joker", alias Eran Backler, a enfermé sa femme, Lauren (tous 2 GBR), dans une bulle qui a duré 1 min et 2,92 s avant d'éclater. Ils ont réalisé le record à Peterborough (Cambridgeshire, GBR), le 22 décembre 2018.

LA PLUS LONGUE SÉRIE DE BULLES SUSPENDUES
Stefano Righi (ITA) a produit une série de 40 bulles suspendues à Empoli, près de Florence (ITA), le 22 février 2017. Cet artiste des bulles avait promis à son fils Thomas qu'il battrait le précédent record (35) – et il a réussi !

LE PLUS GRAND DÔME EN BULLE DE SAVON EXPLOSIF
Le 20 février 2018, Stefano Righi (également ci-dessus) a créé un dôme en bulle de savon de 66 cm de diamètre à Empoli (ITA). Le dôme a été formé sur une surface plane et rempli d'un gaz inflammable (encart ci-dessous). Sa surface a ensuite été allumée avec une flamme nue et le résultat n'a pas tardé. Ce défi est réservé aux pros des bulles !

La plus grande bulle de savon gelée
"Samsam Bubbleman", alias Sam Heath (GBR), a créé une bulle de savon gelée de 4 315,7 cm³ à l'Absolut Vodka Bar de Londres (GBR), le 28 juin 2010.
"Samsam" (en bas à droite), a aussi réalisé **le plus grand nombre de rebonds d'une bulle de savon** au Bubble Daze 5. Équipé d'un gant, il a fait rebondir une bulle 215 fois dans sa main, soit 20 fois plus que le précédent record, établi par Kuo-Sheng Lin (TWN) en 2012.

La plus grosse bulle flottante à l'extérieur
Gary Pearlman (USA) a créé une bulle de 96,27 m³ – soit l'équivalent de 12 900 ballons de basket de NBA – à Cleveland, Ohio (USA), le 20 juin 2015.
Le 19 juin 2017, "Marty McBubble", alias Graeme Denton (AUS), a soufflé **la plus grosse bulle flottante à l'intérieur**, de 19,8 m³, à la Lockleys Primary School d'Adelaide (AUS).

Le plus de personnes enfermées dans des bulles de savon en 30 s
Ce défi a été relevé 2 fois en 2018. Le premier à le réussir a été Eran Backler (GBR), en créant des tubes de bulles autour de 9 personnes en 30 s à Bubble Daze 5. Puis, le 9 novembre 2018, Steven Langley (USA) a augmenté le nombre à 13 personnes à Huntersville, Caroline du Nord (USA). Dans les deux cas, les participants mesuraient au moins 150 cm.

LA PLUS GROSSE BULLE DE SAVON SOUFFLÉE PAR LA MAIN
Mariano Guz (ARG) a plongé ses mains dans du liquide à bulles, puis a soufflé une bulle de 45 510 cm³ entre l'index et le pouce au Bubble Daze 5.

Sans limite de temps, l'artiste Lyudmila Darina (RUS) a enfermé 374 personnes dans une bulle de 2,5 m à Omsk (RUS) le 2 mars 2017 – soit **le plus grand nombre de personnes dans une bulle de savon.**

Le plus de dômes de bulles de savon concentriques
Le 26 avril 2012, Su Chung-Tai (TWN) a placé 15 bulles hémisphériques l'une dans l'autre à Taipei (TWN).
Trois ans plus tard, le 13 janvier 2015, il a soufflé **le plus grand nombre de bulles de savon à l'intérieur d'une grosse bulle** (779) à Jiangyin, Jiangsu (CHN). Pour cela, il a réalisé une grosse bulle, puis a placé ses lèvres à la surface pour souffler des petites bulles à l'intérieur.
Le 28 mars 2018, le prolifique Su a produit **le plus grand dôme en bulle de savon** – d'un diamètre de 1,4 m, d'une hauteur de 0,65 m et d'un volume de 0,644 m³ – dans la ville de Tianjin (CHN).

LA PLUS GRANDE BOUTEILLE À BULLES AVEC BÂTON
Matěj Kodeš (CZE) a présenté une bouteille de liquide à bulles avec bâton de 1,38 m de haut à Lysá nad Labem (CZE), le 25 mars 2018. Cinq mois plus tard, le 6 août 2018, Kodeš a soufflé **le plus de bulles de savons en 1 min** (1 257) au même endroit, sans toutefois utiliser son énorme bouteille.

 MAI 18 En 1968, le joueur de baseball Frank Howard des Washington Senators (tous deux USA) frappe ses 9e et 10e coups de circuit en 7 jours – **le plus de coups de circuit en une semaine.**

 MAI 19 245 alpinistes atteignent le sommet de l'Everest en 2012 – **le plus grand nombre d'ascensions de l'Everest en 1 journée.** Ils provoquent même un bouchon près du sommet.

BUBBLE DAZE 5

Le 23 septembre 2018, le *GWR* retrouve au château de Caernarfon (Pays de Galles, GBR), des "pros des bulles" (encart) lors d'une fête annuelle. Dʳ Zigs Extraordinary Bubbles (GBR) y organise plusieurs activés pour battre des records, dont **le plus de personnes créant simultanément des bulles avec des guirlandes à bulles** (317, ci-dessous) et **le plus de personnes faisant simultanément des bulles avec des baguettes à bulles géantes** (318). Vous en découvrirez d'autres sur ces pages...

LE PLUS LONG ÉCHANGE DE BULLE

"Ray Bubbles", alias Umar Shoaib (GBR), et son fils Rayhaan (FRA) se sont passé 10 fois une bulle de savon à l'École la Grange de Rungis (FRA), le 13 avril 2016. Pour réussir ce défi, ils ont utilisé des "raquettes" couvertes d'un film de liquide à bulles en guise de cordes.

LE PLUS DE REBONDS D'UNE BULLE SUR UN FILM DE SAVON

Après 2 essais moins concluants, Farhaan Shoaib (FRA) a fait rebondir 113 fois une bulle de savon au Bubble Daze 5. L'art des bulles est une passion familiale – le père et le frère de Farhaan ont aussi laissé une trace dans le *GWR* (voir à gauche).

Envie d'essayer chez vous ? C'est délicat ! La bulle peut facilement éclater ou fusionner avec le film sur la raquette.

LE PLUS DE BULLES SOUFFLÉES AVEC UNE SEULE BAGUETTE

Avec une seule baguette, "Samsam Bubbleman", alias Sam Heath, a soufflé 445 bulles de savon au Bubble Daze 5. Il a choisi un défi ne nécessitant ni expérience ni outils particuliers pour encourager les passionnés de bulles de tout âge à essayer eux aussi d'entrer dans le *GWR*.

MAI **20** — En 1927, Charles Lindbergh (USA) effectue **le premier vol transatlantique en solo** en partant de Roosevelt Field à New York, (USA). Il atterrit à Paris (FRA), après un voyage de 33 h 30 min 29 s.

MAI **21** — En 1977, la grenouille à nez pointu (*Ptychadena oxyrhynchus*) "Santjie" réalise **le plus long saut pour une grenouille en compétition** - 10,3 m en 3 bonds - lors d'un concours à Pietersburg (RSA).

91

AU FEU !

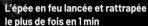

L'ÉCOLE DU FEU
GWR aimerait remercier la *Fire School* pour son aide dans la création de cette rubrique. Le 1er centre britannique des arts du feu se trouve dans l'est de Londres. Il a été fondé en 2012 par l'artiste de cirque, le professeur et la "directrice du feu", Sarah Harman. L'école offre un environnement sûr et professionnel pour maîtriser la jonglerie avec le feu.

L'épée en feu lancée et rattrapée le plus de fois en 1 min
Le 20 avril 2018, Ashrita Furman (USA) a lancé et rattrapé une épée en feu 62 fois, à Jamaica (New York, USA). La lame d'une "épée de feu" est enduite de combustible et enflammée.

Quatre mois plus tard, au même endroit, il est resté **le plus longtemps avec une torche enflammée entre les dents** – 5 min et 1,68 s. Pour ce record, il faut incliner la tête vers l'arrière et placer la torche à l'envers, en partie dans la bouche, en la serrant entre les dents.

 ## Le plus de flammes crachées en 1 min
Le 9 janvier 2015, le cracheur de feu Zhu Jiangao (CHN) a produit 189 flammes en 60 s, sur le plateau de *CCTV - Guinness World Records Special*, à Jiangyin (province du Jiangsu, CHN).

Le 1er août 2015, Tobias Buschick (DEU) a craché 387 flammes consécutives – **le plus de flammes crachées sans reprendre d'alcool** –, à Neuenbürg (DEU). Il n'a mis en bouche qu'une gorgée de fluide combustible avant le record.

Le plus de cerceaux en feu tournant en même temps
Casey Martin (USA) a fait tourner autour d'elle simultanément 4 cerceaux enflammés, au Port Credit Busker Fest, à Mississauga (Ontario, CAN), le 14 août 2014. Chaque cerceau contenait 4 mèches et Casey a réussi à les faire tourner 8 fois autour d'elle.

Pippa Coram "The Ripper" (AUS) a fait tourner **le plus de cerceaux en feu en faisant le grand écart** (3), à Wonderground (Londres, GBR), le 14 septembre 2012. Selon les règles du GWR, les cerceaux devaient tourner autour de ses bras et de son cou 10 s.

Le plus de personnes faisant tourner des bolas en feu
Ameno Signum (DEU) a réuni 250 participants pour faire tourner des bolas en feu (objets liés à une ficelle, dont un bout est enflammé) à Neunburg vorm Wald (DEU), le 1er septembre 2012.

Le plus de ballons éclatés par un cracheur de feu
Le 22 octobre 2017, à Londres (GBR), Colin Llewelyn Chapman (GBR) a fait exploser 131 ballons, en crachant du feu dessus.

La 1re torche humaine faisant du surf
Le 22 juillet 2015, le surfeur professionnel Jamie O'Brien (USA) s'est mué en torche avant de surfer sur l'une des plus grosses vagues à Teahupo'o (Tahiti, PYF), relevant un défi sur Instagram. Il a bravé le feu et l'eau, la vague étant à la fois puissante et dangereuse car elle se brise sur un récif corallien peu profond

Le plus haut saut à l'élastique dans l'eau avec le corps en feu
Le 14 septembre 2012, Yoni Roch (FRA) a sauté d'une hauteur de 65,09 m, le corps en feu, du viaduc de la Souleuvre en Normandie (FRA). Les flammes se sont éteintes quand il est entré dans l'eau de la rivière en contrebas.

LE PLUS DE TORCHES ÉTEINTES PAR UN AVALEUR DE FEU EN 1 MIN
"FireGuy", alias Brant Matthews (CAN), a éteint 101 torches avec la bouche en 60 s, à West Allis (Wisconsin, USA), le 10 août 2018. Il a réalisé cette performance à l'occasion de la foire du Wisconsin.

LE PLUS DE BÂTONS ENFLAMMÉS ÉTEINTS LES YEUX BANDÉS EN 1 MIN
Le 27 janvier 2019, Sarah Harman (GBR) a éteint 91 fois avec la bouche les flammes d'un bâton de feu avec les yeux bandés, à *The Fire School* de Londres (GBR) qu'elle dirige. Elle devait garder une mèche enflammée et l'utiliser pour rallumer le bâton venant d'être éteint.

 ## LA PLUS LONGUE TORCHE HUMAINE (SANS OXYGÈNE)
Josef Tödtling (AUT) est resté sous forme de torche humaine, des chevilles au sommet du crâne, pendant 5 min et 41 s, sans apport d'oxygène, dans le parc de la compagnie de pompiers de Salzbourg (AUT), le 23 novembre 2013. Il portait plusieurs couches d'habits protecteurs et s'était enduit, surtout la tête et le cou, d'un gel résistant à la chaleur pour éviter les brûlures.

LE PLUS DE SALTOS ARRIÈRE EN CRACHANT DU FEU EN 1 MIN
Ryan Luney (GBR) a réalisé 14 saltos arrière en crachant simultanément du feu en 60 s, à la Riverside School d'Antrim (GBR), le 23 juin 2017. La tentative a eu lieu dans le cadre d'une fête marquant la fin de l'année scolaire. Il a eu l'idée de ce record en voyant l'ancienne star de *Jackass*, Steve-O, effectuer cet exploit dans l'émission *Slow Mo Guys* sur YouTube.

⚠ Ne reproduisez pas ces records dangereux chez vous ! Les professionnels dont les performances sont présentées ici s'entraînent des années pour réaliser ces exploits et savent se préparer et se protéger.

Laura et Noelia font des numéros ensemble depuis des années. La confiance est essentielle pour une équipe d'avaleurs de feu.

▶ LE PLUS DE BÂTONS DE FEU ÉTEINTS EN ALTERNANCE EN 1 MIN (ÉQUIPE DE 2)

Lors de cette tentative, une des deux femmes présente une torche enflammée à sa partenaire qui doit l'éteindre avec la bouche et lui donner à éteindre une autre torche enflammée. "Isobel Midnight", alias Laura Sutton (GBR), et "Lady Noelia", alias Noelia Hueso Muñoz (ESP), ont éteint 73 torches en alternance, à *The Fire School*, le 27 janvier 2019.

Au cours de la même séance, Isobel Midnight a **éteint le plus de torches en 1 min (avec 2 bâtons)**, soit 78 (encart).

▶ LE PLUS DE "DOUBLE JELLYFISH" EN 1 MIN

Pour faire un "double jellyfish", il faut soulever 2 torches en feu dans les airs, puis les baisser brusquement. La flamme se détache alors en formant une cloche qui évoque une méduse (*jellyfish*) avant de s'éteindre. Roman Ackley (GBR) a réalisé 24 "double jellyfishes" en 1 min, à *The Fire School*, le 27 janvier 2019. Il a aussi réussi **le plus de "jellyfish" simples en 1 min** (34).

LA PLUS HAUTE FLAMME CRACHÉE PAR UN CRACHEUR DE FEU

Le 11 janvier 2011, Antonio Restivo (USA) a produit une flamme de 8,05 m de haut, dans un entrepôt de Las Vegas (Nevada, USA), en utilisant de la paraffine liquide. La flamme a frôlé le plafond. L'année précédente, il avait présenté ses performances de cracheur de feu lors de la 5ᵉ saison d'*America's Got Talent*. Il était arrivé en demi-finale.

MAI 24 En 1991, un boeing 747 d'El Al transporte **le plus de passagers dans un avion** (près de 1 088), dans le cadre de l'opération Solomon. Les juifs éthiopiens évacués d'Addis-Abeba rejoignent Israël.

MAI 25 **Le rat le plus âgé**, un rat ordinaire baptisé Rodney, meurt à 7 ans et 4 mois, en 1990. Il appartenait à Rodney Mitchell de Tulsa (Oklahoma, USA).

93

PEOPLE ARE AWESOME™

La chaîne YouTube People are Awesome *met en avant tous ceux qui parviennent à repousser les limites humaines et à réaliser ce qui paraît impossible. Elle présente des vidéos qui célèbrent les capacités physiques des hommes et des femmes, leur ambition et leur ingéniosité, et met en lumière les créateurs de vidéos les plus doués. De nombreux records y sont aussi établis – tous les détenteurs d'un record du GWR ont été présentés sur cette chaîne.*

▶ Le plus de noix cassées avec la tête en 1 min
Muhammad Rashid (PAK) a cassé 254 noix avec la tête à Rome (ITA), le 11 novembre 2018.

La plus grande hauteur atteinte après catapultage depuis un coussin gonflable (blobbing)
Le "blobbing" consiste à faire sauter une personne d'une plate-forme sur un coussin partiellement gonflé (le blob) sur lequel sont assis les participants qui se voient alors catapulter dans les airs. Le 7 juin 2012, le "blobber" Christian "Elvis" Guth s'est envolé à 22 m du sol, propulsé par les sauteurs Christian von Cranach et Patrick Baumann (tous

▶ LA PLUS HAUTE PLONGÉE PEU PROFONDE
"Professeur Splash" (alias Darren Taylor, USA) a sauté de 11,56 m de haut dans 30 cm d'eau, à Xiamen (province du Fujian, CHN), le 9 septembre 2014.

Pas assez peur ? Le 21 juin de cette année, il a exécuté **le plus haut plongeon peu profond dans le feu** (8 m). La surface de l'eau avait été embrasée juste avant son saut.

Selon les règles du GWR, les concurrents doivent rester en équilibre sur les mains pendant tout l'essai.

▶ LE PLUS DE MARCHES GRIMPÉES SUR LA TÊTE
Le 5 janvier 2015, Li Longlong (CHN) a grimpé 36 marches sur la tête, à Jiangyin (province du Jiangsu, CHN), battant ainsi son propre record de 2 marches.

DEU). Cet exploit a eu lieu à Hambourg (DEU).

Le plus de barreaux d'échelle gravis avec un bras
Tazio Gavioli (ITA) a gravi 39 barreaux avec le bras gauche, au Heilan International Equestrian Club (province du Jiangsu, CHN), le 9 janvier 2014. (Pour connaître les autres records de Tazio, voir p. 85.)

Le plus rapide à escalader un couloir vertical avec les pieds
Placé entre deux murs, Fang Zhisheng (CHN) s'est propulsé en 28,3 s à plus de 18 m de haut en se servant uniquement de ses pieds, à Pékin (CHN), le 21 novembre 2012.

Le plus de Thomas sur un cheval d'arçons en 1 min
Bien connu des breakers et gymnastes, le Thomas consiste à se tenir en équilibre et à balancer les jambes

LE PLUS RAPIDE À SAUTER SUR 10 BALLONS SUISSES
Neil Whyte (AUS) a sauté sur 10 ballons suisses – séparés de 1 m – en 7,8 s, à Pékin (CHN), le 12 janvier 2016. Après deux essais ratés, il a réussi le 3e, battant ainsi son précédent record de 8,31 s.
Dix ans plus tôt, Neil avait réussi **le plus long saut entre 2 ballons suisses** (2,3 m), au Zest Health Club de Perth (Australie occidentale, AUS), le 25 août 2006.

en cercles. Le 21 avril 2009, Louis Smith (GBR) a exécuté 50 Thomas, à Londres (GBR). Alberto Busnari (ITA) a égalé cet exploit le 10 juillet 2014. Ces 2 hommes sont des gymnastes mondialement célèbres.

Le 10 m le plus rapide en grand écart facial (femmes)
Cette position consiste à étendre les jambes de chaque côté du corps, formant ainsi un angle d'environ 180°. Le 12 mars 2012, Kazumi Kawahara (JPN) a parcouru 10 m en 16,9 s dans cette position à Rome (ITA).

LA PLUS RAPIDE À RENTRER DANS UNE BOÎTE
La contorsionniste Skye Broberg (NZL) est rentrée en 4,78 s dans une boîte de 52 x 45 x 45 cm, à Londres (GBR), le 15 septembre 2011.

Ci-dessous, Skye est passée à travers une raquette de tennis – un exploit qui lui a autrefois valu plusieurs records du GWR. Deux d'entre eux ont depuis été battus par Thaneswar Guragai (NPL) : **le plus de passages à travers une raquette de tennis en 3 min** (96) et **la plus rapide à passer 3 fois à travers une raquette de tennis** (4,91 s).

MAI 26 En 1991, une équipe de 14 étudiants de l'université de Stanford (Californie, USA) parcourt **la plus longue distance à saute-mouton** (1 603,2 km), en 244 h et 43 min.

MAI 27 **La plus longue guirlande de fleurs (équipe)** est réalisée en 1985. Un groupe de 16 villageois de Good Easter près de Chelmsford (Essex, GBR) forme cette guirlande de 2,12 km de long en 7 h.

Qui a eu l'idée de cet audacieux record dans les airs ? Aaron répond : "Je voulais montrer au monde entier que les fauteuils roulants pouvaient voler !"

LE PLUS LONG SAUT EN FAUTEUIL ROULANT DEPUIS UNE RAMPE

Le 20 juillet 2018, Aaron Fotheringham (USA) a exécuté un saut de 21,35 m en fauteuil roulant depuis une rampe, au Woodward West de Tehachapi (Californie, USA). Aaron a établi deux autres records ce jour-là (voir à droite) : **le plus grand drop-in sur un quarter-pipe en fauteuil roulant** et **le plus haut hand plant en fauteuil roulant** (8,4 m chacun).

LE PLUS DE BLOCS DE BÉTON CASSÉS EN 1 MIN

Ali Bahçetepe (TUR) a cassé 1 175 blocs de béton en 60 s, à Datça Cumhuriyet Meydanı (TUR), le 17 novembre 2012. Ali a aussi établi le record du **plus de blocs de béton cassés en 30 s** (683), en 2012, et celui du **plus de blocs de béton cassés en 1 pile** (37), en 2015. (Pour découvrir l'un de ses autres records, voir p. 84.)

LE PLUS RAPIDE À MONTER UNE CORDE DE 5 M

Le 30 septembre 2018, Nick "The KO Ninja" Kostreski (USA, ci-dessus) a monté une corde de 5 m de long – soit la taille d'une girafe adulte –, en 4,11 s, à Santa Monica (Californie, USA).

Le même jour, Natalie Duran (USA, à droite) a été **la plus rapide à monter une corde de 5 m** (7,67 s).

LE PLUS DE POMPES SUR UN DOIGT EN 30 S

Xie Guizhong (CHN) a exécuté 41 pompes sur un doigt en 30 s, à Pékin (CHN), le 8 décembre 2011. Il a ainsi aisément battu son précédent record de 25.

Le 11 décembre 2010, l'homme aux doigts super forts avait été **le plus rapide à pousser une voiture sur 50 m avec un seul doigt** : 47,7 s, à Shenzhen (province du Guangdong, CHN).

MAI 28 En 2006, Xue Chen (CHN, née le 18 février 1989) devient **la plus jeune joueuse à remporter un titre international de beach-volley**, au China Shanghai Jinshan Open, à l'âge de 17 ans et 99 jours.

MAI 29 Rory Blackwell devient **le plus grand homme-orchestre** en 1989 en jouant simultanément de 108 instruments différents (19 mélodies et 89 percussions), à Dawlish (Devon, GBR).

EN REVUE

LE PLUS LONG MARATHON D'ACCORDÉON

Entre les 11 et 13 juillet 2018, Anssi K. Laitinen (FIN) a joué de l'accordéon durant 40 h, 3 min et 10 s, à Kuopio (FIN). Il a interprété 610 morceaux différents, finlandais ainsi que des airs populaires étrangers, entièrement de mémoire.

Il avait déjà battu le record en 2010, avec un marathon de 31 h et 25 min.

Le plus de cartes de jeu mémorisées en 1 h

La jeune Munkhshur Narmandakh (MNG) est la 1re femme à avoir gagné le championnat du monde de mémorisation, à Shenzhen (province du Guangdong, CHN), du 6 au 8 décembre 2017. Elle a mémorisé 1 924 cartes de jeu (37 jeux complets) en 1 h et les a récitées dans l'ordre en 2 h.

Lors du championnat, sa jumelle Enkhshur Narmandakh (MNG) s'est souvenue de 5 445 "1" et "0", soit **le plus de chiffres binaires mémorisés en 30 min.** Enkhtuya Lkhagvadulam (MNG) a fait encore mieux en 2018 en mémorisant 5 597 chiffres binaires.

La plus longue passe de hockey sur glace

Le 20 novembre 2018, Zach Lamppa et l'ancien ailier de la Ligue nationale de hockey Tom Chorske (tous 2 USA) ont uni leurs forces pour faire la plus longue passe de hockey en envoyant le palet à 275,63 m. L'exploit a eu lieu sur le Lake of the Isles, à Minneapolis (Minnesota, USA).

▶ Le but marqué avec un ballon de foot lancé à la plus haute altitude

Le 24 juillet 2018, le footballeur John Farnworth (voir p. 88) et l'ex-vedette de l'English Premier League Jimmy Bullard (tous 2 GBR) ont marqué un but avec un ballon lancé depuis un hélicoptère à une hauteur de 45,72 m. Ce tir extrême a été réalisé sur l'aérodrome White Waltham, à Maidenhead (GBR).

Le marathon en relais le plus rapide

59 athlètes de Kansas City ont parcouru 42,1 km en 1 h, 30 min et 40,31 s, le 15 juin 2018. Le marathon a eu lieu au Johnson County Community College d'Overland Park (Kansas, USA). Il était organisé par Joe et Phil Ratterman (tous 2 USA) pour une œuvre caritative. Les sprinteurs du lycée et de l'université se sont relayés tous les 200 m pour battre ce record resté inégalé durant 20 ans.

Le 1er triple salto arrière sur une slackline

Louis Boniface (FRA) a effectué le 1er triple salto arrière, en partant et en terminant en position assise, le 8 octobre 2018, comme a pu le vérifier l'Association internationale de Slackline. La sangle de 26 m était tendue à 3,10 m du sol à Saint-Lambert (FRA).

▶ LA FEUILLE DE PAPIER PLIÉE EN DEUX LE PLUS DE FOIS

Le 27 janvier 2002, la lycéenne Britney Gallivan (USA) a écrit 2 équations mathématiques afin de plier une feuille de papier en deux, 12 fois de suite. Pour ce record, elle a utilisé un morceau de papier de soie de 1 219 m de long. En parlant de son exploit, elle nous a confié : "J'espère que d'autres le verront... réfléchiront et relèveront de nouveaux défis !"

▶ LE PLUS DE PERSONNES DÉGUISÉES EN DINOSAURES

Le 26 janvier 2019, le célèbre youtubeur Elton Castee (USA) a demandé à 1 000 personnes de l'aider à battre 10 records du GWR au moment du tournage de son clip vidéo *The Fun in Life*, à Los Angeles (Californie, USA). À cette occasion, 252 participants se sont déguisés en dinosaure et **50 personnes de nationalités différentes se sont embrassées en 1 min**, puis **enlacées.**

Dans le clip d'Elton, les dinosaures ont évolué en dansant le "Carniwar" et le "Tyrannasour Twerk".

MAI 30 En 2016, Kyle Lobpries (USA) plane au-dessus de Davis (Californie, USA) durant 8 min et demie. Il parcourt à cette occasion 32,094 km, **la plus longue distance parcourue en wingsuit.**

MAI 31 En 1975, le légendaire gros mangeur Peter Dowdeswell (GBR) est **le plus rapide à boire 1 l de lait.** Il met 3,2 s, au Top Rank Suite de Dudley (Midlands de l'Ouest, GBR).

▶ LE PLUS DE ROTATIONS À 360° VERS LE BAS DANS L'EAU EN 1 MIN

Le 12 décembre 2018, la sirène Ariana Liuzzi (USA) a effectué, en descendant, 32 rotations complètes sous l'eau en 1 min, au Silverton Casino Hotel de Las Vegas (Nevada, USA). Formée à la natation synchronisée, elle passe ses journées dans un aquarium d'eau salée de 442 893 l, où évoluent aussi 4 000 poissons tropicaux, requins et plusieurs pastenagues !

Sa collègue Logan Halverson (USA) a réalisé **le plus de cercles d'air sous l'eau en 1 min (48)**, également le 12 décembre 2018.

Les sirènes de Silverton peuvent rester 15 min sous l'eau. Elles inspirent de l'air à l'aide de "narguilés de plongée" encastrés dans un récif artificiel.

LA PLUS GRANDE POUPÉE DE PORCELAINE

Il a fallu 10 ans aux artistes Wang Chu et Deng Jiaqi (toutes 2 CHN) dans la province du Jiangxi (CHN) pour confectionner une poupée en porcelaine de 172 cm. Leur impressionnante création grandeur nature a un tour de poitrine de 70 cm, un tour de taille de 52 cm et un tour de hanches de 74 cm.

Le véhicule le plus lourd tiré par les cheveux

Mahmood Shamshun Al Arab (UAE) a tiré un camion de 10 380 kg avec ses cheveux à Fujairah (UAE), le 2 décembre 2017.

Le plus grand ensemble de tubas

Les 835 musiciens de l'orchestre symphonique de Kansas City (USA) ont interprété *Douce Nuit* au TUBACHRISTMAS 2018 le 7 décembre à Kansas City (Missouri, USA). L'ensemble était dirigé par Scott Watson et les musiciens étaient âgés de 11 à 86 ans. Pour battre ce record, les cuivres comme le tuba, le baryton et l'euphonium sont autorisés.

▶ Le bateau-dragon le plus long

Le 12 novembre 2018, un bateau-dragon de 87,3 m de long a été dévoilé dans la province de Prey Veng, au Cambodge. Construit par l'Union des fédérations de la jeunesse cambodgienne de la province et financé par l'administration de celle-ci (toutes 2 KHM), il pouvait contenir 179 rameurs.

Le plus rapide pour démonter et assembler une *matriochka* avec les yeux bandés

Le 27 octobre 2018, Kask Georgi (RUS) a démonté et assemblé une poupée russe de 5 pièces en 8,01 s dans le centre Kashirskaya Plaza de Moscou, (RUS). L'événement était organisé par ENKA TC (RUS).

Le plus de personnes empotant des plantes en même temps

Lors d'un nettoyage communautaire à Portsmouth (Ohio, USA), 1 405 bénévoles verte des Amis de Portsmouth (USA) ont empoté des plantes le 18 août 2018.

Le plus de trous joués en 24 heures par un individu (à pied)

Le 23 avril 2019, Eric Byrnes (USA) a parcouru 169 km à pied sur le terrain de golf de Half Moon Bay en Californie (USA). À cette occasion, il a joué 420 trous, améliorant le record de 401 trous resté inégalé pendant 48 ans.

LA PLUS RAPIDE À VISITER TOUS LES PARCS À THÈME DE DISNEY

En 2017, Lindsay Nemeth (CAN) a visité les 12 parcs à thème de Disney en 75 h et 6 min. Elle a commencé par Disneyland (Californie, USA, sur la photo), avant de se rendre en avion dans ceux de Floride (USA), de Paris, de Shanghai et de Hong Kong. Elle a terminé par la visite du Tokyo DisneySea à Urayasu (JPN), le 6 décembre.

JUIN 1 — **Le plus long tunnel de chemin de fer** ouvre en 2016. Le tunnel du Saint-Gothard mesure 57 km de long et passe sous les Alpes entre Göschenen et Airolo (CHE).

JUIN 2 — En 2016, l'homme fort Cosimo Ferrucci (ITA) fait 7 squats en portant une plate-forme sur laquelle 11 personnes sont assises. Il **soulève le plus de personnes en faisant un squat,** à Trani (ITA).

97

SPORTS VIRAUX

Bienvenue dans ce chapitre consacré aux défis amusants, relevés par des gens talentueux, très photogéniques et ultra-partagés ! Ils ont été inspirés par le SkillCon, la fête annuelle des sports atypiques (comme le combat juggling), à Las Vegas (Nevada, USA). En décembre 2018, nos arbitres sont venus y superviser une série de tentatives de records, en partie illustrées dans les pages suivantes, avec d'autres démonstrations impressionnantes de dextérité.

Admirez donc ces individus qui jonglent, retournent des bouteilles et réalisent des prouesses avec un Rubik's Cube ou un pogo stick. Rendez-vous ensuite sur **guinnessworldrecords.com/2020**, afin de découvrir leurs conseils dans des vidéos spécialement réalisées pour vous. Fort de tout cela, pourquoi ne pas relever vous-même certains de ces défis ? Partagez ensuite une vidéo vous montrant en action. Qui sait, vous réaliserez peut-être votre propre "hit viral" – et si vous êtes bon, vous pourrez même figurer dans le GWR 2021 !

Pour plus de vidéos sur les sports viraux : guinnessworldrecords.com/2020

▶ LA PLUS GRANDE COMPÉTITION DE COMBATS AU SABRE LASER

Le 15 décembre 2018, 60 combattants équipés de sabres laser inspirés de ceux de la saga *Star Wars* se sont affrontés au SkillCon. Cang Snow (à droite), fondateur de la Lightspeed Saber League (tous 2 USA), à l'origine de l'événement, a remporté le combat.

En février 2019, cette nouvelle forme de duel a officiellement été reconnue en tant que sport en France, où des clubs d'escrime sont équipés de leurs propres sabres laser en polycarbonate !

Dans un duel au sabre laser, un combattant marque des points lorsque sa "lame" touche son adversaire. Le 1er à réaliser un certain nombre de touches l'emporte. Les combats ont lieu dans une zone délimitée (ou "light box"), des lumières marquant les limites.

SOMMAIRE

DANS LES AIRS

L'art ancien du jonglage améliore, entre autres, la coordination main-œil, la capacité de concentration et la perception spatiale. Il favorise aussi le développement du cerveau et peut être à la fois relaxant et stimulant, tout en étant bien sûr amusant ! Si vous débutez, les bases sont faciles à apprendre. Pour vous encourager, regardez donc ces jongleurs très doués qui utilisent des objets inattendus. Essayez de vous filmer – afin de parfaire votre technique – et mettez votre vidéo en ligne. Vous aurez peut-être du succès – et inciterez d'autres à tenter leur chance !

LE PLUS DE BACK-CROSS EN JONGLANT EN 1 MIN

Les back-cross sont des lancers en continu derrière le dos, alternant gauche et droite Le 16 décembre 2018, Matan Presberg (USA) – champion du monde de l'International Jugglers' Association – a rattrapé ainsi 162 balles en 60 s, au SkillCon de Las Vegas (Nevada, USA).

LE POIDS LE PLUS LOURD JONGLÉ

Denys Ilchenko (UKR) a maintenu en rotation aérienne 3 pneus d'un poids total de 26,98 kg pendant 32,43 s, le 17 juillet 2013. Cet exploit a eu lieu sur le plateau d'*Officially Amazing*, à Nairn (GBR).

LA PERSONNE AYANT MAINTENU EN L'AIR 2 BALLONS AVEC LA TÊTE LE PLUS LONGTEMPS

Jongler, mais différemment... Abhinabha Tangerman (NLD) a gardé 2 ballons en l'air avec la tête pendant 1 min et 9 s, à Leiria (PRT), le 10 juin 2018.

N'essayez pas chez vous ! Le jonglage avec des objets tranchants et lourds est réservé aux professionnels.

JOSH HORTON

Le 6 septembre 2018, Josh Horton, alias "Juggling Josh" (USA, ci-dessus), et sa femme Cassie ont établi le record du **plus de pommes tranchées en jonglant avec des couteaux en 1 min (36)**. Avec Jake Triplett (USA), Josh a réussi le record en **30 s**, fendant 17 pommes en 2, le 4 septembre 2017.

▶ DAVID RUSH

Ce multirecordman américain tente des records pour promouvoir l'éducation STEM (Science, Technology, Engineering and Mathematics). Le 28 octobre 2018, il a rattrapé **le plus de balles en jonglant sur un monocycle (les yeux bandés) (30)**, à la Centennial High School de Boise (Idaho, USA). Le 16 juin, il avait réussi **le plus de jongleries consécutives avec une hache (839)**, au Rhodes Skate Park de Boise. Le 17 août 2018, il a égalé le record 2011 de Milan Roskopf (SVK) du **plus de jongleries avec des boules de bowling (3)**.

 JUIN 3 En 2015, Paul Thompson (GBR) entreprend **le plus long voyage en camionnette de laitier**, parcourant 1 659,29 km en Grande-Bretagne, à une vitesse moyenne de 16 km/h.

 JUIN 4 En 2016, Łukasz Budner (POL) réussit **la frappe de tennis de table la plus rapide** (116 km/h), lors d'une compétition à Częstochowa (POL).

"Elbow Pop" : la balle rebondit près de votre coude ; jonglez à mi-hauteur. Avec les 2 bras, comptez 2 figures !

"Au-dessus des épaules" : un lancer derrière le dos qui peut être exécuté des 2 côtés du corps.

"Sous la jambe" : à faire avec les 2 jambes – on compte une figure par jambe.

Regardez le tutoriel de jonglage de Taylor sur guinnessworldrecords.com/2020

▶ LE PLUS DE FIGURES DE JONGLAGE EN 1 MIN (3 BALLES)

Le 16 décembre 2018, la jongleuse Taylor Glenn (USA) a réalisé 39 figures – dont les 3 illustrées à gauche – avec 3 balles, en 60 s, au SkillCon de Las Vegas. Elle a appris les bases du jonglage à 3 balles à l'âge de 12 ans, puis elle est passée à 4 et 5 balles et à des bâtons à l'adolescence.

À VOUS DE JOUER...

Vous sentez-vous capable de battre les records de Taylor ? Si vous pensez pouvoir faire mieux, suivez les règles du GWR...

- Concentrez-vous sur des figures de jonglage standard.

- Avant votre essai, vous devez fournir une liste complète des figures que vous allez tenter – et de l'ordre de leur exécution.

- Vous pouvez inclure des vidéos ou des photographies montrant comment vous réalisez les figures.

- Vous devez utiliser 3 balles vendues dans le commerce.

- Une fois que vous avez commencé une figure, terminez-la avant de passer à la suivante. Chaque figure ne peut être exécutée qu'une fois.

- Annoncez chaque figure à voix haute lorsque vous l'exécutez.

- Ne faites tomber aucune balle ! Si cela vous arrive, c'en est fini de votre tentative de record.

- Deux témoins indépendants, jongleurs expérimentés, doivent être présents pour vérifier votre tentative. Une preuve de leur compétence doit être fournie avec votre demande.

- Vos témoins doivent revoir la vidéo de votre tentative et confirmer que vous avez terminé toutes les figures dans le bon ordre. Pour connaître les règles officielles du GWR, rendez-vous sur **guinnessworldrecords. com/2020**.

Satyajit Hota (IND) supporte **le poids le plus lourd avec la paupière** (3,51 kg, plus qu'une brique moyenne), en 2013, sur le plateau de *Rekorlar Dünyası*, à Istanbul (TUR).

JUIN 6 Ben, boa arc-en-ciel colombien (né le 31 mai 1974), meurt en 2016, à 42 ans et 6 jours, soit **le plus vieux serpent en captivité de tous les temps**. Il vivait chez la famille Hattermann à Valdosta (Géorgie, USA).

COMME UN PRO

Découvrez des détenteurs de records qui ont transformé leur passe-temps en véritable profession ! Ils sautent avec des bâtons, rebondissent sur des ballons, pratiquent le footbag ou le yo-yo, et ils se sont entraînés pendant des heures pour devenir les meilleurs au monde. Si vous avez aussi une passion, pourquoi ne pas tenter votre chance et établir un record. Inspirez-vous de leurs performances et fixez-vous des objectifs – qui sait, vous aurez peut-être votre nom dans le prochain GWR !

▶ LE PLUS DE HULA-HOOPS SIMULTANÉS

Marawa Ibrahim (AUS) a exécuté 200 hula-hoops simultanés à Los Angeles (Californie, USA), le 25 novembre 2015. Au fil des ans, Marawa a établi de nombreux records de hula-hoop, dont ceux du **50 m le plus rapide en faisant du hula-hoop** (8,76 s) et du **100 m le plus rapide sur rollers avec 3 hula-hoops** (27,26 s).

▶ D'INCROYABLES FOOTBAGGERS

Endurance et rapidité sont nécessaires pour contrôler ces petites balles remplies de billes. Derrick Fogle (USA, à gauche) a couvert **la plus longue distance en 1 h en contrôlant un footbag** (5,05 km). Mathieu Gauthier (CAN, à droite) a donné **le plus de coups de pied consécutifs dans un footbag avec une jambe et 2 footbags** (71). Ces 2 records ont été établis le 15 décembre 2018, au SkillCon de Las Vegas (Nevada, USA).

LE PLUS HAUT SAUT SUR UN POGO STICK

Dmitry Arsenyev (RUS) a atteint 3,4 m – soit à peu près la taille d'un éléphant africain adulte –, à Rome (ITA), le 20 novembre 2018. Le 5 novembre 2017, ce professionnel du Xpogo a aussi réalisé **le plus de saltos consécutifs sur un pogo stick** (26). Pour cette figure, Dmitry fait tourner son bâton par un saut de 360° avant chaque atterrissage !

LA PLUS HAUTE TOUR EN BRIQUES LEGO® EN CROIX CONSTRUITE EN 30 S AVEC UNE MAIN

Silvio Sabba (ITA) a construit une tour de 29 briques LEGO en 30 s, à Milan (ITA), le 3 mars 2017. Il a aussi réalisé **la plus haute tour de capsules de bouteilles en plastique en 1 min** (43) et tenu **le plus de CD en équilibre sur un doigt** (247).

LE 100 M LE PLUS RAPIDE SUR UN BALLON SAUTEUR (FEMMES)

La comédienne star des réseaux sociaux Ali Spagnola (USA) a parcouru 100 m sur un ballon sauteur en 38,22 s, au Drake Track & Field Stadium de UCLA, à Los Angeles (Californie, USA), le 9 mars 2017. Ashrita Furman (USA), détenteur de plusieurs records, a réalisé **le 100 m le plus rapide sur un ballon sauteur**, couvrant cette distance en 30,2 s, le 16 novembre 2004.

 JUIN 7 À Mayence (DEU), en 2015, Christian Schäfer (DEU) **mémorise le plus de cartes à jouer sous l'eau**. Il s'est souvenu de 56 cartes dans l'ordre une fois de retour sur la terre ferme.

 JUIN 8 En 2014, Mario Barth (DEU) achève un sensationnel numéro comique à l'Olympiastadion de Berlin (DEU), vu par 116 498 spectateurs, soit **le plus large public rassemblé par un humoriste en 24 h**.

LE PLUS DE TOUPIES TOURNÉES SIMULTANÉMENT

Le 17 mars 2012, Mark a fait tourner 27 toupies en même temps, au Canal Park Playhouse de New York (USA). Cet exploit faisait partie d'une série de tentatives de records GWR de Mark et de son partenaire de scène, Jonathan Burns, à la fin de leur émission humoristique *Stunt Lab*.

LA PLUS LONGUE DISTANCE PARCOURUE PAR UN YO-YO

L'artiste comique Mark Hayward (USA) est aussi un champion du monde de yo-yo et de toupie. La "promenade de yo-yo" consiste à jeter au sol un yo-yo en train de tourner, afin qu'il roule vers l'avant. Mark a battu ce record au SkillCon, le 15 décembre 2018, lorsque son yo-yo a parcouru 8,28 m.

Mark partage ses conseils sur guinnessworldrecords.com/2020

À VOUS DE JOUER...

Saurez-vous "promener votre yo-yo" plus loin que Mark ? Si vous voulez battre ce record, suivez nos conseils...

• Utilisez un yo-yo acheté dans le commerce, qui n'a subi aucune modification. Faites-vous assister de témoins qui pourront le confirmer.

• Votre tentative de record doit avoir lieu sur une surface plane.

• Le yo-yo doit continuer à tourner pendant tout l'essai. S'il s'arrête, alors il n'est plus question de record !

• Votre témoin doit mesurer la distance horizontale parcourue par le yo-yo et placer un marqueur à l'endroit où il touche en 1er le sol.

• La mesure s'arrête là où le yo-yo quitte le sol pour retrouver votre main. Un témoin doit également marquer cet endroit.

• Lorsque le yo-yo commence à quitter le sol, récupérez-le dans votre main avec un geste contrôlé.

• Chronométrez votre essai et transmettez ce temps avec toutes vos autres preuves.

• Filmez votre essai du début à la fin – y compris la mesure de la distance couverte par le yo-yo. Nous devrons aussi disposer d'un ralenti. Pour connaître toutes les directives officielles du GWR, rendez-vous sur **guinnessworldrecords.com/2020.**

JUIN 9 — Au Skowhegan Moose Festival 2018 du Maine (USA), 1 054 habitants se sont réunis pour battre le record du **plus de personnes à appeler l'orignal en même temps**. Tous ensemble : "Uuuunnnnnnnnggghhhhhhh !"

JUIN 10 — Conçue en 2015, la chambre anéchoïque de Microsoft à Redmond (Washington, USA) est **l'endroit le plus silencieux au monde**, avec un bruit de fond de 20,35 dB, sous le seuil de l'ouïe humaine.

103

ÉQUILIBRISME

Si vous avez la main sûre et la tête froide, une foule de records s'offrent à vous ! Et vous avez certainement chez vous nombre des objets requis. Un jeu de cartes, des bouteilles en plastique et même un range-couverts peuvent permettre de tenter un record – regardez donc ce que ces individus imaginatifs ont réussi à faire ! Qui sait, votre numéro d'équilibriste pourrait rencontrer le succès en ligne, et vos facéties déclencher un engouement médiatique sur les réseaux sociaux...

LE KILOMÈTRE LE PLUS RAPIDE AVEC UNE BOUTEILLE DE LAIT SUR LA TÊTE

En 2004, Ashrita Furman (USA), détenteur de nombreux records, a parcouru 1,6 km en 7 min et 47 s... avec une bouteille de lait sur la tête ! Sept ans plus tard, il a réalisé un nouvel exploit avec une autre bouteille de lait, couvrant **un semi-marathon** en 2 h, 33 min et 28 s.

LE PLUS GRAND CHÂTEAU DE CARTES

L'incroyable Bryan Berg (USA) a construit un château de cartes de 7,86 m de haut, le 16 octobre 2007, à Dallas (Texas, USA). Il a aussi bâti **le plus grand château de cartes en 1 h** (26 étages), sur le plateau de *Live with Kelly and Ryan*, à New York (USA), le 12 septembre 2018.

LE PLUS DE CUILLÈRES EN ÉQUILIBRE SUR LE VISAGE

En 2009, Aaron Caissie (CAN, ci-dessus) a gardé 17 cuillères sur son visage pendant les 5 s requises par les directives du GWR. Avec 31 cuillères, Dalibor Jablanović (SRB) détient le record, établi à Stubica (SRB) le 28 septembre 2013. Seriez-vous capable de faire mieux ?

LE 100 M LE PLUS RAPIDE AVEC UNE BATTE DE BASEBALL SUR LE DOIGT

Il n'est pas qu'un jongleur habile (voir p. 100)... Le 5 octobre 2018, David Rush (USA, ci-dessus et ci-dessous) a couru le 100 m avec une batte de baseball en équilibre sur un doigt en 14,28 s, à la Boise High School (Idaho, USA). La même année, il a aussi battu les records GWR du **100 m** et du **mile les plus rapides avec un œuf dans une cuillère tenue avec la bouche** – respectivement 18,47 s et 8 min 2,44 s –, à Boise (Idaho, USA).

LE PLUS DE GÂTEAUX EN ÉQUILIBRE SUR LE MUSEAU D'UN CHIEN

Même votre toutou peut tenter des records d'équilibre ! Combien de gâteaux arrivera-t-il à garder sur le museau avant que la pile s'effondre (ou qu'il cède à la tentation) ? Ci-contre, l'ancien détenteur du record, Monkey, qui avait gardé en équilibre 26 biscuits pendant le temps minimal requis de 3 s en 2013. Le champion actuel est le croisé husky George, de Dima Yeremenko (GBR), qui a conservé une tour de 29 gâteaux en équilibre, le 9 mai 2015, au London Pet Show (GBR).

JUIN 11 — **Le 1ᵉʳ vol en hovercraft en public** est réalisé par le Saunders-Roe SR.N1 de 4 t, à Cowes (île de Wight, GBR), en 1959. Il atteint une vitesse de 68 nœuds (126 km/h).

JUIN 12 — **La comète à s'approcher au plus près de la Terre** est P/1999 J6. En 1999, elle passe à une distance de 0,012 unité astronomique (1 795,174 km) de notre planète – un peu moins de 5 fois la distance Terre-Lune.

LE PLUS DE CHAMALLOWS ATTRAPÉS AVEC LA BOUCHE EN 1 MIN

Le 17 septembre 2017, Josh (ci-dessous) a attrapé 42 chamallows lancés par Jake Triplett (USA) en 60 s, à Dallas (Texas, USA). Ce record a depuis été battu par Ashrita Furman (voir ci-contre) et Bipin Larkin (tous 2 USA), qui se sont lancé 45 de ces friandises, à Ottawa (Ontario, CAN), le 30 septembre 2018.

LE PLUS DE RETOURNEMENTS DE BOUTEILLE À L'AVEUGLE EN 1 MIN

Le célèbre jongleur et artiste Josh Horton (USA) détient un grand nombre de titres du Guinness World Records. Le 16 décembre 2018, il a retourné une bouteille à 360° 27 fois en 60 s avec un masque sur les yeux. Seules ont été comptées les rotations dans lesquelles la bouteille est retombée sur sa base, conformément aux règles du GWR (voir ci-dessous). Cet exploit a eu lieu au Rio All-Suite Hotel & Casino de Las Vegas (Nevada, USA), lors du SkillCon 2018.

▶ Josh partage ses conseils sur guinnessworldrecords.com/2020

LE PLUS DE ROULEAUX DE PAPIER TOILETTE EN ÉQUILIBRE SUR LA TÊTE EN 30 S

Josh a gardé 12 rouleaux de papier toilette sur sa tête pendant 30 s, à Malibu (Californie, USA), le 16 mai 2017. Son exploit a fait l'objet d'une vidéo en direct sur la page Facebook du GWR.

À VOUS DE JOUER...

Êtes-vous prêt à battre le record de retournements de bouteille à l'aveugle détenu par Josh ? Lisez attentivement les règles du GWR !

- Pour votre tentative, vous pouvez utiliser toute bouteille en plastique de 500 à 590 ml en vente dans le commerce.
- Remplissez la bouteille d'un tiers de liquide environ. (Vous devez fournir une preuve vidéo.)
- Bandez-vous les yeux. Vous ne devez rien voir du tout – un témoin indépendant doit le confirmer.
- Commencez les 2 mains à plat sur une surface dure et plane, la bouteille devant vous.
- Au signal du départ, lancez la bouteille en l'air à 360°. Elle doit atterrir verticalement, sans basculer.

- N'oubliez pas que vous ne pouvez utiliser qu'une seule main et une seule bouteille pour cet exploit.
- Si la bouteille n'atterrit pas verticalement, le retournement n'est pas validé.
- Après chaque retournement, replacez la bouteille pour le prochain essai – pas de tricherie ! Personne ne doit vous aider.
- Seuls les retournements de bouteille réalisés dans le temps imparti, 60 s, seront comptabilisés.
- Pour connaître toutes les directives officielles du GWR, rendez-vous sur **guinnessworldrecords. com/2020**.

JUIN 13 En 2015, Tom Hudson (GBR) et Pete Fletcher (AUS) parcourent **la plus longue distance à la rame en 24 h** (116,76 milles nautiques, soit 216,24 km) lors d'une traversée de l'Atlantique.

JUIN 14 *Spider-Man : Turn Off the Dark*, comédie musicale inspirée de la vie du super-héros de bande dessinée, débute à Broadway en 2011. C'est **la production théâtrale la plus chère** (75 millions $).

105

SPEEDCUBING

En 2020, le Rubik's Cube d'Ernő Rubik (HUN) fête le 40ᵉ anniversaire de son lancement international. Au format d'origine 3 x 3 x 3 s'ajoutent notamment le Megaminx, en forme de dodécaèdre, le Pyraminx et le Clock (à 2 faces, chacune avec 9 horloges à aligner). Grégoire Pfennig (FRA) a même conçu une version 33 x 33 x 33 – **le plus grand Magic Cube**, composé de 6 153 pièces. Si vous débutez, commencez par le modèle le plus simple ! De nombreuses vidéos vous montrent comment résoudre l'emblématique casse-tête 3 x 3 x 3. Une fois que vous aurez réussi, publiez une vidéo vous montrant en pleine action afin d'inspirer peut-être d'autres personnes. Et si vous avez envie d'entrer dans le GWR, voici les records à battre...

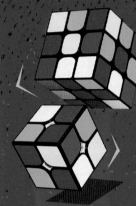

LE PLUS RAPIDE À RÉSOUDRE UN RUBIK'S CUBE

Du Yusheng (CHN) a résolu un Rubik's Cube standard 3 x 3 x 3 en 3,47 s, le 24 novembre 2018, au concours Wuhu Open (province d'Anhui, CHN). Aucune vidéo officielle n'a été filmée, mais on peut voir le moment où Yusheng a résolu le cube sur une vidéosurveillance, observé par un juge officiel (ci-dessus).

ENCORE PLUS FORT !

(Illustrations ci-dessous, de gauche à droite)

Le plus rapide à résoudre...
- **un Rubik's Cube sur un pogo stick** : George Turner (GBR), en 24,13 s ;
- ▶ **3 Rubik's Cubes en jonglant** : Que Jianyu (CHN), en 5 min et 2,43 s ;
- **2 Rubik's Cubes simultanément sous l'eau** : Krishnam Raju Gadiraju (IND), en 53,86 s.

Le plus de Rubik's Cubes résolus...
- **sur un caster board** : 151, par Nikhil Soares (IND) ;
- **d'une main en nageant sur place** : 137, par Shen Weifu (CHN) ;
- **sur un vélo** : 1 010, par P. K. Arumugam (IND) ;
- **sur un monocycle** : 250, par Caleb McEvoy (USA).

LE TEMPS MOYEN LE PLUS COURT POUR RÉSOUDRE UN RUBIK'S CUBE 3 x 3 x 3 LORS D'UN CONCOURS

Feliks Zemdegs (AUS) a réalisé un temps moyen de 5,80 s, le 15 octobre 2017, au Malaysia Cube Open, à Bangi. Il a accompli cet exploit lors du 1ᵉʳ tour du concours, avec des temps individuels de 5,99 s, 5,28 s, 5,25 s, 6,13 s et 9,19 s. Feliks a ensuite remporté la catégorie 3 x 3 x 3.

Il avait auparavant été **le plus rapide à résoudre un Rubik's Cube** (4,22 s), battu par Du Yusheng en novembre 2018 (voir ci-dessus à gauche).

JUIN 15 En 1982, László Kiss inscrit **le triplé le plus rapide en coupe du monde**, en marquant 3 fois en 7 min pour la Hongrie contre l'équipe d'El Salvador, à Elche (ESP).

JUIN 16 En 2009, "Rutt Mysterio", alias Michele Forgione (ITA), sort **le plus long rot au monde** (1 min et 13 s), au concours de rots du 13ᵉ festival annuel Hard Rock Beer, à Reggiolo (ITA).

▶ LE PLUS RAPIDE À RÉSOUDRE UN RUBIK'S CUBE 6 x 6 x 6

Max (voir l'encadré à droite) a terminé un Rubik's Cube 6 x 6 x 6 en 1 min et 13,82 s, au WCA Asian Championship de Taipei, (Taipei chinois), les 17-19 août 2018. Max est aussi le plus rapide à résoudre de nombreux autres Rubik's Cubes, parmi lesquels :

- le 4 x 4 x 4 en 18,42 s ;
- le 5 x 5 x 5 en 37,28 s ;
- le 7 x 7 x 7 en 1 min et 47,89 s.

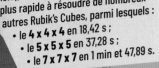

▶ LE TEMPS MOYEN LE PLUS COURT POUR RÉSOUDRE UN RUBIK'S CUBE D'UNE MAIN

En 9,42 s, Max Park (USA) a résolu d'une seule main un Rubik's Cube 3 x 3 x 3, au Berkeley Summer 2018 (Californie, USA), les 15-16 septembre. Il a réalisé des temps individuels de 9,43 s, 11,32 s, 8,80 s, 8,69 s et 10,02 s, les temps les plus bas et les plus hauts n'étant pas comptés pour la moyenne, conformément aux règles de la World Cube Association.

LE PLUS RAPIDE À RÉSOUDRE UN...

3 x 3 x 3	Du Yusheng (CHN, extrême gauche)	3,47 s
2 x 2 x 2	Maciej Czapiewski (POL)	0,49 s
3 x 3 x 3 yeux bandés	Jack Cai (AUS)	16,22 s
3 x 3 x 3 une seule main	Feliks Zemdegs (AUS, à gauche)	6,88 s
3 x 3 x 3 avec les pieds	Daniel Rose-Levine (USA)	16,96 s
Megaminx	Juan Pablo Huanqui Andia (PER)	27,81 s
Pyraminx	Dominik Górny (POL)	0,91 s
Clock	Suen Ming Chi (CHN)	3,29 s
Skewb	Jonatan Kłosko (POL)	1,10 s
Square-1	Vicenzo Guerino Cecchini (BRA)	5 s

Source : World Cube Association, le 12 avril 2019

LE PLUS RAPIDE À RÉSOUDRE UN RUBIK'S CUBE 4 x 4 x 4 LES YEUX BANDÉS

Le 20 mai 2018, Stanley Chapel (USA) a terminé un Rubik's Cube 4 x 4 x 4 les yeux bandés en 1 min et 29 s, à Fort Wayne (Indiana, USA). Il a battu le record au World Cube Association's CubingUSA Great Lakes Championship. Pour connaître les règles de la WCA sur la résolution de cubes, voir à droite.

▶ Stanley partage ses conseils sur guinnessworldrecords.com/2020

▶ Vous trouverez des vidéos de cubing sur guinnessworldrecords.com/2020

À VOUS DE JOUER...

Le GWR suit les règles de la World Cube Association (WCA) pour la résolution rapide. Voici un aperçu de ces règles pour tenter de résoudre des cubes les yeux bandés. Pour plus de détails, rendez-vous sur worldcubeassociation.org.

- Vous devez fournir votre propre bandeau pour la tentative de record.
- Chaque catégorie de résolution rapide a une limite de temps que les organisateurs annoncent avant le début de chaque essai.
- Si vous pensez résoudre le cube en moins de 10 min, un StackMat est utilisé. C'est le chronomètre standard des compétitions WCA. Si vous pensez être plus long, le juge emploie un chronomètre classique.

- Avant que vous commenciez, votre cube est mélangé, puis recouvert.
- Le juge vous demande si vous êtes prêt, puis le cube est découvert selon votre réponse. Si un StackMat est utilisé, le chronomètre est déclenché lorsque vous levez les mains.
- Mémorisez l'apparence du cube avant de vous bander les yeux et de commencer à le résoudre. Vous ne pouvez pas manipuler le cube tant que vos yeux ne sont pas couverts.
- Lorsque vous pensez avoir terminé, posez le cube pour arrêter le chronomètre.

 JUIN 17 — Le très attendu *Finding Dory* (USA) de Pixar sort en 2016. Après 2 jours dans les cinémas américains, il devient **le film d'animation ayant rapporté le plus rapidement 100 millions $.**

 JUIN 18 — En 2007, Jeremy Harper (USA) commence à compter pendant 16 h par jour. Il atteint son objectif – 1 million – le 14 septembre, 88 jours plus tard. C'est **le nombre le plus élevé compté à haute voix.**

107

ESPRIT D'AVENTURE

LE RECORD DE VITESSE À VÉLO EN DRAFTING

Le 16 septembre 2018, Denise Mueller-Korenek (USA) a atteint 296,009 km/h à vélo sur la route de Bonneville Salt Flats, Utah (USA). Tractée par un dragster jusqu'à environ 80,5 km/h, dont elle s'est ensuite détachée pour pédaler, elle a été protégée grâce à l'aspiration du véhicule. (L'encart montre l'intérieur du carénage du dragster.) Denise a non seulement pulvérisé son propre record, mais aussi **le record masculin** (268,831 km/h), établi par Fred Rompelberg (NLD) en 1995.

Denise, en photo ci-contre juste avant de pulvériser son record, aux côtés du conducteur du dragster Shea Holbrook.

Le cadre du vélo en carbone de Denise a été fabriqué par KHS Bicycles. Ses pneus de moto de 43 cm ont amélioré la stabilité à pleine vitesse et la fourche de suspension a réduit les vibrations de surface.

SOMMAIRE

LE PLUS GRAND BALLON HABITÉ

Le 14 octobre 2012, tous les regards étaient braqués sur Felix Baumgartner (AUT). Ce sportif de l'extrême était sur le point de rejoindre la stratosphère dans une capsule suspendue au plus grand ballon ayant jamais transporté un être humain, puis de tenter une chute libre spectaculaire vers la Terre. S'il réussissait, il battrait plusieurs records du monde. Mais s'il échouait...

Sept années de préparation ont été nécessaires pour ce grand jour, l'aboutissement de la mission Red Bull Stratos de saut dans l'espace, un projet destiné à fournir de précieuses données pour la NASA et l'US Air Force... et à pulvériser des records en vigueur depuis plus de 50 ans.

Felix a décollé de Roswell, Nouveau-Mexique (USA), à 9 h 28 heure locale (15 h 28 GMT). Au moment où il a atteint son point de largage – près de 2 h plus tard –, le ballon gonflé à l'hélium, constitué d'une enveloppe en polyéthylène de 0,02 mm d'épaisseur, avait atteint près de 850 000 m³ et 129,2 m de diamètre. **Plus grand ballon habité**, il faisait près de 11 fois le volume du *Virgin Otsuka Pacific Flyer*, piloté par Richard Branson (GBR) et Per Lindstrand (SWE) en 1991 lors de **la 1re traversée du Pacifique en montgolfière**. Il était aussi près de 40 fois plus volumineux que les plus grandes montgolfières actuelles.

S'élançant de sa capsule à 38 969 m, Felix a entamé sa descente vertigineuse, et atteint Mach 1,25 (1 357,6 km/h) – **la chute libre la plus rapide** (voir ci-contre). Il est devenu **le 1er être humain à avoir franchi le mur du son en chute libre**, 65 ans jour pour jour après que l'ancien officier de l'US Air Force Chuck Yeager (USA) a voyagé plus vite que le son – bien qu'il fût à bord d'une fusée Bell X-1 à l'époque !

Nos artistes du numérique ont arrimé cet incroyable ballon à terre, en le plaçant aux côtés du Tower Bridge (Londres, GBR). Comme il est difficile de concevoir comment un objet aussi volumineux est capable de flotter à près de 39 km d'altitude, nous avons pris quelques libertés artistiques pour vous donner un ordre d'idée. En réalité, le ballon n'aurait jamais pu atteindre son volume maximum près du sol. Cela dit, il était plus grand au décollage : 167,6 m contre 101,8 m arrivé à destination.

L'hélium, plus léger que l'air, contenu dans l'enveloppe ne pouvait atteindre une telle expansion qu'au moment de rejoindre la stratosphère, où la pression atmosphérique représente 2 % de celle mesurée au niveau de la mer. À ce stade (dit *float altitude* ou "altitude de flottement"), la densité moyenne de l'air à l'intérieur du ballon étant la même qu'à l'extérieur, le ballon a abandonné sa forme allongée pour prendre une apparence ovoïde, de plus de 2 fois la largeur du pont central du Tower Bridge !

DE GRANDS ESPOIRS : HONORER UN EXPLOIT DÉMESURÉ

C'est avec grand plaisir que le GWR a remis à Felix Baumgartner un certificat pour saluer cet exploit hors du commun. "Notre objectif premier a toujours été d'améliorer la sécurité dans l'espace, a-t-il expliqué. Mais en recevant le certificat du Guinness World Records, j'ai pris conscience que mon rêve supersonique était enfin devenu réalité."

SUR LE POINT D'ENTRER DANS L'HISTOIRE

La capsule de Felix a atteint une telle altitude qu'il a pu observer la courbure de la Terre. "Je sais que le monde entier est en train de me regarder", a-t-il annoncé dans sa radio après avoir atteint son point de lancement. "J'aimerais que vous puissiez voir ce que je vois. Il faut parfois aller très haut pour comprendre à quel point on est petit... Je rentre à la maison maintenant." Puis il s'est jeté dans le vide.

Peu après sa sortie, Felix s'est mis à tourner sur lui-même, mais en professionnel du parachutisme, il a réussi à se stabiliser et à éviter la perte de connaissance. Il est parvenu à contrôler sa descente, bien que sa visière se soit embuée, déployant son parachute à une altitude d'environ 1 525 m, avant de se poser dans le désert, près de Roswell, quelque 9 min après avoir sauté de la capsule.

Deux ans plus tard, le 24 octobre 2014, Alan Eustace (USA) réalisait **la plus longue chute libre** et **le plus haut vol en ballon habité** (41 422 m), devançant Felix.

SUR TERRE

LE VOYAGE LE PLUS RAPIDE À VÉLO À TRAVERS L'EURASIE

Jonas Deichmann (DEU) a traversé l'Eurasie d'ouest en est à vélo – de Cabo da Roca (PRT) à Vladivostok, (RUS) – en 64 jours, 2 h et 26 min du 2 juillet au 4 septembre 2017. Il a connu de nombreux déboires en chemin, notamment la chute subite du cadre de son vélo en République tchèque !

Le plus de continents visités en 1 jour

Le 29 avril 2017, Thor Mikalsen et son fils Sondre Moan Mikalsen (tous 2 NOR) ont visité plusieurs villes sur 5 continents : Istanbul (TUR, Asie), Casablanca (MAR, Afrique), Lisbonne (PRT, Europe), Miami (USA, Amérique du Nord) et Barranquilla (COL, Amérique du Sud).

Ce faisant, ils ont égalé l'exploit de Gunnar Garfors (NOR) et Adrian Butterworth (GBR), qui ont voyagé entre Istanbul et Caracas (VEN, Amérique du Sud) le 18 juin 2012.

Le plus de pays visités à vélo en 7 jours (hommes)

David Haywood (GBR) a traversé 13 pays à vélo, de Mouland (BEL) à Bratislava (SVK), entre le 12 et le 18 octobre 2017.

Le plus long voyage en voiture dans un pays

Greg Cayea et Heather Thompson (tous 2 USA) ont parcouru 58 135,87 km en voiture à travers les États-Unis du 11 juillet au 9 novembre 2016.

Le plus long périple à moto dans un pays est de 115 093,94 km, exploit de Gaurav Siddharth (IND), du 17 septembre 2015 au 27 avril 2017, en Inde.

Le plus rapide pour traverser à vélo le Japon dans la longueur (du nord au sud) (hommes)

Il a fallu seulement 7 jours, 19 h et 37 min à Hiroki Nagaseki (JPN) pour traverser le Japon à vélo. Parti de Cape Sōya sur l'île d'Hokkaidō le 19 juillet 2018, il est arrivé une semaine plus tard au cap Sata, Kyūshū.

La femme détentrice de ce record est Paola Gianotti (ITA). Elle a traversé le Japon en 8 jours, 16 h et 19 min du 24 mai au 1er juin 2017. En 2014, cette cycliste hors pair a aussi fait le tour du monde le plus rapide à vélo (femmes) : 144 jours.

La traversée la plus rapide du désert de Simpson à pied

Avec des températures atteignant les 50 °C, Pat Farmer (AUS) a bouclé sa traversée de 379 km du désert de Simpson – le 4e plus grand désert d'Australie – en 3 jours, 8 h et 36 min, le 26 janvier 1998.

LE PLUS RAPIDE POUR RELIER L'ALASKA À USHUAIA À VÉLO (PANAMÉRICAINE)

Il n'aura fallu que 84 jours, 11 h et 50 min à Michael Strasser (AUT) pour relier à vélo Prudhoe Bay, Alaska (USA), à Ushuaia (ARG), et boucler son périple le 16 octobre 2018. Il a quitté Prudhoe Bay 2 mois après Dean Stott (GBR), qui détenait le record sur cette route. Ce dernier avait fait le voyage du sud vers le nord en 99 jours, 12 h et 56 min entre le 1er février et le 11 mai.

Progressant en moyenne à 4,75 km/h, il a traversé 1 162 dunes.

La traversée la plus rapide du désert de Simpson dans un véhicule terrestre solaire a pris 4 jours, 21 h et 23 min. Les époux Mark et Denny French (tous 2 AUS) ont rejoint Birdsville, dans le Queensland (AUS), le 11 septembre 2017.

Le plus long périple pieds nus

Du 1er mai au 12 août 2016, Eamonn Keaveney (IRL) a parcouru 2 080,14 km à travers l'Irlande sans chaussures.

La plus jeune personne ayant effectué le tour du monde à moto (hommes)

Kane Avellano (GBR, né le 20 janvier 1993) a achevé son tour du monde à moto au South Shields Town Hall, Tyne and Wear, (GBR), le 19 janvier 2017 – un jour avant son 24e anniversaire. Parti le 31 mai 2016, Avellano a traversé 36 pays et 6 continents à moto et parcouru au total 45 161 km au cours de ce voyage épique.

Le voyage le plus rapide de Land's End à John o' Groats sur une tondeuse à gazon

Le 30 juillet 2017, Andy Maxfield (GBR) a traversé le Royaume-Uni dans sa longueur en 5 jours, 8 h et 36 min pour recueillir des fonds destinés à la Fondation Alzheimer.

LE TOUR DU MONDE LE PLUS RAPIDE À VÉLO (FEMMES)

Jenny Graham (GBR) a bouclé son tour du monde à vélo en 124 jours et 11 h entre le 16 juin et le 18 octobre 2018, débuté et achevé à Berlin (DEU). Elle a réalisé cet exploit sans assistance, en transportant son matériel.

Mark Beaumont (GBR) a fait le tour du monde à vélo le plus rapide en 78 jours, 14 h et 40 min. Parti de l'Arc de Triomphe à Paris (FRA) le 2 juillet 2017 pour son "Tour du Monde en 80 Jours", il y est revenu le 18 septembre 2017.

LA TRAVERSÉE LA PLUS RAPIDE DES ÉTATS-UNIS À PIED

Pete Kostelnick (USA) a couru du San Francisco City Hall, Californie, au New York City Hall en 42 jours, 6 h et 30 min du 12 septembre au 24 octobre 2016.

Preuve que cet exploit est difficile, le record de la traversée la plus rapide des États-Unis à pied (femmes) est détenu depuis plus de 40 ans par Mavis Hutchinson (ZAF). Elle a bouclé son périple en 69 jours, 2 h et 40 min, du 12 mars au 21 mai 1978.

JUIN 19 En 1963, la cosmonaute Valentina Tereshkova (URSS) réalise un vol de 2 jours, 22 h et 50 min – 48 orbites autour de la Terre – à bord de *Vostok 6*. **Première femme à être allée dans l'espace**, elle est déclarée "Héroïne de l'URSS".

JUIN 20 L'émeraude des Rockfeller de 18,04 carats devient l'émeraude la plus chère au carat en 2017. Elle s'est vendue au prix de 5 511 500 $ – prime d'acheteur comprise – chez Christie's à New York (USA).

90 MILE STRAIGHT
AUSTRALIA'S LONGEST STRAIGHT ROAD
146.6 km

LE TOUR DU MONDE LE PLUS RAPIDE À VÉLO EN TANDEM (HOMMES)

Les cyclistes John Whybrow (gauche) et George Agate (droite) (tous 2 GBR) ont réalisé le tour du monde en tandem en 290 jours, 7 h et 36 min, débuté et achevé à Canterbury (GBR) du 8 juin 2016 au 25 mars 2017. Surnommés "The Tandem Men", les 2 hommes ont parcouru plus de 29 946, 80 km sur leur vélo Orbit fabriqué sur mesure baptisé "Daisy".

Le duo a récolté des milliers de livres pour 3 associations caritatives : Homeless Charity Porchlight, London's Great Ormond Street Hospital et Water Aid.

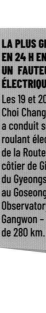

LA PLUS GRANDE DISTANCE EN 24 H EN CONDUISANT UN FAUTEUIL ROULANT ÉLECTRIQUE AVEC LA BOUCHE

Les 19 et 20 avril 2017, Choi Chang-hyun (KOR) a conduit son fauteuil roulant électrique le long de la Route 7, du village côtier de Giseong, Province du Gyeongsang du Nord, au Goseong Unification Observatory, Province du Gangwon – soit une distance de 280 km.

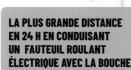

LE PLUS LONG PÉRIPLE VIA LES TRANSPORTS EN COMMUN DANS UN SEUL PAYS

Durga Charan Mishra et son épouse Jotshna (tous 2 IND) ont parcouru 29 119 km à travers l'Inde en utilisant les transports en commun du 18 février au 30 mars 2018. Ayant débuté et achevé leur voyage épique à la gare Puri d'Odisha, ils ont amélioré le précédent record de plus de 19 300 km !

JUIN 21 Manikyam, **la plus petite vache**, mesure 61,1 cm du sabot au garrot (l'arête entre les omoplates) en 2014. Elle appartient à Akshay N. V. (IND) de Kerala, (IND).

JUIN 22 En 2017, Ashrita Furman (USA) parcourt **la plus longue distance en marchant avec une tondeuse à gazon en équilibre sur le menton (en marche)** – 71,5 m – à New York (USA).

DANS LES AIRS

La 1re personne ayant volé à l'horizontale

Le 24 juin 2004, l'aviateur Yves Rossy, alias Jetman (CHE), a volé 4 min à une vitesse de 180 km/h à 1 600 m au-dessus de l'aérodrome d'Yverdon, près du lac de Neuchâtel (CHE). L'engin de Jetman se composait de 2 réacteurs alimentés au kérosène, munis d'ailes pliables en carbone de 3 m d'envergure.

Le saut en wingsuit le plus haut

James Petrolia (USA) a réalisé un saut en wingsuit à 11 407,4 m d'altitude – près de 14 fois la taille du **plus haut building**, le Burj Khalifa de Dubaï (ARE) – au-dessus de Davis en Californie (USA), le 11 novembre 2015.

Le plus haut saut sans parachute

Le 30 juillet 2016, le parachutiste Luke Aikins (USA) a sauté de 7 600 m d'un avion pour atterrir sain et sauf dans un filet de 929 m² à Simi Valley, dans le sud de la Californie (USA). Il avait passé un an et demi à préparer cette cascade baptisée "Saut du ciel", retransmise en direct à la TV. Utilisant un GPS pour le guider vers le filet, Aikins a atteint une vitesse en chute libre de 193 km/h au cours de son plongeon de 2 min.

LE VOL LE PLUS LONG SUR UN HOVERBOARD

Le 30 avril 2016, l'ancien champion de jet-ski Franky Zapata (FRA) a parcouru 2,25 km sur un hoverboard à Sausset-les-Pins (FRA) — une distance 8 fois supérieure à son précédent record. La machine volante de Zapata, le *Flyboard Air*, est propulsée par un réacteur d'une capacité d'environ 1 000 cv. Un appareil de contrôle portable permet de gérer la poussée des moteurs et le pilote utilise le poids de son corps pour se déplacer, comme sur un gyropode.

LE TOUR DU MONDE LE PLUS RAPIDE SUR DES VOLS RÉGULIERS, EN VISITANT 6 CONTINENTS (ÉQUIPE)

Gunnar Garfors (NOR), Ronald Haanstra et Erik de Zwart (tous 2 NLD) – ci-dessus, de gauche à droite – ont survolé tous les continents, à l'exception de l'Antarctique, en 56 h et 56 min entre le 31 janvier et le 2 février 2018. Partis de Sydney (Océanie), ils ont volé jusqu'à Santiago du Chili (Amérique du Sud), Panama (Amérique du Nord), Madrid (Europe), Alger (Afrique) et Dubaï (Asie) avant de revenir à Sydney.

La plus jeune personne ayant réalisé un tour du monde en avion (solo)

Le 27 août 2016, Lachlan Smart (AUS, né le 6 janvier 1998) a bouclé son tour du monde en avion dans un Cirrus SR22 à l'aéroport de Sunshine Coast dans le Queensland (AUS) à l'âge de 18 ans et 234 jours. Au cours de son voyage épique de 7 semaines, commencé le 4 juillet 2016, il aura parcouru 45 000 km et visité 24 sites dans 15 pays.

La chute libre la plus rapide

Le 13 septembre 2016, Henrik Raimer (SWE) a atteint les 601,26 km/h lors des championnats du monde de la Fédération aéronautique internationale (FAI) à Chicago, Illinois (USA). À titre de comparaison, le faucon pèlerin, **l'oiseau le plus rapide en piqué**, atteint une vitesse terminale d'environ 300 km/h.

La plus grande vitesse à l'horizontale en wingsuit

Fraser Corsan (GBR) a volé à 396,88 km/h en wingsuit au-dessus de Davis, Californie (USA), le 22 mai 2017. Il a tenté cet exploit pour sensibiliser le public à la SSAFA, l'association caritative des forces armées.

Le plus haut vol dans un planeur (hommes)

Jim Payne (USA) et son copilote Morgan Sandercock (AUS) ont atteint 15 902 m d'altitude dans leur planeur *Perlan 2* d'Airbus le 3 septembre 2017. Remorqué jusqu'à 3 200 m au-dessus de la Patagonie argentine, le *Perlan 2* a atteint cette altitude grâce aux courants d'air.

La plus longue chute libre en intérieur

Le 10 juillet 2018, Viktor Kozlov et Sergey Dmitriyev (tous 2 RUS) ont réalisé une chute libre de 8 h 33 min et 43 s dans la soufflerie FreeFly Technology de Perm (RUS).

LES PLUS RAPIDES POUR VISITER LES 7 CONTINENTS

Kasey Stewart et Julie Berry (tous 2 USA) ont mis 3 jours, 20 h, 4 min et 19 s pour survoler les 7 continents et atterrir sur l'île du Roi George en Antarctique, le 17 décembre 2017. Ce duo intrépide avait décidé de battre ce record pour s'efforcer de sortir de leur zone de confort et inspirer les autres à faire de même.

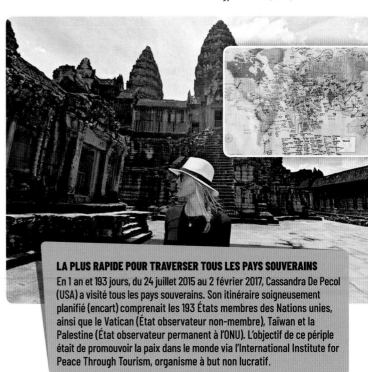

LA PLUS RAPIDE POUR TRAVERSER TOUS LES PAYS SOUVERAINS

En 1 an et 193 jours, du 24 juillet 2015 au 2 février 2017, Cassandra De Pecol (USA) a visité tous les pays souverains. Son itinéraire soigneusement planifié (encart) comprenait les 193 États membres des Nations unies, ainsi que le Vatican (État observateur non-membre), Taïwan et la Palestine (État observateur permanent à l'ONU). L'objectif de ce périple était de promouvoir la paix dans le monde via l'International Institute for Peace Through Tourism, organisme à but non lucratif.

JUIN 23 En 2009, les jeunes mariés Erin Finnegan et Noah Fulmor (tous 2 USA) se disent "oui" en apesanteur à bord du *G-Force One*, un Boeing 727-200 modifié – **le 1er mariage "zéro gravité".**

JUIN 24 Wazir Muhammand Jagirani (PAK) se fait enlever de son rein droit **le calcul rénal le plus lourd**, à Sindh (PAK) en 2008. Il pesait 620 g – l'équivalent du poids d'un ballon de basket.

LA PLUS GRANDE DISTANCE À L'HORIZONTALE EN PARACHUTE

Shinichi Ito (JPN) a parcouru une distance de 46,2 km en parachute au-dessus de Davis, Californie (USA), le 24 février 2018. Après s'être extrait de l'avion, il a ouvert son parachute à environ 7 600 m d'altitude. Lors du vol, Ito a atteint une vitesse horizontale de 279 km/h.

En 2011, Ito a atteint **la plus grande vitesse horizontale en wingsuit** - mais elle a été depuis améliorée de 30 km/h (voir ci-contre).

LE TOUR DU MONDE LE PLUS RAPIDE SUR DES VOLS RÉGULIERS VIA DES POINTS PRESQUE DIAMÉTRALEMENT OPPOSÉS

Le voyage le plus rapide autour du monde en utilisant uniquement des vols réguliers, via des destinations plus ou moins diamétralement opposées, est de 52 h et 34 min, par Andrew Fisher (NZL) du 21 au 23 janvier 2018. Ce dernier a mis le cap sur Shanghai (CHN), Auckland (NZL), Buenos Aires (ARG) et Amsterdam (NLD), avant de revenir à Shanghai.

LE PLUS D'AÉRODROMES VISITÉS EN 24 H EN AVION À VOILURE FIXE

Le 13 juin 2017, Mike Roberts et Nicholas Rogers (tous 2 GBR) ont décollé de Wellesbourne, Warwickshire (GBR), à 3 h 32 et atterri sur la piste de 87 aérodromes, avant de revenir au même endroit à 21 h 38. Ils ont tous deux remis leurs taxes d'atterrissage à l'association caritative Air Ambulance. Roberts avait déjà relevé ce défi en solitaire.

JUIN 25 En 1977, le garde forestier Roy Sullivan (USA) est frappé par la foudre pour la 7e fois - **la personne la plus foudroyée ayant survécu**. Il a tout de même eu les sourcils calcinés, subi une brûlure à l'épaule et perdu un ongle de pied.

JUIN 26 Zeng Jinlian (CHN), **la plus grande femme de tous les temps**, est née en 1964 dans le village de Yujiang, Province du Hunan (CHN). Le jour de son décès, le 13 février 1982, elle mesurait 246,3 cm.

SUR L'EAU

Les 1ʳᵉˢ sœurs ayant traversé ensemble un océan

Le 19 janvier 2018, Camilla et Cornelia Bull (toutes 2 NOR) sont arrivées à Antigua après avoir traversé l'Atlantique à bord d'*Ellida* avec un équipage de 4 femmes. Parties de La Gomera, îles Canaries (ESP), le 14 décembre 2017, elles ont bouclé leur voyage en 36 jours, 9 h et 53 min.

La plus jeune personne ayant traversé un océan en duo

Jude Massey (GBR, né le 6 mars 1999) était âgé de 18 ans et 318 jours au départ de sa traversée de l'Atlantique avec son demi-frère Greg Bailey pour relier la Grande Canarie à la Barbade. Ils ont navigué du 18 janvier au 11 mars 2018 à bord du bateau *Peter*.

La plus jeune personne ayant traversé l'Atlantique en équipe (itinéraire Trade Winds II)

Duncan Roy (GBR, né le 16 août 1990) a commencé sa traversée de Mindelo, Cap-Vert, vers la Guyane le 19 janvier 2018,

à l'âge de 27 ans et 156 jours. Il a bouclé cette traversée de 1 765 milles marins (3 269 km) en 27 jours, 16 h et 50 min, sur le bateau *Rose*, avec un équipage de 5 personnes.

La traversée en solitaire la plus rapide de l'Atlantique d'ouest en est à la rame au départ du Canada

Du 27 juin au 4 août 2018, Bryce Carlson (USA) a relié St John's, Terre-Neuve (CAN), à St Mary's Harbour, Îles Scilly (GBR), à la rame en 38 jours, 6 h et 49 min. Il a parcouru 2 302 milles marins (4 263 km) à une vitesse moyenne de 2,5 nœuds (4,63 km/h) à bord de son bateau open-class *Lucille*.

La 1ʳᵉ personne ayant traversé un océan à la godille

Hervé le Merrer (FRA) a traversé l'Atlantique d'est en ouest d'El Hierro, îles Canaries, à la Martinique en 58 jours du 28 décembre 2017 au 24 février 2018. Il a propulsé son bateau *Eizh an Eizh*, spécialement conçu pour la course, à l'aide d'une seule rame placée à l'arrière de l'embarcation.

La 1ʳᵉ double traversée de la Manche à la nage par une équipe de relais de 2 personnes (hommes)

Le 9 juillet 2018, John Robert Myatt et Mark Leighton (tous 2 GBR) ont relié l'Angleterre à la France à la nage en 10 h et 41 min et effectué la traversée retour en 12 h et 8 min, soit un total de 22 h et 49 min. Les 2 hommes ont alterné des sessions de 1 h.

> Edgley a souffert d'inflammations du cou, de 37 piqûres de méduse et sa langue a été en partie désintégrée par l'exposition à l'eau salée !

LE 1ᵉʳ TOUR DU ROYAUME-UNI À LA NAGE PAR ÉTAPES

Du 1ᵉʳ juin au 4 novembre 2018, Ross Edgley (GBR) a réalisé le 1ᵉʳ tour de l'Angleterre, du Pays de Galles, de l'Irlande et de l'Écosse à la nage avec assistance, commencé et achevé à Margate, Kent (GBR). Nageant en sessions de plusieurs heures, de jour comme de nuit, il a enchaîné jusqu'à 40 000 mouvements de bras par jour. Au cours de ce périple de 157 jours, il aura parcouru 2 884 km ponctués de 209 étapes. Son exploit a été homologué par la World Open Water Swimming Association.

LA PLUS GRANDE VITESSE ATTEINTE EN PLANCHE À VOILE (MILLE MARIN)

Le 21 juillet 2018, le véliplanchiste Vincent Valkenaers (BEL, à gauche) a atteint une vitesse de 42,23 nœuds (78,21 km/h) lors du Speed Sailing Event de La Palme (FRA). Le même jour, Zara Davis (GBR) a atteint **la plus grande vitesse en planche à voile chez les femmes (mille marin)** : 37,29 nœuds (69,06 km/h). Le World Sailing Speed Record Council a homologué ces exploits.

Le 22 juillet 2018, les membres de l'équipe "Sportfanatic" Dezider Pék, Ondrej Pék et Richard Nyary (tous SVK) ont réussi **la 1ʳᵉ double traversée de la Manche par une équipe de relais de 3 personnes**. Ils ont relié l'Angleterre à la France à la nage en 10 h et 14 min et parcouru le chemin retour en 12 h et 20 min – soit 22 h et 34 min au total. Les 2 records ont été établis sous l'égide de la Channel Swimming Association (CSA).

La 1ʳᵉ personne ayant parcouru la longueur de la Manche à la nage

Le 12 juillet 2018, Lewis Pugh (GBR/ZAF) a quitté Land's End, Cornouailles (GBR), et parcouru 560 km à la nage avant de rejoindre l'Admiralty Pier à Douvres, Kent (GBR), le 29 août 2018, temps validé par la CSA. Pugh a nagé entre 10 et 20 km par jour pendant 49 jours.

La personne la plus âgée ayant accompli la "Triple couronne" de nage en eau libre

Le 30 juin 2018, Pat Gallant-Charette (USA, née le 2 février 1951) a bouclé le "20 Bridges", le tour de Manhattan à la nage (45,8 km), à l'âge de 67 ans et 148 jours. Elle avait déjà parcouru le

détroit de Catalina (32,5 km) qui sépare l'île Santa Catalina du sud de la Californie (USA) le 18 octobre 2011, et la Manche (33,7 km) le 17 juin 2017.

La plus haute vague en kitesurf

Le 8 novembre 2017, Nuno Figueiredo (PRT) a surfé une vague de 19 m à Praia do Norte, Nazaré (PRT). Son exploit a été validé par l'International Federation of Kitesports Organisations (IFKO).

La 1ʳᵉ femme ayant remporté une course de voiliers autour du monde

Le 28 juillet 2018, Wendy Tuck (AUS) a conduit son équipage du *Sanya Serenity Coast* sur la ligne d'arrivée et remporté la Clipper Round the World Yacht Race 2017-2018. Ils ont traversé 6 océans et parcouru 40 000 milles marins (74 080 km) en 11 mois.

L'OCEANS SEVEN

L'Oceans Seven est un marathon de natation regroupant 7 traversées de détroit dans le monde : le canal du Nord, la Manche et les détroits de Catalina, de Gibraltar, de Tsugaru, de Molokai et de Cook.

Le 29 août 2013, Darren Miller (USA, né le 13 avril 1983, à droite) a bouclé son 7ᵉ parcours à la nage – le canal du Nord, entre l'Irlande du Nord et l'Écosse – à l'âge de 30 ans et 138 jours, devenant **la plus jeune personne ayant réalisé l'Oceans Seven**. Il a réussi à boucler chaque traversée à la 1ʳᵉ tentative – ce qui n'était jamais arrivé auparavant.

La personne la plus âgée ayant réalisé l'Oceans Seven est Antonio Argüelles Díaz-González (MEX, né le 15 avril 1959, ci-dessous). Le 3 août 2017, il a terminé avec succès sa dernière traversée à l'âge de 58 ans et 110 jours.

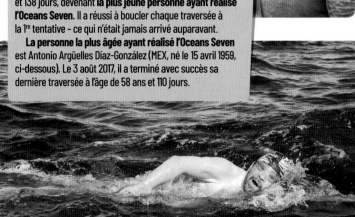

JUIN 27 — Les championnats du monde de charmeurs de vers de terre de Willaston 2009, Cheshire (GBR), sont remportés par Sophie Smith, âgée de 10 ans (GBR). Elle a attiré 567 vers hors du sol en 30 min – **le plus de vers charmés**.

JUIN 28 — En 2005, la chatte Smarty réalise son 79ᵉ vol en avion – **le plus de vols pour un animal de compagnie**. Elle effectue ses voyages entre l'Égypte et Chypre, avec ses propriétaires Peter et Carole Godfrey (tous 2 GBR).

LA TRAVERSÉE LA PLUS RAPIDE DE L'ATLANTIQUE EN SOLO PAR UNE FEMME (ITINÉRAIRE TRADE WINDS I)

Du 1er février au 22 mars 2018, Kiko Matthews (GBR) a ramé de la Grande Canarie, îles Canaries, à Port St Charles, Barbade, en 49 jours, 7 h et 15 min. Elle a parcouru 2 602 milles marins (4 819 km) à une vitesse moyenne de 2,2 nœuds (4 km/h) à bord de *Soma*. Son exploit a été homologué par l'Ocean Rowing Society.

Matthews apprend qu'elle est atteinte de la maladie de Cushing en 2009 et combat 2 tumeurs. Elle navigue pour récolter des fonds destinés à l'hôpital où elle a été traitée.

LES PLUS JEUNES FRÈRES AYANT TRAVERSÉ UN OCÉAN (ÂGE MOYEN)

Du 12 décembre 2017 au 29 janvier 2018, les frères Kiran (GBR, né le 11 septembre 1998, en haut) et Jay Olenicz (GBR, né le 17 juin 1995) ont traversé l'Atlantique d'est en ouest en tandem en 48 jours, 6 h et 31 min à bord de *White Dwarf*. Au départ de leur "Oarsome Odyssey", l'âge moyen du duo était de 20 ans et 318 jours.

LE PLUS RAPIDE POUR TERMINER LA COURSE À LA VOILE SYDNEY HOBART

Lancée en 1945, la Sydney Hobart Yacht Race débute le 26 décembre, le jour du Boxing Day (fête anglo-saxonne). Les voiliers quittent Sydney, Nouvelle-Galles du Sud, pour rejoindre Hobart, Tasmanie (AUS). Les 26–27 décembre 2017, *LDV Comanche* a remporté la course en 1 jour, 9 h, 15 min et 24 s. Il a été déclaré vainqueur après que le gagnant initial, *Wild Oats XI*, a écopé d'une pénalité de 1 heure pour son implication dans une quasi-collision au départ de la course.

LA PLUS RAPIDE POUR ACCOMPLIR DES MARATHONS À LA NAGE DE 10 KM DANS 6 CONTINENTS (FEMMES)

En 2018, Jaimie Monahan (USA) a effectué 6 marathons de 10 km à la nage sur plusieurs continents en 15 jours, 8 h et 19 min. Ayant débuté en Colombie le 13 août 2018, elle a nagé ensuite en Australie, à Singapour, en Égypte et en Suisse/France avant de terminer à New York (USA) le 28 août 2018.

JUIN 29 James Stephens (USA) engloutit **le plus de saucisses en 1 min** (10) sur le plateau de *Guinness World Records Gone Wild !* à Los Angeles, Californie (USA), en 2012.

JUIN 30 Le script de 173 pages du film *Le Parrain* (USA, 1972) appartenant à la star Marlon Brando se vend à 312 800 $ en 2005 – **le script de film le plus cher vendu aux enchères.**

117

SUR LA ROCHE

Le plus d'ascensions de l'Everest en 1 an

La plus haute montagne du monde (8 848 m) a été escaladée 809 fois en 2018, contre 667 ascensions réussies en 2013.

Durant la saison d'escalade du printemps 2018, 18 alpinistes népalaises ont réussi à atteindre le sommet – le plus d'ascensions de l'Everest par des femmes d'un même pays en 1 an.

Le plus de frères et sœurs ayant escaladé l'Everest

Le 23 mai 2018, Dawa Diki Sherpa est devenue le 7e enfant de Chhiring Nurbu Sherpa et Kimjung Sherpa (tous NPL) à avoir gravi le sommet de l'Everest. Six de ses frères l'avaient déjà escaladé. Cette prouesse permet d'égaler le record établi par les enfants de Nima Tsiri Sherpa – le "porteur de messages" d'Edmund Hillary lors de la 1re ascension de l'Everest en 1953 – et Pema Futi Sherpa (tous 2 NPL), dont le 7e fils a atteint le sommet de l'Everest le 23 mai 2007. Ensemble, les enfants de ce dernier ont réalisé le plus d'ascensions de l'Everest par des frères et sœurs (total), soit 63.

Le plus rapide à escalader l'Everest et le K2

Sherpa Mingma Gyabu (NPL) a atteint le sommet de l'Everest le 21 mai 2018 et le K2 (8 611 m), la 2e plus haute montagne, le 21 juillet 2018. Il a ainsi égalé le

record de 61 jours établi par Robert "Rob" Hall (NZL) entre le 9 mai (Everest) et le 9 juillet 1994 (K2). Tous deux ont grimpé à l'aide d'oxygène en bouteille.

La femme la plus rapide pour accomplir cet exploit – également à l'aide d'oxygène – est l'alpiniste He Chang-Juan (CHN). Elle a atteint le sommet de l'Everest le 16 mai 2018 puis celui du K2 66 jours plus tard.

La plus haute montagne indomptée en hiver

En mars 2019, le K2 restait invaincu pendant la saison hivernale, tant calendaire (20 décembre au 20 mars) que météorologique (1er décembre au 28 février). Jusqu'à présent, seules 5 personnes ont tenté l'ascension de la montagne en hiver, sans qu'aucune n'y parvienne.

Le plus d'ascensions du K2 (individuel)

Fazal Ali (PAK) a escaladé le K2 3 fois : le 26 juillet 2014, le 28 juillet 2017 et le 22 juillet 2018. Les 3 ascensions ont été réalisées sans apport d'oxygène.

Le plus d'ascensions du K2 en 1 an est de 64 en 2018, contre 51 en 2004.

Le plus d'ascensions du Kangchenjunga en 1 an

La 3e plus haute montagne (8 586 m) a été escaladée 46 fois lors de la saison d'escalade 2018 – 6 de plus que le précédent record, établi en 1989.

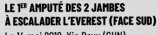

LA 1RE DESCENTE À SKIS DU K2

Le 22 juillet 2018, après avoir escaladé le K2 sans oxygène, Andrzej Bargiel (POL) est devenu la 1re personne à avoir rejoint le camp de base à skis. Il lui a fallu près de 8 h pour réaliser la descente.

La 1re descente à skis du Lhotse

Le 30 septembre 2018, Hilaree Nelson et Jim Morrison (tous 2 USA) ont escaladé le Lhotse, montagne de l'Himalaya (8 516 m) – la 4e plus haute montagne du monde –, et emprunté le couloir à skis du sommet au Camp 2 à 6 400 m.

L'ascension la plus rapide du Lhotse-Everest (femmes)

Le meilleur temps pour escalader le Lhotse et l'Everest par une femme est de 21 h et 30 min par Qu Jiao-Jiao (CHN). Elle a atteint le sommet du Lhotse à 8 h 20 le 20 mai 2018, puis celui de l'Everest à 5 h 50 le lendemain matin.

Le plus d'ascensions à plus de 8 000 m sans oxygène

Ayant commencé par l'Everest le 24 mai 2000, Denis Urubko (KAZ/RUS) a réalisé 20 ascensions de montagnes de plus de 8 000 m sans apport d'oxygène. Son ascension la plus récente est celle du Kangchenjunga, le 19 mai 2014.

L'ASCENSION LA PLUS RAPIDE D'EL CAPITÁN

Le 6 juin 2018, Alex Honnold et Tommy Caldwell (tous 2 USA) ont touché le "Nez" du pic El Capitán dans le parc national de Yosemite (Californie, USA), en 1 h, 58 min et 7 s. C'était la 3e fois en 1 semaine que le duo battait le record de l'ascension la plus rapide du monolithe en granit de 1 095 m de haut, devenant les 1ers à passer sous la barre des 2 h.

LE PLUS D'ASCENSIONS DE L'EVEREST (INDIVIDUEL)

Le 16 mai 2018, Kami Rita Sherpa (alias "Thapkhe", NPL) a réussi l'ascension de l'Everest pour la 22e fois de sa carrière. Ce sherpa de 48 ans partageait jusque-là le record avec Apa Sherpa (NPL) et Phurba Tashi Sherpa (NPL, voir p. 119). Kami Rita a escaladé pour la 1re fois cette montagne le 13 mai 1994.

LE 1ER AMPUTÉ DES 2 JAMBES À ESCALADER L'EVEREST (FACE SUD)

Le 14 mai 2018, Xia Boyu (CHN), 69 ans, a escaladé l'Everest par la face sud. Ses pieds avaient été amputés en 1975 en raison de gelures après avoir tenté d'escalader une 1re fois la montagne, tandis qu'en 1996 ses jambes ont été amputées sous le genou des suites d'un cancer.

Le 1er amputé des 2 jambes à escalader l'Everest est Mark Inglis (NZL). Il est parvenu au sommet via la face nord le 15 mai 2006.

LE PLUS D'ASCENSIONS DE L'EVEREST (INDIVIDUEL, FEMMES)

Lakpa Sherpa (NPL) a atteint le sommet de l'Everest pour la 9e fois le 16 mai 2018. Elle avait escaladé le mont pour la 1re fois le 18 mai 2000 via le versant sud, les 8 autres via la face nord. Entre ses escalades, elle vit dans le Connecticut (USA), où elle travaille comme plongeuse dans un restaurant.

Cherry Yoshitake, alias "Mr Cherry" (JPN), est la personne ayant mangé le plus de haricots blancs à l'aide de baguettes en 1 min (71), dans l'émission *Officially Amazing*, à la RAF Bentwaters (Suffolk, GBR), en 2015.

En 2011, le Juicys Outlaw Grill de Corvallis (Oregon, USA) met en vente le hamburger le plus cher pour 5 000 $. Il pèse 352,44 kg – l'équivalent de 5 hommes.

Plain a imaginé son record "7 en 4" (7 sommets en 4 mois) en 2014 alors qu'il se remettait d'une "fracture du pendu" – cou brisé – survenue en nageant.

▶ LE PLUS RAPIDE À ESCALADER LES 7 SOMMETS, CARSTENSZ INCLUS (HOMMES)

Quand Steven Plain (AUS) a atteint le sommet de l'Everest le 14 mai 2018, il a bouclé son ascension des plus hauts sommets des 7 continents en 117 jours, 6 h et 50 min. Il a débuté le 16 janvier 2018, après avoir escaladé le Vinson en Antarctique (médaillon, à gauche), avant de poursuivre avec l'ascension de l'Aconcagua (Amérique du Sud), du Kilimandjaro (Afrique, médaillon ci-dessous), du Carstensz (Australasie), de l'Elbrouz (Europe), du Denali (Amérique du Nord) et enfin de l'Everest. Le 3 mars, il a aussi escaladé les 2 228 m du Kosciuszko – le point culminant du continent australien.

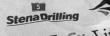

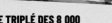

LE 1RE ASCENSION EN HIVER DU GORA POBEDA

Culminant à 3 003 m, le Gora Pobeda (ou Pik Pobeda) est la plus haute montagne de Sibérie, dans le cercle polaire sibérien, ainsi que l'un des endroits les plus froids de la planète. Le 11 février 2018, Tamara Lunger (à gauche) et Simone Moro (à droite, toutes 2 ITA) ont dû affronter des températures de - 40 °C pour atteindre le sommet.

LE TRIPLÉ DES 8 000 LE PLUS RAPIDE (FEMMES)

Nima Jangmu Sherpa (NPL) a escaladé 3 des 5 montagnes de plus de 8 000 m en 23 jours, 18 h et 30 min, entre le 29 avril et le 23 mai 2018. Elle a escaladé le Lhotse et l'Everest avant de parvenir au sommet du Kangchenjunga, la 3e plus haute montagne du monde. Toutes ces ascensions ont été réalisées avec un apport en oxygène.

LE PLUS D'ASCENSIONS À PLUS DE 8 000 M

Le 18 septembre 2017, Phurba Tashi Sherpa (NPL) a réussi sa 35e ascension de l'une des 14 montagnes de plus de 8 000 m quand il a escaladé le Manaslu (8 163 m) au Népal pour la 7e fois. Phurba Tashi a escaladé l'Everest 21 fois en tout – une ascension de moins que Kami Rita Sherpa (voir p. 118).

 JUILL. 3 En 2012, le "Ninja Warrior" et cascadeur Brent Steffensen (USA) réalise un saut de l'ange de 8,8 m de haut dans l'émission *Guinness World Records Gone Wild!*. C'est **le saut le plus haut dans des marshmallows.**

 JUILL. 4 **Le record de la vitesse moyenne la plus élevée lors d'une étape du Tour de France (individuel)** (55,446 km/h) est établi en 2015 par Rohan Dennis (AUS) le jour où il remporte la 1re étape.

119

SUR LA GLACE

LES PREMIERS...

À atteindre le pôle Sud

Le 14 décembre 1911, le capitaine Roald Amundsen et son équipe norvégienne de 5 personnes ont atteint le pôle Sud au terme d'un périple de 53 jours en traîneau à chiens, pour relier la baie des Baleines à la mer de Ross.

À traverser l'Antarctique

L'explorateur Dr Vivian Fuchs (GBR) et son équipe de 12 personnes ont bouclé la 1re traversée de l'Antarctique de part en part le 2 mars 1958. Leur voyage de 3 473 km en tracteur à neige depuis la base Shackleton jusqu'à la base Scott, via le pôle Sud, a duré 99 jours.

Fuchs fut précédé au pôle par une équipe de soutien partie de la base Scott Base chargée du ravitaillement en nourriture et en essence. Elle était dirigée par Sir Edmund Hillary (NZL), à qui l'on doit **la 1re ascension de l'Everest** en 1953 aux côtés de Tenzing Norgay (Tibet/IND).

À traverser l'océan Arctique

Dirigée par Wally Herbert (GBR), l'expédition transarctique britannique a quitté Point Barrow en Alaska (USA) le 21 février 1968 et rejoint l'archipel de Seven Island, au nord-est de Svalbard (NOR), 463 jours plus tard, le 29 mai 1969. Le voyage, effectué en traîneaux tirés par des huskys, couvrait 4 699 km et une dérive de 1 100 km ; la distance en ligne droite était de 2 674 km. Les autres membres de l'expédition étaient Major Ken Hedges, Allan Gill et Dr Roy "Fritz" Koerner (tous GBR).

À atteindre le pôle Nord en solitaire

Le 29 avril 1978, Naomi Uemura (JPN) a atteint le pôle Nord, après avoir parcouru près de 770 km en traîneau à chiens à travers la banquise arctique. Il était parti de l'île d'Ellesmere, à l'extrême nord du Canada, 55 jours plus tôt.

La 1re expédition en solitaire au pôle Sud sans assistance a été réalisée par Erling Kagge (NOR) qui a parcouru 1 400 km à skis. Parti de l'île Berkner, il a atteint le pôle le 7 janvier 1993.

À faire le tour de l'Antarctique en solitaire sur un voilier

C'est à bord du *Trading Network Alye Parusa* que Fedor Konyukhov (RUS) a bouclé le tour de l'Antarctique en 102 jours, 1 h, 35 min et 50 s, et rejoint l'Australie le 7 mai 2008.

Lisa Blair (AUS) a battu **le record féminin** à bord de *Climate Action Now*, atteignant Albany (Australie-Occidentale) le 25 juillet 2017 après 183 jours, 7 h, 21 min et 38 s. Le World Speed Sailing Record Council a validé les 2 records.

LES PLUS RAPIDES...

À nager 1 km dans l'eau glacée (femmes)

Le 6 janvier 2019, Alisa Fatum (DEU) a nagé 1 km dans de l'eau glacée en 12 min et 48,7 s, lors de l'Ice Swimming German Open de Veitsbronn (DEU).

LE 1ER TOUR DE L'ANTARCTIQUE SUR UN VOILIER AU SUD DU 60E PARALLÈLE

Le 23 décembre 2017, le capitaine Mariusz Koper et son équipage de 8 personnes (tous POL) ont quitté Le Cap (ZAF) à bord du voilier *Katharsis II* pour faire le tour de l'Antarctique complètement au sud du 60e parallèle (médaillon). Le 5 avril 2018, au terme d'un périple de 102 jours, 22 h, 59 min et 5 s, ils ont atteint Hobart en Tasmanie (AUS). Ils ont réalisé le tour de l'Antarctique au sud du 60e degré de latitude sud en 72 jours et 6 h, du 7 janvier à 8 h du matin UTC (temps universel coordonné) au 20 mars 2018 à 14 h UTC.

Sven Elfferich (NLD) a décroché **le titre masculin** le 16 février 2019, avec un temps de 11 min et 55,4 s, à Freizeitverein Altenwörth (AUT). Les 2 records ont été homologués par l'International Ice Swimming Association.

À traverser l'Antarctique en solitaire

Børge Ousland (NOR) a achevé un périple de 2 690 km en kite-ski le 19 janvier 1997, 65 jours après être parti de l'île Berkner (mer de Weddell). C'est aussi **la 1re traversée en solitaire de l'Antarctique**. Il a tiré un traîneau de 185 kg de provisions et de matériel jusqu'à la base Scott, non loin de la base McMurdo.

Le 26 décembre 2018, l'athlète d'endurance Colin O'Brady (USA) a annoncé avoir effectué la 1re traversée en solo de l'Antarctique sans assistance, en skiant entre les plateaux de glace de Ronne et de Ross, via le pôle Sud, en 54 jours. Au sein de la communauté des explorateurs polaires, cette annonce a soulevé la polémique autour des règles définissant une vraie traversée de l'Antarctique. Le GWR travaille à une mise à jour du règlement.

À faire un trek au pôle Nord

Le 14 avril 2010, David Pierce Jones (GBR), Richard Weber (CAN), Tessum Weber (CAN) et Howard Fairbank (ZAF) ont atteint le pôle Nord en 41 jours, 18 h et 52 min. Au cours de ces 785 km, l'équipe n'a reçu aucune assistance et n'a été ravitaillée qu'une fois.

LA VITESSE MOYENNE LA PLUS RAPIDE À LA RAME AU LARGE DE L'OCÉAN ARCTIQUE

Du 20 au 27 juillet 2017, l'équipe du *Polar Row* a navigué à une vitesse moyenne de 2,554 nœuds (4,73 km/h) entre Tromsø (NOR) et Longyearbyen (SJM). L'équipe se composait de Fiann Paul (ISL), Tathagata Roy (IND), Jeff Willis (GBR), Carlo Facchino (USA) et Tor Wigum (NOR).

LA PLUS JEUNE PERSONNE À ATTEINDRE LE PÔLE SUD À PIED

Lewis Clarke (GBR, né le 18 novembre 1997) était âgé de 16 ans et 61 jours quand il a atteint le pôle Sud géographique le 18 janvier 2014, aux côtés de son guide Carl Alvey. Ils ont parcouru 1 123,61 km à skis depuis Hercules Inlet, situé à quelque 670 km de la côte Antarctique.

La plus jeune personne à réaliser un trek au pôle Nord est Tessum Weber (CAN, né le 9 mai 1989). Il était âgé de 20 ans et 340 jours quand il a bouclé un périple à pied jusqu'au pôle Nord géographique avec 3 autres personnes, le 14 avril 2010.

LE PARCOURS EN KAYAK À LA PLUS HAUTE ALTITUDE

Le 7 mars 2018, Daniel Bull (AUS) a rejoint en kayak Ojo del Salado, **le volcan actif le plus haut** (sommet : 6 887 m) entre le Chili et l'Argentine. Pour atteindre une altitude de 5 707 m, il a ramé sur un lac semi-gelé sur 2,5 km. Au début 2019, Daniel Bull a cédé son record de **la plus jeune personne à faire l'ascension des 7 sommets et des 7 sommets volcaniques** à Satyarup Siddhanta (IND, né le 29 avril 1983), lequel avait 35 ans et 261 jours quand il est parvenu à son 14e pic, le mont Sidley en Antarctique, le 15 janvier.

JUILL. 5 En 2018, le maestro des marathons musicaux Pandit Sudarshan Das (GBR) réalise **le plus long roulement de tambour en solo**, à Londres (GBR). Il a duré pas moins de... 14 h !

JUILL. 6 En 2012, Jerry Mumma (USA) s'offre **la tarte la plus chère vendue aux enchères**. Il a payé 3 100 $ pour ce dessert au beurre de cacahuètes et à la banane, à Rich Hill (Missouri, USA).

LA 1RE ESCALADE DES CHUTES GLACÉES DU NIAGARA

Le 27 janvier 2015, le célèbre aventurier de l'extrême Will Gadd (CAN) a escaladé la cascade en partie glacée des Horseshoe Falls - la plus grande des chutes d'eau qui composent les chutes du Niagara -, à la frontière américano-canadienne, dans le cadre d'un événement sponsorisé par Red Bull.

Le même jour, Sarah Hueniken (CAN) a réalisé **la 1re escalade sur glace des chutes du Niagara (femmes)**. Les 2 alpinistes ont suivi une bande de glace issue des projections de la chute de 9 m de large, le long de la paroi gauche des Horseshoe Falls. Ci-dessous, le duo intrépide s'étreint après avoir réussi cet exploit.

Se rappelant les sensations de cette escalade sur la glace près de l'une des chutes d'eau les plus puissantes au monde, Gadd a dit : "Cela vous retourne les intestins et on se sent très, très petit..."

LE PLUS DE PISTES PARCOURUES À SKIS EN 8 H

Jimmy DeMartini (USA) a dévalé 70 pistes à skis en 8 h, au Beaver Creek Resort d'Avon (Colorado, USA), le 17 mars 2017. Il a ensuite déclaré en toute modestie qu'il avait réalisé cet exploit en "visant le bas et en laissant la gravité faire le travail".

LA PLUS GRANDE DISTANCE VERTICALE SUR UN SNOWBOARD EN 12 H

Le 12 mars 2017, Keith Hayes (GBR) a descendu 19 000 m sur son snowboard en une demi-journée, au Sun Peaks Resort (Colombie-Britannique, CAN). Hayes a réalisé 40 descentes en 9 h et 48 min, remontant à chaque fois au sommet sur un télésiège. Il s'est entraîné pendant 9 mois pour ce record qui lui a permis de récolter des fonds pour Epilepsy Action.

LA PLUS GRANDE DISTANCE VERTICALE EN SKI-BOB EN 24 H (ÉQUIPE DE 2)

Pour ce record, 2 concurrents réalisent des descentes répétées d'une piste et on calcule la distance totale parcourue. Hermann Koch et Harald Brenter (tous 2 AUT) ont descendu 63 638 m sur leur petit vélo muni de skis, les 11-12 avril 2018, à Obertauern (Salzbourg, AUT) - une distance équivalente à 7 fois l'Everest, **la plus haute montagne**. Pour garder le moral, ils descendaient la plupart du temps l'un à côté de l'autre, se relayant sur un "master" ski-bob. Seule la distance parcourue par ce véhicule comptait pour le total.

Le duo a également battu **le record de distance verticale en ski-bob en 1 h** (3 086 m) **et en 12 h** (32 736 m).

JUILL. 7 Chad Netherland (USA) réussit à **retenir 2 avions le plus longtemps** en 2007. Il empêche le décollage de 2 avions légers Cessna, en les tirant dans la direction opposée, pendant 1 min et 0,6 s.

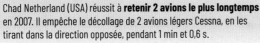
JUILL. 8 En 1990, Pedro Monzón (ARG) est **le 1er joueur à se faire expulser d'une finale de coupe du monde de la FIFA**, à la 65e min d'Allemagne-Argentine. L'Argentine termine le match avec 9 joueurs ; l'Allemagne gagne 1-0.

LA PLUS RAPIDE À COURIR UN ULTRA-MARATHON SUR CHAQUE CONTINENT

Dans le cadre du World Marathon Challenge, Nahila Hernández San Juan (MEX) a participé à 7 courses de 50 km sur plusieurs continents, en 6 jours, 11 h, 29 min et 3 s, du 23 au 30 janvier 2017. Ses épreuves l'ont conduite en Antarctique (encart), au Chili, aux États-Unis, en Espagne, au Maroc, dans les Émirats arabes unis et en Australie (ci-dessus). C'est à Punta Arenas (CHL) qu'elle a couru le plus vite : 5 h, 11 min et 46 s.

LA PLUS GRANDE DISTANCE EN VÉLO ÉLECTRIQUE EN 12 H

Le 26 août 2018, Christopher Ramsey (GBR) a parcouru 286,16 km en vélo électrique, en 12 h, au Grampian Transport Museum d'Alford (Aberdeenshire, GBR). En tant qu'"aventurier du développement durable" autoproclamé, Ramsey voulait tenter ce record pour sensibiliser le public à la réduction des émissions de gaz à effet de serre dans les grandes villes.

Le meilleur temps pour réaliser un marathon dans les 50 États des États-Unis (femmes)

Entre le 3 octobre 1999 et le 20 août 2017, Suzy Seeley (USA) a couru un marathon dans chaque État des États-Unis en un temps global de 176 h, 35 min et 40 s. Elle a terminé toutes ses courses en moins de 4 h.

La traversée à vélo de l'Europe (de Cabo da Roca à Ufa) la plus rapide par un individu

Leigh Timmis (GBR) a relié à vélo le point le plus à l'ouest du Portugal à Ufa (RUS), en 16 jours, 10 h et 45 min, du 10 au 26 septembre 2018. Il a battu le précédent record de 10 jours.

Le record en **équipe** pour cet itinéraire est de 29 jours,

5 h et 25 min. Il a été établi par Helmy Elsaeed (EGY), Måns Möller, Christer Skog, Tony Duberg et Per-Anders Lissollas (tous SWE), du 21 mai au 19 juin 2017.

Le plus long périple à vélo dans un seul pays (individuel)

Benjamin Woods (AUS) a parcouru 18 922,47 km à vélo à travers l'Australie, du 10 juin 2017 au 10 février 2018.

Le plus long périple à vélo dans un seul pays (équipe) a été réalisé 2 mois plus tard. Du 2 octobre 2017 au 3 avril 2018, M.J. Pavan et Bhagyashree Sawant (tous 2 IND) ont parcouru 19 400,83 km en Inde.

La traversée la plus rapide du désert d'Atacama à pied

Parti de San Pedro de Atacama (CHL) le 15 septembre 2018, l'athlète d'ultra-marathon Michele Graglia (ITA) a rejoint le sud de Copiapó à pied en 8 jours, 16 h et 58 min. Au cours de ce périple, il a traversé les quelque 1 200 km du désert aride d'Atacama – **l'endroit le plus sec** sur Terre (voir p. 18). En juillet 2018, Graglia a remporté le Badwater 135 – décrit comme la "course à pied la plus dure au

Le duo a traversé 21 États et 5 territoires de l'Union et visité quelque 600 écoles pour sensibiliser le public à la poliomyélite et à l'importance de l'éducation.

monde" –, un périple reliant la vallée de la Mort au mont Whitney (Californie, USA).

Le plus rapide à visiter tous les pays en utilisant les transports en commun terrestres

L'aventurier Graham Hughes (GBR) a visité 197 pays en 4 ans et 31 jours, sans prendre une seule fois l'avion, entre le 1er janvier 2009 et le 31 janvier 2013. Il s'est notamment rendu dans 193 pays membres de l'ONU, mais aussi au Kosovo, au Vatican, en Palestine et à Taïwan. En chemin, Hughes a pu voir le décollage d'une navette spatiale, mais il a aussi échappé à des pirates aux Seychelles et a été arrêté en Estonie et au Cameroun.

Le plus rapide à visiter tous les pays de l'UE

Parti le 5 septembre 2017 d'Irlande, Sabin Stanescu

(ROM) a traversé les 28 pays de l'Union européenne en 3 jours, 22 h et 39 min, avant de rejoindre la Bulgarie.

Le tour du monde le plus rapide en voiture

Le record du **1er et du plus rapide tour du monde en voiture par un homme et une femme** sur 6 continents, selon les règles en vigueur en 1989 et 1991 qui prévoient une distance parcourue en voiture supérieure à celle de l'équateur (40 075 km), est détenu par Saloo Choudhury et son épouse Neena Choudhury (tous 2 IND). Leur voyage, commencé et achevé à Dehli (IND), a duré 69 jours, 19 h et 5 min, du 9 septembre au 17 novembre 1989. Le couple conduisait une Hindustan "Contessa Classic" de 1989.

▶ LE PLUS HAUT DANS UNE VOITURE ÉLECTRIQUE

Le 24 septembre 2018, Chen Haiyi (CHN) a conduit un SUV électrique ES8 de NIO à 5 715 m d'altitude pour rejoindre le glacier Purog Kangri au Tibet (CHN). L'idée de cette tentative était de démontrer la fiabilité du ES8 dans des conditions extrêmes. Pour se rendre sur le 3e plus grand glacier du monde, le véhicule a dû résister à des températures inférieures à 0 °C.

▶ Vous découvrirez de nombreuses vidéos sur guinnessworldrecords.com/2020

 JUILL. 9 En 2011, le Soudan du Sud (capitale : Djouba) fait sécession avec le Soudan et devient **le pays indépendant le plus récent**. C'est le 1er nouvel État depuis la proclamation d'indépendance du Monténégro en 2006.

 JUILL. 10 Au Brésil, Karoline Mariechen Meyer (BRA) réussit **l'apnée volontaire la plus longue (femmes)** – 18 min et 32,59 s – en 2009. Elle avait inhalé de l'oxygène pendant 24 min avant la tentative de record.

Le plus long voyage en bateau alimenté à l'énergie solaire

MS *TÛRANOR PlanetSolar* a réalisé le tour du globe d'est en ouest, soit 32 410 milles nautiques (60 023 km), du 27 septembre 2010 au 4 mai 2012. Mis à l'eau à Monaco, le bateau a traversé le canal de Panama avant de revenir dans la principauté 1 an et 220 jours plus tard – **le 1er tour du monde en bateau alimenté à l'énergie**

LE PLUS RAPIDE À PARCOURIR 100 000 MILES À VÉLO (HOMOLOGUÉ PAR LA WUCA)

Entre le 15 mai 2016 et le 11 juillet 2017, Amanda Coker (USA) a battu un record vieux de 77 ans en parcourant 160 934 km en 423 jours. Il a été homologué par la World UltraCycling Association (WUCA). Il s'agit notamment de **la plus longue distance parcourue à vélo en 1 an (validée par la WUCA)** : 139 326,34 km.

LA PLUS GRANDE DISTANCE EN SKI NAUTIQUE TRACTÉ PAR UN DIRIGEABLE

Le 13 mars 2018, Kari McCollum (USA) a fait du ski nautique sur le lac Elsinore (Californie, USA), sur 11,1 km, tractée par un dirigeable évoluant à 17 nœuds (31,4 km/h). Cette étudiante de 20 ans a battu tous les autres concurrents lors d'une compétition aquatique organisée par l'opérateur de téléphonie mobile T-Mobile (USA).

solaire. L'équipe était menée par Raphaël Domjan (CHE).

Sur terre, **la plus longue distance parcourue en voiture électrique solaire** est de 29 753 km. Partie le 26 octobre 2011, l'équipe du SolarCar Project Hochschule Bochum (DEU) a en effet parcouru le monde pendant plus d'un an avant de boucler son parcours au mont Barker (AUS), le 15 décembre 2012.

Le plus long voyage en voiture alimentée au carburant alternatif

Tyson Jerry et l'équipe Driven to Sustain (tous 2 CAN) ont parcouru 48 535,5 km dans une voiture alimentée au biodiesel et à l'huile végétale, du 15 novembre 2009 au 4 mai 2010. Jerry a commencé son périple à Columbia (Caroline du Sud, USA) et s'est fourni en carburant dans différents endroits, notamment des fast-foods, pour rejoindre Vancouver (Colombie-Britannique, CAN).

La plus grande distance en bateau électrique, charge unique (non solaire)

Pike a parcouru 220,4 km sans s'arrêter sur la Tamise, à Oxfordshire (GBR), les 20 et 21 août 2001. Le bateau était équipé d'un moteur électrique alimenté par batterie de la Thames Electric Launch Company.

La traversée en paddle la plus rapide des détroits de Floride (femmes)

Les 26 et 27 juin 2018, Victoria Burgess (USA) a surmonté des vents forts pour relier en paddle La Havane (CUB) à Key West (Floride, USA), en 27 h et 48 min. Burgess a tenté ce record pour sensibiliser le public à la préservation des océans et encourager les femmes à la pratique du sport.

La personne la plus âgée ayant traversé la Manche (femmes)

À l'âge de 71 ans et 305 jours, Linda Ashmore (GBR, née le 21 octobre 1946) a relié l'Angleterre à la France à la nage, le 21 août 2018. Elle avait déjà battu ce record en 2007, en traversant la Manche à l'âge de 60 ans et 302 jours.

▶ LA PLUS GRANDE PYRAMIDE HUMAINE À SKI NAUTIQUE

La Mercury Marine Pyramid (USA) a érigé une pyramide humaine de 80 skieurs nautiques, à Janesville (Wisconsin, USA), le 18 août 2018. Disposés en plusieurs pyramides de 4 étages, les membres de la Rock Aqua Jays Water Ski Show Team se sont maintenus sur plus de 350 m, sur la Rock River, à l'aide de bouées de couleur pour marquer la distance.

LE VOYAGE LE PLUS RAPIDE DE LAND'S END À JOHN O' GROATS SUR UNE TRIPLETTE

Du 16 au 22 juin 2018, le trio Harry Fildes (au centre) et les frères Alexander (à droite) et Fergus Gilmour (tous GBR) a parcouru la Grande-Bretagne dans la longueur sur un vélo de 3 places en 6 jours, 13 h et 30 min. Ils se sont lancés dans cette aventure pour récolter des fonds pour Whizz-Kidz, une association caritative aidant les jeunes handicapés, et pour un hôpital de la région.

 JUILL. 11 En 2014, le mangeur de l'extrême Takeru Kobayashi (JPN) engloutit **le plus de hamburgers en 3 min** (12), à Milan (ITA). Il ajoute de la mayonnaise, le seul condiment autorisé.

 JUILL. 12 Lors de la Deja Moo Country Fair de Cowaramup de 2014 (Australie-Occidentale), 1 352 participants réalisent **le plus grand rassemblement de personnes déguisées en vache**.

SOCIÉTÉ

LA CHAÎNE YOUTUBE LA PLUS POPULAIRE D'UN YOUTUBER NÉ APRÈS 2010

Au 1er février 2019, la chaîne Ryan ToysReview avait accumulé 27 143 288 795 vues et 18 052 910 abonnés depuis son lancement, le 16 mars 2015. C'est la plus populaire des chaînes YouTube animées par une personne née après 2010 ("génération alpha"). Le youtubeur s'appelle Ryan, 8 ans (né le 6 octobre 2010 aux USA). Il se met en scène (ou parfois ses parents) dans des vidéos dans lesquelles il commente des jeux et des jouets. Pour protéger la vie privée de l'enfant, les parents ont gardé secret son nom de famille.

Ryan apparaît également dans une 2e chaîne YouTube, Ryan's Family Review. Elle traite d'activités, de voyages et de vacances en famille avec ses parents et ses 2 petites sœurs jumelles, Emma et Kate.

WALKS & STOMPS!
MOTORIZED!
ROARS!
2½ FEET TALL!
STANDS & ROARS!
ROAR!

GUINNESS WORLD RECORDS

SOMMAIRE

プラレール
いっぱいつなげる！
E7系
北陸新幹線かがやき
&ドミカ駅前ロー
SERIES E7 HOKURIKU SHINKANSEN

大地が5編成の
E7系北陸新幹線がやき！

TOMICA
HYPERCITY

Pirate Whale

WINGS FLAP!

LE PLUS RICHE

À la tête d'Amazon – **le plus grand site de vente en ligne** – et propriétaire du quotidien *Washington Post*, Jeff Bezos (USA) est confortablement installé dans son fauteuil de super-riche. Mais riche... comment ? Et cela représente quoi, tout cet argent ?

Avec une fortune estimée à 112 milliards $ au 6 mars 2018, selon la liste Forbes des milliardaires, Jeffrey Preston Bezos est la personne la plus riche du monde. Si l'on en faisait un tas de billets de 1 $, sa fortune formerait une montagne de 77 m de haut, dépassant le palais de Buckingham, à Londres. Pour l'épuiser en un an, il faudrait dépenser 3 550 $ par seconde !

Bezos est né le 12 janvier 1964 à Albuquerque (Nouveau-Mexique, USA). Son inventivité s'est manifestée très tôt : il a démonté son berceau avec un tournevis alors qu'il ne savait pas encore marcher. Adolescent, il a créé une alarme pour dissuader ses frères d'entrer dans sa chambre. Au lycée, il a fondé le Dream Institute, un camp d'été d'un nouveau genre pour étudiants. Il est entré dans la banque d'investissement D. E. Shaw & Co. en 1990, devenant le plus jeune vice-président qu'ait connu la société. Déjà, Bezos était conscient du potentiel illimité des ventes sur Internet et, en 1994, il a démissionné pour créer une librairie en ligne dans un garage à Seattle (Washington, USA). Bezos a baptisé sa société

LE 1ᴱᴿ MILLIARDAIRE EN CENTAINE DE MILLIARDS

Sa fortune de 112 milliards $ place Jeff Bezos d'Amazon dans une catégorie à part. Mais la richesse est relative. Corrigée en fonction de l'inflation, la fortune du patron de Microsoft, Bill Gates (USA), en 1999 correspond à 136 milliards $ actuels. Et le magnat du pétrole John D. Rockefeller (USA) aurait été encore plus riche (voir p. 132).

Il ne s'agit que des fortunes matérielles. Que dire de Genghis Khan, dont l'empire occupait une grande partie de l'Asie ? Ou de l'empereur Mansa Moussa Iᵉʳ du Mali, au XIVᵉ siècle, que le magazine *Time* décrit comme "riche au-delà de toute description" ? On ne peut que deviner leur immense richesse.

Un billet de 1 $ pesant environ 1 g, cette montagne de billets pèserait environ 112 000 t, soit plus de 4 fois que la statue de la Liberté !

Amazon (après avoir hésité avec Cadabra et MakeItSo.com, inspiré par *Star Trek*). Il a vendu son 1ᵉʳ livre en juillet 1995. *Time* a fait de Bezos sa "personnalité de l'année" en 1999 et l'a désigné comme une des 100 personnes les plus influentes du monde en 2018. Amazon a bientôt vendu de la musique, des films et d'autres choses, ajoutant un service de *cloud* en 2006. La liseuse numérique Kindle, des émissions télévisées et des films, puis le service de livraison Amazon Prime ont bientôt suivi. En 2000, Bezos a fondé la société de voyage spatial Blue Origin. En novembre 2015, le véhicule spatial de la société *New Shepard* a effectué **le 1ᵉʳ atterrissage contrôlé d'une fusée suborbitale**. Bien sûr, le propriétaire de Buckingham Palace aurait son mot à dire sur tous ces billets déversés dans sa cour... Aussi surprenant que cela puisse paraître, la fortune de Bezos est 200 fois supérieure à celle de la reine Elizabeth !

LA COUR DU PALAIS DE BUCKINGHAM

Hôtel particulier construit en 1703, le palais de Buckingham fut agrandi dans les années 1820 par deux ailes et une entrée triomphale (Marble Arch), créant un édifice en forme de "U". En 1847, l'arche a été déplacée près de Hyde Park et remplacée par une 4ᵉ aile, créant un rectangle que nous avons rempli avec la fortune de Jeff Bezos !

L'ÉCOLE EN FOLIE

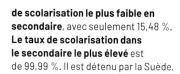

Le taux de scolarisation le plus élevé en primaire
Selon l'Institut de statistique de l'Unesco, en 2015 (date la plus récente offrant des données assez complètes), 99,94 % des enfants du Royaume-Uni en âge de fréquenter l'école primaire y étaient inscrits.
Le pays au **taux de scolarisation en primaire le plus faible** est le Liberia : seulement 37,68 % des enfants en âge de fréquenter le primaire sont scolarisés, selon la même source. Ce pays affichait aussi **le taux** de scolarisation le plus faible en **secondaire**, avec seulement 15,48 %.
Le taux de scolarisation dans le secondaire le plus élevé est de 99,99 %. Il est détenu par la Suède.

Le budget de l'éducation le plus élevé
Selon les chiffres de *The Economist* pour 2018, le Danemark dépense un peu plus de 8 % de son produit national brut (PNB) dans l'éducation. Il est talonné par le Zimbabwe et Malte, qui y consacrent aussi plus de 8 %.

L'enseignant à la carrière la plus longue
Medarda de Jesús León de Uzcátegui (VEN, 8 juin 1899-2002) a commencé à enseigner à l'âge de 12 ans, dans une école qu'elle avait fondée avec ses deux sœurs, à Caracas (VEN). Après s'être mariée en 1942, elle a dirigé sa propre école depuis chez elle. Elle enseignait encore en 1998, 87 ans plus tard.

La personne la plus âgée à s'inscrire dans le primaire
Le 12 janvier 2004, Kimani Ng'ang'a Maruge (KEN), arrière-grand-père, s'est inscrit à l'âge de 84 ans à l'école Standard One, Kapkenduiyo Primary School, Eldoret (KEN). Un an plus tard, il s'est exprimé auprès des Nations unies au sujet de l'importance de l'enseignement gratuit au primaire.

Le plus d'écoles fréquentées
Wilma Williams (USA) a fréquenté 265 écoles différentes de 1933 à 1943. Ses parents travaillaient dans le show business.

L'ÉCOLE DE PÈRE NOËL LA PLUS ANCIENNE ENCORE EN ACTIVITÉ
Nous savons qu'il n'existe qu'un père Noël. Mais ceux qui rêvent de passer son manteau rouge peuvent se tourner vers l'école Charles W. Howard Santa Claus. Fondée à Albion (New York, USA), en octobre 1937, elle était toujours en activité en décembre 2018, après avoir été déplacée à Midland (Michigan, USA). Tous les ans en octobre, l'école propose une session de 3 jours pour découvrir l'univers du père Noël, dont un atelier de jouets et des leçons de traîneau.

Le plus de promotions représentées à une réunion du secondaire
Le 20 octobre 2018, l'Independence High School All Class Reunion 2018 (USA) a rassemblé des élèves de 41 promotions consécutives, à San Jose (Californie, USA).
À cette occasion, les anciens élèves ont apposé **le plus grand nombre de signatures dans un album de promotion en 24 h** (1 902). Bien qu'ils aient eu la journée entière, les anciens élèves ont tous signé en 3 h 30.

La réunion de promo après la plus longue période
En 1999, la promo 1929 du Kindergarten and Continuation School de Bluefield (Virginie-Occidentale, USA) de Miss Blanche Miller a tenu sa 1re réunion 70 ans après. 55 % des anciens élèves y ont participé, bien que 10 d'entre eux soient décédés.

La plus grande réunion de promo
4 268 anciens élèves ont participé à la réunion organisée par Bhashyam Rama Krishna et Bhashyam Educational Institutions (tous 2 IND) à Guntur (Andhra Pradesh, IND), le 24 décembre 2017.

L'ÉCOLE À LA PLUS HAUTE ALTITUDE
Entre 1986 et août 2017, une petite école primaire se situait à 5 022 m d'altitude, à Pumajiangtangxiang (Tibet, CHN). Ses élèves, issus de la communauté nomade locale, étaient une centaine lorsqu'elle a fermé ses portes, notamment en raison du froid extrême, du manque de fournitures et du faible niveau d'oxygène affectant la concentration des enfants.

LA CARRIÈRE LA PLUS LONGUE EN TANT QUE...
Enseignant de langues : Ren Zuyong (CHN, né le 14 mars 1939, ci-dessus, à droite) a enseigné au collège pendant 58 ans, de 1959 au 30 août 2017, à Xinghua (province de Jiangsu, CHN).
Enseignant de musique : Charles Wright (USA, né le 24 mai 1912, ci-dessus à gauche) a commencé à donner des cours de piano, privés et professionnels, en 1931, et a poursuivi pendant 76 ans, jusqu'à son décès le 19 juil. 2007, à 95 ans et 56 jours.

LE PLUS GRAND NOMBRE DE JUMEAUX DANS LA MÊME PROMO
Les étudiants de 1re année de 2016/2017, de la New Trier High School de Winnetka (Illinois, USA), comptait 44 paires de jumeaux (vérifié le 18 mai 2017). Seules 3 paires (toutes des filles) étaient de vraies jumelles, et 2 paires ne sont pas nées le même jour. Cette promo comptait 1 000 élèves : le nombre de jumeaux de l'établissement représentait plus du triple de la moyenne américaine des naissances multiples.

JUILL. 13 En 2015, il n'a fallu que 14,88 s à S. K. Ashraf (IND) pour **saisir les chiffres 1 à 50**, à Hyderabad (IND). Pour valider ce défi, il a dû insérer un point entre chaque nombre.

JUILL. 14 **La plus grande collection de livres de cuisine** compte 2 970 titres (vérifié en 2013). Ils appartiennent à Sue Jimenez (USA/CAN), qui conserve ses ouvrages culinaires chez elle, à Albuquerque (Nouveau-Mexique, USA).

L'Institut Le Rosey détient ce record depuis la 1re édition du Guinness World Records en 1955, les frais de scolarités étant alors de 2 800 $ par élève et par an.

L'ÉCOLE LA PLUS CHÈRE

L'Institut Le Rosey est une école avec internat située à Rolle (CHE), disposant d'un campus dans la station de ski de Gstaad (encadré). Les frais de scolarités annuels sont de 115 500 CHF (101 260 €)/élève. L'établissement ne compte pas plus de 400 élèves, encadrés par 200 personnes. Parmi les anciens élèves, citons des rois et des chefs d'État (comme Juan Carlos Ier d'Espagne), des membres de dynasties dorées comme les Rockefeller et les Rothschild et les enfants de personnalités riches et célèbres.

L'ÉCOLE LA PLUS GRANDE (NOMBRE D'ÉLÈVES)

L'école City Montessori School de Lucknow (IND) comptait 55 547 élèves le 16 janvier 2019. Admis dès 3 ans, les enfants peuvent y suivre leur scolarité jusqu'en terminale. Fondée par les Dr Jagdish et Dr Bharti Gandhi, elle a ouvert en 1959 dans des locaux loués, avec 5 élèves. Elle continue à grandir, compte plus de 1 000 classes et campus en ville, et fête son jubilée de diamant en 2019.

LE PLUS GRAND COURS DE ROBOTIQUE

La St Paul's School Pernambut, la St Joseph's School Pallalakuppam et le Rotary Club of Pernambut (tous IND) ont organisé un cours d'ingénierie robotique avec 1 021 étudiants à Tamil Nadu (IND), le 2 août 2018. Au cours de cette leçon de 1 h et 4 min, les participants ont appris à concevoir et à construire des robots, ainsi que leur utilisation dans la vie quotidienne. Jetez un œil au chapitre sur les robots, p. 146-167.

 JUILL. 15 En 2018, Muhammad Rashid (PAK) a cassé **le plus grand nombre de noix à la main en 1 min** (284) à Karachi (PAK). Il a battu le record établi 2 mois plus tôt, avec 6 noix de plus.

 JUILL. 16 En 2015, Burnaby Q Orbar (CAN) de Monsters of Schlock s'est mis **le plus de clous dans le nez** en 30 s (15), à Saint John (New Brunswick, CAN).

AFFAIRES GRAND FORMAT

La Bourse la plus ancienne

La Bourse d'Amsterdam (NLD) a été fondée en 1602. On y négociait des actions imprimées de la Compagnie des Indes orientales.

L'obligation en cours la plus ancienne a été émise en 1624 par Hoogheemraadschap Lekdijk Bovendams (NLD) pour financer les réparations des digues du Lek. En 2018, l'obligation ne rapportait que 15 € par an, de quoi compenser l'inflation et le taux de change.

Le plus grand parquet de Bourse

Le service financier de la société UBS à Stamford (Connecticut, USA) possédait un parquet de Bourse de 125 × 69 m (8 625 m², soit 33 courts de tennis). Suite à la crise bancaire, le parquet s'est vidé de son personnel, expédié vers des bureaux moins onéreux. Il a finalement été mis en vente en 2016.

LA PLUS GRANDE SOCIÉTÉ EN TERMES D'ACTIFS

Selon les chiffres 2018 de Forbes 2018, l'Industrial and Commercial Bank of China (ICBC) possédait 4 120,9 milliards d'actifs, soit plus que le PNB de l'Allemagne. En tant que l'une des 4 grandes banques étatiques chinoises, l'ICBC a été fondée avec le statut de société limitée en 1984.

Le chimpanzé ayant le mieux réussi à Wall Street

En 1999, Raven, un chimpanzé de 6 ans, s'est placé en 22e position des gestionnaires financiers des États-Unis en choisissant ses actions en lançant des fléchettes sur une liste de 133 sociétés Internet. Son indice, le MonkeyDex, a permis un gain de 213 %, dépassant plus de 6 000 courtiers professionnels.

L'action la plus chère

Le 22 février 2000, le prix intraday d'une action du prestataire de services Internet Yahoo ! Japan (USA/JPN) coûtait 167 899 136 ¥ (1 507 280 $) à la Bourse du JASDAQ. Les prix avaient été entraînés à la hausse par l'optimisme du marché de l'ère .com et le nombre limité d'actions de la société.

La société d'énergie la plus importante en termes de capitalisation boursière

D'après la valeur totale sur le marché de ses actions et autres titres, ExxonMobil (USA) valait 316 milliards $ le 31 mars 2018, selon le rapport annuel *Global Top 100 Companies* de PricewaterhouseCoopers.

Le même rapport désignait JPMorgan Chase (USA) comme **la plus grande banque en termes de capitalisation boursière**, avec une valeur de 375 milliards $. Voir ci-contre à gauche, **la plus grande banque en termes d'actifs**.

LA PLUS GRANDE INTRODUCTION EN BOURSE

Le 19 septembre 2014, les American Depository Shares d'Alibaba Group (CHN ; voir p. 134) cotaient 68 $ par action à la Bourse de New York. Les investisseurs se sont précipités pour acheter une participation au marché en ligne, levant un record de 25 milliards $, après émission d'actions supplémentaires de surallocation. En photo, le fondateur d'Alibaba Group, Jack Ma, brandissant un maillet de cérémonie avant de frapper la cloche lors de l'introduction en Bourse de sa société.

La plus grande offre publique

En février 2002, le conglomérat allemand Mannesmann a fusionné avec Vodafone AirTouch (GBR) pour 112 milliards £.

La plus grande perte boursière

En 2008, Howie Hubler, courtier en obligations hypothécaires travaillant pour la banque américaine Morgan Stanley, a perdu au nom de son employeur environ 9 milliards $ en négociant des contrats d'échange sur défaut de crédits complexes sur le marché des subprimes. Le responsable des finances de la banque a décrit cet événement comme "une leçon d'humilité très onéreuse".

La clôture la plus élevée pour le Dow Jones Industrial Average (DJIA)

Le 3 octobre 2018, le DJIA – un indice boursier fondé sur le prix du jour des actions de 30 grandes sociétés américaines – a clôturé à 26 828,39. Ce record a été suivi d'une baisse brutale, l'index perdant 832 points le 10 octobre.

Le plus grand gain du DJIA en pourcentage en 1 jour est de 15,34 %, le 15 mars 1933. **La plus grande baisse en 1 jour** est de 22,61 %, le 19 octobre 1987 – le fameux "lundi noir".

Le pays le plus favorable aux affaires

Selon le rapport de la Banque mondiale de 2018 *Doing Business*, c'est la Nouvelle-Zélande qui présente le moins d'obstacles pour créer et gérer une société. Elle affiche 86,55 dans le score de distance de la frontière de l'institution.

La Somalie est **le pays dans lequel il est le plus difficile de faire des affaires** : son score est de 45,77 selon le même rapport.

LA PLUS GRANDE ASSEMBLÉE GÉNÉRALE ANNUELLE

Surnommée le "Woodstock du capitalisme", l'assemblée générale annuelle de la société d'investissement Berkshire Hathaway (USA) se tient dans la salle CHI Health Center Omaha (Nebraska, USA), qui offre 18 975 places. Bien que les chiffres officiels de fréquentation ne soient pas publiés, la réunion du 6 mai 2017 aurait rassemblé 42 000 actionnaires.

JUILL. 17 Un cochon vietnamien appelé Ernestine, né à Alberta (CAN) en 1991, a vécu 23 ans et 76 jours – c'est **le plus vieux cochon du monde**. Il est mort le 1er octobre 2014.

130

LA 1ᴿᴱ SOCIÉTÉ PUBLIQUE AUX 1 000 MILLIARDS $

Le 2 août 2018, le géant de la technologie Apple (USA) a franchi la barre des 1 000 milliards lorsque ses actions ont atteint 207,05 $. La valeur d'Apple a été stimulée par les fortes ventes de son iPhone X.

Selon les chiffres publiés par PricewaterhouseCoopers dans son rapport annuel *Global Top 100 Companies*, la valeur d'Apple était de 851 milliards $ le 31 mars 2018 : c'est **la plus grosse société en termes de capitalisation boursière.**

En photo, des clients Apple en Australie (principale) et au Japon (encart) se précipitant pour être les premiers à se procurer un iPhone XS.

LA PERTE LA PLUS ÉLEVÉE EN 1 JOUR À LA BOURSE DE NEW YORK POUR UNE SOCIÉTÉ PUBLIQUE

Le 26 juillet 2018, les actions de Facebook (USA) ont perdu 19 % de leur valeur – soit 119 milliards $ dans la journée. Cela dépasse la chute historique d'Intel de 97 milliards $ le 22 septembre 2000, lors de l'effondrement des .com. La perte record de Facebook a été attribuée à une prévision de croissance très faible dans les rapports de bénéfices de la société.

LE CONSTRUCTEUR AYANT VENDU LE PLUS DE VOITURES DE TOURISME (DÉTAIL)

Selon des recherches sur le volume de vente annuel du 19 novembre 2018, Volkswagen est le constructeur automobile battant le record des ventes, avec une estimation de 10 447 227 unités en 2017. C'est presque 3 millions de plus que Toyota, n° 2 sur la liste. Le groupe Volkswagen possède des marques comme VW, Porsche et Audi.

 JUILL. 19 En 2009, Mauricio Baldivieso (BOL, né le 22 juillet 1996) devient **le plus jeune joueur de football en 1ʳᵉ division nationale** à l'Aurora FC à l'âge de 12 ans et 362 jours, à La Paz (BOL).

 JUILL. 20 Lors des Global Games 2014 de l'International Quidditch Association (IQA), les États-Unis gagnent contre l'Australie à 210-0, **la marge la plus élevée.**

131

LE$ PLU$ RICHE$

GAINS ANNUELS ACTUELS LES PLUS ÉLEVÉS

PROFESSION	NOM	GAINS ESTIMÉS
Joueur de football	Lionel Messi (ARG)	111 millions $
Musicien	Ed Sheeran (GBR)	110 millions $
Animateur radio	Howard Stern (USA)	90 millions $
Auteur	James Patterson (USA)	86 millions $
Magicien	David Copperfield (USA)	62 millions $
Chef cuisinier	Gordon Ramsay (GBR)	62 millions $
Comédien	Jerry Seinfeld (USA)	57 millions $
Coureur automobile	Lewis Hamilton (GBR)	51 millions $
Golfeur	Tiger Woods (USA)	43 millions $

Chiffres de Forbes, du 1er juillet 2017 au 1er juillet 2018

LA PERSONNE LA PLUS RICHE (FEMMES)

Selon la liste 2018 des milliardaires de Forbes, Alice Walton (USA) possédait une fortune de 46 milliards $. Fille de Sam Walton, fondateur de Walmart Inc., Alice est un mécène de renom.

La personne la plus riche de tous les temps (ajusté à l'inflation)

La fortune personnelle du magnat du pétrole John D. Rockefeller (USA) a été estimée à environ 900 millions $ en 1913. C'est l'équivalent d'au moins 189,6 milliards $ actuels, voire 340 milliards $ selon certaines estimations, soit environ 3 fois la fortune de Jeff Bezos (USA), **la personne la plus riche (à date)**, qui possède 112 milliards $. (Voir pages 126-127 pour plus d'infos sur Bezos.)

Le plus de milliardaires (ville)

Des 2 208 milliardaires du monde, 82 habitaient à New York (USA), en mars 2017. Forbes estimait leur fortune cumulée à 397,9 milliards $ – plus que le PIB de l'Iran (376 milliards $) ou des Émirats arabes unis (371 milliards $).

Des 72 pays comptant au moins un milliardaire, les États-Unis comptent **le plus de milliardaires : 585.**

Le milliardaire en vie le plus âgé

Né en 1918, le pionnier des transports maritimes Chang Yun Chung (CHN) est apparu sur la liste des milliardaires 2018 de Forbes à l'âge de 100 ans avec une fortune de 1,9 milliard $. Il a commencé sa carrière dans les transports maritimes à Singapour en 1949 et a cofondé Pacific International Lines en 1967.

LE CRYPTOMILLIARDAIRE LE PLUS RICHE (À DATE)

Selon la toute première liste des personnes riches en cryptomonnaie établie par les experts monétaires de Forbes, le 19 janvier 2018, le cryptomilliardaire le plus riche était Chris Larsen (USA), dont la "cryptofortune" était estimée ce jour-là entre 7,5 et 8 milliards $. Larsen est le cofondateur et ancien P.-D.G. de Ripple. Il possède 5,2 milliards XRP – une cryptomonnaie utilisée par les banques pour transférer des fonds à l'aide du protocole Ripple.

LA PLUS GROSSE ERREUR DE CRÉDIT BANCAIRE

En juin 2013, en se connectant à son compte PayPal, Christopher Reynolds (USA) a constaté qu'il était créditeur de 92 233 720 368 547 800 $. En théorie, ces 92 millions de milliards $ faisaient de lui l'homme le plus riche du monde – il était environ 1 million de fois plus riche que le n° 2. Malheureusement pour lui, l'erreur a été rectifiée quelques instants plus tard.

Account Statement | June 2013 — PayPal
Reynolds, Christopher
Extrait (PayPal Account ID)
Statement period
June 1, 2013 - June 30, 2013
Balance Summary
USD
140.25
Beginning Balance
Ending Balance
-92,233,720,368,547,800.00

La célébrité masculine aux revenus annuels actuels les plus élevés

Le boxeur Floyd "Money" Mayweather (USA) aurait gagné 285 millions $ entre le 1er juillet 2017 et le 1er juillet 2018, selon Forbes. Il a gagné 275 millions $, lors de son fameux combat contre Conor McGregor de l'UFC, le 26 août 2017, dont Mayweather était le promoteur. (Voir ci-contre pour **la célébrité féminine aux revenus annuels actuels les plus élevés**.)

LE TOP DE...

Perte de fortune personnelle

L'investisseur du secteur tech japonais Masayoshi Son a vu sa fortune chuter de 78 milliards $ en février 2000 à 19,4 milliards en juillet de la même année, soit une perte de 58,6 milliards $, après le crash des "point com". Il s'en est suivi l'effondrement de SoftBank, son conglomérat technologique.

Promesse de don

Le 26 juin 2006, l'investisseur et magnat des affaires Warren Buffett (USA) s'est engagé à offrir 10 millions d'actions de classe B de son conglomérat d'investissement Berkshire Hathaway – alors d'une valeur de 30,7 milliards $ – à la Bill & Melinda Gates Foundation. À l'issue de la dernière distribution des paiements, le 16 juillet 2018, Buffett avait déjà cédé 24,5 milliards $ de la somme promise.

Indemnité de départ

En prévision de sa retraite de la multinationale General Electric, le 30 septembre 2001, Jack Welch (USA) avait négocié une indemnité de départ évaluée par GMI Ratings à 417 millions $. Elle comprenait l'utilisation à vie de services financés par l'entreprise comme un jet privé, un chauffeur personnel et un appartement de luxe à Manhattan.

Gains de paris en ligne

Le 1er juin 2018, Lottoland Limited de Gibraltar a versé 90 millions € au gagnant de l'EuroJackpot, une femme de ménage de 36 ans, Christina, de Berlin (DEU). C'était la 2e fois qu'elle jouait au loto. Christina a annoncé qu'elle utiliserait ces gains pour organiser ses vacances de rêve : traverser les États-Unis en camping-car.

LE FABRICANT DE PRODUITS DE LUXE LE PLUS RICHE

Décrit comme le "plus grand instigateur de mode", Bernard Arnault (FRA) contrôle plusieurs des marques les plus prestigieuses du monde en tant que P.-D.G. de LVMH (Louis Vuitton Moët Hennessy). Sa participation de contrôle dans le conglomérat du luxe lui a valu une fortune de 72 milliards $, selon les estimations publiées par Forbes le 6 mars 2018.

LA MILLIARDAIRE LA PLUS JEUNE (À DATE)

Le 3 septembre 2018, la plus jeune milliardaire était Alexandra Andresen, 21 ans (NOR, née le 23 juillet 1996). Sa fortune a été estimée par Forbes à 1,4 milliard $. Elle l'a acquise en héritant de 42 % de Ferd, la société d'investissement détenue par sa famille, au décès de son père Johan Henrik Andresen. Sa sœur Katharina – âgée d'un an de plus – en possède également 42 %.

 JUILL. 21 En 1998, Brian Milton (GBR) effectue **le 1er tour du monde en ULM** à bord d'un Pegasus Quantum 912 Flexwing. Il est parti le 22 mars 1998, avec comme point de départ et d'arrivée Brooklands (Surrey, GBR).

JUILL. 22 Au Delhi Monsoon Open 2018 de Ghaziabad (Uttar Pradesh, IND), Shivam Bansal (IND) a réalisé **le meilleur score de Rubik's Cubes résolus les yeux bandés** – 48 sur 48, en moins d'1 h.

LA CÉLÉBRITÉ FÉMININE AUX REVENUS ANNUELS ACTUELS LES PLUS ÉLEVÉS

Selon les estimations publiées par Forbes le 16 juillet 2018, la star de téléréalité et femme d'affaires Kylie Jenner (USA) aurait gagné 166,5 millions $ entre le 1er juillet 2017 et le 1er juillet 2018 – et cela, avant son 21e anniversaire. Après être devenue célèbre grâce à la série télé *Keeping Up with the Kardashians* (15e saison en 2018), Kylie a accumulé énormément de followers sur les réseaux sociaux pour devenir l'une des personnalités les plus influentes de la mode et de la beauté. Sa société, Kylie Cosmetics – dont elle est propriétaire à 100 % – a été estimée à presque 800 millions $, 3 ans après sa création en 2015.

En novembre 2018, le Year in Fashion Report du moteur de recherche Lyst a déclaré Kylie célébrité la plus influente de la mode – juste devant sa demi-sœur Kim.

LA 1RE MILLIONNAIRE PARTIE DE RIEN

Madam C. J. Walker (USA, née Sarah Breedlove) est née dans une plantation de coton en Louisiane (USA), en 1867. Orpheline à 7 ans, elle a construit sa fortune en développant le Walker System of Beauty Culture – des produits cosmétiques et capillaires pour les Afro-Américaines (voir ci-dessous). En 1919, elle dirigeait une équipe de 25 000 commerciaux.

LE CLUB DE FOOTBALL LE PLUS RICHE

Le 12 juin 2018, le Manchester United (GBR) était la ligue la plus riche avec une fortune estimée à 4,12 milliards $, juste devant le Real Madrid (ESP) avec ses 4,08 milliards $. United affichait un revenu annuel de 737 millions $ et un bénéfice d'exploitation avant impôts de 254 millions $, selon le rapport *The Business of Soccer* de Forbes.

JUILL. 23 En 2015, Stephen Rainey (GBR) a effectué **le plus de rotations manuelles en fauteuil roulant en 1 min** (66), à Liverpool (GBR), pour promouvoir les services accessibles aux utilisateurs de fauteuil roulant.

JUILL. 24 Sous la supervision de Mike Rogiani (CAN), en 1988, Palm Dairies (CAN) a fabriqué **le plus gros sundae**, à Edmonton (Alberta, CAN). Il pesait 24,91 t.

133

SHOPPING

LE PLUS GRAND AQUARIUM DE CENTRE COMMERCIAL

Le centre commercial Dubaï Mall, à Dubaï (ARE), possède une caractéristique inhabituelle. En plus des 1 200 boutiques et de ses 548 127 m² d'espace intérieur, le centre présente un aquarium de 10 millions de litres. Les passants peuvent admirer 140 espèces aquatiques, dont 300 requins et raies, et peuvent même plonger avec les requins !

Le 1er centre commercial

Conçu par Apollodore de Damas et construit en 100-112 apr. J.-C., le forum de Trajan, à Rome (ITA) disposait d'un espace de marché avec 150 boutiques et bureaux sur 6 niveaux de galeries.

La librairie la plus ancienne toujours en activité

La 1re librairie Livraria Bertrand a ouvert en 1732 à Lisbonne (PRT). Elle fait aujourd'hui partie d'une chaîne.

Le plus grand centre commercial (surface commerciale utile)

Inauguré en 2005, le centre commercial New South China Mall de Dongguan (Guangdong, CHN) possède une surface commerciale utile de 600 153 m². C'est plus grand que **le plus petit pays**, la Cité du Vatican (surface : 440 000 m²).

La plus grande rue piétonne commerçante

Zhongyang Dajie, la rue centrale d'Harbin (Heilongjiang, CHN) déborde de boutiques sur 1,21 km ! Elle est devenue piétonne en 1997.

La location d'espace commercial la plus chère

Selon le rapport *Main Streets Across the World 2017* des consultants en propriété Cushman & Wakefield, l'espace commercial sur la 5e avenue, entre la 49e et la 60e rue, à New York (USA), coûte 3 000 $/m²/an.

Le plus grand magasin de vêtements

Le magasin Primark Stores (GBR) de Birmingham (GBR) a une superficie de 14 761 m² (vérifiée le 5 avril 2019). Il s'appelle Primark Pavilions car il se trouve à l'emplacement de l'ancien centre commercial Pavilions.

La 1re boutique de livestream

Entre le 26 et le 30 septembre 2017, les amateurs de fromage se rendant au Kaan's Stream Store pouvaient se connecter en temps réel pour visualiser la boutique et son personnel, tout en discutant en ligne en faisant leurs achats. La boutique livestream résultait d'une collaboration entre Jan Kaan (NLD) et la banque ABN AMRO d'Alkmaar (NLD).

LE PLUS GRAND DÉTAILLANT EN LIGNE (ACHETEURS ACTIFS)

En juin 2018, Alibaba Group, géant de l'e-commerce (CHN), comptait 552 millions d'acheteurs actifs annuels, soit l'équivalent de la population de l'Amérique du Nord. (Amazon en dénombre 310 millions, selon les dernières données disponibles.) Alibaba Group possède plusieurs plateformes d'achat en ligne populaires, comme AliExpress, Alibaba.com et Tmall.

Le 1er rayon de supermarché sans plastique

Le 28 février 2018, Ekoplaza, à Amsterdam (NLD), a inauguré un rayon de supermarché comptant plus de 700 produits d'épicerie, tous emballés dans des matériaux biodégradables et recyclables, comme du métal, du carton et du verre. Parmi ces produits : de la viande, du riz, des produits laitiers, des céréales, des fruits et des légumes.

LE PLUS GRAND DÉTAILLANT (REVENUS)

Le géant de la grande distribution Walmart Inc. (USA) a enregistré un revenu mondial de 500,3 milliards $ pour l'année fiscale 2018, principalement constitué de ventes nettes de 495,8 milliards $. La société a été fondée par Samuel Moore Walton et James Lawrence Walton le 2 juillet 1962. En janvier 2018, Walmart possédait 11 718 magasins dans 28 pays, sous 59 noms.

REVENU ANNUEL LE PLUS ÉLEVÉ POUR UN GRAND MAGASIN

En 2016-2017, le grand magasin Harrods de Londres (GBR) avait vendu pour plus de 2 milliards £, générant un bénéfice avant impôts de 233,2 millions £. Fondé par Charles Henry Harrod en 1849, Harrods compte aujourd'hui 330 boutiques réparties sur plus de 102 000 m². Il est détenu par le fonds souverain du Qatar.

JUILL. 25 Le 1er bébé-éprouvette est né en 1978. Louise Brown (GBR) est née par césarienne à l'hôpital d'Oldham (Lancashire, GBR) et pesait 2,6 kg.

JUILL. 26 L'alpiniste Karl Unterkircher (ITA) a effectué **l'ascension de l'Everest et du K2 la plus rapide sans assistance d'oxygène**. Il a gravi le K2 en 2004, 63 jours seulement après l'Everest.

En 2017, Amazon a expédié plus de 5 milliards d'articles uniquement via son service Prime, soit 158 articles chaque seconde en moyenne.

LE PLUS GRAND MARCHAND EN LIGNE (VALEUR DE MARCHÉ)

Selon des chiffres publiés par PricewaterhouseCoopers dans son rapport annuel *Global Top 100 Companies*, l'entreprise de commerce électronique Amazon (USA) valait 701 milliards $ le 31 mars 2018. Toutefois, son revenu global de 193,2 milliards $ pour l'année fiscale 2017-2018 représente moins de la moitié de celui du leader du marché Walmart (voir ci-contre). En photo, un site de traitement d'Amazon, à Peterborough (Cambridgeshire, GBR), se préparant pour le Cyber Monday – un des jours les plus denses de l'année en termes de vente – en 2013.

Le 22 janvier 2018, la société a ouvert un nouveau magasin pilote à Seattle (USA) : Amazon Go (encart à gauche). Il fonctionne sans caisses ni caissiers. Pour acheter un article, le client scanne le QR code avec l'appli de son smartphone, et le prix est automatiquement facturé sur son compte Amazon.

LE 1er CENTRE COMMERCIAL POUR OBJETS RECYCLÉS

ReTuna Återbruksgalleria à Eskilstuna (SWE) est le 1er centre commercial du monde consacré aux objets réparés, recyclés et revalorisés. Meubles, ordinateurs, matériel audio, vêtements, jouets, vélos, matériel de jardinage et de construction : ces objets usagés sont déposés, puis réhabilités avant d'être revendus.

LE PLUS GRAND MAGASIN LEGO®

Selon LEGO Group, son plus grand magasin serait celui de Leicester Square au cœur de Londres (GBR), avec une surface de 914 m². Les 2 étages dévoilent des sculptures sur le thème de Londres, dont un wagon de métro grandeur nature (ci-dessus), constitué de 637 902 briques. À droite, la mascotte du magasin, Lester, avec son certificat GWR.

JUILL. 27 En 2007, Richard Rodriguez (USA) se lance dans **le plus long marathon en montagnes russes** à Pleasure Beach, à Blackpool (GBR). Il a voyagé sur le Pepsi Max Big One et le Big Dipper pendant 405 h et 40 min.

JUILL. 28 Betty Lou Oliver (USA) a survécu à une chute de 75 étages, soit plus de 300 m, dans l'Empire State Building à New York (USA), en 1945. C'est **la plus grande chute en ascenseur avec survivants**.

LE$ PLU$ CHER$

1. Whisky

Un Macallan 1926 de 60 ans d'âge, une bouteille de whisky single-malt, s'est vendu 848 750 £, frais acheteur compris, à Bonhams (Édimbourg, GBR), le 3 octobre 2018. Il n'existe que 12 exemplaires de cette bouteille. Sa valeur a aussi explosé en raison de son étiquette, conçue par l'artiste Valerio Adami et cosignée par lui-même et le président de Macallan, Allan Shiach.

2. Vin

Une bouteille du Domaine de la Romanée-Conti de 1945, vin de bourgogne rouge, s'est vendue 558 000 $,

frais acheteur compris, chez Sotheby's à New York (USA), le 13 octobre 2018. La bouteille de 73 ans d'âge a été adjugée à plus de 17 fois le prix de départ de 32 000 $.

3. Gin

En novembre 2018, un Morus LXIV, un gin à la mûre noire, a été commercialisé en exclusivité chez Harvey Nichols à Londres (GBR). Pour 4 000 £, les acheteurs recevaient une bouteille en porcelaine de 730 ml et une autre de 30 ml du précieux breuvage, assorties d'une tasse en porcelaine sertie de cuir. Ce gin est distillé avec des feuilles d'un

seul et unique mûrier noir (*Morus nigra*) âgé de plus d'un siècle. Il est produit par la société Jam Jar Gin, détenue par Dan et Faye Thwaites (tous 2 GBR).

▶ 4. Milk-shake

Le 1er juin 2018, le milk-shake LUXE s'est vendu 100 $ au restaurant Serendipity 3 à New York (USA). C'est le fruit d'un partenariat entre le restaurant, Swarovski et le créateur The Crystal Ninja, Kellie DeFries. Il se compose de 3 sortes de crème, de *cremose baldizzone* (une sauce au caramel à base de lait d'ânesse) et d'or comestible 23 carats.

5. Sac à main

Le sac à main Himalaya Birkin 30 d'Hermès a été vendu à 2 940 000 HK$ (377 238 $) à un enchérisseur anonyme le 31 mai 2017. La vente a eu lieu aux enchères Handbags & Accessories, chez Christie's à Hong Kong (CHN). Fabriqué en 2014, le sac à main est incrusté de 10,23 carats de diamants et orné de finitions en or blanc (176,3 g) 18 carats.

6. Porto

Un porto Niepoort de 1863, dans sa carafe en cristal Lalique, s'est vendu 992 000 HK$ (126 706 $) aux enchères, chez Acker Merrall & Condit, au Grand Hyatt de Hong Kong (CHN), le 3 novembre 2018.

7. Cheesecake

Confectionné par le chef Raffaele Ronca (ITA/USA), un cheesecake à la truffe s'est vendu 4 592,42 $ au Ristorante Rafele à New York (USA),

le 30 octobre 2017. Il a été réalisé à base de ricotta de bufflonne, de cognac de 200 ans d'âge, de vanille de Madagascar et de feuilles d'or.

8. Pastèque

Produite par l'Inner Mongolia Green State Fertilizer Co. (CHN), une pastèque de 81,75 kg s'est vendue 51 000 yuans (7 489 $) à la bannière avant droite de Horqin (Mongolie intérieure, CHN), le 26 août 2018.

9. Crabe

Le 7 novembre 2018, le détaillant en fruits de mer Kanemasa-Hamashita Shoten (JPN) a acheté un crabe des neiges (*Chionoecetes opilio*) à 2 millions ¥ (17 648 $) à la préfecture de Tottori (JPN). Le crabe des neiges est un mets recherché au pays du Soleil-Levant. La raréfaction de l'espèce a fait exploser les prix ces dernières années.

10. Appareil photo

Un appareil photo argentique Leica 35 mm a été vendu à

> Le terme de "frais acheteur", souvent rencontré aux ventes aux enchères, désigne un montant supplémentaire destiné à couvrir les frais administratifs, à régler par l'acquéreur.

 JUILL. 29 Aux jeux Olympiques de 2012, le footballeur Ryan Giggs (GBR, né le 29 novembre 1973) a marqué contre les ARE à l'âge de 38 ans et 243 jours – **le buteur le plus âgé aux JO (homme)**. Il a battu un record vieux de 88 ans.

 JUILL. 30 En 2017, 2 325 Ivan ont participé à une fête organisée par Kupreški kosci (BIH) à Kupres (BIH) – **le plus grand rassemblement de personnes portant le même prénom**.

un collectionneur asiatique 2,40 millions € aux enchères de la WestLicht Photographica, à Vienne (AUT), le 10 mars 2018. Connu sous le nom de Leica 0-series No.122, cet exemplaire fait partie des 25 réalisés à titre de test en 1923 – 2 ans avant la commercialisation du 1er appareil photo Leica. Le prix de départ était de 400 000 €.

11. Verre de cognac
Le 21 mars 2018, un verre de 40 ml de Rome de Bellegarde (GBR) a été vendu 10 014 £ à Ranjeeta Dutt McGroarty (IND), au bar de Hyde Kensington, à Londres (GBR). Ce cognac provenait d'une bouteille, trouvée en 2004 dans les chais du domaine Jean Fillioux, datant vraisemblablement de 1894. Le produit de la vente a été reversé à l'association caritative Global's Make Some Noise.

12. Boîte de mouchoirs en papier
Daishowa Paper Products (JPN) a vendu une boîte de mouchoirs en papier 10 000 ¥ (90,39 $). Ce prix a été attesté à Chūō (Tokyo, JPN) le 16 juin 2018. Les mouchoirs Junihitoe se déclinent en 12 couleurs. Leur nom provient de celui d'une robe cérémonielle composée de 12 kimonos superposés.

13. Illustration de livre
Le 10 juillet 2018, l'*Original Map of the Hundred Acre Wood*, dessinée par E. H. Shepard (GBR) pour la page de garde de *Winnie l'ourson* (1926), s'est vendue 430 000 £, frais acheteur compris. Les enchères ont eu lieu chez Sotheby's, à Londres (GBR). L'illustration se présente comme le travail du petit Christopher Robin, et contient des fautes d'orthographe intentionnelles (comme "Big Stones and Rox" et "Nice for Piknicks").

14. Voiture
En mai 2018, l'homme d'affaires et pilote automobile David MacNeil (USA) a acheté une Ferrari 250 GTO de 1963 70 millions $ dans le cadre d'une transaction privée. Ce véhicule a été produit à moins de 40 exemplaires. Ce modèle particulier (n° de châssis 4153 GT) a remporté le Tour de France Automobile en 1964, avec les pilotes Lucien Bianchi et Georges Berger.

Cette 250 GTO à 70 millions $ possède un moteur 3 litres V12 Colombo, la propulsant à la vitesse de pointe de 280 km/h. Chose rare pour une voiture de course de cet âge, elle n'a jamais eu d'accident, ce qui contribue aussi à sa valeur.

▶ Vous trouverez plein de vidéos géniales sur guinnessworldrecords.com/2020

SOCIÉTÉ

JUILL. 31 En 2012, **la plus grande collection de grille-pain** (1 284) a été attestée chez le Dr Kenneth Huggins (USA) à Columbia (Caroline du Sud, USA). Il collectionne aussi les phonographes, les radios et les automobiles.

AOÛT 1 Au cours d'un événement culinaire de 4 jours à Singapour en 2015, l'Indian Chefs & Culinary Association (SGP) a concocté **le plus gros curry** du monde : 15,34 t !

TECHNO AU QUOTIDIEN

L'aéronef à rotors basculants télécommandé le plus rapide

Au 75e festival de vitesse de Goodwood, à Chichester (West Sussex, GBR), le 12 juillet 2018, Luke Bannister (GBR) a piloté un Wingcopter XBR à 240,06 km/h. Cet aéronef à rotors basculants télécommandé a été construit par Vodafone, XBlades Racing (tous 2 GBR) et Wingcopter (DEU ; voir p. 160).

Âgé de 17 ans, Bannister est un pilote de drones expérimenté : il a remporté 250 000 $ au World Drone Prix de Dubaï (ARE), le 12 mars 2016. À la clé pour les gagnants, 1 million $: c'est **le plus gros prix pour un championnat de course de drones**.

Le plus d'enceintes Bluetooth connectées à la même source

Le 25 avril 2017, la société Harman International (USA), spécialisée dans les équipements audio, a fait fonctionner 1 000 enceintes Bluetooth à partir d'une source unique, au Village Underground de Londres (GBR).

Le plus grand écran tactile

Le 7 avril 2017, 2 écrans de 48,77 m² chacun – l'équivalent de 12 lits king-size – ont été dévoilés lors du jeu télévisé Candy Crush, à Los Angeles (Californie, USA). Ils affichaient une version grand format du très populaire jeu pour téléphone portable signé King, qui, dans cette version, exigeait des participants suspendus au moyen de harnais qu'ils alignassent des bonbons colorés affichés sur les écrans.

La plus grande mosaïque animée constituée de téléphones

L'entreprise d'électronique Xiaomi (CHN) a créé une image de sapin de Noël à l'aide de 1 005 téléphones Xiaomi Mi Play, à Pékin (CHN), le 24 décembre 2018. L'animation durait 1 min et 4 s.

En plus de ses prouesses téléphoniques, Xiaomi est aussi **la marque qui vend le plus d'électronique mobile**. D'après les recherches du 3 décembre 2018, Xiaomi aurait vendu 18 643 300 unités d'objets électroniques à porter en 2018.

L'altitude la plus élevée pour un streaming par smartphone

Lors d'un événement organisé par Huawei Suède, le 5 septembre 2016, un smartphone Honor 8 a été fixé à un dirigeable pour étudier son ascension. Le téléphone a envoyé des images de la Terre en direct sur Facebook à une altitude de 18,42 km.

La chaîne de rallonges électriques la plus longue

Lors de la réunion annuelle de leurs dirigeants à Dallas (Texas, USA), le 16 mai 2018, les entrepreneurs électriciens d'IES Residential (USA) ont écrit "IESR" à l'aide de 22,8 km de rallonges électriques.

Ce record à rallonge fait écho à celui du **bloc multiprise le plus long**. L'unité de 3 m de long a été réalisée par Mohammed Nawaz (IND) de l'école d'ingénieurs Aalim Muhammed Salegh. Elle a été mesurée à Tamil Nadu (IND), le 11 octobre 2018. Elle compte 50 sorties fonctionnelles : 26 prises à 3 broches et 24 à 2 broches.

LE PLUS GRAND DÉFILÉ DE VÉHICULES AUTONOMES

Le 28 novembre 2018, la Chongqing Changan Automobile Company (CHN) a organisé un défilé de 55 véhicules autonomes à Chongqing (CHN). Il a fallu 9 min et 7 s aux voitures pour parcourir les 3,2 km de route, sans conducteur au volant. Elles ont battu le convoi de 44 voitures du même jour de l'année précédente, organisé par la même société.

Le plus d'aéronefs sans pilote volant simultanément

Le 15 juillet 2018, Intel Corporation (USA) a fêté son 50e anniversaire avec 2 066 drones survolant Folsom (Californie, USA). Ces drones Shooting Star ont effectué une chorégraphie de 5 min, recréant les logos d'Intel au fil des ans, retraçant ainsi l'histoire de la société.

De l'autre côté du globe, dans la nuit de Dubaï (ARE), une formation de 30 drones a reconstitué les 11 lettres de "Dubai Police", le 3 janvier 2019. Ce **record de formations consécutives de drones** s'inscrit dans le cadre de la commémoration des 50 ans de l'académie de police de Dubaï (ARE).

L'ESPÉRANCE DE VIE LA PLUS LONGUE D'UNE PILE AA

Dans le cadre de tests effectués par les consultants en qualité Intertek Semko AB à Kista (SWE), le 12 octobre 2018, la pile Energizer Ultimate Lithium fabriquée par Energizer (USA) a réalisé une performance moyenne attestée de 229,69. Elle a été soumise à de nombreux tests face aux autres piles lithium AA.

LA PLUS LONGUE DISTANCE PARCOURUE SUR L'EAU PAR UN ROBOT ÉQUIPÉ D'UN SEUL ENSEMBLE DE BATTERIES AA

Pour fêter le 100e anniversaire de Panasonic, un robot de 17 cm de haut, Mr EVOLTA NEO, a ramé sur 3 km, équipé de 2 piles EVOLTA AA. Installé sur un mini-surf, il a effectué la traversée de l'île principale du Japon jusqu'au *torii* du sanctuaire d'Itsukushima (préfecture d'Hiroshima), en 3 h 22 min et 34 s.

LA PLUS LONGUE PERCHE À SELFIE

Le programme de jeunes talents Qatari Sky Climbers a célébré sa 2e cérémonie de remise de diplômes, le 19 septembre 2017, avec une photo prise du bout d'une perche à selfie de 18 m, au Qatar National Convention Centre, à Doha. Il bat de 2 m le précédent record de 2017.

AOÛT 2 En 1917, E. H. Dunning (GBR) réussit **le 1er atterrissage sur un navire en mouvement** tandis qu'il pose son aéronef sur le porte-avions HMS *Furious* à Orkney (GBR). Il meurt le 7 août en tentant de reproduire le même exploit.

AOÛT 3 En 2009, Sarah Outen (GBR, née le 26 mai 1985) accoste à l'île Maurice après être partie de Fremantle (AU). Âgée de 23 ans et 310 jours lors du départ, c'est **la plus jeune personne à avoir navigué dans l'océan Indien en solo.**

LE PLUS DE PERSONNES UTILISANT DES AFFICHAGES DE RÉALITÉ VIRTUELLE (LIEUX MULTIPLES)

Le 10 octobre 2018 – journée mondiale de la santé mentale –, 2 340 personnes situées dans 5 villes chinoises ont regardé un court-métrage de réalité virtuelle intitulé *The World Record of Mr. S*. Le film suit un personnage appelé Mr. S et son processus de guérison de la schizophrénie. Cette tentative de record a été organisée par Xian Janssen Pharmaceutical (CHN) pour attirer l'attention sur la schizophrénie.

Le plus de personnes utilisant un masque de réalité virtuelle (lieu unique) est de 1 867. Ce record a été réalisé par Mobileye (ISR) le 3 mars 2017, à Vancouver (Colombie-Britannique, CAN).

LA MARQUE QUI VEND LE PLUS DE TABLETTES

L'iPad d'Apple (USA) a été vendu à 36 273 000 d'exemplaires selon les estimations 2018, d'après les recherches menées le 3 décembre, soit 12 millions d'appareils de plus que son rival Samsung (KOR), qui en a vendu environ 24 360 900. En 2018, Apple a lancé l'iPad Pro, véritable bête de course, passerelle entre tablette et ordinateur portable.

LA MARQUE QUI VEND LE PLUS DE SMARTPHONES

Selon une recherche menée le 3 décembre 2018, Samsung (KOR) aurait vendu 1 348 911 300 d'appareils entre 2014 et 2018. Il a dépassé l'iPhone – n° 2 avec ses 937 036 100 unités – tous les ans pendant cette période, et a presque atteint le triple des ventes du n° 3, Huawei.

AOÛT 4
Le groupe finnois de heavy-metal Agonizer exécute **le concert le plus profond** en 2007, jouant à 1 271 m sous le niveau de la mer, dans la mine de Pyhäsalmi, à Pyhäjärvi (FIN).

AOÛT 5
En 1971, Al Worden (USA) effectue **la 1re sortie dans l'espace lointain**, récupérant des cassettes de photos dans le module d'instruments scientifiques d'*Apollo 15*, à 320 000 km de la Terre.

139

VIE EN VILLE

LE PARC LE PLUS PETIT

Le Mill Ends Park trône sur un îlot de circulation du SW Naito Parkway à Portland (Oregon, USA). Il occupe un disque de 60,96 cm de diamètre pour une surface de 2 917,15 cm². Il a été créé le 17 mars 1948 à la demande de Dick Fagan, un journaliste local, en tant que parc urbain à destination des courses d'escargots et d'une colonie de leprechauns.

La ville la plus ancienne habitée sans interruption

Les archéologues ont découvert des traces d'habitation à Jéricho, dans les territoires palestiniens, remontant à 9000 av. J.-C. Située sur une rive du Jourdain, en Cisjordanie, la ville abrite aujourd'hui 20 000 habitants. En 8000 av. J.-C., entourée d'un mur de pierre construit par la communauté, la cité comptait 2 000 à 3 000 âmes.

La capitale la plus petite (population)

Melekeok, la capitale de la petite nation archipel des Palaos, dans le Pacifique, ne compte que 277 habitants selon le recensement de 2015. Cette région peu peuplée est reconnue comme capitale par les gouvernements étrangers. Elle abrite un capitole, dans un lieu-dit appelé Ngerulmud.

Le bâtiment d'habitation le plus grand

Inauguré en 2015, le 432 Park Avenue de New York (USA) est la tour à usage exclusivement résidentiel la plus élevée du monde avec ses 425,5 m de haut. L'immeuble en béton compte 85 étages, le niveau le plus élevé se situant à 392,1 m.

La ville la plus chère…

Pour y vivre : l'étude *Worldwide Cost of Living* de 2018 de The Economist Intelligence Unit a classé Singapour comme la ville la plus chère. Basé sur le prix de 400 produits allant de la nourriture aux vêtements en passant par le transport, les services et les écoles, l'indice du coût de la vie à Singapour est de 116, contre 100 pour New York et 26 pour Damas (SYR) - **la moins chère**.
Pour y louer : la location mensuelle d'un deux-pièces à Hong Kong est de 3 737 $. Ces données sont basées sur l'étude *Mapping the World's Prices* 2018 de la Deutsche Bank, qui dresse la liste du coût des biens et des services dans 50 grandes villes.
Pour y manger : selon le même rapport 2018, un repas simple pour deux, dans un restaurant de Zurich (CHE), coûte en moyenne 72,30 $.

LA CAPITALE LA PLUS PEUPLÉE

Selon le *World Urbanization Prospects 2018* de l'ONU, la capitale la plus peuplée serait Tokyo (JPN), avec ses 37 468 302 habitants en zone métropolitaine.

Le plus grand nombre d'escalators dans un métro

Le métro de Washington (USA) compte 618 escalators. Leur maintenance est assurée par le service interne d'entretien des escalators le plus coûteux d'Amérique du Nord, qui compte 90 techniciens.

La ville à la croissance la plus rapide

Selon le *World Urbanization Prospects 2018*, la population de Rupganj (BGD) aura augmenté de 9,35 % en 2020 par rapport à 2015, à la suite de la construction de 2 nouvelles villes, Jolshiri Abashon et Purbachal New Town, aux abords des limites actuelles de Rupganj.

La ville à la croissance la plus faible (ou à la perte la plus rapide) est

Yichun (Heilongjiang, CHN), qui aura perdu 1,35 % de ses habitants en 2020. Sans doute plus important que ne le dévoilent les statistiques, ce déclin est lié à l'effondrement de l'industrie du bois, qui a surexploité les forêts de la région.

Le premier passage piéton

En 1949, au cours d'une semaine de sécurité piétonne, 1 000 passages piétons rayés noir et blanc expérimentaux ont été mis en place au Royaume-Uni. Le premier passage piéton permanent a été peint à Slough (Berkshire, GBR), en 1951.

La plus petite rue

Le 28 octobre 2006, il a été établi que l'Ebenezer Place à Wick (Caithness, GBR) ne mesurait que 2,05 m. La Grande-Bretagne possède également **l'espace le plus court de stationnement interdit** – une zone de 43 cm de long avec double ligne jaune, dans la Stafford Street à Norwich (Norfolk, GBR).

Yonge Street, quittant Toronto (Ontario, CAN) par le nord, est **la rue la plus longue**. La longueur de 1 896 km, bien souvent citée, n'est plus d'actualité, car elle intègre la Highway 11. Toutefois, cette voie urbaine en ligne droite reliant le port de Newmarket, ville-dortoir, mesure quand même 48 km.

La rue la plus étroite est Spreuerhofstrasse à Reutlingen (DEU). Mesurée en février 2006, elle ne fait que 31 cm en son point le plus étroit.

LA VILLE À L'AIR LE PLUS POLLUÉ

Un rapport de l'Organisation mondiale de la santé (OMS) de mai 2018 a révélé que Kanpur (IND) affichait un niveau de PM$_{2,5}$ de 173 µg par m³ en 2016. C'est 17 fois plus élevé que le maximum recommandé par l'OMS (10 µg par m³). Le terme de PM$_{2,5}$ désigne une *particulate matter* (particule) d'un diamètre de moins de 2,5 µm, comme la suie, la poussière et la cendre. Une exposition prolongée à ces polluants peut provoquer des maladies pulmonaires et cardiaques.

LA VILLE LA PLUS APPRÉCIÉE DES TOURISTES

Bangkok (THA) est la destination touristique préférée des voyageurs internationaux, selon l'index *Mastercard Global Destination Cities* de 2018. L'afflux de touristes étrangers a augmenté de 3,3 % pour atteindre 20,05 millions en 2016. La capitale thaïlandaise a ainsi dépassé les grands pôles touristiques tels que Londres (GBR), 19,83 millions de visiteurs, et Paris (France), 17,44 millions.

LA VILLE LA PLUS CHÈRE POUR PASSER UN WEEK-END

Pour passer un week-end dans la capitale danoise Copenhague, le visiteur devra débourser la modique somme de 2 503 $, pour 2 nuits dans un hôtel 5 étoiles, la location d'une voiture, 4 repas pour 2 et un peu de shopping. Ces données sont basées sur le rapport *Mapping the World's Prices* de la Deustche Bank, publié le 22 mai 2018. À titre de comparaison, un week-end similaire à Paris coûterait 1 861 $.

AOÛT 6 **Le premier site Web** est lancé en 1991. Créé par Tim Berners-Lee (GBR) à Genève (CHE), info.cern.ch explique ce qu'est le World Wide Web et comment l'utiliser.

AOÛT 7 En 2012, un jour férié est déclaré à Grenade (109 000 habitants) à la suite de la victoire olympique au 400 m de Kirani James. L'île est **le plus petit pays (population)** à avoir remporté une médaille d'or olympique.

LE SITE LE PLUS ÉLEVÉ HABITÉ EN PERMANENCE

Située sur le mont Ananea au sud-est du Pérou, à 5 100 m d'altitude, La Rinconada compte 50 000 habitants. Avec des températures inférieures à 0 °C, et seulement accessible par des chemins de montagne dangereux, le site est peu fréquenté par les touristes. Il manque d'infrastructures, de réseau d'assainissement, d'hôpitaux et d'hôtels. L'économie est basée sur l'exploitation de l'or des mines proches.

Les mineurs travaillent sans être payés pendant 30 jours, mais ils ont une journée au cours de laquelle ils peuvent conserver l'or qu'ils ont trouvé.

LA PLUS GRANDE POPULATION URBAINE (EN PROPORTION TOTALE)

Le rapport *World Urbanization Prospects 2018* de l'ONU révèle que 12 pays/territoires possèdent 100 % de population urbaine. Il s'agit de Singapour, des îles Caïmans, de Saint-Martin, de Nauru, de Monaco, de Gibraltar, du Koweït, du Vatican, d'Anguilla, des Bermudes, de Macao et de Hong Kong (ci-dessous), le plus peuplé (7,4 millions d'habitants).

LA PLUS GRANDE ZONE URBAINE SANS VOITURE

La médina de Fès (MAR) est entièrement piétonne. Également appelé Fès el-Bali, c'est le quartier le plus vieux de Fès, fondé à la fin du IXe siècle apr. J.-C. La médina abrite plus de 156 000 habitants, mais aucun n'est autorisé à conduire dans le quartier. Les rues anciennes très étroites, ne dépassant parfois pas 60 cm de large, rendent de toute façon impossible toute circulation.

AOÛT 8 En 2010, 102 personnes souhaitant lever des fonds caritatifs utilisent nus la montagne russe de l'Adventure Island de Southend-on-Sea (Essex, GBR) – le plus grand nombre de personnes nues sur un manège.

AOÛT 9 L'aventurier Ed Stafford (GBR) devient **la 1re personne à parcourir le fleuve Amazone** en 2010. Son voyage de 7 226 km dure 2 ans et 129 jours.

Énergie hydroélectrique : les "capacités installées" chinoises de 332 gigawatts (GW) produisent 1 130 TWh d'électricité, soit 28,4 % de l'énergie hydroélectrique du monde. Le terme de "capacités installées" renvoie au maximum d'électricité pouvant être généré dans des conditions optimales.

Énergie éolienne : les États-Unis possèdent une capacité installée de 72,6 GW, produisant 193 TWh d'électricité – soit 23 % de l'énergie éolienne mondiale. Mais le secteur éolien explosant en Chine, il devrait bientôt dépasser celui des États-Unis.

La source des records ci-dessus est le rapport *Key World Energy Statistics* 2017 de l'Agence internationale de l'énergie (IEA). Pour **le plus grand producteur d'électricité solaire,** voir ci-contre.

LE 1er TRAIN DE PASSAGERS À HYDROGÈNE

Développé par Alstom (FRA), le Coradia iLint est un train à zéro émission alimenté par une pile à hydrogène convertissant l'hydrogène et l'oxygène en électricité. Le 16 septembre 2018, deux de ces trains sont entrés en service commercial dans le nord de l'Allemagne, pour relier Buxtehude (banlieue de Hambourg) et les villes proches de Bremerhaven et Cuxhaven.

LE TRAJET LE PLUS LONG EN VÉHICULE ÉLECTRIQUE (AUTONOME, NON SOLAIRE)

Les 16-17 octobre 2017, une voiture électrique construite par IT Asset Partners, Inc. (USA), a parcouru 1 608,54 km en autonomie sur l'Auto Club Speedway à Fontana, Californie (USA). Baptisé *The Phoenix*, ce véhicule est fabriqué à partir de 90 % de déchets électroniques recyclés. Il était piloté par son cocréateur, Eric Lundgren (USA, ci-dessus).

Le plus grand producteur d'électricité à partir de...

Sources renouvelables : la Chine génère environ 25 % de l'énergie renouvelable du monde – soit 1 398 térawatt-heure (TWh) d'électricité. (1 térawatt-heure représente 1 000 milliards de watts pendant 60 min.) Cette énergie suffirait à alimenter 930 millions de ménages chinois pendant 1 an.

Le plus grand four solaire

À Font-Romeu-Odeillo-Via, dans le sud de la France, près de 10 000 miroirs orientables (héliostats) dirigent les rayons du soleil sur une parabole réfléchissante de 2 000 m², qui les concentre sur un point focal, dont la température peut atteindre 3 800 °C. Les scientifiques du site, créé en 1969, utilisent cette énergie à diverses fins : fabrication de piles à hydrogène et expériences, allant de l'ingénierie solaire au test de matériaux pour véhicules spatiaux.

La cellule solaire la plus efficace (prototype)

En 2014, une cellule photovoltaïque expérimentale a été produite pour convertir 46 % de la lumière du soleil en électricité. Elle a été développée par le Fraunhofer Institute for Solar Energy Systems (DEU), l'institut de recherche Leti du CEA et le producteur de matériaux Soitec (tous 2 FRA).

L'installation marémotrice la plus puissante

La centrale marémotrice de Sihwa (UKR) développe une capacité de 254 mégawatts (MW), générée par 10 turbines immergées de 25,4 MW chacune. De quoi alimenter 54 000 foyers.

La turbine éolienne la plus puissante

est la V164-9,5 MW, fabriquée par la société MHI Vestas Offshore Wind (DNK). Lancée le 6 juin 2017, elle peut produire 9,5 MW d'énergie. Cette turbine abrite 3 pales de 80 m, soit l'équivalent de 9 bus à 2 étages chacune.

Le plus grand stade à énergie solaire

Le stade national de Kaohsiung (TWN) est équipé de 8 844 panneaux solaires sur une surface de 14 155 m², pouvant générer 1,14 gigawatt-heure (GWh) chaque année (1 gigawatt = 1 milliard de watts). Cela lui permet de couvrir 80 % de ses besoins. Une centrale conventionnelle rejetterait 660 t de CO_2 dans l'atmosphère tous les ans.

LE PLUS GRAND PARC ÉOLIEN OFFSHORE

Le parc éolien de Walney, d'une capacité de 659 MW, a été inauguré le 8 septembre 2018. Situé en mer d'Irlande, à environ 19 km de l'île de Walney (GBR), il couvre 145 km² – soit 20 000 terrains de football. Ce parc a été développé par la société danoise Ørsted pour un montant de 1 milliard £.

LE TAUX DE RECYCLAGE LE PLUS ÉLEVÉ

L'Allemagne recycle 66,1 % de ses déchets, ainsi que l'a révélé un rapport de 2017 publié par des consultants en recherche environnementale d'Eunomia (GBR) et par le Bureau européen de l'environnement. Ci-dessus, des ouvriers trient les déchets plastiques sur une bande transporteuse dans l'usine ALBA Group de Berlin, qui recycle environ 140 000 t de déchets tous les ans.

Les 189 turbines du parc éolien, de 190 m de haut chacune, produisent assez d'énergie pour alimenter 590 000 foyers par an.

"FireGuy" Brant Matthews (CAN) "allume le feu" à la fête du Wisconsin State Fair 2018 avec **le plus grand nombre de torches éteintes par un avaleur de feu en 1 min** (101) à West Allis (Wisconsin, USA).

En 2014, l'illusionniste et artiste de l'évasion Alexis Arts (ITA, né Danilo Audiello) réussit **l'évasion la plus rapide d'une camisole de force,** en 2,84 s à Foggia (ITA).

LE PLUS GRAND PRODUCTEUR D'ÉLECTRICITÉ À PARTIR D'ÉNERGIE SOLAIRE

Selon le rapport *Key World Energy Statistics* 2017 de l'IEA, la Chine produit environ 45 TWh d'électricité à partir de panneaux photovoltaïques chaque année, soit 43,2 GW de capacité installée. Cela représente 18,3 % de la production mondiale d'énergie solaire.

À l'extrémité gauche, un parc solaire à Chunjiangyuan (Zhejiang, CHN). La photo principale représente le 2ᵉ parc solaire de Chine sur le thème du panda à Guigang (Guangxi, CHN). Ci-dessous, des panneaux solaires sur le site d'Anhui Quanchai Engine Co., dans la province d'Anhui, dans l'est de la Chine.

L'INDICE ENVIRONNEMENTAL LE PLUS ÉLEVÉ (PAYS)

L'édition 2018 de l'*Environmental Performance Index*, produit conjointement par les universités de Yale et de Columbia (toutes deux USA) depuis 2002, classe la Suisse comme pays au meilleur indice environnemental. Elle affiche le score de 87,42. L'indice est fondé sur 24 indicateurs, comme la perte de couvert forestier, les émissions de méthane et de CO_2, le traitement des eaux usées et la pollution aux métaux lourds.

LA PLUS GRANDE QUANTITÉ DE DÉTRITUS EXTRAITS PAR UN COLLECTEUR DE DÉCHETS EN 1 MOIS

Entre le 1ᵉʳ et le 30 avril 2017, Mr. Trash Wheel, un collecteur de déchets flottant géré par le Waterfront Partnership of Baltimore (USA), a extrait 57,4 t de déchets dans l'embouchure du fleuve Jones Falls à Baltimore (Maryland, USA). Ce tapis roulant flottant, activé par énergie solaire et hydraulique, a empêché 847,6 t de déchets flottants (dont 561 180 bouteilles en plastique, selon les estimations) d'atteindre la baie de Chesapeake.

AOÛT 12 — En 2012, 4 514 membres de la famille Porteau-Boileve se sont retrouvés pour **la plus grande réunion de famille**. Cette tradition a été instaurée par Georges Porteau et Madeleine Boileve au XVIIᵉ s.

AOÛT 13 — Mike Newman (GBR) établit **le record de vitesse de conduite d'une voiture les yeux bandés**, soit 322,69 km/h, dans le Yorkshire du Nord (GBR) en 2014. Il est aveugle depuis l'âge de 8 ans.

143

Le PIB le plus élevé

Le produit intérieur brut (PIB) est la valeur de tous les biens et services produits par un pays en une année. Selon la Banque mondiale, les États-Unis sont le pays au PIB le plus élevé. Son économie valait 19,39 trillions $ en 2017. Si l'on ajustait ces chiffres au coût de la vie, la Chine serait la détentrice du record avec un PIB de 23,3 trilliards $.

Le PIB par habitant le plus élevé

Pour exprimer la vitalité économique d'un pays, on divise le PIB par le nombre d'habitants. En 2017, la Banque mondiale estimait que le Luxembourg était le pays au PIB/hab. le plus élevé, avec 104 103 $ par tête. Si l'on ajustait ces chiffres au coût de la vie, le Qatar détiendrait le record avec un PIB par habitant de 128 378 $.

Selon les mêmes sources, le Burundi aurait **le PIB par habitant le plus faible**, avec 320 $. En ajustant ces chiffres au coût de la vie, le PIB/hab. du Burundi augmenterait pour céder sa place à la République centrafricaine, avec 725 $/hab.

Le plus gros excédent commercial annuel (pays)

Lorsque la valeur des exportations d'un pays dépasse celle des importations, il en résulte un excédent commercial : on parle de "balance commerciale excédentaire". Selon les chiffres 2016 de la Banque mondiale (la dernière année pour laquelle des données internationales comparables sont disponibles), l'Allemagne est le pays affichant le plus gros excédent commercial, avec une balance commerciale de 274,7 milliards $.

Selon les chiffres de la même année de la Banque mondiale, les États-Unis souffrent du **plus gros déficit commercial annuel**, soit 504,7 milliards $.

Le taux d'inflation le plus bas

Selon l'édition d'avril 2018 du *World Economic Outlook* du Fonds monétaire international (FMI), l'Arabie saoudite et le Tchad avaient un taux moyen d'inflation de − 0,9 % en 2017.

LE PLUS JEUNE AMBASSADEUR DE BONNE VOLONTÉ DE L'UNICEF

Le 20 novembre 2018 – Journée internationale des droits de l'enfant –, Millie Bobby Brown (GBR, née le 19 février 2004) a été nommée ambassadrice de l'UNICEF à 14 ans et 274 jours. L'actrice est surtout connue pour le rôle d'Eleven dans la série *Stranger Things* (encadré), qui lui a valu une nomination aux Emmy (voir p. 205). Dans son nouveau rôle, Millie défend les droits des enfants et met un coup de projecteur sur les problèmes des jeunes, comme le harcèlement.

Le taux de TVA le plus élevé

Selon des données collectées par le réseau international de cabinets d'audit et de conseil KPMG, la taxe sur la valeur ajoutée (TVA) en Hongrie était de 27 % en 2018.

Aruba, dans les Caraïbes, affiche **le taux d'impôt sur le revenu le plus élevé**, selon les données collectées par KPMG en 2018. Tout contribuable dont le revenu brut annuel dépasse 304 369 florins arubais (168 602 $) est soumis à un taux d'impôt de 59 %.

Les Émirats arabes unis avaient **le taux d'impôt sur les sociétés le plus élevé** en 2018, selon les mêmes sources. Les émirats de Dubaï, Charjah et Abou Dabi prélèvent tous un impôt de 55 % sur les bénéfices des sociétés au-delà de 5 millions de dirhams (1,3 million $).

Le plus de journalistes en prison

272 journalistes étaient emprisonnés en 2017, en raison de leur travail, selon le recensement annuel du Comité pour la protection des journalistes (CPJ), association à but non lucratif basée à New York (USA). 2017 est donc la pire année en la matière depuis le début du recensement par le CPJ, en 1990.

LE PLUS GRAND DRAPEAU DÉPLOYÉ

Le 2 novembre 2017, Trident Support Flagpoles et Sharjah Investment and Development Authority (tous 2 ARE) ont déployé un drapeau de 2 448,56 m², à Charjah (ARE).

Près de 2 fois plus grand, **le plus grand drapeau déployé du ciel** (saut en parachute, encadré) mesurait 4 885,65 m². C'était le 29 novembre 2018, à Dubaï (ARE). C'est environ 10 fois la surface d'un terrain de basket !

LES PRIX RELATIFS LES PLUS ÉLEVÉS

Selon les données de l'Organisation de coopération et de développement économiques (OCDE) pour août 2018, l'Islande connaissait les prix les plus élevés. Un panier de marchandises standard de 100 $ aux États-Unis coûterait l'équivalent de 149 $ en Islande. En appliquant la même comparaison, les pays suivants seraient la Suisse (138 $) et le Danemark (127 $).

AOÛT 14 — Maria Paraskeva (CYP) réalise un rêve d'enfance en portant **le plus long voile de mariée** en 2018, à Larnaca (CYP). Il mesure 6,96 km.

AOÛT 15 — En 2003, Ron Hunt (USA) tombe la tête la première sur un foret de 46 cm et survit. L'élément est extrait par des chirurgiens du Nevada (USA). C'est **le plus gros objet extrait d'un crâne humain**.

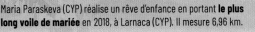

LE BUDGET DE LA DÉFENSE LE PLUS ÉLEVÉ

Aucun pays ne dépense plus pour sa défense que les États-Unis. Selon les derniers chiffres du Stockholm International Peace Research Institute (SIPRI), le Département de la Défense des États-Unis (qui coordonne le budget des forces armées des États-Unis) a reçu 609,758 milliards $ en 2017 – contre 600 milliards $ en 2016.

Le plus de demandes de brevet

Selon les chiffres de l'Organisation mondiale de la propriété intellectuelle, 1 381 594 demandes de brevet ont été déposées en Chine en 2017 (dernière année de données disponibles), dont 1 245 709 brevets en provenance du pays et 135 885 de l'étranger.

La population urbaine la plus faible (en proportion du total)

Selon le rapport *World Urbanization Prospects 2018* des Nations unies, deux pays du Pacifique se partagent le titre de pays le moins urbanisé : les îles de Tokelau et de Wallis-et-Futuna. Aucune des deux ne présente d'implantation assez importante pour répondre à la définition d'agglomération urbaine de l'ONU. En d'autres termes, leur population est entièrement rurale.

La ville la plus chère pour acheter une voiture

Singapour est la ville la plus onéreuse du monde pour acheter une voiture neuve, selon le rapport *2018 Mapping the World's Prices* de la Deutsche Bank, qui recense le coût des biens et services dans 50 grandes villes. Principalement en raison de taxes visant à décourager l'achat de voitures, une voiture coûte en moyenne 86 412 $, soit presque le double de la 2e ville la plus chère, Copenhague (DNK), avec 44 062 $.

Le déchet plastique récupéré le plus profondément en mer

Un sac en plastique a été trouvé à une profondeur de 10 898 m dans la fosse des Marianes, dans la partie ouest du Pacifique, selon une annonce faite dans le journal *Marine Policy* en octobre 2018.

La plus grande mosaïque recyclable (image)

Le 29 juillet 2018, Memories Events Management (ARE) et MTV SAL (LB) ont présenté une mosaïque de 971,37 m², à Dbaiyeh (LBN). Représentant trois bateaux sur la mer, l'œuvre était composée de 10 000 éléments recyclables.

LE PREMIER MINISTRE EN ACTIVITÉ LE PLUS ÂGÉ

Le 10 mai 2018, Mahathir bin Mohamad (MYS, né le 10 juillet 1925) est devenu le Premier ministre de Malaisie à 92 ans et 304 jours, dans la capitale Kuala Lumpur. Mohamad avait déjà été Premier ministre de 1981 à 2003.

La plus grande quantité d'eaux usées retraitées en eau potable en 24 h

Le 16 février 2018, le Groundwater Replenishment System (USA) a retraité 378 541 208 litres d'eaux usées en H_2O suffisamment pure pour être bue, dans le comté d'Orange (Californie, USA).

La carrière la plus longue de...

• Chasseur d'ouragan : Dr James "Jim" McFadden (USA), météorologue, travaille à l'Agence américaine d'observation océanique et atmosphérique depuis 1962. Il vole régulièrement dans des cyclones tropicaux dans le cadre de recherches sur les orages. Sa 1re mission remonte au 6 octobre 1966, au cours de laquelle il a étudié en vol l'ouragan Inez. Sa dernière mission remonte au 10 octobre 2018, avec l'ouragan Michael. Sa carrière active de "chasseur" s'étend sur 52 ans et 4 jours.

• Employé dans la même société : le 2 avril 2018, Walter Orthmann (BRA) avait travaillé chez le fabricant de textiles Industrias Renaux (aujourd'hui RenauxView) à Brusque (Santa Catarina, BRA), pendant 80 ans et 75 jours. Il a commencé le 17 janvier 1938.

LE TAUX D'INFLATION LE PLUS ÉLEVÉ

Selon l'édition d'avril 2018 du *World Economic Outlook* du FMI, le Venezuela détient le taux d'inflation le plus élevé. Il était en moyenne de 1 087,5 % en 2017, pour atteindre 2 818,4 %. Selon les projections du FMI pour 2018, il aurait augmenté de manière exponentielle, avec un taux annuel d'inflation estimé à 13 864,6 %.

LA PLUS GRANDE SOMME D'ARGENT PERDUE AU JEU PAR UN PAYS

Selon les chiffres publiés en mai 2017 par l'organisation du jeu internationale H2 Gambling Capital, un adulte australien moyen a perdu 1 052 $ en pariant en 2016. Singapour arrivait en 2e position, avec une moyenne de 674 $ par habitant et, en 3e, l'Irlande, avec 501 $. Environ 70 % des Australiens joueraient régulièrement, en particulier aux machines de poker omniprésentes.

Le 16 août 2018, lorsque cette photo a été prise, un poulet coûtait 14,6 millions bolívars (2,20 $), à Caracas, la capitale du Venezuela.

 AOÛT 16 — *Star of the King*, comédie musicale de 92 min sur Elvis, a été créée en Hongrie en 2002. Ádám Lörincz (HUN, né le 1er juin 1988) avait alors 14 ans et 76 jours, ce qui en fait **le plus jeune compositeur de comédie musicale**.

 AOÛT 17 — En 1896, Bridget Driscoll (GBR) est devenue **le 1er piéton à être tué par une voiture**, alors qu'elle croisait la route d'une voiture roulant à 6,4 km/h, qui effectuait des parcours d'essai à Londres (GBR).

145

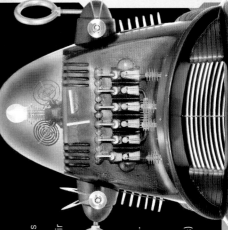

BionicOpter

Int-Ball de JAXA

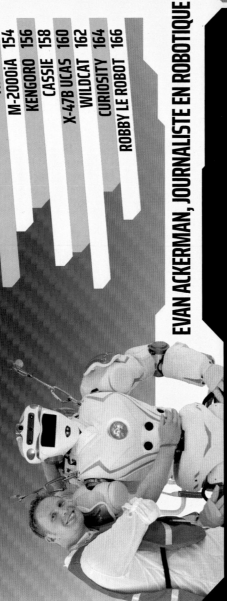

Boston Dynamics

ROBOTS

QU'EST-CE QU'UN ROBOT ?

Au cours de la prochaine décennie, les robots joueront un rôle beaucoup plus actif dans notre vie quotidienne. Grâce à des capteurs et des ordinateurs plus rapides, plus accessibles que jamais, les robots peuvent sortir des laboratoires et pénétrer dans le monde réel. Néanmoins, selon le sens que vous donnez au mot "robot", ces derniers font déjà partie de votre vie depuis des années. Alors, qu'est-ce qu'un robot ?

Il n'existe pas de définition universelle de ce qu'est - et n'est pas - un robot. Cependant, la plupart des gens s'entendraient sûrement sur cette définition : un robot est un appareil capable de détecter, penser et agir. Cela signifie qu'il peut percevoir son environnement, prendre une décision en fonction de ce qu'il voit, puis agir, altérant le monde qui l'entoure.

Au-delà, la définition devient plus délicate. Les robots de science-fiction des années 1950 (voir Robby le Robot, p. 166-167) n'ont pas toujours pas émergé, mais bon nombre de leurs fonctions sont désormais remplies par des dispositifs intelligents autonomes. Même certaines technologies plus anciennes, telles que les thermostats, répondent aux critères de détection, de pensée et d'action autonome. À l'inverse, de nombreux éléments qui ressemblent à ce qu'on attendrait d'un robot – comme la plupart des quadrirotors et des robots militaires – sont en réalité contrôlés à distance par des humains et ne correspondent pas à la définition du robot.

En pratique, le mot "robot" a un sens différent selon le contexte, couvrant les nombreuses manières dont les humains utilisent l'automatisation.

Une bonne analogie serait le mot "animal", qui englobe une large gamme de créatures, de formes microscopiques à l'éléphant.

UN ÉCOSYSTÈME DE ROBOTS

Le monde des robots, comme le monde naturel, est fait de spécialisations. Les roboticiens peuvent être très créatifs en adaptant leurs conceptions aux besoins d'un projet ou en tirant parti d'une nouvelle technologie. Certains robots ressemblent aux humains, d'autres à des animaux, et d'autres encore ne ressemblent à rien d'existant. Les robots peuvent être énormes comme microscopiques. Ils peuvent être plus forts, plus rapides et, à certains égards, plus intelligents que nous.

Malgré les progrès de la technologie (voir ASIMO, ci-dessous), il reste beaucoup à faire. Les robots présentés ici représentent des technologies de pointe qu'on bat tous les records, mais même ces machines n'atteignent pas l'adaptabilité et l'intelligence d'un enfant en bas âge. Toutefois, au cours des prochaines années, les robots actuels seront remplacés par des générations de robots encore plus rapides, puissants et intelligents.

Quelle que soit leur apparence, les robots sont conçus pour nous aider. Ils existent pour faire des choses ennuyeuses, ingrates ou dangereuses. Bien qu'ils ne puissent pas encore exaucer tous nos souhaits, il existe déjà de nombreux robots incroyables qui travaillent dur pour améliorer notre vie.

EVAN ACKERMAN, JOURNALISTE EN ROBOTIQUE

Evan Ackerman, consultant en robotique du GWR, écrit sur les robots depuis plus de 10 ans. Il a lancé son blog en 2007 et écrit dans le magazine IEEE Spectrum.

Quelle a été votre 1re expérience avec les robots ?

Quand j'ai commencé à écrire sur les robots, je n'y connaissais pas grand-chose, mais je me rappelle avoir assisté à ma 1re conférence sur la robotique et avoir été émerveillé par la variété des robots. C'est toujours incroyable, c'est pourquoi je continue d'écrire à ce sujet.

Pourquoi les robots sont-ils mauvais dans des tâches que les humains trouvent faciles ?

Nous, les humains, avons le temps de comprendre le monde qui nous entoure, pas les robots. Ils sont capables d'apprendre à accomplir une tâche à la perfection, mais ils ne sont pas dotés de notre bon

sens. Il est donc très difficile pour eux de s'adapter à de nouvelles situations ou de comprendre des choses pour lesquelles ils n'ont pas été spécifiquement programmés.

Les robots vont-ils me voler mon travail ou conquérir le monde ?

Probablement pas ! Les robots ne sont qu'un autre type de technologie. En fonction de l'évolution de leur utilité, certains emplois seront modifiés, mais les robots ne remplaceront pas les hommes de sitôt. Et ils ne risquent pas de conquérir le monde, à moins d'être programmés pour le faire.

Quel est votre robot préféré ?

J'aime tous les robots, mais certains un peu plus que d'autres... J'apprécie particulièrement Keepon (un robot danseur jaune et spongieux), PR2 (un robot de recherche à 2 bras) et mes 5 Roombas.

Comment puis-je avoir un robot ?

Les aspirateurs robots – comme le Roomba – sont un excellent moyen d'ajouter un robot utile à votre vie. Si vous voulez essayer de fabriquer un robot, commencez avec un kit de robotique qui vous apprendra également à programmer.

CONTRÔLE DE VOL

Un moteur est placé à chaque joint d'aile, contrôlant leur degré de mouvement. Des capteurs dans le corps du BionicOpter l'aident à maintenir sa stabilité et à surveiller son vol. Ils évaluent la position et la torsion des ailes, ainsi que la vitesse et la direction du robot.

15–20 Hz **1**

2 90°

3 50°

4

Les moteurs à chaque joint permettent aux ailes de bouger indépendamment, avec des intensités de poussée variables.

LE BIONICOPTER EN ACTION

Le BionicOpter est piloté par un simple joystick, les actions de l'opérateur modifiant subtilement divers aspects du vol du robot. Il peut **(1)** augmenter ou diminuer le taux de battement, **(2)** modifier l'angle de l'aile, **(3)** augmenter l'amplitude de chaque battement et **(4)** bouger sa tête et sa queue pour équilibrer son poids.

Le corps du robot ne mesure que 44 cm de long, mais contient un microcontrôleur, 9 moteurs et une batterie.

AU CŒUR DU ROBOT

Un mécanisme compact à l'intérieur du BionicOpter traduit le mouvement des 9 moteurs électriques en oscillations complexes d'ailes d'insecte. Un système de contrôle coordonne les changements de rythme des battements et la répartition du poids pour permettre un vol stable.

ISTANTS HUMANOÏDES

HANDLE

Certains robots sont humanoïdes, avec quelques améliorations mécaniques. Les fonctionnalités d'Atlas et ajouté des roues motorisées. Les patins à roulettes intégrés d'Handle lui permettent de se déplacer vite et efficacement sur des surfaces planes, tout en conservant sa capacité à monter des escaliers ou à traverser des terrains accidentés. Conçu pour transporter des colis au sein d'entrepôts ou à notre porte, Handle peut soulever 45 kg.

ASIMO

Le robot ASIMO de Honda a été dévoilé le 20 novembre 2000. Il représentait une grande avancée pour le programme robotique de Honda (voir p. 147), avec sa reconnaissance faciale, son autonomie et une liberté de mouvement de 57 degrés. ASIMO a conservé le titre de **robot humanoïde au plus fort degré de liberté** pendant plus de 10 ans. Il est désormais détenu par Kengoro (voir p. 156-157). Avec ASIMO, Honda a montré que les robots pouvaient fonctionner aux côtés des humains, bien qu'il n'ait pas été conçu pour une utilisation réelle.

E2-DR

En 2018, Honda a annoncé que son programme de développement d'humanoïdes s'éloignerait d'ASIMO pour se concentrer sur des robots plus utiles dans le monde réel. E2-DR est un robot créé pour intervenir en cas de situation d'urgence. Il est conçu pour pénétrer dans des endroits trop dangereux pour l'homme, tels que des réacteurs nucléaires ou des bâtiments endommagés par un séisme. Il est capable de gravir des escaliers et des échelles et de marcher sur des débris, à 4 pattes si nécessaire.

T-HR3 ET SON SYSTÈME DE MANŒUVRE MAÎTRE

La "téléprésence" décrit une situation dans laquelle un humain contrôle un robot à distance. L'humanoïde T-HR3 de Toyota est livré avec un "système de manœuvre maître" qui capte les mouvements d'un téléopérateur humain et les font reproduire par le robot. L'humain partage la vision du robot dans une réalité virtuelle immersive.

Atlas a des caméras en guise de vision stéréo. Il est aussi équipé de la technologie de capteur LIDAR, de la lumière laser réfléchie qui utilise la lumière laser réfléchie pour mesurer la distance d'un objet.

Les poignets modulaires peuvent être équipés de différentes pinces.

Cette main à 3 doigts est conçue pour être fonctionnelle plutôt que comme une réplique de main humaine.

Boston Dynamics

ATLAS

Si nous voulons que les robots nous assistent, nous sauvent ou prennent soin de nous à mesure que nous vieillissons, une forme semblable à la nôtre facilitera leur présence dans des lieux adaptés à l'homme.

À court terme, les robots peuvent être simplifiés par rapport aux humains – par exemple, disposer d'un ou deux doigts est suffisant pour réaliser la plupart des tâches. Les robots présentent par ailleurs des fonctionnalités que les hommes n'ont pas, telles que la possibilité de remplacer certains membres par des outils. Cette adaptation sera cruciale lorsqu'ils seront utilisés dans le monde du travail.

LE 1ᵉʳ BACKFLIP D'UN ROBOT HUMANOÏDE BIPÈDE

Boston Dynamics, la société qui a conçu Atlas, est connue pour ses projets secrets. La plupart de ses avancées récentes ont été présentées par le biais de courtes vidéos mystérieuses sur YouTube. Nous avons vu Atlas trier de lourds cartons dans un entrepôt (à gauche), faire du running sur le campus de Boston Dynamics (ci-dessous, à droite) et, le 17 novembre 2017, effectuer le 1ᵉʳ backflip d'un robot humanoïde grandeur nature (ci-dessous, à gauche). Ce dernier exploit, qui a nécessité de nombreux essais, a montré la vitesse, la force et la coordination d'Atlas.

En 2012, la DARPA (Defense Advanced Research Projects, USA) a annoncé 2 défis destinés à montrer le potentiel de la technologie robotique en cas de catastrophe. Pour remporter ce défi, les robots devaient effectuer des tâches telles que déblayer des débris, utiliser des outils électriques et conduire des véhicules. La DARPA a choisi Boston Dynamics pour créer un robot standard pour la compétition. Le robot Atlas 1ʳᵉ génération a été présenté en 2013. Il utilise des pistons hydrauliques compacts pour mouvoir ses membres, le rendant bien plus puissant que les robots humanoïdes qui utilisent des moteurs électriques. Le dernier Atlas de la DARPA mesurait 1,9 m, pesait 156 kg, et était assez fort pour se relever en cas de chute.

Le DARPA Robotics Challenge a pris fin en 2015, mais Boston Dynamics a poursuivi la mise à niveau du matériel d'Atlas tout en lui apportant de nouvelles choses. Début 2016, ils ont dévoilé une version plus agile d'Atlas, capable de traverser des terrains accidentés, de transporter des objets lourds et de se relever après une chute. Atlas a appris à courir, à sauter et même à exécuter **le 1ᵉʳ backflip d'un robot humanoïde** (voir ci-dessus), faisant de lui l'un des robots humanoïdes les plus dynamiques jamais construits.

Les capteurs des jambes à commande hydraulique aident Atlas à maintenir son équilibre.

Boston Dynamics a utilisé l'impression 3D pour intégrer des systèmes tels que des actionneurs hydrauliques, dans les membres du robot. Cela réduit le nombre de pièces individuelles, rendant Atlas plus léger et compact.

Ses pieds, semblables à des palmes, sont fonctionnels et non conçus pour ressembler à des pieds humains.

LA DÉMARCHE LA PLUS EFFICACE D'UN ROBOT BIPÈDE

DURUS a été développé en 2016 par le laboratoire AMBER (USA), alors installé à l'Institut de technologie de Géorgie. Lors des tests sur tapis de course, le robot a enregistré un coût de transport de 1,02. Un coût de transport bas implique un système efficace, capable d'aller plus loin en consommant moins d'énergie. Le coût de transport moyen d'un humain est d'environ 0,2 pour la marche et 0,8 pour la course.

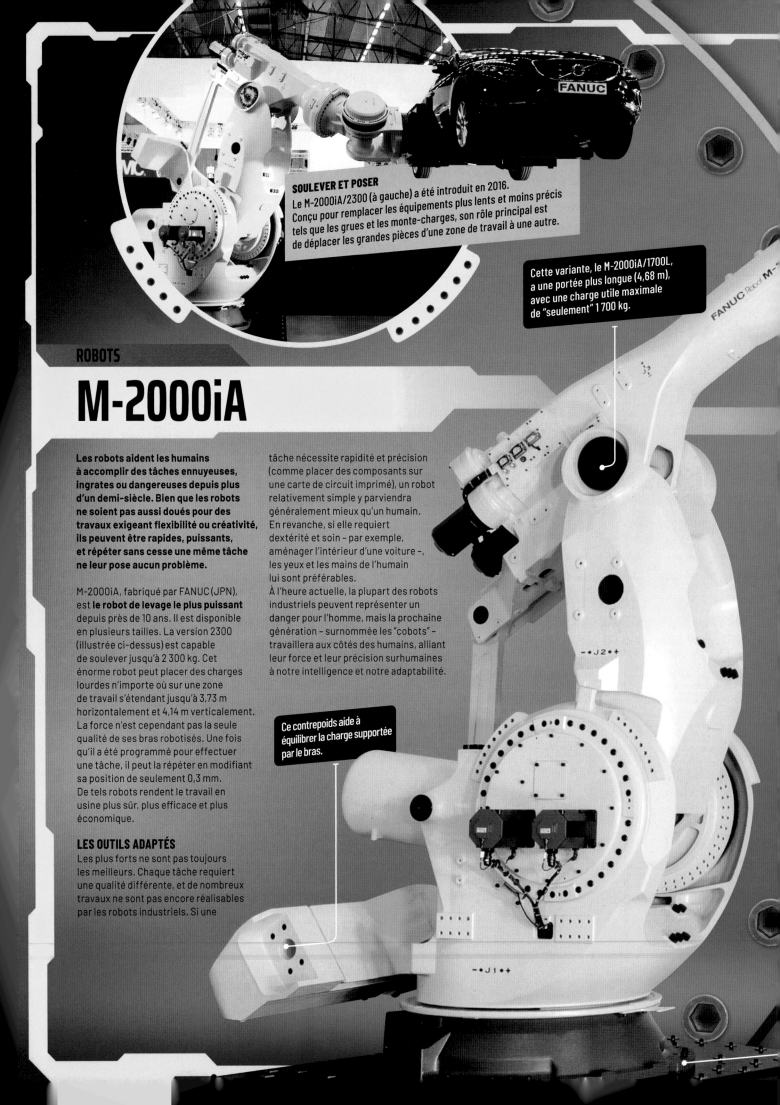

SOULEVER ET POSER
Le M-2000iA/2300 (à gauche) a été introduit en 2016. Conçu pour remplacer les équipements plus lents et moins précis tels que les grues et les monte-charges, son rôle principal est de déplacer les grandes pièces d'une zone de travail à une autre.

Cette variante, le M-2000iA/1700L, a une portée plus longue (4,68 m), avec une charge utile maximale de "seulement" 1 700 kg.

M-2000iA

Les robots aident les humains à accomplir des tâches ennuyeuses, ingrates ou dangereuses depuis plus d'un demi-siècle. Bien que les robots ne soient pas aussi doués pour des travaux exigeant flexibilité ou créativité, ils peuvent être rapides, puissants, et répéter sans cesse une même tâche ne leur pose aucun problème.

M-2000iA, fabriqué par FANUC (JPN), est **le robot de levage le plus puissant** depuis près de 10 ans. Il est disponible en plusieurs tailles. La version 2300 (illustrée ci-dessus) est capable de soulever jusqu'à 2 300 kg. Cet énorme robot peut placer des charges lourdes n'importe où sur une zone de travail s'étendant jusqu'à 3,73 m horizontalement et 4,14 m verticalement. La force n'est cependant pas la seule qualité de ses bras robotisés. Une fois qu'il a été programmé pour effectuer une tâche, il peut la répéter en modifiant sa position de seulement 0,3 mm. De tels robots rendent le travail en usine plus sûr, plus efficace et plus économique.

LES OUTILS ADAPTÉS
Les plus forts ne sont pas toujours les meilleurs. Chaque tâche requiert une qualité différente, et de nombreux travaux ne sont pas encore réalisables par les robots industriels. Si une tâche nécessite rapidité et précision (comme placer des composants sur une carte de circuit imprimé), un robot relativement simple y parviendra généralement mieux qu'un humain. En revanche, si elle requiert dextérité et soin – par exemple, aménager l'intérieur d'une voiture –, les yeux et les mains de l'humain lui sont préférables. À l'heure actuelle, la plupart des robots industriels peuvent représenter un danger pour l'homme, mais la prochaine génération – surnommée les "cobots" – travaillera aux côtés des humains, alliant leur force et leur précision surhumaines à notre intelligence et notre adaptabilité.

Ce contrepoids aide à équilibrer la charge supportée par le bras.

L'avion de combat sans pilote X-47B est propulsé par un turboréacteur à post-combustion F100-PW-220U de Pratt & Whitney.

Bien que l'avion n'ait jamais été armé, il possède une soute pouvant contenir 2 041 kg d'armement.

Le train avant peut être commandé par un appareil portatif quand l'avion est sur le pont.

Une cellule renforcée protège l'avion contre l'air marin salé.

GUERRIER FURTIF
Le X-47B a une allure aplatie d'aile volante qui rappelle le bombardier furtif B-2. Il est donc difficilement détectable par les radars et les capteurs de chaleur.

LA VIE EN MER
Le X-47B a été conçu pour fonctionner en mer. Ses ailes peuvent se replier, réduisant sa largeur de 18,9 à 9,4 m, ce qui lui donne un meilleur "spot factor" – une mesure relative au nombre d'avions pouvant être installés sur le pont d'un porte-avions.

ROBOTS
X–47B UCAS

Les véhicules aériens sans pilote (drones ou UAV) ont dépassé leurs applications militaires initiales et trouvé leur place dans de nombreux domaines de la vie moderne. Leur intelligence évolue plus vite que celle de la plupart des autres robots, et beaucoup sont assez bon marché pour être à la portée des particuliers et petites entreprises.

Les générations précédentes de drones, tel le MQ-9 Reaper de l'armée américaine, ont une autonomie limitée et dépendent d'un pilote au sol pour de nombreuses tâches. À mesure que le coût des capteurs et ordinateurs diminue, même les drones les moins chers sont de plus en plus autonomes. Les drones militaires sont toujours les plus avancés, avec une intelligence artificielle qui leur permet de réaliser d'impressionnantes manœuvres.

Le X-47B UCAS (*Unmanned Combat Air System*) de Northrop Grumman, développé par l'US Navy en 2011, illustre bien le chemin parcouru par les drones. Le 10 juillet 2013, le prototype du X-47B a été **le 1er drone autonome à atterrir sur un porte-avions** – l'USS *George H. W. Bush* au large de la Virginie (USA). Les atterrissages sur porte-avions font partie des manœuvres les plus difficiles. Les pilotes doivent attraper un brin d'arrêt sur un pont en mouvement, 20 % moins large qu'une piste standard.

Bien que les humains restent les meilleurs pilotes, les drones autonomes présentent leurs propres avantages : ils ont des réflexes ultrarapides, restent alertes pendant des jours et ne sont pas affectés par des forces G élevées. Pour l'armée, l'utilisation de drones signifie également que les humains peuvent être tenus à l'écart du danger, en particulier lors d'opérations de routine où la présence d'un pilote hautement qualifié n'est pas nécessaire.

Les petits drones possèdent également des avantages d'un point de vue commercial, leur taille et leur prix abordable leur permettant d'être exploités dans des activités telles que l'agriculture (pour surveiller les cultures ou le bétail) et la médecine (pour effectuer des livraisons qui sauvent des vies).

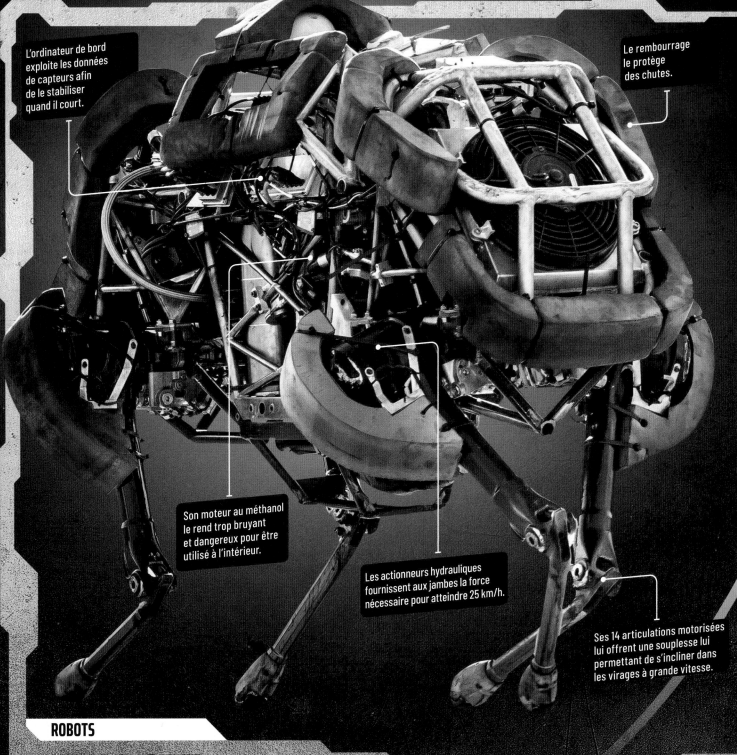

L'ordinateur de bord exploite les données de capteurs afin de le stabiliser quand il court.

Le rembourrage le protège des chutes.

Son moteur au méthanol le rend trop bruyant et dangereux pour être utilisé à l'intérieur.

Les actionneurs hydrauliques fournissent aux jambes la force nécessaire pour atteindre 25 km/h.

Ses 14 articulations motorisées lui offrent une souplesse lui permettant de s'incliner dans les virages à grande vitesse.

ROBOTS

WILDCAT

Les humains ont un penchant pour les robots bipèdes, même si on ne peut pas nier qu'avoir 4 jambes serait plus simple. Avoir plus de jambes simultanément au sol facilite le levage de charges lourdes et le maintien de l'équilibre, notamment sur les terrains accidentés ou lors de déplacements rapides.

Les robots quadrupèdes sont plus polyvalents que les modèles à roues ou à chenilles, et plus stables et fiables que leurs équivalents à 2 jambes. C'est pour cette raison que les robots quadrupèdes seront sûrement parmi les 1ers à sortir des laboratoires et des environnements contrôlés

pour se confronter au monde réel et à son lot d'imprévus. Ils exploreront des zones sinistrées, inspecteront du matériel et livreront même des colis.

GUÉPARD ET CHAT SAUVAGE

De nombreuses innovations en matière de conception quadrupède ont été entreprises par Boston Dynamics (USA). Au cours des années 2000 et 2010, ses équipes se sont inspirées de l'allure d'animaux quadrupèdes pour les adapter à leurs robots. En imitant la marche, le trot ou le galop de ces animaux, ils espéraient atteindre une vitesse et une efficacité de mouvement supérieures.

Le 1er essai de Boston Dynamics en matière de conception d'un quadrupède rapide est le robot câblé Cheetah, capable d'atteindre 45,5 km/h sur un tapis de course. En 2013, ses techniciens ont intégré le système de stabilisation de Cheetah à un robot autonome appelé WildCat, remplaçant l'alimentation externe par un moteur fonctionnant au méthanol. Ce robot de 154 kg était capable de galoper jusqu'à 25 km/h sur un terrain relativement plat, faisant de lui **le robot quadrupède autonome le plus rapide**.

Les robots à 4 pattes ont beaucoup évolué depuis 2013, mais aucune conception n'a encore rivalisé avec Wildcat et sa vitesse incroyable.

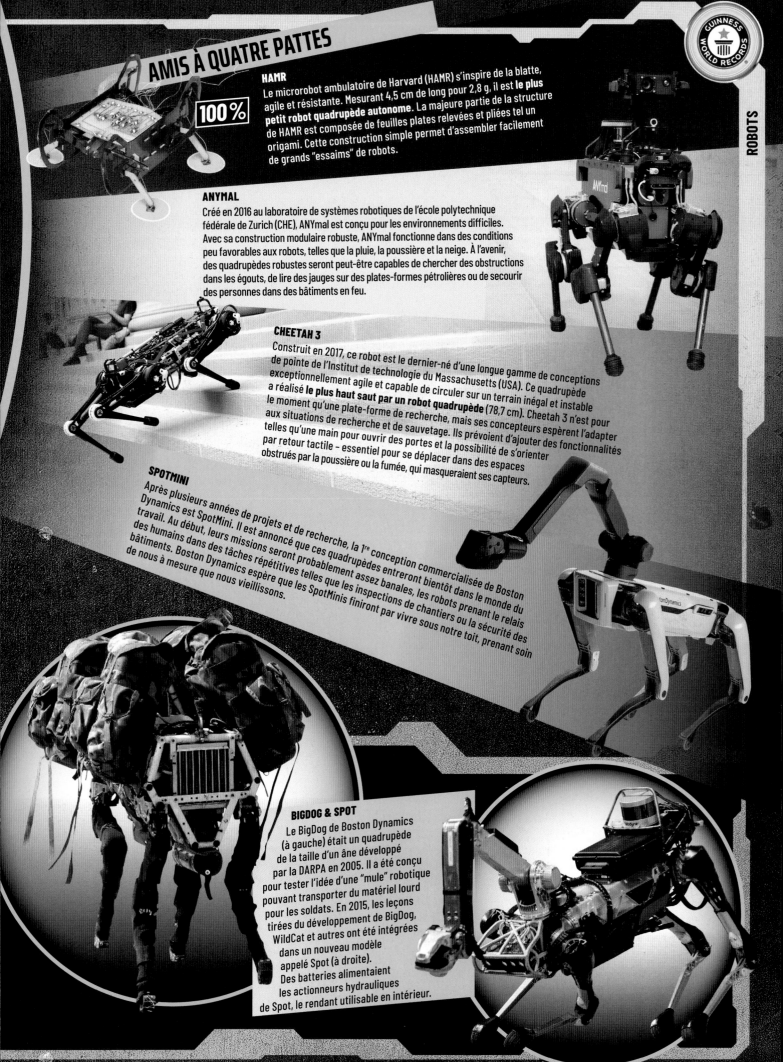

AMIS À QUATRE PATTES

100 %

HAMR

Le microrobot ambulatoire de Harvard (HAMR) s'inspire de la blatte, agile et résistante. Mesurant 4,5 cm de long pour 2,8 g, il est **le plus petit robot quadrupède autonome**. La majeure partie de la structure de HAMR est composée de feuilles plates relevées et pliées tel un origami. Cette construction simple permet d'assembler facilement de grands "essaims" de robots.

ANYMAL

Créé en 2016 au laboratoire de systèmes robotiques de l'école polytechnique fédérale de Zurich (CHE), ANYmal est conçu pour les environnements difficiles. Avec sa construction modulaire robuste, ANYmal fonctionne dans des conditions peu favorables aux robots, telles que la pluie, la poussière et la neige. À l'avenir, des quadrupèdes robustes seront peut-être capables de chercher des obstructions dans les égouts, de lire des jauges sur des plates-formes pétrolières ou de secourir des personnes dans des bâtiments en feu.

CHEETAH 3

Construit en 2017, ce robot est le dernier-né d'une longue gamme de conceptions de pointe de l'Institut de technologie du Massachusetts (USA). Ce quadrupède exceptionnellement agile et capable de circuler sur un terrain inégal et instable a réalisé **le plus haut saut par un robot quadrupède** (78,7 cm). Cheetah 3 n'est pour le moment qu'une plate-forme de recherche, mais ses concepteurs espèrent l'adapter aux situations de recherche et de sauvetage. Ils prévoient d'ajouter des fonctionnalités telles qu'une main pour ouvrir des portes et la possibilité de s'orienter par retour tactile – essentiel pour se déplacer dans des espaces obstrués par la poussière ou la fumée, qui masqueraient ses capteurs.

SPOTMINI

Après plusieurs années de projets et de recherche, la 1ʳᵉ conception commercialisée de Boston Dynamics est SpotMini. Il est annoncé que ces quadrupèdes entreront bientôt dans le monde du travail. Au début, leurs missions seront probablement assez banales, les robots prenant le relais des humains dans des tâches répétitives telles que les inspections de chantiers ou la sécurité des bâtiments. Boston Dynamics espère que les SpotMinis finiront par vivre sous notre toit, prenant soin de nous à mesure que nous vieillissons.

BIGDOG & SPOT

Le BigDog de Boston Dynamics (à gauche) était un quadrupède de la taille d'un âne développé par la DARPA en 2005. Il a été conçu pour tester l'idée d'une "mule" robotique pouvant transporter du matériel lourd pour les soldats. En 2015, les leçons tirées du développement de BigDog, WildCat et autres ont été intégrées dans un nouveau modèle appelé Spot (à droite). Des batteries alimentaient les actionneurs hydrauliques de Spot, le rendant utilisable en intérieur.

ROBOTS DANS L'ESPACE

LUNOKHOD & YUTU-2

Le 1ᵉʳ rover planétaire est Lunokhod 1 (à droite) de l'Union soviétique, qui a atterri sur la Lune le 17 novembre 1970. Bien que simple selon les normes modernes, Lunokhod disposait d'un degré d'autonomie important, avec un système adaptant les commandes reçues de la Terre pour les terrains difficiles. Les leçons qui en ont été tirées ont servi aux rovers suivants, dont Yutu-2 (tout à droite), qui a effectué **le 1ᵉʳ atterrissage sur la face cachée de la Lune** – à l'intérieur de l'atterrisseur du Chang'e-4 – le 3 janvier 2019.

INT-BALL

Les astronautes de la *Station spatiale internationale* (ISS) consacrent environ 10 % de leur journée de travail à prendre des photos et vidéos d'expériences en cours. Pour les aider, le 4 juin 2017, l'Agence d'exploration aérospatiale japonaise (JAXA) a envoyé la caméra interne sphérique JEM ("Int-Ball") – **la 1ʳᵉ caméra autonome sur une station spatiale**. Int-Ball est équipée de minuscules ventilateurs, qui la propulsent autour du module *Kibo*, et utilise des marqueurs visuels pour circuler d'une station expérimentale à une autre.

ROBONAUT 2 & VALKYRIE

Le 1ᵉʳ robot humanoïde dans l'espace est Robonaut 2 (à droite). Robonaut est arrivé à l'*ISS* à bord de la navette spatiale *Discovery* le 26 février 2011, et a été mis en route le 22 août 2011. Après 7 ans dans l'espace, Robonaut est revenu sur Terre en mai 2018 pour être réparé. Afin de poursuivre ses recherches en robotique sur Terre, la NASA a développé en 2013 un robot humanoïde expérimental appelé Valkyrie (tout à droite), dont des copies ont été distribuées à des partenaires dans le monde entier.

SPIRIT & OPPORTUNITY

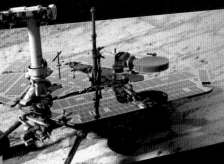

Les rovers jumeaux Opportunity (à gauche) et Spirit ont atterri sur Mars en janvier 2004. Ils étaient nettement plus grands et performants que **le 1ᵉʳ rover sur Mars**, Sojourner, qui a atterri avec la mission Mars Pathfinder en 1997. Les véhicules ont reçu plusieurs mises à jour au cours de leur longue mission (voir p. 184), afin d'augmenter leur autonomie et de tester des systèmes utilisés avec Curiosity.

ATTERRISSAGE EN DOUCEUR

Atterrir sur Mars est compliqué. La NASA a essayé diverses méthodes au fil des années, notamment des fusées à bord et des coussins d'air externes. La plus complexe de toutes est le système de grue volante qui a descendu *Curiosity* d'une plate-forme en vol stationnaire à 20 m au-dessus de la surface.

ROBOTS

CURIOSITY

Nous envoyons des robots explorer l'espace car ils y sont beaucoup mieux adaptés que les humains. Nous sommes fragiles et ne pouvons pas survivre sans nourriture, eau et chaleur. Un jour, les humains retourneront sur la Lune et iront sur Mars, mais tant que nous n'aurons pas la technologie nécessaire pour y parvenir, les robots continueront à prendre notre place dans l'exploration du Système solaire.

Le 6 août 2012, la NASA a fait atterrir sur Mars le rover *Curiosity*. De la taille d'une voiture et pesant 899 kg – dont 80 kg d'instruments scientifiques –, *Curiosity* est **le plus grand rover planétaire**. Depuis plus de 7 ans, ce robot à énergie nucléaire essaie de répondre aux questions non élucidées concernant notre planète voisine.

SE DÉPLACER

Diriger un rover sur Mars n'est pas seulement une question de contrôle à distance. Les signaux terrestres peuvent mettre jusqu'à 24 min à atteindre Mars. Il est donc impossible que *Curiosity* ne s'appuie que sur l'intervention de l'homme pour ses déplacements. La plupart du temps, le rover est ainsi semi-autonome, avec des opérateurs humains qui planifient ses trajets et fixent des objectifs majeurs depuis la Terre. Une fois que ces objectifs ont été relayés au rover, les ordinateurs de bord de *Curiosity* décident des détails de l'itinéraire, du déploiement des bras et du ciblage laser.

Les données recueillies par les caméras et instruments du rover sont transmises à la Terre une ou deux fois par jour. Ces données fournissent aux scientifiques des informations sur Mars et son histoire. Le futur rover de la NASA, *Mars 2020* – qui devrait atterrir dans le cratère Jezero en février 2021 –, sera encore plus grand que *Curiosity*, avec une masse totale de 1 050 kg.

Cette partie du rover s'appelle le "mât". Il contient le système de caméra principal et le laser ChemCam.

Le rover est alimenté par un générateur thermoélectrique à radio-isotope, qui exploite la chaleur provenant des pastilles de plutonium radioactif pour produire de l'électricité.

Parmi les instruments du bras robotique, on compte la caméra MAHLI et le spectromètre à particules alpha et à rayons X.

SÉANCE PHOTO
Le rover *Curiosity* de la NASA compte 17 caméras, dont une au bout de son bras qui a réalisé **le 1er selfie complet sur une autre planète** le 31 octobre 2012. L'image est en fait une mosaïque de 55 images assemblées numériquement de manière à supprimer le bras du premier plan.

Les roues ont souffert sur la surface rocheuse et portent des bosses, des perforations et des déchirures.

GUINNESS WORLD RECORDS

Les moteurs de Robby ont été récupérés dans les tourelles d'un avion-bombardier de la Seconde Guerre mondiale.

Dans *Planète interdite*, cette pièce servait à distribuer de tout, des donuts au whisky.

L'intensité des lumières bleues dans la "bouche" de Robby pulsait au rythme de ses dialogues.

L'opérateur de Robby ouvrait et fermait ses mains en tirant sur des leviers à l'intérieur de ses bras.

L'HISTOIRE DES ROBOTS AU CINÉMA

MASCHINENMENSCH
Les 1res apparitions de robots à l'écran ont précédé l'usage même du mot "robot" (à l'origine, un terme tchèque synonyme de travail forcé, utilisé pour la 1re fois au sens moderne en 1920 par le dramaturge Karel Čapek). On les appelait des "automates". Le 1er à jouer un rôle clé dans un film est l'emblématique Maschinenmensch ("homme-machine") dans Metropolis de Fritz Lang, grand classique de science-fiction sorti en 1927.

C-3PO
Ce droïde protocolaire timide (interprété par Anthony Daniels) a fait **le plus d'apparitions dans la saga *Star Wars***, figurant dans 9 des 10 films de la franchise. Comme Robby avant lui, C-3PO est très intelligent et doté d'une personnalité distincte, tout en étant traité comme une simple machine qu'on achète et qu'on revend.

TERMINATOR
L'infiltrateur T-800, ou "Terminator", dans le blockbuster *Terminator* (1984), est un robot assassin conçu pour ressembler aux humains. Dans le film, le T-800 (interprété par Arnold Schwarzenegger) est envoyé pour tuer le chef des forces humaines anti-robot, un scénario qui joue sur la peur que l'être humain soit un jour renversé par les machines.

ROBOCOP
Le thriller de science-fiction *RoboCop* (1987) met en scène l'hybride humain-robot du même nom, associant un corps de machine quasi indestructible à l'esprit d'un policier récemment tué. Entre explosions et fusillades, le film questionne l'avenir des robots, se demandant si ceux-ci travailleront pour aider l'humanité, ou uniquement leurs propriétaires.

WALL-E
Dans *WALL-E* de Pixar (2008), qui a remporté **le plus de nominations aux Oscars pour un film d'animation** (6), les humains se sont complètement retirés du monde du travail. La gestion de leurs vaisseaux spatiaux et le nettoyage des ruines polluées de la Terre ont été confiés à une armée de robots.

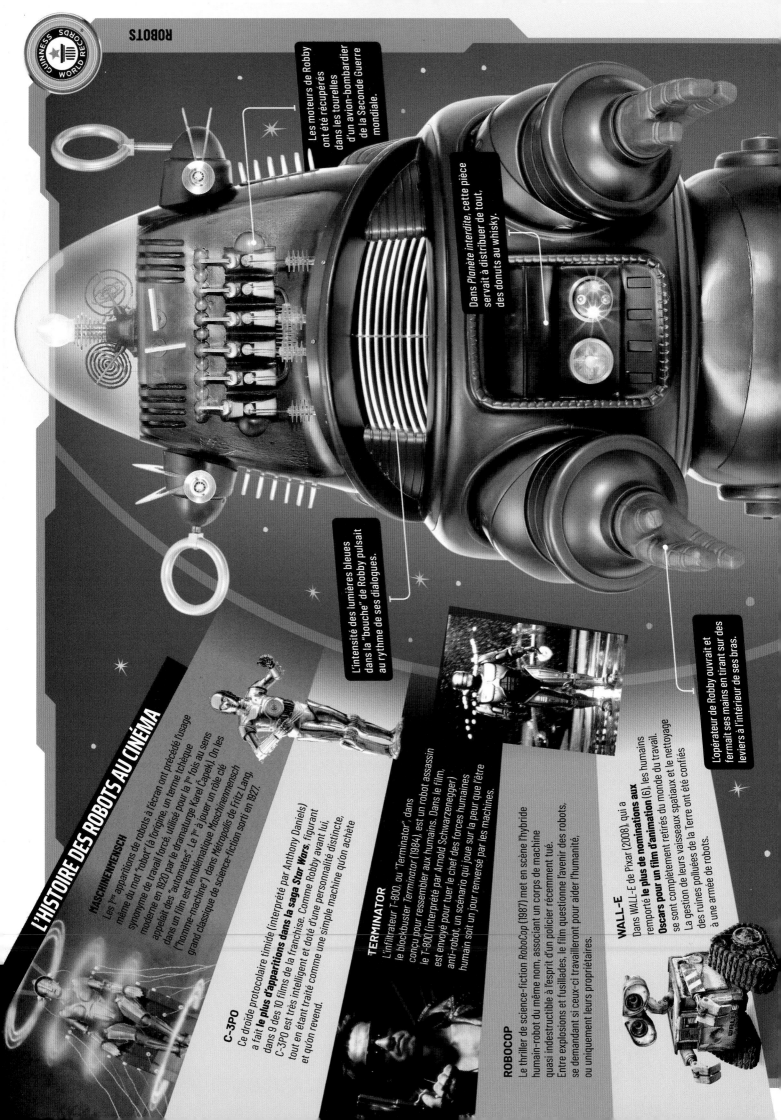

Le corps était fabriqué en plastique ABS, installé sur une structure en métal.

DONNER VIE À ROBBY

L'opérateur qui donnait vie à Robby portait une combinaison de 54 kg sur un harnais en cuir et en métal (à gauche). L'espace étant limité, il devait mesurer 1,60 m maximum et afficher un tour de taille de 76 cm. Un autre opérateur se tenait à proximité et contrôlait le système électrique de la combinaison depuis le tableau de bord présenté ci-dessous.

EAR LAMPS

GENTIL OU MÉCHANT ?

Au cours de sa carrière de plus de 20 ans au cinéma et à la télévision, Robby a joué le rôle d'un serviteur et à la télévision, Robby a joué le rôle d'un serviteur obligeant dans *Planète interdite* (ci-dessus). Il a été l'outil d'un sinistre superordinateur dans *Le Cerveau infernal* (1957). Dans un épisode de *La Quatrième Dimension* de 1964, il jouait un robot dont le rôle était de remplacer à moindre coût les travailleurs humains dans une usine.

ROBOTS

ROBBY LE ROBOT

Le 21 novembre 2017, un enchérisseur anonyme de Bonhams New York a payé la somme stupéfiante de 5 375 000 $ pour acquérir ce robot emblématique – l'accessoire de cinéma le plus cher vendu aux enchères. Alors, que peut bien avoir de si particulier ce viel accessoire?

Pour la majorité des gens, le 1er robot qu'ils voient de leur vie apparaît dans un film, un jeu ou une série. Robby le Robot est un des robots les plus célèbres et les plus reconnaissables de l'histoire du cinéma. Il a été créé pour le film de science-fiction *Planète interdite* (1956), dans lequel il joue le rôle de serviteur et protecteur du mystérieux Dr Edward Morbius et de sa fille.

Son fonctionnement

Contrairement à ses prédécesseurs, tels que Gort dans *Le Jour où la Terre s'arrêta* (1951),

Robby était bien plus qu'un simple acteur dans un costume en métal. Avec ses pièces mobiles et ses lumières éclatantes, Robby était le symbole d'un monde technologique qui rattrapait la fiction.

Ce robot avait besoin d'au moins 2 personnes pour fonctionner. La 1re était l'acteur qui se glissait dans le corps du robot. Celui-ci partageait le costume étroit avec 365 m de câbles électriques. Ses yeux se situaient au niveau des interstices de la grille lumineuse qui formait la "bouche" de Robby. Un 2nd opérateur, hors champ, contrôlait les antennes et lumières qui composaient la tête et le "cœur" de Robby, déclenchant les mouvements nécessaires à chaque scène.

Même si nous vivons dans un monde où les robots font de plus en plus partie de notre quotidien, ce sont ces créations fictives qui ont façonné notre image des robots, suggérant leur potentiel et leur capacité à changer le monde (pour le meilleur ou le pire).

TÊTE D'AFFICHE

Au moment de sa construction en 1955, Robby était l'un des accessoires de cinéma les plus chers jamais fabriqués. Il aurait coûté 125 000 $ – l'équivalent d'environ 1,18 million $ actuels – représentant environ 7 % du budget de *Planète interdite*. Le studio a donc cherché à tirer parti au mieux de sa nouvelle création en l'envoyant en tournée promotionnelle et en le plaçant au centre de l'affiche du film (à droite).

CINEMASCOPE COLOR

FORBIDDEN PLANET

M-G-M PRESENTS

STARRING WALTER PIDGEON · ANNE FRANCIS · LESLIE NIELSEN With WARREN STEVENS And Introducing ROBBY, THE ROBOT

Screen Play by CYRIL HUME · Based on a Story by IRVING BLOCK and ALLEN ADLER · Photographed in EASTMAN COLOR · Directed by FRED McLEOD WILCOX · Produced by NICHOLAS NAYFACK

AMAZING!

TECHNOLOGIE & INGÉNIERIE

▶ LA PLUS HAUTE GRANDE ROUE SANS RAYONS

Du haut de ses 142,5 m, cette grande roue futuriste qui surplombe le fleuve Bailang (province du Shandong, CHN), offre une vue imprenable sur la mer de Bohai et l'intérieur des terres par-delà Weifang.

Cette attraction, qui a ouvert ses portes au public le 16 mai 2018, utilise une structure immobile en acier qui forme la "roue" autour de laquelle tournent 36 cabines montées sur rails. Elle a été construite par la 6ᵉ division d'ingénierie chinoise et équipée par la société de matériel pour attractions Zhejiang Juma pour la Société de gestion du site touristique du fleuve Bailang à Weifang (tous CHN).

En dépit de sa taille, cette roue, s'avère plus petite que la grande roue la plus haute, inaugurée à Las Vegas (Nevada, USA), le 31 mars 2014. Connue sous le nom de High Roller, elle culmine à 167,5 m et emmène ses visiteurs à une altitude supérieure à 3 fois la hauteur de la colonne Nelson à Londres (GBR).

▶ Regardez des vidéos de ses merveilles sur guinnessworldrecords.com/2020

La construction de cette roue a duré 4 ans. La structure, d'un diamètre de 126,25 m, a nécessité à elle seule 4 600 t d'acier.

SOMMAIRE

LA PLUS GRANDE STATION SPATIALE

La Station spatiale internationale, ou *International Space Station* (*ISS*), laboratoire de recherches en microgravité à la pointe de la technologie, tourne en orbite basse autour de la Terre à la vitesse de 27 540 km/h. C'est la **plus grande station spatiale**, avec une masse de 419 725 kg. Ici, on se rend mieux compte de la taille de l'ISS si on l'imagine posée sur l'un des sites les plus visités de Londres : Trafalgar Square.

La construction de l'ISS a commencé le 20 novembre 1998 dans l'espace après le décollage du module *Zarya* depuis le cosmodrome de Baïkonour (KAZ). Des modules pressurisés ont ensuite rejoint une orbite basse avant d'être interconnectés. La phase initiale s'est achevée avec le couplage du module logistique polyvalent *Leonardo* en février 2011. Aujourd'hui, l'ISS compte un volume pressurisé de 932 m³, comparable à celui d'un Boeing 747, bien que plus de la moitié ne soit pas accessible.

L'ISS est un projet mondial, rassemblant les agences spatiales américaine, canadienne, russe, japonaise et européenne. **Le premier équipage permanent de l'ISS** comptait Sergueï Krikaliov, Iouri Pavlovich Guidzenko (tous deux RUS) et William Shepherd (USA), arrivés le 2 novembre 2000 dans le cadre de l'*Expédition 1*. Ils sont restés à bord pendant 136 jours. Depuis, la station a reçu la visite de plus de 200 astronautes, originaires de plus de 18 nations. Bien que la coopération entre membres d'équipage soit essentielle, ils ne partagent pas tout : les cosmonautes russes de l'ISS profitent à bord de 300 plats différents, parmi lesquels purée de pommes de terre, brocolis au fromage, bœuf séché, pêches et noix — **le menu le plus complet dans l'espace**.

Des éléments viennent finaliser la station spatiale et ses 16 modules pressurisés. **Le plus grand module de l'ISS**, *Kibo*, a été développé par l'agence spatiale japonaise JAXA et lancé le 31 mai 2008 à bord de la navette *Discovery*. Il atteint 11,19 m de long, possède un diamètre de 4,39 m et une masse de 14 800 kg. Le module *Cupola* dispose de 7 hublots en forme de dôme, conçus en verre de silice et en verre borosilicate. Sa baie centrale, qui mesure 80 cm de diamètre, est **le plus grand hublot dans l'espace**. Braqué sur la Terre, *Cupola* offre à l'équipage une excellente visibilité pour les opérations dans l'espace, telles que la manipulation du bras robotique *Canadarm2*.

L'ISS devrait rester en service au moins jusqu'en 2028. À ce jour, on estime le coût total de la station spatiale à environ 104,7 milliards € — ce qui en fait **l'objet le plus coûteux créé par l'être humain**.

S'il est amusant d'imaginer l'ISS posée sur Trafalgar Square, quand la station sera réformée, elle quittera son orbite de manière contrôlée pendant une douzaine de mois et s'abîmera dans l'océan, afin que touristes et pigeons n'aient rien à craindre !

On voit ici l'ISS à l'envers, avec le dôme du module *Cupola* tourné vers le ciel. D'une largeur d'environ 110 m, Trafalgar Square ferait une "place de parking" très étroite pour l'ISS, dont la poutre atteint une longueur de 109 m.

LE PLUS GRAND HABITAT SPATIAL GONFLABLE

Le *Bigelow Expandable Activity Module* (BEAM) est un module gonflable expérimental amarré à l'ISS (il n'apparaît pas sur l'image ci-dessous), dont le volume interne atteint 16 m³. Gonflé et pressurisé le 28 mai 2016, il devait subir des tests pendant 2 ans pour estimer sa viabilité en tant qu'habitat gonflable. En octobre 2017, la NASA a annoncé que le *BEAM* pourrait rester attaché à l'ISS jusqu'au début des années 2020.

Des modules gonflables tels que le *BEAM* seraient très utiles pour les missions vers Mars, car ils offrent de grands espaces habitables sans avoir à être lancés par d'énormes fusées.

LE PLUS GRAND NOMBRE DE SORTIES DEPUIS UNE STATION SPATIALE

Au 11 décembre 2018, 213 sorties spatiales — alias activités extravéhiculaires ou *extra-vehicular activities* (EVA) en anglais — ont eu lieu en dehors de l'ISS afin d'assurer sa maintenance et son assemblage. La plupart des sorties empruntent le sas *Quest*, mais d'autres utilisent le compartiment d'amarrage *Pirs* ou le module *Poisk*. Le temps total passé dans l'espace pendant ces 213 EVA atteint 1 335 h 2 min.

VOITURES EN FOLIE

La voiture la plus chevelue
Maria Lucia Mugno et Valentino Stassano (tous 2 ITA) possèdent une Fiat 500 couverte de 120 kg de cheveux humains, record homologué à Padula Scalo (Salerne, ITA), le 15 mars 2014.

La plus haute bicyclette fonctionnelle
Conçue par Richie Trimble (USA) et homologuée à Los Angeles (Californie, USA), le 26 décembre 2013, *Stoopidtaller* mesure 6,15 m. D'où vient ce nom qui signifie "ridiculement plus grand" ? L'un des premiers vélos construits par Richie s'appelait *Stoopidtall*, "ridiculement grand" !

La limousine la plus lourde
Conçue par Michael Machado et Pamela Bartholomew (tous 2 USA), *Midnight Rider* pèse 22,933 t et mesure 21,3 m de long et 4,16 m de haut.

Le poids le plus lourd tiré par une voiture électrique
Le 15 mai 2018, une voiture Model X prêtée par Tesla Australia a tiré un Boeing 787-9

de 130 t sur 30,4 m. Ce record a eu lieu au centre de maintenance de la compagnie Qantas à Melbourne (Victoria, AUS).

Le slalom le plus rapide à bord d'une automobile
Jia Qiang (CHN) a piloté une Chevrolet Camaro RS entre 50 plots en 48,114 s, à Shaoguan (Guangdong, CHN), le 16 décembre 2018. Les plots n'étaient séparés que de 15,2 m. Cet événement a été organisé par Chevrolet China.

La plus grande parade de dépanneuses
L'association de dépanneurs Fier D'être Dépanneur (FRA) a aligné 491 camions de remorquage, à Moulins (FRA), le 13 octobre 2018.

Le plus grand "burn-out" simultané
Pour faire un "burn-out", le pilote accélère et freine en même temps ; le véhicule reste immobile, tandis que les pneus arrière tournent en dégageant de la fumée. 126 voitures en ont réalisé un organisé par Rare Spares, au Street Machine Summernats (AUS), à Canberra (AUS), le 4 janvier 2019.

Le plus de donuts (révolutions) en voiture assis sur le toit
Après avoir lancé sa voiture, Naji Bou Hassan (LBN) s'est assis sur le toit tandis que le véhicule décrivait 52 révolutions, à Aley (LBN), le 26 août 2018.

LA PLUS GRANDE DANSE SYNCHRONISÉE DE VOITURES
Le 23 octobre 2018, 180 véhicules ont réalisé une chorégraphie lors d'un événement organisé par Nissan Middle East (ARE), à Dubaï (ARE). Les voitures ont esquissé la forme d'un faucon sur le sable du désert, un clin d'œil au Patrol Safari Falcon de Nissan.

LA PLUS LONGUE DISTANCE EN BURN-OUT À MOTO
Le cascadeur Maciej "DOP" Bielicki (POL, ci-dessus) a parcouru 4,47 km sur une Harley-Davidson Street Rod de 2017 tout en effectuant un burn-out, à Rzeszów (POL), le 20 mai 2017. Cet exploit a été accompli en collaboration avec Game Over Cycles, le propriétaire de la plus grande concession Harley-Davidson de Pologne, située à Rzeszów.
Quant à **la plus longue distance en burn-out en voiture**, elle atteint 487,07 m. Elle a été réalisée par Ron Buckholz (USA) dans une Chevrolet Malibu de 1964, le 13 octobre 2018. 600 spectateurs ont assisté à cette tentative au Pacific Raceways de Kent (Washington, USA).

Le plus de personnes sur une motocyclette
58 membres de l'équipe motocycliste des Tornadoes appartenant à l'armée indienne ont chevauché une Royal Enfield 500 cc, à Karnataka (IND), le 19 novembre 2017.

LES PLUS RAPIDES...

Tondeuse à gazon
Le 5 novembre 2015, Per-Kristian Lundefaret (NOR) a atteint 214,96 km/h sur sa tondeuse Viking T6 modifiée, à Vestfold (NOR).

Véhicules en salle
Mikko Hirvonen (FIN) a atteint 140 km/h dans un kart-cross Speedcar XTREM, au Helsinki Expo Centre (FIN), le 25 février 2013.

Scooter électrique pour personnes à mobilité réduite
Sven Ohler (DEU) a piloté un scooter gonflé à 180,26 km/h lors d'une course organisée par *GRIP – Das Motormagazin* à Klettwitz (DEU), le 25 mai 2017.

Chariot motorisé
Le 18 août 2013, Matt McKeown (GBR) a conduit un chariot équipé d'un démarreur d'hélicoptère Chinook modifié de 150 CV (111 kW) pour atteindre 113,298 km/h, à Elvington Airfield (Yorkshire, GBR).

Le plus grand chariot motorisé
mesure 8,23 m de long et 4,57 m. Il a été construit par Fred Reifsteck (USA) en 2012. Il est présenté à South Wales (New York, USA).

En 1960, Mickey Thompson (le père de Danny) est devenu le 1er Américain à franchir la barre des 400 mph (643 km/h), à bord de *Challenger I*.

LA VOITURE À MOTEUR À PISTONS LA PLUS RAPIDE
Pilotée par Danny Thompson (USA), *Challenger 2* a atteint une vitesse moyenne de 722,204 km/h, lors d'une course d'un mile (1 609 m) aller et retour, à Bonneville Salt Flats (Utah, USA), les 11-12 août 2018.
Ce qui reste assez loin de **la voiture la plus rapide**. Avec Andy Green (GBR) au volant, *Thrust SSC* a roulé à 1 227,985 km/h sur un mile (1 609 m), dans le désert de Black Rock (Nevada, USA), le 15 octobre 1997.

LA PLUS GRANDE PARADE DE CAMIONS DE GLACES
Le 16 octobre 2018, un défilé de 84 camions de glaces baptisé la "Ice Cream Van Dream Team" a pris la route à Crewe (Cheshire, GBR). Le convoi, organisé par Edward Whitby de Whitby Morrison (tous 2 GBR), a mis 25 min pour couvrir le trajet de 3,2 km. Cette parade annonçait une exposition de 2 jours consacrée à l'industrie de la glace.

 AOÛT 18 En 1984, Arvind Pandya (IND) se lance dans une tentative pour accomplir **la course à pied à reculons la plus rapide à travers les États-Unis**. Il court 2 400 km de Los Angeles (Californie) à New York en 107 jours.

 AOÛT 19 L'auteur-compositeur et interprète français Gérald Genty effectue **le plus de concerts en 12 h** (37), à Bruxelles (BEL), en 2015. Il joue au moins 5 morceaux devant plus de 10 personnes dans chaque salle.

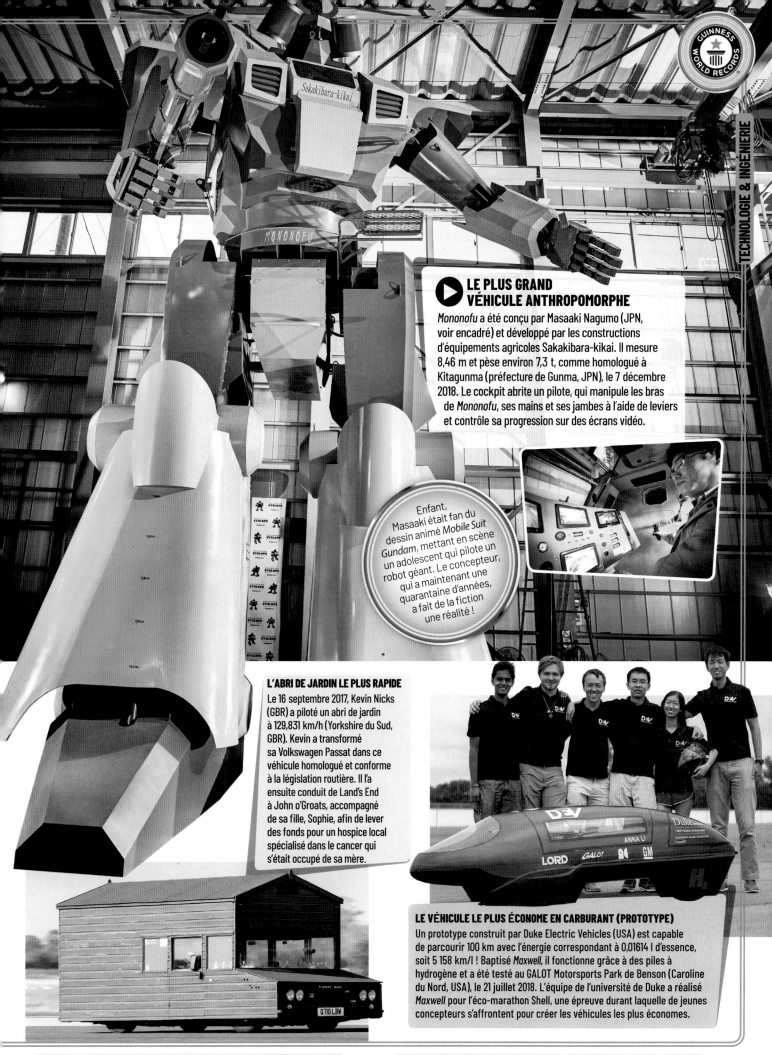

▶ LE PLUS GRAND VÉHICULE ANTHROPOMORPHE

Mononofu a été conçu par Masaaki Nagumo (JPN, voir encadré) et développé par les constructions d'équipements agricoles Sakakibara-kikai. Il mesure 8,46 m et pèse environ 7,3 t, comme homologué à Kitagunma (préfecture de Gunma, JPN), le 7 décembre 2018. Le cockpit abrite un pilote, qui manipule les bras de *Mononofu*, ses mains et ses jambes à l'aide de leviers et contrôle sa progression sur des écrans vidéo.

Enfant, Masaaki était fan du dessin animé *Mobile Suit Gundam*, mettant en scène un adolescent qui pilote un robot géant. Le concepteur, qui a maintenant une quarantaine d'années, a fait de la fiction une réalité !

L'ABRI DE JARDIN LE PLUS RAPIDE

Le 16 septembre 2017, Kevin Nicks (GBR) a piloté un abri de jardin à 129,831 km/h (Yorkshire du Sud, GBR). Kevin a transformé sa Volkswagen Passat dans ce véhicule homologué et conforme à la législation routière. Il l'a ensuite conduit de Land's End à John o'Groats, accompagné de sa fille, Sophie, afin de lever des fonds pour un hospice local spécialisé dans le cancer qui s'était occupé de sa mère.

LE VÉHICULE LE PLUS ÉCONOME EN CARBURANT (PROTOTYPE)

Un prototype construit par Duke Electric Vehicles (USA) est capable de parcourir 100 km avec l'énergie correspondant à 0,01614 l d'essence, soit 5 158 km/l ! Baptisé *Maxwell*, il fonctionne grâce à des piles à hydrogène et a été testé au GALOT Motorsports Park de Benson (Caroline du Nord, USA), le 21 juillet 2018. L'équipe de l'université de Duke a réalisé *Maxwell* pour l'éco-marathon Shell, une épreuve durant laquelle de jeunes concepteurs s'affrontent pour créer les véhicules les plus économes.

AOÛT 20 — En 2009, **le plus grand ensemble de cors des Alpes**, composé de 366 musiciens, se réunit sur le Gornergrat, près de Zermatt (CHE). L'orchestre joue 6 morceaux lors d'un concert de 20 min.

AOÛT 21 — **Le plus de personnes sur un skateboard de taille normale** est de 22. Ce record est réalisé au cours du tournage du clip de *Troublemaker*, du groupe Weezer, à Los Angeles (Californie, USA), en 2008.

SCIENCE XXL

Le laser le plus puissant

Le 6 août 2015, les scientifiques de l'Institut d'ingénierie laser de l'université d'Osaka (JPN) ont expérimenté le Laser for Fast Ignition Experiments, d'une puissance de 2 millions de milliards de watts (2 pétawatts). L'impulsion, qui n'a duré que 1 picoseconde, représente l'équivalent de 1 000 fois toute la puissance électrique consommée quotidiennement dans le monde. Ce laser a pour objectif de générer des faisceaux quantiques à haute énergie qui possèdent de multiples applications potentielles, dont le traitement des cancers.

Le champ magnétique artificiel le plus puissant

En avril 2018, Shojiro Takeyama (JPN) et son équipe de l'université de Tokyo (JPN) ont enregistré le plus grand champ magnétique jamais créé en laboratoire. Il a produit 1 200 teslas et a soufflé les portes en acier de la chambre de confinement où se déroulait l'expérience. Le champ, qui s'est maintenu 40 microsecondes, représentait 400 fois la puissance générée par les aimants utilisés dans les IRM et plus de 50 millions de fois le champ magnétique de la Terre.

Des champs de cette intensité seront peut-être nécessaires pour les réacteurs nucléaires à fusion (tels que le Wendelstein 7-X ci-contre), où les températures du plasma dépassent la tolérance de tous les matériaux connus. Des champs magnétiques pourraient contenir cette substance et ainsi l'empêcher de détruire le réacteur.

▶ Le plus grand accélérateur de particules

Le grand collisionneur de hadrons (*Large Hadron Collider*, LHC) est l'équipement scientifique le plus vaste et le plus complexe. Le collisionneur occupe un tunnel circulaire de 27 km sous Genève (CHE) et pèse 38 000 t. Depuis sa mise en marche le 10 septembre 2008, les travaux au LHC ont mené à d'importantes découvertes scientifiques et à de nombreux records. On notera ainsi **la plus haute température artificielle** :

5 000 milliards de Kelvin (soit 800 millions de fois plus chaud que la surface du Soleil) en 2012, et **la plus haute énergie produite par les collisions d'ions dans un accélérateur de particules** — qui a atteint 1 045 TeV (téraélectronvolts) — en 2015. Ces expériences nécessitent en outre une petite armée de scientifiques. En 2015, l'étude fournissant la mesure de masse la plus précise pour le boson de Higgs, une particule élémentaire, regroupait 5 145 auteurs : **le plus de contributeurs pour un article scientifique**.

L'ordinateur quantique le plus puissant

Lors d'une réunion de l'American Physical Society le 5 mars 2018, les scientifiques de Google (USA) ont dévoilé un ordinateur quantique opérationnel de 72-qubit basé sur un processeur nommé *Bristlecone*. (Un "qubit" est un bit quantique.) À l'heure actuelle, les ordinateurs quantiques font des erreurs qui les rendent beaucoup moins fiables que leurs homologues conventionnels. *Bristlecone* devrait pouvoir fournir aux scientifiques les connaissances qui leur permettront de les améliorer.

La température artificielle la plus basse

Une équipe du Massachusetts Institute of Technology de Cambridge, Massachusetts (USA), conduite par Aaron Leanhardt, a atteint une température de 450 picokelvins (0,000 000 000 45 K au-dessus du zéro absolu, **la température la plus basse possible**). Leur expérience apparaît dans le numéro du 12 septembre 2003 du magazine *Science*.

Le plus grand miroir convexe

En mai 2017, la société allemande Schott a fondu le miroir secondaire (M2) du télescope géant européen, Extremely Large Telescope (ELT), qui devrait être achevé par l'Observatoire européen austral en 2024. Ce miroir d'un diamètre de 4,2 m pèse 3,5 t. Il est conçu dans un verre de type vitrocéramique appelé Zerodur — un matériau au coefficient de dilatation thermique très faible qui le rend indispensable dans les télescopes pour lesquels la qualité de l'image est essentielle. Il lui faut une année pour refroidir après fabrication. Il sera poli et protégé par un revêtement en attendant la construction de l'ELT.

Le plus grand simulateur de séisme 3D

E-Defense est un plateau utilisé pour étudier la résistance aux séismes des immeubles et autres constructions. Situé à Miki, préfecture de Hyōgo (JPN), il mesure 300 m² et peut supporter des structures d'une masse de 1 200 t. Ce plateau peut secouer sa charge en la soumettant à une accélération de 1 *g* horizontalement dans les deux dimensions et de 1,5 *g* verticalement.

LE PLUS GRAND NAVIRE À RETOURNEMENT

Le *FLoating Instrument Platform*, FLIP, est un navire de recherches océaniques de 108 m capable de flotter "à la verticale" en laissant 17 m de sa coque au-dessus de la surface et 91 m immergés. Le navire pivote à 90° en remplissant ses énormes ballasts. En coulant, la partie émergée du FLIP — qui abrite les quartiers des 16 membres d'équipage et leur équipement — se soulève. Il est utilisé par l'institut d'océanographie Scripps de l'université de Californie à San Diego, (USA).

La conception du FLIP offre aux scientifiques une plateforme stable pour étudier météorologie, géophysique et acoustique sous-marine.

LA PLUS GRANDE ENCEINTE À VIDE

La Space Power Facility de la Plum Brook Station de Sandusky, Ohio (USA), appartenant au centre de recherches Glenn de la NASA mesure 30,4 m de diamètre et 37 m de haut. La chambre permet de tester les engins et les équipements spatiaux avant leur lancement. Elle est également capable de simuler les radiations solaires grâce à des rampes d'émetteurs infrarouges atteignant 4 MW et de produire des températures descendant à -195,5 °C.

AOÛT 22 En 1980, Fuatai Solo (FJI) a établi le record **du grimper de cocotier le plus rapide**, en escaladant un arbre de 9 m pieds nus en 4,88 s au concours annuel de grimper de cocotier à Sukuna Park (FJI).

AOÛT 23 Depuis 2007, la jument JJS Summer Breeze détient le record de **la plus longue queue pour un cheval** : 3,81 m. L'animal appartient à Crystal et Casey Socha d'Augusta, Kansas (USA).

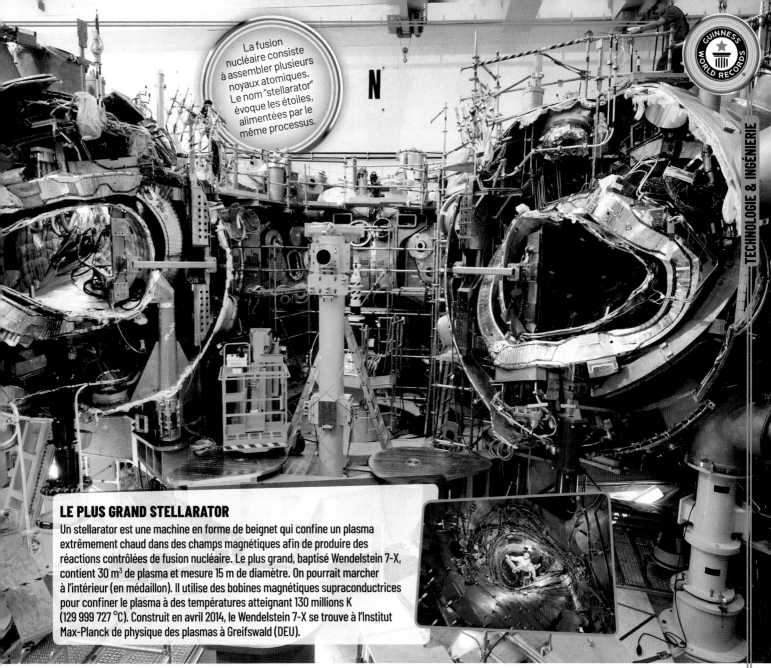

La fusion nucléaire consiste à assembler plusieurs noyaux atomiques. Le nom "stellarator" évoque les étoiles, alimentées par le même processus.

LE PLUS GRAND STELLARATOR

Un stellarator est une machine en forme de beignet qui confine un plasma extrêmement chaud dans des champs magnétiques afin de produire des réactions contrôlées de fusion nucléaire. Le plus grand, baptisé Wendelstein 7-X, contient 30 m³ de plasma et mesure 15 m de diamètre. On pourrait marcher à l'intérieur (en médaillon). Il utilise des bobines magnétiques supraconductrices pour confiner le plasma à des températures atteignant 130 millions K (129 999 727 °C). Construit en avril 2014, le Wendelstein 7-X se trouve à l'Institut Max-Planck de physique des plasmas à Greifswald (DEU).

L'ORDINATEUR LE PLUS RAPIDE

Le 8 juin 2018, le laboratoire national d'Oak Ridge, Tennessee (USA), appartenant au ministère de l'Énergie américain a dévoilé le supercalculateur *Summit*. Construit par IBM, il peut réaliser 143,5 millions de milliards d'opérations en virgule flottante par seconde (143,5 pétaflops). À titre d'exemple, sur les mêmes tests de référence, un ordinateur familial puissant est capable de calculer environ 300 gigaflops — seulement 0,000 2 % de la vitesse de *Summit*.

LA TENSION LA PLUS ÉLEVÉE D'UNE BATTERIE À FRUIT

Le professeur Saiful Islam (PAK/GBR) et son équipe ont généré 1 275,4 V à partir d'une batterie constituée de 2 016 moitiés de citron à l'Institut royal de Londres (GBR). L'expérience, filmée par la BBC dans le cadre des conférences de Noël de l'Institut royal, a été enregistrée le 13 décembre 2016 et diffusée le 29 décembre. La tension délivrée par la batterie a été mesurée grâce à un voltmètre fourni et calibré par le Laboratoire national de physique.

AOÛT 24 En 394 de notre ère, **les derniers hiéroglyphes** — connus sous le nom d'inscription d'Esmet-Akhom — sont gravés dans le temple d'Isis, sur l'île de Philæ, sur le Nil (EGY). La date apparaît dans le texte.

AOÛT 25 Après un voyage de 3 ans depuis Uranus, *Voyager 2* a accompli **le 1er survol de Neptune** en 1989. La sonde s'est rapprochée à moins de 4 800 km des nuages qui couvrent le pôle Nord de la planète.

LA VIE XXL

Le tapis rouge le plus long

Le 25 octobre 2018, Bogaris Retail (ESP) a déroulé un tapis rouge mesurant 6,35 km au Centro Comercial Torrecárdenas d'Almería (ESP). Il est plus long que **la plus longue piste d'atterrissage**, à l'aéroport Qamdo Bamda au Tibet (CHN), qui atteint 5,5 km. Ce tapis rouge commémore l'histoire cinématographique d'Almería, riche de grands classiques tels que *Le Bon, la Brute et le Truand* (ITA, 1966).

Le tapis le plus long

Un tapis long de 10,9 km a été créé par The Children are Painting the World Social Fund (KAZ) et les habitants d'Almaty (KAZ), le 16 septembre 2018.

LE PLUS GRAND PARASOL

Le 24 mars 2018, Khalifa Student Empowerment Program – Aqdar (ARE) a déployé un parasol d'un diamètre de 24,5 m et d'une hauteur de 15,22 m sur la promenade de la corniche à Abu Dhabi (ARE). La toile arborant les couleurs du drapeau des Émirats arabes unis a été créée pour célébrer le programme national du bonheur des Émirats.

Le plus de lumières sur un sapin de Noël artificiel

Les studios Universal du Japon ont rêvé d'un Noël éclatant lorsqu'ils ont suspendu 580 806 lumières sur un sapin de Noël artificiel dans leurs studios d'Osaka (JPN). Le record a été homologué le 23 octobre 2018.

LES PLUS GRANDS...

Attrape-rêves

Le 21 juillet 2018, Vladimir Paranin (LTU) a suspendu un attrape-rêves d'un diamètre de 10,14 m au parc régional d'Asveja (LTU), lors du festival "Masters of Calm". L'attrape-rêves, fabriqué en pin à l'aide de 1 250 m de cordelette synthétique, de

LA PLUS GRANDE DIRNDL

Le 4 septembre 2016, Maria Aberer (AUT) a dévoilé une robe traditionnelle des Alpes longue de 7,03 m devant 8 000 spectateurs à la fête des moissons de Dorfbeuern (AUT). La dirndl mesure 4,20 m à la taille et 5,28 m au niveau de la poitrine. Maria a été inspirée par un reportage radiophonique sur **la plus grande lederhose**, conçue par Gerhard Ritsch (AUT) en 2014.

700 bâtonnets et brindilles, de 319 perles et de 5 plumes, pèse 156 kg.

▶ Pièce d'échecs

Le World Chess Museum (USA) a dévoilé un roi atteignant 6,09 m de haut et 2,79 m de diamètre à sa base, à Saint-Louis (Missouri, USA), le 6 avril 2018. Il mesure 53 fois la taille d'un roi dans un jeu d'échecs classique de type "Champion Staunton".

Fleur en origami

Le 1er septembre 2018, Arbnora Fejza Idrizi (KOS) a réalisé un pliage de fleur de 8,7 m de diamètre, à Skenderaj (KOS). Elle pratique l'art de l'origami depuis plus de 10 ans.

Pot de confiture

Le 4 juin 2018, l'Instituto Tecnológico Superior de Los Reyes (MEX) a présenté un pot de confiture pesant 559,8 kg, à Los Reyes (Michoacán, MEX). Il était rempli d'une confiture faite avec 600 kg de mûres locales.

Pour ouvrir ce pot, il vous faudrait peut-être prendre un peu de masse musculaire grâce au **plus grand pot de protéines en poudre**. Créé par True Nutrition et Douglas Smith (tous 2 USA), il pèse 1 000 kg et a été homologué le 2 mai 2018.

Guitare acoustique à cordes métalliques

Long Yunzhi (CHN) a agrandi une guitare folk Yamaha MG700MS pour en faire un instrument mesurant 4,22 m de long, 1,60 m de large et 33 cm d'épaisseur. Homologuée le 8 septembre 2018, cette guitare pèse 130 kg et deux musiciens doivent être mobilisés pour en jouer correctement.

Rabot fonctionnel

Schreinerei Fust (CHE) a construit un instrument de menuiserie de 7,13 m de long, 4,37 m de haut et 2,10 m de large. Il a été mesuré le 6 mai 2017.

Parmi les autres inventions de Peter, on trouve une maquette d'avion dotée de seaux de fast-food rotatifs en guise d'ailes.

▶ LE PLUS GRAND BRIQUET ALLUME-FEU

Les YouTubers Peter Sripol (ci-dessus) et Samuel Foskuhl (tous 2 USA) font grimper la chaleur grâce à leur briquet géant mesuré officiellement à une longueur de 2,17 m, le 26 octobre 2018, lors d'un barbecue à Beavercreek (Ohio, USA). Il a été conçu à l'aide d'un désherbeur thermique modifié, d'un chalumeau et d'un allumage électrique. Alors, vous les voulez comment vos hamburgers ?

AOÛT 26 En 2013, le cycliste de trial Thomas Öhler (AUT) réalise **le 400 m haies le plus rapide à bicyclette** (44,62 s), lors d'une course contre le double médaillé d'or olympique Félix Sánchez, à Linz (AUT).

AOÛT 27 En 1896, la Grande-Bretagne et Zanzibar (désormais rattaché à la Tanzanie) entrent officiellement en guerre à 9 h. Le conflit s'achève 45 min plus tard — **la guerre la plus courte**. Zanzibar déplore 500 victimes.

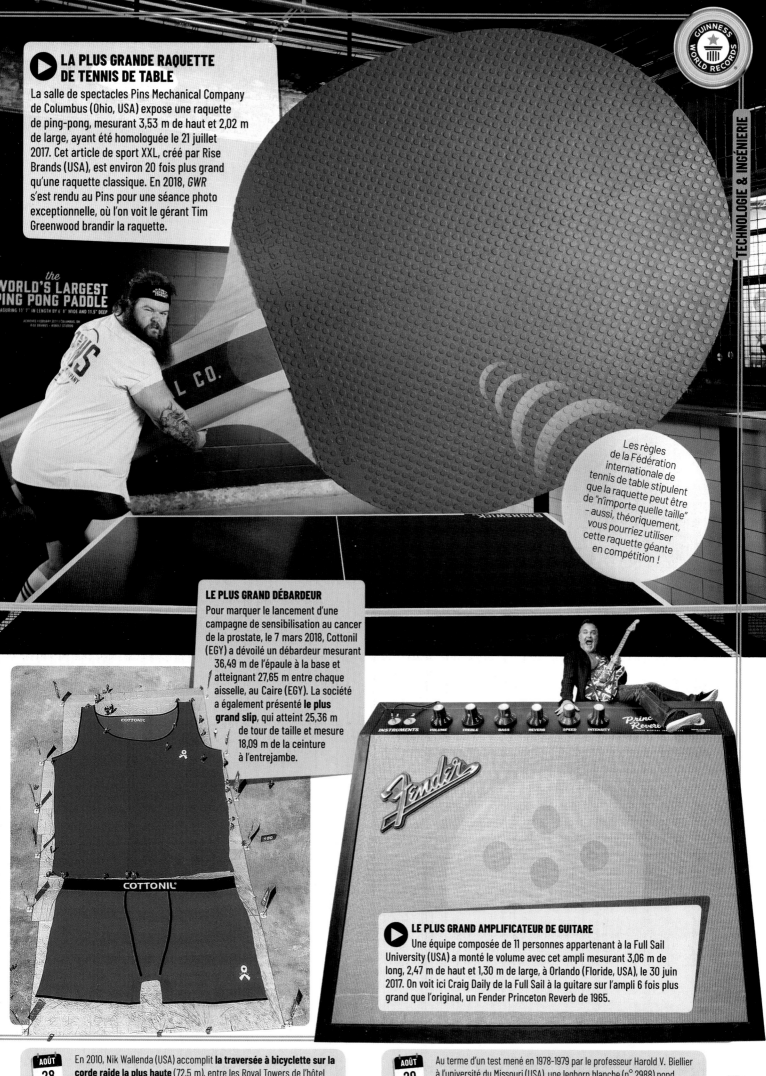

LA PLUS GRANDE RAQUETTE DE TENNIS DE TABLE

La salle de spectacles Pins Mechanical Company de Columbus (Ohio, USA) expose une raquette de ping-pong, mesurant 3,53 m de haut et 2,02 m de large, ayant été homologuée le 21 juillet 2017. Cet article de sport XXL, créé par Rise Brands (USA), est environ 20 fois plus grand qu'une raquette classique. En 2018, *GWR* s'est rendu au Pins pour une séance photo exceptionnelle, où l'on voit le gérant Tim Greenwood brandir la raquette.

the WORLD'S LARGEST PING PONG PADDLE

Les règles de la Fédération internationale de tennis de table stipulent que la raquette peut être de "n'importe quelle taille" – aussi, théoriquement, vous pourriez utiliser cette raquette géante en compétition !

LE PLUS GRAND DÉBARDEUR

Pour marquer le lancement d'une campagne de sensibilisation au cancer de la prostate, le 7 mars 2018, Cottonil (EGY) a dévoilé un débardeur mesurant 36,49 m de l'épaule à la base et atteignant 27,65 m entre chaque aisselle, au Caire (EGY). La société a également présenté **le plus grand slip**, qui atteint 25,36 m de tour de taille et mesure 18,09 m de la ceinture à l'entrejambe.

LE PLUS GRAND AMPLIFICATEUR DE GUITARE

Une équipe composée de 11 personnes appartenant à la Full Sail University (USA) a monté le volume avec cet ampli mesurant 3,06 m de long, 2,47 m de haut et 1,30 m de large, à Orlando (Floride, USA), le 30 juin 2017. On voit ici Craig Daily de la Full Sail à la guitare sur l'ampli 6 fois plus grand que l'original, un Fender Princeton Reverb de 1965.

AOÛT 28 En 2010, Nik Wallenda (USA) accomplit **la traversée à bicyclette sur la corde raide la plus haute** (72,5 m), entre les Royal Towers de l'hôtel Atlantis Paradise Island de Nassau (BHS).

AOÛT 29 Au terme d'un test mené en 1978-1979 par le professeur Harold V. Biellier à l'université du Missouri (USA), une leghorn blanche (n° 2988) pond 371 œufs en 364 jours, ce qui en fait **la poule la plus féconde**.

COFFRE À JOUETS GÉANTS

Le plus long circuit Hot Wheels
La filiale russe de Mattel a monté un circuit Hot Wheels de 560,3 m – plus long qu'une piste de dragsters classique –, à Moscou (RUS), le 25 août 2018.

Le plus grand cheval à bascule
Gao Ming (CHN) a dévoilé un cheval à bascule mesurant 8,20 m de haut pour 12,72 m de long, à Linyi (province du Shandong, CHN), le 7 juillet 2014. Il atteint 3 fois la hauteur d'un bus à impériale Routemaster.

Le plus grand puzzle
Le 7 juillet 2018, DMCC (UAE) a présenté un puzzle de 6 122 m² commémorant feu le cheikh Zayed, à Dubaï (ARE). Il est plus grand que la surface au sol de la Maison-Blanche !

LA PLUS GRANDE ROUE EN BRIQUES LEGO®
Tomáš Kašpařík (CZE) a assemblé une grande roue d'un diamètre de 3,38 m en briques LEGO, homologuée le 22 octobre 2017, à Utrecht (NDL). Elle mesurait 3,64 m de haut et comptait 43 cabines. Il a fallu 200 h et 37 000 briques de plastique à Tomáš pour la concevoir et la construire.

Le plus grand plateau de Monopoly
Hasbro et la Ceres Student Association (tous 2 NLD) ont créé une version du jeu de société atteignant 900 m², à Wageningen (NLD). De la taille de 3 courts de tennis et demi, il a été mesuré le 30 novembre 2016, à l'université locale.

Le plus rapide à disposer un grand jeu d'échecs
Nurzat Turdaliev (KAZ) a mis 46,62 s pour aligner un grand jeu d'échecs sur la place Kashirskaya, à Moscou (RUS), le 28 octobre 2018. Selon le règlement *GWR*, les plus petites pièces (les pions) doivent au minimum mesurer 20 cm de haut.

LA PLUS GRANDE MAQUETTE DE VOITURE FONCTIONNANT AVEC DES MOTEURS LEGO® TECHNIC
LEGO Technic (DNK) a construit une Bugatti Chiron fonctionnelle en briques LEGO mesurant 1,21 m de haut, 2,03 m de large et 4,54 m de long, comme certifié en août 2018, à Kladno (CZE). La maquette compte plus d'un million d'éléments LEGO Technic, a nécessité 13 438 h de construction et atteint 28 km/h.

Le plus grand fusil NERF
L'ingénieur et inventeur Mark Rober (USA) – un ancien de la NASA – a construit un fusil à fléchettes en mousse mesurant 1,82 m de long, homologué à Sunnyvale (Californie, USA), le 22 juin 2016. En 2017, il a également travaillé sur **le plus grand pistolet à eau**, en collaboration avec Ken Glazebrook, Bob Clagett et Dani Yuan (tous USA). Ce pistolet géant mesure 2,22 m de long et 1,22 m de haut.

Les plus grandes constructions en LEGO...
• **Batmobile** : le 28 février 2017, l'artiste Nathan Sawaya (USA) a dévoilé une Batmobile LEGO grandeur nature de 5,51 m. Fabriquée avec environ 500 000 briques, elle faisait partie d'une exposition consacrée à DC Comics, à Londres (GBR).

• ▶ **Caravane** : le 26 septembre 2018, Ben Craig, "The Brick Builder"(AUS), a réalisé une caravane avec 288 630 briques de LEGO, à Brisbane (AUS). Top Parks et Caravanning Queensland (tous 2 AUS) ont financé cette tentative.

• ▶ **Cerisier en fleur (avec support)** : pour son 1er anniversaire, LEGOLAND Japon a construit un cerisier en fleur de 4,38 m avec 881 479 briques, à Nagoya (préfecture d'Aichi, JPN), le 28 mars 2018.

• ▶ **Navire (avec support)** : le 17 août 2016, la compagnie maritime DFDS (DNK) a présenté le *Jubilee Seaways*, navire en LEGO long de 12 m à Copenhague (DNK). Cette maquette comprend plus de 1,2 million de briques en plastique. Pour respecter la tradition, une bouteille de champagne en LEGO a été lancée contre la coque pour baptiser le navire.

LE PLUS GRAND HAND SPINNER
Giovanni Catalano (ITA) a créé un hand spinner de 74 cm de diamètre, comme certifié à Rozzano (Milan, ITA), le 21 novembre 2018. Ce jouet, existant depuis le début des années 1990, a connu une explosion de popularité inexpliquée en 2017.

 AOÛT 30
En 2010, le footballeur américain professionnel et porte-parole d'une marque de shampoing Troy Polamalu (USA) fait assurer sa chevelure pour 1 million $, soit **les cheveux les mieux assurés**.

AOÛT 31
Le chou le plus lourd est pesé à 62,71 kg, lors de l'Alaska State Fair de Palmer (Alaska, USA), en 2012. "Enfin, j'ai atteint le sommet de la montagne !", déclare son producteur Scott A. Robb (USA).

▶ LE PLUS GRAND HULA-HOOP EN ROTATION (FEMMES)

Getti Kehayova (USA) a fait tourner un hula-hoop d'un diamètre de 5,18 m autour d'elle, à Las Vegas (Nevada, USA), le 2 novembre 2018. Elle s'est entraînée quotidiennement pendant 1 an pour préparer cette tentative – et son corps en porte encore les stigmates ! Chaque fois que le lourd cerceau évoluait autour de Getti, elle avait l'impression de recevoir un coup de poing dans les côtes.
Si sa 1re tentative a échoué (le cerceau l'a percutée au visage), la 2de a été homologuée par le GWR !

Quant au cerceau utilisé pour **le plus grand hula-hoop en rotation** toutes catégories, il est à peine plus grand et affiche un diamètre de 5,40 m. Le 19 février 2019, Yuya Yamada (JPN) l'a mis en rotation autour de lui à Yokohama (préfecture de Kanagawa, JPN).

Cette passion pour les cerceaux, c'est de famille. En juillet 1987, la sœur aînée de Getti, Desai, a remporté le titre GWR pour **le plus de hula-hoops en rotation simultanément** (75). Marawa Ibrahim détient le record actuel (voir p. 102).

▶ LE PLUS GRAND COUSSIN PÉTEUR

Cet article de farces et attrapes mesurant 7,62 m de diamètre a été créé par Lee Burgess d'Affordable Moonwalks pour un événement organisé par le pasteur Matt Funk de la First Baptist Church de Covington (tous USA). Près de 30 membres du groupe de jeunes de l'église ont fait équipe pour le dégonfler et produire ainsi le son caractéristique, à Covington (Géorgie, USA), le 5 août 2017.

▶ LE PLUS GRAND RUBIK'S CUBE

Le musée TELUS Spark science (CAN) a produit une version agrandie du célèbre casse-tête, dans laquelle chaque face couvre 2,82 m², homologuée à Calgary (Alberta, CAN), le 24 septembre 2018. Il a fallu à l'équipe 8 semaines pour créer ce cube colossal avant de le mettre à disposition du public volontaire pour le résoudre.

SEPT. 1 En 2007, l'artiste martial Kevin Shelley (USA) pulvérise le record du **plus de lunettes de toilette cassées avec la main en 1 min**, à Cologne (DEU). Les 46 abattants sont tous en bois.

SEPT. 2 En 2017, "Avery & Sylvia" — Avery Chin et Sylvia Lim (tous 2 MYS) — établissent le record du **plus de changements de costume en 1 min**. Sylvia revêt 24 tenues différentes, à Penang (MYS).

ARCHITECTURE

Le plus grand bâtiment en forme d'oiseau

Située à Kembanglimus, Magelang (IDN), Gereja Ayam, ou "l'église poulet", mesure environ 56,41 m du bec à la queue. Construit à l'image d'une colombe par Daniel Alamsjah entre 1988 et 2000, le temple a reçu son surnom de "poulet" quand Alamsjah a déposé une couronne sur la tête de la colombe, ce qui l'a fait malencontreusement ressembler à un coq.

L'extérieur le plus sombre pour un bâtiment provisoire

Le pavillon Hyundai est une structure temporaire mesurant 10 m de haut inaugurée le 9 février 2018 aux JO de Pyeongchang (KOR). Conçu par l'architecte Asif Khan (GBR), l'extérieur du pavillon a été recouvert de Vantablack Vbx2, un revêtement ultra-noir composé de nanotubes de carbone alignés verticalement qui absorbe 99 % de la lumière et crée l'illusion du vide.

Le 1er bâtiment traversé par une autoroute

Les étages 5 à 7 de la Gate Tower d'Osaka (JPN), qui culmine à 71,9 m, présentent un élément de design peu commun : la sortie Umeda de l'autoroute Hanshin y passe. Achevé en 1992, le bâtiment ne touche pas la route sur piles et bénéficie d'une isolation supplémentaire afin de minimiser bruits et vibrations.

Le funiculaire le plus pentu

Un funiculaire est un système sur rails dans lequel les cabines ascendantes et descendantes s'équilibrent. Le funiculaire Schwyz–Stoos de la station de sports d'hiver de Stoos (CHE) affiche une pente de 47,7 ° (110 %) au point le plus raide. Inaugurées en décembre 2017 pour un coût de 52 millions de francs suisses (53 millions $), les 4 cabines accueillant 34 personnes conçues en forme de cylindres rotatifs s'ajustent à la pente et permettent aux passagers de rester debout au cours du trajet de 4 min.

Le plus grand parking automatisé

Emirates Financial Towers à Dubaï (ARE) possède un parking automatisé de 2 314 places, homologué le 21 octobre 2017. Il a été conçu par Robotic Parking Systems (USA) et construit par Mohamed Abdulmohsin Al-Kharafi & Sons (KWT). Le système informatique range et sécurise les voitures laissées dans les sas. Il se souvient de l'historique de stationnement des conducteurs et avance les voitures avant l'heure de départ prévue.

LE PLUS VASTE TOIT RÉTRACTABLE À IRIS

Le Mercedes-Benz Stadium d'Atlanta (Géorgie, USA) — stade de l'équipe de la NFL des Atlanta Falcons — présente un toit rétractable circulaire. Il couvre une surface de 5,8 ha, avec une ouverture ovale atteignant 104,35 m dans sa plus grande largeur. Le toit du stade compte 8 lamelles — mesurant chacune 67 m de long, 23 m de large et pesant 453,5 t — et le système dans son ensemble a nécessité 19 050 t d'acier et utilise 16 moteurs électriques.

Le plus grand panneau d'affichage

Le 5 novembre 2018, Emirates Intellectual Property Association (ARE) a dévoilé un panneau publicitaire mesurant 6 260 m², à Dubaï (ARE). Le panneau affiche des logos publicitaires afin de sensibiliser le public aux droits de la propriété intellectuelle.

L'immeuble le plus haut

Inauguré le 4 janvier 2010, le Burj Khalifa de Dubaï (ARE) comprend 160 étages et atteint 828 m. La construction de cet immeuble développé par Emaar Properties (ARE) a nécessité 22 millions d'heures de travail et 1,5 milliard $.

Quant à **la tour la plus haute**, il s'agit de la Tokyo Skytree (JPN), qui s'élève à 634 m jusqu'au sommet de son mât. Achevée en février 2012, cette tour de radiodiffusion compte 2 plates-formes d'observation.

LE 1ER ASCENSEUR MAGNÉTIQUE

Installé en 2017 par ThyssenKrupp (DEU) dans une tour haute de 246 m permettant de réaliser des tests, à Rottweil (DEU), le prototype MULTI est un système d'ascenseurs utilisant des cabines se déplaçant sur une piste magnétique. Non seulement les cabines sont dépourvues de câbles, mais elles peuvent se mouvoir verticalement ou horizontalement. En changeant de piste, les cabines descendent, montent et vont à gauche ou à droite pour atteindre leur destination.

LE PLUS GRAND CHÂTEAU RÉALISÉ EN BOUTEILLES PLASTIQUE

Le "roi du plastique" Robert Bezeau (CAN) a construit en 2017 un château de 4 étages et 14 m de haut, à Bocas Del Toro (PAN), fabriqué à partir de 40 000 bouteilles en plastique. Il fait partie d'un village écologique en bouteilles plastique et offre 4 chambres, une salle de banquet et une plate-forme d'observation au sommet.

LE PLUS DE GRATTE-CIEL DANS UNE VILLE

Acteur économique majeur de l'Asie du Sud-Est situé sur un territoire de 1 106,34 km², Hong Kong connaît l'une des plus fortes densités de population résidentielle du monde. Pour héberger ses 7 millions de citoyens et travailleurs, le Skyscraper Center estime que la ville comprend 2 580 immeubles d'au moins 100 m de haut en mars 2019. Hong Kong est également **la ville qui présente le plus d'immeubles de plus de 150 m (385).**

SEPT. 3 En 2004, lors de la 3e convention des avaleurs de sabre et des spectacles de foire, Natasha Veruschka (USA) bat le record du **plus d'épées avalées simultanément (femmes)**, soit 13.

SEPT. 4 En 2015, Hunter Ewen (USA) établit le record du **plus de ballons gonflés en 1 h par une personne** (910), un total à couper le souffle, au Wild Basin Lodge Event Center d'Allenspark (Colorado, USA).

Sur le pont, les visiteurs doivent porter des "sur-chaussures" afin de ne pas abîmer les plaques de verre.

LE PLUS LONG PONT EN VERRE

Inauguré en 2017 dans le site touristique de Hongyagu (province du Hebei, CHN), le pont suspendu en verre de la vallée de la Falaise rouge mesure 488 m de long. Conçu par Haim Dotan et composé de 1 077 plaques taillées dans un verre de 40 mm d'épaisseur, il connaît un mouvement d'oscillation qui augmente à la hauteur de l'excitation qu'on éprouve du haut de ses 214 m. Le pont peut supporter le poids de 2 000 personnes, bien que seulement 600 soient admises simultanément.

LE PLUS VASTE MUSÉE DES SCIENCES

Le centre des sciences Guangdong (province du Guangzhou, CHN) s'étend sur une superficie de 126 513 m². Le centre — dont la forme rappelle la fleur de kapokier — abrite 10 pavillons permanents à thème présentant plus de 510 expositions. Inauguré en septembre 2008, il a reçu un titre *GWR* le 7 novembre 2018, à l'occasion de son 10e anniversaire.

LE PLUS HAUT TOBOGGAN À L'EXTÉRIEUR D'UN IMMEUBLE

Sur le flanc de la US Bank Tower de Los Angeles (Californie, USA), le Skyslide se situe à une hauteur de 280 m à son point culminant. Construite en 2016 dans un verre de 32 mm d'épaisseur, cette attraction touristique serpente sur 14 m entre les 70e et 69e étages du gratte-ciel.

SEPT. 5 — En 2008, Herbert Weber (AUT) célèbre ses 30 ans de travail au sein de Moser Holzindustrie, à Salzbourg (AUT). Il détient le record du **plus de cercueils assemblés au cours d'une vie** (707 335), tous réalisés à la main.

SEPT. 6 — Coordinadora de Peñas de Valladolid réunit **le plus de personnes portant des lunettes de soleil dans l'obscurité** (6 774), à Valladolid (ESP), en 2015. Cet exploit se déroule en extérieur, à 22 heures.

ÇA COLLE BIEN !

Le 1er timbre postal
Le Penny Black – le 1er timbre postal au dos adhésif – a été mis à la vente dans les plus grandes agences postales du Royaume-Uni le 1er mai 1840 (bien qu'il n'ait été validé qu'à partir du 6 mai). Ce timbre présente le profil de Victoria, reine d'Angleterre, à l'âge de 15 ans, et a été imprimé jusqu'en février 1841.

La plus grande boule en autocollants
Au 13 janvier 2016, John Fischer (USA) a créé une sphère de 105,05 kg entièrement faite d'autocollants, homologuée à Longmont (Colorado, USA).

La plus grande mosaïque en autocollants (image)
Avant la finale de la coupe du monde 2018 de la FIFA en Russie, CapitaLand Retail (CHN) a dévoilé une mosaïque de 385,3 m² composée de 154 000 autocollants, à Shanghai (CHN), le 15 juillet 2018. Elle représente les footballeurs les plus célèbres des 32 équipes du tournoi.

Le Post-it le plus cher
Une de ces feuilles autoadhésives présentant une œuvre d'art réalisée au pastel et fusain nommée *After Rembrandt* a été adjugée 640 £ (939 $), lors d'une vente aux enchères en ligne, le 20 décembre 2000. L'auteur, R. B. Kitaj (USA), fait partie d'un groupe de célébrités ayant produit de mini-chefs-d'œuvre pour le 20e anniversaire de Post-it. Les bénéfices des enchères ont été reversés à des organisations caritatives.

Le plus de feuilles autoadhésives collées sur le visage en 1 min
Au rythme d'une par seconde, Taylor Maurer (USA) a couvert son visage de 60 Post-its, à Sioux City (Iowa, USA), le 16 novembre 2014.

Le plus grand *sticky toffee pudding* (moelleux au caramel)
Un moelleux de 334 kg a été réalisé par Farmhouse Fare Limited, à Lancashire (GBR), le 17 mars 2012.

Le plus grand lac d'asphalte
Pitch Lake à La Brea ("bitume" en espagnol), à Trinidad, recouvre environ 457 294,8 m², l'équivalent de 62 terrains de football. Ce lac contient plus de 10 millions de tonnes d'asphalte et on estime qu'il atteint 76 m de profondeur au centre.

LE PLUS D'AUTOCOLLANTS SUR UN BUS
STL Sticker Swap (USA) a collé 29 083 stickers sur un bus, à la LouFest de Saint-Louis (Missouri, USA), le 10 septembre 2017. Dans le monde entier, des personnes ont envoyé des autocollants afin de battre ce record, tandis que le maire de Saint-Louis a proclamé le 10 septembre 2017 "STL Sticks Together Day" ("Restons soudés") pour fêter l'événement.

ventre afin de s'agripper aux rochers. Les geckos présentent ces mêmes petites structures sous leurs doigts.

Le poisson le plus collant
Le crampon bariolé (*Gobiesox maeandricus*) est une petite espèce native de la côte Pacifique des États-Unis et du Canada. Il possède une force adhésive représentant 80 à 230 fois son poids selon une étude de 2013. Ce poisson utilise une ventouse modifiée – équipée de minuscules poils appelés setæ – sur son

La plus vieille toile d'araignée contenant une proie piégée
Le plus vieux spécimen de toile d'araignée contenant des insectes piégés remonte au crétacé inférieur, voici 110 millions d'années. Il a été retrouvé à San Just (ESP) et dévoilé en juin 2006. La toile est composée de 26 filaments de soie adhésive préservés dans l'ambre (résine de conifère fossilisée) et révèle un coléoptère, une mite, une mouche et une guêpe parasite désormais éteinte.

L'ADHÉSIF NATUREL LE PLUS FORT
En 2006, des chercheurs de l'université de l'Indiana (USA) ont découvert que les bactéries *Caulobacter crescentus* produisent une substance collante qui leur permet de s'attacher à n'importe quelle surface, y compris sous l'eau. Ce mélange de longues molécules constituées de sucre appelées polysaccharides (ci-dessous) offre une adhérence environ 7 fois plus forte que celle des doigts du gecko. Lors des tests, les scientifiques ont localisé 14 bactéries accrochées sur une base équivalente à du verre. Ils ont calculé que la force nécessaire pour séparer les microbes de cette base atteignait 7 000 newtons par cm² – à peu près 3 fois plus que la force déployée pour arracher 2 surfaces collées par une super-colle du commerce (encadré ci-dessous).

LA PLUS ANCIENNE UTILISATION DE COLLE
Les Néandertaliens fabriquaient des lances en collant une pointe de silex à une hampe de bois grâce à une colle issue de l'écorce de bouleau. Les scientifiques ont d'abord cru que le processus pour extraire cette poix de bouleau était trop avancé pour des Néandertaliens, mais des fouilles archéologiques datant du milieu du pléistocène (environ 200 000 ans) ont révélé qu'ils utilisaient bien cette colle. En 2017, des chercheurs de l'université de Leyde (NLD) ont découvert qu'il suffisait de chauffer des rouleaux d'écorce de bouleau sur un foyer ouvert pour produire cette poix.

LA PLUS ANCIENNE UTILISATION DE COLLE POUR DES OBJETS DÉCORATIFS
La grotte de Nahal Hemar, près de la mer Morte (ISR), a été localisée en 1983 par une équipe de l'université de Harvard (USA) et l'Autorité des antiquités d'Israël. Parmi d'autres découvertes extraordinaires, ils ont trouvé des crânes humains décorés de motifs en croisillons qui remonteraient entre 8310 et 8110 avant notre ère, d'après la datation au carbone. Les motifs ont été créés en utilisant un collagène issu de graisse et de tissus animaux.

LE PLUS DE PARTICIPANTS À UN DÉFILÉ DE MODE DUCK TAPE
Le 14 juin 2014, au 11e festival annuel du Duck Tape, à Avon (Ohio, USA), 340 personnes ont défilé pour présenter des tenues utilisant le célèbre adhésif. Le juge GWR Michael Empric (ci-dessus, à droite) s'est pris au jeu et a exercé ses fonctions en portant une veste en Duck Tape.

 SEPT. 7 Ian Neale (GBR) présente **la betterave la plus lourde** au championnat national des légumes géants 2001 de Shepton Mallet (Somerset, GBR). Elle pèse 23,4 kg.

 SEPT. 8 En 2013, une girafe réticulée nommée Jang-soon met au monde son 18e petit dans la réserve animalière Samsung Everland de Yongin (KOR), soit **le plus de girafons nés en captivité**.

La colle spéciale utilisée pour ce record fond lorsqu'on la chauffe et se solidifie en refroidissant. Les cylindres ont été chauffés à 400 °C et la colle a été appliquée sur chacun d'eux. Après chauffage, ils ont été assemblés.

LE POIDS LE PLUS LOURD SOULEVÉ À L'AIDE D'UNE COLLE (NON DISPONIBLE DANS LE COMMERCE)

Le 22 septembre 2013, une colle super-forte a été employée pour soulever un camion de 16,09 t et le maintenir à 1 m du sol pendant plus de 1 h. Cet exploit a été accompli par le Centre aérospatial allemand (DEU), dans son centre de Cologne (DEU). Au cours de ce test, 2 cylindres d'acier inoxydable ont été collés à l'aide d'une résine thermoplastique appliquée sur 39,6 cm² seulement sur chacun. Un camion a été relié aux cylindres, eux-mêmes attachés au crochet d'une grue. Le véhicule a été soulevé et suspendu de façon que seule la colle sur les cylindres le maintenait en l'air.

LE PLUS DE PERSONNES PRODUISANT DU SLIME SIMULTANÉMENT

Le 1er juillet 2018, une séance de production de masse de slime a réuni 933 personnes, lors d'un événement organisé par la ville de Carson (Californie, USA). Le record s'est déroulé au cours de la Journée de l'amitié entre communautés qui fait partie des célébrations du 4 juillet. Pour réaliser la substance gluante, les participants ont mélangé et malaxé chacun 8 cl de colle, 6 cl d'amidon liquide, du colorant rouge, blanc et bleu et parfois quelques paillettes.

L'HABILLAGE VINYLE DE VOITURE LE PLUS RAPIDE

L'habillage consiste à couvrir la surface d'une voiture d'une feuille de vinyle — parfois simplement pour changer de couleur, bien que l'habillage vinyle serve principalement à des fins publicitaires. Le 15 juillet 2018, une équipe de folien+zubehör (DEU) a habillé une Tesla Model X d'un film vinyle spécial en 22 min et 56,25 s, au Flugplatz Schwarze Heide, à Hünxe (DEU).

L'HABILLAGE VINYLE DU PLUS GRAND SUPER-YACHT

En février 2015, le chantier maritime Rybovich, propriété de Wild Group à Miami (Floride, USA), a habillé de vinyle toute la coque du super-yacht Aviva Abeking & Rasmussen, long de 68 m. Plus de 800 m de vinyle métallique ont été utilisés. La réalisation a pris environ 1 mois ; les couches ne se chevauchent que de 5 mm.

SEPT. 9 En 1917, une lettre de l'amiral John "Jacky" Fisher au ministre de l'Armement Winston Churchill (tous 2 GBR) contient la phrase "O.M.G. (Oh ! My God !)" (Oh ! Mon Dieu !) — **la 1re occurrence d'"OMG" imprimée.**

SEPT. 10 **La dernière utilisation de la guillotine** a lieu en 1977 à la prison des Baumettes, à Marseille (FRA), pour exécuter le meurtrier Hamida Djandoubi. La peine capitale sera abolie en France en 1981.

183

EXPLORATION SPATIALE

Le plus grand nombre de lancements en orbite

L'Union soviétique/la Fédération de Russie a réalisé 3 064 lancements en orbite couronnés de succès au 19 mars 2019, soit plus de la moitié de ces lancements depuis le début de l'ère spatiale. En 1982, l'Union soviétique en a réalisé 101, **le plus grand nombre de lancements en orbite en 1 an.**

Sur les 14 379 débris orbitaux enregistrés par Space-Track.org au 4 janvier 2019, environ 5 075 peuvent être reliés aux activités spatiales soviétiques ou russes, ce qui fait de ce pays **le plus gros contributeur de débris spatiaux.** Ce total comprend des satellites inactifs, des étages de fusées, des équipements perdus et d'autres pièces.

Le plus grand nombre de satellites en orbite

Au 4 janvier 2019, les États-Unis avaient 1 594 satellites en orbite autour de la Terre. Il s'agit de satellites gouvernementaux ou commerciaux appartenant à des entreprises américaines.

Le vaisseau spatial le plus réutilisé

La navette spatiale *Discovery* (NASA) a été lancée pour la 39e et dernière fois le 24 février 2011, lors du vol STS-133 pour la Station spatiale internationale (ISS). Son 1er vol, le STS-41D, date du 30 août 1984.

Le plus grand nombre d'exoplanètes découvertes par un télescope

Au 19 mars 2019, 2 697 exoplanètes (planètes situées en dehors du Système solaire) ont été identifiées et confirmées grâce aux observations du télescope spatial *Kepler*, soit plus des 2 tiers des 3 925 exoplanètes connues.

La plus longue période cumulée en sortie extravéhiculaire

Le cosmonaute Anatoli Iakovlevitch Soloviov (URSS/RUS) a passé 82 h 22 min dans l'espace au cours de ses 5 missions spatiales de 1988 à 1998. Il a réalisé 16 sorties extravéhiculaires à partir de la station *Mir*.

La plus longue période cumulée en sortie extravéhiculaire (femmes) est de 60 h 21 min pour Peggy Whitson (USA), la 3e place dans l'absolu. Le 23 mai 2017, elle a réalisé sa 10e sortie extravéhiculaire et a passé 2 h 46 min hors de l'ISS pour réparer une armoire à relais.

LE PLUS DE LANCEMENTS CONSÉCUTIFS RÉUSSIS POUR UN MODÈLE DE FUSÉE

La fusée Delta II d'United Launch Alliance (USA) a réussi 100 lancements en orbite entre le 5 mai 1997 et le 15 septembre 2018, date du dernier lancement : Delta-381 a lancé *ICESat-2* depuis la base de l'Air Force de Vandenberg en Californie (USA). Les fusées Delta II ont lancé des missions majeures, comme les observatoires spatiaux *Kepler* et *Swift*.

Le 1er alunissage sur le côté sombre de la Lune

Le 3 janvier 2019 à 2 h 26 UTC, l'atterrisseur *Chang'e* 4 (voir p. 164-165) de l'Administration spatiale chinoise a aluni dans le cratère Von Kármán. Ce n'est pas le 1er objet humain à toucher le sol de ce côté de la Lune, mais le 1er à y alunir de manière contrôlée. *Chang'e* 4 transporte des équipements destinés à mieux comprendre cet environnement peu connu, comme des instruments astronomiques, une biosphère scellée contenant des œufs de ver à soie et des graines, ainsi qu'un petit rover à énergie solaire, *Yutu-2*.

La plus longue survie d'un rover sur Mars

Le 10 juin 2018, le rover *Opportunity* (NASA) est passé en alimentation faible d'urgence, une tempête de poussière ayant obscurci ses panneaux solaires. C'était la 1re perte totale de contact depuis son atterrissage en 2004. *Opportunity* et son jumeau *Spirit* avaient été conçus pour fonctionner 90 jours, mais se sont révélés très résistants (*Spirit* s'est éteint en 2010). Le 13 février 2019, la NASA a confirmé que les tentatives de contact avaient échoué et a annoncé la fin de la mission du rover après 15 ans et 19 jours.

LA PLANÈTE VISITÉE PAR LE PLUS DE SONDES

Au 27 novembre 2018, 25 missions concluantes ou partiellement concluantes ont été lancées vers Mars. Elles ont placé 14 orbiteurs autour de la planète rouge et déposé avec un succès au moins partiel 9 atterrisseurs à la surface. La mission martienne la plus récente est l'atterrisseur *InSight* de la NASA (ci-dessus), qui s'est posé le 26 novembre 2018.

Le 1er survol de Pluton

Neuf ans après son décollage en janvier 2006, la sonde *New Horizons* de la NASA est passée à 12 472 km de Pluton le 14 juillet 2015 à 11 h 49 UTC. Elle a ensuite atteint Ultima Thule, dans la ceinture de Kuiper, le 1er janvier 2019 (voir p. 186-187).

La 1re sonde à quitter le Système solaire

La sonde *Voyager 1*, lancée en septembre 1977, devait étudier Jupiter, Saturne, Uranus et Neptune. En août 2012, elle a quitté le Système solaire et est entrée dans l'espace interstellaire. Située à plus de 20,9 milliards de km de la Terre, elle continue de transmettre ses données et n'atteindra pas d'autre étoile avant 40 000 ans.

LE PLUS GRAND SATELLITE DÉPLOYÉ DEPUIS UNE STATION SPATIALE

Construit par Surrey Satellite Technology (GBR), *RemoveDEBRIS* a une masse de 88,47 kg et mesure 79 × 60 × 60 cm. Ce satellite conçu pour ramasser les débris spatiaux a été déployé par le NanoRacks Kaber Microsatellite Deployer (encadré) à bord de la Station spatiale internationale (ISS) le 20 juin 2018.

 SEPT. 11 En 1978, le dissident Georgi Markov (BGR) meurt après qu'un parapluie lui a tiré un microprojectile toxique dans la jambe à Londres (GBR). C'est **le 1er assassinat par empoisonnement à la ricine.**

 SEPT. 12 En 2015, Guennadi Ivanovitch Padalka (RUS) revient sur Terre après sa 5e mission spatiale. Il a passé **la plus longue période de temps dans l'espace (cumulé)** : 878 j, 11 h, 29 min et 24 s.

LE PLUS PROCHE SURVOL DU SOLEIL PAR UN VAISSEAU SPATIAL

À 3 h 27 min 52 s UTC le 6 novembre 2018, la sonde non habitée *Parker Solar Probe* (USA) est passée à 24 122 872 km de la surface du Soleil. Elle se déplaçait à une vitesse héliocentrique (par rapport au Soleil) de 95,32 km/s (343 180 km/h), **la vitesse la plus rapide pour un vaisseau spatial.** Au fil de sa mission, elle devrait le frôler à 6,1 millions de km en 2024.

En route, la *Parker Solar Probe* a atteint le point de son trajet le plus proche de Vénus le 3 octobre 2018 (encart), 52 j, 1 h et 13 min après son départ. C'est **le voyage interplanétaire le plus rapide.**

La sonde peut atteindre une vitesse de 692 000 km/h, de quoi aller de New York à Tokyo en moins de 1 min.

LA PLUS LONGUE DURÉE D'UTILISATION POUR UN OBSERVATOIRE SPATIAL

Le télescope spatial *Hubble* (USA) a été lancé le 24 avril 1990 et était encore actif le 22 janvier 2019, après 28 ans 273 jours de mission. Le 2 avril 2018, un article de *Nature Astronomy* a révélé que *Hubble* avait repéré une supergéante de type B appelée "Icarus" à 9 milliards d'années-lumière de la Terre. C'est **la plus lointaine étoile observée.**

LE TRAJET LE PLUS RAPIDE VERS L'ISS

Le 10 juillet 2018, le véhicule de ravitaillement automatisé *Progress MS-09* s'est amarré à l'ISS après un voyage de 3 h 40 min, moins de la moitié de la durée d'un vol Londres-New York. Il a décollé de Baïkonour (KAZ) le 9 juillet à 21 h 51 et s'est amarré au module *Pirs* de l'ISS à 1 h 31 UTC le lendemain.

SEPT. 13 En 2016, le match de baseball Chicago White Sox vs Cleveland Indians (tous 2 USA) attire 1 122 spectateurs canins lors du "Bark at the Park", **le plus grand nombre de chiens à un événement sportif.**

SEPT. 14 La contorsionniste acrobate Leslie Tipton (USA) établit **le temps le plus rapide pour entrer dans une valise** en s'y enfermant en 5,43 s durant l'émission *LIVE ! with Regis and Kelly* en 2009.

185

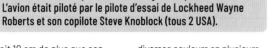

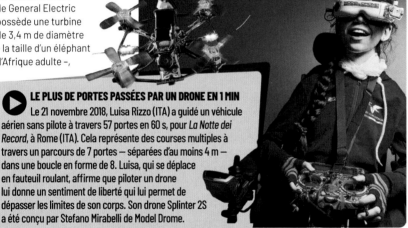

Le 1er verre autoréparant

Le 14 décembre 2017, des scientifiques de l'université de Tokyo (JPN) ont publié un article décrivant la découverte d'un polymère ressemblant à du verre pouvant "s'autoréparer". Le polyéther thiourée est résistant et capable de se ressouder à température ambiante. S'il est cassé, ses éclats peuvent se recoller. Une pression de la main pendant 30 s à 21 °C suffit à réunir les pièces et, quelques heures plus tard, le matériau retrouve sa solidité antérieure.

Le plus grand turboréacteur

Le réacteur GE9X de General Electric possède une turbine de 3,4 m de diamètre – la taille d'un éléphant d'Afrique adulte –, soit 10 cm de plus que son prédécesseur le GE90-115B (qui reste **le turboréacteur le plus puissant**). Il a été homologué pour équiper les nouveaux Boeing 777-9.

La 1re lentille simple concentrant toutes les couleurs en un point unique

Les lentilles en verre ou en plastique concentrent les diverses couleurs en plusieurs points et non en un point unique de l'espace. Le 1er janvier 2018, des scientifiques de l'université d'Harvard (USA) publient un article dans *Nature* décrivant pour la 1re fois une "metalens", ou "méta-lentille" qui concentre toutes les couleurs de l'arc-en-ciel (notre spectre de lumière visible) en même temps en un point unique. Ces lentilles optiques vont peu à peu devenir plus minces, moins chères et plus efficaces que toute lentille classique.

LE PLUS LOURD AÉRONEF À RÉALISER UN LOOPING

Le 18 juillet 2018, un Lockheed-Martin LM-100J pesant 36 740 kg a réalisé un looping lors d'un vol de démonstration au salon aéronautique de Farnborough (Hampshire, GBR). L'avion était piloté par le pilote d'essai de Lockheed Wayne Roberts et son copilote Steve Knoblock (tous 2 USA).

L'ŒUVRE D'ART CRÉÉE PAR UNE IA LA PLUS COÛTEUSE VENDUE AUX ENCHÈRES

Le 25 octobre 2018, *Portrait of Edmond de Belamy* a atteint 432 000 $ chez Christie's, à New York (USA). Ce portrait d'une personne imaginaire a été produit par une forme d'intelligence artificielle nommée réseaux adverses génératifs (en anglais, *GAN*) utilisée par les membres du collectif artistique Obvious Art (FRA). Ce système développe de nouvelles images à partir d'œuvres existantes — en l'occurrence, 15 000 portraits peints entre le XIVe et le XXe siècle. La "signature" (voir le zoom) est l'algorithme employé pour créer cette œuvre.

$$\min_{G} \max_{D} E_x[log(\mathcal{D}(x))] + E_z[log(1-\mathcal{D}(\mathcal{G}(z)))]$$

LE PLUS DE PORTES PASSÉES PAR UN DRONE EN 1 MIN

Le 21 novembre 2018, Luisa Rizzo (ITA) a guidé un véhicule aérien sans pilote à travers 57 portes en 60 s, pour *La Notte dei Record*, à Rome (ITA). Cela représente des courses multiples à travers un parcours de 7 portes — séparées d'au moins 4 m — dans une boucle en forme de 8. Luisa, qui se déplace en fauteuil roulant, affirme que piloter un drone lui donne un sentiment de liberté qui lui permet de dépasser les limites de son corps. Son drone Splinter 2S a été conçu par Stefano Mirabelli de Model Drome.

La 1re centrale électrique à gaz zéro émission

Le 30 mai 2018, Net Power (USA) a présenté la 1re centrale électrique à gaz zéro émission. Il s'agit d'un prototype de centrale électrique de 25 MW, à La Porte (Texas, USA). Ce système fonctionne à l'aide de CO_2 pressurisé et chauffé entraînant une turbine. Le CO_2 est chauffé en brûlant un mélange de gaz naturel et d'oxygène (extrait de l'atmosphère dans une installation annexe). Le CO_2 additionnel produit en brûlant le gaz est alors siphonné pour maintenir l'équilibre du système. Le CO_2 en excès est capturé et non rejeté dans l'atmosphère afin d'éviter toute pollution. Quant aux coûts d'utilisation de la centrale, ils n'excèdent pas ceux des centrales à gaz traditionnelles.

La plus haute altitude atteinte par une fusée propulsée par des comprimés effervescents

BYU Rocketry (USA), équipe d'étudiants de l'université Brigham Young University, a expédié une fusée propulsée par des comprimés effervescents à 269,13 m d'altitude, au Kennedy Space Center Visitor Complex (Floride, USA), le 12 décembre 2018. Le lancement a eu lieu lors du 2e "Alka-Rocket Challenge" annuel de Bayer, durant lequel 5 équipes ont concouru pour remporter un prix de 30 000 $.

Le plus de vaisseaux en activité autour d'une autre planète

Six vaisseaux opérationnels orbitent autour de Mars au 14 novembre 2018. Le dernier arrivé, *ExoMars Trace Gas Orbiter*, a atteint la planète rouge le 19 octobre 2016.

Cette énorme structure a nécessité 420 000 t d'acier — c'est-à-dire environ 8 ponts de Sydney !

LE PLUS LONG PONT-TUNNEL

Le pont-tunnel Hong Kong-Zhuhai-Macao atteint 29,6 km. Reliant Hong Kong à Macao et Zhuhai sur le delta de la rivière des Perles, il compte 4 îles artificielles, 3 ponts à haubans totalisant 22,9 km et 1 tunnel sous-marin de 6,7 km — localisé entre deux îles baignées de lumière, visibles ci-dessus. En incluant les deux accès autoroutiers, la construction mesure 55 km.

SEPT. 15 Lors du Nickelodeon Slimefest annuel de 2012, Nickelodeon organise l'engluage de 3 026 personnes à Sydney (AUS) — **le plus de personnes recouvertes de slime simultanément**.

SEPT. 16 **L'aéroport situé à la plus haute altitude** ouvre en 2013. Daocheng Yading Airport culmine à 4 411 m dans la préfecture autonome du Tibet (province du Sichuan, CHN).

La plus lointaine exploration d'un objet du système solaire
À 5 h 33 temps universel, le 1er janvier 2019, la sonde spatiale *New Horizons* a survolé dans la ceinture de Kuiper l'astéroïde 2014 MU69 (baptisé plus tard "Ultima Thulé", après un vote public). Les images révèlent que cet objet de 31 km de long est un petit corps "binaire à contact", constitué de 2 sphères connectées.

La toupie motorisée fonctionnant le plus longtemps (prototype)
Conçue par Nimrod Back de Fearless Toys (tous 2 ISR) et créée en partenariat avec Breaking Toys (USA), la toupie motorisée *LIMBO* a tourné 27 h, 9 min et 24 s en continu, à Tel-Aviv (ISR), les 18-19 juin 2018.

La plus longue distance en hélicoptère électrique (prototype)
Le 7 décembre 2018, un hélicoptère électrique expérimental alimenté par des batteries a volé 56,82 km, à Los Alamitos (Californie, USA). Créé par Martine Rothblatt, Lung Biotechnology et Tier 1 Engineering, il était piloté par Ric Webb (tous USA).

LE CÂBLE LE PLUS LOURD
Redaelli Tecna (ITA) a produit un câble Flexpack ultrarésistant pesant 488 366 t — plus lourd que la Station spatiale internationale —, à Trieste (ITA), le 30 octobre 2017. Il mesure en tout 4 050 m de long. Le poids total a été extrapolé à partir d'une section d'une longueur de 99,5 cm (voir le zoom).

Cet épais câble en acier est employé dans les secteurs pétrolier et gazier pour des opérations de pose et de récupération de canalisations.

L'ORBITE LA PLUS PROCHE POUR UN ASTÉROÏDE
À 19 h 44, temps universel, le 31 décembre 2018, la sonde *OSIRIS-REx* de la NASA s'est mise en orbite autour de l'astéroïde 101955 Bennu (encart). Son orbite légèrement elliptique a permis au véhicule de se rapprocher à moins de 1 600 m du centre de l'astéroïde.

Le 3 octobre 2018, le vaisseau *Hayabusa2* (JPN) a transporté 3 des 4 sondes ayant atterri à la surface de l'astéroïde 162173 Ryugu, soit **le plus de sondes ayant atterri sur un astéroïde**.

Le plus vieil astrolabe marin
Les astrolabes calculaient en mer la latitude d'un navire en fonction de la position de certaines étoiles. *The International Journal of Nautical Archaeology* a révélé en mars 2019 la découverte par David L. Mearns (GBR) d'un astrolabe de 1498 (+/- 2 ans) dans une épave au large d'Oman, le 8 mai 2014.

La plus petite publicité
Le 21 septembre 2018, la compagnie technologique ASML (NDL) a dévoilé une publicité de 258,19 micromètres-carrés, à Veldhoven (NDL). Gravée et imprimée sur une plaque de silicium, elle indique : "To Truly Go Small You Have To Think Big #Smallest_AD ASML" (Pour faire aussi petit, il faut penser grand #Plus_petite_PUB ASML).

À l'autre bout de l'échelle, la chaîne de restauration rapide US Arby's a exposé **la plus grande affiche publicitaire** — 28 922,10 m² —, à Monowi (Nebraska, USA), le 13 juin 2018, pour marquer son partenariat avec Coca-Cola. Monowi a été sélectionnée, car elle est considérée comme la plus petite ville des États-Unis. Son unique habitant, Elsie Eiler, est à la fois maire, bibliothécaire et barman.

LE VOYAGE LE PLUS LONG D'UN BATEAU-JOUET
Un bateau pirate Playmobil baptisé *Adventure* a parcouru 6 072,47 km entre le 28 mai 2017 et le 12 mai 2018. Les frères Ollie et Harry Ferguson (tous 2 GBR) ont lancé leur jouet à Peterhead (Aberdeenshire, GBR), et les courants marins l'ont fait voguer jusqu'en Scandinavie. Le navire norvégien *Christian Radich* l'a récupéré avant de le remettre à l'eau à 160 km au large des côtes mauritaniennes, d'où il a poursuivi son voyage à travers l'Atlantique-Sud vers La Barbade. Au cours de son périple, un contrepoids permettait de stabiliser l'*Adventure*, tandis que du polystyrène améliorait sa flottabilité et qu'un GPS embarqué le localisait.

En 2017, l'artiste martial Anthony Kelly (AUS) fait preuve de réflexe en accomplissant **l'attrapé de la balle de tennis le plus rapide** (248,09 km/h), lors de l'émission *Officially Amazing* sur CBBC, à Birchgrove (AUS).

En 2014, Ahmed Gabr (EGY) effectue **la plongée sous-marine la plus profonde** (332,35 m) dans la mer Rouge, au large de Dahab (EGY). Sa plongée dure 13 h et 50 min, avec une descente réalisée en 14 min.

ARTS & MÉDIA

ÉDITION GAMER DU GWR 2020

Accro à *Fortnite* ? Nous avons réservé 14 pages à cet emblématique jeu en ligne dans l'édition *Gamer* du *GWR 2020*. Rencontrez les meilleurs youtubeurs et joueurs pros, dont Richard Tyler "Ninja" Blevins, et sa "Map for all Seasons" en perpétuelle mutation. Familiarisez-vous avec les tenues et les armes *Fortnite*, et lancez-vous dans des défis qui mettront votre créativité à contribution. Bien entendu, l'édition *Gamer* réunit aussi les derniers records de tout l'univers du jeu vidéo !

LE PREMIER JEU VIDÉO CROSS PLAY COMPATIBLE SUR PLATEFORMES SONY, MICROSOFT ET NINTENDO

Le 26 septembre 2018, après un changement de politique chez Sony, le jeu FPS phare *Fortnite Battle Royale* (Epic, 2017) est devenu le premier jeu vidéo qui permette aux gamers de jouer ensemble en ligne quelle que soit leur plateforme, que ce soit la PS4 de Sony, la Xbox One de Microsoft, la Nintendo Switch, sans oublier l'environnement PC ou les mobiles sous Android et iOS. Sony avait d'abord refusé de doter *Fortnite* du cross-play sur la PS4, mais sous la pression des joueurs et d'Epic, l'entreprise a finalement trouvé une solution permettant une utilisation compatible avec d'autres consoles. Une version bêta du jeu a été testée à la date mentionnée ci-dessus.

SOMMAIRE

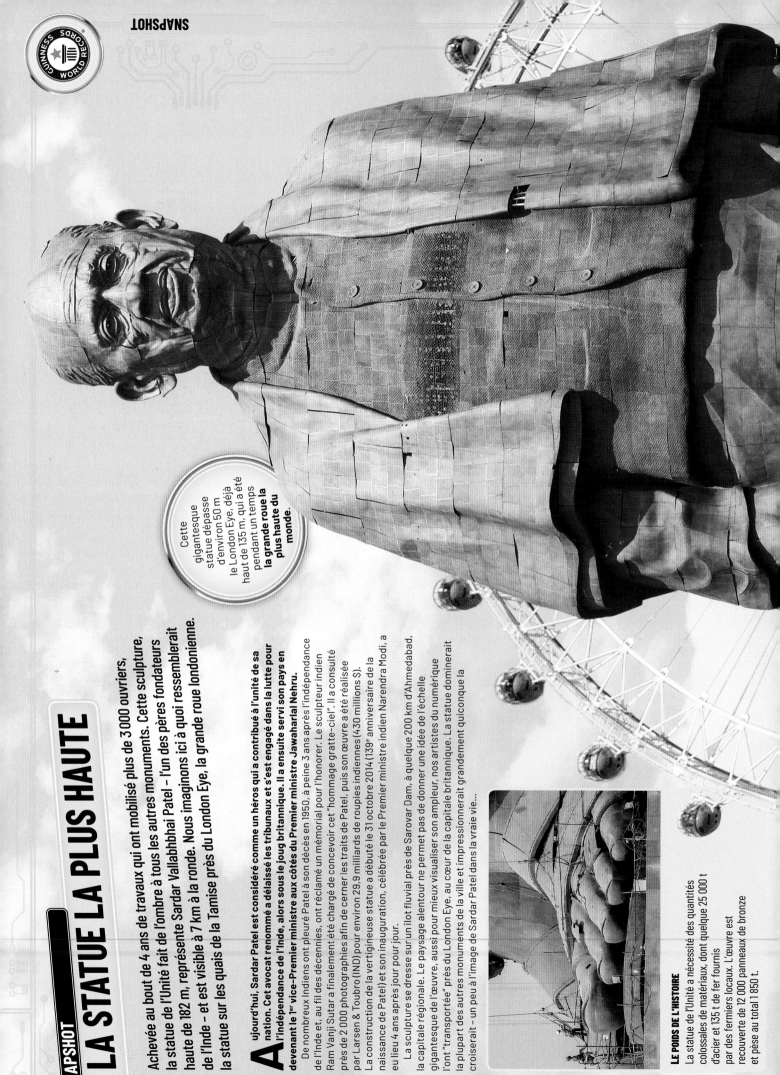

LA STATUE LA PLUS HAUTE

Achevée au bout de 4 ans de travaux qui ont mobilisé plus de 3 000 ouvriers, la statue de l'Unité fait de l'ombre à tous les autres monuments. Cette sculpture, haute de 182 m, représente Sardar Vallabhbhai Patel – l'un des pères fondateurs de l'Inde – et est visible à 7 km à la ronde. Nous imaginons ici à quoi ressemblerait la statue sur les quais de la Tamise près du London Eye, la grande roue londonienne.

Aujourd'hui, Sardar Patel est considéré comme un héros qui a contribué à l'unité de sa nation. Cet avocat renommé a délaissé les tribunaux et s'est engagé dans la lutte pour l'indépendance de l'Inde, alors sous le joug britannique. Il a ensuite servi son pays en devenant le 1er vice-Premier ministre aux côtés du Premier ministre Jawaharlal Nehru.

De nombreux Indiens ont pleuré Patel à son décès en 1950, à peine 3 ans après l'indépendance de l'Inde et, au fil des décennies, ont réclamé un mémorial pour l'honorer. Le sculpteur indien Ram Vanji Sutar a finalement été chargé de concevoir cet "hommage gratte-ciel". Il a consulté près de 2 000 photographies afin de cerner les traits de Patel, puis son œuvre a été réalisée par Larsen & Toubro (IND) pour environ 29,9 milliards de roupies indiennes (430 millions $). La construction de la vertigineuse statue a débuté le 31 octobre 2014 (139e anniversaire de la naissance de Patel) et son inauguration, célébrée par le Premier ministre indien Narendra Modi, a eu lieu 4 ans après jour pour jour.

La sculpture se dresse sur un îlot fluvial près de Sarovar Dam, à quelque 200 km d'Ahmedabad, la capitale régionale. Le paysage alentour ne permet pas de donner une idée de l'échelle gigantesque de l'œuvre, aussi pour mieux visualiser son ampleur, nos artistes du numérique l'ont "transportée" près du London Eye, au cœur de la capitale britannique. La statue dominerait la plupart des autres monuments de la ville et impressionnerait grandement quiconque la croiserait – un peu à l'image de Sardar Patel dans la vraie vie…

Cette gigantesque statue dépasse d'environ 50 m le London Eye, déjà haut de 135 m, qui a été pendant un temps **la grande roue la plus haute du monde.**

LE POIDS DE L'HISTOIRE

La statue de l'Unité a nécessité des quantités colossales de matériaux, dont quelque 25 000 t d'acier et 135 t de fer fournis par des fermiers locaux. L'œuvre est recouverte de 12 000 panneaux de bronze et pèse au total 1 850 t.

La statue de l'Unité a été construite pour durer. Elle peut affronter des vents de 130 km/h et des séismes de 6,5 sur l'échelle de Richter.

UN TRIO TITANESQUE

La statue de l'Unité trône 54 m au-dessus de la précédente sculpture la plus haute du monde – le Bouddha du Temple de la Source dans la province de Henan (CHN). Elle mesure aussi près de 4 fois la taille de la statue de la Liberté new-yorkaise (hors piédestal) – en fait, elle est plus haute que ces 2 célèbres monuments superposés.

182 m

128 m

46 m

AU BOX-OFFICE

LES PLUS RENTABLES...

Film
Avatar (USA/GBR, 2009) reste le plus gros succès de tous les temps, avec des recettes globales de 2 776 345 279 $. Le week-end du 29-30 janvier 2010, le blockbuster de science-fiction de James Cameron est devenu **le 1er film à rapporter 2 milliards $**. Cameron était aussi à la barre du **1er film à générer 1 milliard $** : *Titanic* (USA, 1997).

Film "ethnique" de super-héros
Black Panther (USA, 2018) de Ryan Coogler totalise 1 348 258 224 $ et devient ainsi le 9e film le plus rentable de tous les temps. L'histoire explique comment T'Challa – alias Black Panther, roi de la nation africaine fictive du Wakanda – doit se battre pour son trône.

Le 22 janvier 2019, *Black Panther* est devenu le **1er film de super-héros nommé pour l'Oscar du meilleur film**. S'il s'est incliné devant *Green Book : Sur les routes du Sud* (USA, 2018), il a remporté le trophée de la meilleure musique originale, des meilleurs costumes et des meilleurs décors - **le plus d'Oscars obtenus par un film de super-héros**.

Long-métrage d'animation
La Reine des neiges (USA, 2013) de Disney a généré 1 272 469 910 $. Sa suite, *La Reine des neiges 2 - Le Miroir sacré*, est prévue pour

LA SORTIE EN SALLE LA PLUS LARGE (SUR UN MARCHÉ NATIONAL)
Le chouchou des familles *Moi, moche et méchant 3* (USA, 2017) a été diffusé dans 4 529 salles d'Amérique du Nord le week-end de sa sortie (30 juin-2 juillet). Aux 2e et 3e places, nous retrouvons 2 films de 2018 : *Jurassic World : Fallen Kingdom* (USA), exploité dans 4 475 cinémas, et *Avengers : Infinity War* (USA), dans 4 474 salles.

LE REMAKE LE PLUS RENTABLE
Le remake en prises de vues réelles du dessin animé culte de 1991 de Walt Disney *La Belle et la Bête* sorti en 2017 a généré un total de 1 259 199 706 $. Le film, inspiré du conte de fées français éponyme de 1740 – écrit originellement par Gabrielle-Suzanne Barbot de Villeneuve -, met en scène Emma Watson et Dan Stevens (tous 2 à droite).

LA SÉRIE CINÉMATOGRAPHIQUE LA PLUS LUCRATIVE
Au 4 avril 2019, les films *Star Wars* avaient généré 9 307 186 202 $ à travers le monde. À lui seul, le 7e volet de la franchise de science-fiction à grand succès, *Le Réveil de la Force* (USA, 2015, sur la photo), a rapporté 2 053 311 220 $, devenant le 3e film le plus rentable de tous les temps.

La musique culte est l'œuvre de John Williams (USA, encadré), **le compositeur le plus bankable d'Hollywood**. Au 28 février 2019, sa cote dans l'industrie cinématographique avait été évaluée à 10,7 millions $ par film.

novembre 2019. Le teaser, dévoilé le 13 février 2019, a été vu 116,4 millions de fois en un jour selon Disney – soit **la bande-annonce de dessin animé la plus visionnée en 24 h,** dépassant ainsi *Les Indestructibles 2* (voir à droite).

Dessin animé traditionnel
Le Roi lion (USA, 1994) de Disney a rapporté 986 214 868 $. Dessiné entièrement à la main et réalisé par Roger Allers et Rob Minkoff, il a été le film le plus rentable de 1994.

Le film animé en stop motion le plus rentable reste l'opus d'Aardman Animations *Chicken Run* (USA/GBR/FRA, 2000), avec 227,8 millions $.

Film inspiré d'un jeu vidéo
Avec le concours de Dwayne Johnson (voir p. 194), *Rampage - Hors de contrôle* (USA, 2018) a mis le feu au box-office mondial en générant 428 056 280 $. Ce film est inspiré du jeu d'arcade de 1986 *Rampage* de Bally Midway.

Le film le plus rentable inspiré des jeux vidéo est *Ready Player One* (USA, 2018), qui a totalisé 579 290 136 $.

Film d'horreur
Adapté d'un roman de Stephen King paru en 1986, *Ça* (USA, 2017) a généré 697 457 969 $. La suite, *Ça : Chapitre Deux*, devait sortir sur les écrans en septembre 2019.

Week-end de sortie d'un film original
Comme des bêtes (USA, 2016), scénario inédit non inspiré des intrigues ou personnages déjà existants, a rapporté 104 352 905 $ lors de sa sortie nationale dans les cinémas américains les 8-10 juillet 2016.

L'ANIME LE PLUS RENTABLE
Le long-métrage fantastico-romantique écrit et réalisé par Makoto Shinkai, *Your Name* (*Kimi no na wa*, JPN, 2016, ci-dessus), a rapporté 361 024 012 $ dans le monde. Un autre prétendant au titre, *Spider-Man : New generation 3D* (USA, 2018), l'avait dépassé avec 373 735 455 $ au 4 avril 2019 - certains se demandent néanmoins si ce film peut être considéré comme un véritable *anime*.

so
The-Nu
vérifiés
2019 sau

 SEPT. 19 En 1893, la Nouvelle-Zélande devient **le 1er pays à donner le droit de vote aux femmes**. La loi reçoit l'assentiment de la couronne d'Angleterre par la voix du gouverneur Lord Glasgow.

 SEPT. 20 En 2013, *Grand Theft Auto V* (Rockstar Games) devient **le jeu vidéo ayant atteint le plus vite 1 milliard $ de recettes**. Il lui a suffi de 3 jours pour accomplir cet exploit.

LE DESSIN ANIMÉ ORIGINAL LE PLUS RENTABLE

Les Indestructibles 2 (USA, 2018) ont généré 1 242 532 436 $ au box-office mondial, devenant ainsi le 6e film au scénario original le plus rentable de tous les temps. Cette suite est le 2e film d'animation le plus rentable de tous les temps, derrière *La Reine des neiges* (USA, 2013, voir à gauche), qui est basé sur le conte de fées éponyme écrit en 1844 par Hans Christian Andersen (DNK).

LE PLUS LONG FILM OSCARISÉ

Grâce à *O.J. : Made in America* (USA, 2016), ses créateurs Ezra Edelman et Caroline Waterlow (tous 2 USA) sont repartis de la 89e cérémonie des Oscars avec la statuette du meilleur documentaire, le 26 février 2017. Le film, qui relate l'histoire vraie de l'ascension et de la chute de la star du football américain O. J. Simpson, dure 467 min (7 h et 47 min).

O.J. : MADE IN AMERICA
A FIVE-PART 30 FOR 30 MINI-SERIES EVENT

LE FILM LE PLUS RAPIDE À GÉNÉRER 1 MILLIARD $

Le blockbuster de super-héros de Disney-Marvel *Avengers : Endgame* (USA, 2019) a dépassé 1 milliard $ au box-office mondial tout juste 5 jours après sa sortie entre le 25 et le 29 avril 2019. Le 22e film de Marvel Cinematic Universe a alors généré 1,209 milliard $– **le week-end de sortie mondiale le plus rentable pour un film.**

LE FILM AUTOBIOGRAPHIQUE LE PLUS RENTABLE

Avec Rami Malek dans le rôle de Freddie Mercury, le charismatique chanteur du groupe de rock britannique Queen, *Bohemian Rhapsody* (GBR/USA, 2018) a généré 773 633 838 $. Le film a reçu 4 statuettes à la 91e cérémonie des Oscars le 24 février 2019, dont celui du meilleur acteur pour Malek.

MARVEL STUDIOS
AVENGERS ENDGAME
APRIL 26

CINÉMA

Le plus de nominations aux Oscars pour un film en langue étrangère
Roma (MEX/USA, 2018) a totalisé 10 nominations lors de la 91ᵉ cérémonie des Oscars 2019, égalisant l'exploit de *Tigre et Dragon* (TWN/USA, 2000). Il a finalement remporté 3 statuettes : meilleur film en langue étrangère, meilleure photographie et meilleur réalisateur pour Alfonso Cuarón.

La 1ʳᵉ personne nommée simultanément pour les Oscars de la meilleure actrice et de la meilleure chanson originale
L'actrice-auteur-interprète Lady Gaga, alias Stefani Germanotta (USA), a été nommée 2 fois en 2019 par l'Académie des Oscars : meilleure actrice pour son interprétation de la chanteuse de night-club Ally Maine dans le remake *A Star is Born* (USA, 2018), et meilleure chanson originale pour *Shallow*, qu'elle a écrit avec Mark Ronson pour le même film. Elle a remporté le trophée de la meilleure chanson originale, après une performance sur scène inoubliable avec son partenaire à l'écran Bradley Cooper.

Le plus de nominations aux Oscars sans victoire (actrice)
En 2019, Glenn Close (USA) a quitté la cérémonie des Oscars les mains vides pour la 7ᵉ fois de sa carrière. Elle a reçu 4 nominations pour la meilleure actrice principale – *Liaison fatale* (USA, 1987), *Les Liaisons dangereuses* (USA/GBR, 1988), *Albert Nobbs* (GBR/IRL/FRA/USA, 2011), *The Wife* (GBR/SWE/USA, 2018) –

et 3 pour la meilleure actrice dans un second rôle – *Le Monde selon Garp* (USA, 1982), *Les Copains d'abord* (USA, 1983) et *Le Meilleur* (USA, 1984).
Peter O'Toole (IRL) détient **le plus de nominations aux Oscars sans victoire pour un acteur** (8). Il a cependant reçu un Oscar d'honneur en 2003.

La nommée aux Oscars la plus âgée
Le 4 mars 2018, la réalisatrice Agnès Varda (BEL/FRA, 30 mai 1928-29 mars 2019) a été nommée dans la catégorie meilleur documentaire à l'âge de 89 ans et 279 jours. Son film *Visages Villages* (FRA, 2017) suit Varda et un artiste "photograffeur" nommé JR (identité réelle inconnue) alors qu'ils sillonnent la France rurale pour créer des portraits de personnes qu'ils rencontrent.

Le réalisateur hollywoodien le plus rentable
La cote de Zack Snyder (USA) dans l'industrie cinématographique était évaluée à 15 737 661 $ par film, au 28 février 2019. Les 8 films de Snyder en tant que réalisateur – comprenant les films de super-héros DC *Justice League* (USA, 2017), *Batman v. Superman : L'Aube de la justice* (USA, 2016), *Man of Steel*

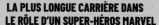

(USA, 2013) et *Watchmen : Les Gardiens* (USA, 2009) – ont rapporté au total 3 165 511 174 $.

Le compositeur de film le plus rentable
Au 23 janvier 2019, les 100 films dont Hans Zimmer (DEU) a composé la musique – dont *Les veuves* (USA, 2018), *Interstellar* (USA/GBR, 2014) et *The Dark Knight Rises* (GBR/USA, 2012) – totalisaient 27 807 884 544 $ au box-office.

L'acteur de Bollywood le mieux rémunéré (à date)
D'après Forbes, l'acteur de Bollywood le mieux rémunéré est Akshay Kumar, alias Rajiv Hari Om Bhatia (CAN, né IND), qui, entre le 1ᵉʳ juin 2017 et le 1ᵉʳ juin 2018, a gagné 40,5 millions $. Kumar est la seule star de Bollywood figurant sur la liste Forbes des 100 personnalités les mieux rémunérées au monde pour cette année.

L'actrice de Bollywood la mieux rémunérée (à date) est Deepika Padukone (IND, née DNK), qui a cumulé environ 112,8 millions de roupies indiennes (15,37 millions $) entre le 1ᵉʳ octobre 2017 et le 30 septembre 2018, selon les chiffres publiés par Forbes India.

Le plus de morts dans une carrière cinématographique
Christopher Lee (GBR, 1922-2015) a "trouvé la mort" dans au moins 61 des plus de 200 films auxquels il a participé. Les personnages de Lee ont été pendus, défenestrés, frappés par la foudre, empalés, poignardés, brûlés, électrocutés, dissous, explosés, décapités et écrasés sur la Lune...

LA PLUS LONGUE CARRIÈRE DANS LE RÔLE D'UN SUPER-HÉROS MARVEL

Hugh Jackman (AUS, à droite) et Patrick Stewart (GBR, à gauche) ont joué le même super-héros Marvel - respectivement Wolverine et Professeur Charles Xavier de X-Men – pendant 16 ans et 232 jours. Ils ont débuté dans la série *X-Men* (USA, 2000) avant de reprendre plus récemment leurs rôles dans *Logan* (USA, ci-dessus) en 2017. Les 2 acteurs ont reçu un certificat GWR pour marquer leur exploit en février 2019.

LES REVENUS LES PLUS ÉLEVÉS POUR UN ACTEUR DE CINÉMA (À DATE)

George Clooney (USA, ci-dessous) a perçu 239 millions $ entre le 1ᵉʳ juillet 2017 et le 1ᵉʳ juillet 2018, selon Forbes. Cette somme provient en grande partie de la vente de l'entreprise de téquila Casamigos, qu'il avait cofondée. Le second acteur le plus rentable est la vedette de *Jumanji : Bienvenue dans la jungle* (USA, 2017), Dwayne Johnson (USA, à gauche), avec 124 millions $.

L'ACTEUR PRINCIPAL LE PLUS RENTABLE

Les 30 films avec Robert Downey Jr (USA) en vedette ou covedette ont totalisé 11 347 917 823 $. En avril 2019, le film le plus rentable de l'acteur était *Avengers : Infinity War* (USA, 2018), qui a généré 2,048 milliards $. Sa partenaire à l'écran Scarlett Johansson (USA) est **l'actrice principale la plus rentable**, ses 25 films cumulant 10 786 897 236 $.

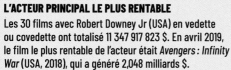

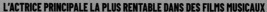

L'ACTRICE PRINCIPALE LA PLUS RENTABLE DANS DES FILMS MUSICAUX

Au 7 février 2019, Meryl Streep (USA, à gauche) avait généré 1 550 488 703 $ grâce à ses 4 rôles musicaux : *Mamma Mia !* (USA, 2008), *Mamma Mia ! Here We Go Again* (SWE/GBR/USA, 2018), *Le Retour de Mary Poppins* (USA, 2018) et *Promenons-nous dans les bois* (USA, 2014). Streep a dépassé sa partenaire de *Mamma Mia !* Amanda Seyfried (USA, à l'extrême-gauche), qui avait touché 1,4 milliard $.

Tom Cruise a été nommé 3 fois aux Oscars pour sa prestation dans *Né un 4 juillet* (USA, 1989), *Jerry Maguire* (USA, 1996) et *Magnolia* (USA, 1999).

L'ARTISTE LE PLUS RENTABLE D'HOLLYWOOD

Au 28 février 2019, l'indice de rentabilité de The Numbers couronnait Tom Cruise (USA), dont la cote dans l'industrie cinématographique était évaluée à 20 934 185 $ par film. En 2018, Cruise a repris le rôle de l'agent spécial Ethan Hunt dans *Mission : Impossible – Fallout* (USA, à droite). Le film a généré 787 456 552 $, devenant le film le plus lucratif de ses 38 ans de carrière.

L'actrice principale hollywoodienne la plus rentable est Sandra Bullock (USA), avec une valeur ajoutée de 14 533 088 $ par film. En 2018, elle a dirigé une équipe de voleuses dans la nouvelle adaptation *Ocean's 8* (USA, en photo ci-contre avec sa partenaire Rihanna).

L'OSCARISÉ LE PLUS ÂGÉ

Le 4 mars 2018, James Ivory (USA, né le 7 juin 1928, à gauche) a remporté l'Oscar du meilleur scénario adapté, à l'âge de 89 ans et 271 jours. Son script pour *Call Me by Your Name* (ITA/FRA/BRA/USA, 2017), adaptation du roman d'André Aciman, relate les relations entre un adolescent précoce de 17 ans, Elio (Timothée Chalamet, ci-dessus, à droite), et un étudiant, Oliver (Armie Hammer, à gauche).

LE PRODUCTEUR LE PLUS RENTABLE D'HOLLYWOOD

La cote de Kathleen Kennedy (USA) dans l'industrie cinématographique était estimée à 15 541 558 $ par film au 28 février 2019. Ses 35 projets en tant que productrice ont généré près de 12 milliards $, provenant en majeure partie de la saga *Star Wars*, notamment *Le Réveil de la Force* (USA, 2015, voir p. 192) et *Rogue One* (USA, 2016).

LA 1RE PERSONNE À REMPORTER UNE MÉDAILLE OLYMPIQUE ET UN OSCAR

Le 4 mars 2018, le double champion olympique Kobe Bryant (USA) a ajouté un Oscar sur son étagère de trophées grâce à la victoire de *Dear Basketball* (USA, 2017) dans la catégorie du meilleur court-métrage d'animation. Il a partagé la récompense avec l'animateur Disney Glen Keane. Le film s'inspire d'un poème que Bryant avait écrit en 2015, annonçant sa retraite.

SEPT. 25 En 2016, l'actrice et chanteuse Selena Gomez (USA) devient **la 1re personne comptant 100 millions de followers sur Instagram** grâce à son hashtag #SelenaBreakTheInternet, devenu viral.

SEPT. 26 En 2016, un débat télévisé opposant Hillary Clinton à Donald Trump (tous 2 USA) attire près de 84 millions de téléspectateurs, devenant ainsi **le débat présidentiel télévisé le plus suivi.**

195

POP RECORDS

LE 1ER ARTISTE À DOMINER EN SIMULTANÉ 5 CHARTS COUNTRY

Le 28 octobre 2017, Kane Brown (USA) s'est hissé simultanément à la 1re place des 5 hit-parades country principaux du *Billboard*. Le single *What Ifs*, avec Lauren Alaina, a régné sur le Hot Country Songs, Country Airplay et Country Streaming Songs, alors que *Heaven* a débuté n° 1 des Country Digital Song Sales. La même semaine, le 1er album éponyme de Brown dominait le Top Country Albums.

La 1re chanson de rap à remporter le Grammy de la chanson de l'année

Lors des 61e Grammy Awards, le 10 février 2019, *This Is America* de Childish Gambino (alias Donald Glover, USA) a remporté 4 trophées, dont celui de la chanson de l'année. Ce titre est également devenu **le 1er titre de rap à obtenir le Grammy Award de l'enregistrement de l'année.**

La plus grande attente pour un single dans le Top 10 US

Robert "Bobby" Helms (US, 1933-1997) s'est retrouvé dans le Top 10 du *Billboard* Hot 100 le 5 janvier 2019, grâce à *Jingle Bell Rock* (n° 8). 60 ans et 140 jours s'étaient écoulés depuis le 1er album de Helms, *Borrowed Dreams*, sorti le 18 août 1958.

Le plus de semaines n° 1 au US Hot Country Songs

Le duo de Nashville Florida Georgia Line (Tyler Hubbard et Brian Kelley, tous 2 USA) a fêté sa 106e semaine non consécutive à la 1re place du Hot Country Songs du *Billboard*, le 17 novembre 2018.

LE PLUS DE SINGLES N° 1 AUX ÉTATS-UNIS POUR UNE RAPPEUSE

Cardi B (USA, née Belcalis Almánzar) compte trois n° 1 dans le *Billboard* Hot 100 : *Bodak Yellow* (Money Moves), le 7 octobre 2017 ; *I Like It* (*feat.* Bad Bunny & J. Balvin), le 7 juillet 2018, et *Girls Like You* (Maroon 5 *feat.* Cardi B), le 29 septembre 2018. Elle a été invitée à participer au remix de *Girls Like You*, sorti à l'origine sur l'album *Red Pill Blues* des Maroon 5 en 2017.

Meant to Be, sa collaboration avec Bebe Rexha, a prolongé son record du **plus de semaines consécutives n° 1 au US Hot Country Songs** : 50, à la même date.

Le plus d'entrées simultanées dans le top singles USA pour un groupe

Le trio de rap Migos (USA) a placé 14 hits dans le *Billboard* Hot 100 en date du 10 février 2018, égalant ainsi l'exploit des Beatles (GBR) du 11 avril 1964.

Le titre le plus streamé sur Spotify pour une chanteuse

Havana, le succès 2017 de Camila Cabello (CUB/USA), en duo avec Young Thug, totalisait 1 182 041 228 streams sur Spotify au 27 mars 2019.

Le titre le plus streamé de Spotify est *Shape of You* d'Ed Sheeran (GBR) – le 1er titre à dépasser les 2 milliards de streams en décembre 2018.

Le titre le plus streamé sur Spotify en 24 h est *All I Want for Christmas Is You* de Mariah Carey (USA, à droite), diffusé 10 819 009 fois le 24 décembre 2018.

Le titre le plus streamé sur Spotify en 24 h (hommes) est *SAD !* de XXXTentacion (USA, né Jahseh Onfroy, 1998-2018), avec 10 415 088 streams le 19 juin 2018. La musique du rappeur floridien avait suscité un regain d'intérêt après son assassinat le jour précédent.

LE PLUS DE VUES SIMULTANÉES POUR UNE VIDÉO MUSICALE SUR YOUTUBE PREMIÈRES

Le 30 novembre 2018, *thank u, next* d'Ariana Grande (USA) a généré 829 000 vues simultanées sur Premières, la fonctionnalité de planification de YouTube.

Grande totalise également **le plus de streams sur Spotify en 1 an pour une musicienne** (3 milliards en 2018), tandis que *7 rings* est devenu **le titre le plus streamé de Spotify en 1 semaine** (71 467 874 fois), entre les 18 et 24 janvier 2019.

Le 23 février 2019, elle est devenue **la 1re artiste solo à occuper simultanément les 3 premières places des palmarès singles USA** avec *thank u, next*, *break up with your girlfriend, i'm bored* et *7 rings*. Elle est également **la 1re artiste féminine à se supplanter elle-même au top des singles GBR** : *break up with your girlfriend, i'm bored* a dépassé *7 rings*, le 21 février 2019.

Le plus de semaines n° 1 au Top Latin Albums du *Billboard* (hommes)

Ozuna (PRI, né Juan Carlos Ozuna Rosado) a dominé le palmarès pendant 46 semaines non consécutives grâce à *Odisea*, du 16 septembre 2017 au 1er septembre 2018.

LA CHANSON DE NOËL LA MIEUX PLACÉE DANS LE HOT 100 POUR UNE ARTISTE SOLO

Initialement sorti en 1994, *All I Want for Christmas Is You* de Mariah Carey (USA) s'est retrouvé n° 3 du *Billboard* Hot 100 daté du 5 janvier 2019. *The Chipmunk Song* des Chipmunks avec David Seville (ci-dessous), n° 1 quasiment 60 ans plus tôt, le 22 décembre 1958, est la seule chanson de Noël à avoir dépassé le succès festif de Carey.

LE PLUS DE TITRES ENREGISTRÉS DANS TOUS LES TOPS LATINOS DU *BILLBOARD*

Le chanteur de salsa Victor Manuelle (PRI, né USA) avait placé 72 titres dans le palmarès des chansons tropicales du *Billboard* au 12 mars 2019. Surnommé El Sonero de la Juventud ("Le chanteur des jeunes"), Manuelle est un représentant immensément populaire de la *salsa romántica*. Il a décroché son 72e hit avec *Con Mi Salsa La Mantengo*, le 16 février 2019.

SEPT. 27 Au Ski Fluid International de 2016, Jacinta Carroll (AUS) exécute **le plus long saut en ski nautique (femmes)** (60,3 m), sur le lac Grew de Polk City (Floride, USA).

SEPT. 28 En 2012, l'artiste de foire "Zoe L'Amore", alias Zoe Ellis (AUS), décroche le record du **plus de souricières libérées avec la langue en 1 min (femmes)** (24), à Londres (GBR).

LE 1ᴱᴿ ALBUM À GÉNÉRER 1 MILLIARD DE STREAMS AUDIO EN 1 SEMAINE

Le 29 juin 2018, Drake (CAN, né Aubrey Drake Graham) a sorti le double album *Scorpion*, dont les 25 titres ont été streamés plus de 1 milliard de fois à travers le monde la semaine qui a suivi. Drake a obtenu **le plus de titres simultanés dans le top singles US pour un artiste solo** – avec 27 chansons placées dans le *Billboard* Hot 100 du 14 juillet 2018. Cet exploit inclut **le plus d'entrées simultanées dans le Top 10 (7)**, toutes tirées de *Scorpion*, dont le n° 1 *Nice for What*.

Les 25 chansons de l'album de Drake *Scorpion* sont entrées dans l'US Hot 100. Les 193 hits de sa carrière (au 9 mars 2019) constituent **le plus d'entrées dans l'US Hot 100 pour un artiste**.

LA CHANTEUSE LA PLUS JEUNE À DOMINER LE TOP ALBUMS GBR

WHEN WE ALL FALL ASLEEP, WHERE DO WE GO ?, le 1ᵉʳ album studio de l'auteur-interprète Billie Eilish (USA, née 18 décembre 2001), est devenu n° 1 du top albums GBR le 11 avril 2019, alors qu'elle avait 17 ans et 114 jours.

Eilish a aussi cumulé **le plus d'entrées simultanées dans le *Billboard* Hot 100 pour une femme (14)** d'après les chiffres datés du 13 avril 2019.

LE SINGLE LE PLUS VENDU AU ROYAUME-UNI

Something About the Way You Look Tonight/ Candle in the Wind 1997 – ce dernier écrit par Elton John et Bernie Taupin (tous 2 GBR) en 1973, mais retravaillé après le décès de Lady Diana (1961-1997) – s'est vendu à 4,9 millions d'exemplaires au Royaume-Uni. Environ 50 ans après son 1ᵉʳ succès au Top 10 GBR (*Your Song*), Sir Elton s'est engagé dans une tournée mondiale de 3 ans, *Farewell Yellow Brick Road*, avec plus de 300 concerts. Un biopic de la star, *Rocketman*, est sorti en mai 2019.

LE DÉLAI LE PLUS LONG ENTRE LA SORTIE D'UN ENREGISTREMENT ORIGINAL ET LE RÉENREGISTREMENT DU MÊME SINGLE PAR UN MÊME ARTISTE

En 1949, sous le nom de scène Joe Bari, Tony Bennett (USA) a fait ses débuts avec une reprise du standard de jazz écrit par George Gershwin *Fascinating Rhythm*. Le 3 août 2018, soit 68 ans et 342 jours plus tard, le chanteur légendaire a sorti une nouvelle version de ce titre, enregistrée avec Diana Krall.

SEPT. 29 Les fans des Kansas City Chiefs (USA) poussent **le rugissement de foule le plus puissant dans un stade**. Ils atteignent un niveau assourdissant de 142,2 dBA durant leur victoire 41-14 contre les New England Patriots en 2014.

SEPT. 30 En 2010, **la chapelle de mariage la plus rapide** atteint 99 km/h, à Shelbyville (Illinois, USA). Le *Best Man* est un camion de pompiers reconverti et doté de vitraux, de bancs d'église et d'une chaire.

197

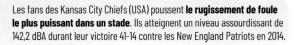

CONCERTS

Le 1er concert de rock 'n' roll
Le Moondog Coronation Ball qui s'est tenu à la Cleveland Arena (Ohio, USA), le 21 mars 1952, est considéré comme le "Big Bang du rock 'n' roll". Organisé par le DJ Alan Freed et le disquaire Leo Mintz, le concert proposait en tête d'affiche le saxophoniste Paul Williams et ses Hucklebuckers (tous USA). L'événement prit fin au bout de 30 min en raison d'une foule trop nombreuse et de désordres.

Le plus de spectateurs pour un concert de rock gratuit
Le 31 décembre 1994, Rod Stewart (GBR) a attiré 4,2 millions de fans pour un concert de la Saint-Sylvestre, sur la plage de Copacabana, à Rio de Janeiro (BRA). Même si certains spectateurs s'étaient peut-être déplacés pour le feu d'artifice de minuit, Stewart a cependant doublé le précédent record d'audience au même emplacement.

La plus forte audience réalisée par un concert de rock télévisé
The Beach Boys, David Bowie et Queen comptaient parmi les artistes qui se sont produits au double concert de charité Live Aid du 13 juillet 1985, et qui a été suivi par 1,9 milliard de téléspectateurs dans 150 pays. Organisé par les musiciens Bob Geldof (IRL) et Midge Ure (GBR), l'événement a été diffusé en simultané depuis le stade Wembley de Londres (GBR) et le stade John F. Kennedy de Philadelphie (Pennsylvanie, USA).

Le plus ancien festival de pop annuel
Le Reading Festival (GBR) a débuté en tant que festival national de jazz (et de blues) itinérant en 1961 avant de s'établir de façon permanente à Reading (Berkshire, GBR), en 1971. Il s'est tenu chaque année sauf en 1984 et 1985, le site n'étant pas disponible.
Le festival de musique pop annuel le plus pérenne (sans interruption) est le Pinkpop Festival, qui a fêté ses 50 ans en juin 2019. Il se tient chaque année dans la province de Limburg (NLD) depuis 1970.

Le festival musical le plus rentable (à date)
L' Outside Lands Music and Arts Festival, qui s'est tenu à San Francisco (Californie, USA) les 10-12 août 2018, a généré plus de 27,7 millions $ selon Pollstar. Le spectacle de 3 jours affichait The Weeknd, Florence + The Machine et Janet Jackson.

LA TOURNÉE MUSICALE LA PLUS RENTABLE POUR UN DUO (À DATE)
La tournée de Beyoncé et Jay-Z (tous 2 USA) *On the Run II Tour* a généré 253,5 millions $ en 48 spectacles en 2018, selon les chiffres du Billboard Boxscore. Le duo (The Carters) a lancé sa 2e tournée des stades le 6 juin et l'a terminée le 4 octobre, au CenturyLink Field de Seattle (Washington, USA).

La tournée musicale la plus rentable pour une artiste (de tous les temps)
Le *Sticky & Sweet Tour* de Madonna (USA) a rapporté 407,7 millions $ en 2008-2009. La tournée de 85 dates, pour promouvoir l'album *Hard Candy*, a débuté au Millennium Stadium de Cardiff (GBR), le 23 août 2008, et s'est achevé au Yarkon Park de Tel Aviv (ISR), le 2 septembre 2009. La tournée a attiré 3,54 millions de fans, chaque spectacle rapportant 4,79 millions $.

Le plus de prestations musicales live en 24 h (villes multiples)
Dans le cadre de son *Never Give Up Tour*, Scott Helmer (USA) a donné 12 concerts de charité les 28-29 novembre 2016. L'auteur-interprète a commencé son marathon musical à San Diego (Californie) et l'a clos à Phoenix (Arizona), le jour du "Giving Tuesday". Depuis 2012, Helmer a levé plus de 2 millions $ pour des bonnes causes dans tous les États-Unis.

La 1re formation musicale à se produire en concert sur chaque continent
Metallica (USA) est devenu le 1er groupe musical à se produire sur les 7 continents lorsqu'ils ont joué devant 120 chercheurs et lauréats de concours à la station Carlini en Antarctique, le 8 décembre 2013. Le spectacle de 1 h a été baptisé *Freeze 'Em All* ("Glacez-les tous").

Le 1er concert de musique live diffusé dans l'espace
Le 12 novembre 2005, Paul McCartney (GBR) a charmé les astronautes de la *Station spatiale internationale* avec 2 chansons – *English Tea* et *Good Day Sunshine* – interprétées en live depuis son concert à Anaheim (Californie, USA).

LE PLUS D'ALBUMS LIVE COMMERCIALISÉS
Sans compter les enregistrements pirates, le groupe de rock Grateful Dead (USA) a sorti 167 albums live complets depuis 1969 – dont 150 commercialisés depuis la séparation de la formation californienne en 1995. Les albums live rétrospectifs comprennent des archives d'enregistrements live des tournées *Dick's Picks* (1993-2005), *Road Trips* (2007-2011) et *Dave's Picks* (depuis 2012).

LA TOURNÉE MUSICALE LA PLUS RENTABLE
Le *U2 360° Tour* (à gauche) du groupe culte irlandais a généré 736,4 millions $ en 110 spectacles organisés entre le 30 juin 2009 et le 30 juillet 2011. Confirmant sa suprématie, entre le 2 mai et le 28 octobre 2018, U2 a touché 119,2 millions $ grâce aux 55 dates de son *eXPERIENCE + iNNOCENCE Tour* – **la tournée musicale la plus rentable pour un groupe (à date)**.

LE PLUS DE SPECTACLES AU MADISON SQUARE GARDEN POUR UN MUSICIEN
Le 18 juillet 2018, Billy Joel (USA) a donné son 100e concert au Madison Square Garden de New York (USA). Il a été rejoint sur scène par Bruce Springsteen pour *Tenth Avenue Freeze-Out* et *Born to Run*. Joel – qui totalisait 107 représentations dans la salle culte au 14 février 2019 – s'y produit une fois par mois depuis le 27 janvier 2014 dans le cadre de sa tournée *Billy Joel in Concert*.

OCT. 1 **Le plus grand village de ballons** ouvre à Jimei (Xiamen, CHN). Composé de 365 000 ballons et imaginé par l'artiste Guido Verhoef (NLD) pour le festival international du Ballon de 2016, il comprend un palais et un jardin à thème panda.

OCT. 2 En 2007, il est établi que Tim Leigh (GBR) possède **la plus grande collection de sachets de sel et de poivre** vérifiée, avec 172 paires assorties. 9 ans de patiente collecte.

LA TOURNÉE MUSICALE LA PLUS RENTABLE SUR UNE ANNÉE

La tournée d'Ed Sheeran (GBR) ÷ [*Divide*] *Tour* de 2018 a généré 429,5 millions $ en 99 concerts et attiré 4 800 441 spectateurs. Il s'agit des revenus les plus élevés pour une tournée musicale sur un an depuis la parution du Billboard Boxscore en 1990, dépassant les 425,1 millions $ de celle des Rolling Stones *A Bigger Bang* en 2006.

La tournée musicale la plus rentable pour une chanteuse (à date) est le *Reputation Stadium Tour* de Taylor Swift (USA, à droite). Son 5e tour de chant a rapporté 345,7 millions $ en 2018.

L'ALBUM LIVE LE PLUS VENDU

Unplugged, l'album d'Eric Clapton (GBR) aux multiples Grammies sorti en 1992, s'est vendu à environ 26 millions d'exemplaires à travers le monde. L'opus a été enregistré en live aux Bray Studios près de Maidenhead (Berkshire, GBR), le 16 janvier 1992, et comprend le single *Tears in Heaven* ainsi qu'une version acoustique de *Layla*. Au 25 janvier 2019, la RIAA (Recording Industry Association of America) avait confirmé la vente de 10 millions d'exemplaires du disque, faisant d'*Unplugged* le 3e album live le plus rentable aux États-Unis.

LES REVENUS ANNUELS LES PLUS ÉLEVÉS POUR UNE MUSICIENNE (À DATE)

D'après les estimations publiées par Forbes, la pop star Katy Perry (USA) a gagné 83 millions $ du 1er juin 2017 au 1er juin 2018. Cette somme provient essentiellement des 80 concerts de son *Witness : The Tour*, qui a généré 1 million $ par soirée.

Le record pour un **musicien** durant la même période revient à Ed Sheeran (GBR, ci-dessus), avec des revenus annuels de 110 millions $ selon Forbes.

Left Shark, devenu célèbre pendant le spectacle de Katy Perry lors de la mi-temps du Super Bowl XLIX, l'a rejointe sur scène durant la tournée.

OCT. 3 En 1967, le pilote d'essai de l'USAF William "Pete" Knight atteint une vitesse de Mach 6,7 (7 274 km/h) en Californie (USA), dans le prototype X-15A-2 - **l'avion-fusée le plus rapide.**

OCT. 4 Le Field Museum de Chicago (Illinois, USA) acquiert un squelette de T. rex nommé "Sue" 8,3 millions $ lors d'une vente aux enchères en 1997. Il s'agit **des ossements de dinosaure les plus chers.**

JEUX VIDÉO

Cette année, le *Guinness World Records Gamer's Edition* – déjà disponible – est consacré aux personnages de jeux vidéo les plus populaires de tous les temps. Nous vous proposons ici un avant-goût des stats et infos – et design – que vous retrouverez dans l'ouvrage dédié aux records de jeux le plus vendu au monde.

Le jeu vidéo Sonic le mieux noté
Au 29 mars 2019, *Sonic Mania* (Sega, 2017) affichait un score moyen de 87,02 % sur GameRankings. Il a surpassé les 86,51 % de *Sonic Adventure* (Sega, 1999), longtemps détenteur du titre. Commercialisé pour marquer le 25e anniversaire du véloce hérisson, le jeu au look vintage *Sonic Mania* a fait un retour aux sources 2D de la série.

La collection de jeux vidéo remastérisés la plus rentable
Uncharted : The Nathan Drake Collection (Sony, 2015) est la réédition sur PS4 des 3 premiers jeux de la série. Ils ont rencontré un immense succès auprès des gamers du monde entier : au 21 mars 2019, 5,7 millions d'exemplaires avaient été vendus selon le site Internet de suivi des ventes VGChartz. Pour cette exclusivité PlayStation, les aventures sur PS3 de Drake ont migré sur PS4, avec un graphisme amélioré, de nouveaux trophées et un mode photo inédit.

Le jeu vidéo d'action-aventure le plus apprécié par la critique
The Legend of Zelda: Ocarina of Time (Nintendo, 1998) totalisait 97,54 % sur GameRankings au 5 février 2019.
L'achèvement le plus rapide de *The Legend of Zelda: Ocarina of Time* est de 17 min et 4 s, exploit réalisé par Torje Amundsen (NOR) le 5 septembre 2018. La partie a été disputée par plus de 5 000 fans dans un speedrun. Même si le jeu a plus de 20 ans, les pilotes chevronnés rivalisent pour trouver des parcours toujours plus rapides.

VOUS CONNAISSEZ LE JEU ? NOMMEZ LE PERSONNAGE !
GameRankings a listé les jeux suivants comme les mieux évalués de leurs franchises respectives au 5 février 2019. Pouvez-vous nommer les principaux protagonistes ? Trouvez les réponses p. 249.

10. Tekken 3 — Antihéros des arts martiaux, son gène diabolique le rend aussi puissant qu'un démon.

Cet agent spécial est en charge des menaces biologiques et des zombies. **9. Resident Evil 4**

8. ------ Arkham City — Une tragédie dans l'enfance le transforme en Chevalier noir.

Une chasseuse de primes ; ses ennemis jurés sont les Pirates de l'Espace. **7. Metroid Prime**

6. Uncharted 2 — Inspiré d'Indiana Jones, ce voyou a des défauts très attachants.

La série de jeux vidéo de tir de science-fiction la plus lucrative
Sans compter les séries spin-off *Halo Wars*, la franchise *Halo* (Microsoft) avait généré des ventes mondiales de 65,08 millions d'exemplaires au 21 mars 2019, selon VGChartz. Le jeu vidéo Halo le plus rentable est *Halo 3* (2007), qui totalisait 12,13 millions d'exemplaires vendus à la même date. Le jeu est également le seul titre de la franchise vendu à plus de 10 millions d'exemplaires.

Le jeu vidéo le plus acclamé par la critique (à date)
Le jeu vidéo préféré des critiques sorti en 2018 (la dernière année complète pour laquelle les évaluations sont disponibles) est *Red Dead Redemption 2* (Rockstar). D'après GameRankings, ce western est devenu instantanément culte, avec un score global de 96,45 % pour 49 évaluations. Son plus proche rival est *God of War* (Sony), avec un score de 94,10 % pour 63 critiques.

OCT. 5 David Kunst (USA) termine le 1er tour du monde à pied (homologué) en 1974. Il avait débuté son expédition plus de 4 ans auparavant, parcourant au total 23 250 km à pied.

OCT. 6 Kurt Hess (CHE) effectue la plus longue ascension verticale en montant des escaliers en 24 h (18 585 m), en 2007. Il gravit et descend 413 fois la tour d'Esterli (CHE).

LE PERSONNAGE DE JEU VIDÉO LE PLUS PRÉSENT

Mario avait participé à 217 titres de jeux vidéo au 5 février 2019, sans compter les remakes et ressorties. Au moins 2 autres opus, *Dr Mario World* et *Mario Kart Tour* (tous 2 Nintendo), étaient prévus en 2019. Le personnage a débuté dans *Donkey Kong* (1981), endossant le rôle d'un menuisier nommé "Jumpman".

Le jeu Mario le plus rentable est le titre sorti sur NES *Super Mario Bros.* (Nintendo, 1985), qui s'était écoulé à 40,24 millions d'exemplaires au 5 février 2019, selon VGChartz. C'est aussi **le jeu de plateforme le plus lucratif**.

INFO : ○ Charles Martinet (USA) a prêté sa voix à Mario dans 100 jeux de 1995 à 2018 – le plus de voix off dans un jeu vidéo pour un même personnage.

Cette brute fait partie d'un gang mais se refait ensuite une conscience.

5. Red Dead Redemption 2

4. SoulCalibur

Connu en tant que "Pirate de l'effroi" et "Pirate immortel", son vrai nom est... ?

Cet immigrant, vétéran de guerre, ne croit plus au rêve américain.

3. Grand Theft Auto IV

2. The Legend of Zelda: Ocarina of Time

Son ennemi est Ganondorf et sa principale alliée, la Princesse Zelda.

Mamma mia ! Mais c'est le plombier préféré du Royaume Champignon !

1. ----- ----- Galaxy

L'héroïne de jeu vidéo la plus rentable

Grâce à des ventes cumulées de 44,5 millions au 21 mars 2019, *Tomb Raider* (Square Enix), avec Lara Croft en vedette, a dépassé toutes les franchises portées par un personnage féminin, selon VGChartz. L'héroïne a inspiré romans, BD et films – y compris une nouvelle adaptation cinématographique avec Alicia Vikander en 2018. Le 1er jeu a été commercialisé par Eidos Interactive le 25 octobre 1996.

Le jeu vidéo le plus "platiné" sur PlayStation

Un trophée platine couronne le plus grand exploit possible dans un jeu vidéo sur PlayStation. Il ne s'obtient qu'après avoir remporté tous les autres trophées du jeu. Au 13 février 2018, les joueurs d'*Assassin's Creed II* (Ubisoft, 2009) sur PS3 totalisaient 156 569 trophées platine, d'après le suivi de plusieurs millions de comptes gamers par PSNProfiles.

OCT. 7 En 1990, les alpinistes Andrej et Marija Štremfelj (SVN) deviennent **le 1er couple marié à conquérir l'Everest**, rejoignant le sommet par le col sud.

OCT. 8 En 2001, David Meenan (USA) parcourt **la plus longue distance en faisant des claquettes**, soit 51,49 km en 7 h et 35 min, au Count Basie Track and Field (New Jersey, USA).

FORTNITE

L'ARME LA PLUS NUISIBLE DANS *FORTNITE* (DPS)

Envie de laisser un souvenir impérissable dans *Fortnite Battle Royale* (Epic, 2017) ? Le fusil à pompe à double canon légendaire (1), le minigun légendaire (2) et le fusil mitraillette rare (3) produisent tous un total inégalé de 228 dégâts par seconde (DPS).

L'arme la plus dévastatrice de *Fortnite* (tir unique) est le fusil de précision lourd légendaire (4). Avec 157 dégâts par tir, cette arme ultra rare offre le plus fort impact par balle. Toutefois, en raison d'une lenteur à la recharge, mieux vaut viser juste dès la 1re fois !

Le 1er jeu vidéo de Battle Royale avec 250 millions de joueurs enregistrés

Si quelqu'un mentionne *Fortnite*, il parle en fait de *Battle Royale*. Le 29 mars 2019, Epic Games (USA) a annoncé officiellement que le jeu comptait 250 millions de joueurs enregistrés – plus que 3,25 fois la population du Royaume-Uni. Epic Games reste discret sur les chiffres *Fortnite* et n'a révélé ses 200 millions de joueurs enregistrés que le 27 novembre 2018 – ce qui correspondait à un bond de 60 % par rapport aux 125 millions annoncés en juin 2018.

Le plus de compétiteurs pour un jeu vidéo

En mars 2019, *Fortnite* enregistrait 10,8 millions de joueurs simultanés. Son succès tient à différents facteurs, notamment sa disponibilité sur consoles, PC et appareils mobiles, ainsi que sa gratuité (voir p. 188).

Le 1er joueur *Fortnite* à atteindre 100 000 éliminations

Le *gamer* américain "HighDistortion", alias Jimmy Moreno, a franchi cette importante étape le 21 janvier 2019. Il comptait aussi **le plus d'éliminations cumulées dans** *Fortnite* : 101 017, au 28 janvier 2019.

La vidéo à thématique *Fortnite* la plus vue sur YouTube

"The Fortnite Rap Battle | #NerdOut ft Ninja, CDNThe3rd, Dakotaz, H2O Delirious & More" de "NerdOut !" affichait 96 097 735 vues au 29 avril 2019. Uploadée sur YouTube le 10 mars 2018, la vidéo consiste en un rap humoristique effectué sur des images de *Fortnite*.

Le 1er skin *Fortnite* avec exclusivité de console

Avoir une PlayStation 4 et être membre PlayStation Plus sont les seuls moyens d'acquérir le skin Blue Team Leader. Il a été commercialisé pour la console de Sony le 14 février 2018, en même temps que le planeur Blue Streak. Microsoft a sorti son skin Eon pour les propriétaires de Xbox One S, et Nintendo a suivi avec son costume Double Helix.

Le 1er personnage Marvel dans *Fortnite*

Le 8 mai 2018, afin de fêter la sortie cinématographique de *Avengers : Infinity War* (USA) des studios Marvel, Thanos le titan fou est venu faire un tour dans *Fortnite*. Le croisement éphémère des 2 univers a été appelé mode du "Gant de l'Infini". Les joueurs pouvaient se transformer en Thanos s'ils trouvaient le Gant de l'Infini, parachuté à un endroit aléatoire au début de la partie. Si Thanos était éliminé, alors le gant tombait à terre et pouvait être ramassé librement par n'importe quel autre personnage. Ce mode a disparu le 15 mai 2018.

Le plus de chaînes Twitch pour un jeu vidéo

Au 29 avril 2019, *Fortnite* avait été streamé par 66 600 chaînes Twitch. Le dauphin était *Apex Legends* (Respawn, 2019), fort de 18 919 chaînes.

La chaîne Twitch la plus suivie

Le streamer et joueur de *Fortnite* "Ninja", alias Richard Tyler Blevins (USA), comptait 14 064 046 followers sur Twitch au 29 avril 2018, selon Social Blade. Son auditoire a bondi de 2 millions en quelques semaines après son stream people, le 14 mars 2018, avec l'icône de football américain "JuJu" Smith-Schuster et les musiciens Drake et Travis Scott, et il ne cesse de croître depuis.

L'ARME *FORTNITE* EN BRIQUES LEGO® LA PLUS GRANDE

Assemblée par le concepteur LEGO et YouTuber "ZaziNombies LEGO Creations", alias Kyle L. Neville (CAN), cette réplique à l'échelle du minigun éventreur de *Fortnite* faisait 140 cm de long, comprenait plus de 5 000 briques LEGO et pesait 8 kg. Sa construction a nécessité 60 h de travail sur 1 semaine. Elle a été présentée sur YouTube le 22 février 2018.

LE PLUS DE PARTICIPANTS DANS UNE EMOTE DE JEU VIDÉO

Les "emotes" sont des mouvements ou des danses qu'un personnage peut effectuer pendant une partie. Le 28 octobre 2018, 383 fans de *Fortnite* ont enfilé des sweats à capuche Cuddle Team Leader pour une emote de masse au cours de la Paris Games Week (FRA). La horde en capuche s'est trémoussée entre autres au son de *Boogie Down*, *Orange Justice* et *Groove Jam*, lors d'un événement organisé par Epic Games.

La vidéo YouTube présentant le minigun record totalisait 812 255 vues au 1er avril 2019.

OCT. 9 Shiko Kurihara (JPN) décroche le record du **plus de baisers reçus en 1 min** (131), en 2014, au stade Differ Ariake de Tokyo (JPN).

OCT. 10 Une version de la *Cosmographie* de Ptolémée datant de 1477 devient **l'atlas le plus cher du monde** lors de sa vente à 2 136 000 £ chez Sotheby's, à Londres (GBR), en 2006.

LE PLUS DE VICTOIRES DANS *FORTNITE*

Ce jeu en ligne gratuit en mode "il n'en restera qu'un" bat tous ses concurrents depuis sa sortie le 26 septembre 2017. Dans ce jeu, 100 joueurs sautent en parachute sur une île pour combattre en solo, en duo ou en équipe.

Au 30 octobre 2018, **le record de victoires** (en solo ou en équipe) était de 5 567 (en 11 746 parties) et appartenait à "ViniciusΔmazing ツ" (BRA). "COOLER eXzacT" (HRV) détenait **la plus longue série de victoires solo** (36 succès consécutifs), tandis que "FeroX M33P_" détenait **la plus longue série de victoires ininterrompue au sein d'une équipe** (66) à la même date. **Le record de victoires en solo** était de 4 351, pour "SoaR PierXBL" (USA), au 13 décembre 2018.

Fin 2018, un nouveau patch pour la saison 6 de *Fortnite* a introduit les "Cube Monsters" (zombies). Pour les gérer, les joueurs ont reçu une nouvelle arme : l'arbalète du chasseur de démons.

LE PLUS DE VICTOIRES ROYALES DANS *FORTNITE* AVEC UNE MANETTE DE JEU QUADSTICK

Tétraplégique à la suite d'une grave chute, "RockyNoHands", alias Rocky Stoutenburgh (USA), s'est entraîné à jouer à des jeux vidéo en utilisant un joystick à commande buccale. Au 26 mars 2019, il avait à son actif 509 victoires royales sur *Fortnite*. Il a également réalisé **le plus d'éliminations dans une seule *Fortnite Battle Royale* avec un QuadStick** (11), le 3 octobre 2018.

LE SKIN LE PLUS RARE DE *FORTNITE*

Si vous apercevez un Recon Expert, faites une capture d'écran. Ce skin de la saison 1 n'a été disponible que pendant 2 semaines, du 27 octobre au 12 novembre 2017. Actuellement, il faut débourser 1 200 V-Bucks pour ce costume assez quelconque. Au 12 novembre 2018, dans la boutique *Fortnite*, il était indisponible à la vente depuis 1 an.

LE SKIN *FORTNITE* LE PLUS POPULAIRE

Les fans de *Fortnite* ont imaginé des centaines de skins, mais aucun n'est aussi haut (perché ?) que le puissant Chicken Trooper (Tender Defender). Créé par Connor, le fils de l'utilisateur Reddit "tfoust10", il manie un fouet en guise de hache, a un sac à dos en forme d'œuf fêlé et se lance dans les combats en chevauchant un autre poulet. Le concept a été posté sur Reddit le 12 septembre 2018 et avait obtenu plus de 44 700 votes positifs au 31 octobre 2018.

OCT. 11 Le 1er plateau-repas en vol est servi en 1919 sur la desserte Londres-Paris assurée par Handley Page Transport (GBR). Il est constitué de sandwichs et de fruits emballés.

OCT. 12 En 2016, **le marathon de DJ radio le plus long** se termine après 205 h, 2 min et 54 s d'antenne sur Radio B.B.S.I., à Alexandrie (ITA). Stefano Venneri (ITA) avait débuté son programme de presque 9 jours le 4 octobre.

TV : LES PLUS DEMANDÉS...

PARROT
ANALYTICS

Afin d'évaluer et comparer la demande multiplateforme des séries télé, GWR s'est associé aux experts de Parrot Analytics. Cette entreprise a inventé un système de "mesure de la demande des contenus télévisés" capable de quantifier le comportement des téléspectateurs envers les séries. Pour cela, il analyse les "Expressions de Demandes" dans le monde entier – depuis la consommation de vidéo (streaming/téléchargements) jusqu'aux réseaux sociaux (hashtags, likes, partages) et requêtes ou commentaires (lecture ou écriture de contenus sur des séries, etc.). Plus l'effort (c'est-à-dire le temps passé) de l'usager est important, plus l'impact l'est. L'intérêt pour un programme est évalué en termes d'"Expressions de Demandes per capita" (EDx/c) – l'implication quotidienne et moyenne globale dans une série pour 100 personnes dans un cadre temporel défini. Tous les records "les plus demandés" présentés ici s'inscrivent dans la période de 12 mois s'achevant le 14 janvier 2019.

LA SÉRIE TV ISSUE D'UNE ADAPTATION LITTÉRAIRE LA PLUS DEMANDÉE : 6,271 EDx/c

Inspiré par les romans fantastiques de George R. R. Martin *Le Trône de fer*, *Game of Thrones* (HBO, USA) a vu le jour en 2011. Durant 8 saisons (la dernière a été diffusée à partir du 14 avril 2019), la série explore les luttes de pouvoir dynastiques au royaume des Sept Couronnes de Westeros et sur le continent d'Essos. Sur la photo se trouve l'acteur Kit Harington, qui joue Jon Snow, meneur du combat contre le Roi de la Nuit et son armée de morts-vivants, les Marcheurs Blancs.

Action et aventure : 5,235 EDx/c
Le drame médiéval *Vikings* (History, CAN ; depuis 2013) raconte les aventures de guerriers scandinaves, notamment leurs raids dans les contrées alentour.

Animation : 2,368 EDx/c
Produit d'une franchise japonaise, *Dragon Ball Super* (Fuji TV, JPN ; 2015-2018) mettait en scène les aventures du guerrier Goku et de ses amis.

Programme pour enfant : 2,561 EDx/c
Fort de son adorable vedette éponyme en forme d'éponge jaune, *Bob l'éponge* (Nickelodeon, USA ; depuis 1999) suscite toujours l'adulation de ses fans.

Documentaire : 1,246 EDx/c
Narrée par David Attenborough, la série *Planète Terre* (BBC, GBR ; 2006) a été le documentaire nature le plus onéreux de la BBC. Plus d'informations sur ce présentateur télé en page 211.

Horreur : 3,016 EDx/c
Chaque saison d'*American Horror Story* (FX, USA ; depuis 2011) constitue une minisérie indépendante. Le top-model Naomi Campbell, la pop-star Lady Gaga et Jyoti Amge, **la plus petite femme du monde** (voir p. 69), ont figuré au générique de la série d'épouvante.

LA SÉRIE DE TÉLÉRÉALITÉ LA PLUS DEMANDÉE : 2,319 EDx/c
The Voice – concours de talents musical avec une évaluation "à l'aveugle" – a vu le jour aux Pays-Bas en 2010 sous le titre *The Voice of Holland*. Plusieurs éditions internationales ont rapidement suivi, ainsi que d'autres variantes comme *The Voice Kids*, *The Voice Teens* et *The Voice Senior*. Le jury actuel américain comprend (ici de gauche à droite) Adam Levine, John Legend, Kelly Clarkson et Blake Shelton.

Drame médical : 3,850 EDx/c
Dans *Grey's Anatomy* (ABC, USA ; depuis 2005), Meredith Grey et son équipe sauvent des vies, tout en découvrant que les relations humaines ne sont jamais manichéennes.

Remake d'une série existante : 3,241 EDx/c
Shameless (Showtime, USA ; depuis 2011) délocalise la comédie dramatique britannique d'une cité de Manchester vers le South Side de Chicago.

Drame romantique : 1,815 EDx/c
Dans *Outlander* (Starz, USA ; depuis 2014), l'infirmière Claire Randall est téléportée de 1945 à 1743, où elle tombe amoureuse d'un guerrier des Highlands.

Drame de science-fiction : 3,680 EDx/c
Westworld (HBO, USA ; depuis 2016) s'inspire du film éponyme de 1973. Ce western futuriste est **la série télé basée sur une adaptation cinématographique la plus demandée**.

Soap opera : 1,311 EDx/c
Dynasty (The CW, USA ; depuis 2017) propose aux nouvelles générations une relecture du soap opera des années 1980.

Série de super-héros : 4,605 EDx/c
Frappé par un éclair, Barry Allen acquiert une vélocité surhumaine dans *Flash* (The CW, USA ; depuis 2014).

Débuts d'une série télé : 2,956 EDx/c
Titans (DC Universe, USA ; depuis 2018) suit des jeunes super-héros menés par Dick Grayson (le 1er Robin de Batman) dans leur combat contre le mal.

Talk-show : 1,640 EDx/c
Le talk-show nocturne *Daily Show with Trevor Noah* (Comedy Central, USA ; depuis 2015) propose des sketches et des entretiens avec des célébrités.

LA SÉRIE TV DRAMATIQUE POUR ADO LA PLUS DEMANDÉE : 3,817 EDx/c
Inspirée des personnages apparus dans *Archie Comics*, la série de Netflix *Riverdale* (The CW, USA) met en scène K. J. Apa (au centre) dans le rôle d'Archie Andrews. La série propose une approche inattendue de la BD originale, explorant le côté surréaliste et sombre d'une ville de province, ce qui lui a valu d'être comparée à *Twin Peaks*, série des années 1990 de David Lynch.

LA SÉRIE TV DRAMATIQUE JURIDIQUE LA PLUS DEMANDÉE : 2,927 EDx/c
Créée par Aaron Korsh en 2011, *Suits* est la série la plus pérenne d'USA Network. Le personnage principal, Mike Ross (Patrick J. Adams, à l'extrême droite), a abandonné les cours et rejoint un cabinet d'avocats new-yorkais malgré son manque d'expérience. Sa petite amie Rachel (2e depuis la droite) était jouée par Meghan Markle avant qu'elle ne s'installe au Royaume-Uni en 2017 après ses fiançailles avec le prince Harry.

OCT. 13 Aux UFC 153 de 2012, Anderson Silva (BRA) bat Stephan Bonnar au 1er round de leur match des poids mi-lourds. C'est sa 16e victoire d'affilée - **le plus de succès UFC consécutifs**.

OCT. 14 En 2013, Pavel Gerasimov (RUS) possède **la plus grande collection homologuée d'objets sur le thème de l'écureuil**. 1 103 articles ont été comptés, dont une statuette d'écureuil en or massif.

LA SÉRIE TV LA PLUS DEMANDÉE : 6,999 EDx/c

The Walking Dead (AMC, USA) suit les aventures du shérif-adjoint Rick Grimes (joué par Andrew Lincoln, sur la photo), qui se réveille d'un coma et découvre un monde dévasté, envahi par les zombies. Après avoir rejoint un groupe de survivants, il affronte des dangers provenant non seulement des morts-vivants (appelés aussi "rôdeurs"), mais aussi d'autres groupes d'humains qui ont adopté des codes moraux très particuliers. La diffusion de la 10e saison de la série est prévue en octobre 2019. Il s'agit aussi de **la série télé issue de l'adaptation d'une bande dessinée la plus demandée**.

The Walking Dead est issue de la série de BD éponyme de Robert Kirkman et Tony Moore. Elle a remporté 2 trophées Eisner depuis ses débuts en 2003.

LA SÉRIE COMIQUE LA PLUS DEMANDÉE : 4,793 EDx/c

The Big Bang Theory (CBS, USA) met en scène 2 physiciens dont le génie est entravé par leur maladresse sociale. D'après Forbes, la vedette Jim Parsons (USA, assis au centre), dont les revenus ont été estimés à 26,5 millions $ entre les 1er juin 2017 et 1er juin 2018, est **l'acteur télé le mieux payé** pour la 4e année consécutive. La série est aussi **la sitcom la plus demandée**.

LA SÉRIE DIGITALE ORIGINALE LA PLUS DEMANDÉE : 3,484 EDx/c

Une "série digitale originale" est une série produite ou mise à disposition pour la 1re fois sur une plate-forme de streaming. Située dans les années 1980, la célèbre série de science-fiction et d'épouvante *Stranger Things* (Netflix, USA) a débuté en 2016. Ci-dessous, en partant de la gauche, nous retrouvons Caleb McLaughlin, Gaten Matarazzo (tous 2 USA), Finn Wolfhard (CAN) et Sadie Sink (USA).

LA SÉRIE TV ANIMÉE LA PLUS DEMANDÉE : 2,794 EDx/c

La création originale de Justin Roiland et Dan Harmon, *Rick et Morty* (USA), a fait ses débuts en décembre 2013 sur Adult Swim, le créneau nocturne de Cartoon Network. La série tourne autour de la famille Smith – Jerry, Beth et leurs enfants, Summer et Morty. Le père de Beth, Rick, un scientifique excentrique, vit avec eux et persuade souvent son petit-fils Morty de l'accompagner dans des voyages délirants à travers l'Univers.

OCT. 15 L'expédition britannique transafricaine en aéroglisseur débute sous la direction de David Smithers (GBR) en 1969. Elle parcourt 8 000 km et traverse 8 pays d'Afrique de l'Ouest – **le plus long voyage en aéroglisseur**.

OCT. 16 En 2013, 2 négociants en vin italiens suspectés d'avoir contrefait au moins 400 bouteilles de romanée-conti sont appréhendés. Estimée à 1,7 million $, il s'agit de **l'escroquerie vinicole la plus lucrative**.

BANDES DESSINÉES

La 1re BD

L'*Histoire de M. Vieux-Bois* du dessinateur suisse Rodolphe Töpffer, créée en 1827 et publiée une décennie plus tard, est la 1er bande dessinée. L'histoire comportait environ 30 planches. Chaque page était divisée en 6 vignettes, avec une légende sous chaque dessin.

La 1re BD avec un personnage principal féminin

Le personnage de Sheena, reine de la jungle, a fait son apparition dans le 1er numéro de *Wags* (GBR, 1937) ; ses débuts américains ont eu lieu dans *Jumbo Comics* en septembre 1938. La bande dessinée *Sheena, reine de la jungle* est arrivée au printemps 1942. *Wonder Woman* a également vu le jour en 1942, mais pas avant l'été.

L'édition la plus rentable pour une BD

X-Men #1 (Marvel Comics, 1991) s'est écoulée à 8,1 millions d'exemplaires. Elle a été créée par Chris Claremont (GBR) et Jim Lee (USA). Ce dernier avait dessiné 4 autres versions de la couverture (1A, 1B, 1C et 1D), portant la date d'octobre 1991. Assemblées, elles formaient une plus grande image, utilisée comme pochette pour 1E, publiée un mois plus tard.

Le plus de couvertures pour une BD de superhéros

The Amazing Spider-Man #666 de Marvel – prologue de l'histoire de Dan Slott "Spider-Island" – était vendu avec 145 couvertures différentes. La plupart d'entre elles étaient personnalisées en fonction des détaillants.

Le plus d'éditions pour une BD

La bande dessinée *Pepín* (MEX) a été publiée pour la 1re fois le 4 mars 1936 sous forme d'anthologie hebdomadaire. La bande dessinée est devenue quotidienne, publiée jusqu'au 23 octobre 1956, avec 7 561 numéros.

Le plus de numéros consécutifs pour une BD illustrée et écrite

Dave Sim (CAN) a créé 300 numéros de sa bande dessinée *Cerebus* – qui retrace les aventures d'un oryctérope – entre décembre 1977 et mars 2004.

Le plus de bandes dessinées publiées par un auteur est de 770 titres (en 500 volumes) et le trophée revient à Shotaro Ishinomori (JPN, 1938-1998).

Le plus gros éditeur de manga

Shueisha (JPN), fondé à Tokyo en 1925, est le plus important éditeur de manga, avec un revenu de 123 milliards ¥ (1,1 milliards $) pour l'année 2016-2017. Son titre phare est *Shōnen Jump*, publié pour la 1re fois en 1968.

LA BD HEBDOMADAIRE LA PLUS PÉRENNE

La bande dessinée *The Beano* (GBR), aujourd'hui intitulée *Beano*) a été lancée le 30 juillet 1938 (ci-dessus à gauche) par D.C. Thomson et, depuis, a paru chaque semaine, excepté pendant la Seconde Guerre mondiale en raison d'une pénurie de papier. Il s'agit de la bande dessinée la plus ancienne avec un nom et un système de numérotation inchangés. Le 3 950e exemplaire, daté du 1er septembre 2018, est représenté ci-dessus à droite.

La BD la plus précieuse

Au 21 janvier 2019, *Action Comics #1* (juin 1938) – produit par DC Comics (USA) – était évaluée à 4 620 000 $, selon le guide de cotation des bandes dessinées Nostomania. Elle marque les débuts de Superman, **le 1er superhéros doté de pouvoirs**.

Superman a également été la vedette de la couverture du 1 000e numéro d'*Action Comics* en avril 2018. L'édition "deluxe" a marqué le 80e anniversaire de **la série de bandes dessinées de superhéros la plus pérenne**.

Le plus de planches publiées pour la même série de manga yonkoma

Le terme "yonkoma" décrit des mangas verticaux de 4 vignettes. Au 23 janvier 2019, Shoji Izumi (JPN) avait créé 15 770 de ces planches pour la série *Jan Ken Pon* débutée le 30 septembre 1969. Le manga apparaît quotidiennement dans *Asahi Shogakusei Shimbun*, un journal destiné aux enfants des classes élémentaires.

L'IMAGE GRAPHIQUE D'UN SEUL TENANT LA PLUS LONGUE DANS UNE BD NUMÉRIQUE

Le 19 avril 2018, Papyless (JPN) a dévoilé une bande dessinée d'un seul volet, *Hitokoma no Kuni no Alice* (*Les aventures d'Alice à Onederland*), d'une largeur de 320 pixels dp et d'une longueur de 163 631 dp. La technologie "dp" préserve les dimensions d'une image quel que soit l'appareil utilisé. Pour voir le panneau entier, les lecteurs doivent faire défiler l'équivalent de 25,56 m. La BD a été créée afin de promouvoir TateComi, un service permettant de lire des mangas numériques par simples glissements de doigt sur l'écran.

LE PLUS GRAND LIVRE DE BD PUBLIÉ

Turma da Mônica (*Monica's Gang*), conçu par Mauricio de Sousa Produções et publié par Panini Brasil (tous 2 BRA), fait 69,9 cm de large sur 99,8 cm de haut une fois refermé, soit une superficie de 6 976 cm². La mesure a été effectuée à São Paulo (BRA), le 5 août 2018. 120 exemplaires de cette édition de 18 pages ont été tirés.

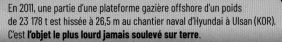

LE PLUS DE TROPHÉES EISNER POUR...*

Meilleure anthologie	5	*Dark Horse Presents*, de Dark Horse Comics (USA ; ci-dessus à gauche)
Meilleur artiste/ dessinateur	4	P. Craig Russell et Steve Rude (tous 2 USA)
Meilleur coloriste/colorisation	9	Dave Stewart (USA)
Meilleur artiste de couverture	6	James Jean (USA)
Meilleure nouvelle série	4	*Saga*, de Brian K. Vaughan (USA ; ci-dessus à droite)
Meilleur auteur	9	Alan Moore (GBR)
Une catégorie	17	Todd Klein (USA), meilleur lettrage

*Au 8 avril 2019

OCT. 17 En 2011, une partie d'une plateforme gazière offshore d'un poids de 23 178 t est hissée à 26,5 m au chantier naval d'Hyundai à Ulsan (KOR). C'est **l'objet le plus lourd jamais soulevé sur terre**.

OCT. 18 En 1998, Ken Thompson (GBR) découvre **la plus grande toile d'araignée (en extérieur)**. Réalisée par des milliers d'araignées porte-bonheur, elle recouvre un terrain de sport de 4,54 ha à Kineton (West Midlands, GBR).

Ce panneau sur mesure a été créé pour le GWR par Nigel Parkinson, dessinateur de Denis la Malice dans Beano depuis 1998.

NIGEL PARKINSON.

LE PLUS GRAND CONCOURS "TERMINEZ LA BD"

723 compétiteurs ont participé à un concours pour achever une bande dessinée inspirée de *Beano* au Festival 3D du musée V&A de Dundee (GBR), les 14–15 septembre 2018. Trois mois plus tard, l'œuvre soumise par Louise Anderson (encadré) a été primée. L'événement multimédia a été organisé pour marquer l'ouverture de la nouvelle antenne du musée londonien Victoria & Albert, dont l'original est situé à Londres (GBR). Les concepteurs de *Beano* ont commémoré leur exploit inégalé avec cette illustration exclusive.

UN HOMMAGE AFFECTUEUX À STAN "THE MAN" LEE

La défunte icône de Marvel Comics, Stan Lee (USA, 1922–2018), détenait plusieurs titres GWR. Le 9 mai 2019, ses exploits incluaient **le plus d'adaptations cinématographiques inspirées de l'œuvre d'un créateur de BD (36)**, **l'acteur de petits rôles cinématographiques le plus rentable (30 milliards $)** et **le producteur exécutif le plus rentable (30,3 milliards $)**. Les autels installés sur l'étoile de Stan du Walk of Fame hollywoodien témoignent de la ferveur des fans pour ce personnage hors du commun.

LA BD LA PLUS LONGUE CONÇUE PAR UNE SEULE PERSONNE

Les 1er-3 novembre 2018, Claudio Sciarrone (ITA) a produit une bande dessinée longue de 297,5 m pour le compte de Walt Disney Company Italia à Lucques (ITA). Claudio est un artiste Disney et a créé l'œuvre (intitulée *Réveille-toi Mickey !*) au festival BD & Jeux de Lucques pour fêter le 90e anniversaire du personnage.

LA PLUS GRANDE COLLECTION D'OBJETS *DRAGON BALL*

Michael Nilsen (USA) avait rassemblé 6 148 articles en lien avec la série de manga/animation *Dragon Ball* au 1er octobre 2012, date du décompte à Duluth (Minnesota, USA). La collection, initiée en 1996, comprend jouets, posters, DVD, figurines, tapis de souris, celluloïds originaux et même un distributeur de mouchoirs à l'effigie du personnage Kamé Sennin.

OCT. 19 Le **1er tournoi de jeu vidéo** – les jeux Olympiques intergalactiques *Spacewar* – se déroule en 1972 dans le laboratoire d'intelligence artificielle de l'université de Stanford en Californie (USA).

OCT. 20 Peter Wehrmann (DEU) entame **le plus long marathon humain de beat box** en 2012 au Best Western Premier Hotel MOA de Berlin (DEU). Il l'achève 25 h et 30 min plus tard.

RÉSEAUX SOCIAUX

LE PLUS DE FOLLOWERS SUR INSTAGRAM POUR UN NATURALISTE TÉLÉ

Bindi Irwin (AUS ; @bindisueirwin) compte 2 334 912 followers. Elle vient d'une longue lignée de naturalistes dont son père, Steve Irwin (1962-2006), sa mère Terri et son frère Robert, photographe de la vie sauvage. La famille Irwin possède l'Australia Zoo dans le Queensland.

Tous les chiffres ont été relevés au 29 avril 2019, sauf mention contraire

LE PLUS DE FOLLOWERS SUR INSTAGRAM

Cristiano Ronaldo (@cristiano) totalise 163 658 939 followers sur le site de partage d'images. Seul Instagram lui-même, fort de ses 296 269 356 followers, compte plus de fans que la vedette de football.
Le plus de followers sur Instagram (femmes) est de 152 882 321, record détenu par la chanteuse Ariana Grande (USA, @arianagrande). On retrouve à la 2e place la chanteuse et actrice Selena Gomez (USA), précédente détentrice du record.

Ariana Grande affiche aussi **le plus d'abonnés pour une musicienne sur YouTube** (35 242 046).

Le plus grand réseau social en ligne

Facebook totalise 2,37 milliards d'utilisateurs actifs par mois (personnes s'étant connectées au site au cours des 30 derniers jours). La plate-forme de réseau social a atteint 2 milliards d'utilisateurs mensuels le 30 juin 2017.

La personne la plus likée sur Facebook est le footballeur de la Juventus Cristiano Ronaldo (PRT), avec 122 308 950 likes. **La femme la plus likée** est la chanteuse Shakira (COL, née Shakira Mebarak Ripoll), avec 101 234 534 likes. Le 18 juillet 2014, Shakira est devenue **la 1re personne à totaliser 100 millions de likes sur Facebook**.

Le plus grand site de réseau social professionnel en ligne

LinkedIn (USA) attire 303 millions d'utilisateurs actifs par mois.

L'utilisateur LinkedIn le plus suivi est Sir Richard Branson (GBR), fondateur de Virgin, avec 15 732 651 followers.

Le plus de followers sur Twitter

La chanteuse pop Katy Perry (USA, née Katheryn Hudson) est à la tête de 107 279 315 followers sur Twitter. Quant à Barack Obama (@barackobama), il compte **le plus de followers sur Twitter (hommes)**, soit 105 946 443.

Le plus de followers pour un…

Lieu : le Museum of Modern Art (USA, @MuseumModernArt) de New York (USA) totalise 5 404 072 followers.
Compte sportif : l'équipe de football du Real Madrid (ESP, @realmadrid) affiche 31 892 268 fans sur Twitter.

La plus rapide à atteindre 1 million de followers sur Twitter

À peine 4 h et 3 min ont suffi à Caitlyn Jenner (USA) pour atteindre la barre du million de fans sur Twitter, le 1er juin 2015.

Le hashtag le plus utilisé sur Twitter en 24 h

Les 16-17 mars 2019, le hashtag #TwitterBestFandom a généré 60 055 339 tweets. Il a permis au public de voter pour les 14es Annual Soompi Awards, qui honorent les meilleurs artistes de la télévision et la musique coréennes.

Le plus de votes négatifs pour un commentaire sur Reddit

Un post mis en ligne par l'éditeur de jeux vidéo Electronic Arts, en réponse aux joueurs qui se plaignaient de devoir débloquer des personnages comme Dark Vador et Luke Skywalker dans *Star Wars Battlefront II* (2017) avec des "coffres à butin aléatoires", totalise 683 000 votes négatifs.

Le plus de followers sur Weibo

L'animatrice télé, chanteuse et actrice Xie Na (CHN) compte 123 810 773 fans sur le site de microblogging chinois. Le 7 avril 2018, elle est devenue **la 1re personne avec 100 millions de followers sur Weibo**.

L'homme le plus suivi sur Weibo est He Jiong (CHN), présentateur télé et célébrité médiatique, avec 111 759 484.

Le plus d'abonnés pour une chaîne animalière sur YouTube

Présenté par l'expert de la vie sauvage Coyote Peterson (USA, né Nathaniel Peterson), "Brave Wilderness" a vu le jour le 8 septembre 2014 et compte 14 264 941 abonnés. C'est aussi **la chaîne**

[certificat] The most liked image on Instagram is an image of an egg and was achieved by the Instagram account 'world_record_egg', posted by the Egg Gang with 52 399 013 likes as of 6 February 2019

L'IMAGE LA PLUS LIKÉE SUR INSTAGRAM

Une simple image d'œuf a recueilli 53 427 655 likes. Elle a été postée le 4 janvier 2019 par le Egg Gang sur le compte @world_record_egg. On a découvert que le Egg Gang utilisait son exploit Instagram comme plate-forme de soutien aux personnes souffrant de stress et d'anxiété déclenchés par la pression des réseaux sociaux.

animalière la plus regardée sur YouTube, avec 2,6 milliards de vues. Peterson interagit avec des animaux dangereux et accepte de se faire piquer ou mordre.

Le clip le plus vu sur YouTube en 24 h pour un artiste solo

Les 26-27 avril 2019, Taylor Swift (USA) a cumulé 65,2 millions de vues pour sa vidéo du titre *ME !*, avec Brendon Urie.

Le plus de blogs de vidéos privées quotidiennes et consécutives postées sur YouTube

Charles Trippy (USA) a uploadé 3 653 vidéos entre les 1er mai 2009 et 2019. Après une décennie de vlogging quotidien, Trippy a cessé sa course aux records pour consacrer plus de temps à sa famille. Ses 1ers vlogs sont apparus sur la chaîne "Internet Killed Television" (alias "CTFxC"), puis il a poursuivi sur "Charles and Allie".

LE PLUS D'ABONNÉS SUR YOUTUBE

La maison de disques indienne T-Series compte 96 321 836 abonnés sur le site de vidéo YouTube. Elle détrône ainsi le comédien et gamer "PewDiePie", alias Felix Arvid Ulf Kjellberg (SWE, ci-dessus), détenteur du record depuis 2013.
Un duel acharné a vu le jour entre les fans des 2 chaînes, les visiteurs ne reculant devant rien – pas même le hacking ou la diffamation – pour inciter les gens à s'abonner à leur chaîne.

OCT. 21 En 2001, Tuomo Kostian (FIN) accomplit **l'ascension inversée à la corde la plus rapide sur 5 m** (13,7 s), à Helsinki (FIN). Il a grimpé à la corde, tête en bas.

OCT. 22 En 1911, durant le conflit italo-turc, le capitaine Carlo Piazza (ITA) effectue un vol de reconnaissance entre Tripoli et El Azizia (LBY) à bord d'un monoplan Blériot. C'est **la 1re utilisation d'un avion pendant une guerre**.

LE CLIP LE PLUS VU SUR YOUTUBE EN 24 H

La vidéo officielle du titre *Boy with Luv* de BTS (KOR) avec Halsey (USA) totalisait 74 600 000 vues les 12-13 avril 2019. BTS a détrôné ses compatriotes pop sud-coréens BLACKPINK (à droite), dont la vidéo du titre *Kill this Love* avait cumulé 56 700 000 vues la semaine précédente, les 4-5 avril.

Les stars des charts BTS (@BTS_twt) comptent également **le plus d'engagements Twitter (moyenne des retweets)** enregistrés (422 228).

LA VIDÉO EN LIGNE LA PLUS REGARDÉE

Le clip de *Despacito* de Luis Fonsi et Daddy Yankee (tous 2 PRI) a été vue 6 159 897 341 fois. Fonsi est photographié ci-dessous avec les certificats GWR couronnant la chanson et la vidéo, notamment pour **la 1re vidéo YouTube à totaliser 5 milliards de vues** (atteint le 4 avril 2018).

LE PLUS RAPIDE À ATTEINDRE 1 MILLION DE FOLLOWERS SUR INSTAGRAM

Il a fallu 5 h et 45 min au duc et à la duchesse de Sussex – alias le prince Harry (GBR) et Meghan Markle (USA) – pour atteindre 1 million de followers sur Instagram le 2 avril 2019. Leur compte joint (@sussexroyal) a largement battu le précédent record de 11 h et 36 min détenu par le chanteur Kang Daniel (KOR), et datant du 2 janvier 2019.

▶ LE PLUS DE FOLLOWERS SUR INSTAGRAM POUR UN CHIEN

Un loulou de Poméranie nommé Jiffpom (@jiffpom) et habitant en Californie (USA) compte 9 018 251 followers sur Instagram. Le compte de Jiffpom présente des photos de lui dans divers costumes, se relaxant chez lui, ou honorant de sa présence cérémonies de remise de prix, studios télé et défilés de mode.

 OCT. 23 Northwest Fudge Factory (CAN) produit **la plus grande plaque de caramel**, en 2010, à Levack (Ontario, CAN). La friandise géante pesait 2,61 t et contenait de la vanille, du chocolat et du sirop d'érable.

 OCT. 24 **La plus grande collection de cornemuses** comprend 105 instruments opérationnels, en 2013, à Cleethorpes (Lincolnshire, GBR). Elles sont à Daniel Fleming (GBR), qui les collectionne depuis l'âge de 10 ans.

£500,000

L'ÉMISSION TV LA PLUS VENDUE

En 2017, il existait 100 versions internationales du jeu de questions à choix multiples *Qui veut gagner des millions ?* (Sony Pictures Television), d'après "Tracking the Giants : The Top 100 Travelling TV Formats 2017-18" des analystes K7 Media. Depuis sa 1re diffusion sur la chaîne britannique ITV, le 4 septembre 1998, l'émission a connu au moins 142 variantes dans plus de 80 langues.

LE SPECTACLE SOLO LE PLUS RENTABLE DE BROADWAY

De l'avant-première du 3 octobre 2017 à la dernière représentation du 15 décembre 2018, *Springsteen on Broadway* a généré 113 058 952 $, à New York (USA). Le spectacle intimiste, dans lequel "The Boss", leader du groupe E. Street Band, livre des souvenirs de sa carrière et chante en solo au piano ou à la guitare, a attiré 223 585 spectateurs en 236 représentations.

Les revenus hebdomadaires les plus élevés au box-office de Broadway

Hamilton, dont la musique, les paroles et le livret ont été écrits par Lin-Manuel Miranda (USA), a rapporté 4 041 493 $ entre les 24 et 30 décembre 2018.

10 766 personnes ont assisté au spectacle cette semaine, déboursant en moyenne 375,39 $ par billet.

Ce succès a contribué aux chiffres de **la semaine la plus fructueuse dans les théâtres de Broadway** :
57,8 millions $ engrangés du 24 au 30 décembre 2018.

La personne la plus jeune à publier un livre (hommes)

Thanuwana Serasinghe (LKA) avait 4 ans et 356 jours quand son livre *Junk Food* a été publié, le 5 janvier 2017. Son ouvrage met en garde contre les dangers d'une mauvaise alimentation.

L'auteur aux revenus les plus élevés (femmes, à date)

J. K. Rowling (GBR) aurait gagné 54 millions $ entre les 1er juillet 2017 et 2018, selon Forbes. Même sans la sortie d'un nouvel *Harry Potter*, Rowling a suffisamment bénéficié des ventes de son fond de catalogue, des productions théâtrales et des parcs à thème pour déposer une somme substantielle sur son compte en banque à Gringotts.

Pour découvrir qui est **l'auteur le mieux rémunéré (à date)**, rendez-vous p. 132.

La présentatrice télé la mieux rémunérée

D'après les estimations publiées par Forbes le 16 juillet 2018, l'animatrice de talk-show Ellen DeGeneres (USA) a gagné 87,5 millions $ entre les 1er juillet 2017 et 2018.

L'animateur télé le mieux rémunéré (hommes) est Dr Phil McGraw (USA), qui aurait perçu 77,5 millions $ sur la même période.

Le programme télé pour enfants le plus pérenne

Blue Peter (BBC, GBR) a célébré son 60e anniversaire avec une émission spéciale live *Big Birthday* le 16 octobre 2018. L'émission enfantine culte a été diffusée pour la 1re fois le 16 octobre 1958.

Le plus de Primetime Emmy Awards pour une série télé

Saturday Night Live (NBC) a remporté 62 Primetime Emmys depuis sa 1re diffusion en 1975. Le show diffusé en nocturne a reçu 3 trophées en 2018, dont celui de la meilleure émission de divertissement à sketches.

En 2018, *The Simpsons* (Fox) ont également été récompensés pour la meilleure prestation individuelle en animation, cumulant ainsi 33 statuettes, soit **le plus d'Emmys pour une série télé animée**.

Le plus de nominations aux Grammys pour une artiste

Beyoncé (USA) a totalisé 66 nominations aux Grammys entre 2000 et 2018. Elle a été nommée 3 fois lors des 61es Grammy Awards annuels, le

Les baleines bleues pèsent environ 136 t – le même poids que la masse de plastique déchargée toutes les 9 min dans les océans.

Monterey Bay Aquarium

OCT. 25 En 2009, Miki Sakabe (JPN) est **le plus rapide à parcourir 100 m sur le fessier** (11 min et 59 s), à Hokkaido (JPN). Il s'est appuyé principalement sur ses grands glutéaux.

OCT. 26 En 2002, la laiterie Edelweiss Käsewerk (DEU) produit **le fromage à pâte molle le plus lourd** (180 kg) – un poids équivalent à celui de 3 adultes –, à Kempten (DEU).

L'ŒUVRE LA PLUS CHÈRE D'UN ARTISTE VIVANT (ENCHÈRES)

Portrait of an Artist (Pool with Two Figures), acrylique sur toile peinte par David Hockney (GBR) en 1972, s'est négocié 90 312 500 $ (commission d'achat incluse), à la salle des ventes Christie's de New York (USA), le 15 novembre 2018. Animé par une créativité débordante, Hockney a peint l'œuvre en 2 semaines, travaillant sur des cycles de 18 h.

10 février 2019, en tant que membre du duo The Carters, le projet musical mené avec son mari Jay-Z (voir p. 198).

Le plus de visionnages d'un même film en salle
Anthony "Nem" Mitchell (USA) avait vu *Avengers : Infinity War* (USA, 2018) en salle 103 fois au 19 juillet 2018. Les réalisateurs ont récompensé le zèle du superfan de super-héros avec des billets gratuits pour la première du nouveau volet de la série sorti en 2019 *Avengers: Endgame* (USA, voir p. 193).

L'enchère la plus élevée pour une figurine *Star Wars*
La figurine en résine d'un prototype de Bib Fortuna utilisé pour créer les jouets dérivés du *Retour du Jedi* (USA, 1983) s'est vendue 36 000 £ (commission comprise), le 30 avril 2019. Cet objet *Star Wars* rare était le plus cher des 3 lots – les 2 autres figurines étant Ewok "Logray" et un garde royal impérial –, tous mis aux enchères chez Vectis, à Thornaby (Yorkshire du Nord, GBR).

LES PLUS GRANDS...

Anaglyphe mural en 3D
Un anaglyphe 3D comprend 2 images en couleurs différemment filtrées qui, lorsqu'on les regarde avec des lunettes spéciales, révèlent une seule image stéréoscopique. Le 14 mars 2018, Jason Tetlak (USA) a dévoilé un anaglyphe mural en 3D du groupe de hip-hop les Beastie Boys de 179,36 m² – soit l'équivalent de 45 matelas king size –, à Jacksonville (Floride, USA).

Tapisserie
Pour célébrer les 100 ans de la ville d'Espinar (PER), le 15 novembre 2018, Planta de Fibra y Lana Convenio Marco de Espinar (PER) a dévoilé une tapisserie de 288,55 m². Douze artisans ont travaillé 3 mois sur l'œuvre, qui est suffisamment grande pour recouvrir un court de tennis. Elle représente l'iconographie et les costumes traditionnels de Cuzco ainsi que des danseurs indigènes K'ana.

▶ Dessin par une seule personne
Alex Dzaghigian (CYP) a dessiné une esquisse au fusain de 323,90 m² représentant une tortue nageant dans des déchets de plastique, le 29 décembre 2018 à Nicosie (CYP).

LA CARRIÈRE LA PLUS PÉRENNE POUR UN PRÉSENTATEUR TÉLÉ

Mise en ligne sur Netflix le 5 avril 2019, *Our Planet* était la dernière série en date narrée par le naturaliste Sir David Attenborough (GBR). Il a fait ses débuts à l'écran le 2 septembre 1953 avec le programme télé pour enfant de la BBC *Animal Disguises* (GBR), soit une carrière de 65 ans et 215 jours à date. Il est le seul à avoir remporté des trophées BAFTA pour des séries en noir et blanc, couleurs, HD et 3D. Son record devrait même être amplifié grâce à la série de 2019 *One Planet, Seven Worlds* (BBC).

Our Planet a été tourné en 4 ans dans 50 pays, avec une équipe technique de plus de 600 personnes.

▶ LA PLUS GRANDE SCULPTURE EN PLASTIQUE RECYCLÉ

En 2018, afin d'alerter l'opinion sur la pollution plastique, le Monterey Bay Aquarium (USA) a fabriqué une baleine bleue à taille réelle avec des déchets en plastique (bouteilles de lait et de détergents, jouets) ramassés dans la baie de San Francisco. La baleine mesurait 25,89 m, le 26 novembre 2018, à San Francisco (Californie, USA).

La sculpture en médailles pour animaux de compagnie la plus grande est intitulée *Sun Spot* (à droite) et a été créée à partir de 90 000 plaques d'identification pour chien en acier inoxydable, en 2011, par les artistes Laura Haddad et Tom Drugan (tous 2 USA). Elle était destinée au Denver Animal Shelter du Colorado (USA).

Le 22 septembre 2018, le Zunyi Culture & Tourism Development Group (CHN) a présenté un dinosaure *Triceratops* fabriqué à partir de 10 variétés de légumes (à l'extrême droite), à Chishui (province du Guizhou, CHN). Le grand "légumo-saurus" de 14,31 m de long et 5,4 m de haut est **la sculpture en légumes variés la plus grande du monde**.

OCT. 27 Steve Fossett (USA) et son copilote Hans-Paul Ströhle (DEU) atteignent **la vitesse la plus rapide en dirigeable** (115 km/h), à bord d'un Zeppelin Luftschifftechnik LZ N07-100, au-dessus de l'Allemagne, en 2004.

OCT. 28 Le gouvernement de l'État mexicain d'Hidalgo dévoile **le plus grand autel de la Toussaint**, à Pachuca, en 2017. Il mesure 846,48 m² et arbore 9 200 tagètes (œillets d'Inde).

SPORTS

LE MARATHON LE PLUS RAPIDE

Le 16 sept. 2018, Eliud Kipchoge (KEN) a terminé le marathon de Berlin (DEU) en 2 h 1 min et 39 s, explosant le record du monde précédent – établi par son compatriote Dennis Kimetto en 2014, également à Berlin – de 1 min et 18 s. C'est la meilleure amélioration du record sur la distance depuis 1967.

Avec les progrès des athlètes, la perspective d'un marathon en moins de 2 h, autrefois jugée impossible, devient probable. Le 6 mai 2017, Kipchoge a enregistré un chrono de 2 h et 25 s au défi "Breaking2" de Nike, bien que cette performance ne soit pas homologuée par l'IAAF en raison de l'utilisation de "lièvres".

La course record de Kipchoge marquait sa 3e victoire à Berlin. En 2013, il avait terminé 2e derrière Wilson Kipsang, qui établissait alors le record en 2'03''32. À ce jour, c'est la seule défaite de Kipchoge en 12 marathons.

LES JO 2020 À LA LOUPE

TOKYO 2020

TOKYO 2020
PARALYMPIC GAMES

Le 24 juill. 2020, la torche sera portée dans l'enceinte du Nouveau stade olympique national de Tokyo (JAP) pour enflammer le chaudron et marquer l'ouverture de la XXXIIᵉ olympiade. Les meilleurs athlètes de la planète s'affronteront dans différentes disciplines, du tir à l'arc à la lutte, en quête d'une médaille d'or. Suivront les jeux Paralympiques (25 août-6 sept.). L'élite mondiale a rendez-vous à Tokyo.

Tokyo organisera les jeux Olympiques d'été pour la 2ᵉ fois, 56 ans après les JO 1964. (La ville aurait dû accueillir les JO d'été 1940, mais cette édition a été annulée quand la Seconde Guerre mondiale a éclaté.) Les Jeux 2020 se dérouleront sur 42 sites regroupés dans deux zones circulaires autour de Tokyo, la "Zone Héritage" et la "Zone de la baie de Tokyo", le village olympique étant situé entre les deux. Plusieurs sites utilisés en 1964 seront le théâtre d'épreuves olympiques pour la deuxième fois, dont le Nippon Budokan (judo) et le Gymnase national de Yoyogi (handball).

Les mascottes ont déjà été dévoilées : il s'agit de deux

super-héros créés par l'artiste Ryo Taniguchi et sélectionnés par des élèves d'écoles élémentaires du pays. La mascotte olympique est Miraitowa (en bleu, en haut à gauche), dont le nom vient des mots japonais signifiant "futur" et "éternité". La mascotte paralympique est Someity (en rose, à droite), qui tire son nom d'une variété de cerisier.

HISTOIRE ANTIQUE
Les premiers jeux Olympiques dont nous ayons une trace ont eu lieu en juillet 776 av. J.-C. dans un sanctuaire religieux à Olympe (GRC). Corèbe, un cuisinier de la cité voisine d'Élis, remporte la course pédestre du stade et reçoit une branche d'olivier

en récompense. Les Jeux ont décliné vers la fin de l'Empire romain avant d'être officiellement interdits, de même que les autres "fêtes païennes", par l'empereur Théodose Iᵉʳ en 393 apr. J.-C. Il faut attendre 1896 avant de voir les Jeux être rétablis par Pierre de Coubertin, fondateur du Comité international olympique. **Les premiers jeux Olympiques modernes** sont organisés à Athènes

(GRC), le 6 avr. 1896. C'était alors une compétition relativement modeste, puisqu'elle regroupait 241 participants issus de 14 pays.

En comparaison, les JO 2020 verront concourir plus de 11 000 athlètes dans 33 disciplines. Ce total comprend cinq nouvelles épreuves olympiques : le karaté, le skateboard, le surf, l'escalade et le

softball/baseball (le softball et le baseball ont déjà été inscrits au programme, mais séparément). Des sports classiques accueillent de nouvelles spécialités – comme le basket-ball à 3, joué sur demi-terrain avec un seul panier, ou le park en BMX freestyle, issu des X-Games –, afin d'attirer un public plus jeune. Des épreuves mixtes en tir, natation ou triathlon seront aussi introduites.

LE PLUS DE MÉDAILLES OLYMPIQUES
Un record qui ne sera pas battu à Tokyo est celui de Michael Phelps (USA), qui a remporté 28 médailles entre 2004 et 2016 : 23 en or, 3 en argent et 2 en bronze. En 2008, il a obtenu le **plus de médailles d'or en une édition** – 8 - et a établi 7 records du monde, dont celui du **400 m 4 nages le plus rapide en grand bassin (hommes)** : 4 min et 3,84 s.

LÉGENDES OLYMPIQUES

LE 1ᵉʳ CHAMPION MODERNE
James Connolly (USA) a remporté le *"hop, skip and jump"* (précurseur du triple saut moderne), aux Jeux d'Athènes (GRC), le 6 avr. 1896. Il a réussi un saut de 13,71 m qui lui a permis de devenir le 1ᵉʳ champion olympique officiel depuis le boxeur arménien Varazdat en 369, 1 527 ans plus tôt.

LE PLUS VIEUX MÉDAILLÉ
Le 27 juill. 1920, le tireur suédois Oscar Swahn (né le 20 oct. 1847) a obtenu l'argent à l'âge de 72 ans et 281 jours au tir sur cerf courant à 100 m (deux coups) par équipe, à Anvers (BEL). Il était déjà **le plus vieux champion olympique** depuis son titre en tir sur cerf courant à 100 m (un coup), à l'âge de 64 ans et 258 jours, en 1912.

LE PLUS DE TITRES EN ATHLÉTISME EN UNE ÉDITION
En 1924, Paavo Nurmi (FIN) a décroché 5 médailles d'or - sur 1 500 m, 5 000 m, 3 000 m par équipe et en cross-country individuel et par équipe -, à Paris (FRA). Il a remporté les épreuves sur 1 500 m et 5 000 m avec 42 min entre les deux finales. Il n'a pas été sélectionné par la Finlande sur 10 000 m.

LE PLUS JEUNE CHAMPION
Marjorie Gestring (USA, née le 18 nov. 1922) a gagné l'or en plongeon féminin à 3 m, à 13 ans et 268 jours, aux JO de Berlin (DEU), le 12 août 1936. Sa carrière olympique a été interrompue par la guerre. Gestring a ensuite terminé 4ᵉ des qualifications américaines pour les JO 1948 et n'a pu défendre son titre.

LE PLUS DE MÉDAILLES OLYMPIQUES (FEMMES)
La gymnaste soviétique Larisa Latynina totalise 18 médailles en 3 Jeux, de 1956 à 1964. Ses 9 sacres constituent le plus de **médailles d'or olympiques (femmes)**. Elle a aussi obtenu 5 médailles d'argent et 4 de bronze. Aucun athlète n'a obtenu plus que ses 18 médailles jusqu'à Michael Phelps (ci-dessus), en 2012, soit 48 ans plus tard.

OCT. 29 Francisco Javier Galán Marín (ESP) réussit le **tir le plus rapide en football** en 2001, à 129 km/h, au studio d'*El Show de los Récords*, à Madrid (ESP).

OCT. 30 **Le plus petit cinéma (nombre de places)** commercial ouvre à Radebeul (DEU), en 2006. Le Palastkino ne compte que 9 sièges. Il se trouve à l'intérieur d'une gare.

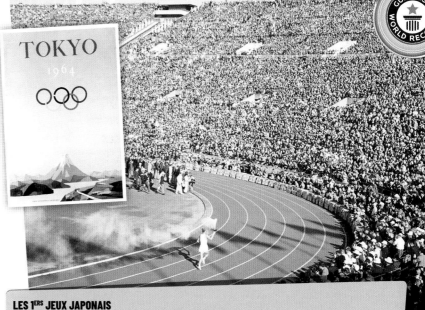

AMBITIONS DORÉES

La judoka Uta Abe (née le 14 juill. 2000) promet d'être l'une des stars des JO 2020. Elle est championne du monde et **la plus jeune vainqueure d'une épreuve de l'IJF World Tour**, titrée en - 52 kg au Grand Prix de Düsseldorf (DEU), à 16 ans et 225 jours, le 24 févr. 2017. Son frère aîné Hifumi – double champion du monde de judo en - 66 kg – est également pressenti pour décrocher l'or.

PRÉCIEUSES MÉDAILLES

Une autre innovation pour les prochains Jeux a été baptisée le Tokyo 2020 Medal Project, qui vise à produire quelque 5 000 médailles d'or, d'argent et de bronze à partir de métal recyclé donné par les citoyens japonais. Lors des premières éditions des Jeux modernes, les champions recevaient des médailles d'argent, l'or étant jugé trop cher. **Les 1ʳᵉˢ médailles d'or olympiques** ont été décernées aux JO de 1904 à Saint-Louis (USA), mais elles ne sont plus en or massif depuis 1912.

À Tokyo, les États-Unis tenteront d'améliorer leur **nombre record de médailles d'or aux Jeux d'été** – 1 022 – et celui **de médailles au total** : 2 520.

Les supporters locaux encourageront bien sûr les athlètes nationaux. De grands espoirs reposent sur Ippei Watanabe, auteur du **200 m brasse le plus rapide en grand bassin (hommes)** – 2 min et 6,67 s –, à Tokyo, le 29 janv. 2017. Les gymnastes Kenzō Shirai (voir p. 231) et Kōhei Uchimura (médaillé 7 fois aux JO) visent également le podium. De son côté, la lutteuse Kaori Icho a une chance d'améliorer son record du **nombre de médailles d'or olympiques consécutives en une épreuve individuelle féminine**. Icho totalise 4 titres entre Athènes 2004 et Rio 2016 – 3 en lutte féminine 63 kg et 1 en 58 kg.

LES 1ᴱᴿˢ JEUX JAPONAIS

Les jeux Olympiques d'été 1964 à Tokyo ont été les 1ᵉʳˢ JO organisés en Asie. L'Éthiopien Abebe Bikila alors établissait un record du monde en conservant son titre en marathon chez les hommes, tandis que Larisa Latynina obtenait sa 18ᵉ médaille olympique (voir en bas à gauche). L'un des succès les plus attendus était celui de l'équipe féminine de volleyball, titré dans le **1ᵉʳ sport collectif féminin olympique**. Après un entraînement intense tous les soirs jusqu'à minuit, les Japonaises emmenées par la centrale Masae Kasai ont battu l'Union soviétique 3-0 en finale et sont devenues les héroïnes de toute une nation.

Les jeux Paralympiques verront 4 400 athlètes – soit potentiellement **le plus de participants à des jeux Paralympiques d'été** après les 4 328 de Rio 2016 – se disputer 537 médailles dans 22 disciplines. Le badminton et le taekwondo feront leurs débuts, et d'autres leur retour, comme le boccia, le volleyball assis et le goalball, joué par des sportifs malvoyants avec une balle contenant des grelots. La flamme paralympique sera éteinte le 6 sept. 2020, ce qui marquera la fin des Jeux et le début d'un nouveau cycle olympique tourné vers Paris 2024.

LE RECORD OLYMPIQUE LE PLUS ANCIEN EN ATHLÉTISME

Enregistré le 18 oct. 1968, à Mexico (MEX), le saut en longueur de Bob Beamon (USA) à 8,90 m n'a jamais été battu aux JO. Le saut en longueur masculin de 2016 – 47 ans et 300 jours plus tard – a été remporté par Jeff Henderson avec un saut d'une cinquantaine de centimètres plus court que celui de Beamon.

LE PLUS DE MÉDAILLES PARALYMPIQUES D'ÉTÉ

La nageuse Trischa Zorn (USA) compte 55 médailles sur 7 jeux Paralympiques, entre 1980 et 2004, dont 41 en or, 9 en argent et 5 en bronze dans 13 spécialités de natation. À Barcelone 1992, Zorn, née aveugle, est arrivée en tête du tableau des médailles paralympiques avec 10 titres et 2 médailles d'argent.

LE PLUS DE MÉDAILLES PARALYMPIQUES D'ÉTÉ (HOMMES)

Jonas Jacobsson (SWE, ci-dessus) a obtenu 30 médailles en épreuves de tir, entre 1980 et 2012 : 17 d'or, 4 d'argent et 9 de bronze. L'athlète en fauteuil Heinz Frei (CHE) compte **le plus de médailles paralympiques en athlétisme (hommes)** (34), mais il en a obtenu 8 aux jeux Paralympiques d'hiver.

LE PLUS DE PARTICIPATIONS

Le cavalier Ian Millar (CAN) a participé à ses 10ᵉ Jeux à Londres 2012. Il avait fait ses débuts en 1972 et a disputé 8 éditions consécutives entre 1984 et 2012. Millar a aussi été sélectionné dans l'équipe canadienne pour Moscou 1980, mais son pays a finalement boycotté les Jeux. Il a remporté sa seule médaille, en argent, en 2008.

LE PLUS DE TITRES SUR 100 M

Usain Bolt (JAM) a été sacré sur 100 m à 3 reprises en 2008-2016. Il a aussi obtenu **le plus de victoires sur 200 m** (3) et 2 titres en relais 4 x 100 m. Bolt a écrit l'histoire avant sa retraite en 2017. Il a notamment signé les records du **100 m le plus rapide** (9,58 s) et du **200 m le plus rapide** (19,19 s) toujours en vigueur.

 OCT. 31 En 2005, 68 vaches jersiaises meurent quand la foudre tombe sur une ferme laitière près de Dorrigo (AUS) – **le plus de têtes de bétail tuées d'un coup par la foudre**.

 NOV. 1 La Jailbreak Society de l'université de Warwick (GBR) a fait tenir **le plus de personnes dans un sous-vêtement** – 314 –, lors d'un événement caritatif à Coventry (GBR), en 2014.

FOOTBALL AMÉRICAIN

LE PLUS DE TITRES AU SUPER BOWL (ÉQUIPE)

Le 3 février 2019, les New England Patriots ont battu les Los Angeles Rams 13-3 lors du **Super Bowl le moins prolifique**. C'était leur 6e victoire dans la grande finale annuelle. Les Patriots font aussi bien que les Pittsburgh Steelers et améliorent leur record du **plus de présences au Super Bowl** (11). Le quarterback Tom Brady (maillot 12, à gauche) a dépassé Charles Haley pour devenir **le joueur le plus titré au Super Bowl** avec 6 victoires. Il a aussi amélioré son record du **plus de passes réussies au Super Bowl** (256) et **de yards gagnés** (2 838).

La meilleure moyenne de yards à la course en 1 match (joueur)

Le 7 octobre 2018, Isaiah Crowell a couru 219 yards en 15 courses – une moyenne de 14,6 yards par course – pour les New York Jets victorieux 34-16 des Denver Broncos.

Le meilleur taux de passes complétées

Le quarterback des Los Angeles Chargers Philip Rivers a terminé la rencontre contre les Arizona Cardinals (45-10), le 25 novembre 2018, avec un taux de 96,6 %. Il explose le record précédent de 92,3 %, établi par Kurt Warner des Cardinals contre les Jacksonville Jaguars, le 20 septembre 2009.

Rivers a réussi 28 passes sur 29 et a signé **le plus de passes complétées à la suite en début de match pour un quarterback** (25). C'est aussi **le plus de passes complétées à la suite**, à égalité avec Nick Foles des Philadelphia Eagles, le 30 décembre 2018.

LE PLUS DE MATCHS CONSÉCUTIFS À RÉUSSIR UN SACK

Du 7 octobre au 23 décembre 2018, Chris Jones, des Kansas City Chiefs, a plaqué un quarterback dans 11 matchs de suite. Le défenseur s'est emparé du record en stoppant Russell Wilson, des Seattle Seahawks. La fin de sa série a sans doute soulagé une partie de son vestiaire, puisque Jones a porté la même paire de gants tout du long… sans les laver !

LE PLUS DE POINTS EN CARRIÈRE

Le kicker Adam Vinatieri a inscrit 2 600 pts avec les New England Patriots (1996-2005) et les Indianapolis Colts (2006-2018). Il a dépassé les 2 544 pts de Morten Andersen (DNK) avec un field goal de 25 yards contre les Oakland Raiders, le 28 octobre 2018. Vinatieri a aussi inscrit **le plus de fields goals en playoffs** (56), à la fin de la saison 2018.

contre les Jacksonville Jaguars, le 6 décembre 2018. Il égale un record vieux de 35 ans, signé Tony Dorsett pour les Dallas Cowboys contre les Minnesota Vikings, le 3 janvier 1983.

Toutes les équipes et tous les joueurs sont américains et évoluent en NFL, sauf mention contraire.

Le plus de points marqués par une équipe perdante

Le 19 novembre 2018, lors du match du lundi soir le plus prolifique de l'histoire, les Kansas City Chiefs ont inscrit 51 pts contre les Los Angeles Rams, mais se sont inclinés 54-51.

Les 2 équipes totalisent 105 pts, mais **le record de points en un match** est de 113, lors de la victoire des Washington Redskins 72-41 contre les New York Giants, le 27 novembre 1966.

La plus longue course depuis le scrimmage

Derrick Henry a réussi un touchdown après une course de 99 yards pour les Tennessee Titans

Le plus de matchs consécutifs à 100 yards reçus en 1 saison (joueur)

Le receveur Adam Thielen des Minnesota Vikings a totalisé 100 yards en réception dans chacun des 8 premiers matchs de la saison 2018, du 9 septembre au 28 octobre. Il égale le record de Calvin Johnson des Detroit Lions en 2012.

Le plus de passes tentées sans interception

Du 30 septembre au 16 décembre 2018, Aaron Rodgers des Green Bay Packers a lancé 402 passes consécutives sans jamais être intercepté.

Le plus jeune entraîneur au Super Bowl

Le coach des Los Angeles Rams Sean McVay (né le 24 janvier 1986) a emmené son équipe jusqu'au Super Bowl LIII, à 33 ans et 10 jours. C'est son homologue des New England Patriots, Bill Belichick (né le 16 avril 1952), qui a gagné, devenant **le plus vieil entraîneur à remporter le Super Bowl**, à 66 ans et 293 jours.

LE PLUS DE RÉCEPTIONS EN 1 SAISON POUR UN RUNNING BACK ROOKIE

Saquon Barkley des New York Giants a réussi 91 réceptions pour sa 1re saison, en 2018. Il fait mieux que les 88 de Reggie Bush pour les New Orleans Saints en 2006.

Le record du **plus de réceptions en 1 saison pour un running back** est aussi tombé en 2018, grâce à Christian McCaffrey des Carolina Panthers (107).

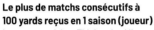

LE PLUS DE YARDS À LA PASSE EN CARRIÈRE

De 2001 à la fin de la saison 2018, Drew Brees avait gagné 74 437 yards à la passe. Il a dépassé les 71 940 yards de Peyton Manning lors du succès 43–19 des New Orleans Saints contre les Washington Redskins le 8 oct. 2018. Brees a réussi 364 passes sur 489 en 2018, le **meilleur taux de passes complétées sur une saison** : 74,4 %.

NOV. 2 En 1996, les Rostrum Clubs de Tasmanie lancent **le plus long débat**, jusqu'au 1er décembre sur le sujet : "Le plus grand atout de la Tasmanie est son peuple." Il a duré 29 jours, 4 h, 3 min et 20 s.

NOV. 3 Le basketteur "Thunder" Law (USA) des Harlem Globetrotters réussit **le tir le plus lointain dos au panier** (25 m), en 2014, à l'US Airways Center de Phoenix (USA).

BASEBALL

LE PLUS DE HOME RUNS EN 1 SAISON (ÉQUIPE)

Les New York Yankees ont frappé 267 home runs en 2018, soit mieux que les 264 réalisés par les Seattle Mariners en 1997. Ils le doivent à Giancarlo Stanton (à gauche), auteur de 38 coups gagnants. Quatre Yankees en ont signé 27 chacun : Didi Gregorius, Aaron Hicks, Miguel Andújar et Aaron Judge.

LE PLUS DE STRIKEOUTS PAR DES LANCEURS EN 1 SAISON

Les lanceurs des Houston Astros ont éliminé 1 687 batteurs en 2018, avec une moyenne de 10,4 strikeouts en 9 manches, la plus haute en MLB. Justin Verlander (à droite) et Gerrit Cole ont signé respectivement 290 et 276 strikeouts, les 2e et 3e meilleurs totaux de la saison, derrière Max Scherzer des Washington Nationals (300).

Toutes les équipes et tous les joueurs sont américains et évoluent en MLB, sauf mention contraire.

Le plus gros contrat de MLB

Le 20 mars 2019, les Los Angeles Angels et Mike Trout ont signé un contrat de 12 ans estimé à 426,5 millions $. C'est plus que le contrat de 13 ans signé par Bryce Harper avec les Philadelphia Phillies quelques jours plus tôt, évalué à 330 millions $. Trout est septuple All-Star de MLB et sextuple lauréat du trophée Silver Slugger.

Le plus de bases touchées en carrière

Le 21 mars 2019, Ichiro Suzuki (JPN) a dit adieu à la MLB lors du match des Seattle Mariners contre les Oakland Athletics, à Tokyo (JPN). Suzuki compte

LE 1ER À SIGNER UN CYCLE (PLAYOFF)

En baseball, un cycle se produit lorsqu'un batteur réussit un simple, un double, un triple et un home run dans le même match. Le 8 octobre 2018, Brock Holt a accompli cet exploit pour les Boston Red Sox dans le match 3 des American League Division Series, au Yankee Stadium de New York (USA). Il a aidé les Red Sox à écraser 16-1 leurs ennemis jurés, les New York Yankees.

---

4 367 bases touchées depuis 1992, que ce soit en Nippon Professional Baseball ou en MLB.

Le moins de matchs pour atteindre 300 sauvetages

Craig Kimbrel a réussi son 300e sauvetage en carrière lors de son 494e match, en lançant pour les Boston Red Sox lors de leur victoire 6-5 face aux Texas Rangers, le 5 mai 2018. Il lui a suffi de 330 tentatives, soit un taux de sauvetage de 90,9 %.

Le plus de strikeouts pour un lanceur en début de match (ère moderne)

Germán Márquez (VEN) des Colorado Rockies a éliminé ses 8 premiers batteurs des Philadelphia Phillies le 26 septembre 2018. Il a fait aussi bien que Jim Deshaies des Houston Astros le 23 septembre 1986 et que Jacob deGrom des New York Mets le 15 septembre 2014.

Le plus de strikeouts pour un batteur dans une double confrontation

Le batteur des New York Yankees Aaron Judge a été éliminé 8 fois en 2 matchs contre les Detroit Tigers, le 4 juin 2018.

Le plus de strikeouts en une saison (équipe) est de 1 594 par les batteurs des Chicago White Sox en 2018. Ils ont fait pire que les 1 571 éliminations des Milwaukee Brewers en 2017.

Le plus de strikeouts en une saison (toutes équipes) est de 41 207, toujours en saison régulière 2018.

Le plus de matchs de playoffs à la suite à frapper un home run (équipe)

Les Houston Astros ont signé des home runs dans 14 matchs

LE SCORE LE PLUS ÉLEVÉ POUR UNE ENTRÉE AU HALL OF FAME

Mariano Rivera (PAN) a fait l'unanimité pour son entrée au panthéon du baseball en 2019, élu par 100 % des 425 votants. Le lanceur a passé 19 saisons avec les New York Yankees, signant **le plus de matchs comme lanceur pour une équipe (1 115)**, **le plus de matchs terminés par un lanceur (952)** et **le plus de sauvetages en carrière (652)**.

de playoffs de suite, du match 6 de l'American League Championship Series (ALCS) 2017 au match 2 de l'ALCS. Ils ont réussi 29 home runs au total.

Le plus de matchs de playoffs à la suite à frapper un home run (joueur) est de 6, par Daniel Murphy pour les New York Mets en 2015.

Le plus de franchises représentées

Le 25 juin 2018, le lanceur Edwin Jackson (né DEU) a porté les couleurs d'une 13e franchise de MLB, les Oakland Athletics. Jackson, qui a débuté en MLB en 2003, a imité Octavio Dotel (DOM) et ses 13 équipes entre 1999 et 2013.

LE MATCH DE WORLD SERIES LE PLUS LONG

Le 27 octobre 2018, les Los Angeles Dodgers ont vaincu les Boston Red Sox 3-2, lors d'un marathon de 18 manches et 7 h et 20 min de jeu. Les 2 équipes ont appelé 46 joueurs - **le plus de joueurs utilisés en un match de World Series (2 équipes)**. Les Dodgers l'ont emporté grâce à un home run final frappé par Max Muncy (au centre), mais les Red Sox ont eu le dernier mot en remportant la série 4-1.

NOV. 4 Les montagnes russes les plus rapides ouvrent en 2010, au Ferrari World d'Abou Dabi (ARE). *Formula Rossa* atteint 240 km/h et atteint sa hauteur maximale de 52 m en 4,9 s.

NOV. 5 En 2013, l'existence du Grand Mur d'Hercule-Couronne boréale est révélée. S'étendant sur plus de 10 milliards d'années-lumière, c'est **la plus grande structure de l'univers**.

217

BASKETBALL

Ces records sont issus de la National Basketball Association (NBA). Tous les joueurs et toutes les équipes sont américains, sauf mention contraire.

Le plus de triples doubles consécutifs

Russell Westbrook a réussi un triple double dans 11 matchs consécutifs pour l'Oklahoma City Thunder, du 22 janvier au 14 février 2019. Le record précédent était de 9, par Wilt Chamberlain des Philadelphia 76ers, les 8-20 mars 1968, et tenait depuis 51 ans. Westbrook tournait à une moyenne de 21,9 points, 13,3 rebonds et 13,5 passes pendant sa série.

Le triple double le plus rapide

Nikola Jokić (SRB) a obtenu des scores à deux chiffres pour les points, les passes et les rebonds en 14 min et 33 s, sur le parquet avec les Denver Nuggets contre les Milwaukee Bucks, le 15 février 2018. Il a terminé avec 30 points, 17 passes et 15 rebonds.

Le plus de 3 points en un match (équipe)

Les Houston Rockets ont converti 27 tirs à 3 points lors de leur victoire 149-113 contre les Phoenix Suns, le 7 avril 2019. Ils ont battu leur propre record de 26, établi le 19 décembre 2018, lors de leur victoire 136-118 face aux Washington Wizards.

Lors de la saison précédente, les Rockets avaient signé **le plus de paniers à 3 points en une saison (équipe)**, soit 1 256.

LE PLUS DE MATCHS À 30 POINTS EN PLAYOFFS

Dans le match 3 des Finales NBA 2018, le 6 juin, LeBron James a inscrit 33 points pour les Cleveland Cavaliers contre les Golden State Warriors – c'était son 110e match de playoff à plus de 30 points, mieux que Michael Jordan.

Depuis 2006, James a inscrit **le plus de points en playoffs** (6 911). Il est le meilleur de l'histoire en playoffs pour **les paniers réussis** (2 457), **les lancers francs tentés** (1 627) et **les interceptions** (419).

LE PLUS DE 3 POINTS EN UN MATCH

Klay Thompson a marqué 14 paniers à 3 points contre les Chicago Bulls dans l'Illinois (USA), le 29 octobre 2018. Il dépasse son coéquipier de Golden State Stephen Curry (13 en 2016).
Dans la première moitié du match contre les Bulls, Thompson a égalé **le plus de 3 points en une mi-temps** (10), comme Chandler Parsons le 24 janvier 2014.

Le plus de 3 points en un match des Finales NBA

Dans le match 2 des Finales NBA 2018, le 3 juin, Stephen Curry a marqué neuf 3 points pour les Golden State Warriors contre les Cleveland Cavaliers, à l'Oracle Arena d'Oakland (USA). Il a inscrit 33 points au total pour mener son équipe à la victoire 122-103.

Dans le match 1, LeBron James (voir en bas à gauche) a marqué 51 points pour Cleveland, malgré la défaite 124-114 – **le plus de points en un match de Finales NBA par un joueur de l'équipe perdante**. Golden State s'est imposé 4-0.

LE PLUS DE SAISONS AVEC LA MÊME FRANCHISE

Le 13 décembre 2018, tout juste remis d'une opération à la cheville, Dirk Nowitzki (DEU) a foulé le parquet pour les Dallas Mavericks pour sa 21e saison. Il a joué plus de 1 400 matchs pour la franchise depuis 1998, remportant le titre en 2011. Nowitzki a surpassé Kobe Bryant et ses 20 saisons chez les LA Lakers.

LE PLUS DE POINTS EN UN MATCH DE WOMEN'S NATIONAL BASKETBALL ASSOCIATION (WNBA)

Le 17 juillet 2018, Liz Cambage (AUS) a inscrit 53 points pour les Dallas Wings contre le New York Liberty, à Arlington (USA). La pivot de 2,03 m a réussi 17 tirs sur 22 dans le jeu et 15 lancers francs sur 16. Elle a battu le record précédent avec un dernier panier à 3 points.

Le plus de matchs en carrière WNBA

Sue Bird a disputé 508 matchs pour le Seattle Storm de 2002 à la fin de la saison 2018. Elle a dépassé les 499 parties de DeLisha Milton-Jones lors de son 500e match, contre l'Atlanta Dream, le 22 juillet 2018.

Le plus de paniers en carrière WNBA

La nonuple All-Star WNBA Diana Taurasi compte 2 721 paniers pour le Phoenix Mercury depuis 2004.

Le plus de rebonds en une saison de WNBA

Sylvia Fowles a repris 404 rebonds pour le Minnesota Lynx en 2018 – un de plus que le record précédent détenu par Jonquel Jones. Ce total inclut **le plus de rebonds défensifs en une saison de WNBA** (282).

Le plus de rebonds en carrière WNBA est de 3 356 par Rebekkah Brunson pour les Sacramento Monarchs et Minnesota Lynx de 2004 à 2018.

Le plus de passes en une saison de WNBA

Courtney Vandersloot a réalisé 258 passes pour le Chicago Sky en 2018. Elle a battu le record de Ticha Penicheiro de 236 passes en 2000.

Le plus de passes en carrière WNBA est de 2 831 par Sue Bird, de 2002 à 2018.

LE TRIPLE DOUBLE AVEC LE PLUS DE POINTS

Le 30 janvier 2018, James Harden des Houston Rockets a marqué 60 points, en plus de ses 10 rebonds et 11 passes, contre l'Orlando Magic.

En 8 rencontres, du 13 au 27 janvier 2019, Harden était en feu et a inscrit **le plus de points sans assistance consécutifs** (304). Aucun de ses coéquipiers n'a été crédité d'une dernière passe sur ces points.

NOV. 6 — Kenichi Ito (JPN) s'adjuge le record du **100 m le plus rapide à quatre pattes** en 2015, avec un chrono de 15,71 s, sur le terrain d'athlétisme du parc olympique Komazawa de Tokyo (JPN).

NOV. 7 — En 2006, **le plus petit chien policier** passe son certificat de chien de détection dans l'Ohio (USA). Midge – un croisé chihuahua/rat terrier – mesure 28 cm de haut et 58 cm de long.

HOCKEY SUR GLACE

LE PLUS DE VICTOIRES AUX TIRS AU BUT POUR UN GARDIEN

Le 30 octobre 2018, le gardien des New York Rangers Henrik Lundqvist (SWE) a remporté sa 60e séance de tirs au but en NHL en stoppant 2 tirs pour une victoire 4-3 contre les San Jose Sharks au SAP Center (USA).

Le 16 janvier de la même année, Lundqvist s'offrait **le plus de saisons consécutives à 20 victoires pour un gardien** (13).

Tous les records sont issus de la National Hockey League (NHL), disputée aux États-Unis et au Canada. Tous les joueurs et toutes les équipes sont américains, sauf mention contraire.

Le plus de matchs consécutifs avec une passe décisive en début de saison

Sebastian Aho (FIN) a offert des passes décisives dans les 12 premiers matchs des Carolina Hurricanes en 2018-2019. En offrant le but à Micheal Ferland (CAN) contre les Boston Bruins,

le 30 octobre 2018, Aho a égalé l'exploit de Wayne Gretzky des Edmonton Oilers (CAN) en 1982-1983 et de Ken Linseman (CAN) des Bruins en 1985-1986.

Le plus de tirs au but en carrière

Frans Nielsen (DNK) a réussi son 49e tir au but le 10 novembre 2018 pour offrir la victoire aux Detroit Red Wings 4-3 contre les Carolina Hurricanes. C'était aussi son 23e but victorieux – **le plus de tirs au but décisifs en carrière**.

Le plus de tirs tentés en un tiers-temps (équipe)

Le 21 octobre 2018, le Tampa Bay Lightning a tiré 33 fois au but dans le 2e tiers-temps contre les Chicago Blackhawks, à l'United Center de Chicago (USA). C'est un record depuis 1997-1998, quand les "tirs par tiers-temps" sont devenus une statistique officielle de la NHL.

Les deux buts les plus rapides (même équipe)

Les Canadiens de Montréal (CAN) ont inscrit 2 buts en 2 s contre les Washington Capitals, au Bell Centre de Québec (Canada), le 1er novembre 2018. Max Domi (CAN) et Joel Armia (FIN) ont été plus rapides que les St Louis Eagles

LE PLUS DE VICTOIRES EN UNE SAISON POUR UNE FRANCHISE PROMUE

Les Vegas Golden Knights ont obtenu 51 victoires en 2017-2018, leur première saison en NHL, améliorant le record de 33 victoires des Anaheim Ducks et Florida Panthers en 1993-1994. Vegas est devenue la 3e nouvelle franchise de l'histoire à se qualifier pour les Finales de Stanley Cup dès sa 1re saison, perdues 4-1 contre les Washington Capitals.

LE PLUS D'ENGAGEMENTS REMPORTÉS EN UNE SAISON

Ryan O'Reilly (CAN) a gagné les mises en jeu à 1 274 reprises avec les Buffalo Sabres pendant la saison 2017-2018. Il a dépassé le record précédent de 1 268, réalisé par Rod Brind'Amour (CAN) des Carolina Hurricanes en 2005-2006. La NHL a commencé à suivre cette statistique en 1997.

le 12 mars 1935 (3 s) et ont égalé les Minnesota Wild en 2004 et les New York Islanders en 2016.

Le plus de matchs consécutifs

Le 13 janvier 2018, la série de 830 matchs consécutifs d'Andrew Cogliano (CAN) en NHL – 4e meilleure série de l'histoire – s'est achevée lorsqu'il a été suspendu pour 2 rencontres. Le record

appartient toujours à Doug Jarvis (CAN) et ses 964 matchs consécutifs pour Montréal (CAN), les Washington Capitals et les Hartford Whalers, du 8 octobre 1975 au 10 octobre 1987.

Le plus de buts en prolongation en saison régulière (carrière)

Alex Ovechkin (RUS, voir ci-dessous) a inscrit son 22e but en prolongation pour les Washington Capitals, tombeurs 5-4 des Carolina Hurricanes, le 2 janvier 2018.

LE PLUS DE TIRS BLOQUÉS EN CARRIÈRE

Au 8 janvier 2019, Dan Girardi (CAN) avait bloqué ou dévié 1 873 tirs pour les New York Rangers et Tampa Bay Lightning depuis la saison 2006-2007. Le défenseur a donné de sa personne tout au long de sa carrière avec un record de 236 tirs bloqués en une saison, en 2010-2011. La NHL a commencé à suivre cette statistique en 1998.

TROPHÉES NHL – LES PLUS TITRÉS

TROPHÉE	DÉCERNÉ POUR	JOUEUR*	VICTOIRES
Art Ross	Le plus de points en saison régulière	Wayne Gretzky	10
Hart Memorial	Le plus d'hommes du match	Wayne Gretzky	9
Lady Byng	Le plus fair-play	Frank Boucher	7
Vezina	Le meilleur gardien	Jacques Plante	7
Jack Adams	Le meilleur apport pour un entraîneur	Pat Burns	3
Conn Smythe	Le plus d'hommes du match en Stanley Cup	Patrick Roy	3

Tous les joueurs sont canadiens.

LE PLUS DE PRIX MAURICE RICHARD

Créé en 1999, le trophée Maurice Richard est attribué chaque année au meilleur buteur de NHL. En 2018, Alex Ovechkin (RUS, à droite) des Washington Capitals a décroché son 7e titre après une saison à 49 buts. C'était son 5e succès en 6 saisons, soit **le plus de saisons comme meilleur buteur de NHL**, à égalité avec Bobby Hull.

NOV. 8 **Le plus grand rosier** – cultivé, forcément, par Christopher Rose (USA) – est mesuré à 5,68 m, à La Puente (Californie, USA), en 2017.

NOV. 9 En 2007, Trever McGhee (CAN) parcourt **la plus longue distance sur du feu** (181,9 m). Il a marché sur des braises d'une température de 853,3 °C, à Calgary (CAN).

FOOTBALL

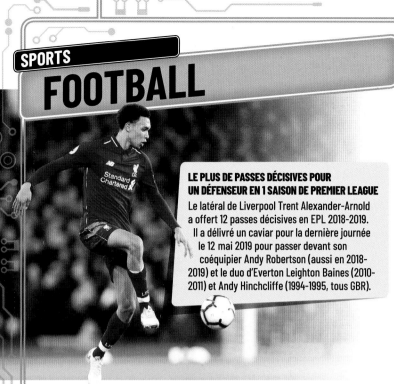

LE PLUS DE PASSES DÉCISIVES POUR UN DÉFENSEUR EN 1 SAISON DE PREMIER LEAGUE

Le latéral de Liverpool Trent Alexander-Arnold a offert 12 passes décisives en EPL 2018-2019. Il a délivré un caviar pour la dernière journée le 12 mai 2019 pour passer devant son coéquipier Andy Robertson (aussi en 2018-2019) et le duo d'Everton Leighton Baines (2010-2011) et Andy Hinchcliffe (1994-1995, tous GBR).

Le plus jeune à remporter la Premier League anglaise (EPL)

Phil Foden (GBR, né le 28 mai 2000) a été sacré avec Manchester City à 17 ans et 350 jours à la fin de la saison 2017-2018. Il a disputé son 5e match de la saison contre Southampton le 13 mai pour être officiellement considéré comme champion.

Le 4 mai 2019, Harvey Elliott (GBR, né le 4 avril 2003) est devenu **le plus jeune joueur d'EPL** en entrant en jeu à 16 ans et 30 jours pour Fulham contre Wolverhampton Wanderers.

Le but le plus rapide en EPL

Le 23 avril 2019, le buteur irlandais de Southampton Shane Long a marqué après 7,69 s de jeu contre Watford, à Vicarage Road (Watford, GBR). C'était le but le plus rapide de l'ère Premier League, devant celui de Ledley King, inscrit en 9,82 s pour Tottenham contre Bradford le 9 décembre 2000.

Le plus de matchs consécutifs à marquer en Serie A (même saison)

Le 26 janvier 2019, l'attaquant de la Sampdoria Fabio Quagliarella (ITA) a inscrit un doublé contre l'Udinese, son 11e match de suite à trouver les filets. Il égale la prouesse de Gabriel Batistuta (ARG) avec la Fiorentina, entre le 4 septembre et le 27 novembre 1994.

Le plus jeune auteur d'un triplé en UEFA Europa League

Le 11 avril 2019, João Félix (PRT, né le 10 novembre 1999) a réussi le coup du chapeau pour Benfica contre l'Eintracht Francfort, à 19 ans et 152 jours, à l'Estádio da Luz de Lisbonne (PRT).

Le plus jeune buteur en Europa League (hors qualifications) est Romelu Lukaku (BEL, né le 13 mai 1993), à 16 ans et 218 jours, le 17 décembre 2009 pour Anderlecht.

La meilleure buteuse en saison régulière de National Women's Soccer League

Samantha Kerr (AUS) a inscrit 63 buts en championnat américain féminin, du 20 avril 2013 au 12 mai 2019, pour 3 clubs différents.

En Australie, Kerr est aussi **la meilleure buteuse en W-League** (70), pour Perth Glory et Sydney FC, entre le 7 décembre 2008 et le 16 février 2019.

Le meilleur buteur en une saison de Major League Soccer (MLS)

Josef Martínez (VEN) a totalisé 28 buts pour l'Atlanta United pendant la saison 2018 de MLS. Du 30 juin au 24 août, il a aussi enchaîné **le plus de matchs de MLS à marquer** (9), autant que Diego Valeri (ARG) du 29 juillet au 24 septembre 2017.

LE PLUS JEUNE JOUEUR NOMMÉ AU BALLON D'OR

Kylian Mbappé (FRA, né le 20 décembre 1998) a été sélectionné pour le Ballon d'Or *France Football* à 18 ans et 293 jours, le 9 octobre 2017. Mbappé a remporté la coupe du monde avec la France en 2018 et est devenu le 2e adolescent à marquer en finale après Pelé (BRA), **le plus jeune buteur en coupe du monde FIFA**, à 17 ans et 249 jours, le 19 juin 1958.

LE CLUB LE PLUS TITRÉ EN COUPE EUROPÉENNE/UEFA CHAMPIONS LEAGUE

Le 26 mai 2018, le Real Madrid (ESP) a décroché son 13e titre en C1 – le 3e de suite – en battant Liverpool 3-1, au Stade olympique de Kiev (UKR). Les Espagnols ont gagné 6 fois la coupe des clubs champions européens entre 1956 et 1966, avec 5 titres consécutifs, et ont remporté la Ligue des champions 7 fois depuis 1998.

LE PLUS DE TRIPLÉS EN EPL

Sergio Agüero (ARG) a signé son 11e triplé en Premier League pour Manchester City lors de la victoire 6-0 contre Chelsea le 10 février 2019. Le buteur argentin a égalé le record d'Alan Shearer (GBR), auteur de 11 coups du chapeau pour Blackburn Rovers et Newcastle United, du 23 novembre 1993 au 19 septembre 1999. Agüero détient toutefois **le plus de triplés en EPL pour un même club**.

LE MEILLEUR BUTEUR EN UNE ÉDITION DE COUPE D'ASIE

Almoez Ali a marqué 9 buts avec le Qatar lors de la coupe d'Asie des nations 2019. Le Soudanais a fait mieux qu'Ali Daei et ses 8 buts en 1996 avec un splendide retourné (photo) en finale contre le Japon, battu 3-1 par le Qatar. Ali a signé un quadruplé contre la Corée du Nord le 13 janvier, **le plus de buts en un match de coupe d'Asie (joueur)**, avec 4 autres joueurs.

NOV. 10 En 2000, Rob Williams (USA) est **le plus rapide à préparer un sandwich avec les pieds**. Il y a mis du saucisson, du fromage et de la salade, et l'a servi avec des olives sur des cure-dents, en 1 min et 57 s.

NOV. 11 Pour fêter le GWR Day 2009, Toufic Daher (LBN) construit **la plus grande maquette en allumettes** : une réplique de la tour Eiffel de 6,53 m de haut. Elle est dévoilée au City Mall de Beyrouth (LBN).

LE MEILLEUR BUTEUR EN LIGA

Au 12 mai 2019, le meneur du FC Barcelone Lionel Messi (ARG) avait inscrit 417 buts en 451 matchs dans le championnat espagnol, soit un taux de 0,92 but par match.

Le 18 septembre 2018, Messi a amélioré son record du **plus de triplés en UEFA Champions League** (8), égalé le 12 mars 2019 par Cristiano Ronaldo.

Le meilleur buteur étranger en Bundesliga

Le record de buts inscrits en Bundesliga par un joueur non allemand est de 202, par Robert Lewandowski (POL), avec le Borussia Dortmund et le Bayern Munich, entre le 19 septembre 2010 et le 4 mai 2019. Lewandowski a surpassé son ancien coéquipier, Claudio Pizarro (PER), avec un doublé le 9 mars 2019. Le 4 mai 2019, Pizarro (né le 3 octobre 1978) a inscrit son 196e but à 40 ans et 213 jours, il est **le plus vieux buteur de Bundesliga**.

Le plus jeune entraîneur en UEFA Champions League

Julian Nagelsmann (DEU, né le 23 juillet 1987) était sur le banc du TSG 1899 Hoffenheim à 31 ans et 58 jours, lors du match contre le Shakhtar Donetsk, le 19 septembre 2018.

Le club le plus titré en UEFA Women's Champions League

L'Olympique Lyonnais Féminin (FRA) a remporté l'UEFA Women's Champions League 5 fois : en 2011, 2012 et 2016-2018. L'OL a obtenu son 5e sacre le 24 mai 2018 en battant le VfL Wolfsburg 4-1 après prolongation, à Kiev (UKR).

Avec 41 buts, Hegerberg s'approche du **plus de buts en UEFA Women's Champions League** (51), par Anja Mittag (DEU).

LA 1RE BALLON D'OR FÉMININE

Récompensant le meilleur joueur de l'année, le Ballon d'Or *France Football* est décerné aux joueurs masculins depuis 1956. Le 3 décembre 2018, le premier Ballon d'Or féminin a été remis à Ada Hegerberg (NOR, en haut à droite). L'attaquante de l'Olympique Lyonnais est **la meilleure buteuse en 1 saison d'UEFA Women's Champions League** (15), en 2017-2018.

FIFA WORLD CUP 2018

COUPE DU MONDE DE LA FIFA 2018

La coupe du monde de la FIFA 2018, organisée en Russie du 14 juin au 15 juillet, a vu la France décrocher sa 2e étoile en battant la Croatie 4-2 en finale. Les Bleus ne sont pas les seuls à avoir fait vibrer le public.

Avant même le début de la compétition, l'Islande était entrée dans l'histoire en devenant **la plus petite nation (nombre d'habitants) qualifiée à la coupe du monde** (337 669 habitants). C'est presque 1 million de moins que le record précédent détenu par Trinité-et-Tobago, en 2006.

Sur la touche, Óscar Tabárez (URY) a égalé **le plus de participations à la Coupe du monde comme entraîneur de la même sélection** (4), comme Walter Winterbottom (GBR) avec l'Angleterre en 1950-1962 et Helmut Schön (DEU) avec la RFA en 1966-1978. L'arbitre Ravshan Irmatov (UZB) a arbitré **le plus de matchs de coupe du monde** avec sa 10e rencontre, la victoire de la Croatie 3-0 contre l'Argentine, le 21 juin.

LE PLUS DE COUPES DU MONDE À MARQUER

Cristiano Ronaldo (PRT) a rejoint un club très fermé en inscrivant un but dans sa 4e phase finale de coupe du monde, comme Miroslav Klose (DEU), Uwe Seeler (RFA) et Pelé (BRA).

Le 15 juin, Ronaldo (né le 5 février 1985) est devenu **le joueur le plus âgé à inscrire un triplé en coupe du monde**, lors du nul 3-3 contre l'Espagne, à 33 ans et 130 jours.

Les joueurs sont aussi entrés au chapitre des records. Le 17 juin, Rafael Márquez disputait **le plus de coupes du monde comme capitaine** pour sa 5e phase finale avec le Mexique depuis 2002. Le 24 juin, Felipe Baloy (PAN) est devenu **le joueur le plus âgé à marquer pour ses débuts en coupe du monde**, à 37 ans et 120 jours, lors de la défaite 6-1 contre l'Angleterre. (**Le joueur le plus âgé à marquer en coupe du monde** reste le Camerounais Roger Milla, à 42 ans et 39 jours, face à la Russie, le 28 juin 1994.)

Le Brésil n'a pas répondu aux attentes en Russie en étant éliminé dès les quarts par la Belgique (2-1), mais a toutefois amélioré son record du **plus de matchs de coupe du monde remportés par une équipe** (73 depuis 1930). Son record du **plus de titres en coupe du monde** (5) n'est pas menacé.

Autre record notable battu en 2018, même si les joueurs concernés s'en seraient passés : **le plus de buts contre son camp marqués en une coupe du monde** (12).

LE JOUEUR LE PLUS ÂGÉ EN COUPE DU MONDE

Le gardien Essam El-Hadary (EGY, né le 15 janvier 1973) a joué contre l'Arabie saoudite à 45 ans et 161 jours, le 25 juin 2018. L'Égypte était déjà éliminée de la compétition, mais El-Hadary a tenu son rang et fêté son record en arrêtant un penalty en 1re période.

 NOV. 12 Lars Clausen (USA) termine **le voyage le plus long en monocycle**, en 2002, à Los Angeles (Californie, USA). Il a parcouru 14 686,82 km pour traverser 2 fois les États-Unis.

 NOV. 13 En 2010, Dominic Cuzzacrea (USA) réussit **le lancer de pancake le plus haut**, avec un saut de 9,47 m, au centre commercial Walden Galleria de Cheektowaga (New York, USA).

221

RUGBY

à Twickenham (GBR), le 16 mars 2019. Les Anglaises ont marqué 45 essais et 278 pts pendant cette édition.

Le plus d'essais en Top 14 (joueur)
Vincent Clerc (FRA) a terminé sa carrière professionnelle en grande pompe en battant le record de Laurent Arbo et de ses 100 essais dans le championnat de France de rugby. Clerc a aplati pour la 101e fois en Top 14 dans son dernier match, lors du succès 38-26 du RC Toulon contre Pau, le 5 mai 2018.

Le plus d'essais inscrits en une saison de Top 14 est de 24, par Chris Ashton (GBR) pour le RC Toulon en 2017/2018.

Le plus d'essais en 1 saison de Super Rugby (joueur)
Ben Lam (NZ) a inscrit 16 essais pour les Hurricanes en Super Rugby 2018. Il a décroché le record à la dernière seconde en aplatissant à la 80e min, en demi-finale face aux Crusaders, le 28 juillet.

Le plus de matchs en Super Rugby
Prop Wyatt Crockett (NZ) a joué 202 matchs de Super Rugby avec les Crusaders de 2006 à 2018. Il a joué son dernier contre les Sharks, le 21 juillet 2018.

LE PLUS DE TITRES EN HEINEKEN CUP CHAMPIONS CUP DE RUGBY (CLUB)
Les Irlandais du Leinster ont décroché leur 4e titre européen lors d'un succès à l'arraché 15-12 contre le Racing 92, le 12 mai 2018, après leurs triomphes en 2009, 2011 et 2012. Ils égalent le record du Stade Toulousain (FRA), champion en 1996, 2003, 2005 et 2010. Les Français ont aussi été finalistes en 2004 et 2008.

Deux semaines plus tard, les Crusaders ont décroché leur 9e sacre - **le plus de titres en Super Rugby**. L'équipe de Christchurch a battu les Lions 37-18, le 4 août 2018.

Le plus de matchs de Rugby Championship gagnés
La Nouvelle-Zélande a gagné 35 de ses 39 matchs dans le tournoi international de l'hémisphère Sud du 18 août 2012 au 6 octobre 2018.

Le plus de points en carrière en National Rugby League (joueur)
Lors de la victoire 18-12 des Melbourne Storm contre les North Queensland Cowboys, le 12 avril 2019, Cameron Smith (AUS) a dépassé Hazem El Masri (LBN) pour devenir le meilleur marqueur de NRL avec 2 422 pts. Il a aussi porté son **record de matchs joués en NRL** à 389.

LE PLUS DE PARTICIPATIONS AU TOURNOI DES 5/6 NATIONS
Sergio Parisse a disputé 69 rencontres pour l'Italie dans le tournoi des 5/6 Nations entre le 15 février 2004 et le 16 mars 2019. Il a battu le record de Brian O'Driscoll (IRL), lors de son 66e match, face à l'Écosse, le 2 février 2019. Parisse n'est sorti victorieux que de 9 de ces rencontres, contre 45 pour O'Driscoll.

Le plus de Grands Chelems aux Six Nations
Le 1er tournoi des Six Nations s'est déroulé en 2000, quand l'Italie a rejoint l'Angleterre, l'Irlande, l'Écosse, le pays de Galles et la France. Le 16 mars 2019, les Gallois ont décroché leur 4e Grand Chelem en battant l'Irlande 25-7, au Millennium Stadium de Cardiff (GBR).

Le plus de titres aux Six Nations (femmes)
L'Angleterre a été sacrée 10 fois dans le tournoi féminin - dont 9 Grands Chelems - avec une victoire totale 80-0 contre l'Écosse

LE PLUS DE TITRES EN WORLD CLUB CHALLENGE
Le 17 février 2019, les Sydney Roosters (AUS) ont battu les Wigan Warriors (GBR) 20-8 pour s'adjuger un 4e titre, comme Wigan, au World Club Challenge. Pour ses débuts à Sydney, Brett Morris (AUS, photo) a inscrit **le plus d'essais en 1 match du World Club Challenge** (3), comme Michael Jennings (AUS) des Roosters en 2014 et Joe Burgess (GBR) de Wigan en 2017.

LE PLUS DE FRANCHISSEMENTS DE LIGNE EN WORLD RUGBY SEVENS SERIES
Au 16 avril 2019, Perry Baker (USA) avait franchi 235 fois les lignes défensives adverses en tournois du World Rugby Sevens Series. L'ailier supersonique est devenu l'un des joueurs les plus dangereux du rugby en inscrivant 179 essais (souvent spectaculaires) en 202 matchs. En 2018, Baker est devenu le 1er à remporter le titre de meilleur joueur du tournoi à 2 reprises.

LE PLUS DE FINALES DE PREMIERSHIP REMPORTÉES (JOUEUR)
Le demi de mêlée Richard Wigglesworth (GBR) a remporté sa 5e finale de Premiership le 26 mai 2018, lors de la victoire des Saracens 27-10 contre les Exeter Chiefs. Il avait déjà été titré en 2011, 2015 et 2016, ainsi qu'en 2006, avec les Sale Sharks.
Le 23 septembre 2018, Wigglesworth est aussi devenu **le joueur comptant le plus d'apparitions en Premiership**. Il avait disputé 237 matchs au 7 mars 2019.

WORLD SEVENS SERIES			
LE PLUS DE...	NOM	PAYS	TOTAL
Matchs (hommes)	D. J. Forbes	Nouvelle-Zélande	512
Essais (hommes)	Dan Norton	Angleterre	332
Points (hommes)	Ben Gollings	Angleterre	2 652
Matchs (femmes)	Sarah Hirini	Nouvelle-Zélande	183
Essais (femmes)	Portia Woodman	Nouvelle-Zélande	195
Points (femmes)	Ghislaine Landry	Canada	1 090

Statistiques au 16 avril 2019

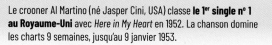

NOV. 14 Le crooner Al Martino (né Jasper Cini, USA) classe **le 1er single n° 1 au Royaume-Uni** avec *Here in My Heart* en 1952. La chanson domine les charts 9 semaines, jusqu'au 9 janvier 1953.

NOV. 15 En 2012, le présentateur météo Steve Jacobs (AUS) se prépare à une vague de froid en récupérant son record du **plus de sous-vêtements enfilés** (266), à Sydney (Nouvelle-Galles du Sud, AUS).

TENNIS

au tour principal d'un Grand Chelem. Les joueurs risquent une pénalité s'ils ne servent pas avant la fin de ces 25 s.

La demi-finale de Grand Chelem la plus longue

Kevin Anderson (ZAF) et John Isner (USA) se sont livrés à un marathon sur le central pendant 6 h et 36 min, en demi-finale de Wimbledon, à Londres (GBR), le 13 juillet 2018. Anderson l'a finalement emporté 7-6, 6-7, 6-7, 6-4, 26-24. Le 5e set a duré à lui seul 2 h et 54 min.

LA 1RE JOUEUSE DES ANNÉES 2000 CHAMPIONNE WTA

Le 29 juillet 2018, Olga Danilović (SRB, née le 23 janvier 2001) a remporté la Moscow River Cup en Russie (RUS) contre Anastasia Potapova, à l'âge de 17 ans et 187 jours. Elle est la 1re joueuse née au XXIe siècle à remporter un tournoi WTA, et la 1re "lucky loser" à remporter un titre en simple en WTA, après avoir été repêchée malgré sa défaite en qualifications.

LE PLUS DE VICTOIRES D'UN GRAND CHELEM EN SIMPLE (ÈRE OPEN)

Le maître de l'ocre Rafael Nadal (ESP) a été sacré pour la 12e fois à Roland Garros le 9 juin 2019 en battant Dominic Thiem (AUT) 6-3, 5-7, 6-1, 6-1, à Paris (FRA).

Nadal avait déjà gagné la finale de l'Open de France en 2005-2008, 2010-2014 et 2017-2018.

Cette victoire en Grand Chelem – sa 18e en date – a permis à Nadal d'obtenir le record **du plus de titres en simple sur terre battue** - 59.

Le plus de matchs gagnés en Grand Chelem en simple

Au 18 janvier 2019, Roger Federer (CHE) avait gagné 342 matchs entre Wimbledon, l'Open d'Australie, Roland Garros et l'US Open. Serena Williams (USA) détient **le record féminin** avec 335 victoires sur les 4 tournois au 21 janvier 2019.

Le 1er joueur de simple à remporter le Master d'or

Le 19 août 2018, aux Masters de Cincinnati, Novak Djokovic (SRB, voir ci-dessous) avait remporté dans sa carrière les 9 Masters 1 000 de l'ATP (Association of Tennis Professionals). Les autres sont Indian Wells, Miami, Monte-Carlo, Madrid, Rome, Montréal/Toronto, Shanghai et Paris.

Djokovic totalise **le plus de gains en carrière en tennis (hommes)** avec 129 000 709 $ depuis 2003.

Le plus de titres en simple en Masters 1 000 en carrière est de 33, par le rival du "Djoker", Rafael Nadal (voir en haut à gauche).

Le plus de Grands Chelems en simple joués à la suite

À l'Open d'Australie 2019, Feliciano López (ESP) avait disputé 68 tournois du Grand Chelem consécutifs depuis 2002. Il a atteint 4 fois les quarts de finale : à Wimbledon en 2005, 2008 et 2011, ainsi qu'à l'US Open en 2015.

Le 1er Grand Chelem à adopter le shot clock au tour principal

À l'US Open 2018 de New York (27 août-9 septembre), une horloge de 25 s était utilisée pour la 1re fois

LE PLUS DE TITRES DU GRAND CHELEM EN FAUTEUIL (HOMMES)

Shingo Kunieda (JPN) a remporté 22 titres en simple : 9 fois l'Open d'Australie (2007-2011, 2013-2015, 2018), 7 fois Roland Garros (2007-2010, 2014-2015, 2018) et 6 fois l'US Open (2007, 2009-2011, 2014-2015). Kunieda a aussi gagné 20 titres en double, dont 8 en Australie (2007-2011, 2013-2015).

LE PLUS DE TITRES À L'OPEN D'AUSTRALIE EN SIMPLE (HOMME)

Le 27 janvier 2019, Novak Djokovic (SRB) a décroché sa 7e couronne sur les courts de Melbourne (AUS), plus que quiconque en 114 ans d'existence du tournoi, après son succès 6-3, 6-2, 6-3 contre Rafael Nadal (ESP). Djokovic s'était déjà imposé à l'Open d'Australie en 2008, 2011-2013 et 2015-2016.

L'ASCENSION LA PLUS RAPIDE DU TOP 10 À LA 1RE PLACE

Naomi Osaka (JPN) n'a eu besoin que de 138 jours pour se hisser au sommet du classement WTA (Women's Tennis Association) après son entrée dans le Top 10, le 10 septembre 2018. Ses titres à l'US Open, le 8 septembre 2018 et à l'Open d'Australie 2019 l'ont propulsée à la 1re place du classement le 26 janvier 2019.

Djokovic a remporté l'Open d'Australie 2012 après la **finale la plus longue en Grand Chelem** – 5 h et 53 min, face à Nadal.

 NOV. 16   En 2010, Magnus Andersson (SWE) fait valider **la plus grande collection de timbres de papes** avec 1 580 timbres, à la bibliothèque publique de Falun (SWE).

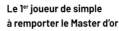 NOV. 17   Art Arfons (USA) ressort de **l'accident de voiture le plus rapide avec survivant** en 1966, quand son véhicule à réacteur s'écrase à 981 km/h, à Bonneville Salt Flats dans l'Utah (USA).

223

SPORTS DE BALLE

La finale de championnat du monde de softball féminin la plus prolifique

Le 12 août 2018, les États-Unis ont vaincu le Japon 7-6 en finale du championnat du monde de softball féminin au ZOZO Marine Stadium de la préfecture de Chiba (JPN). Menées 6-4 à la 10ᵉ manche, elles ont arraché la victoire avec un home-run. C'était la 7ᵉ fois de suite que ces deux nations s'affrontaient en finale.

Les États-Unis comptent désormais 11 sacres – **le plus de titres au championnat du monde de softball féminin**.

Le plus de titres au championnat du monde de la Fédération internationale de Lacrosse (FIL)

L'équipe américaine de Lacrosse a été couronnée à 10 reprises : en 1967, 1974, 1982, 1986, 1990, 1994, 1998, 2002, 2010 et 2018. Elle a obtenu sa dernière victoire avec un succès de justesse de 9-8 contre le Canada, à Netanya (ISR), le 21 juillet 2018.

Le plus de titres au championnat du monde de Lacrosse en salle est de 4, par le Canada en 2003, 2007, 2011 et 2015. Les Canadiens ont remporté toutes les éditions et n'ont jamais perdu un match.

Le plus d'arrêts en saison régulière de Super Netball (joueuse)

La gardienne Geva Mentor (GBR) a terminé la saison 2018 de Super Netball avec 102 arrêts avec les Sunshine Coast Lightning (AUS).

LE PLUS DE BUTS MARQUÉS EN UNE SAISON DE SUPER NETBALL

Jhaniele Fowler (JAM) a réussi ses débuts en Super Netball avec 783 buts pour le West Coast Fever (AUS) en 2018. Elle en a aussi le plus tenté avec 846 tirs, soit un taux de réussite de 92 %.

Aux tours 1 et 8 de la saison, Fowler a inscrit **le plus de buts en un match de Super Netball** (66), chaque fois contre les Adelaide Thunderbirds.

LE 1ᵉʳ TRIPLE CHAMPION D'UNE ÉPREUVE DU TOUR MONDIAL ITTF

Jang Woo-jin (KOR) s'est imposé en individuel, double et double mixte, à l'Open Platinum de Corée comptant pour le Tour mondial de la Fédération internationale de tennis de table (ITTF), à Daejeon (KOR), les 19-22 juillet 2018. Son titre avec Cha Hyo-sim (PRK) était le premier pour une équipe de Corée unifiée sur le tour mondial.

Elle a battu son propre record de 90 arrêts datant de 2017. Mentor a guidé son club à 2 titres de suite avant de s'engager avec les Collingwood Magpies en septembre 2018.

Le plus de titres au championnat du monde masculin de tennis de table

Le 6 mai 2018, la Chine a soulevé sa 21ᵉ coupe Swaythling, le trophée décerné à l'équipe masculine victorieuse du Mondial de tennis de table. La Chine a battu l'Allemagne 3-0 lors de la finale à Halmstad (SWE).

La veille, la Chine avait aussi remporté **le titre féminin** pour la 21ᵉ fois en s'adjugeant la coupe Corbillon avec une victoire 3-1 contre le Japon.

LA PLUS JEUNE MÉDAILLÉE D'OR EN FINALE DU WORLD TOUR DE BEACH-VOLLEY

Le 19 août 2018, Eduarda "Duda" Santos Lisboa (BRA, née le 1ᵉʳ août 1998, en haut à droite) a décroché l'or à 20 ans et 18 jours, en finale du World Tour de beach volley-ball de la Fédération internationale de volley-ball (FIVB). Avec Ágatha Bednarczuk (en haut à gauche), elles sont venues à bout de la paire tchèque 21-15, 21-19, à Hambourg (DEU).

LE PLUS DE VICTOIRES EN COUPE DU MONDE FÉMININE DE HOCKEY

Le 5 août 2018, les Pays-Bas ont obtenu leur 8ᵉ titre mondial de la Fédération internationale de hockey (FIH) depuis 1974 avec une victoire 6-0 contre l'Irlande, à Londres (GBR). Les Néerlandaises ont marqué 4 buts en 7 min pour obtenir **l'écart de points le plus large en finale de coupe du monde féminine de hockey**.

Le 29 juillet 2018, les Pays-Bas ont battu l'Italie 12-1 – **l'écart de points le plus large en coupe du monde féminine de hockey**.

Le plus de buts inscrits au Final Four de Ligue des champions de handball

Organisé à la Lanxess Arena de Cologne (DEU), le Final Four de la Ligue des champions de la Fédération européenne de handball comprend les demi-finales et la finale de la compétition. Kiril Lazarov (MKD) y a inscrit 14 buts en 2 matchs pour le HBC Nantes (FRA) en 2017-2018 et totalise 65 buts depuis 2011.

L'arrière droit a également inscrit **le plus de buts en Ligue des champions EHF** : 1 299 au 26 mars 2019. Sa 1ʳᵉ participation remonte à 1998 et il a joué pour 7 clubs différents.

Le plus de buts en Ligue des champions féminine de handball

Au 26 mars 2019, Anita Görbicz (HUN) a marqué 939 buts en Ligue des champions féminine EHF. Elle a trouvé les filets 70 fois en 2017-2018 pour décrocher un 4ᵉ titre avec le club hongrois Győri Audi ETO KC.

NOV. 18 En 2010, Christian Schäfer (DEU) donne un nouveau sens au "transport aérien" en devenant **le plus rapide à souffler un timbre sur un mile** – en 1 h 57 min et 38 s –, à Netphen (DEU).

NOV. 19 La monocycliste professionnelle Satomi Sakaino (JPN) réussit **le plus de rotations sur un monocycle en 1 min** – 131, plus de 2 par seconde – sur le plateau de *Kinsma*, à Tokyo (JPN), en 2011.

CRICKET

LE PLUS DE TITRES EN CHAMPIONNAT INDIEN (IPL)

Les Chennai Super Kings ont décroché leur 3e titre d'IPL avec une victoire par 8 guichets d'avance sur les Sunrisers Hyderabad, au stade Wankhede de Mumbai, le 27 mai 2018. C'est autant que les Mumbain Indians, champions en 2013, 2015 et 2017. Chennai s'était déjà imposé en 2010 et 2011 et a été 4 fois 2e (2008, 2012-2013, 2015).

Le plus de test-matchs consécutifs disputés

Alastair Cook (GBR) a joué 159 matchs de Test cricket à la suite du 11 mai 2006 au 7 septembre 2018. Au fil de ses 161 matchs internationaux, il n'a raté qu'une seule rencontre, contre l'Inde en mars 2006, en raison de maux d'estomac. Cook a annoncé sa retraite en 2018 après 12 472 courses – **le plus de points en test marqués par un batteur gaucher**. Il a frappé 11 845 courses en tant que n° 1 ou n° 2 – **le plus de courses inscrites par un premier batteur**.

Le plus de balles frappées en Test-match sans une faute

Au 15 février 2019, Ravichandran Ashwin (IND) avait tapé 18 372 balles (3 062 séries) en Test cricket sans commettre une seule faute. Le joueur polyvalent a pris 342 guichets en 65 matchs avec une moyenne de 25,43 courses par guichet.

L'écart de points le plus important en un One Day International (ODI)

L'équipe féminine de Nouvelle-Zélande s'est imposée 491-4 contre l'Irlande, au YMCA Cricket Club de Dublin (IRL), le 8 juin 2018. C'est 10 courses de plus que **l'écart de points le plus important en ODI (hommes)** – 481-6 pour l'Angleterre contre l'Australie, le 19 juin 2018.

Le plus rapide à atteindre 10 000 courses en ODI

Virat Kohli (IND) a eu besoin de 205 manches pour franchir les 10 000 courses en ODI, grâce à son 37e century contre les Indes occidentales, le 24 octobre 2018. Kohli a réussi une année remarquable en remportant les prix de meilleur joueur de l'année en Test et ODI de l'International Cricket Council (ICC) et le trophée Sir Garfield Sobers de joueur de l'année, un triplé inédit.

Le plus jeune à prendre 5 guichets en un ODI

Mujeeb Ur Rahman (AFG, né le 28 mars 2001) a pris 5 guichets en ODI, à 16 ans et 325 jours, contre le Zimbabwe, à Sharjah (ARE), le 16 février 2018.

Le plus de centuries inscrits en ODI (femmes)

Meg Lanning a réussi 12 centuries en ODI pour l'Australie en 69 matchs, du 5 janvier 2011 au 22 octobre 2018. Son meilleur score est un 152 *not out*.

LE PLUS DE GUICHETS PRIS PAR UN LANCEUR RAPIDE EN TEST

Le 11 septembre 2018, James Anderson (GBR) a surpassé Glenn McGrath (AUS) en prenant le 564e guichet de sa carrière en test à la dernière balle contre l'Inde, à The Oval de Londres (GBR). Anderson est le 4e meilleur marqueur de l'histoire derrière 3 spinners. Il en était déjà à 575 guichets au 26 février 2019.

Le plus de victoires en ICC World Twenty20 (T20) féminin

L'Australie s'est adjugé l'ICC World Twenty20 féminin 4 fois : en 2010, 2012, 2014 et 2018. Les Southern Stars ont battu l'Angleterre en finale de la dernière édition à Antigua, le 24 novembre 2018.

Le plus de courses inscrites par un joueur en carrière en T20 (hommes)

Le 8 février 2019, Rohit Sharma (IND) est devenu le meilleur marqueur en T20 masculin grâce à ses 50 points contre la Nouvelle-Zélande, à l'Eden Park d'Auckland (NZL). Au 26 février 2019, il comptait 2 331 courses en carrière dans ce format.

Le plus de courses marquées par un joueur en un match de T20 (hommes) est de 172, par Aaron Finch (AUS) contre le Zimbabwe, au Harare Sports Club (ZWE), le 3 juillet 2018. Il a inscrit 16 quatre et 10 six.

Le score le plus large en un T20 (femmes)

L'équipe féminine d'Angleterre s'est imposée 250-3 contre l'Afrique du Sud au match des Tri-Nations à Taunton (GBR), le 20 juin 2018. C'est mieux que le record de la Nouvelle-Zélande de 216-1 établi plus tôt le même jour, déjà contre l'Afrique du Sud.

Le score le plus large en un T20 international est de 278-3, par l'équipe masculine afghane contre l'Irlande, le 23 février 2019.

Le score le plus faible en un T20 international

Les Mexicaines ont été éliminées avec seulement 18 courses inscrites contre le Brésil, au Los Pinos Polo Club 2 de Bogota (COL), le 24 août 2018. Seules 2 joueuses ont évité le zéro pointé dans ce match de championnat féminin d'Amérique du Sud.

LE PLUS DE GUICHETS INTERNATIONAUX PRIS PAR UN ADOLESCENT

Rashid Khan (AFG, né le 20 septembre 1998) a pris 176 guichets internationaux avant son 20e anniversaire. Le spinner a fait 110 victimes en ODI, 64 en T20 et 2 lors de son seul Test match. Waqar Younis (PAK) est le seul autre joueur à avoir dépassé les 100 guichets internationaux (125) à l'adolescence.

LA PLUS JEUNE À INSCRIRE UN DOUBLE CENTURY INTERNATIONAL

Le 8 juin 2018, Amelia Kerr (NZL, née le 13 octobre 2000) a frappé un 232 *not out*, à 17 ans et 243 jours, face à l'Irlande, au YMCA Cricket Club de Dublin (IRL). Il s'agit du **plus de courses marquées par une joueuse en One Day International (ODI)**. Kerr a notamment signé 31 quatre et 2 six.

NOV. 20 En 2011, **la plus grande collection d'extraterrestres gris** (547) est validée en Floride (USA). Elle appartient à Lisa Vanderperre-Hirsch (USA) et comprend des figurines, des masques et du papier hygiénique.

NOV. 21 En 1783, François Pilâtre de Rozier et le marquis d'Arlandes (tous 2 FRA) réalisent **le 1er vol habité en ballon**, pendant 25 min au-dessus de Paris (FRA).

SPORTS

SPORTS DE COMBAT

depuis 4 ans et 201 jours – **le plus long règne de champion du monde unifié de boxe**.

Le plus de titres individuels aux Mondiaux de l'IBJJF

Marcus Almeida (BRA) a obtenu 11 médailles d'or au championnat du monde de la Fédération internationale de jiu-jitsu brésilien, surnommé le Mundials. Il a décroché sa dernière médaille (en +100 kg extra-lourds) au Mundials 2018 de Long Beach (USA), les 31 mai–3 juin 2018.

Almeida aurait pu en ajouter une autre à sa collection, mais a décidé d'abandonner pour que son adversaire et ami Leandro Lo, souffrant d'une épaule démise, soit sacré dans la finale de la catégorie libre.

Le vainqueur le plus âgé d'une épreuve de l'IJF World Tour

Le 11 août 2018, Miklós Ungvári (HUN, né le 15 octobre 1980) s'est imposé en -73 kg à 37 ans et 300 jours au Grand Prix de Budapest (HUN) de la Fédération internationale de judo (IJF). Ungvári a battu le triple champion du monde Masashi Ebinuma (JPN) en finale.

Le plus de médailles sur l'IJF World Tour

Au 2 avril 2019, Urantsetseg Munkhbat (MNG) totalisait 34 médailles sur l'IJF World Tour depuis le 17 décembre 2010. Elle en a remporté 11 en or, 10 en argent et 13 en bronze en -48 kg et -52 kg.

Le plus de combats UFC

Le 15 décembre 2018, Jim Miller (USA) a disputé son 31e combat en Ultimate Fighting Championship (UFC). Il a été battu au premier round par

LE PLUS JEUNE CHAMPION DU MONDE DE JUDO

Aux mondiaux 2018 de judo à Bakou (AZE), Daria Bilodid (UKR, née le 10 octobre 2000, ci-dessus en bleu) est devenue championne du monde à 17 ans et 345 jours. Dans la finale féminine des -48 kg le 20 septembre, Bilodid a battu Funa Tonaki (JPN) par *ippon* avec un fauchage *ōuchi-gari* de son cru.

LE MOINS DE COMBATS POUR DÉTENIR LES 4 CEINTURES DE BOXE

Le 21 juillet 2018, Oleksandr Usyk (UKR) est devenu le premier champion du monde unifié des lourds-légers après seulement 15 combats professionnels depuis le 9 novembre 2013. Déjà détenteur des ceintures WBO et WBC, Usyk a gagné l'IBF et la WBA contre Murat Gassiev (RUS) en finale du World Boxing Super Series au complexe sportif Olimpiysky de Moscou (RUS).

Le plus de combats sans défaite pour une championne du monde de boxe

Cecilia Brækhus (NOR) a obtenu sa 35e victoire de rang sur décision unanime face à Aleksandra Magdziak Lopes (USA) au StubHub Center de Carson (USA), le 8 décembre 2018. Au 2 avril 2019, la "Première Dame" de la boxe détenait les ceintures WBO, WBC, WBA et IBF en catégorie welters

Charles Oliveira (voir ci-contre), portant son bilan à 18 victoires, 12 défaites et 1 "no contest". Miller a obtenu 17 succès en poids légers, record de la catégorie.

Le plus de victoires en UFC

est de 22, par Donald "Cowboy" Cerrone (USA) du 5 février 2011 au 19 janvier 2019.

La première combattante UFC détenant 2 titres

À l'UFC 232 du 29 décembre 2018, la championne des poids coqs Amanda Nunes (BRA) a battu Cris Cyborg (BRA) par KO en seulement 51 s pour décrocher le titre féminin des poids plumes. Elle est devenue le 3e combattant seulement

LE PLUS DE MÉDAILLES D'OR AUX MONDIAUX DE BOXE DE L'AIBA

Mary Kom (IND) a décroché 6 titres au championnat du monde féminin de l'Association internationale de boxe (AIBA) depuis 2002, soit autant que Félix Savón (CUB) en 1986-1997. Le 24 novembre 2018, Kom a battu Hanna Okhota (UKR) en finale des poids mouches (ci-dessus) pour s'emparer de sa 6e couronne devant son public, à New Delhi (IND).

LA PLUS GRANDE AUDIENCE TÉLÉ EN UFC

Environ 2,4 millions de téléspectateurs ont payé pour voir l'*UFC 229 : Khabib vs McGregor* organisé à la T-Mobile Arena de Las Vegas (USA), le 6 octobre 2018. Le combat très attendu entre Conor McGregor (IRL, à gauche) et Khabib Nurmagomedov (RUS, à droite) pour le titre UFC léger s'est soldé par la victoire du Russe sur soumission au 4e round. Toutefois, le chaos et la controverse ont entaché la fin du combat, avec une rixe violente dans et autour de l'octogone.

NOV. 22 Au marathon de Philadelphie (USA) en 2015, Noël est en avance pour Brian Lang (USA), qui court **le marathon le plus rapide déguisé en père Noël** : 2 h 54 min et 2 s.

NOV. 23 En 2007 à Cologne (DEU), Thomas Blackthorne (GBR) devient **l'avaleur de l'objet le plus lourd** (un marteau-piqueur DeWALT D25980 de 38 kg).

au 2 février 2019. Il a dépassé les 10 succès de Royce Gracie lorsqu'il a contraint Christos Giagos à abdiquer sur étranglement arrière à l'UFC Fight Night 137.

Le plus de défenses du titre en ONE Championship (femmes)

Le 18 mai 2018, Angela Lee (SGP, née CAN) a conservé son titre pour la 3e fois en poids atomes. Elle a battu sa rivale Mei Yamaguchi (JPN) sur décision unanime.

Le plus de médailles d'or pour un pays aux mondiaux d'escrime

L'Italie compte 116 médailles d'or au championnat mondial d'escrime FEI (54 en épreuves individuelles et 62 par équipe). Aux mondiaux 2018 de Wuxi (CHN), l'Italie a ajouté 4 titres à son compteur : en fleuret individuel masculin et féminin, en épée individuelle féminine et en fleuret par équipe masculine.

LE PLUS DE TITRES MONDIAUX DE TAEKWONDO PAR ÉQUIPE (HOMMES)

Le 25 septembre 2018, l'Iran a remporté son 3e titre au championnat du monde de taekwondo par équipe en battant la Russie d'un point à Fujairah (ARE). Créée en 2006, la compétition s'appelait la coupe du monde de taekwondo par équipes.

La Corée du Sud et le champion 2015, la Chine, détiennent **le plus de titres féminins (5)**.

à détenir 2 titres UFC en même temps après Conor McGregor (plumes et légers) et Daniel Cormier (USA ; mi-lourds et lourds). C'est **le plus de titres mondiaux UFC détenus simultanément dans des catégories différentes**.

La victoire de Nunes contre Cyborg était sa 10e en UFC – **le plus de victoires UFC pour une combattante**.

Le plus de victoires par soumission en UFC

Charles Oliveira (BRA) a remporté 13 combats par soumission du 1er août 2010

LE PLUS DE VICTOIRES DANS L'ÉLITE SUMO

Au 25 mars 2019, Hakuhō Shō (MNG, né Munkhbat Davaajargal) avait remporté 1 026 combats en *makuuchi*, la division d'élite des sumos. Il a décroché sa 1 000 e victoire au grand tournoi sumo d'automne 2018 face à Gōeidō le 22 septembre (ci-dessus). Hakuhō a remporté le tournoi de printemps avec un bilan parfait de 15 victoires en 15 combats. Il possède **le plus de titres dans l'élite (42)** et **le plus de titres sans défaite dans l'élite (15)**.

LE MOINS DE COMBATS POUR DEVENIR CHAMPION DU MONDE DE BOXE DANS 3 CATÉGORIES

Pour son 12e combat professionnel seulement, le 12 mai 2018, Vasyl Lomachenko (UKR) a pris la ceinture WBA des légers, alors qu'il détenait déjà les titres en plumes et super-plumes. Il a décroché ce dernier le 11 juin 2016 pour son 7e combat, soit **le moins de combats pour devenir champion du monde de boxe dans 2 catégories**.

Henry Cejudo est le 3e champion olympique à s'engager en UFC après Mark Schultz et Kevin Jackson.

LE 1ER À REMPORTER LE TITRE MONDIAL UFC ET L'OR OLYMPIQUE

Le 4 août 2018, le médaillé d'or olympique Henry Cejudo a battu Demetrious Johnson (tous 2 USA) au Championnat UFC mouches, à l'UFC 227. Cejudo a battu Johnson – qui détenait **le plus de défenses d'un titre UFC consécutives (11)** du 26 janvier 2013 au 7 octobre 2017 – sur décision partagée au Staples Center de Los Angeles (USA). Cejudo avait obtenu l'or aux JO de Pékin 2008 dans la catégorie lutte libre masculine 55 kg (encadré).

NOV. 24 En 1963, les téléspectateurs voient Lee Harvey Oswald, accusé de l'assassinat du président John F. Kennedy, se faire tuer par Jack Ruby (tous USA). C'est **le premier meurtre diffusé en direct**.

NOV. 25 Scouts Australia organise **la plus grande course en portant un partenaire sur le dos** à Pascoe Vale South (AUS), en 2012. Elle rassemble 1 274 participants.

CYCLISME

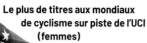

Le plus de titres aux mondiaux de cyclisme sur piste de l'UCI (femmes)

Kristina Vogel (DEU) a rejoint Anna Meares (AUS) et ses 11 médailles d'or après son titre aux sprints individuel et par équipe des mondiaux 2018 de l'UCI, à Apeldoorn (NDL). Le 26 juin 2018, Vogel a dû mettre un terme à sa carrière à la suite d'un accident tragique à l'entraînement qui l'a rendue paraplégique.

La plus longue distance en 1 h – départ arrêté sans entraîneur (femmes)

Le 13 septembre 2018, Vittoria Bussi (ITA) a parcouru 48,007 km en 60 min, à Aguascalientes (MEX). Elle a établi le nouveau record de l'heure le lendemain de sa tentative ratée qui l'avait vue abandonner après 44 min.

La poursuite individuelle 3 km la plus rapide (C4, femmes)*

Les cyclistes handisports capables d'utiliser un vélo classique sont inscrits en catégories C1-C5. Les athlètes C1 ont les mouvements les plus limités ; les C5 répondent aux critères minimaux de handicap. Aux mondiaux de paracyclisme sur piste 2019, le 16 mars, Emily Petricola (AUS) a remporté la poursuite individuelle féminine en 3 min et 43,620 s, soit 10 s

*en attente de validation par l'UCI

LA POURSUITE INDIVIDUELLE 3 KM LA PLUS RAPIDE (FEMMES)

Le 3 mars 2018, Chloé Dygert (USA) a gagné la poursuite individuelle féminine en 3 min et 20,060 s, aux mondiaux de cyclisme sur piste de l'Union cycliste internationale (UCI), à Apeldoorn (NDL). Elle a battu le record de Sarah Hammer 2 fois le même jour, après un temps de 3 min et 20,072 s en qualifications. Dygert totalise désormais 5 médailles d'or aux championnats du monde.

LE SPRINT 200 M DÉPART LANCÉ LE PLUS RAPIDE (B, FEMMES)

La cycliste malvoyante Sophie Thornhill et sa pilote Helen Scott (toutes 2 GBR) ont pris l'or en 10,891 s, aux mondiaux de paracyclisme sur piste de 2018, le 25 mars. Le duo a ensuite réussi un chrono de 10,609 s aux Jeux du Commonwealth, le 5 avril 2018 (ci-dessus), en attente de validation.

de mieux que son record précédent. Petricola souffre de sclérose en plaques.

La poursuite individuelle 4 km la plus rapide (hommes)

Le 31 août 2018, le vététiste devenu cycliste sur piste Ashton Lambie (USA) a signé un chrono de 4 min et 7,251 s en poursuite individuelle masculine aux championnats panaméricains d'Aguascalientes (MEX).

La poursuite par équipe 4 km la plus rapide (hommes)

Sam Welsford, Kelland O'Brien, Leigh Howard et Alex Porter (tous AUS) ont triomphé aux mondiaux de cyclisme sur piste de l'UCI, en 3 min et 48,012 s, le 28 février 2019.

Le plus de participations au Tour de France

En 2018, Sylvain Chavanel (FRA)

a couru son 18e Tour de France à 39 ans, terminant 39e au général. Chavanel, qui avait roulé pour son premier Tour en 2001, a terminé toutes les éditions, sauf en 2007 et 2012, soit autant que Hendrik "Joop" Zoetemelk (NDL, 16) en 1970-1973 et 1975-1986 : **le plus de Tour de France terminés.**

Le plus de titres en descente en coupe du monde de VTT (femmes)

La vététiste Rachel Atherton (GBR) a remporté la coupe du monde de l'UCI 6 fois : en 2008, 2012-2013, 2015-2016 et 2018.

Le plus de titres en coupe du monde de cyclo-cross (femmes)

Le 28 janvier 2018, Sanne Cant (BEL) a décroché sa 3e victoire en cyclo-cross, à Hoogerheide (NDL). Elle fait aussi bien que Daphny van den Brand (NLD) en 2005-2006, 2009-2010 et 2011-2012.

Peter Sagan a aussi décroché le plus de victoires d'étape au Tour de Suisse – 16, de 2011 à 2018.

LE PLUS DE MAILLOTS VERTS AU TOUR DE FRANCE

Peter Sagan (SVK) a remporté le classement par points du Tour de France pour la 6e fois en 2018, soit autant qu'Erik Zabel (DEU) en 1996-2001. Instaurés en 1953, les points sont décernés aux coureurs selon leur classement à chaque étape, avec des bonus pour les sprints intermédiaires. Le leader du classement porte traditionnellement un maillot vert.

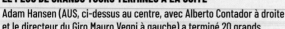

LE PLUS DE GRANDS TOURS TERMINÉS À LA SUITE

Adam Hansen (AUS, ci-dessus au centre, avec Alberto Contador à droite et le directeur du Giro Mauro Vegni à gauche) a terminé 20 grands tours consécutifs – soit le Tour de France, le Giro en Italie et la Vuelta en Espagne –, du 11 septembre 2011 au 27 mai 2018. Son incroyable série d'endurance s'est achevée au Giro 2018, quand il a annoncé qu'il ne prendrait pas part au Tour de France cette année-là.

NOV. 26 Le Dr Vijaypat Singhania (IND) dirige **le vol de montgolfière le plus haut**, à 21 027 m d'altitude, dans un ballon Cameron Z-1600, au-dessus de Mumbai (IND), en 2005.

NOV. 27 En 2014, Norbert Selmaj, alias Norberto Loco (POL), termine **le plus long marathon de DJ**, après 200 h derrière les platines de l'Underground Temple Bar, à Dublin (IRL).

SPORTS MÉCANIQUES

LA 1ʳᵉ CHAMPIONNE DU MONDE DE MOTO

Ana Carrasco (ESP) a remporté le Supersport 300 de la Fédération internationale de motocyclisme (FIM) avec une 13ᵉ place lors de la dernière course, le 30 septembre 2018, pour remporter le titre d'un point. Elle s'est imposée à Imola (ITA) et à Donington Park (Leicestershire, GBR) pour totaliser 93 points.

Le plus de courses gagnées au championnat du monde de Superbike

Jonathan Rea (GBR) a réussi une nouvelle saison record en Superbike avec une 71ᵉ victoire au Qatar, le 26 octobre 2018. Il avait dépassé les 59 succès de Carl Fogarty, qui tenaient depuis 1999, à l'Automotodrom Brno (CZE), le 9 juin 2018.

Rea a décroché le Mondial 2018 avec un record de 11 victoires consécutives. Au passage, il a égalé le record de Fogarty du **plus de titres au championnat du monde de Superbike** (4), mais Rea les a tous remportés à la suite (2015-2018).

Le plus jeune pilote à gagner un Grand prix moto

Le 18 novembre 2018, le pilote de Moto3 Can Öncü (TUR, né le 26 juillet 2003) a passé le drapeau à damiers à 15 ans et 115 jours, au Grand prix d'Espagne, à Valence. Pour sa première course, Öncü est parti de la 4ᵉ place et a remporté une course spectaculaire où plusieurs pilotes ont glissé sur la piste humide du Ricardo Tormo.

La vitesse la plus élevée dans une course de dragsters moto Pro Stock NHRA

Le 11 novembre 2018, Matt Smith (USA) a été flashé à 323,83 km/h en finale de l'Auto Club NHRA, à l'Auto Club Raceway de Pomona (Californie, USA). Smith a décroché son 3ᵉ titre mondial en Pro Stock Moto de la National Hot Rod Association grâce à ce succès face à Eddie Krawiec au dernier tour.

La vitesse la plus élevée dans une course de dragsters Top Fuel (1 000 pieds)

Tony Schumacher (USA) a atteint 541,65 km/h, à l'Arizona Nationals de la NHRA, le 23 février 2018, à Chandler (Arizona, USA).

Le plus de courses gagnées en Truck Series de NASCAR

Le 26 mars 2019, Kyle Busch (USA) comptait 54 victoires en Truck Series de NASCAR. Il a dépassé le record de Ron Hornaday Jr (51) grâce à son succès à l'Ultimate Tailgating 200, le 23 février 2019, à Atlanta (Géorgie, USA).

Le meilleur tour en Grand Prix de F1

Le pilote de Ferrari Kimi Räikkönen (FIN) a signé un tour à une vitesse moyenne de 263,587 km/h, lors des qualifications du Grand Prix d'Italie, le 1ᵉʳ septembre 2018, à l'Autodromo Nazionale Monza. Il a bouclé les 5,7 km du circuit en 1 min et 19,119 s pour s'emparer de la pole.

Le plus de victoires en World Rally Championship (WRC)

Nonuple champion du monde, Sébastien Loeb (FRA) a remporté sa 79ᵉ course WRC au rallye de Catalogne, les 25-28 octobre 2018. À la retraite depuis 2012, Loeb a remporté sa première course en plus de 5 ans pour Citroën Racing.

LE PLUS DE COURSES DE F1 CONSÉCUTIVES DANS LES POINTS

Lewis Hamilton (GBR) a fini dans les points dans 33 courses de suite pour Mercedes, du 9 octobre 2016 au 24 juin 2018. Sa série s'est achevée au Grand Prix d'Autriche le 1ᵉʳ juillet 2018, à cause d'une panne de pression d'essence. En 2018, Hamilton a décroché son 5ᵉ titre et porté son record du **plus de pole positions en F1** à 83.

Le 27 janvier 2019, Citroën a fêté sa 100ᵉ victoire en WRC au rallye de Monte-Carlo - **le plus de courses WRC remportées par un constructeur**.

Le plus de victoires au championnat du monde de rallycross FIA

Pour PSRX Volkswagen, Johan Kristoffersson (SWE) a gagné 11 des 12 épreuves en 2018 pour conserver son titre mondial en rallycross. Il égale l'exploit de Petter Solberg (NOR), sacré champion en 2014-2015.

LA VITESSE ABSOLUE LA PLUS ÉLEVÉE AU TT DE L'ÎLE DE MAN

Peter Hickman (GBR) a signé une vitesse moyenne au tour de 217,989 km/h en Senior TT, le 8 juin 2018. C'était une année particulièrement véloce, où les conditions idéales ont permis de battre des records de vitesse dans plusieurs catégories (voir tableau).

MEILLEURS TOURS AU TT DE L'ÎLE DE MAN			
CLASSES	DATE	PILOTE(S)*	TEMPS
Superbike TT	2 juin 2018	Dean Harrison	16 min et 50,384 s
Superstock TT	4 juin 2018	Peter Hickman	16 min et 50,501 s
Supersport TT	4 juin 2018	Michael Dunlop	17 min et 31,328 s
Lightweight TT	6 juin 2018	Michael Dunlop	18 min et 26,543 s
TT Zero	6 juin 2018	Michael Rutter	18 min et 34,956 s
Sidecar TT	8 juin 2018	Ben et Tom Birchall	18 min et 59,018 s

*Tous GBR

LE PLUS RAPIDE AU PIKES PEAK INTERNATIONAL HILL CLIMB DE BROADMOOR

Le 27 juin 2018, Romain Dumas (FRA) a remporté la "course dans les nuages" en 7 min et 57,148 s. Au volant de sa Volkswagen électrique *I.D. R Pikes Peak*, Dumas a roulé à une vitesse moyenne de plus de 144 km/h sur les 19,98 km du circuit de montagne, qui présente une élévation de 4 302 m et 156 virages.

Blue Water Recoveries (GBR) localise **l'épave la plus profonde** en 1996. Le SS *Rio Grande*, forceur de blocus allemand de la Seconde Guerre mondiale, gît à 5 762 m au fond de l'Atlantique sud.

En 1976, **le 1ᵉʳ crash aérien provoqué par un chien** a lieu quand un berger allemand non attaché interfère avec les commandes d'un Grand Canyon Air Piper 32-300 en Arizona (USA).

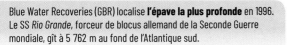

HALTÉROPHILIE

Powerlift handi en -55 kg (femmes)
Le 9 février 2019, Mariana Shevchuk (UKR) a soulevé 131 kg au 10e Fazza World Para Powerlifting World Cup à Dubaï (ARE).

Épaulé-jeté en 55 kg (hommes)
Om Yun-chol (PRK) a soulevé 162 kg au championnat du monde de l'IWF à Achgabat le 2 novembre 2018. Il s'est emparé du titre avec un total de 282 kg.

Épaulé-jeté en 59 kg (femmes)
Le 24 février 2019, Chen Guiming (CHN) a soulevé 136 kg à l'épreuve de coupe du monde de l'IWF organisée à Fuzhou (CHN).

LE POWERLIFT HANDISPORT LE PLUS LOURD EN -50 KG (FEMMES)
Le 10 avril 2018, Esther Oyema (NGA) a soulevé 131 kg pour remporter l'or en catégorie légers aux Jeux du Commonwealth. La Nigériane a décroché les 4 titres en jeu en force athlétique handisport à Gold Coast (AUS). Dans cette discipline, les athlètes n'ont qu'une seule épreuve : le développé-couché.

LE SOULEVÉ TOTAL LE PLUS LOURD EN 59 KG (FEMMES)
Aux mondiaux 2018 de la Fédération internationale d'haltérophilie (IWF) à Achgabat (TKM), Hsing-chun Kuo (TWN) a pris l'or avec 237 kg au total le 4 novembre. Elle a enchaîné **l'arraché le plus lourd en 59 kg (femmes)** (105 kg) et un épaulé-jeté de 132 kg. L'IWF a modifié ses catégories de poids en 2018 et a remis les records du monde à zéro le 1er novembre.

LE SOULEVÉ TOTAL LE PLUS LOURD EN 96 KG (HOMMES)
Sohrab Moradi (IRN) a établi 3 records à Achgabat (TKM) le 7 novembre 2018, avec un total de 416 kg. Il a réussi **l'arraché le plus lourd en 96 kg (hommes)** (186 kg) et **l'épaulé-jeté le plus lourd en 96 kg (hommes)** (230 kg). Trois mois plus tôt, Moradi avait réalisé le dernier record de l'IWF avant la création de la catégorie 94 kg.

Soulevé total en 71 kg (femmes)
Le 6 novembre 2018, Wangli Zhang (CHN) a obtenu le titre de championne du monde à Achgabat (TKM) avec un total de 267 kg. Elle a notamment signé **l'épaulé-jeté le plus lourd en 71 kg (femmes)** (152 kg).

Soulevé total en plus de 109 kg (hommes)
Le 10 novembre 2018, Lasha Talakhadze (GEO) a pris l'or en catégorie superlourds avec un total de 474 kg, lors du championnat du monde de l'IWF à Achgabat (TKM). Il a établi 7 records du monde en une seule journée, dont **l'arraché le plus lourd en plus de 109 kg (hommes)** (217 kg) et **l'épaulé-jeté le plus lourd en plus de 109 kg (hommes)** (257 kg). Talakhadze détenait les 3 records chez les plus de 105 kg avant la nouvelle classification de poids de l'IWF.

Soulevé total en 64 kg (femmes)
Deng Wei (CHN) a soulevé 254 kg au total à Fuzhou, le 25 février 2019, réussissant **l'arraché le plus lourd en 64 kg (femmes)** (113 kg) et **l'épaulé-jeté le plus lourd en 64 kg (femmes)** (141 kg).

LES PLUS LOURDS...

Powerlift handi en -107 kg (hommes)
Sodnompiljee Enkhbayar (MNG) a réussi un développé couché de 244 kg le 12 octobre 2018 aux Jeux asiatiques handisport à Jakarta (IDN). C'était le dernier des 5 records établis dans la compétition.

Yujiao Tan (CHN) a réussi **le powerlift handi le plus lourd en -67 kg (femmes)** (140,5 kg) le 9 octobre 2018 lors de son 4e soulevé supplémentaire de la compétition. Le même jour, Roohallah Rostami (IRN) a décroché l'or avec 229 kg – **le powerlift handi le plus lourd en -72 kg (hommes)**.

Le 10 octobre 2018, Lili Xu (CHN) a réussi **le powerlift handi le plus lourd en -79 kg (femmes)** (141 kg).

Le 11 octobre 2018, Jixiong Ye (CHN) a pris l'or avec 234 kg – **le powerlift handi le plus lourd en -88 kg (hommes)**. Il a battu son propre record de 233,5 kg, établi le mois précédent au Japon.

Les haltérophiles olympiques s'affrontent en arraché et épaulé-jeté. Les épreuves de force athlétique sont le développé-couché, l'arraché et le soulevé de terre.

LE SOULEVÉ À L'ELEPHANT BAR LE PLUS LOURD
Hafþór Björnsson (ISL) a soulevé une elephant bar de 472,1 kg à l'Arnold Strongman Classic 2018 à Columbus (USA) le 3 mars 2018. Il bat le record précédent de Jerry Pritchett (USA) (467,65 kg). Björnsson, connu pour son rôle de Gregor Clegane dans la série de HBO *Game of Thrones*, a réussi une année extraordinaire en remportant l'Arnold Strongman Classic, l'Europe's Strongest Man et le World's Strongest Man.

Records en fonction du poids de l'athlète dans les catégories définies par les organisations compétentes

NOV. 30 En 1954, Ann Hodges, originaire de Sylacauga (USA), devient **la 1re personne blessée par une météorite**, quand un morceau de chondrite de 5,5 kg traverse le toit de sa maison.

DÉC. 1 En 2017, Jonas Livet (FRA) décroche le record du **plus de zoos visités** (1 068). Il s'est rendu dans des parcs et des réserves animaliers de 50 pays depuis 1987.

SPORTS ARTISTIQUES

LE PLUS DE MÉDAILLES AUX MONDIAUX DE PATINAGE SYNCHRONISÉ DE L'INTERNATIONAL SKATING UNION (ÉQUIPE)

Le 7 avril 2018, la Team Surprise (SWE) a décroché sa 12e médaille, en argent, aux mondiaux de patinage synchronisé. L'équipe Marigold IceUnity (FIN) compte aussi 12 podiums, mais la Team Surprise totalise **le plus de médailles d'or (6)**. Autrefois appelé "patinage de précision", le patinage synchronisé a été créé dans les années 1950, et les 1ers mondiaux se sont tenus en 2000.

Le meilleur score en patinage artistique – programme court (femmes)

Rika Kihira (JPN) a obtenu 83,97 points pour son programme court le 11 avril 2019 lors de l'ISU World Team Trophy à Vancouver (CAN). Pour plus de patinage sur glace, voir p. 240-241.

Le meilleur score pour une routine individuelle aux massues en gymnastique rythmique

Le 18 août 2018, Linoy Ashram (ISR) a décroché 20,65 points pour son enchaînement aux massues à la World Challenge Cup de la Fédération internationale de gymnastique (FIG) à Minsk (BLR). Cinq accessoires sont utilisés en gymnastique rythmique : la corde, le cerceau, le ballon, les massues et le ruban.

Le plus de figures portant le nom d'un gymnaste au code de pointage FIG (hommes)

Kenzō Shirai (JPN) a donné son nom à 6 éléments (figures originales) dans le code de pointage 2017-2020 de la FIG : 3 pour des exercices au sol et 3 au saut de cheval. Le dernier intégré est le "Shirai 3", réalisé par Shirai au saut le 25 février 2017.

Le record féminin est de 7, par la gymnaste Nellie Kim (RUS). Elle compte 3 figures au saut de cheval, 2 à la poutre et 2 au sol.

Le plus de médailles sur un même agrès aux mondiaux de gymnastique artistique

Oksana Chusovitina (UZB) a décroché 9 médailles au saut de cheval aux mondiaux de gymnastique artistique de 1991 à 2011 : 1 en or, 4 en argent et 4 en bronze. Aux mondiaux 2018, âgée de 43 ans, elle a terminé à la 4e place.

Chusovitina a l'intention de participer aux JO de Tokyo en 2020. Elle est déjà **la gymnaste olympique la plus âgée (femmes)** depuis sa participation aux Jeux de Rio de Janeiro (BRA) en 2016, à l'âge de 41 ans et 56 jours.

Le plus de titres masculins seniors en patin en ligne aux mondiaux de patinage artistique

Le 4 octobre 2018, Yi-fan Chen (TPE) a obtenu un 4e titre successif en roller artistique en ligne aux mondiaux organisés au Vendéspace, à Mouilleron-le-Captif (FRA).

Le plus de titres féminins seniors est de 11, par Silvia Marangoni (ITA) en 2002, 2004, 2006-2013 et 2015. Elle a aussi obtenu l'argent en 2003, 2005 et 2014.

LE MEILLEUR SCORE AUX WORLD SERIES FINA DE NATATION ARTISTIQUE (FEMMES, SOLO)

Le 11 mars 2018, Svetlana Kolesnichenko (RUS) a obtenu 95,500 points en World Series FINA de natation artistique à Paris (FRA). Elle totalise 13 médailles d'or aux mondiaux, soit 6 de moins que Natalia Ishchenko (RUS), qui détient **le plus de médailles d'or en natation synchronisée aux championnats du monde de natation de la FINA (19)**.

Le plus de titres consécutifs aux mondiaux masculins de trampoline (individuel)

Le 10 novembre 2018, Gao Lei (CHN) a été sacré pour la 3e fois consécutive à Saint-Pétersbourg (RUS), égalant Alexander Moskalenko (RUS), sacré en 1990, 1992 et 1994.

Le plus de titres individuels consécutifs (femmes) est de 5, par Judy Wills Cline (USA) en 1964-1968.

LE MEILLEUR SCORE EN CYCLISME ARTISTIQUE UCI (FEMMES, INDIVIDUEL)

Comparés par l'Union cycliste internationale (UCI) aux patineurs et gymnastes artistiques, les cyclistes présentent un programme de 5 min sur de la musique et des vélos à pignon fixe. Le meilleur score pour une femme en individuel est de 191,86 points, par Iris Schwarzhaupt (DEU) aux masters allemands #1 de Wendlingen, le 8 septembre 2018.

MEILLEURS SCORES EN CYCLISME ARTISTIQUE UCI			
CATÉGORIE	PARTICIPANT(S)	POINTS	DATE
Hommes, individuel	David Schnabel (DEU)	208,91	6 nov. 2011
Femmes, duo	Katrin Schultheis et Sandra Sprinkmeier (toutes 2 DEU)	165,12	21 sept. 2013
Mixte, duo	André Bugner et Benedikt Bugner (tous 2 DEU)	168,68	28 août 2015
Femmes, ACT-4	Céline Burlet, Jennifer Schmid, Melanie Schmid et Flavia Zuber (toutes CHE)	234,44	30 sept. 2017

Informations mises à jour au 1er février 2019

LE PLUS DE MÉDAILLES D'OR AUX MONDIAUX DE GYMNASTIQUE ARTISTIQUE

Aux championnats du monde de gymnastique artistique 2018 de Doha (QAT), Simone Biles (USA) a gagné 4 titres et porté son total à 14, soit 2 de plus que Vitaly Scherbo (BLR). Au passage, elle compte **le plus de titres mondiaux au concours général individuel (4)**, en 2013-2015 et 2018.

Biles détient aussi **le plus de médailles aux mondiaux de gymnastique artistique (femmes) (20)** — autant que Svetlana Khorkina (RUS, de 1994 à 2003).

DÉC. 2 Le plus grand Bouddha est mesuré en 2009. Le Bouddha du Temple de la Source dans le district de Luoshan (CHN) culmine à 127,64 m - presque 3 fois la hauteur de la statue de la Liberté.

DÉC. 3 La sonde de la NASA *Pioneer 10* réalise le 1er survol de Jupiter en 1973. Elle passe à 130 000 km au-dessus des nuages de la géante gazeuse.

231

SPORTS DE CIBLE

Le plus de points en 30 m–36 flèches à l'arc classique en extérieur (hommes)

Le 15 juin 2018, Kim Hyun-jong (KOR) a obtenu un score de 360 (27x), au 36e National Tournament for President Challenge Flag, à Gwangju (KOR). Il a atteint le centre avec ses 36 flèches, dont 27 ont touché la croix centrale. À 18 ans, Hyun-jong fait mieux que son compatriote Kim Woo-jin et son 360 (26x).

Le plus de points à 70 m–72 flèches à l'arc classique en extérieur (femmes)

Kang Chae-young (KOR) a totalisé 691 points en 72 flèches, lors du tour de classement de l'épreuve de coupe du monde, à Antalya (TUR), le 21 mai 2018.

Le plus de points à 60 m–36 flèches à l'arc à poulies en extérieur (femmes)

Le 31 mars 2018, Danelle Wentzel (ZAF) a obtenu 357 points en 36 tirs à 60 m, lors du championnat sud-africain de tir à l'arc au Marks Park Archery Club de Johannesburg. Wentzel a amélioré d'un seul point le record de 356 points de Gladys Willems, qu'elle détenait depuis plus de 10 ans.

Le plus de points en match à 15 flèches à l'arc à poulies en extérieur (femmes)

Linda Ochoa-Anderson (MEX) a enregistré un score de 150 (11x) en 15 flèches, lors d'un match de l'Easton Foundations Gator Cup, à Newberry (Floride, USA), le 12 mai 2018. Elle a mis toutes ses flèches dans le mille, et 11 sur la croix.

LE PLUS DE TITRES MAJEURS DE LA PROFESSIONAL BOWLERS ASSOCIATION (PBA)

Le 21 mars 2019, Jason Belmonte (AUS) a battu Jakob Butturff 236-227, au Thunderbowl Lanes d'Allen Park (USA), décrochant ainsi son 2e titre mondial PBA et son 11e Majeur au total. Belmonte – célèbre pour sa technique à 2 mains – a aussi remporté 2 Players Championships, 4 USBC Masters et 3 tournois des Champions.
Sur les 5 Majeurs PBA, seul l'US Open lui échappait encore en avril 2019.

La plus haute moyenne en finale de Premier League Darts

Le 17 mai 2018, Michael van Gerwen (NLD) a battu Michael Smith 11-4 en finale de la Premier League Darts avec une moyenne à 3 fléchettes de 112,37 points. Il a manqué de peu son propre record de **la meilleure moyenne pour une finale télévisée de fléchettes** (112,49), décroché au Masters le 1er février 2015.

LE PLUS DE TITRES MONDIAUX EN CURLING FÉMININ

Le Canada a été sacré aux championnats du monde de curling féminin 17 fois depuis 1980. Son dernier titre a été obtenu à domicile avec la capitaine Jennifer Jones, en battant la Suède 7-6, le 25 mars 2018, à North Bay (Ontario, CAN).
Le plus de titres mondiaux en curling masculin est de 36, également par le Canada, entre 1959 et 2017.

LE MEILLEUR SCORE EN TIR À LA CARABINE 50 M COUCHÉ SH2

Aux mondiaux 2018 de para-tir sportif, à Cheongju (KOR), Kristina Funkova (SVK), 16 ans, a obtenu 250,7 points en tir à la carabine couché SH2 à 50 m, le 11 mai. L'épreuve fera ses débuts paralympiques à Tokyo en 2020. Les tireurs ont besoin d'un support pour tirer.

Le record masculin de l'épreuve

est 150 (12x), décroché par le sextuple champion du monde Reo Wilde (USA), le 7 mai 2015, à l'épreuve de coupe du monde de Shanghai (CHN).

Le meilleur score en 10 m pistolet à air de l'ISSF (hommes)

Chaudhary Saurabh (IND) a inscrit 245 points, à l'épreuve de coupe du monde de la Fédération internationale de tir sportif (ISSF), à New Delhi (IND), le 24 février 2019. C'était le 1er tournoi senior du tireur de 16 ans.
Le lendemain, la championne des Jeux du Commonwealth Apurvi Chandela (IND) a signé **le meilleur score en 10 m pistolet à air (femmes)** (252,9 points), également à New Delhi.
Veronika Major (HUN) a suivi avec **le meilleur score en 25 m pistolet (femmes)**, en touchant 40 des 50 cibles en finale, le 24 février 2019.

Le meilleur score en trap ISSF (femmes)

Le 5 mars 2018, Ashley Carroll (USA) a touché 48 cibles sur 50, à l'épreuve de coupe du monde de Guadalajara (MEX). Le trap est l'une des disciplines principales du tir au pigeon d'argile. Les cibles sont lancées d'une même machine.

Le plus de victoires aux mondiaux de lancer de fer à cheval (hommes)

Alan Francis (USA) a remporté son 23e titre au tournoi mondial de fer à cheval NHPA 2018. Il a remporté 14 de ses 15 matchs.

Le plus de participations aux mondiaux de croquet

Stephen Mulliner (GBR) a disputé 15 éditions des championnats du monde de croquet depuis 1989. Il a dépassé David Openshaw et Robert Fulford en participant aux mondiaux 2018 à Wellington (NZL), du 3 au 11 février. Mulliner n'a remporté qu'un titre, en 2016.

LE 1ER JOUEUR DE BILLARD À ATTEINDRE 1 000 CENTURIES

Le 10 mars 2019, Ronnie O'Sullivan (GBR) a décroché son 1 000e century en billard professionnel. Il a franchi cette barre avec un break de 134 dans la dernière manche de sa victoire 10-4 contre Neil Robertson, au Coral Players Championship de Lancashire (GBR). Parmi ses centuries, O'Sullivan compte **le plus de breaks maximums** (15) et **le break maximum le plus rapide** (5 min et 8 s), aux mondiaux de billard 1997. Après analyse vidéo, la durée de ce break royal a même été rectifiée à la baisse.

Après une saison 2018-2019 hors norme, O'Sullivan a égalé Stephen Hendry (GBR) pour **le plus de titres classés en billard** (36), au 28 mars 2019.

DÉC. 4 — La "Swish Pie" de Charlie Bigham est lancée au Royaume-Uni en 2013. À 314,16 £, c'est **le plat cuisiné le plus cher**. Il contient du homard, du turbot et des huîtres à la sauce Dom Pérignon.

DÉC. 5 — En 2015, Ratnesh Pandey (IND) effectue **la plus longue distance ininterrompue debout sur une moto**, couvrant 32,3 km sur une Honda Unicorn, à Indore (Madhya Pradesh, IND).

GOLF

LES GAINS LES PLUS ÉLEVÉS SUR LE PGA TOUR

Tiger Woods (USA) totalisait 118 309 570 $ de gains sur le Tour de la Professional Golfers' Association (PGA) au 15 avril 2019. Il a remporté son 1er tournoi en 5 ans le 23 septembre 2018 et décroché le 15e Majeur de sa carrière au Masters, le 14 avril 2019 (ci-dessus). Il a réussi un come-back remarquable après une blessure au dos qui l'avait fait sortir du top 1 000 mondial en 2017. Woods n'est plus qu'à une longueur du **record de victoires sur le PGA Tour** (82), par Sam Snead (USA).

Le plus de victoires sur le PGA Tour pour un gaucher

Le 11 février 2019, Phil "Lefty" Mickelson (USA) a remporté son 44e titre sur le PGA Tour, à l'AT & T Pebble Beach Pro-Am de Californie (USA). C'était son 2e succès de l'année sur le circuit. Mickelson, qui a appris son swing en se plaçant face à son père, est droitier, sauf en golf.

Mickelson a terminé 2018 avec **le plus de participations à la Ryder Cup** – 12, sans interruption depuis 1995. Choix du capitaine pour l'édition 2018 au Golf national de Guyancourt (FRA), il a perdu ses 2 matchs.

Le plus de birdies consécutifs en tournoi professionnel

Le 7 février 2019, James Nitties (AUS) a passé 9 birdies de rang à l'ISPS Handa Vic Open de Geelong (Victoria, AUS). C'est autant que Mark Calcavecchia (USA) à l'Open du Canada le 25 juillet 2009, égalé par Amy Yang (KOR), Beth Daniel, Omar Uresti (tous 2 USA), Rayhan Thomas (IND) et Bronte Law (GBR).

Le plus de gains sur le Tour européen PGA

Lee Westwood (GBR) avait amassé 36 499 627 € sur le circuit européen au 15 avril 2019. Le 11 novembre 2018, il a remporté son 1er titre en 4 ans sur le Tour européen, au Nedbank Golf Challenge de Sun City (ZAF), avec sa compagne comme caddie. Westwood, qui a disputé son 1e tournoi du Tour en 1994, a gagné 24 tournois et a terminé dans les places primées 451 fois.

LE SCORE CUMULÉ LE PLUS BAS AU LPGA TOUR

Les 5-8 juillet 2018, Kim Sei-young (KOR) a balayé tous les records au Thornberry Creek Ladies Professional Golf Association (LPGA) Classic d'Oneida (Wisconsin, USA). Elle a rendu des cartes de 63, 65, 64 et 65 pour un total record de 257 coups, soit 31 sous le par – **le score sous le par le plus bas en 72 trous LPGA**. Kim a aussi signé **le plus de birdies en 72 trous LPGA (31)**.

Le plus long drive sur le PGA Tour

Officiellement, le plus long drive de PGA à l'ère du ShotLink est de 476 yards, par Davis Love III (USA), au Mercedes Championships de Kapalua (Hawaï, USA), le 11 janvier 2004. Le ShotLink est un système laser utilisé par la PGA pour mesurer la distance des coups depuis 2003.

Le 23 mars 2018, Dustin Johnson a frappé un drive de 489 yards, au WGC-Dell Technologies Match Play, à l'Austin Country Club (Texas, USA). Toutefois, le record n'est pas homologué puisqu'il s'agissait de match-play et non de stroke-play classique.

LE SCORE LE PLUS BAS EN UNE MANCHE DU TOUR EUROPÉEN PGA

Le 21 septembre 2018, Oliver Fisher (GBR) est devenu le 1er joueur à passer sous la barre des 60 sur le circuit européen avec un 59 au Portugal Masters, à Vilamoura. Il a rentré 10 birdies et un eagle pendant son 2e tour. Du jamais vu en près de 700 000 tours disputés dans l'histoire du Tour européen.

LE SCORE CUMULÉ LE PLUS BAS À L'USPGA CHAMPIONSHIP

Brooks Koepka (USA) a remporté l'USPGA 2018 au Bellerive Country Club du Missouri (USA) avec une carte finale de 264 en 4 tours (69, 63, 66, 66 ; 16 sous le par). Son tour à 63 est **le score le plus bas en un tour du PGA Championship**, un record qu'il partage avec 15 autres golfeurs.

Le score le plus bas en un tour de l'US Open

Le 17 juin 2018, Tommy Fleetwood (GBR) a rendu une carte de 63 au dernier tour de l'US Open à Shinnecock Hills (USA). Il a égalé les exploits de Johnny Miller en 1973, Jack Nicklaus et Tom Weiskopf (tous USA) en 1980, Vijay Singh (FJI) en 2003 et Justin Thomas (USA) en 2017. Sur le dernier green, Fleetwood a manqué un putt à 2,7 m qui lui aurait assuré le record.

Le plus de Majeurs disputés avant de remporter un titre

Angela Stanford (USA) a décroché sa 1re victoire en Majeur à sa 76e participation, à l'Evian Championship 2018, les 13-16 septembre. Son meilleur résultat jusque-là était une 2e place à l'US Open féminin 2003. Elle a éclipsé le record de Sergio García, champion en 2017 après 74 tentatives.

LE PLUS DE POINTS GAGNÉS PAR UN GOLFEUR EN RYDER CUP

Sergio García (ESP) a offert 25,5 points à l'Europe en 9 participations à la Ryder Cup, de 1999 à 2018. Son bilan personnel est de 22 victoires, 12 défaites et 7 nuls. Invité de dernière minute au tournoi 2018, García a gagné 3 matchs, dépassant ainsi le record précédent de 25 points de Nick Faldo.

 DÉC. 6 En 2002, **le bébé le plus petit** est autorisé à quitter l'hôpital de Minneapolis (Minnesota, USA). À sa naissance avec 108 jours d'avance, le 20 juillet, Nisa Juarez (USA) ne mesurait que 24 cm.

 DÉC. 7 En 1995, une sonde larguée par *Galileo* entame sa descente dans l'atmosphère de Jupiter, atteignant 170 000 km/h – **l'entrée atmosphérique la plus rapide**.

233

ATHLÉTISME

LE PLUS DE POINTS EN DÉCATHLON

Les 15-16 septembre 2018, Kevin Mayer (FRA) a enregistré 9 126 points au Décastar des épreuves combinées IAAF, à Talence (FRA). Mayer, qui avait décidé de prendre part à la compétition pour effacer son échec aux championnats d'Europe d'athlétisme le mois précédent, est devenu le 1er décathlète à dépasser 9 100 points.

LES PLUS RAPIDES...

Mile en salle (hommes)*

Le 3 mars 2019, Yomif Kejelcha (ETH) a battu un record vieux de 22 ans avec un chrono de 3 min et 47,01 s, au Bruce Lehane Invitational Mile de Boston (USA). Il a amélioré de 1,44 s le record établi par Hicham El Guerrouj (MAR), le 12 février 1997.

El Guerrouj a aussi perdu son record du **1 500 m en salle le plus rapide (hommes)*** en

En attente de validation par l'IAAF

2019 quand Samuel Tefera (ETH) l'a couru en 3 min et 31,04 s le 16 février, au meeting de Birmingham du Circuit mondial IAAF.

400 m en salle (hommes)*

Michael Norman (USA) a remporté le 400 m en salle en 44,52 s, le 10 mars 2018, au championnat d'athlétisme en salle de 1re division masculine NCAA, à College Station (USA). À 20 ans, sous les couleurs de l'université

de Californie du Sud, il a battu le record de 44,57 s de Kerron Clement (USA), qui tenait depuis presque 13 ans.

Le même jour, Norman a couru la dernière partie du relais 4 x 400 m par équipe, en décrochant le meilleur temps mondial en 3 min et 0,77 s. Toutefois, le record n'a pas été homologué par l'IAAF, puisque les coureurs doivent être de la même nationalité et que Rai Benjamin n'était pas qualifié pour représenter les USA au 3 octobre 2018, ayant couru pour Antigua en junior. Ce sont donc leurs dauphins, Texas A & M – Ilolo Izu, Robert Grant, Devin Dixon et Mylik Kerley (tous USA) – qui ont établi le record du **relais 4 x 400 m en salle le plus rapide (hommes)***, en 3 min et 1,39 s.

4 x 800 m en salle (hommes)

Le 25 février 2018, l'équipe Hoka NJ/NY Track Club – représentée par Joe McAsey, Kyle Merber, Chris Giesting et Jesse Garn (tous USA) – a remporté le relais masculin 4 x 800 m en 7 min et 11,30 s, au 2018 Boston University Last Chance Meet (USA).

100 m fauteuil (T34, femmes)

Le 22 juillet 2018, Kare Adenegan (GBR) a remporté le 100 m T34 féminin en 16,80 s, aux Anniversary Games de Londres (GBR).

LE PLUS DE TITRES À LA DIAMOND RACE (FEMMES)

Les 30-31 août 2018, Caterine Ibargüen (COL) a été sacrée championne en triple saut et saut en longueur, pour un total de 6 victoires en Diamond Race. Elle égale ainsi Sandra Perković (HRV), championne en disque en 2012-2017 (voir à droite). Ibargüen a été nommée Athlète IAAF de l'année le 4 décembre 2018 : une année remarquable.

Âgée de 17 ans, elle est devenue la 1re femme T34 à passer sous la barre des 17 s.

Le **100 m en fauteuil roulant (T34, hommes) le plus rapide** est établi à 14,80 s, par Rheed McCracken (AUS), au Grand prix mondial d'athlétisme handisport, à Nottwil (CHE), le 26 mai 2018. Il a battu son propre record (14,92 s) établi sur la même épreuve l'année d'avant.

400 m (T11, femmes)

Cuiqing Liu (CHN) a survolé le 400 m en 56 s, au Grand prix mondial d'athlétisme handisport de Pékin (CHN), le 13 mai 2018. Elle améliore le record de 2007 de Terezinha Guilhermina (56,14 s). La catégorie T11 regroupe les athlètes malvoyants.

LE PLUS LOIN...

Saut en longueur (T64, femmes)

Marie-Amélie Le Fur (FRA) a pris l'or avec un saut à 6,01 m, le 26 août 2018, au championnat d'Europe d'athlétisme handisport organisé à Berlin (DEU).

Le Fur, amputée de la jambe gauche à la suite d'un accident de scooter en 2004, détient aussi le record du **400 m le plus rapide (T64, femmes)** – 59,27 s – enregistré aux jeux Paralympiques 2016.

LE 3 000 M STEEPLE LE PLUS RAPIDE (FEMMES)

Beatrice Chepkoech (KEN) a remporté le 3 000 m steeple, au meeting de Monaco de la Diamond League IAAF, en 8 min et 44,32 s, le 20 juillet 2018. Elle a battu le record précédent de plus de 8 s, devenant la 1re Kényane à détenir le record du monde dans cette épreuve.

LE PLUS JEUNE À COURIR 1 MILE EN MOINS DE 4 MIN

Le 27 mai 2017, le demi-fondeur norvégien Jakob Ingebrigtsen (né le 19 septembre 2000) a couru 1 mile en 3 min et 58,07 s, à 16 ans et 250 jours, à Eugene (USA). En 2018, il a décroché l'or sur 1 500 m et 5 000 m (ci-dessus), aux championnats d'Europe d'athlétisme, à seulement 17 ans.

DÉC. 8 Procter & Gamble (BRA) diffuse **la plus longue publicité télévisée** en 2018. D'une durée de 14 h, elle vante les mérites du déodorant Old Spice sur la chaîne Woohoo, à Sao Paulo, entre 6 h et 20 h.

DÉC. 9 En 1989, *Le Départ des Argonautes*, par "un maître de 1487" (probablement l'Italien Pietro del Donzello), se vend à Sotheby's (Londres, GBR) 4,2 millions £ - **la peinture anonyme la plus chère**.

LE 4 X 800 M EN SALLE LE PLUS RAPIDE (FEMMES)
Le 3 février 2018, l'équipe américaine composée de Chrishuna Williams, Raevyn Rogers, Charlene Lipsey et Ajeé Wilson a remporté le relais féminin 4 x 800 m en 8 min et 5,89 s au New York Road Runners Millrose Games de New York (USA), améliorant le record qui tenait depuis 2011. Wilson (2e en partant de la droite) a réussi le 800 m le plus rapide en 1 min et 58,37 s.

LE PLUS DE...

Médailles remportées aux Mondiaux en salle de l'IAAF (pays)
Depuis 1985, les États-Unis ont empoché 257 médailles en salle – 114 en or, 77 en argent et 66 en bronze. Sur ce total, 18 ont été glanées aux Mondiaux 2018 les 1er–4 mars, établissant 4 nouveaux records dans la compétition.

Le plus grand nombre de médailles remportées aux Mondiaux en salle de l'IAAF (individuel) est de 9, par Maria Mutola (MOZ), sur 800 m, entre 1993 et 2008, et Natalya Nazarova (RUS) sur 400 m et relais 4 x 400 m, entre 1999 et 2010.

Victoires en Diamond League
La lanceuse de disque croate Sandra Perković a remporté 42 épreuves de Diamond League, entre le 12 juin 2010 et le 22 juillet 2018 – plus que tout autre athlète, homme ou femme. Elle a remporté 4 épreuves sur 4 en 2018 avant de subir une défaite surprise en finale.

LA PLUS JEUNE VAINQUEUR AT AU DIAMOND LEAGUE (FEMMES)
Le 3 mai 2019, lors du meeting l'IAAF Diamond League de Doha (Qatar), Yaroslava Mahuchikh (UKR, née le 19 sept. 2001) a réalisé le plus haut saut en hauteur féminin, à l'âge de 17 ans et 226 jours. Déjà médaillée d'or aux JO d'été de la jeunesse, elle a établi un record personnel avec un saut de 1,96 m.

Lancer de disque (F53, femmes)
Le 20 août 2018, Iana Lebiedieva (GBRR) a décroché l'or au championnat d'Europe d'athlétisme handisport avec un lancer à 14,93 m. Elle bat le record vieux de 23 ans de 14,46 m établi par Cristeen Smith 2 fois dans la même compétition, avec des lancers records aux 5e et 6e tours.

Lancer de disque (F11, hommes)
Oney Tapia (ITA, né CUB) a réussi un lancer à 46,07 m, au championnat d'Europe d'athlétisme handisport, le 22 août 2018. Il a battu son propre record de 45,65 m réalisé à Chiuro (ITA), le 28 avril 2018. Cet arboriculteur a perdu la vue en 2011 après avoir été heurté par une branche. En 2017, il s'est fait connaître en remportant la version italienne de *Danse avec les stars*.

Lancer de massue (F51, hommes)
Le 13 mai 2018, le double champion paralympique Željko Dimitrijević (SRB) a lancé sa massue à 32,90 m, à Split (HRV). La catégorie F51-57 regroupe les athlètes en fauteuil.

Participations à la Diamond League
Au 30 août 2018, Blessing Okagbare-Ighoteguonor (NGA) avait disputé 67 meetings de Diamond League depuis le 3 juillet 2010. Elle a disputé le 100 m, 200 m et le saut en longueur, obtenant au passage 10 victoires.

Victoires au Challenge IAAF du lancer de marteau
Anita Włodarczyk (POL) a remporté le Challenge IAAF 6 fois de suite, en 2013-2018. Elle a glané son 6e titre avec un score de 228,12 points.

Le plus grand nombre de victoires au Challenge IAAF du lancer de marteau (hommes) est de 4, par Paweł Fajdek (POL), en 2013, 2015, 2016 et 2017.

LE SAUT EN LONGUEUR LE PLUS LONG (T64, HOMMES)
Le 25 août 2018, "Blade Jumper" Markus Rehm (DEU) a remporté l'or au championnat d'Europe d'athlétisme handisport à Berlin (DEU), avec un saut de 8,48 m. Il bat son propre record de 1 cm. Son saut égale celui réalisé par l'athlète valide Luvo Manyonga qui lui a valu la médaille d'or aux Mondiaux de l'IAAF l'année précédente.

 DÉC. 10 En 2017, Dzmitry Dudarau (BLR) établit **un record de temps en restant accroché par une dent** de tout son poids pendant 7 min et 15 s, à Jimo (CHN).

 DÉC. 11 En 2004, plus de 5 millions de personnes se donnent la main pour former **la plus longue chaîne humaine**, sur 1 050 km, de Teknaf à Tentulia, dans le nord-ouest du Bangladesh.

MARATHONS

LE PLUS DE VICTOIRES AU GREAT NORTH RUN

Le 9 septembre 2018, Mo Farah (GBR, né SOM) a décroché son 5e titre consécutif au semi-marathon Great North Run, à Newcastle (GBR). Il partageait auparavant le record de titres avec le quadruple vainqueur Benson Masya (KEN). Un mois plus tard, l'ancienne star des pistes a remporté le marathon de Chicago en 2 h, 5 min et 11 s – son 1er succès sur la distance.

LONDON MARATHON 2019
Virgin money

Le plus de victoires en World Marathon Majors (hommes)

Créé en 2006, le World Marathon Majors est une compétition par points qui regroupe les marathons annuels de Boston, Tokyo (depuis 2013), Berlin, Chicago, Londres et New York, ainsi que les marathons du championnat du monde IAAF et des jeux Olympiques. Les 5 premiers obtiennent des points. En 2018, Eliud Kipchoge (KEN) a confirmé sa domination sur la distance en décrochant son 3e titre consécutif chez les hommes.

Le plus de titres (femmes) est aussi de 3, par Irina Mikitenko (DEU, née KAZ) de 2007-2008 à 2009-2010, et Mary Keitany (KEN) en 2011-2012, 2015-2016 et 2017-2018.

Le plus de victoires au marathon de Londres (hommes)

Le 28 avril 2019, Eliud Kipchoge a été sacré pour la 4e fois à Londres après ses titres en 2015-2016 et 2018. Son chrono victorieux de 2 h, 2 min et 37 s est **le marathon de Londres le plus rapide (hommes)** et le 2e temps de l'histoire, à 58 s de son propre record du monde (voir p. 213).

Le plus de victoires au marathon de Londres (femmes) est de 4, par Ingrid Kristiansen (NOR) en 1984-1985 et 1987-1988.

LA PLUS RAPIDE AU CHAMPIONNAT DU MONDE IRONMAN® (FEMMES)

Daniela Ryf (CHE) a remporté le championnat du monde IRONMAN® en 8 h, 26 min et 18 s, le 13 octobre 2018, à Hawaï (USA). Elle s'est rétablie d'une piqûre de méduse juste avant le départ, et a amélioré son propre record, établi en 2016, de 20 min et 28 s. Ryf a terminé le parcours de natation de 3,8 km en 57 min et 27 s, les 180 km de vélo en un temps record de 4 h, 26 min et 7 s (encadré) et le marathon de 42,1 km en 2 h, 57 min et 5 s. C'était sa 4e victoire consécutive au championnat du monde IRONMAN®.

Le plus de victoires à l'Ultra-Trail du Mont-Blanc (hommes)

Organisé depuis 2003, l'Ultra-Trail du Mont-Blanc est un parcours d'environ 167 km à travers les Alpes françaises, suisses et italiennes. Trois athlètes l'ont emporté 3 fois : Kilian Jornet (ESP) en 2008-2009 et 2011 ; François D'Haene (FRA) en 2012, 2014 et 2017 ; et Xavier Thévenard (FRA) en 2013, 2015 et 2018.

LES PLUS RAPIDES...

Championnat du monde IRONMAN® (hommes)

Le 13 octobre 2018, Patrick Lange (DEU) est devenu le 1er athlète à passer sous la barre des 8 h au championnat du monde IRONMAN®, avec un temps de 7 h, 52 min et 39 s. C'était sa 2e victoire consécutive à Hawaï (USA).

1er marathon

Le 25 janvier 2019, Getaneh Molla (ETH) s'est imposé à Dubaï (ARE) pour son tout 1er marathon officiel. Il a franchi la ligne en 2 h, 3 min et 34 s. C'était non seulement **le marathon de Dubaï le plus rapide (hommes)** – améliorant de 26 s le précédent record –, mais aussi le 9e meilleur temps de l'histoire sur une course officielle.

Ruth Chepngetich (KEN) a réalisé **le marathon de Dubaï le plus rapide (femmes)** en 2 h, 17 min et 8 s. C'était le 3e meilleur temps de l'histoire

Le 28 avril 2019, quelque 43 000 coureurs ont pris le départ du 39e marathon de Londres (GBR). Le GWR était partenaire de l'événement pour la 12e année et a vu de nombreux records tomber dans les mains de coureurs déguisés (tous GBR, sauf mention contraire) :

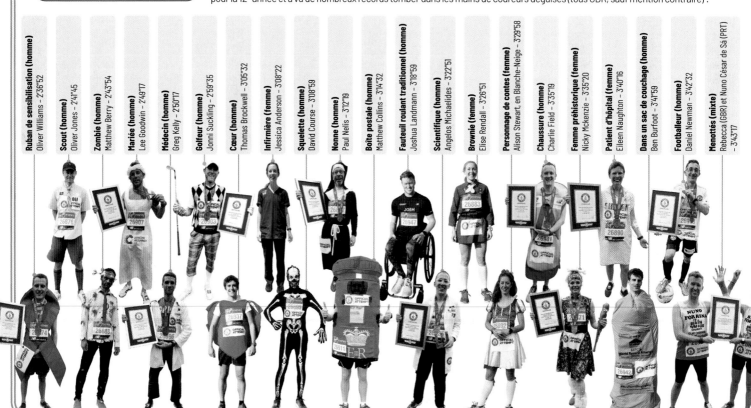

Ruban de sensibilisation (homme) Oliver Williams – 2'36"52
Scout (homme) Oliver Jones – 2'41"45
Zombie (homme) Matthew Berry – 2'43"54
Mariée (homme) Lee Goodwin – 2'49"17
Médecin (homme) Greg Kelly – 2'50"17
Golfeur (homme) Jonni Suckling – 2'59"35
Cœur (homme) Thomas Brockwell – 3'05"32
Infirmière (femme) Jessica Anderson – 3'08"22
Squelette (homme) David Course – 3'08"59
Nonne (homme) Paul Nelis – 3'12"19
Boîte postale (homme) Matthew Collins – 3'14"32
Fauteuil roulant traditionnel (homme) Joshua Landmann – 3'18"59
Scientifique (homme) Angelos Michaelides – 3'22"51
Brownie (femme) Elise Rendall – 3'26"51
Personnage de contes (femme) Alison Stewart, en Blanche-Neige – 3'29"58
Chaussure (homme) Charlie Field – 3'35"19
Femme préhistorique (femme) Nicky McKenzie – 3'35"20
Patient d'hôpital (femme) Eileen Naughton – 3'40"16
Dans un sac de couchage (homme) Ben Burfoot – 3'41"59
Footballeur (homme) Daniel Newman – 3'42"32
Menottés (mixte) Rebecca (GBR) et Nuno César de Sá (PRT) – 3'43"17

DÉC. 12 Après exactement 24 h, Richard Glover conclut **la plus longue interview radio** avec l'auteur Peter FitzSimons (tous AUS) en 2011. Le duo a discuté dans un studio éphémère installé dans une boutique de Sydney (AUS).

DÉC. 13 En 1972, Eugene Cernan et Harrison Schmitt (tous 2 USA) établissent **le record de vitesse lunaire** en pilotant le rover d'Apollo 17 à 18 km/h, à l'est du site d'atterrissage sur la Lune.

11 s. Gudeta a battu le record de Lornah Kiplagat de 1 h, 6 min et 25 s, établi aux mondiaux de course sur route en 2007 – le 1er record féminin unisexe ratifié par l'IAAF sur la distance.

Le semi-marathon le plus rapide (femmes) est de 1 h, 4 min et 51 s, par Joyciline Jepkosgei (KEN), le 22 octobre 2017, lors d'une course mixte à Valence (ESP).

Marathon de Berlin (femmes)
Gladys Cherono (KEN) a pris l'or en 2018 en 2 h, 18 min et 11 s, le 16 septembre. C'était la 3e victoire de Cherono à Berlin et le 8e temps féminin de l'histoire.

Marathon de Rotterdam (hommes)
Marius Kipserem (KEN) a franchi la ligne à Rotterdam (NLD) en 2 h, 4 min et 11 s, le 7 avril 2019. Il a battu le record de la course de son compatriote Duncan

Kibet, fixé à 2 h, 4 min et 27 s, 10 ans plus tôt.

100 miles (femmes)
Camille Herron (USA) continue de faire tomber les records en ultradistance. En novembre 2018, son temps de 12 h, 42 min et 40 s – enregistré le 11 novembre 2017 au Tunnel Hill 100 de Vienna (Illinois, USA) – a été ratifié par l'IAU. Elle a ajouté à son palmarès **la course la plus longue en 24 h (femmes)** (262,193 km), au Desert Solstice Track Invitational, les 8-9 décembre 2018, à Phoenix (Arizona, USA).

Herron détient aussi le record **du marathon le plus rapide déguisée en super-héros (femmes)**. Le 18 novembre 2012, elle a terminé le marathon de la Route 66 avec un costume de Spider-Man rose en 2 h, 48 min et 51 s, à Tulsa (Oklahoma, USA). Elle est arrivée 1re chez les femmes.

LE 100 KM SUR ROUTE LE PLUS RAPIDE
Le 24 juin 2018, Nao Kazami (JPN) a remporté l'ultramarathon de 100 km de Lake Saroma en 6 h, 9 min et 14 s, à Kitami City (JPN). Il a amélioré le record précédent de 4 min, lequel avait été établi par son compatriote Takahiro Sunada 20 ans plus tôt.

Il s'agit aussi **du 100 km ultradistance le plus rapide** – validé par l'International Association of Ultrarunners (IAU). Kazami a fait mieux que les 6 h, 10 min et 20 s de l'athlète Don Ritchie (GBR, 1944-2018), à Londres (GBR), le 28 octobre 1978.

derrière Mary Keitany (2 h, 17 min et 1 s, au marathon de Londres 2017) et Paula Radcliffe (GBR), dont **le marathon le plus rapide (femmes)** en 2 h, 15 min et 25 s, réalisé également à Londres le 13 avril 2003, reste inégalé.

Semi-marathon (femmes, course unisexe)
Aux mondiaux de semi-marathon de l'IAAF à Valence (ESP), le 24 mars 2018, Netsanet Gudeta (ETH) s'est imposée dans l'épreuve féminine en 1 h, 6 min et

LE MARATHON EN FAUTEUIL T54 LE PLUS RAPIDE (FEMMES)
Le 16 septembre 2018, Manuela Schär (CHE) a réalisé le marathon en fauteuil le plus rapide sur un parcours officiel en 1 h, 36 min et 53 s, au marathon de Berlin (DEU). Elle a battu le record précédent de plus de 1 min.

Le record masculin est de 1 h, 20 min et 14 s, par Heinz Frei (CHE), le 31 octobre 1999, à Ôita (JPN).

LA PLUS JEUNE CHAMPIONNE DU MARATHON DE LONDRES
Brigid Kosgei (KEN, née le 20 février 1994) a gagné le marathon féminin de Londres à 25 ans et 67 jours, le 28 avril 2019, en 2 h, 18 min et 20 s – le 9e meilleur temps féminin sur la distance –, après avoir réalisé la 2nde moitié d'un marathon la plus rapide de l'histoire (femmes), en 1 h, 6 min et 42 s.

Arbre de Noël (homme) Laurence Mumford – 3'43'41

Arbre (homme) Alan Dean – 3'48'17

Costume d'animal intégral (femme) Kate Carter, en panda – 3'48'32

Elvis (femme) Elizabeth Sampson – 3'49'53

Produit de beauté (femme) Katie Simpson, en dentifrice – 3'51'17

Dent (femme) Fiona Henderson – 3'51'17

Corps céleste (homme) Philip Rose, en Soleil – 3'52'40

Fourniture de bureau (femme) Belinda Neild, en crayon – 3'54'25

Personnage de jeu vidéo (femme) Shaolin Loke, en Chun-Li – 3'56'18

Dans une tente (homme) Oscar White – 3'57'05

Créature mythologique (homme) Andy Taylor, en licorne – 3'58'05

Œuf (femme) Katy Garnham-Lee – 3'58'43

Momie (homme) Pardip Singh Minhas – 3'59'04

Noix (femme) Sally Orange – 4'09'51

ADN (femme) Marie Evans – 4'20'07

Dragon (homme) James Cook – 4'46'50

Snowboarder (homme) James Williams – 5'21'50

En bottes de ski (homme) Paul Harnett – 5'30'27

Costume à 6 personnes Charlotte Farge, Cey Uzun, Rob Jones, Helen Smith, Andy Moulden et David Brennan, en Thunderbirds – 5'59'33

DÉC. 14 En 1952, le Dr Jac Geller termine **la 1re séparation réussie de jumeaux siamois**, sur des filles xiphopages (réunies par le sternum), à l'hôpital Mount Sinai de Cleveland (Ohio, USA).

DÉC. 15 La goélette à 7 mâts *Thomas W. Lawson* s'échoue au large des îles Scilly (GBR) en 1907. Construit en 1902 à Quincy (Massachusetts, USA), le *Lawson* était **le voilier comptant le plus de mâts**.

NATATION

LE PLUS DE TITRES EN FINA MARATHON WORLD SERIES (FEMMES)

Ana Marcela Cunha (BRA) a remporté le FINA Marathon Swim World Series 4 fois : en 2010, 2012, 2014 et 2018. Pendant l'épreuve 2018, elle a remporté 2 des 8 courses – à Balatonfüred (HUN) et au lac Saint-Jean de Québec (CAN) –, améliorant son record du **plus de courses remportées en World Series (femmes)** - 20.

LES PLUS RAPIDES...

1 500 m nage libre en grand bassin (femmes)

Katie Ledecky (USA) a amélioré son propre record de 5 s en touchant le mur en 15 min et 20,48 s, à Indianapolis (USA), le 16 mai 2018.

50 m papillon en grand bassin (hommes)

Andriy Govorov (UKR) a battu un record "en combinaison" de 2009 (voir ci-dessus à droite) en parcourant le 50 m en 22,27 s, au Trophée Sette Colli de Rome (ITA), le 1er juillet 2018.

50 m dos en grand bassin (femmes)

Liu Xiang (CHN) a remporté le 50 m dos féminin en 26,98 s, aux 18es Jeux asiatiques, à Jakarta (IDN), le 21 août 2018.

100 m brasse en grand bassin (hommes)

Le 4 août 2018, Adam Peaty (GBR) a triomphé au 100 m brasse en 57,10 s, au championnat d'Europe de natation, à Glasgow (GBR). Il détient les 14 temps les plus rapides de l'épreuve.

Relais 4 x 100 m nage libre en grand bassin (femmes)

L'équipe australienne composée de Cate Campbell, Emma McKeon, Bronte Campbell et Shayna Jack a subjugué son public aux Jeux du Commonwealth 2018 en remportant le relais 4 x 100 m en 3 min et 30,05 s, le 5 avril.

50 m brasse en petit bassin (femmes)

Au meeting de Budapest (HUN) de la coupe du monde de la FINA 2018, le 6 octobre, Alia Atkinson (JAM) s'est imposée au 50 m brasse en 28,56 s. Elle a battu son propre record de 0,08 s.

Le même jour, Nicholas Santos (BRA) a fait tomber un autre record en combinaison avec **le 50 m papillon le plus rapide en petit bassin (hommes)**, en 21,75 s.

Lors du meeting du 11 novembre 2018 à Tokyo (JPN), Xu Jiayu (CHN) a réussi **le 100 m dos le plus rapide en petit bassin (hommes)**, en 48,88 s.

LE 50 M DOS LE PLUS RAPIDE EN GRAND BASSIN (HOMMES)

Kliment Kolesnikov (RUS) a pris l'or en 24 s au championnat d'Europe de natation, à Glasgow (GBR), le 4 août 2018. Le nageur de 18 ans a battu le record de Liam Tancock (24,04 s) établi en 2009, à l'époque où les nageurs portaient des combinaisons synthétiques high-tech (désormais interdites) qui ont fait tomber tous les records.

LE PLUS DE MÉDAILLES D'OR EN UN MONDIAL DE LA FINA (INDIVIDUEL)

Olivia Smoliga (USA) a décroché 8 titres aux 14es mondiaux de la FINA (25 m), les 11-16 décembre 2018, à Hangzhou (CHN). Elle a remporté les 50 m et 100 m dos féminins ainsi que 6 relais (4 féminins et 2 mixtes). Le record précédent en une édition du championnat du monde était de 7 médailles d'or, par Caeleb Dressel en 2017 et Michael Phelps en 2007.

LE 100 M 4 NAGES LE PLUS RAPIDE EN PETIT BASSIN (HOMMES)

En coupe du monde de la FINA 2018, Vladimir Morozov (RUS) a remporté le 100 m 4 nages en 50,26 s à 2 reprises : le 28 septembre, à Eindhoven (NLD), et le 9 novembre, à Tokyo (JPN). Morozov a remporté 88 courses et n'est devancé que par Chad le Clos (ZAF, 143 victoires) pour **le plus de médailles d'or en coupe du monde de la FINA (hommes)**.

400 m nage libre S11 (femmes)

Liesette Bruinsma (NLD) a battu un record vieux de 8 ans de presque 6 s en remportant le 400 m nage libre en 5 min et 4,74 s, au championnat d'Europe de paranatation à Dublin (IRL), le 15 août 2018. La catégorie S11 concerne les nageurs malvoyants.

Toujours à Dublin, Bruinsma a réussi **le 100 m nage libre S11 le plus rapide (femme)**, en 1 min et 5,14 s, et **le 200 m 4 nages SM11 le plus rapide (femme)**, en 2 min et 46,58 s.

100 m brasse SB14 (hommes)

Scott Quin (GBR) a nagé le 100 m brasse en 1 min et 5,28 s, aux championnats du monde de paranatation de Glasgow (GBR), le 27 avril 2019. La catégorie SB14 est réservée aux nageurs déficients intellectuellement.

LE 200 M 4 NAGES SM6 LE PLUS RAPIDE (FEMMES)

Le 25 avril 2019, Maisie Summers-Newton (GBR), âgée de 16 ans, a réalisé le 200 m 4 nages en 2 min et 57,99 s aux championnats du monde de paranatation de Glasgow (GBR). Elle a battu son propre record de 2 min 59,60 s établi le 14 août 2018 (ci-dessus).

Summers-Newton, qui est de petite taille, a aussi établi **le record du 100 m brasse SB6 le plus rapide (femmes)**, en 1 min et 33,63 s, le 15 août 2018.

 DÉC. 16 En 2016, Todd Simpson (CAN) construit **le plus petit bonhomme de neige** – de 3 micromètres de haut –, au Western University Nanofabrication Facility (Ontario, CAN).

 DÉC. 17 A. J. Hackett (NZL) réalise **le saut à l'élastique le plus haut depuis un immeuble**, en plongeant d'une plate-forme de 199 m installée sur la tour Macao, à Macao (CHN), en 2006.

SPORTS NAUTIQUES

LE MEILLEUR SCORE EN SLALOM EN SKI NAUTIQUE (FEMMES)

Le 16 juillet 2018, Regina Jaquess (USA) a passé 4 bouées sur une corde de 10,25 m, à 55 km/h, au July Heat de Floride (USA). C'était son 8e record en slalom, approuvé par la Fédération internationale de ski nautique et wakeboard. Les skieurs doivent suivre un parcours autour de 6 bouées ; à chaque bouée passée, le bateau accélère et la longueur de la corde est progressivement réduite.

Le plus de points en ski nautique (hommes)

Le 16 juillet 2018, Adam Sedlmajer (CZE) a obtenu 2 819,76 points au July Heat. Il a passé 3 bouées avec une corde de 10,25 m, à 58 km/h, inscrit 10 750 points de figures et sauté 66,3 m au total. Le record a été approuvé par la Fédération internationale de ski nautique et wakeboard.

Le 6 octobre 2018, Erika Lang (USA) a inscrit **le plus de points en figures en ski nautique (femmes)**, soit 10 850, au Sunset Fall Classic de Groveland (Floride, USA).

La plus jeune surfeuse qualifiée pour le Championship Tour de la World Surf League

Caroline Marks (USA, née le 14 février 2002) a validé son billet pour le Championship Tour de la WSL 2018 à 15 ans et 264 jours, au terme des qualifications féminines organisées le 5 novembre 2017. Elle a achevé sa 1re saison à la 7e place, ce qui lui a valu le titre de meilleure débutante de l'année.

La plus grande vague surfée (femmes)

Maya Gabeira (BRA) a glissé sur une vague de 20,72 m de haut, à Praia do Norte, à Nazaré (PRT), le 18 janvier 2018. La vague de 7 étages a été mesurée par le groupe Big Wave Award de la WSL.

La vitesse la plus élevée en kitesurf masculin (mille nautique)

Christophe Ballois (FRA) a atteint 35,78 nœuds (66,26 km/h) sur un mille nautique (1,8 km), au Speed Challenge de La Palme (FRA), le 21 juillet 2018. Le record a été ratifié par le World Sailing Speed Record Council (WSSRC). Privé d'avant-bras gauche depuis la naissance, Ballois a appris à naviguer avec un bras, mais il a utilisé une prothèse pour ce record.

La plus rapide sur un mille nautique

Toujours au Speed Challenge de La Palme le 21 juillet 2018, la windsurfeuse Zara Davis (GBR) a atteint 37,29 nœuds (69,06 km/h), comme l'a vérifié le WSSRC.

LE 2 000 M SKIFF DE PARA-AVIRON LE PLUS RAPIDE (FEMMES)

Birgit Skarstein (NOR) a remporté le skiff féminin PR1 en 10 min et 13,630 s, aux championnats du monde d'aviron, à Plovdiv (BUL), le 16 septembre 2018. Elle a battu son propre record du monde de plus de 10 s. Skarstein a aussi représenté la Norvège en ski de fond aux Jeux paralympiques d'hiver 2014 et 2018.

Le 2 000 m le plus rapide en skiff (hommes)

Le 9 septembre 2018, Jason Osborne (DEU) a remporté sa course de qualification en skiff en 6 min 41,030 s aux championnats du monde d'aviron à Plovdiv (BGR).

La plongée en apnée dynamique avec palmes la plus profonde (femmes)

Magdalena Solich-Talanda (POL) a plongé à 243 m avec des palmes en une seule inspiration à Belgrade (SRB), le 29 juin 2018. Elle a battu le record précédent (237 m) détenu depuis 4 ans par Natalia Molchanova.

LE 1 000 M C1 DE L'ICF LE PLUS RAPIDE (HOMMES)

Le 26 mai 2018, Martin Fuksa (CZE) a remporté l'épreuve de C1 (canoë monoplace) sur 1 000 m, en 3 min et 42,385 s, aux mondiaux de course en ligne, à Duisburg (DEU).

Six jours plus tôt, Fuksa avait accompli **le 500 m C1 le plus rapide (hommes)**, en 1 min et 43,669 s, à l'épreuve des mondiaux tenue à Szeged (HUN).

L'APNÉE EN POIDS CONSTANT LA PLUS PROFONDE (HOMMES)

Le 18 juillet 2018, Alexey Molchanov (RUS) a plongé à 130 m, à la compétition d'apnée Vertical Blue de Dean's Blue Hole, aux Bahamas. C'est la plongée sans aide la plus profonde jamais réalisée. Lors de ce Vertical Blue marqué par plusieurs records, Molchanov a aussi réalisé **l'apnée en immersion libre la plus profonde (hommes)**, soit 125 m, le 24 juillet 2018.

LE PLUS DE TITRES MONDIAUX ASP/WORLD SURF LEAGUE (FEMMES)

Stephanie Gilmore (AUS) a remporté la World Surf League 2018, décrochant ainsi son 7e titre mondial. Elle égale Layne Beachley (AUS), championne en 1998-2003 et 2006. Gilmore s'était qualifiée en 2007 pour le World Tour de l'Association of Surfing Professionals (ASP), qu'elle a remporté dès sa 1re saison, ainsi qu'en 2008-2010, 2012 et 2014. La World Surf League a remplacé l'ASP World Tour en 2015.

> Gilmore s'est imposée en Australie, au Brésil et en Afrique du Sud avant de remporter le titre WSL 2018.

DÉC. 18 En 1898, Gaston de Chasseloup-Laubat (FRA) établit **le 1er record de vitesse terrestre reconnu**, à Achères (Yvelines, FRA), en atteignant 63,15 km/h dans sa Jeantaud *Duc* électrique.

DÉC. 19 En 2014, Puskar Nepal (NPL) enchaîne **le plus de coups de pied contre sa propre tête en 1 min** (134), à Katmandou (NPL), devant des invités triés sur le volet.

239

SPORTS D'HIVER

LE 3 000 M EN PATINAGE DE VITESSE LE PLUS RAPIDE (FEMMES)

Martina Sáblíková (CZE) a remporté la finale de coupe du monde ISU de patinage de vitesse en 3 min et 52,02 s, le 9 mars 2019 à Salt Lake City (Utah, USA). Elle a battu son propre record, 3 min et 53,31 s, établi 1 semaine avant aux mondiaux toutes épreuves, où elle a aussi réalisé **le 5 000 m le plus rapide (femmes)** (6 min et 42,01 s).

LE 500 M SUR PISTE COURTE LE PLUS RAPIDE (HOMMES)

Le 11 novembre 2018, Wu Dajing (CHN) a gagné le 500 m masculin en 39,505 s, à la coupe du monde ISU de patinage de vitesse sur piste courte, à Salt Lake City (Utah, USA). Il a profité pleinement de l'altitude de l'Utah Olympic Oval, où l'air oppose moins de résistance et la glace contient moins d'oxygène, ce qui la rend plus dure et rapide.

Le 500 m en patinage de vitesse le plus rapide (hommes)

Organisée les 9-10 mars 2019, à Salt Lake City (Utah, USA), la finale de coupe du monde ISU de patinage de vitesse a battu tous les records. Pavel Kulizhnikov (RUS) a couru sa 1re course sur 500 m en 33,61 s, le 9 mars. Le même jour, Brittany Bowe (USA) a réalisé **le 1 000 m le plus rapide (femmes)** (1 min et 11,61 s).

Le 10 mars, Miho Takagi (JPN) a signé **le 1 500 m le plus rapide (femmes)** (1 min et 49,83 s) et Kjeld Nuis (NLD) **le 1 500 m le plus rapide (hommes)** (1 min et 40,17 s).

Le moins de points en mini-combiné sur piste longue (femmes)

Le mini-combiné comprend 4 courses sur 500 m, 1 000 m, 1 500 m et 3 000 m. Grâce au système samalog, les temps sur chaque distance sont convertis en points, le score le plus bas remportant l'épreuve. Les 9-10 mars 2018, aux mondiaux juniors de patinage de vitesse à Salt Lake City (Utah, USA), Joy Beune (NLD) a obtenu un score total de 153,776 points. Elle a aussi établi le record junior dans 3 des 4 distances.

Le relais 5 000 m le plus rapide sur piste courte (hommes)

L'équipe hongroise – composée de Csaba Burján, de l'ancien patineur américain Cole Krueger et des frères Shaoang Liu et Shaolin Sándor Liu – a couvert les 45 tours du relais masculin 5 000 m en 6 min et 28,625 s, le 4 novembre 2018, lors de la coupe du monde ISU sur piste courte, à Calgary (Alberta, CAN).

LE PLUS DE TITRES AUX MONDIAUX DE LUGE (FEMMES)

Lors des mondiaux de luge 2019, à Winterberg (DEU), Natalie Geisenberger (DEU) a décroché ses 8e et 9e titres mondiaux. Elle s'est imposée en individuel et en sprint, après ses 4 titres en relais et 3 en individuels.

Geisenberger compte aussi **le plus de titres en coupe du monde féminine de luge** (7 consécutifs), de 2012-2013 à 2018-2019.

Le quadruple lutz de Chen aux mondiaux lui a valu la meilleure note en exécution pour un saut : 4,76.

PATINAGE : UNE NOUVELLE ÈRE

Au début de la saison 2018-2019, l'International Skating Union (ISU) a élargi son système de notes d'exécution de -3/3 à -5/5 et remis à zéro tous les scores de patinage artistique. Les records du monde ont été redéfinis tout au long de la saison dans les 4 disciplines, notamment lors d'une édition spectaculaire des championnats du monde 2019, à Saitama (JPN).

MEILLEURS SCORES EN PATINAGE ARTISTIQUE

HOMMES	ATHLÈTE	POINTS	LIEU	DATE
Programme court	Yuzuru Hanyu (JPN)	110,53	Moscou (RUS)	16 nov. 2018
Libre	Nathan Chen (USA, à droite)	216,02	Saitama (JPN)	23 mars 2019
Total combiné	Nathan Chen	323,42	Saitama (JPN)	23 mars 2019
FEMMES				
Programme court	Rika Kihira (JPN)	83,97	Fukuoka (JPN)	11 avril 2019
Libre	Alina Zagitova (RUS)	158,50	Oberstdorf (DEU)	28 sept. 2018
Total combiné	Alina Zagitova	238,43	Oberstdorf (DEU)	28 sept. 2018
COUPLES				
Programme court	Evgenia Tarasova et Vladimir Morozov (RUS)	81,21	Saitama (JPN)	20 mars 2019
Libre	Sui Wenjing et Han Cong (CHN, à gauche)	155,60	Saitama (JPN)	21 mars 2019
Total combiné	Sui Wenjing et Han Cong	234,84	Saitama (JPN)	21 mars 2019
DANSE				
Rythmique	Gabriella Papadakis et Guillaume Cizeron (FRA)	88,42	Saitama (JPN)	22 mars 2019
Libre	Gabriella Papadakis et Guillaume Cizeron	135,82	Fukuoka (JPN)	12 avril 2019
Total combiné	Gabriella Papadakis et Guillaume Cizeron	223,13	Fukuoka (JPN)	12 avril 2019

Chiffres actualisés au 12 avril 2019

DÉC. 20 Le cracker de Noël le plus long (63,1 m) est fabriqué par les parents des élèves de Ley Hill School & Pre-School à Chesham (Buckinghamshire, GBR) en 2001. Il contient des ballons, des jouets et des blagues.

DÉC. 21 En 2012, le clip de *Gangnam Style*, de PSY (KOR), devient **la 1re vidéo vue 1 milliard de fois**, seulement 159 jours après avoir été postée sur YouTube en juillet.

LE PLUS DE COURSES GAGNÉES EN COUPE DU MONDE FIS

Aucun skieur n'a remporté plus de courses de coupe du monde de la Fédération internationale de ski (FIS) qu'Amélie Wenger-Reymond (CHE). Elle a décroché sa 141e victoire en télémark le 17 février 2019. Deux autres skieurs ont dépassé les 100 victoires : Marit Bjørgen (114, ski de fond) et Conny Kissling (106, ski acrobatique).

Elle compte **le plus de victoires en descente (femmes)** (43) et **le plus de victoires en Super-G (femmes)** (28). Poussée à la retraite par des blessures en 2018-2019, Vonn n'était qu'à 4 longueurs du **record absolu de victoires en coupe du monde** (86), établi par la légende Ingemar Stenmark (SWE) en 1974-1989.

Le médaillé le plus âgé aux mondiaux FIS de ski alpin

Le 6 février 2019, Johan Clarey (FRA, né le 8 janvier 1981) a gagné l'argent aux mondiaux, à 38 ans et 29 jours, dans le Super-G masculin, à Åre (SWE). Clarey a fait l'essentiel de sa carrière en descente. Le 19 janvier 2013, il signe **la vitesse la plus élevée en coupe du monde de descente** (161,9 km/h), à Wengen (CHE). Il était le 1er skieur à franchir la barre des 100 miles par heure (100,6 mph) en compétition.

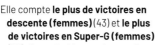

LE PLUS DE VICTOIRES EN COUPE DU MONDE DE SKI ACROBATIQUE (HOMMES)

Mikaël Kingsbury (CAN) a décroché 8 titres consécutifs en freestyle depuis 2011-2012. En 2018-2019, il a gagné 7 des 9 épreuves de coupe du monde, obtenant ainsi le globe de cristal de ski acrobatique pour la 8e année de suite. Le total de 56 victoires de Kingsbury représente aussi **le plus de courses gagnées en coupe du monde de ski acrobatique**.

Le plus de victoires individuelles en coupe du monde de saut à ski (femmes)

Sara Takanashi (JPN) a gagné 56 épreuves en coupe du monde de saut, du 3 mars 2012 au 10 février 2019.

Le plus de victoires en skeleton en coupe du monde IBSF (hommes)

Le 18 janvier 2019, Martins Dukurs (LVA) a obtenu son 51e succès en skeleton en coupe du monde de la Fédération internationale de bobsleigh et skeleton (IBSF), à Innsbruck (AUT).

Le plus de pays aux mondiaux de bandy

Semblable au hockey sur glace, le bandy se joue par équipes de 11 sur une patinoire de la taille d'un terrain de foot et avec un ballon. Vingt pays, dont la Chine, la Grande-Bretagne et la Somalie, ont participé aux mondiaux de bandy du 21 janvier au 2 février 2019, à Vänersborg (SWE).

Le plus de victoires aux mondiaux de bandy (hommes) est de 14, par l'Union soviétique, entre 1957 et 1991. La Suède et la Russie comptent 12 titres. **Chez les femmes**, le record est de 8, par la Suède, entre 2004 et 2018, avec un seul échec en 2014.

Le plus de victoires au championnat canadien de curling

La compétition provinciale The Brier est organisée depuis 1927. Le 10 mars 2019, l'Alberta a remporté son 28e titre en battant la Team Wild Card, à Brandon (Manitoba, CAN).

LE PLUS DE COURSES GAGNÉES EN UNE SAISON DE SKI ALPIN

Mikaela Shiffrin (USA) a survolé la saison 2018-2019 avec 17 victoires lors de la coupe du monde de ski alpin. C'est 3 de plus que le record précédent, établi par Vreni Schneider en 1988-1989. Shiffrin est la 1re athlète à gagner les titres en slalom, géant, Super-G et général au cours de la même saison. Parmi ses 60 victoires en carrière, elle compte **le plus de courses gagnées en slalom (femmes)** (40).

Le plus de titres aux mondiaux ISU de simple distance (hommes)

Sven Kramer (NLD) a décroché son 20e titre en carrière aux mondiaux ISU de patinage de vitesse simple distance 2019. Il compte 8 titres sur 5 000 m, 5 sur 10 000 m et 7 en poursuite par équipe.

Le plus de titres féminins est de 15, par Martina Sáblíková (en haut à gauche) entre 2007 et 2019. Elle totalise 5 titres sur 3 000 m et 10 sur 5 000 m.

Le plus de victoires en coupe du monde FIS de ski alpin (femmes)

Lindsey Vonn (USA) a remporté 82 courses de coupe du monde FIS de ski alpin, du 3 décembre 2004 au 14 mars 2018.

LE PLUS DE TITRES AU GÉNÉRAL EN SKI ALPIN (HOMMES)

Marcel Hirscher (AUT) a été sacré 8 fois de suite au général en coupe du monde FIS de ski alpin, de 2011-2012 à 2018-2019. Il a gagné 67 courses : 32 slaloms, 31 géants, 3 parallèles et 1 Super-G. En 2017-2018, Hirscher a gagné 13 courses – **le plus de courses gagnées en 1 saison de ski alpin (hommes)** –, autant qu'Ingemar Stenmark (SWE, 1978-1979) et Hermann Maier (AUT, 2000-2001).

DÉC. 22 Wilhelm Röntgen (DEU) dévoile la **1re radiographie publiée**, de la main de sa femme, à l'université de Würzburg (DEU), en 1895. En voyant ses os, elle s'est exclamée : "J'ai vu ma mort !"

DÉC. 23 En 2013, Pabba Soujanya (IND) réalise **le plus de claquements de doigts par un individu** (1 233), en Andhra Pradesh (IND). Il ne lui a fallu que 3 min et 59 s pour battre le record.

241

SPORTS EXTRÊMES

Le 25 janv. 2019, Kelly Sildaru a remporté l'or en slopestyle avec **le score le plus élevé aux Winter X-Games** – 99,00.

La plus longue séquence de formations à 4 en chute libre indoor (femmes)

Les Aerodyne Weembi Girls – Clémentine Le Bohec, Paméla Lissajoux, Christine Malnis et Sophia Pécout (toutes FRA) – ont enchaîné 45 formations au championnat d'Europe de chute libre indoor, à Voss (NOR), le 13 avril 2018.

Le score combiné le plus bas en paraski

Le paraski associe 2 sports : le slalom géant et le parachute de précision. Le score total le plus bas après 2 descentes et 6 sauts est de **7 pour les hommes**, par Sebastian Graser (AUT), à Bad Leonfelden (AUT), le 16 février 2019.

Le record féminin est de 10, par Magdalena Schwertl (AUT), au cours du même événement.

La descente d'escaliers à vélo la plus longue

Du sommet d'une colline qui surplombe Bogota (COL), le Devotos de Monserrate, s'initie une descente de 2,40 km le long de chemins étroits comprenant 1 060 marches. La dernière édition de la course – organisée par Red Bull Colombia – a été remportée par Marcelo Gutiérrez en 4 min et 42,48 s, le 16 février 2019.

LA VITESSE LA PLUS ÉLEVÉE EN PILOTAGE SOUS VOILE (FEMMES)

Le 4 juillet 2018, Cornelia Mihai (ARE, née ROU) a parcouru 70 m en 2,273 s, aux championnats du monde de pilotage sous voile à Wrocław (POL), soit une vitesse moyenne de 110,86 km/h.

Le record masculin est de 2,019 s, par Mohammed Baker (ARE), à Dubaï (ARE), le 24 avril 2015, avec une vitesse moyenne de 124,81 km/h. Les 2 records ont été ratifiés par la Fédération aéronautique internationale (FAI).

Le plus haut saut en monocycle (hommes)

Le triple champion du monde de monocycle Mike Taylor (GBR) a sauté sur une plate-forme, à 148,5 cm de hauteur, à l'Unicon XIX d'Ansan (KOR), le 3 août 2018.

Toujours en 2018, Lisa-Maria Hanny (DEU) a réalisé **le saut le plus lointain en monocycle (femmes)** (à 3,35 m), le 16 juin, à Warendorf (DEU). Les 2 records ont été validés par la Fédération internationale de monocycle.

LE PLUS DE MÉDAILLES EN UNE ÉDITION DES WINTER X-GAMES (FEMMES)

Aux Winter X-Games 2019, sur les pistes de Buttermilk, à Aspen (Colorado, USA), la skieuse freestyle Kelly Sildaru (EST) a remporté 3 médailles en 25 h : l'or en slopestyle, l'argent en superpipe et le bronze en big air. Elle égale le total de la snowboardeuse Jennie Waara (SWE) en 1997, qui avait pris l'or en boardercross, l'argent en halfpipe et le bronze en slopestyle, à Big Bear Lake (Californie, USA).

La plus jeune championne aux Winter X-Games

Le 19 mai 2018, Kokomo Murase (JPN, née le 7 novembre 2004) a remporté l'or en big air de snowboard aux X-Games de Norvège à 13 ans et 193 jours. Elle est la 1re femme à plaquer un backside double-cork 1260 en compétition, ce qui lui a valu un 49,66 sur 50.

Le plus de médailles gagnées aux X-Games (femmes)

La snowboardeuse Jamie Anderson (USA) a décroché 16 médailles aux Winter X-Games entre 2006 et 2019 : 14 en slopestyle (5 en or, 7 en argent, 2 en bronze) et 2 en big air (en bronze).

Le plus de participations aux Winter X-Games

Le 26 janvier 2019, la septuple championne Kelly Clark (USA) a participé à ses 22es et derniers Winter X-Games.

LE PLUS DE VICTOIRES EN BEST TRICK DE MOTO X AUX SUMMER X-GAMES

Jackson Strong (AUS) a survolé la catégorie Best Trick de Moto X à 4 reprises : en 2011-2012, 2016 et 2018. Il a décroché son 4e titre le 21 juillet 2018 avec un no-handed front flip dès son 1er run qui lui a valu un score de 93,00. Strong a aussi obtenu l'argent en Best Trick de Snow Bike aux Winter X-Games de 2018.

LA PLUS JEUNE DOUBLE CHAMPIONNE AUX X-GAMES

Aux X-Games 2018 de Minneapolis (Minnesota, USA), Brighton Zeuner (USA, née le 14 juillet 2004) a conservé son titre en skateboard park à 14 ans et 8 jours. Son score de 90,33 a suffi à lui offrir sa 2e médaille d'or. Elle avait remporté la 1re le 15 juillet 2017, à 13 ans et 1 jour, devenant **la plus jeune championne aux X-Games**.

LE PLUS DE VICTOIRES AU RED BULL CLIFF DIVING WORLD SERIES (HOMMES)

Gary Hunt (GBR) a remporté la compétition de plongeon de haut vol 7 fois : en 2010-2012, 2014-2016 et 2018. Son dernier titre, glané à Polignano a Mare (ITA) le 23 septembre (à droite), marquait sa 34e victoire en 72 épreuves individuelles.

Le plus de victoires (femmes) est de 3, par Rhiannan Iffland (AUS) en 2016-2018.

DÉC. 24 En 1968, l'équipage d'*Apollo 8* en orbite autour de la Lune – Frank Borman, Bill Anders et James Lovell (tous USA) – assiste au **1er lever de Terre vu par l'Homme**.

DÉC. 25 En 2017, Beijing Hyundai et l'office du tourisme de Mohe (tous CHN) mettent la touche finale à **la plus longue liste de Noël**, à Mohe (province du Heilongjiang, CHN), avec 124 969 vœux.

MONDE DU SPORT

LE PLUS DE VICTOIRES EN SEPAK TAKRAW AUX JEUX ASIATIQUES (HOMMES)

Les joueurs de sepak takraw utilisent leur tête, leur poitrine et leurs pieds pour pousser une balle en rotin au-dessus d'un filet de volley. La Thaïlande a remporté le *regu* (à 3 joueurs) masculin aux Jeux asiatiques 6 fois : en 1998, 2002, 2006, 2010, 2014 et 2018. Le dernier titre a été acquis après une victoire en 2 sets contre la Malaisie, le 22 août 2018, au Ranau Hall (Palembang, IDN).

LE PLUS DE VICTOIRES AUX MONDIAUX DE LUTTE DANS LE JUS DE VIANDE

La compétition la plus juteuse du monde se tient tous les ans depuis 2007 devant le pub Rose 'n' Bowl de Stacksteads (Lancashire, GBR). Les combats de 2 min sont jugés sur les tenues, le divertissement et les talents de lutte. Joel Hicks (ci-dessus) détient **le record masculin** avec 5 succès. **Le record féminin** est de 2, par Roxy Afzal, alias "The Oxo Fox" ou "Foxy Roxy" (encadré), et Emma Slater (toutes GBR).

Le tournoi de lutte des doigts le plus ancien

La lutte de doigts, appelée "fingerhakeln", fait l'objet d'un tournoi en Bavière (DEU) depuis le XIVe siècle. Les participants choisissent un doigt (souvent le majeur), lequel est attaché à celui de l'adversaire par une bande de cuir. L'objectif est de tirer l'autre par-dessus une table.

Le plus de victoires aux mondiaux de lutte d'orteils

Alan "Nasty" Nash (GBR) a obtenu son 15e titre en lutte d'orteils masculine – son 7e consécutif – en battant Ben Woodroffe en finale de l'édition 2018, le 22 juin, à Fenny Bentley (Derbyshire, GBR).

Le plus rapide à terminer les mondiaux de snorkelling en tourbière

Le 26 août 2018, Neil Rutter (GBR) a nagé jusqu'à la victoire en 1 min et 18,81 s, au Llanwrtyd Wells de Powys (GBR). Les participants doivent faire 2 longueurs dans un marais de 55 m.

LE PLUS D'ÉQUIPES EN COUPE DU MONDE DE QUIDDITCH

Vingt-neuf équipes, dont le Vietnam, la Slovénie et la Catalogne, ont participé à la coupe du monde 2018 de quidditch, organisée les 27 juin-2 juillet, à Florence (ITA). Les États-Unis ont obtenu leur 3e titre - **le plus de victoires en coupe du monde de quidditch** - en battant la Belgique 120-70 en finale. L'attrapeur Harry Greenhouse a pris le vif d'or des Belges pour l'emporter. Le seul autre pays champion est l'Australie, en 2016.

Le meilleur chrono féminin est de 1 min et 22,56 s, par Kirsty Johnson (GBR), le 24 août 2014.

Le saut de canal le plus long (hommes)

La distance la plus longue pour sauter par-dessus un canal avec une perche en fierljeppen ("long saut"), dans le Frison occidental, est de 22,21 m, par Jaco de Groot (NLD), le 12 août 2017, à Zegveld (NLD).

Le record féminin est de 17,58 m, par Marrit van der Wal (NLD), le 16 juillet 2016, à Burgum (NLD).

La plus longue rotation à 360° en kiiking (hommes)

Dans ce sport estonien, l'objectif est de faire des tours complets sur des balançoires géantes. Le 25 août 2018, Sven Saarpere (EST) a fait sa révolution avec une balançoire longue de 7,38 m, à Tallinn (EST).

La 1re championne du monde de footgolf (femmes)

Sophie Brown (GBR) a remporté la 1re coupe du monde féminine organisée par la Fédération internationale de footgolf (FIFG), les 9-16 décembre 2018, à Marrakech (MAR). Brown a fini avec 280 coups en 4 tours, 6 coups sous le par. Les joueurs suivent un parcours de golf avec un ballon de foot à rentrer dans un trou de 53 cm.

Le plus de championnats All-Ireland Senior de camogie

Le camogie est un sport collectif féminin semblable au hurling. Les "Rebelettes" de Cork ont décroché leur 28e titre depuis 1934 le 9 septembre 2018 en battant Kilkenny 0-14 à 0-13 en prolongation, au Croke Park de Dublin (IRL).

Le plus de titres mondiaux en rodéo

Le 15 décembre 2018, Trevor Brazile (USA) a attaché sa 24e boucle de ceinture en or, au championnat du monde de la Professional Rodeo Cowboys Association. Il compte **le plus de titres mondiaux all-around** (14). Ceux-ci sont décernés chaque saison au meilleur vainqueur d'au moins 2 épreuves.

Le plus de titres nationaux de NATwA

Le légendaire Larry Kahn (USA) a obtenu 30 titres en simple et 25 en duo au championnat américain du jeu de puces de la NATwA entre 1976 et 2018.

LE PLUS DE VICTOIRES AUX MONDIAUX FÉMININS DE FISTBALL

Le 28 juillet 2018, l'Allemagne a obtenu son 3e titre consécutif - le 6e au total - aux championnats du monde féminins de fistball, en battant la Suisse 4-1, à l'ÖBV Arena de Linz (AUT). Les Allemandes avaient déjà gagné en 1994, 1998, 2006, 2014 et 2016.

LE PLUS DE LANCERS DE TRONCS EN 3 MIN

Le 20 juillet 2018, Daniel Frame (CAN) a lancé le tronc 16 fois en 180 s, au Middleton Heart du Valley Festival (Nouvelle-Écosse, CAN). Il a décroché le record à sa seconde tentative, un tronc s'étant brisé lors de la première. **Le record féminin** est de 15, par Heather Boundy (CAN), le 10 septembre 2016 à Trenton (Ontario, CAN).

DÉC. 26 Cranston Chipperfield (GBR), 3 ans, devient **le plus jeune Monsieur Loyal**, en 2005, au Circus Royale de Strathclyde Country Park (Lanarkshire, GBR).

DÉC. 27 Maria Leijerstam (GBR) atteint le pôle Sud en 2013 après être partie du bord de la barrière de Ross dans l'Antarctique sur un tricycle couché. Elle est **la 1re personne à pédaler au pôle Sud**.

Les 1ers championnats d'orientation ont été organisés en 1966. Ils ont désormais lieu tous les ans.

LE PLUS DE TITRES EN COUPE DU MONDE FÉMININE DE BASEBALL

En 2018, le Japon a remporté la coupe du monde féminine de baseball pour la 6e fois de suite grâce à une victoire 6-0 contre le Taipei chinois, le 31 août, à Viera (Floride, USA). Les Japonaises ont remporté leurs 9 matchs en ne concédant que 4 points pour 63 inscrits. Elles ont enchaîné 30 victoires sans la moindre défaite depuis les mondiaux 2012.

LES PLUS RAPIDES À...

Escalader 15 m (femmes)

Le 26 avril 2019, Song Yi Ling (CHN) a remporté l'escalade de vitesse en quart de finale en 7,101 s aux mondiaux de la Fédération internationale d'escalade sportive, à Chongqing (CHN). Elle a battu le précédent record féminin, détenu par 2 escaladeuses, de 0,219 s.

L'escalade de vitesse la plus rapide sur 15 m (hommes) est de 5,48 s par Reza Alipour (IRN), le 30 avril 2017.

Atteindre 2 000 m sur rameur d'intérieur Concept2 (hommes)

Le 10 mars 2018, Josh Dunkley-Smith (AUS) a ramé 2 km sur un rameur d'intérieur Concept2 en 5 min et 35,8 s, à l'entraînement de l'équipe d'aviron australienne. Il a battu le record de Rob Waddell (NZL) établi 10 ans plus tôt – 5 min et 36,6 s.

Toujours en 2018, le 10 juillet, Jennifer Casson (CAN) a réalisé **le 2 000 m sur Concept2 le plus rapide (femmes, poids légers)** en 6 min et 53,8 s, au Rowing Canada Aviron National Training Centre, à Victoria (CAN).

Nager sur 400 m en bipalme (femmes)

Le 18 juillet 2018, Maria Patlasova (RUS) a décroché l'or en 3 min et 44,92 s, aux mondiaux de nage avec palmes, à Belgrade (SRB). C'était son 2e record du monde en 3 jours, après avoir fait partie de l'équipe russe qui a signé **le relais 4 x 100 en nage en bipalme le plus rapide (mixte)**, en 2 min et 58,04 s, le 16 juillet. Patlasova était accompagnée de Lev Shtraikh, Aleksey Fedkin et Vitalina Simonova.

Toujours le 16 juillet, Yi Ting Sun (CHN) a réussi **le 400 m nage avec palmes en surface le plus rapide (femmes)**, en 3 min et 12,10 s.

Remorquer un mannequin sur 100 m avec palmes (hommes)

Dans cette épreuve de la Fédération internationale de sauvetage (ILSF), les participants nagent 50 m, remontent un mannequin immergé et le ramènent jusqu'à la ligne d'arrivée. Jan Malkowski (DEU) y est parvenu en 44,21 s, à l'épreuve de DLRG Cup Pool 2018, à Warendorf (DEU), le 23 septembre 2018.

Le record féminin est de 50,43 s, par Lucrezia Fabretti (ITA), à l'Open d'Italie, à Milan (ITA), le 16 décembre 2018. Elle a battu son propre record de 50,78 s, établi le 12 septembre 2018 aux championnats d'Europe junior.

LE PLUS DE...

Titres en World League de water-polo (femmes)

Les États-Unis ont remporté la World League féminine de la FINA 12 fois : en 2004, 2006-2007, 2009-2012 et 2014-2018. La compétition se tient tous les ans depuis 2004 et regroupe les meilleures nations du monde dans un format de championnat.

Le record masculin est de 11 titres, par la Serbie, en 2005-2008, 2010-2011 et 2013-2017.

LE PLUS DE TITRES AUX MONDIAUX D'ORIENTATION LONGUE DISTANCE (HOMMES)

Olav Lundanes (NOR) a remporté son 5e titre longue distance aux mondiaux d'orientation en 2018. Il est arrivé en tête le 11 août, en 1 h, 37 min et 43 s, à Riga (LVA). C'était sa 3e victoire consécutive dans l'épreuve, en plus de ses titres obtenus en 2010 et 2012.

LE PLUS DE MONDIAUX DE TRIAL INDOOR ET OUTDOOR

Antoni Bou (ESP) domine son sport comme peu d'autres. Il a remporté le championnat du monde FIM de trial (image principale) et le X-Trial (encadré) tous les ans entre 2007 et le 9 mars 2019, soit 25 titres. Bou a remporté 104 épreuves outdoor et 61 indoor. Le trial n'est pas une discipline de vitesse : les pilotes de moto doivent franchir une série d'obstacles sans poser pied à terre.

DÉC. 28 En 2010, Thomas Müller et Heiko Becher (tous 2 DEU) parcourent **la plus grande distance en raquettes en 24 h** (94,41 km), entre Gräfenwarth et Saalburg (DEU).

DÉC. 29 **Le pont le plus haut** est inauguré en 2016 à Dugexiang (province de Guizhou, CHN). Le pont du Beipanjiang se dresse à 565 m au-dessus de la rivière Beipan.

LE PLUS DE COURSES DE GROUPE 1 GAGNÉES PAR UN CHEVAL

Le 13 avril 2019, la jument Winx a remporté sa 25ᵉ épreuve dans le Groupe 1, au Queen Elizabeth Stakes, à Sydney (AUS). Elle avait dépassé le record de 22 victoires détenu par Hurricane Fly's lors de sa victoire au Chipping Norton Stakes, le 2 mars 2019. Winx a été mise à la retraite pour se reproduire après son triomphe au Queen Elizabeth Stakes, sa 33ᵉ victoire consécutive.

Speedway (Colorado, USA). Le pilote de 69 ans a aussi amélioré son record du **plus de finales NHRA** (251).

Titres en Champions Trophy de hockey sur gazon (hommes)

L'Australie a obtenu un 15ᵉ sacre lors de la dernière édition, le 1ᵉʳ juillet 2018, en battant l'Inde 3-1 aux tirs au but.

Le plus de titres en Champions Trophy (femmes) est de 7, par l'Argentine et les Pays-Bas, champions 2018. Pour plus de hockey, voir p. 224.

Victoires au Prix de l'Arc de Triomphe (jockey)

Frankie Dettori (ITA) a triomphé dans la course hippique la mieux dotée pour la 6ᵉ fois en 2018, chevauchant Enable pour la 2ᵉ année consécutive. Dettori a aussi gagné avec Lammtarra (1995), Sakhee (2001), Marienbard (2002) et Golden Horn (2015).

Médailles d'or en coupe du monde de voile (hommes)

Au 1ᵉʳ mars 2019, l'Australie totalisait 53 médailles d'or en épreuves masculines de coupe du monde de voile depuis 2008.

Le plus de médailles d'or (femmes) est de 26, pour la Grande-Bretagne, une de plus que la Chine et 2 de plus que les Pays-Bas.

LE PLUS DE TITRES EN INDIVIDUEL AUX MONDIAUX DE BADMINTON (FEMMES)

Le 5 août 2018, Carolina Marín (ESP) a été sacrée pour la 3ᵉ fois en individuel, aux mondiaux de la Fédération mondiale de badminton, à Nankin (CHN). Comme lors de la finale olympique 2016, Marín a battu P. V. Sindhu (IND) en finale, sur le score de 21-19, 21-10. Elle s'était aussi imposée en 2014 et 2015.

Titres aux mondiaux de squash (femmes)

Nicol David (MYS) a annoncé sa retraite sportive en 2019 après une carrière brillante. Elle a passé 9 ans en tant que n° 1 mondiale (2006-2015), un record représentant 81 titres sur le tour et 8 sacres aux championnats du monde individuels (en 2005-2006, 2008-2012 et 2014).

LES MEILLEURS...

Score pour des figures en ski nautique pieds nus (hommes)

Le 14 août 2018, David Small (GBR) a glané 13 350 points aux mondiaux de ski nautique pieds nus organisés sur le Dream Lake, à Napanee (Ontario, CAN).

Small a aussi réalisé **le plus long saut en ski nautique pieds nus (hommes)**, soit 29,9 m, à Brandenburg (DEU), le 11 août 2010.

Éditions du Rallye Dakar (consécutives)

Yoshimasa Sugawara (JPN) a couru son 36ᵉ Dakar consécutif en 2019. Cette série ne comprend pas l'édition 2008, qui a été annulée, mais pour laquelle il était enregistré.

Victoires en National Hot Rod Association (NHRA)

Le 22 juillet 2018, John Force (USA) a décroché sa 149ᵉ victoire en Funny Car depuis 1979, au Dodge Mile-High NHRA Nationals, organisé sur le Bandimere

LA PLUS RAPIDE SUR LA MONTANE SPINE RACE

Le 16 janvier 2019, Jasmin Paris (GBR) est devenue la 1ʳᵉ femme à remporter la Montane Spine Race, en franchissant la ligne d'arrivée en 83 h, 12 min et 23 s. L'ultramarathon hivernal de 431 km sans assistance, qui traverse le Derbyshire jusqu'à la frontière écossaise, représente un dénivelé positif de 13 106 m.

Ioseba Fernández a aussi accompli **le 200 m le plus rapide en rollers de vitesse sur route (hommes)**, soit 15,879 s, le 9 décembre 2012.

LE 100 M LE PLUS RAPIDE EN ROLLERS DE VITESSE SUR ROUTE (HOMMES)

Aux mondiaux 2018 de rollers de vitesse, à Arnhem (NLD), Ioseba Fernández (ESP, à droite) a gagné sa demi-finale du 100 m masculin sur route en 9,684 s, le 7 juillet. En plus du record du monde, il est reparti avec la médaille d'or en battant Edwin Estrada (COL, à gauche) en finale.

DÉC. 30 **Le plus grand piano** est utilisé lors d'un concert en Pologne en 2010. Construit par Daniel Czapiewski (POL), il comporte 156 touches et mesure 2,49 m de large, 6,07 m de long et 1,9 m de haut.

DÉC. 31 En 2008, la Sun Bowl Association fête le Nouvel An en organisant **la plus grande danse YMCA**, au Texas (USA). Quelque 40 148 participants se sont déhanchés sur le titre des Village People.

245

INDEX

Les entrées en **gras** dans l'index se réfèrent à des thématiques principales ; les entrées en **CAPITALES GRAS** correspondent aux chapitres.

CONSULTANTS

CONSULTANTS

Le contenu du *Guinness World Records 2020* est issu non seulement des candidatures aux records réalisées par le grand public, mais aussi de l'apport d'un réseau mondial de consultants et de contributeurs, que nous tenons à remercier ici.

L'École des fourmis : le Dr Kirsti Abbott, spécialiste des fourmis, dirige The School of Ants en Australie, un projet de sciences participatives destiné à étudier la diversité et la répartition des fourmis au sein des paysages urbains. Elle fait découvrir aux jeunes générations le monde passionnant des fourmis. *www.schoolofants.net.au*

Le Centre d'étude des montagnes : Martin Price est directeur du Centre d'étude des montagnes de Perth College, University of the Highlands and Islands (GBR). Son équipe mène des recherches et des missions de conseil variées en Écosse et dans le monde entier. Elle organise également des conférences. Le professeur Price occupe actuellement une chaire de développement durable en montagne à l'Unesco. *www.perth.uhi.ac.uk/mountainstudies*

L'université de Liverpool : le Dr João Pedro de Magalhães dirige le Groupe de génomique intégrative des personnes âgées de l'université de Liverpool (GBR), où sont effectuées des recherches sur les mécanismes génétiques, cellulaires et moléculaires du vieillissement. Il a également créé *AnAge*, une base de données ciblée sur le vieillissement et le déroulement de la vie des animaux ; y sont inclus les records de longévité. *pcwww.liv.ac.uk/~aging/*

Le Laboratoire de sismologie de Berkeley : le professeur Michael Manga est le président du département des Sciences terrestres et planétaires de l'université de Californie à Berkeley (USA). Il est spécialiste des éruptions volcaniques et des geysers sur la Terre comme sur d'autres planètes. Ses recherches ont été reconnues par le prix MacArthur et son élection à l'Académie nationale des sciences des États-Unis. *seismo.berkeley.edu/~manga*

La Société américaine des ichtyologistes et herpétologistes (ASIH) : cette société fondée en 1913 se consacre à l'étude scientifique des poissons, des amphibiens et des reptiles. Son objectif est d'améliorer la connaissance de ces animaux, de partager son savoir et de soutenir les jeunes scientifiques qui feront avancer la recherche dans ce domaine. *www.asih.org*

La Société nationale américaine de spéléologie (NSS) : Scott Engel est le vice-président exécutif de la NSS, une organisation à but non lucratif consacrée à l'étude scientifique, à l'exploration, à la protection et à la conservation des grottes et du karst. La NSS prône également une exploration et une gestion responsable des grottes. Fondée en 1941 aux États-Unis, elle est la plus grande organisation de ce type dans le monde. *caves.org*

Le Centre de recherches Jane Goodall : le Dr Craig Stanford, primatologue, est professeur d'anthropologie et de biologie à l'université de Californie du Sud, où il est également le codirecteur du centre de recherches Jane Goodall. Il a mené des recherches approfondies sur les grands singes, les singes et d'autres animaux d'Afrique orientale, d'Asie, ainsi que d'Amérique centrale et du Sud. Il est l'auteur de plus d'une dizaine d'ouvrages et d'une centaine d'articles scientifiques. *dornsife.usc.edu/labs/janegoodall*

La Société internationale de limnologie (SIL) : le Dr Tamar Zohary mène des recherches au Laboratoire limnologique Kinneret de l'Institut de recherche océanographique & limnologique d'Israël. Elle s'intéresse à l'écologie du phytoplancton et à l'impact des fluctuations du niveau de l'eau sur l'écologie des lacs. Depuis 2013, elle est également secrétaire générale-trésorière de la Société internationale de limnologie (SIL), organisme consacré à l'étude des eaux intérieures. *limnology.org*

L'Institut de recherche sur le désert (DRI) : le Dr Nick Lancaster est professeur émérite au DRI (Nevada, USA). Il est spécialisé dans la géomorphologie du désert et les impacts des changements climatiques sur les régions désertiques. Il est également membre de la Société royale de géographie et de la Société géologique d'Amérique. Le DRI joue un rôle majeur dans la recherche interdisciplinaire fondamentale et appliquée. *www.dri.edu*

Le site MonumentalTrees.com : Tim Bekaert est l'administrateur du site Internet MonumentalTrees.com, site communautaire recensant des dizaines de milliers de photos d'arbres monumentaux, indiquant leur circonférence et leur hauteur, ainsi que la localisation d'arbres remarquables non documentés par ailleurs. *www.monumentaltrees.com*

Le site www.ultimateungulate.com : Brent Huffman, zoologiste de Toronto (Ontario, CAN), est spécialiste de la biologie des ongulés (mammifères à sabots). Il a contribué à diverses publications spécialisées et grand public, mais il est aussi connu pour la création du site Internet www.ultimateungulate.com en 1996. Il s'agit du premier site consacré aux ongulés. *ultimateungulate.com*

L'Union internationale des ornithologues (International Ornithologists' Union, IOU) : le Dr Dominique Homberger est professeur émérite à l'université de Louisiane (USA) et président de l'IOU. Elle effectue des recherches sur l'anatomie comparée, qui permet de répondre à des questions fonctionnelles et évolutionnistes. Elle s'intéresse particulièrement à l'ordre des Psittaciformes (dont font partie les perroquets et les cacatoès). L'IOU compte près de 200 experts se réunissant dans le cadre d'un congrès international tous les quatre ans. Le premier congrès a eu lieu en 1884. *www.internationalornithology.org*

La Société royale britannique d'entomologie (Royal Entomological Society, RES) : le Dr Luke Tilley est directeur du programme de sensibilisation et de développement de la RES, fondée en 1833 pour promouvoir la connaissance des insectes. L'organisme soutient la collaboration, la recherche et les publications internationales. Il vise à favoriser l'excellence dans sa discipline et à démontrer l'importance de l'étude des insectes. *www.royensoc.co.uk*

L'Organisation météorologique mondiale (World Meteorological Organization, WMO) : le Dr Randall Cerveny est professeur en sciences géographiques spécialisé dans la météorologie et le climat au sein de l'École des Sciences géographiques et de l'Urbanisme de l'université d'État d'Arizona. Il est également rapporteur sur les questions de phénomènes météorologiques et climatiques extrêmes auprès de la WMO depuis 2007. *wmo.asu.edu*

Le Muséum d'histoire naturelle de Vienne : le Dr Ludovic Ferrière est géologue et expert dans le domaine des météorites et des impacts de cratères. Il est conservateur en chef des prestigieuses collections de météorites et de roches du Muséum d'histoire naturelle de Vienne en Autriche. Avec ses collègues, il a validé l'existence de quatre cratères d'impact : Keurusselkä en Finlande, Luizi en République démocratique du Congo, Hummeln en Suède et Yallalie en Australie. *www.nhm-wien.ac.at*

La Société écologique britannique : le professeur Richard Bardgett est président de la Société écologique britannique. Il est aussi professeur d'écologie à l'université de Manchester (GBR). Ses domaines d'expertise sont l'interaction plante-sol et les écosystèmes des prairies. Rédacteur en chef du *Journal of ecology*, il a publié plus de 260 articles scientifiques et plusieurs ouvrages, dont *Earth Matters: How Soil Underpins Civilization* (2016). *www.britishecologicalsociety.org*

Les Jardins botaniques royaux de Kew : les Jardins botaniques royaux de Kew abritent une organisation scientifique mondialement réputée et respectée pour ses collections exceptionnelles. Cette organisation est experte dans le domaine de la diversité et de la conservation des espèces végétales, ainsi que du développement durable au Royaume-Uni et dans le monde. Elle mène des recherches approfondies dans les domaines de la botanique et des champignons. Ses départements spécialisés sont consacrés à l'identification des espèces, à l'information sur la biodiversité et à la biologie comparée des plantes et des champignons. Les jardins de Kew à Londres sont un site touristique très réputé, classé au patrimoine mondial de l'Unesco en 2003. *www.kew.org*

Le laboratoire Cornell : dirigé par le Dr Holger Klinck, le Programme de recherche sur la bioacoustique (BRP) du Laboratoire Cornell d'ornithologie de New York réunit une équipe interdisciplinaire de scientifiques, d'ingénieurs, d'étudiants et de chercheurs travaillant sur une grande variété de projets de bioacoustique terrestre, aquatique et marine. Ce programme a pour mission de recueillir et d'interpréter les sons de la nature tout en développant et en mettant en œuvre des technologies de sauvegarde innovantes au sein de plusieurs échelles écologiques pour inciter à la préservation de la faune et des habitats. *brp.cornell.edu*

L'université du Maryland : le Dr Andrew Baldwin est professeur au département des Sciences environnementales et de la technologie de l'université du Maryland (USA). Il donne des conférences sur l'écologie et la restauration des zones humides, et mène des recherches sur ce sujet et sur les changements environnementaux planétaires. Il est membre et ancien président de la Société internationale des scientifiques des zones humides. *www.enst.umd.edu*

L'Association internationale d'étude et de gestion des ours (IBA) : l'IBA est une association internationale à but non lucratif ouverte aux biologistes professionnels, aux gestionnaires de la faune et à toute personne se consacrant à la préservation des espèces d'ours. Elle compte plus de 550 membres au sein de 60 pays et soutient la gestion des ours en conduisant des recherches et en diffusant l'information. *www.bearbiology.org*

L'Institut Scott de recherche polaire (SPRI) : le SPRI de l'université de Cambridge au Royaume-Uni a été fondé en 1920 en mémoire des hommes qui ont trouvé la mort durant l'expédition du capitaine Scott au pôle Sud en 1910-1913. Sa documentation couvre la totalité de l'Arctique et de l'Antarctique. Il abrite une grande bibliothèque et des archives, des départements de recherche sur plusieurs spécialités polaires et un petit musée public. L'Institut est aujourd'hui un centre international d'histoire, de géographie et de recherche sur le terrain et en laboratoire concernant les deux régions. *www.spri.cam.ac.uk*

L'École vétérinaire royale de Londres (Royal Veterinary College) : Alan Wilson est professeur de biomécanique de la locomotion et responsable du laboratoire de la Structure et du Mouvement de l'École vétérinaire royale de l'université de Londres. Il est chirurgien vétérinaire et physiologiste de l'université de Glasgow et a obtenu son doctorat de mécanique des blessures du tendon à l'université de Bristol. Ses recherches ont trait aux limites mécaniques et physiologiques de la performance locomotrice d'espèces allant des pigeons aux guépards. Il étudie actuellement des mammifères emblématiques d'Afrique, tels que le lion et le gnou au Botswana, à l'aide d'équipements GPS et de suivi innovants des animaux. *www.rvc.ac.uk*

La Société internationale des pierres précieuses (International Gem Society, ou IGS) : Donald Clark a fondé en 1998 l'IGS, dont la mission consiste à informer un large public. Cette société compte des membres sur tous les continents (excepté l'Antarctique), qui peuvent être des professionnels chevronnés ou de simples amateurs. Elle propose une abondante documentation, dont une bibliographie mise à jour chaque semaine et des formations certifiantes en gemmologie. *www.gemsociety.org*

L'Agence américaine d'observation océanique et atmosphérique (NOAA) : le champ d'étude de la NOAA s'étend de la surface du Soleil au fond des océans. L'Agence informe le public des changements environnementaux. Elle réalise quotidiennement des bulletins météorologiques, annonce les grosses tempêtes et surveille le climat tout en veillant à la gestion de la pêche, à la préservation des côtes et au soutien du commerce maritime. *www.noaa.gov*

Le Service de recherches sur le corail, université de l'Essex : professeur de biologie marine à l'université d'Essex, GBR, David Smith s'intéresse à l'écologie des récifs de coraux et à leur conservation depuis 20 ans. Il est rédacteur en chef adjoint du journal *Global Change Biology* et conseille gouvernements et organi-

University of the Highlands and Islands Perth College | Centre for Mountain Studies

UNIVERSITY OF LIVERPOOL

Berkeley Seismology Lab

BRITISH ECOLOGICAL SOCIETY

phm naturhistorisches museum wien

SCHOOL of ANTS AUSTRALIA

Royal Botanic Gardens Kew

WORLD SURF LEAGUE EST. 1976

NATIONAL SPELEOLOGICAL SOCIETY

WHALE AND DOLPHIN CONSERVATION WDC

WOWSA

THE NUMBERS Where Data and the Movie Business Meet

TheCornellLab Bioacoustics Research Program

Channel Swimming Association

USC University of Southern California

International Mineralogical Association IMA

sations en matière de stratégies de recherche et de solutions de conservation. *www.essex.ac.uk/departments/biological-sciences/research/coral-reef-research-unit*

L'Association internationale de minéralogie (IMA) : l'IMA s'est réunie pour la première fois en avril 1958. Elle compte aujourd'hui 39 sociétés membres représentant les six continents habités. Finançant et organisant des conférences, elle facilite aussi les échanges au sein de la communauté minéralogique mondiale par le biais des activités de ses commissions, comités et groupes de travail. Elle a pour mission la simplification de la nomenclature et de la classification des minéraux, ainsi que la conservation du patrimoine minéralogique. *www.ima-mineralogy.org*

La société de préservation des baleines et des dauphins (Whale and Dolphin Conservation, WDC) : la WDC est une association internationale consacrée à la préservation et à la protection des baleines et des dauphins. Elle défend les cétacés contre les nombreuses menaces auxquelles ils font face en organisant des campagnes, des actions de lobbying, des projets de protection, des recherches sur le terrain, des sauvetages et en conseillant les gouvernements. Selon la WDC, les dauphins et les baleines ne doivent pas être tenus en captivité pour le plaisir des humains. Ceux qui partagent cet avis peuvent la rejoindre. *whales.org*

L'Association internationale de nage en eau libre (World Open Water Swimming Association, WOWSA) : la WOWSA est un organisme international régissant la nage en eau libre. Elle propose des programmes d'adhésion et de certification, ainsi que des publications et de la documentation en ligne destinées à encourager sa communauté et à mettre en valeur les performances. Elle codifie également la réglementation, les records et la terminologie propres au sport pour favoriser son développement. *www.worldopenwaterswimmingassociation.com*

L'Association de traversée de la Manche à la nage (Channel Swimming Association, CSA) : la CSA réglemente la traversée à la nage de la Manche et apporte son aide aux nageurs depuis sa création en 1927. Elle ne reconnaît que les traversées conformes à ses règles et accompagnées par des observateurs compétents. *www.channelswimmingassociation.com*

Le Conseil des records mondiaux à la voile (World Sailing Speed Record Council, WSSRC) : le WSSRC a été créé en 1972 par la Fédération internationale de voile (World Sailing, appelée Yacht Racing Union à l'époque). Très tôt, la décision a été prise d'homologuer les records sur une distance de 500 m (une seconde catégorie pour les distances d'un mille nautique a été créée ultérieurement). Le Conseil compte des membres en Australie, en France, en Grande-Bretagne et aux États-Unis. *www.sailspeedrecords.com*

La Ligue mondiale de surf (World Surf League, WSL) : la WSL est destinée à célébrer le meilleur du surf mondial sur les plus belles vagues du monde grâce à des plateformes publiques représentant les meilleures catégories. La WSL défend le surf depuis 1976, en organisant chaque année plus de 180 événements internationaux, dont le championnat du monde de surf, le circuit mondial de grosses vagues (*Big Wave Tour*), le circuit *Longboard*, la ligue d'accès à l'élite (*Qualifying Series*) et le circuit Junior, ainsi que le prix *WSL Big Wave Awards*. Elle possède une connaissance approfondie de l'héritage de ce sport, au sein duquel elle promeut le progrès, l'innovation et la performance au plus haut niveau, et figure systématiquement en tête du championnat du monde. *www.worldsurfleague.com*

The Numbers : The-Numbers.com est la plus grande base de données d'Internet regroupant des informations financières sur l'industrie cinématographique. Elle fournit des chiffres sur plus de 38 000 films et 160 000 personnes de ce secteur. Elle a été créée en 1997 et compte plus de 8 millions de visiteurs chaque année. Le site est consulté non seulement par les amateurs de cinéma, mais aussi les grands studios, les compagnies de production indépendantes et les investisseurs qui peuvent ainsi décider quel type de film réaliser et à quel moment les sortir. Les données proviennent des studios de cinéma, de la distribution, de supports d'information et d'autres sources. La base de données, exhaustive, est baptisée OpusData. Elle recense plus de 14 millions d'informations sur l'industrie du cinéma. *www.the-numbers.com*

Le Conseil des édifices en hauteur et de l'habitat urbain (Council on Tall Buildings and Urban Habitat, CTBUH) : le CTBUH, situé à Chicago, (Illinois, USA), est le principal centre de documentation mondial des professionnels en matière de création, conception, construction et fonctionnement des édifices en hauteur et des villes de demain. Il constitue une source d'informations actuelles grâce à ses publications, à ses recherches, à sa documentation en ligne, aux événements qu'il organise et à sa représentation à l'international. *www.ctbuh.org*

Le site 8000ers.com : Eberhard Jurgalski est fasciné par les montagnes depuis son enfance. En 1981, il a commencé à rédiger des chroniques sur les hauts sommets d'Asie. Il a conçu le système Elevation Quality, méthode universelle de classement des chaînes de montagne et des sommets. Son site Internet, *8000ers.com*, est aujourd'hui une source majeure de données concernant l'altitude de l'Himalaya et du Karakorum. Il est également coauteur du livre *Herausforderung 8000er*, guide de référence sur les 14 sommets dépassant 8 000 m dans le monde. *www.8000ers.com*

Ocean Rowing Society, ORS : L'ORS a été fondée en 1983 par Kenneth F. Crutchlow et Peter Bird, rejoints ensuite par Tom Lynch et Tatiana Rezvaya-Crutchlow. Elle répertorie les tentatives de traversée à la rame des océans et des grandes étendues d'eau (comme la mer de Tasman et la mer des Caraïbes), ainsi que les expéditions à la rame autour de la Grande-Bretagne. Elle classe, vérifie et arbitre les performances. *www.oceanrowing.com*

Great Pumpkin Commonwealth, GPC : la GPC se consacre à la culture de potirons géants et d'autres légumes surdimensionnés et établit des normes et des réglementations pour garantir leur qualité, l'équité de la compétition, décerner des prix, recruter des membres, informer les participants et contrôler les sites des concours. *gpc1.org*

Le Championnat national britannique CANNA de légumes géants : en septembre, sur le champ de foire *Three Counties* de Malvern (Worcestershire, GBR), Martyn Davis, juge de la Société nationale britannique des Légumes, accueille des cultivateurs spécialisés lors du championnat national britannique CANNA, organisé conjointement avec la cidrerie Westons. Martyn vérifie que les légumes respectent les critères stricts de la compétition et qu'ils sont correctement pesés et décrits. *www.malvernautumn.co.uk*

L'Association mondiale d'ultracyclisme (World UltraCycling Association, WUCA) : la WUCA (ex-UMCA) est une organisation à but non lucratif destinée à soutenir le cyclisme dans le monde entier. Elle possède la plus grande base de données de records liés au cyclisme pour tous les types de vélos et homologue des records pour ses membres, lesquels participent à des défis annuels et se soutiennent mutuellement lors des épreuves. *worldultracycling.com*

L'École d'architecture Bartlett : Iain Borden est professeur d'architecture & de culture urbaine, et vice-doyen de l'École au sein de l'University College de Londres, université internationale. Skateur, photographe, amateur de films et de promenades urbaines, il est l'auteur de plus de 100 livres et articles sur ces sujets, ainsi que d'ouvrages sur les architectes, les édifices et les villes. *www.ucl.ac.uk/bartlett/architecture*

The Penguin Lady : Dyan deNapoli est spécialiste des pingouins, conférencière TEDx et a été primée pour son ouvrage intitulé *The Great Penguin Rescue* (2011), chronique d'un sauvetage mouvementé de 40 000 pingouins touchés par la nappe de pétrole échappée du *Treasure* au large de l'Afrique du Sud, en 2000. Elle donne des conférences en Antarctique pour *National Geographic* et possède un site Internet intitulé The Penguin Lady. *thepenguinlady.com*

Mark O'Shea : Mark est professeur d'herpétologie à l'université de Wolverhampton et conseiller en protection des reptiles au parc de safari West Midland (GBR). Il a plus de 50 ans d'expérience des reptiles sauvages ou en captivité, et sa carrière s'est déroulée dans 40 pays différents sur 6 continents. Il est l'auteur de 6 ouvrages, dont *The Book of Snakes* (2018), qui présente 600 des 3 700 espèces et quelques de serpents. Mark est aussi présentateur d'émissions télévisées sur la nature, dont 40 documentaires et l'émission *O'Shea's Big Adventure* sur les chaînes *Animal Planet* et *Channel 4* (GBR). *www.markoshea.info*

Mark Aston est consultant en sciences et technologies pour Guinness World Records depuis 2010. Fort de 30 ans d'expérience dans le domaine des sciences et de l'ingénierie liées aux hautes technologies, il veille à la précision et à l'exactitude des records. Son parcours universitaire et en entreprise lui ont valu une carrière bien remplie dans le développement optique.

Tom Beckerlegge est un écrivain primé, dont les livres ont été traduits dans le monde entier. Consultant sportif pour GWR, il a depuis des années analysé toutes sortes de sports et s'est documenté à leur propos. Il a collaboré à 5 de nos éditions et étudié des centaines de records dans des domaines sportifs divers.

David Fischer est notre principal consultant pour les sports américains depuis 2006. Il a écrit pour le *New York Times* et *Sports Illustrated for Kids*, et a travaillé pour *Sports Illustrated*, *The National Sports Daily* et NBC Sports. Il est l'auteur de 2 ouvrages, *The Super Bowl: The First Fifty Years of America's Greatest Game* (2015) et *Derek Jeter #2: Thanks for the Memories* (2014). Il a également publié *Facing Mariano Rivera* (2014).

Rory Flood possède une licence de géographie, une maîtrise de sciences environnementales et un doctorat en géographie physique. Il est maître de conférences en géographie physique à l'université de la Reine à Belfast (Irlande du Nord). Il a publié des articles sur la géomorphologie, la sédimentologie et la géochimie, dans l'univers des environnements marins et terrestres. Il s'intéresse tout particulièrement à la formation des paysages côtiers et des reliefs et à la façon dont ils se modifient sous les influences marines, climatiques et humaines.

Jonathan McDowell est astrophysicien au Centre Harvard-Smithsonian d'Astrophysique (USA), où il fait partie de l'équipe qui gère l'observatoire Chandra X-ray. Il administre un site Internet traitant de l'histoire de l'exploration spatiale (*planet4589.org*) et publie une lettre d'information mensuelle intitulée *Jonathan's Space Report* depuis 1998.

James Proud est écrivain et chercheur spécialisé dans les faits et histoires insolites du monde entier, en particulier quand ils ont trait à la technologie ou aux exploits extrêmes. Il est l'auteur de plusieurs livres sur des sujets très variés, dont les anecdotes historiques, les légendes urbaines et la culture pop.

Karl P. N. Shuker possède un doctorat en zoologie et physiologie comparée de l'université de Birmingham. Il est membre de la Société zoologique de Londres, de la Société royale britannique d'entomologie et de la Société des auteurs du Royaume-Uni. Il a écrit 25 livres et des centaines d'articles traitant de divers thèmes d'histoire naturelle. Son œuvre traite d'animaux extraordinaires, ainsi que de nouvelles espèces, d'espèces redécouvertes et d'autres non identifiées.

Matthew White est consultant pour GWR dans les domaines de la musique, du cricket et du tennis. De 2009 à 2019, il a examiné avec soin un nombre de records publiés estimé à 40 000 en qualité de relecteur de 12 éditions de la **publication annuelle la plus vendue** dans le monde.

Robert D. Young est le principal consultant de GWR en matière de gérontologie – l'étude des différents aspects du vieillissement. Il recense les personnes les plus âgées du monde pour le Groupe de recherche en gérontologie américain (Gerontology Research Group, GRG ; *grg.org*) depuis 1999 et a travaillé en collaboration avec l'Institut Max Planck de démographie et avec la Base de données internationale sur la longévité (International Database on Longevity). Il est directeur du Département de recherche du GRG sur les supercentenaires depuis 2015.

GWR 2020

Éditeur en chef
Craig Glenday

Mise en page
Tom Beckerlegge, Rob Dimery

Responsable éditorial
Adam Millward

Éditeur
Ben Hollingum

Éditeur Jeux vidéo
Mike Plant

Révision-correction
Matthew White

Responsable Édition et Production
Jane Boatfield

Responsable de l'iconographie et du graphisme
Fran Morales

Recherches iconographiques
Alice Jessop

Graphiste
Billy Waqar

Création graphique
Paul Wylie-Deacon et Rob Wilson de 55design.co.uk

Conception graphique de la couverture
Paul Wylie-Deacon, Edward Dillon

Design 3D
Joseph O'Neil

Responsable Produit
Lucy Acfield

Responsable du contenu visuel
Michael Whitty

Producteur de contenu
Jenny Langridge

Directeur de production
Patricia Magill

Coordinateur de production
Thomas McCurdy

Consultants de production
Roger Hawkins, Florian Seyfert, Tobias Wrona

Reprographie
Res Kahraman et Honor Flowerday de Born Group

Photographies originales
James Ellerker, Jon Enoch, Paul Michael Hughes, Prakash Mathema, Kevin Scott Ramos, Alex Rumford, Ryan Schude, Trevor Traynor

Indexation
Marie Lorimer

Recherches
Ben Way

Impression et façonnage
MOHN Media Mohndruck GmbH, Gütersloh, Allemagne

55-2688-5 I ISBN : 978-1-912286-90-4
Dépôt légal : septembre 2019
Les records sont faits pour être battus ; en effet, c'est l'un des critères clés pour composer une catégorie de record. Aussi, si vous pensez pouvoir battre un record, informez-nous en et présentez votre candidature. Contactez-nous toujours avant de vous lancer dans une tentative de record. Retrouvez régulièrement sur le site www.guinnessworldrecords.com des informations sur les records et des vidéos des tentatives de record. Rejoignez la communauté en ligne GWR et participez.
Pour l'édition française
Responsable éditoriale : Anne Le Meur
Réalisation : Dédicace/NordCompo (Villeneuve-d'Ascq)
Traduction : Stéphanie Alglave, Olivier Cechman, Karine Descamps, Charlotte Faraday, Alice Gallori, Cécile Giroldi, Laurent Laget, Agnès Letourneur, Guillaume Marlière, Christine Mignot, Ghislaine Tamisier
Relecture : Anne-Fleur Drillon et Odile Raoul
L'éditeur remercie Lou Brugère pour son aide précieuse.
Développement durable
Les arbres utilisés pour la production du papier destiné à l'impression du Guinness World Records 2020 sont soigneusement sélectionnés à partir de forêts gérées dans le respect du paysage.

Le papier de cette édition a été fabriqué par Stora Enso Veitsiluoto, en Finlande. Le site de production bénéficie d'une certification forestière et ses activités de la certification ISO14001 pour s'assurer d'une production durable.

Guinness World Records Limited a recours à des méthodes de vérification très précises pour certifier les records. Malgré ses efforts, des erreurs peuvent subsister. Guinness World Records Limited ne peut être tenu pour responsable des erreurs ou omissions que comporterait cette édition. Toute correction ou précision de la part des lecteurs est bienvenue.

Guinness World Records Limited utilise le système métrique dans cette édition. Pour la conversion des monnaies, lorsqu'une date précise est indiquée, nous appliquons le taux de change en vigueur à l'époque. Si seule l'année est mentionnée, nous appliquons le taux de change au 31 décembre de l'année.

Il est important de prendre conseil auprès de personnes compétentes préalablement à toute tentative de record. Les candidats agissent à leurs risques et périls. Guinness World Records Limited conserve l'entière liberté d'inclure ou non un record dans ses ouvrages. Être détenteur d'un record ne garantit pas sa mention dans une publication de Guinness World Records.

OFFICIALLY AMAZING

THE JIM PATTISON GROUP

SIÈGE SOCIAL

Président-directeur général : Alistair Richards

Administration
Alison Ozanne
Gestion des catégories : Benjamin Backhouse, Jason Fernandes, Sheila Mella Suárez, Will Munford, Shane Murphy, Luke Wakeham
Finance : Tobi Amusan, Jusna Begum, Elizabeth Bishop, Jess Blake, Yusuf Gafar, Lisa Gibbs, Kimberley Jones, Nhan Nguyen, Sutharsan Ramachandran, Jamie Sheppard, Scott Shore, Andrew Wood
Ressources humaines : Jackie Angus, Alexandra Ledin, Farrella Ryan-Coker, Monika Tilani
DSI : Céline Bacon, Ashleigh Bair, John Cvitanovic, Diogo Gomes, Rob Howe, Benjamin Mclean, Cenk Selim, Alpha Serrant-Defoe
Juridique : Catherine Loughran, Raymond Marshall, Kaori Minami, Mehreen Moghul

Stratégie de marque, Contenu & Produit, Création
Sam Fay, Katie Forde, Paul O'Neill
Partenariats de marque : Juliet Dawson
Design : Edward Dillon, Alisa Zaytseva
Numérique : Veronica Irons, Alex Waldu
Marketing : Lucy Acfield, Rebecca Lam, Emily Osborn, Mawa Rodriguez, Louise Toms
Contenu visuel : Sam Birch-Machin, Karen Gilchrist, Jenny Langridge, Matthew Musson, Joseph O'Neil, Catherine Pearce, Alan Pixsley, Jonathan Whitton, Michael Whitty
Site Internet et réseaux sociaux : David Stubbings, Dan Thorne

EMEA & APAC

Nadine Causey

Marque & Contenu
Marketing & RP : Nicholas Brookes, Lauren Cochrane, Jessica Dawes, Imelda Ekpo, Amber Georgina Gill, Lauren Johns, Doug Male, Connie Suggitt
Ventes Édition : Caroline Lake, Helene Navarre, Joel Smith
Gestion des records : Lewis Blakeman, Adam Brown, Tara El Kashef, Daniel Kidane, Mark McKinley

Consultants - UKROW
Neil Foster
Services comptes clients : Sonia Chadha-Nihal, Fay Edwards, Samuel Evanson, Andrew Fanning, William Hume-Humphreys, Soma Huy, Irina Nohailic, Sam Prosser, Nikhil Shukla, Sadie Smith
Production événementielle : Fiona Gruchy-Craven, Danny Hickson
Marketing & RP : Lisa Lambert, Iliyan Stoychev, Amanda Tang
Gestion des records : Matilda Hagne, Paul Hillman, Christopher Lynch, Maria Raggi

Consultants - MENA
Talal Omar
Services comptes clients : Naser Batat, Mohammad Kiswani, Kamel Yassin
Ressources humaines : Monisha Bimal
Marketing & RP : Aya Ali, Leila Issa
Gestion des records : Hoda Khachab, Samer Khallouf

ASIE DE L'EST

Marco Frigatti

Chine
Services comptes clients : Blythe Fitzwilliam, Catherine Gao, Chloe Liu, Tina Ran, Amelia Wang, Elaine Wang, Ivy Wang, Jin Yu, Jacky Yuan
Ressources humaines : Tina Shi, Crystal Xu
Juridique : Paul Nightingale, Jiayi Teng
Marketing & RP : Tracy Cui, Karen Pan, Vanessa Tao, Angela Wu, Echo Zhan, Naomi Zhang, Yvonne Zhang, Delling Zhao, Emily Zeng
Gestion des records : Fay Jiang, Ted Li, Reggy Lu, Charles Wharton, Winnie Zhang, Alicia Zhao

Japon
Erika Ogawa
Services comptes clients : Blythe Fitzwilliam, Wei Liang, Takuro Maruyama, Yuki Morishita, Yumiko Nakagawa, Masamichi Yazaki
Ressources humaines : Emiko Yamamoto
Marketing & RP : Kazami Kamioka, Vihag Kulshrestha, Aya McMillan, Momoko Satou, Masakazu Senda, Yumi Uota, Eri Yuhira
Gestion des records : Aki Ichikawa, Kaoru Ishikawa, Momoko Omori, Koma Satoh, Lala Teranishi, Yuki Uebo

AMÉRIQUES

Alistair Richards

Amérique du Nord
Services comptes clients : Alex Angert, Mackenzie Berry, David Canela, Danielle Levy, Nicole Pando, Kimberly Partrick, Michelle Santucci
Ressources humaines : Vincent Acevedo, Jennifer Olson
Marketing, RP & ventes édition : Valerie Esposito, Lauren Festa, Michael Furnari, Rachel Gluck, Elizabeth Montoya, Morganna Nickoff, Rachel Silver, Kristen Stephenson, Sonja Valenta
Gestion des records : Spencer Cammarano, Christine Fernandez, Hannah Ortman, Callie Smith, Claire Stephens, Kaitlin Vesper

Amérique latine
Carlos Martinez
Services comptes clients : Carolina Guanabara-Hall, Ralph Hannah, Jaime Rodriguez
Marketing & RP : Laura Angel, Alice Marie Pagán-Sánchez
Gestion des records : Raquel Assis, Jaime Oquendo

JUGES OFFICIELS

Camila Borenstain, Joanne Brent, Jack Brockbank, Sarah Casson, Dong Cheng, Christina Conlon, Swapnil Dangarikar, Casey DeSantis, Brittany Dunn, Michael Empric, Pete Fairbairn, Victor Fenes, Fumika Fujibuchi, Ahmed Gabr, John Garland, Şeyda Subaşı Gemici, Andy Glass, Sofia Greenacre, Iris Hou, Rei Iwashita, Louis Jelinek, Kazuyoshi Kirimura, Mariko Koike, Lena Kuhlmann, Maggie Luo, Solvej Malouf, Mike Marcotte, Mai McMillan, Rishi Nath, Chika Onaka, Anna Orford, Douglas Palau, Kellie Parise, Pravin Patel, Justin Patterson, Glenn Pollard, Natalia Ramirez, Stephanie Randall, Cassie Ren, Philip Robertson, Paulina Sapinska, Tomomi Sekioka, Hiroaki Shino, Lucia Sinigagliesi, Brian Sobel, Kevin Southam, Richard Stenning, Carlos Tapia, Lorenzo Veltri, Xiong Wen, Peter Yang

Crédits iconographiques

1 Shinsuke Kamioka/GWR, Shutterstock ; 2 Alamy, Jon Enoch/GWR, Paul Michael Hughes/GWR, Shutterstock ; 3 Boston Dynamics, NASA, Shutterstock ; 4 Shutterstock ; 6 Getty, Prince of Speed ; 7 Shutterstock, Alamy ; 14 Roger Culos ; 15 Alamy, Shutterstock ; 16 Shutterstock, Alamy ; 17 Shutterstock, Alamy, SPL ; 18 Shutterstock, Alamy ; 19 Shutterstock ; 20 Shutterstock, Alamy ; 21 Alamy, Shutterstock ; 22 Shutterstock, Karl Brodowsky, M. San Félix ; 23 Shutterstock, Alamy ; 24 Alamy, Shutterstock ; 25 Shutterstock, Getty, Alamy, Robin Brooks ; 26 Shutterstock, Mick Petroff/NASA, Alamy ; 27 Shutterstock, Alamy ; 28 Shutterstock, Alamy, SPL, Jason Edwards/National Geographic ; 29 Shutterstock, Alamy ; 30 Shutterstock, Alamy ; 31 Alamy, Robbie Shone, Neckton ; 32 Jon Enoch/GWR ; 34 Shutterstock, Science Source/ARDEA, Nobu Tamura, Alamy ; 35 Shutterstock, Alamy ; 36 Alamy ; 37 Alamy, Shutterstock ; 38 Alamy, Shutterstock ; 39 Alamy, Shutterstock ; 40 Nature PL, Shutterstock ; 41 Shutterstock, Nature PL, Ardea, Alamy ; 42 Alamy, Shutterstock ; 43 Alamy, Shutterstock ; 44 Shutterstock, Alamy ; 45 Alamy, Shutterstock ; 46 Shutterstock, Ardea, Alamy, Getty ; 47 Shutterstock ; 48 Shutterstock, Alamy ; 49 Alamy, Shutterstock ; 50 Shutterstock, Alamy ; 51 Shutterstock, Alamy ; 52 Jon Enoch/GWR, Kevin Scott Ramos/GWR ; 53 Shutterstock, Paul Michael Hughes/GWR ; 54 Alamy, Shutterstock, Clay Bolt: claybolt.com ; 55 Ardea, Alamy ; 56 Jon Enoch/GWR ; 58 Paul Michael Hughes/GWR ; 59 Tim Anderson/GWR ; 60 Reuters, Alamy, Kevin Scott Ramos/GWR ; 61 Getty, Shinsuke Kamioka/GWR ; 62 John Wright/GWR, Paul Michael Hughes/GWR, Richard Bradbury/GWR, NBC/NBCU Photo Bank ; 63 Chris Granger/GWR, John Wright/GWR, Paul Michael Hughes/GWR ; 64 Alamy, Aleksandar Terzic, Harvey Nichols ; 65 Kevin Scott Ramos/GWR, Shutterstock, Al Diaz/GWR ; 66 Reuters, Shutterstock, Ortiz-Catalan et al ; 67 Paul Michael Hughes/GWR, Fernanda Figueiredo ; 68 UGLY Enterprises LTD, Paul Michael Hughes/GWR, Getty, Evgeny Nikolaev ; 69 Paul Michael Hughes/GWR, Shutterstock ; 70 Paul Michael Hughes/GWR, John Wright/GWR, Kimberly Cook/GWR ; 71 Kevin Scott Ramos/GWR, Reuters, Ranald Mackechnie/GWR ; 72 Paul Michael Hughes/GWR ; 74 Shutterstock ; 75 Shutterstock, Craig Glenday ; 77 Jon Enoch/GWR ; 79 Brian Braun/GWR ; 80 Alamy, Richard Bradbury, Sam Christmas/GWR, Shutterstock ; 81 Ryan Schude/GWR ; 82 Getty, GWR, Karen Wade/GWR ; 83 Marvel/Sony/GWR ; 84 Kevin Scott Ramos/GWR, Paul Michael Hughes/GWR, GWR ; 85 Alex Rumford/GWR, Jon Enoch/GWR ; 87 James Ellerker/GWR, Alex Rumford/GWR ; 88 Christian Houdek/GWR ; 89 James Ellerker/GWR, Ryan Schude/GWR ; 90 Paul Michael Hughes/GWR, Jon Enoch/GWR ; 91 Paul Michael Hughes/GWR ; 92 Richard Bradbury/GWR, Paul Michael Hughes/GWR ; 93 Ryan Schude/GWR, Paul Michael Hughes/GWR ; 94 Richard Bradbury/GWR, Paul Michael Hughes/GWR, John Wright/GWR ; 95 Trevor Traynor/GWR, Paul Michael Hughes/GWR, John Wright/GWR ; 97 Ryan Schude/GWR, Jenna Henderson ; 98 Ryan Schude/GWR ; 100 Ryan Schude/GWR, Ranald Mackechnie/GWR, Kevin Scott Ramos/GWR, James Ellerker/GWR ; 101 Ryan Schude/GWR, Shutterstock ; 102 Ryan Schude/GWR, Paul Michael Hughes/GWR, James Ellerker/GWR ; 103 Ryan Schude/GWR, Shutterstock ; 104 James Ellerker/GWR, Drew Gardner/GWR, John Wright/GWR ; 105 Ryan Schude/GWR, Kevin Scott Ramos/GWR ; 106 Shutterstock, Mark Dadswell/GWR, Maria Marin ; 107 Ryan Schude/GWR, Shutterstock ; 108 Matt Ben Stone ; 109 Alamy ; 110 Red Bull/GWR, Jörg Mitter/Red Bull Content Pool ; 111 Shutterstock, Jay Nemeth/Red Bull Content Pool ; 112 Samuel Renner ; 116 Raphael Thomas/Prince of Speed, Alex Broadway/Red Bull Content Pool, Dan Speicher ; 117 Anthony Ball, Reuters, Shutterstock ; 118 Samuel Crossley, Shutterstock, Marek Ogień/Red Bull Content Pool, Getty ; 119 Matteo Zanga ; 120 Christian Pondella/Red Bull Content Pool, Keith Ladzinski/Red Bull Content Pool ; 123 AP Images for T-Mobile US, Jenna Henderson ; 124 Kevin Scott Ramos/GWR ; 126 Shutterstock ; 127 Shutterstock, Alamy ; 128 Alamy, Getty ; 129 Iwan Baan, Getty ; 130 Shutterstock, Getty ; 131 Shutterstock, Alamy ; 132 Alamy, Courtesy Chris Reynolds, Frédéric Boudin/Ferd, Shutterstock ; 133 Alamy, Shutterstock ; 134 Alamy, Shutterstock ; 135 Shutterstock ; 136 Courtesy Bonhams, Alamy, Shutterstock ; 137 Alamy, Raphaël Dauvergne, Shutterstock ; 139 Shutterstock ; 140 Getty, Shutterstock ; 141 Alamy, Shutterstock ; 142 Shutterstock, Alamy ; 143 Shutterstock ; 144 Shutterstock, Alamy ; 145 Lt. Chad Dulac, Shutterstock, Getty, Reuters ; 146 JAXA, Boston Dynamics, Roborace ; 147 Festo AG & Co.KG, JSK Lab/University of Tokyo, Bonhams, Honda ; 148 DARPA, Roborace ; 149 Roborace, DARPA, Shutterstock ; 150 University of Pennsylvania, TU Delft, Kevin Ma and Pakpong Chirarattananon/Harvard University, Adam Lau/Berkeley Engineering ; 151 Adam Lau/Berkeley Engineering, Festo AG & Co.KG, Shutterstock ; 152 Boston Dynamics, Honda, Toyota ; 153 Shutterstock ; 154 FANUC, Karen Ladenheim ; 155 Christian Sprogoe, The Henry Ford, NASA, Shutterstock ; 156 Hiroshi Ishiguro Laboratory, IIT-Istituto Italiano di Tecnologia, Shutterstock, Kibo Robot Project ; 157 Honda Motor Co, JSK Lab/University of Tokyo ; 158 Shutterstock, Boston Dynamics, Ethan Schaler ; 159 Shutterstock, Joseph Xu/Michigan University College of Engineering ; 160 NASA, Airbus, DHL, Getty, Northrop Grumman Corporation ; 161 Northrop Grumman Corporation, U.S. Navy ; 162 Boston Dynamics ; 163 Wyss Institute/Harvard University, ANYbotics, MIT, Boston Dynamics, Alamy ; 164 Alamy, CNSA, JAXA, NASA ; 165 NASA ; 166 Shutterstock, Alamy, Bonhams ; 167 Bonhams, Shutterstock ; 168 VCG/Getty ; 169 Alamy ; 170 Alamy ; 171 NASA/BEAM, NASA ; 172 Jon Enoch/GWR, Holly Martin/MetalAndSpeed, Paul Michael Hughes/GWR ; 173 Shinsuke Kamioka/GWR, Shutterstock ; 174 NASA, U.S. Navy ; 175 Alamy, ORNL & Carlos Jones ; 176 Kevin Scott Ramos/GWR ; 177 Kevin Scott Ramos/GWR, Shutterstock ; 178 Paul Michael Hughes/GWR ; 179 Ryan Schude/GWR, Kevin Scott Ramos/GWR ; 180 Getty, Thyssenkrupp, Marcus Ingram/dreamstime, Plastic Bottle Village, Shutterstock ; 181 Shutterstock ; 182 Alamy, Shutterstock, Diederik Pomstra/Leiden University ; 184 Lockheed Martin Corporation, NASA, NanoRacks ; 185 NASA ; 186 Alamy, Christies, Getty, Paul Michael Hughes/GWR, Shutterstock ; 187 NASA ; 190 Shutterstock ; 191 Shutterstock ; 192 David James/Lucasfilm Ltd, Shutterstock ; 193 Walt Disney Pictures, Marvel Studios, ESPN Films, 20th Century Fox ; 194 Ken McKay/ITV/Rex Features/Shutterstock ; 195 Alamy, Shutterstock, Believe Entertainment Group ; 196 Shutterstock ; 197 Universal Music Group, Shutterstock ; 198 Alamy, Shutterstock ; 199 Alamy, Shutterstock ; 204 NBCUniversal Media, Alamy, Ian Watson/USA Network, Warner Bros ; 205 AMC, Warner Bros, Shutterstock, Alamy ; 206 Beano, Todd Klein, Image Comics ; 207 Nigel Parkinson/Beano, Shutterstock, Alamy ; 208 Getty ; 209 Kevin Scott Ramos/GWR, Shutterstock ; 210 Getty, Sony Pictures Television ; 211 Shutterstock, AMC/BBC ; 212 Shutterstock ; 213 Shutterstock ; 214 Alamy, Shutterstock, Getty ; 215 Alamy, Getty, Shutterstock ; 216 Getty, Alamy ; 217 Getty, Shutterstock ; 218 Getty ; 219 Getty, Shutterstock ; 220 Shutterstock, Getty ; 221 Alamy, Shutterstock ; 222 Shutterstock, Mike Lee/KLC Fotos, Getty ; 223 Shutterstock, Alamy, Getty ; 224 Getty, Shutterstock, PA ; 225 Shutterstock ; 226 Alamy, Shutterstock ; 227 World Taekwondo, Getty, Shutterstock ; 228 Shutterstock, Getty ; 229 Alamy, Shutterstock, Volkswagen AG ; 230 International Weightlifting Federation, Shutterstock, Arnold Sports Festival ; 231 Getty, Leo Zhukov, Alamy ; 232 PBA LLC, Jeffrey Au/WCF, Getty ; 233 Getty, Shutterstock ; 234 Getty, Alamy, Shutterstock ; 235 Shutterstock, Alamy ; 236 Getty, Shutterstock ; 237 Saroma 100km Ultra Marathon Organising Committee, Shutterstock ; 238 FINA, Alamy, Shutterstock, Seb Daly/Sportsfile ; 239 USA Water Ski & Wake Sport, Balint Vekassy, Shutterstock, World Surf League/Sloane, Alex St. Jean ; 240 Shutterstock, Alamy, Getty ; 241 Shutterstock ; 242 Christian Pondella/Red Bull Content Pool, Peter Morning/Red Bull Content Pool, Michal Rotko, Getty, Ricardo Nascimento/Red Bull Content Pool ; 243 Alamy, Getty, Reuters, Wolfgang Benedik ; 244 Torben Utzon, Alamy, Getty ; 245 Getty, Shutterstock, Eline Hooghiemstra ; 254 Shutterstock, EHT Collaboration, Anthony Upton

GWR 2020

GWR voudrait remercier : Stuart Ackland (Bodleian Library), David C Agle (NASA JPL), American Society of Ichthyologists and Herpetologists (Bruce Collette, JP Fontenelle, Kirsten Hechtbender, David Smith, Leo Smith, Milton Tan, Tierney Thys, Luke Tornabene, Peter Wainwright), ATN Event Staffing, Baltimore City Department of Public Works (Jeffrey Raymond, Muriel Rich), British Aerobatic Association (Alan Cassidy, Steve Todd, Graeme Fudge), Jochen Brocks (Australian National University), Peter Brown (Rocky Mountain Tree-Ring Research), Benson Brownies, Buena Vista Television, Michael Caldwell (University of Alberta), Steve Campbell, Canada Running Series, CBS Interactive, Che John Connon (Newcastle University), John Corcoran, Jon Custer (International Energy Agency), Adriene Davis Kalugyer (Lilly Family School of Philanthropy), Ryan DeSear, Suzanne DeSear, Disney ABC Home Entertainment and TV Distribution, Dude Perfect, Christopher Duggan, Péter Fankhauser (ANYBotics), Matias Faral, Corrine Finch (King's School Canterbury), FJT Logistics Ltd (Ray Harper, Gavin Hennessy), Marshall Gerometta (Council on Tall Buildings and Urban Habitat), Emily D Gilman, Megan Goldrick, Jessy Grizzle (University of Michigan), Götz Haferburg (Freiburg University of Mining and Technology), Nora Hartel (Foundation for Environmental Education), Timothy Hoellein (Loyola University Chicago), Joe Hollins, Paul Holmes, Kelly Holmes, Marsha K Hoover, Chuanmin Hu (University of South Florida), Integrated Colour Editions Europe (Roger Hawkins, Susie Hawkins), International Association for Bear Research and Management (Djuro Huber, Svitlana Kudrenko, Martyn Obbard, Bernie Peyton, Ioan-Mihai Pop, Hasan Rahman, Agnieszka Sergiel, Siew Te Wong, Jennapher Teunissen van Manen, Renee Ward), IUCN (Craig Hilton-Taylor, Dan Laffoley), Johns Hopkins University Applied Physics Laboratory (Geoffrey F Brown, Justyna Surowiec), Carol Kaelson, Almut Kelber (Lund University), Priya Kissoon (University of the West Indies), KWP Studios Inc., Robert D Leighton, Brian Levy (Metropolitan Water Reclamation District of Greater Chicago), Roy Longbottom, Stefano Mammola (University of Turin), Mastercard, Amanda McCabe (Port Lympne Hotel & Reserve), Gary McCracken (University of Tennessee), Lisa McGrath, Giorgio Metta (Istituto Italiano di Tecnologia), William C Meyers, Mohn Media (Anke Frosch, Theo Loechter, Marina Rempe, Reinhild Regragui, Jeanette Sio, Dennis Thon, Christin Moeck, Jens Pähler), Michael Moreau (NASA Goddard Space Flight Center), Shon Mosier (Elastec), Carolina Muñoz-Saez (University of Chile), Adriaan Olivier (Klein Karoo International), William Pérez (Universidad de la República), Simon Pierce (Marine Megafauna Foundation), Print Force, Xinpei Qitong, Rachael Ray, Rick Richmond, Ripley Entertainment, Kieran Robson, Royal Botanic Gardens, Kew (Martin Cheek, Elizabeth Dauncey, Aljos Farjon, Michael Fay, Peter Gasson, Christina Harrison, Heather McCleod, William Milliken, Paul Rees, Chelsea Snell), Kate Sanders (The University of Adelaide), Etsuro Sawai (Ocean Sunfishes Information Storage Museum / Hiroshima University), Scott Polar Research Institute (Peter Clarkson, Robert Headland), Robert Sieland (Wismut GmbH), John Sinton (University of Hawai'i at Mānoa), Southern California Timing Association (Dan Warner, JoAnn Carlson), StackOverflow (Sarah Caputo, Khalid El Khatib), Stephanie Stinn (Lockheed Martin), Stora Enso Veitsiluoto, Mike Szczys (Hackaday), Andy Taylor, Ginnie Titterton (Chronicle of Philanthropy), University of Arizona LPL (Erin Morton, Dante Lauretta), University of Birmingham (Rebecca Lockwood, Stuart Hillmansen), University of Tokyo (Yuki Asano, Rohan Mehra), Beverley Wiley, Beverley Williams, Eddie Wilson, Alexandra Wilson (Foreign and Commonwealth Office), WTA Networks Inc., XG Group, Liam Yon (St Helena Government), Xuexia Zhang (Southwest Jiaotong University), Paul Zimnisky Diamond Analytics (paulzimnisky.com), ZSL (James Hansford, Samuel Turvey), 55 Design (Hugh Doug Wylie, Linda Wylie, Hayley Wylie-Deacon, Tobias Wylie-Deacon, Rueben Wylie-Deacon, Anthony "Dad" Deacon, Vidette Burniston, Lewis Burniston)

Pages de garde

Garde avant, rangée 1 : la plus grande image humaine représentant un stylo, le plus de plaques d'immatriculation tordues en 1 min, le tiltrotor miniature contrôlé à distance le plus rapide, la plus grande sculpture en papier mâché, le plus haut lancement d'une fusée effervescente, le plus grand *cheerleading*.

Garde avant, rangée 2 : le plus long voyage à vélo elliptique dans un seul pays, le plus long équilibre d'une chaise sur une corde raide, le plus grand château gonflable, le parcours à la rame le plus rapide en Atlantique au départ du Canada, la plus grande collection de souvenirs de la série *Happy Days*, le vaisseau spatial le plus actif en orbite autour d'une autre planète.

Garde avant, rangée 3 : le premier implant météo barométrique, le vol le plus rapide d'un hélicoptère électrique (prototype), record de temps pour passer sous 10 barres en limbo skate, la tenue en équilibre la plus longue d'un ballon de basket sur une brosse à dents, le semimarathon le plus rapide habillé en tenue de baseball (homme), la plus haute montée d'escaliers en 1 h (homme).

Garde avant, rangée 4 : la 1re descente à ski du Lhotse, la plus grande mosaïque animée de téléphones portables, la plus grande paire de jeans, le plus grand attrape-rêve, le plus grand rassemblement de personnes habillées en lapin, le plus grand parking automatisé, la plus grande collection de souvenirs *Muppets*.

Garde arrière, rangée 1 : le plus de personnes donnant des coups de sifflets de gare en même temps, temps record pour faire tourner un spinner sur un orteil, le plus grand scone, le voyage le plus rapide de Land's End à John o' Groats sur une tondeuse à gazon, le plus de maquillage réalisé en 1 h (équipe de 5), le plus de moissonneuses-batteuses travaillant en même temps.

Garde arrière, rangée 2 : la plus longue tenue en équilibre d'un ballon sur le genou, la plus grande bataille d'oreillers, la plus grande planche de charcuteries, la plus grande guitare acoustique avec cordes en acier, la plus grande pièce de jeu d'échec, le plus grand plat de beshbarmak, le plus de chiens-guides entraînés par une association.

Garde arrière, rangée 3 : le plus long circuit de petites voitures, le plus de notes adhésives collées sur le visage en 30 s, la plus longue chaîne de rallonges électriques, le plus grand T-shirt, le plus de séances d'*escape rooms* réalisées en 1 jour, la personne la plus jeune à avoir traversé l'Atlantique à la rame, en équipe (Trade Winds II).

Garde arrière, rangée 4 : le plus grand défilé de dépanneuses, la plus grande mêlée de rugby, le plus de rebonds de balles de ping-pong contre un mur réalisés avec la bouche en 30 s, record de temps passé dans une bulle, la plus grande collection de cravates, la plus grande mosaïque en stickers (image).

Codes pays

Code	Pays
ABW	Aruba
AFG	Afghanistan
AGO	Angola
AIA	Anguilla
ALB	Albanie
AND	Andorre
ARE	Émirats arabes unis
ARG	Argentine
ARM	Arménie
ASM	Samoa américaines
ATA	Antarctique
ATF	Terres australes et antarctiques françaises
ATG	Antigua-et-Barbuda
AUS	Australie
AUT	Autriche
AZE	Azerbaïdjan
BDI	Burundi
BEL	Belgique
BEN	Bénin
BFA	Burkina Faso
BGD	Bangladesh
BGR	Bulgarie
BHR	Bahreïn
BHS	Bahamas
BIH	Bosnie-Herzégovine
BLR	Biélorussie
BLZ	Belize
BMU	Bermudes
BOL	Bolivie
BRA	Brésil
BRB	Barbade
BRN	Brunei
BTN	Bhoutan
BVT	Île Bouvet
BWA	Botswana
CAF	République centrafricaine
CAN	Canada
CCK	Îles Cocos
CHE	Suisse
CHL	Chili
CHN	Chine
CIV	Côte d'Ivoire
CMR	Cameroun
COD	République démocratique du Congo
COG	République du Congo
COK	Îles Cook
COL	Colombie
COM	Comores (pays)
CPV	Cap-Vert
CRI	Costa Rica
CUB	Cuba
CXR	Île Christmas
CYM	Îles Caïmans
CYP	Chypre (pays)
CZE	Tchéquie
DEU	Allemagne
DJI	Djibouti
DMA	Dominique
DNK	Danemark
DOM	République dominicaine
DZA	Algérie
ECU	Équateur (pays)
EGY	Égypte
ERI	Érythrée
ESH	République arabe sahraouie démocratique
ESP	Espagne
EST	Estonie
ETH	Éthiopie
FIN	Finlande
FJI	Fidji
FLK	Malouines
FRA	France
FRO	Îles Féroé
FSM	Micronésie (États fédérés de)
GAB	Gabon
GBR	Royaume-Uni
GEO	Géorgie (pays)
GHA	Ghana
GIB	Gibraltar
GIN	Guinée
GLP	Guadeloupe
GMB	Gambie
GNB	Guinée-Bissau
GNQ	Guinée équatoriale
GRC	Grèce
GRD	Grenade
GRL	Groenland
GTM	Guatemala
GUF	Guyane
GUM	Guam
GUY	Guyana
HKG	Hong Kong
HMD	Îles Heard-et-MacDonald
HND	Honduras
HRV	Croatie
HTI	Haïti
HUN	Hongrie
IDN	Indonésie
IND	Inde
IOT	Territoire britannique de l'océan Indien
IRL	Irlande (pays)
IRN	Iran
IRQ	Irak
ISL	Islande
ISR	Israël
ITA	Italie
JAM	Jamaïque
JOR	Jordanie
JPN	Japon
KAZ	Kazakhstan
KEN	Kenya
KGZ	Kirghizistan
KHM	Cambodge
KIR	Kiribati
KNA	Saint-Christophe-et-Niévès
KOR	Corée du Sud
KWT	Koweït
LAO	Laos
LBN	Liban
LBR	Liberia
LBY	Libye
LCA	Sainte-Lucie
LIE	Liechtenstein
LKA	Sri Lanka
LSO	Lesotho
LTU	Lituanie
LUX	Luxembourg
LVA	Lettonie
MAC	Macao
MAR	Maroc
MCO	Monaco
MDA	Moldavie
MDG	Madagascar
MDV	Maldives
MEX	Mexique
MHL	Îles Marshall
MKD	République de Macédoine (pays)
MLI	Mali
MLT	Malte
MMR	Birmanie
MNE	Monténégro
MNG	Mongolie
MNP	Îles Mariannes du Nord
MOZ	Mozambique
MRT	Mauritanie
MSR	Montserrat
MTQ	Martinique
MUS	Maurice (pays)
MWI	Malawi
MYS	Malaisie
MYT	Mayotte
NAM	Namibie
NCL	Nouvelle-Calédonie
NER	Niger
NFK	Île Norfolk
NGA	Nigeria
NIC	Nicaragua
NIU	Niue
NLD	Pays-Bas
NOR	Norvège
NPL	Népal
NRU	Nauru
NZL	Nouvelle-Zélande
OMN	Oman
PAK	Pakistan
PAN	Panama
PCN	Îles Pitcairn
PER	Pérou
PHL	Philippines
PLW	Palaos
PNG	Papouasie-Nouvelle-Guinée
POL	Pologne
PRI	Porto Rico
PRK	Corée du Nord
PRT	Portugal
PRY	Paraguay
PSE	Palestine
PYF	Polynésie française
QAT	Qatar
REU	La Réunion
ROU	Roumanie
RUS	Russie
RWA	Rwanda
SAU	Arabie saoudite
SDN	Soudan
SEN	Sénégal
SGP	Singapour
SGS	Géorgie du Sud-et-les îles Sandwich du Sud
SHN	Sainte-Hélène, Ascension et Tristan da Cunha
SJM	Svalbard et île Jan-Mayen
SLB	Salomon
SLE	Sierra Leone
SLV	Salvador
SMR	Saint-Marin
SOM	Somalie
SPM	Saint-Pierre-et-Miquelon
SRB	Serbie
SSD	Soudan du Sud
STP	Sao Tomé-et-Principe
SUR	Suriname
SVK	Slovaquie
SVN	Slovénie
SWE	Suède
SWZ	Swaziland
SXM	Saint-Martin
SYC	Seychelles
SYR	Syrie
TCA	Îles Turques-et-Caïques
TCD	Tchad
TGO	Togo
THA	Thaïlande
TJK	Tadjikistan
TKL	Tokelau
TKM	Turkménistan
TLS	Timor oriental
TON	Tonga
TTO	Trinité-et-Tobago
TUN	Tunisie
TUR	Turquie
TUV	Tuvalu
TZA	Tanzanie
UGA	Ouganda
UKR	Ukraine
UMI	Îles mineures éloignées des États-Unis
URY	Uruguay
USA	États-Unis
UZB	Ouzbékistan
VAT	Saint-Siège (État de la Cité du Vatican)
VCT	Saint-Vincent-et-les Grenadines
VEN	Venezuela
VGB	Îles Vierges britanniques
VIR	Îles Vierges des États-Unis
VNM	Viêt Nam
VUT	Vanuatu
WLF	Wallis-et-Futuna
WSM	Samoa
YEM	Yémen
ZAF	Afrique du Sud
ZMB	Zambie
ZWE	Zimbabwe

DERNIÈRE MINUTE

Ces records ont été certifiés et intégrés à notre base après la date limite fixée pour les contributions de l'année.

Le plus de tornades observées par une personne
Le chasseur de tornades professionnel Roger Hill (USA) a observé 676 tornades entre le 7 juillet 1987 et le 13 juillet 2017, nombre vérifié le 15 février 2018.

La plus longue chaîne de chenilles cure-pipes
Le 9 mars 2018, des élèves de l'école élémentaire Brookman de Las Vegas (Nevada, USA) ont élaboré, avec leur institutrice Alana London et son mari Adam, magicien (tous 2 USA), une chaîne de chenilles cure-pipes de 18,09 km. Il s'agissait d'inciter les enfants à la lecture : à chaque livre lu, ils gagnaient un cure-pipe.

La plus haute pyramide de rouleaux de papier toilette
Pour l'inauguration d'un hypermarché à Appleton (Wisconsin, USA), une pyramide de rouleaux de papier toilette de 4,36 m a été réalisée le 24 mai 2018 par Kimberly-Clark Corporation et Meijer (tous 2 USA) : 10 h ont été nécessaires à 14 personnes pour ériger cette ziggourat composée de 25 585 rouleaux.

Le 1ᵉʳ serpent embryonnaire conservé dans l'ambre
Les restes d'un embryon de serpent conservés dans l'ambre, estimés à environ 99 millions d'années, ont été mis au jour dans l'État Kachin (MYN). Le spécimen, une nouvelle espèce baptisée *Xiaophis myanmarensis*, mesurait 4,75 cm et son crâne était manquant ; entier, le serpent devait atteindre 8 cm. La découverte a été rapportée dans la revue *Sciences Advances* le 18 juillet 2018.

▶ La plus grande couverture tricotée (hors crochet)
Valery Larkin (IRL) et Knitters of the World ont tricoté une couverture de 1 994,81 m², soit la dimension d'environ 4 terrains de basket, selon des mesures effectuées le 26 août 2018 à Ennis (IRL). Plus de 1 000 personnes ont confectionné la couverture, qui a été découpée et offerte à la Croix-Rouge.

L'empilement 3-3-3 le plus rapide en sport stacking (individuel)
Le 4 novembre 2018, Hyeon Jong-choi (KOR) a réalisé un empilement 3-3-3 en 1,322 s, au 1ᵉʳ championnats du monde de sport stacking, à Séoul (KOR). Il a battu son record du 16 septembre 2018 de 0,005 s.

La projection sur le plus grand écran d'eau
Le 20 septembre 2018, le festival international Circle of Light de Moscou incluait un spectacle son et lumière sur un écran d'eau de 3 099,24 m². L'événement, coordonné par LBL Communication Group (RUS), a également été le cadre du **record de projections de flammes déclenchées simultanément** (162).

La plus grande image humaine d'un pays
Le 29 septembre 2018, 4 807 personnes ont célébré le 100ᵉ jour de l'Union en formant une image de leur pays dans une citadelle restaurée du XVIIᵉ siècle, à Alba Iulia (ROU). L'événement a été organisé par Asociația 11even, Primăria Alba Iulia et Kaufland (tous ROU).

La plus grande leçon de hurling
Pour ses 20 ans, le 30 septembre 2018, le musée de l'Association athlétique gaélique (IRL) a organisé un cours de hurling (sorte de hockey sur gazon) pour 1 772 personnes, au Croke Park de Dublin (IRL). Le cours était dirigé par Martin Fogarty, chargé du développement de ce sport.

Le plus d'*escape games* en 1 journée
Le 3 octobre 2018, Richard Bragg, Daniel Egnor, Amanda Harris (tous USA) et Ana Ulin (ESP), membres de la "Bloody Boris's Burning Bluelight Brigade", ont exploré 22 salles d'*escape games* en 24 h, à Moscou (RUS). Ils ont pu s'échapper de toutes les salles sauf une dans le temps imparti.

La plus jeune personne à réaliser une circumnavigation en avion (solo)
Mason Andrews (USA, né le 26 avril 2000) a fait le tour du monde dans un Piper PA-32 monomoteur en 76 jours. Il a achevé son voyage le 6 octobre 2018, à Monroe (Louisiane, USA), à l'âge de 18 ans et 163 jours.

Le plus de personnes préparant des packs contre la famine (plusieurs sites)
Le 16 octobre 2018, l'association Rise Against Hunger (USA) a préparé des packs contre la famine avec l'aide de 832 participants. Plus de 4 500 packs ont été assemblés dans différents lieux des États-Unis, d'Inde, d'Italie, des Philippines et d'Afrique du Sud.

Le parcours de 10 m le plus rapide debout (chien)
Le 11 novembre 2018, un cavapoo de 3 ans baptisé Oliver a parcouru 10 m sur ses pattes arrière en 3,21 s, à Nashville (Tennessee, USA). Oliver était accompagné de son propriétaire et entraîneur Rayner Fredrick (USA).

Le plus d'empanadas servies en 8 h
Le 11 novembre 2018, l'Asociación de Propietarios de Pizzerías y Casas de Empanadas (ARG) a battu 2 records à Buenos Aires (ARG). Ce jour-là, 11 472 empanadas ont été servies en 8 h ainsi que 11 089 pizzas en 12 h – **le plus de pizzas confectionnées en 12 h (en équipe)**.

Le plus de personnes soufflant des bougies simultanément
Le 18 novembre 2018, à Bangkok (THA), King Power International (THA), partenaire de Disney, a réuni 1 765 personnes pour souffler des bougies simultanément en l'honneur du 90ᵉ anniversaire de Mickey.

Le plus petit aspirateur
Talabathula Sai (IND) a créé un aspirateur miniature de 5,4 cm, à Peddapuram (IND), record homologué le 10 décembre 2018. L'aspirateur était composé d'un bouchon de stylo, d'un moteur à courant continu et d'une petite feuille de cuivre.

Le plus de personnes écrasant des canettes simultanément
463 personnes ont écrasé des canettes simultanément dans le cadre d'un événement organisé par Coca-Cola HBC Ireland & Northern Ireland Ltd à Belfast (GBR), le 17 janvier 2019.

▶ Le rattrapage de la plus haute balle de cricket
Le 31 janvier 2019, la gardienne de guichet Alyssa Healy (AUS) a rattrapé avec précision une balle de cricket lâchée d'un drone de 82,5 m d'altitude, à Melbourne (Victoria, AUS). Sa tentative de record était destinée à promouvoir les compétitions internationales féminines et masculines T20 de cricket de l'ICC en 2020.
La promotion de ces compétitions a aussi donné lieu à **un record de signatures sur un objet de collection sportif**, avec 1 033 signatures comptabilisées à Melbourne, le 8 mars 2019, sur un maillot de cricket géant.

Le plus grand jean
Le 19 fév. 2019, la société Paris Perú (PER) a présenté un jean de 65,5 m de long et

---

L'AVION À LA PLUS GRANDE ENVERGURE
Imaginé par le cofondateur de Microsoft Paul Allen (1953-2018) et l'ingénieur en aérospatiale Burt Rutan (tous 2 USA), le *Stratolaunch* a une envergure de 117,35 m. Le 13 avril 2019, il a effectué un vol inaugural depuis l'aéroport et port spatial de Mojave (Californie, USA). Il est conçu pour transporter des fusées spatiales qui seront lancées depuis les confins de l'atmosphère.

LA 1ᴿᴱ IMAGE DIRECTE D'UN TROU NOIR
Le 10 avril 2019, le réseau de télescopes *Event Horizon Telescope* a dévoilé cette image d'un trou noir situé au cœur de la galaxie M87. On peut y voir un disque de matière surchauffée formant une spirale autour de la zone sombre de l'horizon des événements - limite du trou noir au-delà de laquelle sa force gravitationnelle ne laisse plus échapper la lumière.

DE SPECTACULAIRES TRAVERSÉES À LA RAME (2018-2019)

Source: Ocean Rowing Society

La traversée en solitaire la plus rapide d'Europe en Amérique du Sud	60 jours, 16 h et 6 min pour Lee Spencer alias "Frank" (GBR) sur le *Rowing Marine* (photo à droite)	26 janv.- 11 mars 2019
La 1re traversée en solo (amputé)	Lee Spencer alias "Franck" (voir ci-dessus)	Voir ci-dessus
La traversée d'un océan par la plus jeune équipe de 4 hommes	22 ans et 246 jours (moyenne d'âge) pour Lee Gordon, Cole Barnard, Matthew Boynton et Grant Soll (les "Mad4Waves", tous ZAF) sur *Jasmine 2*	12 déc. 2018- 20 janv. 2019
La 1re équipe familiale de 4 personnes (traversée Atlantique d'est en ouest)	Caspar Thorp, Toby Thorp, George Blandford et Justin Evelegh (les "Oar Inspiring", tous GBR), sur *Lionheart*	12 déc. 2018- 16 janv. 2019
Le 1er binôme masculin (Atlantique depuis l'Europe continentale)	John Wilson et Ricky Reina (les "Atlantic Avengers", tous 2 GBR) sur *Sic Parvis Magna*	27 nov. 2018- 23 févr. 2019
La traversée Atlantique d'est en ouest en binôme, route des alizés (toutes catégories) la plus rapide	2,875 nœuds (5,32 km/h) par Alex Simpson et Jamie Gordon (tous 2 GBR) sur *Hyperion Atlantic Challenge*	29 janv.- 8 mars 2019
La plus jeune personne à accomplir 3 traversées de l'océan	27 ans et 4 jours pour Alex Simpson (né le 25 janvier 1992)	Voir ci-dessus
La personne la plus âgée à accomplir 3 traversées de l'océan	Fedor Konyukhov (RUS, né le 12 décembre 1951) à 66 ans et 359 jours, de Nouvelle-Zélande en Amér. du Sud sur *Akros*	6 déc. 2018- 9 mai 2019
Le 1er équipage multiple à traverser l'Atlantique et la mer des Caraïbes	Isaac Giesen (NZL), Jógvan Clementsen, Niclas Olsen et Jákup Jacobsen (tous FRO) sur *SAGA*	12 mars- 13 mai 2018

42,7 m de large, au centre commercial del Sur de Lima (PER). Le pantalon pesait 4,8 t et a nécessité le travail de 50 personnes durant 6 mois.

La table périodique reconstituée le plus vite
Le 25 fév. 2019, Ali Ghaddar (LBN) a réuni une série d'images mélangées des éléments et les a placées dans l'ordre de la table périodique en 6 min et 44 s, au lycée Safir de Saïda (LBN). Sa tentative de record a eu lieu à l'occasion de la célébration internationale du 150e anniversaire de la 1re version de la table périodique de Mendeleïev (1869).

Le score le plus élevé en cyclisme artistique de l'UCI (femmes, solo)
Milena Slupina (DEU) a obtenu 194,31 points lors de la coupe du monde de cyclisme artistique de l'UCI, à Prague (CZE), le 9 mars 2019. Elle a battu le record de sa compatriote Iris Schwarzhaupt (voir p. 231).

La marche de 50 km la plus rapide sur route (femmes)
Le 9 mars 2019, Hong Liu (CHN) est devenue la 1re femme à effectuer une marche sportive de 50 km en moins de 4 h. Elle a achevé le Grand Prix de marche sportive de Chine en 3 h 59 min et 15 s, à Huangshan (CHN), battant ainsi le record de sa compatriote Rui Liang (4 h 4 min et 36 s). Son temps doit toutefois être ratifié par l'IAAF.

Le plus de personnes se passant un œuf
Le 10 mars 2019, 353 habitants de Misaki à Kume (Préfecture d'Okayama, JPN) ont utilisé des cuillères à café pour se passer un œuf frais et cru sans le casser.

Le plus rapide dans une course de dragsters de la NHRA (catégorie Pro Stock Motorcycle)
Le 17 mars 2019, Andrew Hines (USA) a remporté une course de 402 m dans la catégorie Pro Stock Motorcycle en 6,720 s, lors des 50es Amalie Motor Oil Gatornationals de la NHRA sur le circuit de Gainesville (Floride, USA).

Le pigeon le plus cher
Le pigeon de course Armando a été adjugé 1 252 000 €, au cours d'une vente aux enchères de la maison PIPA, le 17 mars 2019. Plusieurs oiseaux avaient été mis en vente par l'éleveur de pigeons Joël Verschoot (BEL), directeur à la retraite d'un abattoir. Armando ne concourt plus depuis quelque temps, mais il a un passé de champion, ayant remporté ses 3 dernières compétitions : le championnat as-pigeon de 2018, l'olympiade pigeon de 2019 et

l'Angoulême. Les enchères se sont envolées lorsque deux Chinois ont enchéri l'un contre l'autre à la dernière minute.

Le record de profondeur pour un serpent de mer
Selon un article d'*Austral Ecology* du 18 mars 2019, un serpent de mer du genre *Hydrophis* (espèce indéterminée) a été filmé le 16 novembre 2014, à 245 m de profondeur, par un véhicule sous-marin téléguidé du bassin de Browse, au large du nord-ouest de l'Australie. Un autre véhicule sous-marin a également filmé un serpent de mer *Hydrophis* explorant le fond marin au même endroit, le 18 juillet 2017, à 239 m de profondeur.

La note sifflée la plus aiguë
Le 20 mars 2019, Andrew Stanford (USA) a sifflé une note d'une fréquence de 8 372,019 Hz (ut^9), à Hanover (New Hampshire, USA). Il a été enregistré dans une cabine acoustique au Dartmouth College.

LE TAPIR EN CAPTIVITÉ LE PLUS ÂGÉ
Le 13 mars 2019, l'âge d'un tapir malais (*Tapirus indicus*) baptisé Kingut (né le 27 janvier 1978), soit 41 ans et 45 jours, a été vérifié au Port Lympne Hôtel & Reserve dans le Kent (GBR). Kingut est né à Jakarta (IDN) et s'appelait à l'origine Huta, avant d'être acclimaté au Royaume-Uni. Il aime être brossé par Alice Elliot (à gauche), chargée de le soigner, et a une prédilection pour les friandises comme les bananes.

L'âge combiné le plus élevé de 2 frères
Albano et Alberto Andrade (PRT, nés le 14 décembre 1909 et le 2 décembre 1911) ont un âge combiné de 216 ans et 230 jours, selon des vérifications effectuées le 2 avr. 2019, à Santa Maria da Feira (district d'Aveiro, PRT).

Le participant le plus âgé à une course de bateaux universitaire
James Cracknell (GBR, né le 5 mai 1972), âgé de 46 ans et 337 jours, a ramé pour Cambridge lors de la 165e course de bateau universitaire du 7 avril 2019. Il a terminé dans le bateau de tête, Cambridge ayant battu Oxford en 16 min et 57 s. Il avait 8 ans de plus que le précédent participant le plus âgé (le barreur Andrew Probert, en 1992) et 10 ans de plus que le 3e rameur le plus âgé (Mike Wherley, d'Oxford, en 2008).

Le plus grand assemblage de figurines LEGO® Star Wars
Pour l'anniversaire de *Star Wars*, le 11 avr. 2019, LEGO (USA) a assemblé à Chicago (Illinois, USA) 36 440 figurines *Star Wars* disposées pour former l'image d'un casque de Stormtroopers. L'image mesurait 6,93 m de large sur 6,88 m de haut et sa réalisation a occupé 12 personnes durant 38 h, dont 16 h uniquement dédiées à l'assemblage.

La plus grande dégustation de whisky
Le 13 avril 2019, Nigab (SWE) et Bruichladdich (GBR) ont organisé une dégustation de whisky pour 2 283 personnes, à Göteborg (SWE).

La plus grande distance à vélo en 1 h (sans abri coupe-vent, départ arrêté)
Le 16 avril 2019, Victor Campenaerts (BEL) a parcouru 55,089 km en 60 min, à Aguascalientes (MEX). Située à une altitude de 1 800 m, la ville a aussi accueilli le record féminin sur 60 min de Vittoria Bussi (voir p. 228).

La langue la plus large (hommes)
La langue de Brian Thompson (USA), mesurée à La Cañada Flintridge (Californie, USA), le 30 juillet 2018, atteignait 8,88 cm à son point le plus large, un record homologué le 16 avril 2019. Brian a donc battu le précédent détenteur du record, Byron Schlenker (voir p. 70).

La plus grande baignoire en or
Le 22 avril 2019, le parc à thème Huis Ten Bosch de Sasebo (préfecture de Nagasaki, JPN) a accueilli une baignoire en or de 18 carats pesant 154,2 kg. La baignoire d'un diamètre de 1,3 m et d'une profondeur de 55 cm est assez grande pour accueillir 2 adultes.